COMMERCIAL AND INTELLECTUAL PROPERTY LAW AND PRACTICE

University of Law

COMMERCIAL AND INTELLECTUAL PROPERTY LAW AND PRACTICE

Judith Embley, Keir Bamford and Nick Hancock

Published by

College of Law Publishing,
Braboeuf Manor, Portsmouth Road, St Catherines, Guildford GU3 1HA

British Library Cataloguing-in-Publication Data
A catalogue record for this book is available from the British Library.

ISBN 978 1 915469 20 5

Typeset by Style Photosetting Ltd, Mayfield, East Sussex
Tables and index by Moira Greenhalgh, Arnside, Cumbria

Preface

This book is intended to reflect modern vocational training practice. It is hoped that the level of detail and analysis of the cases and statutes will be suited to both vocational study and to the early years of practice. Clearly, with such a diverse range of discrete topics, many limitations are imposed upon such a work, but it is intended that the reader should be assisted in gaining a firm grasp of the general principles and a flavour of the current state of legislation and case law.

In the interest of brevity, the masculine pronoun is used throughout to include the feminine.

Judith Embley would like to thank her colleagues at Bloomsbury, Susan Sang, Alex Laski and Mary Medyckyj, who reviewed and contributed invaluable suggestions to the Sale of Goods and Marketing chapters.

JUDITH EMBLEY
KEIR BAMFORD
NICK HANCOCK
The University of Law

Further Study

The following books may be of interest to readers wishing to pursue a particular topic further. In addition, there are some references to Internet sources in the text, as well as the obvious ones such as the European Commission sites and the UK legislation ones.

Sale of Goods

Canavan et al, *Atiyah and Adams' Sale of Goods* (14th edn, Pearson, 2020)

Bridge, *Benjamin's Sale of Goods* (11th edn, Sweet & Maxwell, 2020)

Encyclopedia of Forms and Precedents (2011 reissue 5th edn, LexisNexis Butterworths), vol 34 on Sale of Goods

Rosenberg, *Practical Commercial Precedents* (Sweet & Maxwell), section on Sale of Goods

(The above works have useful sections on exclusion of liability.)

Drafting

Beale, *Chitty on Contracts* (34th edn, Sweet & Maxwell, 2021)

Christou, *Drafting Commercial Agreements* (6th edn, Sweet & Maxwell, 2016)

Christou, *Boilerplate: Practical Clauses* (8th edn, Sweet & Maxwell, 2019)

Marketing Agreements

Practical Commercial Precedents and the *Encyclopedia of Forms and Precedents* have useful sections on agency distribution and other types of marketing agreement. See also:

Christou, *International Agency, Distribution and Licensing Agreements* (6th edn, Sweet & Maxwell, 2011)

Commercial Law

Byles on Bills of Exchange and Cheques (30th edn, Sweet & Maxwell, 2019)

Carr, *International Trade Law* (6th edn, Routledge, 2017)

Goode, *Commercial Law* (6th edn, LexisNexis Butterworths, 2021)

International Chambers of Commerce, *Incoterms 2020* (ICC Publishing, 2019)

Murray, Holloway, Timson-Hunt and Dixon, *Schmitthoff's Export Trade* (12th edn, Sweet & Maxwell, 2012)

Sealy and Hooley, *Commercial Law* (6th edn, Oxford University Press, 2020)

Wilson, *Carriage of Goods by Sea* (7th edn, Pearson Educational, 2010)

Competition Law

Whish and Bailey, *Competition Law* (10th edn, Oxford University Press, 2021)

Bellamy and Child, *European Union Law of Competition* (8th edn, Oxford University Press, 2018)

Intellectual Property

Cornish and Llewelyn, *Intellectual Property* (9th edn, Sweet & Maxwell, 2019)

CIPA Guide to the Patents Acts (9th edn, Sweet & Maxwell, 2019)

Bainbridge, *Intellectual Property* (10th edn, Pearson, 2018)

Information Technology

Reed and Angel, *Computer Law* (7th edn, Oxford University Press, 2011)

Susskind, *Transforming the Law* (Oxford University Press, 2004)

Todd, *E-Commerce Law* (Routledge-Cavendish, 2005)

Contents

Table of Cases

Table of Primary Legislation

Table of Secondary Legislation

Table of Abbreviations

ALCS	Authors' Licensing and Collecting Society
BEA 1882	Bills of Exchange Act 1882
CA 1998	Competition Act 1998
CDPA 1988	Copyright, Designs and Patents Act 1988
CESL	Common European Sales Law
CISG	United Nations Convention on the International Sale of Goods
CFR	Cost and Freight
CIF	Cost, Insurance and Freight
CIP	Carriage and Insurance Paid To
CJEU	Court of Justice of the European Union
CLA	Copyright Licensing Agency Ltd
CPT	Carriage Paid To
CRA 2015	Consumer Rights Act 2015
DAF	Delivered at Frontier
DAP	Delivered at Place
DC	documentary credit
DDP	Delivered Duty Paid
DPU	Delivered at Place Unloaded
ECJ	European Court of Justice
EEA	European Economic Area
EFTA	European Free Trade Area
EPC 1973	European Patent Convention 1973
EPO	European Patents Office
EUTM	European Union Trade Mark
EXW	Ex Works
FAS	Free Alongside
FCA	Free Carrier
FOB	Free On Board
FSR	*Fleet Street Reports*
HRA 1998	Human Rights Act 1998
ICANN	Internet Corporation for Assigned Names and Numbers
ICC	International Chamber of Commerce
IP	intellectual property
IPO	Intellectual Property Office
ISP	Internet Service Provider
ISS	information society service
ISSP	information society service provider
IT	information technology
MCPS	Mechanical Copyright Protection Society
NAOMI	Notice on Agreements of Minor Importance
NLA	Newspaper Licensing Agency Ltd
PA 1977	Patents Act 1977

PECL	Principles of European Contract Law
PCT	Patent Cooperation Treaty
PICC	UNIDROIT Principles of International Commercial Contracts
PLS	Publishers Licensing Society
PPL	Phonographic Performance Ltd
RDA 1949	Registered Designs Act 1949
RPC	*Reports of Patent, Design and Trade Mark Cases*
ROT	retention of title
SGA 1979	Sale of Goods Act 1979
SGSA 1982	Supply of Goods and Services Act 1982
TEU	Treaty on European Union
TFEU	Treaty on the Functioning of the European Union
TTBER	Technology Transfer Block Exemption Regulation
UCC	Uniform Commercial Code
UNIDROIT	International Institute for the Unification of Private Law
UNCITRAL	United National Commission on International Trade
UCP	Uniform Customs and Practice for Documentary Credits
UCTA 1977	Unfair Contract Terms Act 1977
VPL	Video Performance Ltd
VRBE	Vertical Restraints Block Exemption
WIPO	World Intellectual Property Organisation

PART I

COMMERCIAL AGREEMENTS

INTRODUCTION TO COMMERCIAL CONTRACTS

LEARNING OUTCOMES

After reading this chapter you will be able to:

- explain the role of a commercial lawyer
- describe the stages of a supply chain and the contracts involved
- prepare a checklist for a commercial agreement
- summarise the main provisions in standard terms and conditions of sale between a commercial seller and a commercial buyer.

1.1 INTRODUCTION

This book will deal with some of the legal issues that arise in relation to commercial transactions which govern everyday business activity. The term 'commercial law' covers a large number of interconnecting areas of law and practice (both domestic and international), including the sale of goods, marketing agreements, transport, finance and credit arrangements, competition law, intellectual property, insurance and related areas, such as banking or tax law. Clearly it will not be possible to cover all aspects of commercial law. However, the thread which links together all of these interconnecting areas of law is the use of commercial contracts. All of the topic areas which will be considered are in some way related to commercial contracts, either very obviously, for example the drafting of standard terms and conditions for the supply of goods, or indirectly, for example the application of competition law to distribution agreements or the exploitation of intellectual property rights by the use of licensing agreements. This reflects the realities of commercial practice.

It is extremely difficult to generalise on the role of a commercial solicitor which will, inevitably, be varied and depend on the type of firm in which they practise. In smaller firms in the UK, combined company/commercial departments (so-called 'CoCo' departments) may deal with a range of matters, from the setting up of companies and partnerships to consumer issues. In a large international corporate firm, there will be a far higher degree of specialisation within discrete areas, for example shipping law or the competition aspects of distribution agreements. However, any commercial lawyer will be routinely involved with either the drafting or interpretation of contracts.

In this book, we have brought together some typical kinds of commercial contract. You will see that the topics include:

(a)   sale of goods, both domestic and international;

(b)   carriage arrangements;

(c)   payment and security for international transactions;

(d)   agency; and

(e)   the use of conventions such as Incoterms and Uniform Customs and Practice for documentary credits.

These topics have been chosen to illustrate the main areas of commercial contract law that an international lawyer could reasonably expect to come across in practice. We now need to see what ties these disparate areas together.

Part I on Commercial Contracts will cover the content and drafting of contracts for the sale of goods and marketing agreements domestically. It will also consider briefly other types of contract under which goods may pass, such as hire purchase and leasing. It is designed to bring together most of the basic legal considerations that must be addressed in order to understand the nature of these types of commercial contracts. Part II will go on to deal with the extra considerations required where such contracts involve international aspects.

The emphasis throughout this book will be on business-to-business contracts (B2B contracts) focusing on the position and protection of the commercial supplier. Most manufacturers do not themselves sell directly to end users, so contracts which govern the supply of goods to consumers (B2C contracts) are outside the scope of this book, although there are some areas of overlap, for example the drafting of exclusion clauses, and the chapter on e-commerce (**Chapter 26**) will touch on some aspects of consumer protection.

1.2   SOURCES OF COMMERCIAL LAW IN THE UK

Where do you look to find the legal principles on which commercial law in the UK is based? The main sources of commercial law are:

(a)   the law of contract;

(b)   established custom and usage of the trade;

(c)   national legislation;

(d)   European Union law; and

(e)   international conventions.

If you are dealing with a commercial contract matter in practice, the sources which are likely to cause the most difficulty are custom and usage of the trade and international conventions. Legal databases are ideal for sourcing legislation, but the 'soft' material can be harder to track down. Indeed, half the problem is knowing that it exists in the first place. As regards the custom and usage of the trade, a lawyer will be often be reliant on the client for information on this aspect, as the client's knowledge of the market will often be far greater.

The sources of commercial law internationally will be explored in **Chapter 2**.

Brexit

On 31 January 2020, the UK left the European Union following a withdrawal agreement with the EU, implemented by the European Union (Withdrawal Agreement) Act 2020. Following the end of the transition period at 11pm on 31 December 2020, EU law and regulation ceased to apply to the UK. However, there is a body of 'retained EU law', in other words EU-derived legislation, rules and principles, which have, in effect, been transposed into UK law, and which entered into force at the same time. This body of law will remain in effect in the UK until the government decides to repeal or amend it.

In the future, as English contract law is not EU-derived, except in certain areas, for example, consumer law (see **Chapter 7**) and agency regulation (see **Chapter 11**), Brexit will not have a significant impact on the legal aspects of most commercial contracts. However, Brexit will undoubtedly have significant commercial implications, and there are other considerations, for example in relation to the interpretation of contracts (see **Chapter 3**) and choice of law and the enforcement of judgments of the English courts (see **Chapter 14**), which mean that parties to commercial contracts may seek to review their contracts.

1.3 THE SUPPLY CHAIN

The fundamental concern of a commercial supplier is how to get his goods to the ultimate consumer in the most efficient and cost-effective manner. Most of the contracts that are covered in this book are designed to achieve this goal, so it is important to understand the steps in the supply chain. This is illustrated in **Figure 1.1** below.

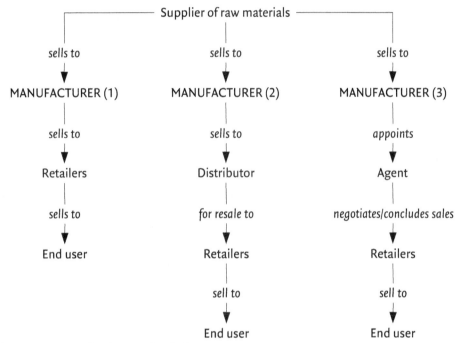

Figure 1.1 Steps in the supply chain

One possibility is for a manufacturer (Manufacturer 1) to sell his goods direct to retailers, who will sell on to other retailers or direct to the end user. This is, however, not the most usual arrangement, and often a 'middle man' in the form of either a distributor (see Manufacturer 2) or an agent (see Manufacturer 3) will be involved.

The choice of marketing arrangement will be dictated by commercial factors, and the appropriate form of contract must be drafted. This will be considered in **Chapter 10**.

A manufacturer will also be concerned with producing the goods as efficiently and cheaply as possible. One aspect of the manufacturing process is the sourcing of the raw materials, goods, services and utilities necessary to produce the goods and enable the business to function effectively. (This is referred to as 'supply chain procurement'.) Commercial contracts are sometimes classified into two types: 'upstream' and 'downstream' contracts.

(a)   Upstream contracts are typically those which provide the client with the resources needed in order to carry on his business, for example contracts for the supply of goods or services to the business, the supply of funds through loan agreements, permission to manufacture through intellectual property licences and the variety of contracts that come under the heading 'overheads', such as utilities, employees, IT, maintenance, security etc – in other words, contracts which require some sort of financial outlay by the business. These are outside the scope of this book, but a commercial lawyer will need to be aware of their existence.

(b)   Downstream contracts are those under which the client passes on and exploits the fruits of his labour, contracts for the supply of goods and services by the business – in other words, contracts which generate income for the business. It is these contracts which will be considered in this book.

When acting for a manufacturer, it is important to remember that the client's objectives, and thus the drafting considerations, will be very different depending on whether it is buying or selling.

At the time of writing, the aftermath of the coronavirus pandemic and geopolitical factors, such as the war in Ukraine and the US–China trade war, have had a devastating effect on both national and global supply chains. Factory shutdowns, reduced workforces, inability to access essential raw materials, inflationary pressures and the insolvency of essential suppliers are all contributing to disruption and uncertainty. This creates considerable legal risk and potential for disputes as to who will bear the loss, which to an extent may be managed in the future by careful drafting of supply contracts. However, attention has been focused on the need to move away from the linear supply chain model described above. Increasingly, it is thought that companies will look to digital supply networks (DSNs) which, using advanced technologies, enable companies to connect to their complete supply network and anticipate and meet problems.

1.4 STANDARD TERMS AND CONDITIONS

An important consideration for the client will be whether to use standard terms and conditions or individually negotiated contracts. In practice, it is very common for a set of terms to be put into a standard contract which a business will use for all transactions. Whether the contract between the buyer and seller is based on the seller's standard terms and conditions or the buyer's will depend on the relative bargaining positions of the parties.

There are advantages and disadvantages to the use of standard terms and conditions (see the table below).

In any transaction for the sale of goods, the seller and buyer have very different agendas. At the very least, the buyer:

(a)   will want the goods to be delivered on time, preferably to its own premises; and

(b)   will want the seller to be liable for any defects.

The seller:

(a)   will want flexibility for late delivery if, for example, it is let down by its own suppliers;

(b)   will want the buyer preferably to collect the goods from its factory; and

(c)   whilst it might be willing to accept some liability for defects, will not want to be liable for every trivial problem.

The use of standard terms ensures that the final contract suits the needs of whichever party has been able to insist on their use. Not all transactions are the same, and standard terms are never going to be suitable for every occasion. However, they can provide a useful starting point for negotiation, and differences may be resolved without the need for major revision. Standard terms and conditions have the added advantage of ensuring commercial certainty.

A commercial contract is a long and complex document, and so the cost of drafting individual contracts will be high. Although some transactions may require individually negotiated contracts to be drafted, generally the parties will want to avoid incurring these costs for each sale. Such costs would have an impact throughout the supply chain. A seller will invariably try to pass the additional cost on to a buyer, and this will eventually impact on the ultimate consumer.

In addition, there are practical and administrative considerations in the use of standard terms and conditions. They create standardised procedures which enable sales or purchasing representatives or junior staff, with proper training and instruction, to safely use the standard terms and conditions to enter into contracts without having to refer back to managers or solicitors every time. It is, however, essential that clients understand the need for proper training and procedures to ensure that staff do not use standard terms inappropriately. One major practical difficulty is the need to ensure that the terms are properly incorporated into the sales contract, and the so-called 'battle of the forms'. Staff must be trained to ensure that their company's terms are the ones that are incorporated into the contract (see **3.3.3**).

It is important that standard terms and conditions are reviewed regularly to ensure that they take account of any legislative changes or new case law, and that they reflect any changes in the way that the client does business.

Standard terms and conditions are subject to greater regulation than individually negotiated contracts. Most importantly, in B2B contracts in the UK, s 3 of the Unfair Contracts Terms Act 1977 (UCTA 1977) subjects any exclusion of liability contained in standard terms to the test of reasonableness. The implications of this will be considered in **Chapter 8**. Note that s 26 excludes international sale of goods contracts from the provisions of the Act (see **Chapter 9**).

Standard Terms and Conditions	
Advantages	**Disadvantages**
Contract on terms favourable to client	Lack of flexibility
Standardised procedures	Effective training and procedures essential
Commercial certainty	Incorporation difficulties/'battle of the forms'
Cheaper	Need for regular review
Starting point for negotiation	Legal constraints, eg UCTA 1977

1.5 DRAFTING AND CONTENT OF A COMMERCIAL CONTRACT

1.5.1 The structure of a commercial agreement

The choice of commercial agreement dictates the type of contract. However, most commercial contracts, whether on standard terms or individually negotiated, follow the same basic structure. It is the specific provisions which differ, according to the type of agreement reached and the underlying commercial factors.

Key factors in drafting a commercial agreement are:

(a)   analysis of the client's instructions;
(b)   establishing the client's objectives;
(c)   not losing sight of the client's commercial aims;
(d)   adapting precedents to fit the client's instructions, and not adapting the client's instructions to fit the precedents.

In practice, this is easier said than done.

A basic checklist for a commercial agreement will be as follows:

(a)   commencement and date;
(b)   the parties;
(c)   the recitals, if any;
(d)   definitions and interpretation;
(e)   conditions precedent, if any;
(f)   agreements;
(g)   representations and warranties; } 'operative part'
(h)   indemnities;
(i)   limitations and exclusions;

(j)   'boiler-plate' clauses;

(k)   execution clause and signature; and

(l)   schedules.

1.5.1.1   Recitals

Recitals are not essential, but can be useful to help put a contract in context or explain the reason for a contract being entered into. Alternatively, recitals may set out the factual background to an exclusion clause by explaining the decision of the parties to impose the risk of loss on one party rather than the other, for example because it is more economical from an insurance point of view. This may help the party excluding liability to establish that it was reasonable to do so. However, recitals must be used with care to ensure that they do not introduce ambiguity into a document.

1.5.1.2   Definitions clause

There are a few basic rules to follow when drafting a definitions clause:

(a)   A definitions clause should do no more than give a clear meaning to defined terms. A definition should not be operative, ie impose obligations on the parties, as this may lead to ambiguity.

(b)   All defined terms should start with a capital letter. If the same word or phrase is used in the agreement without being capitalised then the inference is that something different from the defined term is intended.

(c)   Defined terms should be listed alphabetically for ease of reference.

(d)   Defined terms should be used only where they are recurrent in the body of the agreement, or where there is a danger of ambiguity if no clear definition is given.

(e)   All defined terms in the agreement should be defined in the definitions section. (In some complex agreements, the entry in the definitions section will merely be a cross-reference, possibly to an appendix or other part of the agreement.)

(f)   The definitions must meet the requirements of the agreement, for example, should the definition of 'Territory' include the whole of the UK or just England and Wales? As the agreement progresses through negotiations with the other side and a number of drafts are drawn up, continual checks should be made to ensure the definitions still work satisfactorily and reflect any changes to the agreement. (In practice, changes will be 'tracked' on the document, so it should be clear where such changes have been made.)

(g)   Care should be taken in defining things which might be subject to change during the contract, such as 'the Contract Goods'. This definition would need to cover different goods at different periods under the contract, and would need to be expressed accordingly.

1.5.1.3   Interpretation clause

This section should be non-controversial. It covers the basics of interpretation, for example by providing that the headings do not form part of the agreement (as if they did, lawyers would feel the need to draft them more comprehensively, which would detract from their usefulness).

1.5.1.4   The operative part

Conditions precedent

Conditions precedent are conditions that have to be satisfied before the agreement comes into effect. For example, in an international sale of goods contract, the contract may specify that the supply of the goods is conditional on the buyer obtaining a letter of credit. If the condition is not satisfied, there will be no binding contract.

Agreements

Agreements define the rights and obligations of the parties. In a sale of goods contract, the seller will be promising to sell and deliver goods of a certain description and quality. The buyer will be promising to pay the price. In addition, there will be provisions covering what happens if the seller fails to deliver or the buyer fails to pay, and exclusions of one or other party's rights or liability in these circumstances.

This part of the contract is the key section of a commercial agreement. Most of the key operative provisions will be considered throughout Part I of this book.

Representations and warranties

These are statements of factual and legal matters which one of the parties requires to be made to it in a legally binding way. Warranties are promises that a given statement or fact is true. They tend to be of less importance in sale of goods contracts, where any specification or description of the goods is a condition of the contract, than in contracts for the sale of businesses, where the buyer will want some assurance that, for example, profit figures are accurate. However, the warranties section can provide for remedies in addition to the usual remedy of contract damages, for example, they may make provision for repair or replacement. Representations and remedies for misrepresentation will be covered in **Chapter 3**.

Indemnities

Indemnities are different from warranties in that here one party promises to make good another's loss. The contract may provide that if one party (A) incurs loss as a result of the happening of a particular event, then the other (B) will indemnify A. They can be used where the parties have done a risk assessment and decided that should that event occur, one party should bear the cost. In sale of goods contracts, for example, an indemnity for intellectual property infringement claims relating to the goods may be included.

Limitation and exclusion of liability in contracts

This is an important area of commercial contracts and is dealt with in **Chapter 8**. An important aspect of limitation, exclusion and transfer of liability clauses in commercial contracts is the question whether the clause is liable to come within the scope and effect of the Unfair Contract Terms Act 1977 (UCTA 1977), and this is also dealt with in **Chapter 9**.

1.5.2   Introduction to boiler-plate clauses

So-called 'boiler-plate' clauses (often simply referred to as the 'boiler-plate') are standard clauses which are included as a matter of course into all agreements of a certain type. They often remain as drafted in the precedent which is being used. They are not usually individually negotiated, as they are relatively uncontroversial. Nevertheless, you must of course check that they are not contrary to your client's interests when negotiating an agreement. It can be a bad mistake to assume that boiler-plate clauses can just be copied out of a precedent. For example, in *Oxonica Energy Ltd v Neuftec Ltd* [2008] EWHC 2127 (Pat) the High Court attacked an agreement where standard paragraphs had been bolted together to make a 'nonsensical agreement'. Mr Peter Prescott QC, sitting as a Deputy High Court Judge, stated that 'Bits of legal phraseology have been lifted from I know not what precedents and assembled in a strange way'.

There is no precise definition of 'boiler-plate clauses', nor do they have to appear at a given point in the agreement. However, it is common to have a group of boiler-plate clauses at or towards the end of an agreement. Typical boiler-plate clauses are as follows:

1.5.2.1   Prevail clauses

A prevail clause states that, in the event of a dispute, one party's (eg the seller's) terms shall prevail.

1.5.2.2   Entire or whole agreement clauses

An entire or whole agreement clause provides that all of the obligations of the parties are recorded in one document. They seek to avoid the evidential difficulties associated with oral representations and discussions.

1.5.2.3   'No authority' clauses

A 'no authority' clause states that variation of the contract will be effective only if made by certain people (eg directors) or in a certain way (eg evidenced in writing). It makes clear which terms certain employees, eg sales staff, have no authority to agree on behalf of the company. Sometimes, a seller will want to give other employees, for example sales representatives, limited discretion (eg to agree discounts) and, if so, the clause will need to be amended appropriately.

Prevail, whole agreement and 'no authority' clauses are attempts to keep out extraneous terms and to prevent unauthorised variation of the terms of the contract. The effectiveness of such clauses in the UK will be dealt with in **Chapter 3**.

1.5.2.4   Waiver

There may also be a clause trying to prevent any waiver arising as a result of one party agreeing to a relaxation of a contractual provision, for example an express delivery date. Again, these clauses will be considered in **Chapter 3**.

1.5.2.5   Insolvency

This is a standard provision relating to the operation of the agreement. It makes provision for what happens if one of the parties becomes insolvent. This clause is often linked to the retention of title clause in a sale of goods agreement, as retention of title clauses are typically used when the buyer is going insolvent (see **Chapter 6**). It will normally make payment obligations immediate, and historically has allowed for termination.

However, under the Corporate Insolvency and Governance Act 2020, from June 2020 suppliers can no longer rely on provisions providing for termination in the event of a corporate customer becoming insolvent or entering an insolvency process. Clauses providing for the facility to terminate the contract in case of insolvency proceedings of one of the parties will be invalid.

1.5.2.6   Choice of law and jurisdiction

It is important that the contract includes an express choice of the law and the jurisdiction which will govern the contract in the event of a dispute. In the UK, this will normally be the law of England and Wales and the jurisdiction of the English courts. Generally, where one of the parties is domiciled in the EU, if for any reason this clause had been omitted then the courts of all EU Member States will apply Regulation 593/2008 ('Rome I') in relation to law. However, in relation to jurisdiction, there is considerable uncertainty. The relevant Convention (Regulation 1215/2012 – the recast 'Brussels I') no longer applies to the UK post-Brexit, and, in absence of choice, jurisdiction will be governed by complex common law rules (see **14.2**).

1.5.2.7   Service of notices

A notice clause has to provide for the places where notice is to be served, the method of service and the time at which the notice is deemed to be served. Such clauses have become more complex with the increase in the number of ways in which notice could be given (eg, fax and email). Most notice clauses will not permit oral notice but rather will require it to be in writing. They will specify the address(es) to which, and the person (eg, the company secretary for a corporate party to the contract) to whom, notice is to be sent.

Notice clauses will typically require notice to be served during business hours if served in person. If notice is permitted to be sent by fax or email then it could be deemed served when received. If sent by post then it could be deemed served two days after posting. It will all depend on the wording agreed by the parties.

Internationally, the rules in the Principles of European Contract Law (PECL) concerning formal notices in contracts include the following:

(a)   Notice may be given by any means, whether in writing or otherwise, as appropriate to the circumstances.

(b)   Any notice becomes effective when it reaches the addressee.

(c)   A notice reaches the addressee when it is delivered to him or to his place of business or mailing address, or, if there is not a place of business or mailing address, to his habitual residence.

(d)   A delay or inaccuracy in the transmission of the notice or its failure to arrive does not prevent it from having effect.

(e)   The notice shall have effect from the time at which it would have arrived in normal circumstances.

(f)   A notice has no effect if a withdrawal of it reaches the addressee before or at the same time as the notice.

1.5.2.8   Force majeure

A force majeure clause is intended to suspend or terminate the contractual obligations in the event of an occurrence outside the control of the parties (eg fire, flood, storm etc). A force majeure clause is usually for the benefit of the seller or deliverer of the goods, as it is the party obliged to supply and/or deliver the goods.

If one or more of the specified events occurs then contractual performance will be suspended for a specified period. If the event is still continuing at the end of that period then the contract will be considered to be terminated. Whether one or both parties will have the right to terminate the contract will depend on the bargaining strength of the parties.

The force majeure events must be defined in the contract. The list of events can cause some discussion. The usual ones are so-called Acts of God, adverse weather such as floods or snow, war, riot, government action, embargoes or strikes by third parties and, in light of coronavirus, epidemics and pandemics.

The effectiveness of force majeure clauses will be discussed in **Chapter 9**.

1.5.2.9   'No partnership' clauses

This type of clause seeks to ensure that the agreement cannot be construed as a partnership between the parties to the agreement. There are obvious disadvantages to partnership law, such as being liable for a partner's debts. However, the factor that determines whether or not a partnership is in existence is the definition of 'partnership' in the Partnership Act 1890, s 1, not the wording of a 'no partnership' clause.

1.5.2.10   'No assignment, no subcontracting' clauses

If a buyer has selected a specific supplier, it will not want that supplier to subcontract the work to an unknown third party. Similarly, the buyer may not want the contract to be assigned to another supplier. Thus, a clause to cover both these possibilities is often included in commercial contracts.

The Business Contracts Terms (Assignment of Receivables) Regulations 2018 (SI 2018/1254) now invalidate restrictions on the assignment of 'receivables' in contracts for the supply of goods, services or intangible assets. A receivable is the right to be paid under such a contract.

The purpose of the Regulations is to make it easier for businesses to raise finance by, for example, factoring (see **4.7.7**).

1.5.2.11   Dispute resolution

Particularly where there is a long-term supply contract, a dispute resolution clause may be included in the contract. These are sometimes called 'midnight clauses', as they tend to be the last clauses negotiated between the parties, often as an afterthought, without careful thought to the drafting. A poorly drafted clause can have costly implications for the parties. Traditionally, the options for dispute resolution were litigation or arbitration, both of which are expensive for the parties. However, more and more parties are using combined or multi-tiered clauses, which provide for negotiation, then mediation and finally arbitration or litigation. This provides a structure for the parties to follow in the event of a dispute, enabling the parties to avoid the time and expense involved in arguing about dispute procedure, or being left with no option but to resort to litigation. A well drafted clause can also help to maintain a good commercial relationship between the parties.

1.5.2.12   Severance

Some agreements may include a severance clause purporting to allow the court to strike out any clause or part of a clause which is for some reason illegal or invalid. The purpose of the clause is to ensure that once the offending provisions have been severed, the remainder of the agreement will be enforceable.

Severance clauses are sometimes said to be of limited value. It is important to realise that the courts will not use severance to rewrite the contract or alter its basic nature. The court will ignore the clause if the offending provisions go to the root of the contract. On the other hand, the court has the power to sever a clause, whether or not a severance clause is included in the agreement.

1.5.2.13   Termination

Where there is a long-term supply contract, it is important to think carefully about the duration of the contract and termination provisions. It is surprising in practice that parties do forget to include these provisions – and no-one notices until something goes wrong, when they discover that there is no way to get out of the contract. If the contract is for an indefinite duration, the contract will normally provide for a termination period on notice and list events, for example material breach, that would entitle one or other of the parties to terminate, and also provide for the consequences of termination.

Note that under the Corporate Insolvency and Governance Act 2020, a term providing for automatic termination as the result of the buyer's insolvency will be invalid (see **1.5.2.5**).

1.5.3   Schedules

Schedules are a way of removing unnecessary detail from the body of an agreement and thereby improving its readability. In a large agreement, representations and warranties would also be removed to the schedules. Schedules can also be used to annex other documents to the contract.

SUMMARY

We have considered the role of a commercial lawyer, the concerns of commercial sellers supplying goods to the ultimate consumer, and the main terms and provisions in standard terms and conditions of sale.

We are now going to look at some of the international conventions that govern commercial contracts.

CHAPTER 2

INTERNATIONAL ASPECTS OF COMMERCIAL CONTRACTS

LEARNING OUTCOMES

After reading this chapter you will be able to:

- locate sources of commercial law internationally
- appreciate the main differences between common law and civil jurisdictions.

2.1 INTRODUCTION

This chapter introduces some of the main principles of commercial law internationally, and highlights the main differences between civil and common law legal systems.

In **Chapter 1**, you considered the main sources of commercial law in the UK. Internationally, commercial law is governed by important treaties and conventions.

2.2 INTERNATIONAL CONVENTIONS AND AGREEMENTS

2.2.1 Background

It is widely accepted by developing and developed countries that trade creates wealth and is essential to the economic health of the world.

When world trade began to expand dramatically in the 1960s, national governments began to realise the need for a global set of standards and rules to harmonise and modernise the worldwide assortment of national and regional regulations which, until then, largely governed international trade.

2.2.1.1 UNCITRAL

In 1966 the United Nations, recognising the need for it to play a more active role in removing legal obstacles to the flow of international trade, established the United Nations Commission on International Trade Law (UNCITRAL). UNCITRAL has since become the core legal body of the United Nations system in the field of international trade law.

Much of the complex network of international legal rules and agreements that affects today's commercial arrangements has been reached through long and detailed consultations and negotiations organised by UNCITRAL. As well as the removal of legal obstacles to the flow of international trade, its aim is to progressively modernise and harmonise trade laws. It also seeks to coordinate the work of organisations active in this type of work and promote wider acceptance and use of the rules and legal texts it develops.

Over nearly 40 years, UNCITRAL has completed major international texts on sale of goods, transport, dispute resolution, procurement and infrastructure development, international payments, e-commerce and insolvency. International arbitration, transport law, e-commerce, insolvency law, security interests and public procurement are the focus of current work.

The most significant international convention produced by UNCITRAL is the United Nations Convention on Contracts for the International Sale of Goods (the 'Vienna Convention' or CISG) (see **2.2.3**). It forms part of the domestic law of the nations which have signed up to the Convention, and governs the sale of goods internationally.

2.2.1.2   UNIDROIT

The International Institute for the Unification of Private Law, also known as UNIDROIT, is an independent intergovernmental organisation. The current Institute was established in 1940, on the basis of a multinational agreement, the UNIDROIT Statute, to which its members must accede. It currently has 63 Member States from five continents, including the UK and the US.

Its purpose is to study needs and methods for modernising and harmonising private international law and in particular commercial law between States, and to draft international conventions to address the needs. The first edition of the UNIDROIT Principles of International Commercial Contracts (PICC), intended to harmonise international commercial contracts law, was produced in 1994 (see **2.2.4**). The PICC were most recently updated in 2016. They are a set of voluntary principles, which the parties can choose to incorporate into an international commercial contract. They have the widest geographical scope of all the instruments we shall look at, in that they are intended to apply to commercial contracts globally.

2.2.1.3   Role of the EU

In Europe, there has been great interest in developing a common European civil and commercial law. The European Commission has long maintained that the diversity of legal systems within the European Union is discouraging businesses from making sales across borders and proposed to remedy this by the introduction of a Europe-wide law of contract.

Following a resolution of the European Parliament in 1989, the Commission on European Contract Law, better known as the Lando Commission, was set up. It was an independent body of experts from each of the then 12 Member States of the European Union, and produced a general contract code: the Principles of European Contract Law (PECL) (see **2.2.5**). Parts I and II were published in 1999 and Part III in 2003. Again, these are voluntary principles, which the parties can incorporate into the contract if they wish. They are primarily intended to provide general rules of contract within the EU.

However, following considerable opposition, a proposal for a Common European Sales Law (CESL) was withdrawn by the European Commission in December 2014 and replaced as part of the EU Digital Single Market (DSM) strategy, adopted on 6 May 2015. Based on three 'pillars' – 'access', 'environment' and 'economy and society' – it aims to provide better access to online activities for individuals and businesses under conditions of fair competition, thus maximising the growth potential of the digital economy within the EU. It is, in effect, a series of wide-ranging legislative proposals, many of which have now been either agreed or implemented by the Parliament of the EU, the Council of the EU and the European Commission.

Importantly, in April 2019, the Council adopted two directives: the Digital Content Directive (2019/770/EU) and the Sale of Goods Directive (2019/771/EU) (see **8.2.2.2**). Both directives are aimed at fully harmonising key aspects of the sale of digital content and goods across the EU. Member States were required to transpose these directives into national law and apply them by 1 January 2022.

More recently, the Commission proposed two further pieces of legislation designed to upgrade the rules covering digital services in the EU: the Digital Markets Act (DMA) and the

Digital Services Act (DSA). The DMA has now been approved by the European Parliament and the Council of Ministers. The DSA, with some significant amendments, has been approved by the Parliament but, at the time of writing, awaits approval by the Council.

Closely aligned to this is the 'New Deal for Consumers' initiative, which the Council adopted in 2018. This is aimed at strengthening consumer rights online and giving consumers more effective means of enforcement. This has resulted in the Enforcement and Modernisation Directive (2019/2161/EU) (see **8.10.2.2**).

Post-Brexit, the UK no longer participates in the DSM, but UK businesses trading within the EU will remain subject to its regulations.

2.2.1.4 Uniform laws in the US

In the US, both the federal government and the individual states have the power to pass statutes. In addition, there are some areas of law which are still governed by the common law. Particularly in the field of commerce, it is desirable that there should be uniformity of law on particular subjects, which is applicable in all states. As a result, in 1892, the National Conference of Commissioners on Uniform State Laws (NCUSL), a body of lawyers chosen by the states, was formed. It oversees the preparation of proposed 'uniform laws', which all the US states are encouraged to adopt. Since its formation, it has produced over 200 uniform laws, one of the best known of which is the Uniform Commercial Code (UCC), first published in 1952.

Once a uniform law is drawn up, it is not a law as such. It is simply a legislative proposal addressed to the states, which they can adopt in whole or in part, or with specific amendments. Once enacted by a state, it is codified into that state's code of statutes. The versions that the various states adopt are not necessarily identical. For example, although Louisiana has adopted parts of the UCC, it did not adopt it all (eg Article 2, which you will consider below, is not included in Louisiana state law).

Where an area of the law is governed by common law, the American Law Institute has produced 'Restatements'. These are codifications or restatements of the law in that area, eg the Restatement (Second) of the Law of Contract intended to 'codify, simplify and unify' the common law in relation to contract.

2.2.1.5 'Lex mercatoria'

The *lex mercatoria* stems from the medieval 'law merchant', the body of commercial law which evolved through custom and trade usage and was used by European merchants throughout Europe in the Middle Ages, but which was gradually subsumed as the legal systems of States were codified and nationalised. As trade has evolved, however, it has been recognised that there is a need for a transnational law, consisting of a common code of rules and principles which would provide a common frame of reference for negotiations or when disputes arose between commercial parties from different legal backgrounds. This provides a more flexible and workable system than adapting national laws for international transactions.

At its very simplest, the modern *lex mercatoria* can seen as a growing body of 'spontaneous' law which has evolved from the customs, practices and trade usages of international trade, and which integrates the principles, conventions and institutions which are common to States involved in international trade. It is a transnational uniform law without a state, which parties can choose to use to govern international transactions and disputes.

Where the parties to a contract choose the *lex mercatoria* to govern a dispute, and the rules which are common to States involved in international trade are not easily identifiable, the arbitrator will consider the law of different legal systems and find that which they consider most appropriate to settle that dispute fairly. These decisions are then integrated into the *lex mercatoria*.

You should be aware that despite the *lex mercatoria* having very distinguished proponents, for example Professor Ole Lando, who chaired the Lando Commission (see **2.2.1.3**), there is still much academic debate as to whether there is a sufficiently identifiable and developed body of international law which is capable of being applied to complex international transactions, with lawyers particularly from common law systems arguing against the concept, for example Lord Mustill, a former Appeal Court judge. This debate is outside the scope of this book. However, in practical terms, the somewhat nebulous nature of the *lex mercatoria* means that there can be some uncertainty as a result of the parties choosing it to govern their contracts. This is addressed to an extent by the PICC and the PECL (see **2.2.3.1** and **2.2.4.1**).

2.2.2 United Nations Convention on Contracts for the International Sale of Goods (CISG)

The CISG, adopted by a diplomatic conference on 11 April 1980, is a multinational accord which establishes a comprehensive set of civil code provisions, applicable to transactions for the sale of goods in international commerce. As of April 2021, the United States and 93 other nations in Europe, Asia, Africa and Latin America have ratified and implemented the CISG. However, the United Kingdom is not a party.

2.2.2.1 When does the CISG apply?

The effect of Article 1 of the CISG is that it will apply if:

(a) the contract is for the sale of goods (commercial rather than personal); and

(b) both parties are in different Contracting States; or

(c) the parties have agreed that their contract will be subject to the law of a Contracting State; or

(d) the parties agree that the CISG will govern their contract; or

(e) the court of a country where a dispute has broken out finds that the applicable law is the law of a Contracting State; and

(f) the parties have not opted out of the CISG.

The nationality or residence of the parties is not relevant.

The following are examples of when the CISG might apply. Assume in each case that the parties have not opted out of the Convention.

EXAMPLE 1

The parties to a sale of goods contract have places of business in Austria and Germany respectively. Both parties have places of business in different Contracting States, so the CISG will apply.

EXAMPLE 2

The parties to a sale of goods contract have places of business in Austria and the UK respectively. The parties have agreed that Austrian law will govern the contract. Although the UK is not a Contracting State, the CISG will apply.

EXAMPLE 3

The parties to a sale of goods contract have places of business in Austria and the UK respectively, and the contract does not contain a choice of law clause. Prima facie, the CISG will not apply as the UK is not a Contracting State and the parties have not chosen the law of a Contracting State.

> However, a dispute has broken out, and proceedings are commenced in the French courts. If the French court, applying its own private international law (the Rome I Regulation) finds that Austrian law is the law applicable to the contract, the CISG will apply. However, if the French court finds that the applicable law is English law, the CISG will not apply, as the UK is not a Contracting State. (For the rules on applicable law under the Rome I Regulation, see **Chapter 14**.)

2.2.2.2 What does the CISG cover?

If applicable to a given transaction, the CISG supplies default, or 'gap filling', rules that govern sale of goods contracts, including:

(a) contract formation;

(b) rights of the buyer and seller;

(c) obligations of the buyer and seller;

(d) passing of risk;

(e) remedies.

Unlike the PICC and PECL, it does not deal with issues such as mistake, misrepresentation or agency.

The CISG recognises the principle of contractual autonomy and provides that express contractual provisions take precedence over the default provisions of the Convention. Thus, contracting parties remain free to specify whatever law or terms they wish to apply to their transaction, and may exclude altogether the application of the CISG to their contractual relationship (Article 6).

2.2.2.3 Trade usage

The rules of the CISG operate in conjunction with international trade usages. The purpose of the CISG is not only to create new, State-sanctioned law, but also to give recognition to the rules born of commercial practice and to encourage national courts to apply them.

Accepted trade usages constitute the major part of *lex mercatoria*. It has long been recognised that these usages in fact have a greater impact on international contracts than domestic laws. The CISG acknowledges unequivocally the paramount importance of usages as a source of law for transactions. Article 9 deals with the question of usages, providing that the parties are bound by any usage to which they have agreed or established between themselves, and by established usages about which they knew or ought to have known.

2.2.3 The UNIDROIT Principles of International Commercial Contracts (PICC)

The most recent edition of the PICC is the 2016 edition, which is a set of non-binding, 'soft' laws that contain a set of rules applicable in international commercial contracts. The objective of the PICC is to establish a balanced set of rules designed for use throughout the world irrespective of the legal traditions, and the economic and political conditions of the countries in which they are to be applied.

2.2.3.17 When do the PICC apply?

It should be noted that, unlike the CISG, which only applies to contracts for the sale of goods, the PICC are applicable to any commercial contract.

The Preamble to the PICC states that they:

(a) *will* apply to an international commercial contract when the parties have incorporated them;

(b) *may* apply to an international commercial contract when the parties have agreed that the contract be governed by general principles of law, the *lex mercatoria*, or 'the like', or if the parties have not chosen any law to govern their contract;

(c)   may also be used to interpret or supplement other international law instruments or domestic law.

The PICC can be used to interpret or fill gaps where either there is uncertainty arising as a result of the parties choosing, eg, the *lex mercatoria*, or where the domestic or other international law does not provide a solution.

As the Principles can be incorporated for different purposes, in 2013, UNIDROIT adopted new model clauses which can be incorporated into the contract to show more precisely how the parties wish the Principles to be used, for example Model Clause 1 is used where the parties wish to choose the Principles as the rules of law governing the contract, and Model Clause 2 is for use where the parties choose the Principles as the terms of the contract.

2.2.3.2   What do the PICC cover?

The PICC cover issues such as contract formation, authority of agents, validity (including illegality), interpretation, contents, performance, non-performance (breach) and remedies, set-off, assignment and plurality of parties.

They have wide application and, as a result, lack the specific terms which the CISG contains on specific sales issues, such as delivery and quality of goods. For example, the parties under the Principles are only obliged to 'render a performance of a quality that is reasonable and not less than average in the circumstances' (Article 5.1.6).

2.2.4   The Principles of European Contract Law (PECL)

Like the PICC, the PECL are non-binding, 'soft' laws. As we have seen, the object of the PECL is the harmonisation of European contract law, so in that respect they are narrower than the PICC. In other respects, the PECL are wider, in that they apply to any contract, not just commercial contracts.

2.2.4.1   When do the PECL apply?

Article 1:101 is similar to the Preamble to the PICC, and states that the PECL are intended to be applied as general rules of contract law in the European Union, and they:

(a)   will apply if the parties have agreed to incorporate them;

(b)   may apply when the parties have agreed that the contract be governed by general principles of law, the *lex mercatoria*, or 'the like', or if the parties have not chosen any law to govern their contract;

(c)   may also be used as a 'solution to the issue raised' where the applicable law does not provide one.

Like the PICC, the PECL therefore fulfil a 'gap filling' role, where the parties have not provided for certain eventualities in the contract.

2.2.4.2   What do the PECL cover?

The PECL are similar in structure and content to the PICC, and contain some identical provisions:

(a)   Parts I and II of the PECL cover the rules of contract formation, authority of agents, validity (including mistake and 'incorrect information'), interpretation, contents, performance, non-performance (breach) and remedies.

(b)   Part III covers plurality of parties, assignment of claims, substitution of new debt, transfer of contract, set-off, prescription, illegality, conditions and capitalisation of interest.

Although, again, the PECL have wide application, they also lack specific terms in relation to issues such as delivery and quality, eg under Article 6:108 performance must be 'of an average quality'.

2.2.5   The Uniform Commercial Code (UCC)

As we have seen, the UCC is one of the uniform acts that has been promulgated in the US in an attempt to harmonise the law of sales and other commercial transactions in all 50 states. It has eleven Articles covering many important types of commercial transactions, for example sales, leases, bank deposits, fund transfers and securities. Article 2 contains the provisions in relation to sales of goods.

The Code has been adopted (in one form or another) in all US states, and so whilst there may be minor variations from state to state, eg on sales laws, there is a great degree of consistency.

2.2.5.1   When does the UCC apply?

It may be relevant in an international contract if the parties either:

(a)   choose to incorporate it; or

(b)   choose the law of a US state as the law of the contract.

2.2.5.2   What does the UCC cover?

Article 2 is divided into seven sections dealing with, broadly:

(a)   scope and definitions;

(b)   form, formation and variation of the contract, including assignment;

(c)   obligations and construction, including delivery and quality;

(d)   title, including retention of title;

(e)   performance;

(f)   breach and repudiation;

(g)   remedies.

Both the UCC (in Article 2) and the CISG deal specifically with agreements for the sale of goods, and as a result share certain similarities. However, the UCC's conceptual scope is broader. In addition, it is more precise. For example, when specifying the obligations of the parties, there are implied warranties in relation to merchantability (Section 2-314) and fitness for purpose (Section 2-315).

All references to the UCC will be to Article 2 unless otherwise stated.

2.3   CIVIL LAW AND COMMON LAW

In dealing with international commercial transactions, it should be appreciated that legal jurisdictions may be classified as either civil law or common law jurisdictions. Whilst the fundamental aspects of the two jurisdictions are not poles apart, they each have characteristics with which a commercial lawyer must be familiar.

A further complication for UK-based lawyers is that, whilst their jurisdiction is a common law one, where their clients are trading within the EU (a jurisdiction which bears most similarities to civil law jurisdictions) they must have a working knowledge of how civil law systems operate. Even post-Brexit, EU law will continue to have a significant influence. Equally, lawyers from civil law jurisdictions who are involved in international trade must be familiar with how common law systems work, as many international transactions are governed by UK or American law (another common law jurisdiction).

Civil law countries – eg many European countries such as France, Belgium, Luxembourg, Spain, Italy, Germany and Switzerland, most Arab countries, former French Indo-China, Latin and South America, Russia, Japan, Turkey, South Korea, China, South Africa and Sri Lanka. In North America and Canada, Louisiana and Quebec have civil law systems. Note that the similarities between the civil laws used by these countries vary.

Common law countries – eg England and Wales and former British colonies, eg USA (except for Louisiana), Canada (except for Quebec), Australia, New Zealand, India, Pakistan, Ireland, some African countries, Hong Kong, Cayman Islands and Gibraltar.

2.3.1 Characteristics of civil law jurisdictions

Civil laws are intended to be accessible to the people. They are therefore often simply drafted and contain general statements. Detailed regulation is left to governmental regulations and decrees. Interpretation is on the basis of general principles and the purposive intent of the legislature, rather than in a dissection of the precise wording. For example, in the Treaty on the Functioning of the European Union, there is an article which says there must be freedom of movement of workers from State to State. How this is achieved is left to secondary legislation and interpretation by the courts.

The interpretative approach applied to legislation applies also to contracts. As judges have the freedom to interpret a contract in a way which makes it effective, there is less temptation to cover every single detail when drafting it. In addition, an overriding principle of good faith in the formation and performance of contracts (see **2.3.6** below) and other civil law concepts makes the way in which contracts work legally very different to common law jurisdictions.

There is rarely a system of precedent in civil law jurisdictions, and so judges can make decisions without having to take into account the impact on later decisions and are more able to decide cases on their merits. This arguably leads to a greater degree of inconsistency in decision-making, but perhaps also leads to decisions which are more tailored to the particular situation.

A further characteristic of civil law cases is that the judgments are short, without lengthy reasoning. This means that the interpretation put on them by academic writers is of greater importance than in common law jurisdictions, where the judgment is usually lengthy enough to be clear and not open to a wide variety of meaning.

2.3.2 Characteristics of common law jurisdictions

By contrast, common laws are intended to be self-contained. An Act of Parliament in a common law jurisdiction is intended to tell you everything you need to know about that particular law, in such a detailed way as to leave little freedom of interpretation for judges. Apart from any rights or obligations specifically imposed by statute, the parties can only rely on the content of clauses in the contract. This leads to contracts being very carefully (and lengthily) drafted to accurately reflect exactly what has been agreed.

It is rare for common law jurisdictions to use general principles which guide the direction in which the law goes. Statutes, which are detailed and specific, guide the direction of the law. Perhaps one of the main areas in which overriding general principles are used in common law is in the field of human rights. UK lawyers, for example, have had to get to grips with the fact that UK statutes may be subject to challenge if they offend human rights. It is unusual, however, for other principles to apply, eg contracts having to be fair (although statute imposes this for consumer contracts).

Precedent is an important aspect of common law systems. Courts are typically bound by the decisions of higher courts. Higher courts therefore have to consider that decisions they make may affect thousands of cases taking place in courts below them. Whilst this seems an onerous responsibility, it should be remembered that the specific nature of common law statutes, and also contracts, tends to mean that logic dictates the decision. So judges are more constrained by what the law or the contract specifically says, rather than by what they feel is the correct application of general principles to the situation.

2.3.3 Categorisation of contracts

Civil law systems have essentially three categories of contract: *public law* (regulating relationships between the State and the individual or private bodies), *civil law* (regulating relationships between individuals) and *commercial law* (part of civil law but with separate rules for the relationship between businesses). Common law systems, however, typically see all contracts as within one category (although it should be remembered that there may be specific statutes regulating particular contracts, eg for the sale of goods).

The three categories of contract in civil systems have different rules which apply to them. It is therefore vital to decide which type of contract it is, so that the correct set of rules can be applied. A seemingly small change to a contract may radically change it because, after the change, a different set of rules may apply to the contract as a whole.

2.3.4 Consideration

Common law jurisdictions typically have a requirement of consideration for a contract to exist (see **3.2.3.1**). This is the quid pro quo – you do X and I will do Y. There is no requirement that the quid pro quo be equal – in English law there is the concept of the 'peppercorn', being a virtually valueless consideration but enough for a contract to be created. English law takes the view that it is for the parties to make their bargain and to assess whether a good deal is being obtained. So a court will not challenge whether what either party to the contract is getting out of it is enough.

There is no concept of consideration in civil law systems. In many systems, however, eg French law, a contract has to have a 'cause' in order to exist. A party must have a motive or purpose in entering the contract and what he gets out of it must be realistic. However, in some civil systems, eg Germany, a cause is not necessary, and a contract is valid as long as the parties intend it to be.

2.3.5 Substance or form?

Common law systems tend to favour form over substance. That is, whatever the law specifically says applies, irrespective of overriding principles. So it is common for lawyers to see their task as 'drafting around the law' to ensure their client fits within a loophole, or gains a slightly favourable situation. This, however, does not work in civil systems, where attempts to get around rules will fail for public policy reasons. Whilst a lawyer in a common law jurisdiction may come up with a highly complex way of structuring a deal to make it, for example, tax efficient, a civil lawyer will know that such an attempt is pointless.

Following on from the example given above regarding UK lawyers having to get to grips with civil law concepts in the form of EU law, EU competition rules favour substance over form, so that clever drafting does not help one escape penalties for, eg, anti-competitive behaviour. Interestingly, when the UK revamped its own, form-based competition laws, which could be drafted around, it followed the EU system, and created a substance-based competition statute (the Competition Act 1998), which looks at the nature of what parties have agreed rather than the way the terms are expressed in the contract.

Civil law systems often have rules as to equality and fairness, as general principles. So it may be that a contract is void because of an inequality as to what the parties get from the contract, and sometimes the price agreed must reflect the market value for the goods.

2.3.6 Good faith

2.3.6.1 Civil law systems

A further principle common to civil law systems is that of good faith, in other words an obligation to act reasonably towards the other party to the transaction. This, in particular, affects the length of, and levels of detail in, civil law contracts. As the parties are under a duty to act in good faith, there is less need to 'cover all the bases' in terms of exactly what each party must do to fulfil its obligations. This extends to a principle, often called 'abuse of right', whereby it may be unlawful to insist upon the performance of an obligation to its letter if it would be an undue burden on the other party, for example in circumstances where an event has radically changed the situation. If performance of obligations becomes difficult or impossible, the courts may render the contract void.

As an example of good faith appearing in a civil jurisdiction, in the Dutch Civil Code, good faith overrides not only the wording of a contract, but also the effect of custom and indeed statutes impacting on the contract.

2.3.6.2   Common law systems

Generally, there is no equivalent principle in common law systems. For example, historically, there has been no doctrine of good faith in English contract law. However, there is some evidence from recent cases that the English courts are moving towards recognising the importance of the doctrine of good faith and fair dealing.

(a)   Express duty of good faith

Increasingly, parties are including express duties of good faith in commercial contracts, eg, to act 'with good faith' or 'with the utmost/absolute good faith'. The problem here is that good faith has no generally accepted meaning and so whether or not such a term is enforceable will very much depend on the commercial context and the wording of the contract itself. A duty to perform a specific contractual obligation with good faith is more likely to be upheld than an obligation to perform the contract as a whole in good faith. See, for example, *Mid Essex Hospital Services NHS Trust v Compass Group UK and Ireland (t/a Medirest)* [2013] EWCA Civ 200.

(b)   Implied duty of good faith

The starting point here is that there is no general implied duty of good faith in English contract law. See, for example, *MSC Mediterranean Shipping Company SA v Cottonex Anstalt* [2016] EWCA Civ 789. However, over the last decade, the courts have started to recognise that an implied obligation of good faith may arise in certain limited circumstances. The decision in *Yam Seng Pte (a company registered in Singapore) v International Trade Corporation* [2013] EWHC 111 (QB) established that where there is a 'relational' contract, the courts may be prepared to imply a duty of good faith. What amounts to a relational contract depends on the contract itself and its business context. This issue was considered in *Bates v Post Office Ltd (No 3)* [2019] EWHC 606 (QB). The courts will consider factors such as whether the contract is long term, requires collaboration between the parties and/or involves significant investment.

(c)   The 'Braganza duty'

The 'Braganza duty', or duty of rationality, is an aspect of good faith, so-called after the Supreme Court decision in *Braganza v BP Shipping Ltd* [2015] EWSC 17. It is a now well-established principle, which applies where a contract gives a party a contractual discretion which will affect both parties to the contract. In the absence of agreement to the contrary, it is recognised that the parties have a duty to exercise the contractual discretion rationally, in good faith and not capriciously or arbitrarily.

The conclusion seems to be that an obligation of good faith may be implied in particular circumstances, but it will not be implied as a general rule, and if the parties want ensure that such an obligation is included in an English contract, it should be clearly stated.

2.3.6.3   International conventions and treaties

All the international private law instruments that we have looked at make reference to good faith, which is, however, not defined in any of these instruments:

(a)   CISG. There is no positive obligation of good faith imposed on the parties. However, Article 7 provides that in its interpretation, regard is to be had to the observance of good faith in international trade.

(b)   PICC. Article 1.7 states that the parties must act in accordance with good faith and fair dealing, and cannot contract out of this obligation.

(c)   PECL. Article 1:201 again states that the parties must act in accordance with good faith and fair dealing and cannot exclude or limit the duty.

(d)   UCC. Although the USA is a common law jurisdiction, Section 1-302 of the UCC refers to the parties' obligation of good faith, and they cannot contract out of this. However, the parties are able to set good faith standards amongst themselves unless such standards are manifestly unreasonable.

So as a rule of thumb, in a common law jurisdiction, it is more likely that in a contract between commercial parties, the law will allow them to make their own provisions (subject to any specific statutes), whereas, in a civil law jurisdiction, there is more chance that general principles will override certain aspects of what the parties have agreed.

2.4   THE HIERARCHY OF INTERNATIONAL COMMERCIAL LAWS

Many different types of laws have been mentioned in this chapter. The question which arises is which prevails in the event of conflict? As a general rule, the order to follow is:

(1)   Look to fundamental basic principles. In common law jurisdictions, these may be few, but they are likely to be more prevalent in civil jurisdictions, such as the duty of good faith.

(2)   Look for international treaties of a *mandatory* nature. This type of law may be limited to contracts between parties in Contracting States. These are few but can be significant, eg the Treaty on the Functioning of the European Union.

(3)   Look to domestic laws covering the specific type of situation in question. For example, in the UK, the Sale of Goods Act 1979 covers domestic sales. For an international sale, check which country's laws have been chosen to cover the contract. Within this third category are international treaties which make Contracting States change their domestic legislation in order to comply with their obligations. For example, within Europe, the content of many domestic statutes is dictated by the content of EU directives, which Member States have an obligation to implement.

(4)   Look for customs or practices in that particular area of law.

(5)   Look for treaty rules of an *optional* nature, which the parties may have chosen to adopt (or not to opt out of). An example would be the CISG, which can be excluded if the parties wish.

(6)   Look for general principles (to be distinguished from fundamental principles mentioned above). These will not override what the parties have agreed, but may guide the court in interpreting what has been agreed. An example would be the common law notion of *contra proferentem*, whereby a clause limiting a seller's liability would be construed, in cases of doubt, against the seller.

SUMMARY

We have considered some important aspects and issues in relation to international commercial contracts, and we are now going to look at some basic principles of UK contract law and their application to commercial contracts. Where there are important issues which are likely to arise in practice, we will compare how the various international instruments studied in this chapter deal with these.

CHAPTER 3

NEGOTIATION, CONTRACT FORMATION AND POST-CONTRACTUAL CONSIDERATIONS

LEARNING OUTCOMES

After reading this chapter you will be able to:

- describe the phases in the lifespan of a commercial contract
- recognise the issues that affect the negotiation phase of a contract
- identify whether a contract has been formed validly
- explain circumstances which may prevent performance of a contract
- summarise the main rules relating to interpretation of contract terms
- identify when a contract has been discharged.

3.1 INTRODUCTION

From the list of sources of law in **1.2** above, it is clear that a basic understanding of the law of contract is essential for a commercial lawyer. In addition, where sales of goods are involved, s 62(2) of the Sale of Goods Act 1979 (SGA 1979) states:

> The rules of common law, including the law merchant, except in so far as they are inconsistent with the provisions of this Act, and in particular the rules relating to the law of principal and agent and the effect of fraud, misrepresentation, duress or coercion, mistake, or other invalidating cause, apply to contracts for the sale of goods.

This chapter considers the underlying principles of contract law as they affect a contract from the negotiation stage to the conclusion and discharge of the contract. The 'lifespan' of a contract can be broken down into distinct phases:

(a) negotiation;

(b) entry into the contract;

(c) performance;

(d) discharge.

Although the focus of this chapter will be on the principles of UK contract law, for the purposes of comparison you will also consider how some of the issues that arise are dealt with by the international instruments that you looked at in **Chapter 2**.

Each phase raises different issues and problems, as illustrated in **Figure 3.1** below.

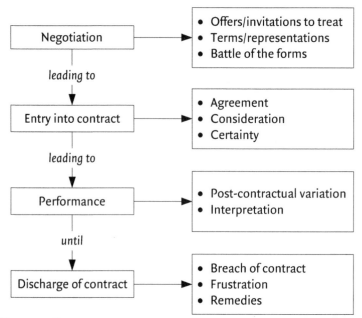

Figure 3.1 The 'lifespan' of a contract

3.2 UK CONTRACT PRINCIPLES

3.2.1 Formation of the contract

Before there can be a contract, one party (the offeror) must make an identifiable offer on certain terms, showing intention to be bound, and the other party (the offeree) must accept those terms unconditionally, ie, the terms of the acceptance must be a 'mirror image' of the offer. This agreement must be supported by consideration, and there must be intention to be legally bound by the terms of the contract. At that point the contract comes into existence. Where the contract is in writing and signed by the parties, it will be obvious when this occurs. However, it may not always be clear exactly when the contract was made, especially if the parties did not sign any form of written document.

3.2.2 The negotiation phase

In all but the simplest of commercial contracts, the entry into the contract will be preceded by a period of negotiation, either oral or written. The length and complexity of the negotiations (and the resulting documentation) will depend on a number of factors, for example whether this is the first time the parties have dealt with each other, the subject matter of the contract, and whether or not the parties are using standard terms and conditions. In a simple sale of goods contract, the only negotiations may be a discussion of the quantity and the price, but in many contracts the negotiations will be more complex. However long or short the negotiations, some of the same issues and problems can arise.

Where several offers have been made and refused, or met with counter-offers, it can be difficult to decide exactly when the parties have moved from negotiation to conclusion of the contract and whether or not unwanted terms have been 'accidentally' included in the contract. All documentation should be carefully monitored throughout the negotiating process to prevent this from happening. Factors to consider include the following.

3.2.2.1 Offers

An offer must be distinguished from an invitation to treat, where there is no intention to be legally bound. Generally, the following will not be offers:

(a) advertisements;

(b)   estimates;

(c)   brochures;

(d)   price lists;

(e)   enquiries or requests for information;

(f)   letters of intent/heads of terms/memoranda of understanding (these are documents which outline the terms on which the parties intend to contract with each other in the future).

However, these are general rules, and whether a communication is an offer or an invitation to treat will always depend on the facts of each case. Particular issues can arise, for example, with letters of intent/heads of terms. If the intended terms of the contract are set out in too much detail or, in a goods and services contract, include requests for work to commence, then they may be construed as an offer.

In practice, the words 'subject to contract' indicate that the parties do not intend to be bound by the terms of any informal agreement or pre-contractual negotiations, and this qualification will usually rebut the usual presumption that, in commercial contracts, the parties do intend to be legally bound. However, the courts will look at the conduct of the parties during negotiations, so, to be absolutely certain, the parties should also include an express statement to the effect that they do not intend to be legally bound.

Throughout the negotiation process, it is important to ensure that any offer remains on the table. An offer can be ended by rejection, counter-offer, lapse of time, death of the other party or by revocation before it has been accepted. If any of these has occurred, then there will be no offer capable of acceptance.

3.2.2.2   Terms and representations

Pre-contractual statements can cause difficulties between the parties, particularly if they subsequently turn out to be untrue. There are three types of pre-contractual statement:

(a)   terms;

(b)   representations; and

(c)   mere advertising puff.

The last will never have an effect on the contract, but the first two may. It is important to distinguish between terms and representations, as the remedies where problems arise are different for each.

A pre-contractual statement which amounts to a term will form part of the contract, and breach will give the injured party the usual contractual remedies, including the right to terminate the contract and sue for damages as of right, depending on the status of the term. To decide whether a statement amounts to a term or not, the courts will look at the common intention of the parties and, in the absence of clear intent, will apply various guidelines, looking at, for example, the importance of the statement to the contract and the skill and knowledge of the party making it.

Not all pre-contractual statements made during negotiations will end up as terms of the contract: some may be representations. A representation is a statement of fact made by one party to the contract to the other which induces the contract (although it need not be the sole inducement). If it turns out to be untrue it will be a misrepresentation. There are three types of misrepresentation: fraudulent, negligent and innocent. The primary remedy for misrepresentation is rescission, although it may be possible to claim damages under s 2(1) of the Misrepresentation Act 1967. However, if the maker of the statement can show that he honestly believed that the statement was true at the time that it was made, and that he had reasonable grounds for that belief, then the innocent party may lose his right to damages. The right to rescission may be lost where one of the equitable bars, such as delay or affirmation, applies.

Depending on its bargaining strength, the buyer may insist that any pre-contractual representations form part of the express terms of the contract, and they may be included as warranties (see **1.5.1.4**). A warranty is a promise given by one or other party to the contract that a given statement or set of facts is true, for example that a business makes a specified annual profit. In the event of a breach, the buyer would then be entitled to contractual damages as of right. The only time when a claim for damages for misrepresentation may be appropriate is if there is a problem with remoteness (see **3.2.6.3**). However the parties describe them, the test as to whether a statement is a term or a representation is objective.

3.2.2.3   Battle of the forms

Where both parties seek to impose their own terms on the other, it may not be clear whose standard terms apply. A battle of the forms may occur, for example where the seller provides the buyer with an invitation to treat, containing the seller's standard terms and conditions, and the buyer then makes an offer, introducing his own terms. If the seller does not accept the buyer's terms, and insists instead on reinstating its own terms, the seller has made a counter-offer. Another possibility is that the seller makes the original offer, which the buyer purports to 'accept' but with the introduction of new terms, thereby itself making a counter-offer.

If the contract is dealt with by the seller's sales representatives or untrained administrative staff, who may not be aware of the rules relating to offer and acceptance, there is always a possibility that the wrong set of terms may be accepted by accident. The offer may be accepted by the conduct of the parties, eg by the seller delivering the goods or the buyer accepting delivery. In *Butler Machine Tool Co Ltd v Ex-Cell-O Corporation (England) Ltd* [1979] 1 WLR 401, CA, the return of a signed acknowledgement slip amounted to acceptance of the buyer's terms. Where negotiations are protracted, there may be several sets of terms and conditions put forward. In the event of a dispute, the court will consider whose terms and conditions were on the table at the time of acceptance, and apply 'the last shot wins' doctrine. In *Tekdata Interconnections Ltd v Amphenol Ltd* [2009] EWCA Civ 1209 the Court of Appeal confirmed that the courts should use the traditional offer and acceptance analysis to decide on a battle of forms dispute, rather the relationship and conduct of the parties.

3.2.2.4   Prevention

As discussed in **1.5.2**, the parties may attempt to keep out extraneous terms, eg statements by sales representatives in relation to the goods which may amount to terms of the contract. The problem is that these attempts are not always effective.

Prevail clauses

A prevail clause provides in effect that if there is a battle of the forms then the seller's terms will prevail. Legally, the clause is ineffective, as any later set of terms which is introduced will act as a counter-offer and override an earlier set. However, a prevail clause is often included for bluff value.

Entire or whole agreement clauses

The seller may include an 'entire' or 'whole agreement' clause. This is intended to prevent any statements made by sales representatives, or statements included in sales literature, brochures and the like, forming terms of the contract. The clause will state that the seller's terms and conditions form the whole agreement between the seller and the buyer and cannot be varied in any way. It will also usually include a statement that no other express terms, written or oral, shall be included as part of the contract, thus avoiding the evidential difficulties associated with oral representations and discussions.

In the absence of a whole agreement clause, the parties would have to rely on the parol evidence rule which provides that outside, or extrinsic, evidence should not be adduced to vary the written contract. However, it may be possible for a contract to be part written and part oral, if this is what the parties intended. A whole agreement clause avoids oral terms being included in the contract.

Although the inclusion of an entire agreement clause may solve the problem of extrinsic evidence, as far as the battle of the forms is concerned, it is open to the same objections as a prevail clause. If the buyer makes an offer or counter-offer on different terms, this clause will be destroyed along with all the seller's other terms.

A further danger of a whole agreement clause is that it might exclude other documents which the parties do wish to have taken into account, for example a price list.

Where the clause attempts also to exclude liability for misrepresentation, it can also be seen as an exclusion clause. To be effective, the wording must be clear, and it must be reasonable under s 3 of the Misrepresentation Act 1967. In *Thomas Witter v TBP Industries* [1996] 2 All ER 573, such a clause was held to have excluded liability for fraudulent misrepresentation and was therefore void. One way around this is for the clause also to include a statement of non-reliance, with an express carve-out for fraudulent misrepresentation. However, in *HIH Casualty and General Insurance Ltd and Others v Chase Manhattan Bank and Others* [2003] UKHL 6, the House of Lords made it clear that an express carve-out for fraudulent misrepresentation was not necessary, as in the absence of words referring directly to dishonesty, there is an assumption that the parties will behave honestly.

In *First Tower Trustees v CDS Superstores Ltd* [2018] EWCA Civ 1396, the Court of Appeal confirmed that a non-reliance clause generally acts as an exclusion of liability for misrepresentation and is subject to reasonableness.

'No authority' clauses

These are attempts by the seller:

(a) to put a limit on the extent to which its sales representatives, or other employees, are permitted to negotiate individual terms with the buyer; and

(b) to exclude any extravagant claims made by the sales representatives to induce the buyer to enter into the contract.

To some extent there is an overlap with whole agreement clauses, and they are subject to the same difficulties.

Importance of staff training

The best way to avoid a battle of the forms problem is to ensure that all staff are effectively trained so that they know what they may and may not say in negotiations. Administrative staff should be warned not to send anything to the other side which could be interpreted as acceptance of an offer, without referring the matter on to managers or higher authority.

3.2.3 Entry into the contract

The essence of a contract, therefore, is that there should be valid agreement between the parties. All parties must have been agreeing to the same thing, and must not have been talking at cross-purposes. The existence, or otherwise, of agreement is judged objectively. We have already seen that there must be a genuine offer, as opposed to an invitation to treat, which has been accepted in its entirety. Usually, an identifiable offer and acceptance have to be made and communicated to the other party and, generally, actual communication is needed. However, a contract can come into existence by means of performance, although this must be clear from the conduct of the parties.

3.2.3.1 Consideration

In many jurisdictions (particularly common law jurisdictions), there has to be consideration for the contract (or, in some jurisdictions, it has to be drafted as a deed). The courts will not look at the value of the consideration (this is not the case in some civil law jurisdictions). The consideration in a commercial contract will usually be money, goods or services, or the promise of these. However, some types of act or promise are not regarded by law as being valid consideration, for example past consideration or performance of an existing duty. In commercial contracts, consideration will not generally be a problem when the contract is entered into, as there is usually the exchange of goods for payment, or the promise of payment of the price. Problems tend to arise when there is a variation of the terms of the contract, which will be dealt with at **3.2.4.1** below.

3.2.3.2   Certainty

One of the key concepts in the law of contract is that there must be contractual certainty, that is the parties must be specific about the terms of the contract. An agreement which fails to address a key area, for example the price, will be void for uncertainty unless it can be saved by using a statutory provision such as s 8 of the SGA 1979 (see **5.2**). The general approach adopted by the courts is that it is the responsibility of the parties to make their agreement, and if they do so incompetently then that is their problem. However, the courts can fix a badly drafted contract if there is other evidence of the intent of the parties which can be used to plug the gaps, or the court may agree to sever an irrelevant or badly drafted clause, provided that the rest of the contract is still commercially workable.

Agreements to agree

The courts will not enforce an 'agreement to agree'. So an agreement to enter into a contract at a later date, or an agreement that a certain provision will be agreed between the parties after the commencement of the contract would be void for uncertainty. These are both fairly obvious examples of uncertainty, but there are provisions where the position is less clear (see, eg, *Courtney & Fairbairn Ltd v Tolaini Bros (Hotels) Ltd* [1975] 1 WLR 297; cf the older case of *Foley v Classique Coaches Ltd* [1934] 2 KB 1, where there was an arbitration clause if the parties could not agree on the price and the contract was upheld).

However, agreements to agree remain a commercial fact of life and, as a result, continue to be litigated, see, for example, *Morris v Swanton Care & Community Ltd* [2018] EWCA Civ 2763. In this case, the Court of Appeal made it clear that there is a distinction between unenforceable agreements where the parties have deferred their agreement on contractual terms and enforceable agreements, where the parties have reached agreement but left gaps which can be resolved by reference to objective criteria which are capable of assessment by the court. Much will depend on the wording used in each specific contract, so it is important for lawyers to draft a contract bearing these distinctions in mind, for example by including a provision for arbitration or the adoption of a specific procedure or formula in the event of disagreement.

Lock-out and lock-in agreements

A lock-out agreement is one in which one party, for example a manufacturer (A), agrees with another, a distributor (B), not to negotiate with anyone other than B. It is essentially a negative promise. From a commercial point of view, if a manufacturer approaches a potential distributor, the distributor may not want to commit to the arrangement until he has carried out some market research to establish whether there is a viable market. In the meantime, he wants to be sure that the manufacturer will not enter into negotiations with anyone else. Such agreements may be enforceable provided that B gives consideration for the promise not to negotiate with anyone else.

A lock-in agreement, where one party agrees to negotiate with another, is different from a lock-out agreement. In a lock-out agreement, A is not obliged to negotiate with B; A simply agrees not to negotiate with anyone else. In a lock-in agreement, there is such an obligation. Such agreements are too uncertain and therefore unenforceable. In *Walford v Miles* [1992] 1 All ER 453, HL, Lord Ackner thought that such agreements would be 'unworkable in practice'.

Cancellation clauses

Both the buyer and the seller might want to have a let-out clause, allowing them to withdraw from the contract without liability in certain circumstances, particularly during periods of economic uncertainty where it may be uneconomic to continue with the contract. The parties may therefore include a cancellation clause in the contract. The content of the clause will depend on the bargaining strength of the parties, but typically a clause may provide that one or other party (often the seller) can cancel in a wide variety of circumstances.

However, if the cancellation clause is too wide, it may have the effect of invalidating the contract altogether, as it may mean that the seller is simply making mere statements of intention to perform but is not, in effect, under any obligation to perform its obligations under the contract.

A further possibility is that the clause will provide that the buyer can cancel only with the seller's written consent and must pay a percentage of the purchase price (eg 10% of the contract price). Here the parties must be careful to ensure that the clause does not amount to a penalty clause or it will be unenforceable.

3.2.3.3 Mistake

A mistake may mean that the parties have failed to reach agreement, because, for example, unknown to the parties, the subject matter of the contract does not exist or has perished. To have an effect on the contract, the mistake must have occurred before the contract was made. In practice, the doctrine of mistake is quite narrow and very few mistakes will affect the validity of a contract, but where they do, the effect is to render the contract void. Innocent third parties may find themselves out of pocket as a result. Note that in the case of sale of goods contracts, where there is a contract for the sale of specific goods, if the goods have perished before the contract is made, s 6 of the SGA 1979 provides that the contract is void and there is no need to rely on the common law doctrine of mistake.

3.2.4 Performance of the contract

3.2.4.1 Post-contractual variation

Once the contract is in existence, it is important that the terms of the contract are not inadvertently varied by sales representatives or other staff. An example would be where the parties have contracted on standard terms and conditions which state that all delivery dates are approximate, thus avoiding liability for late delivery, but, after the contract is entered into, a sales representative agrees that the goods will be delivered on a particular date. There are two problems here: the general principle that any variation of the contract must be supported by consideration and the sales representative's authority to bind the seller.

Where one party agrees to do something over and above the terms of an existing contract, the other party must provide consideration for that promise, either by providing something extra over and above his existing contractual duty, as in *Hartley v Ponsonby* (1857) 7 EB 872, or by conferring a benefit on the promisor, as in *Williams v Roffey Bros* [1990] 1 All ER 512, CA. However, such a promise might be enforceable even though no consideration has been provided for it in the two following situations.

The doctrine of waiver

Where the promise in question is a promise not to enforce the other party's obligations under the contract (ie a negative promise), the courts of equity may give limited effect to the promise. An example would be where a delivery date has been agreed, but the seller finds that he is unable to deliver. Normally the buyer can refuse to accept late delivery, but if the buyer agrees to it, the court will usually decide that the buyer has waived its right to terminate the contract for late delivery.

However, the limit on this exception is that the buyer always has the right to reinstate the original terms by reasonable notice. So if the original delivery date was 22 June, but the buyer has agreed to accept delivery on 31 July, if nothing more is said, the buyer will be unable to refuse delivery on that date. If, however, the buyer contacts the seller in the first week of July and says that he now wants delivery, say within seven days, the seller will have to deliver within that seven-day period or the buyer's right to termination will be reinstated (provided that the seven-day notice period is reasonable in the circumstances).

Promissory estoppel

The doctrine of promissory estoppel applies to promises not to claim sums of money which would otherwise be due under a contract. This is of limited application in practice, and its scope is unclear. The main application of the doctrine has been in relation to contracts where there are continuing obligations, for example as in the leading case of *Central London Property Trust v High Trees House* [1947] KB 130, where the obligation concerned payments of rent during the Second World War. How far the doctrine applies to one-off payments under a contract is unclear. In a sale of goods context, if a buyer agrees to buy goods for £10,000 but then tells the seller that it cannot afford the full price and the seller agrees to accept £8,000, it seems that the seller can change its mind and, on reasonable notice, sue for the outstanding £2,000.

Prevention

In the same way that the parties can attempt to draft the contract to solve 'battle of the forms' problems, they may also attempt to prevent unauthorised variation of the terms of the contract, by extending the no-authority clause (see **3.3.4.3**) into the contract to restrict the grant of variations or waivers to senior staff or providing that a variation or waiver will only be valid if agreed in writing (a no oral modification (or NOM) clause). Alternatively, a statement may be included that any variation or waiver does not affect the seller's strict rights under the contract, or that sales representatives and other staff have no authority to vary the contract.

In *MWB Business Exchange Centres Ltd v Rock Advertising Ltd* [2018] UKSC 24, the Supreme Court held that a NOM clause is legally effective, thus ending a period of uncertainty as to the effectiveness of such clauses. Where a contract includes a NOM clause, the parties must comply with the formalities set out in the clause if they wish to vary the contract.

Economic duress

Even if a variation is supported by consideration, it may not be valid if it is brought about by economic duress, where one party threatens to break its side of the contract unless the other side promises to pay more than originally agreed.

An example would be where a food supplier agrees with a catering company to deliver food for a wedding. The day before the wedding, the supplier tells the caterer that it will not deliver unless the buyer pays an extra £1,000. The supplier agrees that, for the extra money, it will deliver king prawns instead of ordinary freshwater prawns (thus providing consideration at minimal cost to itself). The caterer is unable to source the food from anywhere else in time for the wedding and so agrees to pay the extra money. This would clearly amount to economic duress as there is an unlawful threat by the supplier not to perform its side of the contract, and there is no practical alternative for the caterer but to agree to pay more. It must, however, have been left with no practical alternative – mere commercial pressure will not be enough.

The variation of the contract will be voidable and the only remedy is rescission. The buyer may refuse to pay the extra money, or, if he has already paid, he may recover the money, provided that he does not delay too long or there is no other evidence that he has affirmed the contract.

3.2.5   Interpretation (or construction) of contracts and implied terms

When drawing up a contract, sometimes the parties will overlook terms which should be included, or will include terms which are vague or incomplete. In such cases, the courts will be called upon to fill in the gaps, or interpret the meaning of these vague or incomplete terms. Recent Supreme Court decisions dealing with implied terms and construction of contracts make it clear that the courts will respect the deal that the parties have made, and will not rewrite the contract, however disastrous the result for one or other of those parties. In *Marks and Spencer plc v BNP Paribas Securities Services Trust Company (Jersey) Ltd and another* [2015] UKSC 72 the Court confirmed that contractual interpretation and the implication of terms are separate processes, governed by different rules.

3.2.5.1   Interpretation

At its very simplest, interpretation (often referred to as construction) is deciding the meaning of the words of the contract. In *Arnold v Britton* [2015] UKSC 36 the Supreme Court supported a literal approach to identify the intended meaning of the words through the eyes of a reasonable person, and made it clear that the starting point is the language that the parties have chosen. Only if the language is unclear or there are clear drafting problems should the court be prepared to depart from the natural meaning of the words, or invoke business common sense as advocated by Lord Hoffmann in *Investors Compensation Scheme Ltd v West Bromwich Building Society* [1998] 1 WLR 898.

The decision in *Arnold* suggested that the courts were moving towards a more literal approach, with commercial common sense assuming less importance. However, in *Wood v Capita Insurance* [2017] UKSC 24, the Supreme Court confirmed that commercial common sense is still a relevant factor. The extent to which each is used will depend on the facts of the case and the type of contract.

Brexit

One of the consequences of Brexit could be uncertainty as to the meaning of certain contractual provisions. Questions arise as to whether references to the EU in existing contracts will include the UK, eg in relation to territory or legislation. The problem is whether 'the EU' means the EU at the time of the contract or at the time of performance of the contract. This will depend on the wording and the context in which it is used. Going forward, commercial parties should now review their contracts to identify and amend any ambiguous provisions.

3.2.5.2   Implied terms

In *Marks and Spencer v BNP Paribas*, the Supreme Court returned to the traditional tests in relation to implied terms and confirmed that a term will only be implied into a contract if either it is necessary to give business efficacy to the contract (the 'business efficacy test') or it is so obvious that it should be included that it goes without saying (the 'officious bystander test'). Commenting on *Attorney General of Belize v Belize Telecom Ltd* [2009] UKPC 10, the court stated that Lord Hoffmann's judgment was an 'inspired discussion' on implied terms, and should not be interpreted as having diluted these traditional tests. A term cannot be implied simply because it is reasonable to do so.

3.2.6   Discharge of contracts

A contract comes to an end when it has been discharged by:

(a)   performance of the contract (which will be the usual situation);

(b)   agreement between the parties;

(c)   frustration, if the contract can no longer be performed in the manner intended by the parties;

(d)   breach, if it is a repudiatory breach, ie breach of a condition not of a warranty, and that repudiation is accepted by the innocent party.

The first two are unlikely to cause any problems. The remainder of this chapter will look at the last two matters.

3.2.6.1   Frustration

A contract is frustrated when, after the contract is made, and without the fault of either party, an unforeseen event makes the contract becomes impossible or radically different to perform, eg because the subject matter of the contract has been destroyed (*Davis Contractors v Fareham Urban DC* [1956] AC 696). The result is that the contract automatically comes to an end and both parties are relieved of their obligations under the contract. Unlike mistake (see **3.2.3.3**), the event must occur after the formation of the contract, and before performance.

If the contract is frustrated, the provisions of the Law Reform (Frustrated Contracts) Act 1943 will come into operation. Prima facie, the buyer can recover any payments it made before frustration (s 1(2)), and any sums which are due before the frustration date will cease to be payable. The court, however, has the discretion to allow the seller to keep all or some of any advance payment if it considers that this will be just, having regard to any expenses which the seller may have incurred in preparing to perform the contract. If one party has conferred a valuable benefit on the other, the court may allow the first party to claim a just sum in respect of that benefit (s 1(3)), although this is less likely to be relevant in a supply of goods case. It might be more relevant in a services contract, where the supplier has done some of the work but has been unable to finish it due to a frustrating event.

The doctrine is rarely invoked and, where it is, claims are very rarely successful. In *Canary Wharf (BP4) T1 Ltd v European Medicines Agency* [2019] EWHC 921 (Ch), the court held that Brexit was not a frustrating event. However, in the absence of a force majeure clause, it may be possible that the coronavirus pandemic, or at least its effect, is. Although the pandemic itself was arguably foreseeable, the far-reaching government restrictions throughout the world were not.

In sale of goods contracts, to a limited extent, the problem is dealt with by the SGA 1979. Where there is a contract for the sale of specific goods, if (again without the fault of either party) the goods perish before risk has passed to the buyer, under s 7 the contract is avoided, and the Law Reform (Frustrated Contracts) Act 1943 will not generally apply (s 2(5)). However, the common law doctrine is still of considerable significance, especially for shipping contracts.

3.2.6.2   Remedies for breach of contract

Not all breaches of contract will give the innocent party the right to bring the contract to an end. It is important to decide whether the term that has been breached is a condition or a warranty.

(a)   Breach of a condition will give the innocent party the right to repudiate or terminate the contract. Termination means that the innocent party is discharged from all future obligations under the contract, and may recover any property transferred under the contract (including the price paid for any goods or services) and claim damages. Alternatively, the innocent party can chose to affirm the contract, in other words to hold the other party to its obligations under the contract (although this will not always be practically possible).

(b)   Breach of warranty only gives the innocent party the right to claim damages (provided that it can show that it has suffered a loss). The innocent party does not have the option to terminate the contract.

3.2.6.3   Contractual damages

Damages are the 'usual' remedy for breach of contract and, provided that the claimant can show that it has suffered a loss, are available as of right. The purpose of contractual damages is compensatory, not punitive. Most damages in contract are assessed on an expectation basis – the aim is to put the claimant into the position that he would have been if the contract had been performed as intended. However, they are subject to certain restrictions.

Remoteness of damage

Not all loss which the claimant suffers will arise as a direct result of the breach. Damages cannot be claimed for losses that are too remote. The remoteness rule was set out in *Hadley v Baxendale* (1854) 9 Exch 341. Claims for damages are limited to:

(a)   losses that flow naturally from the breach (the so-called 'first limb' of *Hadley v Baxendale* which covers all direct loss/damage). Whether or not the loss comes within this limb is an objective test, but it is important to note that ordinary loss of profit can come within this limb;

(b)   losses that may reasonably be supposed to have been in the contemplation of the parties at the time they made the contract, as a result either of actual knowledge (the 'second limb'). Some loss of profit, or indirect and consequential loss will fall within this limb. For example, in *Victoria Laundry v Newman Industries* [1949] 1 All ER 997, CA, 'exceptional profit' arising as a result of a lucrative dyeing contract which had not been drawn to the attention of the defendant was too remote. It is the knowledge of the parties at the time the contract is made, not at the time of the breach, which is relevant when applying this test.

In many jurisdictions, consequential loss is recoverable only in limited circumstances.

In commercial contracts, most sellers will want to exclude indirect or consequential loss, although in the UK this will always be subject to UCTA 1977. However, it is not always clear whether loss of profit falls within the first or second limb. As we have seen, ordinary loss of profit can come within the first limb, but more recent cases, such as *Brown v KMR Services Ltd* [1955] 4 All ER 598 and *Transfield Shipping Inc v Mercator Shipping Inc* [2008] UKHL 48, have looked at the situation where there are exceptional losses. *Brown* involved the Lloyd's underwriting losses, and *Transfield* involved loss of profit as a result of the late delivery under a charterparty in an extremely volatile market. In *Brown*, the losses were not too remote, but in *Transfield* the House of Lords held that the loss was too remote. It is clear that the courts were drawing a distinction between different kinds of loss of profit. However, the Court of Appeal in *Supershield Ltd v Siemens Building Technologies FE Ltd* [2010] EWCA Civ 7 confirmed that the *Hadley v Baxendale* test remains the 'standard rule', but held that, looking at the commercial context, the reasonable expectations and intentions of the parties may cause the court to depart from this rule. From a drafting point of view, it is important clearly to allocate responsibility for the consequences of breach in order to avoid these uncertainties (see **Chapter 9**).

Mitigation

The claimant must have made a reasonable attempt to mitigate its loss. It cannot claim for loss which it failed to mitigate. The burden of proof is on the defendant to show that the claimant did not make a reasonable attempt to mitigate.

Restitution and restitutionary damages

The aim of restitution is to prevent unjust enrichment, eg where an advance payment has been made for a service and there has been a total failure of consideration, in the sense that no benefit at all has been provided under the contract. Commercially, restitution can useful where no contractual relationship exists, and includes quasi-contractual claims for the return of money paid, or quantum meruit where work has been carried out under a contract which has never come into existence, for example as a result of mistake.

Restitutionary damages are different from other restitutionary remedies in that that they are an equitable remedy. Such damages are sometimes referred to as *Wrotham Park* damages, following the case of *Wrotham Park Estates v Parkside Homes Limited* [1974] 1 WLR 798, which established that damages might not always be based on financial loss to the claimant. Normally, as discussed at **3.7.3** above, the aim of contractual damages is to compensate the claimant for the loss suffered, not to punish the defendant for breaching the contract. There is some academic debate as to whether restitutionary damages sit outside this general purpose and so may be awarded when the defendant has made gains at the expense of the claimant, making such damages more akin to a claim for account of profit. The case law, particularly on the rationale for an award of restitutionary damages, is complex and outside the scope of this book.

Restitutionary remedies are an alternative to contractual remedies, and the claimant will not receive both. They are awarded rarely, and never where contractual remedies would produce a satisfactory result.

3.3   INTERNATIONAL CONSIDERATIONS

3.3.1   Formation of the contract

The CISG, the PICC, the PECL and the UCC all deal with the formation of the contract. A definite offer must be accepted by words or conduct, together with intention to be bound. As a general rule, they adopt the 'mirror image' principle. However, in all of these instruments, to avoid situations where the small modifications would preclude acceptance, there are similar rules which allow contract formation even if minor, non-material alterations are included in the acceptance (see **3.3.2.1**). Consideration is not a requirement in the CISG, PICC, PECL or UCC.

There are equivalent provisions for revocation of offers and communication of acceptance. Unlike English law, where a promise to keep an offer open must be supported by consideration, and, if not, can be revoked at any time, the CISG (Article 16), the PICC (Article 2.1.4) and the PECL (Article 2:202) provide that an offer cannot be revoked if it states a time for acceptance or it was unreasonable to revoke it. The UCC (Section 2-205) has an equivalent provision.

3.3.2   The negotiation phase

As we have seen (at **2.3.6.2**), the parties to a contract in the UK are not under a duty to negotiate in good faith. The PICC (Article 2.1.15) and the PECL (Article 2:301) impose an express obligation to do so. Under both sets of Principles, a party who breaks off negotiations in bad faith is liable for losses caused to the other party. Both state that it is contrary to good faith to enter into or continue negotiations with no real intention of concluding an agreement with the other party.

The PICC, the PECL and the UCC deal with pre-contractual issues involving the validity of the contract, such as mistake, fraud and illegality. The CISG does not.

3.3.2.1   'Battle of the forms'

The approach of the English courts to the 'battle of the forms' is to apply the 'last shot wins' doctrine (see **3.2.2.3**). Internationally, it is more common to find that the courts use what is known as the 'knock-out' doctrine. Effectively, where there are two sets of standard terms and conditions on the table, the doctrine allows a contract to be formed on the basis of any agreed terms and any terms in each set of standard terms and conditions which are common in substance. Any conflicting terms in the parties' standard terms and conditions are 'knocked out'.

(a)   CISG. Article 19(2) provides that an acceptance which introduces new or different terms can still be an acceptance if the offeree intended it to be an acceptance, the terms do not materially alter the terms of the offer, and the offeror does not object to these terms. Article 19(3) gives a non-exhaustive list of terms that would materially alter the terms of the offer, including terms relating to price, payment, delivery and liability of the parties. The effect of Article 19(3) is that most terms that the offeree may seek to introduce are likely to be material, and thus the court will be obliged to adopt the 'last shot' approach.

(b)   PICC. Article 2.11 contains a similar provision to Article 19(2) of the CISG in relation to non-material additions or alterations, without the restrictions introduced by Article 19(3). In addition, Article 2.22 specifically deals with the 'battle of the forms', and adopts the 'knock-out' doctrine, unless the doctrine has clearly been excluded by one party in advance or without undue delay after the contract has been concluded.

(c)   PECL. Article 2:208 provides that a reply to an offer which gives definite acceptance can amount to acceptance provided any additional or different terms do not manifestly alter the terms of the offer. Article 2:209 adopts the 'knock-out' doctrine in relation to 'conflicting general conditions of a contract', providing that a contract can be formed on the basis of the terms which are common in substance. Again, the parties can derogate from the doctrine by one party excluding it in advance or without delay after the contract has been concluded.

(d)   UCC. Section 2-207(1) allows for a statement of different or additional terms to those of the offer to act as an acceptance, provided that the offeror has not stipulated that acceptance must be on the terms of the offer, the new terms do not materially alter the terms of the offer, or no objection is made at the time or within a reasonable time thereafter. Provided that the conditions are met, the knock-out doctrine operates.

3.3.2.2   Entire agreement or 'merger' clauses

The rules of interpretation of contracts, under the CISG, the PICC and the PECL, which look to the intention of the parties, effectively exclude the application of the parol evidence rule (see **3.2.2.4** and **3.3.5**). Section 2-202 of the UCC provides a 'let out' to strict interpretation of the rule. Thus, international contracts will often contain an entire agreement clause (referred to internationally as a 'merger' clause), which is intended to demonstrate that the written contract is the final agreement of the parties and no prior or contemporaneous oral representations by salesmen or others should be admissible.

Merger clauses are expressly dealt with in both the PICC and the PECL, but not in the CISG or the UCC.

(a)   PICC. Article 2.1.17 provides that where a merger clause is included in the contract, and states that the document is the entire agreement between the parties, it cannot be contradicted or supplemented by evidence of prior statements or agreement. However, such statements can be used in interpreting the contract (see **3.3.5**).

(b)   PECL. Article 2:105 distinguishes between individually negotiated merger clauses and those which have not been individually negotiated. In the former case, the document will be the entire agreement between the parties, but if it has not been individually negotiated, there is merely a presumption to that effect.

3.3.3   Performance

Because the CISG and Article 2 of the UCC deal specifically with the sale of goods, both spell out the performance rights and obligations of the parties. In general, these correspond to the rights and obligations of the buyer and seller under the UK SGA 1979 (see **Chapters 4** and **5**).

The main obligations of the seller are to deliver the goods and ensure that those goods conform to the contract (CISG, Article 30 and UCC, Section 2-301). The main obligations of the buyer are to take delivery and pay the price (CISG, Article 53 and UCC, Section 2-301). Both instruments contain default provisions where the parties have not provided for these in the contract. The PICC and the PECL are broader in scope, and contain default provisions in relation to price determination, quality of performance (although in broad terms), and time, place and order of performance.

3.3.4   Entry into the contract

Consideration is not a requirement in the CISG, PICC, PECL or UCC. The important element is intention to be bound. The CISG and UCC contain express provisions stating that a contract may be modified by mere agreement of the parties. In addition, both the CISG and UCC provide that a contract may still come into existence where terms are left open, if the parties have intended to conclude a contract.

3.3.5   Interpretation

The CISG (Article 7), the PICC (Article 1.6) and the PECL (Article 1:106) expressly state that, as a general rule, in their interpretation regard is to be had to their international character and the need to promote uniformity in their application. In addition, the terms will be construed in accordance with the overriding principles of good faith and fair dealing. Internationally, the starting point is the common intention of the parties, and, unlike under English law, prior negotiations between the parties will be taken into account.

(a)   *CISG.* Article 8 provides that contracts are to be interpreted according to common intent. Where it is not possible to establish subjective intent, then statements and conduct will be looked at from the point of view of a reasonable person. This will take into account all the circumstances, including negotiations, practices and usages and the conduct and performance of the parties.

(b)   *PICC.* Article 4 contains similar provisions on interpretation and looks to the common intention of the parties, subjective or objective. In establishing this, regard is to be had to all the circumstances, including extrinsic evidence, as under the CISG.

(c)   *PECL.* Article 5 again provides that a contract is to be interpreted according to the common intent of the parties, even if this differs from the literal meaning of the words used. It contains similar provisions in relation to extrinsic evidence as the PICC.

(d)   *UCC.* Section 2-202 precludes the use of parol or extrinsic evidence to contradict the terms of the written document which the parties intended to be the final agreement of the parties. The court may consider evidence of consistent, additional terms unless it finds the writing to have been intended as a complete and exclusive statement of the terms of the agreement.

3.3.6   Discharge of contracts and remedies

Where there has been a failure to perform the obligations under the contract, there is some difference in terminology between the various instruments. The CISG and the UCC refer to 'breach' of contract, the PICC and the PECL to 'non-performance'. All set out a system of reciprocal remedies, which are available unless the non-performing party is excused from performance of its obligations, eg as a result of impossibility of performance.

3.3.6.1   Frustration

The doctrine of frustration is a common law doctrine which is not recognised in civil law systems. Civil law systems have the doctrine of 'force majeure', or equivalents. Both deal with situations where performance has become impossible, as a result of events outside the control of the parties. Although the international instruments deal with situations where performance has become impossible, they do not cover identical doctrines. They all deal with 'impediments' to performance. The PICC, the PECL and the UCC deal respectively with circumstances of 'hardship', situations where a contract has become 'excessively onerous', and 'impracticability', where performance is possible but has become unduly burdensome or would cause commercial hardship. The provisions of the CIGS are limited to those 'impediments' that result in impossibility of performance but not impracticability.

(a)   *CISG.* Article 79 provides for non-performance by either party, where non-performance is the result of an unforeseen and unavoidable impediment. It provides for an exemption from damages, but all the other remedies remain available. The parties' obligations are not discharged.

(b)   *PICC.* Article 6 deals with 'hardship', which is where there is a change of circumstances which is so severe and fundamental that the parties cannot be held to the contract. Here the parties are under an obligation to negotiate in good faith to resolve the situation, although if this proves impossible after a reasonable time, the court may terminate the contract. Article 7 deals with 'force majeure' and, like the CISG, contains an exemption where there is an unforeseen and unavoidable 'impediment' to performance. Again, this prevents a claim in damages against the non-performing party, but the other party can still terminate the contract and claim interest on money due.

(c)   *PECL.* Article 6:111 provides for 'change of circumstances' which render the performance of the contract 'excessively onerous', and a similar obligation on the parties to renegotiate in good faith. Article 8:108 covers 'excuse due to an Impediment' and contains an identical provision to Article 7 of the PICC. This excludes the right to damages and the right to claim performance.

(d)   *UCC.* Section 2-613 deals with 'casualty to the goods' and Section 2-615 deals with impracticability. Both these are limited in scope in that they only deal with delay and non-delivery by the seller:

   (i)   Where goods in existence at the time of the contract suffer 'casualty' without fault of either party before the risk of loss passes to the buyer, if the loss is total then the contract is avoided. There are also provisions for partial loss.

   (ii)   Where delivery is made impossible by the 'occurrence of a contingency the non-occurrence of which was a basic assumption on which the contract was made', the seller only is excused performance.

3.3.6.2   Remedies

Unlike common law systems, which tend to regard damages as the primary remedy for breach of contract, and where specific performance is only granted where damages would not be an adequate remedy, civil law systems regard specific performance as the primary remedy. Thus there is some variation in the remedies provided under the various international instruments. The emphasis in the CISG, PICC and PECL is on preservation of the contract, rather than termination, and all three include provisions intended to do this.

(a)   *CISG.* The main remedies of the buyer if the seller fails to perform are set out in Articles 45–52 and are specific performance, damages, reduction in the price and termination. The main remedies of the seller, set out in Articles 61–65 are equivalent, but the buyer does not have the remedy of price reduction. Specific performance is the primary remedy, available for both the buyer and the seller. The buyer is entitled to delivery, substitute delivery or repair. The seller is entitled to require the buyer to pay the price, take delivery or perform his other obligations. Other provisions include giving the non-performing party the right to an additional period to perform, and the seller a right to attempt to 'cure', or remedy, the non-conformity.

Under Article 74, damages consist of a sum equal to the loss, including loss of profit, suffered as a result of the breach. They are limited by foreseeability, in the light of what the parties knew or ought to have known at the time of conclusion of the contract.

Despite the reference to foreseeability rather than reasonable contemplation, this is roughly equivalent to the remoteness rule under *Hadley v Baxendale*. The parties are also under an obligation to take reasonable measures to mitigate the loss.

(b)   *PICC.* Under Article 7 the main remedies for both parties are specific performance, termination and damages. Again, the primary remedy for both parties is specific performance: a party who has not paid may be obliged to pay, and where a party has failed to perform a non-monetary obligation, the other party may require performance. The right to performance may give the right to repair, replacement or 'other cure' of defective performance.

Damages consist of 'full compensation for harm sustained as a result of the non-performance', including any gain of which the innocent party was deprived, and non-pecuniary harm such as physical suffering and emotional distress (Article 7.4.2). They are limited by lack of certainty, foreseeability and mitigation.

(c)   *PECL.* Under Article 9, the main remedies are specific performance, damages, the right to withhold performance and termination. The provisions in relation to specific performance, which is the primary remedy, are similar to those in the PICC. The general measure of damages is similar to the measure under English law, being 'such sum as will put the aggrieved party as nearly as possible into the position which it would have been if the contract has been duly performed' (Article 9:502). They include loss, including non-pecuniary loss and future loss which is reasonably likely to occur, and any gain of which the injured party has been deprived. They are limited by foreseeability.

(d)   UCC. The provisions of the UCC reflect the common law, and provide for damages as the main remedy. The seller's remedies include the right to withhold the delivery, stoppage of the goods in transit, an action for the price, resale of the goods (with a right to sue for the difference in the price), damages for lost profit and incidental damages. The buyer's rights include rejection, 'cover' damages for non-delivery (ie the right to recover the difference between the contract price and the price of substitute goods), damages for breach of warranty (the right to recover the difference between the value of the goods delivered and the goods as warranted), incidental and consequential damages. There are similarities with the rights of the unpaid seller and the buyer's remedies under the UK SGA 1979 (see **5.5** and **5.6**).

SUMMARY

We have seen that there are distinct phases in the lifespan of a commercial contract: negotiation, formation, performance and final discharge. When drafting commercial contracts, lawyers should always think about the how the main principles of black-letter contract law affect each phase. We are now going to consider the statutory regulation of domestic contracts for the sale of goods and supply of services.

SALE OF GOODS: INTRODUCTION

> **LEARNING OUTCOMES**
>
> After reading this chapter you will be able to:
>
> - appreciate how the UK Sale of Goods Act 1979 (SGA 1979) applies to contracts at each stage of the supply chain
> - identify the relevant legislation that governs all sale of goods contracts
> - understand the statutory definitions relating to sales of goods
> - summarise the main rights and duties which the UK SGA 1979 imposes on a seller and buyer of goods, how and when they apply, and whether or not these may be excluded
> - explain the effects of a sale of goods contract
> - identify other types of contract under which goods may pass.

4.1 INTRODUCTION

The next four chapters will examine direct sales of goods from manufacturer to retailer. A brief reminder of the supply chain (see **Chapter 1**) shows the relevant contracts which will be governed by the SGA 1979.

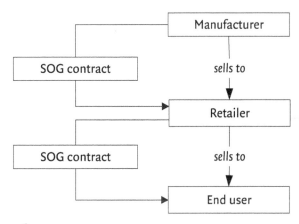

Figure 4.1 Sale of goods contracts

The sale of goods contract is probably the most commonly occurring contract type of all, with countless numbers of contracts being entered into every day. This is a vast area of law and the purpose of this chapter is to introduce you to the legal framework within which such contracts are created, and to provide a summary of the structure of the SGA 1979.

4.2   RELEVANT LEGISLATION

In the UK, all commercial (B2B) sales of goods are governed by the SGA 1979, as amended by:

(a)   the Sale and Supply of Goods Act 1994;

(b)   the Sale of Goods (Amendment) Act 1994;

(c)   the Sale of Goods (Amendment) Act 1995.

Where goods are supplied along with services, eg a contract to decorate a house, the Supply of Goods and Services Act 1982 (SGSA 1982) applies.

The Unfair Contract Terms Act 1977 (UCTA 1977) deals with exclusion clauses, including exclusion of the implied terms under the SGA 1979.

In this chapter, all references are to the UK SGA 1979, the UK SGSA 1982 and the effect of the provisions of UCTA 1977 within the UK, unless otherwise stated.

4.3   SALE OF GOODS TO CONSUMERS

Consumer contracts are largely beyond the scope of this book, although they are clearly important in practice. Many commercial clients will have dealings with consumers, and will need to consider the particular issues raised by dealings with this type of buyer.

Between 2014 and 2016, consumer legislation underwent a major overhaul as a result, first, of the introduction of the Consumer Rights Act 2015 (CRA 2015), which came into force in October 2015, and, secondly, the implementation of the Consumer Rights Directive in the summer of 2014 by the Consumer Contracts (Information, Cancellation and Additional Charges) Regulations 2013 (SI 2013/3134) ('Consumer Contracts Regulations 2013').

The purpose of the CRA 2015 was to simplify, consolidate and expand the existing consumer legislation relating to the provision of goods and services, and to introduce measures in relation to digital content. In summary, it governs all contracts between 'traders' and 'consumers' (B2C). It deals with the rights and remedies of consumers, giving consumers greater potential for effective redress and enhances consumer protection from unfair contract terms. (Note that the CRA 2015 does not cover C2C contracts, so where protection exists, consumers will still have to rely on the SGA 1979, eg, sales by description.)

It amended or repealed a number of consumer protection statutes, including the SGA 1979, the Supply of Goods and Services Act 1982, UCTA 1977, the Unfair Terms in Consumer Contracts Regulations 1999 and the Misrepresentation Act 1967, amongst others, consolidating the consumer protection measures from these in one statute (see **Chapters 7 and 8**).

From 13 June 2014, the Consumer Contracts Regulations 2013 replaced the Consumer Protection (Distance Selling) Regulations 2000 (SI 2000/2334) and introduced important changes to the statutory regulation of distance, off-premises and some on-premises sales. The Electronic Commerce (EC Directive) Regulations 2002 (SI 2002/2013) which regulate both B2B and B2C contracts in relation to e-commerce remain in force. The application of these Regulations in relation to e-commerce will be discussed in **Chapter 26**.

Further legislation has been introduced to implement other provisions of the Consumer Rights Directive which will not be covered by the CRA 2015 or the Consumer Contracts Regulations 2013:

(a)   The Consumer Protection from Unfair Trading (Amendment) Regulations 2014 (SI 2014/870) came into force on 13 June 2014. They extend the Consumer Protection from Unfair Trading Regulations 2008 (SI 2008/1277). The Regulations give consumers greater protection by introducing new rights of redress in relation to misleading and aggressive demands for payment and 'inertia' selling, ie sales of unsolicited goods, which do not have to be paid for and can be retained.

(b)   The Consumer Rights (Payment Surcharges) Regulations 2012 (SI 2012/3110) came into force on 6 April 2013. These Regulations ban credit or debit card surcharges which exceed the cost to the business of using such credit or debit card facilities. The Regulations only apply to consumer contracts.

4.3.1   Brexit

Much of UK consumer law is UK-derived or inspired by UK law and is largely unchanged as a result of Brexit. At least in the short term, where UK law derives from the EU, UK consumer law will remain aligned to EU consumer law. The body of 'retained EU law' contains a raft of consumer protection measures that will remain in force. It is not thought that the government will make any significant changes, particularly given the relatively recent overhaul of consumer law. However, in the longer term, it is thought likely that EU and UK consumer protection law will begin to diverge, with inevitable problems for UK suppliers with markets within the EU.

4.3.2   Proposals for reform

The government recognises that, even since the Consumer Rights Act came into force in 2015, new technologies and the exponential growth of data have meant that trading practices and the way people shop have changed. In July 2021, the government launched a consultation on its Green Paper, 'Reforming Competition and Consumer Policy', with an emphasis on modernising the UK's regulatory framework to reflect these developments and impose stronger penalties for enforcement of consumer law. Following the response to the consultation, the Digital Markets, Competition and Consumer Bill was announced in the 2022 Queen's Speech, but no timetable for its introduction has yet been put forward. These aims broadly reflect the aims of the EU's 'New Deal for Consumers' (see **2.2.1.3**).

4.4   DEFINITIONS

4.4.1   What is 'sale of goods'?

The SGA 1979, s 2(1) defines a contract for the sale of goods as:

> ... a contract by which the seller transfers or agrees to transfer the property in goods to the buyer for a money consideration, called the price.

Section 2(4) defines a sale as follows:

> Where under a contract of sale the property in the goods is transferred from the seller to the buyer the contract is called a sale.

These subsections indicate how a sale of goods differs, for example, from a contract for hire of goods because the property in the goods (the title to the goods) changes hands. It differs from a gift of the goods because the buyer pays the seller money for the goods in a sale contract. It also differs from a contract of barter, in which goods are exchanged for goods or a combination of goods and money. Whether a contract amounts to a sale of goods contract will be a question of fact in each case. For example, see *PST Energy Shipping 7 LLC and Product Shipping and Trading SA v OW Bunker Malta Ltd and ING Bank SA (Res Cogitans)* [2016] UKSC 23, where the Supreme Court has confirmed that despite the expectations of the parties, a contract for the supply of marine bunkers (marine fuel), where the parties know and intend that the bunkers will be consumed prior to payment, is not a sale of goods contract (and see **6.1.3**).

4.4.2   What are 'goods'?

Usually it is perfectly obvious whether the subject matter of the contract is goods (eg buying a chocolate bar in a shop). The SGA 1979, s 61 defines goods as including 'all personal chattels other than things in action and money'. An example of a thing in action is a cheque, which is in effect a promise to pay money. Land is not included, but crops and 'things attached to and forming part of the land which are agreed to be severed before sale or under the contract of sale' are within the definition of goods.

Section 5(1) differentiates between present and future goods:

> The goods which form the subject of a contract of sale may be either existing goods, owned or possessed by the seller, or goods to be manufactured or acquired by him after the making of the contract of sale, in this Act called future goods.

Existing goods may be:

(a)   specific goods, which under s 62 are goods which 'can be identified and agreed upon at the time of the contract', eg 'my 2007 sky blue Mercedes SLK registration number T15 SHR';

(b)   unascertained purely generic goods, eg 100 tons of potatoes;

(c)   a specified quantity of goods from an identified bulk, eg 100 tons of potatoes from 200,000 tonnes currently stored in Allpress Distribution Ltd's warehouse in Chatteris.

Future goods are goods which do not yet exist, eg next year's potato crop, or goods which the seller does not yet own. Future goods can never be specific goods.

The distinction between the various types of goods is important when considering when title or property in the goods passes (see **6.2**).

Section 6 provides that where specific goods have perished, the contract is void (see **3.4.3**).

One area where there has been uncertainty is computer programs. Are they goods or services? (The point is that the implied terms in the contract would be different for goods and for services.) In *St Albans City and District Council v International Computers Ltd* [1996] 4 All ER 481, it was held *obiter* that programs were goods when they were supplied on a disk. Increasingly, as most digital content is now delivered electronically, and legislation such as the Consumer Rights Act 2015 specifically governs digital content (and see **8.10.2.2**), this will become of less relevance. However, the issue was considered in *Computer Associates (UK) Ltd v Software Incubator Ltd* [2018] EWCA Civ 518. Following the Court of Appeal decision that electronically delivered software cannot constitute goods, the Supreme Court referred the matter to the CJEU.

4.5 STRUCTURE OF THE UK SGA 1979

The SGA 1979 imposes duties on the buyer and the seller, with corresponding rights and remedies for each party, relating to transfer of ownership and performance of the contract. Under s 27, for example, the buyer's duty to pay for the goods is concurrent with the seller's duty to deliver them, and failure to perform these duties gives rise to statutory remedies over and above the ordinary contractual remedies discussed in **Chapter 3**.

The effect of a sale of goods is that ownership of, and risk in, the goods passes to the buyer. This is fundamental, but, in addition, each party to a sale of goods contract will have particular commercial concerns, which have been touched on in **Chapter 1**. For example:

(a)   The main concern for both parties will be that the contract works for them financially. The seller will want to ensure that the price is right and that payment is prompt in order to avoid cash-flow problems. In relation to payment, the buyer will be looking for favourable credit periods and will be more concerned to see that delivery is prompt. The terms relating to these issues of price, payment and delivery are the 'core' terms of the contract, because they define the parties' principal obligations: the seller's obligation to deliver the goods; and the buyer's obligation to accept and pay for them.

(b)   Once the goods are delivered, the buyer will want to ensure that it has got what it paid for, in the sense that the goods are exactly as described and that they are in perfect condition. The seller will be concerned to minimise its liability in relation to the buyer in the event that the goods turn out to be defective or unsuitable for any reason.

The SGA 1979 deals with these issues. Surprisingly, however, the SGA 1979 imposes very little control on a commercial sale agreement. The SGA 1979 acts, in some circumstances, to fill in voids and omissions to which the parties have not turned their minds, or where they have simply relied upon the Act. In addition, in certain circumstance the parties can opt out of some of these controls.

Provisions as to ownership and the 'core' duties, rights and remedies of both parties are summarised in **Table 4.1** below.

Duties of Seller	Duties of Buyer

• To deliver the goods (s 29)
• To deliver the correct quantity (s 30)
• To pass good title (s 12)
• To deliver goods which:
  – correspond with description (s 13)
  – are of satisfactory quality and fit for purpose (s 14)
  – correspond with sample (s 15)
	• To accept delivery (s 27)
	• To pay for the goods (s 27)

Rights/Remedies of Seller	**Rights/Remedies of Buyer**

• To terminate/repudiate the contract for breach of condition
• Action for the price (s 49)
• Damages for non-acceptance (s 50)
• Rights of the unpaid seller:
  – lien (s 41)
  – stoppage in transit (ss 44, 45)
  – resale (s 48)
• To retain title to the goods until paid (ss 17 and 19)
	• To inspect the goods (s 34)
	• To reject the goods and refuse payment for breach of condition
	• To damages for non-delivery (s 51)
	• To damages when the goods are accepted (s 53)
	• To request specific performance (s 52)

Table 4.1 **Rights and remedies of parties to a contract**

The main performance obligations can be divided, albeit loosely, into three categories, as set out below.

4.5.1 Default provisions

Many of the implied terms are safety-net terms, implied only if the parties have not made their own provision. They would often be unsuitable for a commercial contract, eg s 28 implies cash on delivery, which will not be appropriate for most commercial transactions, where a buyer will normally be buying on credit.

4.5.2 Implied terms which can be excluded by agreement between the parties

Section 55 provides that some of the terms implied into a contract for the sale of goods by the 1979 Act can be excluded by the agreement of the parties, subject to UCTA 1977 (see **Chapters 8** and **9**). It may be perfectly valid and desirable to exclude them, but the problem usually is to what extent UCTA 1977 permits this.

4.5.3 Implied terms which can never be excluded

Under UCTA 1977, the obligation of the seller to pass good title to the buyer can never be excluded. Any attempt to do so will be void.

Figure 4.2 below shows into which categories the main performance obligations fall. Each of these obligations will be discussed in more detail in **Chapters 5, 6** and **7**.

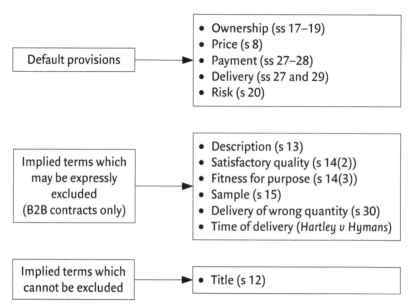

Figure 4.2 Categories of performance obligations

4.5.4 International sales of goods

Internationally, the extent to which statutes relating to the sale of goods can be excluded varies from state to state. The CISG, the UCC, the PICC and the PECL envisage liability under domestic sale of goods legislation being excluded.

4.6 EFFECTS OF A SALE OF GOODS CONTRACT

The effects of a sale of goods contract are that:

(a)   ownership of the goods is transferred to the buyer;

(b)   the risk in the goods passes to the buyer; and

(c)   the seller is paid.

4.7 OTHER TYPES OF CONTRACT UNDER WHICH GOODS MAY PASS

Contracts for goods and services clearly involve the sale of goods but do not fall within the ambit of the SGA 1979. Many of the legal controls on the 'goods' part are in effect the same as for the sale of goods, but in addition there are controls on the 'services' component.

Other contracts under which goods may pass include conditional sale, hire purchase, leasing, bailment and factoring.

4.7.1 Contracts for services

Many businesses supplying services also provide goods as well, and to further complicate things, businesses supplying goods often provide a service, eg installation. Sometimes, it is quite difficult to know whether there is a sale of goods contract (to which the SGA 1979 only would apply) or a supply of goods and services contract, sometimes known as a work and materials contract (to which the SGSA 1982 would apply). In *Samuels v Davis* [1943] KB 526, the Court of Appeal suggested that it did not much matter how the agreement was categorised, as long as the correct terms were implied. In essence, there are three types of contract involving services:

4.7.1.1 Contracts for services only

Examples of contracts for services only are contracts for legal or accountancy advice. These are governed by the Supply of Goods and Services Act 1982 (SGSA 1982). The main terms implied are:

(a)   the service will be performed with reasonable skill and care (s 13);

(b)   the work will be carried out within a reasonable time, but only if no time for performance has been fixed by the contract (s 14); and

(c)   a reasonable charge will be paid, but only if no price is fixed by the contract (s 15).

4.7.1.2 Contracts for work and materials

A good example of a contract for work and materials (ie, goods and services) is a contract for repair, where the repairer supplies not only his own labour but also the necessary parts. These contracts are governed by the SGSA 1982. It is important to remember that it is *not* the SGA 1979 itself which applies in such cases (SGSA 1982, s 1).

4.7.1.3 Contracts for finished products

An example of this type of contract would be where a carpenter agrees to construct a kitchen unit on site. These types of contract are governed by the SGSA 1982.

Note that, in all these cases, consumer contracts are governed by the CRA 2015. Where businesses are selling goods to consumers within the EU, the Sale of Goods Directive (2019/771/EU) will apply.

4.7.2 Exchange and barter

Contracts of exchange and barter are found relatively rarely in practice. In the past, they have been most frequently encountered in dealings with businesses in developing countries, where foreign currency may not be available to allow the buyer to pay in cash. There is evidence that they are now also being used in some forms of online trading.

4.7.3 Hire purchase

In a hire purchase agreement, the buyer obtains immediate possession of the goods, in return for making regular payments. However, ownership remains with the other party to the agreement. The buyer has an option to obtain ownership by paying a final instalment. The buyer 'buys' the goods not from the 'seller' but from the finance house, pursuant to the hire purchase agreement.

In the UK, hire purchase agreements are regulated under the Consumer Credit Act 1974. However, the 1974 Act does not deal with implied terms relating to title to the goods or quality. These are governed by the Supply of Goods (Implied Terms) Act 1973, which implies terms similar to those implied into sale of goods agreements by ss 12–15 of the SGA 1979.

4.7.4 Conditional sale

A conditional sale agreement achieves a very similar result to a hire purchase agreement. Again, the buyer obtains immediate possession and makes regular payments in return. Again, ownership remains with the other party, although the buyer can obtain ownership by making a final payment. However, the agreement is structured rather differently in that there is no option to purchase. Instead, it is a sale of goods agreement under which ownership does not pass until the final payment is made.

Conditional sale is often used to finance consumer purchases in exactly the same way as a hire purchase agreement. When used in this way it is regulated by the UK Consumer Credit Act 1974. Because they are sale of goods agreements, the SGA 1979 applies to conditional sale agreements in the normal way and so, for example, ss 12 to 15 imply terms regarding title to the goods, quality, etc.

4.7.5   Hire agreements

A hire agreement differs from a sale of goods agreement in that ownership of the goods does not pass as the hirer obtains only possession, not title to the goods. In some situations, hire agreements with consumers are regulated by the UK Consumer Credit Act 1974.

The SGA 1979 does not apply to hire agreements. Instead, terms relating to the right to transfer possession and quality are implied by the SGSA 1982, ss 6–11. The terms are very similar to those implied in sale of goods agreements by the SGA 1979, ss 12–15. Exceptions are that s 7 of the SGSA 1982 implies a term that the owner, referred to as the 'bailor', has the right to transfer possession rather than a right to sell the goods. In a hire agreement, of course, it is only possession of the goods which is being transferred, not the title to them, so that is the important thing here.

4.7.6   Leases of goods

A lease is the contract between a lessor and a lessee for the hire of an asset. Today, this would be an expensive item of equipment, perhaps industrial machinery, a computer system, lorries or other motor vehicles. The lessor need not necessarily be the manufacturer or a seller of the equipment. It could instead be a finance company. The lessor is the owner of the equipment, and keeps the ownership. The lessee has the right to possess and use the equipment during the term of the lease. The lessee pays the lessor rental payments as specified in the lease contract. At the end of the lease, the equipment is returned to the lessor, which may lease it out again or more usually sell it. If the equipment is sold to the lessee, the danger is that the contract may instead be construed as a hire purchase contract and therefore be subject to the legislation on hire purchase.

There are two basic categories of lease:

(a)   Operating leases. With an operating lease, the equipment is hired out to the user (the lessee) for a short period of time, returned to the lessor and then hired out to another user. This is, for example, how a tool hire shop would normally operate.

(b)   Finance leases. With a finance lease, the equipment is supplied to one user only, which retains possession of it for substantially the whole of its working life. Most computer leases are finance leases. With a finance lease, there is no contractual relationship between the user and the supplier of the hardware. The lessor will be a finance house, which has purchased the equipment from the supplier.

4.7.7   Factoring

Factoring is where a supplier of goods sells its unpaid invoices (debts) to a third party, the factor. The supplier will not receive the full book value for the debts, as the factor will charge a fee and interest, and will also take into account the risk of the debtor defaulting. However, there are considerable advantages for the business in that it releases cash and improves cash flow. Customers will deal direct with the factor in the collection of the factored debts.

4.7.8   Bailment

Bailment is where the owner of goods (the bailor) transfers possession of the goods to another party, the bailee. The bailee will keep the goods on behalf of the bailor, subject to any express or implied conditions of the bailment contract, for example the goods may be used for a specified purpose. The bailment contract will normally provide for the eventual return of the goods to the bailor. The bailee, therefore, does not own the goods but simply has possession of them, and must take reasonable care of them, until the bailor reclaims them.

Bailment does not always depend on the existence of a bailment contract. It may arise as a result of one party assuming voluntary possession of another's goods. The bailee will still have an implied duty to take reasonable care of the goods whilst they are in his possession.

SUMMARY

This chapter has introduced the legislation governing the sale of goods, in particular the SGA 1979. We have seen how the SGA 1979 imposes corresponding rights and duties on both seller and buyer, and how ownership of and risk in the goods pass from seller to buyer in return for payment. We are now going to consider the main terms of a sale of goods contract.

CHAPTER 5

SALE OF GOODS: CORE TERMS – PRICE, PAYMENT AND DELIVERY

LEARNING OUTCOMES

After reading this chapter you will be able to:

- recognise that the 'core' terms in a sale of goods contract are those relating to price, payment and delivery, and their importance to a commercial client
- define what is meant by price, payment and delivery
- summarise the duties of a buyer in relation to payment of the price and the duties of the seller in relation to delivery of the goods
- explain the main drafting considerations governing the price of the goods, payment provisions and delivery of the goods
- advise on the rights and remedies of the parties where there has been a breach of core terms.

5.1 INTRODUCTION

In a commercial context, it is unusual for the parties not to make provision about the essential terms of the contract: price, payment and delivery. Clearly, the seller and the buyer will have different agendas on these issues. Initially, each of the parties' solicitors will want to include terms which are favourable to their client in the draft contract. This will often be followed by a period of negotiation until the issues are resolved. How they are dealt with will ultimately depend on the bargaining strength of the parties.

In the UK, the SGA 1979 contains default, or fallback, provisions which will be implied into the contract only where the parties have not made their own provision. In addition, in relation to delivery, there are implied duties imposed on each party, which are fundamental to the performance of the contract. These are the duty of the seller to deliver the goods and the duty of the buyer to accept delivery. Clearly, without these, the contract will not be performed at all. Finally, there are further delivery obligations imposed on the seller which will be implied into the contract as conditions, either by statute or by the common law. These are the duty to deliver the right quantity, and the duty to deliver on time where there is a specified delivery date. These implied conditions can be excluded only by agreement between the parties, in domestic B2B sale of goods contracts, and subject to UCTA 1977.

In this chapter each of the core provisions will be dealt with in turn, concentrating on the default provisions and drafting considerations relevant to each of these. The implied terms will be dealt with in more detail in **Chapter 7**.

International conventions contain similar provisions in relation to price, payment and delivery. Some of these will be considered in outline in this chapter. Remember that only the CISG and Article 2 of the UCC deal directly with sale of goods. The PICC and the PECL deal with general contract principles.

5.2   THE PRICE

5.2.1   UK provisions

5.2.1.1   Definition of 'price' (UK SGA 1979, s 8)

Section 8 provides:

(1)   The price in a contract of sale may be fixed by the contract, or may be left to be fixed in a manner agreed by the contract, or may be determined by the course of dealing between the parties.

(2)   Where the price is not determined as mentioned in subsection (1) above the buyer must pay a reasonable price.

(3)   What is a reasonable price is a question of fact dependent on the circumstances of each particular case.

The basic position is that the parties are free to fix their own price. The fallback position is that if they fail to do so, the price will be a reasonable one. It is clearly preferable to have a specific provision as to price to avoid uncertainty. One problem with s 8 is that, if the parties have not agreed such a basic term of the contract as the price of the goods, it is debatable whether or not they have concluded a contract at all. Alternatively, the parties may conclude the contract but agree that the price will be fixed at some point in the future. This is an 'agreement to agree' which, as discussed in **Chapter 3**, will be unenforceable, unless the parties have agreed on a specific mechanism for fixing the price.

5.2.1.2   Agreeing the price (UK SGA 1979, ss 8 and 9)

In most circumstances, the parties will agree the price. This may be done in one of several ways:

(a)   The price may be fixed by use of a price list or by quotation.

(b)   The price may have been agreed during negotiation. If so, it is important that such agreement should be documented.

(c)   The price may also be determined by a consistent course of dealing between the parties.

(d)   A further possibility is that the parties leave the price to be fixed by the valuation of a third party. If this does not happen, the contract is void (s 9).

5.2.2   International provisions

Article 55 of the CISG contains a similar provision to s 8 of the SGA 1979 regarding price – with reference to 'the price generally charged … for such goods sold under comparable circumstances in the trade concerned'. Article 5.1.7 of the PICC refers to 'the price generally charged … in comparable circumstances in the trade concerned or, if no such price is available, a reasonable price'. Article 6:103 of the PECL states that the parties are to be treated as 'having agreed on a reasonable price'. The UCC, simply refers to a 'reasonable price'.

5.2.3   Price – drafting considerations

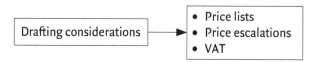

5.2.3.1 Price lists and quotations

Where the price is fixed by reference to a price list or quotation, it is important to specify the length of time for which any quoted price or price list will remain valid. Price lists and quotations should include a statement that such a price must be accepted within a specified time period, for example 28 days.

It is also important to specify clearly what is included in the price, for example whether the price includes delivery costs or insurance.

5.2.3.2 Price escalation clauses

If there is a likelihood of the cost of raw materials or labour increasing between the signing of the contract and delivery, it is advisable to put in a specific price escalation clause. In the absence of such a clause, the seller will not be able to change the price.

In a B2B contract, any provision allowing the seller to increase its price may be subject to reasonableness under s 3 of UCTA 1977, as it can render its performance under the contract substantially different from that which was reasonably expected.

5.2.4 Value added tax

A price in a contract is taken as including value added tax (VAT) unless otherwise specified (Value Added Tax Act 1994, s 19(2)). If the price is to be exclusive of VAT, that must be expressly stated. Failure to do this will result in the seller having to bear the VAT itself and not being able to pass it on to the buyer.

5.3 PAYMENT

5.3.1 Duty to pay the price (UK SGA 1979, ss 27–28)

In the UK, under s 27 of the SGA 1979, it is the buyer's duty to pay the price. Where the contract provides for cash on delivery, the buyer cannot claim possession of the goods unless it is able to pay the price in accordance with the terms of the contract. Only payment in full will discharge the buyer's liability, unless a discount has been agreed. In most commercial contracts, the buyer will want a credit period.

5.3.2 International provisions

The buyer's obligation to pay is contained within Article 53 of the CISG. In the UCC, this obligation is contained in Article 2-301. In the PICC, there is no direct obligation to pay; however, for a sale transaction, it is likely to be construed as an implied (at least) obligation under Article 5.1.2. The PECL leaves the obligation to pay to be implied into the circumstances of the contract.

5.3.3 Payment – drafting considerations

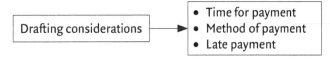

5.3.3.1 Time for payment

Unless the parties agree otherwise, s 28 of the SGA 1979 states that the time for payment is when the goods are delivered. Obviously, this is the normal position when buying goods in a shop. Delivery and payment will take place when the goods are paid for and handed over to the customer. In other commercial situations, however, this may not be the most suitable arrangement. Payment is generally linked to the issue of an invoice. The parties may wish to agree that:

(a) payment be made in advance. This is more common, for example, in international sales or where the seller is uncertain of the buyer's ability to pay;

(b) the buyer be given a credit period, say 30 days from the delivery of an invoice. It will then be important that the contract not only addresses the credit period, but also specifies when the seller has the right to issue an invoice, eg on delivery or after delivery has taken place.

Section 10(1) provides:

> Unless a different intention appears from the terms of the contract, stipulations as to time of payment are not of the essence of a contract of sale.

This has been interpreted as meaning that failure to pay is not a breach of condition entitling the seller to treat the contract as repudiated and to sell the goods elsewhere. It limits the seller's right to the price and to damages, if any, for late payment. This has been criticised, for example in Adams, JN and MacQueen, H, *Atiyah's Sale of Goods*, 12th edn (Longman, 2010), as providing a 'compulsory credit which the seller has to extend to the buyer'. The seller should therefore ensure that the contract does make time for payment of the essence.

For timing of payment under the PECL, see **5.3.2** above.

5.3.3.2 Method of payment

Under s 28 of the SGA 1979, subject to contrary agreement between the parties, the seller is entitled to be paid in cash. Again, in ordinary retail sales, the customer gives the shopkeeper the money and takes the goods away. However, this may not always be the most practical commercial scenario:

(a) If a seller accepts a cheque or other negotiable instrument, this is treated as a conditional payment. If the cheque is not honoured, the seller may sue for the price either as breach of the sale of goods contract, or on the cheque as being a contract in itself. It is advisable to include a provision ensuring that payment takes place only when the cheque has been cleared, and that the buyer will allow for the time it will take for the cheque to clear when meeting any payment deadline.

(b) Payment by credit card will usually be treated as an absolute payment. Therefore, failure by the credit card company to pay the seller does not entitle the seller to sue the customer. The customer's only liability is to pay the credit card company, but failure to do so does not mean that it will be liable to the seller.

5.3.3.3 Late payment (UK provisions)

In the absence of contrary agreement, damages for late payment may be awarded by the English courts for additional costs caused to the seller. Interest can be awarded under:

(a) the Law Reform (Miscellaneous Provisions) Act 1934;

(b) the Late Payment of Commercial Debts (Interest) Act 1998 (see **6.6.4**); and

(c) the Late Payment of Commercial Debts Regulations 2013 (SI 2013/395), which implement Directive 2011/7/EU (see **5.3.3.4**).

It is obviously sensible to provide in the contract for interest for late payment, as this avoids having to rely on these statutory provisions. Any contractual arrangement to recover, by way of damages or interest, for late payment must not 'amount to a penalty' but must be based upon a genuine pre-estimate of loss.

Clearly, prevention is better than cure, and an alternative to encourage the buyer to pay promptly would be to include a discount for prompt payment.

5.3.3.4 Late payment (EU provisions)

Directive 2011/7/EU on Combating Late Payment in Commercial Transactions (replacing Directive 2000/35/EC) applies to all commercial transactions, ie to all transactions carried out between undertakings or between undertakings and public authorities or bodies forming part of the public sector, which lead to the delivery of goods or the provision of services for remuneration. The Directive does not apply to transactions with consumers.

The 2011 Directive sets an absolute cap on late payment permitted in commercial contracts at 60 days. It also contains default provisions; they apply only if the parties have not agreed something else in the contract. Thus the principle of contractual freedom, which is recognised in all Member States, still applies. According to this, parties can fix longer payment periods than the ones provided for in the Directive. The Directive defines a reference period, fixed at 30 days. This reference period begins on the date of receipt of the invoice or at the date of receipt of the goods. In cases where the parties have agreed a procedure for acceptance or verification of the goods, it starts upon completion of this process.

The payment period can be extended (up to 60 days) by agreement of the parties. Any agreement on the payment period is not enforceable if it is grossly unfair to the creditor. In this respect, all circumstances of the case, including good commercial practice and the nature of the product, will have to be considered.

The Directive provides for a penalty interest of 7 percentage points above the European Central Bank rate, or equivalent rates for Member States outside the Eurozone or the European Economic Area members. Furthermore, the Directive gives the right to sellers to claim full compensation for all relevant recovery costs incurred when trying to obtain payment from their customers.

Brexit

The Late Payment of Commercial Debts Regulations 2013 derive from EU legislation, but the Regulations to a large extent replicated existing UK law. Post-Brexit, the Government may decide to amend or repeal the Regulations, but again this is unlikely to be a priority.

5.3.3.5 International provisions

(a) *CISG.* Under Article 58, the general rule is that the buyer must pay the price when the goods, or documents representing the goods, are placed at his disposal. However, the buyer is not bound to pay the price until he has had an opportunity to examine the goods. There is no provision in relation to the method of payment. Article 78 provides for the payment of interest in the event of late payment.

(b) *PICC.* Article 6.1.4 states that all obligations must take place simultaneously, so it will be implied that payment and delivery, the main (implied) obligations of a buyer and seller in a sale of goods contract, are simultaneous obligations. There are specific provisions in relation to the method of payment. Under Article 6.1.7, payment may be made 'in any form used in the ordinary course of business'. If a party accepts payment by cheque, this is conditional on the cheque being honoured. There are also provisions in relation to the currency of payment.

(c) *PECL.* Article 7:104 provides that, where possible, performance should be rendered simultaneously, thus payment and delivery would be simultaneous obligations. Article 7:107 provides that payment may be in 'in any form used in the ordinary course of business'. Again, acceptance of payment by cheque is conditional on the cheque being honoured. There are also provisions in relation to the currency of payment.

(d) *UCC.* Section 2-310 contains a similar provision to the CISG, providing that payment is due at the time and place that the buyer is to receive the goods, subject to the buyer's right in Section 2-513 to inspect the goods before payment. Section 2-511 provides that tender of payment is sufficient 'when made by any means or in any manner current in the ordinary course of business', but where nothing is agreed to the contrary, the seller has the right to demand 'legal tender' (ie cash). Payment by cheque is conditional on the cheque being honoured.

5.3.4 Action for the price

Section 49 of the SGA 1979 provides that the unpaid seller has the right to sue for the price (see **5.5.2.1**).

5.3.5 Right of resale (UK SGA 1979, s 48)

Where the buyer fails to pay, the seller has a statutory right of resale under s 48(3). However, this is limited in scope (see **5.5.1.5**) so it is advisable for the seller to reserve the right of resale in the contract in the event of undue delay in payment by the buyer. This prevents the buyer from taking advantage of the 'compulsory credit' period created by s 10(1) (see **5.3.3.1**).

5.4 DELIVERY

5.4.1 Duties of the seller and buyer (UK SGA 1979, ss 27, 28)

The SGA 1979 imposes corresponding duties on the seller and the buyer in relation to delivery. To understand the delivery provisions, the starting point is to consider three aspects of delivery, namely:

(a)   definition of the word 'delivery';

(b)   the duties of the seller and buyer in relation to delivery; and

(c)   methods of delivery.

5.4.2 What is 'delivery'?

'Delivery' is defined in s 61(1) as the 'voluntary transfer of possession from one person to another'. It is, if you like, handing over the goods. However, it is important to distinguish between 'legal' and 'physical' delivery. 'Delivery' in the sense used in sale of goods does not mean the physical transportation of the goods from the seller's premises to another location, eg the buyer's premises. ('Physical transportation' is usually referred to as 'carriage of goods'.) Nor is delivery confined to the transfer of physical possession of the goods, as there are various ways in which goods may be 'delivered' (see **5.4.4**). It really means the point in time and space at which the parties can be seen to have agreed that the legal right to possession of the goods passes from the seller to the buyer. It is important to understand from the outset that delivery does not necessarily occur at the same point at which ownership passes – the two are separate legal issues. A clear distinction must be made between 'delivery' (ie the transfer of possession) and the passing of title (ie ownership).

5.4.3 Duties of the seller in respect of delivery

5.4.3.1 Duty of the seller to deliver the goods

UK provisions

Under s 27 of the SGA 1979, it is the duty of the seller to deliver, in the legal sense, the goods. There is no general duty to transport the goods to the buyer.

The seller must deliver goods which comply with the contract and which comply with the implied conditions under ss 12, 13, 14 and 15. Failure to do so will give the buyer the right to reject delivery (see **Chapter 7**).

International provisions

Both the CISG (Article 30) and the UCC (Section 2-301) place an obligation on the seller to deliver the goods. There is no express delivery obligation in either the PICC or the PECL, but in a sale of goods contract this would nevertheless be implied.

5.4.3.2   Duty to deliver the right quantity

UK provisions

The seller is required to deliver goods of the right quantity:

(a)   Under s 30(1), the buyer may reject the goods if the quantity is less than the contract quantity. However, if it accepts them, it must pay for them at the contract rate.

(b)   If the seller delivers a quantity greater than the contracted quantity, the buyer may accept the contract quantity and reject the rest, or may reject the whole (s 30(2)). If the buyer accepts the whole quantity, it must pay for the excess quantity at the contract rate (s 30(3)). If the variation from the contract quantity is slight then the buyer may not reject the goods, unless the buyer is a consumer (s 30(2A)).

(c)   Section 31(1) provides that the buyer is not obliged to accept delivery in instalments. This means that the seller cannot deliver some of the goods and promise to deliver the remainder later. In these circumstances, the buyer will be entitled to reject the goods.

International provisions

Under Article 35 of the CISG, delivery of the wrong quantity would amount to delivering goods which do not conform with the contract. This must be remedied within a reasonable time. Article 7.1.4 of the UNIDROIT Principles contains a similar provision. In the UCC, quantity fits within an implied obligation of merchantability in Article 2-314. With the PECL, if the wrong quantity is delivered, it would be seen as non-performance which is remediable under Article 8.104 unless the court saw it as a fundamental breach.

5.4.4   Duties of the buyer in respect of delivery

5.4.4.1   Duty of the buyer to take delivery

UK provisions

Under s 27 of the SGA 1979, it is the duty of the buyer to accept and pay for the goods in accordance with the terms of the contract of sale. Failure to do so gives the seller statutory rights and remedies (see **5.4.6** and **5.5**).

International provisions

Under the CISG, the buyer has an obligation under Article 53 to take delivery. Under the UCC, the obligation appears in Article 2-301. In the PICC and the PECL, again there are no obligations placed on the buyer to take delivery; however, the obligation to take delivery is likely to be construed as an implied obligation under Article 5.1 and Article 6:102 respectively.

5.4.4.2   Delivery and payment

As discussed at **5.3.2**, s 28 of the SGA 1979 (and equivalent international provisions) provide that delivery of the goods and payment should happen at the same time, subject to contrary agreement, but as it is commercially unlikely that the parties will want to rely on these provisions, these aspects of delivery should be provided for in the contract.

5.4.4.3   Delivery and acceptance

Under the UK SGA 1979, although s 27 refers to the duty of the buyer to 'accept' the goods, it is important to realise that the SGA 1979 distinguishes between taking delivery of the goods and acceptance, in the legal sense, of the goods. Taking delivery of the goods does not mean that the buyer has agreed that the goods comply with the contract, ie the buyer has not yet necessarily accepted them. Acceptance is dealt with in s 35.

Under s 35(1), the buyer is deemed to have accepted the goods when:

(a)   it tells the seller that it has accepted them; or

(b)   it does any act in relation to them which is inconsistent with the ownership of the seller, eg uses them or sells them to a third party.

Section 35(2) provides that acceptance will not take place until the buyer has had a reasonable period to examine the goods to ensure that they conform with the contract. To give a simple example, if A agrees to sell a car to B and that the method of delivery will be the handing over of the registration documents, then B will take delivery when it collects the documents. However, B will still have the opportunity to inspect the car before the buyer is deemed to have accepted the goods.

Section 35(4) is particularly important in commercial contracts. The buyer is deemed to have accepted the goods if it fails to notify the seller within a reasonable time that it wishes to reject them. Thus, if goods for some reason do not comply with the contract, eg they are faulty or do not match the description, then the buyer must notify the seller within a reasonable timescale that it wishes to reject. The problem here is that what amounts to a 'reasonable time' will be a question of fact in each case (see **Chapter** 7). The seller may therefore wish expressly to provide the number of days after which the buyer may no longer reject the goods.

5.4.5   Methods of delivery

There are various methods of delivery. The most obvious is actual delivery, ie physically handing over the goods, as would happen when a consumer is buying goods in a shop. Other methods of delivery include:

(a)   transfer of a document (eg, a bill of lading: see **15.3.1**);

(b)   delivery of an object giving control (eg giving the keys to premises where the goods are stored, or even the keys to a motor car);

(c)   the buyer's continuance of possession (eg where the buyer already holds the goods as bailee of the seller, and then on the sale there is a notional delivery of the goods to the buyer);

(d)   delivery to a carrier (see **5.4.6.1**);

(e)   'attornment', where a seller or a third party acknowledges that goods which were held by the seller, or on its behalf, are now held on behalf of the buyer.

The contract should expressly deal with how the goods are to be delivered.

5.4.6   Delivery – drafting considerations

The fallback delivery provisions of the UK SGA 1979 raise a number of issues which should be considered when drafting the contract.

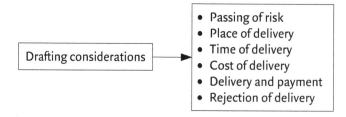

Drafting considerations →
- Passing of risk
- Place of delivery
- Time of delivery
- Cost of delivery
- Delivery and payment
- Rejection of delivery

5.4.6.1   Passing of risk

UK provisions

Prima facie, the risk of loss or damage to the goods does not automatically pass with delivery, ie with physical possession of the goods. Under s 20(1), risk passes with the property in the goods, that is with the title to/ownership of the goods. So, it is perfectly possible for the goods to be in the buyer's (physical) possession but still be at the seller's risk, if the seller still has title to them. The seller would therefore have the trouble and expense of insuring goods that are no longer in its possession. The seller will usually want the contract to be drafted so that the risk of the goods passes to the buyer with physical possession of the goods, so that the buyer has both control of the goods and the obligation to insure them. This is particularly important in retention of title sales (see **Chapter 6**).

An example of where problems could arise is the installation of a new computer system. The buyer will not want to pay the whole price until the system is running properly, yet the goods are on the buyer's premises and under its control whilst they are being installed. In such circumstances, the contract should provide that the risk in the goods passes to the buyer when the goods arrive at the buyer's premises. It is then up to the buyer to insure the goods, for example against theft or fire.

Where goods are delivered to a carrier, the contract should deal with the passing of risk. Section 32(1) provides that where the seller is authorised or required to send the goods to the buyer, transfer of possession to the carrier constitutes delivery to the buyer. The goods are at the buyer's risk from the point at which they are in the carrier's possession. The buyer should insure them against damage or loss from that point. However, this is not invariably the case and, in any event, this arrangement is often varied by express provision in the contract.

Under s 20(2), if there is a delay in delivery then, during the period of the delay, the goods are at the risk of whichever party to the contract caused the delay. Again, this may be varied by the contract. Where the delay is beyond the control of the parties, the issue can be dealt with by the inclusion of a force majeure clause (see **Chapter 9**).

International provisions

The passing of risk is also an important consideration in international sale of goods contracts. As, unlike the PICC and PECL, both the CISG (Articles 66–70) and the UCC (Section 2-509) deal with sale of goods, they also deal with the passing of risk in the goods. Under the CISG, the general rule is that risk passes when the seller has performed his obligations. If the contract involves carriage, once the goods are handed over to the carrier, as specified in the CISG, risk passes to the buyer. There are also provisions for goods in transit. If carriage or transit is not involved, then risk passes to the buyer when he takes over the goods or when the goods are placed at his disposal. Under the UCC again, risk mostly passes with carriage, as specified in Section 2-509(1). There are arrangements for bailees. Otherwise, the UCC makes a distinction between the position where the seller is a merchant (risk passes on receipt of the goods) and a non-merchant (risk passes on tender of delivery).

These are default provisions, in the absence of contrary agreement. In international sales, it is likely that the parties may choose to use an Incoterm, which will govern delivery and the passing of risk, and replace these provisions (see **Chapter 15**).

5.4.6.2   Place of delivery

In the absence of a contrary agreement, the default position under s 29(2) is that the place of delivery will be at the seller's place of business or residence. The contract between the seller and buyer should therefore specify where delivery is to occur. Alternatives include that:

(a)   the seller will deliver the goods to the buyer's premises;

(b)   the buyer will collect the goods from the seller's premises; or

(c)   the goods will be delivered to a carrier.

5.4.6.3   Date and time of delivery

Where no provision has been made as to the date and time of delivery, the default position under s 29(3) is that delivery should take place within a reasonable time. What constitutes a 'reasonable time' depends on the facts and the circumstances at the time of delivery. To avoid commercial uncertainty, the contract should deal with the issue. The form of clause will vary, depending on what has been agreed in relation to the place of delivery:

(a)   Where the seller is to deliver the goods, the time of delivery will usually be the moment when the goods are handed over to the buyer. It may be worth considering whether the seller should be given the right to deliver before any agreed delivery date, by giving reasonable notice to the buyer.

(b)   Where the buyer is to collect the goods, delivery could take place when the buyer physically removes the goods from the seller's premises. An alternative is to provide that delivery takes place when the seller authorises the buyer to collect the goods.

(c)   Where delivery is to a carrier, delivery will usually be when the seller hands the goods to the carrier.

Delivery must be made at a 'reasonable hour' (s 29(5)).

5.4.6.4   Express delivery dates

As discussed at **5.3.3.1**, s 10(1) states that time of payment is not of the essence in a sale of goods contract, unless the parties agree otherwise. Section 10(2) then provides that the parties can agree whether or not time is of the essence with regard to any other terms of the contract. The default position is, therefore, that time will not be of the essence, unless agreed otherwise by the parties.

With delivery, the exception to this general rule is that, in commercial contracts only, whether or not time is of the essence is governed by case law. In *Hartley v Hymans* [1920] 3 KB 475, it was held that in ordinary commercial contracts for the sale of goods, where a delivery date has been specified, time of delivery is prima facie of the essence. This has the effect of making the obligation to deliver on the specified date a condition, breach of which will give the buyer the right to repudiate the contract as well as sue for damages. This prima facie rule may be rebutted by the facts in a particular case.

In most commercial contracts, a delivery date will usually have been specifically agreed. Thus, under the common law rules, there is usually an implied condition that time will be of the essence for delivery. This clearly works in favour of the buyer, and the seller will want to ensure that the contract is drafted to avoid making time of the essence for delivery. It is important to remember that this is one of the implied conditions that may be excluded by agreement between the parties, but any attempt to do so will be subject to s 3 of UCTA 1977 (see **Chapter 8**).

Waiver

If the buyer waives the original delivery date before the goods are delivered, the buyer is entitled to give the seller reasonable notice that it will not accept the goods after a certain date. See *Charles Rickards Ltd v Oppenheim* [1950] 1 KB 616, where the buyer waived the original delivery date but then gave the seller reasonable notice of a revised date. The seller failed to meet even the revised date and the buyer was held to be entitled to refuse to accept the goods. A 'no authority clause' could be included to avoid 'accidental' waiver, eg by unauthorised employees (see **3.5.1.3**).

Force majeure

Even if there is an agreed delivery date, the duty to deliver by the agreed date could be suspended or extinguished. This is typically dealt with in a force majeure clause in the contract, which concerns events beyond the control of the parties. Again, a force majeure clause amounts to an exclusion of liability and will be subject to s 3 of UCTA 1977, and the implications will be considered in **Chapter 9**.

5.4.6.5   Cost of delivery

The parties should agree, and provision should be made in the contract, as to who will bear the costs of delivery. Usually, this will be the buyer. The only default provision is s 29(6), which relates to goods which are not yet in a deliverable state. In the absence of contrary agreement, the seller is responsible for the costs of putting the goods into a deliverable state.

5.4.6.6   Rejection of delivery

Section 36 of the SGA 1979 states that where the goods have been delivered to the buyer and the buyer rightfully rejects them, the buyer is not obliged to return them to the seller. The seller must therefore arrange for collection of the goods. This may cost the seller both time and expense, particularly where there are considerable distances involved, both in checking that rejection is justified (eg because the goods really are defective) and in arranging collection. The seller may therefore wish to include a non-rejection clause. However, this may be subject to s 6 or s 3 of UCTA 1977 (see **8.7**).

Under s 37 the buyer is liable for costs incurred by the seller due to the buyer's neglect or refusal to take delivery, ie wrongful rejection of delivery. Any attempt to make the seller pay for storage charges in this instance would be subject to s 3 of UCTA 1977, as it is an attempt to limit the buyer's liability for breach of the implied duty to accept delivery of the goods.

5.5   RIGHTS AND REMEDIES OF THE SELLER

The seller's primary right for breach of a condition of a contract by the buyer is to terminate the contract and/or to sue for damages. In addition, the seller has the right to sue for damages for breach of warranty. Damages will always be subject to the common law rules on remoteness, in particular *Hadley v Baxendale*, and measure (see **Chapter 3**).

Where the buyer fails to accept delivery of the goods and/or to pay for them, the seller has statutory remedies under the SGA 1979 as well as the usual contract remedies. These may be divided loosely into two categories:

(a)   the unpaid seller's rights against the goods ('real rights');

(b)   the unpaid seller's personal rights/remedies.

5.5.1   Seller's rights against the goods

5.5.1.1   Definition of an 'unpaid seller' (s 38)

Section 38(1) of the 1979 Act defines an unpaid seller in the following manner:

> The seller of goods is an unpaid seller within the meaning of this Act—
>
> (a)   when the whole of the price has not been paid or tendered;
>
> (b)   when a bill of exchange or other negotiable instrument has been received as conditional payment, and the condition on which it was received has not been fulfilled by reason of the dishonour of the instrument or otherwise.

5.5.1.2   Rights of the unpaid seller under the SGA 1979, s 39

Section 39(1) gives the unpaid seller the following rights:

(a)   a right of lien on the goods;

(b)   a right of stopping the goods in transit;

(c)   a right of re-sale.

It is important to remember that the seller is able to exercise these rights only in limited circumstances:

(a)   the seller must come within the definition of an unpaid seller; and

(b)   the seller has to have possession of, or at least control over, the goods.

In most circumstances, it will be unwise for the seller to rely solely on its statutory rights, and a retention of title clause should be included in the contract as a matter of course (see **Chapter 6**).

Seller's lien (ss 41, 43)

Section 41 states that an unpaid seller who is in possession of the goods is entitled to retain possession of them:

(a)   until paid;

(b)   where any credit period has expired; or

(c)   where the buyer has become insolvent.

Under s 43, the right of lien is lost if the goods are paid for, or when the goods are consigned to a carrier without retaining title to the goods, or when the buyer has possession of the goods, or by waiver by the seller.

Stoppage in transit (ss 44–46)

Sections 44 to 46 state that the seller may stop the goods in transit where the buyer has become insolvent, and retain them until paid. Under s 46(1), the stopping could be either by:

(a)   taking actual possession of the goods; or

(b)   by giving notice of the seller's claim to the carrier.

Again the right is limited. It can be used only where the buyer becomes insolvent, and can be lost if the buyer manages to intercept the goods before the seller has an opportunity to exercise its right. It cannot be used if the carrier is the agent of the buyer.

Re-sale by seller (s 48)

Section 48(3) provides that an unpaid seller can re-sell the goods where:

(a)   the goods are perishable; or

(b)   the seller gives notice to the buyer of its intention to do so.

The limit on the right of re-sale is that the seller must give notice to the buyer of its intention to re-sell and wait to see whether the buyer tenders the price within a reasonable time. Where the goods are perishable, however, the seller does not need to serve a notice.

The unpaid seller who re-sells the goods to another buyer (ie a third party) passes good title to the goods. To do so, however, the seller must be in possession of the goods, ie must still have a lien on them or have the right to stop the goods in transit (ss 48(2), (3) and s 25).

Where the unpaid seller remains in possession of the goods and re-sells them, the original contract of sale is rescinded and the buyer is discharged from further liability to pay the price. The seller is entitled to keep the proceeds of the re-sale and to sue the original buyer for damages for non-acceptance if the seller makes any loss on the re-sale (including the expense of re-selling) as against the original price (see *RV Ward v Bignall* [1967] 2 All ER 449, CA). However, the seller is entitled to keep any profit which it makes on the re-sale.

5.5.2   Personal rights of the unpaid seller

5.5.2.1   Action for the price (s 49)

The unpaid seller can sue the buyer for the price of the goods where the buyer has the property in the goods, ie ownership of the goods, but has not paid for them, or where the price is due on 'a day certain' (s 49). The advantage is that actions for the price are debt actions, so the seller does not need to worry about remoteness, mitigation, or how damages will be assessed. However, this does not help if the buyer is insolvent or likely to become so, as there is no point in taking action against an 'empty vessel'.

This right is subject to statutory limitations.

(a)   Under s 49(1) the seller can bring an action for the price if, and only if, ownership in the goods has passed, and the buyer fails or refuses to pay. This subsection cannot therefore be used where, for example, the goods are subject to a retention of title clause.

(b)   Section 49(2) gives the seller a limited right to bring an action for the price, irrespective of whether ownership of the goods has passed, where the price is payable on 'a day certain' and the buyer refuses to pay. The wording of this subsection is complex, but it only deals with cases where the price is payable 'irrespective of delivery'. There is no problem if payment is due on a specified date after delivery. Once the date for payment has passed, the seller can bring an action for the price.

The result is that failure by the buyer to pay on time does not necessarily give the seller the right to bring an action for the price, and the seller may have to rely on a claim for damages instead. In addition, recent cases have shown that problems may arise where the contract includes a retention of title clause. It is therefore advisable to include a clause in the contract giving the seller a right to bring an action for the price as soon as the date for payment has passed, irrespective of whether or not ownership has passed or title has been retained.

5.5.2.2 Non-acceptance of the goods – assessment of damages (s 50)

Where the buyer has wrongfully refused to accept and pay for the goods, the seller can sue the buyer for damages (s 50). Section 50(2) mirrors the first limb of *Hadley v Baxendale* (see **3.2.6.3**) and provides that the measure of damages is the estimated loss directly and naturally resulting from the breach. The basis for assessment of damages is laid down in s 50(3):

> Where there is an available market for the goods in question the measure of damages is prima facie to be ascertained by the difference between the contract price and the market or current price at the time or times when the goods ought to have been accepted or (if no time was fixed for acceptance) at the time of the refusal to accept.

Presumably, where there is no available market, the measure of damages is the contract value of the goods plus any additional direct expenses caused to the seller.

A problem area is consequential loss. Such loss recovery is contemplated as 'special damages' by s 54. Beyond the prima facie measure provided by s 50(3), 'special damages' (ie damages for consequential loss recoverable under the second limb of *Hadley v Baxendale*) are recoverable.

5.5.3 The seller who is not in possession of the goods (ss 17 and 19)

As discussed, the rights of the unpaid seller against the goods apply where the seller still has possession, or at least physical control, of the goods. A more difficult situation is where the goods are in the possession or control of the buyer, but the seller has still not been paid. This is a major concern for the seller, especially where the buyer is going insolvent. The danger is that the goods will be sold by a liquidator. The seller would be only an unsecured creditor and would be unlikely to be paid much, if anything, by the liquidator, and damages would not be an appropriate remedy.

There is a right under ss 17 and 19 of the SGA 1979 to reserve title to the goods. This can be done in a contract of sale by inserting a retention of title (ROT) clause (also called a *Romalpa* clause after *Aluminium Industrie Vaassen BV v Romalpa Aluminium* [1976] 1 WLR 676). The idea behind this is to allow the seller to recover the goods if the buyer fails to pay or becomes insolvent, as the seller remains the owner of the goods which are the subject to the ROT clause. These clauses will be considered in **Chapter 6**.

5.5.4 International aspects

Under the CISG, if the buyer does not pay on time, the seller may allocate a further period for payment, after which he may avoid the contract. This would mean that (provided he was in possession of them) the seller would be able to dispose of the goods as he wished without liability to the buyer.

In the PICC, Article 7.1.3 states that, where performance is to take place simultaneously, either party may withhold performance until the other party is ready to perform. If this does not take place, termination is an option. This would mean that the seller may retain the goods until payment is made. This is replicated in the PECL in Article 9:201.

Article 2-703 of the UCC allows a seller, in the event of non-payment, to withhold delivery, stop delivery, reclaim the goods, resell them, or alternatively recover damages.

5.6 RIGHTS AND REMEDIES OF THE BUYER

As with the seller, a breach of condition will always entitle the buyer to reject the goods, repudiate the contract and/or sue for damages. In addition, the buyer has the right to sue for damages for breach of warranty. Thus, the buyer will generally have the right to repudiate the contract for:

(a)   non-delivery;

(b)   late delivery, if time is of the essence;

(c)   delivery of the wrong quantity, subject to s 30(2A).

5.6.1 Claim for damages (s 53)

The buyer can sue for damages for breach of a contract term, either express or implied (s 53). This is either where the term in question is classified as a warranty, or where it is a condition but the buyer has elected not to reject the goods.

Section 51 lays down the principles for calculating damages for non-delivery of the goods, and in particular s 51(3) states:

> Where there is an available market for the goods in question the measure of damages is prima facie to be ascertained by the difference between the contract price and the market or current price of the goods at the time or times when they ought to have been delivered or (if no time was fixed) at the time of the refusal to deliver.

In other words, the buyer's loss is any increase in the price of equivalent goods obtained from another source.

Where the buyer has suffered consequential loss, it too can claim for 'further damage' under s 53(4) and 'special damages' under s 54, which, as discussed above, represent damages under the second limb of *Hadley v Baxendale* (see **5.5.2.2**).

Limitation and/or exclusion clauses in sale of goods contracts are often aimed at limiting or excluding consequential loss, subject to being disallowed under UCTA 1977. The seller will not want to take on liabilities that might far exceed its profit on the sale. Such exclusions will be considered in **Chapter 7**.

5.6.2 Specific performance (s 52)

The buyer's right to apply for specific performance is regulated by s 52. The right is only for specific or ascertained goods, that is goods identified and agreed upon at the time the contract is made. It does not extend to unascertained goods, eg 5 kilos of potatoes (not yet identified) (see **Chapter 4**). The right applies whether or not the property in the goods (title to the goods) has already passed to the buyer. Whether or not specific performance is ordered is a matter within the discretion of the court. It will not be awarded in respect of goods which can be bought elsewhere by the buyer, or where damages would provide an adequate remedy.

5.6.3 International provisions

Under the CISG, remedies for the buyer are contained in Articles 46 to 52, and include specific performance, repair or replacement, damages, and avoidance of the contract. In the PICC, Articles 7.2.2 to 7.3.1 includes similar remedies, as does Article 2-711 of the UCC. Article 9 of the PECL contains remedies including specific performance, damages and termination. (See **3.3.6.2**.)

SUMMARY

The core terms of a sale of goods contract are those relating to price, payment and delivery. These are default terms which will apply only where the parties have not made their own arrangements as to these matters. We have looked at the main considerations in relation to each of these, and the remedies available where one or other of the parties to a sale of goods contract is in breach of the core terms. We are now going to consider how a commercial seller may protect itself against non-payment.

SALE OF GOODS: OWNERSHIP AND RETENTION OF TITLE

LEARNING OUTCOMES

After reading this chapter you will be able to:

- understand the default provisions of the SGA 1979 in relation to the transfer of ownership (or title) and the passing of risk in the goods
- appreciate that the main concern of a commercial seller of goods is ensuring that it is protected in the event of non-payment
- explain the purpose of a retention of title clause
- describe the legal and practical effect of typical provisions in a retention of title clause
- prepare a checklist for a retention of title clause
- give practical advice on the measures that a seller should take to back up a retention of title clause.

6.1 INTRODUCTION

The effect of a sale of goods contract is that ownership of the goods passes to the buyer, so the next issue to consider is the transfer of ownership in the goods. Before looking at the rules relating to ownership, it is worth briefly thinking about the terminology. The SGA 1979 refers to both 'title to goods' and 'property in goods'. Both of these terms are used to mean the same thing: 'ownership' (although this is not a term that is used in the Act itself).

The rules on ownership are complicated by the fact that the SGA 1979 provides separate rules for specific (or ascertained) goods and unascertained goods (see **Chapter 4** and **6.2.2**). Sales of specific goods are the most common in practice, but the transfer of ownership of unascertained goods gives more scope for problems to arise, particularly where the parties have not made provision for this.

It is also important to remember that the SGA 1979 itself separates ownership, possession and the passing of risk, and as discussed in **Chapter 5**, the parties can provide for each of these separately. The result is that it is perfectly possible for one party, often the buyer, to have possession but not ownership of the goods. Deciding who has ownership of the goods, and when, is important for a number of reasons.

The rules relating to ownership and retention of title in the UK are dealt with at **6.1–6.6**. International aspects of retention of title clauses are considered at **6.7**.

6.1.1   Insolvency

In the event of the insolvency of either of the parties, the goods come under the control of the liquidator, administrator or trustee in bankruptcy, and there is a risk that they may be sold. If the seller has delivered the goods, it would only have a claim to the proceeds as an unsecured creditor. However, if the seller has a valid retention of title over the goods (ie ownership has not passed) then it may be able to reclaim them before they are sold and thus recover the full value of the goods. Equally, where the buyer has paid for the goods but these have not been physically delivered, again its only claim will be as an unsecured creditor. If, however, the buyer has acquired ownership before the goods have been physically delivered, it can claim the goods before they are sold.

6.1.2   Risk

Under s 20, prima facie risk passes with ownership, so where the parties have not made specific provision for the passing of risk, and the goods are damaged or destroyed, it is important to know who has ownership of the goods to establish liability. If the goods are damaged or destroyed by a third party, eg a carrier, it will be necessary to establish who has the right to bring a claim against the carrier.

6.1.3   Seller's action for the price

Retention of title clauses can create difficulties in relation to the application of s 49 of the SGA 1979. In *PST Energy Shipping 7 LLC and Product Shipping and Trading SA v OW Bunker Malta Ltd and ING Bank SA (Res Cogitans)* [2016] UKSC 23 (see **4.4.1**), the Supreme Court held that the SGA 1979 did not apply to the contract, and hence the buyer could not rely on s 49 as a defence to an action for the price. The court identified three features of a supply contract that were important in reaching this decision:

(a)   the contract contained a credit period; and

(b)   the contract contained a retention of title clause; and

(c)   the contract gave permission for the buyer to consume the goods prior to the end of the credit period, and before title had passed. (It seems that such permission can be express or implied.)

This is a decision which will have wide-reaching consequences for many types of supply contract, particularly commodities which are likely to be used before title has passed, and suppliers may need to consider carefully whether it is necessary to include a retention of title clause.

Where a contract includes a retention of title clause, the Court of Appeal decision in *Caterpillar (NI) (formerly FG Wilson (Engineering) Ltd) v John Holt & Co (Liverpool) Ltd* [2013] EWCA Civ 1232 created considerable uncertainty as to the application of s 49 of the SGA 1979. In that case, the Court held that an action for the price could only brought under the precise circumstances set out in s 49(1) (or s 49(2), which is in effect an exception to the strictness of the rule in s 49(1) – see **5.5.2.1**). The retention of title clause prevented the seller (Caterpillar) from bringing an action for the price, as title to the goods had not passed to the seller.

In the *OW Bunker* case, the Supreme Court commented on whether an action for the price could be brought where there is a valid retention of title clause, as a result of which ownership has not passed to the buyer. Had the OW Bunker contract been a sale of goods contract, Lord Mance, who delivered the judgment of the Court, considered that the Court would have overruled the decision of the Court of Appeal in the *Caterpillar* case. In his view, s 49 is not a 'complete code of situations' where the price of the goods may be recoverable. Although these comments were obiter, they are likely to be persuasive in deciding when s 49 applies. There still remains a degree of uncertainty, as he commented that the precise circumstances where it would apply 'must be left for determination at some future date'.

6.2 TRANSFER OF OWNERSHIP

6.2.1 Specific or ascertained goods

Ascertained goods are goods that can be identified at the time of the contract. Specific goods are goods which have been agreed on at the time of the contract. Section 17 of the SGA 1979 provides that the property in ascertained goods passes when the parties intend it to pass. This leaves the parties free to decide when ownership of the goods will pass. Their decision is often bound up with what they have agreed about delivery and payment.

6.2.2 Unascertained goods

Unascertained goods are goods which have not yet been identified. Unascertained goods may be generic goods, for example 100 kilos of potatoes or goods forming part of a bulk, or 100 kilos of potatoes out of 500 kilos. As far as unascertained goods are concerned, s 16 makes it clear that property cannot pass until the goods are ascertained. This section applies regardless of the intention of the parties, so it is not possible to make provision for the passing of ownership until the goods are ascertained. This can present serious problems for the buyer if the seller becomes insolvent.

6.2.3 Default provisions

Where the parties have failed to make provision for the passing of ownership, there are default provisions in s 18. The SGA 1979 does not really contemplate the possibility that the parties did not have any intention in relation to the transfer of ownership, and so s 18 contains complex rules for ascertaining their intention. The reason that it is important to deal with transfer of ownership as an express provision is that unintended effects can arise out of the application of the s 18 rules.

Rules 1–4 relate to specific goods. Rule 5 relates to unascertained or future goods:

(a) Rule 1 deals with unconditional contracts for the sale of specific goods in a deliverable state. Property passes when the contract is made. A simple example is when a customer buys a chocolate bar in a shop. Ownership passes when the money is handed over and the customer receives the chocolate bar.

(b) Rule 2 deals with conditional contracts where the goods exist but the seller is bound to do something to put the goods into a deliverable state, eg the buyer agrees to buy 100 kilos of potatoes (specific goods), but the seller has to package them into 1 kilo bags before delivery. Property passes once the seller has done this and given notice to the buyer.

(c) Rule 3 deals with conditional contracts where the goods exist in a deliverable state but the seller has to weigh, measure, test the goods or 'do some other act' to ascertain the price. Property passes when the seller has done this and given notice to the buyer.

(d) Rule 4 deals with goods delivered on approval or sale and return. Property passes when the buyer approves, accepts the goods, 'otherwise adopts the transaction' or retains them beyond any fixed time for their return (or if none, beyond a reasonable time).

(e) Rule 5 provides that property in unascertained goods passes in two situations, either when:

(i) unascertained goods are unconditionally appropriated to the contract by one party and the other party assents to this, either expressly or impliedly, for example 100 kilos of potatoes are weighed and put into a container for transportation; or

(ii) the seller delivers the goods (either to the buyer or a carrier) and the buyer assents to this, either expressly or impliedly.

The obvious danger with Rule 5 is that is that the property might pass to the buyer long before the seller wishes that to happen, ie before the seller is paid. Another serious consequence is that the risk of the goods will pass over to the buyer (under s 20(1), see **5.4.6.1**) at a time when they could easily still be in the possession of the seller. Again, this may not be the desired result at all; see *Wardars (Import & Export) Co Ltd v W Norwood & Sons Ltd* [1968] 2 QB 663, CA.

6.2.4   The basis for retention of title clauses

Section 19 provides the basis for retention of title. It provides that a seller may 'reserve the right of disposal of goods until certain conditions are fulfilled'. Therefore a seller who is allowing its buyer a credit period can stipulate that ownership will not pass to the buyer until the buyer pays for the goods. The seller retains ownership until that condition is fulfilled.

6.2.5   Proposals for reform

The rules in relation to transfer of ownership, which apply to both businesses and consumers, have remained largely unchanged since the 19th century. The language is outdated and unclear, and the rules are generally recognised to be unsuitable for today's trading conditions, particularly in relation to online sales to consumers. In 2021, the Law Commission published a draft bill that would introduce new provisions into the Consumer Rights Act 2015 to modernise the rules on when consumers acquire ownership of goods under sales of goods contracts, but no further progress has been made on this.

6.3   INTRODUCTION TO RETENTION OF TITLE

The effect of ss 17 and 19 (**6.2** above), therefore, is to give the seller the right to reserve title to the goods. This can be done in a contract of sale by inserting a retention of title (ROT) clause (also called a *Romalpa* clause after *Aluminium Industrie Vaassen BV v Romalpa Aluminium* [1976] 1 WLR 676). The idea of retaining title to the goods until they are paid for, or until they are sold on or used up (as with components/ingredients, etc), is that, in the last resort, the seller can recover its own goods and prevent a liquidator or trustee in bankruptcy of the buyer disposing of the goods.

The advantage for the buyer is that, up until such time as the seller might need to rely upon its ROT clause, the buyer is free to sell or deal with the goods as it wishes. In *Fairfax Gerrard Holdings Ltd v Capital Bank plc* [2007] EWCA Civ 1226, it was held that there is no inconsistency between the inclusion of a ROT clause and an implied or even express right to sell the goods. In practice, many ROT clauses include a provision which states that the buyer has right to sell the goods. This does no more than restate the legal position, but it provides reassurance for inexperienced buyers who are not familiar with ROT provisions.

The validity of ROT clauses has been upheld where the goods remain identifiable (see eg *Clough Mill Ltd v Martin* [1985] 1 WLR 111 and *Armour v Thyssen Edelstahlwerke AG* [1991] 2 AC 339). In *Clough Mill*, yarn had been sold to a manufacturer of fabrics. The seller was held to have title to the unused yarn.

6.3.1   Creation of charges

A charge is a right granted over an asset or assets to secure a debt. It gives the charge holder priority to be paid ahead of unsecured creditors in the event of insolvency. Under s 859A of the Companies Act 2006, charges may be registered at Companies House within 21 days of creation. Registration is not compulsory. If the charge is not registered, s 859H provides that it will be void against a liquidator or an administrator, and also against other unsecured creditors. However, it is important to note that it will still be valid as between the parties themselves. For a full discussion of charges, see **Chapter 11** of *Business Law and Practice*.

Simple ROT clauses do not generally create registrable charges over the buyer's assets. Such clauses operate by preventing the property in the goods from passing to the buyer in the first place, ie the seller still owns them until he is paid. A seller cannot (and would not) take a charge over its own property by way of security. Problems only arise where the clause attempts to go further than simply retaining title to the goods and gives the seller rights over the buyer's property. These include attempts to retain title to either the proceeds of sale of the original goods, or products which have been mixed with or manufactured into other goods. Any such attempt would create a charge, which would be void against a liquidator, an administrator or a third party unless registered.

In practice, it is not going to be practical to register these charges. A new charge would come into existence each time the buyer resold the goods, in the case of a proceeds of sale clause, or mixed them with others, in the case of a mixed/manufactured goods clause. The seller would find it very hard to police this. It would also be onerous to complete the necessary registration forms each time, identifying the property over which the charge had been created. Registering numerous charges could also lead to adverse credit ratings for the buyer if it is a company, because the buyer's file at Companies House would show all these charges registered against it. This would discourage anyone thinking of lending money to the buyer. The effect of such actions by the seller would be to put off the buyer from contracting with the seller in the first place. In practice, therefore, the seller will not usually attempt to register any charge which an ROT clause might create.

6.3.2   Proceeds of sale

Where the goods have been sold on to an innocent third party, under s 25 of the SGA 1979 an innocent third party will get good title to the goods. If a buyer of the goods sells them on, the sub-buyer will get good title to those goods. The proceeds of the sub-sale sale will belong to the buyer, and not to the seller. Any attempt by the seller to claim or trace the proceeds would therefore amount to an attempt to claim the buyer's property and so would amount to a charge.

Tracing has been done successfully only once, in *Aluminium Industrie Vaassen BV v Romalpa Aluminium* [1976] 1 WLR 676. The sellers there tried to claim the proceeds of sale of the goods once the goods themselves had been sold on. The Court of Appeal allowed this on the grounds that there was an express fiduciary relationship between the sellers and the buyers (with the buyers selling the goods on to a third party as agents for the sellers rather than in their own right). Subsequently, the courts have been unwilling to recognise this fiduciary relationship, which seems to have been based, in *Romalpa*, upon concessions made by one party, probably unnecessarily.

Over the years, there have been many attempts to draft ROT clauses to permit the seller to claim sale proceeds. Very simple clauses entitling the seller to the proceeds are almost certain to be construed as charges over the proceeds. It seems from the case law that the courts will take exactly the same view of more complex attempts (eg elaborate clauses describing the existence of a fiduciary relationship between the parties).

In *Compaq Computer Ltd v Abercorn Group Ltd (t/a Osiris) and Others* [1991] BCC 484, Abercorn was appointed as an authorised dealer of Compaq's computers. The agreement contained a clause that the goods were held by Abercorn as 'bailee and agent' and proceeds of sub-sales were to be accounted for to Compaq. The court held that the relationship was a commercial buyer/seller relationship, and not a bailment, agency or fiduciary relationship. The arrangement was held to be a charge over the proceeds of the sub-sales, which was void for want of registration. It seems that even a very carefully worded clause will create only a charge.

6.3.3   Separation of proceeds

The clause may also provide that where the buyer sells the goods on, it will pay the proceeds of sale into a separate bank account, which it will hold on trust for the seller. The idea is to stop the money generated by the sale of the seller's goods from becoming mixed up with other money the buyer may have which is nothing to do with the seller. The problem here is that, whilst the clause is legally effective as between the buyer and the seller, a buyer in financial difficulties is unlikely to comply with such a provision, and may use the money to stave off creditors or to pay off its overdraft. Basic banking principles mean that once money is paid into an overdrawn account, it will be absorbed by the overdraft. Tracing will not be possible. It is therefore common to provide that the money should not be paid into an overdrawn bank account, but this is difficult to police and the seller's only remedy for breach is damages.

It is quite common to find that the clause also requires the buyer to assign the debts arising from any credit sub-sales that it makes to the seller. The problem with such a clause is that if the sub-buyer fails to comply with this or does it when it is insolvent, the seller will not usually recover the money. The rights are merely contractual and of little use in insolvency. See *Fairfax Gerrard Holdings Ltd v Capital Bank plc* [2007] EWCA Civ 1226.

6.3.4   Mixed, manufactured or altered goods

Problems also arise where the original goods have been used in a manufacturing process and have lost their original identity. Where the goods have been incorporated into other products, the original goods are considered to have been subsumed into the new products and the seller has no right to the new products. The buyer will have incurred additional costs of the manufacturing process, eg the cost of other materials and labour. The manufactured goods belong to the buyer and incorporate its profit. Again, any attempt by the seller to claim a right over the new product belonging to the buyer would create a charge.

This point was considered in *Clough Mill Ltd v Martin* [1985] 1 WLR 111, where the seller supplied yarn to a manufacturer of fabrics. Lord Goff stated:

> I find it impossible to believe that it was the intention of the parties that the plaintiff would thereby gain the windfall of the full value of the new product, deriving as it may well do not merely from the labour of the buyer but also from materials that were the buyer's without any duty to account to the buyer for any surplus of the proceeds of sale above the outstanding balance of the price due by the buyer to the plaintiff.

The seller was held not to have title to the finished fabric, only to the unused yarn.

In *Borden (UK) Ltd v Scottish Timber Products Ltd* [1981] Ch 25, the sellers sold resin to manufacturers of chipboard. It was held that they did not have title to the chipboard, or to the proceeds of its sale. It is interesting to note that in *the OW Bunker* case (see **4.4.1**), the Supreme Court suggested that it may have been wrongly assumed in this case that there was a sale of goods contract, although it would not have affected the outcome.

Sometimes it may not be quite so clear whether the goods have been incorporated during the manufacturing process. In *Re Peachdart Ltd* [1984] Ch 131, leather hides had been made into handbags. It was held that 'once the process of manufacture had started ... work and materials provided by the company would result in the leather being converted into ... other goods of a distinctive character'. A slightly more gruesome example is *Chaigley Farms Ltd v Crawford Kay and Grayshire* [1996] BCC 957, where the retention of title was over animals which were sent for slaughter. The judge held that there was 'an inescapable difference between a live animal and a dead one'. The result was the title had passed to the buyer, and the seller did not own the carcasses.

6.3.5   Detachable goods

It is important to distinguish between manufactured goods and goods which have simply been attached to other goods. Where the goods are readily detachable then it is appropriate to have a clause reserving the right of the seller to detach its goods and remove them. For example, in *Hendy Lennox (Industrial Engines) Ltd v Graham Puttick Ltd* [1984] 1 WLR 485, the seller had sold diesel engines to the buyer. The buyer had bolted the engines to electrical generators. It was therefore feasible to detach the engines without damaging the generators. A clause allowing the seller to separate and remove detachable goods will not create a charge and is likely to be upheld by the court.

6.3.6 Goods which cannot be identified

Where the goods have been mixed with other goods and are no longer identifiable, the goods will belong to the buyer. In *Re Andrabell Ltd (In Liquidation); Airborne Accessories Ltd v Goodman* [1984] 3 All ER 407, the seller sold travel bags in a number of consignments. The contracts did not have an 'all moneys' clause (see **6.4.2.1**) so any rights attached only to the consignment for which the seller had not been paid. The seller was not able to identify those bags from all the other bags, so could not recover any bags. It was also not allowed to trace the proceeds of sale through the buyer's general bank account.

6.3.7 Bulk storage

Where the seller's goods are of a type that can be stored, typically in bulk, along with the goods of the same type which belong to other suppliers or even of the buyer, eg diesel oil or grain, it may be possible to retain title to a share of the bulk. The goods must all be of the same type and specification. In such a 'commingled' mass, title does not pass to the buyer but, instead, all contributors become owners in common, generally, in proportion to their contributions to the bulk.

Glencore International AG v Metro Trading International Inc (No 2) [2001] 1 Lloyd's Rep 284 involved the storage of oil from different suppliers. The oil was all of the same type and grade, and had been stored by the buyer mixed, or co-mingled, in bulk containers. It was held that upon commingling during storage, Glencore would become an owner of the whole of the commingled bulk in common with Metro and any other persons whose oil had contributed to the bulk. Each party's share would be in proportion to the quantity of oil contributed by each of them. This illustrates the problems that such cases throw up. The big difference between this case and the earlier 'mixed goods' cases is that, in the bulk storage cases, it can be seen that the goods have not lost their identifiable nature and title does not pass to the buyer. Nevertheless, slight differences in grade or specification between the separate quantities supplied would easily cause a mixing or blending into a bulk, in which the separate sellers had lost their titles and property.

6.4 DRAFTING A RETENTION OF TITLE CLAUSE: A BASIC CHECKLIST

It is important to appreciate at this stage that no clause can always be guaranteed to be appropriate in all situations. The solicitor drafting the clause should always check when using a precedent that it fits in with the client's needs and instructions. The following suggested provisions aim to cover the basic situation of retaining title to the goods, but also to go further and cover some of the problems mentioned above.

Any ROT checklist should deal with:

(a) provisions which are essential to ensure that the clause is legally effective;

(b) provisions which are not legally essential, but which are desirable to make the clause work practically for the seller;

(c) clauses which may not be legally effective, but which may be included for 'bluff' value.

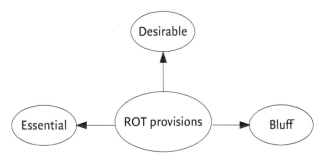

6.4.1 Essential provisions

6.4.1.1 Reserving title – simple retention of title

The seller should make it clear that it will remain the owner of the goods and that (legal) ownership will not pass to the buyer until full payment is received. This is a simple ROT clause. To be legally effective, an ROT clause must retain legal title to the goods, although it is not necessary to provide specifically for 'legal title' or 'legal ownership' to be retained; wording such as 'ownership', or 'title' will suffice. What is not sufficient is to retain 'equitable and beneficial ownership' as in *Re Bond Worth* [1980] Ch 228, where the seller was held to have passed title to the goods. The clause created an equitable charge which was then void for lack of registration.

It is important to remember the seller cannot recover more than it is owed. Where the seller recovers the goods and resells them under a simple ROT clause, it must reimburse the buyer the amount of any advance or part payment which it has made. However, where the seller makes a profit on the sale, it is entitled to keep any profit which it has made, as it is selling as the owner of the goods.

6.4.1.2 Rights of entry, seizure and sale

The seller must make sure that the clause specifically provides for the right to go on to the buyer's premises (or the seller will commit trespass in doing so) to recover the goods (which would otherwise be conversion) and also to re-sell them. Clearly the seller cannot do this on a whim. The clause should contain 'triggers': events that will enable the seller to exercise these rights. The rights could be expressed as arising when the buyer is overdue in paying for the goods (ie, the consignment actually sold under this agreement, or any other goods which the seller has supplied to the buyer). This could be linked through to a clause in the agreement making the price become due immediately on the buyer becoming insolvent.

6.4.2 Desirable provisions

The following provisions are not essential but are desirable from the seller's point of view. All these clauses will be legally effective, although practically it may not always be possible to enforce them.

6.4.2.1 All moneys clause

Often an ROT clause will provide that ownership will not pass to the buyer until the buyer has paid all amounts owing to the seller in respect of all goods which the seller has supplied to the buyer (ie, paid for not just this consignment of goods but any others which the buyer has bought previously). This is called an 'all moneys' (or 'all monies') clause. It aims to retain ownership of the goods until all outstanding debts owed to the seller have been paid. Many precedents are likely to include an 'all moneys' provision. It is not necessary for an ROT clause to include this provision, but it is potentially a very useful protection where the seller is dealing with repeat orders, as it avoids the seller having to identify particular goods from particular consignments.

Such clauses have been upheld as legally effective, eg in *Armour v Thyssen Edelstahlwerke AG* [1991] 2 AC 339. However, the clause must be consistent with the parties' overall trading relationship. Where finished goods are sold for immediate onward resale, the clause may be at odds with this relationship (see *Sandhu (t/a Isher Fashions UK) v Jet Star Retail Ltd (In Administration)* [2011] EWCA Civ 459, although in this case there were a number of additional reasons why the court found that the clause was ineffective). An all moneys clause should be carefully drafted and included as a separate sub-clause to allow for severance in the event that it is found to be ineffective.

6.4.2.2 Sales to sub-buyers

The clause may also provide that title will pass when the buyer sells the goods on to a sub-buyer in accordance with the agreement. This acknowledges s 25 of SGA 1979, which states that an innocent third party gets good title to the goods when the goods are sold on to it by the original buyer (see **6.3.2**).

It has also been suggested that, where the buyer resells the goods to a sub-buyer pending transfer of title, the agreement should state that it does so as principal and not as agent for the seller. Although, in the absence of any case law on this point, the position is far from certain, this may help to preserve the seller's right to an action for the price (see **6.1.3**).

6.4.2.3 Separate storage of the seller's goods while in the buyer's possession

An ROT clause will be practically effective only if the seller can identify its goods once it goes to collect them. The seller needs to decide whether anything can or should be done to maximise the chances of being able to recover the goods (or at least getting some money back if something happens to them while in the buyer's possession). So, a clause could be included to provide for separate storage in order to maximise the chances that the seller can identify its own goods when trying to recover them.

A further possibility for protection of the goods is the seller marking its goods to make them easily identifiable. Where practicable, this can be a useful back-up to a separate storage clause (which the buyer may disobey). Obviously this will not always work – for example, 100 tons of gravel is impossible to mark. Note that the seller will sometimes reserve the right to inspect the buyer's premises to check if separate storage provisions are being complied with. Although this may be a useful power to have, the reality is often that separate storage provisions are impossible to police. If the buyer does disobey it will obviously be in breach of contract, the remedy for which is damages. This may be of no use to the seller (eg if the buyer is in financial difficulties or has become insolvent).

6.4.2.4 Passing of risk

It is important for sale of goods agreements to provide expressly for the passing of the risk of accidental loss of, or damage to, the goods. This may be done in a separate clause, but is often found in a retention of title clause.

Under s 20 of the SGA 1979, goods remain at the seller's risk until the property in them (ie, ownership) is transferred to the buyer, unless the parties agree otherwise (see **5.4.6.1**). This is not the desired situation in a contract with a retention of title clause, so a clause is added which displaces s 20 by contrary agreement. The seller will usually stipulate that risk passes on delivery. This will often be linked to a requirement that the buyer insures the goods and holds any proceeds of the policy on trust for the seller (see **6.4.2.5**).

6.4.2.5 Insurance

If the goods are destroyed before they can be reclaimed, the seller will want recompense. So a clause should be included to require the buyer to insure the seller's goods and to hold the proceeds on trust for the seller. (Unlike a tracing clause (see **6.3.1**), this does not create a charge, as the ownership of the goods will not have passed when the goods are destroyed and the insurance payment becomes due.)

6.4.2.6 Detachable goods

A detachable goods clause will provide that if the goods supplied to the buyer are readily detachable without damage to the buyer's products, the seller's goods can be recovered, as in *Hendy Lennox (Industrial Engines) Ltd v Graham Puttick Ltd* [1984] 1 WLR 485 (see **6.3.1**). Such a clause should not be confused with mixed or manufactured goods clauses.

6.4.3 Bluff value clauses

Some of the tactics used by sellers are not going to be succeed because, as discussed at **6.3.1,** certain clauses create charges which are void as against liquidators, administrators or third parties if not registered. However, this does not stop such clauses being included, if only in the hope that they might serve to exert commercial pressure, even though enforcement is unlikely to succeed. These include:

(a) tracing into the proceeds of sale, separation of proceeds and assignment of debts;

(b) claiming ownership of 'mixed' or manufactured goods.

It is important to remember that each of these clauses will be valid as between the buyer and the seller, and enforceable until the buyer becomes insolvent. Thus, if the seller acts quickly it may have some chance of success, especially as against smaller companies which may not have taken legal advice. However, once the buyer is insolvent, a seller will not succeed in trying to enforce an unregistered charge against battle-hardened liquidators or administrators.

6.5 EXAMPLES

Table 6.1 below gives examples of some clauses that may be included in an ROT clause. (These are not intended to be exhaustive, nor are they intended to be watertight. They are simply examples of the types of clause that may be encountered in practice.)

Type of clause	Example	Effectiveness
'Simple' retention of title	'Ownership of the Goods shall not pass until the Buyer has paid the purchase price in full.'	Valid. Must be supported by right of entry, seizure and sale.
All monies clause	'Ownership of the Goods shall not pass until the Buyer has paid all amounts owing to the Seller and no amounts remain outstanding.'	Valid. Usual type of commercial ROT clause. Must be supported by right of entry, seizure and sale.
Detachable goods clause	'The Seller may enter the Buyer's premises to repossess the Goods and may, if necessary, detach or remove the Goods from any other goods.'	Valid, provided goods can be identified and detached without damaging the buyer's property. [Not to be confused with mixed/manufactured/altered goods clause.]
Separate storage/ marking	'The Buyer must store the Goods separately from any other goods in its possession.'	Valid. Difficult to police. Seller's only remedy for breach is damages, which may not be helpful once buyer is insolvent.
Insurance proceeds	'If the Goods are destroyed by an insured risk before the Buyer has paid for them, the Buyer must hold any proceeds of insurance on trust for the Seller.'	Valid, provided ownership of goods has not passed to buyer at time of claim. Must require the buyer to insure at least up to amount owing to seller.
Fiduciary relationship	'The Buyer shall hold the Goods on a fiduciary basis as the Seller's bailee.'	Creates charge. Void against a liquidator or administrator or third party without notice unless registered. Valid as between the parties. Ineffective once the buyer is insolvent. Usually used with tracing.

Type of clause	Example	Effectiveness
Tracing clause	[On sale to a sub-buyer at any time before payment]: 'The Seller may trace any proceeds of sale which the Buyer receives into the [separate] bank account or any other bank account which the Buyer maintains.'	As above, void against a liquidator, etc unless registered, but valid as between the parties. Usually supported by a clause providing that the Buyer should pay any proceeds of sale into a separate bank account.
Mixed goods clause	'If the Goods are incorporated in or used as material for other goods, ownership in the whole of such goods shall be and remain with the Seller [until payment or resale].'	As above, void against a liquidator, etc unless registered, but valid as between the parties

Table 6.1 ROT provisions

6.6 'BACKING UP' A RETENTION OF TITLE CLAUSE

Even the best drafted ROT clauses will not always be effective, and may not be appropriate commercially. There are practical and legal limitations, which need to be considered:

(a) Practically, the effectiveness of ROT clauses depends on the nature of the goods. They will work only if the goods remain unaltered and can be identified. They will not be suitable if the goods are perishable or of low value.

(b) Legally, the clause will work only if it has been incorporated into the contract by signature, notice or previous course of dealing.

(c) A clause may be effective as between the buyer and the seller, eg a separate storage clause, but the seller's only remedy for breach will be a claim for damages, which will be useless where the buyer is in financial difficulties or insolvent.

(d) Experienced liquidators will use every opportunity to challenge a clause, and watertight drafting is not always possible. Very often, a seller will find that it is obliged to obtain a court order to enforce its ROT clause.

(e) A further consideration, where the buyer has gone into administration, is that the Insolvency Act 1986 provides that the administrator's consent is needed to reclaim the goods. Where a company is subject to the new standalone moratorium introduced by the Corporate Insolvency and Governance Act 2020, the consent of the court is required to reclaim the goods. The retention of title is effectively 'frozen' during the period of the administration or moratorium.

(f) Speed is of the essence once a buyer enters liquidation or administration. Recent case law suggests that failure to notify a liquidator/administrator of a claim under an ROT clause can render what would otherwise be a legally enforceable ROT clause invalid (*Sandhu v Jet Star Retail Ltd*). Once they are aware of the claim, however, a liquidator/administrator can be personally liable in the tort of conversion if they sell the goods which they are aware are subject to a valid ROT clause.

It is worth encouraging a seller to back up any ROT clause by taking practical steps either to minimise the chances of dealing with buyers who may not pay, or to provide an incentive for the buyer to pay up, or both. The possibilities include the following.

6.6.1 Checks on the buyer/controlling the credit the buyer is given

This is likely to be a useful practical back-up to retention of title. In an ideal world, it would include the following measures:

(a)   The seller should run a tight system of credit control, with frequent checks on buyers' creditworthiness. The seller should take steps to ensure that buyers always pay by the due date, send out invoices on time and chase debts before they start to become a problem. It should ensure that all relevant staff know precisely the limit of the credit that the buyer is allowed.

(b)   If buyers start to fall behind in paying for the goods, the seller may want to consider reducing any credit period allowed, or even move on to demanding cash on delivery or 'up front'. Obviously, whether this is a practical solution will vary from case to case. The buyer may not agree to the new terms being imposed on it.

(c)   If the contract permits, the seller should consider removing its goods from the buyer's premises at the first hint of trouble rather than waiting for a receiver or liquidator to be appointed. Once creditors become twitchy, things can happen very quickly indeed and, in practice, the goods may simply 'disappear' before they can be reclaimed.

(d)   If a buyer persistently pays late, there is always the option of refusing to deal with the buyer in future.

(e)   If the contract is still subsisting, the threat of termination may serve to concentrate the buyer's mind. However, such threats should be used with care, not least because the seller will not want to be sued for damages for breach of contract. Appropriate notice periods should be given. However, it may be more efficient for the seller to pay the damages and cut his losses on an uneconomic contract, rather than continue with it. (This is sometimes referred to as 'efficient' or 'economic' breach.) Again, careful thought must be given to the likely amount of any damages which the buyer may claim.

6.6.2   Debt factoring

Factoring is where the debts are sold to someone else who will then collect them (see **4.7.8**). This is an alternative to retention of title, rather than a supplement to it. Obviously, the debts cannot be sold for 100% of their value, as the factor has to make a profit. The discount can vary considerably, according to the credit period and/or the creditworthiness of the debtor.

6.6.3   Credit risk insurance

A seller may also be able to insure against the risk of the buyer not paying. Credit risk insurance may sometimes be too expensive to be worthwhile, but in the last few years it has become cheaper and more widely available. Sellers are able to obtain policies tailored to their precise needs rather than on an 'all debts' basis, which would be very expensive.

6.6.4   Providing for interest

The seller may charge interest on sums which become overdue. This may act as an incentive to the buyer to pay on time, and will give the seller some recompense if the payment is late. Normally, the best way to deal with interest is to provide for it expressly in the contract. The seller must not go over the top when providing for the amount of interest, as a provision which claimed excessive interest could be struck down as a penalty.

The Late Payment of Commercial Debts (Interest) Act 1998 (as amended) provides specifically for the payment of interest in certain commercial situations. The 1998 Act works in the following way:

(a)   it implies into applicable contracts a term relating to interest (basically it will apply to commercial contracts for the supply of goods or services);

(b)   the term is to the effect that any 'qualifying debt' created by the contract carries simple interest in accordance with the Act, known as 'statutory interest', currently 8% above the Bank of England base rate; and

(c)   in certain circumstances, this right to interest may be ousted by contract terms if there is another 'substantial contractual remedy' for late payment, but the contract may not provide that late payment carries no remedy at all.

Many businesses which might benefit under the Act are becoming more aware of its existence, and there is some evidence that it is beginning to have an impact.

In *Banham Marshalls Services Unlimited v Lincolnshire CC* [2007] EWHC 402 (QB), the Act was even applied to payments which were being withheld because of a genuine legal dispute, where one party had delayed the commencement of proceedings.

Even if there is no express provision in the contract and the Act does not apply, there are statutory provisions for claiming interest in both the High Court and county court. This has the disadvantage that technically any award of interest is in the discretion of the court (although this is rarely a problem). Also, to be certain of its entitlement to interest, the seller must incur the cost of proceedings and wait for judgment. Debtors routinely rely on this loophole and refuse to pay interest unless proceedings are commenced.

6.7   INTERNATIONAL ASPECTS OF RETENTION OF TITLE CLAUSES

There is no international harmonisation of the rules relating to retention of title clauses. The result is that there may be variations from state to state as to whether retention of title is allowed at all and, if it is, what the specific rules are in relation to clause validity and application.

As a general rule, watch for variety in the following areas:

(a)   *Whether the clause needs to be in writing.* In some countries, for example Belgium, a retention clause is ineffective unless in writing, whereas in Australia and Greece it may be implied into the contract. In some countries, such as Denmark, it must also be signed. In other countries, such as France, the clause must be in larger writing than the rest of the contract, so that it is easier to spot.

(b)   *Registration.* The formalities to be observed vary from country to country. In Brazil, the sale contract should be translated into Portuguese and registered. In Switzerland, the ROT clause must be registered. In other countries, such as the UK, Australia and Greece, the clause may create a charge, which will not be valid unless registered.

(c)   *Whether mixing or selling the goods ends the retention rights.* This again varies from country to country. For example, in the US, the Netherlands, South Africa, Spain and Germany, rights can exist in the finished product, but this is not possible in the UK and most other countries. In Belgium and many other countries, only a clause which operates between the parties to the sale is permitted, so it cannot affect the rights of third parties who gain possession of the goods. In Ireland, tracing into the proceeds of sale is possible.

As far as the international conventions are concerned, the CISG does not deal with retention of title, and provides for risk to pass when the goods are handed over. The timing of the handing over of title is not dealt with (apart from saying that it is to be 'in accordance with the contract': the implication being that the parties are free to set the timing of this themselves).

As the PICC are not specifically concerned with sales of goods, the issue of the timing of the passing of title and risk is not dealt with, apart from in Article 6.1.1, which states that a party must perform its obligations 'if a time is fixed by or determinable by the contract, at that time'. So it seems that the parties would be free to include a retention of title clause if they wished. A similar provision is contained in Article 7:102 of the PECL.

In the UCC, retention of title is specifically dealt with; retention of title clauses are permitted by Article 2-401. In the US (and under the UCC), they are called 'security interests' and, where relevant, must be filed in accordance with the UCC (except in Louisiana).

SUMMARY

In most commercial sale of goods contracts, the parties will provide when ownership of the goods will pass. Often the contract will include an ROT clause to protect the seller where the buyer fails to pay for the goods. This chapter has introduced and analysed some typical provisions you are likely to find in such a clause. We are now going to consider how the seller may protect itself from liability to the buyer.

CHAPTER 7

SALE OF GOODS: IMPLIED TERMS – TITLE AND QUALITY PROVISIONS

LEARNING OUTCOMES

After reading this chapter you will be able to:

- explain how the implied terms under ss 12–15 of the SGA 1979 impose liability on the seller
- recognise the overlap between ss 13, 14 and 15 of the SGA 1979, and the relationship between s 13 of the SGA 1979 and the rules relating to misrepresentation
- advise on the rights and remedies of the buyer where the seller is in breach of the implied terms
- appreciate that in certain circumstances a buyer may have an alternative claim for misrepresentation.

7.1 INTRODUCTION

In this chapter we consider the implied terms of the SGA 1979 in relation to title and quality, and equivalent provisions from international conventions.

The main concerns of the seller and the buyer will be the payment and delivery provisions, and, as discussed in **Chapter 5**, it is unlikely that commercial parties would not make express provision in relation to these 'core' terms. Underlying any express provisions are the implied duty of the seller to deliver (and to deliver the right quantity) and the implied duty of the buyer to accept and pay for delivery.

In the UK, ss 12–15 of the SGA 1979 impose further implied duties on the seller over and above its duty to deliver the goods. Commercial parties should be aware of these duties which relate to:

(a)   title (s 12);

(b)   correspondence with description (s 13);

(c)   quality and fitness for purpose (s 14); and

(d)   correspondence with sample (s 15).

Again, this chapter will consider some of the more important equivalent aspects of the international conventions and instruments studied in earlier chapters.

These terms will be implied into all commercial contracts, but, with the exception of s 12, the parties may expressly agree to the contrary. Section 55 provides that various implied terms can be excluded, but any exclusion of liability will be subject to UCTA 1977. However, effective exclusion will depend on the seller knowing the extent of its liability and, in the light of that liability, anticipating what could go wrong. This chapter is intended as a reminder of the liability which arises under the implied terms. Exclusion of liability will be considered in **Chapters 8** and **9**.

Sections 13, 14 and 15 of the SGA 1979 are all implied into commercial contracts as strict conditions, as is the duty to pass good title under s 12(1). Any breach will, prima facie, give the buyer the right to reject the goods and terminate the contract without the need for the buyer to prove that the seller is at fault and to claim damages for any loss arising as a result of the breach. Consumer contracts are considered at **7.9**.

Table 7.1 below gives a summary of how these sections operate.

Section	Duty of seller in relation to:	Condition/warranty	Remedy
s 12(1)	Title	Condition (s 12(5A))	Rejection and/or damages
s 12(2)	Freedom from charges and encumbrances	Warranty (s 12(5A))	Damages only
s 12(2)	Quiet possession	Warranty (s 12(5A))	Damages only
s 13(1)	Description	Condition (s 13(1A))	Rejection and/or damages
s 14(2)	Satisfactory quality	Condition (s 14(6))	Rejection and/or damages
s 14(3)	Fitness for purpose	Condition (s 14(6))	Rejection and/or damages
s 15(1)	Sample	Condition (s 15(3))	Rejection and/or damages

Table 7.1 Operation of the SGA 1979, ss 12–15

7.2 THE SELLER'S DUTY TO PASS GOOD TITLE TO THE GOODS

7.2.1 UK provisions

Section 12(1) implies into the contract a term that the seller has the right to sell the goods. In other words, it has good title to the goods. This is a condition of the contract.

In addition (and closely linked to the duty to pass good title), s 12(2) provides that there is an implied warranty:

(a)   that the goods are free from any charge or encumbrance not already known to the buyer; and

(b)   that the buyer will enjoy quiet possession of the goods.

For example, in *Rubicon Computer Systems Ltd v United Paints Ltd* [2000] 2 TCLR 453, it was held that the seller attaching a time lock to a computer system in order to deny access to the buyer was in breach of the 'quiet possession' term under s 12(2)(b).

7.2.2 International provisions

Under Article 41 the CISG, the seller must deliver goods which are free from any claims of third parties. This effectively means good title must be passed. The UCC contains, in Article 2-312, an implied warranty that the seller will pass good title to the buyer.

Neither the PICC nor the PECL specifically provide that title must be passed; however, to attempt to sell without holding good title would first be implied and secondly an infringement of the duty of good faith which both impose. This is a good example of rules which are based on civil law systems solving a problem via a general principle rather than a specific rule.

7.3 SALE BY DESCRIPTION

7.3.1 UK provisions

Section 13(1) implies a term that the goods sold should comply with their description. This might apply to goods bought from websites, catalogues, brochures or advertisements, for example. Commercially, such sales are common, so in practice it is extremely important that commercial sellers should be aware of this duty.

In order to be a sale by description, the words used must be words of description rather than simply words identifying the goods. The description may go further than simply describing the goods themselves, eg any description of the packaging of the goods will be covered by s 13. In *Re Moore v Landauer & Co* [1921] 2 KB 519, the goods were not packed as had been described in the contract, which was held to be breach of description entitling the buyer to reject the entire shipment.

Section 13(1A) states that s 13(1) is a condition.

7.3.2 International provisions

Article 35 of the CISG imposes an obligation for the goods supplied to comply with their description unless the parties have agreed otherwise. Under the UCC, again, goods would not be merchantable under Article 2-314 unless they complied with description. Under the PICC, a lack of compliance with a description would be seen as the supply of non-conforming goods, which must be remedied under Article 7.1.4, and under the PECL it would be seen as non-performance which is remediable under Article 8.104 unless the court saw it as a fundamental breach.

7.3.3 Reliance on the description

The buyer must know of and must have relied on the description. Where the buyer does not rely on the seller's description but on his own skill and judgement, s 13 will not apply. Whether or not the buyer has relied on the description will depend on the facts of the particular case, and will depend on factors such as the expertise of the buyer. The fact that the buyer has examined the goods will not necessarily mean that the buyer has relied on its own skill and judgement. In *Beale v Taylor* [1967] 1 WLR 1193, a car was described as a 1961 Triumph Herald. Two parts of different cars had been welded together, and only one was from the 1961 model. The sale was held to be a sale by description even though the buyer inspected the car after having seen the advertisement for it in the local paper.

7.3.4 Overlap between description and misrepresentation

A breach of s 13 may also amount to a misrepresentation. This gives the buyer the option to bring a claim for misrepresentation, although usually it will achieve a better outcome by suing for breach of contract (see **7.8.4** and **Chapter 3**).

7.4 SATISFACTORY QUALITY

7.4.1 UK provisions

Section 14(2) of the SGA 1979 implies a term that, in a sale in the course of a business, the goods are to be, objectively, of satisfactory quality. Under s 14(2A) the price and description of the goods will be taken into account in deciding whether or not the goods are of satisfactory quality. Section 14(2B) lists further factors which will be taken into account. These include:

(a)   fitness for the common purposes of the goods;

(b)   appearance and finish;

(c)   freedom from minor defects;

(d)   safety; and

(e)   durability.

Whether or not goods are of satisfactory quality will depend on the facts of each particular case, taking into account factors such as the price of the goods, whether the goods are new or second hand and their expected durability, which can be a particular problem. If goods are fundamentally defective, for example they do not work at all or are unsafe, they will very clearly not be of satisfactory quality. However, where the defect is not fundamental or not immediately obvious (ie latent defects) then the position may not be so clear.

Britvic Soft Drinks Ltd v Messer UK Ltd [2002] EWCA Civ 548 involved the contamination of carbon dioxide gas, supplied for making soft drinks. The evidence showed that the contaminating substance, benzene, was not present in high enough quantity to be a danger to human health, but would have damaged the saleability of the drinks. This was enough for the court to hold that the gas was not of satisfactory quality for manufacturing drinks.

By contrast, in *Thain v Anniesland Trade Centre* [1997] SCLR 991, a six-year-old car, sold for £2,995, was held to be of satisfactory quality, even though the gearbox failed two weeks after purchase of the car.

Durability was an important factor in *Friarwood Ltd v Champagne Cattier SA* [2006] EWCA Civ 1105, in deciding whether or not champagne was of satisfactory quality. The champagne was alleged to have aged prematurely, resulting in 'much reduced fizz'. In this case, a retrial was ordered after the court disapproved a judge's approach in deciding that the wine was not of satisfactory quality. He had decided that the issue should be looked at from the point of view of an average, rather than a sophisticated, customer and had rejected expert evidence which should have been taken into account.

The seller will not be liable if the defect has been specifically drawn to the buyer's attention before the contract is made, or if it should have been obvious on examination of the goods (s 14(2C)).

7.4.2   International provisions

Article 35 of the CISG imposes an obligation for the goods to be 'of the quality ... required by the contract'. Whilst it goes on to describe a specific obligation for the goods to be fit for purpose, it does not describe quality. For this reason, it is sensible, if using CISG terms, for the buyer to ensure that quality standards are included in the contract. Under Article 2-314 of the UCC, goods (in order to be 'merchantable') must be of 'fair average quality'.

Article 5.1.6 of the PICC states that, where the standard of performance for the parties is not stated in the contract, each party must perform their obligations to a 'reasonable' standard. This is likely to mean that the goods must be of reasonable quality.

Article 6.108 of the PECL states that if a party's required standard of performance is not mentioned in the contract, the party must at least tender performance which is of 'adequate quality'. This is likely to mean that the goods must be at least functional.

7.5   FITNESS FOR PURPOSE

7.5.1   UK provisions

In addition to the s 14(2) requirement that the goods should be fit for their common purpose, where goods are sold in the course of a business s 14(3) implies a term that the goods are fit for any particular purpose which the buyer makes known to the seller, either expressly or by implication. In the absence of any information to the contrary, the seller is entitled to assume that the goods will be used for their normal purpose. Where a buyer requires goods for a particular (non-normal) purpose, it must inform the seller before the contract is made. For example, in *Micron Computer Systems Ltd v Wang (UK) Ltd* (HC, 9 May 1990), the buyer of a computer system failed to tell the seller of the particular purpose in question and was therefore unsuccessful in its claim.

This term does not apply where the circumstances show that the buyer does not rely upon, or it is unreasonable to rely upon, the skill or judgement of the seller.

7.5.1.1 Relationship between s 14(2) and s 14(3)

One problem is the overlap between s 14(2) and s 14(3). The issue is complex, but, as a rule of thumb, where goods are not of satisfactory quality, it is unlikely that they will be fit for common purpose. This would therefore be a breach of s 14(2B)(a). However, it is perfectly possible for the goods to be unfit for a particular purpose under s 14(3), but still to be fit for common purpose and therefore of satisfactory quality under s 14(2). For example, if a buyer specifies that he needs specialist trainers for running, but the seller supplies ordinary trainers, the goods may not be fit for the specified purpose, but they will still be of satisfactory quality as they are fit for their common purpose under s 14(2B)(a).

The issue was dealt with in *Jewson v Kelly* [2003] EWCA Civ 1030, where the seller was held by the Court of Appeal not to be liable for breach of the SGA 1979 in relation to the supply of electrical heating equipment. The buyers alleged that the sale was in breach of s 14(2) and (3), as the equipment had reduced the energy efficiency ratings of the flat conversions in question. The Court held:

> Although there was considerable overlap between s 14(2) and s 14(3), the function of s 14(2) was to establish a general standard, and the function of s 14(3) was to impose a particular standard tailored to the individual circumstances of the case.

The equipment did work as heating equipment, so s 14(2) was held not to be applicable. As regards s 14(3), the buyer was held not to have relied on the sellers as regards the question of the 'particular' fitness for purpose, which was the effect of the heating equipment on the flats' energy efficiency ratings. There was therefore no breach of s 14(3).

Section 14(6) provides that s 14(2) and s 14(3) are conditions.

7.5.1.2 Trade usage (s 14(4))

The SGA 1979, s 14(4) states that an implied condition or warranty about quality or fitness for a particular purpose may be annexed to a contract of sale by usage in the course of a particular trade. The requirements are that the usage or custom must be reasonable, universally accepted by the particular trade or profession, be certain, be lawful, and be consistent with the express or implied terms of the contract .

7.5.2 International provisions

As mentioned above, Article 35 of the CISG requires the goods to be fit for purpose. Under Article 2-314 of the UCC, the goods must be 'fit for the ordinary purposes for which goods of that description are used'.

Again, in the PICC, the obligation to perform obligations to a reasonable standard may (but not necessarily must) be interpreted as imposing an obligation that the goods are fit for their purpose. This is more likely to be the case where the purpose has been made known to the seller. If he supplies goods which do not conform, it could be said that he has not performed his obligation to a reasonable standard.

In the PECL, again, performance of an obligation has to be to an adequate standard, which may be interpreted as encompassing a need for the goods to be fit for their purpose, although it may be that the purpose must be made known for this interpretation to be put on it.

7.6   SALE BY SAMPLE

7.6.1   UK provisions

Section 15(2) implies a term that where the sale is by sample then the bulk of the goods will correspond with the sample in quality. The goods are also to be free of any defect, not apparent on reasonable examination, which would render the quality unsatisfactory. Section 15(1) defines a sale by sample.

In *Godley v Perry* [1960] 1 WLR 9, a retailer bought plastic catapults from a wholesaler. He tested one sample catapult and it worked satisfactorily, so he bought a consignment of them. However, a catapult sold to a customer broke, hitting the child using it, and as a result the child lost an eye. The goods were held not to comply with the sample, in breach of s 15. There had been reasonable examination of the sample which had not shown up any defects.

Section 15(3) states that s 15(2) is a condition.

7.6.2   International provisions

Article 35 of the CISG requires goods to comply with samples given. Article 2-313 of the UCC imposes a similar obligation.

In the PICC, there is no direct obligation to supply goods which correspond with description; however, if they do not correspond, it may be construed as a failure to perform to a reasonable standard, as mentioned above. Civil law jurisdictions in particular are unlikely to have difficulty construing the wording in this way.

In the PECL, there is no mention of sale by sample. Again, the obligation to render adequate performance may include the obligation to deliver goods which correspond with samples given.

7.7   OVERLAP BETWEEN ss 13, 14 AND 15 OF THE SGA 1979

Often a sale by description may raise quality issues, eg a statement that goods are more durable than turns out to be the case (note that this could also amount to a misrepresentation).

A sale by sample will normally also amount to a sale by description. Failure to match the sample may also mean that the goods are not of satisfactory quality or fit for their purpose, as in *Godley v Perry* (**7.6** above).

7.8   BUYER'S REMEDIES FOR BREACH OF THE IMPLIED TERMS

7.8.1   Breach of condition

As discussed, all of the implied terms, with the exception of s 12(2), are conditions. Breach of any of these terms will therefore entitle the buyer to reject the goods, repudiate the contract and recover the price from the seller, as well as to claim damages if it has suffered further loss, eg loss of profit.

The buyer is not obliged to reject the goods. It may elect not to reject the goods, treat the breach as a breach of warranty and sue for damages.

7.8.2   Limits on the right to reject

In certain circumstances, the buyer will lose the right to reject the goods, although its right to claim damages will not be affected.

7.8.2.1   Slight breach (s 15A)

The Sale and Supply of Goods Act 1994 introduced s 15A into the SGA 1979. Section 15A provides that the right to reject is lost where the sale is not a consumer sale and the breach is so slight that it would be unreasonable for the buyer to reject the goods. Section 15A applies only to breach of ss 13–15 and not, for example, to breach of a stipulation concerning time of delivery.

7.8.2.2 Acceptance by the buyer (ss 34–36)

As discussed in the context of delivery, s 34 states that the buyer has a right to have a reasonable opportunity, on request, to examine the goods (see **5.4.4.3**).

Section 35 deals with the loss of the right to reject. So, for example, the buyer loses the right where it tells the seller that it has accepted the goods, or does something inconsistent with the seller's ownership after the goods have been delivered to it. The buyer also loses the right to reject if it retains the goods beyond a reasonable period of time (s 35(4)).

Whether or not the buyer has accepted the goods will be a question of fact in each case. *Clegg v Olle Andersson (t/a Nordic Marine)* [2003] EWCA Civ 320 concerned an ocean-going yacht. The buyer took three weeks to assess the situation before rejecting the goods. This was in fact many months after delivery, as the seller had been slow to respond to requests for information. The Court of Appeal held that the Sale and Supply of Goods Act 1994 (which amended the SGA 1979) allowed the buyer to have time to ascertain the actions needed to modify or repair the goods, and the buyer's rejection was upheld.

7.8.3 Breach of warranty

Section 61 of the SGA 1979 states that breach of a term which is a warranty gives rise only to a claim for damages. It does not give the buyer the right to reject the goods and treat the contract as repudiated, only a right to damages. This simply confirms the common law rules on breach of warranty. As for delivery, the relevant provision in relation to damages is s 54 (see **5.6.1**). The problem for the buyer is that there are situations where it may be unclear whether the term breached is a strict condition or not. Section 15A means that careful judgement is needed before rejection – a breach of, say, s 14 may be so slight as to preclude rejection.

7.8.4 Buyer's remedies for misrepresentation

In the UK, these are now controlled by the Misrepresentation Act 1967 (see **3.3.2**). If a pre-contractual misrepresentation has become a term of the contract, eg as a result of s 13 of the SGA 1979, or the contract has been performed, then the buyer may still rescind the contract (Misrepresentation Act 1967, s 1). Rescission is possible for innocent misrepresentation. The buyer does not have to rely on an allegation of fraud or negligence, although rescission is also available in those circumstances. See *Shogun Finance Ltd v Hudson* [2004] 1 AC 919.

Rescission for misrepresentation is barred by affirmation, lapse of time, inability to restore the parties to their original position, or the goods being acquired by an innocent third party.

Damages for misrepresentation are also a possibility, but there can be no double recovery, ie the buyer cannot recover damages for breach of contract in respect of the same loss. (Note. It is no defence for the seller to say that a reasonable person would not have relied on the representation if he should have known that the buyer would rely on it – *Ronastone Ltd v Indigo International Holdings Ltd* [2003] All ER (D) 332 (Dec).)

7.9 CONSUMER RIGHTS ACT 2015

As discussed in **Chapter 4,** the Consumer Rights Act 2015 (CRA 2015) came into force in October 2015. This governs all contracts between 'traders' and 'consumers', ie B2C contracts, and replaced the consumer provisions of the UK SGA 1979 and SGSA 1982. Although the summary below concentrates on the sale of goods, bear in mind that the CRA 2015 also governs the provision of services and the provision of digital content (which will be given equivalent protection to physical goods).

'Statutory rights' in relation to title, description, quality, fitness for purpose and sample are implied into B2C contracts for the sale of goods. These are equivalent to the SGA 1979 implied terms. There are additional implied terms: certain pre-contractual information as required by the Consumer Contracts Regulations 2013 are incorporated into the contract as implied terms, the goods must match any model which the consumer has seen or examined, and where the contract provides for installation, the goods will not conform to the contract if they are not installed correctly.

There are also 'other rules' in relation to delivery and passing of risk. In the absence of an agreed delivery period, goods must be delivered without undue delay, and in any event within 30 days from the date when the contract was entered into. As a general rule, risk remains with the trader until the goods are in the physical possession of the consumer.

The CRA 2015 provides for a new remedy structure for consumers in relation to defective goods. Where there is a breach of the statutory implied terms, there is effectively a three-tier system:

(a)   A short-term right to reject. Within a 30-day mandatory period, a trader must allow the consumer to reject the goods.

(b)   The right to repair or replacement. The consumer may require the trader to repair or replace the goods at the trader's cost, if possible and provided that the cost is not disproportionate. If a trader fails to repair or replace the goods on the first attempt, or refuses to do so, the consumer may move to the next remedy.

(c)   The right to a price reduction or the final right to reject. Where it is not possible to repair or replace the goods, the consumer may demand a discount or return the goods and demand a refund. Traders may make a deduction for any use which the consumer has had of the goods.

We shall consider the provisions of the CRA 2015 in relation to exclusion of the statutory implied terms and other exclusion clauses in **Chapter 8**.

Table 7.2 shows the equivalent provisions in the CRA 2015 and SGA 1979.

Sale of Goods		
	CRA 2015 Statutory Rights	**SGA 1979 Implied Terms**
Satisfactory quality	s 9	s 14(2)
Goods to be fit for particular purpose	s 10	s 14(3)
Goods to be as described	s 11	s 13
Other pre-contract information included in contract	s 12	n/a
Goods to match sample	s 13	s 15
Goods to match model seen or examined	s 14	n/a
Installation as part of conformity with contract	s 15	n/a
Title	s 17	s 12
Other Rules		
Delivery of goods (includes 30-day delivery period)	s 28	n/a
Passing of risk. (Goods at trader's risk until in physical possession of consumer)	s 29	n/a

Remedies		
Short-term right to reject	ss 19, 20 and 22	These remedies replaced the remedy structure of the SGA 1979 in relation to consumers.
Repair or replacement	ss 19 and 23	
Right to reduction or final right to reject	ss 19, 20 and 24	

Table 7.2   Implied terms and remedies under the CRA 2015 and SGA 1979

SUMMARY

This chapter has given you an outline of the obligations imposed on a seller of goods by the implied terms of the SGA 1979 and under international conventions and agreements. These terms relate to the seller's obligations in relation to title, description, quality and sample, and provide for the buyer's remedies in the event of breach. Under the UK SGA 1979, these are not default terms; they will be implied into all sale of goods contracts unless they are expressly, and validly, excluded by the contract. We shall now consider whether these terms may be validly excluded and, if so, how.

Exclusion Clauses: General Principles

LEARNING OUTCOMES

After reading this chapter you will be able to:

- appreciate that there are basic rules to follow in drafting an exclusion clause effectively to protect a commercial seller of goods
- identify different types of exclusion clause
- appreciate the importance of a client's commercial background when drafting exclusion clauses
- adopt a structured approach when testing the validity of an exclusion clause and dealing with problems in relation to exclusions of liability
- summarise the common law rules which govern the validity of exclusion clauses
- summarise the main provisions and scope of the Unfair Contracts Terms Act (UCTA) 1979, and its effect on exclusion clauses
- recognise when the provisions of the Consumer Rights Act 2015 might apply to an exclusion clause.

8.1 INTRODUCTION

Commercial clients will always be concerned about the liability they may incur in performing their contracts, and in most cases their instinct will be to try to reduce their exposure as much as possible. Such liability may arise as the result of express terms in the contract, eg in relation to time of delivery, or terms implied by the SGA 1979 such as the implied terms in relation to quality. The solicitor is likely to be approached for advice in two respects:

(a) drafting an agreement to minimise the client's liability if things should go wrong;

(b) advising on the protection given by exclusions in an agreement once problems have arisen.

Most of this chapter deals with the first point, looking at the position under English law. (International provisions are dealt with at the end of the chapter.) It considers the various matters which the solicitor should bear in mind when drafting (or reviewing) an agreement. The use of exclusion and limitation clauses, particularly in commercial contracts, is part of the process by which the parties agree to allocate risk, liability and responsibility for performance as between themselves. Much like other clauses in the contract, the exclusions will usually reflect the nature and context of the contract, as well as the relative needs and bargaining power of the parties.

Exclusion of liability from the point of view of a solicitor drafting on behalf of a commercial seller which is entering into agreements with other commercial parties is considered at **8.2**–**8.7**. The rules in relation to consumer buyers are considered at **8.8** and **8.9**.

8.2 BASIC RULES FOR SUCCESSFUL DRAFTING OF EXCLUSION CLAUSES

Three points are particularly important:

(a)   know the commercial background;

(b)   know the law;

(c)   know the drafting principles.

8.2.1 Know the commercial background

Although this may seem obvious, the solicitor needs to anticipate the sort of liability that may arise in that type of business, so that they know what to exclude. Therefore it is essential to know how a client's business operates, and the potential risks it faces, before it is possible to draft effectively for exclusion of liability on behalf of the client. In addition, exclusion clauses in commercial contracts are in many cases subject to the reasonableness test under UCTA 1977, and many of the factors which are relevant in deciding whether or not a clause passes the reasonableness test are specific to the circumstances of each contract. Basic questions to ask would include:

(a)   What sort of customers does the client normally deal with?

(b)   What type of products does the client sell and what can go wrong with them?

(c)   Which of the client's employees actually make the contracts (and therefore 'operate' the exclusion clauses)?

(d)   How, if at all, are any exclusions introduced to the customers?

(e)   Are certain exclusions/limitations or standard-form contracts common within that type of industry?

The final consideration is that, although the solicitor must try to achieve what the client has requested, the client must also be advised (as constructively as possible) that no exclusion clause can be guaranteed to work in all circumstances.

8.2.2 Tactics – drafting to litigate or to negotiate?

Once the solicitor has an idea of the commercial background, it is a good idea to consider tactics with the client. In most cases, a solicitor will be drafting to negotiate, rather than to litigate, should problems arise with the agreement in the future. It is therefore often valid to draft a clause which a court might hold unreasonable, if litigation is in fact unlikely and the clause achieves the right result for the client (eg the client deals with the type of customer which is unlikely to claim, or which will tend to settle any claim on suitable terms). Obviously, the client should be informed of what the solicitor is doing (and why) and warned that it is impossible to guarantee that the clause will achieve this result. Note that any attempt to exclude liability for breach of s 12 of the SGA 1979 or liability for death or personal injury caused by negligence will be void.

In some circumstances, it is worth drafting positively rather than (as is traditional with exclusion clauses) negatively. It could be worthwhile, for example, in a contract for the performance of services, for the supplier to promise to exercise reasonable care and skill in carrying out the work under the contract, and to accept full liability for any personal injury or death caused by breach of its promise. This gives the other party no more than its legal rights, but creates the impression that the supplier is being generous. Onerous exclusions will achieve the opposite effect.

8.2.3 Know the law

Relevant areas include:

(a) the implied terms that may affect the contract, eg the implied terms in relation to delivery, title and quality;

(b) the likely remedies for breach of express or implied terms;

(c) the common law rules relating to incorporation and construction;

(d) the rules in UCTA 1977; and

(e) the factors which determine whether a clause will pass the reasonableness test or not.

8.2.4 Know the drafting principles

Although the client's instructions, or the circumstances in which the clause is to operate, may in practice limit how a clause can be put together, the way in which an exclusion clause has been drafted may have a profound influence on its effectiveness. You should bear in mind the following.

8.2.4.1 Use of precedents

Because the effectiveness of an exclusion clause will depend to a large extent on its own individual context, precedents for exclusion clauses need to be used with some caution. The solicitor should always consider how a clause might work in a particular business context, and think carefully before simply copying a precedent which appears to be suitable on paper. Having said that, precedents can be very useful in this context as a source of inspiration, or as a guide to how the layout of the exclusions within the contract might be organised.

8.2.4.2 Drafting for severance

Instead of drafting one clause to cover all the exclusions under the contract (which carries the risk that the clause may then be struck down in its entirety as unreasonable), it is usually more appropriate to draft a series of clauses or sub-clauses. If one sub-clause is found to be unreasonable, the others may still survive if the court is able to apply the normal principles of severance. To reinforce the point, the series can end with a statement that each clause or sub-clause is to be treated as separate and independent.

8.3 PREPARING TO DRAFT

Before beginning to draft, there are several general considerations which the solicitor should have in mind, which will relate to the likely effectiveness of the finished clauses.

8.3.1 What is an 'exclusion clause'?

There is no really comprehensive legal definition of what constitutes an 'exclusion' or 'exemption' clause. The closest approach to a full definition is probably contained in s 13 of UCTA 1977, which defines very widely the type of clause to which that Act applies. In addition, all the relevant sections of UCTA 1977 refer to 'exclusion or restriction of liability', so the Act clearly covers limitation clauses as well as strict exclusion clauses. However, bear in mind that UCTA 1977 does not cover every case of exclusion or limitation of liability (see **8.7.1**). For the sake of simplicity, this chapter uses the expression 'exclusion clause' to cover both exclusion and limitation clauses, unless the context requires otherwise.

Practically, an exclusion clause is a clause which attempts to exclude or limit the availability of the remedies arising as the result of the happening (or more often non-happening) of a specified event, generally a breach of contract by one of the parties.

8.3.2 Ways of excluding liability

8.3.2.1 Trying to exclude everything

Sometimes, the client may want the solicitor to exclude all liability which could arise from breach of any contractual obligation. Tempting as this may be, it cannot be done:

(a)   Some liability is non-excludable because of UCTA 1977 (see **8.2.1**).

(b)   A contract which purports to exclude one party's liability for breach in respect of all its contractual obligations would not be a contract at all. That party would not be binding itself to do anything, and the 'contract' would be no more than a declaration of intent. Either the contract would be void for uncertainty, or a court faced with this situation would probably assume that the parties had made a mistake, and attempt to construe the contract in such a way that it does not exclude liability for everything.

(c)   Commercially, this is unlikely to be practical. Customers are unlikely to want to do business where there is no prospect of recompense if things go wrong.

The solicitor will have to judge carefully how far it is possible to go if the client requests as much exclusion as possible, and advise accordingly.

8.3.2.2 Fundamental breach

A problem may arise where a client seeks to exclude liability for its own fundamental, repudiatory breach of contract. This is possible to achieve, but the scope for excluding liability in such circumstances is very narrow and will turn upon the construction of the exclusion. If the wording is clear, a clause may cover a serious repudiatory breach (see *PhotoProductions Ltd v Securicor Transport Ltd* [1980] AC 827, HL). However, following the *NetTV* case (*Internet Broadcasting Corporation (t/a NetTV) v MAR LLC (t/a MARHedge)* [2009] EWHC 844 (Ch)), there is now a rebuttable presumption that an exclusion clause does not apply to a deliberate personal repudiatory breach.

8.3.2.3 Types of exclusion clause

Table 8.1 below lists some of the main types of exclusion clause. The examples given are not intended to be watertight provisions; they are simple illustrations of the type of clause that could be encountered in practice. In a commercial contract, all of these would be subject to reasonableness under either s 3 or s 6 of UCTA 1977, and their effectiveness will be considered in **8.7.2**.

Type of clause	Effect of clause	Example
Exclusion of liability	Excludes liability altogether.	'The Seller accepts no liability for the late delivery of the Goods.'
Limitation of liability	Limits the extent of liability.	'The Seller's liability is limited to the contract price of the Goods.'
Exclusion of remedies	Limits the remedies which are available to the buyer, eg the right to terminate or the right to damages. Includes non-rejection clauses. (An alternative is to provide for substitute remedies, eg repair or replacement.)	'Where the Seller is in breach of any terms of this Agreement the Buyer may not reject the goods or terminate the contact and any claim is limited to damages.'

Type of clause	Effect of clause	Example
Exclusion of types of loss	Limits liability for a particular type of loss, eg loss of profit or consequential loss.	'The Seller accepts no liability for indirect or consequential loss or damage (whether loss of profit, loss of business or otherwise), costs, expenses or other claims for consequential compensation whatsoever (howsoever caused) which arise out of or in connection with this Agreement.'
Time bar	Excludes liability unless notice of breach is given within a specified time period.	'The Seller will not be liable for any defect in the quality of the Goods unless such defect is notified to the Seller within 7 days beginning with the date of delivery.'
Duty defining	Prevents liability arising in the first place.	'Any delivery dates specified are approximate only and whereas every attempt will be made to meet these dates the Seller cannot promise to do so.'
Force majeure	Excludes liability for failure to perform the contract as a result of events outside the seller's control.	'The Seller is not liable for any delay in performing or failure to perform any of the Seller's obligations in relation to the Goods if the delay or failure was due to circumstances outside the Seller's reasonable control.' (A non-exhaustive list of the force majeure circumstances, eg war, riot, flood, fire, abnormal weather, etc, should be included.)

Table 8.1 Exclusion clauses

8.4 TESTING THE CLAUSE

Although this chapter deals with the drafting of exclusion clauses, rather than the more general contractual background against which they will operate, it is often helpful at the drafting stage to consider that contractual background; this can be an extremely useful way of assessing a draft clause's potential strength. The solicitor should try to anticipate what problems may arise, and whether, if they do, a customer will be able to establish a cause of action. If it seems likely that the customer will succeed, the solicitor should then consider whether the clause will work to protect the client against such a claim. To test the clause the solicitor should consider the following.

8.4.1 Contractual background

(a)   Identify the terms of the contract, both express and implied, which are likely to be relevant, ie those terms which may lead to liability if breached. (It is tempting to think that the exclusion clause is a 'relevant' term, but at this stage the solicitor is simply assessing their client's potential liability and so does not need to consider any exclusions yet.)

(b)   Decide whether those terms are likely to be breached and the likely events which will lead to breach.

(c)   Anticipate what remedy the injured party will be seeking and decide whether or not that remedy is legally available, eg rejection of the goods will not be available for breach of warranty.

These points will form an integral part of the process of applying the clause if problems occur, and will often provide important information at the drafting stage as to how well the clause is likely to work.

8.4.2   Three stages for effectiveness

Once the claimant has established a cause of action, the burden of proof will shift to the defendant to show that its exclusion clause is valid. A party who wishes to claim the protection of an exclusion clause must prove three things:

(a)   *incorporation*: that the clause forms part of the contract;

(b)   *construction*: that the wording of the clause is wide enough that, on its true construction, it covers the breach which has occurred;

(c)   UCTA 1977: that the clause is not invalidated by UCTA 1977 (if applicable).

8.5   INCORPORATION

To be effective, a clause must form part of the contract. This rule applies to all contractual terms, but the courts apply it particularly strictly in relation to exclusion clauses. A clause may be incorporated in one of three ways:

(a)   by signature;

(b)   by notice; and

(c)   by previous course of dealing.

There may be practical problems in relation to each of these methods of incorporation which the solicitor must consider.

8.5.1   Signed or unsigned documents?

If a clause is contained in a contractual document which the client's customers will sign, the chances of incorporation are very good (the normal contractual rule is that a customer will be bound by signature, whether or not he has read or understood the document). If, however, the clause is in an unsigned document, it will form part of the contract only if reasonable steps are taken to bring it to the customer's attention before the contract is made. Putting the clause into a document which is to be signed should, therefore, be less risky as far as incorporation is concerned. However, this may not be the best solution if it does not fit in with the client's normal business practices, eg where sales are concluded online. There may also be problems over signature itself:

(a)   What if the clause is in a document which should be signed but which the customer does not sign?

(b)   What if a regular customer normally signs a contractual document but fails to sign on one or more occasions?

(c)   Is it possible to draft and locate the clause so that it will be incorporated even if the document is not signed?

There can be no general answers to these questions; in each case, the solicitor must obtain full instructions and then draft to meet the needs of the client's particular business. The case of *Kingsway Hall Hotel Ltd v Red Sky IT (Hounslow) Ltd* [2010] EWHC 965 (TCC) illustrates the importance of ensuring that standard terms and conditions and procedures for incorporation reflect sales practices. Operating documents for Red Sky's software were supplied to the customer after the system had been installed. These operating documents contained exclusions of liability for quality and fitness for purpose. The clauses had not been supplied to the customer before the contract was signed and therefore the exclusions did not apply.

8.5.2 Notice and timing

If the clause is contained in a document which is not intended to be signed, it will be incorporated provided that reasonable steps have been taken to bring it to the customer's attention *before* the contract is made. It is important to look at the background to the contract. If the parties have negotiated the terms, particularly the exclusions, of if the buyer has queried these, it will be difficult for the buyer to deny that it had no knowledge of the exclusions, or that these had not been brought to its attention. However, problems may arise if there is normally an interval between drawing the buyer's attention to the clause and the contract being made. Again, it will help to find out how the client's business operates, but the solicitor may in practice be unable to resolve this problem. There may be problems if it is intended to incorporate exclusion clauses by reference to other documents (see **9.2.5.7** below).

It is important that exclusion clauses should not be 'hidden away' in the body of the agreement. The more unusual or onerous the clause, the greater the need to draw this to the attention of the other side (the so-called 'red hand rule'). Particularly in a long and complex document, it is advisable to include a limitation of liability warning at the beginning, eg the 'The Buyer's attention is drawn in particular to the provisions of Clause X.' This could also be included on order forms and other contractual documentation.

Particular care should be taken to ensure incorporation of terms and conditions when selling online. Before the buyer proceeds to payment, the website should incorporate the client's standard terms and conditions of sale. Customers should be asked to read the terms and conditions, and tick a box confirming that they accept them ('click wrap' acceptance). The website should be programmed in such a way that the buyer should not be able to proceed to the next stage of the transaction without signifying its consent to the seller's terms and conditions, having had the opportunity to read them (whether or not it does so).

8.5.3 Course of dealings

If the clause is in an unsigned document, it may be incorporated into the contract by way of a regular and consistent course of dealings. Once again, the solicitor needs to know how the client's business works in order to decide whether this is likely. Questions to ask are:

(a) Does the client do a lot of business with regular customers?

(b) Is it involved mainly in 'one-off' transactions?

(c) Are there a variety of different dealings? (This is perhaps most likely.)

Incorporation by course of dealings is far more likely to happen with contracts made between commercial parties than with contracts between a commercial party and a consumer, but it may be unwise to depend too much upon a course of dealing as a reliable method of incorporation because exclusion clauses and, particularly, limitation clauses do tend to vary over time, and should in any event be regularly updated.

8.5.4 Preventing incorporation problems

If the solicitor has acquired a background knowledge of how the client actually makes contracts, it should be possible to spot potential incorporation problems and take action before they arise. This could, for example, take the form of advice to the client (eg about staff training in relation to how contracts should be entered into), or building in safeguards when drafting (eg paying particular attention to the layout of the contract and the location of the clause). Whatever method is chosen, the client should always be made aware of the dangers; in particular, that its employees' actions when making contracts on the client's behalf could actually prevent exclusions in the contract from working.

8.6 CONSTRUCTION

8.6.1 Does the clause cover the breach?

Even if the clause is incorporated into the contract, it will be effective only if, on its true construction by the court, it is worded to do two things:

(a)   to cover the breach which actually occurs; and

(b)   to exclude the seller's liability for that breach.

As with incorporation, this poses problems when drafting; the solicitor must be aware of the sort of things that can go wrong, so that the exclusion can be drafted to cover such eventualities. The problem is how far the solicitor can foresee the circumstances in which the clause will eventually operate, or what breaches might occur. Once again, knowing the client's business as thoroughly as possible and taking full instructions will help, particularly in trading contexts, such as insurance and freight contracts, where disputes and litigation arise with some frequency.

An awareness of the basic contractual principles of construction is also important. Unfortunately, this is a widely misunderstood area of the law. However, the basic principle is straightforward: when looking at the construction of a clause, the court is looking at the wording to see whether the clause does what it is intended to do, which, in the case of an exclusion clause, is to exclude liability in the event of a specified breach. So the clause must specify the breach that is likely to occur (cover the breach) and specify the liability which the client wants to exclude. The following simple examples of some poorly-drafted terms illustrate this.

EXAMPLE 1

Clause: 'The Seller will not be liable for any loss suffered as a result of failure to deliver the Goods.'

Breach: The seller delivers the goods late.

Construction: The clause does not cover the breach which has occurred, as failure to deliver (non-delivery) is not the same thing as late delivery.

EXAMPLE 2

Clause: 'The Seller will not be liable for loss of profit or consequential loss resulting from late delivery of the Goods.'

Breach: The seller delivers the goods late, and the buyer wants to reject the goods and recover the price.

Construction: The clause does cover the breach (late delivery), but it has not excluded the buyer's right to reject the goods and reclaim the price. It has only protected the seller from a claim for damages for indirect loss.

8.6.2 Contra proferentem

Historically, exclusion clauses have been construed strictly *contra proferentem* (ie any ambiguity will be construed against the person attempting to rely on it), especially in relation to exclusions of liability for negligence. The general rule was that a clause seeking to exclude liability for negligence should refer clearly to negligence or other appropriate synonym, such as 'howsoever caused'. However, recent case law has cast doubt on this traditional approach. In *Persimmon Homes Ltd v Ove Arup and Partners* [2017] EWCA Civ 373, the Court of Appeal emphasised that in commercial contracts negotiated between two parties of equal bargaining power, the *contra proferentem* rule now has a very limited role.

8.6.3   Other principles of construction

In construing an exclusion clause, the court may apply various other principles to decide whether or not the clause covers the breach, for example:

(a)   *Expressio unius est exclusio alterius*: by this principle, if a contract expressly mentions one or more matters, those not mentioned are automatically excluded. For example, if a clause lists claims which are to be barred, it will not apply to claims not mentioned.

(b)   *Ejusdem generis*: this is a general aid to construction, which is sometimes seen as being more appropriate to property documents than to commercial contracts. The principle is that general words which follow two or more specific words are restricted to the same type of item or situation as the preceding specific words. (Note that this principle does not apply to a force majeure clause; see further **9.3.2**.)

8.6.4   Avoiding loose terminology

If words or phrases are used inappropriately, this may mean that a clause does not cover the breach which it was intended to cover. In particular, jargon may be misused (even by lawyers). For example, the words 'rescission', 'condition' and 'warranty' are all often used in commercial contracts in ways which pervert their strict legal meaning. A similar problem arises from the use of words which may mean different things to different readers of the contract (eg, 'consequential loss'). When drafting, therefore, the solicitor should either try to avoid expressions which may cause problems, or define clearly what a particular expression means in context (for further discussion of this point in relation to the expression 'consequential loss', see **9.3.5**). Note that even if loose terminology does not prevent the clause from covering the breach, it may make the clause less likely to pass the reasonableness test if, for example, the effect is to make it difficult to understand (see further **9.2.5** and the discussion of *Regus (UK) Ltd v Epcot Solutions* at **8.6.2** above)).

8.7   UNFAIR CONTRACT TERMS ACT 1977

The solicitor will obviously need to be aware of statutory controls on the drafting of exclusion clauses. By far the most important of these is UCTA 1977. Note that the consumer provisions of UCTA 1977 have been replaced by equivalent provisions in the CRA 2015.

8.7.1   Scope of UCTA 1977

Section 13 of UCTA 1977 gives the Act a wide scope in respect of the type of clause to which it applies, but it will by no means apply in every case. In particular, by s 1(3), the Act applies only to business liability, ie to breach of obligations arising 'in the course of a business' (or use of business premises), so it will not cover the contracts where the seller is a consumer. Business is defined in s 14 to include a profession, government department or public authority.

8.7.1.1   Contracts to which UCTA 1977 does not apply

The most important examples of this are:

(a)   contracts listed in Sch 1 to UCTA 1977. By this Schedule, ss 2–4 (and to a limited extent s 7) do not apply to certain types of contract, including insurance contracts, contracts relating to land and contracts relating to intellectual property rights;

(b)   international supply contracts. By s 26(2), the reasonableness test under ss 3 and 4 of UCTA 1977 does not apply to an international supply contract.

Note also that, by s 27 of UCTA 1977, if the applicable law of the contract is that of some part of the UK only because of the choice of parties (and would, apart from that choice, be the law of a country outside the UK), then ss 2–7 and 16–21 of UCTA 1977 do not operate as part of the law applicable to the contract. Thus where both parties to the contract are based outside of the UK, they will not be subject to UCTA 1977 simply because they have chosen UK law to govern their contract (see **Chapter 14**).

8.7.1.2 Clauses to which UCTA 1977 does not apply

Even if UCTA 1977 can apply generally to a particular type of contract, it may not apply to certain individual clauses within that contract. For example, in B2B contracts, s 3 of UCTA 1977 applies only if the parties are using standard terms. So if two businesses enter into a tailor-made (ie not standard-form) contract for the sale of goods and the seller inserts a clause into the contract excluding liability for late delivery of the goods, s 3 will not apply to this clause because the buyer deals neither as consumer nor on the other party's written standard terms of business: no other section of UCTA 1977 is relevant to the clause either. However, a term in the same contract excluding liability for breach of one or more of the implied terms in ss 13–15 will be subject to reasonableness by virtue of s 6 of the 1977 Act.

8.7.2 A reminder of the effect of UCTA 1977 on contractual terms in commercial contracts

Clauses purporting to exclude or limit liability for negligence will be subject to s 2 of UCTA 1977. Clauses purporting to exclude or limit liability for losses and some clauses purporting to replace common law or statutory remedies with contractual ones will, depending on circumstances, be subject to either s 6 or s 3 of UCTA 1977.

If a clause falls within the scope of UCTA 1977, the effect of the Act is that either:

(a)   the clause will be void; or

(b)   the clause will be subject to the test of reasonableness.

The following is a brief reminder into which of these two categories certain types of clause will fall. (Although the word 'void' is used here to describe the effect of the relevant sections of UCTA 1977 on exclusion clauses, and is a convenient shorthand description, none of the sections of the Act actually uses this word. Instead, each section provides that the relevant liability cannot be excluded or restricted.)

8.7.2.1 Void clauses

Section 2(1)

By s 2(1) of UCTA 1977, a person cannot, by reference either to a contract term or to a notice, exclude or restrict his liability for personal injury or death resulting from negligence.

Section 6(1)

By s 6(1) of UCTA 1977, liability for breach of the implied condition of title under either s 12 of the SGA 1979 or s 8 of the Supply of Goods (Implied Terms) Act 1973 cannot be excluded or restricted by reference to any contract term.

8.7.2.2 Clauses subject to the reasonableness test

The two ways in which the contractual reasonableness test (see **9.1.1**) is most likely to apply are as follows.

Section 3

Section 3 of UCTA 1977 applies where one party deals on the other party's written standard terms of business, and the clause attempts to exclude or restrict liability for breach of contract. It imposes the reasonableness test on a wide variety of clauses.

Section 6(1A)

Any attempt to exclude the liability arising under ss 13–15 of the SGA 1979 against a person who does not deal as consumer is subject to the reasonableness test.

Table **8.2** below gives a summary of these provisions.

Exclusion of liability for	Effect (B2B contract)	UCTA 1977
Death or PI caused by negligence	Void	s 2(1)
Damage to property caused by negligence	Subject to reasonableness	s 2(2)
Breach of express term	Subject to reasonableness (if dealing on STC)	s 3
s 12 SGA (title)	Void	s 6(1)
s 13 SGA (description)	Subject to reasonableness	s 6(1A)
s 14 SGA (quality/fitness for purpose)	Subject to reasonableness	s 6(1A)
s 15 SGA (sample)	Subject to reasonableness	s 6(1A)

Table 8.2 Summary of the reasonableness test

The diagram in **Figure 8.1** below provides a summary of the six-stage 'exclusion clause checklist' which the solicitor should work through before starting to draft any exclusion clauses. It will also be useful for assessing their validity once problems have arisen. Provided that it is established that the clause is not void, the next stage is to think about whether the clause will pass the reasonableness test.

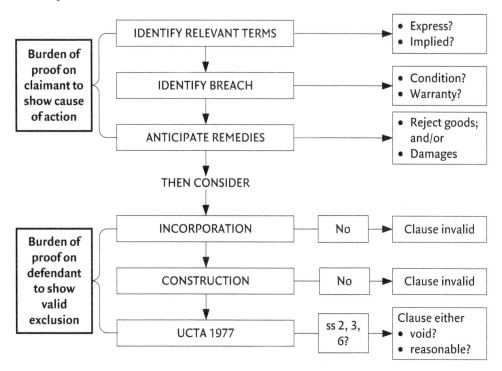

Figure 8.1 Exclusion clause checklist

8.8 CONSUMER RIGHTS ACT 2015

The implementation of the Consumer Rights Act 2015 (CRA 2015) means that the consumer provisions of UCTA 1977 were repealed, the Unfair Terms in Consumer Contracts Regulations 1999 (UTCCR 1999) were repealed in their entirety, and s 3 of the Misrepresentation Act 1967 no longer applied to terms in consumer contracts. The CRA 2015 consolidates these provisions, and contains equivalent provisions in relation to B2C contracts:

(a)   Certain statutory rights can never be excluded, and any attempt to do so will render the clause void. In a sale of goods contract, s 31 is equivalent to s 6 of UCTA 1977. Examples include attempts to exclude the implied terms of title, description, satisfactory quality or fitness for purpose. Such clauses may be regarded as 'blacklisted'.

(b)   Section 65 is the equivalent of s 2(1) of UCTA 1977. A trader cannot exclude or restrict liability for death or personal injury either by a term of the contract or a consumer notice.

(c)   Certain clauses and notices are subject to a test of fairness, breach of which will render the clause unenforceable. This is the equivalent to the test of fairness in the UTCCR 1999. Schedule 2 to the CRA 2015 contains a similar list of terms which may be regarded as unfair (see **8.9.1.1**).

Note that with the repeal of the consumer provisions of UCTA 1977, the test of reasonableness will no longer apply to consumer contracts.

Table 8.3 below shows the position under the CRA 2015.

Exclusion of liability for	Effect	CRA	UCTA 1977
Death or personal injury caused by negligence	Void	s 65(1)	s 2(1)
Damage to property caused by negligence	Subject to fairness	s 62(1)	s 2(2)
Breach of express term	Subject to fairness	s 62(1)	s 3
s 9 (satisfactory quality)	Void	s 31(1)(a)	s 6(2)
s 10 (fitness for purpose)	Void	s 31(1)(b)	s 6(2)
s 11 (description)	Void	s 31(1)(c)	s 6(2)
s 12 (other pre-contract information)	Void	s 31(1)(d)	n/a
s 13 (sample)	Void	s 31(1)(e)	s 6(2)
s 14 (model)	Void	s 31(1)(f)	n/a
s 15 (installation)	Void	s 31(1)(g)	n/a
s 17 (title)	Void	s 31(1)(i)	s 6(1)
s 28 (delivery)	Void	s 31(1)(j)	n/a
s 29 (risk)	Void	s 31(1)(k)	n/a
Misrepresentation	Subject to fairness	s 62	MA 1967, s 3

Table 8.3   **Effect of exclusion clauses under the CRA 2015**

8.9   UNFAIR TERMS IN CONSUMER CONTRACTS

Until October 2015, unfair terms in consumer contracts were governed by the UTCCR 1999. These Regulations have been repealed in their entirety and replaced with the provisions of Part 2 of the CRA 2015.

8.9.1   Definitions and scope of Part 2

Section 61 provides that Part 2 applies to a 'consumer contract' and a 'consumer notice'. A consumer contract is 'a contract between a trader and a consumer', as defined in s 2 of the Act. A consumer notice is caught:

to the extent that it:

(a)   relates to rights or obligations as between a trader and a consumer, or

(b)   purports to exclude or restrict a trader's liability to a consumer.

Section 62 imposes a requirement for contract terms and notices to be fair. A term or notice is 'unfair' if, contrary to the requirement of good faith, it causes a significant imbalance in the parties' rights and obligations to the detriment of the consumer.

An 'indicative and non-exhaustive list of terms that may be regarded as unfair' is given in Part 1 of Sch 2 to the Act. The list is the equivalent of the list of 'grey terms' from the UTCCR 1999, but has been expanded to include, eg, disproportionately high cancellation charges and attempts to determine the price after the contract has been entered into.

Under s 62, the effect of an unfair term or notice is that it is not binding on the consumer, although under s 67, where an unfair term is not binding, the rest of the contract remains in effect, so far as is practicable.

8.9.2 The requirement for 'transparency'

By s 68 a trader must ensure that a written term in a consumer contract or notice is transparent. To be transparent, it must be expressed in 'plain and intelligible language' and be legible. This is the equivalent of the requirement in reg 7 of the UTCCR 1999 on the use of plain and intelligible language, but has been expanded to impose an obligation ensuring appropriate prominence. This gives statutory force to the common law 'red hand rule' (see **8.5.2**). Section 69 also provides that if a term in a consumer contract or notice 'could have different meanings, the meaning that is most favourable to the consumer shall prevail'.

8.9.3 Enforcement

The Competition and Markets Authority is the main regulator responsible for the enforcement of Part 2. Its powers and those of other regulators are set out in Sch 3.

8.10 INTERNATIONAL PROVISIONS

8.10.1 Introduction

When dealing with international contracts, it is very important to pay special attention to the existence of mandatory rules capable of affecting the contract. This is particularly important when dealing with exclusion clauses.

For instance, the European Union has adopted directives containing rights and obligations which, once in force in the Member States, are of mandatory application to certain commercial relations, relating to specific contracts or sectors.

When dealing with contract law in the European Union, the following elements need to be taken into account:

(a) Member States have adopted, through their national legislations, mandatory provisions in contract law, which may differ from State to State.

(b) The European Union has sought to eliminate obstacles to free circulation, and by doing so has adopted directives aimed at eliminating the referred obstacles. Some of those directives contain mandatory provisions which cannot be waived via exclusion clauses.

(c) The directives seek the harmonisation of the internal market but leave certain margin to the Member States when adopting the directives. As a consequence, differences exist in certain aspects, such as degrees of protection, ways of exercising the rights, etc.

8.10.2 Directives

8.10.2.1 Directive 85/374/EEC on Liability for Defective Products

This Directive establishes the principle of objective liability (liability without fault).

Producers of a defective movable must compensate any damage caused to the physical well-being or property of individuals regardless of the existence of negligence of the producer (or importer).

The liability of the producer may not be limited or excluded in relation to the injured person.

8.10.2.2   Community legislation relating to consumer protection

The following directives are aimed at harmonising consumer protection measures throughout the EU. There are two types of harmonisation measures:

- Maximum protection measures, where, in implementing them, Member States cannot give consumers greater or lesser protection than given by the directive, unless provided for in the directive itself. The Unfair Commercial Practices Directive and the information and cancellation requirements of the Consumer Rights Directive (see below) are examples.

- Minimum protection measures, where the Member States can adopt higher degrees of protection. The Unfair Contract Terms Directive (see below) is an example.

Directive 2011/83/EC on consumer rights (Consumer Rights Directive)

The Consumer Rights Directive is intended to harmonise the rules on consumer protection. It replaces two of the main consumer protection Directives, Directive 97/7/EC on Distance Selling and Directive 85/557/EC (the so-called 'Doorstep Selling' Directive). It applies to almost all contracts for goods and services between 'traders' and 'consumers', including on-premises contracts (those made in a shop, unless they are 'day to day' contracts and performed immediately), off-premises contracts (eg doorstep sales) and distance contracts (online, telephone and catalogue sales).

The Directive also gives the consumer specific rights and imposes obligations and restrictions on the seller. It provides a list of information requirements for both on-premises and distance contracts which must be given to consumers, including, in distance contracts, the right to cancel and the costs of cancellation These rights and obligations cannot be waived.

For implementation in the UK, see **4.3**.

The Directive operates in conjunction with the following Directives, which remain in force.

Directive 93/13/EEC on unfair terms in consumer contracts (Unfair Contract Terms Directive)

This Directive seeks to prevent significant imbalances in the rights and obligations of the contracts dealing with commercial relations between consumers on the one hand and suppliers on the other hand.

The Directive requires contract terms to be drafted in plain and intelligible language.

Unfair terms (as defined in the Directive) are not binding for consumers.

Directive 98/6/EC on the indication of the prices of products (Price Indication Directive)

This Directive requires the selling price and price by unit to be clearly indicated to enable consumers to make price comparisons.

Directive 2005/29/EC on unfair commercial practices (Unfair Commercial Practices Directive)

This Directive seeks to clarify consumers' rights and to harmonise the Internal Market's rules on 'business to consumer' commercial practices.

The Directive bans misleading or aggressive practices used by business in their dealings with consumers (pressure selling, unfair advertising, etc), setting up a 'blacklist' of unfair commercial practices.

Directive 2019/2161/EU on better enforcement and modernisation of Union consumer protection (Enforcement and Modernisation Directive)

As part of the EU's 'New Deal for Consumers' initiative (see **2.2.1.3**), the Enforcement and Modernisation Directive (or the 'Omnibus' Directive) was adopted by the European Council in November 2019. It must be implemented in EU Member States by May 2022. The Directive amends four consumer directives: the Consumer Rights Directive, the Unfair Contract Terms Directive, the Price Indication Directive and the Unfair Commercial Practices Directive. It aims to harmonise and guarantee higher standards of protection for EU consumers when they buy products or services online and to provide for stronger protection against unfair or misleading trade practices across the EU.

The main provisions include the expansion of the definition of goods to include digital content and services, and protection for consumers in relation to 'free' digital content and services (provided in exchange for data), increased transparency obligations on online traders with the introduction of additional information requirements, the introduction of turnover based fines (up to 4% of annual turnover) for breaches of consumer protection measures, and new provisions in relation to misleading actions and omissions.

Directive 2019/770/EU on contracts for the supply of digital content and digital services (Digital Content Directive)

This Directive seeks to harmonise rules governing business-to-consumer supply of digital content (such as computer programs, applications, video files or electronic books) and digital services (such as SaaS (Software as a Service), including video and audio sharing and other forms of file hosting). It also extends to digital content or digital services provided in exchange for personal data from consumers (such as social media), whereas the Sale of Goods Directive applies only where a price is paid.

Directive 2019/771/EU on contracts for the sale of goods (Sale of Goods Directive)

This Directive seeks to harmonise the rules, previously contained in the Sales and Guarantees Directive (99/44/EC) which is revoked, as to the quality of goods, remedies for goods and consumer guarantees. The rules affect all business-to-consumer sales of goods, whether face-to-face (in shops), online or distance sales. Goods with a digital component (for example, smart phones, smart TVs or fitness trackers) are also covered.

The 2019 directives were intended to introduce maximum harmonisation principles, although some derogations have been agreed to allow Member States to retain some key consumer legislation.

The UK was not obliged to implement these directives as the transition periods ended before the implementation deadline. However, UK-based companies that trade within the EU will need to be compliant with these directives (and the local implementing legislation applicable in the relevant EU Member State(s)).

8.10.3 Product liability

Be aware that, in some countries, product liability laws can imply terms into a contract and can alter the effectiveness of exclusion clauses. This may particularly be the case where goods are manufactured negligently, and/or where it is a sale to a consumer. Throughout the European Union, Directive 85/374/EEC on Liability for Defective Products imposes strict liability (ie irrespective of fault) for death or personal injury or damage to consumer goods on the producers or importers of defective products. This Directive does not affect other laws already in place in the individual Member States.

8.10.4 International agreements

Some of the international agreements (treaties, conventions etc) mentioned in earlier chapters contain provisions on exclusions of liability.

(a)   PICC. Under Article 7.1.6, an exclusion clause may not be invoked if it would be 'grossly unfair to do so'. This provision, however, can be varied by the parties.

(b)   PECL. Article 8:109 states that exclusion clauses are permissible unless they are contrary to 'good faith and fair dealing'. This may be interpreted as saying the clause must be reasonable in the circumstances.

(c)   UCC. Under Article 2-316, an exclusion of liability is permissible if it is deemed reasonable.

(d)   The CISG, however, does not make provision for exclusion clauses.

8.10.5 Dos and Don'ts

When drafting exclusion clauses in international contracts:

Do

*   Check if there is mandatory legislation applicable to the contract.

*   Check if the exclusion clause waives any rights and obligations contained in the mandatory legislation.

Don't

*   Copy and paste exclusion clauses from previous contracts – they may not be valid for your contract.

*   When dealing with a Member State of the EU, examine only a EU Directive without checking how the Member State has transposed the Directive (Member States may have adopted more stringent provisions).

SUMMARY

We have looked at the reasons why a commercial seller of goods might want to exclude liability to a buyer, the problems lawyers face in attempting to do so, and the importance of adopting a structured approach and careful drafting in order to achieve this. You have seen that in order to be effective an exclusion clause must be properly incorporated and constructed, and must be UCTA compliant. In the UK, many commercial contracts will also be subject to the UCTA 1977 test of reasonableness. We are now going to analyse this test in more detail.

CHAPTER 9

EXCLUSION CLAUSES: DRAFTING FOR REASONABLENESS

LEARNING OUTCOMES

After reading this chapter you will be able to:

- appreciate the importance of the application of the UCTA 1977 test of reasonableness to an exclusion clause in a commercial contract
- identify the main factors which affect the reasonableness of an exclusion clause and the drafting considerations in relation to each of these
- analyse the effectiveness of different types of exclusion clause.

This chapter concentrates on the effect of UCTA 1977 within the UK. Section 26 of UCTA 1977 provides that the Act does not apply to 'international supply contracts'. An international supply contract includes a contract for sale of goods where the buyer and seller are in different jurisdictions and where *one* of three additional criteria apply:

(a) the goods are to be carried from one state to another; or

(b) the offer and acceptance have been made in different territories; or

(c) the goods are to be delivered to a territory other than that in which the offer and acceptance took place.

9.1 GENERAL PRINCIPLES

9.1.1 The contractual reasonableness test

In practice, where UCTA 1977 applies to a commercial agreement, most (if not all) of the agreement's exclusion clauses will be subject to the reasonableness test, so it is usually against this test that the solicitor will need to assess a clause.

Section 11(1) of UCTA 1977 states that:

> In relation to a contract term, the requirement of reasonableness ... is that the term shall have been a fair and reasonable one to be included having regard to the circumstances which were, or ought reasonably to have been, known to or in the contemplation of the parties when the contract was made.

It is, therefore, a test of reasonableness of incorporation, not reasonableness of reliance. If (in the light of the actual and constructive knowledge of the parties at the time) it is reasonable to include a particular clause when the contract is made, it should pass the reasonableness test. The court should not look at whether it was reasonable for the 'guilty' party to rely on the clause in the light of the breach (although it has to be said that it is not uncommon in practice for courts to do this). It is for the party claiming that a term satisfies the reasonableness test to show that it does (s 11(5)).

9.1.2 The Sch 2 guidelines

The court will look at the Sch 2 guidelines to assess whether the clause is reasonable. The guidelines include:

- the relative bargaining power of the parties (Sch 2(a));
- whether any choice was available (eg could the buyer have acquired the goods elsewhere without the clause?) (Sch 2(a));
- whether the buyer was offered any inducement to accept the clause (Sch 2(b));
- the extent of the parties' knowledge of the existence and effect of the terms (Sch 2(c));
- whether it was practicable to comply with any condition imposed on bringing a claim (Sch 2(d));
- whether the goods were manufactured to special order (Sch 2(e)).

The list is not intended to be exhaustive and, strictly speaking, applies only when the court is assessing reasonableness under s 6(1A) and s 7(1A) of UCTA 1977. However, the courts often apply the guidelines by analogy when considering the reasonableness test in relation to other sections, notably s 3. This approach was confirmed as appropriate by the Court of Appeal in *Overseas Medical Supplies Ltd v Orient Transport Services Ltd* [1999] 2 Lloyd's Rep 273 and, more recently, in *Regus (UK) Ltd v Epcot Solutions Ltd* [2008] EWCA Civ 361. The former case also contains a useful discussion and summary of the factors which are generally relevant to assessing the reasonableness of a clause.

It is unusual for one factor alone to be conclusive on reasonableness; in drafting, the solicitor must take into account all the factors (often conflicting) which could apply, and try to assess on balance whether the clause is likely to be held reasonable.

The Schedule 2 guidelines are not the only factors the court will consider to decide whether a clause is reasonable. The clause must be a reasonable one to include in the particular circumstances in relation to that particular contract. One of the most important factors therefore is the type of contract.

9.1.3 Is it a consumer contract or a commercial contract?

In determining whether a clause will survive, a crucial factor is often whether the contract is a consumer contract or a commercial contract. As discussed, a clause which excludes liability for breach of ss 13–15 of SGA 1979 is subject to the reasonableness test only against a commercial buyer; under s 31 of the CRA 2015, a clause which excludes liability for breach of ss 9–17, 28 and 29 is void against a buyer who deals as a consumer (see **8.8**).

Attempts to exclude liability for damage to property caused by negligence, or for breach of an express term, will be subject to the test of fairness under s 65 of the CRA 2015, which may be stricter in its application than the test of reasonableness (see **8.9**).

If the client deals with both commercial and consumer buyers, it is important for the solicitor to recognise this when drafting. There may be several different ways of dealing with the problem, depending on how the client does business and the other relevant circumstances. For example, the solicitor may decide to draft two different forms of contract, with the 'consumer' version either omitting certain exclusion clauses, or containing only modified versions. However, this may be risky; it would then be necessary to ensure that those operating the contract are able to distinguish between the two versions (perhaps by printing them on different coloured paper).

9.2 DRAFTING FOR REASONABLENESS: RELEVANT FACTORS

9.2.1 Introduction

Looking at the cases in which the courts have applied the contractual reasonableness test, it is possible to identify a number of factors which have been held to have a bearing on reasonableness. However, even if a clause has been interpreted in a particular way or held to be reasonable on one occasion, this is no guarantee that a court will react in the same way when faced with the same clause in a different case. As a result, it is not possible to produce an exhaustive list of relevant factors on reasonableness. However, the following are factors that the court will consider in relation to each of the Sch 2 guidelines.

It is important to bear in mind that in practice there is considerable overlap between the Sch 2 guidelines. For example, the parties' knowledge of the market in which they operate and the nature of the goods will clearly affect their understanding of a particular clause, but it will also be relevant when assessing their relationship – a well-informed buyer will be in a much stronger position than one who is new to the market.

9.2.2 Case law

It is not possible to summarise the extensive case law on the subject of reasonableness, but an awareness of some of the leading cases to which reference will be made in this section is essential before considering the reasonableness factors.

Arguably, still by far the most important case in relation to reasonableness is *Watford Electronics Ltd v Sanderson CFL Ltd* [2001] EWCA Civ 317. In this case, the seller had supplied the buyer with computer hardware and software; the supply was on the seller's standard terms, which contained the following provisions:

(a)   a clause limiting the seller's liability to the contract price and excluding liability for consequential or indirect losses;

(b)   a clause providing that neither party relied on any representation by the other party in entering the contract; and

(c)   an addendum to the contract (the 'side letter') in which the seller agreed to use its best endeavours to allocate appropriate resources to the contract to minimise any losses which might arise from its performance of the contract.

The software did not perform to the buyer's satisfaction, and the buyer sued for damages for breach of contract. The Court of Appeal held that the limitation clause passed the reasonableness test, noting generally that the parties were both experienced commercial parties and of roughly equal bargaining power; this clearly influenced the court's decision. In addition, the parties would (or should) have taken into account the risk of the software failing to perform when settling the contract price. The buyer also appeared to have taken a conscious decision to live with the exclusion clauses in return for various concessions from the seller (in particular the addendum referred to at (c) above, the side letter obliging the seller to use its best endeavours to allocate resources so as to minimise the effect of any failure). As a matter of construction, the limitation clause did not deprive the buyer of the chance to recover damages for breach of contract in all situations, and the seller's ability to rely on it was further qualified by the addendum to the contract. In the circumstances, and having regard to the Sch 2 guidelines, the clause satisfied the reasonableness test.

By contrast, the 'soft drinks' cases – *Britvic Soft Drinks Ltd v Messer UK Ltd* [2002] EWCA Civ 548 and *Bacardi-Martini v Thomas Hardy Packaging* [2002] EWCA Civ 549 – involved the contamination of carbon dioxide supplied to drinks manufacturers. In both cases, the exclusion of liability for breach of the implied terms relating to quality and fitness for purpose was found to be unreasonable.

More recently, the Court of Appeal has considered the issue again in *Goodlife Foods Ltd v Hall Fire Protection Ltd* [2018] EWCA Civ 1371. Goodlife challenged a broadly drafted exclusion clause which excluded liability for loss arising from defects in fire suppression equipment. The Court upheld the clause on the basis that the terms had been freely agreed between two commercial parties of equal bargaining power. Goodlife could have obtained the equipment from other suppliers, the clause had been brought to the attention of Goodlife at the time that the contract was made, the risk of fire was one that Goodlife could have anticipated and insured against, and the clause itself drew Goodlife's attention to the availability of insurance for the type of loss excluded by the clause.

The decision is indicative of the courts' willingness to uphold even broadly drafted clauses where the parties are commercial parties of equal bargaining strength. As in *Watford Electronics*, the availability of insurance and the ability to contract elsewhere were important factors in considering bargaining strength.

However, it is also worth noting that the Court of Appeal emphasised that an exclusion clause must be considered in its contractual and factual context, so that some clauses will be reasonable whilst others are not. It is impossible to lay down prescriptive rules on whether a clause will fall on one side of the line or the other.

9.2.3   Bargaining strength and the relationship between the parties

The first of the Sch 2 guidelines is the relationship between the parties and the strength of their bargaining positions. Where the parties are both businesses, size alone will not always be the determining factor. The court will look at the relationship between the parties and consider some of the factors set out below.

Drafting considerations →
- Negotiated/standard-form contract
- Market of operations
- Nature of goods
- Financial pressure
- Age/experience of buyer
- Legal advice

9.2.3.1   Negotiated or standard-form contract?

If the contract was individually negotiated, so that both sides were able to influence its contents, the courts may be more likely to decide that exclusions are reasonable than they would if one party had simply imposed terms on the other (as in a standard-form contract). Note, however, that a contract may not necessarily fall neatly into one particular category. An example of this is where the original 'framework' of the contract is negotiated between the trade associations of the parties, but, by the time it goes into operation, the contract is in effect standard-form.

9.2.3.2   Market in which the parties operate

This raises a number of issues on reasonableness and bargaining power. The courts tend to hold that commercial parties which are operating in the same market may be taken to know exactly how that market works; if they have provided for this accordingly in their contracts, the courts are likely to assume that those provisions are reasonable and neither is at an unfair advantage. This conclusion may be reinforced where both parties are known to have used the same or similar clauses in their own standard-form contracts. See, for example, *Watford v Sanderson* and *Regus v Epcot* (**9.2.2** above). However, the use of an industry standard clause will not necessarily point to reasonableness. In some cases, the courts have suggested that a distinction can be drawn between types of standard-form contract which have been settled over the years to reflect the realities of a particular business operation, such as bills of lading and charterparties, and standard-form contracts which are simply imposed by the strong on the weak. If there is a very considerable imbalance of bargaining power, the courts may still be prepared to hold that a clause imposed by the stronger party is unreasonable, even if both parties operate in the same market. The court will also consider this factor when assessing the knowledge and understanding of the parties under Sch 2(c) (see **9.2.5**).

9.2.3.3 Financial pressure

One party may have been forced to accept an exclusion because its financial situation at the time of the contract means that it cannot afford to turn down the deal which the other side is offering, despite the presence of an exclusion. This may make the exclusion unreasonable.

9.2.3.4 Age and experience of the buyer

The courts may hold that an experienced buyer (whether individual or commercial) should know what it is doing when it enters into contracts, and therefore be more likely to decide that an exclusion clause against such a buyer is reasonable. Compare, for example, two cases on property surveys. In *Stevenson v Nationwide Building Society* (1984) 272 EG 663, the buyer was an estate agent, and an exclusion in the contract relating to the negligent performance of a survey was held to be reasonable. In *Smith v Bush (Eric S) (a firm); Harris v Wyre Forest District Council* [1989] 2 All ER 514, however, the buyer was inexperienced in buying property, and a similar exclusion was held to be unreasonable against him.

9.2.3.5 Effect of legal advice

If the 'victim' of the clause received legal advice, any exclusion stands a better chance of being held reasonable. However, in *Walker v Boyle* [1982] 1 All ER 634, the 'victim', the buyer in a conveyancing transaction, was legally advised (as was the seller) and the clause was a standard term in the then edition of the National Conditions of Sale. Nevertheless, it was still held to be unreasonable.

9.2.3.6 Drafting techniques

In a tailor-made (ie fully-negotiated) contract, it may be useful to include a preamble to the exclusion, referring to as many of the above factors as are relevant, and stating whether and, if so, how those factors have been taken into account in drafting the exclusion. If the court appreciates the background, it may be more likely to hold that the exclusion is reasonable.

9.2.3.7 Attitude of the courts

To sum up, as a general proposition, it seems that if the buyer is a consumer, any exclusion clause is more likely to fail the reasonableness test; if the contract is between commercial parties, it is more likely to pass.

In a commercial contract where there is no great inequality of bargaining power, and particularly where the parties have had the opportunity to identify the risks under the contract and cover them by insurance, the courts have often taken the view that they should not interfere with what the parties have done. In *Watford v Sanderson* (see **9.2.2**), Chadwick LJ stated:

> Where experienced businessmen representing substantial companies of equal bargaining power negotiate an agreement, they may be taken to have had regard to the matters known to them. They should, in my view, be taken to be the best judge of the commercial fairness of the agreement which they have made; including the fairness of each of the terms in that agreement. They should be taken to be the best judge on the question of whether the terms of the agreement are reasonable ... Unless satisfied that one party has, in effect, taken unfair advantage of the other – or a term is so unreasonable that it cannot properly have been understood or considered – the court should not interfere.

However, it must be stressed that there is no guarantee that a court will always take this view; each case must turn on its own facts. There may be particular or additional factors that will mitigate either for or against reasonableness. For example, the factor that clearly influenced the Court of Appeal in both *Watford Electronics Ltd v Sanderson CFL Ltd* and the later case of *Regus (UK) Ltd v Epcot Solutions Ltd* [2008] EWCA Civ 361 was that both parties in each case had used the same terms before in their respective standard-form contracts (**9.2.2** above).

9.2.4   Choice

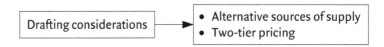

9.2.4.1   Do other suppliers use the clause?

Could the buyer have obtained the goods or services from another supplier which does not impose the exclusion clause in question? This factor may point in either direction. If the buyer could have gone elsewhere without having the clause imposed, and yet chose to make this particular contract, this may mean that the clause is more likely to be reasonable. However, if all suppliers use a similar exclusion, lack of choice may make the exclusion unreasonable. If the supplier is the only one in a particular line of business using a particular exclusion clause, and is, therefore, out of step with its competitors, this again may be evidence that it is unreasonable to use the clause at all. The buyer's knowledge of the existence and extent of the clause (see **9.2.5**) is also likely to be relevant in these circumstances.

9.2.4.2   Two-tier pricing

In a clause of this type, the supplier of the goods or services charges a lower price if the buyer accepts the exclusion clause, and a higher price if the contract contains either a modified version of the clause or no clause at all. Using two-tier pricing can help the clause to pass the reasonableness test. For example, in *RW Green Ltd v Cade Brothers Farm* [1987] Lloyd's Rep 602, the seller in a commercial sale of goods contract used an exclusion with two-tier pricing, and the clause passed the reasonableness test.

9.2.5   Buyer's knowledge and understanding of the clause

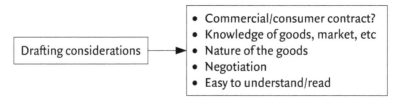

It is important to remember that it is the knowledge and understanding of the parties at the time that the contract was made that will be relevant here.

In a contract between commercial parties, to assess the knowledge and understanding of the parties the courts will look at factors such as the nature of the goods, their awareness of market conditions, and whether or not the parties have used the same standard terms and conditions themselves.

Where the buyer is a consumer, knowledge and understanding is particularly important, as the buyer is unlikely to have inside knowledge of the market. In this context, it is essential to ensure that the clauses are both readable and comprehensible, although this requirement is by no means confined to consumer contracts. Consider, for example, the following comments of Staughton J in the commercial case of *Stag Line v Tyne Ship Repair Group (The Zinnia)* [1984] 2 Lloyd's Rep 211:

> I would have been tempted to hold that all of the conditions are unfair and unreasonable for two reasons; first, they are in such small print that one can barely read them; secondly, the draftsmanship is so convoluted and prolix that one almost needs an LLB to understand them.

9.2.5.1   Nature of the goods

In *Watford v Sanderson* (see **9.2.2**) the Court of Appeal, in finding the exclusion clauses in issue to be reasonable, was clearly influenced by the nature of the product (computer software) as being likely to give rise to predictable problems (and, potentially, to extreme liability). Both parties were aware of this. In *Britvic Soft Drinks Ltd v Messer UK Ltd* (see **9.2.2**), the Court found the exclusions unreasonable and noted that the goods in question (carbon dioxide for use in manufacturing soft drinks) were not ones where the end-user of the goods would reasonably anticipate difficulties or expect to have to test them for compliance with the contract. Again, the court will also consider the nature of the goods when assessing the bargaining strength of the parties.

9.2.5.2 Negotiation

Clearly, if the parties have negotiated on the nature and extent of the term, they can be taken to know and understand its implications. This was an important factor in *Watford v Sanderson* (see **9.2.2**). In *Regus v Epcot* (see above), the attempt by the 'buyer' (an experienced commercial tenant) to renegotiate other terms of the contract, but not the exclusion clause, was seen by the Court as a significant indication of the reasonableness of the clause.

9.2.5.3 Short and simple drafting

This can be difficult to achieve, but is worth aiming for. The solicitor should, in particular, consider the likely reading abilities of those involved with the contract, both customers and employees of the client.

9.2.5.4 Size of print, layout and appearance

Wherever possible, the solicitor should advise the client to use easily readable print, and to set documents out in a way which assists reading (if this can be done without wasting space). Devices such as different typefaces, bold type, underlining and boxes are all useful for drawing attention to significant parts of a contract.

9.2.5.5 Position of the clause

The solicitor will also need to consider where and how the exclusion should appear in the contract. There is no single correct way of doing this; it is often helpful to look at several sets of precedents to get a feel for the different methods. For example, some contracts will place each exclusion immediately after the clause to which it relates; some will have a separate section for the exclusions, cross-referring to other relevant clauses where necessary. The way in which the exclusions are presented may have a bearing on the victim's knowledge and understanding of them, and therefore affect their reasonableness.

9.2.5.6 Practical problems

Following these guidelines should increase the chances of a clause being held reasonable, but it may also create practical difficulties. For example, a clause which is well laid out and clearly expressed may not fit onto the back of an order form. Sometimes 'wall-to-wall' layout (where the print covers virtually the entire surface of the paper, without margins or adequate space between lines) is essential because space is limited. In this case it will be worth considering whether space can be increased by getting rid of redundant clauses, or deleting clauses which cover contingencies so remote that they are not worth providing for (or which would cause few problems if they did occur). It is also possible that a document written in 'plain' English may turn out to be shorter than the same thing expressed in traditional 'legal' English.

9.2.5.7 Incorporation by reference

Incorporation by reference is a common practice in both consumer and business contracts. For example, the supplier under a sale of goods agreement may wish to use standard terms laid down by its trade association as the basis of any contracts it makes. To save space, the agreement can state that the goods are sold subject to the relevant trade association's standard terms, and that the supplier will provide the buyer with a copy of the terms. This may be a useful space-saving device, but there can be problems with both incorporation and reasonableness.

9.2.5.8   Tactics

The solicitor must also be aware of tactical considerations. The client may not want the finished document to be too clear. It may be valid to obscure the meaning of a clause for tactical reasons (and some clients may be uncomfortable with a document which is not written in what they perceive to be 'legal' English). There are no clear-cut solutions to the problems which this raises: solicitor and client must discuss the pros and cons of each approach in each individual case.

9.2.5.9   Conclusion

Because of the numerous considerations, this factor will often be difficult to weigh up; solicitor and client will have to decide what the priority is in each particular case. On the one hand, if a contract is drafted and set out clearly, clauses which are subject to the reasonableness test are more likely to pass the test. On the other hand, fitting a contract into a set amount of space (eg the back of the client's order form) may be seen as more important, even though this may require a compression of drafting and layout which could render a clause unreasonable. However, there may be some room for compromise; just because a contract must fit onto an order form, it does not necessarily also have to be drafted 'wall-to-wall', difficult to read and full of jargon.

9.2.6   Compliance with conditions

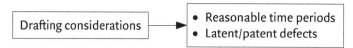

The court will consider whether it was reasonable to expect compliance with any condition for bringing action imposed by the contract, for example a time bar clause stating that the right to reject is lost if defects are not notified to the seller within a specified period. It may be reasonable to state that obvious defects should be notified within a relatively short period, but such a requirement will not be reasonable in respect of latent defects which are not likely to become apparent immediately. Again, the condition must have been reasonable at the time of the contract. Before drafting such a clause, it is therefore important that the solicitor has as much information as possible about the product to establish the type of defect likely to occur, and how quickly the buyer might be expected to notice it.

9.2.7   Goods manufactured to special order

Whether it is reasonable to exclude liability in these circumstances will depend on the facts of the case. Where a seller has expended considerable time and money in manufacturing a 'one-off' product to the order of a particular customer, eg heavy industrial plant, it may find that if it is rejected by the buyer for any reason, it will be difficult to sell on to anyone else. The seller will therefore wish to exclude the buyer's right to reject. A buyer, on the other hand, may have incurred considerable expenditure in order to ensure that a product is unique or free from defects, eg where a consumer buyer commissions an item of furniture from a cabinet maker. If the product turns out to be defective, he will want to be able to return it, and it may be unreasonable to exclude the right to do so.

Tactics

Where there is a particular commercial reason to exclude liability, again, it is advisable to include a preamble explaining why the clause has been included.

9.2.8 Other factors

The Sch 2 guidelines can be seen as a starting point for assessing the reasonableness of the clause. However, there are further factors which the court will consider, and it is important not to overlook these.

9.2.8.1 Price

If the loss which may result from breach of contract is wholly disproportionate to the contract price, it may be reasonable for the contract to contain an exclusion (or limitation) clause. If both parties are aware of this from the outset, the chances of the clause being reasonable may be enhanced. In a tailor-made contract, a preamble can be used to set out the basis on which the parties are contracting.

9.2.8.2 Allocation of risk and insurance

The parties to a commercial contract will usually be in the best position to decide what the risks under the contract are, and how to deal with them. The court may attach considerable significance to how the parties have identified and dealt with the risks under the contract. If an exclusion or limitation clause has the effect of passing the risk of loss or damage from one party to the other, it has more chance of surviving the reasonableness test if it is clear that the contract has provided for this. Examples include:

(a) reflecting the degree of risk in the contract price, then backing this up with a limitation clause;

(b) imposing an obligation on the party with the risk to take out appropriate insurance;

(c) prefacing any insurance clause with a preamble explaining how the insurance arrangements and the exclusions have been arrived at.

Even if there is no obligation to insure, the courts place considerable emphasis on the availability of insurance to the parties respectively. For example, in *George Mitchell (Chesterhall) Ltd v Finney Lock Seeds Ltd* [1983] 2 AC 803, where defective cabbage seed was sold to a farmer, the House of Lords was obviously impressed by evidence that it would have been easy and inexpensive for the supplier to cover itself against the risk of supplying defective seed. This was one of several reasons for finding that a clause limiting liability to the price of the seed was unreasonable.

It may be worthwhile obtaining expert evidence on insurance before drafting the contract and its exclusions. The courts will not always be in the best position to assess what the risks and the most suitable insurance arrangements are, and may, therefore, in the absence of suitable evidence, make an inappropriate decision on the reasonableness of any exclusion.

Note that where a limitation clause is concerned, UCTA 1977, s 11(4)(b) specifically mentions the availability of insurance as a factor in assessing reasonableness (see further **9.3.1.2**).

9.2.8.3 Trade associations

Approval by a trade association (or similar body) may help an exclusion clause to pass the reasonableness test. For example, in *RW Green Ltd v Cade Brothers Farm* [1987] Lloyd's Rep 602, a case involving the sale of defective potato seed, the parties used a standard-form contract which had originally been negotiated between the National Farmers' Union and the National Association of Seed Potato Merchants. The limitation clause was found to be reasonable.

9.3   EFFECTIVENESS OF DIFFERENT TYPES OF EXCLUSION CLAUSE

In deciding whether the clause is reasonable, the court will also look at the clause itself. The extent of the exclusion and the type of clause will be relevant factors. This chapter ends with a closer look at the effectiveness of some of the different types of exclusion clause commonly found in commercial contracts:

(a)   limitation clauses;

(b)   force majeure clauses;

(c)   time bar clauses;

(d)   non-rejection clauses;

(e)   exclusions and limitations of consequential loss.

9.3.1   Exclusion or limitation?

9.3.1.1   General principle

The House of Lords has held on a number of occasions that a clause which limits liability is more likely to pass the reasonableness test than one which excludes it altogether (see eg *Ailsa Craig Fishing Co Ltd v Malvern Fishing Co Ltd* [1983] 1 WLR 964). However, this principle should be treated with caution; arguably, what is important is the difference in the degree of exclusion, not simply in the type of clause. A clause which limits the supplier's liability to the contract price, where the damage likely to be caused is far in excess of this, may be as unreasonable as a total exclusion, especially if the contract price in the latter case is low.

9.3.1.2   UCTA 1977 guidelines

Note that UCTA 1977, s 11(4) contains two guidelines which apply only where a term is designed to limit liability to a specified sum of money rather than to exclude it altogether:

(a)   by s 11(4)(a), the court should take account of the resources available to the person relying on the limitation to meet liability, should it arise; and

(b)   by s 11(4)(b), the court should have regard to how far it was open to that person to cover himself by insurance.

In *St Albans City and District Council v ICL* [1996] 4 All ER 481, the Court of Appeal looked at the bargaining strength of the parties, and held that a limitation clause in a contract between a multinational company with substantial resources and a local authority was unreasonable. Other factors which the Court took into account were the fact that ICL was covered by product liability insurance of £50 million yet had limited its liability to £100,000, and the limited choice of similar products available to the local authority. Had the limitation clause been upheld, the cost of the loss would have been borne by the local taxpayers, so it was fairer to allocate the risk to ICL. As discussed at **9.2.2**, the Court of Appeal considered the reasonableness of a limitation clause in *Watford v Sanderson CFL Ltd* and concluded that the clause did not deprive the buyer of the right to damages in all circumstances.

9.3.2   Force majeure clauses

A force majeure clause is designed to apply where contractual performance has become impossible because of circumstances unforeseen by the parties and outside their control. In a sale of goods contract, it will normally seek to excuse the seller for failure to deliver the goods on time (or even at all) in these circumstances. A force majeure clause is normally classified as part of the boiler-plate of an agreement (see **1.5.2.8**). 'Force majeure' clauses have been, of course, hugely relevant in the light of the coronavirus pandemic and are again of importance following Russia's invasion of Ukraine.

9.3.2.1 Meaning of 'force majeure'

The expression 'force majeure' has been interpreted by the courts to cover a range of events, including act of God, war, strikes, embargoes, government refusal to grant licences and abnormal weather conditions. The common factor in each case is that the event is outside the contracting parties' control. However, it is usual for a force majeure clause to do more than simply state that the supplier will not be liable for non-performance caused by 'force majeure'. Instead, it will normally set out a (non-exhaustive) list of specific events which the clause is intended to cover and the consequences of any of those events arising, so that both parties know exactly where they stand. (As noted at **8.6.3**, the *ejusdem generis* rule does not apply to force majeure clauses; specifying events does not cut down the meaning of any general words which follow.)

9.3.2.2 Frustration of the contract

As discussed in **Chapter 3** (see **3.7.1**), where performance has become impossible due to unforeseen events beyond the parties' control, in the absence of express provision the contract may be frustrated. Thus, for example, a contract for supply of goods will be frustrated if it becomes clear that any delivery of the goods will be so late that performance of the contract will be radically different from that envisaged by the parties. As noted at **3.7.1**, it is possible that the coronavirus pandemic, or at least its effect, may be a frustrating event. The war in Ukraine is a further example.

9.3.2.3 Advantages of a specific provision in the contract

The problem with frustration is that it is rather uncertain (how long must the buyer wait before the performance of the contract will become radically different from that which the parties envisaged?), and its effects under the Law Reform (Frustrated Contracts) Act 1943 are rather arbitrary. Thus, although it will act as a kind of 'safety net' if the parties do not turn their attention to what will happen if unforeseen events occur, it is generally preferable to have a specific provision (ie, a force majeure clause) in the contract dealing with this situation. The parties can then agree that when the disrupting circumstances have been in existence for a specific time, either party may cancel the agreement by giving the other a certain period of written notice. The contract can also make specific provision for the financial consequences of such a cancellation.

9.3.2.4 Application of UCTA 1977

As long as one party deals on the other party's written standard terms of business, a force majeure clause will be subject to the reasonableness test under s 3 of UCTA 1977, as an attempt by the party relying on the clause to render no contractual performance at all (s 3(2)(b)(ii)). Although this may appear to be a rather drastic type of exclusion at first sight, courts often are prepared to treat force majeure clauses favourably (ie hold that they are reasonable) if care is taken over drafting.

9.3.2.5 Drafting points to consider

(a) The force majeure events should be clearly defined. Knowledge of the client's business is therefore essential to anticipate the type of events to be included. Certainly, the list of events should now include 'pandemic' or the imposition of economic sanctions.

(b) If a force majeure event occurs, should the contract to be suspended or cancelled (or suspended for a certain period followed by cancellation)? Which is appropriate will depend on the client's instructions and the circumstances.

(c) If cancellation is chosen, is it more appropriate to have automatic cancellation of the contract if a force majeure event occurs, or should the party relying on the force majeure give notice of cancellation to the other? The latter will usually be preferable. (Note that the party relying on force majeure will have to prove that the event in question has arisen.)

(d)   Should the party relying on force majeure refund any payments which the other party has already made to it? Providing for a refund should help to ensure that the clause is reasonable. It need not always be a full refund; a partial refund may be appropriate, especially if the supplier has already incurred expense.

9.3.3 Time bar clauses

A client who is involved in the supply of goods or services may wish to reduce the limitation period which would normally apply to claims arising from breach of the contract (the basic contractual limitation period is six years). This may be justifiable: long before the statutory limitation period expires, evidence of a breach of contract may become hard to pin down, and perishable goods will have lost any market value they may have had. In addition, a supplier will probably want to close its books on a particular contract reasonably soon after performance. In a commercial contract, therefore, it may be appropriate to include a 'time bar' clause (eg, in a sale of goods contract, stating that the buyer cannot claim in respect of defects in the goods unless it notifies those defects to the supplier within a certain period of time).

Time bar clauses will usually be effective (and reasonable) if they are included for good commercial reasons, particularly if they result from insurance consequences or requirements (see *Super Chem Products Ltd v American Life and General Insurance Co Ltd* [2004] UKPC 2).

9.3.3.1 Application of UCTA 1977

If (as will usually be the case) the effect of the time bar clause is to exclude liability for breach of the implied conditions under the SGA 1979 then s 6 of UCTA 1977 will apply, and the clause will be subject to the reasonableness test. Otherwise, s 3 of UCTA 1977 will apply (as long as one party deals on the other party's written standard terms of business); the clause is an attempt by one party to exclude or restrict its liability when in breach of contract (s 3(2)(a)).

9.3.3.2 Drafting points to consider

(a)   Does the party relying on the clause want to be notified of defects (ie, of the possible existence of a claim) or of the claim itself within a specified period, or to impose a time-limit for bringing proceedings, or all of these? A clause which raises too many barriers or is too complex may fail the reasonableness test.

(b)   It is often sensible to distinguish between patent and latent defects, giving a longer time period for notification in respect of defects which are not immediately apparent on delivery. This is more likely to be reasonable than having the same time period for notification of both types of defect.

(c)   The clause should state whether it is a particular remedy (eg rejection, damages) or the claim itself which is to be barred. If only the remedy is barred, the buyer might be able to use the claim as a defence to an action for the price by the seller.

If the contract is between members of the same trade association, a time bar clause probably has a better chance of passing the reasonableness test. Parties operating in the same market should know and accept the problems likely to arise in that market, and it may then be possible to make the clause stricter (eg, cut down the notification period) than if the other contracting party is unfamiliar with the problems of the trade.

9.3.4 Non-rejection clauses

There are two main reasons why a seller may consider a non-rejection clause:

As discussed in **Chapter 5**, for his own convenience, a seller may want to prevent SGA 1979, s 36 from applying to the contract (see **5.4.6.6**).

The seller may want to stop its buyer from taking advantage of a fall in the price of the contract goods by finding a technical breach of contract, rejecting the goods (with a view to getting its money back from the seller, or not having to pay at all) and then buying replacement goods more cheaply at the new, lower market price.

9.3.4.1   Application of UCTA 1977

A non-rejection clause may, depending on the circumstances, be subject to either s 6 or s 3 of UCTA 1977.

9.3.4.2   Drafting points to consider

(a)   As there may be different reasons for including a non-rejection clause (see above), different types of clause will be necessary according to the client's needs. Again, it is important to be aware of the commercial background before drafting the clause.

(b)   It may be worth using a preamble to explain why the clause has been included.

(c)   Sometimes a simple reversal of s 36 of SGA 1979 will meet the seller's needs (eg allowing the buyer to reject but making it clear that, following rejection, the buyer must return the goods to the seller).

(d)   Alternatively, the seller may wish to go further and state that the buyer cannot reject at all. This will also prevent the buyer claiming restitution of the purchase price, but not from suing for damages for breach of contract.

9.3.5   Loss of profits, indirect and consequential loss clauses

A common drafting technique with exclusion or limitation clauses is to try to limit liability to 'direct loss' and exclude liability for all or any of the following: 'loss of profits' or 'indirect loss' or 'consequential loss'. However, there may be problems with construction, and the terms are frequently misunderstood by clients and consequently misused. The starting point is therefore to take a brief look at terminology, as this will have a bearing on construction of the clause. The traditional approach is as follows:

(a)   '*Loss of profits*'. Clients tend to assume that all 'loss of profits' is indirect or consequential loss. However, contracts are designed to achieve profits, so loss of ordinary profits can be direct loss. In legal terms, these profits would fall within the first limb of *Hadley v Baxendale* (see **3.7.3.1**) as arising naturally from the breach. Thus, a clause excluding consequential loss or indirect loss will not exclude normal loss of profit. Clearly, ordinarily contemplated re-sale profits (as in distribution or wholesale contracts) would naturally fall within normal loss of profits; it may be more problematic where the goods are likely to be used by the seller in a way not directly linked to profit making, rather than being simply sold on.

(b)   '*Indirect*' or '*consequential*' *loss*. Consequential or indirect loss is all loss other than direct loss. In legal terms, it is loss which falls under the second limb of *Hadley v Baxendale*, so these terms will not cover ordinary loss of profits. The term does not, therefore, cover all financial loss. Thus, a clause excluding indirect or consequential loss will not preclude a claim for direct loss. See *Markerstudy Insurance Co Ltd v Endsleigh Insurance Services Ltd* [2010] EWHC 281 (Comm).

More recently, however, there are indications that the courts are moving away from the traditional approach and recognising the need to adopt a case-by-case approach which considers the natural meaning of the words within the context of the agreement as a whole. See, for example, 2 *Entertainment Video Ltd v Sony DADC Europe Ltd* [2020] EWHC 972 (TCC).

It is perfectly acceptable to exclude liability both for loss of profits and for indirect or consequential loss. For example, in *Watford v Sanderson* (see **9.2.2**), the Court of Appeal held that where the parties were of equal bargaining power and were aware of the potential risks, 'it is reasonable to expect that the contract will make provision for the risk of indirect or consequential loss to fall on one party or the other'. The problem is just how wide the exclusion is. Clearly it is not acceptable to exclude all liability, so as to leave the buyer with no remedy at all (see, eg, *Regus v Epcot* (at **9.2.2**) and the *NetTV* case (at **8.3.2.2**)). In *Regus*, the court held that, on true construction of the clause, the exclusion of consequential loss, although wide-reaching, did not prevent recovery of direct loss.

9.3.5.1 Application of UCTA 1977

Exclusion or limitation of liability for loss of profits and indirect or consequential loss may be subject to s 3 or s 6 of UCTA 1977.

9.3.5.2 Drafting points to consider

(a) When excluding liability for loss of profits, list what types of profit are contemplated and separate loss of profits from indirect or consequential loss; otherwise 'ordinary' profits, eg anticipated re-sale profits, might well not be covered by the clause.

(b) With clauses dealing with indirect or consequential losses, the scale and type of matters within reasonable contemplation of the parties should be considered. Again, it is important to have a good grasp of the commercial background and, if necessary, investigate with the client the types of loss which could arise. The clause should specify the types of loss excluded, eg loss of contracts, loss of goodwill, loss of anticipated earnings, etc. However, the list should not be a veiled disguise for effectively excluding all types of financial loss.

(c) Consider the nature of the goods. The clause should not exclude the type of consequential loss that is always likely to result from defects in the particular type of goods, eg computer programs, leaving the buyer without any remedy.

(d) Consider including a cap on liability rather than a total exclusion, and take out insurance to cover this. The cap could be related to the extent of the seller's product liability insurance, and a preamble included explaining that this is the reason for the limit. The cap should not be set too low (see *St Albans v ICL* discussed at **9.3.1.2**). A further possibility is to link the cap to the price of the goods.

SUMMARY

We have considered the importance of the UCTA 1977 test of reasonableness in assessing the validity of an exclusion clause in a commercial contract in the UK. There are a number of factors which the courts will consider when deciding whether or not such a clause is reasonable, but it is important to appreciate that in the event of a dispute, the outcome will be notoriously difficult to predict and will often depend on the facts of a particular case. We are now moving away from direct sales of goods, to look at other types of marketing agreement.

CHAPTER 10

MARKETING AGREEMENTS: INTRODUCTION TO AGENCY AND DISTRIBUTION

LEARNING OUTCOMES

After reading this chapter you will be able to:

- explain the main characteristics of an agency and a distribution agreement
- recognise the main differences between an agency and a distribution agreement
- advise on the advantages and disadvantages of each type of agreement.

10.1 INTRODUCTION

The previous chapters have concentrated on the contractual arrangements into which commercial manufacturers may enter to make direct sales to retailers or the end users of the goods. However, commercial suppliers may decide, for a variety of reasons, not to market the goods themselves but to appoint an intermediary. They may lack the resources to market the goods effectively, or they may wish to break into a new and unfamiliar market where they require the expertise of a third party.

The topic of agreements for the marketing of goods and services is introduced in **Chapters 34** and **35** of **Business Law and Practice**. This chapter gives a brief reminder of two of the most commonly encountered marketing agreements: agency and distribution. **Chapter 11** will then goes on to consider how each type of agreement might be put together.

10.2 AGENCY

10.2.1 What is agency?

Agency is the relationship which arises where one party, the principal, gives another (the agent) authority to act on his behalf. Any contract concluded by the agent is binding on the third party with whom the contract is made. However, to create a binding contract between the principle and the third party, the agent must generally have authority. The agent may be liable to the principal and to the third party if the agent exceeds that authority.

10.2.2 Types of agency

The term 'agency' is often used very loosely in relation to commercial activities to cover a number of different types of business relationship, and it is extremely important not to take at face value the label which the parties have put on their arrangement; always check carefully the actual nature of the relationship.

A true sales agency agreement is one where the agent makes contracts with customers on behalf of its principal; in other words, the agent binds the principal, so there is a contract between the principal and the customer (but none between the agent and the customer). At this stage the agent 'drops out' of the process. However, the principal is liable for the acts of his agent.

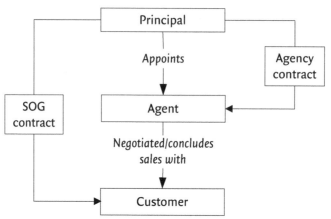

Figure 10.1 Sales agency agreement

The agent does not hold stocks of the goods, although it may have samples to show to prospective customers. When the goods are sold, title to the goods passes direct from the principal to the customer. The agent never owns the goods – it is simply an intermediary, and so will not generally incur liability, for example, if the goods are defective.

Other types of agency agreement are possible; for example marketing or 'introducing' agency. This term normally covers the situation where the agent simply finds customers and introduces them to the principal, which then negotiates and makes the contract for itself; however, it is also used where the agent finds customers and negotiates terms on the principal's behalf but without having the authority to make the contract on the principal's behalf.

In any dispute, the court is likely to attach little weight to the labelling of an agreement but will look at the relationship between the parties. In *Mercantile International Group plc v Chuan Soon Huant Industrial Group Ltd* [2002] EWCA Civ 288 the arrangement between the parties was described as an 'agency agreement'. However, the claimant was not paid by commission but (like a distributor) was remunerated by mark-up. The Court of Appeal looked at the substance of the agreement itself. Under the agreement, the claimant clearly had authority to negotiate in the principal's name, the principal delivered direct to customers and the claimant never held any stock. The Court decided that, despite the way that the claimant was paid, the agreement was in fact an agency agreement.

10.2.3 How is agency created?

10.2.3.1 Express actual authority

By far the most usual way that the agency relationship is created is by an agreement under which the principal gives the agent authority to do specific things, for example to negotiate contracts on his behalf. The agent has been given express actual authority to do these specific things, but no more, and no less. The agent who has been given express actual authority to negotiate contracts will not have authority to conclude contracts on the principal's behalf.

10.2.3.2 Implied actual or usual authority

Implied actual authority may arise in one of two ways:

(a) The agent will have implied actual authority to do such things as are incidental to the performance of his duties, eg an agent who has express actual authority to sell cosmetics on behalf of the principal will have implied actual authority to receive payment on the principal's behalf.

(b) Implied actual or usual authority may arise out of the customs of a particular trade, profession or business, eg partners in a firm have implied authority to do all the usual things which partners do, such a employing staff or buying office equipment.

10.2.3.3 Apparent or ostensible authority

Apparent (or ostensible) authority arises where the principal has given the distinct but false impression that the agent had authority to enter into a particular contract. Such authority is said to arise from estoppel, because the principal is deemed to have acted in such a way that he is estopped from denying that the agent had authority.

There are three criteria which must be met for an agency by estoppel to arise. These come from the case of *Freeman & Lockyer v Buckhurst Park Properties (Mangal) Ltd* [1964] 2 QB 480:

(a) the principal must at some stage have represented (by words or by conduct) that the agent had authority;

(b) the third party must rely on that representation, believing that the agent had authority; and

(c) the third party must alter his position, eg by entering into the transaction.

Apparent authority is particularly important where an agent has been expressly told not to make contracts of a type that someone in his position would normally have authority to make. However, where the third party has reason to believe that the agent does not have actual authority and fails to make the relevant inquiries that a reasonable person would, it cannot rely on apparent authority (see, for example, *East Asia Company Co Ltd v PT Satria* [2019] UKPC 30).

10.2.3.4 Ratification

Where someone purports to act as an agent, but has no authority, or has exceeded his authority, then, subject to certain restrictions, the principal may ratify the unauthorised acts of the agent. Ratification retrospectively creates actual authority, and goes back to when the unauthorised acts were carried out.

10.2.4 Effects of agency

10.2.4.1 Where the agent had actual authority

(a) *As between the principal and the third party:* There is a contract between the principal and the third party and each party can sue the other on it.

(b) *As between the agent and the third party:* The contract made by the agent is the contract of the principal. The agent drops out of the picture, in other words acquires no rights or liabilities under the contract, and the contract takes effect between the principal and the third party.

10.2.4.2 Where the agent had apparent authority

(a) *As between the principal and the third party:* There is a contract between the principal and the third party, and each party can sue the other on it. The principal will be estopped from denying that there was a contract.

(b) *As between the agent and the third party:* as above, there is a contract between the principal and the third party, and the agent drops out of the picture.

(c) *As between the principal and the agent:* the principal may be able to bring an action against the agent if the agent has acted outside of his authority.

10.2.4.3   Where the agent had no authority

(a)   *As between the principal and the third party:* there is no contract between the principal and the third party, because the agent did not have authority to bind the principal.

(b)   *As between the agent and the third party:* the third party may sue the agent in deceit, where the agent knew that he had no authority, or for breach of warranty of authority, ie the third party can bring an action for damages against the agent. The third party cannot sue the agent for breach of contract, as he has purported to contract on behalf of the principal, and not on his own behalf.

(c)   *As between the principal and the agent:* the agent may be liable to the principal if the principal suffers loss as a result.

10.2.4.4   Undisclosed principal

Under most circumstances, the agent will disclose the name of the principal and that he is acting as an agent. Where he does not, the third party can hold the agent liable as though he were the principal, but has the option to hold the principal liable. The principal may in turn hold the third party liable on the contract.

10.3   DISTRIBUTION

In a distribution agreement, the supplier sells goods to the distributor, which buys them in order to re-sell on its own behalf. A common example of a distribution agreement is where a manufacturer sells its products to a wholesaler, which buys them to sell to its own customers to retail onwards; the relationship between manufacturer and wholesaler is a distribution agreement.

The distributor owns the goods which it sells, and title to the goods passes from the distributor to its customers. The supplier has no contractual relationship with the distributor's customers, and so will have no contractual liability, for example under ss 13–15 of the SGA 1979 (see **Chapter 7**). If the goods are defective, the supplier may, however, be liable to end users in tort or for product liability, eg in the UK under the Consumer Protection Act 1987.

Note that a distribution agreement is sometimes referred to as a 'distributorship agreement' (or simply 'distributorship'). Some commentators prefer this term, on the ground that, in practice, 'distribution agreement' is sometimes used loosely to refer to an agreement for the carriage of goods.

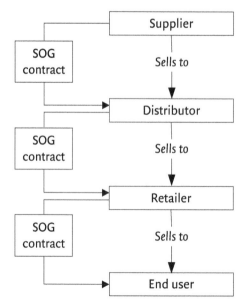

Figure 10.2 Distribution agreement

10.4 ADVANTAGES AND DISADVANTAGES OF EACH TYPE OF AGREEMENT

Table 10.1 below contains a reminder of the commercial factors to consider when deciding whether an agency or a distribution agreement would be more suitable. For a more detailed discussion, see **Chapter 35** of *Business Law and Practice*.

Agency	Distribution
Agent (A) appointed by principal (P) under agency agreement. A receives commission (usually agreed percentage of sales or introductions). Can be used for marketing services as well as goods.	Supplier (S) enters distribution agreement with distributor (D). D buys the goods from S for resale, and retains all profits from resale. Generally only suitable for marketing goods.
Requires close supervision by P. Less suitable if A and P are based in different countries or P has limited time for this. More suitable for bespoke products, products requiring close contact or after-sales service. Useful to protect brand/goodwill.	Requires limited supervision. D decides how and where to market goods. More suitable for mass-produced products or where S is likely to encounter unfamiliar markets/language problems. More difficult to protect brand/goodwill.
P remains contractually liable to his customers. A has limited financial risk, and has no initial outlay on stock, although A will probably earn less through payment of commission than profit from re-sale.	No contractual liability between S and D's customers, although S may be liable in tort or under product liability legislation. D bears the risk of non-payment, claims from customers and unsold stock.
Often more expensive for P to set up and operate.	More expensive for D to set up and operate, but can be more lucrative for D. D may have more incentive to exploit market to generate profit.
Agency agreements are unlikely to infringe UK or EU competition law (see **11.1.3.2** and **Chapter 28**).	Can give rise to competition law problems. The grant of territorial protection may infringe Article 101 of the TFEU or the Chapter I Prohibition (see **Chapter 28**).
Agency agreements in the UK are subject to the Commercial Agents (Council Directive) Regulations 1993 (SI 1993/3053), which govern areas such as payment of duties of A and P, commission, and payment on termination of the agreement (see **11.3**). Equivalent provisions apply throughout the EU (see **10.2**).	No equivalent legislation for distribution.
Where P and A are based in separate jurisdictions, they may be regarded as one undertaking for corporation tax purposes, which may have adverse tax consequences for P. P will be liable for VAT on products supplied in its name.	D will generally pay all tax on profits and VAT.

Table 10.1 Advantages of agency and distribution agrements

10.5 EXCLUSIVITY

Whether the manufacturer decides to appoint an agent or a distributor, it will be important to decide the extent to which the agent/distributor will be protected from competition within the territory where it is operating. There are three options:

(a) Exclusive agency/distributorship. The manufacturer agrees not to appoint any other agents/distributors within the territory and will not sell the products within the territory itself.

(b) Sole agency/distributorship. The manufacturer agrees not to appoint any other agents/distributors within the territory, but remains free to sell the products within the territory itself.

(c) Non-exclusive agency/distributorship. The manufacturer can appoint other agents/distributors within the territory, and can sell the products within the territory itself.

Again, in practice, clients tend to use the terminology loosely. In particular, the legal and commercial meanings of the terms 'sole' and 'exclusive' have become confused, and may even mean different things in different product markets, so it is important to establish the exact nature of the relationship between the parties.

The choice will depend on various factors, including the bargaining power of the parties. Clearly, exclusivity is preferable for the agent or distributor, and may be important to allow a new appointee to establish itself within a territory. Businesses often regard territorial exclusivity as a fundamental term, particularly in a distribution agreement, in order to benefit as much as possible from their initial investment. Without the grant of exclusivity, a potential distributor might not agree to take on the distributorship at all.

Where exclusivity is granted, the manufacturer should put in place measures to ensure that the territory is fully exploited, such as minimum target obligations.

10.6 BASIC RULES FOR SUCCESSFUL DRAFTING OF MARKETING AGREEMENTS

The three basic rules in relation to drafting mentioned in **Chapter 8** (know the commercial background, know the law, and know the drafting principles) are equally important in this context:

(a) Commercial background is essential to advise the client on the most appropriate type of marketing agreement.

(b) Lawyers should be aware of the common law rules in relation to authority of agents.

(c) Agency agreements are regulated by the Commercial Agents (Council Directive) Regulations 1993, and distribution agreements may be subject to both EU and UK competition law, so it is vital for the solicitor drafting the agreement to have an awareness of both of these areas of law. A cautionary tale in relation to agency is *Berry v Laytons* [2009] ECC 34, where an agent was awarded £192,189 plus interest in damages as a result of his solicitor's negligent failure to advise on his entitlement under the Regulations on termination of the agency agreement. The consequences could be a great deal worse where parties can be fined up to 10% of worldwide turnover for breach of relevant EU or UK competition provisions.

(d) Lastly, the usual health warning applies to the use of precedents, but it is important that the agreement does not fall foul of the Commercial Agents (Council Directive) Regulations 1993 or competition law respectively, so a precedent may be helpful in deciding whether or not a clause complies.

SUMMARY

Commercial suppliers may chose to use an intermediary to market their goods, rather than selling direct to the end user. The two main types of marketing agreement are agency agreements and distribution agreements. You have considered the main characteristics of each type of agreement, and the advantages and disadvantages of both, concentrating on agreements within the EU. The next chapter will concentrate on the drafting considerations in relation to both type of agreement.

CHAPTER 11

MARKETING AGREEMENTS: DRAFTING AGENCY AND DISTRIBUTION AGREEMENTS

LEARNING OUTCOMES

After reading this chapter you will be able to:

- recognise the main constraints, both legal and practical, that affect the drafting of agency and distribution agreements in the UK
- summarise the structure and content of a typical agency agreement
- summarise the structure and content of a typical distribution agreement
- understand the importance and scope of the Commercial Agents (Council Directive) Regulations 1993 (the Regulations) when drafting an agency agreement in the UK
- apply the provisions of the Regulations to an agency agreement
- identify the main EU competition law issues which should be taken into account when drafting a distribution agreement.

11.1 DRAFTING AN AGENCY AGREEMENT

11.1.1 Introduction

To help in considering how to approach an agency agreement, this section will refer to an expanded version of the agency example described in *Business Law and Practice* at **35.6**.

EXAMPLE

Wood Magic Ltd is a medium-sized company in the UK city of Chester. It has been established for about 20 years, and has built up a thriving business making custom-designed furniture in luxury woods such as yew and cherry. Its sales have been largely confined to the North of England, where it has built up an excellent reputation. However, following a recent change of management and an injection of new capital, the directors plan to expand the business. In particular, they want to target London and the South-East, but have not yet decided how best to do this. Up to now, Wood Magic has carried out its own marketing, and there are no plans to change the set-up for the existing Northern operations.

> The directors now feel that Wood Magic needs to find a 'trading partner' with a presence in the target market to help the furniture become established in that market. They are prepared to commit at least one director to be permanently engaged in developing this side of the business and establishing good relations with the trading partner. This commitment will be a long-term one and, despite having the trading partner to find customers for it, Wood Magic needs to maintain customer contact itself to ensure that customers get the products they need.
>
> The directors would like to know how the involvement of a trading partner might affect Wood Magic's liability to customers, but see no problem in being liable to customers if things go wrong, as they are proud of the company's reputation.

11.1.2   Initial advice

At this stage of the proposed transaction, the solicitor is likely to be asked to advise on two related areas:

(a)   What sort of marketing arrangement is most suitable for Wood Magic?

(b)   What factors should it take into account when looking for a trading partner?

The facts indicate that some form of agency agreement would be most appropriate:

(a)   Wood Magic needs to be able to supervise its trading partner quite closely, and is prepared to commit resources to this supervision.

(b)   Wood Magic needs to have some sort of contact with the buyers of its furniture to give them the products they need.

(c)   Wood Magic is not concerned about being liable to its ultimate customers.

(d)   The target market is in the UK, so supervision of the trading partner should be easier.

Either marketing or sales agency may be suitable, depending on whether the directors simply want the agent to find customers, or whether they want to give the agent authority to make contracts on Wood Magic's behalf. In both cases (but particularly the second), Wood Magic should be looking for a reliable, well-organised and creditworthy business, preferably with an established reputation.

11.1.3   Preliminary considerations

Assume now that Wood Magic's directors have found a suitable trading partner, a company called Lynwood Ltd, which is based in Kingston-upon-Thames near London. They have checked Lynwood's business credentials and are satisfied that it will make a suitable trading partner. In particular, Wood Magic is satisfied that using Lynwood will give Wood Magic an appropriate level of customer contact. The prospective parties are now negotiating the agency agreement, and have provisionally agreed certain terms, including the following:

(a)   Lynwood will have authority to find customers and make contracts on Wood Magic's behalf.

(b)   Wood Magic will deliver the finished furniture direct to customers.

(c)   Wood Magic will pay Lynwood a monthly commission.

(d)   Wood Magic will set the prices for the furniture (as it is custom-made, Wood Magic will supply Lynwood with a detailed 'pricing menu' which will allow Lynwood to work out the price for each order).

(e)   Lynwood will keep certain display items of Wood Magic's furniture at its premises to show potential customers what can be achieved. Wood Magic will supply Lynwood with these items free of charge and will remain the owner of the items.

On the basis of these instructions, the solicitor is ready to begin drafting the agreement. However, there are several preliminary considerations which should be taken into account.

11.1.3.1   Statutory restrictions on drafting

Many agency agreements are now subject to the 1993 Regulations. The impact of these Regulations will be considered in detail at **11.3** below.

11.1.3.2   How far will the agreement be affected by competition law?

If the law of the contract is to be English law, English competition law is potentially applicable (for choice of law, see **Chapter 14**). The Competition Act 1998 contains a basic prohibition (the Chapter I prohibition) on anti-competitive agreements between two or more undertakings if they have the potential to affect trade in the UK and have as their object or effect the prevention, restriction or distortion of competition within the UK (Competition Act 1998, s 2) (see **28.2.7**).

Theoretically, agency (and distribution) agreements within the UK can be in breach of the Chapter I prohibition if they contain provisions which (inter alia):

(a)   control selling prices;

(b)   restrict markets;

(c)   restrict customers;

(d)   limit production.

In practice, agency agreements will fall outside the scope of the Chapter I prohibition. The Chapter I prohibition applies to agreements between two or more undertakings. Generally, as a result of the principal–agent relationship, the agent will be treated as being part of the same undertaking as the principal and so will not fall foul of the prohibition. However, post-Brexit, the UK competition authorities will enforce rules which are based on those which apply within the EU. Guidance on vertical restraints was set out in the Commission Notice of May 2010. In relation to agency agreements, under the guidelines, if the agent assumes a significant amount of 'financial or commercial risk', it will be considered to be an independent undertaking, and so the agreement may infringe the prohibition if it contains anti-competitive terms. Indications that the agent is assuming significant financial or commercial risk are, for example, that:

(i)   the principal requires the agent to contribute towards the supply of the contract goods;

(ii)   the agent is maintaining stocks of the goods at its own cost;

(iii)   the agent is required to contribute to advertising and sales promotion itself; or

(iv)   the agent operates and is required to pay for after-sales, repair or warranty service.

On the basis of the terms agreed in principle, there seems a good chance that Wood Magic's proposed agreement will fall outside the scope of the Chapter I prohibition, as Lynwood does not appear to be accepting financial or commercial risks. In particular:

(a)   There is no evidence that Lynwood will ever be the owner of the contract goods, and although Lynwood keeps display items of furniture at its premises, these are not 'stocks' in the normal sense (Lynwood has not paid for them and does not own them).

(b)   There is no evidence of Lynwood providing promotional or after-sales services.

11.1.3.3   How far should the agreement expressly refer to the basic principles of agency law?

(Again, this discussion assumes that the proper law of the agreement is to be English law.)

This will depend upon the relationship of the parties and how familiar they are with the principles of agency law generally. If they are new to one another and have little experience of agency agreements (this would seem to apply to Wood Magic and Lynwood), setting out the principles could be beneficial; both parties will know exactly where they stand. If, however, the parties are both experienced and already have a long-standing relationship, express inclusion of basic agency principles may only offend both sides. If the agency falls within the ambit of the Regulations, wide fiduciary duties are imposed upon the parties (see **11.3.2**).

11.2 PLANNING, FORM AND CONTENT OF AN AGENCY AGREEMENT

For many years, there was comparatively little statutory provision in English law which could affect the contents of an agency agreement. However, many agency agreements in the UK are now subject to the Commercial Agents (Council Directive) Regulations 1993 (SI 1993/3053) ('the Regulations'), which came into force on 1 January 1994 and enacted into English law the requirements of the EC Directive on the Co-ordination of Laws of Member States relating to Self-Employed Commercial Agents (Directive 86/653/EEC). The existence of this Directive means that agency rules are very similar across Europe, as each Member State of the EU has implemented the Directive into its national law.

The next step is to plan the structure of the agreement. Whilst doing so, it is essential to consider how the Regulations affect each part of the agreement. An agency agreement is likely to follow the structure set out in **Table 11.1** below. The regulations relevant to each part of this structure are shown in the right-hand column.

Structure of agency agreement	Relevant regulations
(a) Date, parties, recitals	(a) None
(b) Interpretation clause	(b) reg 2
(c) Appointment of agent	(c) regs 1 and 2, 14
(d) Agent's rights and duties	(d) reg 3
(e) Principal's rights and duties	(e) reg 4
(f) Financial provisions	(f) regs 6–12
(g) Termination (if not dealt with elsewhere)	(g) regs 5, 16–20
(h) Boiler-plate clauses	(h) regs 21 and 22
(i) Signatures	(i) reg 13
(j) Schedules	(j) None

Table 11.1 Structure of an agency agreement

Note that there is no requirement under the Regulations that the agreement should be in writing or signed, but under reg 13 either party has the right to request a signed written document from the other. Clearly it would be unusual for a commercial agency agreement not be in writing.

This section will look at the content of a simple agency agreement, and then the effect of the Regulations will be discussed in **11.3**.

11.2.1 Introduction to the agreement

This section of the agreement is likely to cover the following areas:

(a)   a preliminary clause setting out the date of the agreement, the parties and any recitals which are felt to be necessary;

(b)   a definitions and interpretation clause; and

(c)   a clause dealing with the appointment of the agent.

11.2.1.1 Date, parties, recitals

The date of the agreement should cause few problems, but the description of the parties may need some thought. The principal will often be a manufacturer (as with Wood Magic), but, as agency can be created at any stage of the marketing chain, it could be, for example, a wholesaler.

Recitals may be useful for setting out the basis on which the parties are making their agreement. For example, Wood Magic and Lynwood might use a recital to show that their relationship is such that the agent (Lynwood) is not accepting significant financial or commercial risk, and to indicate therefore that the parties believe that the agreement will not be affected by competition law.

11.2.1.2 Definitions and interpretation

Two definitions which are likely to require some thought are 'Products' and 'Territory'.

'Products'

It is useful for the agreement to contain a comprehensive definition of the products which the agent is marketing on the principal's behalf. In the case of the agreement under consideration, this is clearly Wood Magic's furniture, but a more precise definition is likely to be needed. For example, will the agent handle the principal's whole product range, or only some of the principal's products? Will it handle all products of a particular type which the principal manufactures? This is often best dealt with by listing the relevant products in a schedule to the agreement.

Often the main problem in a continuing relationship is how to handle changes which may occur (eg what will happen if the principal ceases to manufacture a particular product or begins to manufacture a new one?). To cover this, the parties should decide matters such as:

(a)   whether the agreement should include provision for a mutually agreed variation;

(b)   whether the principal will force the agent to take up a new product (either with or without notice);

(c)   whether any changes to the product range should be made only with the agent's consent.

The answers will obviously depend upon the relationship between the parties, their relative needs and their bargaining strengths.

'Territory'

Where will the agent market the goods? In Lynwood's case, the relevant area is to be London and the South-East of England. In many cases, defining 'territory' will be straightforward, but it should be expressed as precisely as possible. If this is not made clear, it may lead to disputes over territorial rights between different agents and between agent and principal. This may also involve disputes over exclusivity of the agency (see **11.2.1.3**, 'Agent's authority', below).

11.2.1.3 Appointment of the agent

The appointment clause defines the agent's role in the agreement, and is perhaps the single most important clause in an agency agreement. In particular, it defines the extent of the agent's authority to bind the principal, which in turn will determine a number of other matters. It is likely to cover the following areas.

Agent's authority

In a sales agency agreement, the agent is given authority to enter contracts on the principal's behalf for the sale of the products. As the agent binds the principal, the principal must honour any contracts which the agent has made on its behalf. As noted previously, a marketing agent's authority will be more restricted; it will either be limited to finding customers and introducing them to the principal, or to finding customers and conducting some negotiation on the principal's behalf without, however, binding the principal. Whatever the parties decide is best for them, the appointment clause should always make clear the extent of the agent's authority.

Agent's operations

In attempting to define the geographical limits of the agent's operations and the extent to which the agent will be protected from competition by others within this territory, the clause should be as clear as possible. As discussed in **Chapter 10,** a particular problem arises with the use of the expressions 'sole' agency and 'exclusive' agency. It is, therefore, unsafe to define the scope of the agent's protection from competition in the territory simply by using the words 'sole' or 'exclusive' in the agreement.

It is better to state clearly whether the principal can appoint other agents or market the products in the territory itself (and in what circumstances). It is also sensible to make clear how far (if at all) the agent can extend its operations beyond the territory. On this last point, note that forbidding the agent to accept unsolicited orders from outside the territory can cause real problems if Article 101 TFEU does apply to the agreement (see **11.1.3.2**).

Duration and termination

The appointment clause often also deals with duration and termination of the agreement. The parties may consider entering into a fixed-term agreement. It may be desirable to grant the agent a reasonably long initial fixed term, in order to give it an incentive to build up the business. However, there are, of course, other possibilities. If the parties want an indefinite term, or a fixed term followed by an indefinite term, a suitable notice provision should be included. (Note that under reg 15 of the 1993 Regulations, the agent is entitled to certain minimum periods of notice – see **11.3.5.1**.)

Del credere agency

If the agency is to be a del credere agency (ie, where the agent agrees to guarantee the customer's performance of the contract in return for an additional commission), this is likely to be an appropriate part of the agreement in which to include the del credere provision.

In the proposed agreement between Wood Magic and Lynwood, the solicitor will need to take instructions on most of the preceding matters, as there is no evidence that the parties have yet considered any of them (except the matter of Lynwood's authority).

11.2.2   The agent's rights and duties

11.2.2.1   Introduction

The principal needs to have an appropriate amount of control over its sales agent's activities, so the section on agent's duties is likely to be the longest of the agreement. Broadly speaking, the principal will want to ensure (as far as possible) that the agent observes certain limitations (eg, in a sales agency, that the agent does not make unsuitable contracts on the principal's behalf), while still encouraging the agent to exploit the agency to its full potential. It may be appropriate when drafting the agreement to have a clause relating to general duties, followed by individual clauses covering particular duties (such as advertising and promotion).

11.2.2.2   General duties

The principal may want to provide that the agent uses its 'best endeavours' in promoting and marketing the products. 'Best endeavours' does, however, put a considerable burden upon the agent (it means that the agent must make every effort possible to find customers and make contracts), and the agent may consider this duty too strict.

11.2.2.3   Specific duties

Licences and permits

It may sometimes be necessary to obtain a licence for the sale of the products in the territory, or to comply with local regulations. Clearly, this is unlikely to be a problem for Wood Magic and Lynwood. However, if this is the case, the agreement should allocate responsibility for doing so. The solicitor should consider which party is best placed to obtain any licence or comply with any regulations, and draft accordingly. It is often sensible to make the agent responsible for getting permits and licences for the sale of the products and in respect of its own performance. It is also customary to provide that the agent must comply with laws and regulations concerning the sale of the products, but not those concerning the nature of the products or their packaging; this will normally be for the principal to do.

Promotion and marketing

The principal will want the agent to promote the principal's business and to keep up good relations with customers. It is clear, for example, in the agreement under consideration, that Wood Magic and its products already enjoy an excellent reputation, and Wood Magic will obviously want this to continue. The principal may want to make this duty more specific, for example by requiring the agent's staff to be available when needed for meetings with the principal or potential customers, or for attending trade fairs and other relevant marketing events. The principal may also require the agent to provide premises which the principal considers suitable (it may also want the right to inspect these premises from time to time), and to set up proper office facilities and a suitable organisation for the efficient operation of the agency.

The parties need to agree which of them will have the responsibility and expense of advertising. It is common to find a clause which requires the agent to pay for the advertising, but to use only material which has either been supplied or approved by the principal, thus allowing the principal to keep considerable control of the agent's activities. For example, Wood Magic may want Lynwood to use advertising and promotional tactics which Wood Magic knows to be effective from its own marketing experience.

However, if the agent is either directly or indirectly obliged to invest in sales promotion (eg, by contributing to the principal's advertising budget), this may amount to incurring a 'risk' which would bring the agreement within the ambit of the Chapter I prohibition (see **11.1.3.2**). Caution may therefore be required.

Stock

Principal and agent may agree that the agent will itself keep stocks of the principal's products in order to fulfil the contracts it makes on the principal's behalf. If the parties have agreed, however, that the principal will supply customers direct, the stock clause could be much simpler, or perhaps omitted altogether. If the agent is to keep stocks of the products, the agreement should deal with the level of stock which the agent is to carry and what is to happen to stock while it is on the agent's premises.

The principal will not want the stock to be counted as part of the agent's assets, and therefore claimable by the agent's creditors if the agent becomes insolvent, so it is desirable to provide, for example, that the stock is clearly marked as being the principal's and is stored separately from other goods while on the agent's premises. The principal may want to add the right to inspect the agent's premises from time to time to ensure that the agent is complying with this.

Note that if it is clear that the agent bears the risk of loss while the stock is on its premises, competition law problems might arise (see **11.1.3.2**). Similarly, if there is any requirement for the agency to provide specialised premises or handling facilities, etc, there is the possibility that it may be considered to be an independent undertaking. However, Wood Magic and Lynwood will not have problems in this respect: Wood Magic will deliver direct to customers.

Duty to supply information

It may be useful (eg, in order to plan future products, or to improve existing ones) for the principal to receive feedback from the agent on how customers are reacting to the products. How much information the principal wants from the agent, and on what matters, will obviously vary from case to case; for example, some principals may be satisfied with a clause which requires the agent to report 'from time to time', others may want the agent to report on a regular basis and at definite times. The principal may also wish to restrict the agent's right to get involved in disputes or proceedings concerning the products without the principal's written consent.

Confidentiality

An agency agreement will not always require highly sophisticated confidentiality provisions; if the agent is simply finding customers and making contracts, it may not be privy to any information or process which could be described as confidential. If, however, the agent will be handling confidential material, the principal will need to consider how best to protect its interests. This is usually done by making clear what information is confidential, and what the agent is and is not entitled to do in relation to confidential information. In the agreement under consideration, Wood Magic will need to decide if Lynwood needs any confidential information (eg about how the furniture is made) to be able to fulfil its role as sales agent. For more on the law of confidence (and, in particular, the implied duty of confidentiality), see **Chapter 24**.

Intellectual property

This section of the agreement is likely to vary considerably and will not be necessary at all if the agent does not 'handle' any intellectual property (IP) rights under the agreement. If such a clause is necessary, its specific nature and extent will vary according to the circumstances and the type of intellectual property involved. Generally speaking, however, the clause will be designed to protect the principal's rights in the intellectual property and prevent the agent from getting any interest in it. It may be necessary to include clauses which:

(a)   require the agent to inform the principal of any infringement of the principal's rights in the territory, or any claim by a third party that the principal has infringed its rights;

(b)   require the agent to act on the principal's instructions and at the principal's request to institute or defend proceedings, or to do whatever else is necessary to maintain the validity and enforceability of the principal's rights;

(c)   state that the agent is not to have, or seek to gain, any interest in the principal's rights (eg, trade marks on products, goodwill);

(d)   require the agent not to damage the principal's goodwill by using confusingly similar trade names or trade marks, or behaving in any way that would invalidate the principal's rights or be inconsistent with them. A clause of this type would in most agreements need to be made subject to the rights of the agent and any third party to challenge the validity of the principal's intellectual property, or competition law problems could arise (see **Chapter 29** for a fuller discussion of the relationship of intellectual property and competition law, and how this may affect the drafting of commercial agreements).

The solicitor will need to take full instructions from Wood Magic about IP rights which may be involved in the marketing (eg, any trade mark which Wood Magic uses, and any registered or unregistered design rights relevant to the furniture).

Miscellaneous clauses relating to the agent's duties

It is quite common to find a clause in the 'Agent's Duties' section which gathers together clauses which do not fall under any other heading. Obviously, the solicitor will need to decide whether this is appropriate or necessary in the light of Wood Magic's instructions, but a 'Miscellaneous Provisions' clause could include the following terms:

(a)   that the agent will meet targets set by the principal. Depending on the nature of the agency, these might be for numbers of customers found and introduced, or numbers of contracts made on the principal's behalf;

(b)   that the agent will not pledge the principal's credit;

(c)   that the agent will not become involved in or try to settle any dispute about the products without first obtaining the principal's permission to do so;

(d)   that the agent will not do anything which might prejudice the principal's business or the marketing of its products;

(e)   that where the agent makes contracts on the principal's behalf, the contracts will be made on the principal's standard terms;

(f)   that the agent will not become involved in any way with goods which compete with the products which are the subject of the agency agreement.

Note that the Regulations impose mandatory duties on the agent (see **11.3.2**).

11.2.3   The principal's rights and duties

These are often less onerous than the agent's duties to the principal. Again, the solicitor will need to take instructions from Wood Magic as to what it intends its rights and duties as principal to be. However, the following provisions are commonly encountered (note how many of them complement duties which have already been imposed on the agent):

(a)   the right for the principal to amend the listed products which are the subject of the agreement;

(b)   the duty for the principal to pay commission to the agent. It is customary for an agent to be remunerated by commission; the duty to pay it may be stated as part of the principal's rights and duties, or it may be included as part of a complete financial provisions clause (see **11.3.4**);

(c)   the duty of the principal to comply with all relevant laws relating to the composition, packaging and labelling of the goods; this is likely to make sense, as these matters will be under the principal's control;

(d)   the duty for the principal to supply advertising and promotional material;

(e)   the duty for the principal to pass on to the agent any information which might assist the agent in marketing the goods;

(f)   if the agreement requires the agent to hold stock, the duty for the principal to supply stock (this should also encompass how and when stock is to be supplied, ordering procedure, returns and so on);

(g)   the duty for the principal to provide an after-sales service for the products;

(h)   the duty for the principal to indemnify the agent against any liability which the agent incurs as a result of being held out as the principal's agent (eg, costs and expenses which the agent may incur in relation to claims arising out of the agency).

Again, the Regulations impose mandatory duties on the principal (see **11.3.3**).

11.2.4   Financial provisions

This section of the agreement is likely to vary considerably in content and layout. The parties are obviously free to choose the form of agreement which suits them best, and could combine the financial provisions with the principal's and the agent's duties respectively, if appropriate. However (especially where the financial provisions in the agreement are elaborate), it will often make sense to deal with them in a separate section relating to both parties.

11.2.4.1   Commission

Most genuine agency agreements deal expressly with matters such as how the commission is to be calculated, and when it is to be paid. All Wood Magic and Lynwood have agreed so far is that Wood Magic will pay Lynwood a monthly commission, so the solicitor will clearly need to take full instructions on the precise requirements. In practice, there may be considerable variation in the way commission can be dealt with, but it is important to note that under the

1993 Regulations there are mandatory provisions in relation to commission, and the parties may not always be completely free to make their own arrangements (see **11.3.4**).

11.2.4.2 Accounting arrangements for commission

The agreement should also deal with how the agent is to receive the commission. A number of possibilities arise. For example, the agent may collect payment for the goods from customers, and then account to the principal after deducting its commission. If the agent collects money, the parties may prefer the agent to pay the gross sum to the principal, which then pays commission over to the agent. Alternatively, the principal may collect payment from customers and then pay the agent a regular amount of commission. If the parties are based in different countries, it is also particularly important that the agreement should state the currency in which the commission is to be paid.

11.2.4.3 Deductions

If the agent does collect money from customers on behalf of the principal, it may sometimes be obliged to deduct certain sums (eg in respect of local taxes) before handing over the balance. If this is the case, the parties should deal with the deductions expressly in the agreement.

11.2.4.4 General accounting arrangements

The parties may wish to provide, where appropriate, for the payment of interest on any sums outstanding if either side fails to account to the other (the agent in respect of money collected from customers, the principal in respect of commission). The agreement should also provide for the keeping of accounts and other financial records. This should cover not only which records each party is to keep, but also whether either party has the right to inspect or ask for copies of the other side's records.

11.2.5 Termination

11.2.5.1 What circumstances will allow either party to terminate?

Circumstances in which either side may want the right to terminate the agreement will normally include:

(a)   either side getting into financial difficulties, such as receivership, winding up or making a voluntary arrangement;

(b)   breach of the agreement (consider drafting a notice procedure under which the party in breach can be required to remedy the breach where possible); and

(c)   change in control of the agent if the agent is a company.

It is normally desirable to set out the circumstances expressly in the agreement. See also **11.3.5.1** on notice requirements in cases within the Commercial Agents Regulations 1993.

11.2.5.2 What will the effects of termination be?

The agreement should state how termination will affect the following:

(a)   any stocks of the product, samples and advertising material held by the agent;

(b)   sales which the agent has already negotiated, but in respect of which no moneys have been paid over;

(c)   the agent's authority to negotiate on behalf of the principal;

(d)   the agent's duty of confidentiality;

(e)   the agent's right to compensation on termination.

11.2.5.3 Does the principal need to pay anything to the agent on termination?

This will normally be a matter for agreement between the parties. However, there are mandatory provisions under the Regulations in relation to termination which require the principal to give the agent a 'pay off' on termination of the agreement in the form of either indemnity or compensation (see **11.3.5.2**). If the Regulations apply to the agreement, it is important that the client should be advised of the options. There is still considerable debate in practice as to whether an agreement should go for indemnity or compensation, how far the agreement should deal expressly with the point (in most cases, the agent will be entitled to a pay-off regardless of what the agreement says) and how any termination payment clause should be worded.

11.2.6 Miscellaneous

An agency agreement will usually have a 'boiler-plate', containing a number of miscellaneous clauses (eg arbitration, notices, choice of law and jurisdiction). Boiler-plate clauses in general are considered in **Chapter 1**.

11.2.7 Particular points to consider when drafting a marketing agency agreement

A standard marketing agency agreement will be substantially similar in content and layout to a sales agency agreement; the main differences will result from the fact that a marketing agent has no authority to conclude contracts on the principal's behalf.

11.2.7.1 Appointment

The agreement should define the nature of the agent's operations, with a clear statement that the agent is not authorised to enter into contracts on the principal's behalf. Normally, the agent also agrees not to describe itself as a sales agent.

Care needs to be taken about defining the exact limits of the agent's authority: is it to have authority only to find potential customers and pass them on to the principal; or is it to have authority to do at least some negotiating on the principal's behalf (without actually making any contract)? Although the terms 'marketing' and 'introducing' agency are widely used, they have no legally exact meaning, and so should not be used without additional explanation to make the extent of the agent's authority clear.

Note that an agent which does not have 'continuing authority' to negotiate on the principal's behalf is not a 'commercial agent' within the meaning of the Commercial Agents Regulations 1993 (see **11.3.1.1**).

11.2.7.2 Introducing potential customers

The agreement should provide that the agent is to pass on all orders and enquiries promptly to the principal.

11.2.7.3 Principal's response to potential customers

Is it desirable or possible to provide that the principal should comply with all orders generated by the agent's efforts? A marketing agent does not bind its principal. If the principal refuses to accept an order from a particular customer introduced by the agent, however, this could damage the agent's reputation, and possibly make it more difficult for the agent to earn commission in future. The parties may be able to agree some sort of compromise, for example that the principal will comply with orders from all customers, as long as it is satisfied that they are good credit risks.

11.2.7.4 Agent's duties

A marketing agent is very unlikely to carry stock or collect payments on the principal's behalf.

11.3 COMMERCIAL AGENTS (COUNCIL DIRECTIVE) REGULATIONS 1993

As discussed at **10.2**, agency agreements in the UK are governed by the Regulations, which lay down rules in relation to a number of important areas of an agency agreement, in particular:

(a)   the rights and obligations of both parties;

(b)   the agent's remuneration; and

(c)   the conclusion and termination of the agency contract.

Many, but not all, agency agreements will be subject to these Regulations. Where they do apply, it is essential when drafting or analysing an agency agreement to ensure that it complies with the Regulations. Provisions which do not comply will be unenforceable.

11.3.1 Scope of the 1993 Regulations

Before starting to draft the agreement, the solicitor should consider whether the Regulations do, in fact, apply to the agreement. The Regulations 'govern the relations between commercial agents and their principals ... in relation to the activities of commercial agents in Great Britain' (reg 1(2)). Provision is made in reg 1(3) (as amended) for agreements which are to be governed by the law of another Member State. Thus the agent must conduct his activities within Great Britain. Note that the Regulations do not extend to Northern Ireland (reg 2(5)).

11.3.1.1 Meaning of 'commercial agent'

'Commercial agent' is defined in reg 2(1) as:

> a self-employed intermediary who has continuing authority to negotiate the sale or purchase of goods on behalf of another person (the 'principal') or to negotiate and conclude the sale or purchase of goods on behalf of and in the name of that principal ...

This definition means that the type of 'marketing' agent which only has authority to find customers and is not authorised to 'negotiate' on the principal's behalf will not be a 'commercial agent'. Whether an agent falls within this definition is not always straightforward. Note that a company can be a self-employed intermediary.

In *Mercantile International Group plc v Chuan Soon Huant Industrial Group Ltd* [2002] EWCA Civ 288, because the claimant clearly had authority to negotiate in the principal's name, the Court of Appeal held the agreement was consistent with the agent being a 'commercial agent', and the Regulations therefore applied.

By contrast, see *Sagal (t/a Bunz UK) v Atelier Bunz GmbH* [2008] EWHC 789 (Comm), where, in a complex contractual relationship, the claimant was held not be a commercial agent. Despite all other appearances, the claimant did not negotiate the sale of jewellery as an intermediary; he negotiated the sale on his own behalf.

11.3.1.2 Meaning of 'negotiate'

In *PJ Pipe & Valve Co Ltd v Audco India Ltd* [2005] EWHC 1904 (QB), the claimant's role consisted of identifying opportunities for the defendant, advising it of those opportunities and promoting it to potential customers, rather than negotiating specific terms on the defendant's behalf. The High Court gave the words 'to negotiate' a broad meaning, ruling that if the agent spent time and resources on developing the principal's goodwill, and it was in the principal's commercial interest for the agent to do this, this could amount to 'negotiation', just as much as negotiating specific terms of the contract between principal and customer.

11.3.1.3 Situations in which the Regulations will *not* apply

The Regulations will not apply:

(a)   where the agent's activities are not within Great Britain, (although equivalent regulations apply throughout the EEA);

(b)   where the agent does not come within the definition of 'commercial agent' (reg 2(1));

(c)   where the agent is an agent of a type listed in reg 2(2);

(d)   where the agent's activities as a commercial agent are to be considered secondary under reg 2(3), (4) and the Schedule. The drafting of the Schedule is extremely complex, and it is not always clear when an agent is involved in secondary activities. Examples include part-time agents or agents who sell through mail order catalogues or brochures. From *Light v Ty Europe Ltd* [2004] 1 CLC 71, it seems that sub-agents who do not have a contractual relationship with the principal to a sales agency agreement would fall within this category;

(e)   where the contract covers the supply of services rather than goods. Note that in *Computer Associates (UK) Ltd v Software Incubator Ltd* [2018] EWCA Civ 518, the Court of Appeal has held that software supplied in the form of a download is not 'goods' for the purposes of the Regulations.

Assuming that Lynwood falls within the definition of 'commercial agent' (which it will, as long as it has in practice 'continuing authority to negotiate and conclude the sale ... of goods on behalf of another person'), the Regulations will apply to its agreement with Wood Magic.

The checklist below summarises the steps to consider to help decide whether the 1993 Regulations apply.

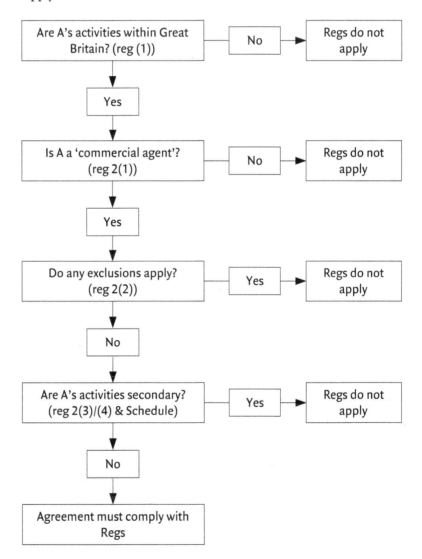

11.3.2 Agent's duties

Regulation 3 of the 1993 Regulations governs the agent's duties:

(a)   By reg 3(1), a commercial agent must look after the interests of his principal and act dutifully and in good faith.

(b)   Regulation 3(2) deals with a number of specific developments of these general duties; for example reg 3(2)(c) requires the agent to comply with reasonable instructions.

11.3.3 Principal's duties

Regulation 4 governs the principal's duties:

(a)   By reg 4(1), a principal must act dutifully and in good faith in its relations with its commercial agent.

(b)   Regulation 4(2) and (3) deal with specific aspects of these general duties, for example there is a mandatory duty to notify the agent within a reasonable period once the principal anticipates that the value of commercial transactions will be significantly lower than normal expectations (see reg 4(2)(b)).

(c)   Under reg 15 there is a duty to give minimum periods of notice to terminate the agreement, except where immediate termination would be justified by conduct or other exceptional circumstances (eg repudiatory breach or frustration, etc). Note that this provision applies to either party (see **11.3.5.1**).

11.3.4 Financial provisions

The principal must ensure that the remuneration provisions in the agreements are consistent with the Regulations:

(a)   Regulation 7 provides for the agent's right to commission on transactions which are concluded during the agency agreement.

(b)   Regulation 8 gives the agent certain rights to commission even after the agency agreement has ended. Regulation 8(a) provides that the agent will be entitled to post-termination commission if the transaction is 'mainly attributable' to its efforts whilst the agency agreement was still subsisting and the contract is concluded within 'a reasonable time' after termination. The problem here is that both phrases are somewhat vague. In *Tigana Ltd v Decoro Ltd* [2003] EWHC 23 (QB) the agent was awarded the equivalent of nine months' commission in relation to such transactions, and the court considered the circumstances where the transaction could be said to be 'mainly attributable' to the agent's efforts.

(c)   Regulation 9 deals with the situation where a new agent is appointed and under reg 7 the new agent would be entitled to commission on the same transaction as the previous agent. The claim of the 'old' agent will prevail over the new agent, unless it can be shown that it is 'equitable' for them to share. Again, the terminology is vague, and it is not always clear what the new agent would have to do to meet this requirement.

(d)   Regulation 10 controls when commission becomes due and when it must be paid. The agreement should deal with this.

   (i)   *Payment due.* There are three options available to the parties, but they should bear in mind that payment will become due at the latest when the customer 'executes' (or performs) its part of the transaction.

   (ii)   *Payment made.* Payment must then be made at the latest at the end of the month following the quarter on which it became due.

(e)   The agent's right to commission can be extinguished only in the circumstances described in reg 11, ie broadly, that the contract arranged by the agent will not be carried out but that this is not the principal's fault.

(f)   Regulation 12 obliges the principal to supply the agent with a statement of commission, and entitles the agent to demand the information it needs (including 'an extract from the books' to check the amount of commission due to it).

11.3.5   Termination

11.3.5.1   Notice provisions

Regulation 15(2) provides for minimum notice periods to be given by the parties:

(a)   one month's notice for the first year;

(b)   two month's notice for the second year;

(c)   three month's notice for the third and subsequent years.

Under reg 15(3), the parties can agree to longer notice periods, but the agreement can never provide a shorter notice period for the principal than the agent. Unless there is contrary provision in the contract, the notice period must expire at the end of a calendar month.

11.3.5.2   Termination payments

The provisions of the 1993 Regulations in relation to termination payments are complex, but are of crucial importance when drafting the agreement. In most cases, reg 17 obliges the principal to give the agent a 'pay-off' on termination of the agreement. This right arises automatically on termination of the agreement, not simply when the principal is in breach of contract. The pay-off may take the form of indemnity or compensation, depending on the circumstances, but the principal cannot contract out of its obligation to pay.

The position under reg 17 may be briefly summarised as follows:

(a)   Regulation 17(1) provides that, on termination of the agency contract, the agent is entitled either to be 'indemnified' in accordance with reg 17(3)–(5), or to be 'compensated for damage' in accordance with reg 17(6)–(7).

(b)   Regulation 17(2) states that except where the agreement provides otherwise, the agent is entitled to be compensated rather than indemnified.

(c)   Regulation 18 gives the grounds for excluding the payment of either indemnity or compensation, broadly speaking, where the termination is due to the agent's conduct (which would justify termination under reg 16, eg repudiatory breach) or the agent has itself terminated the agreement or assigned its rights and duties under the agreement. The grounds for excluding payment are extremely limited. The agent will still be entitled to compensation if, for example, the agreement comes to an end as a result of:

    (i)   effluxion of time; see, eg, *Cooper v Pure Fishing (UK) Ltd* [2004] 2 Lloyd's Rep 518; or

    (ii)   age, illness or infirmity of the agent (reg 18(b)(ii)).

(d)   Regulation 19 states that the parties cannot derogate from regs 17 or 18, which are consequently mandatory provisions. Any provision in the agreement which removes or cuts down the agent's right to a pay-off will be of no effect. See *Crane v Sky In-Home Service Ltd* [2007] EWHC 66 (Ch).

(e)   Under reg 17(9) the agent must inform the principal of its intention to claim (either for indemnity or compensation) within one year from termination of the agreement, or the agent will lose its right to claim.

The indemnity option is based on German law (it is sometimes referred to as the 'German model') and may seem attractive to principals because it provides a limit on the payment the agent can get, ie no more than one year's commission, based on the agent's actual annual remuneration over the past five years (see reg 17(4)). There is also some evidence in practice that the actual payment will often be less than this.

The 1993 Regulations are considerably less clear about what 'compensation for damage' is. As far as the Directive is concerned, 'compensation' in this context is based on French agency law (sometimes referred to as the 'French model'), and often, in practice, French law allows the agent on termination a sum equivalent to two years' commission.

Authority on the meaning of 'compensation for damage' was somewhat scarce and contradictory, and it remained unclear for over a decade whether the French model would be followed in the UK. However, since July 2007 there has been House of Lords' authority on the calculation of compensation for damage: *Lonsdale v Howard & Hallam Ltd* [2007] UKHL 32. The House of Lords confirmed the approach previously taken by the Court of Appeal:

(a)   It was inappropriate in the UK to apply the French law which exists in this area; in particular, there was no reason why courts in the UK should use two years' commission as a basis for calculating compensation for damage. French and English practices on damages differed, not because their respective courts were applying different rules of law but because they were operating in different markets.

(b)   The House of Lords noted that, in *Honyvem Informazioni Commerciali Srl v Mariella de Zotti* (Case C-465/04) [2006] OJ C131/19, the ECJ had made it clear that the method of calculation of the damage which the agent suffers as a result of termination is a matter for the law of each Member State, as long as calculation is done consistently with the Directive. The purpose of reg 17 was to compensate for damage to the agent's business as a result of the termination.

(c)   Compensation should be calculated on the value of the agency business to the agent (including goodwill) at the date of termination of the agency. In giving the leading opinion in the House of Lords' judgment, Lord Hoffmann noted that this should be assessed on the basis of what a buyer would be prepared to pay to 'stand in the shoes' of the agent.

Although there has been some controversy as to the impact of the ruling in the long term, most commentators agree that it brings clarity to a complex area of law. However, there is some concern that the decision favours principals at the expense of agents, especially where (as in *Lonsdale* itself) the agency business is declining. In *Green Deal Marketing Ltd v Economy Energy Trading & Others* [2019] EWHC 507 (Ch), the High Court looked in detail at the calculation of compensation and the role of expert evidence in the valuation of compensation. The court applied the principles established by the House of Lords in *Lonsdale*, confirming that the basis of the calculation is the loss to the agent of the goodwill in the business, retained by the principal after termination.

Note that reg 17(5) expressly provides that the grant of an indemnity 'shall not prevent the commercial agent from seeking damages'. It is generally assumed here that 'damages' refers to normal contractual damages, and that this provision would be relevant where, for example, the agreement has been unjustifiably terminated with no or insufficient notice. There is no express equivalent of this provision in relation to compensation for damage. In *Green Deal Marketing Ltd v Economy Energy Trading*, the High Court acknowledged that contractual damages and compensation under the Regulations are two different remedies. Compensation can be awarded under the Regulations where there is no breach of contract and the Regulations themselves do not exclude the right to damages for breach of contract. However, double recovery will not be permitted. This will depend on the facts in each case. In *Green Deal*, the court held that to award damages as well as compensation would result in two awards for the same loss.

Note that a principal cannot 'hedge its bets' on the choice of indemnity or compensation. In *Shearman (t/a Charles Shearman Agencies) v Hunter Boot Ltd* [2014] EWHC 47 (QB), the court held that a clause which provided that on termination the agent would not be entitled to compensation but would be indemnified, unless the amount of compensation was less than the amount of the indemnity, was not permitted under reg 17. This would defeat the purpose of the Regulations, which is to 'protect agents not principals'.

11.3.6 Derogation

A final consideration is how far it is possible to derogate from the 1993 Regulations. Some of the Regulations contain non-derogation provisions, others do not. The literal approach would be to consider that where no derogation provision is included, it may be possible to derogate. However, in *Graham Page v Combined Shipping and Trading Co Ltd* [1997] 3 All ER 656 the Court of Appeal did emphasise that because the Regulations are implementing legislation, courts must adopt a purposive approach to their interpretation. Lord Justice Staughton was in no doubt that the main purpose of the Commercial Agents Directive was to protect the agent: 'commercial agents are a downtrodden race, and need and should be afforded protection against their principals'. Thus, if the Regulations are interpreted purposively, then derogation would not be possible.

In *Ingmar v Eaton Leonard* (Case C-381/98) [2000] ECR I-9305, the ECJ was of the opinion that derogation from reg 8 would be possible only in so far as it does not thwart the purpose of the Directive. In *Computer Associates (UK) Ltd v Software Incubator Ltd*, at first instance, the judge stated that reg 8 could be excluded. The Court of Appeal, having held that the Regulations did not apply to the agreement (see **11.3.1.3**), did not therefore deal with this issue so the position is still far from clear. The solicitor should always advise the client of the risks of any attempt at derogation. How far the UK courts will follow the purposive approach post-Brexit remains to be seen.

Derogation	
Regulations with non-derogation provisions	**Derogation not mentioned**
Regs 3 and 4 (reg 5)	Reg 6
Reg 10 (reg 10(4))	Reg 7
Reg 11 (reg 11(3))	Reg 8
Reg 12 (reg 12(3))	Reg 9
Reg 13 (reg 13(2))	Reg 14
Reg 15 (reg 15(2))	Reg 20
Regs 17 and 18 (reg 19)	

Table 11.2 Derogation

11.3.7 Brexit

The 1993 Regulations are an example of 'retained EU law', so it is possible that the government might consider repealing the Regulations, which are often criticised as being overprotective of agents. However, it is generally considered that this would lead to some uncertainty as far as existing agency agreements are concerned, with particular problems arising where an agreement provides for indemnity or compensation on termination. On the other hand, the removal of regulation, particularly in relation to termination payments, could encourage greater use of agency as a marketing arrangement.

11.4 INTERNATIONAL AGENCY AGREEMENTS

It is very important to adapt international agency agreements to the particular foreign market in which they will be employed. The definitions and clear articulation of the nature of the relationship is, if possible, even more important in international agreements than it is in domestic cases, since there are no unified concepts or rules regarding international agency and distribution agreements. By drafting the contractual clauses carefully and in detail, serious misunderstandings (as well as possible litigation, damage to working relationships, and injury to the principal's reputation in a foreign market) may often be avoided.

Clear definitions also exclude the potential risk of considering the agent as an employee of the principal. Ambiguous agency agreements or subsequent written and oral communications between the principal and the agent may transform an agency agreement into an employment contract in the eyes of courts in some jurisdictions. This is particularly the case when the agent is an individual rather than a company. In the event that employment laws should apply for example in the event of termination of the agreement, these laws frequently impose heavy financial compensation and extended advance notice requirements exceeding those applicable to agents.

Another problem due to the lack of uniform, international rules regarding agency agreements is that the parties are obliged to apply national legislation into international agreements, which do not take into account the special characteristics of international sales. The discrepancies between the parties will be normally resolved according to the laws of the home country of the agent, which may cause surprises for an unprepared principal.

While businesses in the United States are generally given freedom to determine all of the essential terms of their agency relationship, European countries have often protected the interests of the weaker party (the agent) by imperative legislation that declares void all the agreements in contradiction with its contents. The principal should always seek legal advice regarding the existence of such rules in the home country of the agent especially regarding termination and the possible obligation to pay compensation and/or indemnities.

In the European Union, agency agreements are somewhat harmonised by Directive 86/653 (the Commercial Agents Directive) even if all the countries have not transposed the Directive into national legislation in an identical form. The Directive is only a 'minimum requirements harmonisation' and the Member States are entitled to impose more (stricter) rules applying in their territory. It is important to carry out specific research into the relevant local legislation when drafting agency agreements or attempting to enforce agents' rights in such countries.

In principle, the applicable law and the jurisdiction for claims (see **Chapter 14**) may be agreed between the parties. Some laws though declare invalid any clause that takes the jurisdiction away from the tribunals of the home country of the agent. The parties may normally choose the application of *lex mercatoria*, ie the legal principles, that are generally recognised in international commerce.

11.5 DRAFTING A DISTRIBUTION AGREEMENT

11.5.1 Introduction

This section continues with the Wood Magic example (see **11.1.1**), but in relation to a different aspect of Wood Magic's business.

> **EXAMPLE**
>
> Assume that Wood Magic has, for the past five years, carried on a small sideline business of manufacturing ready-made furniture (such as coffee tables, dining tables and chairs). The directors feel that this side of the business is now ready to be developed much further. Wood Magic recently rented a stand at a trade fair in Paris to show this furniture. The response was such that the directors believe that there is an important market in France, consisting of wealthy French customers with second homes and English 'ex-pats' who have settled in France.

In the short term, the directors believe that Wood Magic can spare the time and commitment needed to establish relations with a 'trading partner' in France; the directors who attended the trade fair made some promising contacts and believe that one company in particular, Bois Massif SA, could be the partner Wood Magic is looking for. However, assuming that they do establish relations with a partner they can trust, the directors would, in the long term, seek to market Wood Magic's goods in France in a way which does not require close day-to-day supervision. They believe that if they give the right training to the French partner at the outset, it will be easy for the partner to sell the ready-made furniture, without major involvement from Wood Magic.

The difficulty for Wood Magic in its expansion is that it has little experience in the export trade, and it admits that its collective knowledge of the French language and of French business practices is negligible.

11.5.2 Initial advice

At this stage (as with an agency agreement) the solicitor is likely to be asked to advise on two related areas:

(a)   What sort of marketing arrangement is most suitable for Wood Magic?

(b)   What factors should it take into account when looking for a trading partner?

This time, the facts indicate that a distribution agreement would be appropriate:

(a)   The goods can be marketed in France in the same form in which Wood Magic sells them (eg, no customising is necessary).

(b)   Wood Magic needs the help of a trading partner based in the target territory, because it is not familiar with that territory's language or business practices.

(c)   The marketing of the goods does not require much supervision by Wood Magic (after initial training has been given).

(d)   Wood Magic will not be liable in contract to the ultimate customers.

Note that whereas some of these factors would not necessarily make an agency agreement unsuitable, they indicate that the main advantages of that type of agreement (ie supervision of agent, contact with customers: see **10.4**) are not really needed here. A distribution agreement is likely to be the cheapest and most efficient way to market these goods.

Wood Magic will need to be aware, however, that, depending on the terms which are included in the agreement with Bois Massif and the circumstances in which the agreement operates, competition law problems may arise (see **11.7** and **Chapter 28**).

As with the agency agreement, Wood Magic should check out any potential trading partner very carefully; for example, creditworthiness is even more important here than in the agency agreement, as the distributor will actually be buying the goods from Wood Magic, and therefore Wood Magic is directly at risk of non-payment by its trading partner.

11.5.3 Preliminary considerations

Assume now that Wood Magic's directors are satisfied that Bois Massif is the right trading partner for them in France, and have begun detailed negotiations over the terms of the distribution agreement which the parties will enter. They have still to decide how to deal with many areas of the agreement, but have agreed the following in principle:

(a)   In order to give Bois Massif the best possible chance of getting the distributorship established, Wood Magic has agreed that it will not appoint any other distributors (or agents) for the sale of its goods in France, and that it will not sell any of its own goods in France.

(b)   In return, Bois Massif has agreed to concentrate on the French market only: it will not actively seek customers from outside France (although it will be free to fulfil unsolicited orders).

What considerations arise for the solicitor in drafting the agreement?

11.5.3.1   Agency and distribution agreements: similarities and differences

It is important to note that the relationship of distributor and supplier is created and defined by the distribution agreement. Many of the clauses already discussed in relation to agency agreements are equally relevant to distribution agreements: these include interpretation, appointment, duration and many of the 'duties' clauses (allowing for some necessary modifications: see below). However, a distribution agreement is essentially an agreement for the sale of goods from the supplier to the distributor, and so matters relevant to drafting a sale of goods agreement must be considered (see **Chapter 3**).

11.5.3.2   Distribution agreements and EU competition law

Even though the UK has fully withdrawn from the EU, EU competition law applies to conduct, practices and agreements which have an 'appreciable effect' within the EU, regardless of the domicile of the parties. The relevant factor in deciding whether EU competition law applies is where the anti-competitive behaviour takes place, not whose behaviour it is. Thus, clients, like Wood Magic, who trade within Europe will still be bound by EU competition law. For a full discussion of the application of EU competition law in the UK post-Brexit, see **Chapter 28**.

Briefly, however, a distribution agreement is more likely than an agency agreement to infringe Article 101(1) TFEU as, depending on the terms which the parties include and the circumstances in which the agreement operates, its potential for affecting trade and competition is greater. However, there are several ways of avoiding the impact of Article 101(1) TFEU. For example, the agreement may be ignored by the Commission if it falls within the Notice on Agreements of Minor Importance (to advise on this, it would be necessary to know the parties' market shares; see **28.5.1**). Even if this does not apply, it may be possible to draft the agreement to comply with a relevant block exemption.

In the agreement under consideration, Wood Magic is offering Bois Massif 'exclusive territory' and Bois Massif will agree not to sell actively outside that territory. Both parties are therefore limiting their commercial freedom, and (in theory at least) doing so in a way which may affect trade and competition (eg French buyers will have only one authorised source of supply within France) and infringe Article 101(1) TFEU. However, if in practice the agreement contained only these two restrictions, the block exemption contained in Regulation 330/2010 would apply to the agreement, and therefore Article 101(1) TFEU would not. This block exemption is discussed in more detail at **28.5.2.1**.

11.6   PLANNING, FORM AND CONTENT OF A DISTRIBUTION AGREEMENT

Again, the solicitor will need to plan the structure of the agreement and look at the competition elements, and consider how they affect each part of the agreement. A distribution agreement is likely to follow the structure set out in **Table 11.3** below. Likely anti-competitive terms relevant to each part of this structure are shown in the right-hand column:

Structure of Distribution Agreement	Anti-competitive terms
(a) Date, parties, recitals	(a) not relevant (n/r)
(b) Interpretation clause	(b) n/r
(c) Appointment of distributor	(c) Exclusivity, especially if in conjunction with territorial restrictions
(d) Standard terms of sale (may be in Schedule)	(d) n/r

Structure of Distribution Agreement	Anti-competitive terms
(e) Distributor's rights and duties	(e) Price-fixing, export bans, non-compete obligations, no-challenge clauses (IP)
(f) Supplier's rights and duties	(f) n/r
(g) Termination (if not dealt with elsewhere)	(g) Post-termination non-compete obligations
(h) Boiler-plate clauses	(h) n/r
(i) Signatures	(i) n/r
(j) Schedules	(j) n/r

Table 11.3 Structure of a distribution agreement

11.6.1 Date, parties, recitals, interpretation

This part of the agreement is likely to be very similar to the corresponding section of a sales agency agreement (see **11.2.1.1**). In particular, similar points are likely to arise in relation to 'Products'.

11.6.2 Appointment

The appointment clause will be vitally important, in particular the question of exclusivity. How much protection will the distributor get against competition from others in its territory? The distributor may want such protection (eg against the supplier appointing other distributors or agents, or against the supplier selling within the territory) in order to benefit as much as possible from its investment in the distributorship.

It is always desirable to define the extent of the distributor's protection from competition as clearly as possible, rather than relying on the words 'sole' or 'exclusive' territory or distribution, which raise problems in the same way as they do in an agency agreement (see **11.2.1.3**). The agreement should also define the limits of the distributor's freedom to operate outside the defined territory.

The appointment clause may also deal with the duration of the agreement, although this can be done elsewhere in the agreement. Whichever method is chosen, note that an initial fixed term may be even more appropriate here than in an agency agreement, as it will give the distributor (which may have taken risks by making a large investment in the distributorship) both security and an incentive to build up the business. If this is what the parties require, the agreement must state when the fixed term is to commence. If the parties require an indefinite term, the agreement must include suitably drafted notice provisions.

11.6.3 The distributor's duties

Some of the distributor's duties will be similar to those in an agency agreement (eg in relation to confidentiality, transmission of information, training and availability of the distributor's representatives). However, other duties are likely to be significantly different because of the different nature of the agreement.

11.6.3.1 Minimum target obligations

The supplier will normally want to impose some form of minimum target obligation on the distributor to ensure that the distributor exploits the relevant market to the full, especially where the distributor has been granted exclusivity. The supplier will often see this as justifiable in return for giving the distributor an initial fixed term. A minimum target obligation can be either for:

(a)   a minimum level of sales by the distributor to its customers; or

(b)   a minimum level of purchases by the distributor from the supplier.

It is sometimes suggested that the latter may be more commercially flexible. For example, with a minimum purchase target, the distributor can buy extra goods from the supplier to meet the targets, and so perhaps cover a temporary bad patch more easily; purchase targets are also easier for the supplier to monitor.

If targets of either sort are imposed, the supplier must decide what is to happen if the distributor does not comply with them. The supplier may want either to end the distributor's freedom from competition in the territory, or to terminate the agreement itself. The former may appear to be less drastic from the distributor's point of view, but could be as devastating as termination of the entire agreement in the long run.

In practice, ending territorial protection for failure to meet targets is not always seen as being commercially sensible; if the distributor is finding it hard to succeed with the help of sole or exclusive territory, presumably its task will be even more difficult without it, and the supplier may not benefit in any way. The supplier should therefore consider doing this only if it is certain that matters will improve if the distributor's protection from competition is ended (eg it will encourage the distributor to make greater efforts, or the supplier will benefit by being able to appoint another distributor or market the goods itself).

11.6.3.2   Advertising and promotion

The distributor is normally made responsible for advertising and promotion. It will often be better placed than the supplier to know what sort of advertising and promotional campaigns will succeed in the territory. Wood Magic may see this as a valuable contribution which Bois Massif can make to the success of Wood Magic's furniture in France. However, the supplier may wish to reserve the right to vet the distributor's activities, especially if it wants to keep a reasonably uniform brand image over several different territories. The supplier may also wish to provide that the distributor spends a minimum sum each year (or quarter, or month as the case may be) on advertising and promotion.

11.6.3.3   Stock

The distributor will inevitably hold stock – it has actually bought the products from the supplier. The agreement will therefore need to provide for numerous matters relating to stock, including the following:

(a)   How much stock should the distributor carry?

(b)   What procedure should the distributor follow when it orders and pays for the goods?

(c)   What procedure should the distributor follow for returning unsatisfactory goods?

(d)   When are title and risk in the goods to pass to the distributor?

(e)   Is it necessary to insure the products (eg, while they are in transit from supplier to distributor)? If so, who should do this?

(f)   What is to happen to stock if the agreement is terminated. The supplier often faces a dilemma here, especially when Article 101 TFEU or the Chapter I prohibition could apply to the agreement. If the distributor is still holding stock after termination, it may deal with it in ways which could damage the brand's reputation (eg, sell it cut-price in markets or through discount shops). However, because the stock is the distributor's own property, to deal with as it sees fit, any clause in the agreement which obliges the distributor to sell the stock back to the supplier on termination potentially restricts competition, and could infringe competition law. In most cases, the supplier will have to decide whether the risk of competition law problems is greater than that of harm to the supplier's reputation. However, note that a clause which gives the distributor the option of selling the stock back to the supplier (rather than forcing the distributor to do this) should not cause competition law problems, as the distributor is not then obliged to deal with its own property in a particular way. Subject to these points, any clause dealing with the fate of stock on termination is more likely to be an aid to negotiation than anything else.

(g) What is to happen to any advertising or promotional material on termination?

(h) What is to happen to obsolete stock? If the agreement requires the distributor to sell it back to the supplier, competition law problems may arise (in the same way as in (f) above). The parties should try to come to a workable compromise which will prevent obsolete stock affecting the market for new stock.

11.6.3.4 Confidentiality and intellectual property

The areas of confidentiality and intellectual property may be more relevant in a distribution agreement than in an agency agreement. As the distributor is actually buying the products and then selling them on, it may be necessary to supply the distributor with confidential information relating to the products, or to allow the distributor to use the supplier's intellectual property.

11.6.3.5 Competing products

The supplier may want the distributor to agree not to handle products which could compete with the products being supplied under the agreement.

11.6.4 The supplier's duties

If dealt with separately, the list of supplier's duties is likely to be comparatively small. It may be appropriate to deal with the following:

(a) Will the supplier need to supply any promotional literature, models or samples of the goods to allow the distributor to market them properly?

(b) Should the supplier be obliged to supply the distributor with information which may help the distributor to market the goods?

(c) Is the supplier prepared to offer the distributor an indemnity against defects in the products? If so, what liabilities will it cover? In addition, does the supplier wish to give limited warranties to the distributor (eg, to cut down the protection given by s 14 of the SGA 1979 if English law applies – see **7.4** and **7.5**)?

11.6.5 Sale of goods terms

Because the supplier will be selling goods to the distributor, it will be necessary to include in the agreement suitable terms to cover this sale of goods. For discussion of the basic terms which will be included in a sale of goods agreement in the UK, see **Chapters 4–8**. Consider, particularly in relation to a distribution agreement, the following:

(a) Are the supplier's sales to the distributor to be on the supplier's standard terms? If so, the agreement should make clear what these are. Perhaps the best way of doing this is to set them out in a schedule to the agreement, so that both parties are certain which terms apply.

(b) Which basic sale of goods terms (such as price, payment, delivery, description and quality) need to be included in the distribution agreement? Note that the term relating to price will be of particular importance to the distributor; it will make its money from the difference between the price at which it buys the goods from the supplier and the price at which it can sell them to its customers.

11.6.6 Termination

The termination of the agreement and the consequences of termination may be handled in a number of ways. One matter which will require particular care (for the reasons outlined in

11.6.3.3) is disposal of stock on termination, which the solicitor may feel is better dealt with here than in the 'stock' clause.

Note that it is relatively rare for distributors to be entitled by law to compensation on termination (compare the position of agents under the 1993 Regulations; see **11.3.5.2**), but this may be relevant in certain jurisdictions (not the UK). The supplier may, however, be prepared to agree to include a term in the agreement providing for compensation.

11.6.7 Miscellaneous

Like an agency agreement, a distribution agreement usually has a 'boiler-plate'. Many of the miscellaneous clauses will be the same as those in an agency agreement (eg force majeure, arbitration, choice of law and notices).

11.7 COMPETITION ISSUES IN DISTRIBUTION AGREEMENTS

The impact of competition law on distribution agreements in the EU is dealt with in detail in **Chapter 28**. The following is a brief summary of some of the issues that arise in relation to the provisions discussed above.

11.7.1 Exclusivity

European case law indicates that exclusivity on its own will not necessarily cause competition problems, unless accompanied by territorial restrictions (see *Établissements Consten SA and Grundig GmbH v Commission* (Cases 56 and 58/64) [1966] ECR 299). The agreement must not forbid the distributor from exporting the goods from the territory, as this is likely to infringe Article 101(1) TFEU (and will not get the benefit of Regulation 330/2010). It is, however, possible in certain circumstances to provide that the distributor must not actively solicit orders from outside the territory, a provision that Wood Magic and Bois Massif have in mind. They could still benefit from Regulation 330/2010: see **28.5.2**.

11.7.2 Minimum target obligations

Although target obligations are often acceptable from a competition law point of view, care may be needed if the target is so exacting that it effectively limits the distributor's commercial freedom. The result may be that the distributor has to concentrate on promoting the supplier's products to the exclusion of others, and some purchase targets (over 80% of the distributor's total purchases of the contract goods) automatically amount to non-compete obligations. (For more on the potential competition law implications, see **Chapter 28**.)

11.7.3 Confidentiality and intellectual property

Provided that the provisions allowing the distributor to use the IP rights are not the 'primary object' of the agreement, these will not cause competition problems. However, a clause imposing a restriction on the right of the distributor to challenge the validity of the supplier's IP rights (a no-challenge clause) may be restrictive of competition.

11.7.4 Non-compete obligations

Both restrictions on handling competing products and post-termination restraint of trade clauses may amount to non-compete obligations, which may cause problems as being potentially restrictive of competition. For more detail on how these might be handled to avoid the impact of competition law, see **28.5.2.1**.

11.7.5 Severance

It is advisable to include a severance clause which will ensure that any anti-competitive (or other illegal) clause can be severed from the agreement. Clauses should be drafted for severance, using a series of clauses and sub-clauses, so that if one is found to be anti-competitive, the remainder of the agreement can survive (but see **28.5.2.1**).

11.8 OTHER FORMS OF MARKETING ARRANGEMENT

Given the nature of Wood Magic's business operations, it is unlikely that the directors will need to consider anything other than agency and distribution. A further alternative would a joint venture scheme. The nature of joint ventures and their likely advantages and disadvantages are dealt with in **Appendix 3** to *Business Law and Practice*. A joint venture may become relevant if Wood Magic's directors come up with a project which requires input from another business with different but complementary skills. For example, assume that the directors decide to develop a range of upholstered furniture: they may seek to set up a joint venture with a company specialising in furnishing fabrics. If they did so, the two businesses could pool their resources to set up a separate joint venture company to carry out the project.

SUMMARY

This chapter has introduced the main terms and conditions you will find in both a typical agency agreement and a typical distribution agreement. In the UK, it is essential to ensure that when drafting an agency agreement, it complies with the provisions of the Commercial Agents (Council Directive) Regulations 1993; and that when drafting a distribution agreement, it does not fall foul of European or UK competition provisions.

As the final part of this section on marketing, we shall look at how a supplier may exploit and market its intellectual property rights.

CHAPTER 12

MARKETING AGREEMENTS: DRAFTING LICENSING, MERCHANDISING AND FRANCHISING AGREEMENTS

LEARNING OUTCOMES

After reading this chapter you will be able to:

- explain how a client may exploit its intellectual property (IP) rights
- summarise the structure and content of a typical IP licensing agreement
- advise when a franchising agreement might be a suitable arrangement for a client
- identify the formalities required for licences and assignments of different IP rights.

12.1 INTRODUCTION

Chapter 11 considered the most common marketing arrangements, agency and distribution. Many businesses will not need to consider other arrangements. However, if a business continues to be successful and develops, other marketing opportunities may arise. It may, for example, be in a position to exploit its intellectual property (IP) rights. Intellectual property rights (as the name suggests) are intangible property rights which may, like any other form of property, be sold, assigned, licensed or used as security. This chapter deals with IP licences, looking at the basic structure of a licence agreement. It then goes on to give a brief introduction to other types of marketing arrangement which involve the exploitation of IP rights.

12.2 LICENSING

The rules governing intellectual property rights, both in the UK and internationally, are dealt with in **Chapters 17–24**. Clearly, when acting for a client who is seeking to exploit his IP rights outside the jurisdiction, it is essential to be aware of the local rules governing those rights. This chapter looks at IP licensing within the UK.

As discussed in these chapters, an owner of intellectual property will have certain exclusive rights over that property, eg in the UK the owner of a literary copyright has the exclusive right to copy that work; and the owner of a registered trade mark has the exclusive right to use the mark on the goods and services covered by the registration. If anyone else copies the work or uses the mark, they will infringe these rights. However, the owner may wish to license, or grant permission to, a third party to exploit these rights. The licence may cover all of the rights of the licensor, or it may be limited in its scope, so that the licensee only has the right to exploit some of these rights. For example, if a trade mark is licensed to a third party, it may only have the right to manufacture products to which the mark has been applied, but not to sell them. The scope of the licence will depend on the bargaining position of the parties.

Continuing with the example used in **Chapter 11**, assume that Wood Magic comes up with a potentially very popular design for a range of furniture, but that it does not have the resources to manufacture and distribute enough of the new product to satisfy customer demand. It is therefore considering granting a licence to a much larger furniture manufacturing business, 'Ottoman' Empire Ltd, allowing that business to use Wood Magic's designs to make and sell the furniture, initially within the UK. Very broadly, the licence agreement will permit the licensee to do this in return for payment to Wood Magic (possibly a one-off licence fee, but more likely continuing payments of royalties on chairs manufactured and sold).

Wood Magic may own design rights (see **Chapter 22**) in relation to the furniture, which it will license to the furniture manufacturer. The most suitable form of licence will be a licence of its industrial designs. However, Wood Magic may also want the furniture to be marketed using any trade mark which it may own (the Wood Magic name may not qualify for trade mark protection, but it may have registered a logo or brand name). Wood Magic may also own the copyright in any drawings of the furniture or logo. In addition, there may be trade secrets or know-how attached to the manufacturing process for Wood Magic's furniture. All these should be considered.

12.2.1 Basic rules for successful drafting of licence agreements

Again, it is extremely important to consider the three basic drafting rules, as discussed in **Chapters 8** and **11**.

12.2.1.1 Commercial background

Researching the commercial background is important to establish what IP rights will be relevant. The solicitor may be told, for example, that the client uses a logo as a trade mark. The first thing to check is whether the mark has in fact been registered at the Intellectual Property Office. Protection is not automatic and, if not registered, the mark will only be protected by the law of passing off (see **Chapter 18**). The client may not be aware of all the relevant rights that attach to a particular item, eg is it aware that there may be copyright attached to any drawing of the logo, or the possibility of registering a design right?

12.2.1.2 Legal background

Care must be taken to check the following legal issues, which can cause difficulties in the context of IP licensing:

(a) *Ownership.* There may be problems if the right has been created by employees or commissioned from an independent contractor. Each IP right has its own rules in relation to ownership. Not only should the solicitor be aware of these, but they should also check all relevant employment contracts or commissions to satisfy themselves that the rights have not been assigned to third parties.

(b) *Infringement.* The statutory rights arising in relation to each item of intellectual property are different. For example, the Trade Mark Act 1994 and the Patents Act 1977 both grant a monopoly right to the owner to use the mark or exploit the invention, but under the Copyright, Designs and Patents Act 1988, a copyright owner has more limited rights, ie only to prevent copying. In order to license the rights effectively, the licence will need to mirror the infringement provisions of the relevant statute, granting corresponding rights to the licensee.

12.2.1.3 Precedents

Extreme care is needed when using precedents, which must be carefully adapted to the requirements of the particular client. In a recent case, *Oxonica Energy Ltd v Neuftec Ltd* [2009] EWCA Civ 668, the Court of Appeal remarked on an 'appallingly drafted' patent licence and stressed the importance of giving careful thought to all the terms, rather than blindly copying from precedents.

12.2.2 Planning, form and content of the agreement

All of the rights may be included in one licence, or there may be separate licences for each right. There are advantages and disadvantages to each approach. A simple licensing agreement is likely to follow the structure below.

Structure of licence agreement
(a) Date, parties, recitals
(b) Interpretation clause
(c) Grant of licence
(d) Quality control
(e) Marketing
(f) Financial provisions
(g) Protection of IP rights
(h) Termination (if not dealt with elsewhere)
(i) Post-termination provisions
(j) [Warranties and indemnities]
(k) Boiler-plate clauses
(l) Signatures
(m) Schedules

The terms of the licence will depend to a certain extent on the bargaining position of the parties. In our example, it appears that Wood Magic is dealing with a large manufacturing company, and so may not be able to call all the shots.

12.2.2.1 Recitals

The recitals in IP licences are of particular importance. Although it may seem an obvious point, it is important that the licensor is, in fact, the owner of the particular right, and therefore has the right to license it. Problems can arise, for example, where the intellectual property is created by an employee or had been commissioned from a third party (see **12.2.1.2**). Recitals provide the background to the agreement, and can be used to set out the licensor's title to the right and that he has the right to license it. They can also be used to explain the intention of the parties, which may help to clarify the operative provisions, eg the scope of the licence.

12.2.2.2 Definitions

A clear definition of the IP rights to be licensed should be given. For example, if Wood Magic decides to license its design rights (both registered and unregistered) in the furniture, it could include these in a general definition of 'Intellectual Property Rights' or give separate definitions of each. If the licence is to include any trade marks or copyright, these should be clearly defined. The definition should also include the registration number of any registered right. The trade marks may, alternatively, be the subject of a separate licence. The rights are often defined by reference to a schedule.

The definitions should also identify the products to which the IP rights can be applied. A consideration is how broad the definition should be. Should it include the entire furniture range, or just some of it? Initially, it is probably in Wood Magic's interest to keep the definition narrow, eg chairs, as it will then be able to negotiate separate terms for other items if this product proves successful. The same is true in relation to the territory into which, for example, the licensee can sell, which should also be clearly defined. If potential markets open up outside the UK, further licences can be granted to exploit these markets.

12.2.2.3   Scope of the licence

The scope of the licence should be clearly set out. It should make clear what the licensee has the right to do, in relation to what product, where and for how long:

(a)   The licence could be exclusive, sole or non-exclusive. The same considerations apply to the use of these terms as discussed in relation to agency and distribution. So far, Wood Magic appears not to have considered this point.

(b)   Is the licensee to be given the right both to manufacture and to sell, or simply to manufacture the product? Here Wood Magic appears to want to give Ottoman Empire the right to both manufacture and sell the product, but the solicitor will need to check that this is what they have agreed.

(c)   If the right to sell the product is included, can Ottoman Empire sell the products throughout the UK or simply in a particular region of the UK?

(d)   The duration of the licence could be dealt with here, although this may be dealt with in a separate clause. The licence could be for a fixed or indefinite term.

The clause may also deal with registration. Requirements for registration (at the Intellectual Property Office) of IP licences vary depending on the right involved and whether the licence is exclusive or non-exclusive. These are set out in the table at **12.5**.

12.2.2.4   Quality control

The licence should place controls on the quality of the product and contain provisions for Wood Magic to police these. These may include a right to inspect samples and/or visit the licensee's premises to inspect the quality control systems in place.

Where trade marks are to licensed, these will often be the subject of a separate licence. Quality control provisions will be very important for the mark owner to be able to defend the integrity of any mark which is being licensed out; this is to protect the goodwill of the mark and prevent its reputation from being diluted or damaged by, say, inappropriate use by the licensee. Clearly this would affect the value of the mark.

The quality control provisions should reflect the risk of the mark being revoked, so the licence will usually provide that the licensee must not use the mark in a misleading or deceptive way, or do anything leading to loss of the mark's distinctiveness. The licensee should be required to describe the mark as a registered mark belonging to the licensor, and to specify that it is used under licence. This will ensure that the benefit of the mark's goodwill continues to accrue to the licensor.

12.2.2.5   Marketing

The licence will contain marketing requirements, for example in relation to advertising and promotion, and may require the licensor to provide marketing support to the licensee.

Furthermore, the licensee may be obliged to clear all advertising, promotional and marketing material featuring trade-marked goods/services with the licensor before use.

12.2.2.6   Financial matters

Wood Magic may want to charge a one-off flat fee for use of the rights, but more commonly will wish to charge a royalty based on a particular formula (eg based on number of items manufactured/sold by the licensee). If royalties are charged then the agreement should establish a system for record-keeping and allow for verification of the licensee's accounts by the licensor at regular intervals. Alternatives would be to provide for the licensor to take a share of the profits, an annual fee or 'milestone payments', ie the payment of fixed amounts paid on fixed dates throughout the agreement.

It is a good idea to include a minimum royalty provision, particularly if the licence is exclusive, as this will give the licensee the incentive to market the product effectively. Where a trade mark is used, this will also ensure that the mark does not become vulnerable to revocation for non-use. The consequences of failing to meet the target should be dealt with. For example, will failure to meet the target give the licensor the right to terminate the agreement?

The agreement should also provide for interest charges for late payment.

12.2.2.7   Protection of the IP rights

Provision should be made for the protection of the IP rights from infringement by third parties. In particular, the parties should decide who will have the right to bring any proceedings. In the event that the parties do not provide for this in the contract, licensees have differing statutory rights in relation to their right to bring proceedings, depending on the type of licence. These are set out in the table at **12.5**. Usually the licensor will want to retain control of infringement proceedings, but, again, whether it will be able to do so will depend on its bargaining strength.

12.2.2.8   Warranties and indemnities

The licensee will want to be sure that the use of the intellectual property does not infringe the rights of any third party, and that the rights granted are valid. Ottoman Empire is probably in a strong enough bargaining position to be able to require the Wood Magic to give express warranties (or assurances) on validity, and that the use is lawful and does not infringe any third parties' rights. Wood Magic may also be required to indemnify the licensee against liability in the event of any successful claim for infringement. A licensor will usually try to avoid giving such warranties and indemnities, but where it does, care should be taken that they are accurate.

12.2.2.9   Termination and post-termination provisions

The licence should set out the circumstances in which the agreement can be terminated, for example in the event of breach of the agreement, insolvency, or change of control of one or both of the parties. This is crucial. Surprisingly, termination provisions are often overlooked by licensors of IP rights, who fail to consider what will happen if things go wrong. Change of control provisions are particularly important to consider. A licensor should be aware that there is the possibility of its IP rights ending up in the hands of a competitor which has gained control of a licensee company. Whether the termination provisions are reciprocal will depend on the bargaining strengths of the parties.

Provision should also be made for what is to happen to the licensed products if the licence is terminated. For example, will the licensee have to deliver up any unsold stock or be given a limited period to dispose of the products, which would prevent them having to be destroyed.

Intellectual property licences may also involve competition law considerations (see **Chapter 29**).

12.2.2.10 Execution

Different statutory rules apply to execution of a licence agreement, depending again on the type of agreement and whether or not it is an exclusive licence. Again, these are set out in the table at **11.5**.

12.3 MERCHANDISING AGREEMENTS

A merchandising agreement is a form of licence agreement. It is used by media organisations to exploit their IP rights (in particular copyright and trade marks) by licensing rights for the merchandising of toys and other products based on films, television programmes, etc. The licensee is granted the right to produce products and market products based on the licensor's IP rights in return for payment, usually in the form of royalties. Merchandising agreements are of increasing importance given the huge earning potential for both the licensor and licensee. For example, Reuters reported that the *Toy Story 3* film had generated more merchandise in the US than any other recent film. Tracking of shipments (using official bills of lading – see **15.3.1**) into the US showed that 724 cargo size containers of *Toy Story* merchandise had been imported, mostly from China. Over and above this, there would be sales of home-produced merchandise, and this figure relates only to the merchandising of these products within the US.

A merchandising agreement will follow the same basic structure as the IP licence considered at **12.2**. It is likely to be a non-exclusive licence, and so the licensor has the right to grant licences to other licensees.

12.4 FRANCHISING

A franchise is where a business allows a third party to use its name, concept, business format and experience. There is ongoing and close control by the franchisor over its franchisees, but they remain legally and financially separate undertakings. Well-known examples include McDonalds, KFC and the Body Shop. The most usual arrangement is between a manufacturer and retailers, but a franchise can operate at other levels of the supply chain. A franchise agreement involves the franchisor giving the franchisee the right to use the franchisor's IP rights. There may also be competition law considerations (see **Chapter 29**).

In the example given in **Chapter 11**, Wood Magic decided to extend its custom-made furniture business by opting for an agency agreement. Another way of extending this business format would be to franchise the Wood Magic 'concept' of furniture making. This would mean that Wood Magic (the franchisor) would establish a 'Wood Magic' uniform business format, which it would then authorise other businesses (the franchisees) to use in return for payment, usually an initial fee and royalties based on a percentage of turnover or profit on the product. In the franchise agreement, Wood Magic would lay down operating conditions and specifications for the franchisees to meet (eg what their premises should look like, how they should offer the furniture-making service to customers). This would allow Wood Magic to extend this part of its business without having to raise capital to do so, while still retaining considerable control over what the franchisee does with the business.

In the UK, there are no legal requirements as such governing franchising, and the agreement will simply be based on normal contractual principles. However, although not legally binding, it is advisable that the agreement should comply with the European Code of Ethics for Franchising which has been adopted by the British Franchise Association.

The franchise agreement will contain many of the same terms which have been considered when looking at other marketing and licence agreements. The exact content will depend on the type of franchise, but will generally include the following: a grant of the rights, including any IP rights, obligations of the parties, payment provisions, duration, termination provisions, provisions for the protection of and warranties in relation to the IP, plus usual boiler-plate clauses. As the franchisee will be relying on the franchisor's business expertise and concept, the franchisor's obligations may include training provisions and the obligation to provide all the necessary stock and materials to set up the franchise. In addition, the agreement will impose operating obligations on the franchisee and obligations in respect of the premises, from which it will be operating, eg that it will not alter the premises or its layout or fixtures and fittings in any way.

12.5 LICENCES AND ASSIGNMENTS OF IP RIGHTS – FORMALITIES AND CONSEQUENCES

Right	Assignment	Exclusive licence	Non-exclusive licence
Registered trade mark	In writing and signed by or on behalf of assignor: TMA 1994, s 24(3). Prudent to register: TMA 1994, s 25.	In writing and signed by or on behalf of licensor: TMA 1994, s 28(2). Prudent to register: TMA 1994, s 25. Licensee can sue for infringement if licence agreement allows: TMA 1994, s 31(1), but must join proprietor of trade mark in action: TMA 1994, s 31(4). Licensee can call on proprietor of trade mark to sue for infringement: TMA 1994, s 30(2).	In writing and signed by or on behalf of licensor: TMA 1994, s 28(2). Prudent to register: TMA 1994, s 25. Licensee can call on proprietor of trade mark to sue for infringement: TMA 1994, s 30(2).
Copyright	In writing and signed by or on behalf of assignor: CDPA 1988, s 90(3).	In writing and signed by or on behalf of licensor: CDPA 1988, s 92(1). Licensee can sue for infringement: CDPA 1988, s 101(1), but must join the copyright owner in the action or obtain leave of the court: CDPA 1988, s 102(1).	No formalities. In certain circumstances , if the licence is in writing, the licensee can sue: CDPA 1988, s 101A.
Patent	In writing and signed by or on behalf of all parties: PA 1977, s 30(6). Prudent to register: PA 1977, s 33(3).	Prudent to register: PA 1977, s 33(3). Licensee can sue for infringement: PA 1977, s 67.	Prudent to register: PA 1977, s 33(3).
Unregistered design right	In writing and signed by or on behalf of assignor: CDPA 1988, s 222(3).	In writing and signed by or on behalf of licensor: CDPA 1988, s 225. Licensee can sue for infringement.	No formalities.

Right	Assignment	Exclusive licence	Non-exclusive licence
Registered design right	In writing and signed by or on behalf of assignor: RDA 1949, s 15B(3).	In writing and signed by or on behalf of proprietor of design (otherwise will not bind successors in title): RDA 1949, s 15C.	In writing: *Jewitt v Eckhardt* (1878) 8 Ch D 404.
	Must be registered: RDA 1949, 19(1).	Must be registered: RDA 1949, s 19(1). Licensee can sue for infringement: RDA 1949, s 24F(1), but must join proprietor of design in the action: RDA 1949, s 24F(4).	Must be registered: RDA 1949, s 19(1).

SUMMARY

There is a variety of options open to a client who wishes to exploit his IP rights. We have considered when licensing, merchandising and franchising agreements may be suitable options.

This is the final part of the section on marketing agreements. In Part II, we shall look at international sale of goods agreements.

COMMERCIAL AGREEMENTS

Topic	Summary
Definition	There is no single definition of what constitutes a 'commercial agreement' or 'commercial contract', although a basic starting point would normally be 'a deal made between two (or more) parties, both or all of whom are in business'.
Scope	A variety of elements might be relevant in a commercial agreement: the principles of commercial drafting, contracts for the sale of goods, exclusion and restriction of liability, other types of contract under which goods pass, agency and distribution agreements and the principles of consumer credit.
Contracts for the sale of goods	These are, broadly speaking, contracts between a buyer and seller, under which the ownership of goods changes hands in return for the payment of a money consideration known as the price, and where the buyer is not intending to resell the goods (cf 'Distribution agreements' below).
UK Sale of Goods Act 1979 (as amended)	Although normal principles of freedom of contract apply to commercial agreements, in the UK the Sale of Goods Act 1979 provides a type of regulatory framework for sale of goods agreements.
Implied terms	In the UK, the Sale of Goods Act 1979 implies a variety of terms into commercial contracts for the sale of goods; which terms will be implied depend on the circumstances of the contract (for example, some implied terms, such as those relating to price, are implied only where the parties have not expressly or impliedly decided the matter for themselves).
Duties of the parties	The UK Sale of Goods Act 1979 outlines the duties of the buyer and seller under a commercial sale of goods agreement; however, virtually all these duties can be modified or excluded by agreement between the parties.
Rights of the parties	The UK SGA 1979 also sets out the rights of commercial parties (eg, the buyer's right to reject the goods; the seller's rights if the buyer fails to pay for the goods).
Remedies	The UK SGA 1979 also outlines the remedies which are available if either party breaches the contract.
Retention of title	This is a particularly important device in a commercial agreement for the sale of goods: the right of the seller to retain ownership of the goods until the buyer has paid for them.

Topic	Summary
Exclusion and restriction of liability	This is another important device: the ability of either party to exclude or restrict liability for breach of contract. In the UK, normal contractual principles of incorporation and construction apply to exemption clauses in commercial contracts; so does the Unfair Contract Terms Act 1977.
UCTA 1977	UCTA 1977 generally allows parties to commercial contracts more freedom to use exemption clauses than is allowed for consumer contracts. With a very few exceptions (eg, purported exclusion of the implied condition relating to title, which is always void) liability can generally be excluded in a commercial agreement in so far as it is reasonable. Note that s 26 of UCTA 1977 excludes 'international supply contracts' from the provisions of UCTA 1977.
Other contracts under which goods pass	These include contracts of exchange, barter, hire purchase, conditional sale, work and materials and contracts of hire. They are governed by a variety of statutory provisions, all of which are closely modelled on the Sale of Goods Act 1979, so the points made above concerning implied terms are also relevant here.
Contracts for services	These are governed by the UK Supply of Goods and Services Act 1982; the Act implies a small number of terms into contracts for the supply of services, including a term that the services will be provided with reasonable skill and care.
Marketing agreements	Some agreements involving goods concentrate on getting the goods to a wider market. Examples include agency agreements and distribution agreements.
Agency agreements	Although agency agreements come in a number of different types, the classic sales agency agreement involves one party (the principal) giving authority to the other party (the agent) to take actions on the principal's behalf to find customers for the principal's goods or services.
Commercial Agents Regulations 1993	Agency agreements are to a large extent governed by the normal law of contract and law of agency. However, a substantial number of agency agreements in the UK are also subject to the Commercial Agents (Council Directive) Regulations 1993, which lay down a framework of rules concerning the rights and duties of each party (notably the agent's right to a payment on termination of the agency agreement). Equivalent provisions apply throughout the EU.
Distribution agreements	A distribution agreement is fundamentally based on a sale of goods agreement. However, in a distribution agreement the parties specifically agree that the buyer of the goods (the distributor) is buying them for the purpose of re-selling them, rather than for end-use in its own business. Distribution agreements are chiefly subject to the ordinary law of contract (and sale of goods), but may have competition law implications.

Topic	Summary
International conventions	A number of important conventions and agreements govern commercial contracts internationally. The most important are: • the United Nations Convention on Contracts for the International Sale of Goods (the 'Vienna Convention' or CISG) • the Uniform Commercial Code (UCC) • the Principles of European Contract Law (PECL) • the UNIDROIT Principles (PICC)

INTERNATIONAL SALE AGREEMENTS

INTRODUCTION TO INTERNATIONAL SALE AGREEMENTS

> **LEARNING OUTCOMES**
>
> After reading this chapter you will be able to:
>
> - appreciate the similarities and differences between domestic and international sale of goods agreements
> - explain the practical and legal problems that affect international sale of goods agreements
> - realise that in any international sale of goods transaction a series of contracts is involved: sale of goods, freight, insurance and finance contracts
> - identify the main legislation governing these contracts.

An international sale of goods contract will need to cover the same type of issues as a domestic agreement (eg transfer of ownership, price, payment, and delivery). Generally, if the contract is subject to English law, the UK SGA 1979 will apply to an international contract. However, there are added complications, both legal and practical. For example, UCTA 1977 does not generally apply to international sales contracts (see s 26), and the use of exclusion clauses is prohibited in some international contracts of carriage.

The most obvious practical problem is that arrangements have to be made for transportation of the goods, often over long distances. The result, clearly, will be increased delivery periods and the associated cost of long-distance freight carriage. The parties need to decide who will arrange, and more importantly, pay for this. Language problems may cause complications and misunderstandings. Some problems can be solved by the parties using a standard contract drawn up by a trade association, or by an international body. The ones at which we shall look in Part II of this book are the Incoterms, produced by the International Chamber of Commerce. These are a set of standard form rules, produced in a variety of languages, relating to the transport arrangements. These will be considered in **Chapter 15**.

The seller will be particularly concerned with the payment arrangements. The method of payment will need to be considered. In an international sale, cash payment will usually be impractical. It may be possible to arrange for payment in advance, but more usually the buyer will demand a credit period, so payment may not take place until some time after the goods have been shipped, resulting in obvious cash flow problems. In addition, the seller will want to put in place arrangements for facilitating and guaranteeing payment. This will require complex contractual arrangements, to be put in place through a bank or banks, to which the seller can look for payment if the buyer defaults. The finance arrangements will be considered in **Chapter 16**.

Then there are various additional, or increased, risks, for example:

(a)   physical risk of damage to the goods associated with sea or air transport and the associated extra handling;

(b)   financial risks, for example due to changes in currency exchange rates;

(c)   increased risks of not being paid, or being paid late, possibly by reason of buyer insolvency;

(d)   political/geopolitical risks, possibly even of war, terrorist attack or blockades (a recent example is the problems for shippers caused by government restrictions imposed during the coronavirus pandemic);

(e)   legal risks if the contract is subject to foreign law (are you qualified to advise on foreign law?); and

(f)   the difficulties associated with litigation, or enforcing contractual remedies outside of the seller's jurisdiction (eg how practical is it to attempt to enforce a retention of title clause?).

Some of these risks can be covered by insurance, although this may be expensive and it may not be economically viable for the seller to purchase it.

The starting point for any international sale of goods transaction will be the sale of goods contract itself but, because of these additional risks and complications, international sale of goods contracts commonly include terms dealing with international transport arrangements, insurance provision, complex financing and credit provision, and closely related payment provisions. As a result, there will be a series of additional contracts with third parties, which are essential to ensure that the parties fulfil their obligations under the principal sale of goods contract. Each contract will be governed by legislation and international conventions relevant to each area of law (international conventions are beyond the scope of this book, but an awareness of their existence is important):

(a)   The freight contract between the shipper and the carrier. The party arranging (and paying for) the contract is the 'shipper'. Whether this is the buyer or seller will depend on the bargaining strength of the parties, and will be provided for in the sale contract, usually by incorporation of the relevant Incoterm. Under English law, these contracts are governed by the Carriage of Goods by Sea Acts 1971 and 1992. These Acts implement various international conventions into English law, such as the Hague and Hague-Visby rules, and regulate the rights and duties of carriers.

(b)   The contract of marine insurance. Whether the buyer or seller arranges for insurance will again depend on what has been agreed between the parties and will be normally provided for in the sale contract. Where the seller is obliged to insure, the obligation will often be created by incorporation of the relevant Incoterm. Not all Incoterms oblige the seller to insure, so the buyer may need to make its own arrangements. If English law applies, the insurance contract will be governed by the Marine Insurance Act 1906.

(c)   Again, the finance arrangements will be provided for in the sale of goods contract, and the method and the degree of security for payment will again depend on the relationship between the parties. The implementation of these arrangements will involve the buyer making the appropriate contractual arrangements with his bank, to which the seller and the seller's bank may be party. If the method of payment is to be a bill of exchange then, under English law, this will be governed by the Bills of Exchange Act 1882. The contract may require that the buyer sets up a documentary credit to guarantee payment. This is governed by the Uniform Customs and Practice for Documentary Credits (UCP) published by the ICC. (The current version is UCP 600 (2007 revision), which came into effect on 1 July 2007; a supplement, 'eUCP', updated in 2019, deals with electronic documents.)

These additional contracts are illustrated by **Figure 13.1** below, which assumes that the goods are to be shipped by sea and that the governing law of the contract is English law.

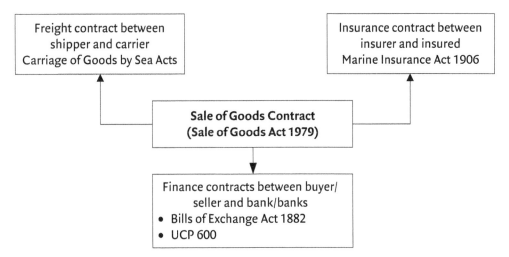

Figure 13.1 Additional contracts with third parties

Finally, it is important for lawyers involved in international sale contracts to be aware of some of the terminology, especially as some terms are given a different meaning from the one which you might commonly use. The following are the most important:

(a)   *Shipper.* This is the person who arranges for goods to be sent by ship, and will usually be the seller itself but may also be the seller's agent.

(b)   *Shipment.* This is the act of putting the goods onto the ship before it sails. The word is used differently to everyday language, where you might talk about 'sending a shipment of bananas', which actually means 'sending a *consignment* of bananas'. In the same way, if you say 'When were the goods shipped?', this does not mean 'When did the ship sail?'. It means 'When were the goods put onto the ship?'.

(c)   *Carrier.* This is the shipping company on whose ship the goods are transported.

(d)   *Consignee.* The person collecting the goods at their destination (which will often be the buyer itself but may also be the buyer's agent).

(e)   *Freight.* This is the cost of carriage, not the goods themselves (the *cargo*).

(f)   *Freight forwarder.* Freight forwarders, or forwarding agents, are logistics specialists who arrange for the transport of goods to the final destination on behalf of the seller. They deal with all aspects of the delivery of the goods, including the carriage and the freight, insurance and customs clearance as well as transport.

(g)   *P&I Clubs.* Group of 13 independent, non-profit-making, mutual insurance associations which provide insurance and advice for shipowners and charterers against liability arising from the use and operation of ships.

SUMMARY

An international sale of goods contract is similar to a domestic sale of goods contract, but there are additional practical and legal problems which affect these transactions. The most important issues are those relating to choice of jurisdiction and law, transport and finance arrangements. The remainder of Part II will consider how these problems may be resolved.

CHAPTER 14

CHOICE OF JURISDICTION AND LAW

LEARNING OUTCOMES

After reading this chapter you will be able to:

- explain issues that may arise in relation to choice of jurisdiction and law
- appreciate that choice of jurisdiction and choice of law are separate issues
- understand the default position where the parties fail to make a choice of either jurisdiction or law in their agreement
- summarise the main provisions of EU Regulation 44/2001 (Brussels I) which govern jurisdiction
- summarise the main provisions of EU Regulation 593/2008 (Rome I) which govern law.

14.1 INTRODUCTION

The whole area of jurisdiction, and of law, has been given a boost in the minds of commercial lawyers by the advent of e-commerce. Today, international contracts can be concluded at the click of a mouse. The collision of opposing jurisdictions is therefore an increasingly important issue (see further **Chapter 26**).

This chapter concentrates on what happens when a contract goes wrong. In which jurisdiction can a client sue and be sued, and which country's laws are applicable to the contract?

Jurisdiction means the courts which would hear the dispute. Choice of law obviously means choosing which law would apply to the contract. Normally, both law and jurisdiction would be decided by a clause in the contract. If that has not been done in respect of a contract, then problems may arise.

Within the EU, until the end of the transition period, these problems were, in general, resolved by applying two EU Conventions: EU Regulation 593/2008 ('Rome I'), which deals with governing law, and the recast Regulation 1215/212 ('Brussels I'), which deals with jurisdiction within the EU. The non-EU EFTA states, Iceland, Norway and Switzerland, come under the 2007 Lugano Convention, which contains similar provisions to those in Brussels I.

Rome I has been incorporated into domestic law and so forms part of the body of 'retained EU law' (under the Law Applicable to Contractual Obligations and Non-Contractual Obligations (Amendment etc) (EU Exit) Regulations 2019 (SI 2019/834) as amended by the Jurisdiction, Judgments and Applicable Law (Amendment) (EU Exit) Regulations 2020 (SI 2020/1574)).

However, Brexit has brought about a fundamental change in the rules on jurisdiction. From the date of the end of the transition period, Brussels I ceased to apply to the UK, except to proceedings instituted before 1 January 2021. The UK has applied to join the Lugano Convention. Despite the fact that Iceland, Norway and Switzerland support its application, the EU Commission has recommended that the EU states should not consent to its accession to the Convention. The Council of the EU will now make the final decision. At the time of writing (August 2022), it seems that the Member States are split on the issue. For the application to succeed, the UK would need the support of 55% of the Member States representing 65% of the EU's population. As yet, there is no date set for a decision.

It has always been desirable that commercial agreements should include a choice of both law and jurisdiction (see **1.5.2.6**). The considerable uncertainty created by the current situation now makes this absolutely essential.

14.2 JURISDICTION

14.2.1 Suing in the English courts

The effect of Brussels I ceasing to apply is that, rather than looking to a single Convention, jurisdiction is now governed by a combination of existing common law and statute and the Hague Convention on Choice of Court Agreements (the Hague Convention).

14.2.1.1 The common law rules

The common law rules which govern whether the English courts have jurisdiction are based on the principles of international law which have been derived from case law over the years. The outcome depends on whether the defendant can be served with proceedings either within the jurisdiction or outside the jurisdiction, with the permission of the court.

There are three circumstances in which the English courts may have jurisdiction to hear a claim:

(a)   if a claim form is served on the defendant whilst they are physically present within the jurisdiction (however briefly);

(b)   if the defendant submits to the jurisdiction of the English courts; or

(c)   if the courts authorise service of a claim form out of the jurisdiction.

14.2.1.2 The Hague Convention

Like the Lugano Convention, the UK was a party to the 2005 Hague Convention as a result of its membership of the EU. Unlike the Lugano Convention, the UK's application to accede to the Hague Convention was approved by the other contracting states and, following the end of the transition period, it re-acceded in its own right. The other contracting states are the EU (including Denmark), Mexico, Montenegro and Singapore, but not any of the EFTA states.

Under the Convention, where commercial parties have agreed that the courts of a state which is a party to the Hague Convention shall have exclusive jurisdiction to hear their disputes, the courts of other contracting states will uphold that agreement. As all EU Member States and the UK are party to the Convention, if parties agree to an exclusive jurisdiction clause in favour of the English courts, any English court judgment arising from that contract will be enforceable in the courts of other EU Member States.

However, the Convention has its limitations, which make it absolutely essential that commercial agreements should include a choice of (exclusive) jurisdiction:

(a)   There must be an exclusive jurisdiction agreement where the court is designated in the agreement.

(b)   Arguably, it does not apply to so-called asymmetrical jurisdiction clauses. (An asymmetrical jurisdiction clause provides that one party must sue the other in a particular jurisdiction (say the English courts) whereas the other can sue in the courts of any jurisdiction.)

(c)   It excludes various claims from its scope. Most importantly for our purposes, these include consumer claims, claims relating to carriage by air or sea and various intellectual property matters.

(d)   Crucially, it only applies where the parties have made a choice of exclusive jurisdiction. Unlike Brussels I, it does not contain any rules for determining which courts have jurisdiction where the parties have not done so.

14.2.1.3   Consumers

The Jurisdiction, Judgments and Applicable Law (Amendment) (EU Exit) Regulations 2020 (SI 2020/1574) amend the Civil Jurisdiction and Judgments Act 1982 to include ss 15A–15E which relate to jurisdiction in consumer and employment matters.

Section 15B provides for special jurisdiction rules for disputes relating to consumer contracts, which effectively mirror the rules in Brussels I which relate to consumers (Articles 17–19). A consumer domiciled in the UK can only be sued in their own courts but can chose to bring proceedings against the other party to the contract either in their own courts or in the other party's courts (regardless of the domicile of the other party).

Note that these rules only apply to consumer contracts as defined in s 15E. The definition includes contracts where the other party 'directs [commercial or professional] activities to that part or to other parts of the United Kingdom including that part [where the consumer is domiciled]'. This means that s 15B will protect consumers who have entered into contracts online by requiring that the consumer only be sued in their own courts, whilst giving them a choice of where they can sue the other party.

14.2.2   Being sued abroad

Other than the Hague Convention, England is not a party to any other convention on jurisdiction. The question of whether an English defendant can be sued in a foreign country depends on that country's jurisdiction rules.

14.3   ROME I – REGULATION 593/2008

This Regulation applies to Member States of the EU and to the UK as retained law. It deals with the choice of laws, that is, the question of which law applies to the contract.

14.3.1   The basic position under Regulation 593/2008

Article 1(2) specifies the matters to which the Regulation does not apply, for example wills and probate, and matters governed by company law. There is no need for the parties to be nationals of, or domiciled within, the EU. A court within the EU must apply Rome I where it has to determine which law applies to a contract.

Article 3(1) allows the parties to choose the law of the contract, either expressly or impliedly. If they have done so, then that is the applicable law that governs the contract.

If no such choice has been made then the rules in Article 4 apply. Typically, in a sale of goods contract, this means that the law of the country where the seller has his habitual residence will apply, unless the buyer is a consumer, who cannot be denied the use of laws which cannot be derogated from in his own jurisdiction.

Article 4(1) sets out a list of different types of contract, and states whose law will apply to each type of contract. Looking at the contracts that we have covered in the preceding chapters:

(a)   In a sale of goods contract, the law of the country where the seller has his place of habitual residence is the law that will apply (Article 4(1)(a)).

(b)   In a contract for the supply of services, the law of the country where the service provider has his place of habitual residence is the law that will apply (Article 4(1)(b)).

(c)   In a franchise agreement, the law of the country where the franchisor has his place of habitual residence is the law that will apply (Article 4(1)(e)).

(d)   In a distribution agreement, the law of the country where the distributor has his place of habitual residence is the law that will apply (Article 4(1)(f)).

Habitual residence means, for companies, the place where the company has its central administration and, for individuals acting in the course of business, the principal place of business. There is an exception for contracts with local/branch offices (Article 19).

This establishes a presumption only that for each type of contract the law stated in Article 4(1) will apply, but this presumption can be rebutted by showing that the contract is 'manifestly more closely connected' with another country. Recital 20 of the Regulation states that this would be the case where the contract has a 'very close relationship with another contract or contracts', eg, where there is a network of connected contracts. An example would be the network of contracts set up by a documentary credit (see **16.3.5**), where it would not be practical for each of the different contracts involved to be subject to the laws of separate countries.

Where a contract does not fall into one of the categories set out in Article 4(1) or is a hybrid of several types of contract, Article 4(2) provides that the contract will be governed by the law of the country where the party required to effect the characteristic performance of the contract has his habitual residence. Characteristic performance is a concept from the old Rome Convention, which Rome I replaced. Generally, the party who is *not* under an obligation to pay is the party effecting characteristic performance. (Although not stated in those terms, Article 4(1) effectively gives a list of the parties effecting characteristic performance under each particular type of contract.)

If the applicable law cannot be determined under Article 4(1) or 4(2), then the contract will be governed by the law of the country with which it is most closely connected (Article 4(4)).

14.3.2   Other exceptions to the seller's law applying

Article 4(1)(c) deals with a right in 'immovable property'. The presumption here is that the contract is governed by the law of the country where the immovable property is situated. This does not apply to contracts for repair or construction of immovable property.

Article 5(1) provides that, in a contract for the carriage of goods (not *sale* of goods), it is the country where the carrier has its place of business if that is also the country of loading or discharging the goods, or if it is also the country where the consignor has its principal place of business.

Article 4(4) provides that the court may decide that the contract is more closely connected with another country and apply that country's laws.

14.3.3   Local 'mandatory rules'

There are limitations on the use of the applicable law. If any provisions of the applicable law conflict with local laws of the jurisdiction where the dispute is heard, relating to the contract, those conflicting provisions of the applicable law cannot validly be used. These local law provisions are the 'mandatory rules' which are referred to in Article 9 of the Regulation. These are 'rules' which cannot be derogated from (eg, in the case of the UK, the Financial Services and Markets Act 2000, the Consumer Rights Act (when implemented), etc). Article 9 provides that the choice of foreign law by the parties will not prejudice the application of the mandatory rules of the home country to the contract. So, even if the applicable law was held to be, say, Austrian law, the Financial Services and Markets Act 2000 could also apply to a relevant dispute heard by a court in England and Wales, and would override any inconsistent provisions in Austrian law.

14.3.4 Exceptions for consumer and employment contracts

Articles 6 and 8 are intended to give protection to the weaker party to a contract.

Article 6 deals with certain types of consumer contract. Where no choice has been made, such contracts are governed by the law of the consumer's habitual residence. Where a choice has been made, the chosen law operates subject to any rules for the protection of the consumer applicable in the consumer's country of habitual residence.

Article 8 deals with individual contracts of employment. Where there is no choice of law in the contract then the presumption is that contained in Article 8(2). This is basically that the law is that of the country where the work takes place, or where the business is situated if the work takes place in a different country. However, a contractual choice of law cannot operate so as to deprive the employee of the protection of the mandatory rules which would apply under Article 8(2).

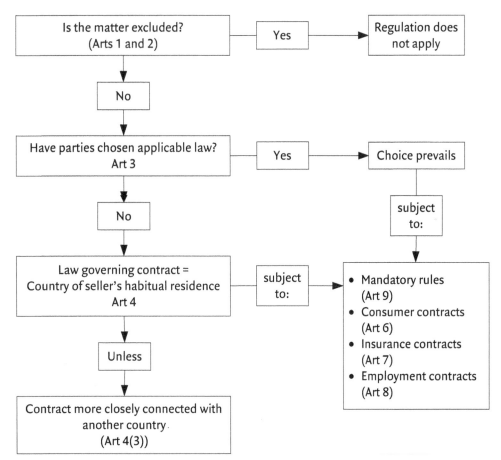

Figure 14.2 Regulation 593/2008 (Rome I): sale of goods contracts

---

SUMMARY

In the event of a dispute arising from an international commercial agreement, the parties need to know which courts will have jurisdiction to hear the dispute and whose law will apply to the contract. The parties are free to choose both jurisdiction and law, but they must be aware of the Regulations which govern this choice. These EU Regulations also dictate the position where the contract is silent on the issues of choice of law or jurisdiction.

CHAPTER 15

INTERNATIONAL SALE OF GOODS

LEARNING OUTCOMES

After reading this chapter you will be able to:

- identify the main documents involved in an international sale of goods transaction
- explain the function of the relevant documents
- recognise the importance of Incoterms in resolving practical and legal issues in relation to transport arrangements
- summarise the function of each of the main Incoterms
- advise on the choice of Incoterm and the consequences of that choice
- identify some specific international rules governing international sales transactions.

15.1 INTRODUCTION

The typical international sale of goods transaction is one where the goods are shipped by sea over a long distance. This means there could be a considerable time delay between the goods being supplied and the seller being paid for them. The seller would ideally like to be paid when the goods are dispatched. The buyer would ideally want to pay only when he has received the goods and had a chance to inspect them.

The seller's desire to be paid is not just wishful thinking. The seller will have to pay his own suppliers, his employees and other business expenses. This is a cash flow problem that happens in all business, but the situation is exacerbated in international sale contracts because of the distances over which the goods are shipped.

In addition to the possible delay in payment, there are increased costs of insurance, to cover the sea voyage and possibly other risks.

To solve the problems of slow payment, the documents involved in an international sale have been elevated to a special status. In effect, they come to represent the goods themselves for the purposes of contract law. So, for example, delivery of the goods, in the legal sense, is performed by handing over documents, which are delivered via the international banking system (see **16.3.3.3**).

15.2 THE DOCUMENTS

The key documents are:

(a) the bill of lading (or alternatives – see **15.2.2** and **15.2.4**);
(b) the commercial invoice;

(c)   the policy of marine, or air, insurance;

(d)   documents relating to trade finance, eg documentary credit (see **16.3**);

(e)   documents relating to border clearance, eg export/import licences and a certificate of origin.

The shipping 'paper trail' begins when the arrangements are made for a cargo to be shipped and ends with payment. There are often very large numbers of lengthy documents which have to be filled in and checked before a ship can enter or leave a port which makes the process cumbersome and expensive.

It has been estimated that, even in normal circumstances, up to 50% of shipping documents are late. To give an example of the process, the shipping line, Maersk, tracked a refrigerated container, containing roses and avocados, from a farm in Kenya to its final destination in the Netherlands to assess the impact of the multitude of documents. Over 30 people and organisations (eg, banks) were involved in the process. It took 34 days for the consignment to reach its destination, including 10 days waiting for documents to be processed. One document was lost and retrieved from a pile of other papers.

The coronavirus pandemic further highlighted the problem: documents could potentially be a source of infection and, with the banks closed, there was no-one to examine them. As a result, ships backed up outside ports, unable to unload their cargoes.

Although a great deal of progress is still to be made, the industry is exploring new technologies, such as smart contracts, blockchain and distributed ledger technology (DLT), which have the potential to simplify and thus revolutionise the documentation and finance arrangements involved in international trade.

15.2.1   The bill of lading

The bill of lading (BoL or B/L) is given by the carrier of the goods to the consignor of the goods, at the time of the goods being loaded.

The bill of lading serves three purposes:

(a)   it is a receipt for the goods and provides evidence that they are in good condition at loading;

(b)   it contains the terms of contract of carriage; and

(c)   it is evidence of title to the goods, and a right to possess them.

Thus, at the destination the goods will be handed over to the person holding the bill of lading. The bill is given to the carrier in exchange for the goods. It should arrive before the goods, as the goods travel by sea but the bill is sent by airmail. A key property of a bill of lading is that its holder has title to the goods.

Only an original bill of lading will suffice. A photocopy, faxed or email copy is no good. This means that the original bill must be couriered to the recipient. Where a bill of lading is used in conjunction with a documentary credit, it must be 'conforming', ie conform with the terms of the documentary credit (see **16.3.6.1**).

There are disadvantages to bills of lading. They are expensive to arrange and administer, but the main disadvantage is that bills of lading were intended for the sale of bulk commodities which were shipped, slowly, a considerable distance by sea. Today, most goods are containerised, air transport is used more, and ships have become faster. Especially for short (international) journeys, the cargo can often reach the destination before the bill of lading does.

An additional complication is that it is common practice to issue bills of lading in sets of three. Only one copy needs to be presented to claim the goods from the carrier. The practice was originally devised to enable the resale of goods whilst at sea, even though criticised then (see *Glyn Mills Currie & Co v East and West India Dock Co* (1882) 7 App Cas 591). Today, this practice can lead to fraud. The use of bills of lading has decreased dramatically as alternatives that are more amenable to electronic communication have gained acceptance (see **15.2.2**).

Where the goods may arrive before the bill of lading or have discrepancies, the carrier will usually deliver the goods to the buyer in return for a letter of indemnity (LOI) from the seller, but this is risky for the carrier and the buyer.

As a result, sea waybills (see **15.2.2**) and freight forwarders receipts are often preferred to bills of lading, as they can be sent by fax or email. Although they give less legal protection, the buyer can collect the goods from the carrier by giving proof of their identity without having to produce a bill of lading, as such. With advances in technology, electronic bills of lading are now being used more widely (see **15.2.3**).

Bills of lading are governed in the UK by the Carriage of Goods by Sea Act 1992.

There are three types of bills of lading – inland, ocean and through bill:

(a)   Inland bill of lading – this is a contract between a shipper and transportation company used when transporting goods overland to an exporter's international carrier.

(b)   Ocean bill of lading – this is a contract between an exporter and an international carrier for transport of merchandise to a specified foreign market overseas.

(c)   Through bill of lading – this is a document that establishes the terms between a shipper and transportation company covering both the domestic and international transport of export goods between specified points for a specified charge. For example, an air shipment can be covered with a through bill of lading; however, ocean shipments require both an inland bill of lading (for domestic transport) and an ocean bill of lading (for international transport).

15.2.2   An alternative to bills of lading – waybills

A waybill is an alternative to a bill of lading. A waybill is a receipt for the goods and evidence of the carriage contract, but it does not constitute a document of title to the goods. It also specifies the person to whom delivery should be made. The original does not have to be sent to the buyer for him to be able to collect the goods from the carrier. Its disadvantage is that it does not enable the buyer to sell the goods on before he has possession of them, as he can with a bill of lading.

An advantage of waybills is that they can be sent electronically (or by fax). The transaction may thus be undertaken as e-commerce, with the payment being sent from the buyer to the seller by electronic means.

Although waybills have traditionally been used for air freight, they are nowadays also used for sea freight with increasing frequency.

15.2.3   Electronic bills of lading

Despite the difficulties with bills of lading, they are still favoured in the transport of bulk cargoes, eg grain, coal, or metal ores, and a bill of lading will usually be required to secure payment under a documentary credit (see **16.3.6.1**). Since the 1980s, there have been attempts to produce electronic bills of lading (e-bills), which have considerable advantages over paper bills: an electronic bill can pass through the banking system quickly, there are fewer administrative costs and the potential for fraud is reduced, although there are concerns about cybercrime. Until recently, they had not been widely used.

Electonic Trading Systems (ETS) are online platforms by which bills of lading can be created and traded. There are now four ETS which have been approved by the P&I clubs and other shipping associations, and as a result e-bills are becoming more popular. These systems are BOLERO (Bills of Lading Electronic Registry Organisation), essDOCS, e-title and edoxOnline.

These require all users to sign up to the relevant ETS in advance so that the e-bill can be transferred and traded between them. The parties enter into a multi-party contract which means the systems replicate, by contract, the law governing bills of exchange and implement all the rights and obligations of a bill of exchange.

Although there are still legal and practical hurdles in relation to the use of e-bills, this would seem to be where the future lies for bills of lading.

Proposals for reform

One of the main problems has been that although some jurisdictions, for example Singapore and Spain, do now accept the legal status of e-bills, many jurisdictions, including the English courts, do not.

English law does not recognise the 'possession' of electronic documents and, consequently, does not recognise an e-bill as a document of title. Following a consultation on the legal status of e-bills, the Law Commission has now published a report with draft legislation which will allow for the recognition of e-bills in electronic form. The Electronic Trade Documents Bill was announced in the 2022 Queen's Speech but, at the time of writing, there is no timetable for its introduction.

15.2.4 Road, rail or air transport

There is no equivalent to the bill of lading in air transport. An 'air waybill' is normally used. This would be made out to the buyer as consignee. Often, the basis is an 'FOB airport' contract (see **15.4.4.3**). The seller's duties end when the goods are delivered at the destination airport to the carrier or buyer's agent.

For road and rail transport, the contract would usually be made with a firm that undertakes the whole transport chain, normally using containerised transport for the goods. The contract document is a 'combined transport document'. There are various standard-form contracts from the International Chamber of Commerce (ICC) that deal with these arrangements (see **15.4**).

For a discussion of the problems of multi-modal transport, see Faber [1996] LMCLQ 503.

15.2.5 The commercial invoice

This lists and describes the contract goods (eg, '20 cases of Adams Baked Beans, each comprising 30 tins of 100g size'). It will also usually constitute a demand for payment by the buyer.

15.2.6 The policy of marine (or air) insurance

This should be worded so as to cover the goods specified in the commercial invoice for the journey described in the bill of lading. The policy would be transferred from one party to another along with the bill of lading (and would obviously need to be a transferable policy).

15.3 EFFECT OF TRANSFER OF THE DOCUMENTS

The Carriage of Goods by Sea Act 1992 provides a solution to any problems of privity of contract which would occur when the bill of lading is transferred from one holder to another. The Act provides that anyone who holds the bill of lading is entitled to sue the carrier on the contract of carriage. A holder also assumes the contractual burdens. (The Act also applies to other documents such as waybills, which are mentioned at **15.2.2** and **15.2.4**.) The holder also has rights in tort in relation to the goods (eg, for negligent damage).

The buyer who is in possession of the shipping documents can enforce his:

(a)   contractual rights against the person who sold to him, under the contract of sale;

(b)   contractual rights against the carrier under the contract of carriage; and

(c)   rights against the insurer under the terms of the policy of which he is the assignee.

Motis Exports Ltd v Dampskibsselskabet AF 1912 (No 1), A/S and Another [2000] 1 All ER (Comm) 91 is an example of the problems of bills of lading. In that case, the defendant carrier delivered goods against a forged bill of lading. The owner of the goods successfully sued the carrier, as the Court of Appeal affirmed that a forged bill of lading was simply a worthless piece of paper. Delivery of the goods against a forged bill of lading was held to be misdelivery of the goods, and the carrier's general exclusion of liability for loss in transit did not cover the situation.

15.4   ARRANGING TRANSPORTATION OF THE GOODS – INCOTERMS

In an international sale of goods, there will be various stages in the transport chain. For example, if the goods are being exported to Korea from a factory in Manchester, they will first of all have to be taken by road or rail from Manchester in the UK to a British port, possibly Liverpool or Hull. They will then need to be loaded on to a ship and be taken by the ship from the British port to a port in Korea. Once they reach there, they will then be taken by road or rail from the Korean port to the premises of the buyer.

15.4.1   Multi-modal transport and container transport

Nowadays, it is usual for the parties to arrange so-called multi-modal transport, where the goods are transported under a single contract of carriage, using a combination of two or more modes of transport, eg road, rail, air or sea. Where, for example, the parties are based in the UK and Korea, the goods will be transported by road in the UK, by sea and then by road in Korea. Although not all multi-modal transport involves the use of containers, this will most often be the case. The goods will be loaded into a container, either directly at the manufacturer's premises or at a carrier's depot in the seller's country (in the UK), and transported to a depot in the buyer's country (in Korea). Rather than a series of contracts of carriage covering the carriage by road in the UK, loading onto the ship, the sea voyage, the unloading and the carriage by road in Korea, one contract with the carrier covers all these aspects. The carrier who arranges the transport is the 'contractual carrier', which will normally arrange a series of sub-contracts to cover different aspects of the entire journey, eg the shipping arrangements. The sub-contractors are known as the 'actual carriers'. Very often the arrangements are made on behalf of the shipper by freight forwarding companies.

The method of transportation will be agreed between the parties and provided for in the sale contract.

15.4.2   Legal and practical considerations

As between the seller and the buyer, there are legal and practical issues to be considered. The major ones are:

(a)   who pays for each stage of the journey; and

(b)   which party is responsible for the goods at each stage?

So, how do you draft the contract to take care of this?

One way is to use a standard contract. Since 1936, the ICC has published Incoterms, which are sets of standard terms, setting out the obligations of each party and laid out in simple terms in a standard book. These are now updated every 10 years, and the latest version is the Incoterms 2020 (which came into force on 1 January 2020). In addition, many contracts will continue to be in place which are based on the previous edition, the Incoterms 2010, and the parties are free to choose previous versions if they wish.

Incoterms are published in more than 30 languages. This means that each party to a carriage contract can look up the relevant Incoterm in their own language, and see the buyers' and sellers' obligations laid out in simple steps. This helps to avoid misunderstandings, especially when the parties are separated by distance and by language. It thus helps to avoid disputes and litigation, with the consequent cost and time involved.

It should be realised that the Incoterms are not statutory provisions. An Incoterm will only form part of a sale of goods contract if it is expressly incorporated by reference into it, eg 'This contract is to be FOB Hull and is governed by Incoterms 2020'. Once incorporated, they do not deal with the terms of the carriage contract but merely provide which party is to arrange and pay for each of the stages of carriage. In particular, they do provide for the delivery, in the legal sense, of the goods and the passing of the risk in the goods (ie the obligation to insure the goods:). They also cover the obligation to obtain export or import clearance (not relevant for deals entirely within the EU), the buyer's obligation to take delivery, and the obligation to provide proof that the various obligations have been complied with. However, Incoterms do not attempt to cover all the terms of the sale of goods contract. They do not deal with the passing of ownership which the parties should address in the sale of goods contract.

It is also worth adding that the Incoterms use the word 'delivery' both in the legal sense of voluntary transfer of possession of the goods and in the commercial sense of transporting the goods to the buyer.

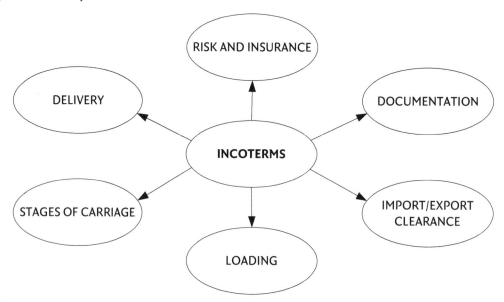

The choice of Incoterm will depend partly on the bargaining strength of the parties and partly on commercial convenience. The use of a particular Incoterm does have implications for the other contracts between the parties. For example, if the parties choose a CIF or CFR contract (see below) the mode of transport must be sea transport for these terms to work.

There is information on the ICC site at www.iccwbo.org.

Incoterms are classified into two groups:

Group I: Rules for Any Mode of Transport

EXW	Ex Works
CIP	Carriage and Insurance Paid
CPT	Carriage Paid To
DAP	Delivered at Place
DPU	Delivered at Place Unloaded
DDP	Delivered Duty Paid
FCA	Free Carrier

Group II: Rules for Sea and Inland Waterway Transport Only

| CFR | Cost and Freight |

CIF   Cost, Insurance and Freight
FAS   Free Alongside Ship
FOB   Free On Board

The Group II terms are nowadays generally only used for unpacked bulk cargoes, like coal, grain, ore, sugar etc, or other non-containerised cargoes. These are transported in the holds of ships known as bulk carrier ships. Liquid cargoes such as oil or liquified gas are transported in the holds of tanker ships. Manufactured goods are more suited to being containerised, and one of the Group I terms will normally be used. The containers are transported on container ships. Some of the largest ships in the world are container ships. (The Chinese ship, the HMM Algeciras, is 400 metres long and 200 metres wide. To put this into perspective, the Eiffel Tower in Paris is 300 metres high.)

The lightest burden on the seller is when the goods are delivered to the buyer 'ex works', that is at the seller's premises. The heaviest is when they have to be delivered to the buyer's premises with the relevant duty paid. These burdens on the seller are reflected in the price agreed for the deal. The less the burden, the less the price. However, it does mean that the buyer has to arrange and pay for the other parts of the chain of transport.

The Incoterms beginning with 'F' or 'C' are contracts where the seller fulfils its obligations in the country of shipment, ie the country of departure of the goods. Those beginning with 'D' are different in nature from those beginning with 'F' and 'C', in that the seller is responsible for the arrival of the goods in the country of destination and must bear all the risks and costs of achieving it.

The traditional sets of terms could not always be adapted for modern shipping practice. For example, as discussed at **15.4.1**, the typical situation today is not of the ship lying at the dockside waiting for cargo to be loaded. Rather, the aim is to minimise the time spent in port. The goods are therefore in shipping containers which are stored in the docks pending arrival of the appropriate ship. It would also be typical today for goods to be put into shipping containers at the sellers' premises, or at a depot run by the carrier. They would stay in the container until they reached either the buyer, or a carrier's depot in the country of destination. The Incoterms were revised in 2010 to take into account this practice, and to deal with issues such as security arrangements. The Incoterms 2020 have made further revisions to reflect what the ICC describes as 'ever-evolving' commercial practice. The revisions in the latest version include clearer guidance for buyers and sellers on the costs for each party at each stage of the journey and more detailed security arrangements. They also provide for the situation where no carrier is involved but the seller uses its own means of transport or the buyer collects direct from the seller's premises.

The most commonly used contracts nowadays are FCA (Free Carrier), CFR (Cost and Freight), and to a lesser extent CIP (Carriage and Insurance Paid), although some sellers do still use FOB for containerised cargoes.

Some terms which are used for the container trade are as follows:

(a)   full container load (FCL);

(b)   less than full container load (LCL);

(c)   free carrier (equivalent to FOB);

(d)   freight, carriage paid (equivalent to CFR); and

(e)   freight carriage and insurance paid (equivalent to CIF).

15.4.3   Examples of Incoterms – ex works (EXW)

The burden is lightest on the seller and heaviest on the buyer, in that the buyer has to arrange and pay for collection at the seller's premises.

The seller delivers the goods when he places the goods at the disposal of the buyer at the seller's premises (or other named location, eg a warehouse).

The first point is that the place where the 'works' are has to be specified. So, it could be 'ex works Adams Waste Recycling, Pepper Street, London', for example.

The obligations on the two parties are as follows:

(a)   Seller is required to:

    (i)   supply goods conforming to the contract, measured and packed;

    (ii)   supply the invoice and any other documents;

    (iii)   deliver the goods (in the legal sense of transfer of possession) by placing them at the buyer's disposal;

    (iv)   pay for any costs incidental to placing the goods at the buyer's disposal; and

    (v)   provide further assistance to the buyer for the buyer to obtain necessary licences or insurance.

(b)   Buyer is required to:

    (i)   accept delivery of the goods and pay for them;

    (ii)   obtain appropriate licences and customs clearances; and

    (iii)   pay any costs incidental to the export of the goods.

Under EXW, the seller does not arrange for export clearance (which is, of course, only relevant to sales to a buyer located outside the EU). If the buyer were unable to arrange export clearance, then the FCA set of terms should be used instead (see **15.4.4**), providing that the seller is also willing to take on the burden and risk of loading the goods.

The purchase price would always become due on delivery of the goods unless the parties agreed otherwise.

15.4.4   Examples of Incoterms – 'F' terms: main carriage unpaid

These impose more responsibility on the seller than under the ex works terms (see **15.4.3**). Incoterms beginning with 'F' require the seller to deliver the goods for the main carriage (usually sea or air transportation) as required by the buyer. The buyer will usually arrange and pay for the main carriage and the insurance for that journey. With 'F' terms, risk in the goods passes with delivery. There is a variety of 'F' terms. The difference between the 'F' terms is the hand-over point for the goods (ie, the point of legal delivery of the goods).

15.4.4.1   Free carrier (FCA) (named place)

The seller fulfils his obligations when he delivers the goods to the carrier chosen by the buyer at the named point. The risk of loss or damage is transferred at that point. The hand-over point could be the seller's premises, or it could be the carrier's depot, especially if the goods are to be sent by container. The term is frequently used when goods are shipped by container. It can also be used for air freight. It may also be used if the seller or the buyer wishes to use their own transport.

One of the problems with using an FCA term is that the buyer arranges the sea carriage and therefore the seller does not have a bill of lading. However, documentary credits normally stipulate that the seller must produce what is known as a clean, 'on board' bill of lading as evidence that the goods have been shipped in good condition before payment can be made under the documentary credit (see **16.3.6.1**). The 2020 Incoterms now provide for the parties to agree that the buyer will instruct the carrier to issue an on-board bill of lading to the seller once the goods have been loaded on board, and for the seller then to tender the document to the buyer (often through the banks).

15.4.4.2 Free alongside ship (FAS) (named port of shipment)

Here, the seller fulfils his obligations when he delivers the goods alongside the ship (ie, on the dockside) at the named port of shipment (ie, the port of departure). The buyer will have arranged for the ship, and be paying for the sea carriage and insurance. The costs of loading the goods on to the ship will also be the buyer's expense. Given the need for tight security arrangements at ports, this is rarely used.

15.4.4.3 Free on board (FOB) (named port of shipment)

These terms impose higher obligations on the seller than FAS. Here, the seller undertakes to place the goods on board a specified ship in a specified port of shipment. All charges up to and including loading the goods on to the ship are the seller's expense. The buyer has to pay the subsequent charges, including sea freight, marine insurance, unloading charges and import duties.

Under Incoterms 2020, 'free on board' means the seller delivers the goods when the goods 'pass over the ship's rail' at the port of shipment. (If this is not suitable then FCA or FAS should be used.) The buyer has the task of making the shipping arrangements and the insurance arrangements. This delivery point in FOB is the same as for CFR and CIF (see **15.4.5**). The 'over the ship's rail' provision does not always accord with modern shipping practice, that is containerised transport and roll-on, roll-off ferries. Incoterms 2010 therefore revised the point of delivery for FOB, CFR and CIF to when the goods are 'on board' the vessel.

The risk in the goods passes with delivery, that is the goods are at the seller's risk until they cross the ship's rail in Incoterms 2000, or are 'on board' in Incoterms 2010 and 2020.

Under FOB, the following are the obligations on the seller and buyer:

(a) Seller is required to:
  (i)   supply goods conforming to the sale of goods contract;
  (ii) deliver the goods to the buyer by placing them on board the ship;
  (iii) place them on board in the position required;
  (iv) pay any costs incidental to delivery of the goods;
  (v)   obtain an export licence; and
  (vi) provide to the buyer proof of delivery to the ship.
(b) Buyer is required to:
  (i)   give sufficient notice to the seller of the time and location of the delivery point (the buyer having contracted with a carrier for the sea journey, and insured the goods from the port of shipment);
  (ii) obtain any appropriate licences;
  (iii) pay costs incidental to the importation of the goods; and
  (iv) pay for the goods.

You should be aware that there are many varieties of FOB contract used in international trade. You have to be sure which one you are using (eg, Incoterms 2010 FOB Hull).

FOB is not recommended for containerised transport.

15.4.5 Examples of Incoterms – the 'C' terms: main carriage paid

These sets of terms have more onerous obligations on the seller than the 'F' terms. In the 'C' terms, the seller arranges and pays for the main carriage, usually the sea freight. Therefore, the point up to which the seller is responsible for transport costs needs to be stated after the relevant 'C' term (eg, CIF Sydney). In the CIF and CIP terms, the seller is also responsible for arranging and paying for the insurance. However, the 'C' terms are still contracts where the goods are at the seller's risk only until completion of the first leg of the journey, before the main carriage (like in 'F' terms). So, under the 'C' terms the passing of risk differs from the place to which the seller arranges transport (it is one stage earlier in the journey). It will always be in the seller's country.

Under the 'D' terms, the risk will not pass until the goods reach their destination (see **15.4.6**).

15.4.5.1   Cost, insurance, freight (CIF) (named port of destination)

This is the typical contract where payment against documents would be used, usually on presentation of a bill of lading. In a CIF contract, the seller is in effect undertaking to arrange for the goods to be supplied and transported to the buyer's country.

The seller is required to:

(a)   ship goods conforming to the description in the contract;

(b)   clear the goods for export;

(c)   arrange a contract for sea carriage to the port of destination;

(d)   obtain a bill of lading or waybill when the goods are loaded;

(e)   arrange and pay for insurance under which the buyer can claim, and provide insurance documents to the buyer;

(f)   provide an invoice for the cost of the goods and carriage and insurance; and

(g)   transmit to the buyer the bill of lading, insurance documents and invoice, and any other documents needed.

The buyer is required to:

(a)   accept the documents tendered by the seller if they are in order;

(b)   pay the contract price;

(c)   receive the goods at the port of destination;

(d)   pay any ancillary costs of the sea voyage, and costs of unloading and land transport to the buyer's premises;

(e)   bear all risks of the goods after their passing over the ship's rail at the port of shipment;

(f)   pay all customs dues and taxes; and

(g)   obtain any import licences.

Under CIF, the price quoted to the buyer for the goods includes insurance and freight to the buyer's home port. This increases the certainty of the price for the buyer. Under an FOB contract, the buyer bears the risk of fluctuations in freight and insurance rates. The use of payment against documents means the seller will be paid quickly, and that the goods can be sold on by the buyer whilst they are still on the high seas.

Depending on what the parties have agreed, the property in the goods may pass when the buyer pays for them and accepts the documents. However, the risk in the goods has already passed to the buyer when the goods were loaded on to the ship in the port of shipment (ie, in the seller's country). Thus, CIF is an exception to SGA 1979, s 20, where prima facie risk passes with the property in the goods.

A CIF contract is always an export contract, and can be used only for sea or inland waterway transport. CIF is not recommended for containerised transport.

As with FOB, there are many variations of CIF used in the commercial world. CIF and FOB are the two commonest sets of Incoterms in commercial use.

15.4.5.2   Cost and freight (CFR) (named port of destination)

The seller has to arrange and pay for the carriage of the goods to the foreign port. He is not obliged to take out insurance for the sea voyage, which is the buyer's responsibility both to arrange and to pay for, unlike CIF. If the seller fails to give the buyer enough notice for the buyer to be able to insure the goods, the goods could be regarded as travelling at the seller's risk, under SGA 1979, s 32(3).

The CFR terms lead to a rather artificial division between the arrangements for carriage and those for insurance. As such, they are not frequently used. They may be of use where the buyer's country requires its importers to insure at home, possibly for foreign exchange reasons.

15.4.5.3 Carriage and insurance paid to (CIP) (named place of destination)

CIP tends to be used for more valuable cargoes where the buyer is able to negotiate for the seller to pay for insurance.

CIP is suitable for any mode of transport, including multimodal transport. The seller pays the freight to the named place of destination (which could be a port, as with CIF), but in addition the seller arranges and pays for insurance to that place of destination for the buyer's benefit. The risk in the goods passes when the goods are handed over to the carrier in the seller's country.

15.4.5.4 Carriage paid to (CPT) (named place of destination)

This differs from CIP in that the seller is not obliged to obtain insurance cover for the transport.

15.4.5.5 Insurance under CIF and CIP Incoterms

It is important for a buyer to be aware that the insurance arranged by the seller under a CIF contract will not necessarily cover all risks and losses, eg the goods being washed overboard. Unless otherwise agreed, the seller's insurance obligation is to provide minimum cover (essentially 'named peril' cover for 110% of the CIF invoice price). This may not be adequate to cover all situations, and the buyer should arrange any additional cover which it anticipates might be needed.

The 2020 Incoterms changed the insurance requirements in relation to CIF contracts. Here the seller is obliged to provide higher 'all risks' cover, ie, all risks that are not specifically excluded. (Bear in mind that 'all risks' is an insurance term. It does not mean that every risk is covered.) The rationale behind this is that manufactured goods, for which a CIP contract is more suitable, generally require a higher level of cover.

In neither case is cover for consequential loss included, eg for the effect of a delay which causes a buyer to miss a contract deadline. The parties may agree that the cover can be extended to include such losses, although this will be at additional cost to the seller.

15.4.6 Examples of Incoterms – the 'D' Incoterms: arrival

'D' terms impose the highest burden on the seller.

In the 'D' Incoterms, the passing of risk and delivery of the goods occur at the same time. The goods are delivered, in the legal sense, to the buyer at the place of arrival in the buyer's country, at which point risk passes as well. This is in contrast to the 'C' terms, where (legal) delivery takes place in the country of shipment (see **15.4.5**). In the case of 'D' contracts, payment by the buyer is made against the goods arriving, not against documents. However, the seller would hand over a bill of lading or a waybill to the buyer to enable the buyer to obtain delivery of the goods from the carrier.

15.4.6.1 Delivered at place (DAP) (named place of destination)

Typically under this term, delivery is at the buyer's premises but the goods are not cleared for import. Importation formalities must be therefore arranged by the buyer, including payment of any import charges.

15.4.6.2 Delivered at place unloaded (DPU) (named place of destination)

This is a new Incoterm introduced in Incoterms 2020. It replaces DAT (delivered at terminal) as it was not clear exactly what was meant by 'terminal'. Under this term, the goods are delivered, unloaded, to any named place, which could be a port or terminal or all the way to the buyer's premises. Other than the fact that it could be any place, it operates in the same way as DAP.

15.4.6.3 Delivered duty paid (DDP) (named place of destination)

These terms place the highest burden of all the Incoterms on the seller. They would normally be used only for the supply of a small quantity of goods by air.

The goods are at the seller's risk and expense until the buyer takes delivery at the place of destination in the buyer's country. Under DDP, the seller pays all charges, including import duties and carriage in the buyer's country.

There is no obligation on the seller to insure the goods under DDP.

15.5 UCC MERCANTILE OR SHIPPING TERMS

Although a detailed analysis of the UCC shipping terms is outside the scope of this book, it is worth noting that the UCC contains its own domestic delivery terms, which are commonly used in domestic transactions. Section 2-319 deals with FOB and FAS terms, Section 2-320 with CIF and C&F terms, and Section 2-322 with Delivery Ex-ship. These set out the obligations of the seller and buyer where each one is used. It is not obligatory for the parties to a contract governed by the UCC to use one of the UCC delivery terms. These can be replaced with, eg, equivalent Incoterms. Although similar, the UCC terms are not exactly the same as the equivalent Incoterms, and it is important that the differences are understood before deciding which to use.

Section 2-235 deals with Letters of Credit, and provides that a failure by the buyer to provide an agreed letter of credit amounts to a breach of contract.

SUMMARY

This chapter has introduced the shipping documents used in resolving some of the legal and practical difficulties caused by the distances involved in international sales. It has also considered the importance of Incoterms in resolving issues in relation to the transport of the goods. Next we shall consider how to resolve the problems that arise in relation to payment.

CHAPTER 16

FINANCING AND SECURITY ARRANGEMENTS IN INTERNATIONAL SALE OF GOODS

LEARNING OUTCOMES

After reading this chapter you will be able to:

- recognise the different priorities of the parties to an international sale agreement in relation to payment
- explain the nature and function of a bill of exchange
- explain the nature and function of a documentary credit
- describe the steps involved where a seller collects payment from an international buyer using a documentary credit (collection arrangements)
- explain the role and duties of the banks in facilitating payment under a documentary credit.

16.1 INTRODUCTION

An international sale of goods contract, like a domestic sale contract, will set out the payment provisions agreed between the parties. However, as discussed in **Chapter 13**, there are two main problems for the seller because of the longer payment periods involved:

(a) it needs money as soon as possible to meet its own outgoings incurred in performance of the contract, eg the costs of raw materials, labour, transport, etc; and

(b) it needs some sort of security that it will actually get paid, because the commercial risks in international sale agreements are far higher. In the event of non-payment by the buyer, the chances of recovering the goods are extremely remote once they are offshore.

If the seller is in a strong enough bargaining position, it may be able to demand payment in advance or, at the latest, before the time of shipment of the goods, but this is very much an exceptional situation. In most cases, the buyer will want to arrange for a credit period, especially as it may be some time before the goods arrive at their ultimate destination. In practice, the seller may take the length of the credit period into account in setting the price of the goods, but the economic reality for the seller is that it may still encounter cash-flow problems while waiting for payment.

These problems can be resolved by the use of negotiable instruments, eg bills of exchange, or drafts, and by the use of documentary credits. These are used in conjunction with the delivery of the shipping documents by the seller as described in **Chapter 15**. The documents are used to trigger the obligation to pay on the part of the buyer. The importance of the delivery of documents in order to facilitate payment was illustrated when the Icelandic volcano erupted, grounding flights throughout northern Europe. The ICC reported that payments under the documentary collection system were being delayed as courier companies were prevented from delivering documents.

The law relating to bills of exchange and documentary credits has developed over centuries and involves complex networks of contractual relationships between the seller, buyer and the parties' respective banks. This chapter gives an introduction to bills of exchange and documentary credits, and some of the contractual relationships involved are discussed in more detail below. However, given the complexity of this area of law, only a broad outline is possible.

Although the emphasis of this chapter is on the firmly entrenched paper based systems, again, as discussed in **Chapter 16**, the banks, shipping lines and others involved in the process are increasingly aware that these can be cumbersome, slow, prone to error and consequently expensive. New technologies, such as blockchain, are beginning to impact on trade finance. In the same way that digitalising bills of lading will reduce delays and inefficiencies, the digitalising of documentary credits and bank guarantees will provide similar benefits. The ICC estimates that it could provide a potential $1.5 trillion boost to international trade.

16.1.1   Methods of payment

There are three main methods of payment available in an international transaction:

(a)   Cash in advance. The seller may insist on payment in advance, particularly where he has not dealt with the buyer before or lacks confidence in the buyer's creditworthiness. In practice, this is unusual, and insistence on cash in advance may cause the buyer to seek the goods from other suppliers.

(b)   Payment on 'open account'. Where the parties have dealt with each other on a regular basis and the seller has complete faith in the creditworthiness of the buyer, the seller may agree to 'open account' terms. This is more favourable to the buyer than insistence on cash in advance. There are advantages for both parties, as it is cheaper than the use of a bill of exchange since bank charges will be lower. Once the seller has delivered the goods to the buyer, he will invoice the buyer. The invoice may provide for a credit period, depending on what has been agreed between the parties. There is a variety of actual payment methods, eg cheque, banker's draft, inter-bank transfer or international direct debit. Payment on 'open account' is more usual where the sale is within Europe.

(c)   Bill of exchange. Where the seller is unsure of the buyer's creditworthiness, the parties may agree for payment to be made under a bill of exchange, which is a form of negotiable instrument. This method of payment is more likely to be used if the sale is outside of the EU, as it will be more difficult to enforce payment or reclaim the goods. Payment is arranged through the international banking system. The mechanics of payment under a bill of exchange will be considered at **16.2.4**. As payment is arranged through the banking system, it is a more expensive method than using 'open account' methods.

The method of payment will be agreed between the parties and will depend on a variety of factors, including the bargaining strength of the parties. It will be provided for in the sale contract.

16.1.2   Guarantee of payment

Whichever method of payment is chosen, it does not always guarantee payment. To secure the seller's position, it is possible for the buyer to arrange for a third party, generally a bank, to provide documentary credits. These are contractual undertakings by which the bank itself will guarantee payment, provided that the seller complies with the terms of the credit (usually by providing specified documents). As above, payment may be by any method agreed by the parties. See **16.3.6.5**. The advantage of a documentary credit is that the seller can be guaranteed payment before it ships the goods. Clearly, the promise of payment by the bank to the seller is dependent on the buyer's agreement to reimburse the bank. In addition, such guarantees come at a price, and the buyer will incur considerable expense in putting in place the necessary arrangements for a documentary credit.

16.1.3 Relationship between bills of exchange and documentary credits

Documentary credits and bills of exchange have very different uses and functions; they are very different entities in law, aimed at solving very different problems.

(a) The primary function of the bill of exchange is as a means of providing payment to the seller, by way of an easily transferable document rather than the straightforward payment of cash.

(b) The main function of a documentary credit is to help guarantee that the seller will be paid. It is a promise provided by a third party bank, or financial institution, that the seller will be paid, even if the buyer defaults. Although similar to a bank guarantee, the two should not be confused as the obligations of the parties differ.

The provision of a documentary credit will be required where the seller is unwilling to contract with the buyer without one, eg because it has no knowledge of the credit history of the buyer, and where it is powerful enough to get its own way. Where a documentary credit has been agreed, the sale contract will oblige the buyer to open the credit within a specified time from the date of the contract. A documentary credit creates separate contractual obligations on the part of the bank additional to and independent of the sale contract and the buyer's obligation to pay for the goods.

16.2 BILLS OF EXCHANGE

Bills of exchange (or 'drafts') are defined in s 3(1) of the UK Bills of Exchange Act 1882 (BEA 1882) as follows:

> A bill of exchange is an unconditional order in writing, addressed by one person to another, signed by the person giving it, requiring the person to whom it is addressed to pay on demand or at a fixed or determinable future time, a sum certain in money to or to the order of a specified person, or to a bearer.

In other words, a bill of exchange is a document under which one party (the 'drawer') orders another party, usually a bank or financier (the 'drawee') to pay a specified sum of money to a third party (the 'payee') or to bearer. A bill of exchange will specify the place of payment (eg, 'payable in Rio de Janeiro at XY bank').

A cheque is defined as a 'bill of exchange drawn on a banker, payable on demand' (BEA 1882, s 73). A cheque is therefore a sub-species of a bill of exchange.

Typical characteristics of a bill of exchange are:

(a) every obligation in the bill must be expressed in writing;

(b) the order to pay must be unconditional;

(c) it is addressed by one person to another;

(d) it is payable on demand or at a fixed time in the future (see **16.2.1**);

(e) it is for a specific sum of money;

(f) the drawer, or his agent, must have signed it;

(g) the obligations, typically payment, may be transferred by 'negotiation', usually at a discount (see **16.2.2.1**); and

(h) performance of the obligations (eg payment) may be demanded only by the person holding the bill.

Before considering the mechanics of how payment will be made under a bill of exchange, it is useful to look at some of the terminology involved.

16.2.1 Types of bill

16.2.1.1 Sight bills and term bills

The type of bill determines when it will be paid:

(a) 'Sight' bills are payable on demand, ie on presentation to the drawee, usually a bank, so payment is immediate. They are less important commercially than term bills. A cheque is an example of a sight bill. It is payable when it is presented to the drawer's bank.

(b) 'Term' bills provide for payment at some specified date in the future. This is usually 90 or 180 days from the date of presentation, eg '90 days after sight'. The advantage of a term bill is that it can be used to provide the buyer with a credit period. The rest of this chapter will deal with term, rather than sight, bills.

16.2.1.2 Bearer bills and order bills

A bill may either be payable to 'bearer', or may direct payment to, or to the order of, a specified person.

(a) Bearer bills may be transferred merely by delivery, like a bank note. The drawee (see **16.2.3**) is simply obliged to pay out to whoever happens to possess the bill at the relevant time. There is no obligation on the drawee to check how the holder has obtained the bill. Bearer bills are clearly very insecure and are not used much in practice.

(b) Order bills specify payment to a particular person or to his order, like a cheque. In order to make a bill non-transferable, it is essential to state this specifically, eg 'pay X only'.

An order bill may be 'opened up' into a bearer bill by the present holder indorsing it in blank (ie signing his name only on the back), and then 'closed down' again by indorsing it to a particular person (ie the holder signing his name with the words 'pay X or order'). A bearer bill, however, cannot be 'closed down'. (Cheques used to be widely negotiable but, as a fraud prevention measure, most cheques are now printed with crossing lines and 'a/c payee', which prevents them being transferable by endorsement.)

16.2.1.3 Documentary, clean and claused bills

Where payment of the bill is stated to be against documents, ie the seller must provide stipulated shipping documents, it is known as a 'documentary bill'. If payment is not against documents, ie the bank will pay simply on presentation of the bill, it is described as a 'clean' bill.

A bill of exchange is not normally set out as simply as a personal cheque – it has 'clauses'. There could be provisions, for example, dealing with exchange rates for currencies, or stating that the bill is payable with bankers' charges. If a bill does not stipulate that incidental charges are borne by the drawee (the bank) then they are borne by the drawer (buyer of the goods). An example of a simple draft bill of exchange (without clauses) is set out on p 198.

16.2.2 Negotiable instruments

A bill of exchange is a type of negotiable instrument. Negotiable instruments include:

(a) cheques;
(b) bills of exchange;
(c) bank notes;
(d) banker's drafts; and
(e) promissory notes (in some circumstances).

An 'instrument' is a document which evidences the holder's right to enforce a legal right, such as a promise to pay a sum of money (a 'promissory note') or an order to someone else to pay out a sum of money (a bill of exchange).

In this context, 'negotiation' means the giving and receiving of documents which evidence promises to pay and to receive money, as a 'substitute' for handing over the money itself. Where the documents are freely transferable, the documents are said to be 'negotiable'.

One significant advantage of a bill of exchange is that the document itself, the bill, is transferable, so that payment may be demanded not only by the original payee, but also by anyone who has possession of it at the relevant time for payment. Thus a bill of exchange may be bought and sold like any other commodity. The way in which a bill is transferred is by the holder 'indorsing' it (ie signing his name on the back of the bill).

16.2.2.1 Discounting

This ability to transfer a bill of exchange means that term bills can be used by the seller to raise money before payment becomes due, by selling the bill on to a third party. Whoever buys the bill will be able to present the bill for payment (unless he sells it on to someone else). The buyer will pay less than the face value of the bill to take into account the delay in receiving payment. This is known as 'discounting'. This use of a bill gives considerable flexibility to the seller in its need to raise interim finance.

For discounting to work, it is important that the buyer knows that the drawee of the bill (usually a bank) will pay up when the payment date is due. Term bills are therefore presented to the drawee which will indorse its 'acceptance' on the face of the bill, thus guaranteeing payment of the bill in the future (see **16.2.4**). When payment is due, the bill is re-presented to the drawee for payment. Thus, a term bill must be presented twice to the bank, and payment is due on the second occasion.

16.2.2.2 The 'holder in due course'

The problem for the ultimate holder is that the bill might have been stolen, or one of the previous holders of the bill might have had some other defect in his title to the bill. However, rules have developed to protect the 'holder in due course'. Under s 29(1) of the BEA 1882, a holder in due course is anyone who gives value for a bill which is still current and which appears to be perfectly regular on the face of it. Provided a holder in due course has taken the bill in good faith, and without knowledge of any defects in the title to the bill, he will take the bill 'free from equities'. This means that he can ignore any defects in the title of anyone who had held the bill before him. There is a presumption in favour of a holder that he is a holder in due course.

There are two other types of holder under the 1882 Act: 'holders for value', and mere 'holders'. They have fewer rights than a holder in due course, and are beyond the scope of this chapter.

16.2.3 Parties to the bill of exchange

There are three original parties to a bill of exchange:

(a)   drawer;

(b)   drawee; and

(c)   payee.

Perhaps the analogy of a personal cheque is the easiest one to visualise. Here, you would be the drawer of the cheque, your bank would be the drawee (eg, Barclays Bank) and the payee would be the person you are paying (eg, your landlord). The biggest difference from a personal cheque is that with a term bill, the drawee must 'accept' the bill by signing it in order to become liable to pay out on it (see **16.2.4**). Once it has done so, it becomes known as the 'acceptor'.

16.2.4 Collection arrangements

The term 'collection arrangements' or 'documentary collection' describes the mechanics by which the seller collects payment under a documentary bill. A bill of exchange is normally drawn either against (or guaranteed by) a documentary credit, or alternatively against the documents themselves, when it will be known as a 'documentary bill'. A documentary bill is used where the seller wishes to guard against the possibility of not getting paid, but is not in a strong enough bargaining position to be able to demand a documentary credit (see **16.3**). The problem about delivering documents of title, such as a bill of lading (see **15.3.1**), direct to the buyer is that there is a serious risk of non-payment for the seller. Often the buyer sells the goods on (and transfers the bill of lading) to a third party whilst the goods are still at sea, and the seller loses control of the goods. The advantage of a documentary bill is that it uses the banking system to safeguard the seller's position so it can be reduce the risk of non-payment.

Given the analogy of a cheque (see **16.2.3**), it would be logical to assume that the basic position would be that the drawer is the buyer, the drawee is the buyer's bank, and the payee is the seller of the goods. However, with a bill of exchange, the position is as follows:

(a)   the seller is the drawer;

(b)   the buyer or his bank is the drawee; and

(c)   the seller is the payee, ie the drawer and the payee are the same.

To see how the collection arrangements work, assume that a UK seller, Wood Magic, has entered into a CIF contract with an Australian buyer, Franklin Furnishings Ltd. The parties have agreed a 90-day credit period. The sale contract will provide for a term bill of exchange, and that the documents will be tendered against acceptance. (This is usually abbreviated in the contact to 'D/A' ('documents against acceptance').) The buyer has made the necessary arrangements through its bank in Australia.

(The law and practice in this area can be complex. The following account is simplified. You may wish to make reference to works on this subject, particularly if you come across this area in practice.)

(a)   Wood Magic ships the goods as agreed in the sale contract, and forwards the bill of exchange with the shipping documents (commercial invoice, bill of lading and the insurance policy) to its own bank in the UK (known as the 'remitting bank').

(b)   Wood Magic's bank will then pass the shipping documents together with the bill of exchange to Franklin's bank in Australia (known as the 'collecting bank'). The safeguard for Wood Magic is that the documents do not go directly to the buyer.

(c)   The collecting bank will either forward the bill of exchange to Franklin for acceptance, or, more usually, accept the bill on behalf of the buyer. A bill is accepted by signing the front of the bill. If the bank does this, it will become the 'acceptor'. At this stage, Wood Magic can discount the bill. If the bill is not accepted it is 'dishonoured', and Wood Magic can immediately sue Franklin.

(d)   The documents will be released to Franklin only on acceptance of the bill of exchange. Once Franklin has the documents, it will be able to use them to obtain possession of the goods from the carrier (or to sell them on whilst still in transit), as it now has the documents of title. A further safeguard for Wood Magic is that the collecting bank should not release the documents to Franklin until acceptance has taken place or it will be liable, even if it is not the acceptor.

(e)   The collecting bank will either advise the seller of acceptance and hold the bill until the end of the credit period, or return it to Wood Magic. If Wood Magic has discounted the bill, it will transfer it to any subsequent holder of the bill.

(f)   When the bill matures, the Australian bank will pay out on the bill and recover the money from Franklin.

These arrangements may be varied by the agreement of the parties, usually to suit commercial convenience. A commonly agreed practice is for the seller to draw up the bill and to present it to its own bank for acceptance. The seller's bank acts as both remitting and collecting bank. This will be the case, for example, where the parties have agreed that payment will be guaranteed by a confirmed documentary credit. (see **16.3.4.2**). This has the advantage of keeping the bill of exchange in the seller's country, which makes it easier to enforce payment. Clearly, the seller's bank will be prepared to accept the bill only if it has already agreed with the buyer's bank that the buyer's bank will reimburse it in return for the documents required to perform the sale of goods contract.

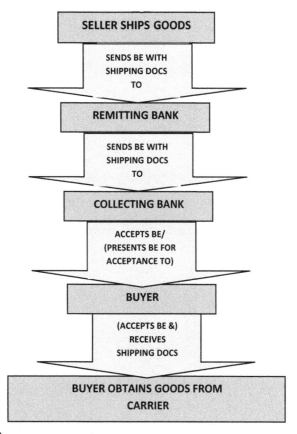

Figure 16.1 Collection arrangements

16.2.5   The relationship of the bill of exchange and underlying sales contracts

The obligation to pay on a bill of exchange is unconditional, and will not be affected by any defect or breach of the underlying sales contract on the part of the seller. Thus the obligation to pay under the bill of exchange is the result of a separate contract and remains unaffected, even if the goods are defective. In other words, a bill of exchange has an autonomy of its own.

The only real exception to this is if there is complete or partial failure of consideration by the seller. If the seller sues for payment, the buyer can raise the breach as a defence to a claim for refusal to pay the bill. The claim is a claim on the bill of exchange, on a promise that the paper could be turned into cash. It is not a claim for breach of the payment obligations under the underlying sales contract.

16.2.6   Liability on a bill of exchange

With our example (at **16.2.4**), the primary liability is clearly intended to be on the Australian bank as acceptor of the bill. If the bank refuses to accept, ie 'dishonours', the bill then Franklin will be secondarily liable. As discussed above, Wood Magic can immediately sue Franklin.

BILL OF EXCHANGE

(DRAFT)

No ....

Exchange for .... [AMOUNT] [6] .... [DATE] .... 20 ....

.... [AT SIGHT/90 DAYS AFTER DATE] [5] .... of this BILL OF EXCHANGE

pay to the order of [4] .... [OURSELVES] .... the sum of ....

[AMOUNT IN WORDS] ....

To   NORTH EAST BANK plc[2]   FOR AND ON BEHALF OF
      COMMERCIAL ROAD, DALEBY,   NORTHERN SPINNERS LTD[1,3]
      EAST YORKSHIRE, DN1 72Y

                                               _____
                                               DIRECTOR

1. addressed by one person (the drawer)
2. to another (the drawee), here the seller's bank
3. signed by the person giving it (the drawer)
4. requiring the person to whom it is addressed to pay to the order of a specified person or to bearer (the payee)
5. on demand, or at a fixed or determinable future time
6. a certain sum in money.

[Note: acceptance by signature will be required with a 'term bill' (see point 5 in this example and **16.2.1**); it is quite normal to insert words of acceptance on the face of the bill, but this is not essential as signature will suffice without more. With a sight or demand bill, no signature is required.]

On maturity, at the end of the credit period, the bill in the Wood Magic example above will be expressed to be payable at the Australian bank. The bill will be exchanged for payment. If payment is 'in due course', the bill will be discharged and no longer be legally operative.

Under s 59(1) payment 'in due course' means payment to the holder on the date the bill matures or some time afterwards, in good faith and without notice of any defect in the holder's title. If the Australian bank does not pay, the holder of the bill may sue the bank.

This is a very general statement of the liability situation, and reference should be made to other texts for dealing with detailed questions, such as liability and indemnity between different parties.

16.2.7 The function of the bill of exchange in international trade

The bill of exchange performs many functions in international trade including the following:

(a)   It facilitates the granting of trade credit in a legal format by permitting payments on agreed future dates.

(b)   It provides formal evidence of the demand for payment from a seller to a buyer.

(c)   It provides the seller with access to finance by permitting them to transfer their debts to a bank or other financier by merely indorsing the bill of exchange to that bank or financier.

(d)   It permits the banker or financier to retain a valid legal claim on both the buyer and the seller. In certain circumstances, a bank or financier may have a stronger legal claim under a bill than the party that sold them the debt.

(e)   It permits a seller to obtain greater security over the payment by enabling a bank to guarantee a drawee's acceptance (guarantee to pay on the due date) by signing or endorsing the bill.

(f)   It allows a seller to protect his access to the legal system in the event of problems, while providing easier access to that legal system.

16.2.8 UNCITRAL Convention on International Bills of Exchange and International Promissory Notes (1988)

The UNCITRAL Convention on International Bills of Exchange and International Promissory Notes was adopted in 1988. It is designed to harmonise the rules relating to bills of exchange and negotiable instruments, by setting out a new set of rules for optional use in international transactions. The Convention is not yet in force as it has not yet been ratified by the necessary 10 states, but parties may choose to use negotiable instruments which are governed by its provisions.

In order to apply, the bill of exchange must be headed 'International bill of exchange (UNCITRAL Convention)' or, in the case of a promissory note, 'International promissory note (UNCITRAL Convention)', and this wording must be included in the wording of the bill or note (Article 1). It does not apply to cheques.

16.3 DOCUMENTARY CREDITS

We have just looked at the use of bills of exchange and other ways to facilitate the payment to the seller, but payment may never be made at all if the buyer refuses to, or cannot, pay for the goods, for example because of insolvency. In international (and sometimes in domestic) sales of goods, it is quite common for the seller to require a documentary credit ('letter of credit') to be opened, as a guarantee that the buyer will comply with its payment obligations once it presents the documents specified in the credit to the bank. See **16.3.6.5**.

Where the parties have agreed that a documentary credit will be opened, the contract of sale will provide that the buyer will arrange (and pay for) the credit. The buyer will enter into an agreement with a bank (often its own bank), under which the bank provides a written assurance (the documentary credit) that, if the seller properly performs its side of the contract, the bank will pay the seller. The bank acts directly as principal towards the seller, and not simply as a guarantor if the buyer does not pay. Therefore the bank, rather than the buyer, pays the seller, and the seller's rights are directly enforceable against it.

Documentary credit

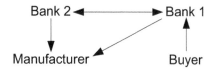

1.   Bank 1 guarantees the buyer will pay.
2.   With a confirmed DC, Bank 2 guaranteees as well.
3.   Revocable can be cancelled, irrevocable cannot.

16.3.1 What is a documentary credit?

Almost all documentary credits are regulated by the Uniform Customs and Practice for Documentary Credits (UCP) published by the ICC. The current version is UCP 600 (2007 revision, which came into effect on 1 July 2007), which consists of 39 articles which regulate documentary credits. (Note that the UCP rules are not statutory rules. Like Incoterms (see **15.4**), they must be incorporated into the contract to be effective. Usually, the credit itself will state that it is subject to the UCP 600.)

The definition of a 'documentary credit' in Art 2 of UCP 600 is:

> Any arrangement, however named or described, ... that is irrevocable and thereby constitutes a definite undertaking of the issuing bank to honour a complying presentation.

To 'honour' means to fulfil the credit arrangement by one or another of the payment methods discussed in **16.1.1**. A 'complying presentation' of documents is one that is in accordance with the terms and conditions of the credit, the applicable provisions of the UCP and with international standard banking practice.

The ICC has also produced a supplement to the UCP 600, the Uniform Customs Practice for Documentary Credits (Supplement for Electronic Presentation), the eUCP, which is designed to address issues arising from the increasing use of electronic letters of credit and electronic presentation of documents.

Like the UCP 600, the eUCP must be incorporated into the contract if the parties wish to present documents electronically.

A specimen documentary credit is reproduced below. This will be used to illustrate how a documentary credit works.

16.3.2 Advantages and disadvantages of documentary credits

The use of a documentary credit has advantages for all the parties, as set out in **Table 16.1** below. The main disadvantage is the cost to the buyer of using letters of credit. These are very expensive to arrange, and the less creditworthy the buyer, the more expensive the credit, because of the risk to the credit supplier. Clearly, a seller is able to obtain a documentary credit only if it has enough bargaining power. However, the buyer may be compensated by a reduction in the price of the goods.

Advantages for the seller	Advantages for the buyer	Advantages for the bank
Insolvency of B is less of a risk	Added security for the seller is likely to be reflected in price of goods.	Possession of documents protects its position if B fails to refund

Advantages for the seller	Advantages for the buyer	Advantages for the bank
Guarantees payment from an early stage in transaction	Documents examined by professional staff at bank(s) so more likely to be in order.	
Can deal with a bank in its own country		
Further protection can be offered by 'confirmed' credit		

Table 16.1 Advantages and disadvantages of a documentary credit

16.3.3   How a documentary credit works

To illustrate how a documentary credit works, assume that as well as agreeing to payment by means of a 90-day bill of exchange, Wood Magic and Franklin (see **6.2.4**) have agreed to a confirmed irrevocable letter of credit.

Lloyds TSB
Commercial

an irrevocable letter of credit

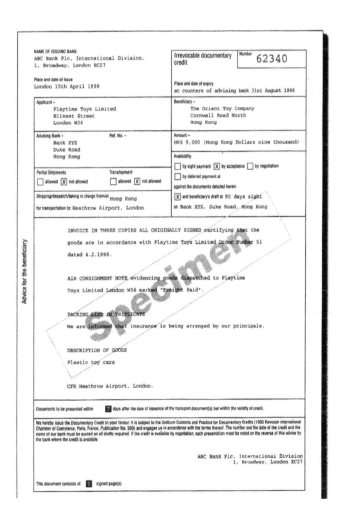

16.3.3.1   Arranging the credit

The buyer, Franklin, will go to a bank in its own country and ask the bank to set up a documentary credit in favour of the seller, Wood Magic. In practice, the bank to be used will have been agreed between the parties. The buyer is the 'Applicant' and the seller is the 'Beneficiary'. Clearly, the buyer will have to pay for this service, and the provision of a documentary credit, particularly a confirmed credit, is expensive. This is why it has to be a term of the sale contract between the buyer and the seller, and, as discussed, the buyer is unlikely to agree unless it is in a weak bargaining position.

16.3.3.2   Notification of the credit

Once the Australian bank has agreed to the credit being opened, it will issue the letter of credit (the bank will clearly be unwilling to do so unless it is assured that the buyer has the funds to reimburse it, so generally the buyer will either deposit funds to cover this, or have sufficient credit with the bank). It will ask another bank in the UK to advise Wood Magic that the credit has been opened. The Australian bank is the 'Issuing Bank' and the UK bank is the 'Advising Bank'. The Advising Bank is usually a bank with which the Issuing Bank has a special arrangement. (If the seller banks at one of the major international banks, it will usually be able to arrange for its own bank to be the Advising Bank.) As this is a confirmed credit, the Advising Bank will add its confirmation to the credit, thus becoming the 'Confirming Bank' (see **16.3.3.3**). **Figure 16.2** below illustrates how the transaction works.

16.3.3.3   Role of the banks in relation to the documents

Once Wood Magic has been notified of the credit, it will ship the goods and send the bank the documents stipulated in the credit. The documents are examined for 'strict compliance' to ensure that they comply with the terms of the credit (see **16.3.6.2**). This will often involve two detailed examinations, one by the Advising/Confirming Bank and another by the Issuing Bank upon transfer to it of the documents. This is because either bank may be liable for wrongfully accepting or rejecting documents. If the documents comply with the credit, the Advising/Confirming Bank will pay out the seller in accordance with the chosen payment method shown on the credit itself. (Again, the transaction has been simplified.)

16.3.4   Types of documentary credit

Documentary credits can be of different types. The type of credit will be agreed between the parties and provided for in contract of sale.

16.3.4.1   Revocable and irrevocable credits

A revocable credit may be cancelled or 'revoked' by the buyer at any time. Thus it is, to all intents and purposes, useless in guaranteeing payment. Once an irrevocable letter of credit has been notified to the seller, the buyer is powerless to countermand it. Under the UCP 600, all credits are now irrevocable, unless the parties state otherwise. (The previous version, UCP 500, did extend to revocable credits, and the parties can agree to make the agreement subject to the UCP 500 rather than the UCP 600.)

The use of revocable credits is rare, and so the rest of this chapter will concentrate on irrevocable credits.

16.3.4.2   Confirmed and unconfirmed letters of credit

Even an irrevocable credit is not the ideal arrangement for the seller. If the buyer's bank does not pay for any reason, the seller will have to take action against a foreign bank in a different country. The best arrangement for the seller is to insist that the credit is 'confirmed'. Here the Advising Bank (in the seller's country) will add its own undertaking to that of the Issuing Bank that it will pay under the terms of the credit, ie it confirms the credit (and becomes the 'Confirming Bank').

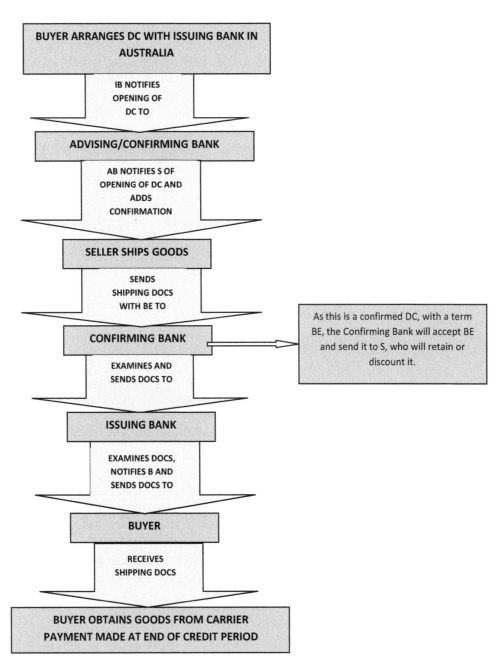

Figure 16.2 Documentary credit transaction

16.3.5 Contractual relationships

The relationships of the parties with the banks involved depends on which type of credit is used:

(a)   With an unconfirmed letter of credit, the Advising Bank is simply an agent of the Issuing Bank, and its only function is to notify the seller and receive the documents. Other banking arrangements may be entered into, eg there may be a Nominated Bank, authorised by the Issuing Bank to pay, negotiate, issue a different payment undertaking or accept drafts under the documentary credit. This facilitates collection and payment in the seller's country.

(b)   With a confirmed letter of credit, the Confirming Bank is adding its own guarantee of payment. It is, in effect, entering into a separate banking contract (as principal, not as an agent) with the seller to pay, provided that the seller provides the documents stipulated in the letter of credit. If the Confirming Bank fails to pay, the seller can sue it direct without needing to claim against the Issuing Bank.

Thus the setting up of a documentary credit gives rise to a complex network of contractual relationships. In relation to a confirmed documentary credit, these were summarised by Lord Diplock in *United City Merchants (Investments) Ltd v Royal Bank of Canada* [1938] 1 AC 168: 'It is trite law that there are four autonomous though interconnected contractual relationships involved.' In fact, as Malek and Quest point out in *Jack: Documentary Credits* (4th edn, Bloomsbury Professional, 2009), there are in fact five separate contracts, as Lord Diplock overlooked the contract between the confirming bank and the beneficiary. These are between:

(a)   Buyer and Seller (ie the sale contract);
(b)   Buyer and Issuing Bank;
(c)   Issuing Bank and Confirming Bank;
(d)   Issuing Bank and Beneficiary;
(e)   Confirming Bank and Beneficiary.

The exact nature of these contracts is beyond the scope of this book, but the case illustrates the complexity of the relationships involved.

16.3.6   Practical considerations

Where the documentary credit does not comply with the provisions of the sale contract, the buyer will be in breach of contract. In addition, the obligations of the buyer and the seller in relation to the documentary credit are regulated by the UCP 600.

16.3.6.1   What documents must be presented under a documentary credit?

As well as specifying what type of credit the buyer must arrange (eg irrevocable and unconfirmed), the sale contract will also have to specify what documents have to be presented in order to receive payment under the credit. The documents required will also be set out in the credit itself (see the specimen credit on p 201 for an example of this). This will depend on the Incoterm agreed between the parties (see **15.4**). For example, in a CIF contract, the documents will be a clean bill of lading, the insurance policy and a commercial invoice. Further documentation, eg a packing list or certificate of inspection, may be agreed between the parties. The seller must present documents that comply exactly with the terms of the credit in order to be paid (see **16.3.7.2**).

16.3.6.2   When is the credit to be provided?

The sale contract will normally specify when the credit is to be provided. If nothing is mentioned in the contract, generally the credit should be opened no later than the earliest shipping date under the contract. (If no opening date is specified in the sale contract, there will be an implied term that the credit will open and be advised to the seller within a reasonable period before the shipment date.) The seller will not be under an obligation to ship the goods unless the buyer has opened a credit in accordance with the terms of the contract. Failure to do so within the specified time period gives the seller the right to terminate the contract, or waive the breach and sue for damages.

16.3.6.3   How long must the credit last?

The sale contract will specify for how long the credit is to be opened, and this will also appear in the credit itself. Under Art 6 of UCP 600, all credits must stipulate an expiry date and a place for presentation of documents. The specimen documentary credit above has a clear issue and expiry date. The seller thus knows exactly for how long he is covered by the credit.

16.3.6.4   Presentation of the documents

The documents must be presented before the expiry date of the credit. The credit should also state a period of time after shipment within which the documents should be tendered by the seller. Under Art 14 of UCP 600, if no such period is stated, 21 days only is allowed. So, the longstop date for presenting documents is either the expiry date of the credit, or 21 days after shipment, whichever occurs first.

16.3.6.5   Methods of payment under a documentary credit

In the Wood Magic example above, the method payment chosen by the parties is a term bill of exchange. The documentary credit could provide for any one of four methods of payment:

(a)   Cash on presentation of the documents by the seller – 'payment at sight'. Here the Advising/Confirming Bank will make immediate payment on receipt (or 'sight') of the documents.

(b)   Cash at some future time, eg after 90 days – 'deferred payment'. The bank will examine the specified documents, but it will not make payment until the date specified in the credit.

(c)   A bill of exchange drawn by the seller, probably a term bill payable at a future date – 'acceptance credit'. Here the seller presents the bill of exchange with the stipulated documents, and the bank accepts the bill of exchange. If the credit is unconfirmed, the Issuing Bank will accept the bill. If the credit is confirmed, the Confirming Bank will accept the bill. Once the bank has accepted the bill of exchange, there will be no further obligation under the terms of the documentary credit.

(d)   Negotiating a bill of exchange drawn by the seller – 'negotiation credit'. Once the seller has produced the correct documentation, and the bill has been accepted, the seller can negotiate the bill.

The sale contract will specify which method of payment is to be used. In addition, the method of payment will be specified in the credit itself. The specimen credit sets out four options shown on it: payment in cash on sight of the documents; by acceptance of a bill of exchange; by negotiating a bill of exchange; and by a deferred cash payment. The acceptance option has been chosen on the specimen.

It is important to remember that a documentary credit is not generally a method of payment. 'Payment' in this context does not necessarily mean that the seller will receive cash in return for the documentary credit. If the method of payment is an accepted term bill of exchange, the seller may not be paid until the bill matures. The bill itself will set out how the seller will be paid and when. The purpose of obtaining the documentary credit in this example will be to ensure that the bill of exchange is accepted.

16.3.6.6   Reimbursement

Clearly, where a bank has undertaken to pay out on the documentary credit, it will want to be reimbursed. Where the Confirming Bank has made the payment, the UCP 600 provides that it is entitled to be reimbursed by the Issuing Bank. The Issuing Bank is then entitled to be reimbursed by the buyer. The Issuing Bank can protect its position by retaining the documents until it is certain of payment from the buyer. As between the banks themselves, further protection is given by the Uniform Rules for Bank-to-Bank Reimbursement under Documentary Credits (URR 725).

16.3.7   Duties of the banks in relation to the documents

There are two fundamental principles of documentary credits, which affect the position of the banks involved. These are:

(a)   the autonomy of the documentary credit; and

(b) the doctrine of strict compliance.

16.3.7.1 The autonomy of the documentary credit

Once in place, the credit contract is autonomous and has a separate life of its own. Although the sale contract is the contract which imposes the obligation for the documentary credit to be opened, the documentary credit itself is completely independent from the underlying sale of goods contract. It is also generally independent of any contracts arising out of the associated use of bills of exchange. The banks involved are not concerned with issues relating to either of these. For example, once an irrevocable documentary credit has been opened, the buyer cannot instruct the Issuing Bank to withdraw the credit, even if the seller has shipped goods which do not comply with the contract. Under Art 4 of UCP 600, 'banks are in no way concerned' with the underlying contracts for sale. Banks only need to ensure that the documents provided by the seller are in accordance with the instructions of the buyer. Article 5 specifically states: 'Banks deal with documents and not with goods, services or performance to which the documents may relate.'

16.3.7.2 The doctrine of strict compliance

As discussed above (**16.3.6.1**), in order to be paid the seller must present the documents to the relevant bank for examination. (In the Wood Magic example it would be the Advising/Confirming Bank which would then forward the documents to the Issuing Bank.) Under Art 14 of UCP 600, the purpose of the examination is to see whether the documents comply with the terms of the credit. The bank must only pay over the money if the seller provides exactly the right documents which strictly comply with the terms of the credit. If, for example, the documentary credit stipulates that a clean bill of lading must be provided, a claused bill will not suffice.

In *Equitable Trust Company of New York v Dawson Partners Ltd* (1927) 27 Ll L Rep 49, which concerned a fraudulent seller and a contract to buy vanilla beans from Indonesia, Sumner LJ summed up the position: 'There is no room for documents which are almost the same or which will do just as well.'

The bank is under a duty to take 'reasonable care' in the examination of the documents. As long as the documents appear, on their face, to comply with the terms of the credit, the bank will be protected. It does not need to go 'digging' for defects. An example of this is *Gian Singh & Co Ltd v Banque de l'Indochine* [1974] 1 WLR 1234. The Privy Council allowed the defence of a bank that used reasonable care in complying with the prima facie requirements of a documentary credit, notwithstanding that one of the specified documents was in fact a forgery. Thus the visual appearance of compliance is all that needs to be determined on presentation of the documents.

If the bank wrongly accepts or rejects documents, it will be liable for the loss.

16.3.7.3 The fraud exception to acceptance of complying documents

The only exception to the doctrine of strict compliance is fraud. The likely scenarios are that one or more of the documents is a forgery (or has been altered in a material matter), or that the beneficiary or his agent is a party to a fraudulent transaction involving the goods. Even so, the fraud has to be pretty clear-cut before the bank could be restrained from making payment (*Czarnikow-Rionda Sugar Trading Inc v Standard Bank London Ltd and Others* [1999] 1 All ER (Comm) 890). That case is a good illustration of the general reluctance of judges in commercial law cases to interfere with established commercial practices, in this case reliance upon documentary credits (letters of credit). Thus, Rix J held:

> ... even if I assume for the sake of argument that Rionda [the buyer] has otherwise brought itself within the fraud exception, its claim against Standard [the bank] for a pre-trial injunction must fail on the balance of convenience alone. I would seek to put the matter in the following way.

(1) The interest in the integrity of banking contracts is so great that not even fraud can be allowed to intervene unless the fraud comes to the notice of the bank (a) in time, ie in any event before the beneficiary is paid, and (b) in such a way that it can be said that the bank had knowledge of the fraud.

... Unless the banking commitment can be insulated from disputes between merchants, international trade would become impossible.

(2) ... Once, however, a letter of credit arrangement has been set up, the special rule that only the fraud exception permits interference comes into play.

(3) Thus, in the absence of the fraud exception, a buyer can no more seek to prevent his seller from drawing on the letter of credit for which the seller has stipulated, than the buyer can seek to prevent his bank from making the payment under it. The reason is that otherwise the special rule could be subverted, and the integrity and insulation of banking contracts could be overthrown, simply by the device of injuncting the beneficiary rather than the bank.

So, Rix J would not allow an injunction to prevent the bank from paying out on the documentary credit, or an injunction to prevent the seller from drawing on the documentary credit. Instead, he suggested that the claimant could seek a freezing ('Mareva') order against the seller's bank accounts, so that the proceeds of the alleged fraud could not be disposed of before the dispute was resolved.

SUMMARY

The parties to international sale of goods agreements have different priorities in relation to payment. The seller will want to be assured of payment before it parts with the goods, and the buyer will not want to pay until the goods arrive in good condition. These differences may be resolved by the use of bills of exchange and documentary credits. We have considered how these work in practice and the mechanics of the collection arrangements. This concludes the overview of international sale of goods contracts. Part III deals with intellectual property rights and their importance in a commercial contract.

INTERNATIONAL SALE AGREEMENTS

Topic	Summary
Jurisdiction	This term means that a court has the constitutional power to hear and decide a legal matter between parties. These powers extend to geographical limits as well as to the range of persons and issues which fall within the legal competence of any particular court or system of courts. Any attempt by a court to give a legal ruling outside of its jurisdiction will result in a nullity, both in the place for which the court has jurisdiction, as well as elsewhere in the world. Many nations and States recognise the jurisdictions and judgments of other countries as a matter of international convention.
	Since 1 January 2021, when EU Regulation 1215/2012 ('Brussels I') ceased to apply, jurisdiction is governed by a combination of existing common law rules, statute and the Hague Convention on Choice of Court Agreements. This has created a degree of uncertainty, and it is therefore important that a contract should include an express choice of jurisdiction.
Choice of applicable law	When any court has to decide a civil legal dispute, it also has to decide what national system of law should be applied to decide the issues. In the areas with which this text deals, these are mainly contractual issues and the question is of which national law is applicable to the contract or, if more than one system is applied to different parts of the contract, which systems should be applied. Generally, if the parties have made an express choice in a contract, that choice will be respected and applied by the court.
	This is governed by Regulation 593/2008 ('Rome I') which forms part of EU retained law. This provides a system of prima facie rules which help a court decide which country's law is applicable for a particular contract. The rules may result in the court applying the law of a country which either or both of the parties would not have chosen. It is therefore important that the contract should include an express choice of law.
Bill of lading	This is a document provided by a carrier of goods over water to the person who is shipping the goods, ie sending them off to somewhere else. Its function is to show that the goods have been received by the carrier, to show their quantity and condition, to show the terms under which the goods are being carried and, if necessary, to act as a document of title to show the right to sell the goods or to take possession of them from the carrier, at the end of the journey.

Topic	Summary
Multimodal transport	This term refers to the method of transporting goods from one place to another where the goods, typically packed into steel containers, may easily be carried by a succession of different vehicles and vessels. Such a trip might initially involve road transport, then cargo air transport, then further road or inland waterway transport, to its ultimate destination.
Incoterms	These are a comprehensive set of standard-form contracts, drawn up by the International Chamber of Commerce, to allow for international transport of goods. They are based on long-settled mercantile practices and provide contracts under which the rights and responsibilities of the parties are very clearly laid out and recognised. The terms deal particularly with demarcation of responsibility for timing and place of delivery, responsibility for cost allocation and arrangement of the different stages of the transport process, insurance obligations, etc. They are designed to be incorporated by simple reference within sale of goods contracts, with or without express modification.
Negotiable instrument	This refers to a variety of written documents, which are intended to form the subject matter of contractual promises to exchange money for the written document itself. The paper is treated as being equivalent to a certain amount of money, and the right to the money represented by the paper may be transferred by the transfer of the paper document, from one person to another, by whatever method the particular type of instrument requires, in law. Bills of exchange, cheques, banker's drafts and promissory notes are all negotiable instruments.
Bill of exchange	This is a type of negotiable instrument in which one person instructs someone else to pay money to, or to the order of, a specified person. Although these may be drawn against and addressed to private persons, they are much more commonly drawn against and payable by a person's bank ('the drawee'). Typically, they are used by a buyer of goods, who has arranged to pay the seller by the use of a bill of exchange. They are much used in international commerce. Primary liability to pay out on the bill arises upon 'acceptance', by the signature of the drawee (eg the buyer's bank).
Term bill	This is a bill of exchange which is designed to be paid out not on the day of acceptance but at some period later. This is often used to provide a credit period to a buyer, who can get his bill accepted and with it the acceptor's promise to pay up. In the alternative, he could take the accepted bill and attempt to negotiate it on (at a small discount) to someone else who is prepared to wait for the term to expire, in order to cash it at full face value.
Sight bill	This is a bill of exchange which is designed to be paid immediately upon acceptance ('on sight'), at full face value.

Topic	Summary
Documentary credit	This is a written contractual promise that the person to whom it is intended to give a benefit will be guaranteed to be paid out, provided that that beneficiary performs his part of a contractual arrangement properly. The idea is to provide a solvent and reliable assurance, independent of the buyer of goods, that the seller will be paid. Usually, the credit will be raised by a bank ('the issuing bank'), instructed and paid by the buyer, at the buyer's expense. Most documentary credits are issued under the Uniform Customs and Practice for Documentary Credits. The contract of credit itself is a separate contract from the sale of goods, so failure or insolvency of the buyer would not affect the seller, once the contract is under way. The credit may, quite independently, be confirmed by another bank, eg an offshore issuing bank and an onshore 'confirming bank'.

PART III

INTELLECTUAL PROPERTY

CHAPTER 17

INTRODUCTION TO INTELLECTUAL PROPERTY

LEARNING OUTCOMES

After reading this chapter you will be able to:

- explain what intellectual property is
- identify the main types of intellectual property
- understand the role of public registration in the administration of intellectual property rights.

17.1 WHAT IS INTELLECTUAL PROPERTY?

The basic concept of intellectual property (IP) is that of protecting the products, results and rewards of the exercise of human intellectual and commercial endeavour. The property rights in these matters are a form of intangible property, comprising the legal right to stop others using the owner's property without permission and, in some cases, to give a monopoly right to exploit that property commercially.

A problem with protecting things that originate in a person's mind is that much of the subject matter comprised in IP gets dangerously close to claiming, as private property, some things which, at least in theory, should belong to humanity in common. Matters such as use of words of the language, shapes and forms, colours, ideas, ways of thinking and doing things, methods of manufacture, even geographical locations can form the subject matter of such rights. It follows from this that the legal framework for identifying the existence and scope of a private IP right must be very precise and technically ascertainable, if private rights are not to interfere in the free and normal conduct of a civilised society. This has become an ever-increasing problem as we have moved away from an object-based world towards a much more information-based existence, where by making a few electronic connections, a person may use and engage the IP of many different owners, possibly in many different places.

Only a limited treatment of these extensive areas of law is possible in this work and the matters are approached as follows.

The question of protection of business reputation is dealt with in **Chapters 18** and **19**, which deal with passing off and trade marks. Business exists to make profits, and the surest way to make a profit is to become known and identified as a reliable and reputable supplier of whatever a market requires. It is this protection of the identity of the mark of an organisation with its own particular reputation and output, particularly through the eyes of customers, that is the binding connection between trade mark law and passing off.

The second area of protection is that given to creative expression and the right of a creative person to develop property rights in the tangible results of creative talents, so as to be able to stop other persons from making free use of that property without the permission of the creator, by way of copying or otherwise, whether for gain or not. This is dealt with in **Chapters 20** and **21**, on copyright and database right protection.

A third area of protection, similar to protection of creativity, is that given to designs for shapes (both internal and external shapes) and appearances of objects, which are intended to be created to that design, typically by way of manufacture. This is a vital area for protection and one calling for some very fine distinctions, if freedom of design and manufacture is to be generally available to anyone who wishes to make use of it. **Chapter 22** deals with this area. The general idea, here, is to prevent unauthorised commercial exploitation of the designs, rather than simple copying for non-commercial purposes.

The fourth area of protection is that which allows persons of an inventive nature (in terms of being able to do or make things) to be able to take advantage of a limited time period in which they are able to exploit the commercial possibilities of their invention, in a monopolistic way, by the use of registered patents. Even during this limited time period, the underlying inventive thinking must be available to the public at large, so as to enter the collective body of human knowledge, in exchange for the monopoly right of exploitation. This area is dealt with in **Chapter 23**.

These areas of law, along with other concepts such as the protection of confidential information and 'know-how' protection (dealt with in **Chapter 24**), provide the framework within which individuals, businesses and the general public are able to benefit from a principled, reasonably predictable and equitable sharing of human intellectual output. This framework gives protection to those who create and think; it allows the public to benefit and develop from steps taken by innovators and designers; it encourages and stimulates business growth and entrepreneurial spirit; lastly, it prevents an unseemly and ultimately destructive free-for-all in the unlimited and unscrupulous use and misuse of other people's property.

A consequence of the ownership of IP is that it can come to represent much, if not all, of the real asset value of many businesses. Like most other property it can be dealt in, sold, bought, licensed or charged by way of security. Modern giants, such as the Microsoft organisation, could not have come into existence so quickly, on such a titanic, financial scale, unless they consisted primarily of IP assets.

17.2   TYPES OF INTELLECTUAL PROPERTY

Intellectual property rights are now primarily statutory, supported by considerable case law. Some common law rights still exist, however, mainly passing off and breach of confidence. The main IP rights are as follows.

17.2.1   Trade marks

A trade mark is a brand name or other mark of trade origin, for example Coca-Cola for soft drinks, BMW for cars and motorcycles, or Levi's for jeans. It is a highly commercial right. Trade marks are best protected by registration (and all well-known trade marks are registered). This gives the owner of the trade mark statutory rights, under the Trade Marks Act 1994 (TMA 1994), to defend its trade mark against infringers who are using the same mark or a similar one.

The registration of a trade mark can be renewed indefinitely, provided the trade mark does not run foul of some restrictions under the TMA 1994. The oldest trade mark in the UK is the Bass red triangle for beer. It was registered in the 1870s and is still valid today.

In 1905, a pine tree logo, still in use by Fisons plc for chemicals, became the first registered trade mark in Australia. In Hong Kong, the first registered trade mark was Nestle's 'Eagle' Brand, granted in 1874 for condensed milk. The first registered trade mark in Japan was a design of a seated figure, registered for pills and wound dressings, issued around 1884. The first US registration was granted in 1870 for an eagle logo used for paints by Averill Paints (this is no longer in use). The oldest registered mark still in use in the US is 'Samson', with the design of a man and a lion, registered on 27 May 1884 for use on cords, line and rope.

Contenders for the oldest continuously used trade mark in the world are 'Lowenbrau', which claims use since 1383, and 'Stella Artois', which claims use since 1366.

Most countries, including the US, have a similar trade mark registration system. Each of the 50 States of the US, however, has its own statewide trade mark registration system, which is independent of the US national system. Trade marks registered in one (or more) States have priority over subsequently registered national (federal) rights.

If a trade mark is not registered then it can only be protected by the law of passing off; except that in the US, statute expressly provides protection for unregistered trade marks as explained at **17.2.2**.

17.2.2 Passing off

This is a common law tort which enables a business to defend itself from someone who is trying to take unfair advantage of the trading reputation of that business, for example by using its name or selling goods in packaging that looks similar. Passing off is less important than trade mark law, and also less certain as regards the outcome. It has also been diminished by the increased scope of registered designs (see **17.2.4**). Nevertheless, there are many situations in which the scope of passing off can reach further than trade mark protection, so the two rights can complement each other as they are not mutually exclusive, often being pleaded in the same proceedings.

Other common law jurisdictions, such as New Zealand and Australia, also have a law of passing off, whereas civil law jurisdictions tend to approach the issue by way of a statutory law of unfair competition. This often achieves similar aims. There is an international obligation to ensure effective protection against unfair competition in the Paris Convention (signed by 171 States worldwide).

US trade mark law contains a special provision which provides protection for both registered and unregistered (called common law) trade marks if the use by the second entrant into the market is likely to cause confusion, mistake or deception as to source, origin and/or affiliation with the prior user of the mark. The same law also makes false or misleading designations relative to the goods actionable. All of this falls within the concept that the consumer should be free to select goods based upon the reputation of the original, bona fide purveyor of those goods, not the activities of the unlicensed copier. However, purely functional aspects of the goods are not protected.

17.2.3 Copyright

Copyright is a right to prevent copying of creative expression, such as writing, art, music, architecture, film and even computer software.

It is an unregistered system, and for an infringement to occur it has to involve 'copying'. Copyright does not stop you writing an exciting book about wizards just because JK Rowling has produced many such books. However, it does stop you copying the works and detailed plots of JK Rowling.

Copyright extends to pictorial and photographic creation, industrial plans, sculpture, recorded music and films. These media are 'artistic' but also highly commercial, if you think about the money involved in a major film, such as the James Bond films. It is the principal IP right in computer programs and therefore of great importance today. Nevertheless, the right is not registrable and comes into existence when the work is first created.

The common law concept to prohibit copying has been eliminated in the US – copyright protection is based solely on the Copyright Act of 1976.

All major jurisdictions worldwide have a law of copyright, and are signatories to the Berne Convention which protects copyrighted works internationally.

17.2.4   Designs

Designs that relate to the appearance of an object can be registered, but ones that relate solely to its technical function (ie to how it works) cannot. Registration gives statutory protection for up to 25 years.

There is also statutory unregistered design right protecting features of shape or configuration of articles which are intended to be made available commercially. This protection can extend for between 10 and 15 years, according to circumstances.

Most countries, however, including the US, have statutes specifically relating to designs. In the US, the statute is part of the Patent Act. In the US, 'design' patent protection is limited to the non-functional appearance of the goods. There is no protection for the functional aspect of the goods, or their appearance or packaging.

17.2.5   Patents

Patents are a commercial IP right. A patent is protection for an invention. The invention could be a better mousetrap, or a wonder drug to treat cancer, or anything in between. A patent is a registered right, administered by the Patents Office.

A patent gives the holder the right to a monopoly for 20 years over the technology revealed in the patent. 'Revealed' is an important concept. The description of the invention is made public in return for the grant by the Crown of the period of protection. Thus, after the 20-year period expires, the invention is then public property. Anybody can use it because the technology is revealed in the patent document, known as a patent specification.

The philosophy is that inventors, and those who employ or sponsor them, should have this 20-year period in which to exploit their monopoly. Were it otherwise, it would never be worth the financial risk of the huge research and testing regimes needed for many modern inventions or patented ideas undertaken by, say, drug manufacturers.

Virtually all countries have a similar Patent Act and permit protection of similar scope and duration. A distinction must be made, however, with the US Patent Act. While the UK Act provides the 20-year affirmative 'monopoly', in the US the Patent Act is a negative right, specifically, the right to exclude others from practising the invention.

You can protect your invention in many international jurisdictions by making an application under the Patent Cooperation Treaty. This involves making an initial single application through the World Intellectual Property Organization (WIPO) or the European Patent Office (EPO). Unfortunately, in the case of worldwide protection, the application then progresses as an application in each jurisdiction.

Another possible means of exploiting a patent is by commercial exploitation of any confidential information concerning the most efficient way to make the patented invention or process work. The registered patent specification will show the world the inventive concept itself and how it broadly works, but that is very different from showing the best and most cost-effective way to make it work. Such additional information is termed 'know-how' and is, itself, highly valuable and exploitable material, as long as it remains confidential. Typically, it is not independently protected as a patent but is often ancillary to the patent, so that a patent licence will be accompanied by a know-how licence, to give the licensee the best chance of using the patent efficiently.

17.2.6 Confidential information

The law of confidence is not an IP right in a pure sense, but is often classified with the mainstream rights as it is sometimes associated with them. For example, maintaining confidentiality before submitting a patent application is vital to avoid destruction of the invention's novelty.

Case law rather than statute governs the law of confidence and, as you would expect, the vast majority of cases relate to circumstances where express obligations of confidence are lacking and implied duties of confidentiality have to be considered. It is, however, important to remember that express obligations can (and often should) be imposed (eg, on key employees or independent contractors). Where confidentiality cannot be protected by contractual means, eg once it gets to third parties, the courts may use trust principles to restrict its use.

Most jurisdictions protect confidential information based upon case law. The US has a dual system of case law and adoption in each State of a version of a Model Law known as the 'Uniform Trade Secrets Act'.

17.2.7 What else is there?

There are various other IP rights. For example:

The IP right	What does it protect against?
Database right	Copying of information
Semiconductor topography	Copying of computer 'chips'
Plant varieties	Anyone else selling the registered new variety of plant
Moral rights	Inappropriate treatment of an artist's work
Performers rights	Copying of live performances

17.3 PUBLIC REGISTRATION AND ADMINISTRATION

It can be seen that much IP is protected by the use of registration of rights in public registers. This is the work of what is now entitled the Intellectual Property Office ('the IPO') (www.ipo.gov.uk), which covers the formerly more separated functions of registration of trade marks, designs and patents and various other matters connected with different types of IP within the UK. Additionally, IP issues which have an EU component are likely to come into contact with the Office for the Harmonisation of the Internal Market ('OHIM'), based in Alicante, Spain. There is an almost seamless joint between the registration process and the way in which courts, both national and EU, deal with IP actions and proceedings, in that harmonisation and approximation of national IP legal frameworks, within the EU, has gone much further than in many other areas of business and property law. This has followed upon a long-established international tradition of according reciprocal rights to some IP, in the interests of fostering world trade and development; see **19.13** and **20.10**.

17.4 THE UK'S WITHDRAWAL FROM THE EU

Brexit has necessitated a review of the relationship between EU IP rights and UK IP rights. The main UK legislative provisions which were introduced essentially have the aim of maintaining the status quo, so for example providing for those with EU rights to be allowed to exercise equivalent UK rights in the UK (as the EU right itself will no longer apply). Where appropriate in the chapters that follow, these provisions will be explained.

UK lawyers will still need to know about EU intellectual property systems, as clients are often multinational or at least operate within the EU. For this reason, the following chapters will, where relevant, make reference to EU systems.

17.5 SUMMARY OF INTELLECTUAL PROPERTY RIGHTS

17.5.1 Trade marks

What is protected?	a brand name and/or a logo for goods or services (also, in limited circumstances, shapes)
What benefit is there?	exclusive right to the use of the trade mark with statutory protection
How is it obtained?	registration
How long does it last?	indefinitely

17.5.2 Passing off

What is protected?	goodwill (eg, a logo or a name or associated 'get up')
What benefit is there?	gives protection against unfair imitation
How is it obtained?	arises automatically (no registration)
How long does it last?	indefinitely

17.5.3 Copyright

What is protected?	'artistic output'; creative expression
What benefit is there?	preventing copying
How is it obtained?	arises automatically (no registration)
How long does it last?	70 years from death (usually)

17.5.4 Database right

What is protected?	collections of information
What benefit is there?	protects against unauthorised copying
How is it obtained?	arises automatically (no registration)
How long does it last?	15 years from creation or revision of the database

17.5.5 Registered design right

What is protected?	new designs for products
What benefit is there?	monopoly right to use and benefit from the design commercially
How is it obtained?	registration
How long does it last?	25 years from registration (maximum)

17.5.6 Unregistered design right

What is protected?	three-dimensional shapes of articles
What benefit is there?	prevents commercial copying of articles
How is it obtained?	arises automatically (no registration)
How long does it last?	10 years in most cases (maximum of 15)

17.5.7 Patents

What is protected?	new invention or process
What benefit is there?	monopoly right to apply the technology
How is it obtained?	registration
How long does it last?	20 years from application

17.5.8 Confidential information

What is protected?	secret information
What benefit is there?	protects against unauthorised disclosure
How is it obtained?	arises automatically (no registration)
How long does it last?	indefinitely

17.6 INTRODUCTION TO INTERNATIONAL PROPERTY RIGHTS TREATIES

Strong protection for intellectual property rights (IPR) worldwide is vital to the future economic growth and development of all countries. As they create common rules and regulations, international IPR treaties are essential to achieving the robust intellectual property protection that spurs global economic expansion and the growth of new technologies.

The international community, however, did not have a single source for intellectual property obligations until the 1994 Uruguay Round of the General Agreement on Tariffs and Trade created the World Trade Organization (WTO) and the Agreement on Trade Related Aspects of Intellectual Property Rights (TRIPS).

The significance of TRIPS is three-fold:

(a) it was the first single, truly international agreement to establish minimum standards of protection for several forms of intellectual property;

(b) it was the first international intellectual property agreement to mandate detailed civil, criminal, and border enforcement provisions; and

(c) it was the first international intellectual property agreement subject to binding, enforceable dispute settlement.

In effect, TRIPS laid the groundwork for a strong and modern IPR infrastructure for the world community.

As a strong adherent of TRIPS and all other international IPR treaties, discussed below, the US government encourages other countries to join and implement them.

17.6.1 TRIPS

TRIPS came into force in 1995. It incorporates and builds upon the latest versions of the primary IP agreements administered by the World Intellectual Property Organization (WIPO), the Paris Convention for the Protection of Industrial Property, and the Berne Convention for the Protection of Literary and Artistic Works, agreements that go back to the 1880s.

TRIPS is unique among these IPR accords because membership of the WTO is a 'package deal', meaning that WTO members are not free to pick and choose among agreements. They are subject to all the WTO's multilateral agreements, including TRIPS.

TRIPS applies basic international trade principles to member States regarding IP, including national treatment and most-favoured-nation treatment. TRIPS establishes minimum standards for the availability, scope, and use of seven forms of IP: copyrights, trade marks, geographical indications, industrial designs, patents, layout designs for integrated circuits, and undisclosed information (trade secrets). It spells out permissible limitations and exceptions in order to balance the interests of IP with interests in other areas, such as public health and economic development.

Because TRIPS is over 25 years old, however, it does not address several new developments, such as the Internet and digital copyright issues, advanced biotechnology, and international harmonisation, the process of creating uniform global standards of laws or practice. It sets the floor for minimum IPR protection, not the ceiling. Since the conclusion of TRIPS, the WIPO has addressed digital copyright issues in the so-called Internet Treaties, namely the WIPO Copyright Treaty (WCT) and the WIPO Performances and Phonograms Treaty (WPPT).

What follows are summaries of other WIPO treaties that complement TRIPS, particularly in addressing new technological developments.

17.6.2 The Singapore Treaty on the Law of Trademarks

The Singapore Treaty on the Law of Trademarks (SLT), which came into force in March 2009, was enacted to revamp and replace the Trademark Law Treaty (TLT) of 1994.

The TLT was enacted to simplify procedures in the application and registration process, and to harmonise trade mark procedures in different countries. The TLT harmonised procedures of national trade mark offices by establishing the maximum requirements a contracting party can impose.

The TLT gave service marks – the distinctive identifiers of businesses that offer a service, as opposed to goods – 'equal' status with trade marks. Previously, many countries treated trade marks and service marks differently. The TLT required member nations to register service marks and treat them as they would trade marks.

The SLT carries on this work by incorporating provisions necessary due to the growth of electronic communications.

From the trade mark owner's perspective, the SLT saves time and money in the preparation and filing of documents for the application. It streamlines the process for post-registration renewals, recording assignments, changes of name and address, and powers of attorney. Member countries to the SLT are required to permit the use of multi-class applications, enabling trade mark owners to file a single application covering multiple classes of goods and services.

Another significant feature of the SLT that benefits trade mark owners is its prohibition of requirements by national offices for authentication or certification of documents as well as signatures on trade mark applications and correspondence. Many countries had required that any signatures submitted in support of registration of a mark be notarised or otherwise legalised in accordance with the laws of that nation. Under the SLT, it is no longer necessary in most instances to go through these procedures. This feature enables trade mark owners to complete and file trade mark documents more quickly, at less cost.

An additional advantage of the SLT is the harmonisation of the initial and renewal terms of trade mark registration among signatory countries. The SLT provides for an initial 10-year term, with 10-year renewals. Other key features of the SLT include an intent-to-use application system (with proof of use prior to registration); streamlined renewal procedures; minimisation of the elements to obtain an application filing date; and simplified procedures for recording changes in name and ownership of trade mark applications and registrations.

Overall, the SLT is intended to facilitate international trade. It is of particular importance to individuals and small businesses looking for markets in other countries.

17.6.3 Patent Law Treaty

The Patent Law Treaty (PLT), adopted by WIPO in June of 2000, entered into force on 28 April 2005. The PLT is the product of several years of multilateral negotiations on harmonising global patent systems. The PLT harmonises certain patent application procedures in order to reduce or eliminate formalities and the potential for loss of rights. The PLT does not harmonise substantive patent law, that is, the laws of each country that set forth the conditions that must be met in order to receive a patent for an invention in that country. WIPO is, however, holding discussions regarding harmonisation of substantive patent law.

The PLT makes it easier for patent applicants and patent owners to obtain and maintain patents throughout the world by simplifying and, to a large degree, merging national and international formal requirements associated with patent applications and patents.

The PLT:

(a)   simplifies and minimises patent application requirements to obtain a filing date;

(b)   imposes a limit on the formal requirements that contracting parties may impose;

(c)   eases representation requirements for formal matters;

(d)   provides a basis for the electronic filing of applications;

(e)   provides relief with respect to time limits that may be imposed by the Office of a Contracting Party, and reinstatement of rights where an applicant or owner has failed to comply with a time limit and that failure has the direct consequence of causing a loss of rights; and

(f)   provides for correction or addition of priority claims and restoration of priority rights.

17.6.4 Patent Cooperation Treaty System

The roots of the Patent Cooperation Treaty (PCT) go back to 1966, when the Executive Committee of the Paris Convention for the Protection of Intellectual Property called for a study of how to reduce, for applicants and patent offices, the duplication of effort involved in filing and obtaining patent applications for the same invention in different countries. The resulting WIPO treaty, the PCT, was signed in Washington, DC, in 1970 and entered into force in 1978. The Treaty was amended in 1979, 1984, 2001, and 2004. There are 156 contracting parties to the PCT.

By simplifying patent application filing, the PCT assists innovators in obtaining patent protection throughout the world. It also encourages small businesses and individuals to seek patent protection abroad.

Under this WIPO-administered treaty, nationals or residents of a contracting State file a single patent application, called an 'international' application, with their national patent office or with WIPO as a receiving office. This automatically lodges the application for patent protection in all contracting parties to the PCT.

The Treaty provides a longer period of time, 30 months, before applicants must commit themselves to undertake the expenses of translation, national filing fees, and prosecution in every country in which they want protection. By providing applicants with more time and information to evaluate the strength of their potential patent and to determine marketing plans, the 30-month period allows applicants to be more selective as to the countries in which they will file. This is a major improvement over the 12-month priority period provided under the Paris Convention for patent applicants.

Under the PCT, WIPO publishes the 'international application', together with a non-binding indication as to the potential patentability of the invention. This non-binding indication is a preliminary search and/or examination by an 'International Authority', one of 11 patent offices designated by WIPO that currently meet the Treaty's minimum staffing and documentation requirements. The non-binding indication helps applicants decide whether to proceed with their patent applications in national or regional offices. Patent offices also benefit from these non-binding indications of patentability when deciding whether to grant national or regional patents based upon PCT applications. Foreign search reports identify relevant documents that help patent offices to conserve resources in the examination process and to improve the quality of examination.

17.6.5   Madrid System for the international registration of marks

The Protocol Relating to the Madrid Agreement Concerning the International Registration of Marks – the Madrid Protocol – was adopted in Spain's capital on 27 June 1989, and entered into force on 1 December 1995. The Protocol is one of two treaties comprising the Madrid System for international registration of trade marks. The first Treaty, the 1891 Madrid Agreement, provides for the registration of trade marks in several countries through the filing of one international trade mark registration with WIPO in Geneva.

The Madrid Protocol, developed because some countries had problems with the operation of the Madrid Agreement, is seen as an improvement to the system for international registration of trade marks. As a result, more and more trade mark owners are using the Madrid Protocol every year to protect their trade marks in foreign countries. There are 128 countries which are party to the Madrid Protocol.

The Madrid Protocol is a filing treaty and not a substantive harmonisation treaty. It provides a cost-effective and efficient way for trade mark holders – individuals and businesses – to ensure protection for their marks in multiple countries through the filing of one application with a single office, in one language, with one set of fees, in one currency. Moreover, no local agent is needed to file the application. Applications may be filed in English, French, or Spanish. An application for international registration has the same effect as a national application for registration of the mark in each of the countries designated by the applicant. Once the trade mark office in a designated country grants protection, the mark is protected just as if that office had registered it.

The Madrid Protocol also simplifies the subsequent management of the mark, since a simple, single procedural step serves to record subsequent changes in ownership or in the name or address of the holder with WIPO's International Bureau.

Before the Protocol was enacted, burdensome administrative requirements for the normal transfer of business assets often made it difficult for trade mark owners to carry out valid assignments of their marks internationally. The Protocol allows the holder of an international registration to file a single request with a single payment, in order to record the assignment of a trade mark with all the member countries. Registration renewal also involves a simple, single procedural step. International registration lasts 10 years, with 10-year renewal periods.

Trade mark owners may designate additional countries if they decide to seek protection in more member countries, or if new countries accede to the Protocol.

If the basic application – or registration upon which the international registration is based – is cancelled for any reason in the first five years, the Madrid Protocol gives the holder of the international registration the opportunity to turn the international registration into a series of national applications in each designated country. This series of applications keeps the priority date of the original international registration in each country. The holder also preserves the rights acquired in each member country, even if international registration fails.

17.6.6 The Hague System for the international deposit of industrial designs

The Hague System is an international registration system that enables owners to obtain protection for their industrial designs with a minimum of formality and expense. A single international application filed with WIPO's International Bureau replaces a whole series of applications previously required in a number of States and/or intergovernmental organisations party to the Hague System. The subsequent management of the international registration is considerably easier under this system. For example, one single step is all that is needed to record a change in the name or address of the holder, or a change in ownership for some or for all of the designated contracting parties.

The Hague System currently has 77 contracting parties.

17.6.7 Conclusion

In the information age, with technology advancing at an accelerating rate, simply implementing TRIPS is not enough to establish a robust intellectual property system. While it was the first comprehensive IPR agreement of its time, TRIPS is over 25 years old and reflects a 'snapshot' in time. Technological advances in information technology, biotechnology and other fields require the updating of national and international laws that protect IP. Fortunately, WIPO has led the way in developing new international norms to meet these challenges.

WIPO has also led the way in simplifying and streamlining the procedures for seeking, obtaining and maintaining rights in multiple countries. Through its 'Global Protection Services' and its harmonisation treaties, it saves creators and national IP offices a great deal of time and effort. WIPO also makes available its excellent technical assistance for establishing and improving IPR systems worldwide. Countries should look to both the WTO and to WIPO when crafting their IPR systems.

SUMMARY

Intellectual property consists of a collection of legal rights. Whilst there are typical characteristics which are common to most of the rights, there are significant differences. This chapter will have helped you to appreciate what the main rights are and generally how they work. This will give you a sound basic understanding, which you may develop as you read the following chapters dealing with each right in detail.

PASSING OFF

LEARNING OUTCOMES

After reading this chapter you will be able to:

- explain the key highlights of the law of passing off
- identify the three main elements of passing off
- apply relevant defences
- explain the remedies available for breach
- understand how passing off works in other countries.

18.1 INTRODUCTION

Passing off is about stopping the infringer from selling his goods or services by making unfair use of the claimant's reputation. Passing off can happen in a number of different ways. Typically, passing-off cases concern the 'get-up' of goods (ie, their packaging and presentation as seen by the consumer). Passing off is often used as an additional remedy to trade mark infringement claims, and will sometimes succeed where the trade mark claim does not as it is more flexible in approach than the registered trade mark system.

The classic quote, which sums up passing off, is from Lord Halsbury in *Reddaway and Frank Reddaway & Co Ltd v Banham and George Banham & Co Ltd* [1896] AC 199: '... nobody has any right to represent his goods as the goods of somebody else'. If you make a potential buyer or recipient of your services think you are another party, that person has a right to claim compensation for losses suffered by the deception.

Passing off has to be in relation to a commercial activity. In *Kean v McGivan* [1982] FSR 119, an action concerning the name of a political party (the Social Democratic Party) did not succeed. Usually, something must be happening that is capable of causing people to spend money.

In the classic case of passing off, the defendant adopts some mark, or sign or other distinguishing feature (eg, the appearance of the packaging of the goods) which customers associate with the claimant. He uses this, or something confusingly similar to it, for his own goods/services, with the result that customers are fooled into thinking they are buying the claimant's product. In one of the most famous passing-off cases, *Reckitt & Colman Products Ltd v Borden Inc and Others* [1990] 1 WLR 491, the distinguishing feature of the claimants' goods was that their lemon juice was sold in a plastic lemon. The defendant also started selling lemon juice in a plastic lemon. Reckitt & Colman succeeded in stopping the defendant using this shape of container. Today, the claimants could also use trade mark infringement as, under the TMA 1994, they have been able to register the shape of their lemon as a registered trade mark (see **Chapter 19**).

Modern marketing methods have created many hugely ingenious ways of free-riding on the business reputations and goodwill created by others. In *British Sky Broadcasting Group plc v Sky Home Services Ltd* [2006] EWHC 3165 (Ch), various defendants had made use of the SKY word in corporate names, as well as in marketing material and telephone sales methods used for selling extended warranties for maintenance of satellite TV reception equipment. Passing off was established fairly easily in the circumstances of such a widely-known organisation as the claimant.

Although at the time of writing no actions are known to have been commenced in respect of it, news stories of unofficial Apple stores opening in China, where the whole shop is branded and has the look and feel of an Apple Store, show how far alleged infringers are prepared to go.

What is protected?	goodwill, eg logo or name, 'get-up'
What benefit is there?	protects against unfair use of, or damage to, business reputation
How is it obtained?	arises automatically (no registration)
How long does it last?	indefinitely

18.2 THE THREE ELEMENTS OF PASSING OFF

In *Consorzio del Prosciutto di Parma v Marks & Spencer plc* [1991] RPC 351, the House of Lords judgment of Lord Oliver in *Reckitt & Colman* is quoted as a good exposition of the elements of passing off:

> More specifically, it may be expressed in terms of the elements which the plaintiff in such an action has to prove in order to succeed. These are three in number. First, he must establish a *goodwill* or reputation attached to the goods or services which he supplies in the mind of the purchasing public by association with the identifying get-up (whether it consists simply of a brand name or a trade description, or the individual features of labelling or packaging) under which his particular goods or services are offered to the public, such that the get-up is recognised by the public as distinctive specifically of the plaintiff's goods or services. Secondly, he must demonstrate a *misrepresentation* by the defendant to the public (whether or not intentional) leading or likely to lead the public to believe that goods or services offered by him are the goods or services of the plaintiff ... Thirdly, he must demonstrate that he suffers or ... that he is likely to suffer *damage* by reason of the erroneous belief engendered by the defendant's misrepresentation that the source of the defendant's goods or services is the same as the source of those offered by the plaintiff. (emphasis added)

18.2.1 First element: goodwill

Goodwill means business reputation. The reputation must be among customers, or prospective customers (ie, buyers, or prospective buyers of lemon juice, for example).

The reputation also needs to be in relation to some distinguishing feature, eg, in the plastic lemon. What the claimant needs to show is not only that customers associate the plastic lemon with the claimant, but also that they understand the plastic lemon as an indication or sign that the lemon juice comes from the claimant. The claimant generally demonstrates his reputation to the court by showing sales figures and expenditure on advertising (using the distinguishing feature in question), by witness evidence and survey evidence.

The distinguishing feature could be:

(a) logos, shape or style of packaging, get up, colour (eg, Heinz beans tin (colour, shape of label, name); the classic Coca-Cola bottle (shape, name); Body Shop bottle (the rounded shape and lettering); Penguin (six-pack wrapper)); or

(b) a name (eg, 'Neutrogena', where the defendant was restrained from using the similar name 'Neutralia' (*Neutrogena Corporation and Another v Golden Ltd and Another* [1996] RPC 473), or 'Harrods' (*Harrods Ltd v Harrodian School Ltd* [1996] RPC 697), although Harrods were unsuccessful in stopping the school using the same name because they could not show that this would result in damage).

In *Riddle v United Service Organisation Ltd* [2004] LTL AC9100218, the claimant was the son of the late Nelson Riddle, a composer and orchestra leader. Riddle senior and his orchestra had last toured the UK in the 1960s. It was held that there was no goodwill remaining after 40 years, so the son could not maintain a passing-off claim against defendants who ran an orchestra called the Nelson Riddle Orchestra UK. This can also be a problem for new businesses or ventures, where the goodwill has yet to become established.

The category of things in which the claimant can have reputation is not closed and cannot be conclusively defined or limited. Being common law based, the limits of the tort are potentially very wide. Reputation as a diary writer was able to be protected in *Clark (Alan Kenneth McKenzie) v Associated Newspapers* [1998] RPC 261, where parodied versions of Alan Clark's diaries were held to be passing off. Scents of products can be another tricky area, as seen in *L'Oréal SA v Bellure NV* [2006] EWHC 2355 (Ch), where the scent of a fine perfume, although important to the customer, was held to be not protected, on the facts of that case, although there were trade mark infringements of other features.

18.2.2   Second element: misrepresentation, leading to confusion

There must be a misrepresentation made by the defendant in the course of trade. In the Jif lemon case (see **18.1**) the misrepresentation was the use of the plastic lemon. In most passing-off cases the misrepresentation is deliberate. In other words, there is a deliberate attempt by the defendant to 'ride on the back' of the claimant's success. For example, consider the 'Penguin and Puffin' case, *United Biscuits (UK) Ltd v Asda Stores Ltd* [1997] RPC 513, which concerned the similarity in packaging for the two brands of chocolate biscuit. Asda produced the Puffin biscuit. They had designed packaging that was very similar to that of the Penguin biscuit. They even ran an advertising campaign with the slogan 'pick up a Puffin'. This rather suggested deliberate reference to Penguin, and did not help Asda's case in court, as passing off was easily established.

However, a misrepresentation could be innocent but still actionable. The defendant need not even be aware of the claimant's products, as intention to misrepresent is not an essential element. It would, though, be likely to severely affect the award of damages.

The misrepresentation must lead to confusion of customers or potential customers, and generally it must be confusion as to trade source. The customers must be fooled into thinking that the defendant's products come from the claimant, or that they are associated with the claimant (eg, that they are made/supplied by a company within the same group, or by a licensee). A classic example of such misrepresentation may be seen in *First Conference Services Ltd v Bracchi* [2009] EWHC 2176 (Ch), [2009] All ER (D) 56 (Oct), where a former employee of the claimant attempted to pass off conferences organised by him as those of his old employer. He did this by stating that the speakers would be 'previous speakers', ie those at conferences organised by the claimant the year before. He also misled the speakers themselves as to the identity of the true organiser of the conference.

The general rule is that confusion must be at the point of sale, or before it (however, see below for a High Court case which departed from this).In *Bostik Ltd v Sellotape GB Ltd* [1994] RPC 556, the makers of Blu-tack failed to obtain an injunction in passing off against a rival manufacturer of a similar looking product. The similarity in the product could be realised only when the packaging was removed. There was no possibility of confusion by the customer at the point of sale. So far, English courts which set a precedent (ie the Court of Appeal or Supreme Court) have refused to follow other jurisdictions where post-sale confusion is enough. However, in the High Court case of *Freddy SPA v Hugz Clothing and others* (Intellectual Property Enterprise Court, 19 November 2020), the court accepted that 'post-sale confusion' can form the basis of a passing off claim. In this case, the claimant, a successful fashion brand, argued that the defendants were selling body-enhancing jeans which imitated its product. Consumers generally knew they were buying the 'unofficial' version but hoped that people seeing them wearing them would assume they were the more expensive genuine jeans. The court followed an earlier New Zealand case in which it was accepted that the owner of goodwill is entitled to passing off protection during the life of the product and not just at the point of sale. As the court in the *Freddy* case is part of the High Court, it has not set a precedent which has changed the law, so it will be interesting to see whether a higher court follows its logic when the opportunity arises.

It is not enough that there is confusion between the claimant's and the defendant's product. Customers must believe that the defendant's products are associated with the claimant. This was illustrated in the case of *HFC Bank plc v Midland Bank plc* [2000] FSR 176. When Midland was taken over by HSBC and changed its name to HSBC, HFC Bank objected. They argued that customers would confuse HSBC with HFC. However, among other things, HFC were not able to show they had achieved sufficient brand name recognition in relation to the letters HFC. Even if customers did confuse the two acronyms, they would not necessarily think HSBC was a reference to HFC.

The removal of a distinguishing feature can result in unintentional misrepresentation. In *Sir Robert McAlpine Ltd v Alfred McAlpine plc* [2004] EWHC 630 (Ch), [2004] RPC 36, it was held that the defendant's dropping of the first name 'Alfred', so that it used the name McAlpine alone, did amount to a misrepresentation. In other words, it caused confusion with the claimant's name.

There needs to be overlap between the alleged infringer and the proprietor in that there is a 'common field of activity', in the following respects:

(a)   type of goods or services: would someone confuse a bicycle maker with a law firm?

(b)   geographical area: a restaurant in Aberdeen is unlikely to take away trade from one in Plymouth; and

(c)   time: the overlap must be more or less contemporaneous.

Unless there is a common field of activity, it will be difficult (but not impossible) to show confusion or, indeed, damage to goodwill in many cases. Nevertheless, as large national or multinational organisations, such as Tesco or BP etc, are commonly known to be involved in a hugely diverse range of goods and services, it would be very easy for passing off to take place without a common activity taking place at all, but it would still be open to the claimant to have a good chance of stopping the activity, as can be seen from the case law.

18.2.2.1   Evidence of confusion

A passing-off case will not succeed without evidence of confusion. Customer confusion is a question of fact, and it is always very difficult to predict the outcome of a passing-off claim. It is difficult to generalise about the type of thing that will lead to confusion, but the confusion must be as to trade source.

The usual evidence might be survey evidence (ie a survey of a sample of members of the public is taken, often by marketing analysts) or witness evidence, preferably from people employed in the relevant trade. In effect, they become expert witnesses on the question of likely confusion. The burden on the claimant is heavy and is often difficult to discharge. In *Julius Sämaan v Tetrosyl Ltd* (see **19.8.2**), a passing-off claim failed for lack of evidence of confusion, even though there was a clear trade mark infringement.

The courts are sceptical about survey evidence, but nevertheless it is frequently presented. Often what will be conclusive is placing the two products before the judge. Do they think customers are likely to be confused? If they agree, they are more likely to accept the survey evidence. If they do not, they are likely to reject it.

Although the defendant may use the claimant's distinctive feature in some way, there might not be confusion if either the claimant or the defendant has clearly distinguished their products in some way. In *Arsenal Football Club plc v Reed* [2001] RPC 922, a long-standing trader in unofficial Arsenal club memorabilia was not found to have created any confusion in the minds of customers, merely by using the club's logo and name (not least, because of a clear disclaimer). The passing-off action failed (but see the trade mark case at **19.9**).

If people merely recognise the look-alike as being a cheaper copy of the branded product then this is not going to be enough for passing off. There is then no confusion as to the trade source of the goods or services. Some allowance is made for the circumstances under which the customer will look at and decide about buying the material. A quick selection from a shelf is very different from a considered examination of the matter, perhaps over days. For there to be a likelihood of confusion, it would need to confuse a more alert customer than 'a moron in a hurry' (*Morning Star v Express Newspapers* [1979] FSR 113). Next time you are in a supermarket, see if you can spot examples of where the 'own brand' supermarket version of a product is made to look similar to the well-known household name. Consider whether you are actually confused as to origin (but only glance at the shelf – the point here is that the court recognises that customers do not stare at the products, trying to spot the differences).

18.2.3 Third element: damage

The claimant must show damage, or the likelihood of damage. Often, because of the likelihood of damage, the claimant will generally be seeking an interim injunction. In the ordinary case, where the claimant and defendant are trading in the same line of business, once goodwill and misrepresentation have been established the court is usually willing to infer damage.

The main types of damage are:

(a) loss of profits – people buy the infringing product instead of the claimant's product; and

(b) loss of reputation – usually because the infringing product is of inferior quality, and customers think the infringing product is made by the claimant.

If the infringer is in a different field of activity, the claimant might not succeed because he cannot show damage. For example, in *Stringfellow and Another v McCain Foods GB Ltd and Another* [1984] RPC 501, the nightclub was not able to stop oven chips being sold under the name 'Stringfellows'. In *Wombles Ltd v Wombles Skips Ltd* [1977] RPC 99, the copyright owners of the Wombles books and television series could not stop rubbish skips being hired out under the name 'Wombles'.

However, in other cases, claimants have been able to establish damage as a result of not being able to expand into a new market. The manufacturer of 'Marigold' rubber gloves was able to stop a toilet tissue being called 'Marigold' (*LRC International Ltd and Another v Lilla Edets Sales Co Ltd* [1973] RPC 560). Also, if the infringer's product is in a field that brings disrepute on the claimant then this can be a ground of damage. In the case of *Annabel's (Berkeley Square) Ltd v Schock (t/a Annabel's Escort Agency)* [1972] RPC 838, the use in question could have created an assumption that a well-known nightclub had started an escort agency. See **18.2.2** on the significance of large organisations and common field of activity problems.

In *Global Projects Management Ltd v Citigroup Inc* [2005] EWHC 2663 (Ch), the judge, in giving summary judgment for Citigroup, was prepared to accept that a domain owner, in using 'citigroup.co.uk', had created such a risk of e-mails going to unintended recipients that damage was self-evident, even if unquantifiable.

In *Irvine and Others v Talksport Ltd* [2003] EWCA Civ 423, [2003] 2 All ER 881, the matter concerned Eddie Irvine, a well-known racing driver. A photograph of him holding a mobile phone was altered so as to replace the mobile phone with a radio with the words 'Talk Radio' on it, and was then used by the defendants on a promotional leaflet for their activities. In short, they used him to advertise their product without paying him to endorse it. The Court of Appeal held that this was passing off, and that the measure of damages for a false product endorsement was the typical fee which the claimant would usually have sought.

18.3   DEFENCES TO PASSING OFF

There are a number of defences to passing off which have developed through the case law, in a random and somewhat overlapping manner. The principal ones are as follows:

(a)   careful and honest use of defendant's own name, mark or get-up;

(b)   defendant's or claimant's use otherwise than in trade;

(c)   claimant has no goodwill or the goodwill is owned by someone else;

(d)   claimant's acquiescence, encouragement or consent to use;

(e)   no provable damage or loss to claimant.

18.4   REMEDIES FOR PASSING OFF

Remedies for passing off can include:

(a)   an injunction;

(b)   damages (nominal, if innocent passing off);

(c)   an account of profits;

(d)   an order to cover up marks or repackage;

(e)   an order for delivery up or destruction of the offending items;

(f)   declarations as to rights.

Note: remedies (b) and (c) are normally mutually exclusive.

18.5   INTERNATIONAL ASPECTS

Other common law countries, such as Australia and New Zealand, also have laws of passing off, but their case law has developed differently on some points. Civil law countries, for example most European ones, have the law of unfair competition, which sometimes overlaps with passing off, but it is not the same in all respects. The US has the statutory claim of 'palming off', which is similar to passing off.

18.5.1   Paris Convention for the Protection of Industrial Property of 1883

The main source of international obligations in the field of unfair competition is the Paris Convention for the Protection of Industrial Property of 1883, as revised most recently in 1979. Its main highlights are as follows:

(a)   Countries which are signatories to the Convention (currently running at 171) are bound to assure to nationals of such countries effective protection against unfair competition.

(b)   Any act of competition contrary to honest practices in industrial or commercial matters constitutes an act of unfair competition.

(c)   The following in particular shall be prohibited:

(i)   all acts of such a nature as to create confusion by any means whatever with the establishment, the goods, or the industrial or commercial activities of a competitor; and

(ii)   false allegations in the course of trade of such a nature as to discredit the establishment, the goods, or the industrial or commercial activities of a competitor.

In the EU, Directive 2005/29 covers Member States' obligations deriving from the Convention. Among other things, it prohibits behaviour which is likely to distort the economic behaviour of consumers. This may include using a commercial practice to appreciably impair the consumer's ability to make an informed decision: this is very similar to passing off.

> **SUMMARY**
>
> Passing off is the first IP right we have looked at in detail. It is an unregistered right, so there is no public register in which you are able to record the existence of your right. It is a very flexible right, but not always easy to establish.

CHAPTER 19

TRADE MARKS

LEARNING OUTCOMES

After reading this chapter you will be able to:

- explain the key highlights of the law of trade marks
- apply the law to decide whether a mark would be prevented from registration for policy reasons
- apply the law to decide whether a mark would be prevented from registration due to similarity with other marks
- explain the consequences of infringement of a trade mark
- explain what remedies are available for breach
- categorise marks into classes used in the public register.

19.1 FUNCTIONS AND PURPOSES OF TRADE MARKS

A trade mark is simply a badge or indication of the trade origin of goods or services from a particular supplier. The legislative framework for registered marks in the United Kingdom is primarily the Trade Marks Act 1994 (TMA 1994), which has to date been moulded by harmonisation of trade mark laws across Europe.

Harmonisation has occurred not just at an EU level: international conventions, such as the Singapore Trade Mark Law Treaty and the Agreement on Trade Related Aspects of International Property Rights (TRIPs), have ensured that trade mark law does not vary widely around the world.

It may be said that the main functions of a registered trade mark are as follows:

(a) to indicate the trade origin of the goods or services with a particular supplier; see the definition in s 1(1) of the TMA 1994:

In this Act a 'trade mark' means any sign which is capable—

(a)   of being represented in the register in a manner which enables the registrar and other competent authorities and the public to determine the clear and precise subject matter of the protection afforded to the proprietor, and

(b)   of distinguishing goods or services of one undertaking from those of other undertakings.

(b)   as a likely indication of the quality of product associated with that supplier;

(c)   as a measure of the ongoing and changing value of the particular brand image of particular products, or of the image of the supplier as a whole;

(d)   as a useful and commercially exploitable piece of property, in itself.

19.2   ADVANTAGES AND CONSEQUENCES OF REGISTRATION

The two greatest advantages of registration of trade marks are that the period of protection given by registration is, potentially, unlimited and that the scope of protection is equivalent to an exclusive right to use the mark in trade for most commercial purposes permitted by the particular registration. Almost all other advantages and consequences stem from these two incidents of registration as can be seen from the brief following analysis.

19.2.1   Duration

The period of registration is an initial 10 years, with the option to renew the mark for subsequent 10-year periods, without limit in time. Provided that the mark does not lose its ability to distinguish the particular goods or services in question and is kept in (at least limited) use, it can remain in registration. The Bass red triangle trade mark for beer has been in use for more than 130 years and still retains its validity. An incidental gain from such long use is the possibility to develop wide and immediate recognition for a good brand, possibly at international level, and, additionally, a very strong presumption that the mark was validly registered in the first place. It is possible for registered trade marks to lose their validity by various means in due course, but this is discussed at **19.8**.

19.2.2   Exclusive rights

The starting point, here, is s 9(1) of the TMA 1994:

> The proprietor of a registered trade mark has exclusive rights in the trade mark which are infringed by use of the trade mark in the United Kingdom without his consent.

The infringing acts are then set out exhaustively in ss 10 and 11. All the various infringing acts involve use of the trade mark, 'in trade', without consent, in some way or another.

19.2.3   Other reasons to register

Other advantages to registering a trade mark are as follows:

(a)   *Easier to sue for infringement of a trade mark.* It is much quicker, cheaper, and less uncertain than a passing-off action. With a registered trade mark, there is an initial presumption of validity and the claimant usually starts off in quite a strong position. There is no need for the claimant to prove reputation in the mark.

(b)   *You can register a trade mark before you start using it.* Usually the trade mark is 'bagged' by making an application before the product is launched. This is a major advantage. In the US, such an application for registration is based on 'intent to use' but the actual registration itself will not be finalised until use occurs.

(c)   *There is a public record for trade marks.* This records both applications and registered trade marks. If somebody is intending to launch a new product (or to name a new company) then he will usually search the trade mark register to check whether anybody else has registered or applied for the same or a similar name. If it has been registered then he will think twice about using the name. In practice this is a very important reason for registering a mark – warning others off.

(d) *Danger that somebody else will register.* If you rely on building up rights in a mark through use, you run a risk that somebody else will register the same mark and even be able to stop you using it. However, a mark can be struck off for non-use in relation to the specified goods or services, so a purely defensive registration can be problematic. In the UK, for example, a mark can be struck off after five years' non-use. If 'BMW' was registered for, say, hair dryers but not used for five years, it could be struck off in relation to hair dryers, but not of course in relation to cars and whatever else it is actually used on.

A trade mark registration can last indefinitely if it retains its ability to distinguish the goods or services in question. The Bass red triangle for beer has been in existence for some 130 years and is still valid today.

In the US, however, a registration will not extinguish the rights of a prior user of a trade mark to continue use indefinitely. The registration will serve, however, to prevent the prior user from engaging in geographic and/or product expansion of the use of the mark. In the US this is referred to as the common law right of the first user.

19.3 THE REGISTRATION SYSTEM, ITS PROBLEMS AND RECENT CHANGES

Very widespread and far-reaching changes have been made to the system of registration and dealing with trade marks in the United Kingdom. For a very long time, the UK Trade Mark Registry ('the Registry') applied three quite different tests in considering whether any trade mark should be registered or not; if the mark failed to comply with any of them, registration was refused. It considered:

(a) whether the mark was capable of being a trade mark within the s 1(1) definition at all;

(b) whether, if it was, it should be refused registration under any of the absolute grounds under s 3 of the TMA 1994 (including the law on passing off); and

(c) whether it should be refused registration for any of the relative grounds in s 5 of the TMA 1994.

These steps are discussed in more detail below and at **19.4–19.6**. This system long had the advantage that trade marks registered here were seen as having a very strong presumption of validity because of the care with which the Registry formerly investigated prior registrations and, indeed, unregistered marks before allowing a mark to be registered.

The difficulty was that this was not the general practice in most of Europe, and what brought the matter into sharp focus was the very large expansion in the EU Trade Mark (EUTM) system (see **19.13.1**). The broad rule for EUTMs and trade marks throughout much of the EU (other than in the UK until recently) is that it is for objectors to registration to raise the objection themselves, rather than for the registrars to search. The registrar does, however, retain the discretion to search for prior registrations under the Trade Mark Rules 2000 (SI 2000/136), r 11A.

This created such a problem that the UK Registry has now adopted the technique of relying upon objections being raised by persons adversely affected by an application for a UK trade mark. This may well create great expense and difficulty, especially for the smaller undertaking, in protecting registered trade marks (as well as unregistered matters which might be passed off). The following description deals with the practice followed in registration. The new approach to dealing with relative grounds objections is dealt with at **19.7.3**.

Anyone can apply to register a trade mark in the UK, whether they own the trade mark or not, provided that they are using the mark for goods or services, or intend to do so. It does not matter where the applicant comes from. There is a fairly large number of formalities, which are not extensively reviewed here, but which can fairly easily be ascertained by a visit to the website at <www.ipo.gov.uk>. The main legal source of these requirements is the TMA 1994 and the Trade Mark Rules 2000 made under the Act. The formal and procedural stages of the registration process are not dealt with further, but they may be seen on the website mentioned above and in the Trade Mark Rules 2000.

A trade mark has to be registered in relation to named goods or services, in that a class or classes of goods or services must be chosen. Trade marks are registered in one or more of 45 classes (see **19.16**). The main purpose of the classes is to facilitate searching for trade mark registrations. A trade mark will often be registered in more than one class. For example, the trade mark for a beer would be registered in class 32, but the same trade mark could also be registered in class 25 for clothing, as the name might be used on clothing to promote the beer.

As well as the Nice Agreement for classification of products, the figurative elements of marks are classified according to the Vienna Agreement Establishing an International Classification of the Figurative Elements of Marks. This was adopted on 12 June 1973 by a conference held in Vienna. The Agreement in fact only entered into force on 9 August 1985. Use of the Vienna Classification by national offices has the advantage of filing the figurative elements of marks with reference to a single classification system. This procedure facilitates trade mark anticipation searches and obviates substantial reclassification work when documents are exchanged at the international level.

The Vienna Classification constitutes a hierarchical system that proceeds from the general to the particular, dividing all figurative elements into categories, divisions and sections. Explanatory notes have been introduced where appropriate. The classification comprises a total of 29 categories, 144 divisions and 1,887 sections in which the figurative elements of marks are classified. There are at present only 28 contracting States, but many others use the classification system without having signed the agreement.

Further, in the US, it is not an infringement to use a trade mark of another in a descriptive, ie non-trade mark, way. This defence is limited, however, to those trade marks which themselves are somewhat weak.

19.4 CAN THE TRADE MARK MEET THE STATUTORY DEFINITION?

There are two distinct issues within this question. Can the sign be represented on the register? Can it distinguish the goods or services of the applicant from those of other undertakings?

19.4.1 Capable of being represented in the register

In order to be registered, a mark must be capable of being represented in the register in a manner which enables the registrar and other competent authorities and the public to determine the clear and precise subject matter of the protection afforded to the proprietor (TMA 1994, s 1(1)). This replaced the previous requirement (until January 2019) that the mark must be 'capable of being represented graphically'. It is thought that the wider definition in the revised Act will allow more scope for sounds and smells to be registered, subject to s 3 (discussed below). Sounds previously suffered from the need to represent them in musical notation (ie graphically), and so sound recordings may not have been registered if they were not recordings of music. Now a computer-recorded file may be submitted, and so we may see an increase in the registration of, for example, advertisement jingles or catchphrases in sound form. Smells would previously struggle for registration unless they could be represented by a chemical formula. It is unclear how the new definition will change that, but see the discussion of s 3 below for further issues which may cause smells registration problems.

19.4.2 Capable of distinguishing

Many signs and words are so commonplace in everyday use as to be incapable of having a distinctive quality in isolation. There is a strong overlap between the general limitations of the s 1(1) definition and the absolute bars to registration in s 3, so most of the discussion on the distinctiveness requirement follows in **19.5**, but it should be borne in mind that what needs to be distinctive is the mark, as a whole, rather than particular features within it. It is, therefore, quite normal to find imaginative combinations of rather commonplace symbols, words or colours achieving registration as trade marks; all that matters is to find something distinctive about the overall arrangement. A well-known example is the 'Finish' title, combined with the red 'powerball' device mark for dishwasher products. None of the component parts of the mark is particularly distinctive, but in aggregate they become highly distinctive and recognisable.

The word mark 'Deliberately Innovative' was found to lack any distinctive character in *Interactive Intelligence Inc's Registration No 873858* [2007] WL 1180.

19.5 ABSOLUTE GROUNDS FOR REFUSAL

In s 3 of the TMA 1994, the absolute grounds for refusal to register are laid down. The most common ones are in s 3(1):

> The following shall not be registered—
>
> (a) signs which do not satisfy the requirements of section 1(1),
>
> (b) trade marks that are devoid of distinctive character,
>
> (c) trade marks which consist exclusively of signs or indications which may serve, in trade, to designate the kind, quality, quantity, intended purpose, value, geographical origin, the time of production of goods or of rendering of services, or other characteristics of goods or services,
>
> (d) trade marks that consist exclusively of signs or indications which have become customary in the current language or in the bona fide and established practices of the trade:
>
> Provided that, a trade mark shall not be refused registration by virtue of paragraph (b), (c) or (d) above if, before the date of application for registration, it has in fact acquired a distinctive character as a result of the use made of it.

After implementation of the Trade Mark Directive, the following grounds were added as absolute grounds: designations of origin, geographical indications, traditional terms for wine, traditional specialities guaranteed and plant varieties.

Distinctiveness, in the eyes of the customer, is the idea that lies behind all the paragraphs of s 3(1). A mark will undoubtedly be distinctive if it is a made-up name. The ones usually quoted are 'Kodak' or 'Exxon'. Beware of words that are merely phonetic spellings of ordinary words so that they look distinctive until pronounced (eg, 'Orlwoola' for all wool (see **19.5.5**), or 'Writs' for a sandwich bar (ie, potential problems with the Ritz restaurant)).

Clearly, the bars to registration in s 3(1)(b) to (d) can largely be bypassed by the proviso that distinctiveness has been acquired by extensive use of the trade mark. That will not, however, cure any objections under paragraph (a), such as that the sign fails the s 1(1) requirement that the mark can be represented on the register; no amount of use can get over that hurdle and that sign will remain unregistrable. Distinctiveness acquired through use is discussed in more depth at **19.6**.

The main s 3(1) problem areas in registration tend to be associated with:

(a) the use of names of individuals or businesses;

(b) aspects of the goods or services on offer; and

(c) geographical origins of the goods or services.

These matters are dealt with at **19.5.1**, **19.5.2** and **19.5.3**. The difficult question of shape marks (s 3(2)) is dealt with at **19.5.4** and public policy objections (s 3(3)) at **19.5.5**.

Intellectual property lawyers will tell you that it is very common for a client to come up with a name for a product or business which falls foul of (b) above: it sums up the product or business too accurately. For example, 'Shine' may be a great name for a cleaning product, but it stands little chance of registration, at least not until a reputation is built up in the name. Note that this does not mean that it cannot be used to sell the product: the client simply has no protection in the name. Often clients like their idea so much that they press ahead with the name, accepting that, at least initially, there is a risk that others will also choose to use it.

19.5.1   Use of names as trade marks

It is long established that any person is entitled to use his own personal or business name and address, fairly and honestly, without it comprising an infringement; see s 11(2) of the TMA 1994. It does not follow from this that everyone can register their own name, in that way. Many names are so common as to be unable to distinguish goods or services for the purposes of s 3(1)(b), so that the name, standing alone, is unregistrable; combine it with an address or some other distinctive feature, however, and that may solve the problem. Nevertheless, people like short, catchy trade marks. An unusual name is unlikely to create such distinctiveness problems, but common names, even if presented in an eye-catching way, can be difficult to register, although sometimes personal signatures are trade marked (consider the 'Ford' signature mark). Often, the problem is that there are already prior registered marks, using the same name.

The former Registry practice was to use a simple rule of thumb, based on the statistical incidence of the name in the London telephone directory, as a guide. This was held, with reason, to be so arbitrary as to be useless in deciding the question of distinctiveness, in the ECJ decision in *Nichols plc v The Registrar of Trade Marks* (Case C-404/02) [2004] All ER (D) 114. The approach of the ECJ was that an individual assessment needs to be made on the facts of each application, taking into account the likely scope of use of the mark, as to area of use, range of products marked and likely customer group, allowing for a certain level of reasonably informed and aware customers; see *Koninklijke Philips Electronics v Remington Consumer Products Ltd* (Case C-299/99) [2002] 2 CMLR 52, [2003] Ch 159. This approach seems now to have been adopted by the IPO, but it should still be borne in mind that even common names can acquire distinctiveness through use; see *El Du Pont de Nemours & Co v ST Dupont* [2004] FSR 15.

The trade mark use of names, other than that of the provider of the goods or services, raises different considerations such as arise in character merchandising, franchising and IP licensing. Those matters are beyond the scope of this part of the text.

19.5.2   Aspects of the goods or services themselves within s 3(1)(c)

This is a vital protection against unfair monopolisation of descriptive signs or indications by any particular person. The paragraph only strikes at trade marks consisting exclusively of such indications (which are usually terms common in the trade). In *Timken Co's Application No 2418442* (Trade Mark Registry 18/09/07) [2007] WL 2817814, the Registry refused 'friction management solutions' as far too descriptive of the services offered to be registered, as other people offering friction management solutions would not have been able to advertise what they do. If the descriptive aspect is used in combination with more distinctive features, there is usually no problem.

Signs only serving to describe the type of good cannot be registered by themselves: orange juice, cornflakes or crisps are obviously unregistrable, but even more imaginative signs may still fail for descriptiveness. 'Tastee-Freez' for ice cream and 'Weldmesh' for reinforcing mesh were too descriptive to register, whereas 'Twiglets' has long been registered for snack-type biscuits for both humans and animals. The obvious difference is that although the snacks look like twigs, they are, in fact, completely different things; the mark is not descriptive of the kind of good, only suggestive of its appearance. This imaginative mark is highly distinctive among biscuits. Put simply, coming up with the name 'Twiglets' took some ingenuity, whereas coming up with the name 'Snacks' or even 'Snax' does not.

Words of quality or value are, likewise, unregistrable, by themselves, particularly 'laudatory' words such as 'magic', 'supreme', etc. Some imagination, though, can change the situation considerably; there are very large numbers of registrations, in all sorts of classes, for variations on 'exel', 'excell', 'XL' etc. Some of the most imaginative trade mark concepts have come from the confectionery world, with imagery such as 'Mars', 'Galaxy', 'Smarties', 'Quality Street', etc. The list is endless but all have the same aspect: they do not directly, or in many cases indirectly, suggest the nature of the good itself, but may, indirectly, suggest qualities and connotations beyond the mundane and mediocre. A case that is very close to the line is *Bostik Ltd v Henkel KGAA* (Trade Mark Registry 3/09/07) [2007] WL 2573891, where the applications to register 'Hyper Glue' and 'Hypaglue' were upheld, because 'hyper' was not found to be synonymous with 'super' (which would not have been registrable). Similarly, with words or signs showing the intended purpose of the good, one needs to go beyond mere descriptiveness to achieve registration: the 'Walkman' personal stereo and 'Workmate' portable work bench illustrate the successful registration and use of such marks.

The case of *Procter & Gamble Co v Office for Harmonisation in the Internal Market (Trade Marks and Designs)* [2002] RPC 17 has widened the scope for businesses that want to use trade marks which could be descriptive. This was a case before the ECJ. The applicant appealed from a decision of the OHIM (the predecessor to the EU Intellectual Property Office). The application was for registration as a European trade mark of 'Baby-Dry' for 'disposable diapers made out of paper or cellulose and diapers made out of textile'. The application had been rejected by OHIM as being the combination of two descriptive words, that is 'baby' and 'dry'. However, the ECJ held that while each word on its own was not distinctive, the use of the two words together produced an unusual combination which was not in common English usage.

In contrast, in *DKV Deutsche Krankenversicherung AG v Office for Harmonisation in the Internal Market* [2002] ECR I-7561, the appeal against the refusal of OHIM to allow 'Companyline' to be registered as a Community trade mark for insurance and financial advice was rejected by the ECJ. The judgment of the Court of First Instance, and therefore the refusal to register, was upheld. The ECJ held that coupling together two such general words as 'company' and 'line' created nothing distinctive in the factual circumstance. In *Easynet Group plc v Easygroup IP Licensing Ltd* [2006] EWHC 1872, Mann J confirmed that the correct approach was an overall assessment of the composite expression as to whether it is descriptive or not. If it is not, it is likely to be distinctive and registrable. The registration of 'easy.com' for a range of goods and services was upheld.

In the case of the 'Doublemint' trade mark for chewing gum, the ECJ held that the trade mark was descriptive, ambiguous and therefore deceptive, and could not be registered. Part of the reason for distinguishing this application from Baby-Dry was that Baby-Dry was an unusual combination of two ordinary words, in the reverse order from any common usage of the terms. This was not the case with 'Doublemint' (*OHIM (Doublemint) v Wrigley* (Case C-191/01) (ECJ, 23 October 2003)). The judgment followed the *Chiemsee* case, in that the ECJ held that this was a trade expression that should be kept free for other businesses to use if they so wish (see **19.5**).

19.5.3 Marks suggesting geographical origin

In the majority of cases, geographical names will not be acceptable as trade marks.

In the leading case of *Windsurfing Chiemsee Produktions und Vertriebs GmbH v Boots und Segelzubehör Walter Huber and Another* [2000] Ch 523, the ECJ refused to allow the geographical name to be registered. It held that a geographical name had to be left available for other traders to use in the future, particularly those actually located at Chiemsee (a holiday lake in Bavaria). A geographical name which did not indicate the origin of the goods would be unregistrable for being deceptive. For example, 'Swiss Miss' was refused as the chocolate was not produced in Switzerland. However, if it is totally fanciful it could succeed, for example 'Sahara' for ice cream. An objection on grounds of deceptiveness could not be overcome by any amount of use of the mark.

There are some indications that a more relaxed attitude is being taken towards geographical marks in Community trade mark applications (see **19.13.1**), particularly so with small geographical locations (see *Peek & Cloppenburg v OHIM* [2006] ETMR 35).

The problem of geographical indications can be cured, for trade marks purposes, by making certain that the mark is not exclusively geographical, eg, 'Grants of St James's', although high-class areas are not easy to use in this way because of the possibility of deceptiveness.

Another possible protection, one that often overlaps with geographical indications, is the use of 'collective marks'. These can be registered under s 49 of and Sch 1 to the TMA 1994 and comprise marks which show that the goods or services are provided by a member of a particular trade association, so as to distinguish them from those of other organisations or persons. These can be registered and frequently contain indications of geographical origins (subject to most relevant traders in that product and location being willing to join the association, as with the Melton Mowbray Pork Pie Association, which has 'AUTHENTIC . MELTON MOWBRAY' as its mark); this is permitted by the Schedule, but the collective trade mark cannot be used to prevent other persons (typically, those local traders who do not wish to join up), who would be following normal, honest business practice, from using that geographical indication in their business. In a similar way, 'certification marks' may be registered under s 50 of and Sch 2 to the TMA 1994 to show other highly descriptive characteristics of goods or services that would normally be caught by s 3(1)(c); things like the 'Woolmark' for textiles and 'Stilton' for cheese are registered.

There are further levels of protection available to geographical indications at the EU level by way of 'protected designations of origin' ('PDO') and 'protected geographical indications' ('PGI'), as well as at international level, where there are World Intellectual Property Organisation 'appellations of origin'. The general idea of most of this protection is to allow persons to use and register official logos and titles to show that certain products (and only those products) are designated by and linked to particular geographical origins and locations. In *Consorzio del Prosciutto di Parma v Asda Stores Ltd* (Case C-108/01) [2001] UKHL 7, the Parma Ham Association attempted to prevent Asda from further processing Parma ham, protected by a PDO, by way of slicing, labelling and packaging it in the UK. The ECJ, on a reference from the House of Lords, found that this further protection for the ham was justified by its protection under the PDO and was a valid Community right, directly enforceable in Member States (subject to its being properly publicised to the Community). The Melton Mowbray Pork Pie Association has now achieved PGI status for a range of its products. Further discussion of geographical indications is, however, beyond the scope of this book.

Many jurisdictions have been required to amend their trade mark legislation in order to accommodate the requirement of protection of collective marks under TRIPS. Article 7 *bis* of the Paris Convention also requires signatories 'to accept for filing and to protect collective marks belonging to associations the existence of which is not contrary to the law of the country of origin, even if such organisations do not possess an industrial or commercial establishment'.

As mentioned above, designations of origin and geographical indications were added as absolute grounds upon implementation of the Trade Marks Directive.

19.5.4 Shape marks or those involving characteristics of the goods (s 3(2))

It is not possible to register trade marks which consist exclusively of:

(a)   the shape or other characteristics which result from the goods themselves;

(b)   the shape or other characteristics of goods which is necessary to achieve a technical result; or

(c)   the shape or other characteristics which gives substantial value to the goods.

Again, the key to these exclusions is that what needs to be shown is that the mark is distinctive, eye-catching and memorable in some way and, additionally, raises the association with a particular trade source. The main problem with allowing registration of shape marks is that the potentially unlimited duration of the mark contrasts so vividly with the limited protection period (25 years maximum) of other industrial and commercial designs (see **Chapter 22**). It is very dangerous to allow anyone a monopoly on shapes – that is why they were not capable of trade mark protection until 1994 – and it is still not easy to achieve shape mark registration.

The case law is often quite speculative in its interpretation of s 3(2) and Council Directive 89/104 EEC, to which it gives effect. (Section 3(2) was further amended, due to EU Directive 2015/2436, to add 'characteristics of the goods'.) It is quite clear that there is a substantial overlap between the three excluded cases in s 3(2); it is also clear that the s 3(1) provision for distinctiveness, acquired by use, does not apply to shape marks which are excluded by s 3(2), although it could apply to marks comprising, in part, matters restricted by s 3(2). That explains how the Coca-Cola bottle achieved its registration.

The key to understanding much of the case law on s 3(2) lies in the fact that to exclude a shape mark from registration, that mark must consist 'exclusively' of the proscribed shape. Many marks will consist of other things beyond mere shape. Some indication of the judicial approach is seen as follows.

19.5.4.1   The shape of the goods themselves

The Court of Appeal upheld the Registrar's refusal to register the shape of the shaver heads of the Philishave razor (*Philips Electronics NV v Remington Consumer Products Ltd (No 2)* [1999] RPC 809). On a reference to the ECJ on construction of the Directive on the Approximation of the Laws of Member States about Trade Marks (Directive 89/104/EC) from which TMA 1994 derives, the ECJ held that a shape determined by technical function of the product was not registrable as a trade mark (Case C-299/99).

In effect, the logic behind the s 3(2) exclusion is that the shape of products should be given a lesser protection as a registered design if the shape is new and has individual character (see **22.2.1**). A registered trade mark is not the appropriate right.

In *Dyson Ltd v Registrar of Trade Marks* (Case C-321/03) [2003] EWHC 1062 (Ch) Dyson attempted to achieve a very wide-ranging protection for all conceivable shapes and configurations of the external face of part of its vacuum cleaner. This was treated by the High Court, as well as the ECJ on reference, as not being a shape mark application at all, but simply a feature, which had a function and a potentially variable appearance. The ECJ was also asked whether public association of such features with Dyson was enough for it to be registrable. The ECJ found that such an infinitely variable shape could not be graphically represented so as to constitute a distinctive trade mark, because it was simply not a 'sign' in the first place. The question of distinctiveness by use did not arise on those facts.

In *Société des Produits Nestlé SA v Unilever plc* [2002] EWHC 2709 (Ch), [2003] RPC 35, it was held that it was arguable that the shape of Vienetta ice cream resulted from the nature of the product itself, which of course would render it unregistrable as a trade mark. It was also held that there was insufficient evidence that the public recognised the shape of Vienetta as a badge of origin of the goods (ie, as emanating from Unilever), which also renders it unregistrable. In *Société des Produits Nestlé SA v Mars UK Ltd* [2004] EWCA Civ 1008, the Court of Appeal confirmed the refusal of an application to register as a trade mark the three-dimensional shape of a 'Polo' mint, which did not have the word 'Polo' embossed on it. The Registrar would have allowed registration if the application had been for mint-flavoured confectionery only, and had been for the colour white and only for the size of a standard 'Polo' mint. The Court upheld his opinion.

Guidance from the ECJ came in 2018 in Case C-84/17 P *Société des produits Nestlé SA v Mondelez UK Holdings & Services Ltd*, formerly Cadbury Holdings Ltd, in which Nestlé and Cadbury fought over whether a four-finger Kitkat was capable of being trade marked as an EU trade mark. The ECJ said that Nestlé had failed to establish that the shape had gained a distinctive character throughout the EU. It should be noted that it was accepted by the Court that the product had gained a distinctive character in several Member States; however, this was insufficient for an EU trade mark. It is therefore possible that local registrations in various countries would be valid.

19.5.4.2   The shape of the goods which is necessary to achieve a technical result

This was the real basis of the result in the *Philips* case (see **19.5.4.1**); the 3-rotor configuration gave the technical superiority to the shaver in the first place, and the ECJ made it clear that the exclusion was not limited to situations where the shape in question was the only available shape to achieve that particular technical result. As long as the shape is important to the technical outcome, that is likely to prevent its registration. One solid advantage of this is that interesting shapes might be registrable in other applications, where they are not technically necessary, technically, eg, a small pistol as a trade mark for '*femme fatale*' scent.

19.5.4.3   The shape which gives substantial value to the goods

This seems to be a rather difficult exclusion to apply, and it gave difficulties to the High Court and the Court of Appeal in attempting to rationalise its meaning in the *Philips* case (see **19.5.4.1**). It may well be that a shape which makes goods substantially more valuable to the user, but which is protected by way neither of patent nor design, is what is really being aimed at here. In that case, it would be a retrograde step to allow anyone to have a permanent monopoly by way of trade mark over it. Possibly, things like pistol-grip shapes, spout shapes etc, which do not fit easily into the other exclusions but are intensely used and valued by buyers, might be caught here.

In *Benetton Group SpA v G-Star International BV* (Case C-371/06) [2008] ETMR 5, ECJ, the Court held that a jeans manufacturer should not have been given registration of two shape marks for jeans where the public recognition was based upon extensive advertising of the interesting shapes. The rule in the *Philips* case was applicable, and distinctiveness acquired by use could not cure the statutory bar to registration. The marks were annulled.

19.5.4.4   Other characteristics of the goods

Directive 2015/2436, when implemented in the UK in January 2019, added 'or another characteristic' to each subsection of s 3(2) of the TMA 1994, so applications will be unsuccessful if such a characteristic of the goods arises from the nature of the goods, is necessary to achieve a technical result, or gives substantial value to the goods. At the time of writing it is too early to have examples where applications have been rejected; however, it may be the case that smells of, eg, perfumes would not be registrable under the revised section, as the smell is a characteristic of the goods, and adds value to them.

19.5.5   Public interest objections (s 3(3)) and bad faith applications (s 3(6))

An application will not succeed if the trade mark in question is contrary to public policy or morality (s 3(3)(a)), is likely to deceive (s 3(3)(b)) or is made in bad faith (s 3(6)).

19.5.5.1   Likely to deceive

For example, 'Orlwoola' for clothes would be deceptive if the clothes were not made entirely of wool (and if they were, it would be descriptive). 'Instant dip' for cleaning materials was refused on the basis that some of the materials were not in fact dips (*In the matter of Application No 713,406 by Otto Seligmann for the Registration of a Trade Mark* (1954) 71 RPC 52).

Often, a significant limitation to such objections can arise if a mark has been registered for use in only particular colours. The use of a similar mark in quite different colours may not necessarily be deceptive (see *Phones 4u Ltd and Another v Phone4u.co.uk Internet Ltd* [2006] EWCA Civ 244).

19.5.5.2 Bad faith applications

An example of an existing trade mark registration being struck off as being in bad faith occurred in *Byford v Oliver and Another* [2003] EWHC 295 (Ch), [2003] All ER (D) 345 (Feb). This concerned a number of registrations obtained in 1999 by the defendants for the name 'Saxon', which was a 1980s heavy metal band that is still performing – very loudly. The membership of the band had changed over the years but the claimant had always been a member. The defendants had been members for only part of the period. The defendants were held not to own the name and goodwill of the band 'Saxon' in its various guises. There appear to be other disputes concerning the reformation of earlier successful bands and the use of associated names and marks, so more legislation is likely, shortly.

In *Jules Rimet Cup Ltd v Football Association Ltd* [2007] EWHC 2376 (Ch), the court held that the claimant had acted, both subjectively and objectively, in bad faith, in seeking to register the 'World Cup Willie' logo and words as trade marks. The claimant must have known that there was still valuable residual goodwill in the UK for such a familiar mark.

An application to strike off a mark as being deceptive was made in *Zakritoe Aktsionernoe Obchtechestvo Torgovy Dom Potomkov Postavechtchika Dvora Ego Imperatorskago Velitschestva PA Smirnova v Diageo North America Inc* [2003] All ER (D) 99 (Apr). The (Russian) appellant's argument was that the (American) respondent's 14 registrations of the word 'Smirnoff' implied an unjustified connection with the Russian Federation. Smirnoff vodka has been sold since 1952 and is described as the world's leading brand. The appeal failed, as there was held to be no deception as to the origin of the goods. The registrations for 'Smirnoff' were upheld.

19.5.5.3 Public policy or morality

In *Ghazilian's Trade Mark Application* [2002] RPC 23, the applicant appealed the refusal of the Registrar of Trade Marks to register as a trade mark for clothing the words 'Tiny Penis'. Not surprisingly, the judge agreed with the Registrar and refused registration. The judge held that the hearing officer had to consider objectively how a right-thinking, but open-minded, member of the public would view the mark in question, as in *Re Masterman's Design* [1991] RPC 89. (This concerned a Scottish doll wearing a kilt but nothing under it. Registration of the design was allowed.)

An attempt to have the FCUK registration declared invalid on public policy grounds failed; the mark had been properly registered and any objectionable use of the mark by third parties could not affect its continued validity (see *French Connection Ltd's Trade Mark Application (No 81862)* [2005] WL 3734085). This reasoning can be seen in the successful registration of many highly suggestive marks.

19.6 EVIDENCE OF USE TO OVERCOME ABSOLUTE GROUNDS

In **19.5** we saw how the criteria for absolute grounds work. However, there are lots of registered trade marks which would offend these criteria. The registration system would therefore unfairly deprive the proprietors of the protection of registration, when in fact the trade marks are already well known in the trade or to the public. Examples of trade marks which prima facie offend the criteria for absolute grounds but yet have been registered include the 'York' trailer trade mark (geographical objections) and 'Premier' luggage (laudatory description). The reason is that lack of distinctiveness can often be overcome by publicly recognised use, that is, by building up goodwill in the mark. If an applicant can show that it has built up a reputation in, say, a descriptive mark by using it, then it may have acquired distinctiveness in fact through use and it can be registered. The Coca-Cola bottle shape was universally associated, by use, with the company, although the bottle shape had some distinctive features anyway. The applicant will establish reputation in the mark by sending a statutory declaration to the Trade Mark Registry giving evidence of advertising spend, turnover in the goods and length of use. (Also it needs to be use as an indicator of origin of the goods or services, sometimes referred to as 'trade mark use'.) An informal minimum number of years' use is five. If you do not have five years of use, it is not generally worth trying. Usually the client does better to choose a mark that is registrable from the outset without use, but valuable marks do often arise over time.

Very few colours are registered, but the colour of Heinz tins of baked beans has now been registered on the basis of use. Usually, for colour to be considered it has to be a combination of colours, not just a single shade. See *Smith Kline & French Laboratories Ltd v Sterling-Winthrop Group Ltd* [1975] 2 All ER 578, where a complex of colours for a pharmaceutical capsule was accepted on evidence of wide recognition of the complex as distinguishing the goods. (Be aware that this case was under the old Trade Marks Act 1938.) Nevertheless, in *BP Amoco plc v John Kelly Ltd* [2002] FSR 5, it was held that BP's trade mark registration of a single colour was valid. The trade mark consisted of the shade of green defined in colour charts as Pantone 348C, which BP used as the livery for their petrol filling stations. In *Libertel Group BV v Benelux-Merkenbureau Case* (C-104/01) [2004] 2 WLR 1081, the ECJ held that in order to be capable of being registered as a trade mark, a colour had to be defined by reference to an international identification system. It was not sufficient to lodge a sample with the trade mark office in question. The colour also had to have distinctive character (ie, to have been used in relation to the goods or services in question).

A type of mark that often arises over time is in the recognised use of slogans; these can become very well known indicators of trade origin. But they have their own problems. The long-running attempt to register 'HAVE A BREAK', quite independently of the well-known 'have a break ... have a Kit Kat', has produced an ECJ reference by the Court of Appeal that appears to give support for the proposition that long use and recognition of the mark, in association with a registered trade mark, even as part of a more extensive slogan, can give the necessary distinctiveness of trade origin for registration; see *Société des Produits Nestlé SA v Mars UK Ltd* (Case C-353/03) [2005] 3 CMLR 12, [2006] All ER (EC) 348, ECJ. The problem, up to the stage of the reference, was the High Court view, supporting the refusal to register, that 'have a break', standing alone, was a common phrase that had no distinctive quality in itself.

Generally, with slogans, the more curious the expression and the less related to the particular goods or services, the greater the likelihood of registration, the downside being that the promotional value must, necessarily, be very indirect. Established use is very helpful in trying to register slogans as trade marks, in part because it allows a trial period to see whether the slogan is effective, in a commercial sense, before trying to register.

19.7   RELATIVE GROUNDS FOR REFUSING AN APPLICATION

19.7.1   What does 'relative grounds' mean?

'Relative grounds' means a conflict with an existing registered trade mark, belonging to someone else, which is identical or similar to the one being applied for. In TMA 1994, s 5, the relative grounds for refusal are laid down. The most common ones are as follows:

(1)   A trade mark shall not be registered if it is identical with an earlier trade mark and the goods or services for which the trade mark is applied for are identical with the goods or services for which the earlier trade mark is protected.

(2)   A trade mark shall not be registered if because—

(a)   it is identical with an earlier trade mark and is to be registered for goods or services similar to those for which the earlier trade mark is protected, or

(b)   it is similar to an earlier trade mark and is to be registered for goods or services identical with or similar to those for which the earlier trade mark is protected,

there exists a likelihood of confusion on the part of the public, which includes the likelihood of association with the earlier trade mark.

(3)   A trade mark which—

(a)   is identical with or similar to an earlier trade mark, ...

(b)   ...

shall not be registered if, or to the extent that, the earlier trade mark has a reputation in the United Kingdom (or, in the case of an EU trade mark, in the European Union) and the use of the later mark without due cause would take unfair advantage of, or be detrimental to, the distinctive character or the repute of the earlier trade mark.

Following implementation of the Trade Marks Directive, the owner of a designation of origin or a geographical indication will now be able to rely on those rights to prevent the registration of a mark.

How do you find out whether your client's proposed trade mark is going to run foul of an existing registration? The answer is to do a trade mark search. Most firms have facilities for doing this online; alternatively, you can get one through an agency like Compumark. If you are inexperienced in this kind of work then it is best to go to an agency because they will analyse it for you to some extent. If you really don't know what you are doing, you instruct a trade mark agent. Beware that the results of a trade mark search are never completely up to date. The search facilities available on www.ipo.gov.uk are admirably easy to use.

Because trade marks are registered in relation to specified goods or services, the starting point is to look for trade marks registered for the same types of goods and services, that is, in the relevant classes (see **19.3** and **19.16**).

Note that 'without due cause' in s 5(3) was recently interpreted by the ECJ in the context of the use of the wording in Directive 2008/95 (a harmonising directive on trade marks which the TMA 1994 complies with). Case C-65/12 *Leidseplein Beheer BV, Hendrikus de Vries v Red Bull GmbH* concerned a trade mark infringement allegation made by Red Bull against the manufacturer of the 'Bulldog' energy drink, Hendrikus de Fries. De Fries had used the mark for many years prior to Red Bull's 1983 registration, for other commercial activities such as coffee shops and hotels. In 1983 he registered it as a mark for non-alcoholic drinks but only began using it for energy drinks in 1997.

The ECJ said that 'due cause' means that the proprietor of the mark has to tolerate the use by a third party of a sign similar to that mark in relation to a product which is identical to that for which that mark was registered, if it is demonstrated that the sign was being used before that mark was filed and that the use of that sign in relation to the identical product is in good faith. In order to determine whether that is so, the national court must take account, in particular, of:

•   how that sign has been accepted by, and what its reputation is with, the relevant public;

•   the degree of proximity between the goods and services for which that sign was originally used and the product for which the mark with a reputation was registered; and

•   the economic and commercial significance of the use for that product of the sign which is similar to that mark.

It is for the national courts to apply this ruling to the facts before them.

A trade mark application can also be refused on the grounds that it is likely to be the subject of a passing-off action (TMA 1994, s 5(4) and see **18.1**). To check for earlier rights in passing off, you can do a common law search by looking in telephone directories and journals (eg, in magazines on mountain bikes for marks used in connection with push bikes), etc. This common law search cannot, of course, be comprehensive. Some earlier rights may well be obvious, even without a search. See *Jules Rimet Cup Ltd v Football Association Ltd* (at **19.5.5.2**), concerning an application to register the 'World Cup Willie' logo and words.

The starting point, then, with relative ground objections, is to show an identical or similar pre-existing registration; dissimilar marks usually create few problems. The same concepts and case law come into play when considering infringements under s 10, which are discussed at **18.9**, and the same matters need to be considered. It is very important, therefore, to consider how identity and similarity are assessed in this circumstance and it is not at all easy to summarise the approaches taken. Generally, the test is one for the registration authorities and the courts, according to legal principles, a brief summary of which now follows.

19.7.1.1 Identical marks

The broad approach is for the court to put itself in the position of a reasonable, well-informed and alert customer, seeing the mark and having all the usual imperfections of recall of earlier marks that would be normal in such a person. It follows that tactile, visual and aural perceptions are important and it is probably only going to be clearly an identical mark if, without much modification, the essential elements of the earlier mark, as registered, are reproduced in the later one.

Usually, the difficulties come where someone has used only part of an earlier mark, or has used all of an earlier mark and added more to it to create a larger, more complex mark, eg, if someone used the famous 'Smartie' mark in a larger composition. Generally, anyone doing the latter would be at risk of infringing the earlier mark, because they have reproduced it in its entirety, albeit as part of a mark; that could be done by extending a trade marked word into a longer word or phrase; see *Decon Laboratories Ltd v Fred Baker Scientific Ltd* [2001] RPC 293 and *System 3R International AB v Erowa AG and Erowa Nordic AB* [2003] ETMR 916 where the marks were 'Decon-Phase', 'Decon-Phene', 'Decon-Ahol' and 'Decon-Clean'. It was felt that the additions were merely variations of the mark, and so did not take away meaning. However, the Court of Appeal came to a contrary conclusion in *Reed Executive and Reed Solutions v Reed Business Information and Elsevier* [2004] EWCA Civ 159, [2004] RPC 40. There, the claimant argued that 'Reed Business Information' was identical under s 10(1) to its registered trade mark 'Reed'. In other words, if the registered trade mark cropped up in only part of another business name, that was use of an identical sign. The Court rejected this argument and held that the words 'Business Information' were part of the defendant's business name. Consequently, 'Reed Business Information' was not identical to 'Reed', so the issue was not use of an identical sign in s 10(1), but rather of a 'similar' sign under s 10(2). In other words, you have to look at the whole of the allegedly infringing sign or mark.

It would also seem that stylising the word in a different way may still amount to using an identical mark. The advantage of finding an identical mark, as compared with a similar one, is that, if used on identical goods, nothing more needs to be established to prevent registration (compare s 5(1) with s 5(2)).

19.7.1.2 Identical goods or services

This can be a problem area in some respects. It is certainly not enough that the goods or services are within the same registration class; the goods or services need to have a considerable identity in terms of what they are, in themselves, as well as with respect to what the customer is expecting to obtain. There is no requirement for direct identity between the particular appearance or other aspects of the compared matters; a square, red ceramic floor tile is identical, for these purposes, to a round, blue one.

19.7.1.3 Similarity of marks

Here, somewhat different considerations apply, because the point has been visited on many occasions and there is now a fairly well-established approach, as shown by the ECJ in *Sabel BV v Puma AG, Rudolf Dassler Sport* (Case C-251/95) [1998] ETMR 1. A court should take an overall impression of the visual, aural and conceptual similarities of the marks, looking in particular at distinctive and dominant features. To this list, scents and smells must now be added. The whole point about this test is that it concentrates upon similarities, rather than distinctions. One might well add all sorts of fancy differences on top of someone else's registered mark, but if the 'distinctive and dominant' features of the prior registered mark are still discernible enough to lead to the necessary confusion in the mind of the customer, causing him to associate the mark before him with a completely different trade source that he already associates with of those features, it will be a similar mark; see *Sir Terence Orby Conran v Mean Fiddler Holdings Ltd* [1997] FSR 856, where the 'Zinc' mark was successfully protected in opposition proceedings. The question of similarity cannot really be divorced from the question of confusion as to trade source, and similarity, in the absence of confusion or, at least, association with the registered mark, is not a relevant consideration.

In *Alticor Inc v Nutrigreen Health Products Ltd* (Trade Mark Registry 09/11/07) [2007] WL 4368242, an application was upheld to register 'NUTRILIFE' as a trade mark over opposition from the owner of the registration of 'NUTRILITE'. The mark applied for comprised 'NUTRI' and 'LIFE' on different lines, and the words were linked by other graphic imagery. Taking the totality of each mark into consideration, the differences far outweighed the similarities.

19.7.1.4 Similarity of goods and services

Here, much more emphasis is placed upon the fact that, to deny registration, there must be demonstrable confusion and wrong association of the trade source of the goods or services to be marketed under the sign for which registration is sought. Everything, here, is likely to turn upon what, exactly, the likely users of goods or services might expect to find on offer under a particular registered trade mark (bearing in mind the uses for which the trade mark is registered) and where or when those goods or services might be expected to be offered. Clearly, the closer the range and type of goods and/or services to be marketed under the new application, where they are to be marketed, and the closer the marketing techniques used are to those under the existing registration, the more likely it is that there will be found to be similarity. The conclusion to be drawn from the many cases in this area seems to be that the greater the reputation and public goodwill in the prior registered trade mark, the more the emphasis of the comparison by the court tends to shift, noticeably, from the question of similarity of the goods or services offered towards the question of confusion or wrong association of the trade source. It is a subtle point, but it is necessary in order to understand the judicial and registration approach.

For an example of a judicial decision as to whether goods are similar, see *British Sugar plc v James Robertson & Sons Ltd* [1996] RPC 281, commonly known as the 'Treat' case. In 1992 British Sugar registered the mark TREAT in Class 30 for 'dessert sauces and syrups'. The mark was used on 'Silver Spoon Treat', a syrup to be poured over desserts and, in particular, ice cream. In 1995 James Robertson produced a spread known as 'Robertson's Toffee Treat', which was sold along with Robertson's traditional jams and preservatives. British Sugar brought an action for trade mark infringement against James Robertson on the basis of the inclusion of the mark TREAT in the name of its product.

Once the court had decided that the goods were not identical (in fact spreads were registrable in Class 29, and so they were not even in the same class), it was crucial to decide whether the goods were similar, so that there might be an infringement under s 10(2).

On the issue of similarity of goods, the court said that the relevant factors are:

- a comparison of the use, users, and physical nature of the goods;
- the way in which the goods are sold; and
- the extent to which the goods are competitive.

In the case, it was held that Robertson's spread was not similar to Silver Spoon's syrup, and so the action was unsuccessful under s 10(2). Note that s 10(3) was not in the legislation at the time, and so an action could not be brought which was based on the goods being dissimilar.

19.7.2 Relative grounds, registration and specific examples

Someone trying to register 'Coca-Cola' for fizzy drinks would find it impossible on relative grounds because of the existing registrations for the real 'Coca-Cola' (ie 'identical' goods (s 5(1))). However, this could also be the case for someone trying to register 'Coca-Cola' for cars, lavatory brushes or other 'dissimilar' goods. In the case of the use in relation to cars, it would be held as obtaining an unfair advantage from the reputation of the existing trade mark. In the case of goods such as lavatory brushes, it could be held to be detrimental to the existing mark, as well as taking unfair advantage (s 5(3)).

In *Enterprise Rent-a-car Co v Eurodrive Car Rental Ltd* [2005] Lawtel 2/3/2005, the case concerned an application for a trade mark stylised letter 'E' for car rental services. The appellant objected, as it was the proprietor of various trade marks beginning with the letter 'E'. It was held that there was no likelihood of confusion under s 5(2)(b).

In *Intel Corporation v Sihra* [2003] EWHC 17 (Ch), [2003] All ER (D) 212 (Jan), registration of 'Intel-Play' was refused as it was held that it would take unfair advantage of, or be detrimental to the character and repute of the existing registered trade mark 'Intel', under s 5(3). The application was for use on constructional toys, whereas the Intel registration was for computer components.

The situation with relative grounds is very close to that under s 10 for infringement (see **19.9**), and for most purposes ss 5 and 10 can be treated as equivalent provisions. In other words, the rules on whether you can register a mark are virtually the same as the rules on whether you will infringe an existing mark if you use your mark. I cannot register 'Coca-Cola', and I shall infringe it if I try to use it.

19.7.3 When might relative grounds show themselves?

The relative grounds are likely in some cases to show themselves at the first stage of application to register, where there is an initial examination and search of the Register to ensure the application complies with the substantive requirements of a trade mark and that there are no absolute or relative grounds of objection, as discussed above at **19.7.1**. The Trade Mark Manual of the IPO shows that, since October 2007, the Registrar has only been able to refuse registration on relative grounds if there is a successful objection by a proprietor of an existing trade mark or sign. If the examiner's preliminary search shows up a potential relevant ground opposition, the result of this is notified to the applicant for the new registration, so that the applicant can withdraw or amend, at this early stage. This initial check is relevant only to objections under s 5(1) and (2). Grounds of objection based upon the other parts of s 5 – s 5(3) and (4) – would not be apparent to the examiner on his initial examination.

If the relative ground difficulty has not been spotted by the examiner, or if the applicant decides to press ahead, notwithstanding potential opposition, the application is then published in the *Trade Marks Journal*, as discussed earlier at **19.4.1**. At the same time as the new application is published, the owners of the prior-registered trade mark(s) that have been identified by the initial examination will be notified of the new application. That triggers a three-month period in which any person objecting on relative grounds, in respect of prior registered marks, can bring opposition proceedings. These commence with a hearing between the parties by a hearing officer at the Registry, with available appeals either to an

'Appointed Person', appointed by the Lord Chancellor (usually a very senior practitioner), or to the Chancery Division of the High Court.

Under this more modern practice, whereby the Registrar cannot simply, on their own initiative, refuse registration on relative grounds, opposition proceedings are bound to become more frequent.

A useful case to examine the proper approach to opposition proceedings on relative grounds is seen in *Esure Insurance Ltd v Direct Line Insurance plc* [2008] EWCA Civ 842. Here, the owners of the well known 'red telephone on wheels' device trade mark for insurance objected to the application to register a computer mouse on wheels as a device mark for insurance and financial services. The Hearing Officer upheld the objection, on grounds of similarity and likelihood of confusion. On appeal to a judge, the judge disallowed the objection, mainly because of the approach to similarity taken by the Officer. The Court of Appeal, allowing the appeal from the judge below and upholding the objection, gave some useful pointers on s 5(1) and (2). First, confusion was ascertained from the point of view of the average consumer in the light of all factors, and there was no need to apply a strict threshold of similarity, completely independently of confusion. Provided that the Hearing Officer had seen evidence of the marks themselves and the class of registration, that was enough for him to come to his view. It was said that little would be gained by the use of expert evidence in such cases, except where the particular market in question might be one with which the general consumer was unfamiliar.

These changes have necessitated some amendments to the TMA 1994, and these may be seen in the Trade Marks (Earlier Trade Marks) Regulations 2008 (SI 2008/1067). The changes also include giving better protection to 'well-known' trade marks (see **19.10**) as against later registered national trade marks.

19.7.4 Summary

It can be seen, by examining the extract from s 5 shown at **19.7.1**, that all different combinations of identity/similarity of both the marks and the relevant goods/services may now be objected to on relative grounds. This is extended by s 5(3), to deal with the circumstance of identical/similar marks being used even on dissimilar goods. The position is summarised in the table below.

Goods or services	Trade mark identical	Trade mark similar
Identical	no proof of confusion needed (s 5(1))	likelihood of confusion needed (s 5(2)(b))
Similar	likelihood of confusion needed (s 5(2)(a))	likelihood of confusion needed (s 5(2)(b))
Identical, similar, dissimilar	unfair advantage or detriment needed (s 5(3))	unfair advantage or detriment needed (s 5(3))

19.8 PROTECTING THE MARK, ONCE REGISTERED

Once the client has the registration, he needs advice on protecting the mark. If it is not protected it can become subject to misuse, including infringement, and ultimately to revocation. The most important grounds of revocation to be aware of are as follows.

19.8.1 Non-use

If the mark has not been used for five years following registration, or any subsequent five-year period, it can be struck off for non-use in that category of goods or services. It is a matter of 'use it or lose it' (ss 46(1)(a) and 6A). This happened in the *United Biscuits* case, discussed at

18.2.2, where the successful claimants nevertheless had four trade mark registrations revoked for non-use.

19.8.2 Has become generic

A trade mark becomes generic if, as a result of action or inaction by the proprietor, it has become a common mark in the trade for a product or service for which it is registered. So, under s 1(1) of the TMA 1994, the trade mark no longer distinguishes the goods or services of one business from those of another business and would not be registrable because of s 3(1)(d). This may lead to a revocation application under s 46 of the TMA 1994; see **19.8.3**.

In *Julius Sämaan v Tetrosyl Ltd* [2006] EWHC 529 (Ch), owners of fir tree marks for cardboard strip air fresheners were able to show infringement by Tetrosyl, which made similar items for use in cars. A defence that 'tree' marks were now generic was rejected as the only other relevant 'tree' mark in the market showed an oak tree.

Biro, Linoleum, Refrigerator and Launderette have become generic terms. These were once registered trade marks, but they have lost their ability to identify the goods of one business and are now simply part of the language.

How do you avoid your trade mark becoming generic? You should:

(a)   use it as an adjective and not as a noun, eg, 'Gordons gin and tonic', not 'Gordons and tonic';

(b)   distinguish it from the surrounding writing, eg, by putting it in bold, or in capitals or quotation marks; or

(c)   acknowledge it as a trade mark (use ® if registered; but do not use ® if it is not registered because this is a criminal offence – TMA 1994, s 95).

19.8.3 Has become misleading

A trade mark can be revoked if it has become misleading because of the way the proprietor has used it, or allowed it to be used (s 46(1)(d)). One concern here is that if the mark is licensed to others then they may not produce goods of the same quality as the trade mark proprietor, or as each other. For this reason, it is essential to include quality control provisions in any licence to manufacture goods under a trade mark and to make certain that they are applied by the licensee.

19.9   INFRINGEMENT OF A REGISTERED TRADE MARK

Under s 14, infringement of a registered trade mark is actionable by the proprietor of the trade mark. This is because s 9(1) says the proprietor has exclusive rights in the mark which are infringed by the use of it in the UK without his consent. It is important to realise that not every use of someone else's mark will be an infringement for these purposes. There must be a use of the mark in the course of trade, as distinct from use for non-trading purposes, eg, painting the Mercedes badge onto your wall at home out of enthusiasm. There must also be use of the mark as a trade mark, as a badge of trade origin, as distinct from serving some other purpose. These matters are discussed in more detail below.

There can only be infringement of the trade mark as actually registered. Any limits on the registration are strictly observed, as in *Phones 4u Ltd and Another v Phone4u.co.uk Internet Ltd* [2006] EWCA Civ 244. There, the registered colours of the mark limited the scope of infringement.

To constitute infringement, use of the offending mark (or 'sign', as it is referred to in s 10, to distinguish it from the mark being infringed) must be 'in the course of trade'. Thus, a painting by Andy Warhol of a can of soup did not infringe Campbells' trade mark as Andy Warhol was not in the business of making soup. The s 9 territorial limit on trade mark use within the UK may sometimes create problems involving importing and exporting trade-marked goods.

The issue of use of the mark as a badge of trade origin came up in the case of *Arsenal Football Club plc v Reed* [2003] EWCA Civ 696. Mr Reed sold football merchandise outside the ground of Arsenal Football Club on match days. He had a notice on his stall to the effect that the goods were not official Arsenal regalia. However, the goods did bear the Arsenal logo. At first instance, there was some doubt as to whether this use was use as a trade mark at all. Was the Arsenal badge being used as a trade mark, or was it just an indication of loyalty to a football team? The ECJ held that the badge was a trade mark (*Arsenal Football Club plc v Reed* (Case C-206/01) [2002] All ER (EC) 1). Professional football clubs such as Arsenal are multi-million pound businesses. They register trade marks to protect their commercial rights. The ECJ held that this was use of an identical mark on identical goods. The Court of Appeal followed the reasoning in the ECJ judgment. Aldous LJ explained that the unauthorised goods sold by Mr Reed affected the ability of the trade marks to guarantee the origin of the goods.

A different problem occurred in *R v Johnstone* [2003] UKHL 28, [2003] 3 All ER 884. In this case, the defendant dealt in bootleg copies of music CDs. Various of the artists concerned had registered their names as trade marks. Was the existence of such an artist's name on a CD merely an indication of the identity of the performer, or was it use of the name in a trade mark sense? The House of Lords held that to come within the criminal offence under s 92 of the TMA 1994, the use of the artist's name had to be use of a trade mark as an indication of trade origin of the CDs. Whilst the use of a trade mark such as 'Sony' or 'EMI' would be such a use, this was not the case with the name of an artist. Consequently, the defendant's actions did not fall within s 92.

19.9.1 The methods of infringement

The TMA 1994 now specifies three types of infringement; here you should consider the points on identical similar signs, goods/services, etc at **19.7**:

(a) Use of an identical sign for identical goods or services (as determined by the statement of goods or services with which the mark was registered) (s 10(1)).

(b) Use of an identical or similar sign for similar goods or services, or a similar sign for identical goods or services, if there is a likelihood of confusion (s 10(2)). This is a higher hurdle for the trademark proprietor to overcome, hence the argument at (a) above in the *Reed* case. Confusion must be as to the trade origin of the goods and services.

(c) Use of an identical or similar sign for goods or services, whether identical, similar or dissimilar, if the use is detrimental to, or takes unfair advantage of, the distinctive character or repute of the mark (s 10(3)). In *Conroy v SmithKline Beecham plc* (Trade Marks Registry 0-085-03, 3 April 2003), the applicant had applied to register 'Nit Nurse' in class 3 for oils and shampoos for the control of head lice. The opponents objected, successfully. They held registrations in class 5 for respiratory decongestants under the trade marks 'Night Nurse'. There were arguments that a consumer could confuse the two products, with unfortunate results. In contrast, see also *Premier Brands UK Ltd v Typhoon Europe Ltd* [2000] FSR 767, where the proprietors of 'Typhoo' for tea, objected unsuccessfully to a registration of 'Typhoon' for kitchen utensils. It should be noted that the tests in ss 5(3) and 10(3) were amended by the Trade Marks (Proof of Use) Etc Regulations 2004 (SI 2004/946). This was to fill a gap in these subsections; originally they did not extend to unfair use of a mark on similar or identical goods, only dissimilar ones. See *Adidas-Salomon AG v Fitnessworld Trading Ltd* (Case C-408/01) [2004] 1 CMLR 14, [2004] Ch 120.

It is not sufficient to show that the alleged infringer has gained an advantage; what must be shown is that the advantage was gained because the registered mark was highly distinctive, and that the reminder of it given to the public by the infringer's use of the sign is strong. The claimant was unable to show this in *Whirlpool Corporation Ltd v Kenwood Ltd* [2009] EWCA Civ 753 (application alleging infringement of a EUTM shape mark, in form of a kitchen mixer, causing detriment and taking unfair advantage, was dismissed). See also the important development concerning unfair advantage claims discussed at **19.9.2** below.

These grounds are much the same as the relative grounds for invalidity (see **19.7**).

The proprietor of a registered trade mark would usually have to produce evidence of confusion, or unfair advantage or detriment, as the case may be. This could be in the form of survey evidence, or expert witnesses from the trade in question, but the nature of the required evidence must be considered now in the light of the ECJ ruling in *L'Oréal SA v Bellure NV*, discussed in **19.9.2** below.

19.9.2   Detrimental or unfairly advantageous use

Very significant guidance has recently been given by the ECJ in *L'Oréal SA v Bellure NV* (Case C-487/07) [2009] All ER (D) 225 (Jun), on the evidential and legal requirements of an infringement claim under s 10(3) (see (c) at **19.9.1** above) and of Article 5(2) of Directive 89/104. Here, the claimant manufacturer of high-quality beauty products sought remedies, inter alia, for trade mark infringements against 'smell-alike' importers using packaging and comparison lists from which the alleged infringements arose. There were issues concerning the scope of taking unfair advantage of the reputation of a trade mark, both for the purposes of trade mark infringement and for the closely connected question of permissible comparative advertising under EC law on misleading advertisements. The matter went to the Court of Appeal, from which the following questions were referred to the ECJ (summarised here, for simplicity, as the ECJ dealt with them in a slightly different way from that in which the Court of Appeal referred them) for preliminary rulings:

(a)   *Whether a third party using a sign, identical to a trade mark with a reputation, in comparative advertising in relation to identical goods, could be held to take unfair advantage where the third party gained a marketing advantage, but without causing confusion to the public as to trade origin, or causing detriment to the mark or its proprietor.* The ECJ ruled that unfair advantage could be taken of the distinctive character or the repute of the mark, without requiring a likelihood of confusion or detriment. The unfairness of the advantage lay in the third party riding 'on the coat-tails' of the trade mark, to exploit the marketing effort and expense needed to maintain the registered mark's image, without paying any compensation for it.

(b)   *Whether the proprietor of a well-known registered mark could prevent such a use in comparative advertising as is described in (a) above, by a third party, where such use is not capable of jeopardising the essential function of the trade mark as an indicator of trade origin.* The ECJ ruled that the proprietor of the mark could prevent such use, even in those circumstances, provided that such use was liable to affect some other function of the mark (examples were given, in particular, of the functions of guaranteeing quality, of communication, investment or advertising). It would be for the referring court (in this case, the Court of Appeal) to determine whether the use made of the infringing sign was liable to affect one or more of the functions of the trade mark. The case law showed that the proprietor cannot oppose the use of an identical sign, if that use is not liable to cause detriment to any of the functions of the trade mark. Nevertheless, the ECJ made very clear that an advertiser, in a comparative advertisement that satisfied all the requirements of Article 3a(1) of Directive 84/450 (the Directive covering misleading advertising, which extends to comparative advertising: see further **19.9.4** below) could not be prevented from honest use of the mark by the proprietor of it. (See **19.9.4** on the point of regulation of misleading advertisements.)

(c)   *Whether Article 3a(1) of Directive 84/450 means that where an advertiser indicates through a comparison list, without in any way causing confusion or deception, that his product has a major characteristic similar to that of a product marketed under a well-known trade mark, of which the advertiser's product constitutes an imitation, that advertiser takes unfair advantage of the trade mark (for the purposes of Article 3a(1) of Directive 84/50), or presents 'goods or services as imitations or replicas' for the purposes of Article 3a(1)(h)*. The ECJ ruled that such an advertiser would be both taking unfair advantage of the reputation of the mark and presenting the goods or services as imitations or replicas within the meaning of Directive 84/450. It appears to follow from this ruling, and the view of the Court of Appeal in the case, that because such a use was impermissible and would be inconsistent with fair competition or honest practice, it was unlawful, and must be regarded as taking unfair advantage of the reputation of the mark, for trade mark infringement purposes, too (this point was not referred to the ECJ as being self-evident).

It seems very likely that this guidance will figure prominently in future cases on comparative advertising, both with respect to trade mark infringements per se and with respect to questions of permissible use of signs and marks in comparative advertising within Directive 84/450, as amended (now Directive 2006/114) (see **19.9.4**).

19.9.3 Trade marks and the Internet

Trade marks are national rights (but see **19.13** below for the international dimension), so the use has to be within the UK. Thus, on the Internet, pre-emptive registration of a domain name that is similar to a registered trade mark might not necessarily be use in the course of trade within the UK. However, the Court of Appeal held it was so likely to lead to infringement that an injunction was granted (*British Telecommunications plc and Others v One in a Million Ltd and Others* [1999] 1 WLR 903). In that case, someone had registered as Internet domain names the names of various well-known businesses, including BT and Virgin. The aim presumably was to sell the domain name to the rightful owner for large sums of money. See also *Tesco Stores Ltd v Elogicom Ltd* [2006] EWHC 403 (Ch), where use of the 'Tesco' mark, as part of several domain names, constituted serious infringement of the trade mark.

A website can be accessed from anywhere in the world; this does not always mean that for trade mark purposes the trade marks are being used in the course of trade in a particular jurisdiction (see *800 Flowers, Trade Mark Application; 1-800 Flowers Incorporated v Phonenames Ltd* [2001] EWCA Civ 721, [2002] FSR 288 and *Euromarket Designs Inc v Peters and Trade & Barrel Ltd* [2001] FSR 288, where the mere possibility of accessing a site from the UK did not necessarily mean that there was infringement of a UK trade mark). In the *Euromarket* case, Jonathan Parker LJ said:

> So I think that the mere fact that websites can be accessed anywhere in the world does not mean, for trade mark purposes, that the law should regard them as being used everywhere in the world. It all depends upon the circumstances, particularly the intention of the website owner and what the reader will understand if he accesses the site. In other fields of law, publication on a website may well amount to a universal publication, but I am not concerned with that.

In *Wilson v Yahoo! UK Ltd* [2008] EWHC 361 (Ch), the defendant was granted summary judgment to strike out a claim that it had infringed the claimant's trade mark via two sponsored links on its Internet search engine. It was held that the trade mark had not been used by the defendant but only by the browser. This happened when the browser put the word mark in as a search term.

Thus, in *Bonnier Media Ltd v Greg Lloyd Smith* [2002] ETMR 86, the Scottish Court of Session held that the defendants could be sued in Scotland in regard to material accessed on the Internet, even though the originating site was outside the UK. The defendants intended to set up a website with a domain name similar to Bonnier's trade mark. It was held that the defendants' activities were aimed at damaging Bonnier's business, which was based in Scotland. In other words, the defendants' intentions are a key part in deciding whether or not there is trade mark infringement (or passing off).

Another aspect of the international dimension of trade marks is the interface with competition law. A trade mark proprietor could not use national trade mark rights to prevent parallel importation of his goods from another EU Member State. However, he can use trade mark rights to prevent importation of goods he has produced and has sold for resale on to a non-EU market. This was the case in *Zino Davidoff SA v A & G Imports Ltd; Levi Strauss & Co and Another v Tesco Stores Ltd and Another; Levi Strauss & Co and Another v Costco Wholesale UK* (Joined Cases C-414/99, C-415/99 and C-416/99) [2002] All ER (EC) 55. Here, the claimants succeeded in preventing Tesco from continuing to import supplies of the Levi Strauss goods from North America and Mexico. The goods were for resale in the Tesco stores in the UK at lower prices than the goods officially released on to the UK market by Levi Strauss (see also the *Silhouette* case at **19.11**). In the case of *Glaxo Group v Dowelhurst Ltd* [2004] EWCA Civ 290, [2004] WL 412961, CA, pharmaceutical products were sold to the defendant company for sale in Africa but were in fact sold within the UK. An injunction was granted to prevent this activity.

Further discussion of trade mark use in Internet trading can be found at **26.5.3** below.

19.9.4 Honest and fair use of a trade mark

All the infringing acts within s 10 are subject to the proviso within the Business Protection from Misleading Marketing Regulations 2008 (SI 2008/1276), namely that any honest and fair use of another person's registered trade mark for the purpose of identifying any goods or services as being those of the proprietor or a licensee of the mark is to be allowed. This is essential, of course, to the widespread modern practice of comparative advertising, ie comparing a range of competing products on price, performance etc. This is very important, because the infringing acts include use of the mark on business papers or in advertising. Whether comparative advertising is honest and fair is a question of degree.

The 2008 Regulations permit referring to another's trade mark in advertisements provided:

- it is not misleading;
- it compares goods or services meeting the same needs or intended for the same purpose;
- it objectively compares one or more material, relevant, verifiable and representative feature which may include price;
- it does not denigrate the mark;
- it does not take unfair advantage or cause detriment to the mark;
- it does not present goods or services as imitations or replicas of those protected; and
- it does not create confusion.

Even with the 'green light' which the 2008 Regulations give to advertisers to make comparisons on things such as price and service without fear of infringing a mark, the UK is still far away from allowing a US-style system of comparative advertising, where traders are generally allowed to openly criticise their competitors, and use their mark in doing so.

19.10 THE USE OF 'WELL-KNOWN' NON-UK TRADE MARKS IN THE UK

Section 56 was introduced as part of the UK implementation of the Paris Convention. If a foreign trade mark is well known in the UK, the foreign proprietor will be able to get an injunction to restrain the use of that mark in the UK where the use would cause confusion. This measure is to protect foreign trade marks that are not registered in the UK. The most likely instance is that of a famous shop, or restaurant or hotel which has no branches in the UK. The section limits the remedy available to injunction but, no doubt, a passing-off claim would be available if further remedies are sought.

These marks are now given better protection under the Trade Marks (Earlier Trade Marks) Regulations 2008 (see **19.7.3**).

19.11   DEFENCES TO INFRINGEMENT

The first line of defence to a trade mark infringement action is that the trade mark is not validly registered and should be removed from the register under s 47 of the TMA 1994. The basis of the invalidity must be that one or more of the absolute grounds for refusing registration (s 3) can be shown.

In *A&E Television Networks LLC and AETN UK v Discovery Communications Europe Ltd* [2013] EWHC 109 (Ch), the claimant owned the trademark 'The History Channel' in relation to satellite TV channels. It took action against the defendant for use of the mark 'Discovery History' in relation to its satellite channel which was devoted to history. The judge, in finding for the defendant, said that he had 'struggled to find any more appropriate word to describe the contents of a channel which is specifically created to show programmes of a historical nature'.

The next line of defence to consider is s 11, which limits the scope of a registered trade mark and therefore provides some defences. For example, s 11(2)(a) allows the honest use of a person's own name or address. In *Reed Executive and Reed Solutions v Reed Business Information and Elsevier* [2004] EWCA Civ 159, [2004] RPC 40, the case concerned two businesses with similar names but operating in different fields of activity. It was held that a company could avail itself of the 'own name defence', and that the existence of the word 'Limited' was not relevant. Section 11(2)(b) allows use for the purposes of indicating the nature of the goods or services, so, for example, allowing an independent business to indicate that it supplied parts for BMW cars (*Bayerische Motorenwerke AG (BMW) and Another v Deenik* (Case 63/97) [1999] All ER (EC) 235).

However, in *Aktiebolaget Volvo v Heritage (Leicester) Ltd* [2000] FSR 253, the defendant motor trader had not made it sufficiently clear that it was no longer an authorised Volvo dealer. Consequently, its use of the Volvo trade mark was held not to fall within s 11, and it had infringed the trade mark registration by using an identical mark on identical goods.

Section 12 deals with the exhaustion of rights. Goods put on to the market elsewhere in the EU by the trade mark proprietor can be legitimately sold under that trade mark in the UK. Note that this does not cover goods put on to the market elsewhere in the world (*Silhouette International Schmied GmbH and Co KG v Hartlauer Handelsgesellschaft mbH* (Case C-355/96) [1999] Ch 77 and see the *Zino Davidoff* case at **19.9**). To exhaust the rights, the owner must have actually consented to the product being placed on the market within the EEA, or there must be a strong implication of such consent. The mere fact that packaging was printed in three European languages was not enough to raise that implication in *Roche Products Ltd v Kent Pharmaceuticals Ltd* [2006] EWHC 335 (Ch).

An interesting case that shows how the implication of consent can arise is *Honda Motor Co Ltd v Neesam* [2008] EWHC 338 (Ch). Here, sales by Honda to its Australian subsidiary, which sold the motor bikes to a dealer who was known to deal in the UK market, were held to show an implied consent, sufficient to exhaust the right.

Section 48 deals with the question of acquiescence. If a proprietor of an earlier mark acquiesces in someone else's use of the registered mark for a continuous period of five years, the right is lost to apply for invalidity of the later mark or to oppose its use. See *Budejovicki Budvar Narodni Podnik v Anheuser-Busch Inc* [2008] EWHC 263 (Ch). In this recent round in the lengthy litigation over the 'Budweiser' and 'Bud' marks (in which both parties have legitimate interests), an acquiescence defence was upheld, in part.

Following implementation of the Trade Marks Directive, three changes have been made to the available defences:

- Using a trade mark for reference purposes is not an infringement: this allows the use of a mark to identify or refer to goods or services.

- The 'own name' defence is limited to natural persons, so it is not available for companies.
- Alleged infringers are now able to insist that owners of marks for more than five years prove use (or proper reasons for non-use) during the five years prior to the proceedings.

19.12 REMEDIES FOR INFRINGEMENT

Section 14(2) provides that the usual remedies of 'damages, injunction, accounts or otherwise' are as available as 'in respect of the infringement of any other property right'. To this are added:

(a)   orders against an infringer to erase or remove the offending sign or, if that is not possible, to destroy the goods or materials (s 15);

(b)   the availability of an order to deliver up infringing goods or materials held in the course of business (s 16);

(c)   orders concerning the disposal of matter delivered up under (b) (s 19);

(d)   relief, including damages, declaration and injunction, against groundless threats of infringement proceedings (s 21).

There are also criminal law sanctions under ss 92–98, creating offences involving unauthorised use of trade marks, subject to defences of reasonable belief that no infringement was involved. There is also the possibility of forfeiture of counterfeit goods, in connection with such offences, under s 97. Further, there is the possibility of injunction and criminal prosecution at the instance of enforcement authorities under the Business Protection from Misleading Marketing Regulations 2008.

19.13 INTERNATIONAL TRADE MARKS

We have been looking at the law of UK trade marks. If you apply for a UK trade mark, this will give you the right to stop infringements only in the UK. If you want protection in other countries (eg, US, Japan, Hong Kong) then you have to make a separate application there. So if you want to protect your mark world-wide, this will be a very expensive process.

Within Europe, two processes allow the applicant to get wider protection on the basis of a single application.

19.13.1 European Union Trade Mark (EUTM)

The EUTM is a single trade mark, effective throughout the European Union (for the avoidance of doubt, this excludes the UK). You apply to the EU Intellectual Property Office (EUIPO) at Alicante. If you can get a EUTM then this will give you protection throughout the Union on the basis of one registration. The difficulty is that the registration can be defeated by similar prior marks anywhere in the European Union. Many well-known UK marks would not be able to achieve a Union-wide registration for this reason. However, the EUTM system does not carry out extensive investigation of existing marks but rather leaves the proprietors of existing marks to object to published applications. This happened in *Mülhens GmbH & Co KG v OHIM and Zirh International Corp* (Case C-206/04P) [2006] ETMR 57, where the owners of the earlier EUTM 'Sir' were able to block the registration of 'ZIRH' for the same class of goods, on grounds of similarity.

If an applicant is unsuccessful, it is then left with the possibility of applying in each of those countries where there is no problem in order to get a bundle of national registered trade marks.

Even if an applicant does not apply for an EUTM, but instead applies for a series of national trade marks in some Member States of the European Union, there is a level of harmonisation of trade mark laws throughout Europe due to the Trade Mark Harmonisation Directive, and so there are significant similarities in both the laws and the application processes.

Following the UK's withdrawal from the EU, holders of EUTMs were, from January 2021, granted an equivalent UK trade mark to ensure that their rights were not weakened. In essence, their EUTM, which covered all EU states including the UK, became an EUTM plus a UK trade mark which has a filing date which is the same as the original EUTM filing date. Moving forwards, applicants for new trade marks who want the same protection will need to apply for a EUTM and a UK trade mark.

Information required to file an application
The full name and address of the applicant
The country and, if appropriate, the State of incorporation of the applicant (needed in the case of federal States such as Australia, Canada and the US)
Full details of the trade mark
A good representation of the logo or design
An indication of the goods and services sold or to be sold under the trade mark (there are 45 classes of trade marks, described with explanatory notes by EUIPO)
Details of the application on which Convention priority is to be claimed

19.13.2   Madrid Protocol

This is a system that allows you to make one application in one country initially. Then an application can be made for registrations in all the other countries listed on the application form, and which are Member States of the Madrid Protocol. The system is run by the World Intellectual Property Organisation (WIPO). A UK trade mark can thus be used as a basis for an international application to obtain trade mark protection.

Prior to the widespread adoption of the system, it was not possible to obtain an 'international trade mark', where a single trade mark registration would automatically apply around the world. The Madrid Protocol now permits the filing, registration and maintenance of trade mark rights in more than one jurisdiction on a global basis. Many countries have had to modify or consider modifying their trade mark laws in order to adhere to the Protocol, which can therefore be said to have helped harmonise trade mark laws globally.

19.13.3   Other international aspects

19.13.3.1   Paris Convention

The Paris Convention for the Protection of Industrial Property, signed in Paris on 20 March 1883, was one of the first IP treaties. Because of this Treaty, IP systems of any contracting State are accessible to the nationals of other States party to the Convention. The Convention now has 179 contracting member countries, which makes it one of the most widely adopted treaties worldwide.

The Convention provides for the right of priority in the case of patents (and utility models, where they exist), marks and industrial designs. This right means that, on the basis of a regular first application filed in one of the contracting States, the applicant may, within a certain period of time (12 months for patents and utility models; six months for industrial designs and marks), apply for protection in any of the other contracting States. These later applications will then be regarded as if they had been filed on the same day as the first application, ie these later applications will have priority (hence the expression 'right of priority') over applications which may have been filed during the said period of time by other persons for the same invention, utility model, mark or industrial design. Moreover, these later applications, being based on the first application, will not be affected by any event that may have taken place in the interim, such as publication of the invention or sale of articles bearing the mark or incorporating the industrial design. One of the great practical advantages of this provision is that, when an applicant desires protection in several countries, he is not required to present all his applications at the same time but has six or 12 months at his disposal to decide in which countries he wishes to arrange protection and to organise with due care the steps he must take to secure that protection.

The Paris Convention does not regulate the conditions for the filing and registration of marks, which are therefore determined in each contracting State by the domestic law. Consequently, no application for the registration of a mark filed by a national of a contracting State may be refused, nor may a registration be invalidated, on the ground that filing, registration or renewal has not been effected in the country of origin. Once the registration of a mark is obtained in a contracting State, it is independent of its possible registration in any other country, including the country of origin. Therefore, the lapse or annulment of the registration of a mark in one contracting State will not affect the validity of registration in other contracting States.

Where a mark has been duly registered in the country of origin, it must, on request, be accepted for filing and protected in its original form in the other contracting States. Nevertheless, registration may be refused in well-defined cases, such as when the mark would infringe acquired rights of third parties, when it is devoid of distinctive character, when it is contrary to morality or public order, or when it is of such a nature as to be liable to deceive the public.

19.13.3.2 TRIPS

The Agreement on Trade Related Aspects of Intellectual Property Rights (TRIPS) contains important provisions on trade marks, which define what member countries must recognise as registrable marks. In particular, Article 15 states:

> any sign … capable of distinguishing the goods and services of one undertaking from those of other undertakings, must be eligible for registration as a trade mark.

This is similar to the rules in the UK (in the TMA 1994).

In terms of infringement, TRIPS prevents the use of:

> identical or similar signs for goods or services which are identical or similar to those in respect of which the trademark is registered where such use would result in a likelihood of confusion. In case of the use of an identical sign for identical goods or services, a likelihood of confusion must be presumed.

Again, the TMA 1994 mirrors this, as does the legislation of many jurisdictions.

19.13.3.3 The Singapore Treaty on the Law of Trademarks

The Singapore Treaty on the Law of Trademarks (and its predecessor, the Trademark Law Treaty) streamlines the process for obtaining a trade mark in many jurisdictions, imposes maximum requirements which can be asked of an applicant before registration is granted, and harmonises the period for registration at 10 years (with subsequent 10-year periods upon the payment of renewal fees). See further **17.6.2** above.

19.14 CLASSES USED IN THE REGISTER OF TRADE MARKS: NICE CLASSIFICATION SYSTEM

CLASSIFICATION OF GOODS (CLASS 1–34)

CLASS 1

Chemicals used in industry, science and photography, as well as in agriculture, horticulture and forestry; unprocessed artificial resins, unprocessed plastics; manures; fire extinguishing compositions; tempering and soldering preparations; chemical substances for preserving foodstuffs; tanning substances; adhesives used in industry

CLASS 2

Paints, varnishes, lacquers; preservatives against rust and against deterioration of wood; colorants; mordants; raw natural resins; metals in foil and powder form for use in painting, decorating, printing and art

CLASS 3

Bleaching preparations and other substances for laundry use; cleaning, polishing, scouring and abrasive preparations; non-medicated soaps; perfumery, essential oils, non-medicated cosmetics, non-medicated hair lotions; non-medicated dentifrices

CLASS 4

Industrial oils and greases; lubricants; dust absorbing, wetting and binding compositions; fuels (including motor spirit) and illuminants; candles and wicks for lighting

CLASS 5

Pharmaceuticals, medical and veterinary preparations; sanitary preparations for medical purposes; dietetic food and substances adapted for medical or veterinary use, food for babies; dietary supplements for humans and animals; plasters, materials for dressings; material for stopping teeth, dental wax; disinfectants; preparations for destroying vermin; fungicides, herbicides

CLASS 6

Common metals and their alloys, ores; metal materials for building and construction; transportable buildings of metal; non-electric cables and wires of common metal; small items of metal hardware; metal containers for storage or transport; safes

CLASS 7

Machines and machine tools; motors and engines (except for land vehicles); machine coupling and transmission components (except for land vehicles); agricultural implements other than hand-operated; incubators for eggs; automatic vending machines

CLASS 8

Hand tools and implements (hand-operated); cutlery; side arms; razors

CLASS 9

Scientific, nautical, surveying, photographic, cinematographic, optical, weighing, measuring, signalling, checking (supervision), life-saving and teaching apparatus and instruments; apparatus and instruments for conducting, switching, transforming, accumulating, regulating or controlling electricity; apparatus for recording, transmission or reproduction of sound or images; magnetic data carriers, recording discs; compact discs, DVDs and other digital recording media; mechanisms for coin-operated apparatus; cash registers, calculating machines, data processing equipment, computers; computer software; fire-extinguishing apparatus

CLASS 10

Surgical, medical, dental and veterinary apparatus and instruments; artificial limbs, eyes and teeth; orthopaedic articles; suture materials; therapeutic and assistive devices adapted for the disabled; massage apparatus; apparatus, devices and articles for nursing infants; sexual activity apparatus, devices and articles

CLASS 11

Apparatus for lighting, heating, steam generating, cooking, refrigerating, drying, ventilating, water supply and sanitary purposes

CLASS 12

Vehicles; apparatus for locomotion by land, air or water

CLASS 13

Firearms; ammunition and projectiles; explosives; fireworks

CLASS 14

Precious metals and their alloys; jewellery, precious and semi-precious stones; horological and chronometric instruments

CLASS 15

Musical instruments

CLASS 16

Paper and cardboard; printed matter; bookbinding material; photographs; stationery and office requisites, except furniture; adhesives for stationery or household purposes; artists' and drawing materials; paintbrushes; instructional and teaching materials; plastic sheets, films and bags for wrapping and packaging; printers' type, printing blocks

CLASS 17

Unprocessed and semi-processed rubber, gutta-percha, gum, asbestos, mica and substitutes for all these materials; plastics and resins in extruded form for use in manufacture; packing, stopping and insulating materials; flexible pipes, tubes and hoses, not of metal

CLASS 18

Leather and imitations of leather; animal skins and hides; luggage and carrying bags; umbrellas and parasols; walking sticks; whips, harness and saddlery; collars, leashes and clothing for animals

CLASS 19

Building materials (non-metallic); non-metallic rigid pipes for building; asphalt, pitch and bitumen; non-metallic transportable buildings; monuments, not of metal

CLASS 20

Furniture, mirrors, picture frames; containers, not of metal, for storage or transport; unworked or semi-worked bone, horn, whalebone or mother-of pearl; shells; meerschaum; yellow amber

CLASS 21

Household or kitchen utensils and containers; combs and sponges; brushes, except paintbrushes; brush-making materials; articles for cleaning purposes; unworked or semi-worked glass, except building glass; glassware, porcelain and earthenware

CLASS 22

Ropes and string; nets; tents and tarpaulins; awnings of textile or synthetic materials; sails; sacks for the transport and storage of materials in bulk; padding, cushioning and stuffing materials, except of paper, cardboard, rubber or plastics; raw fibrous textile materials and substitutes therefor

CLASS 23

Yarns and threads, for textile use

CLASS 24

Textiles and substitutes for textiles; household linen; curtains of textile or plastic

CLASS 25

Clothing, footwear, headgear

CLASS 26

Lace and embroidery, ribbons and braid; buttons, hooks and eyes, pins and needles; artificial flowers; hair decorations; false hair

CLASS 27

Carpets, rugs, mats and matting, linoleum and other materials for covering existing floors; wall hangings (non-textile)

CLASS 28

Games, toys and playthings; video game apparatus; gymnastic and sporting articles; decorations for Christmas trees

CLASS 29

Meat, fish, poultry and game; meat extracts; preserved, frozen, dried and cooked fruits and vegetables; jellies, jams, compotes; eggs; milk and milk products; edible oils and fats

CLASS 30

Coffee, tea, cocoa and artificial coffee; rice; tapioca and sago; flour and preparations made from cereals; bread, pastries and confectionery; edible ices; sugar, honey, treacle; yeast, baking-powder; salt; mustard; vinegar, sauces(condiments); spices; ice

CLASS 31

Raw and unprocessed agricultural, aquacultural, horticultural and forestry products; raw and unprocessed grains and seeds; fresh fruits and vegetables, fresh herbs; natural plants and flowers; bulbs, seedlings and seeds for planting; live animals; foodstuffs and beverages for animals; malt

CLASS 32

Beers; mineral and aerated waters and other non-alcoholic beverages; fruit beverages and fruit juices; syrups and other preparations for making beverages

CLASS 33

Alcoholic beverages (except beers)

CLASS 34

Tobacco; smokers' articles; matches

CLASSIFICATION OF SERVICES (CLASS 35–45)

CLASS 35

Advertising; business management; business administration; office functions

CLASS 36

Insurance; financial affairs; monetary affairs; real estate affairs

CLASS 37

Building construction; repair; installation services

CLASS 38

Telecommunications

CLASS 39

Transport; packaging and storage of goods; travel arrangement

CLASS 40

Treatment of materials

CLASS 41

Education; providing of training; entertainment; sporting and cultural activities

CLASS 42

Scientific and technological services and research and design relating thereto; industrial analysis and research services; design and development of computer hardware and software

CLASS 43

Services for providing food and drink; temporary accommodation

CLASS 44

Medical services; veterinary services; hygienic and beauty care for human beings or animals; agriculture, horticulture and forestry services

CLASS 45

Legal services; security services for the physical protection of tangible property and individuals; personal and social services rendered by others to meet the needs of individuals

---

SUMMARY

One of the most important registered rights is the right to protect your trade mark. Businesses spend millions of pounds on their names and logos, and so are willing to spend large amounts of money to ensure they have the legal right to claim against someone who uses their mark or something confusingly similar. Intellectual property lawyers therefore carry out legal work for their clients to register their trade marks, and to protect them after registration has been obtained.

In this chapter we have examined how to register trade marks, what objections may be raised to prevent a registration, and how to take steps to enforce a registration.

COPYRIGHT

LEARNING OUTCOMES

After reading this chapter you will be able to:

- explain what copyright is
- identify the main types of copyright
- apply the law to decide whether copyright has been infringed
- explain which remedies are available for copyright breaches
- identify impending changes in the law of copyright.

20.1 WHAT IS COPYRIGHT? AN INTRODUCTION

The law of copyright protects the results and expressions of creative ability. No formality is involved; the right comes into existence as the tangible results of that creativity appear. Copyright is said to arise 'before the ink is dry upon the paper'. It is this simple arising of property rights, concurrent with the creation of the protected copyright material, that makes copyright such a valuable protection for the creative person against intentional or unintentional, unauthorised copying. The downside of such informal creation of copyright in a piece of creative work is that it is very easy to use, without realising it, elements of other people's copyright material in creating your own new work. There is no UK 'registry' of copyright material to guide you on this and, in an age of unlimited electronic access to information and imagery of all sorts (including the computer programs that permit you to access other material), the danger of infringement is ever present. The law has, therefore, to achieve a balance between the protection of creative persons and the freedom of others to create new works.

What is protected?	creative output
What benefit is there?	prevents copying
How is it obtained?	arises automatically (no registration)
How long does it last?	70 years from death of creator (in most cases)

There is a great deal of harmonisation of copyright due to international conventions and agreements, most notably the Berne Convention (see **20.9.1**). For simplicity, therefore, we shall concentrate on UK law for the purposes of this chapter, but will note differences with other jurisdictions where appropriate.

The first statutory copyright in England was the Statute of Anne 1709, although the history of copyright goes back much further. The Statute was passed at the request of book publishers, because they were unable to protect their rights effectively against copyists under the common law. The first items protected were therefore books. Over the years, other artistic items have been added, including music and paintings. In the 20th century, new technology allowed the development of new aspects of artistic works, such as film versions of books and plays, and protection became available to the sort of works that lie behind such creations: music, sounds, visual effects etc. This led, via technological progression, to copyright protection of the computer programs that lie behind most modern inventions.

The main legislation on copyright is the Copyright, Designs and Patents Act 1988 (CDPA 1988). In the period before the CDPA 1988, there were attempts to use copyright for industrial items (eg, *British Leyland Motor Corp Ltd v Armstrong Patents Co Ltd* [1986] 1 AC 577 on spare parts for cars) – see **22.1.1**. The philosophy behind the relevant parts of the CDPA 1988 was to push industrial items in the direction of registered and unregistered design right (which the CDPA 1988 respectively strengthened and created), and to restrict copyright to more artistic three-dimensional items. The reason was that copyright would otherwise have given a period of protection of at least 70 years for an industrial item, whereas the duration of a registered design right is 25 years.

The 'classic' copyrights are original literary, dramatic, musical, and artistic (LDMA) works.

The 'entrepreneurial' copyrights are films, sound recordings, published editions, broadcasts and cablecasts.

These copyrights protect the type of creative expression that is necessary if a work is to be made available to the wider public, recognising the effort and investment usually involved in such ventures.

It is important to be able to distinguish between the different categories of copyright, for the following reasons:

(a)   If you cannot find a category for the item, copyright will not subsist in it. A good example of this is the position of computer programs, which are now in s 1 of the CDPA 1988. Until the Berne Convention (see **20.9**) clarified the position by defining software as a literary work, there was some uncertainty about whether copyright subsisted in it at all, although there had been some cases suggesting it did.

(b)   The rules relating to the subsistence, duration, ownership and infringement of the copyright can vary considerably for the different types of work.

(c)   If there is more than one type of work in relation to an item, the different copyright works will often be owned by different people. A film or TV production might need to take account of large numbers of copyright owners, usually by licensing or purchase of the various rights.

In the US, while copyright exists automatically upon creation of the work, formal registration is a prerequisite to bringing an enforcement action. Further, as will be noted below, US law does not make the informal distinction between 'classic' and 'entrepreneurial' works, but merely lists or identifies the types of works.

Let us look at the classic copyrights.

20.2 LITERARY, DRAMATIC, MUSICAL AND ARTISTIC WORKS

These are the 'classic' copyrights, that is, the authors' and artists' rights that most people associate with copyright. These rights have many things in common, so we are going to deal with them together.

The CDPA 1988 provides as follows:

1   Copyright and copyright works

(1)   Copyright is a property right which subsists in accordance with this Part in the following descriptions of work—

(a)   original literary, dramatic, musical or artistic works,

(b)   sound recordings, films, broadcasts or cable programmes, and

(c)   the typographical arrangement of published editions.

...

3   Literary, dramatic and musical works

(1)   In this Part—

'literary work' means any work, other than a dramatic or musical work, which is written, spoken or sung, and accordingly includes—

(a)   a table or compilation other than a database,

(b)   a computer program,

(c)   preparatory design material for a computer program, and (d) a database;

'dramatic work' includes a work of dance or mime; and

'musical work' means a work consisting of music, exclusive of any words or action intended to be sung, spoken or performed with the music.

4   Artistic works

(1)   In this Part "artistic work" means—

(a)   a graphic work, photograph, sculpture or collage, irrespective of artistic quality,

(b)   a work of architecture being a building or a model for a building, or

(c)   a work of artistic craftsmanship.

(2)   In this Part—

'building' includes any fixed structure, and a part of a building or fixed structure;

'graphic work' includes—

(a)   any painting, drawing, diagram, map, chart or plan, and

(b)   any engraving, etching, lithograph, woodcut or similar work;

'photograph' means a recording of light or other radiation on any medium on which an image is produced or from which an image may by any means be produced, and which is not part of a film;

'sculpture' includes a cast or model made for purposes of sculpture.

The definition of 'literary work' in s 3(1) excludes dramatic or musical works. Thus, a play or script for a film will have dramatic copyright, not literary copyright. There are special rules for songs in s 10A of the CDPA 1988. This says that 'a "work of co-authorship" means a work produced by the collaboration of the author of a musical work and the author of a literary work where the two works are created in order to be used together'. So, where one artist creates the music and another creates the lyrics, such as was the arrangement between Elton John and Bernie Taupin, the effect of this definition is that a song written according to this arrangement will be jointly owned, and will have a duration linked to the death of the last of the joint authors to survive.

A 'dramatic' work might be a play, but it might also be dance or mime. So a ballet is a dramatic work, but the music is a musical work. Again, the usual situation would be that the dramatic and musical copyrights are owned separately.

20.2.1   Originality

For LDMA works, copyright will not subsist unless the work is 'original' (see s 1(1)(a)). 'Originality' here means that the work must be the author's own work, not copied from anything else. It is very difficult to come up with completely novel expressions of creativity without borrowing something from elsewhere. Copyright in an organ solo from 'A Whiter Shade of Pale' was considered in *Fisher v Brooker* [2006] EWHC 3239 (Ch). The claimant's contribution to the musical arrangement arose out of an earlier arrangement by the first defendant (which itself was based on an original theme dating back at least three centuries!). The claimant was held, nevertheless, to have created an original arrangement because of its highly distinctive quality. The finding that the claimant was a co-author of the work was upheld by the Court of Appeal (but see the reference to this case at **20.2.5** on the question of ownership of the copyright) ([2008] EWCA Civ 287). Further declarations by the judge concerning the claimant's right to assert his copyright (after 38 years) were struck down by the Court of Appeal but subsequently restored on an appeal to the House of Lords (see **20.4.5** below).

It is originality of expression and form, not of idea or content, that is required. For example, someone could not legally copy a book by John Grisham without his consent, but he has no monopoly over thrillers based on the exciting lives of lawyers, so you could write your own. The distinction between idea and expression has received much attention in recent times in the context of the 'Da Vinci Code' case, *Baigent v Random House Group Ltd* [2006] EWHC 719 (Ch) (discussed at **20.4**), and, to a lesser degree, in musical arrangements (see *Hyperion Records Ltd v Sawkins* [2005] EWCA Civ 565).

20.2.2   Minimum effort

A work may be an original work, but it may be completely trivial. Does it still enjoy copyright protection? There will be no copyright unless a certain minimum amount of effort has gone into the work. The amount of effort required is generally low. But the exact amount depends on the category of work.

To be a joint author, a significant creative contribution as an author has to be made to the production of the work. A joint author has to do more than merely contribute ideas and has to participate actively in the writing or creation of the work (see *Ray v Classic FM plc* [1998] FSR 622).

20.2.2.1   Literary works

Generally, the level of effort required is very low. Any level of writing might attract copyright. For example, there is literary copyright in a junior school pupil's essay, or in an ordinary business letter. In *University of London Press v University Tutorial Press* [1916] 2 Ch 601, 608 it was suggested by Peterson J that almost any 'work which is expressed in print or writing, irrespective of the question whether the quality or style is high', might have the necessary minimum effort. This is slightly circular but it shows that the threshold of minimum effort and quality is quite low. The subject matter is irrelevant; the work could be highly-polished literature or a mundane memorandum or timetable.

However, the writing has to be substantial enough to constitute a 'work'. Consequently, an advertising jingle or a title will not usually be protected by copyright. The courts have been reluctant to grant copyright in single words. For example, EXXON was refused copyright protection (though it would of course get trade mark protection if validly registered) (*Exxon Corpn and Others v Exxon Insurance Consultants International Ltd* [1981] 3 All ER 241).

'Compilations', ie collections of information, are one aspect of literary copyright. Generally the English courts have been willing in the past to grant copyright in almost any compilation, eg, television listings, a directory of solicitors' names and addresses, and football pool coupons. It is likely, for example, that an ordinary, alphabetical telephone directory would have been protected by copyright under English law. However, following the adoption of the Copyrights and Rights in Database Regulations 1997 (SI 1997/3032), there is now a question mark over whether courts will in the future allow copyright in such commonplace compilations where there is nothing special about the selection or arrangement of the contents (see **20.2**). Commentators seem to think it is likely that the alphabetical telephone directory would now no longer be protected by copyright. This is because it would fall within the definition of a 'database' in the Regulations (databases do not have to be electronic) for which the Regulations impose a slightly higher standard of originality for copyright to apply. It may well be, for example, that the *Yellow Pages* would still be protected by copyright, because of the extra effort involved in dividing and classifying its contents. However, the key point is that the database right will apply and protect such collections of mundane information, and copyright will probably be largely irrelevant (see **20.5**, **21.1**).

20.2.2.2   Artistic

Artistic works divide into:

(a)   those that fall under s 4, which are protected 'irrespective of artistic quality', that is, graphic works, photographs, sculptures and collages (s 4(1)(a)); and

(b)   those for which a degree of artistic quality is required, that is, architecture and works of artistic craftsmanship (s 4(1)(b) and (c)).

For the first category, the standard of effort required is low. For example, copyright has been found to subsist in a very simple picture of a hand pointing, as used at a polling station to guide people round the corner. A straight line or circle would not normally be protected. In any event, it would not be substantial enough to constitute a 'work', and would be unlikely to be original. The English law approach is quite different to that applied to artistic works in some other legal systems; see *Blau v BBC* [2002] ECDR 34, where the Swiss law provided a result somewhat different to what might have followed in an English court.

Some artistic merit is required for architecture, as the words 'irrespective of artistic quality' do not appear in s 4(1)(b). Cornish and Llewelyn, in *Intellectual Property* (5th edn, Sweet & Maxwell, 2003), suggest that the artistic merit must be 'something more than the common stock'. Perhaps a mass-produced estate of similar mundane houses might not qualify, but a small development of individual 'executive' homes might. Architectural works are limited to buildings themselves, and models for buildings. Architectural drawings would be protected as graphic works, so a different standard would apply to determine copyright in the drawing to that in the building itself.

20.2.2.3   Works of artistic craftsmanship

This is a topic much beloved by academic writers but of negligible practical relevance. A work of artistic craftsmanship is a three-dimensional item which is not a sculpture, but which results from a combination of artistic and craft skills. Examples could be seen in hand-made musical instruments, furniture or wooden boats etc, provided there is evidence of both artistry and craftsmanship. For works of artistic craftsmanship, it seems that a significant degree of artistic merit is required before copyright protection will be given. The policy reason behind this is that most three-dimensional items that are not sculptures tend to be made to industrial designs, and should normally be protected by the law on designs rather than by copyright.

Unfortunately, the cases on works of artistic craftsmanship do not tell us how much artistic merit is needed for something to qualify as a work of artistic craftsmanship. In *Hensher (George) Ltd v Restawile Upholstery (Lancs)* [1976] AC 64, it was held that a mass-produced suite of furniture did not have enough artistic merit. In *Merlet and Another v Mothercare plc* [1986] RPC 115, it was held that a rain cape made by Mrs Merlet to protect her baby from the weather in

Scotland did not have enough artistic merit. Most industrially manufactured articles will also lack any craft skills.

A key factor in deciding whether an item is a work of artistic craftmanship is to ask: did the author consciously intend to create a work of art? In *Guild v Eskandar Ltd* [2001] FSR 38, the claimant alleged breach of copyright in garments which she had designed for mass-production. These were held not to be works of artistic craftsmanship, because of lack of evidence of craft skills used in the manufacture, but were protected by unregistered design right as they were original and not commonplace (see **22.3.1**).

In practice, one should never rely on there being copyright in three-dimensional objects other than sculptures, but instead advise the client to register a design.

20.2.3   Recorded

For literary, dramatic and musical works, copyright will subsist only if the work is recorded (s 3(2)). This can be in writing or otherwise. Recording can be in any medium, so recording on tape, or typing into a word processor is fine.

There is no express requirement as such in the CDPA 1988 that an artistic work must be recorded, but of course it is difficult to conceive of an artistic work that is not recorded. How else could you create a drawing or a sculpture, for example, and not record it?

20.2.4   Duration of copyright (CDPA 1988, s 12)

The normal duration is life of the author plus 70 years. The 70 years runs from the end of the year of the author's death. If copyright vests in the employer because the author was an employee, the duration of the employer's copyright is the employee's life plus 70 years. The same situation applies if the rights have been assigned. For example, in the copyright in the songs of Buddy Holly (now owned by Sir Paul McCartney), the period is 70 years from the death of Buddy Holly (ie, it expires in 1959 + 70 = 2029).

For songs the 70-year period runs from the death of the last of the author of the lyrics and the composer of the music. Thus there is a single expiry date for both the words and the music.

The basic term for copyright used to be life plus 50 years. The Directive on Copyright Duration (93/98/EC) increased it to 70 years. This not only extended the life of existing copyright works, but also even revived lapsed copyright if the work was still in copyright anywhere within the EU on 1 July 1995. This would have been so at that date in Germany, where the copyright term then was life plus 70 years.

If the work is of unknown authorship, the period of 70 years runs from the year of creation, or the year of first publication, whichever is the later.

For a computer-generated work, the period is 50 years from creation.

20.2.5   Ownership of copyright in LDMA works

As copyright arises 'before the ink is dry on the page', the initial copyright is owned by the author or co-authors (CDPA 1988, s 11(1)). The main exception is if the author is an employee, in which case the copyright is owned by the employer (s 11(2)). The provisos are that the work was done in the course of the employee's employment, and that there was no contrary agreement. In *Noah v Shuba and Another* [1991] FSR 14, it was held that an employed government epidemiologist had not written a document entitled 'A Guide to Hygienic Skin Piercing' in the course of his employment. He therefore owned the copyright, not his employer.

Be aware that if the work has been commissioned then the copyright rests with the author (s 11(1)), not with the person commissioning the work. A properly drafted agreement would include a clause providing for an assignment, or licence, of the copyright to the commissioner. In the absence of such a clause, a licence would usually be implied (*Blair v Alan S Tomkins and Frank Osborne (t/a Osborne & Tomkins (A Firm)) and Another* [1971] 1 All ER 468), as otherwise the commissioner would be prevented from using the work he had paid for. Thus, the copyright in a photograph of Elvis Costello, taken at a photo shoot where the photographer had not been commissioned, was owned by the photographer (*Gabrin v Universal Music Operations Ltd* [2003] EWHC 1335 (Ch)). Some years before, a similar dispute was settled during litigation about the artwork and photographs for the famous 'Sergeant Pepper' album cover. Where a photograph or a film has been commissioned for private and domestic purposes (eg, a wedding), the person commissioning the material will have the right to prevent publication of the material (s 85).

In *R Griggs Group Ltd v Evans* [2005] EWCA Civ 11, the defendant designer was a freelance engaged by an advertising agency. The agency had been commissioned by the claimants to produce drawings for a new combined logo for their 'Dr Martens' range of footwear. The designer fulfilled the commission, but subsequently also sold the designs to an Australian rival of the claimants. It was held that the claimants were entitled in equity to the beneficial title, as a mere licence would not give them enough rights to stop the work being used by a rival. On the basis of this, it looks as if the courts are prepared to rectify the situation, save where a bona fide third party acquires title in the interim.

20.2.6 Moral rights

These are a Continental concept brought into English law by the CDPA 1988. It is the idea that the creative author or artist should retain certain rights in relation to their creation, even after they have sold the copyright to somebody else. In fact, moral rights have slightly wider implications.

The moral rights are as follows:

(a)   The right to be identified ('right of paternity') (s 77). This applies only if the right has been asserted by the author. This is usually done in the copyright assignment or licence.

(b)   The right to object to derogatory treatment (s 80). For example, a novelist might object if their novel were abridged in a way that compromised its artistic integrity. In *Morrison Leahy Music Ltd v Lightbond Ltd* [1993] EMLR 144, the claimants obtained an injunction to restrain the release of a recording consisting of the claimants' music interspersed with other music, as they felt this altered the character of their music. In the unusual German case of *Re Lenin's Monument* [1992] ECC 202, the son of the sculptor of a statue of Lenin failed in his attempt to assert the moral right akin to s 80. The City of Berlin was held not to be planning to destroy the statue, which could have been derogatory treatment, but merely 'to preserve it by burying it', following the demise of the former communist State of East Germany. An interesting claim to derogatory treatment of a sound recording by adding a rap line failed in *Confetti Records and Others v Warner Music UK Ltd* [2003] EWHC 1274 (Ch) because there was nothing prejudicial to the honour and reputation of the author of the original work.

(c)   The right against false attribution of a work (s 84). A novel use of this right was in *Clark v Associated Newspapers* [1998] RPC 261. This concerned the *London Evening Standard*, which was then running a spoof political column called 'Alan Clark's Secret Election Diary'. Mr Clark succeeded on the basis that some people might believe that the views expressed in the column were his.

(d)   The right to privacy in private photographs and films (s 85).

If the author still owns the copyright then they should not normally need to rely on these moral rights as they can control all copying of the work; for example, they can insist on being credited as a condition of allowing the work to be used. The importance of moral rights is in a situation where the author has assigned the copyright to somebody else.

Moral rights are inalienable rights, in that they cannot be assigned (s 94). However, they can be waived. Anyone acting for the assignee of copyright should always consider whether it is appropriate to insist on a waiver. You probably would not expect somebody who has produced a real work of art to waive their moral rights. However, in many commercial situations it will be appropriate (eg, for advertising copy, or designs for use on fabrics or products).

Moral rights apply only to literary, dramatic, musical and artistic works, and also to films (where the director enjoys moral rights). The most important exceptions to be aware of are computer programs and employees. In most situations employees do not enjoy moral rights.

In terms of duration, most of the moral rights will last as long as the copyright itself (s 86(1)). The exception is the paternity right, which lasts for only 20 years after the death of the author (s 86(2)).

20.3 ENTREPRENEURIAL COPYRIGHTS

The descriptions 'classic' and 'entrepreneurial' copyright are not terms of art. However, the distinction is often made between:

(a)   the classic LDMA copyrights, that is, the traditional authors' rights which protect creativity (see **20.2**); and

(b)   the entrepreneurial copyrights which, broadly, protect people who invest in creativity, that is, production companies, broadcasters, publishers, etc.

The entrepreneurial copyrights serve the same purpose as the classic rights. That is, they give a right to stop copying of the relevant 'work'.

20.3.1 Differences between classic and entrepreneurial copyrights

The rules are slightly different for the entrepreneurial copyrights, in particular:

(a)   There is no general requirement of originality and minimum effort (see **20.2.1** and **20.2.2**). Instead there are various detailed rules for each right, which have the broad aim of ensuring that there is no copyright in a mere copy. For example, if I copy somebody else's tape, with or without their permission, I have no copyright in the copy I make. These rules are beyond the scope of this book, but their broad effect can be seen in ss 5A(2), 5B(4), 6(6) and 8(2). (Note that in the case of *Norowzian v Arks Ltd and Others* (No 2) [2000] FSR 363, the claimant failed in his assertion that copyright existed in an editing process for films. The case concerned an advert for Guinness produced by the defendant by a technique devised by the claimant, termed 'jump cutting'.)

(b)   Of the entrepreneurial copyrights, only films have moral rights. These vest in the director. The thinking behind this is, of course, that it is the director who has given the artistic input. The director is the person who might want to defend their artistic integrity. (The director is the one who sits in the canvas chair behind the camera operator and tells the actors what to do.)

(c)   The rules about ownership of the entrepreneurial rights vary (see **20.3.3**).

(d)   The duration of the entrepreneurial rights varies (see **20.3.4**).

The rules are designed to give effect to the commercial, artistic and financial realities of creativity in the modern world.

Under US law, there is no distinction between 'classic copyright' and the 'entrepreneurial rights'. The rules of ownership and duration are the same as for the type of rights referred to above as 'classic'.

20.3.2 Definitions of some entrepreneurial rights

The following definitions are taken from the CDPA 1988:

5A   Sound recordings

(1)   In this Part 'sound recording' means—

    (a)   a recording of sounds, from which the sounds may be reproduced, or

    (b)   a recording of the whole or any part of a literary, dramatic or musical work, from which sounds reproducing the work or part may be produced,

regardless of the medium on which the recording is made or the method by which the sounds are reproduced or produced.

(2)   Copyright does not subsist in a sound recording which is, or to the extent that it is, a copy taken from a previous sound recording.

5B   Films

(1)   In this Part 'film' means a recording on any medium from which a moving image may by any means be produced.

(2)   The sound track accompanying a film shall be treated as part of the film for the purposes of this Part.

. . .

(4)   Copyright does not exist in a film which is, or to the extent that it is, a copy taken from a previous film.

. . .

6   Broadcasts

(1)   In this Part a 'broadcast' means an electronic transmission of visual images, sounds or other information which—

    (a)   is transmitted for simultaneous reception by members of the public and is capable of being lawfully received by them, or

    (b)   is transmitted at a time determined solely by the person making the transmission for presentation to members of the public,

and which is not excepted by subsection (1A); and references to broadcasting shall be construed accordingly.

(1A)   Excepted from the definition of 'broadcast' is any internet transmission unless it is—

    (a)   a transmission taking place simultaneously on the internet and by other means,

    (b)   a concurrent transmission of a live event, or

    (c)   a transmission of recorded moving images or sounds forming part of a programme service offered by the person responsible for making the transmission, being a service in which programmes are transmitted at scheduled times determined by that person.

(2)   An encrypted transmission shall be regarded as capable of being lawfully received by members of the public only if decoding equipment has been made available to members of the public by or with the authority of the person making the transmission or the person providing the contents of the transmission.

(3)   References in this Part to the person making a broadcast or a transmission which is a broadcast are—

    (a)   to the person transmitting the programme, if he has responsibility to any extent for its contents, and

    (b)   to any person providing the programme who makes with the person transmitting it the arrangements necessary for its transmission;

and references in this Part to a programme, in the context of broadcasting, are to any item included in a broadcast.

(4)   For the purposes of this Part, the place from which a wireless broadcast is made is the place where, under the control and responsibility of the person making the broadcast, the programme-carrying signals are introduced into an uninterrupted chain of communication (including, in the case of a satellite transmission, the chain leading to the satellite and down towards the earth).

(4A)   Subsections (3) and (4) have effect subject to section 6A (safeguards in case of certain satellite broadcasts).

(5)   References in this Part to the reception of a broadcast include reception of a broadcast relayed by means of a telecommunications system.

(5A)   The relaying of a broadcast by reception and immediate re-transmission shall be regarded for the purposes of this Part as a separate act of broadcasting from the making of the broadcast which is so re-transmitted.

(6)   Copyright does not subsist in a broadcast which infringes, or to the extent that it infringes, the copyright in another broadcast.

8   Published editions

(1)   In this Part 'published edition', in the context of copyright in the typographical arrangement of a published edition, means a published edition of the whole or any part of one or more literary, dramatic or musical works.

(2)   Copyright does not subsist in the typographical arrangement of a published edition if, or to the extent that, it reproduces the typographical arrangement of a previous edition.

You should be aware of the following points from the above definitions of the entrepreneurial copyrights:

(a)   An attempt has been made to make the definitions of 'film', 'sound recording', etc technology neutral so that they will cover future technological developments. So, for example, 'film' includes any recordings on any medium from which a moving image can be produced. It will include, for example, videos, DVDs and many 'multi-media' recordings (like computer games and websites) where you have moving images. These can be 'films' even though they may be interactive.

(b)   A 'broadcast' has been redefined to make the definition generic, so as to include not only terrestrial broadcasts (BBC and ITV, etc), but also satellite (Sky) and cable broadcasts (NTL) and some Internet transmissions.

(c)   The soundtrack of a film is protected by film copyright unless it is issued as a stand-alone entity, when it would be protected as a sound recording.

20.3.3   Ownership of the entrepreneurial copyrights (s 9)

The first ownership goes to the 'creator' of the copyright work (see the table, 'Ownership of entrepreneurial rights', below). So, for example, the owner of the copyright in a broadcast would be:

(a)   the person providing the programme; and

(b)   the person transmitting who has responsibility for its content.

This could mean that the independent television company and the broadcasting authority could jointly own the copyright.

Entrepreneurial Right	Ownership
Sound recording	Producer
Film	Producer and principal director
Broadcast	Person making the broadcast
Typographical arrangement	Publisher

Establishing the identity of the 'creator' of the work can become a problem, especially for commissioned works (see also **20.2.5**). Thus, the management company of the skaters Torville and Dean commissioned a recording of music for one of their skating routines. The company was held to be the 'maker' of the sound recording, as it had thought of the idea and taken the financial risk, not the person with whom it had contracted to organise the musicians and the studio (see *A & M Records v Video Collection* [1995] EMLR 25).

20.3.4 Duration of the entrepreneurial copyrights (ss 13A, 13B, 14)

The duration of the entrepreneurial copyrights is a bit more complex than the standard period of life of the creator plus 70 years that applies to the classic copyrights. The duration depends on the type of entrepreneurial right concerned. Thus:

(a)   Sound recording – 70 years from being published (50 years from recording if not published).

(b)   Film – 70 years from end of life of last to die of principal director, author of screenplay, author of dialogue, or composer of specially written music.

(c)   Broadcast – 50 years from first broadcast.

(d)   Typographical arrangement – 25 years from end of year of publication.

20.4 INFRINGEMENT OF COPYRIGHT

The starting point is s 16, which gives the copyright owner the exclusive right to copy, publish, perform or show in public and/or to adapt the work. If anyone else does any of those things within the UK without permission, it will be likely to infringe.

There are two types of infringement: primary infringement and secondary infringement. The primary infringer is liable regardless of his state of mind, whereas the secondary infringer is liable only if he knew, or had reason to believe, that he was dealing with an infringing copy. It is certainly not the case that the part that is copied would, standing by itself, have necessarily qualified for copyright protection, so a person might be quite unaware of any infringement. The reason for this is explained below.

Copying need not be of the whole work. The copyright is infringed if a 'substantial part' is taken. The question of what is a substantial part is considered qualitatively. So, even if you take only one line of a poem, the copyright will be infringed if it is a significant line. Similarly, a parody of a work will infringe the copyright if it amounts to a substantial copy of it. The dangers for the infringer are thus twofold: first, he may not realise that he is using a copyright work; secondly, he may not realise that he is using a legally 'substantial' part of the work.

Section 17 shows that copying of literary, dramatic, musical or artistic works means reproducing the work in any material form. That would include storing the work in any medium by electronic means. Artistic copyright can be infringed, for example, by turning a two-dimensional image into a three-dimensional solid object, and vice versa (s 17(3)).

Copyright in a literary or dramatic work will be infringed by translating it into another language, by making it into a play (or vice versa), or by making it into a cartoon. Copyright in a musical work will be infringed by making a different arrangement. These are 'adaptations' of works within s 21.

Some guidance on the judicial approach may be seen in the following cases:

(a)   *Designer's Guild Ltd v Russell Williams (Textiles) Ltd* [2001] FSR 803

Here, the dispute was about alleged infringement of fabric designs, combining stripes and flowers. The House of Lords, allowing the claimants' appeal, said that the first instance finding, after comparing similarities and differences, that copying had taken place should not have been rejected by the Court of Appeal. That is the first stage of the process. Only after that should the inquiry turn to the question whether what was copied represented a qualitatively substantial part of the claimants' created output. The Court of Appeal's approach had been wrong.

(b)   *Baigent v Random House Group Ltd* [2006] EWHC 719 (Ch)

In this case the writers of *The Holy Blood and the Holy Grail* ('HBHG') sued Dan Brown for breach of copyright in *The Da Vinci Code* ('DVC'). The claim was that DVC had used the central theme from HBHG and so breached copyright. The defence was that, although HBHG had been used along with many other sources, only information and general ideas had been used, not detailed copyright expression. The court held that there could be such a concept as a non-literal copying (a concept well known in software copyright claims), but where the purported copyright material largely comprised factual statements and hypotheses, this could only be protected by copyright if there was a discernible 'architecture' in the way it had been used and arranged. In this case, the supposed central theme of HBHG was at too general a level of abstraction to be protected; the claim failed. The Court of Appeal ([2007] EWCA Civ 247) confirmed the broad conclusions of Smith J, but found some faults with his approach. The judgments are very helpful in explaining the judicial approach to qualitatively substantial copying.

(c)   *Newspaper Licensing Agency Ltd v Marks & Spencer plc* [2003] 1 AC 551

The House of Lords had to decide whether selective copying of cuttings from parts of newspaper editions breached, substantially, the copyright in the typographical arrangements of the editions. Although the CDPA 1988, s 8 definition extended to 'any part' of a work, what comprised a substantial part had to be decided qualitatively, not simply by reference to quantity and proportion to the whole. As none of the copied cutting sections reproduced anything like the layout of entire pages, it was not a substantial copying and the claim failed.

(d)   *Nova Productions Ltd v Mazooma Games Ltd* [2007] EWCA Civ 219

In another case which turns on the distinction between idea and expression, the Court of Appeal dismissed claims that the defendant's computer game about pool infringed the claimant's copyright in its game. There were three substantial issues, all of which are helpful to an understanding of infringement. The first point was the claimant's assertion that a sequence of graphic images showed some similarity in both games. The Court said that the starting point was that each frame comprised a separate graphic; the fact of a sequence of them added nothing to that (ie, the sequence is not a graphic work in itself). There was no substantial copying of the individual graphics. The second issue was that although there was some evidence of the copying and taking of ideas, that did not mean that a substantial part of the defendant's creative form and expression had been copied (similarly with the 'Da Vinci Code' case, above). The third issue related to the alleged copying of the computer program. The mere creation of a computer code that gave a similar effect to another one, without copying the computer code of that other, was more to do with protecting ideas than expression. The claimant's ideas had inspired the defendant, but at too general a level to constitute substantial copying.

From these cases, it can be seen that it may be possible to imitate a certain style or way of expressing things, without necessarily infringing the original. Much of today's surreal imagery can be seen to be influenced by the works of Salvador Dali, without close copying. Dali's works, in their time, were heavily influenced by the much earlier work of Hieronymus Bosch. The distinction between copying and reflecting an influence is a hard one to draw.

Copyright is not normally infringed simply by using the work. For example, you do not infringe the copyright in a book by reading it. You do not infringe a recording by playing it. This is because using it does not normally involve making copies of it. However, if you read or play it in public you do infringe. The CDPA 1988 specifically provides that performing or showing a work in public will infringe the copyright, and this is primary infringement (s 19). Similarly, including a work in a broadcast or cablecast will normally be primary infringement (s 20). So the permission (ie, the licence) of the copyright owner is necessary in these circumstances.

20.4.1 Special position of computer programs (software) (s 17(6))

Although the normal position is that you do not infringe by using a work, such as by reading it, a computer program is different in this respect. When a program is run in a computer, the computer has to make at least a transient copy of it in order to run it. This transient copying will infringe the copyright without the copyright owner's permission (s 17(6)). It is not possible, therefore, to use a program without a licence. Often this licence is express. For example, you get a licence with any program you buy off the shelf. Sometimes, this licence may be implied by the circumstances. If someone is a lawful licensee then he is also entitled to make one back-up copy of the software (s 50A).

Further, under US law, the appearance of the program on the computer screen, the 'screen shot', is considered to be part of the software copyright, which is extremely important commercially with respect to computer games.

20.4.2 Primary infringement (ss 16–21)

The most usual act of primary infringement is copying. Copyright is not a monopoly right. As its name implies, it is the right not to be copied. Independently produced items cannot be objected to. It follows that you cannot infringe copyright if you have never had any access to the original. So in a copyright infringement action, if the defendant had no opportunity to copy, he will not be liable. On the other hand, if the defendant did have the opportunity to copy and the defendant's work is so similar to the claimant's that the most likely explanation is that he has copied, then there will be an inference of copying. The defendant will have to prove that he did not copy.

Having said that, copying can be indirect. Copying can occur as a result of seeing not the original work itself but a copy of it, or something derived from it. For example, if a novel has been adapted to make a play, you infringe the copyright in the novel by copying the play. (In that case the separate copyright in the play is also infringed.)

The late George Harrison was sued in the US, as it was alleged that his song 'My Sweet Lord' was a subconscious copy of an earlier work. The song which was the subject of the alleged copying was 'He's So Fine', composed by Ronald Mack and sung by The Chiffons. It was a minor hit in the UK in 1963 and a major one in the US. The Harrison song was held to have infringed the earlier song. Ultimately, George Harrison is reputed to have bought the copyright to the earlier song, so solving the problem.

In *Sony Music Entertainment (UK) Ltd and Others v Easyinternetcafé Ltd* [2003] EWHC 62 (Ch), [2003] FSR 48, the claimants obtained an injunction against the operators of some Internet cafés. They recorded music from the Internet on to CDs for their customers for a fee. This was held to be breach of ss 17 and 18. In *Independiente Ltd and Others v Music Trading On-line (HK) Ltd and Others* [2003] EWHC 470 (Ch), the claimants were seeking to stop the defendants from supplying sound recordings via the Internet to the UK, when those recordings had been licensed for use only outside the EU. (They failed because they did not have the consent of the copyright holders; although the matter was ultimately settled, there has been further litigation about the terms upon which the matter was settled.)

Although US law does not distinguish between primary and secondary infringement, the test for infringement is the same.

20.4.3 Secondary infringement (ss 22–26)

This is all about dealing with or facilitating the manufacture of 'infringing copies'. These are copies made without the copyright owner's permission. So, the trader who imports copies into the UK may be liable for secondary infringement, as will the trader who sells, distributes or stores such copies. It will extend to persons who provide the means to make the copy, or who provide premises or equipment for infringing public performances. Section 27 defines the wide range of meaning given to 'infringing copy'.

In the typical infringement situation, there will be more than one infringer. However, the main culprit will be the person who manufactures the goods. He will be the primary infringer, because he is actually copying the work in order to make the goods.

Then there will be the dealers who buy or import the goods. Maybe this is a wholesaler who buys from the manufacturer and the retailers who buy from the wholesaler. The wholesaler and retailers will be secondary infringers, but only if they knew or had reason to believe that they were dealing with infringing copies. Usually, the copyright owner is mainly concerned with stopping the manufacture. He will normally write to the retailers and the wholesalers (if known) enclosing evidence of his copyright title and asking them to stop selling the goods. If they then carry on, they will be liable for secondary infringement, because from this point on at least they will not be able to argue that they were innocent.

In *Bloomsbury Publishing Group Ltd and Another v News Group Newspapers Ltd and Others* [2003] EWHC 1205 (Ch), [2003] 3 All ER 736, the publisher and author of the 'Harry Potter' books obtained an injunction to restrain unauthorised publication of the fifth book in the series. A copy had been stolen from the printers and was being offered to some national newspapers, in advance of its official release date. The CDPA 1988, s 23 concerns 'possessing or dealing with an infringing copy'. In *Nouveau Fabrics Ltd v Voyage Decoration Ltd* [2004] EWHC 895 (Ch), the claimant's lawyers had written a letter before action informing the defendant of the claimant's copyright. The defendant was thus held to have had reason to believe that the fabrics it was importing were copies which infringed the claimant's copyright.

Under US law, what is referred to above as secondary infringement is considered to be the same as what is referred to above as primary infringement, ie US law does not make any distinction between the two types of infringement.

20.4.4   Defences – 'fair dealing'

In certain circumstances some use of a copyright work is allowed without the permission of the copyright owner. The approach usually followed by the courts is, first, to ascertain whether the defendant's act falls within the particular statutory purpose, and then, even if it is within that purpose, to see that the copying has not gone any further than necessary to comprise 'fair dealing' (*Hyde Park Residence Ltd v Yelland and Others* [2000] RPC 604). The important ones to be aware of are as follows.

20.4.4.1   Fair dealing for the purposes of research or private study (s 29)

This applies to LDMA works and to published editions. It basically allows the taking of copies of pages of books in the course of non-commercial studying or researching. It does not allow the librarian to take lots of copies, one for each student. In practice it must be read together with the provisions about librarians and archives and about schools, which are very complicated.

In *HM Stationery Office v Green Amps Ltd* [2007] EWHC 2755 (Ch), a private company, which had obtained unlicensed access to a mapping database which HMSO made available for licensed research, made use of the data for commercial purposes. The unlicensed infringement was not protected by s 29.

Implementation of Directive 2001/29/EC on copyright and related rights in the information society has inserted the words 'non-commercial' into this defence in relation to research, thus restricting it severely.

20.4.4.2   Fair dealing for the purpose of criticism and review (s 30(1))

If one wished to comment in an article on, say, the quality of a textbook on intellectual property, this fair dealing provision will permit copied extracts from the book to be used without the author's permission. The question whether this use is within the exception depends mainly on:

(a)   the purpose of the use of the quote – if I copy what the textbook says in order to tell people about the law rather than in order to comment on the textbook then I am just letting the textbook do my work for me and this would not be within the exception; and

(b)   how much I quote.

The Publishers' Association publishes guidelines on how much you can quote.

20.4.4.3   Fair dealing for the purpose of reporting current events (s 30(2))

This allows all works, other than photographs, to be used for reporting current events. If the report is in a newspaper or magazine there must be acknowledgement. If the report is on television, radio, etc then no acknowledgement is required (though in practice an acknowledgement is often given). Again, the question whether the dealing is fair depends on:

(a)   the purpose; and

(b)   how much is taken.

The purpose must truly be for reporting current events and not simply using something that has become of interest because of a particular current event. For example, the death of the Duchess of Windsor did not justify the publication of an exchange of letters between her and the Duke of Windsor without the permission of the copyright holder (*Associated Newspapers Group plc v News Group Newspapers Ltd* [1986] RPC 515). It also did not come under fair dealing for criticism and review (see **20.4.4.2**).

20.4.4.4   Artistic works on public display (s 62)

Section 62 provides an important general provision that making graphic or photographic images, broadcasts or films of buildings, sculptures, models for buildings and works of artistic craftsmanship is not an infringement of any copyright in those things. This applies to things which can be seen, permanently sited, in public places or premises open to the public. This provision also protects any further publication or copying of images or representations of those things.

20.4.5   Other defences and licensing

In proceedings for infringement of an IP right, the defendant will often argue that the right in question is not valid and/or the claimant does not have the right to sue for infringement. Another defence is that the copying has been done with the consent of the copyright holder (ie, there is a licence). Such a licence could be express or implied from the circumstances of the case. A licence might be implied, if it were necessary to give business efficacy to or to reflect the true intentions of parties to an agreement, but only to the minimum extent necessary.

20.5   REMEDIES

By s 96(2) of the CDPA 1988, 'in an action for infringement of copyright all such relief by way of damages, injunctions, accounts or otherwise is available to the plaintiff as is available in respect of any other property right'. This range of remedies is open to the copyright owner and, to the extent that licensed material is infringed, it is also open to an exclusive licensee against third parties, concurrently with the copyright owner. A non-exclusive licensee of copyright may have that range of remedies if the licence is in writing and expressly grants the non-exclusive licensee a right of action (ss 101, 101A). Where the rights of action are held concurrently between the owner and the exclusive licensee, usually whichever one initiates the action will need to join the other as second claimant or as defendant, according to the circumstances (s 102).

Damages are available, usually based upon the tortious, compensatory measure, often (but not always) based upon what the infringer would have had to pay for a notional licence to achieve what he has attempted to do without permission. Damages are not available against an innocent infringer, or someone has no knowledge of or reason to believe in the existence of copyright in the material (s 97(1)), although that does not prejudice the availability of other remedies. Under s 97(2), there is a provision for 'additional damages' to be awarded according to the circumstances, particularly the flagrancy of the infringement and the likely benefit accruing to the defendant. This usually depends upon some seriously questionable behaviour by the defendant, over and beyond the simple question of copying (see *Cantor Fitzgerald International v Tradition (UK) Ltd* [2000] RPC 95).

Injunctions, particularly interim ones, are fairly widely used in copyright disputes, the courts deciding the matter upon the weight of the issues and consequences for each party. The test for the court, in interim matters, is usually one of whether there is a serious triable issue. If damages could fairly easily restore the position, without more, an injunction application is unlikely to succeed.

Account of profit is a broad alternative to damages in an appropriate case against any infringer, knowing or innocent. The usual problem applies, in that if the court orders an account to be taken and it turns out that little or no profit has accrued, it will not be possible to fall back upon a substantial damages claim; only nominal damages would be available. The claimant will need to think long and hard about his election.

Orders are available for delivery up of infringing copies or articles held in the reasonable knowledge or belief that they are used, or have been used, for infringement purposes, both in civil and in criminal proceedings (ss 99, 108). This is supported by forfeiture of such similar copies and articles as are found during criminal investigations or proceedings under s114A. There can also be orders to forfeit such articles to the copyright owner, for destruction or whatever the court may think fit as to disposal (s 114).

The CDPA 1988, s 100 allows a copyright owner to seize offending articles. However, the right is in fact very weak. It can be used only against market or street traders as the right excludes business premises. The police also have to be informed beforehand. Section 107 provides for criminal liability for making or dealing with infringing articles. Sections 108 and 114 allow for the delivery up or destruction of infringing copies. Section 111 allows for an order to prevent the importation of infringing copies.

20.6 DATABASES

The Copyright and Rights in Database Regulations 1997 implemented the Directive on the Legal Protection of Databases (Directive 96/9/EC) ('Database Directive') and introduced a new 'database right' which is not the same as copyright but which gives some safeguards which are similar to copyright (see **Chapter 21**).

The new right was introduced to protect the interests of database owners (eg, news agencies), though it applies both to electronic and paper databases. Under English law, many such databases would generally have qualified for copyright as compilations in the past, but in many European countries they might not have been protected by copyright (because they would not be regarded as sufficiently original – see **20.2.2.1**). Even where there was copyright protection, if somebody extracted just one or two pieces of information then this might not amount to substantial copying, so might not be an infringement. See how the database right deals with this at **21.6**.

The individual items from which the database was composed could each also get copyright as a literary work, if substantial enough to constitute a 'work'.

20.7 COPYRIGHT AND INFORMATION TECHNOLOGY

An enormous practical problem in respect of information technology (IT) and the law is that technological advances constantly outstrip the law. For example, it was suggested at the time that the CDPA 1988 was going through Parliament that parts of it were already out of date.

Arguably, copyright is the most important of the 'general' IP rights in relation to IT matters. It is of more direct significance than either trade marks or patents (see also **Chapter 25**).

20.7.1   Computer programs

Perhaps the most important aspect of the application of copyright to IT is that computer programs are protected by literary copyright (see **20.4.1**). Unauthorised copying (including simple down-loading) of a program therefore amounts to breach of copyright (that is, basically, normal rules and remedies apply). So, the resulting anomaly is that something functional is protected by a literary right. It is also more likely that non-literal copying can be shown to infringe software copyright than other forms of literary copyright. This problem has been much considered under US copyright law.

The CDPA 1988, s 3(1), and the Copyright (Computer Programs) Regulations 1992 (SI 1992/3233) provide that software is protected as a literary work. (Note that there are also proposals to give patent protection to at least some computer programs; see **23.3.4**.)

20.7.2   The Internet

There seems to be a strongly-held view in some quarters that the law cannot apply to or control the Internet at all. Nevertheless, the law undoubtedly does apply to the Internet. The fact is that copyright infringement is no less of an infringement simply because it involves the Internet. The only real issues concern the most effective method of dealing with jurisdictional and evidential problems that arise in pursuing large numbers of people in different countries.

Most Internet use, where the material is available to the public in the UK, will fall within s 20 of the CDPA 1988 as a 'communication to the public'; any unauthorised use of copyright material may, therefore, infringe. The section is expressed to apply to making works available by 'electronic transmission'. This sweeps up the former s 7 of the CDPA 1988, which dealt with 'cablecasts'. It does not matter where the host website is located.

In a reference made to the European Court of Justice in *ITV et al v TVCatchup Ltd* (Case C-607/11), the defendant offered an Internet television broadcasting service. This service permitted its users to receive, via the Internet, 'live' streams of free-to-air television broadcasts. The defendant ensured that its subscribers could obtain access only to content which they were already legally entitled to watch in the United Kingdom by virtue of their television licence. The terms to which users must agree included the possession of a valid TV licence and a restriction of use of the defendant's services to the United Kingdom alone. The defendant's website had the facility to authenticate the user's location and thereby to refuse access where the conditions imposed on users were not satisfied. The ECJ was asked to consider whether the defendant's actions amounted to infringement by way of communication to the public of the broadcasts under EU Directive 2001/29 (covered in the UK by s 20 of the CDPA 1988). The Court gave guidance to the effect that the making of works available through the retransmission of a terrestrial television broadcast over the Internet used a technical means different from the original transmission, and so must be considered a communication. As such, it could only be done with the permission of the broadcaster.

There have been cases which have decided that unauthorised use of material from the Internet can amount to breach of copyright (see, eg, *Shetland Times Ltd v Wills and Another* [1997] FSR 604, discussed at **25.6.2**). There is also the opposite situation where copyright material is used on the Internet without permission. For example, in January 1999, a considerable number of musicians and pop singers took out advertisements in newspapers to protest against the unauthorised Internet use of their material, and to demand tighter legal controls. You may be familiar with the litigation in the USA on the 'Napster' site, which various record companies sued for breach of copyright in their recordings. Napster has returned as a licensed site, where you have to pay money to download the recordings. However, other sites have sprung up, such as Pirate Bay. These do not use a centralised server so it is harder to take action against them. They use P2P, software which enables one computer to communicate with another computer without going through a centralised server (P2P stands for 'peer to peer').

See the case of *Sony Music Entertainment (UK) Ltd and Others v Easyinternetcafé Ltd* at **20.4.2** for an instance of copyright infringement on the Internet.

More recently, the Recording Industry Association of America (RIAA) has instituted proceedings against many people in the United States for allegedly using P2P copying, and this policy has also been pursued in the United Kingdom.

Despite these steps in defence of their rights, it does seem as if the emphasis is beginning to shift away from attempts to enforce IP rights against mass users of the Internet, towards a recognition by producers of mass media/entertainment that they will have to live with widespread publication of their products. Many have embraced it by allowing their music to be streamed by companies like Spotify, Deezer and Apple, albeit for fees. The way forward in combating infringement is more likely to be by way of court orders that force ISPs to block sites that have been used to distribute copyrighted work illegally. As at the end of 2014, court orders in the UK had forced the five main ISPs to block a total of 93 sites.

Not all uses of copyrighted material on the Internet are infringements. In *Public Relations Consultants Association Ltd v The Newspaper Licensing Agency Ltd and Others* (Case C-360/13) (otherwise known as the 'Meltwater' case), the ECJ gave its view that temporary copies made automatically when browsing the Internet would not normally infringe copyright as long as Article 5(1) of the Copyright Directive (2001/29/EC) was complied with, namely that the act of reproduction must:

- be temporary;
- be transient or incidental;
- be an integral and essential part of a technological process;
- have the sole purpose of enabling a transmission or lawful use of a work to be made; and
- have no independent economic significance.

20.8 PUBLIC PERFORMANCES – THE COLLECTING SOCIETIES

It would be very difficult for the creators of music and songs, in particular, to enforce their rights acting individually, not least as their copyright could be infringed by a public performance anywhere in the country. To overcome this problem, the collecting societies have existed for many years. They operate either as licensees of the relevant copyrights, or as agents acting on behalf of the copyright holders. They employ staff to travel round the country to find places where public performances are taking place without a licence from one of the collecting societies. The typical problem locations are pubs and restaurants.

The Performing Rights Society (PRS) and the Mechanical Copyright Protection Society (MCPS) act for writers of music and lyrics and their publishers. The MCPS acts on behalf of its composer and publisher members. It negotiates agreements with those who wish to record the music of its members. It collects and distributes the 'mechanical' royalties which are generated from recording of the music on to many different formats. The PRS collects licence fees on behalf of composers, lyricists and music publishers for public performance or broadcast of their works. They co-operate closely under the name 'PRS for Music'. Phonographic Performance Limited (PPL) acts for over 3,000 record companies, both large and small, and deals primarily with the copyright in sound recordings. Video Performance Limited (VPL) is responsible for music videos.

In the US, there are similar societies, such as Broadcast Music Inc (BMI) and the American Society of Composers, Authors and Performers (ASCAP), which enforce copyrights and distribute royalties to the copyright owners.

As well as their policing role, the collecting societies license performance of their works, including to broadcasters such as the BBC, ITV and Sky. All the societies cooperate closely to ensure that the copyright holders in each aspect of a work receive their fair share of a licence fee from a user. Disputes about the terms and other aspects of this system are heard by the Copyright Tribunal, formerly the Performing Right Tribunal. See *Phonographic Performance Ltd v Candy Rock Recording Ltd* [2000] EMLR 618, CA.

In the publishing world, the Copyright Licensing Agency Ltd (CLA) seeks to enforce its members' copyright in their works. It licenses businesses to copy protected works. The CLA is owned by the Authors Licensing and Collecting Society (ALCS) and the Publishers Licensing Society (PLS). The Newspaper Licensing Agency Ltd (NLA) was set up in 1996 to enforce newspaper proprietors' rights in their copyright. It licenses businesses to copy newspapers, and was involved in a high-profile case with Marks & Spencer (see **20.4** and **20.4.4.3**).

20.9 INTERNATIONAL COPYRIGHT PROTECTION

Internationally, there are two distinct levels of recognition and protection of copyright material. The first lies in the various measures taken by the European Community; the second is seen in international treaty obligations of the UK. It is only possible to give a brief outline of these matters here, but they can be summarised as follows.

Within the EU, the matter has been dealt with by directives, leading to national legislation, showing some degree of harmonisation. Examples are seen in computer programs (Directive 91/250/EEC), rental and lending rights in copyright (Directive 92/100/EEC), and database protection (Directive 96/9/EC). The general effect of all this legislation is that most national legislation within the EU is fairly consistent in its effect and application, but there are still anomalous situations, particularly with respect to performance and moral rights. Brexit has not immediately affected UK laws on copyright, although they may diverge from EU harmonised rules over time.

On the broader international stage, the UK is a signatory to two major treaties, the Berne Copyright Convention and the Universal Copyright Convention. Both treaties have a similar effect: they provide assurance, as between the signatory nations, that mutual recognition, availability of jurisdiction and national legal remedies will be given to the owners of copyright within the different signatory states. It is a sort of copyright club arrangement.

20.9.1 Berne Convention

The Berne Convention for the Protection of Literary and Artistic Works, usually known just as the Berne Convention, is an international agreement about copyright, which was first adopted in Berne, Switzerland in 1886.

Prior to the adoption of the Berne Convention, national copyright laws would usually only apply for works created within each country. Consequently, a work published in London by a British national would be covered by copyright in the UK, but could be copied and sold by anyone in France; likewise, a work published in Paris by a French national would be covered by copyright in France, but could be copied and sold by anyone in the UK.

The Berne Convention followed in the footsteps of the Paris Convention of 1883, which in the same way had created a framework for international integration of the other kinds of intellectual property: patents, trademarks and industrial designs.

The Berne Convention was revised in Paris in 1896 and in Berlin in 1908, completed in Berne in 1914, revised in Rome in 1928, in Brussels in 1948, in Stockholm in 1967 and in Paris in 1971, and was amended in 1979. The UK signed the Berne Convention in 1887, but did not implement large parts of it until 100 years later with the passage of the CDPA 1988.

The US initially refused to become a party to the Convention, since it would have required major changes in its copyright law (particularly with regard to moral rights, removal of the general requirement for registration of copyright works, as well as elimination of mandatory copyright notice). However, on 1 March 1989, the US 'Berne Convention Implementation Act of 1988' came into force and the US became a party to the Berne Convention.

Since almost all nations are members of the WTO, the TRIPS Agreement requires non-members to accept almost all of the conditions of the Berne Convention.

There are currently 179 countries that are parties to the Berne Convention. It requires its signatories to recognise the copyright of works of authors from other signatory countries (known as members of the Berne Union) in the same way they recognise the copyright of their own nationals, which means that, for instance, French copyright law applies to anything published or performed in France, regardless of where or by whom it was originally created.

In addition to establishing a system of equal treatment that internationalised copyright amongst signatories, the Convention also required member States to provide strong minimum standards for copyright law.

Copyright under the Berne Convention must be automatic; it is prohibited to require formal registration.

20.9.2   Universal Copyright Convention

The Universal Copyright Convention (UCC) was first created in 1952 as a result of some countries – in particular the US (see **20.9.1** above) – disagreeing with certain articles of the Berne Convention. The UCC was created to give international protection to authors even in countries that would not sign the Berne Convention. However, as most countries are now parties to Berne, the UCC is of limited importance. It was last revised in 1971.

To ensure that the UCC did not lead to conflict with the Berne Convention, Article 17 of the UCC states that it does not affect the operation of Berne for those countries which are signatories to both.

The UCC details the following points:

(a)   Contracting States provide the same cover to foreign published works as they do to their own citizens.

(b)   States that require formal registration should treat works from foreign States that are signatories to the UCC as though they had been registered in the State, provided that they carry a notice which includes the © symbol and states the name of the owner.

(c)   It sets a minimum duration for copyright protection at 25 years from the date of publication, and typically not less that 25 years from the author's death (with the notable exception of photographic and applied arts work which has a minimum protection of 10 years).

(d)   It recognises the economic rights of the author (the right to authorise reproduction, public performance, broadcasting, etc).

(e)   It recognises the author's right to make translations of the work.

(f)   It also specifies particular exceptions which may be applied to developing countries.

20.9.3   TRIPS

The Agreement on Trade Related Aspects of Intellectual Property Rights (TRIPS), discussed earlier in relation to trade marks (see **19.13.3.3**), lays down minimum standards of protection in all areas of intellectual property, including copyright and related rights.

It provides a certain level or harmonisation as it lays down certain minimum standards for the enforcement of copyright, as follows:

(a)   Copyright terms must extend to at least 50 years after the death of the author, although films and photographs are only required to have fixed 50- and 25-year terms, respectively.

(b)   Copyright must be granted automatically, and not be based upon any 'formality', such as registrations or systems of renewal.

(c) Computer programs must be regarded as 'literary works' under copyright law and receive the same terms of protection.

(d) National exceptions to copyright (such as 'fair use' in the US) must be tightly constrained.

(e) In each State, IP laws may not offer any benefits to local citizens which are not available to citizens of other TRIPS signatories by the principles of national treatment.

20.9.4 Rome Convention

The International Convention for the Protection of Performers, Producers of Phonograms and Broadcasting Organisations (the Rome Convention) extended copyright protection for the first time from the author of a work to the creators and owners of particular, physical manifestations of IP, such as audiocassettes or DVDs.

Nations drew up the Convention in response to new technologies, such as tape recorders, that had made the reproduction of sounds and images easier and cheaper than ever before.

Whereas earlier copyright law, including international agreements like the Berne Convention, had been written to regulate the circulation of printed materials, the Rome Convention responded to the new circumstance of ideas variously represented in easily reproduced units by covering performers and producers of recordings under copyright.

The Rome Convention allows the following exceptions in national laws to the above-mentioned rights:

(a) private use;

(b) use of short excerpts in connection with the reporting of current events;

(c) ephemeral fixation by a broadcasting organisation by means of its own facilities and for its own broadcasts;

(d) use solely for the purpose of teaching or scientific research;

(e) in any other cases – except for compulsory licences that would be incompatible with the Berne Convention – where the national law provides exceptions to copyright in literary and artistic works.

Furthermore, once a performer has consented to the incorporation of their performance in a visual or audiovisual fixation, the provisions on performers' rights have no further application.

20.10 OTHER UK RULES RELATED TO COPYRIGHT

20.10.1 Digital Economy Act 2010

The Digital Economy Act 2010 brought in provisions intended to combat the online infringement of copyrighted material. It aims to make it easier to track down infringers, and ultimately to deny them the use of the Internet.

The procedure begins with a harmed copyright owner gathering IP addresses of alleged infringers, following which he contacts the relevant Internet Service Provider (ISP). The ISP has an obligation to contact the alleged infringer to notify him that it has been contacted by the copyright owner. If the number of notifications received by an individual exceeds a threshold to be set by the Internet regulator (Ofcom), the copyright owner can gain a court order to discover the alleged infringer's identity from the ISP. The result would be that the copyright owner has all the information he needs to take legal action against the alleged infringer.

The Act also contains provisions which allow the possibility of a court injunction being granted to prevent ISPs from allowing access to a location on the Internet which is responsible for copyright infringements. Essentially, therefore, websites can be made inaccessible via ISPs, but such court orders are expected to be difficult to obtain because of their draconian nature.

The Digital Economy Act 2010 is controversial, not least because of the difficult situation in which it places ISPs. As a result, despite being passed in 2010, its implementation was delayed until 27 April 2017 by legal challenges.

The Act does not appear to be particularly 'future-proof' against technological developments. For example, a growing number of websites offer encrypted 'cyberlocker' facilities, allowing the swapping of files without their contents being publicly visible. Furthermore, the use of proxy servers, which hide the identity of file sharers by making it appear that they are operating from a different location, is on the increase.

20.10.2 The Hargreaves Review

In May 2011, an independent report was published by Professor Ian Hargreaves entitled *Digital Opportunity: A Review of Intellectual Property and Growth*. It was commissioned by the Government with one main question: 'Could it be true that laws designed more than three centuries ago with the express purpose of creating economic incentives for innovation by protecting creators' rights are today obstructing innovation and economic growth?'

The Report led the Government to make a series of proposals, which have been implemented by way of regulations.

20.10.2.1 Orphaned works

The Government has set up an 'orphaned works' scheme. Orphaned works are those works of which it is unclear who the copyright owners are. The scheme allows the works to be used, but also protects the rights of the owners. It involves setting up a central database of works believed to be orphaned. This enables rights holders to check whether their work is on the register, and to apply for their removal. Prior to this register, it was believed that works were commonly 'lost' to society as people avoided exploiting them because they did not know whom to pay for their use. The register encourages these works to be exploited, since the body controlling the register can authorise use of material on it.

Details of the orphaned works scheme can be found at https://www.gov.uk/copyright-orphan-works.

20.10.2.2 Extended collective licensing

The Government has recently simplified the rights clearance system (for music) through the introduction of a voluntary extended collective licensing (ECL) scheme, which allows authorised collecting societies to license on behalf of all rights holders in a particular sector, except where the rights holders choose to opt out of the scheme. This is an attempt to solve the problem that collecting societies may represent only some rights holders, and so obtaining permission for a series of works otherwise would be expensive and time-consuming as applicants may have to deal with several different collecting societies.

20.10.2.3 Exceptions to copyright

The Government has recently created additional exceptions to copyright as follows:

- limited private copying (allowing people to copy works for which they have paid to other forms of media, eg music onto a PC, iPod, CD, phone, tablet, even uploading to a private space on the Internet such as a cloud). This has been brought in by adding a s 28B to the Copyright Designs and Patents Act 1988;
- the use of quotations for criticism, comment or review as long as such use is fair and does not undermine commercial rights;
- the use of information for data analysis; and
- parody, caricature and pastiche (imitation).

20.10.2.4   Copyright notices

Lastly, the Government recently introduced a Copyright Notice Service, which gives the Intellectual Property Office a statutory function to publish formal opinions on UK copyright law and its application. It recognises that copyright is complex, and believes that an advisory service would be useful for creators and users of copyrighted material. Details can be found at https://www.gov.uk/copyright-notices.

20.10.3   Directive on Copyright in the Digital Single Market

At the time of writing, a controversial Copyright Directive has just come into force for EU countries (not the UK following Brexit). There are three provisions which are controversial in the field of copyright:

- Article 15: Anyone using small amounts of journalistic online content will need to obtain a licence from the publisher. This will impact on services such as Google, Facebook and Twitter, who currently include small summaries of articles as part of a link to the full article. The intention is to provide more income to the journalists who write the articles, but it is being viewed negatively by many as an attack on online linking.

- Article 17: Internet platforms hosting large amounts of user content must monitor user behaviour and filter contributions to identify and prevent copyright infringement. The intent is to protect the music industry from the threat posed by illegal downloads; however, the move is controversial as legal content may be caught in the crossfire as platforms use increasingly aggressive filters to ensure compliance. It arguably will also prohibit start-up companies from entering the market due to the huge cost of compliance.

- Article 3: A text and data mining exception will be created but only for research institutions and for the purposes of scientific research. Text and data mining is a technology for tasks such as analysing big data sets and training artificial intelligence systems. Critics argue that this exception is too limited and does not include, for example, independent researchers or journalists.

SUMMARY

One of the main IP laws often in the news is copyright. Whether because of illegal downloads of music and films, songs which sound like other songs, or videos uploaded to websites without the creator's permission, copyright is often the topic of discussion. This chapter will have enabled you to discuss the key challenges faced by the law of copyright, and allowed you to form a view as to whether impending changes to the law will be a success.

CHAPTER 21

THE DATABASE RIGHT

LEARNING OUTCOMES

After reading this chapter you will be able to:

- define a database
- apply the law relating to database rights
- identify the owner of a database
- explain exceptions and identify infringements.

21.1 BACKGROUND AND INTRODUCTION

There has been a difference of approach between English law and the Continental civil law systems on the protection of utilitarian information such as lists of customers' names and addresses, or entries in a phone directory. The English approach has been to grant copyright protection, but the Continental view was that such functional documents were not literary works and therefore could not be protected by copyright. This difference of approach was resolved by Directive 96/9/EC on the Legal Protection of Databases ('the Database Directive'). This was implemented by the Copyright and Rights in Databases Regulations 1997 ('the 1997 Regulations') (SI 1997/3032). These amended the CDPA 1988. The protection given by the 1997 Regulations is known as the 'database right'.

What is protected?	collections of information
What benefit is there?	protects against unauthorised copying
How is it obtained?	arises automatically (no registration)
How long does it last?	15 years from creation or substantial revision of the database

There remains a class of databases that is protected by copyright (see **20.2** and **21.2**). This class will, in almost all cases, be protected by both copyright and the database right under the 1997 Regulations. The problem that commonly arose for copyright database owners, prior to the 1997 Regulations, was that copying often took the form of repeated, low level use of the material, which usually failed to be a 'substantial' copying for infringement purposes. This gap has now been filled by reg 16(2) (see **21.6**).

Database rights that existed in the UK or EEA before 1 January 2021 (whether held by UK or EEA persons or businesses) continue to exist in the UK and EEA for the rest of their duration. UK citizens, residents and businesses will not be eligible to receive or hold database rights in the EEA for databases created after then. Only UK citizens, residents and businesses are eligible for database rights in the UK for databases created on or after 1 January 2021. Note that copyright protection in databases (if any) is not affected by Brexit as it is guaranteed by international convention.

21.2 DEFINITION OF A DATABASE

A database is defined in the CDPA 1988, s 3A, as follows:

> **3A**   **Databases**
>
> (1)   In this Part 'database' means a collection of independent works, data or other materials which—
>
>   (a)   are arranged in a systematic or methodical way, and
>
>   (b)   are individually accessible by electronic or other means.
>
> (2)   For the purposes of this Part a literary work consisting of a database is original if, and only if, by reason of the selection or arrangement of the contents of the database the database constitutes the author's own intellectual creation.

The definition of a 'database' covers information held in electronic form and also that held only as paper documents. This definition is also applied by the 1997 Regulations.

In practice, a database could, for example, be information on the daily price of stocks and shares, a telephone directory, Lexis or the CD-ROM law reports. Copyright protection may also be afforded to a database specifically as a literary work, although the standard is not only that of originality, but also that it is the 'author's own intellectual creation'. This seems to be a higher standard than for copyright in literary works in general, and so a database is unlikely to have copyright protection.

Whether or not it is protected by copyright, a database attracts the database right, which arises automatically. The database right runs for 15 years from the end of the year of completion. It prevents unauthorised use of the database or a substantial part of it.

Under reg 13 of the 1997 Regulations, the database right exists where there is 'substantial investment in obtaining, verifying or presenting the contents of the database.' Thus, data arrangements have the protection of the database right if there is a substantial investment (including any investment, whether of financial, human or technical resources):

(a)   in quality or quantity; or

(b)   in obtaining, verifying or presenting the data.

Further points to consider in relation to database right are discussed below.

21.3 QUALIFICATIONS FOR THE DATABASE RIGHT

There are copyright-style qualification requirements (1997 Regulations, reg 18) based on nationality, or corporate seat.

21.4 OWNERSHIP OF THE DATABASE RIGHT

The maker of a database protected by the database right is the person who takes the initiative in obtaining, verifying or presenting the contents of the database and who assumes the risk of investing in that obtaining (see 1997 Regulations, reg 14).

The maker is the first owner of the database right (reg 15).

Care is needed in asserting ownership of database rights. In *Google Inc v Copiepresse SCRL* [2007] ECDR 5, a database right infringement claim by a management company failed, simply because the company did not hold the database right but only managed copyright on behalf of various newspapers which were subjected to automatic searches by Google. Copyright infringements were upheld by the Belgian court.

21.5 DURATION OF DATABASE PROTECTION

The database right lasts for the longer of 15 years from the end of the calendar year:

(a) of completion of the database; or

(b) during which the database was first made available to the public (reg 17).

A 'substantial new investment', under s 17(3) will 'top up' the right so the period starts again. So, a telephone directory would in effect have a rolling 15-year protection, as a new edition is produced every year.

21.6 INFRINGEMENT OF THE DATABASE RIGHT

Infringement is the extraction or re-utilisation of all or a substantial part of the contents of a database without the consent of the owner (reg 16).

'Extraction' means the permanent or temporary transfer of the contents of a database to another medium by any means, or in any form.

'Re-utilisation' means making those contents available to the public by any means.

'Substantial' is in terms of quality, or quantity or both.

'Substantial part' can include repeated extraction and/or re-utilisation of insubstantial parts (reg 16(2)). This is the most useful aspect of the right, in that it may prevent repeated, low-level use of the database by unauthorised persons.

21.7 EXCEPTIONS FROM THE DATABASE RIGHT

Database rights are not infringed (regs 19 and 20):

(a) by fair dealing with a substantial part of a database made available to the public if:
    (i) such dealing is for illustration in teaching or research; and
    (ii) sufficient acknowledgement is given; or
(b) generally, by copying or use with the authority of the keeper of a database available for public inspection as a statutory record.

The database right may be licensed or assigned (as may the copyright in the database).

21.8 APPLICATION OF THE DATABASE RIGHT

The database right was introduced to give the database owner an action against people who extract information from the database without its permission, whether or not this would constitute copyright infringement.

In *British Horseracing Board v William Hill*, the British Horseracing Board operated a computerised database containing the details of horse owners, trainers and jockeys, racing colours, horses and other information relating to races to be run in Great Britain. Information on the database was updated after each race. William Hill, a bookmaker with 1,500 licensed betting shops in the UK, legitimately used information from the British Horseracing Board service. In 2000, William Hill started an Internet betting service which used information from the British Horseracing Board service. This was outside the terms of William Hill's licence agreement. The British Horseracing Board therefore sued for breach of the database right, and the case was referred to the ECJ.

In essence, the ECJ held that there needed to be economic investment in resources used to create a database in order for the database right to arise. This was distinct from re-presenting existing materials, which was held to be the case here. The British Horseracing Board would have had to collect the information on runners and riders in any event for its own purposes as the supervisor of horseracing in the UK. The view of the ECJ was therefore that the database in question did not benefit from the database right, and so William Hill could not have infringed it.

An interesting point was considered in *Cantor Gaming Ltd v Gameaccount Global Ltd* [2007] EWHC 1914 (QB). The claimant had inserted a clause in its online game licence that if any use of its intellectual property were made by third party bookmakers, via the defendant, that would be a material breach of the licence. It was decided that the claimant's database, even though not used in a conventional way, had been stored, backed up, reproduced and accessed. That was sufficient to constitute an unlawful use of the database.

In *Cureton v Mark Insulations Ltd* [2006] EWHC 2279 (QB), an agent who had been given the task of selling insulation to his principal's customers began to collate more information about them for his own private purposes, unrelated to the agency function. In a termination dispute, the principal claimed ownership of the database. The court held that although the principal was justified in summarily dismissing the agent, the work in creating the database had been done by the agent and he was, therefore, the owner under reg 14 (see **21.4**).

SUMMARY

Copyright has traditionally been the right which deals with the written word, but there are some written works which may not satisfy some of the requirements for copyright; some works are mundane and may not display much originality or effort in their creation. Nevertheless their creators may view them as valuable and would want the right to take action if someone did copy their work. This is where the law of databases is useful.

This chapter has examined what qualifies as a database, how protection is obtained, and how the law relating to databases can be enforced.

CHAPTER 22

DESIGN RIGHTS

> **LEARNING OUTCOMES**
>
> After reading this chapter you will be able to:
>
> - explain the key highlights of registered design right
> - explain the key highlights of unregistered design right
> - identify what semiconductors are, and what rights may exist over them
> - apply exceptions to design right protection
> - explain the remedies that may be obtained from someone who breaches design rights.

22.1 INTRODUCTION TO DESIGN PROTECTION

So far, in looking at IP rights, we have examined the protection of business reputation and creative expression through trade marks, passing off and copyright, all areas which provide clear and obvious examples of matters that require legal protection. The creator or owner of a business or a copyright work really does look like an owner of property in some form. In dealing with designs, however, somewhat different considerations come into play. Here, we are dealing with the way things look and with the shape and appearance of manufactured articles – often, the quite mundane objects that surround us in our everyday world. It is not so easy or practicable to accept that shapes and appearances of things should remain the monopoly of any particular person for any extensive length of time. Nevertheless, successful shapes and appearances cost money to design and are worth a great deal to their owner, commercially. In consequence, the law has had to develop to give a range of more limited rights to owners of designs, in terms both of period of protection and the scope of the protection offered, than those you have seen in the IP rights studied so far. There is a delicate balancing act here, between over-protection of design owners and the maintenance of general design freedom for other competing designers and manufacturers, who wish to use similar design features on the same, or even on different, types of article.

A simple example illustrates the point: a person buys an article, perhaps a motor cycle, and then decides it is so good that he wishes to keep it for a long time. If the manufacturer changes models after a short while and ceases to make spare parts for the earlier bike, can the enthusiastic owner go to someone else who is willing to make and sell a spare part to that design? It would be a great problem if the original manufacturer could exercise design rights to prevent such a thing permanently, or even stop other manufacturers, as competitors, from making the millions of genuine spare parts used in the everyday world. Design protection has to be able to deal with this practicality; the law has to recognise that where there is plenty of design freedom, an interesting design will merit protection for a period. Where there is little or no room to vary the design (such as with many spare parts, or in interfaces between component parts, or between scart, 3-pin or other cable connections, etc), the law will usually not provide protection for those design features.

The protections we look at below fall into two categories: the most protected category is achieved by initial registration of a design and maintenance of that registration up to a maximum of 25 years, this protection being limited to external shapes and appearances ('registered design right' or 'RDR'); a lesser, unregistered design right will give a shorter period of protection to shapes and forms, but is capable of dealing with the often invisible internal shapes and forms of articles which cannot be protected by registration ('unregistered design right' or 'UDR'). It should be understood though, that it is not always the whole of an article that will be protected; the protection will apply only to those features which are capable of meeting the requirements of the relevant legislation, which tends to exclude many features as being unprotectable.

It is important to realise that RDR and UDR are not mutually exclusive; it is often the case that both rights may co-exist in the same design features or, alternatively, that the separate rights exist in separate features of the same article – eg, RDR protecting the surface decoration of it (to which UDR cannot apply, see **22.1.1** below), while UDR protects inner, unseen shapes and configurations (to which RDR cannot apply, see **22.1.2** below).

22.1.1   Registered design right (RDR) – overview

Registered designs have existed in England since at least the 1830s. They were bolstered at that time to protect the designs of fabrics from being copied by cheap imports. Registered design right was strengthened in the CDPA 1988, with the aim of promoting its use for a wider range of articles. At the same time, copyright was pushed in the direction of artistic output, not least to resist the trend that had developed of trying to use copyright for industrial items such as, say, spare parts for cars, etc, to gain longer periods of protection. The interface between copyright and design protection is discussed at **22.3.7** below. Directive 98/71/EC on the Legal Protection of Design (the Design Directive), implemented by the Registered Design Regulations 2001 (SI 2001/3949), made further amendments to the legislation governing registered designs, the Registered Designs Act 1949 (RDA) 1949, effective from 9 December 2001. Regulation 6/2002 EC set up the framework of the Community Design Scheme (see **22.2.11** and **22.3.9**).

Registered design right protects the visible, external appearance, during ordinary use, of all or part of a product, 'product' being very widely defined so as to include consumer or industrial products.

A visit to the IPO website (www.ipo.gov.uk) and its registered designs search area, under 'products', will reveal designs for just about anything that can be manufactured, from the most artistically designed consumer articles to the most functional industrial items. The range is very wide, from tools, to clothes, to transport, so the protection has come a long way from fabric designs and purely consumer articles. The form of protection given is similar to other registered IP rights: the fact of registration gives notice to the world at large of the existence of the right, so that any commercial use or exploitation of the design, or of articles made to that design, with or without knowledge or intention, is within the scope of the protection (see infringements and remedies at **22.3.5** and **22.3.6**). In effect, RDR gives the owner of the design a monopoly period of up to 25 years (an initial five-year period, renewable in subsequent five-year periods) in which to use and exploit the design.

What is protected?	new designs for manufactured items
What benefit is there?	monopoly right
How is it obtained?	registration
How long does it last?	25 years from registration

22.1.2   Unregistered design right (UDR) – origins and overview

Unregistered design right is a relatively modern form of protection for designs. One of the essential components of most replicable designs is some sort of design document. Such a document is almost sure to be protected by the law of copyright, potentially for a long period, and prior to the CDPA 1988, most industrial and manufacturer's design documents had artistic/graphic protection, capable of preventing unauthorised replication of the designs for the long periods associated with artistic copyright. More significantly, unauthorised reproduction of articles from those design documents also infringed the copyright, under the 2D to 3D transformation, as the law then stood. This was even more dangerous as, because of the informal nature of copyright creation and protection, no registration was required and a person could easily infringe copyright without knowing it.

What the 1988 Act did was to eradicate this long-term copyright protection of designs by the creation of UDR, the effect being that to reproduce the design document, without permission, will certainly infringe any copyright in it (but the period of protection will typically be only for a maximum of 25 years); if the document is reproduced for the purpose of the unauthorised creation of articles to that design, that reproduction will also be an infringement of any UDR in the design (but protection is only for the maximum period of up to 15 years, more typically 10). The most significant change, though, is that any unauthorised making of articles from that infringing copy of the design document will not be an infringement of copyright but will be an infringement of any UDR in the design. The whole idea of this change was effectively to suppress the extensive copyright protection in favour of the much more limited UDR protection (the relationship between copyright and UDR, in a manufacturing, design or production context, is quite complex and more detail is given below, see **22.3.7**). So if I photocopy your design document, I have infringed your copyright, but if I look at your design document and make the object represented in it, I have not infringed your copyright but I have infringed your UDR.

The scope of the protection given by UDR is quite wide, as it protects designs of the shape or configuration, internal or external, of all or part of an article. It can be seen, at once, that this goes further than RDR in protecting internal shapes; but, as will be seen, it is more limited than RDR in that it cannot protect surface decoration. Both RDR and UDR therefore have their individual characteristics. To maximise protection, use of both may be necessary.

What is protected?	3-dimensional shapes and configurations
What benefit is there?	prevents copying
How is it obtained?	arises automatically (no registration)
How long does it last?	10 years in most cases (15 years maximum)

22.2   REGISTERED DESIGN RIGHT

22.2.1   Definitions – 'new' and 'individual character'

'Registered design' is defined in RDA 1949, s 1(2) as:

> ... the appearance of the whole or part of a product resulting from the features of, in particular, the lines, contours, shape, texture and/or materials of the product itself and/or its ornamentation.

'Product' is defined in s 1(3) as:

any industrial or handicraft item other than a computer program; and in particular, includes packaging, get-up, graphic symbols, typographic type-faces and parts intended to be assembled into a complex product.

This definition now includes things that were not covered before (the amendments referred to at **22.1**), perhaps most notably the packaging and get-up (presentation) of goods. Thus, it would now be possible to register the appearance of packaging as a registered design. This would give such items the increased protection of a registered right.

A design must be '*new*' and have '*individual character*', which terms are defined as follows:

1B   Requirement of novelty and individual character

(1)   A design shall be protected by a right in a registered design to the extent that the design is new and has individual character.

(2)   For the purposes of subsection (1) above, a design is new if no identical design or no design whose features differ only in immaterial details has been made available to the public before the relevant date.

(3)   For the purposes of subsection (1) above, a design has individual character if the overall impression it produces on the informed user differs from the overall impression produced on such a user by any design which has been made available to the public before the relevant date.

As to the requirement for novelty, the test in s 1B(2) is clearly one of whether that design is available to the public, which raises further subordinate questions as to what is meant by 'available to the public' in terms of time, geographical scope and purpose of exposure of the design. The answers to these questions can be found in further examination of the rest of s 1B, particularly s 1B(5), (6) and (7). In broad terms, the time at which the novelty test must be met is when the application to register is first filed. The 'public' in question is probably now somewhat wider than the previous statutory test of the public within the UK. Section 1B(6)(a) indicates that the likely scope may well be as large as the purchasing public and the business community throughout the European Economic Area (EEA). Note that this has not been changed by Brexit.

The question whether the design is new, at that date, is one of whether any largely identical design already exists in 'the prior art in the sector concerned'; that is the sort of designs which are already known of or in use at that date, both by buyers and by 'persons carrying on business . . . and specialising in the sector concerned' (s 1B(6)(a)). So, much depends upon what 'the sector' means. According to Lewison J, in *Green Lane Products Ltd v PMS International Group Ltd* [2007] EWHC 1712 (Pat), 'the sector concerned' is the sector in which the 'prior art' is located rather than the particular product sector for which the new registration was applied. That is an important finding, if it is right, in that it means that a design cannot be pirated simply by trying to use that design in a different product sector, as was being attempted in that case. This view has now been upheld by the Court of Appeal ([2008] EWCA Civ 358). This decision suggests that registration of a design for, say, a car, could prevent use of that design on a cake or a toy. The extent of 'the prior art' probably extends to almost any design, wherever located in the world, that is 'available' within the EEA. Registrations will not usually be invalidated by earlier designs in remote places, of which European industry would be unlikely to be aware. The Design Registry will not search prior art but will rely on third parties to object to the application when it is published.

The question of 'individual character' in s 1B(3) is also determined as at the date of first filing and really boils down to a question of evidence as to the overall impression made upon an 'informed user', presumably a person familiar with the designs used in the sector in question. In *J Choo (Jersey) Ltd v Towerstone Ltd* [2008] EWHC 346 (Ch), in a pirated handbag claim, the 'informed user' was said to be neither the woman in the street nor a handbag designer, but rather someone with knowledge of handbag design. The real question is usually whether the creator of the new design has taken advantage of any freedom of design that is available to him to make his new design different from what is already available; if he has not, it is likely that the new design will not have individual character. This is given statutory force in s 1B(4). It should be borne in mind that the different overall impression test might be passed by combining features from several different products to give a completely new amalgam of those features – see *In the Matter of Registered Design No 2044802 in the Name of Household Articles Ltd*, Ch D (Patents Ct) 22/1/98, [1998] FSR 676, a case under the old law, but one which would probably be decided the same way now. There are suggestions in the cases that evidence of both novelty and individual character should be limited to that of purchasers of or traders in the product in question. There is little room for any expert evidence and the court will not usually require it.

It appears, in many cases, that 'individual character' might not add much to the basic requirement that the design be new.

Some helpful guidance on the 'overall different impression' test for individual character has now been given by the Court of Appeal in *Procter & Gamble Co v Reckitt Benckiser (UK) Ltd* [2007] EWCA Civ 936. In the context of a CRD infringement claim, concerning air freshener spray containers, the Court gave some general guidance as follows:

(a) The first point is that a different overall impression is sufficient and it does not need to be 'clearly' different.

(b) The notional informed user would be taken as being fairly familiar with design issues.

(c) Protection would be correspondingly greater for products which were novel, as compared to those only incrementally different from the prior art.

(d) The test for validity of the registered design remained 'Is the overall impression different?'.

(e) The court needed to identify the 'overall impression' with some care.

(f) The level of generality was very important and should be that of the notional informed user, rather than the casual customer.

(g) The court should than repeat this exercise with the alleged infringing design.

(h) The court should ask finally whether the overall impression of each design was different.

In the instant case, the judge had taken the similarities at too general a level and had come to a finding that there had been infringement. The Court of Appeal held that the informed user would have formed different overall impressions of the products and that therefore there was no infringement. Also, on the appeal, the claimant's original registration was upheld.

22.2.2 'Grace period' of 12 months

The amended RDA 1949 now provides a grace period of 12 months during which a designer may disclose the design to others without affecting the design's novelty, or the assessment of its individual character in an application for registration by the end of the 12-month period (s 1B(5), (6)). There is no right to claim for infringement before the design has been granted registration (s 7A(6)). The very point was in issue in *Oakley Inc v Animal Ltd*, because the disclosure date created problems as to which law and tests applied. There are other provisions in s 1B(6) to protect against unauthorised or abusive disclosures of the design during the grace period.

It would still be important to keep evidence of the date of creation of the design (eg, by storing original drawings which should be dated and signed). Thus, if someone else claimed during the 12-month grace period that he had created the design in question, there would be evidence available to refute that claim. Once the design has been registered, any such disputes would be resolved by the registration, if it is valid.

22.2.3 Design features that cannot be protected

22.2.3.1 Technical function (s 1C)

There is an exclusion from registrability for features dictated 'solely by the product's technical function'. The requirement of 'solely' dictated raises the question of how much design freedom is available (see **22.2.3.2**); if there is some freedom to give a different appearance to the design, it is probably registrable, provided it is new and has individual character.

Section 1C(1) states: 'A right in a registered design shall not subsist in features of appearance of a product which are solely dictated by the product's technical function.' An example of such a feature would be the serrated blades of a dressmaker's crimping shears, which create a sawtooth edge on what is cut.

22.2.3.2 Interface features (s 1C(2))

Section 1C(2) excludes registration for any features of the design of a product which are *compelled* to be of a certain exact shape in order to be able to fit into, around or up against some other product so that either or both of the products can perform their proper function. The remaining features of either product may well be registrable, but the interface features are not. If it had to be that design then no design flair has been shown, so why should it gain protection?

One of the more pervasive features of modern designs has been the increasing use of modular ranges (ie things designed to lock together) of products of all types – tools, furniture, utensils, household and vehicle fittings. By itself, s 1C(2) would create a problem for protecting the many ingenious designs for the interfaces between modular items. Section 1C(3) removes this problem by stating that s 1C(2) does not apply to features that allow for assembly or connection of mutually interchangeable products within a modular system; such features can now be registered and protected (although they would still need to be new and of individual character). That tends to cut back the rigour of both s 1C(2) and the earlier case law rule (seen in *Amp Inc v Utilux Pty Ltd* [1971] RPC 397) that such interface connections could never be registered. So, for example, stacking chairs are not automatically excluded from registration (but may fail on other grounds).

22.2.4 Designs that can now be protected

Under the law pre-December 2001, it was not possible to have a design registration for a spare part (see *R v Registered Designs Appeal Tribunal, ex p Ford Motor Co* [1995] 1 WLR 18). However, it is now possible to have such a registration, provided the part is visible during the normal use of the whole product. For example, a new design of radio aerial for a car would be registrable as it would be visible, but a new design for an oil filter for a car would not, as it would be hidden during normal use. Thus, s 1B(8), (9) provide:

> (8)   For the purposes of this section, a design applied to or incorporated in a product which constitutes a component part of a complex product shall only be considered to be new and to have individual character—
>
> > (a)   if the component part, once it has been incorporated into the complex product, remains visible during normal use of the complex product; and
> >
> > (b)   to the extent that those visible features of the component part are in themselves new and have individual character.
>
> (9)   In subsection (8) above "normal use" means use by the end user; but does not include any maintenance, servicing or repair work in relation to the product.

'Normal use' means that the visible parts of a wing mirror, in the *Ford* case, could now be registered as they are visible in the ordinary use of a car.

A design registration cannot be used against someone supplying a spare part for the repair of a complex product, 'so as to restore its original appearance' (eg, the car radio aerial mentioned above (s 7A(5)). So, while the registration can be used to stop another manufacturer from using that design for a car radio aerial on its make of car, it cannot be used to stop someone supplying spare aerials so as to restore the appearance of a car, made by the owner of the registered design. Care would be needed, of course, to avoid reproducing any logos or marks that had any separate rights, such as trade marks or passing off protection; licences would be needed to reproduce those.

22.2.5   The scope of the right

The proprietor has the exclusive right (subject to any compulsory licensing by the Crown under the RDA 1949, Sch 1) to use the design and 'any design which does not produce on the informed user a different overall impression' (s 7(1)). This in effect includes use of the design on any product. It will extend to manufacture, dealing in, importing, exporting, stocking and use of a product incorporating the design (see **22.2.9**).

Unlike the situation under the old law, designs no longer have to be registered in regard to certain types of product. So, use of a design intended for crockery on, say, tee shirts would be infringement of the design registration. That can be seen from an examination of the *Green Lane Products Ltd* case discussed at **22.2.1** above.

22.2.6   Duration of protection

The duration of protection is a maximum of 25 years (s 8). This is achieved by an initial registration of five years, renewable in five-year periods.

22.2.7   Ownership of registered designs (s 2)

The prima facie rule is that first ownership of the design rests in the 'author', ie the actual designer (s 2(1)). However, if the design is created in the course of someone's employment, the ownership of the design belongs to the employer (s 2(1B)). This in effect is the same as copyright (see **20.2.5**).

22.2.8   Exhaustion of rights

Registered design right cannot be used to hinder parallel importing (s 7A(4)), where the product has been put on the market within the EEA by the registered proprietor, or with his consent. So if you sell your product in France, you cannot use RDR to stop it being imported and sold in the UK.

22.2.9   Infringement of registered designs

Knowledge or intention is not required for infringement. The fact of registration gives notice to all, regardless of knowledge. Knowledge becomes relevant only in considering what remedies are available (see **22.2.10**).

The registration of a design gives the registered proprietor the exclusive right to use the design and 'any design which does not produce on the informed user a different overall impression' (s 7(1)). Care is needed, here, to distinguish between an overall design concept and the particular features of the design that are protected by registration. These are quite different things, as can be seen in *Rowlawn Ltd v Turfmech Machinery Ltd* [2008] EWHC 989 (Pat). The defendant had clearly followed much of the broad concept of the claimant's registered design, but that was not what was protected by the registration. In the finer detail of the machinery (a type of mowing machine) the defendant's design differed and had been developed without copying.

'Using' the design is defined in s 7(2), including a reference to '... the making, offering, putting on the market, importing, exporting or using of a product in which the design is incorporated or to which it is applied'.

'Infringement' is defined in s 7A as doing anything that is the exclusive right of the proprietor without its consent. Exceptions in s 7A(2) include:

(a)   an act which is done privately and for purposes which are not commercial;

(b)   an act which is done for experimental purposes;

(c)   an act of reproduction for teaching purposes ...;

(d)   ...

(e)   [these concern foreign ships and aircraft but which are temporarily in the UK]

(f)   ...

Reliance on the exceptions in s 7A(2) requires compliance with s 7A(3), so the exceptions only apply if:

(a)   the act of reproduction is compatible with fair trade practice and does not unduly prejudice the normal exploitation of the design, and

(b)   mention is made of the source.

There can be no infringement before the date of the certificate of registration (s 7A(6)).

The Intellectual Property Act 2014 added a further exception via a new s 7B. It contains a limited defence where a third party acts in good faith in the use of a design that was subsequently registered by another. This will allow third parties to continue to use the design after registration, although only in respect of the use they have already made of the design, and there is no right to sell the design to another.

22.2.10   Remedies

Damages may not be awarded against an infringer who had no knowledge that the design was registered (despite the existence of the public register) (s 24B). It is not enough to mark a design with the word 'registered' to overcome this; rather, the registration number of the design must also be marked on the product in question. Apart from this concession to a lack of awareness, the rest of the remedies are available without regard to knowledge of infringement. The position seems to be different where infringement of a Community design is concerned. In *J Choo (Jersey) Ltd v Towerstone Ltd* [2008] EWHC 346 (Ch), Floyd J held that s 24B, although effective in a claim under the RDA 1949, had no application to a claim based on a Community right.

Remedies can include:

(a)   an injunction;

(b)   damages;

(c)   an account of profits; and

(d)   an order for delivery up or destruction of the offending items.

The RDA 1949, s 26 provides for a remedy for groundless threats of infringement proceedings. This comprises a declaration, damages and an injunction. The reason for these types of provisions in the legislation governing IP rights is that the threat of infringement proceedings is a severe danger to a business.

There are also criminal offences of falsely representing a design as registered, both against individuals and against corporate bodies. Also, the Intellectual Property Act 2014 added a crime of deliberately copying a registered design (RDA 1949, s 35ZA), although there is a defence of reasonably believing one was not infringing.

22.2.11   EU-registered design right – the Community registered design

Regulation 6/2002 set up an EU-registered design system, which deals with CRD registration. The system has been registering CRDs since 2003 under the Regulation. It is run by the EU Trade Marks Office (OHIM) in Alicante.

Community registered designs are similar in many respects to RDR examined at **22.2** above. The broad tests of novelty and individual character are very much the same, and a maximum 25-year term of protection is available. The big difference is that a CRD is effective throughout the EU, and is recognised by all Member States. There is no search mechanism before registration and it is for third parties, Member States or the Commission itself to appeal against registration to the OHIM, with an ultimate appeal to the ECJ.

At the end of the Brexit transitional period (so from 1 January 2021), an existing holder of a CRD was automatically granted an equivalent UK RDR, to ensure that their rights were not weakened. So moving forwards, they will have a CRD covering mainland Europe, and a UK RDR. The duration of the automatically granted UK right matches the remaining period of their CRD. Applicants with new designs will need to apply for both of these if they require EU and UK protection.

22.2.12   The Locarno Classification system

The Locarno Classification system is used as a means of classification for industrial designs. Designs are divided up into classes based on what goods they will be applied to. The system is based on a multilateral treaty administered by the World Intellectual Property Organization (WIPO). This treaty is called the Locarno Agreement Establishing an International Classification for Industrial Designs, which came into being in 1968. The Agreement is open to those States who are party to the Paris Convention for the Protection of Industrial Property (see **18.5.1**).

The design registries of the contracting States of the Locarno Agreement are required to include in the official documents reflecting the deposit or registration of industrial designs the numbers of the classes and subclasses of the Classification into which the goods incorporating the designs belong. They must do the same in any publication which the registries issue in respect of the deposit or registration.

Use of the Locarno Classification by national registries has the advantage of filing industrial designs with reference to a single classification system. This procedure facilitates industrial design searches and obviates substantial reclassification work when documents are exchanged at the international level.

At present, 54 States are party to the Locarno Agreement. They have adopted and apply the Locarno Classification for Industrial Designs.

The Locarno Classification comprises a list of 32 classes and 223 subclasses, with explanatory notes and an alphabetical list of goods in which industrial designs are incorporated, and with an indication of the classes and subclasses into which they fall. This list contains some 6,831 indications of different kinds of goods.

22.2.13   The Hague System

A major advance in the international protection of industrial designs came in the form of the Hague System for the International Deposit of Industrial Designs. The Hague System allows the possibility of obtaining protection for industrial designs in several of the 66 Contracting Parties by means of a single international application filed with the International Bureau of the WIPO in Geneva, Switzerland. Thus, under the Hague System, one international application replaces a whole series of applications which would otherwise have to be effected with different national offices.

Unlike the Madrid Protocol on Trade Marks, the filing of an international application does not require any prior national application or registration. Protection for an industrial design can therefore be applied for at the international level through the Hague System for the first time.

Upon receipt of the international application, the International Bureau checks that it complies with the prescribed formal requirements. The International Bureau does not appraise or concern itself in any way with the novelty of the design and it is therefore not entitled to reject an international application on this or any other substantive ground. Then, publication of the design takes place in the International Designs Bulletin, a publication which appears on the website of the WIPO. This gives other designers the chance to object to the registration of the design.

Following this step, a substantive examination is carried out by the relevant design registry of each signatory country. At this stage the application takes the form of a bundle of national applications. If a country refuses to register the design, it does not affect the applications in other countries. So whilst it is a single initial application, once it is passed to signatory countries the applications do not depend on each other.

The UK joined the Hague system on 13 June 2018.

22.3   UNREGISTERED DESIGN RIGHT

This is referred to in the CDPA 1988 as 'design right'. 'Design' is defined in s 213(2) as 'the shape or configuration (whether internal or external) of the whole or part of an article'. The design must be 'original' (s 213(1)), which is further explained as being 'not commonplace in a qualifying country in the design field in question'.

No right subsists unless the design is recorded in a document, or an article has been made to the design (s 213(6)).

A further complication of the UDR regime is the necessity for the work to 'qualify' for protection within s 217. This depends upon the design having a qualifying connection to a qualifying country (see below) via specified qualifying persons (including designers and employers).

22.3.1   Originality

The requirement of originality for UDR has two aspects:

(a)   that it should be original, in the copyright sense of not itself being a copy; and

(b)   that it should not be 'commonplace in a qualifying country in the design field in question' (s 213(4)). A qualifying country is the UK, Hong Kong, New Zealand and UK dependent territories.

There have been some cases which have considered what it means to be 'commonplace'. The idea is that UDR protects a design against copying. For that concept to work, the design in question has to be distinguishable from all the other goods of that type in the marketplace. For example, see the following cases.

In *Farmers Build Ltd v Carrier Bulk Materials Handling Ltd* [1999] RPC 461, concerning a slurry separator, it was held that putting a number of different commonplace features together in a new way can result in a design that is not commonplace.

In *Jo-Y-Jo Ltd v Matalan Retail Ltd* [1999] EIPR 627, it was held that flowers embroidered on vests were commonplace.

In *Ocular Sciences Ltd and Another v Aspect Vision Care Ltd and Others; Galley v Ocular Sciences Ltd (No 2)* [1997] RPC 289, a design for contact lenses was held to be commonplace if trite, common-or-garden, or hackneyed. In that case, many features of the contact lenses were held to be commonplace, or subject to the 'must fit' exclusion (ie must fit the eye – see **22.3.2**).

In *Lambretta Clothing Company Ltd v Teddy Smith (UK) Ltd & Next Retail plc* [2004] EWCA Civ 886, the subject matter was a 'retro-vintage' track top. On the existence of UDR, it was held that:

(a)   the outline shape of the track top was not original as it had itself been copied from another garment;

(b)   the Lambretta logos were surface decoration and therefore excluded from UDR (see **22.3.2.4**);

(c)   mere juxtaposition of patches of colour on the garment did not fall within the meaning of 'configuration' in s 213(2), so did not attract UDR; and

(d)   two-dimensional colour applied to the garment did not generate an original three-dimensional design.

Overall, there was no UDR existing in the garment.

In *A Fulton Co Ltd v Grant Barnett & Co Ltd* [2001] RPC 16, there was held to be UDR in the handle of an umbrella, which had been designed by a director of the claimant company. The designs were held to be original and not to be commonplace. They were also held to have been infringed by the defendant.

In *Guild v Eskandar Ltd* [2001] FSR 38, UDR was held to exist in garments based on Iranian ethnic clothing, that is, there was sufficient originality in the designs in question (see **20.2.2.3**).

22.3.2   Exclusions

The CDPA 1988, ss 213(3), 244A and 244B set out the exclusions from UDR.

22.3.2.1   Methods or principles of construction (s 213(3)(a))

These are excluded on the basis that methods of construction are the subject of patent law rather than design law. 'Method of construction' has been defined as a process or operation by which a shape is produced, as opposed to the design of the shape itself. In *Landor & Hawa International Ltd v Azure Designs Ltd* [2006] EWCA Civ 1285, this principle was applied to 'piping' arrangements, which cloaked the expanding joint in luggage when unexpanded. It was held not to be part of a method of construction and copying it was an infringement.

In *Christopher Tasker's Design Right References; Re Patent Office* [2001] RPC 3, various aspects of sliding doors for wardrobes were held to be subject to UDR, and therefore to come within s 213(2). However, the hiding from view of aluminium runners by the use of wooden mouldings was a method of construction, and excluded from UDR by s 213(3).

22.3.2.2   Must fit (s 213(3)(b)(i))

This is similar to the interface exclusion for RDR (see **22.2.3.2**). Functional designs are not excluded from UDR; indeed, one of the main purposes of this right is to protect more functional designs. There is, however, an exclusion for those aspects of the design which 'must fit' with other articles in order that either article may perform its function. It is only the 'interface' that is excluded from protection, ie the bits that have to fit into, up to or around the other object. Again, attention will focus on whether the designer truly has any freedom of design open to him. If the shape had to be like that to fit something else, then no design flair has been used and protection should not be granted. The exclusion applies only to the interface connections between objects which are designed to be connected at some stage.

This exclusion would also apply to human spare parts (prostheses), or contact lenses (*Ocular Sciences Ltd and Another v Aspect Vision Care Ltd and Others; Galley v Ocular Sciences Ltd (No 2)* [1997] RPC 289). Another instance concerned a holder for a mobile phone, many features of which did not get UDR as its shape was dictated by the phone (*Parker v Tidball* [1997] FSR 680).

22.3.2.3   Must match (s 213(3)(b)(ii))

Unregistered design right cannot apply to design features of an article if the appearance of those features is dependent on that of a larger article of which it is intended to form an integral part. There could, for example, be no UDR in spare parts (for cars or prostheses for people, eg artificial limbs) where shapes are dependent on the larger object.

The scope of the exclusion was considered in *Dyson Ltd v Qualtex (UK) Ltd* [2004] EWHC 2981 (Ch). Here, Dyson was seeking to prevent the sale of spare parts made by Qualtex to fit and match Dyson vacuum cleaners. The Qualtex spares in question were intended to resemble closely the Dyson spares, not least as they were visible in the normal use of the vacuum cleaners. It was held that the 'must match' exclusion will not apply if the design of the spare part could be itself be changed without radically changing the overall appearance of the whole article, ie a vacuum cleaner in this case. In other words, it was not necessary for the Qualtex spares to be identical in appearance to the Dyson ones, so the must match exclusion did not save Qualtex from infringement of Dyson's unregistered design right.

In *Dyson Ltd v Qualtex (UK) Ltd* [2006] EWCA Civ 166, the Court of Appeal broadly upheld the judge's approach and confirmed that it was for the spare parts dealer or manufacturer to show that, as a practical matter, there was a real need to copy some feature of shape or configuration (because the appearance of the entire article was dependent upon the relevant design feature of the spare part). If there was no such dependence, the consequence would be that any UDR subsisting in that feature of the original design and article could properly be protected; it would not be excluded by 'must match' and the spare part would constitute an infringing article.

22.3.2.4 Surface decoration (s 213(3)(c))

Surface decoration is excluded from UDR. This is really part of the definition, as UDR protects only the shape of a product (see the *Lambretta* case at **22.3.1**). There can be some difficulty in distinguishing surface decoration from 3-dimensional features of an article.

An interesting case on this problem is *Helmet Integrated Systems Ltd v Mitchell Tunnard*, PCC 10/2/2006, LTL 15/12/2006, [2006] FSR 41. The dispute was about design features of a modular, state-of-the-art fire helmet and, in particular, scalloping features along the sides of the helmet. The evidence showed that scalloping had resulted in some advantages of strength, but the features had not been designed for anything other than appearance's sake. The feature was held to be surface decoration and fell within the exclusion.

22.3.2.5 Other exceptions

The Intellectual Property Act 2014 inserted a new s 244A which mirrors the registered designs exceptions of infringement for private acts, experiments and teaching. This brings UDR in line with not only RDR but the EU system for UDR, and also copyright.

New s 244B creates an exception relating to equipment for use on overseas ships and aircraft which are temporarily located in the UK.

22.3.3 Ownership of unregistered designs

If the design is created in the course of someone's employment, the ownership of the design belongs to the employer (s 215). This in effect is the same as copyright (see **20.2.5**).

In *Ultraframe (UK) Ltd v Clayton and Others; Ultraframe (UK) Ltd v Fielding and Others* [2002] EWHC 1964 (Ch), the claimant company was held to be the owner of unregistered designs created by the person who had been managing director and major shareholder. In *A Fulton Co Ltd v Grant Barnett & Co Ltd* [2001] RPC 16, the claimant company was also held to own an unregistered design created by a director, despite the lack of a service contract between company and director.

22.3.4 Duration of protection

Unregistered design right lasts for 15 years from the end of the calendar year in which the design was first created, or 10 years from being made available for sale or hire (s 216).

22.3.5 Infringement of unregistered designs

Unregistered design right follows copyright in that there is primary and secondary infringement. Secondary infringement requires knowledge.

The owner of UDR has the exclusive right to reproduce the design for commercial purposes by making articles to that design, or by reproducing his design document for the purpose of making articles to that design (s 226(1)). The latter is seen in *Societa Esplosivi Industriali Spa v Ordnance Technologies (UK) Ltd* [2007] EWHC 2875 (Ch). Here, the defendant had used the designs for multiple warhead systems, which it had obtained in a collaborative enterprise with the claimant, for purposes different from those originally contemplated by the parties. The end result would have been that weapons would have been made to those designs by third parties. That did not protect the defendant. It did not need to make the weapons itself, to infringe the UDR.

Primary infringement is, therefore, for commercial purposes, directly or indirectly making articles to the design, or making a design document for the purpose of enabling such articles to be made, without the UDR owner's permission, or authorising anyone else to do so (s 226(3)).

Secondary infringement includes importation, possessing for commercial purposes, selling and hiring, but is relevant only if the person had knowledge or reason to believe that the items were infringing items (s 227).

22.3.6 Remedies

Remedies are damages, injunctions, accounts of profits (s 229(1)), order for delivery up of infringing articles (s 230), and an order for disposal of infringing articles (s 231). Damages are not available against an innocent primary infringer (s 233), although other remedies are available. Innocence requires an absence of knowledge of the existence of the UDR and no reason to believe in its existence.

There is a provision providing remedies against groundless threats of infringement proceedings (s 253). The remedies are a declaration, injunction and damages.

By contrast with RDR, exclusive licensees have the same remedies available, concurrently with the owner of UDR.

22.3.7 Overlap with copyright

As we have seen in **Chapter 20**, a three-dimensional article cannot be protected by copyright unless it is itself an artistic object, typically either a sculpture or a 'work of artistic craftsmanship', or an engraving. The intention of the CDPA 1988 is to exclude from copyright protection any industrial or manufactured object that would itself not be protected by copyright. Thus, s 51 also excludes, from copyright protection, the use of any design *document* where an article has been made from that design. In other words, it is not possible to use copyright by the back door to protect the article in question by asserting the copyright in the design drawings (see **22.1.2**). It is simply not an infringement of any copyright that might exist in the design document (s 51(1)).

Instead, the creation of a three-dimensional article can only be protected by UDR, or by registered design right. It would, of course, have to meet the criteria for the design right in question. The overall effect is that copyright protection is suppressed in favour of UDR protection.

Section 236 provides that any UDR that subsists in the article will be ignored if the article is protected by copyright. This would be the case if the article were, say, a sculpture. So, in this situation, copyright prevails (if in fact copyright does apply to the article – see s 51). The combined effect of s 51 and s 236 is to prevent overlap between copyright and design right protection.

By contrast, any registered design right can co-exist with the copyright in a three-dimensional article.

An interesting case that shows the working of s 51 is *Flashing Badge Co Ltd v Groves* [2007] EWHC 1372 (Ch). Here, the defendant had imported flat, flashing badges which were virtually identical to badges made by the claimant. The claimant owned copyright in the surface decoration on the badges. When this was asserted in infringement proceedings, the defendant raised s 51 as a defence, saying that the drawings on the face of the badges were designs for the creation of an article, the badge, and therefore protected by s 51(1). Rimer J held that the designs were surface decoration caught by s 51(3), which removed the disputed material outside the reach of being a 'design document' for the purposes of s 51(1). It was a straightforward copyright infringement.

22.3.8   Licences of right

In the last five years of the term of an unregistered design, anyone can apply for a licence to use the unregistered design (s 237). If terms cannot be agreed between the parties, then the terms are settled by the Designs Registry, which is part of the UK Intellectual Property Office (IPO).

22.3.9   Community unregistered design right – the CUD

Regulation 6/2002 introduced a Community unregistered design (CUD) right. This right lasts for three years. However, it seems that the right is merely intended to protect registrable designs in the period before registration is applied for. In *Landor & Hawa International v Azure Designs* (see **22.3.2.1**), there was infringement of both design right and the CUD right.

In many respects, the CUD can be seen to be a short-term, interim form of protection with a dual purpose. It gives a short period of informal protection to many short-lived designs with commercial lives of not much more than three years. It also gives initial protection to many designs of longer commercial life, while consideration is given to obtaining more long-term protection by registration.

At the end of the Brexit transitional period (so from January 2021), an existing holder of a CUD was automatically granted an equivalent UK UDR, to ensure that their rights were not weakened. So moving forwards, they will have a CUD covering mainland Europe, and a UK UDR. The duration of the UK right matches the remaining period of their CUD. It should be noted that for new designs created after 1 January 2021, there is no reciprocal arrangement in place between the UK and the EU to allow new CUDs to cover the UK, or for designs disclosed within the UK to gain CUD protection.

22.4   SEMICONDUCTOR TOPOGRAPHY DESIGN RIGHT

It is no exaggeration to claim that the modern developed world is largely built around the computer. You will already realise that computer programs get literary copyright protection (see **20.2**). At the heart of computer operation is the integrated circuit or micro-chip, which is a tiny, complex pattern of hairsbreadth electrical circuits, formed by etching within a sandwich of insulating ('semiconducting') material. Under impetus from the USA, the EU turned its attention to the necessity to offer some protection to the designs of the circuits within these vital components, resulting in a European Council Directive on the matter in 1987.

The designs of the chips and their functioning manner had largely been patent-protected, but once that stage was achieved, the precise patterns of etched circuits would not be suitable for patent protection, as there is no inventive step involved in simply using chips to make the computers carry out different operations. Copyright protection is also largely removed by the effect of s 51 of the CDPA 1988. Design protection was the obvious solution, and the result is that a specialised application of informal protection by UDR is given to these circuits, by protecting the topography (the 'map') of the circuits.

The solution eventually arrived at is found in the Design Right (Semiconductor Topographies) Regulations 1989 (SI 1989/1100). The way protection is achieved is to use the framework of the UDR provisions in the CDPA 1988 and to make such amendments as are necessary for precise application to microchips. The basis for protection is, as with UDR, originality, not being commonplace and a qualifying situation for protection. The infringing and permitted acts are, however, rather different from those applicable to UDR and resemble, in many ways, the 'fair dealing' provisions that apply to copyright material. This is clearly in contemplation of the need for a general freedom to use the technology to its limits by encouraging analysis and further development. Ownership and duration are very similar to UDR.

22.5 REGISTERED AND UNREGISTERED DESIGNS

A summary of registered and unregistered designs is provided in the table below.

	RDR	UDR
Statute	RDA 1949 as amended by Registered Designs Regulations 2001	CDPA 1988
Definition	Appearance of whole or part of a product resulting from features of, in particular: (a) lines (b) contours (c) colours (d) shape (e) texture or materials (f) ornamentation 'Product' includes packaging, get up, graphic symbols, typographic type-faces and visible parts	The: (a) shape, or (b) configuration of the whole or part of an article NB no right subsists unless the design is recorded in a document or an article has been made to the design
Originality	**New:** no identical design/design differing in only immaterial details has previously been made available to public, *and* **Individual character:** overall impression to informed user differs from that of any other design that has been made available to public, and **The design has not been made available to public:** ie not published, exhibited or used in the trade NB 12 months grace period	Must be **original**, ie must be: (a) **the result of independent effort** ie not copied, and (b) **not commonplace** in design field in question (in the EU)

	RDR	UDR
Exclusions	(a) features solely dictated by technical function (b) interface (mechanical fittings only) (but modular designs are registrable)	(a) methods of construction (b) must fit (c) must match (d) surface decoration and see **22.3.2.5**
Ownership	The employer; the designer, in that order	The employer; the designer, in that order
Duration	25 years in total (maximum)	The shorter of: (a) 15 years from the end of the year of creation/recording; or (b) 10 years from the end of the year of first sale/hire
Infringement	Making, offering, putting on market, importing or exporting any product incorporating the design or any design which does not produce a different overall impression. No need to prove copying NB private non-commercial acts are excluded	Primary: making articles to the design/making document for purposes of making articles. Need to prove copying: substantial similarity is enough. Secondary: import, sell, hire, offer, possess with knowledge/reason to believe is an infringing article.

SUMMARY

Intellectual property rights tend to protect items produced by people who show flair. This is never more true than with respect to design rights. Whether it be a piece of artwork or a garden tool, those who have shown flair in creating items would want their efforts to be rewarded, and equally would want to be protected against others copying their designs. This chapter has dealt with the registered and unregistered rights enjoyed by designers, and has explored some of the changes made by the Intellectual Property Act 2014.

PATENTS

LEARNING OUTCOMES

After reading this chapter you will be able to:

- explain what a patent is
- apply the law of patents to decide whether articles are patentable
- identify the key aspects of a patent specification
- explain who is entitled to the grant of a patent
- apply patent law to decide whether an infringement has occurred
- apply defences, and explain what remedies are available for breach.

23.1 INTRODUCTION

Patents are monopoly rights granted by the Government to protect inventions under the Patents Act 1977 (PA 1977). If a patent is granted, the inventor gets a monopoly over use of his invention for (generally) 20 years (ie, he can stop anybody else using it for this time). The quid pro quo of getting a patent so far as the inventor is concerned is that before the patent is granted, details of the invention go on a public register at the Intellectual Property Office which everyone may study. So, a patented invention cannot be kept secret. The idea is that others should be able to learn from the patent. It contributes to the general body of technological understanding. After the 20 years are up, the invention is available for anyone to use, but the general thinking behind the new invention will have been available to the rest of the world for those 20 years, during which time the knowledge of how the invention works may have sparked ideas in the minds of other inventors.

The main justification for patents is that if there were no patents, commercial organisations would not invest in the research needed to produce new inventions or would keep the invention a secret. They need to have a chance to recoup their expenditure on the invention that is a success, as well as the time spent on abortive projects. The estimated cost of putting a new pharmaceutical product on the market is £200 million, and it takes about 12 years. A business will need to recover this cost from its product, hence patent protection is very important in the business world.

What is protected?	new invention
What benefit is there?	monopoly right
How is it obtained?	registration
How long does it last?	20 years from application

There is a great deal of international harmonisation on what it patentable. For this reason, this chapter begins with an overview of UK law and then covers general international issues.

23.2 OBTAINING A PATENT

The patent system is a 'first to file' system, not a 'first to invent'. In other words, the crucial step is the bureaucratic step of filing the application at the Intellectual Property Office. You may recall the tale of Elisha Gray, who filed his application for the telephone four hours later than Alexander Graham Bell. Bell therefore was awarded the patent by the US Supreme Court and became famous. Gray has been largely forgotten by history (but he in fact patented a telegraph system and founded the Western Electric Company, so do not feel too sorry for him).

A patent for the UK may be obtained:

(a)   by applying to the UK Intellectual Property Office;

(b)   by applying to the European Patent Office under the European Patent Convention ('EPC'); or

(c)   via an international application under the Patent Co-operation Treaty 1970 ('PCT').

The PCT would be used, for example, if the proprietor of a US or Japanese patent was also seeking to apply for a patent in the UK. It would then be assigned the priority date of the non-UK patent (see **23.4.1**), which is one big advantage of an application through either the PCT or EPC. There are more than 100 countries which are members of the PCT, including most major centres of technology.

The EPC does not provide a true European Patent (but see below for developments on this aspect). It awards a bundle of national patents for countries which are parties to the EPC. Not all EPC patent applications will specify all the countries of the EPC. It is a European system, not an EU one, and encompasses countries that are not EU Member States (eg, Switzerland), though all the EU Member States are individual members of the EPC.

The cost of a European patent (EPC) is high, being about £31,000, as opposed to perhaps £2,000 plus VAT for drafting and filing a UK patent. The headquarters of the European Patent Office (EPO) are in Munich and its search branch is in The Hague.

The PCT 1970 is administered by the WIPO in Geneva. It provides for a single application and preliminary search. The WIPO then sends the application on to national offices for them to decide whether to award a patent for their territory.

23.3 PATENTABILITY

An invention will be patentable if it satisfies four conditions. It must:

(a)   be *new* (PA 1977, s (1)(a));

(b)   constitute an *inventive step* (s 1(1)(b));

(c)   be capable of *industrial application* (s 1(1)(c)); and

(d)   not be within any of the *exclusions* in s 1(2).

23.3.1 New

Novelty is judged by reference to the 'state of the art' at the 'priority date' (see **23.4.1**). In essence, the question is: 'Is this new information, or can we find the information in an existing source?' Under Article 54(2) of the EPC:

The state of the art shall be held to compromise everything made available to the public by means of a written or oral description, by use, or in any way, before the date of filing of the European patent application.

The information sources utilised would be:

(a) other granted patents or published applications, both UK and relevant foreign jurisdictions;

(b) published descriptions of relevant technology, eg in scientific journals or PhD theses; and

(c) existing products or processes that are in the public domain.

As a matter of practicality, these are matters known about within, or are accessible from, the jurisdiction. Third parties can bring material to the attention of the Intellectual Property Office when the application is published (see below).

So this involves a factual investigation (ie, has the invention been thought of before and has it been made public?). The investigation will be carried out by the Intellectual Property Office in its initial examination of the patent application. Third parties can also object after publication of the application by the Intellectual Property Office. The whole topic of novelty is also highly relevant in patent infringement actions, when the usual defence of the alleged infringer is to challenge the validity of the patent. This means that the topic of the prior art is examined again, but this time in retrospect, perhaps 20 years or more after the original patent application (see **23.8**). A common-form defence to infringement claims is that the patent should never have been granted in the first place and is invalid.

A problem that has arisen more significantly, since the EPC and the European patent system, is the uneasy relationship between the test for novelty and the exclusion, within s 1(2)(a) of the PA 1977, of the patentability of 'discoveries' (see **23.3.4**). Perhaps the greatest gain arising from (particularly) medical or pharmaceutical patents is that surprising and unexpected results can arise from their actual use; great progress can be achieved this way. Sometimes it is achieved by discoveries that radically different dosages bring about different effects. Is such a new development patentable? Is it an excluded 'discovery'? The EPC and the national courts have really taken the bull by the horns on this, and it is clear that many such developments are patentable, despite the prior disclosure of the drugs, etc in earlier patents. In *Actavis Ltd v Merck & Co Inc* [2008] EWCA Civ 444, the Court of Appeal held that novelty could be conferred by new dosage regimes or other forms of administration of a substance (known as 'Swiss-type' claims). This was in line with Article 52(4) of the EPC, and such claims were not simply excluded as discoveries or methods of treatment. Although this was a European patent matter, it is probably in line with the established English court approach, that a claim directed to the practical application of the technical effect of a discovery may well be patentable, as distinct from trying to patent the discovery itself.

The question is one of whether the invention has been 'disclosed' to the public before the date of filing of the application (or the priority date). It will only be treated as having been previously disclosed if there has been an 'enabling disclosure'. If there has been an enabling disclosure, the applicant will fail. As the term suggests, an enabling disclosure means a disclosure that would enable somebody to make the product, or work the process, as the case may be. The question the Intellectual Property Office asks is whether, at the priority date, a skilled worker could by observation or analysis reproduce the applicant's invention from the disclosure in question. So, if a newspaper reports that Professor X has created a new process for cloning sheep, this would not be an enabling disclosure. For it to be an enabling disclosure the report would have to describe the process in a way that would allow others to reproduce the invention. (A detailed scientific paper would undoubtedly give such information.)

In what circumstances might an enabling disclosure arise? In the case of product patents, disclosure of the product will usually be an enabling disclosure, especially where the invention is a mechanical device. An obvious example is where there is already a product on the market which discloses the invention. For example, if the patent application is for a bagless vacuum cleaner and there is already a bagless vacuum cleaner on the market. This is clearly an enabling disclosure, because anyone taking the vacuum cleaner apart can see how the invention works. Similarly, if a vacuum cleaner embodying the invention had been exhibited at a trade fair then this would be an enabling disclosure (but some trade fairs are specifically excluded under PA 1977). The enabling disclosure could arise from a third-party product where the third party had thought of the idea first. Alternatively, it could be the applicant for the patent marketing/exhibiting his invention before the filing date. This is called 'self-publication'. So you can defeat your own application by showing the invention to the public prior to making your patent application.

In *Synthon BV v Smithklein Beecham plc* [2006] 1 All ER 685, HL, an interesting enabling disclosure was seen where the claimant had disclosed the nature of a chemical compound in an earlier initial patent application, which was not proceeded with. It was enough to have the defendant's later patent declared invalid.

In one case, the invention was a hay-raking machine in which the rake wheels were turned by contact with the ground rather than by an engine (*C Van der Lely NV v Bamfords Ltd* [1963] RPC 61). A photograph of the machine was printed in a newspaper. The question was whether the photograph was clear enough to show how the invention worked. If so, it was an enabling disclosure, and in this case it was held to be so.

In some cases the product may not disclose the invention. This would often be the case in relation to process patents. The end product of the patented process will not necessarily reveal the process itself. A consequence is that it may be possible to disclose the existence of a new product without showing how the process works. An example is *Quantel Ltd v Spaceward Microsystems Ltd* [1990] RPC 83, where the demonstration at an exhibition of a complex computer for creating visual effects on television would not have enabled someone to work out how it operated. Falconer J said in relation to this aspect:

> Demonstration of a prototype of the claimed invention at an exhibition where no-one was allowed near the actual machine and no engineering description was given, although individuals were allowed to use the stylus to draw a picture, could not possibly have been an enabling disclosure so as to anticipate any claim.

23.3.2 Inventive step

An invention might be new but it also needs to be a quantum leap over the existing technology. This second criterion for patentability is that the invention should involve an 'inventive step' (ie, it shows thinking which has not been seen before). The question asked here is whether the invention would be obvious to a somewhat unimaginative person skilled in the art, taking into account the state of the art at the priority date (see the *Vericore* case at **23.3.1**). The person skilled in the art here refers to the 'uninventive technician'. This is someone who is knowledgeable, but lacking that inventive spark. In the *Rockwater* case (see **23.6.3**), Jacobs LJ described the uninventive skilled man thus: 'It is settled that this man, if real, would be very boring – a nerd.'

In using the 'uninventive technician', the following limitation was referred to by Aldous LJ in *Amersham Pharmacia Biotech AB v Amicon Ltd and Others* [2001] EWCA Civ 1042:

> A fiction in patent law is that the notional uninventive skilled man in the art is deemed to have read and assimilated any piece of prior art pleaded by the party attacking the patent claim ...

> The more distant a prior art document is from the field of technology covered by the patent, the greater the chance that an intelligent but uninventive person skilled in the art will fail to make the jump to the solution found by the patentee.

In other words, the prior art being used in an attempt to strike out a patent has to be highly relevant to the patent in question, rather than just anything, anywhere that just happens to cover the same matter but in a different application or use.

A widely-cited test is in *Windsurfing International Inc v Tabur Marine* [1985] RPC 59. Here, Oliver LJ described the test as having four stages:

(a)   the court must identify the inventive concept embodied in the patent;

(b)   it must assume the mantle of the normally skilled but unimaginative addressee in the art at the priority date and impute to him what was, at that date, common general knowledge in the art in question;

(c)   it must identify what, if any, differences exist between the matters cited as being 'known or used' and the alleged invention; and

(d)   it must ask itself whether, viewed without any knowledge of the alleged invention, those differences constituted steps which would have been obvious to the skilled man, or whether they required any degree of invention.

Put simply, what you have to do is, first, identify what the invention adds to the state of the art. If this new bit is not obvious to the uninventive technician then you have an inventive step.

Some useful guidance on this area is to be seen in *Generics (UK) Ltd v Lundbeck A/S* [2008] EWCA Civ 311, where a patentee brought infringement proceedings and the respondent generic drug manufacturer had raised defences of lack of novelty and inventive step. The Court of Appeal held that in ordinary product patents (as distinct from process patents), where the application satisfied the requirements of s 1, the product itself was the invention and the technical contribution to the world art is the product itself, rather than the process by which it was made. This was so, even if that process provided the only inventive step. In other words, the inventive step taken was in being able to make, for the first time, that new product. It did not matter if that manufacturing process had been used to make a thousand different earlier products; the first-instance judge had taken his eyes off the real invention, which was the new drug itself. The patentee's appeal succeeded.

The classic case was the 'sausage machine case' (*Williams v Nye* (1890) 7 RPC 62, CA). A patent was struck out for lack of inventive step because it was simply the combination of two known machines, a mincing machine and a sausage-filling machine. There were also arguments along these lines in the case of *Hickman v Andrews and Others* [1983] RPC 174, concerning infringement of the patent for the Black and Decker 'Workmate', invented by Ron Hickman. Clamping arrangements of this type were known before Ron Hickman invented the Workmate. However, the Court of Appeal upheld the patent.

In *IDA Ltd v Southampton University* [2006] EWCA Civ 145, the question of inventive step also decided the identity of the 'sole deviser' (and ownership) of a type of insect trap. Two fairly similar designs were only distinguishable because one inventor had used a new and different material. That was the inventive step.

Commercial success of the product is taken as being a good indicator of the patent having an inventive step. So is fulfilling a 'long felt want', that is, plugging a gap in the market. In other words, if it was such an obvious step from the existing technology, why had no one done it before the patentee had come up with his invention?

In *Biogen v Medeva* [1997] RPC 1, the House of Lords held:

> Anything inventive done for the first time was the result of adding a new idea to the existing stock of knowledge. If it was the idea of using established techniques to do something which no one had previously thought of doing, the inventive idea would be doing the new thing.

The question of inventive step is, of course, a question of fact in each case, and if there is no inventive step, the application will fail for 'obviousness' (see *Pozzoli SpA v BDMO SA* [2007] EWCA Civ 588 – an application for a storage device for CDs which failed for obviousness).

23.3.3   Industrial application

It must be possible to make the product/carry out the process. Patents are not about abstract ideas. The invention must be able to be put into practice. In effect, this requirement is taken care of by the exclusions in the PA 1977, s 1(2) and (3) (see **23.3.4**). There is a temptation to avoid disclosing too much detail about the invention, which may cause objections based upon insufficiency, as in *Rex v Arkwright* (1785) 1 WPC 64. There may also be objections that the device cannot be built or made to work at all. In *Duckett v Patent Office* [2005] EWHC 3140 (Pat), a perpetual motion device was rejected because its energy principle was contrary to all accepted views of physics. Its mechanical arrangement, linking a generator with a battery, failed for obviousness.

The desire to avoid too much information being disclosed at the early stage of a patent application often can cause problems of revocation applications, both on insufficiency (s 72(1)(c)), and on grounds of 'added material', (s 72(1)(d)). The latter happens where the matter disclosed in the specification extends beyond that disclosed in the filed application for the patent, ie 'drip-feeding' the information to the registry.

23.3.4   Exclusions

The exclusions are listed in s 1(2) and (3) of the 1977 Act:

> (2)   It is hereby declared that the following (among other things) are not inventions for the purposes of this Act, that is to say, anything which consists of—
>
> (a)   a discovery, scientific theory or mathematical method;
>
> (b)   a literary, dramatic, musical or artistic work or any other aesthetic creation whatsoever;
>
> (c)   a scheme, rule or method for performing a mental act, playing a game or doing business, or a program for a computer;
>
> (d)   the presentation of information;
>
> but the foregoing provision shall prevent anything from being treated as an invention for the purposes of this Act only to the extent that a patent or application for a patent relates to that thing as such.
>
> (3)   A patent shall not be granted for an invention the commercial exploitation of which would be contrary to public policy or morality.

Section 1(2)(a) deals with discoveries of natural phenomena. These have not been invented by any human, so are not patentable. The paragraph also excludes methods of doing things. In *Citibank NA v Comptroller-General of Patents* (ChD, 9 June 2006), a computerised method for checking, statistically, the accuracy of data inputted into systems was not excluded as a 'business method' within s 1(2)(c). It was, however, excluded as a 'mathematical method' by s 1(2)(a). The rationale for excluding methodology is to prevent attempts at monopolising the thinking process itself.

In the US, judicial interpretation of patent law excludes the patenting of the discovery of a natural phenomenon.

Section 1(2)(b) deals with aesthetic creations which are protected by another IP right, that is copyright (see **Chapter 20**).

Section 1(2)(c) deals with mental acts, as explained above. How would you know if someone else was performing the mental act in question? Obviously, you could not, so making such matters patentable would be impractical as well as undesirable.

The borderline between a non-patentable method and a patentable technical contribution to the known art is hard to discern. In *Aerotel Ltd v Telco Holdings Ltd; Macrossan's Patent Application*

(*No* 0314464.9) [2006] EWCA Civ 1371, in a conjoined appeal, the Court held that an automated method of assembling documents required to incorporate a company was excluded methodology. By contrast, the other appeal was successful because it involved a new physical combination of hardware items. That comprised a technical contribution and was patentable. It brought about the effect of making a computer run at a higher speed.

Computer programs are also in theory excluded (s 1(2)(c). However, this does not actually mean that computer programs can never be patented. The tendency in recent years has been to grant patents to more and more computer programs. Very broadly, the test is whether the program has a 'technical effect', that is, has it a practical application? One example is *Vicom's Application* [1987] OJ EPO 14, where a program for doing computer-aided design (CAD) of engineering products was held to be patentable. This case has greatly influenced the approach to computer program patents in both European and UK applications. This is a very complex area, but it might be summarised by saying that, for a computer program to form part of a patent, it must bring about some effect or consequence that, itself, as distinct from the computer program, is new and shows an inventive step. This was applied to exclude *Macrossan's Patent Application*, referred to above.

The approach of the EPO has been more inclined toward granting computer patents since its decisions in two cases – *IBM/Computer Programs* (Case T-935/97) [1999] EPOR 301 and *IBM/Computer Programs* (Case T-1173/97) [1999] EPOR 219. The EPO technical board of appeal held that the 'technical effect' requirement simply meant that to be patentable, the application had to go beyond the mere routine operation of a computer.

As matters presently stand, the UK Intellectual Property Office considers that the correct and definitive approach has been expressed by the Court of Appeal in the *Aerotel Ltd/Macrossan* appeals case discussed above, because the Court considered and evaluated all relevant UK and EPO authorities. The Court took the view that the EPO practice to exclusions had not stabilised sufficiently to be a firm guide in itself. Jacob LJ, after considering the decisions of the EPO boards of appeal, had suggested a four-step approach to dealing with the exclusions within s 1(2). The steps are:

(a)   properly construe the claim;

(b)   identify the actual contribution to the known art;

(c)   ask whether it falls solely within the excluded subject matter (if it does, that would exclude the application);

(d)   check whether the actual or alleged contribution is actually technical in nature (if it is not, that would exclude it).

The Intellectual Property Office considers this to replace all previous tests applied to exclusion issues under s 1(2); it has been used in many applications since and seems to work well.

Section 1(2)(d) deals with presentation of information. This could not constitute an 'invention' in itself, but a new mechanism or process of presentation could be patented. However, in the US there is no such exclusion.

Genetic engineering inventions are patentable, and indeed are a major area of activity for patent agents and lawyers (see **23.3.2**). Also, producing new varieties of plants is protectable under the Plant Varieties Act 1997, which is outside the scope of this book. In the US case on gene engineering (*Diamond v Chakrabarty* 65 Law Ed (2d) 144 (1980)), the Supreme Court held that 'anything under the sun', apart from a human being, should be regarded as patentable. Directive 98/44/EC on legal protection of biotechnological inventions led to changes to the PA 1977, by way of the Patent Regulations 2000 (SI 2000/2037), to take account of technical progress in this field.

23.4 THE PATENT SPECIFICATION

The documents required for filing an application are a request for grant and the patent specification. A request for grant is what it says it is: a document asking for a patent to be granted. The specification contains three sections: an abstract, the description and the claims.

The abstract is a summary which is used for reference purposes (essentially this allows the Intellectual Property Office to decide who has the specialism to deal with the application). The description must disclose the invention sufficiently for it to be performed by a skilled person. Obviously, this may be a very lengthy section where the invention is complex.

The claims indicate the extent of the patent applied for. It is this section which will be used in the event of the patent (assuming it is granted) being enforced in court: the patent owner has protection only over the matters listed in the claims.

The description and the claims must be a consistent match for each other. A case needs to be shown for the grant of a patent, in particular that there has been an inventive step above and beyond the existing technology.

A patent specification is a complex technical and legal document. A patent agent normally drafts it. This is someone with a scientific or engineering qualification, depending on the particular field they are working in. The costs of drafting a specification and dealing with the initial filing of the application are about £2,000 plus VAT. If there are queries from the patent examiner in the Intellectual Property Office then this will increase that cost.

If the patent is granted then it is the claims that define the scope of the monopoly granted to the inventor. The analogy of a fence is sometimes used. The idea is that the claims form a fence that surrounds the area which the inventor claims as his own. For someone to be liable for patent infringement, it is enough to infringe one claim in the patent specification (ie, to have crossed the fence in only one place).

In drafting the claims, the aim is to include all possible alternatives, whilst excluding those that already exist or are obvious. If an alternative is omitted, a competitor could claim that to be their own invention, or could use the gap to exploit the technology themselves. On the other hand, if too much is said in the claims, one danger is that improvements in the technology may not be patentable when they arise in the future. The reason is that a patent specification itself becomes part of the state of the art once it is published, so a new application would have to show that it has achieved an inventive step over the previous patent.

The first claim will be the widest. It will state the invention claimed in fairly general terms. Subsequent claims refine the first claim. Each claim usually narrows the invention down a bit. The final claims usually describe the commercial product that is going to be on the market.

The idea is that the wider the area of technology which is claimed, the further away the patent owner can keep rival inventors. In patent litigation, an inevitable area of dispute is that some of the patent claims are too wide and need to be narrowed, or struck out, as being unjustifiable.

The invention must be described in enough detail to allow a person with the requisite skills to carry out the invention. So, if the patent is for interleaving chocolate and ice-cream, the specification must describe the process in sufficient detail to allow a skilled ice cream maker to set up the process. See the cases on 'sufficiency' at **23.3.3** and also *Schering-Plough Ltd v Norbrook Laboratories Ltd* [2005] EWHC 2532 (Pat), where a patent was revoked because much more research was needed to make the invention work. A patent specification which is refused on this ground is said to lack 'sufficiency'. In *European Central Bank v Document Security Systems Inc* [2008] EWCA Civ 192, a European patent for producing security documents, such as shares or banknotes, that were copy-proof, was held to be invalid. It was only possible to work the invention by adding material not disclosed by the original application.

You should be aware of the difference between this and manufacturing 'know-how'. Manufacturing know-how is the extra tricks of the trade that help you make the process run with greatest efficiency. For example, it might be the speed of the production line to get the most cost-effective results, how much air to blow into the ice-cream, or the temperature at which the room should be maintained. So, even though the patent specification describes the basic invention, the know-how is often also needed for a licensee because it makes it economically feasible to set up and run the process.

23.4.1 The priority date

The 'first to file' basis of the patent system increases the pressure to be the first person to reach the Intellectual Property Office with an application.

Normally, the application or 'filing' date is the patent's priority date. The priority date is the date on which we judge whether the invention is new. The usual reason for the priority date being earlier than the date the papers were filed is that the proprietor is claiming priority from an earlier overseas patent under one of the international conventions (see **23.2**). (An alternative reason, which is much less common, is that the PA 1977, s 15 allows the inventor to file an 'outline application' at an early stage in order to secure an early priority date. The outline application will be less detailed than a full application. A full application must be filed within 12 months.)

23.4.2 Timescale

The Intellectual Property Office takes about 18 months to do the initial examination. It is then published as an application and is on the public register (ie, the invention can no longer be kept secret). Third parties then have the opportunity to object to the grant of the patent. If there are no major problems then the patent will be granted six months or so after publication, that is two years after filing the papers. This period counts as part of the 20-year period for the life of the patent. If there is a major problem that delays grant of the patent, the useful life of the patent once granted could be severely reduced. However, the maximum period between publication and grant of the patent is now 36 months. In addition, there can be other regulatory problems which reduce the useful life of the patent, such as obtaining permission to market a new pharmaceutical product, or plant protection product. There are EU provisions which allow for an extension of up to five years to the life of a pharmaceutical patent (Regulation 1768/92), or to the life of a patent for a plant protection product (Regulation 1610/96). These are intended to compensate for the regulatory delays.

23.5 WHO IS ENTITLED TO GRANT OF A PATENT?

The general rule is that the inventor is the first person entitled (s 7(2)). The inventor is the person who devised the invention. This can be more complicated than it seems, for example if there are multiple parties involved (eg, *Henry Bros (Magherafelt) Ltd v Ministry of Defence* [1999] RPC 442, where the Court of Appeal held that the test was to determine who had contributed to the main concept of the invention). This was applied in *IDA Ltd v Southampton University* [2006] EWCA Civ 145 (see **23.3.2**).

23.5.1 Employees

Under the PA 1977, s 39(1), if the inventor is an employee, the patent will belong to the employer if the invention is made in the course of the employee's normal duties, provided an invention might reasonably be expected to result from the employee's duties. This is also the outcome if the employee owes the employer a special duty (eg, a director's duty to their company). In *Greater Glasgow Health Board's Application* [1996] RPC 207, it was held that a hospital doctor who had invented a new device for examining eyes owned the invention himself. He was employed to treat patients, not to invent, so the invention did not belong to his employer.

The rule is slightly different from the rule for ownership of copyright (see **20.2.5**) but the result is similar. Copyright also does not have any equivalent of the provision relating to employees with a special duty (PA 1977, s 39(1)(b)).

Another important difference is that PA 1977, s 42 does not allow contracting out of these provisions. With copyright there is nothing to stop the employer from putting a provision in the contract of employment that all copyright relevant to the employer's business will belong to the employer. With patents, any such provision would be void. However, there is nothing to stop the employer drafting the job description to emphasise that the employee is employed to make inventions. Also, the employer is still entitled to enforce contractual or common law confidentiality requirements (s 42(3)).

23.5.2   Compensation for employee inventors

Under the PA 1977, s 40, an employee who invents something may be entitled to compensation where the patent belongs to the employer. This is the case if:

(a)   having regard among other things to the size and nature of the employer's undertaking, the invention or the patent for it (or the combination of both) is of outstanding benefit to the employer; and

(b)   it is just that compensation is awarded.

The statutory test is awkward to apply in practice because the criterion is the benefit of the patent or the invention, not the benefit the product which was sold in the marketplace. In the US case of *Garrison's Patent*, an invention which provided 2%–3% of the turnover of a small company was held not to be of outstanding benefit, and therefore no compensation was awarded.

In determining the amount of compensation, s 41 gives guidance, including factors listed in s 41(3) (eg, the nature of the employee's duties and the amount of his remuneration).

Disputes of this type are often settled, and recorded cases are rare.

Under US law, however, there is no such obligation unless expressly set forth in an employment agreement between the employer and the employee.

23.6   INFRINGEMENT

23.6.1   Definition of infringment

Infringement arises where a third party engages in the acts prohibited under the PA 1977, s 60. As patents are national rights, to infringe a UK patent the prohibited acts have to occur within the UK:

> **60   Meaning of infringement**
>
> (1)   Subject to the provisions of this section, a person infringes a patent for an invention if, but only if, while the patent is in force, he does any of the following things in the United Kingdom in relation to the invention without the consent of the proprietor of the patent, that is to say—
>
> > (a)   where the invention is a product, he makes, disposes of, offers to dispose of, uses or imports the product or keeps it whether for disposal or otherwise;
> >
> > (b)   where the invention is a process, he uses the process or he offers it for use in the United Kingdom when he knows, or it is obvious to a reasonable person in the circumstances, that its use there without the consent of the proprietor would be an infringement of the patent;
> >
> > (c)   where the invention is a process, he disposes of, offers to dispose of, uses or imports any product obtained directly by means of that process or keeps any such product whether for disposal or otherwise.

You should note the distinction between infringing acts for a product patent and for a process patent; s 60(1)(b) requires actual or imputed knowledge of infringement, whereas s 60(1)(a) and (c) do not. However, even with a process patent, dealing with the products of that process will be infringement even though the products themselves are not patented.

Section 60(2) makes it an offence to supply or offer to supply 'any means ... for putting the invention into effect'. So, in *Lacroix Duarib SA v Kwikform (UK) Ltd* [1998] FSR 493, the supply of a kit of parts would have infringed the claims in a patent for the completed article.

23.6.2 How do you judge if infringement has occurred?

The first thing to establish is whether the allegedly infringing product or process comes within one of the claims in the patent specification. That is, has the third party crossed the 'fence line' which is constituted by the claims and stepped on to the patentee's monopoly? It is enough for patent infringement if one of the patent claims is infringed.

Sometimes a supposed infringement is not what it seems to be. In *Novartis AG v Ivax Pharmaceuticals UK Ltd* [2007] EWCA Civ 971, the patentee had a patent for making a 'microemulsion' of a drug which was very resistant to solution in water. The defendant was not an infringer when it managed to achieve the same effect by dispersing tiny particles of the drug in a liquid which was not a microemulsion (ie there was no 'oil in water' carrier).

The first claim is often the most important as it will be the broadest. So a patent for a Dyson vacuum cleaner might have as its first claim that it sucks up dust and other particles using a cyclone of air. Later claims would then be more specific about how it achieves this. So why bother with the other claims that narrow this first claim down? The reason is that when you sue somebody for patent infringement, they will invariably counterclaim by saying that the patent is invalid. The patentee then has to defend his claims, particularly in relation to novelty and inventive step (see **23.3**). (The 'infringer' will go digging round in the prior art to try to find reasons why the patent should never have been granted in the first place.) The broader the claim, the more difficult it is to defend. So that is why you have the narrower claims too. If claim 1 falls by the wayside, you may still be able to defend one of the later claims. It is only necessary to show infringement of one claim to succeed against the infringer.

23.6.3 Interpreting the claims in the patent specification

How does the court approach the interpretation of the claims? The court takes a 'middle road' between interpreting the claims strictly, ie literally, and taking into account what the patentee must have intended. Although the courts are said to be taking the 'purposive' approach from *Catnic Components Ltd and Another v Hill & Smith Ltd* [1982] RPC 183, they tend to be a lot less generous to patentees than this might suggest. In effect, the courts tend to hold the view that if the patentee meant to cover a particular variation then he should have claimed it expressly. (It should be remembered that *Catnic* was decided under the PA 1949. It concerned a patent for steel lintels for use above doors and windows. The patent claimed a right angle in the cross-sectional shape of the lintel. The defendant's lintel was 4–5 degrees away from a right angle, but was still held to infringe.)

Improver Corporation and Others v Remington Consumer Products Ltd and Others [1990] FSR 181 was a case which reformulated the test. This was the case about the 'Epilady' device for removing hair. Here, the patented device featured a rotating spring mechanism. The defendant's device performed the same task, but a rubber tube mechanism with slits removed the hairs.

Hoffmann J restated the issues as two of fact and one of construction:

(a) Does the variant have a material effect upon the way the invention works? If so, the variant is outside the claim. If not ...

(b) Would this (ie, that the variant had no material effect) have been obvious at the date of publication of the patent to a reader skilled in the art? If not, the variant is outside the claim. If so ...

(c)   Would the reader skilled in the art nevertheless have understood from the language of the claim that the patentee intended that strict compliance with the primary meaning was an essential requirement of the invention? If so, the variant is outside the claim.

There was held to be no infringement. It is regarded as an example of poor drafting by the patent agent, who apparently did not draft the first claim widely enough to catch the rubber tube variation but restricted it to a helical spring. This is a good illustration of how patent infringement litigation hinges on the precise wording of the claims in the patent specification (see also *Vericore* at **23.3.1**).

In *Kirin-Amgen Inc v Hoechst Marion Roussel Ltd* [2004] UKHL 46, a case concerning genetic engineering, Lord Hoffmann said that it was important to distinguish between two matters. On the one hand, there were the guidelines set out in *Improver Corp* for deciding whether or not equivalent technology fell within the scope of the relevant patent claims. On the other hand, there was the principle of purposive construction established by *Catnic*. *Catnic* was expressed to be the bedrock of patent construction. It was important that the patentee be given the full extent, but no more than that, of the monopoly which the person skilled in the art would think he was intending to claim in the patent specification.

This question, of the precise range of monopoly claimed by the patentee, came up in the *Novartis AG* case mentioned in **23.6.2**. In *M-Systems Flash Disk Pioneers Ltd v Trek 2000 International Ltd* [2008] EWHC 102 (Pat), Kitchin J confirmed that the correct approach to interpretation of a patent specification is that it is to be read, as a whole, through the eyes of a skilled person, giving the words a purposive construction. See this case at **23.6.4** on revocation.

Further guidance came from the Supreme Court in *Actavis v Eli Lilly* [2017] UKSC 48. Lilly is the proprietor of a patent that claims the use of pemetrexed disodium in the manufacture of a cancer drug. Actavis sought declarations for non-infringements of its proposed products. The High Court decided that none of Actavis's products directly infringed the claims, and the Court of Appeal decided that there was an indirect infringement, a point which was appealed to the Supreme Court.

The Supreme Court reviewed *Catnic*, *Improver* and *Kirin-Amgen* and concluded that the issue of infringement should in future be best dealt with by asking three questions:

•   Notwithstanding that it is not within the literal meaning of the relevant claim(s) of the patent, does the variant achieve substantially the same result in substantially the same way as the invention, ie the inventive concept revealed by the patent?

•   Would it be obvious to the person skilled in the art, reading the patent at the priority date, but knowing that the variant achieves substantially the same result as the invention, that it does so in substantially the same way as the invention?

•   Would such a reader of the patent have concluded that the patentee nonetheless intended that strict compliance with the literal meaning of the relevant claim(s) of the patent was an essential requirement of the invention?

Although similar to the *Improver* questions, the first question has been revised to focus on the problem underlying the invention, and the second question has been revised to remove the requirement that the person skilled in the art has to figure out whether the variant would work.

23.6.4   Amendments to the specification, invalidity and revocation

There is a very close connection between a patentee claiming infringement and the possibility of counterclaims that the patent is invalid for some reason and should be revoked. If the patent is invalid, it should not have been granted, and consequently there cannot have been an infringement. It does not follow that revocation proceedings cannot take place without infringement claims, but the two claims often go together; also, the Comptroller of Patents may revoke a patent on their own initiative, under s 73.

The only grounds for revocation are found s 72(1) and are:

(a)   the invention is not a patentable invention (failure to comply with ss 1–4);

(b)   the patent was granted to a person who was not entitled to that patent (failure to comply with s 7);

(c)   the specification of the patent did not disclose the invention clearly enough and completely enough for it to be performed by a person skilled in the art (insufficiency);

(d)   the matter disclosed in the specification extends beyond that disclosed in the patent application as filed ('added matter', forbidden by s 76);

(e)   the protection conferred by the patent has been extended by an amendment which should not have been allowed (also forbidden by s 76).

These are the only grounds on which the validity of a patent may be 'put in issue' (s 74(3)), and the only proceedings in which validity can be raised are limited by s 74(1). It is not possible, for example, simply to seek only a declaration as to the validity or invalidity of a patent (s 74(2)). Validity can be put in issue in infringement cases (by way of defence), in proceedings for groundless threats of infringement or declarations of non-infringement, in revocation proceedings or in disputes as to Crown use under s 58. This greatly reduces the possibilities for unjustified claims or proceedings.

In infringement or revocation proceedings where validity is in issue, there is a limited power, under s 75, to allow the proprietor of the patent to amend the specification to try to bring the patent to a state of validity. In no circumstances can an amendment be permitted that results in the specification disclosing added matter, or which extends the protection conferred by the patent (s 76(3)). Many recent cases have involved disputes about material added on amendments (usually to try to overcome 'inventive step' or 'sufficiency' problems).

23.7   INFRINGERS

The acts listed in s 60 (see **23.6.1**) would cover those making a product, using a process or disposing of the product of a process. Section 60 covers disposing and keeping, so would cover all the parties in a supply chain, even including the ultimate customer. Do not forget that the acts have to take place in the UK for there to be infringement of a UK patent. In the case of *Stena Rederi Aktiebolag and Another v Irish Ferries Ltd* [2002] EWHC 737 (Ch), [2002] RPC 990; [2003] EWCA Civ 66, [2003] RPC 36, the infringing article, a high-speed passenger ship, came into UK waters for periods of only three hours at a time. The defendants were able to use the provisions in the PA 1977, s 60(5)(d), which give exemptions for temporary entry into the UK of ships and aircraft.

If protection outside of the UK is required, applications in other countries should be made for foreign patents (there are of course the options of applying for a European Patent or patents under the PCT).

23.8   DEFENCES

The first possible defence is that the patentee has consented to the use by granting a licence.

The chief line of defence is an attack on the validity of the patent, in part or in total, as described at **23.6.4**. If the patent can be proved to be invalid, or at least some claims can be struck out, then the defendant could not be liable for having infringed an invalid claim.

Patent litigation can, however, become extremely complex and costly, and a very good example of this can be seen in *Edwards Lifesciences AG v Cook Biotech Incorporated* [2009] EWHC 1304 (Pat), and the subsequent costs hearing at [2009] EWHC 1443. This case illustrates how revocation proceedings and infringement claims interact, often at great expense to the parties, and also shows how easy it is for litigation to get somewhat out of control. Edwards ('E') initially sought revocation of a patent registered to Cook ('C'). C counterclaimed that E had infringed its patent by manufacturing a bio-prosthetic, implantable heart valve (C did not manufacture such things). A preliminary issue was ordered to be tried as to whether a product description, which accompanied the sold valves, could properly be described as confidential. The reason for this was that E was being asked to disclose this material for the purposes of the litigation to independent experts acting for C. The court gave its directions on this matter at [2008] All ER (D) 368 (Jul), broadly protecting the material. During the trial of the claim and counterclaim, C originally maintained that all 34 of its claims made in respect of the invention had independent validity; on being required to serve the details of these by the court, the number was reduced to 25. Eventually, just nine claims were considered by the court. The consequence of this was to greatly increase the costs incurred by E.

During the trial, C persisted in seeking disclosure of many documents, which the court subsequently held were irrelevant to the issues, further increasing the legal costs incurred by E. Subsequently, it was held that much of this disclosure was neither necessary nor proportionate. E won on its main points, that C's patent was not valid and that therefore E could not have infringed it, so C's counterclaim failed. Nevertheless, E was held to have failed on a number of the points that it had made, or had withdrawn them. The judge in the costs hearing ordered a reduction of 20% in the costs awarded to E, to reflect those points argued unsuccessfully by E.

A major use for trainees in an IP department is to have them spend weeks in the bowels of the libraries looking for documents on the topic in question which have been date stamped with a date earlier than the priority date. The patentee is fixed with such knowledge in any language, provided the document is within the jurisdiction. The documents may help to strike out some or all of the claims of the patent.

Another defence is that the alleged infringer is in fact a co-owner of the patent, and therefore is entitled to work the patent himself (PA 1977, s 36).

The use in question could be the subject of an implied licence under the patent. Likewise, repair of a patented product is not infringement of the patent. However, reconditioning the patented article may be regarded as going too far and be an infringing act.

Defences may be raised, relying on EU rules for free movement of goods. Goods sold on other markets by the patentee or its licensees may be parallel imported into the UK from other EU Member States, under Articles 34 and 36 of the Treaty on the Functioning of the European Union. The cases that arise usually concern pharmaceuticals, which are high-value items and often have their price regulated by national governments (eg, *Centrafarm BV and Adrian de Peijper v Sterling Drug Inc* (Case 15/74) [1974] ECR 1147). The exercise of patent rights was held to be incompatible with the free movement of goods in that case. (Centrafarm bought a Sterling product in the UK and re-sold it in The Netherlands for twice the UK price.) In such circumstances, the patentee's rights are said to be exhausted. See generally **29.6.4**.

The PA 1977 provides for two general defences in s 60(5):

> An act which, apart from this subsection, would constitute an infringement of a patent for an invention shall not do so if—
>
> (a)   it is done privately and for purposes which are not commercial;
>
> (b)   it is done for experimental purposes relating to the subject matter of the invention.

The activities in s 60(5) are regarded as being for the public good, and therefore the patent system should not be a restraint. The type of activities covered include research by scientists in universities and research institutes.

Section 64 allows a defence of prior use where the defendant was using the relevant technology before the priority date. In practice, this is a very limited defence, as you cannot expand your use, only go on using the process or product exactly as you did before the priority date.

The Intellectual Property Act 2014 added a further defence to the PA 1977: Continuing programmes of research intended for future publication (PA 1977, s 60).

23.9 REMEDIES

Under s 61, the claimant may seek:

(a)   an injunction restraining the defendant;

(b)   an order for delivery up or destruction of the offending goods;

(c)   damages;

(d)   an account of profits (but not as well as damages); or

(e)   a declaration that the patent is valid and has been infringed by the defendant.

Section 62 states that damages may not be awarded against an innocent infringer. See s 62(1) for the rules on notice to persons who claim innocent infringement.

Section 72 allows the court or the Intellectual Property Office to revoke a patent on the grounds of failing to meet the criteria for patentability in s 1(1). Section 75 allows for the amendment of patents under the control of the court or the Intellectual Property Office (see **23.6.4**).

You need to beware of a threats action under the PA 1977, s 70. This is where the patentee may be held liable for a threat to sue someone for patent infringement if the threat turns out to be unjustified. The person threatened may sue for a declaration (that the threats are not justifiable), injunction and damages. An example of such an action is *Cintec International v Parkes* [2003] EWHC 2328 (Ch). There, the patent proprietor alleged, without justification, that C's process infringed P's patents for water-filled bags for suppressing the effects of explosions. C was granted an order restraining P. Consequently, initial letters in patent disputes are very restrained! There is also a similar provision in relation to various IP rights (see **19.12**, **22.2.10** and **22.3.6**).

23.10 GENERAL INTERNATIONAL ASPECTS

23.10.1 International Patent Classification

The Strasbourg Agreement (of 1971) concerning the International Patent Classification (IPC) provides for a common classification for patents for invention including published patent applications, utility models and utility certificates. The IPC is a hierarchical system in which the whole area of technology is divided into a range of sections, classes, subclasses and groups. This system is indispensable for the retrieval of patent documents in the search for establishing the novelty of an invention, or in determining the state of the art in a particular area of technology.

23.10.2 The European Patent Organisation

Established by the Convention on the Grant of European Patents (EPC), signed in Munich in 1973 and entering into force on 7 October 1977, the European Patent Organisation is the outcome of the European countries' collective political determination to establish a uniform patent system in Europe.

As a centralised patent grant system administered by the European Patent Office on behalf of all contracting States, it is a model of successful cooperation in Europe.

23.10.2.1 The European Patent Office

The European Patent Office (EPO) grants European patents for the contracting States to the EPC. It is the executive arm of the European Patent Organisation, an intergovernmental body set up under the EPC, whose members are the EPC contracting States. The activities of the

EPO are supervised by the Organisation's Administrative Council, composed of delegates from the contracting States.

The EPO was set up by the contracting States to the EPC with the aim of strengthening cooperation between the countries of Europe in the protection of inventions. This was achieved by adopting the EPC, which makes it possible to obtain such protection in several or all of the contracting States by a single patent grant procedure, and establishes standard rules governing the treatment of patents granted by this procedure.

More than three decades have clearly demonstrated the advantages of this approach. Looking to the future, the EPO is continuing its efforts to optimise the European patent system by making it more efficient and cost effective, and better adapted to the applicants' needs.

The mission of the EPO is to support innovation, competitiveness and economic growth for the benefit of the citizens of Europe. Its task is to grant European patents for inventions, on the basis of a centralised procedure. By filing a single application in one of the three official languages (English, French and German) it is possible to obtain patent protection in some or all of the EPC contracting States.

In view of the increasing interest in obtaining patent protection in central and eastern European countries, the European Patent Organisation has concluded bilateral agreements with Albania, Croatia, Latvia, Lithuania and the former Yugoslav Republic of Macedonia, allowing the protection conferred by a European patent to be extended to these countries at the applicant's request.

The EPC is linked to the Patent Cooperation Treaty (PCT), an international treaty which offers a unitary, simplified filing procedure, followed by an international search and, at the applicant's option, an international preliminary examination, for over 100 countries. The PCT is administered by the World Intellectual Property Organization (WIPO) in Geneva. See further **17.6.4**.

By agreement with WIPO, the EPO acts under the PCT as a receiving office, an international searching authority and a preliminary examining authority. European patents may be granted on the basis of international applications filed under the PCT.

23.10.3   Paris Convention for the Protection of Industrial Property

The Paris Convention for the Protection of Industrial Property of 1883 covers several intellectual property rights, including patents. In the field of patents, the most notable thing about the Paris Convention is that it offers a right of priority. If you apply for a patent in one contracting State, you can subsequently apply for a patent in any of the 177 other contracting States within one year, and your application will take priority over those of others in respect of the same invention.

This period of grace is particularly useful if you are attempting to obtain protection in several jurisdictions, as will often be the case. Without priority, your own patent in one country could, ironically, help to defeat your own patent application in another country. This is because, in order to be patentable in any country, it must not be part of known technologies anywhere else in the world. Without priority, applying for registration in one country would release details of the invention, so making it part of known technology for the purposes of applications elsewhere.

Another aspect of the Convention is that each contracting State agrees to give equal protection to inventors who obtain patents there, irrespective of their nationality. So a country who gave better treatment in respect of patents to its own nationals – for example, a longer duration for the patent – would be in breach of the Convention.

23.11 THE UNITARY PATENT

The Unitary Patent is a new type of EU patent which at the time of writing is at an advanced stage of adoption but is not yet in force. When it is available, it will be an option for parties to apply for a single EU patent rather than a bundle of national patents. The intention is that disputes as to unitary patents will be heard by a new court, the Unified Patent Court, and that revocation and infringement proceedings would be in relation to the unitary patent as a whole and not each country to which it applies individually.

Attempts to set up the Unitary Patent system have been dogged by delays, with the legislation finally being signed on 19 February 2013. Since then, there has been a slow process of ratification which has been necessary before the system could commence. Current predictions are that the system may begin in early 2023. It should be noted that the UK has confirmed that, despite initially ratifying, it will not be joining the system.

SUMMARY

One of the most famous, but misunderstood, IP rights is the patent. If a client is not adequately advised, he may take steps that would deny him the chance ever to register a patent for his idea. It is important, therefore, to appreciate what is patentable and how to apply for a patent, but also what actions must be avoided if the chance to gain a patent is not going to be lost. This chapter has examined all these issues.

CHAPTER 24

BASICS OF THE LAW OF CONFIDENTIAL INFORMATION

LEARNING OUTCOMES

After reading this chapter you will be able to:

- explain the key elements of the law of confidential information
- apply the law to decide whether a breach has occurred
- identify the possible remedies for breach
- explain the law's relationship with privacy and human rights.

24.1 INTRODUCTION TO THE LAW OF CONFIDENTIAL INFORMATION

Basically, the law will uphold a person's obligation to keep a secret, in certain circumstances. The law of confidence is not an IP right in a pure sense but is often classified with some of the mainstream rights. For example, maintaining confidentiality before submitting a patent application is vital to avoid destruction of the invention's novelty.

On the other hand, the law here can give protection in its own right. For example, the owner of confidential information relating to a product or process may decide to keep this 'know-how' secret, rather than formalise matters by seeking patent protection. The benefit of this is that a well-guarded secret may be protected indefinitely, rather than simply for the limited period afforded to IP rights (eg, 20 years for patents).

Case law rather than statute has historically governed and shaped the law of confidence (although see **24.5** on an EU Trade Secrets Directive), and as you would expect, the vast majority of cases relate to circumstances where express obligations of confidence are lacking and implied duties of confidentiality have to be considered. It is, however, important to remember that express obligations may (and often should) be imposed (eg, on key employees or independent contractors). However, even an express confidentiality agreement may not be upheld by the court. For example, in *London Regional Transport v Mayor of London* [2003] EMLR 4, the Court of Appeal upheld the decision not to prevent publication of the report in question, as publication was held to be in the public interest.

So, what is the legal basis for giving such valuable protection? The principle arises from the equitable jurisdiction of the court to restrain unconscionable behaviour, where such behaviour may result in damage to a person. An early example is seen in the well-known case of *Prince Albert v Strange* (1849) 1 Mac & G 25, where an attempt was made by unscrupulous persons to show to the public some etchings, which were committed to a printer for the private purposes of Queen Victoria and the Prince Consort. This case set an early precedent by showing a readiness to injunct third-party recipients of confidential information or matter, within the court's discretion. The courts have been ready, ever since, to entertain such proceedings and to give a remedy, in appropriate cases.

Another factor that has supervened upon this area has been the way in which the European Convention on Human Rights has required English courts, via the Human Rights Act 1998 (HRA 1998), to deal with the Convention rights of respect for private life and freedom of expression (Articles 8 and 10). These matters have certainly made a subtle alteration to the way in which such applications to the court are dealt with, and pleaded, in the first place, but this chapter will attempt to give an overview of the way in which the courts deal with purely commercial-type disputes about confidentiality, rather than extending to a broad survey of the more rights-based claims (see **24.4** for these matters). The fairly consistent approach of the English courts in commercial/business confidence matters is somewhat easier to grasp and to explain than the more contentious interplay between individual rights and freedoms shown in the HRA 1998 claims.

The whole area has been given considerable publicity, in recent times, by the Michael Douglas and Catherine Zeta-Jones wedding photographs litigation, which raised the interesting point of whether there could be an analogous type of confidential material in photographs, intended for mass publication, but through only one intended publicity outlet (see **24.4** and *Douglas and Others v Hello! Ltd and Others (No 3)* [2007] 2 WLR 920). A person obtained surreptitiously taken photographs, knowing that this was in breach of all rules concerning the occasion. Aspects of this case will be mentioned at points where some of the basic elements of confidentiality are discussed below.

What is protected?	secret information
What benefit is there?	protects against unauthorised disclosure
How is it obtained?	arises automatically (no registration)
How long does it last?	indefinitely

Trade secret protection in the US is based on State law rather than federal law. Each of the States has adopted a version of the Uniform Trade Secrets Act. The essence of Act is that confidential information, which has commercial value, is to be protected against unauthorised disclosure and against unauthorised use, eg use by a former employee in competition with the former employer. The standards for determining the existence of a protectable trade secret, and the type of protection afforded, are essentially the same in the UK and the US.

24.2 THE ELEMENTS OF CONFIDENTIALITY

The case of *De Maudsley v Palumbo and Others* [1996] FSR 447 demonstrates the difficulties faced by a claimant where no express obligation of confidentiality has been imposed. The facts related to the Ministry of Sound, the celebrated nightclub in Southeast London. The case report states:

> At a supper party held on November 1, 1989 between the plaintiff, the first defendant and the latter's girlfriend, the plaintiff communicated to the first defendant his idea for a night club which he claimed had five novel features:
>
> (1) it would be legally open all night long;
>
> (2) of large size with decor of a 'high tech industrial' warehouse style;
>
> (3) it would have separate areas for dancing, resting and socialising, and a VIP lounge;
>
> (4) an enclosed dance area of acoustic design ensuring excellent sound quality, light and atmosphere, with no leakage of those elements beyond its environment; and
>
> (5) it would employ top disc jockeys from the United Kingdom and around the world.

In the autumn of 1991 the defendants opened a nightclub called the Ministry of Sound, featuring some but not all of the plaintiff's ideas. The plaintiff was excluded from the project and subsequently sued for (inter alia) breach of confidence.

The judge (Knox J) relied on the three-point test from *Coco v AN Clark (Engineers) Ltd* [1969] RPC 41, which will be analysed in the paragraphs which follow:

(a)   Did the information have the necessary quality of confidence about it? (**24.2.1**)

(b)   Was the information imparted in circumstances importing an obligation of confidence? (**24.2.2**)

(c)   Was there any unauthorised use of the information? (**24.2.3**)

24.2.1   Did the information have the necessary quality of confidence about it?

In the *De Maudsley* case (see **24.2** above), Knox J stated:

> Before the status of confidential information can be achieved by a concept or an idea, it is necessary to have gone far beyond identifying a desirable goal. A considerable degree of preliminary development of a definite product needs to be shown.

He found that the plaintiff's ideas were too vague to constitute confidential information.

He also found that, in order to merit protection, the idea must contain some element of originality. He took each element of the plaintiff's proposal, and criticised them for lack of novelty and/or vagueness.

Knox J accepted Hirst J's analysis in *Fraser and Others v Thames Television Ltd and Others* [1984] 1 QB 44 of the requirements for a literary, creative or entertainment idea to be protected as confidential information. This case concerned use of the law of confidential information to protect an idea for a television series about a female pop group. (Copyright will not protect a mere idea in these circumstances, see *Green v Broadcasting Corporation of New Zealand* [1989] 2 All ER 1086, which concerned the format for a game show.)

Hirst J said that the idea must:

(a)   contain some element of originality;

(b)   be clearly identifiable (as an idea of the confider);

(c)   be of potential commercial attractiveness; and

(d)   be sufficiently well developed to be capable of actual realisation.

In the *Douglas* case (see **24.1**), the highly valuable photographic rights to the wedding, and the resulting photographs, were held to be proper matters in which a quality of confidence would arise. This would extend to the wedding occasion itself having an obligation of confidence, so far as photography was concerned. All guests were under strict obligation in this respect, and this was enforced by security staff.

In *Thomas Marshall (Exports) Ltd v Guinle* [1979] Ch 227, Megarry VC suggested that four elements were necessary when considering the 'quality of confidence':

(a)   the release of the information would be injurious to the owner of it or of advantage to rivals;

(b)   the owner must believe that the information is confidential, ie not in the public domain;

(c)   the owner's belief in the above is reasonable; and

(d)   the information must be judged in the light of the usage and practices of the industry concerned.

24.2.2   Was the information imparted in circumstances importing an obligation of confidence?

The problem here for the plaintiff in *De Maudsley* was that the relevant occasion on which he had imparted the information was a social one, not a business context. The plaintiff acknowledged in his evidence that he had deliberately refrained from explaining that the information was confidential, 'because [he] did not want to blow the deal there and then'. Lastly, there was no accepted trade practice in this area to substantiate the plaintiff's claim.

Failure to make confidentiality clear also caused the claimant's case to fail in *Shaw v API Group plc* (QBD District Registry (Manchester)), 10 April 2008, WL.

See *Vitof Ltd v Altoft* [2006] EWHC 1678, where computer source code, created in contemplation of the incorporation of a company which would exploit the code commercially, was held to have been imparted under an obligation of confidence.

This requirement can also extend to persons who obtain information in circumstances where they know or have reason to believe that they should not have it. This can be seen in cases such as the *Douglas* case and *Prince Albert v Strange* (see **24.1**). In the case of the photographer at the Douglas wedding, he knew at all times that what he was doing was a serious breach of trust.

In *Northern Rock plc v Financial Times Ltd* [2007] EWHC 2677 (QB), a highly confidential memorandum came into the hands of various publishing organisations. Financial Times Ltd published the whole memorandum, but others published only extracts. Northern Rock contended that the memorandum had been leaked by an employee in breach of his or her contract. An injunction was granted to prevent further publication of the full memorandum but not of the small, extracted parts that had already been widely circulated. There was detailed commercial information in the full document, and the public interest lay in enforcing the duties of confidence in the report.

Whether the obligation can be extinguished was discussed in the case of *Thomas Marshall (Exports) Ltd v Guinle*. The defendant was a managing director who resigned before the end of his contractual term. There was an express clause in his contract prohibiting the use or disclosure of confidential information during or after the duration of the contract. He argued that the resignation was a repudiation of the contract which ended obligations arising from it, and so he should not be liable for breach for disclosure of the information. The judge in the case, Sir Robert Megarry VC, considered the power of a court to prevent a wrongdoer from benefiting from his wrong:

> Above all, I think the courts must be astute to prevent a wrongdoer from profiting too greatly from his wrong. If without just cause a servant who has contracted to serve for a term of years refuses to do so, it is easy to see that the court is powerless to make him do what he has contracted to do .... But why should the court's inability to make a servant work for his employer mean that as soon as the servant refuses to do so the court is forthwith disabled from restraining him from committing any breach, however flagrant, of his other obligations during the period of his contract? I would wholly reject the doctrine of automatic determination, whether in its wide form or in its narrowed version.

24.2.3 Was there any unauthorised use of the information?

Here, the judge in *De Maudsley* held that the plaintiff's ideas and the defendants' club did not overlap to a sufficient degree to constitute unauthorised use.

The plaintiff's action therefore failed on all three counts. However, the judge summarised the situation as follows:

> Mr de Maudsley was in my view rather shabbily treated in that he was encouraged to think that he would be part of the enterprise but was only told that this would not be so, long after Mr Palumbo and Mr Waterhouse had decided, almost certainly justifiably because of Mr de Maudsley's rather difficult character and limited abilities, that he would not be included in their project.

The moral of the story is not to rely upon an implied duty of confidence. It is far better to inject certainty into the situation with the use of a written confidentiality agreement.

In *Cray Valley Ltd v Deltech Europe Ltd and Others* [2003] EWHC 728 (Ch), an action for breach of confidence in relation to the manufacture of industrial resins failed. There were no express undertakings of confidence by the former employees in question. It was held that the information did not have the necessary quality of confidence, not least as much of it had been published already and was easy to reverse engineer. It was not imparted in circumstances importing an obligation of confidence, but merely in the normal running of a factory, without any express instructions to employees to treat it as confidential. A claim for breach of copyright did succeed.

24.3 REMEDIES AND THEIR AVAILABILITY

The most important measure will often be an injunction to prevent disclosure of the information, that is, a restraining order in advance. Once the information has been released it is usually too late to seek an injunction (but see *Northern Rock plc v Financial Times Ltd* at **24.2.2**). However, an injunction may be granted in regard to confidential information that is of commercial value where:

(a)   there are two rival businesses and not to grant an injunction would give the wrong-doer an advantage (eg, *Speed Seal Products Ltd v Paddington and Another* [1986] 1 All ER 91); or

(b)   the 'springboard' doctrine applies, ie where one business would gain an unfair advantage over its rivals because of unauthorised disclosure to it of commercial information (eg, *Terrapin Ltd v Builders' Supply Co (Hayes) Ltd* [1967] RPC 375; *Roger Bullivant v Ellis* [1987] FSR 172). The court will try to prevent such advantage, by injunction, where appropriate (see **24.3.1**). This kind of injunction, granted against a rival in receipt of the information rather than the taker of the information, is called a 'springboard' injunction.

Compensatory damages are available for breach of confidence (see *Seager v Copydex Ltd* [1967] 2 All ER 415).

An account of the defendant's profits is also possible (see *Peter Pan Manufacturing Corporation v Corsets Silhouette Ltd* [1964] 1 WLR 96).

An order for delivery up, or destruction under oath, of the offending document or articles made by use of the information is also possible (see *Industrial Furnaces Ltd v Reaves and Another* [1970] RPC 605).

24.3.1 Whether remedy is available

It will be clear, by now, that the law of confidential information rests upon the equitable jurisdiction to prevent unconscionable use of confidential information; any remedies or reliefs are available only as a matter of the court's discretion, not as of right. Nevertheless, the courts try to exercise their jurisdiction consistently, and a very helpful exposition of the principles involved is given by Arnold J in *Vestergaard Frandsen A/S v Bestnet Europe Ltd* [2009] EWHC 1456 (Ch), [2009] All ER (D) 57 (Oct).

The case arose out of the defendants' (former employees of the claimant) misuse of the claimant's trade secrets to develop a polytex mosquito net, which incorporated an insecticide in the material. The information came to them from their knowledge of the claimant's process for making a protective cattle net, also incorporating an insecticide. The court (at [2009] EWHC 657 (Ch)) held that the defendants had breached the confidentiality of the information, having applied the *Coco v AN Clark* three-point test discussed in **24.2**. The question then became one of how the court should exercise its discretion in granting the remedies sought. The following list is a summary of the valuable guidance given:

(a)   *The general principles involved*. Where the claimant establishes that the defendant had acted in breach of confidence and that there was a sufficient risk of repetition, if there were no specific discretionary reasons to refuse an injunction, one would normally be granted, save in exceptional circumstances.

(b)   *Where information had only a limited degree of confidence.* Here, as, for example, in circumstances where the information might be obtained by research in the public domain, an injunction could be ordered only for a limited period.

(c)   *Whether an injunction could be granted to prevent a defendant from benefiting from a past misuse of confidential information.* In general, it was not clear that such an injunction could be granted, as the primary remedy should be financial. Great care should be exercised, in granting such an injunction, to ensure that the claimant was not thereby put in a position better than if there had been no misuse at all. The duration of such an injunction should not go beyond the period for which the defendant's illegitimate advantage could be expected to last.

(d)   *Where a product derived from, or was manufactured using, confidential information.* An injunction could be granted to restrain the manufacture or sale of such product, where the manufacture represented a continued use of the information, always having regard to the extent and importance of the use of it. Otherwise, the appropriate remedy in respect of manufacture and sale of products derived from a past misuse of information was a financial one.

The resulting orders for the claimant were that the defendants should be restrained from using or disclosing the claimant's trade secrets (except any information which was now in the public domain). An injunction restrained any further production or sale of the first derived product, but did not extend to later developed products, where the derivation from the original information was not so clearly illustrated.

See also *First Conference Services Ltd v Bracchi* [2009] EWHC 2176 (Ch), where an employee, having decided that he would leave his job, e-mailed confidential information to a company that he himself had set up. He was held to have misappropriated the information; he had also involved himself in passing off. The court ordered injunctive relief.

24.3.2   The position of former employees

The majority of breach of confidence claims involve former employees as defendants, and it is important to realise that certain considerations should be added to those already examined where an employment situation is involved. The first point is that it is open to an employer to secure some protection for his secrets or other confidential information by requiring the employee to enter into a covenant in restraint of trade and confidentiality agreements. If the employer fails to do this, it loses control of the situation and is left relying on a court imposing implied obligations.

The second point is that there is considerable judicial guidance as to the different types of information that might come to an employee during his employment. The widely-cited analysis by Goulding J, at first instance, in *Faccenda Chicken v Fowler* [1985] 1 All ER 724, is instructive and helpful here. The judge categorised the types of information and consequent confidentiality status as falling into three groups:

(a)   *Class 1* – mundane, easily obtained information (for all that it might be very technical) that is already in the public domain; <u>such information is not confidential and cannot be protected</u>.

(b)   *Class 2* – confidential information that the employee knows, or ought to know, is confidential; <u>this will normally remain confidential during the term of employment, but will not usually be protected after termination in the absence of an express covenant</u>.

(c)   *Class 3* – highly confidential information in the nature of trade secrets, customer information, etc; <u>this type of information would be protected under an implied term of good faith between the parties, both during the employment and after termination, regardless of the absence of a restrictive covenant</u>.

The main issue in such cases is often about whether the confidential information is easily isolated from other information that the employee is free to use; that will always depend upon the facts of the case. Within the information categorised as Class 3 above (trade secrets), for example, a distinction still needs to be made between the general experience of the employee, and the protectable information belonging to their employer. If, for example, I am a lawyer, I will have in my head the experience of using various firm precedents. To what extent is my knowledge of these precedents something I can exploit when going to work for another firm? My ex-employer may say that the content of the precedents is a trade secret and so cannot be exploited, whereas I would say that knowledge of how to word certain legal clauses (as in those clauses) is part of my wealth of experience. I cannot of course be expected to refrain from exploiting everything I have learnt during my time working for a business.

The distinction between experience and trade secrets is not an easy one to make, and so cases in this area often rest on their particular facts and the court's judgement of the nature of the information in question. Factors such as whether the information was in the form of definable data (eg the results of research), and the quantity of information, will be relevant. On the latter point, where the information is of such high volume that it is not retained in the employee's head (eg it is contained in documents which the employee takes from the workplace), a court will generally see this as beyond mere experience.

24.4 A RIGHT OF PRIVACY AND THE HUMAN RIGHTS ACT 1998?

In the somewhat unusual case of *Douglas and Others v Hello! Ltd and Others* [2003] EWHC 786 (Ch), [2003] All ER (D) 209 (Apr); [2005] EWCA Civ 595, breach of confidence was used to prevent publication by a rival magazine of wedding coverage granted by two film stars to a magazine. It was held that the photographs of the event had the necessary quality of confidence about them, and deserved protection as a trade secret. The illicit photographer from the rival magazine (the defendant) had been under a duty of confidentiality when attending the wedding. The defendant knew of the arrangement between the couple and the other magazine, but had deliberately ignored it and took covert photographs. The law of confidence was held to have protected the claimants' right to respect for private life under the HRA 1998, Sch 1, Pt I, Art 8. It was therefore held that it was unnecessary to consider whether the Act had created a new right of privacy. The wedding and the party were private events held on private property. These were key factors in the Douglases succeeding. The Lords appeal concerned the nature and protectability of the obligation of confidence, rather than the privacy issue. In another case, the privacy of Princess Caroline of Monaco was protected by the European Convention on Human Rights under Article 8, even though the invasion of her privacy occurred in a public place (*von Hanover v Germany*, Application No 59320/00).

In *A v B (A Company) and Another* [2002] EWCA Civ 337, [2002] 2 All ER 545, the Court of Appeal refused to uphold an injunction under the 'respect for private life' provisions of the Act restraining two newspapers from publishing details of the extra-marital affairs of the claimant, a professional footballer.

In *Campbell v MGN Ltd* [2002] EWCA Civ 1373, [2003] QB 633, the Court of Appeal refused to uphold an injunction against a newspaper restraining publication of sensitive information about a well-known media personality, Naomi Campbell. She had been having treatment for drug addiction, having previously denied drug abuse. The Court held that the public interest in publishing the story overrode her privacy rights under the Human Rights Act 1998. However, the House of Lords overruled the Court of Appeal ([2004] 2 All ER 995). It held that the information about Ms Campbell seeking treatment for drug addiction and photographs of Ms Campbell attending treatment were unnecessary intrusions into her private life. Ms Campbell's right to respect for her private life under the HRA 1998, Sch 1, Pt I, Art 8, was held to outweigh M's freedom of expression under Article 10. A similar result followed in *HRH Prince of Wales v Associated Newspapers Ltd* [2007] EWHC 1685 (Ch), where the Prince of Wales was able to obtain summary judgment in his claims for breach of confidence and privacy, and infrigement of the copyright in his private journals.

24.5 TRADE SECRETS REGULATIONS

The UK Government implemented an EU Directive on Trade Secrets, via the Trade Secrets (Enforcement, etc) Regulations 2018 (SI 2018/597). The Regulations define a trade secret as information which:

- is secret in the sense that it is not, as a body or in the precise configuration and assembly of its components, generally known among, or readily accessible to, persons within the circles that normally deal with the kind of information in question;
- has commercial value because it is secret; and
- has been subject to reasonable steps under the circumstances, by the person lawfully in control of the information, to keep it secret.

The Regulations make it unlawful to acquire, use or disclose a trade secret where it would be a breach of confidence in confidential information. This is largely a codification of the existing law of confidential information into regulations (indeed see reg 3 where a breach only occurs if it is a breach of the law of confidential information). This is because it was felt that the UK law already essentially complied with the Trade Secrets Directive. It has not repealed the common law, however, so claimants will have a choice of actions. It remains to be seen whether there will be specific advantages to either claim.

SUMMARY

There are three possible forms of protection for a secret: patent it (if possible), do not tell anybody about it, and assert rights brought about by the law of confidentiality. The last law is often used in circumstances where you have told a secret to someone doing work for you, who would need to know the information in order to do the work. Thus it is commonly used in employment situations, or in circumstances when you might use a consultant.

In this chapter we have seen how the law of confidentiality arises, how it can be enforced, and its limitations. It is an area of law which is ripe for development in view of the way in which the media and electronic communications (such as Twitter) work today.

CHAPTER 25

INFORMATION TECHNOLOGY

LEARNING OUTCOMES

After reading this chapter you will be able to:

- identify which IP rights studied so far are applicable to information technology
- explain which other rights are applicable to information technology
- apply contractual principles to contracts relating to hardware and software
- explain legal issues relating to the Internet.

25.1 INTRODUCTION

This chapter deals primarily with the position in the UK. However, as many rights and obligations derive from EU legislation, there is a great deal of similarity in the rules throughout Europe.

The computer is a universal presence in offices, homes and schools throughout the developed world. The increase in computer use in the last 20 years or so has come about through the amazing reduction in the price of computing power. For comparison, if a new car had decreased in price to the same degree that computers have over the 20-year period, the car would now cost something less than a tankful of petrol.

However, it should not be forgotten that a computer is basically a calculating machine with a very large memory. It needs to be told what to do. This chapter addresses some of the main legal and related issues which this raises:

(a) IP issues;

(b) semiconductor chip protection;

(c) hardware contracts;

(d) software contracts;

(e) the Internet;

(f) computer crime;

(g) data protection; and

(h) rights in databases.

Many of these issues are relevant to areas of law already covered elsewhere in this book, so, where appropriate, this chapter is cross-referenced to that material.

25.2 INFORMATION TECHNOLOGY AND INTELLECTUAL PROPERTY RIGHTS

All the major forms of legal protection of IP rights pre-date the electronic computer by a century or more. As they were not developed with the computer in mind, there have therefore been many problems in deciding whether a particular activity comes within the remit of the existing IP law. Indeed, there has been a considerable need to produce new forms of legal protection to deal with problems that have emerged. The following paragraphs summarise the way in which the various IP rights may be relevant to computer software and hardware.

25.2.1 Copyright

For the main points on the law of copyright itself, see **Chapter 20**. The relevance of copyright to computers is as protection for the software; in other words, the instructions required to enable the computer to perform the desired task. In order to be protected, the software would have to have been 'written down' on some medium at some stage of its existence, although of course when bought by the customer, the software will usually be on floppy disks or a CD. (For the avoidance of doubt, note that 'software' = 'computer programs'.)

A computer program is a series of written instructions telling a computer what to do. It will contain thousands of lines of instructions, each one of which relates to a simple step; but put together as a program, it enables the computer to be used, for example, for word processing. As already noted in **Chapter 20**, copyright exists in software as a literary work (CDPA 1988, s 3(1)); see further **25.5.2**.

Unauthorised use of a computer program (which includes simple down-loading) is therefore breach of copyright. The commercial arrangement for use of software is usually a licence, ie, a copyright licence.

(For the law on copyright in databases, and database right, see **Chapters 20** and **21**.)

25.2.2 Patents

As noted in **Chapter 23**, the PA 1977, s 1(2) excludes 'computer programs' from the remit of the patent system (although, as indicated in **23.3.4**, this does not necessarily mean that a program can never be patented).

The reality is that patents for computer programs are being granted in increasing numbers. The attitude of the UK Intellectual Property Office and the European Patent Office has become more relaxed over recent years, though not to the extent of the 'open doors' policy of the US Patent Office. The patent is really being granted for the technical effect brought about by the use of the program, as distinct from the program itself.

Patents do, of course, have relevance to protection of inventions in relation to computer hardware (ie, the electronics) if the necessary conditions for patentability are satisfied.

25.2.3 Trade marks

Trade marks are covered in **Chapter 19**. This becomes particularly relevant in the context of Internet 'domain' names, where trade mark infringement and passing off are the relevant causes of action (see further, **25.6**).

(Trade marks are, of course, also relevant in the usual context of being used in relation to goods and services, for example Microsoft, Dell, Compaq and so on will have various registered and unregistered marks which they use in connection with their businesses.)

25.2.4 Design rights

Registered and unregistered design rights (see **Chapter 22**) are intended to protect the outward appearance of items. The design rights are not often directly relevant to information technology (IT) (although they may be used to protect the outward appearance of a piece of hardware). However, note that the right which protects semiconductor chips is akin to a design right (see **25.3**).

25.3 SEMICONDUCTOR CHIP PROTECTION

The chip is the brain of the computer. It is made up of millions of transistors and other electronic components, yet is only 2cm by 2cm or so in size.

Obviously, such a marvel of miniaturisation could not be made by sitting at a work bench and soldering all the bits together. Rather, chips are made by a special type of photographic process, whereby the design of the circuit is etched on to the blank chip. As it is made by such a process, it can be copied in a similar manner.

The design of chips is protected in the EU by Directive 87/54/EEC. This has been implemented in the UK by the Design Right (Semiconductor Topographies) Regulations 1989 (SI 1989/1100). Regulation 2(1) defines a semiconductor topography as a design within s 213 of the CDPA 1988 and which relates to a semiconductor product or component thereof. The design has to be recorded in a design document (see **22.4**).

Under the 1989 Regulations, there is prohibition on:

(a)   unauthorised copying of a chip; and

(b)   importation into, or sale in, the UK of unauthorised copy chips.

Note that reverse engineering is not prohibited, so it is permissible for a third party to work out from the chip topography how it works, and then to produce a chip that performs the same function, without copying the topography or 'map' of the original.

The right lasts for 15 years from creation of the design, or 10 years from first sale of objects made to that design, whichever is the shorter (cf the period for UDR; see further **Chapter 22**).

25.4 HARDWARE CONTRACTS

The 'hardware' is the computer equipment. If you buy a computer, you are simply buying electrical equipment; therefore the contract for the purchase of computer hardware is a contract for sale of goods, and is in principle the same as, for example, buying a fridge from Comet. However, there is one important practical difference: it is fairly obvious when a fridge is not working properly, but it is more debatable whether or not a particular computer is doing all the things it is supposed to. Part of this problem is that it is the software which tells the hardware what to do (for more detail on software, see **25.5**).

Consequently, it is suggested that in producing a specification for a new computer system, it is better to specify the software first and then that the hardware to be supplied has to be able to run it (ie, make the buyer's particular purpose expressly known). Many of the contractual disputes in this area arise from a lack of clarity in specifying the performance requirements of the equipment.

Note that, in practice, it is possible either to buy or to lease hardware. With the decrease in the cost of hardware, buying has become more common in recent years. However, if the system is a major installation, leasing would still be encountered. In this case, the contract would be of a different type (see **25.4.2**).

The remainder of this section considers some of the legal issues which may arise in relation to computer hardware. Where sale of goods legislation is referred to, the references given are to business-to-business legislation (eg the Sale of Goods Act 1979) rather than business-to-consumer legislation (eg the Consumer Rights Act 2015) to reflect the likely context for a hardware contract.

25.4.1   Pre-contract issues: negotiation

In *Mackenzie Patten & Co v British Olivetti Ltd* (1984) 1 CL&P 92, a firm of solicitors bought a computer system to run their accounts. The sales representative made various claims for the system. However, there was an exclusion clause in the contract in relation to his statements. The firm signed the contract. The system proved to be slow and hard to use. It was held that Olivetti were bound by the representative's claims, on the basis of a collateral contract. See *Watford Electronics Ltd v Sanderson* at **9.2.2**.

25.4.2   Leasing

With a lease of computer hardware, the lessee has the right to use the equipment but the lessor remains the owner of it. The SGSA 1982 is relevant here (the 1982 Act characterises a contract of this type as a contract of hire, but the term 'lease' is more commercially usual in practice).

Most computer leases will be 'finance leases'. This is a commercial term used to distinguish such a lease from an 'operating lease'. With an operating lease, the equipment is hired out to the user (the lessee) for a short period of time, returned to the lessor and then hired out to another user (this is, eg, how a tool-hire shop would normally operate). With a finance lease, the equipment is supplied to one user only, who retains possession of it for substantially the whole of its working life.

A finance lease basically works as follows. The finance company (lessor) acquires the computer hardware by buying it from a supplier. The finance company pays the supplier for the hardware. It then leases the hardware to the user, and the user pays the finance company a leasing payment, probably monthly. At the end of the lease, the hardware will have little residual value and will be sold off by the lessor. The lessor may credit the user with the sale proceeds (depending on the terms of the lease), but the user must not have the right to acquire title to the hardware, otherwise it will be a hire purchase contract, not a lease.

25.4.3   Sale

As noted at **25.4**, a contract for the sale of hardware is in principle the same as for the sale of any other electrical item. However, the following points will require particular care.

25.4.3.1   Delivery

Depending on the terms of a sale of goods contract, non-delivery or late delivery may entitle the buyer of goods to reject them (see **5.4.6.6**). Remember, however, that this is possible only if the time for delivery is of the essence (ie a condition of the contract: see **5.6**). Problems with hardware contracts can arise if the equipment is being specially produced or modified, or because the supplier is itself waiting for supplies of parts. In such cases, it may not be feasible for the parties to nominate a specific delivery date. It then has to be decided whether the goods have been delivered within a reasonable time. If the delay means that the intended use is no longer practicable then a reasonable time has elapsed. It is advisable for the buyer to inform the supplier at the outset of the intended uses of the equipment. However, it would be best also for the buyer to specify an end-stop date after which the equipment will not be accepted.

25.4.3.2   Payment and changes of specification

Terms on price and payment will need careful consideration.

In major hardware contracts, some changes of specification are likely (eg, it emerges in discussions between the supplier and the buyer that the buyer's future business plans make it advisable to increase the number of file servers, or the specification of the desktop computers). Changes should be categorised as those which are at the buyer's expense and those which are at the seller's expense.

25.4.3.3 Passing of risk and property

The SGA 1979, s 20(1) provides that risk (of accidental loss or damage to the goods) passes at the same time as property (ie, ownership). Sections 16–19 dictate when the property in the goods passes. The issue is important in deciding which party should bear the risk, and therefore the cost of insurance, so remember that ss 16–20 can be ousted by contrary agreement. The parties should consider what is important to them, and provide accordingly.

25.4.3.4 Retention of title

A properly drafted retention of title clause provides added protection for the seller, particularly where standard, non-bespoke equipment is being supplied (see **Chapter 6**).

25.4.3.5 Seller's obligations

Remember that in a sale of goods agreement, various conditions will be implied into the agreement by the SGA 1979:

(a)   s 12 – that the seller will give good title and quiet possession (eg, the hardware will be free of third-party IP rights);

(b)   s 13 – sale by description (the Misrepresentation Act 1967 could also be relevant);

(c)   s 14(2) – satisfactory quality (it is, however, normally better to define 'quality' in the contract than to rely on the statutory implied condition); and

(d)   s 14(3) – reasonable fitness for buyer's purpose (remember that the buyer has to make his purpose known to the seller).

Note that because the functioning of hardware is controlled by the software (ie, the program), it is often difficult to assess the hardware independently in relation to quality issues.

The implied terms in ss 13 and 14 can be excluded from the contract subject to UCTA 1977. This would often be done in computer supply contracts. In their place, the supplier would offer a warranty that the system complies with the specification agreed with the customer.

25.4.3.6 Buyer's remedies

Under the SGA 1979, s 11(3), the buyer can reject the goods for breach of condition (see **5.6**).

Rejection of the goods is the buyer's primary remedy if the seller commits breach of condition. However, this may not be feasible commercially (eg, if the hardware is specially adapted, or made so that it would be difficult for the buyer to find an alternative supplier at short notice, or possibly at all).

In any event, the right to reject is lost if the goods have been accepted (see SGA 1979, s 35). Acceptance may arise in the following ways:

(a)   Hardware contracts will contain acceptance-testing clauses, which would require that the hardware is able to perform certain defined tasks which demonstrate its capabilities. Passing the tests constitutes acceptance. Ordering more hardware from the same seller would normally also constitute acceptance.

(b)   Using the goods beyond mere testing may also constitute acceptance.

(c)   Retaining the goods beyond a reasonable time could also be acceptance. This could happen if the hardware is delivered in instalments.

Note that a buyer may elect not to reject the goods and may claim damages instead (SGA 1979, s 11(2)). A buyer might waive his right to reject, for example, where the hardware is not delivered on time and the buyer presses the seller to make delivery as soon as possible.

25.4.3.7   Seller's remedies

If the buyer refuses to accept the goods, the seller can sue for the price, but will have to mitigate by trying to re-sell the hardware. The question will then arise: is there a market for this particular hardware, and will the seller be able to get the same price? The seller could be awarded his lost profit under SGA 1979, s 50(2), if he can show that there are few alternative buyers.

25.4.3.8   Exclusion clauses

In many cases, UCTA 1977 will apply to a hardware contract. The most likely application is in relation to attempted exclusions of the SGA 1979, ss 13–14 (ie, the implied conditions of description, satisfactory quality and reasonable fitness for purpose). In a commercial sale, the test will be one of 'reasonableness' (UCTA 1977, s 6).

The leading computer case on exclusion clauses is *St Albans City and District Council v ICL* [1996] 4 All ER 481. The loss suffered by St Albans District Council as a result of the computer system supplied by ICL failing to work properly was £1.3m, but the contract contained an exclusion of loss clause for losses over £100,000 (ie, compensation for loss caused was limited to this sum). This was held to be unreasonable because:

(a)   ICL had more resources than the council did;

(b)   ICL had product liability insurance of £50m worldwide;

(c)   ICL could not justify the £100,000 limit;

(d)   the contract was signed on superseded standard terms;

(e)   local authorities are limited in what they can insure against;

(f)   St Albans received no inducement to agree; and

(g)   ICL had said that negotiation over terms would delay implementation of the deal.

The tide has gone the other way to an extent with the case of *Watford Electronics Ltd v Sanderson CFL Ltd* [2001] EWCA Civ 317, [2001] 1 All ER (Comm) 696. An interesting point that went against the claimants is that they themselves used a similar limitation of liability clause in their own terms. They were therefore held to be aware of the commercial considerations and the effect on the price agreed for the job.

25.4.4   Maintenance agreements

Computer hardware will normally come with a guarantee (usually called a warranty) – an express promise from the supplier that it will do or provide certain things if the hardware goes wrong.

After the warranty expires, it makes sense for a buyer to set up a maintenance agreement for commercial hardware.

The key points for the owner of the hardware and the provider of the maintenance to consider when setting up such an agreement are:

(a)   should it provide for repair on site, or return to base?

(b)   the desired response time from the provider (the faster it is, the more expensive it is);

(c)   is replacement equipment to be provided in the interim whilst repair is carried out?

(d)   duration of the contract – the older the equipment, the more repairs it will need and the more it will cost to maintain; and

(e)   is transfer of the agreement to a new owner of the hardware permitted, as this will increase the second-hand value of the hardware?

25.4.5   System supply contracts

A system supply contract is where the buyer receives some or all of the following:

(a)   hardware;

(b)   software;

(c)   cabling, power supply;

(d)   services (eg, installation, maintenance, support, systems integration).

Note that in a 'turnkey' contract (where the system is supplied ready to run, usually with all software and peripherals such as printers), the supplier may buy in various aspects of the goods or services, almost certainly including the software. This would be licensed direct to the user, rather than by licence to the supplier and sub-licence from him to the user. It is important that the user evaluates the terms of the licences to see if they are suitable for his purposes.

25.5   SOFTWARE

Software can be 'off the peg' (ie, a standard package), or 'made to order'. Standard package software will be cheaper than made to order, but may not fulfil the user's requirements adequately. A middle way for the buyer of software to choose is to adapt standard software, in effect customising it. The trend is toward increased sales of standard software.

There is also a distinction between system software, which organises the way the hardware operates, and applications software, which performs the function required by the user (eg, 'Word' or 'Powerpoint' are applications software). System software is normally supplied by the maker of the hardware (eg, the BIOS – the Basic Input/Output System).

25.5.1   Software licensing

Software supply contracts are basically copyright licences (see **Chapter 20**), but also contain terms dealing with the supply of the physical manifestations of the software (eg, sometimes retaining title to the disks, or forbidding the possession of more than one set of back-up disks, or forbidding use other than on specified hardware).

As noted at **25.2.1,** there is specific legal provision on the IP position for software. Under s 17(2) of the CDPA 1988, unauthorised storage of a program in a computer is copyright infringement. Directive 91/250/EEC specifies further legal protection for software. It is implemented in the UK by the Copyright (Computer Programs) Regulations 1992 (SI 1992/ 3233).

Even where software is sold over the counter, licensing is still relevant. In this case, the software house tries to impose a licence on the user by specifying that opening the cellophane in which the software is wrapped constitutes acceptance of the terms of the standard-form licence visible through the wrapper (this is known as a 'shrink-wrap' licence, and is considered further at **25.5.2**).

(What will in practice happen in this sort of 'consumer' sale of software and shrink-wrap licence is that the software creator (eg, Microsoft) will sell the software to a retailer (eg, computer shop). The shop sells the software on to the customer; it is, however, Microsoft which imposes the shrink-wrap licence on the customer.)

25.5.2   Shrink-wrap or click-wrap licensing

Most software today is bought off the shelf; that is, the software is a standard product, such as the 'Word' program used to create this document. As noted at **25.5.1** above, in order to create a licence between the software creator and the user, the device known as a 'shrink-wrap licence' is used (there would otherwise be a contractual link only between the user and the retailer). This means that terms of use can therefore be imposed by the software creator on the user.

The terms of the licence are set out on the outside of the packaging and are visible through the clear wrapping. The licence purportedly comes into being when the user opens the packaging, supposedly having read the terms and agreed to them.

A licensing method which has become more common in recent years, both with software downloaded through the Internet and being downloaded from a CD-ROM, is that of the 'click-wrap' licence. This is where customers are faced with the text of a licence agreement on screen. The customers have to click on the 'I agree' button before they are allowed access to the software.

25.5.2.1   Terms

Typical terms in a consumer licence include that:

(a)   the licence is for use on one computer only;

(b)   the software must not be copied (save for one back-up copy);

(c)   the software must not be altered; and

(d)   the licensor will replace defective disks and supply updates.

All other warranties or conditions are excluded (subject, of course, to the impact of UCTA 1977, or other provisions controlling exclusion or restriction of liability). As the licence will be a pure licence of the software creator's IP rights, the only heads of liability for the software creator are likely to be negligence or product liability. (Remember that exclusion of negligence will be subject to UCTA 1977, s 2; product liability cannot be excluded under s 7 of the Consumer Protection Act 1987.)

If the sale of software is a consumer sale, the Consumer Transactions (Restrictions on Statements) Order 1976 (SI 1976/1813) will apply. This requires there to be a statement that any warranty given does not affect the consumer's statutory rights. The Unfair Terms in Consumer Contracts Regulations 1999 (SI 1999/2083) may also be relevant in this situation (as noted in **Chapter 8**, these Regulations can only apply to consumer agreements).

25.5.3   Bespoke software

Bespoke software (ie, software 'tailored' to the precise needs of a particular user) is expensive, and will be the subject of a specific contract negotiated between the software house and the user, who in legal terms is the commissioner of the software (this is relevant to the ownership of the IP rights in the software; see below).

In this case, software is written to fulfil the functional specification put forward by the user. The software house will depend on the user supplying information on its business and how it is run in order to create a satisfactory program.

The specification may change during the design of the program, and the costs of such alterations need to be allocated between the parties.

Acceptance tests will need to be devised. The user will not accept the software until these have been passed.

A key problem will be that of ownership of the copyright in the program. As noted in **Chapter 20**, the copyright will (subject, of course, to any contrary agreement) vest in the creator (ie author) of the work, not in the person who commissions it. However, this may not fulfil the desires of the parties to the agreement here; the user might ideally want to have exclusive rights to the program which it paid the creator to devise, even if only to prevent third parties from benefiting from the program. The creator, on the other hand, would want to have the right to use at least some aspects of the program in future programs which it may write, not least because it regards it as part of its evolving expertise. In practice, this is another matter which will be determined by bargaining power; basically, users are unlikely to get exclusivity unless they are prepared to pay a substantial amount for it.

25.6 THE INTERNET

It goes without saying that IP laws have been tested quite heavily by the advance of the Internet and, as with the growth of computing generally since their introduction, have had to adapt quickly to react to the new challenges it brings.

25.6.1 Using a name

In order to send a message over the Internet, it has to have an address to go to. An Internet Protocol address has the form '130.132.59.234'. As the Internet Protocol addresses are essentially forgettable, the Domain Name System (DNS) was devised. 'Domain names' are names rather than numbers, and are translated into Internet Protocol addresses by some of the computers in the Internet. An example of a domain name is 'law.ac.uk'. So, for example, a message could be sent to John.Smith@law.ac.uk.

Domain names have different 'levels'; for example, the top-level domain name in the above example is 'uk'. Obviously, this is the country where the relevant party is located. Other examples of top-level domain names are '.com', '.gov' or '.org'. There is little dispute about these. Rather, the problems which arise in relation to domain names usually concern the second-level names, especially where that name is the trade mark, registered or not, of a commercial product or organisation (eg, 'McDonalds.com'). Clearly, unauthorised use of that domain name would upset a certain chain of burger restaurants.

In the UK, the organisation known as Nominet allocates domain names and does so on the basis of first come, first served. It is located at www.nominet.org.uk.

In the United States, and in effect internationally as well, the body known as the Internet Corporation for Assigned Names and Numbers (ICANN) deals with many domain name issues also, and is located at www.icann.org. It has set up some new top-level domain names, for example '.pro' for lawyers and accountants. WIPO also has an input into domain name issues, especially from the trade mark perspective, and runs a dispute resolution procedure.

In England, in the case of *British Telecommunications plc and Others v One in a Million Ltd and Others* [1999] 1 WLR 903, the Court of Appeal held that the use of various business names as domain names without consent was passing off and infringement of the registered trade marks under the TMA 1994. The claimants were BT, Sainsbury's, Virgin, Ladbrokes and Marks & Spencer. Following this case, it seems clear that unauthorised use of a business name as a domain name will be taken by the English courts as constituting passing off and trade mark infringement (assuming that there is a valid trade mark registration). In *Bonnier Media Ltd v Greg Lloyd Smith* [2002] ETMR 86 (see **19.9**), it was held by the Scottish Court of Session that the intent of the infringer was a critical factor, ie were they intending to defraud the legitimate user of the trade mark?

If a domain name is a registered trade mark, the criteria used to decide if there is infringement are those under the TMA 1994. In particular, the criteria identified in the case of *British Sugar plc v James Robertson & Sons Ltd* [1996] RPC 281, concerning the use of the word 'Treat' in relation to sweet sauces and syrups, where it was held that it was not necessary for the infringing use to be use as a trade mark as such, provided it was use in the course of trade. See, at **19.9**, *Wilson v Yahoo! UK Ltd* [2008] EWHC 361 (Ch), on the non-infringing use of trade marks in sponsored links in Internet search engines.

Even if the trade mark is not in use in the UK, it may be protected in the UK as a 'well known mark' under s 56 of the 1994 Act (see **19.10**).

25.6.2 Copyright issues

In the case of *Shetland Times Ltd v Wills and Another* [1997] FSR 604, the Shetland News Internet site had a link which enabled the reader to access pages from the *Shetland Times*, but without seeing the front page of the *Times*. Such unauthorised use of the *Times* pages was held to be breach of copyright. Unauthorised use of copyright material on the Internet now falls within s 20 of the CDPA 1988, which covers infringement by communication to the pubic within the UK, by electronic means.

The BBC has undertaken similar action with regard to infringement via the Internet of its copyright in the Teletubbies.

See also **20.7.2** for further issues relating to copyright on the Internet, including an explanation of the *ITV et al v TVCatchup Ltd* case and the Meltwater case.

25.6.3   Trade mark issues

A recent issue which the courts have had to deal with is the selling of keyword terms by search engines such as Google, and its implications for the application of trade mark rules. In *Interflora Inc and Another v Marks and Spencer plc and Another* [2013] EWHC 1291 (Ch), Interflora alleged that Marks and Spencer bought keywords from Google that referenced Interflora and advertised its own flower service on the back of them. The judge said that Marks and Spencer had failed to make it clear enough that the services it was promoting did not belong to Interflora. He said a 'reasonably well-informed and reasonably observant internet user' would have been confused as to which company was behind the adverts.

25.6.4   Intercepting communications

The Regulation of Investigatory Powers Act 2000 makes it illegal for a business to intercept communications without the consent of both the sender and recipient. Permitted interceptions may be allowed under the Telecommunications (Lawful Business Practice) (Interception of Communications) Regulations 2000 (SI 2000/2699). However, even permitted interceptions may fall foul of the Human Rights Act 1998, or the Data Protection Act 1998. See *Copland v United Kingdom*, Application No 62617/00, (2007) 45 EHRR 37.

See also the offences under the Computer Misuse Act 1990 at **25.7**.

25.6.5   The Defamation Act 2013

The Defamation Act 2013 made changes to the operation of defamation laws in the UK which may be relevant for information and comments placed on the Internet. The Act includes a requirement the claimants show that they have suffered serious harm, which for for-profit bodies is restricted to serious financial loss. It also protects website operators that host user-generated content, providing they comply with a procedure to enable the complainant to resolve disputes directly with the author of the material concerned. Finally, it introduces defences of truth, honest opinion, and 'publication on a matter of public interest'.

25.7   COMPUTER CRIME

There have been attempts in the past to use the law of theft and criminal damage in relation to problems related to computers (eg, problems caused by hackers, people who attempt to gain unauthorised access to computer systems). The problems in using the conventional law proved to be immense; what has been stolen, or what has been damaged? The Computer Misuse Act 1990 seeks to avoid such esoteric questions by creating offences that are specific to computers.

25.7.1   Section 1 – unauthorised access, hacking and like activities

Section 1 of the Computer Misuse Act 1990 makes it an offence to obtain unauthorised access to a computer system, as follows:

    (1)   A person is guilty of an offence if—

        (a)   he causes a computer to perform any function with intent to secure access to any program or data held in any computer;

        (b)   the access he intends to secure is unauthorised; and

(c)   he knows at the time when he causes the computer to perform the function that that is the case.

The punishment is a maximum of six months' imprisonment and/or a fine.

25.7.2   Section 2 – the ulterior intent offence

This is committed by a person who secures unauthorised access to a computer system with the intent of using that access to facilitate the commission of a further serious criminal offence. Such offences are those where the sentence is fixed by law (eg, murder), or where a first offender aged over 18 years could be sentenced to five years in jail. For example, a case has been reported in France where access was sought to medical records in order to blackmail sufferers of AIDS. If such facts arose within the UK, they would be capable of giving rise to the s 2 offence.

The offence in s 2 is triable either way. The maximum sentence is five years' imprisonment.

25.7.3   Section 3 – modification of computer material

The act must be intended to impair the operation of a computer, or to prevent or hinder access to any programs or data, or to impair the operation of any program or reliability of the data. Sending out a computer virus would come within s 3, as would deleting or altering data, or indeed adding jocular comments to the Duke of Edinburgh's e-mail (R v Gold [1988] 2 WLR 984, where the prosecution failed under the then law).

The offence in s 3 is triable either way. The maximum sentence is five years' imprisonment.

25.7.4   Jurisdiction

The Computer Misuse Act 1990 introduced the concept of a 'significant link' with one of the UK jurisdictions. In the case of the s 1 or s 3 offences, it is enough that either the offender or the victim was located within the jurisdiction. For the s 2 offence, the court has jurisdiction only if the further act would be an offence in the country where it was intended that it should occur.

25.8   DATA PROTECTION

The Data Protection Act 2018 deals with the law in this area. See **Chapter 27** for more detailed discussion.

The 2018 Act imposes rules for the processing of individuals' personal data by 'controllers' or 'processors' (those processing data on behalf of controllers). 'Processing' includes collecting, storing, altering, use, and disclosing. The Act expects data to be processed using six principles of good practice:

(1)   fairly and lawfully processed;

(2)   processed for specified, explicit and legitimate purposes;

(3)   adequate, relevant and not excessive;

(4)   accurate and up-to-date;

(5)   not kept longer than necessary; and

(6)   processed in a secure way.

Other provisions in the Act (set out in more detail at **27.2.2**) include obligations for consent to be obtained before data is processed, for processing to be limited to what is necessary, and for the data subject to have certain rights over the data such as the right of access, rectification and erasure.

25.9   THE DATABASE RIGHT

As noted in **Chapter 21**, this is a right relating to the keeping of information. The Copyright and Rights in Databases Regulations 1997 (SI 1997/3032) implement Directive 96/9/EC on the Legal Protection of Databases by amending the Copyright Designs and Patents Act 1988 (CDPA 1988).

A 'database' is defined in the CDPA 1988, s 3A(1) (see **21.2**). In practice, a database could, for example, be information on the daily price of stocks and shares, a telephone directory, LexisLibrary or Lawtel. Copyright protection is also afforded to a database specifically as a literary work, although the standard is not only that of originality, but also that it is the 'author's intellectual creation'. To obtain 'database right' protection, only s 3A(1) needs to be met. For copyright protection, both s 3A(1) and (2) must be met.

Whether or not it is protected by copyright, a database also attracts a new database right, which arises automatically. The database right runs for 15 years from the end of the year of completion. It prevents unauthorised use of the database, or a substantial part of it.

As noted in **21.2**, data arrangements have the protection of database right if there is a substantial investment (including any investment, whether of financial, human or technical resources):

(a)   in quality or quantity;

(b)   in obtaining, verifying or presenting the data.

Further points to consider in relation to the database right are as follows.

25.9.1   Qualifications for the database right

There are copyright-style qualification requirements (Copyright and Rights in Databases Regulations 1997, reg 18) based on nationality or corporate seat.

25.9.2   Ownership of the database right

The maker of a database protected by the database right is the person who takes the initiative in obtaining, verifying or presenting the contents of the database and who assumes the risk of investing in that obtaining. (See Copyright and Rights in Databases Regulations 1997, reg 14.)

The maker is the first owner of the database right (reg 15).

25.9.3   Duration of lesser protection

The database right lasts for the longer of 15 years from the end of the calendar year:

(a)   of completion of the database; or

(b)   during which the database was first made available to the public (reg 17).

A 'substantial new investment' (see **25.9**) will 'top up' the right so the period starts again.

25.9.4   Infringement of the database right

Infringement is the extraction or re-utilisation of all or a substantial part of the contents of a database without the consent of the owner (reg 16).

'Extraction' means the permanent or temporary transfer of the contents of a database to another medium by any means, or in any form.

'Re-utilisation' means making those contents available to the public by any means.

'Substantial' is in terms of quality, or quantity or both.

'Substantial part' can include repeated extraction and/or re-utilisation of insubstantial parts (reg 16(2)). This is very important, as it means that copying of small extracts, which would not comprise a qualitatively sufficient copying for copyright infringement purposes, may still comprise a database right infringement, if done often enough.

25.9.5 Exceptions from the database right

Database rights are not infringed (regs 19 and 20):

(a) by fair dealing with a substantial part of a database made available to the public if:

    (i) such dealing is for illustration in teaching or research; and

    (ii) sufficient acknowledgement is given;

(b) generally, by copying or use with the authority of the keeper of a database available for public inspection as a statutory record.

The database right may be licensed or assigned (as can the copyright in the database).

SUMMARY

Developments in information technology come quickly, and they present the greatest test of whether IP laws are adequate and effective. There is no overall body of law called 'information technology law'; instead, we use a range of laws, mainly IP laws, to provide protection for those who produce hardware, software, or distribute their work over the Internet. This chapter has looked at the key issues presented by information technology, and how IP laws may be used to deal with them.

CHAPTER 26

E-COMMERCE

LEARNING OUTCOMES

After reading this chapter you will be able to:

- explain how contracts work when arranged electronically
- identify jurisdictional issues relating to electronic commerce (e-commerce)
- identify IP issues relating to e-commerce
- explain the differences between business and consumer electronic contracts
- explain the liability of ISPs for actions carried out over their networks.

26.1 INTRODUCTION

This chapter deals primarily with the situation in the UK. However, as many rights and obligations derive from EU legislation, there is a great deal of similarity in the rules throughout Europe.

The exponential growth in the commercial use of the Internet in the last decade and a half, the developments in Internet shopping, and the general adaptation to online contracting by commercial parties and the consumer alike, arguably may be the most fundamental change to commercial activity in centuries. But is it such a change? At first sight one might think so, but the reality is that much of this, from the point of view of the lawyer, is a case of adapting existing, well-known principles to suit new fact situations. A good example of this is the way in which encryption and digital signatures have been introduced to give the legal certainty that would otherwise reside in a confidential agreement, signed by the parties, with a pen. That is not to say that this area of law is easy to understand and to apply; it is not, for the simple reason that the pace of technological and commercial developments has caused the courts and legislators to struggle to keep up. What follows is a summary of the main areas of legal issues and recent developments.

The term 'e-commerce' is used here to describe both contracts between business parties (B2B) and those between businesses and consumers (B2C). To arrive at a satisfactory definition of e-commerce, it is probably not necessary to go much further than to say that it covers business transactions in goods and services between remote parties, who communicate with each other by electronic means. Often, there will also be questions about the use of the Internet for advertising, and these are dealt with at **26.5** below. The aim of this chapter is to provide a preliminary understanding of some of the legal aspects of e-commerce for the budding commercial lawyer, and to highlight problem areas.

26.2 THE LEGAL FRAMEWORK

The very real difficulty with e-commerce is that parties can come to agreements without regard to national frontiers or distance; so can the parties simply forget about law and have a fine old time dealing together? Clearly that would never work, because there would be no legal way in which the parties could either enforce the contract or settle disputes. Consequently, all the major trading countries of the world have had to wrestle with the problem of applying legal systems to e-commerce, but there are still very wide differences in the approaches taken under different national legal systems. For the purposes of this chapter, the main focus will be on the harmonised laws of the EU and English domestic law; much of the law derives from the so-called E-commerce Directive, ie Council Directive 2000/31 EC. This is given effect in the UK by the Electronic Commerce (EC Directive) Regulations 2002 (SI 2002/2013) ('the 2002 Regulations') and is discussed in more depth at **26.7**.

While the Directive is generally about the provision of electronic services by Internet Service Providers (ISPs), it can extend out towards most types of commercial provision of electronic information. It can cover, in particular, website selling of goods and services, but the type of e-commerce that is concluded by parties using an exchange of e-mails is generally not affected by it. Nevertheless, by Article 9(1), Member States are required to ensure that national legal systems effectively facilitate the making of valid contracts by electronic means. The particular position of the consumer in a B2C contract is dealt with at **26.7**.

A distinction that should be raised at the outset is between the use of websites and the use of simple communication between parties by electronic means, such as e-mails. Most of the controlling legislation in this area is aimed at the former, by reference to 'information society services' (ISSs), which covers most of the business activity carried out by the use of websites. The general approach followed below is to deal with this distinction as and when required by the particular point being examined.

26.3 FORMATION AND PROOF OF CONTRACT

26.3.1 Offer and acceptance

Although the Internet is supra-national, every contract requires an applicable law before it can be legally analysed. The issues of law and jurisdiction of e-commerce contracts are dealt with at **26.4** below but, for the purposes of this chapter, it is assumed that the contract will be governed by English law. In essence, the law of offer and acceptance in contract, with which you are already familiar, is applied by analogy to e-commerce; the point to remember is that the familiar steps and distinctions have to be looked at in the light of the particular way in which online transactional communications work. Thus:

(a) *Offer or invitation to treat?* This vital distinction applies just as much in e-commerce as when contracting elsewhere; the point of departure comes when one considers that e-commerce might be entered into either by a simple exchange of e-mails, or by using a website. If the matter is transacted by e-mail, the question will be dealt with exactly as with a traditional exchange of letters, ie whether the communication is an expression of willingness to contract on specified terms, made with the intention that it becomes binding as soon as it is accepted by the person to whom it is addressed. If it is anything less than this, it may be an invitation to treat but is not an offer.

With a website, however, the details displayed by the supplier are much more likely to have been designed so as to constitute an invitation to treat. The reason for that is that the customer is required to make the offer, usually establishing his identity and payment assurance, before the seller will enter the contract by acceptance. The statutory assumption in the 2002 Regulations, reg 12, is that the customer's order will usually comprise the contractual offer, the supplier's acknowledgement being the acceptance.

(b)   *Acceptance.* With regard to e-commerce by exchanges of e-mail, a High Court case (*Thomas v BPE Solicitors* [2010] EWHC 306 (Ch)) decided that acceptance by e-mail does not become effective when sent but rather when it is received. This differs from the 'postal rule' which applies to letters (acceptances are valid when posted). Whether acceptance is valid when received outside of office hours seems to be a question which depends on the facts of the situation: in the *Thomas* case, an acceptance which arrived at 6pm on a Friday was held to be valid, but in coming to this conclusion, the judge referred to the fact that the solicitors involved in the transaction were constantly communicating by e-mail and had been operating on the assumption that the deal would be concluded on the Friday in question.

Where the acceptance taking place is by the use of a website in a transaction to which the 2002 Regulations apply, the recipient of a service must have had explained to him by the provider, prior to placing an order, 'the different technical steps to follow to conclude the contract' (reg 9(1)(a)); additionally, 'the order and acknowledgement of receipt will be deemed to be received when the parties to whom they are addressed are able to access them' (reg 11(2)(a)), but note that parties who are non-consumers are free to agree other arrangements. That suggests that acceptance may take place at the earliest time at which the customer can access the supplier's acknowledgement of the order/offer, regardless of whether the customer actually does so. There seems to be no particular reason why the special telex rule in *Entores Ltd v Miles Far East Corporation* [1955] 2 QB 327 should apply to e-commerce transactions.

(c)   *Incorporation of terms.* In general, the same rules are likely to be applied to the incorporation of terms as in other contractual circumstances, including the court's jurisdiction to decide about the 'battle of forms' where standard-form contract terms are involved.

26.3.2   Electronic execution of documents, encryption and security

Most commercial transactions do not require formal execution by signature as a matter of law, but there are circumstances in which a signature may be required, either by the terms of the contract, or by the common law or by statute. The Electronic Signatures Regulations 2002 (SI 2002/318), made in response to Directive 1999/93 EC, constitute the United Kingdom's framework for providing for the supervision and liability of signature-certification service providers, related data protection measures and admissibility into evidence of electronic signatures (see also Pt II of the Electronic Communications Act 2000). Some statutory requirements for a 'signature' and 'writing' can, it seems, be met by e-mail exchanges (see *Mehta v J Pereira Fernandes SA* [2006] EWHC 813 (Ch), although on the facts of the case an e-mail address not contained in the body of the message did not comprise a 'signature' for the purpose of the Statute of Frauds 1677, s 4).

The security aspects of many online contractual arrangements and negotiations can be of extreme importance, and the problem may become even greater where bank details or the availability of a person's electronic signature are concerned. The ingenuity of fraudsters and computer hackers has no limit, and e-commerce would not be possible without the ability of encryption techniques to help safeguard the confidentiality of much of the material that is transmitted electronically. Such technical questions raise no particular legal problems, but you should be aware of the part that encryption plays in the role of certification providers, and in the use of card and bank details in commercial and consumer transactions.

26.4   LAW AND JURISDICTION, CHOICES AND APPLICATION

In many respects, the question of the system of law properly applicable to an e-commerce contract is very similar to what you have already looked at in **Chapter 14, 14.3,** on the Rome

Convention and its replacement, Regulation (EC) No 593/2008 (note that the substance of this Regulation still applies to the UK post-Brexit due to the Contractual Obligations and Non-Contractual Obligations (Amendment etc) (EU Exit) Regulations 2019). Primacy is given to the choice of law of the parties, subject only to the interposition of mandatory rules of law. Special provision is made to protect the positions of consumers and employees, and a most important provision is in place to deal with Internet selling to consumers; under Regulation (EC) 593/2008, Article 6.1(b), where any person exercising his trade or profession directs his activities by any means (including the Internet) at a Member State where the consumer has his habitual residence, the governing law of the contract will be that of the particular Member State.

As regards choice or determination of jurisdiction, this again is dealt with in **Chapter 14**; and the special rules for determining the jurisdiction in consumer cases, particularly the rule on Internet selling to consumers in Member States, are explained at **14.2**.

In situations where, for whatever reason, none of the above provisions applies, the questions of jurisdiction and applicable law will be determined by the rules on jurisdiction and conflict of laws of the forum where the dispute is heard.

26.5 THE APPLICATION OF INTELLECTUAL PROPERTY LAW TO E-COMMERCE

This is a highly complex and technical matter, some of which has already been been discussed, briefly, when looking at the separate types of IP rights in earlier chapters. A summary of the main areas relating to IP disputes is given below.

26.5.1 Domain name disputes

There have probably been more squabbles about the right to use domain names as such, or about IP-related claims that have a domain name angle to them, than about most other areas of e-commerce, so that a brief examination of the problem is called for. In respect of the right to the 'ownership' and use of any particular domain name, without any additional claim that someone's IP rights are infringed, this will sometimes involve a claimant who claims the right to use a domain name or stop others from using it; the defendants will often be the bodies concerned with the allocation or registration of such names, such as ICANN (US-based allocation system) and Nominet (the UK allocation body). These disputes are essentially contractual. Such a matter may be resolved by litigation, as in *Pitman Training Ltd v Nominet UK* [1997] FSR 797, but nowadays the issue will more usually be dealt with by recourse to the dispute resolution mechanism used by the particular allocation body.

Such disputes, often with an international aspect, can involve difficult constitutional law problems at times, as in *Pocket Kings Ltd v Safenames Ltd* [2009] EWHC 2529 (Ch), [2009] All ER (D) 205 (Oct), where the High Court refused to enforce a penal forfeiture order against a domain name, made by the State of Kentucky, USA (the order was made on the basis that the activities promoted by the site were illegal in that state).

The other main problem area with domain names lies in the potential infringement of IP rights, where the domain name is the same as, or close to, a word trade mark which is owned by someone else. These issues are examined below.

26.5.2 Passing off

There are many cases where the use of a domain name allegedly passes off the user's products or services as those of another. The law on this is very much the same as with any other form of passing off. A very clear example is seen in *Phones 4u Ltd and Another v Phone4u.co.uk Internet Ltd* [2006] EWCA Civ 244, where the defendant, having registered the domain name 'Phone4u.co.uk' at a time when a chain of shops owned by the claimant had established a thriving business using the 'Phones 4u' mark, was held to have passed off its products as those of the claimant. From the date of acquisition of the domain name, there could not be any realistic use of the name without deception; to register and use the name of a well-known company as a domain name to draw in custom was fraudulent.

Beyond the mere use of the domain name, the way in which any e-commerce transmission, or website, uses or displays material may constitute a passing off of someone else's good or services, provided that the classic indicia of the tort – reputation, misrepresentation leading to confusion and damage – can be established. Indeed, the very width of the common law tort (relating to 'get up', display and promotional technique, etc, as well as marks) makes passing off a serious possibility in e-commerce.

26.5.3 Trade marks

Again, the potential infringement of a registered trade mark, either in the domain name or in the other transmitted material, arises in the same way as with any other circumstance, by coming within the statutory acts of infringement. You will have seen already (at **14.9**) that there are very many trade mark cases involving the use of websites, so it is not necessary to repeat that material here.

An interesting issue which the courts have had to wrestle with in recent years, however, is whether keyword advertising is a trade mark infringement. Search engines adopted a practice of selling trademarked words and phrases to competitors of the trade mark owner. The mark owners were unhappy because they believed it led to confusion among consumers. When consumers search for keywords that fall under that trade mark, they see those words on websites that do not relate to the actual brand. Infringement via keyword advertising only occurs when the search engine links the actual words within a trade mark to a competitor.

An important ECJ case is *L'Oréal SA v eBay International AG* (Case C-324/09) (2011), which held that the operator of an online marketplace could be liable for the unlawful sale on its website of goods in breach of the rights of a trade mark proprietor, even though it had not played an active role in promoting such sales, if it was aware of facts on the basis of which a diligent economic operator should have realised that the offers for sale were unlawful and it failed to act promptly to remove the data or disable access to them. This awareness and failure to act raises the liability of the online marketplace above and beyond that of an ISP.

26.5.4 Copyright

This is a vast topic, and a couple of paragraphs can do no more than skim over its surface; nevertheless, you should be aware of the enormous potential for problems from this direction. Almost everything that ever gets onto a website or into an electronic transmission has some sort of copyright in it, or would have were the material not out of its copyright period. The rules for the substantive existence and infringement of copyrights of different types have been explored in **Chapter 20**; in particular, you will have realised that the simple downloading of material by a computer will constitute a copying which, if it is not licensed by the owner of the right, may comprise an infringing act. You will also know that there are many defences to copying, such as 'fair use' for various purposes, as well as transient copying as part of a technological process under s 28A of the CDPA 1988.

The most widespread defence available to the users of websites is that they use the site under the licence of the copyright owner, but that can avail them nothing where the person who put the material on the site did not own the copyright in it in the first place – he might have infringed the copyright and, theoretically, the person downloading it might become a secondary infringer (and, if he passes it on, a primary infringer). That has led to enormous problems involving 'framing' (placing material on a website so that it is displayed on a different site), 'deep linking' (linking one site to the inside pages on another site) and 'peer to peer/information/file sharing' sites.

All sorts of counter-measures have been tried to deal with unauthorised use of copyright material, but the one potent extension of legal powers in this area is probably the Copyright and Related Rights Regulations 2003 (SI 2003/2498), which aim to prevent the circumvention of technological measures which are in place to protect the copyright (and other IP rights such as the database right, etc), where copyright works are made available to the public by electronic means. This has led, inter alia, to the amendment of s 296 and the insertion of ss 296ZA–296ZG of the CDPA 1988. Nevertheless, copyright issues are likely to provide the greatest IP challenge to the future development of the information society, the Internet and e-commerce; time alone will tell whether there is any achievable and practical answer. In the meantime, the courts and enforcement authorities wrestle with the problem using the tools currently available to them, on a case-by-case basis.

26.6 BUSINESS TO BUSINESS E-COMMERCE

As explained at **26.1** above, most of the legislation in this area is aimed at the use of websites by consumers to obtain goods and services, not two businesses arranging a contract by e-mail, except in one crucial respect – almost all of this legislation is based upon the European Union requirement for a level playing field in respect of the conduct of business and commerce. Vital to that end are the requirements for fair consumer practice, for freedom of movement of goods and services, for rights of establishment and for fair competition practices. It would therefore be a great mistake to assume that the use of e-commerce would somehow release the parties from any of these requirements, if the contract could potentially generate any EU Member State effects at all. When one adds in the fact that electronic communications leave an indelible trail for the skilled investigator to follow (who may have impressive powers of investigation and enforcement where these EU or domestic matters are involved), it becomes clear that the apparent freedom from legislation is a dangerous trap for the unwary. The speed with which transactions can be entered into electronically only adds to the danger. The parties to a B2B arrangement, set up without the use of a public access website, should take very great care about the content and legal effect of all of their electronic communications.

Some of the likely risks for B2B arrangements come from competition law (dangers of 'concerted practices' arising out of frequent communications, even if there are no express agreements, for Article 101 TFEU purposes); from impermissible use of confidential information, or copyright or other protected material in e-mails or attachments; and from failing to deal with important points (such as law or jurisdiction points, or incorporation of terms) given the pressure, as regards pace and time, to enter a deal. If B2B contracts are entered into using a website, consideration has to be given to whether there is any way that one party (who must be a natural person) might be seen as acting as a 'consumer' in the transaction; although it will be a rare occurrence, that is not an impossibility, and it could make a great deal of difference as to statutory rules governing the contract (see **26.7** below).

26.7 BUSINESS TO CONSUMER E-COMMERCE

Here, the emphasis moves to the consumer (in an extended sense) protection requirements of European and domestic law. This section is premised on the assumption that the consumer purchase of goods and/or services is via a website. The three main areas of statutory regulation that should be considered are set out in **26.7.1** to **26.7.3** below.

26.7.1 The Electronic Commerce (EC Directive) Regulations 2002

The 2002 Regulations were enacted, in response to the E-commerce Directive, to regulate the provision of goods, services and information to consumers by electronic means by 'information society service providers' (ISSPs). This is mainly aimed at the Internet, although it can extend to other means of electronic communication. The definition of an ISS, given in reg 2 (see the **Appendix** to this work), is:

> any service normally provided for remuneration, at a distance, by means of electronic equipment for the processing ... and storage of data, and at the individual request of the recipient of the service.

'Consumer' is defined as 'any natural person who is acting for purposes other than his trade, business or profession'. 'Recipient of the service' extends, by contrast, to 'any person who, *for professional ends or otherwise*, uses an information society service, in particular for the purposes of seeking information or making it accessible'(emphasis added). You will see, from this last definition, that the reach of the 2002 Regulations goes beyond mere consumer protection.

Regulation 6 (see **Appendix**) governs the detailed information that must be provided by the ISSP. Regulation 6(1) deals with the requirement for transparency regarding the identity, location and contact details of the ISSP, and other professional and regulatory information, including the ISSP's VAT identification number (reg 6(1)(g)). Regulation 6(2) requires, vitally, that where an ISS refers to prices, they must be indicated clearly, unambiguously and indicate, in particular, whether they are inclusive of tax and delivery costs.

Regulation 7 deals with the required attributes and content of 'commercial communications'. A commercial communication is defined in reg 2 as:

> a communication, in any form, designed to promote, directly or indirectly, the goods, services or image of any person pursuing a commercial, industrial or craft activity or exercising a regulated profession ...

This is a very wide definition indeed, clearly extending to advertising. Where such a communication is made, it must be identifiable as such, it must identify the person on whose behalf it is made, it must clearly identify any promotional offer as such, and it must ensure that any conditions are made accessible and are clear and unambiguous (reg 7(a)–(d)).

Regulations 9 and 11 are concerned with the provision of information and the placing of the order where a contract is to be concluded by electronic means (see **Appendix**). Where a consumer is involved, reg 9 requires that, *prior* to the placing of an order, certain information that is vital to the interests of the consumer must be provided in a clear and unambiguous form by the ISSP. Of fundamental importance, where the ISSP provides terms and conditions applicable to the contract, it must make these available to the service recipient in a way that allows for their storage and reproduction (reg 9(3)); this last provision is mandatory, even if the contract is concluded by individual e-mail exchange, whereas the other requirements of reg 9 do not apply in such non-website contracting situations. Regulation 11 deals with the requirements where an order is placed by 'technological means' (not defined); the ISSP must acknowledge receipt to the service recipient, without undue delay and by electronic means.

Non-compliance with the requirements of the 2002 Regulations is actionable at the instance of enforcement authorities (which may involve civil or criminal law proceedings) and at the instance of ISS recipients, whether parties to a contract covered by the 2002 Regulations or not. The principal statutory remedies are:

(a)   a claim for damages for breach of statutory duty (reg 13);

(b)   a court order to require the supply of contract terms or conditions to comply with reg 9(3) (reg 14);

(c)   the right to apply to the court for rescission, if the ISSP does not provide the means for correcting input errors required by reg 11(1)(b) (reg 15);

(d)   protection of the right of any person to seek court relief to stop infringement of any rights (reg 20).

26.7.2   The Consumer Contracts (Information, Cancellation and Additional Charges) Regulations 2013

These Regulations (SI 2013/3134) implement the EU Consumer Rights Directive. They came into force on 13 June 2014 and create new consumer protection rules relating to distance selling and the supply of digital content.

Under these rules, goods bought over the Internet can be cancelled during a minimum 14-day period from receipt. If cancellation occurs, the selling business must issue a refund 'without undue delay' including basic delivery charges it had originally imposed. Before sale, traders are obliged to provide consumers with a clear and comprehensible list of information, including:

- a description of the main characteristics of the product
- the name, address and phone number of their business
- the total price
- payment and delivery arrangements
- details of 'the conditions, time limit and procedures' that apply to cancellations.

The Regulations make specific provision for digital downloads. Retailers must not supply digital content during the 14-day cooling-off period unless the consumer has given specific consent. If he has, once the download starts he will lose his right to cancel.

Physical delivery of goods must be made under the Regulations within any time frame agreed. If none is agreed, supply must be made 'without undue delay' and at the very latest within 30 days. The goods are at the seller's risk until delivered.

Finally, the Regulations prohibit high rate phone charges when a consumer phones to discuss his order – a basic rate number must be supplied.

26.7.3   The Privacy and Electronic Communications (EC Directive) Regulations 2003

The Privacy and Electronic Communications (EC Directive) Regulations 2003 (SI 2003/2426) ('the 2003 Regulations') came into being as a result of Directive 2002/58/EC. They provide a specialised and focused regime of data protection in the realm of electronic communications, which are, of course, essential to the functioning of e-commerce. The 2003 Regulations have wider application than just to e-commerce, in that many of the provisions concern both Internet use and telephone network applications. The main provisions, for present purposes are regs 4–8 and 22–23.

Regulation 4 provides that nothing in the 2003 Regulations relieves a person of obligations under the Data Protection Act 1998 in respect of personal data. Really, the only concern, for present purposes, is with personal data, which is discussed at **27.2.1**. A good deal of the Act is concerned with the security and regulation of public electronic communications, which is beyond the direct relevance of this chapter.

Regulation 5 requires the provider of a public electronic communications service and the provider of any communications network by means of which that service is provided, between them to take appropriate measures to safeguard the security of that service.

Regulation 6 deals with confidentiality of information, and prevents the accessing or storing of information from a subscriber's or user's computer terminal, except where that person is told about the purpose for the access or storage and is given the opportunity to refuse access or storage. This is the basis of the famous 'cookie' box on websites. Regulation 7 deals with the necessary limitations on 'traffic data', the normal electronic nuts and bolts that make the whole electronic communication transmission work. These data must be erased or modified so they cease to be 'personal' data, when no longer required for transmission purposes,

unless the subscriber has given permission for their retention for the time necessary for specific marketing or 'value-adding' purposes. Regulation 8 further expands upon the scope of activities for which such permission may be sought, but provides the usual saving for provision of traffic data to competent authorities acting under statutory powers, or under any provision relating to the settlement of disputes (reg 8(4)).

Regulations 22 and 23 deal with transmission of unsolicited communications and for direct marketing, where the identity or address of the sender is concealed. They really are dealing with spam/junk. In both cases, the practices are forbidden by the Regulations, except that there is a provision in reg 22(3) which allows transmissions, for direct marketing purposes, of unsolicited communications where the recipient has 'opted in' to such communications.

An amendment was made to the 2003 Regulations on 26 May 2011 regarding the use of cookies on webpages. A cookie is a small piece of data sent from a website and stored in a user's web browser while a user is browsing a website. When the user browses the same website in the future, the data stored in the cookie may be retrieved by the website to notify the website of the user's previous activity. Cookies were designed to be a reliable mechanism for websites to remember the state of the website or the activity the user had undertaken in the past. This might include clicking particular buttons, logging in, or a record of which pages were visited by the user even months or years ago.

Before the change, the Regulations stated that cookies might be stored on a user's machine only if the user was able to turn them off and provided it was explained somewhere on the site what the cookies did. Following the amendment, cookies may be stored only if the user has given consent. (You may have noticed pop-ups appearing on screen the first time you visit a site, to ask you if you consent to cookies being stored on your computer.)

26.8 PAYMENT ASPECTS OF E-COMMERCE TRANSACTIONS

Again, it is necessary to draw distinctions between B2B e-commerce, using e-mails etc, and the use of website selling, the latter having far more B2C use. With B2B e-commerce, the risk of fraud (which is usually in obtaining something, without any intention of paying for it) can often be minimised where the supplier is in a strong enough bargaining position to obtain independent credit guarantees or money 'up front'. Where the supplier is not in such a strong position, there are considerable risks, but some of these might be reduced, at the supplier's expense, by credit insurance.

With B2C transactions, using websites, the situation can be better for the supplier, and particularly so for the consumer. A great deal of electronic selling involves credit card payment, and the supplier is largely safeguarded against fraudulent customers by the fact that the cost of any card fraud falls back on the credit supplier, the supplier's position being enhanced, in most cases, by the requirement that the credit/payment is available before any performance is made. The risk for a consumer of a fraudulent supplier trying to obtain either money or the customer's details is, nevertheless, quite high. A fair measure of protection for loss of money is provided by the Consumer Credit Act 1974 (CCA 1974), ss 83 and 84, to limit losses to £50 prior to notification to the bank that the card is lost, stolen or being misused. Further protection is given by the Distance Selling Regulations 2000, reg 21, which provides that consumers can cancel a payment where fraudulent use is made of credit cards in contracts covered by the Distance Selling Regulations; the consumer is then entitled to be re-credited, or to have money returned to him. The burden is on the card issuer to show that any use of the card was authorised by the card holder (reg 21(3)). Regulation 21 does not apply to any contract falling within s 83 of CCA 1974; these two mutually-exclusive provisions, between them, provide quite comprehensive protection to the consumer.

26.9 LIABILITIES OF ISPs AND OTHERS

You will have already come across many instances of liability during your reading of this chapter, and it will perhaps help if a short summary of the position is offered. This is a rapidly developing field, and the courts will be likely to have to react to new techniques and novel legal questions with some rapidity over the coming years.

26.9.1 The position with contracts arranged by exchange of electronic mail

Normally, the situation here is as with any paper or oral contract: provided the parties have restricted their communications to what was necessary for the contract, the only liabilities to arise will usually be as between the parties. It would still be possible for liability to third parties to arise, under normal legal principles, if the arrangement created any tort (such as publishing defamatory statements, procuring breaches of contract or other economic torts, or breaches of trust, etc). Nevertheless, potential third-party liability is probably much less than where widely accessible websites are concerned.

26.9.2 The position with website e-commerce

Here, the situation is very different: the whole idea of a person being provided with virtually free access to a site from which links and connections may lead to an almost unlimited amount of data, belonging to and referring to all sorts of legal entities, is truly a modern Pandora's box. The potential for legal liability to arise is, frankly, immense, particularly if one considers the further possibilities of defamation, IP infringements etc, associated with many sites.

The position of the ISP's liability has been discussed already in various contexts; it might be summed up by saying that whatever it provides or facilitates is designed to be part of the information society, and there is no particular reason why it should not be responsible for whatever harms ensue to others, within the limits permissible under whatever laws are in place at the particular time. The material discussed at **26.7.1**, concerning the E-commerce Directive and the 2002 Regulations, shows that the liability of the ISP can be very wide, but that we should be in a better position to understand the matter, and the position with regard to statutory hosting defences, once the ECJ has delivered rulings and guidance on the cases before it at the moment. Probably the greatest immediate problems arise from the use of link/keyword practices (although the ECJ has decided that Google cannot be held liable for trade mark infringements of advertisers on its webpages that select trade mark keywords without permission of the trade mark owner), and from the questions concerning accessory liability for torts and other wrongs committed by service users using interactive sites.

The position between the ISP and its own users is normally contractual, so that is probably easier to analyse than third-party liability; it will simply depend upon the terms of the contract between the parties, subject to the power of the governing legislation to affect or to invalidate those terms, including the effects of UCTA 1977.

26.10 CONCLUSION

As you will have seen, a body of law and practice has had to be created and applied with completely unprecedented rapidity, to deal with the growth of the information society and e-commerce. There are probably many more questions still to be asked and answered than have already been considered by the legislators and the courts, but the general framework of workable legal systems for e-commerce is discernible on both sides of the Atlantic. The real challenge will come as the giant nations of Asia begin to make their influence and impact felt – upon commerce generally, upon e-commerce in particular, and upon the world of the commercial lawyer. The emphasis is clearly becoming one of globalisation, so that the budding commercial lawyer is well advised to keep abreast of the information available from sources relevant to the growth in world trade. Some useful source locations are given below:

- International Chamber of Commerce – www.iccwbo.org
- ICANN (Internet Corporation for Assigned Names and Numbers) – www.icann.com
- Nominet UK – www.nominet.org.uk
- World Intellectual Property organisation – www.wipo.org
- World Trade Organisation – www.wto.org

SUMMARY

Over the last 20 years, the way in which we do business has changed. More and more people conclude their business by electronic means. Just as laws have had to keep pace with electronic issues generally, laws have had to be developed – and adapted where appropriate – to deal with the conclusion of contracts using webpages and e-mail. This chapter has examined the key issues of e-commerce, and has explained which laws are applicable to it.

CHAPTER 27

DATA PROTECTION AND FREEDOM OF INFORMATION

LEARNING OUTCOMES

After reading this chapter you will be able to:

- explain the key highlights of data protection legislation
- identify data controllers
- apply data protection law to decide what obligations are imposed on those who deal with data
- explain the consequences for failure to comply with data protection obligations, and the remedies which may be sought by those whose data are misused
- identify the key issues relating to freedom of information.

27.1 INTRODUCTION

This chapter deals with the position in the UK, but due to harmonisation the rules throughout the EU are similar.

Data about persons or businesses has always been a valuable and sensitive commodity, but in the last 30 years or so, the exponential growth and availability of computer systems to assemble, arrange and transfer data have posed a challenge for legal systems worldwide. The demand for such data is insatiable, and to allow unrestricted holding of, and access to, it would rapidly lead to chaos and criminality. The only applicable English law, prior to the recent information explosion, worked on the basis of the protection of confidence (see **Chapter 24**), and there was little statutory control of data beyond that. That case law has the broad effect of treating certain confidential information as being within the reach and protection of the equitable jurisdiction. This was completely inadequate to deal with the huge proliferation of potentially accessible databases, containing mundane but highly valuable information. After major investigations and various government reports, coupled with the need to have legal protections compatible with those of the rest of the EU, the Data Protection Act 1984 was enacted. This Act was regulatory in effect and it could not cover paper-based systems; it set out certain guiding principles and its enforcement was largely in the hands of a Data Protection Registrar, with some compensation available for affected individuals. Its effect was to make the handling of personal information subject to controls which had not existed before.

After the 1984 Act came the Data Protection Act 1998, which was enacted pursuant to the European Data Protection Directive of 1995 (95/46/EC). The aim of the Directive (and thus the Act) was to give no more protection to data processing than was commensurate with a balance between the rights of natural persons and the maintenance of a free market within the EU, by harmonising national legal rules. The Directive was replaced by the General Data Protection Regulation (GDPR) in 2018. The GDPR was designed to reshape the way in which data is used across Europe, with a greater emphasis on the privacy of the individual.

The GDPR, as with all EU Regulations, applies across Europe; however, it allows Member States limited opportunities to make provision for how it applies in their countries. It is therefore backed up in most Member States by national legislation. In the UK, this comes in the form of the Data Protection Act 2018. This 1998 Act has one eye on Brexit (which at the time of writing is being negotiated) as, to a large extent, it brings the GDPR into UK legislation in a way which would not be necessary were we to remain part of the EU (as we would be subject to the GDPR itself). It also goes beyond the GDPR, however, as it applies a broadly equivalent regime to certain types of data processing to which the GDPR does not apply.

27.1.1 Data Protection Act (DPA) 2018

The aim of the GDPR (and thus the 2018 Act) is to protect the public from privacy and data breaches in an increasingly data-driven world. The level of data use in 2018 is way above its use in 1998, and so the legislation needed to be modernised to face the challenge which the increase in use poses.

The 2018 Act is split into seven parts:

* Part 1: Preliminary issues.
* Part 2: General processing. It is this part that we will centre on in this chapter as it covers the ways in which individuals' data are processed by commercial entities.
* Part 3: Law enforcement processing. Whilst important, this is beyond the scope of this book.
* Part 4: Intelligence services processing. Again this is beyond the scope of this book.
* Part 5: The Information Commissioner. See below for more on this.
* Part 6: Enforcement. See below for more on this.
* Part 7: Supplementary issues.

27.1.2 Freedom of Information Act (FOIA) 2000

The emergence of data protection legislation has been mainly about protecting the individual's expectation to the privacy of personal data. Over the same period of time, another public expectation has arisen: that of open government and freedom of information about the acts of public authorities. Always a contentious matter, the 'right to know' was not particularly European in origin but has developed more in the common law nations of the world over the last half century. English public law and criminal law show many cases in which the relationship between public access to information and the privacy of the decision-making process is hard to discern with clarity. There was a clear public demand and need for more to be done. Following a period from 1994 during which the Government used a voluntary 'Code of Practice on Public Access to Government Information' (overseen by the Parliamentary Ombudsman), the FOIA 2000 was passed.

The big difference between the DPA 2018 and the FOIA 2000 is that the former deals with the private protection of personal data, whereas the latter is concerned with public access to government information. Nevertheless, there can be overlap because public authorities, for FOIA 2000 purposes, may also be controllers for the purpose of the DPA 2018. However, detailed discussion of that overlap is beyond the scope of this book. This chapter deals first with data protection and then with freedom of information.

27.2 OVERVIEW AND SCOPE OF THE DPA 2018

As mentioned above, for the purposes of this chapter we will concentrate on the provisions of the DPA 2018 as they affect the relationship between the individual and those who process our personal data in the commercial world. In this regard the effects of the DPA 2018 fall into two categories. The first is to allow individuals access to information held about them, for example the information held about people by credit reference agencies. This may be inaccurate and a person would probably want to correct such inaccuracies. The second effect is to protect information about individuals from being disclosed improperly. So, if you give your bank or gas supplier certain information, you might not want them to disclose that information to another business, for example an insurance company, without your consent. Such information is very valuable commercially, and it should not be available for sale without your consent.

To understand the workings of the 2018 Act, it is necessary first to look at some definitions which are closely interdependent, and then to examine the principles of good practice (see **27.2.2**).

27.2.1 The definitions of 'controller', 'processor' 'personal data' and 'processing'

'Controller' means the natural or legal person, public authority, agency or other body which, alone or jointly with others, determines the purposes and means of the processing of personal data.

'Processor' means a natural or legal person, public authority, agency or other body which processes personal data on behalf of the controller.

'Personal data' means any information relating to an identified or identifiable living individual.

'Processing', in relation to information, means an operation or set of operations which is performed on information, or on sets of information, such as—

(a)   collection, recording, organisation, structuring or storage,

(b)   adaptation or alteration,

(c)   retrieval, consultation or use,

(d)   disclosure by transmission, dissemination or otherwise making available,

(e)   alignment or combination, or

(f)   restriction, erasure or destruction.

So, it is fairly easy to see the general scheme of the 2018 Act from the connection of these interpretative definitions; the controller becomes responsible to the individual from the first moment of dealing with any personal data that could identify the individual, even if the data is processed by its processor.

27.2.2 The six principles of good practice

Anyone processing personal information must comply with six enforceable principles of good information handling practice. These principles, which are taken from the GDPR, state that data must be:

(1)   fairly and lawfully processed;

(2)   processed for specified, explicit and legitimate purposes;

(3)   adequate, relevant and not excessive;

(4)   accurate and up-to-date;

(5)   not kept longer than necessary; and

(6)   processed in a secure way.

Processing will be lawful only if and to the extent that one of the following applies (GDPR, Article 6):

(a)   the data subject has given consent to the processing of his or her personal data for one or more specific purposes;

(b)   processing is necessary for the performance of a contract to which the data subject is party or in order to take steps at the request of the data subject prior to entering into a contract;

(c)   processing is necessary for compliance with a legal obligation to which the controller is subject;

(d)   processing is necessary in order to protect the vital interests of the data subject or of another natural person;

(e)   processing is necessary for the performance of a task carried out in the public interest or in the exercise of official authority vested in the controller;

(f)   processing is necessary for the purposes of the legitimate interests pursued by the controller or by a third party, except where such interests are overridden by the interests or fundamental rights and freedoms of the data subject which require protection of personal data, in particular where the data subject is a child.

Where processing is based on consent, the controller must be able to demonstrate that the data subject has consented to the processing of his or her personal data. You may remember that in the run-up to the introduction of the DPA 2018, many traders believed that the best way to establish this was to email previous customers whom they wished to continue to contact with sales offers, etc and either ask for express permission to keep the individual on their mailing list or point out that they believed they did have permission from previous correspondence (with an opt-out option being included in the email for future correspondence).

It is important to appreciate that individuals may withdraw their consent at any time, and it must be as easy to withdraw consent as to give it in the first place. This is an attempt to place the individual more in control of the data about them which is processed.

Special rules regarding consent apply to children and 'information society services', ie online services or shopping. Consent of a child will only be valid where the child is 13 and above. Below this, the consent of the holder of parental responsibility for the child is required. It should be noted that in the GDPR the relevant age is 16, but it allows Member States to reduce this to 13 (post-Brexit of course the DPA 2018 could be amended to apply a lower age if Parliament wished).

27.2.3   Special categories of personal data

There are categories of personal data, the processing of which are prohibited due to their sensitive nature. Data concerning racial or ethnic origin, political opinions, religious or philosophical beliefs, trade union membership, and the processing of genetic data, biometric data for the purpose of uniquely identifying a natural person, data concerning health or data concerning a natural person's sex life or sexual orientation may not be processed. However, exceptions include (inter alia):

•   consent having been obtained;

•   necessary processing in the field of employment and social security in so far as it is lawful;

•   processing is necessary to protect the vital interests of the data subject;

•   processing involves data manifestly made public by the data subject;

•   processing is necessary for reasons of substantial public interest (where proportionate).

27.3 THE RIGHTS OF THE DATA SUBJECT UNDER THE DPA 2018

Again, in the field of commerce, the DPA 2018 largely adheres to the provisions of the GDPR in terms of the rights of the data subject. Therefore, in the discussion below, reference has been made where appropriate to the relevant articles of the GDPR which are applied via Part 2, Chapter 2 of the DPA 2018.

There are eight rights which data subjects have under Chapter 3 of the GDPR:

(1) *The right to be informed.* Individuals have the right to be informed about the collection and use of their personal data. At the time the data is collected, the individual must be provided with information including the purpose for processing it, the retention period for it, and who it will be shared with. If information on an individual is obtained from another source, the controller/processor must provide the individual with privacy information within a maximum of a month.

(2) *The right of access.* Individuals have a right to access their personal data, and this request may be made verbally or in writing. Requests must be responded to within a month, and in most cases no fee can be charged.

(3) *The right to rectification.* An individual may make a request either verbally or in writing for inaccurate information about them to be amended, or completed if it is incomplete. Again requests must be responded to within a month.

(4) *The right to erasure.* This has commonly become known as the right to be forgotten. A request can be made (again verbally or in writing) for data to be deleted. The right is not absolute and only applies in certain circumstances. It has come to the public's attention recently as Google now has a form which can be completed to have data, which would ordinarily be revealed on a Google search about an individual, removed.

(5) *The right to restrict processing.* In some circumstances the individual has the right to restrict the processing of information about them. This is possible where the accuracy of the data is contested (the restriction being to allow a period for the data to be verified), the processing is unlawful, the controller no longer needs the data but it is required by the individual to use in legal claims, or the individual has objected to processing pending the verification of whether the legitimate grounds of the controller override those of the individual.

(6) *The right to data portability.* This right allows individuals to obtain and reuse their data for their own purposes across different services. This allows them to take advantage of applications and services that can use this data to find them a better deal, etc.

(7) *The right to object.* Individuals have the right to object to the processing of their data in certain circumstances, such as for direct marketing. Individuals must be told of their right to object. You may be aware of this: when ordering goods or services online, it is now usual to be asked whether you consent to your data being used for, eg, marketing.

(8) *Rights in relation to automated decision-making and profiling.* An individual has the right not to be subject to a decision based solely on automated processing, including profiling. This does not apply if the decision is necessary for entering into or performing a contract between the individual and controller, is lawful, or is based on the individual's explicit consent.

27.4 THE OBLIGATIONS OF THE DATA CONTROLLER AND PROCESSOR

As we saw at **27.2.2**, data controllers must abide by the data protection principles. The two principles of most concern in regard to disclosure of personal data are the first two, namely that data must be fairly and lawfully processed, and processed for legitimate purposes. In addition, the controller must implement appropriate technical and organisational measures to ensure and to be able to demonstrate that processing is performed in accordance with the GDPR (GDPR, Article 24). This obligation essentially requires a data controller to be able to show that its systems are robust and demonstrably able to comply with the principles. Controllers need to have systems which ensure that only personal data which is necessary for each specific purpose of the processing is processed. These systems must control the amount of personal data collected, the extent of the processing, the period of storage and its accessibility. There are recommendations in the GDPR for national codes of conduct and certification schemes to encourage best practice in the handling of data.

The GDPR specifically envisages controllers using processors, who carry out processing on behalf of the controller. According to Article 28, the controller shall use only processors who provide sufficient guarantees to implement appropriate technical and organisational measures that will meet the demands of the GDPR. The GDPR is very clear that the processor should not process data except on the instructions of the controller (unless the law directs otherwise).

The controller, or its processor, must keep accurate records (according to GDPR, Article 30) covering (inter alia):

(a)   the purposes of the processing;

(b)   a description of the categories of data subjects and of the categories of personal data;

(c)   the categories of recipients to whom the personal data has been or will be disclosed, including recipients in third countries or international organisations;

(d)   where applicable, transfers of personal data to a third country or an international organisation, including the identification of that third country or international organisation and the documentation of suitable safeguards;

(e)   where possible, the envisaged time limits for erasure of the different categories of data.

One of the key reasons for the creation of the GDPR was a desire to increase the security of the handling of data, following some high-profile examples of data breaches by large retailers where credit card details of thousands of customers were accessed illegally, or even put on websites by mistake. Article 32 of the GDPR requires the controller and processor to implement appropriate technical and organisational measures to ensure a level of security appropriate to the risk. This may include: the pseudonymisation and encryption of personal data; the ability to ensure the ongoing confidentiality, integrity, availability and resilience of processing systems and services; the ability to restore the availability and access to personal data in a timely manner in the event of a physical or technical incident; and a process for regularly testing, assessing and evaluating the effectiveness of technical and organisational measures for ensuring the security of the processing. Risks which should be envisaged include accidental or unlawful destruction and unauthorised disclosure of, or access to, the data.

In the event of a data breach, the controller must within 72 hours notify the national supervisory authority, unless the breach is unlikely to result in a risk to the rights of the individuals whose data is held. This notification must identify the nature of the breach, the approximate number of individuals affected, the likely consequences, and the measures taken or proposed to be taken to remedy (if possible) the situation. When the personal data breach is likely to result in a high risk to the rights and freedoms of natural persons, the controller must communicate the personal data breach to the data subject without undue delay. As an example, if a person's credit card details had been accidentally disclosed or unlawfully accessed, the controller should notify both the supervisory authority and also the individuals concerned. This would enable the individuals to take action such as suspending their credit cards, hopefully before they are illegally used.

27.5 TRANSFERS OF PERSONAL DATA TO THIRD COUNTRIES OR INTERNATIONAL ORGANISATIONS

Chapter 5 of the GDPR deals with transfers outside of the EU or to international organisations. For such a transfer to take place by the controller, the rules in the Chapter must be adhered to.

The first rule is that such a transfer can only take place to third countries or international organisations which are approved by the UK Information Commissioner as having an adequate level of protection. Following Brexit, the UK will of course be a 'third country' and so the UK Government is, where possible, incorporating the GDPR into national law via the DPA 2018 to ensure that we are recognised as having adequate levels of protection.

When assessing whether a country or organisation has an adequate level of protection, the following elements (inter alia) may be taken into account:

(a)   the rule of law, respect for human rights and fundamental freedoms, relevant legislation, both general and sectoral, including that concerning public security, defence, national security and criminal law and the access of public authorities to personal data, as well as the implementation of such legislation, data protection rules, professional rules and security measures, including rules for the onward transfer of personal data to another third country or international organisation which are complied with in that country or international organisation;

(b)   the existence and effective functioning of one or more independent supervisory authorities in the third country or to which an international organisation is subject, with responsibility for ensuring and enforcing compliance with the data protection rules;

(c)   the international commitments the third country or international organisation concerned has entered into, or other obligations arising from legally binding conventions or instruments as well as from its participation in multilateral or regional systems, in particular in relation to the protection of personal data.

If the EU Commission decides that a country or organisation should be recognised as having an adequate level of protection, it can pass an implementing act, which will provide a mechanism for review every four years. If such an act is passed, data controllers are free to transfer data to those countries or international organisations provided that all other obligations in the GDPR are complied with. In the absence of such an act, the controller may still transfer the data but only if the controller (or its processor) has provided adequate safeguards, and on condition that enforceable data subject rights and effective legal remedies for data subjects are available.

27.6   ENFORCEMENT, LIABILITY AND PENALTIES

The Information Commissioner may issue to controllers or processors an 'information notice', which requires them to provide such information as the Commissioner may reasonably require for the purposes of carrying out the Commissioner's functions. This notice may request such information as the Commissioner may need to decide whether a breach of the DPA 2018 has occurred. If, on the application of the Commissioner, a court decides that a person has failed to comply with an information notice, the court may make an order requiring the person to supply the information required in the information notice.

The Information Commissioner may also (or subsequently) issue an 'assessment notice' which requires a controller or processor to permit the Commissioner to carry out an assessment of whether either of them has complied with the DPA 2018 (and, consequently, the GDPR). An assessment notice may require the controller or processor to do any of the following (DPA 2018, s 146(2)):

(a)   permit the Commissioner to enter specified premises;

(b)   direct the Commissioner to documents on the premises that are of a specified description;

(c)   assist the Commissioner to view information of a specified description that is capable of being viewed using equipment on the premises;

(d)   comply with a request from the Commissioner for a copy (in such form as may be requested) of—

      (i)   the documents to which the Commissioner is directed;

      (ii)   the information which the Commissioner is assisted to view;

(e)   direct the Commissioner to equipment or other material on the premises which is of a specified description;

(f)   permit the Commissioner to inspect or examine the documents, information, equipment or material to which the Commissioner is directed or which the Commissioner is assisted to view;

(g)   provide the Commissioner with an explanation of such documents, information, equipment or material;

(h)   permit the Commissioner to observe the processing of personal data that takes place on the premises;

(i)   make available for interview by the Commissioner a specified number of people of a specified description who process personal data on behalf of the controller, not exceeding the number who are willing to be interviewed.

Failure to comply with an information notice or assessment notice may lead to the Information Commissioner issuing an 'enforcement notice', failure to comply with which may lead to a 'penalty notice', which requires the controller or processor to pay a sum (as discussed below) to the Information Commissioner. Penalty notices may also be issued for any breach of any of the obligations imposed on controllers or processors by the DPA 2018.

When considering whether to issue a penalty notice, and, if so, when considering what level of penalty to impose, the Information Commissioner must bear in mind the following matters (DPA 2018, s 155(3)):

(a)   the nature, gravity and duration of the failure;

(b)   the intentional or negligent character of the failure;

(c)   any action taken by the controller or processor to mitigate the damage or distress suffered by data subjects;

(d)   the degree of responsibility of the controller or processor;

(e)   any relevant previous failures by the controller or processor;

(f)   the degree of co-operation with the Commissioner, in order to remedy the failure and mitigate the possible adverse effects of the failure;

(g)   the categories of personal data affected by the failure;

(h)   the manner in which the infringement became known to the Commissioner, including whether, and if so to what extent, the controller or processor notified the Commissioner of the failure;

(i)   the extent to which the controller or processor has complied with previous enforcement notices or penalty notices;

(j)   adherence to approved codes of conduct or certification mechanisms;

(k)   any other aggravating or mitigating factor applicable to the case, including financial benefits gained, or losses avoided, as a result of the failure (whether directly or indirectly);

(l)   whether the penalty would be effective, proportionate and dissuasive.

The maximum fine under the DPA 1998 was £500,000 for serious breaches. Under the GDPR and consequently under the DPA 2018, the maximum fine is €20 million, or 4% of annual global turnover, whichever is the highest. This significant increase in the level of fine reflects the perceived increase in importance of compliance in an economy which is much more data driven than when the previous legislation was passed. It also reflects the growth in the size of organisations which handle data – a fine of £500,000 would simply not be felt heavily enough by major companies.

Whilst the €20 million or 4% of annual global turnover fine has grabbed the headlines, there are in fact two levels of fines. As well as the €20 million/4% figure, there is a lower 'maximum' of €10 million or 2% of annual global turnover. The former is called the 'higher maximum amount' and the latter is called the 'standard maximum amount'. The higher maximum amount applies to failure to comply with an information notice, an assessment notice, an enforcement notice, or failure to comply with the principles contained in the DPA 2018. For more minor breaches, the standard maximum amount applies.

The DPA 2018 contains criminal sanctions in s 148 for any person who destroys, conceals, blocks or falsifies information when an information or assessment notice has been issued if it is done with the intention of preventing the Information Commissioner from viewing the relevant information. Further criminal sanctions appear in s 170 (knowingly or recklessly obtaining or disclosing personal data without the consent of the controller), s 171 (knowingly or recklessly re-identifying information that was previously de-identified) and s 173 (deliberately altering or concealing information which should be provided in response to a data subject access request).

As well as fines and criminal sanctions, compensation may be awarded to the data subject by a court for loss suffered due to breach of the GDPR.

27.7 CONCLUSION ON DATA PROTECTION

There have been valuable and practical benefits to the general public being able to prevent, for example, utility providers – or anyone else with vast amounts of commercially valuable personal data – simply selling that data to the highest bidder. It has also been of the greatest importance that individuals have been able to find out just what personal data is held by data controllers, and to what end.

The legal framework seems to be reasonably applicable and workable, considering the exceptional difficulties in regulating the holding and processing of data in an information-based society. Robust systems are needed to protect (as far as possible) against the difficult problem of keeping data processing systems secure against fraudsters, theft and negligence. There have recently been some massive failures of security around data held by government departments and other large organisations. It is hoped that the new legislation will minimise such incidents.

27.8 FREEDOM OF INFORMATION

Freedom of information appears, at first glance, to be quite the opposite of data protection, but there is no fundamental reason for the two concepts to be incompatible. All that is necessary is for public authority users and holders of information to be aware of the difference between duties owed to the general public and those duties owed to the private individual. The Information Commissioner is responsible for both data protection and freedom of information; a very wide range of further information can be found at ico.org.uk.

The basic approach of British bureaucracy, up until the last 20 years or so, was to deal with most information on a strict 'need to know' basis, usually claiming that it was covered by the Official Secrets Act and therefore protected from disclosure. Even very mundane information was treated in a similar way. This became an ever more pressing problem with the growth in number and powers of public agencies and local government authorities. There were many piecemeal initiatives and steps taken to widen access in various areas, such as access to medical records, housing records, meetings of local authorities, etc, but a much more general advance was demanded, so the FOIA 2000 was enacted, coming fully into force on 1 January 2005. The 2000 Act has enhanced many of the existing statutory access rights, but many of those earlier rights still remain and, where this is the case, the FOIA 2000 is not applicable (FOIA 2000, s 21). The philosophy of the 2000 Act is to allow much wider citizen participation in the development of public policy and the decision-making process. It also has the merit of increasing the public awareness and accountability of public bodies.

An important limitation on public access under the 2000 Act is that it applies only to recorded information held by a public body. So, matters which are not so recorded, but which may well be known to public servants, are beyond the reach of the Act; other methods will need to be employed to find out about those matters. Another considerable limitation is that any request by the data subject which involves any of his or her personal data can be made only under the DPA 2018. Such a matter is exempted under s 40(1) of the FOIA 2000. It is possible to obtain data concerning individuals other than the applicant in very restricted circumstances set out in s 40(2)–(4).

27.8.1   Application of the Freedom of Information Act 2000

The 2000 Act applies only to information held by 'public authorities', as defined in s 3(1). These include:

(a)   central government departments and agencies;

(b)   local government;

(c)   the police;

(d)   the NHS;

(e)   State schools, colleges and universities; and

(f)   publicly-owned companies such as the Royal Mail.

The Secretary of State is empowered under s 5 to designate an entity as a public authority. The above list can therefore be added to by that means. This could apply, for example, to a contractor providing services on behalf of a government department. The Act also provides that certain public authorities come within it only in respect of information of a specified description (s 7). See *BBC v Sugar* [2008] EWCA Civ 191.

27.8.2   Accessible information

Section 1 of the 2000 Act defines the right to information. Section 1(1) deals with the basic right:

(1)   Any person making a request for information to a public authority is entitled—

   (a)   to be informed in writing by the public authority whether it holds information of the description specified in the request, and

   (b)   if that is the case, to have that information communicated to him.

The provisions of para (a) are referred to as the 'duty to confirm or deny'. 'Awareness Guidance No 21' from the Information Commissioner deals with this matter. In essence, the thinking behind these provisions is quite straightforward. If information has been requested but is not held by the authority in question, it would normally be reasonable to inform the applicant of that fact. However, there may be some exceptional cases where it would not even be right to confirm or deny that information requested is held. An obvious example is the area of policing, where it would not make sense to allow criminals to discover whether they are under suspicion or not.

Basically, all information held by a public authority is available to an individual under the provisions of the 2000 Act, but there are seven absolute exemptions and 16 qualified exemptions from the general right (see **27.8.5**). The right is to 'information', not to documents or to a file. The public authority can therefore edit documents or files, where they also contain information that would be subject to an exemption. The public authority should not refuse a request for access on the basis that there is exempt information as well as accessible information in the document or file. Considerable editing may result, in practice.

The 2000 Act has given rise to a very wide range and complexity of requests, and there is some concern in public bodies about the cost of compliance. There is a discretion, where the cost of compliance would exceed a statutory limit, to require the applicant to agree to pay the actual cost, or part of it, in advance. The response time allowed is normally a maximum of 20 days, but this may be extended by notice to the applicant, where reasonable to do so.

The accessible information is that 'held' by the public authority, not that 'created' by the authority. Thus, information from or about businesses which is held by a public authority is accessible to the public, if it is not subject to an exemption. This could cover, for example, details of a bid made for government work under the Public–Private Partnership. This aspect of the 2000 Act is a key concern to businesses and their lawyers.

The 2000 Act applies to information obtained by a public authority before the Act came into force (s 1(4)). In other words, information is not exempted from disclosure because it was obtained before the implementation date of the Act.

27.8.3 Publication schemes

All public authorities which are subject to the FOIA 2000 have been obliged to operate approved publication schemes since 30 June 2004, under s 19. These schemes have to be approved by the Information Commissioner. The schemes must have regard to the public interest in, for example, the publication of reasons for decisions which have been made by a public authority. There is a wide range of schemes under the 2000 Act, including, for example, a number for the NHS. A publication scheme will usually comprise four sections:

(a)   information about the public authority, its responsibilities and the scheme;

(b)   classes of information published or to be published;

(c)   the manner in which the information is to be published;

(d)   whether the publication is to be free of charge or not.

The presence of a publication scheme does not, of itself, prevent successful applications for further, more detailed information under the 2000 Act. In *Corporate Officer of the House of Commons v Information Commissioner* [2008] EWHC 1084 (Admin), the decisions of the Information Commissioner and Information Tribunal, to order the provision of detailed breakdowns of claims for accommodation allowances by 14 Members of Parliament, were upheld by the Divisional Court. The consideration of the publication of private addresses had been properly dealt with and had been found to be outweighed by the deeply flawed allowances system; public scrutiny was justified.

27.8.4 Codes for access to information and for management of information

Under s 45 of the 2000 Act, the Secretary of State is required to issue a code of practice giving guidance to public authorities. The Information Commissioner has to be consulted, and the code must be approved by Parliament. This code gives guidance relating to the following:

(a)   the provision of advice by public authorities to applicants – public authorities must provide advice and assistance;

(b)   the transfer of requests by a public authority to another authority which may be the holder of the information;

(c)   consultation with persons to whom the information relates, or whose interests are likely to be affected;

(d)   the inclusion in contracts entered into by public authorities of terms relating to the disclosure of information;

(e)   the provision by public authorities of procedures for dealing with complaints about requests for information.

This code is available at www.dca.gov.uk/foi/reference/imprep/codepafunc.htm.

Under s 46, the Lord Chancellor is obliged to issue a code for public authorities relating to the keeping, management and destruction of their records. This is available at www.dca.gov.uk/foi/reference/imprep/codemanrec.htm. Once a record has been destroyed, there is no access to the information that was contained within it. In some other jurisdictions, the recollections of civil servants are treated as accessible information, but this is not the case in the UK system under the FOIA 2000.

27.8.5   Absolute and qualified exemptions

Section 2 of the FOIA 2000 sets out the circumstances in which a public authority may refuse a request for information. These fall into two categories, namely, absolute exemptions and qualified exemptions. If an absolute exemption applies, there is no legal right of access at all, for example information relating to public security matters. If a qualified exemption applies, a public authority must consider whether there is a greater public interest in, first, confirming or denying the existence of the information requested and, secondly, providing the information to the applicant or not.

The *absolute exemptions* are:

(a)   information accessible by other means (s 21);

(b)   information supplied by, or relating to, bodies dealing with security matters (s 23);

(c)   court records (s 32);

(d)   Parliamentary privilege (s 34);

(e)   personal information (s 40);

(f)   information provided in confidence (s 41); and

(g)   information the disclosure of which is prohibited by law (s 44).

An example of (d) above is seen in *Office of Government Commerce v Information Commissioner* [2008] EWHC 737 (Admin). Here, Parliamentary privilege was held to apply to review documents prepared for the use of Parliament in connection with the Government's identity card programme. The court allowed an appeal against the Information Commissioner's decision to order disclosure.

Examples of (f) are seen in *Secretary of State for the Home Office v British Union for the Abolition of Vivisection* [2008] EWHC 892 (QB) and *Bluck v Information Commissioner* (2007) 98 BMLR 1, Information Tribunal. In the first case, the High Court allowed an appeal against a decision of the Information Tribunal that information held by the Home Office should be disclosed. The information that had been obtained by the Home Office was commercially sensitive and had been obtained under statutory powers, with a very strong implication of confidentiality; the Tribunal's approach had been wrong in law. In the *Bluck* case, a father lost his appeal against a decision of the Information Commissioner that medical records concerning his daughter should not be disclosed without the consent of her husband. The daughter had died in hospital, the hospital had admitted liability and a settlement had been reached with the husband. The Tribunal held that the public interest – that patients retained trust in the confidentiality of their records – greatly outweighed any public interest in their disclosure. Interestingly, the Tribunal took the view that the right to enforce and protect confidentiality, relating to medical records, probably passed to personal representatives, despite earlier authorities to the contrary.

Note that much personal information is exempted from the FOIA 2000, and can only be accessed via the DPA 1998.

The *qualified exemptions* are:

(a)   information intended for future publication (s 22);

(b)   national security (ss 23–24);

(c)   defence (s 26);

(d)   international relations (s 27);

(e)   relations within the UK (s 28);

(f)   the economy (s 29);

(g)   investigations and proceedings (s 30);

(h)   law enforcement (s 31);

(i)   audit functions (s 33);

(j)   formulation of government policy (s 35);

(k)   prejudice to effective conduct of public affairs (s 36);

(l)   communications with Her Majesty (s 37);

(m)   health and safety (s 38);

(n)   some personal information (s 40);

(o)   legal professional privilege (s 42); and

(p)   commercial interests (s 43).

Qualified exemptions may be class-based, or not. Class exemptions under the Act are intended to give protection to *all* information falling within a particular category, for example legal professional privilege.

On the other hand, a qualified exemption could be prejudice-based. Such exemptions come into force only if a disclosure of particular information would cause prejudice to that category of activity, for example prejudice to international relations. If it does not then the information must be disclosed. This applies in relation to the following qualified exemptions:

(a)   defence;

(b)   international relations;

(c)   relations within the UK;

(d)   the economy;

(e)   law enforcement;

(f)   audit functions; and

(g)   commercial interests.

In addition, two sections use alternative words for 'prejudice'. These are:

(a)   prejudice to effective conduct of public affairs (s 36), where 'inhibit' is used in s 36(2)(b); and

(b)   health and safety (s 38).

Both class- and prejudice-based exemptions are subject to the public interest test, unless the Act states that they are absolute exemptions.

27.8.6 Policing the 2000 Act

The Information Commissioner enforces the 2000 Act and is required to promote good practice (s 18). She was previously the Data Protection Commissioner, but now combines that role with her role under the FOIA 2000. She is also responsible for enforcement of the Environmental Information Regulations 2004, which operate separately from the FOIA 2000.

Under s 50, a dissatisfied applicant can apply to the Information Commissioner for a decision. The applicant must have exhausted any complaints procedure which is provided by the public authority. (Such a procedure is required by the access code – see **27.8.4**.)

If the Information Commissioner believes that the public authority has failed to abide by the Act, she can issue an enforcement notice. Under s 54, if the public authority fails to comply with the notice, the Information Commissioner may apply to the court. If the court agrees with the notice, failure to comply is contempt of court. There is an appeal from the decision of the Commissioner to the Information Tribunal under s 57 by either the complainant or the public authority, or both. These appeals apply to decision notices, information notices and enforcement notices. This is a complex area, and in some circumstances it can appear that the Commissioner has reached a decision, whereas the reality is that what she has decided is that the matter complained of is beyond her jurisdiction under the Act. That happened in the *BBC v*

Sugar case (see **27.8.1**). In this circumstance, the appropriate recourse would be to seek judicial review of the Commissioner's decision, rather than to appeal under the 2000 Act.

27.8.7 Interface with the Human Rights Act 1998

Under s 6 of the HRA 1998, it is unlawful for a public authority to act in a way which is incompatible with a Convention right. Under s 12, the right to free speech is upheld. So, suppose that a business wished to obtain an injunction to stop a public authority from releasing confidential information which had originally been obtained from that business, eg a tender for a contract. The business would have to show, in effect, that it was likely to succeed at the full trial. This is a very heavy evidential burden. The court must in any event consider whether it would be in the public interest for the information to be disclosed. (For a case on the public interest in disclosing information, see *London Regional Transport v Mayor of London* [2001] EWCA Civ 1491.)

A more recent case which involved consideration of the situation where data protection, freedom of information and human rights are engaged is *Stone v South East Coast Strategic Health Authority and Others* [2006] EWHC 1668 (Admin). Here, the decision to publish a report following an independent inquiry into the care, treatment and supervision of Michael Stone prior to his committing two murders and attempting another was upheld. The public interest justified the decision, and the publication was not in breach of the claimant's human rights or his rights under the DPA 1998.

There are hints in the *Corporate Officer of the House of Commons v Information Commissioner* case, discussed at **27.8.3**, that the privacy of private addresses would need to be of a very pressing nature to defeat the public interest in freedom of information in matters which disclose serious shortfalls in the conduct of public bodies.

SUMMARY

We live in an information society. It is virtually impossible to carry out our lives without innumerable bodies and businesses holding information about us: who we are, what our financial details are, what we buy, where we go on holiday, how healthy we are, what insurance risks we pose, etc. With so much information being held on us, it is important that the law protects us against misuse of this information, but also makes information readily available when appropriate. This balancing act is performed by data protection laws, and those relating to freedom of information.

In this chapter we have looked at the rights of individuals, and the obligations imposed upon organisations, under the Data Protection Act 2018, and the enforcement measures which may be taken. There is a delicate balance to be struck between protecting individuals' private information, and freedom of information. Whilst the recent phone hacking scandal clearly involved criminal activity, only time will tell whether it will lead to tighter legislation being passed which will shift the balance to allow the individual greater ability to keep information about him or her private.

INTELLECTUAL PROPERTY

Topic	Summary
Passing off	This is a common law tort, in which a person misrepresents his goods or services as being those of some other person, or one of numerous variations on that theme. For a person to succeed in proving passing off, he must show that he has some discernible goodwill in some particular aspect of his own goods or services, that the defendant is misrepresenting that aspect, in some way, so that customers are likely to be confused as to the trade origin of the goods or services that they are purchasing, and that there is some identifiable damage to the claimant's business.
Trade mark	This is a sign that is capable of distinguishing the goods and services of one undertaking from those of another. It must be capable of performing its feature of providing distinctiveness if it is to be registered. Without registration, the mark will not get the statutory protection and the right to a potentially permanent monopoly over that mark in the form in which it is registered.
Descriptive marks	Trade marks which only serve to describe aspects of the type, origin, quality or quantity of the goods are not usually registrable. Often, combining these aspects with other non-excluded matters, such as a logo or different wording, will get around the problem, as might distinctiveness acquired through use of the mark.
Shape marks	There is a limited possibility for registration of trade marks which comprise shapes, but in general it is quite difficult to obtain long-term protection by trade mark for shape marks.
Generic marks	These are trade marks which, over time, have lost their ability to distinguish the objects bearing them from similar objects emanating from different trade sources. If a registered trade mark becomes generic, the registration may be revoked. The term simply becomes part of general trade usage.
EU Trade Mark	This is trade mark registration system that applies right across the EU and which is available provided there is no ground of objection arising in any one of the Member States. The system is administered by the EUIPO.

Topic	Summary
Registered Design Right	This is available to protect aspects of the visible external appearance of objects for a limited period of up to 25 years. The main limitation is that the design feature requiring protection must be new (not available before) and of individual character (creating a different overall impression to what had previously been available to the public).
Unregistered Design Right	This is a residual form of protection that applies to features of the shape or configuration of manufactured articles, internally or externally. The protection is available for up to a maximum of 15 years, more usually 10. To get protection, the feature must be original, in the sense of not being copied, and not commonplace in the design field in question.
Exhaustion of rights	This term describes the process by which the owner of intellectual property rights such as trade marks, patents or design rights loses the power to prevent the further marketing of objects within the EU, once the first dealing in or importation into the EU of the object has taken place, with the right owner's express or implied permission. His rights are said to be exhausted.
Copyright	This is a property right comprising the right to prevent a person copying, for other than a very limited group of 'fair dealing' purposes, an original work of literature, drama, music or art. The right comes into being upon the creation of the work itself and, in most cases, lasts for 70 years from the year in which the creator dies.
Moral rights	These are statutory rights which exist in parallel with the original copyright in most literary, dramatic, musical and artistic works and films. They are designed to remain to the advantage, use and protection of the creator of the work, in the event that he assigns his copyright to someone else.
Entrepreneurial copyright	This is a class of rights that arise out of the exploitation and commercialisation of original copyright works. In the main, they arise as a second generation of rights and are more limited in duration than the original copyright works from which they come. Matters such as films, broadcasts and sound recordings can fall within this category.
Database right	This is a statutory protection that can arise on the creation of databases, that is collections of data or other material that are arranged in a systematic way and which are individually accessible. It applies to both copyright-protected databases as well as non-copyright protected databases. The difference is that, to be copyright protected, the database must have had some human intellectual input in arranging and selecting the material; this is not necessary for non-copyright databases and could be computer created. The right arises automatically on creation and does not need registration. It lasts for 15 years from creation or substantial revision.

Topic	Summary
Patent	The grant of a patent is the giving of a monopoly right to use and exploit an invention of some sort. The right is given in exchange for the invention being made public, so that whatever inventive step is comprised within the idea can enter the 'world art' and become known to all. The effect is that the inventor has a 'lead time' of 20 years in which to exploit his invention to the full, but the rest of the world is able to see, throughout that period, what he has developed and is free to build upon the inventor's thinking, for further developments and inventions. The invention, to be patentable, must be new, comprise some inventive step, be capable of industrial application and not be caught by any statutory exclusion.
Inventive step	This means some new aspect of an invention that, at the time of applying for a patent for it, would not be obvious to a person reasonably skilled in the relevant field of invention and development, but who was not of a particularly imaginative or intuitive mind.
Patent claims	These are a part of the patent specification that must be provided by applicants for grant of patent. They comprise a series of numbered paragraphs, in which the inventor describes features of his invention which are, arguably, things or ways of doing things that no person has done or thought about before. The approach is normally to claim, as the first claim, the widest and most general feature of the invention and then, progressively, to narrow and refine the features and qualities claimed as being new to the world art. A person only needs to infringe any one of the claims to infringe a patent.
Confidential information	Some types of confidential information can be protected from disclosure, even though the information is not intellectual property in itself. Material that has been disclosed to someone else, under circumstances where that other person has reason to believe that he has received it under an obligation of confidentiality, can sometimes be the subject of restraining injunctions as well as compensatory damages for unauthorised disclosure. The legal principles involved are trust and fiduciary in nature. Often, the matter is expressly covered in contractual non-disclosure clauses, but where these are not present or applicable the court must be approached.
Data protection	This is a statutory form of protection which applies where persons obtain or deal with information about individuals, identifiable from the data, in a systematic way. Where this is the case, the persons who are creating, holding or dealing with the information, become subject to six statutory principles of good practice. The individual who is the data subject has a number of statutory rights available, with respect to the processing of the data relating to him or her.

PART IV

COMPETITION LAW

CHAPTER 28

COMPETITION LAW AND COMMERCIAL AGREEMENTS

LEARNING OUTCOMES

After reading this chapter you will be able to:

- describe the structure of the EU and UK rules regulating anti-competitive agreements and the abuse of a dominant position
- identify whether an agreement or abuse may be subject to EU competition law, UK competition law or both
- adopt a structured approach to analyse an agreement in order to decide how it is affected by EU or UK competition law
- identify the potential consequences of a breach of EU or UK competition law
- advise on how to avoid breaching the EU and UK rules on anti-competitive agreements, particularly by applying the Notice on Agreements of Minor Importance and the Vertical Restraints Block Exemption.

28.1 INTRODUCTION

In this chapter we shall consider the treatment of commercial agreements under EU and UK competition law. The UK has now left the EU, and the implementation period which ran until the end of December 2020 has expired. EU law no longer applies directly within the UK. Nonetheless, EU competition law is still important for UK lawyers, as their clients will often be multinational and/or operate within Europe. It is also possible that a future agreement with the EU will contain provisions governing the continued application, investigation and/or enforcement of EU competition law in the UK.

Moreover, and as you may know from previous study of competition law, at present there is a huge degree of overlap between the UK and EU systems. This is no surprise, as the substantive law under the domestic UK system is currently based on that of the EU.

Section 60A of the UK's Competition Act 1998 requires that UK courts and authorities avoid inconsistencies between UK competition law and pre-exit EU case law. The principles underlying EU competition law are therefore important in domestic UK law, and it is likely that they will remain important for many years to come.

However, there is no equivalent requirement for post-exit EU case law. Also, s 60A does allow UK courts and authorities to depart from even pre-exit EU case law if they consider it appropriate to do so. And the UK courts can no longer refer questions of interpretation of competition law to the Court of Justice of the European Union. As you will see later in this chapter and in **Chapter 29**, the detail of UK competition law is beginning to diverge from EU competition law. However, the essential underlying principles are likely to remain the same for the foreseeable future.

Both the UK and EU systems are 'effects based', which means that the law is concerned with the effect that an arrangement may have upon the competitive dynamic of a market. A commercial lawyer must understand the basics of the law, as it can impact on commercial arrangements in numerous ways.

In this chapter we shall again visit the relevant EU and UK legislation. However, here we are going to use the relevant legislation to provide a structure by which you can analyse a commercial agreement in order to determine:

(a)   whether an agreement potentially breaches the law;

(b)   what sanctions can be imposed for breach; and

(c)   how an agreement can be amended, or how it can take advantage of exemptions, so as to be compliant.

Given the degree of overlap between the two systems under discussion here, the approach of this chapter will be to outline the position under EU law and then highlight (where necessary) any additional points which arise under UK law. This approach has been taken to avoid unnecessary repetition, so far as possible, and because of the requirement in s 60A of the Competition Act 1998 (CA 1998) that UK courts and authorities avoid inconsistencies between UK competition law and pre-exit case law.

28.1.1   Who investigates?

Before we look at how to analyse an agreement, let us deal with a couple of issues that can cause some confusion when studying competition law:

(a)   which competition authority will investigate; and

(b)   what is the legal basis for its investigation and prosecution?

Looking at the first of these questions, here we are concerned with two of the major regulating bodies: in the EU context, the regulator is the Competition Directorate of the European Commission (Commission). The main regulatory body in the UK is the Competition and Markets Authority. Under the UK system, other public bodies responsible for the regulation of particular sectors – for example, electricity and gas markets – also have authority to apply competition rules; however, these are beyond the scope of this book.

The national competition authorities – NCAs – of EU Member States have the power to apply EU law as well as national competition rules. This delegation of powers from the Commission (or, more correctly, the sharing of power) was prompted by the expansion of the EU and the fact that the Commission simply does not have the resources to investigate all breaches of EU competition law in the 28 Member States. The sharing of power to investigate and prosecute infringements of EU law has freed the Commission to concentrate on the most serious, pan-European infringements of the rules.

The Commission no longer has direct powers of investigation and enforcement in the UK. Its ability to investigate possible breaches of EU competition law in the UK is limited to addressing written requests for information to the UK authorities. Similarly, the UK authorities can investigate and enforce only UK competition law. However, any analysis of an agreement under either EU or UK competition rules is almost identical.

As a final introductory point, most commercial arrangements fall to be considered under rules relating to anti-competitive agreements. Consequently, this chapter will concentrate on

Article 101 of the Treaty of the Functioning of the European Union (TFEU) (previously Article 81 EC Treaty) and the corresponding UK legislation, known as the Chapter I prohibition. However, it will also briefly deal with Article 102 TFEU (previously, Article 82 EC Treaty) relating to abuse of market power and the UK's Chapter II prohibition.

28.2 ARTICLE 101/CHAPTER I PROHIBITION

28.2.1 EU competition law

Article 101(1) TFEU relates to anti-competitive agreements and prohibits:

> agreements between undertakings, decisions by associations of undertakings and concerted practices which may affect trade between Member States and which have as their object or effect the prevention, restriction or distortion of competition within the internal market.

As you can see, this is a complex provision. We shall look at each element separately, and this will provide a structure by which we can analyse a commercial agreement under either EU or UK competition rules relating to anti-competitive agreements.

28.2.2 'Agreement(s)'

The term 'agreements' has been interpreted widely by the European courts and covers all types of commercial arrangements, whether they are in writing or agreed verbally. The interpretation is wide enough also to include arrangements that are not legally binding and includes so-called 'gentlemen's agreements'. Accordingly, outside a traditional understanding of the term 'agreements', it is sufficient that the undertakings concerned have expressed their joint intention to conduct themselves on the market in a specified way for the definition to be satisfied.

28.2.3 'Between undertakings'

The term 'undertakings' covers virtually all legal or natural persons carrying on economic or commercial activities. It therefore covers companies, partnerships and sole traders. It also includes non-profit making organisations (such as FIFA, the governing body of football).

28.2.3.1 Parent and subsidiary

For an agreement to come within Article 101(1), it must be between two or more separate undertakings (plural). Competition law looks at whether the undertakings form *separate economic entities*. This differs from most systems of company law, under which each company forms a separate legal entity.

As such, parent and subsidiary companies will generally be considered as one and the same economic entity, and therefore agreements between them will not be 'agreements between undertakings' for the purposes of Article 101(1).

28.2.3.2 Agency agreements

Applying the same principle, pure agency agreements will generally fall outside Article 101(1) (see 'Guidelines on Vertical Restraints' in the **Appendix**). A pure agency agreement is one where the financial or commercial risk associated with the agency agreement is borne by the principal. Here the agent is not a separate economic undertaking (as it is not accepting any individual economic risk), so the arrangement between agent and principal in this case will fall outside Article 101(1).

The Guidelines on Vertical Restraints in the **Appendix** were replaced by an updated version on 1 June 2022. The treatment of agency agreements in the revised version is very similar to that in the old one. The main difference is the treatment of online platforms – for example, platforms selling travel services, or insurance. Under the new Guidelines they will always be treated as distributors, even if they purport to be acting as agents.

28.2.4   'Decisions by associations of undertakings'

This category would include decisions taken by, for example, a trade association. Such decisions could provide the potential for anti-competitive conduct by facilitating the co-ordination of market behaviour through, for example, price fixing.

28.2.5   'Concerted practices'

By adding concerted practices to the prohibition in Article 101(1), the legislation extends to include conduct that impacts on competition but is made outside an agreement or decision. Although a concerted practice will breach Article 101(1) (if the other elements of Article 101(1) are satisfied), the problem with establishing a concerted practice is one of evidence and intent. This is a specialist area of competition law and will not be considered further here.

28.2.6   'Affect trade between Member States'

28.2.6.1   EU law

For Article 101(1) to apply, there must be an effect on trade *between Member States*. If there is no such effect then Article 101(1) simply does not apply.

As power to investigate and pursue breaches of EU competition law is shared between the Commission and the national competition authorities, it is particularly important to establish when a national competition authority can apply EU rules and when it can apply national rules. The requirement that an agreement should have an effect on trade between Member States defines the boundaries between conduct which is subject to EU rules under Articles 101 and 102 and conduct which is subject to the domestic competition law of the Member States. In essence this is an issue of jurisdiction.

To ensure that the concept of effect on trade is fully understood and applied consistently between the Member States, the Commission has published *Guidelines on the effect on trade concept contained in Articles 81 and 82 of the Treaty*, Commission Notice [2004] OJ C101/81 ('the Effect on Trade Guidelines'). The Effect on Trade Guidelines provide guidance under the following three heads:

(a)   the concept of 'trade between Member States':

(b)   the notion of 'may affect'; and

(c)   the concept of 'appreciability'.

Of particular interest in the Effect on Trade Guidelines is the 'not capable of appreciably affecting trade' or 'NAAT' rule, whereby agreements are regarded by the Commission, in principle, not to affect trade between Member States if the combined market shares of the parties to the agreement are less than 5% on the relevant market, provided that, in the case of horizontal agreements, the parties' aggregate turnover in the EU is below €40 million. In the case of vertical agreements, the seller's turnover in the EU must be below €40 million for the NAAT rule to apply.

28.2.6.2   UK law

Thus far, we have considered only EU law. Effect on trade is the most obvious difference between EU and UK law. Section 2(1) of the CA 1998 applies to:

> agreements between undertakings, decisions by associations of undertakings or concerted practices which (a) may affect trade within the *United Kingdom* ... (emphasis added)

This is referred to as the Chapter I prohibition.

As you can see, s 2(1) of the CA 1998 is almost identical to Article 101(1) (**28.2.1**), the main difference being the requirement that there must be an effect on trade within the UK.

Even after the UK's departure from the EU, there is potential for an overlap between EU and UK competition law. Where the impact of an agreement is felt both within the UK and also in EU Member States, it is possible that the UK authorities will apply the Chapter I prohibition and that the EU authorities (or the national competition authorities in the Member States concerned) will apply Article 101, as there will be an effect on trade between Member States. The Trade and Cooperation Agreement concluded between the UK and the EU in December 2020 requires the UK and EU authorities (and the NCAs in the Member States) to 'endeavour to cooperate and coordinate with respect to their competition enforcement activities', including the exchange of information.

28.2.7 'Object or effect the prevention, restriction or distortion of competition within the internal market'

If an agreement has as its object or effect the prevention, restriction or distortion of competition within the EU's internal market, it will be caught by Article 101(1). (Under s 2(1) of the CA 1998, the test is whether the object or effect is the prevention, restriction or distortion of competition within the UK.) The distinction between object and effect is an important one in relation to the prosecution of an infringement.

28.2.7.1 Object

A relatively limited number of anti-competitive behaviours will be classified as 'object infringements'. These will include the most serious types of behaviour, and will be dependent on whether the relationship between the parties is horizontal or vertical. The most significant difference in the prosecution of an object infringement is that the competition authorities do not have to prove that there would have been an effect on competition; the mere existence of the infringement is enough to establish liability.

In a staff working document issued in June 2014, the European Commission published a set of guidelines on restrictions of competition 'by object'. Strictly, these guidelines are intended to assist only when applying the Notice on Agreements of Minor Importance (see **28.5.1**), but it is possible that they may be used more widely, and they certainly provide a useful indication of the Commission's thinking.

According to these guidelines, 'by object' restrictions include:

(a) in agreements between competitors (usually horizontal agreements):
- price-fixing;
- any arrangement by which competitors allocate markets or customers;
- agreements between competitors to reduce the volume of their supply or production capacity;
- bid-rigging (an agreement that as part of a tender process one or more competitors will not submit a bid, or will withdraw a bid, or will submit an artificially high bid);
- an agreement between competitors to boycott an actual or potential competitor;
- sharing information regarding intended future prices or quantities; and
- restrictions on research and development or the use of the parties' own technology; and

(b) in agreements between non-competitors (usually vertical agreements):
- restrictions on the territories in which, or the customers to whom, a buyer may sell products;
- sales restrictions on licensees;
- restrictions on the ability of a supplier to supply components as spare parts to end users or repairers; and
- restrictions on the ability of a buyer (eg a distributor) to determine its minimum selling price.

There are detailed exceptions to many of these 'by object' restrictions.

28.2.7.2 Effect

As indicated above, if an arrangement is not classified as an object infringement, the competition authorities must show that the infringement has an appreciable effect on competition before liability can be imposed.

In the absence of an appreciable effect on competition, the agreement will fall outside Article 101(1). This is considered in more detail below at **28.5.1**.

28.3 ANALYSING AN AGREEMENT

Now that we have outlined the elements of Article 101(1) (and, by implication, the elements of the Chapter I prohibition), we can analyse an agreement to see whether it potentially falls within the sanction. We can then consider whether we can 'save' the arrangement.

> **PRACTICAL EXAMPLE**
>
> A German company, X GmbH (X), manufactures widgets. It is very successful and enjoys a market share of 20% of the widgets market in the EU. X has traditionally focused its sales in Germany, but has sold directly to customers all over the EU. Although this has been successful, X's sales have levelled out over the past few years. X believes that it can increase sales elsewhere in the EU (and particularly France) by appointing a company with detailed knowledge of the French market. Consequently, X has been in negotiation with Y (an unconnected company) with the aim of appointing Y as its exclusive distributor in France.
>
> The proposed terms of the agreement are as follows:
>
> * Y will be X's exclusive distributor in France. In order to achieve this, X will not appoint any other distributor in France and it will not itself make any sales there;
> * Y will distribute only in France – it will not be allowed to supply any customer outside France; and
> * Y can only sell at prices set by X – Y is thus prevented from discounting.
>
> Using the legislation as a structure, we can quickly come to a preliminary conclusion as to whether the proposed arrangement might (if entered into) potentially breach Article 101(1) (and/or the Chapter I prohibition).
>
> | Agreement? | Yes | Clearly the distribution agreement satisfies this element of the test. Note that the agreement does not even need to be written down. So no need to consider: (a) decisions by association of undertakings; or (b) concerted practices. |
> |---|---|---|
> | Between undertakings? | Yes | We are told that the two businesses are unconnected – so this is not a parent or subsidiary relationship, nor is the arrangement an agency agreement. |

Effect on trade between Member States?	Yes – the agreement is between a German supplier and a French distributor. It also appears to prevent the sale of goods outside France, including into other EU Member States – so it would appear there is some effect on trade between Member States. In practice you would consult the Effect on Trade Guidelines to finalise this point – however, given the fact that X's market share is 20%, it exceeds the NAAT limits (and so an effect on trade between Member States is likely to be established).	As there is a cross-border effect, Article 101 is likely to apply – however, there may also be an effect on trade within the UK. For example, what if a UK consumer wanted to purchase widgets from the French distributor because it was cheaper? The UK consumer will be compelled instead to purchase from a non-French source; French-sourced widgets will not be available on the UK market. This may affect the operation of the UK market. The Chapter I prohibition may therefore also apply here.
Object or effect, etc?	Yes – there are potential object infringements as the agreement contains an export ban and resale price maintenance. The most obvious anti-competitive activity is price fixing. Clearly, if X dictates the price at which the goods can be sold by Y, Y is not able to discount the goods. Each of Y's buyers will have to pay the same (presumably) inflated price. It is a fundamental principle of competition that price should be set by the market and not artificially. The export ban can also have serious implications for competition. Let us assume that X sells the goods directly to customers in Germany. It does so at very high prices. A consumer, angered by the price she has to pay for widgets in Germany, does some research and finds that she can buy widgets more cheaply from Y in France. However, as Y is prevented from selling outside France, Y cannot supply potential customers in Germany, allowing X to continue to charge very high prices. X's position in Germany is protected from potential competition. Such an arrangement is also sometimes referred to as 'market sharing', because the market is being shared out, or allocated, between the German supplier and the French distributor.	As object infringements there is no need to consider whether there is an anti-competitive effect.

> The appointment of Y as X's exclusive distributor may appear anti-competitive. However, the grant of exclusive rights is not an 'object' infringement and so does not automatically breach Article 101(1). However, it may still infringe, if it has an anti-competitive *effect*. This will require a full investigation. There is likely to be an anti-competitive effect, in particular, if steps are taken to prevent the goods getting into the distributor's territory by other routes – for example, if X gets its other distributors to agree not to sell to anyone who is likely to import the goods into France.

From the above analysis, there is clearly a competition law issue here. Given this fact, this is now a suitable point to look at the consequences of breaching the rules.

28.4 THE SANCTIONS

As we have seen, the substantive law is very similar in both the EU and UK systems. However, some differences exist when it comes to the issue of sanctions for breach. As a general point, the UK competition authorities have a far greater range of sanctions at their disposal (many of which are derived from US competition law).

28.4.1 Fines

28.4.1.1 EU law

This is by far the most well-known sanction. The Commission can impose fines not exceeding 10% of the worldwide turnover of the undertaking for breaches of Article 101 and/or Article 102. This power, as with many of the Commission's powers of enforcement, is contained in the Modernisation Regulation 1/2003 [2004] OJ L1/1 (in this case Article 23(2)). The fact that fines can relate to turnover (rather than profit) means that the level of fines may be very high. For example, in July 2018, Google was fined €4.34 billion (the largest individual fine to date) for breaching Article 102 by requiring mobile phone manufacturers to include various Google products in its Android operating system.

28.4.1.2 UK law

The UK competition authorities also have the power to impose a fine of up to 10% of an undertaking's worldwide turnover.

Under s 39 of the CA 1998, there is 'limited immunity' from the Chapter I prohibition for what it refers to as 'small agreements'. This means that the agreement is immune from penalties (ie fines). A 'small agreement' is one where the parties' joint turnover does not exceed £20 million. It is very important to note, however, that a 'price-fixing agreement' cannot be a small agreement (s 39(1)(b)). Immunity under s 39 does not protect an agreement from the other sanctions for breach of the Chapter I prohibition.

28.4.2 Cease and desist

28.4.2.1 EU law

Article 7 of the Modernisation Regulation allows the Commission to order that the infringement is stopped immediately. In practice, most undertakings that become subject to enforcement proceedings will stop the infringement in any event.

28.4.2.2 UK law

The UK competition authorities can address directions to a party that has or parties that have breached the CA 1998. These directions may involve the requirement to cease the activity in question, and can also require a party to modify its conduct.

28.4.3 Voidness

28.4.3.1 EU law

Agreements that infringe Article 101(1) are automatically void under Article 101(2). Although rarely an issue in a serious infringement case (as it is highly unlikely that a party would attempt to uphold an agreement that was clearly anti-competitive), voidness is more likely to be raised where there is a commercial dispute. For example, if a party to an agreement is being sued for breach, a possible defence to that claim would be to argue that the agreement (or a particular term of the agreement) was in fact void as it breached EU (or indeed UK) competition rules.

28.4.3.2 UK law

Under UK law, the corresponding sanction rendering agreements automatically void for infringements of the Chapter I prohibition is outlined in s 2(4) of the CA 1998.

28.4.4 Other consequences of breach

28.4.4.1 Third party actions

So far we have considered the sanctions that may be imposed by the competition authorities. These sanctions will form part of the public enforcement procedure. Outside public enforcement, private parties and businesses can take action against the infringing business for breaches of EU or UK competition law. So far as EU law is concerned, this is because Articles 101 and 102 are directly effective within the EU (although they no longer have direct effect in the UK). These private actions normally concern a claim for damages – either after the public enforcement process has been completed or, more rarely, independently of public enforcement actions.

Both the EU and UK systems allow the possibility of third party 'class actions' to enable consumer organisations to recover losses suffered by consumers. The Consumer Rights Act 2015 contains provisions to make it easier for aggrieved parties to bring claims for breach of competition law by way of class action. The intention is that all aggrieved parties will obtain the benefit of any judgment unless they expressly opt out. The precise requirements for the UK class action regime are being worked out in the *Mastercard* litigation (see below).

Directive 2014/104/EU, adopted in November 2014, obliges EU Member States to ensure that anyone who has suffered harm caused by an infringement of EU competition law is able to obtain full compensation. It sets out minimum procedural requirements for claims before Member State courts. In the UK, it was implemented by the Claims in respect of Loss or Damage arising from Competition Infringements (Competition Act 1998 and Other Enactments (Amendment)) Regulations 2017 (SI 2017/385). These Regulations lay down rules in the areas of limitation, burden of proof, limitations on liability and rights of contribution, which do not affect the principles described in this chapter. They remain in force following the UK's departure from the EU.

It is also well established in English law that an injunction can be obtained in the English courts to restrain a breach of competition law: *Garden Cottage Foods Ltd v Milk Marketing Board* [1984] AC 130; *Cutsforth v Mansfield Inns Ltd* [1986] 1 All ER 577.

The Consumer Rights Act 2015 has established the Competition Appeal Tribunal as a principal forum to hear claims arising from breaches of competition law.

A private action could result in an award of damages that exceeds the level of any fine imposed by the competition authorities. In *2 Travel Group PLC v Cardiff City Transport Services Ltd* [2012] CAT 19, exemplary damages were awarded for a breach of the UK Competition Act 1998, on the ground that the defendant company had been reckless as to whether its conduct would breach the Act.

The most notable award of damages to date has been in favour of the supermarket J Sainsbury in its litigation against MasterCard, the credit card processing company. The Competition Appeal Tribunal found that the agreements between MasterCard and the banks which issue credit and debit cards breached Article 101(1) TFEU by setting card processing fees at an anti-competitively high level. The fees had been paid by Sainsbury's (and other supermarkets), and Sainsbury's was awarded damages of over £68 million. In June 2020, the Supreme Court confirmed that the agreements restricted competition (see *Sainsbury's Supermarkets v Mastercard Incorporated* [2020] UKSC 24). It referred various questions back to the courts below, including whether Mastercard might be able to rely on an exemption under Article 101(3) TFEU (see **28.5**), and questions of quantification.

The Sainsbury's action was withdrawn in August 2021 after a settlement was reached. Other actions against Mastercard continue. In particular, parallel proceedings are being pursued on behalf of a representative group of consumers who claim that they were affected by the uncompetitive fees. In August 2021, the Competition Appeals Tribunal gave permission for the most important of these, *Walter Hugh Merricks and Others v Mastercard Incorporated and Others*, to proceed, in a landmark judgment on the UK class action regime. Since then, there has been a steady stream of new competition-related class actions in the UK courts.

Following the end of the implementation period, the UK courts can no longer have regard to decisions of the European Commission, and it is difficult, if not impossible, to obtain remedies in the UK courts for infringements of EU competition law. Remedies for infringements of UK competition law are not affected.

28.4.4.2   Management time/publicity

Although not sanctions as such, the breach of competition law will result in a number of additional consequences for the business. First, an investigation launched by the competition authorities will take up a huge amount of management and staff time. A typical investigation could take a number of years to conclude. Secondly, although it is sometimes said that 'all publicity is good publicity', the fact that a business has been found to have breached competition rules is unlikely to endear it to the general public. This possible impact on the company's image/brand is like to be magnified in the event that the breach concerns the fact that customers have been charged higher prices due to the infringement.

28.4.5   UK law – the criminal cartel offence – the Enterprise Act 2002

Under the EA 2002, criminal penalties may be imposed on an individual for serious cartels taking effect within the UK which breach the Chapter I prohibition (or Article 101, until the end of the implementation period). An individual may be imprisoned for up to five years for the most serious anti-competitive behaviour, such as price fixing, limitation of supply or production, market sharing or bid rigging. In addition, the individual may be subject to an unlimited fine.

The important thing to note here is that it is only the UK competition authorities that can apply for these sanctions – the Commission has no power to impose criminal sanctions on an individual. It is not necessary to prove that the defendant acted dishonestly. However, a defendant may have a defence if certain information about the cartel arrangement is disclosed to its customers.

Director disqualification

A director found to have breached the competition rules may be disqualified from acting as a director for up to 15 years by the court, on an application by the UK competition authorities. Disqualification orders may be made in respect of any type of anti-competitive behaviour and not just the infringements which could give rise to imprisonment or the imposition of a fine as described above.

28.5 SAVING THE AGREEMENT

When looking at how to save an agreement that potentially falls within Article 101/the Chapter I prohibition, there are effectively three methods that may be employed:

(a) to establish that, although the agreement in hand may have an effect on competition, the effect is not appreciable (see **28.5.1**);

(b) to ensure that the agreement conforms with a relevant block exemption (see **28.5.2**); or

(c) if the two methods above are not available, to establish whether the agreement might be exempt (under Article 101(3) in the case of EU law, or s 9 of the CA 1998 in the case of UK rules) (see **28.5.3**).

Before we look at these potential ways to 'save' an agreement, it is important to note as a general point that these methods are not available where there is a 'hardcore' infringement of the rules (explained in more detail below). Therefore, as an initial step in most cases, the legal adviser will have to remove or amend hardcore restrictions within the agreement to avoid the possibility of breaching competition rules.

It is essential to consider separately the two questions of (i) whether there has been an infringement; and (ii) whether the agreement can be saved. The concepts arising under each question may be similar, and there is a real risk of confusion if they are mixed up.

28.5.1 Appreciable effect on competition/Notice on Agreements of Minor Importance (NAOMI)

A legal adviser looking to save an agreement will first aim to establish whether or not the agreement is likely to have an appreciable effect on competition.

As we have seen (**28.2.7.2**), EU and UK competition law will impose liability only where any effect on competition is appreciable. In order to assess whether an agreement has an appreciable effect on competition (or otherwise), a legal adviser should refer to the Commission's Notice on Agreements of Minor Importance. The current version of NAOMI was published on 25 June 2014. NAOMI is a Commission Notice, but the UK competition authorities have indicated that they will use the same principles contained within NAOMI when analysing the CA 1998.

28.5.1.1 Object restrictions

Broadly, NAOMI can apply to any type of agreement that does not have the prevention, restriction or distortion of competition as its *object*, if the parties are within the market share limits set out below. Paragraph 13 of NAOMI states that agreements which have the prevention, restriction or distortion of competition as their object *include*:

(1) agreements between competitors which have as their object the fixing of selling prices charged to third parties, the limitation of outputs or sales or the allocation of markets or customers; and

(2)   agreements which contain 'hardcore' restrictions listed in any current or future block exemption regulation (see **28.5.2**).

Vertical agreements are not usually concluded between competitors, and so it is point (2) above which is likely to be important in relation to vertical agreements. In other words, the Commission will look to the 'hardcore' restrictions in any relevant block exemption regulation to determine whether or not a restriction in a vertical agreement is an 'object' restriction.

However, strictly speaking, other restrictions may also be classed as 'object' restrictions. The Commission's guidance on 'object' restrictions (see **28.2.7.1**) is relevant here. The exact relationship between the 'object' restrictions identified in this guidance and the 'hardcore' restrictions is not entirely clear, although the guidance does seem to draw a clear link between them. It is therefore possible – if perhaps unlikely – that a restriction in a vertical agreement which is not caught as a 'hardcore' restriction in a block exemption regulation, or which is expressly excluded from the 'hardcore' restrictions, will still be treated as an 'object' restriction. It is also possible that the Commission will look to more than one block exemption regulation to determine whether a restriction is a 'hardcore' restriction preventing the agreement from benefiting from NAOMI.

28.5.1.2 Market share

For an agreement to qualify under NAOMI, the parties' market shares must be below the following limits:

(a)   agreements between competitors (usually horizontal agreements) – the *aggregate* market share of the parties to the agreement does not exceed 10%; or

(b)   agreements between non-competitors (usually vertical agreements) – the market share *held by each* of the parties to the agreement does not exceed 15%.

(emphasis added)

As can been seen from the above, the limits for vertical agreements are usually much more generous than those for horizontal agreements, which generally give rise to greater competition concerns.

NAOMI is a very useful place to start when looking to save an agreement. However, the market share limits contained within NAOMI are relatively low. Accordingly, only parties with low market share will be able to take advantage of the Notice. In addition, the market share of parties to an arrangement may increase over time, so although the arrangement may be able to take advantage of NAOMI initially, changes in the parties' market share later may preclude its application. In any event, the legal adviser should always inform the client that market share needs to be kept under review to ensure continued reliance on NAOMI.

28.5.2 Block exemptions

The next option for the legal adviser is to assess whether the agreement might benefit from an EU or UK block exemption. Block exemptions, which are produced by the EU Commission and the UK government, provide a 'safe harbour' for agreements. If an agreement comes within certain criteria it will be exempted from Article 101(1) or the Chapter I prohibition. As such, block exemptions provide a very useful device for avoiding infringements of that provision. They recognise that certain agreements, although technically within Article 101(1) or the Chapter I prohibition, should be exempted as the pro-competitive effects of the arrangements outweigh their anti-competitive effects. In this section we examine how one block exemption attempts to achieve this balance.

First, a few more introductory points need to be made:

(1)   It is important that the legal adviser identifies the correct block exemption for the agreement under consideration.

(2) When assessing a block exemption, the legal adviser should also consult any accompanying guidelines published by the Commission.

(3) Block exemptions generally have higher market share limits than NAOMI.

(4) As with NAOMI, and as a general point, block exemptions will not apply where the agreement contains hardcore restrictions.

(5) Unlike NAOMI, block exemptions are capable of exempting agreements containing 'object' restrictions, as long as they are not listed as hardcore restrictions or excluded from the block exemption.

(6) Given all the above, an agreement is more likely to fall under a block exemption than it is to be saved by NAOMI.

(7) However, there may be benefits in bringing the agreement under NAOMI if this can be done, instead of relying on a block exemption. For example, there are certain restrictions which, although they are not hardcore restrictions, may be excluded from a block exemption and therefore not exempted by it (see **28.5.2.1(b)** for examples and an explanation). If the agreement can be brought under NAOMI then it will be taken outside competition law altogether.

Until 31 May 2022, the block exemption applicable to most distribution agreements was Commission Regulation 330/2010 on the application of Article 101(3) of the Treaty on the Functioning of the European Union to categories of vertical agreements and concerted practices. With effect from 1 June 2022, that Regulation has been replaced by Regulation 2022/720. The block exemption is more commonly referred to as the Vertical Restraints Block Exemption (VRBE), and in this chapter we shall refer to the two Regulations as the 'Old VRBE' and the 'New VRBE'. The commentary in this chapter is based on the Old VRBE, but it will also explain how the rules that it describes have been changed in the New VRBE.

The VRBE (both the old and the new version) proceeds on the assumption that distribution agreements may be beneficial for competition. This is because they provide a route by which more goods can reach the market – meaning more consumer choice and therefore more competition. The VRBE recognises that it may be necessary for the parties to impose some restrictions on each other's conduct, in order to encourage distributors to invest in marketing the product and setting up and maintaining their distribution networks. Distributors may not be prepared to make this investment if they are not afforded some protection against competition, for example from other distributors or from free-riders seeking to benefit from their marketing efforts. Thus the VRBE attempts a balancing exercise, allowing certain restrictions, but prohibiting others which are considered too seriously anti-competitive.

What is the position under UK law? As we have seen, NAOMI will apply to an analysis of an agreement under the Chapter I prohibition in the UK Competition Act 1998. A UK analysis under Chapter I may also benefit from a block exemption, but precisely how that works changed with the introduction of the New VRBE.

Section 10 of the CA 1998 expressly provides an exemption from Chapter I if an agreement complies with a Commission regulation. Since the end of the implementation period, s 10 has referred to exemptions contained in Commission regulations as 'retained exemptions'. Retained exemptions continue to have effect in the UK unless and until the UK government removes them or changes them. For UK purposes, all references in the retained exemptions to EU law are replaced by references to UK law. The Old VRBE was a retained exemption until it expired on 31 May 2022.

The Competition Act 1998 allows the UK government to create its own block exemptions from the Chapter I prohibition. When the Old VRBE expired, it did so by passing the Competition Act 1998 (Vertical Agreements Block Exemption) Order 2022 (SI 2022/516) as a replacement (referred to in this chapter as the 'VABEO'). The VABEO is similar to the New VRBE in most respects, but there are some differences of detail.

28.5.2.1   The VRBE

The Old VRBE (reproduced in the **Appendix**) applies to vertical agreements which were in force before 31 May 2022. Agreements coming into force before 31 May 2022 which were exempt under the Old VRBE will continue to be exempt until 31 May 2023. From then on, they will be exempt only if they fulfil the requirements of the New VRBE (if EU law applies) or the VABEO (if UK law applies).

Below, we consider the specific rules contained in the Old VRBE and how these rules balance the pro- and anti-competitive effects of the vertical agreements which we considered above. We then go on to consider how the New VRBE and the VABEO differ from the Old VRBE.

The exemption

The exemption from Article 101(1) is contained in Article 2(1) of the Old VRBE.

The type of agreement

As with all block exemptions, the Old VRBE relates to a fairly narrow sphere of commercial activity. It will apply only to vertical agreements, which are defined in Article 1(1)(a). Clearly, a legal adviser must ensure that the agreement they are considering comes within the block exemption they intend to use. This may sound obvious, but many commercial arrangements do not neatly fit within the definition given by a block exemption.

The entry requirements

In addition to the type of agreement, the Old VRBE sets out (as with other block exemptions) other conditions that must be met before it will apply. These conditions are contained in Article 2(2) to (4) and Article 3. For our purposes, Article 3 is the most important; it outlines the market share limits above which the parties cannot use the Old VRBE. Both the supplier's and buyer's market share are relevant here. The Old VRBE states that the exemption will apply only where:

> ... the market share held by the supplier does not exceed 30% of the relevant market on which it sells the contract goods or services and the market share held by the buyer does not exceed 30% of the relevant market on which it purchases the contract goods or services. (Article 3(1))

The substantive rules

Once the type of agreement is established and the entry requirements are satisfied then the substantive terms of the agreement must be assessed by reference to the Old VRBE's conditions. The main conditions contained in the Old VRBE are found in Articles 4 and 5 (and these will be considered in the context of distribution agreements).

(a)   Article 4 – hardcore restrictions

This Article applies to hardcore restrictions contained within a vertical agreement. The Article states that the exemption contained in Article 2 of the Old VRBE 'shall not apply to *vertical agreements* which, directly or indirectly ... have as their object' any of the restrictions contained in Article 4 (emphasis added).

Accordingly, if a restriction prohibited in Article 4 is contained within the agreement then the *whole* agreement falls outside the Old VRBE. In this event, the only option left to 'save' the agreement is by exemption under Article 101(3) TFEU (see **28.5.3**). However, given that an agreement containing hardcore restrictions is highly unlikely to be exempt under Article 101(3), legal advisers will ensure that no hardcore restrictions, as outlined in Article 4, remain within the agreement. Some of the restrictions contained in Article 4 are examined in a little more detail below.

(i)   *Pricing restrictions*

Article 4(a) prevents any restriction on the ability of the buyer (the distributor in a distribution agreement) to set its sale price – in particular the setting of a fixed or minimum price. In the context of a distribution agreement, and as we saw in the example at **27.3** above, the supplier cannot dictate to the distributor the price at which it sells the goods to retailers. This activity will clearly restrict price competition. This type of infringement is referred to as 'resale price maintenance', which is a form of price fixing.

(ii)   *Territorial restrictions*

Another way in which competition may be severely restricted or removed is by the imposition of territorial restrictions. This is particularly sensitive in the context of the EU, as free movement of goods and services is one of its founding principles.

Article 4(b) is a good example of how the Old VRBE attempts to balance the pro- and anti-competitive effects of vertical agreements. The starting point under Article 4(b) is that no restriction may be placed on the buyer as regards the customers to whom or territories in which it can sell the goods or services which are the subject of the vertical agreement.

However, such a wide-ranging prohibition could cause as many problems as it attempts to solve. Whilst on first impression it might seem a good thing for competition, it would expose other distributors to the full force of competition from goods imported from elsewhere. If distributors could not be protected (to some extent), they might simply not wish to make the necessary investment, and consumers within the EU would be denied access to a new product. Accordingly, Article 4(b) attempts to reach a compromise between restrictions on buyers and protection for distributors. In this regard, the Old VRBE makes a distinction between active and passive selling. 'Active selling' describes the process where a seller (in our case, the distributor) approaches potential buyers. 'Passive selling' describes the process where consumers approach the seller. This is outlined in **Figure 28.1** below.

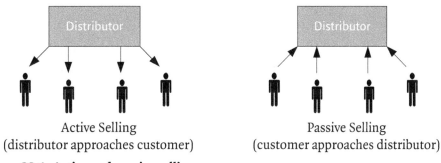

Active Selling
(distributor approaches customer)

Passive Selling
(customer approaches distributor)

Figure 28.1 Active and passive selling

So, whilst the starting point is that no restriction may be placed on the distributor regarding the customers to whom or the territories in which it may sell the goods or services, Article 4(b)(i) allows restrictions to be placed on distributors, preventing them from actively seeking customers in territories that have been awarded on an exclusive basis to another distributor (or reserved to the supplier). Remember that Article 4(b)(i) is an exception to the general prohibition contained in Article 4(b) (you need to read the last word of Article 4(b) to appreciate this – see **Appendix**).

Accordingly, a supplier can provide protection for an exclusive distributor by placing in *other* distribution agreements a restriction which prevents those distributors from actively seeking orders in the exclusive territory. Given this protection, the distributor will be more willing to make the necessary investment (and consumers will get access to the product).

PRACTICAL EXAMPLE

This can be confusing, so let us look at this by way of an example. Assume that a supplier appoints distributors in four territories (A, B, C and D). One of these territories has been awarded on an exclusive basis, Territory C. In these circumstances, the supplier can place restrictions in the agreements of the distributors in Territories A, B and D, preventing them from actively seeking customers in Territory C (see **Figure 28.2** below).

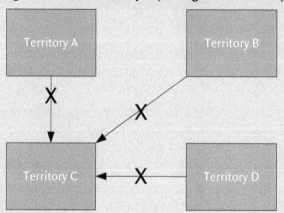

Figure 28.2 Territory C appointed on an exclusive basis – restriction of active selling

As the exclusive distributor in Territory C is protected from other distributors actively attempting to take away its customers, the distributor is more likely to make the necessary investment that an exclusive distributor would be required to make.

Note that Article 4(b)(i) only provides for a (partial) restriction on *active* selling – it does not allow a restriction on *passive* sales. Accordingly, a customer in Territory C cannot be prevented from approaching the distributors in Territories A, B and D to source the product (see **Figure 28.3** below). In theory, the distributor in Territory C, aware that customers are able to source the product elsewhere, will not charge excessive prices.

As the restrictions on the distributors in Territories A, B and D can apply only to active sales into Territory C – and restrictions on passive sales are prohibited altogether – total export bans and other similar restrictions will be prohibited.

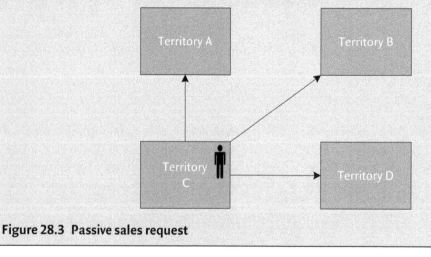

Figure 28.3 Passive sales request

The above discussion deals with the most common instance of territorial restrictions contained in the Old VRBE. Note that Article 4 contains other rules relating to territorial and customer groups, and which ones apply will be dependent on the type of agreement in contemplation. A detailed discussion of these rules is beyond the scope of this book.

(b) Article 5 – non-hardcore restrictions

There is an important difference between the restrictions in Article 4 and Article 5. If an agreement contains any of the restrictions set out in Article 5, the Old VRBE will not apply to *that obligation*, but the rest of the agreement can still benefit from the block exemption, as long as the infringing restrictions are severable from the 'legitimate' parts of the agreement as a matter of the governing law of the contract.

Article 5 is generally concerned with non-compete provisions. A non-compete obligation can take many forms and will clearly impact on the competitive dynamic. A definition of 'non-compete' may be found at Article 1(1)(d) (see **Appendix**).

Again, the Old VRBE attempts to balance the interests of the supplier (for example, by permitting restrictions on competition by the buyer) with the wider need to ensure that the supplier is not completely immune from competition. The Old VRBE therefore allows non-compete clauses, but only for a limited period. During the term of any vertical agreement, a non-compete obligation cannot exceed five years (Article 5(1)(a)). However, a non-compete obligation in such an agreement may be renewed before the five-year limit (and thereby give the supplier a longer period of protection) as long as the obligation does not simply roll over but is subject to some form of negotiation (see the last paragraph of Article 5(1)).

In terms of post-termination non-compete obligations, the general rule is that these cannot be longer than one year from the date of termination of the agreement, although additional conditions also apply (see Article 5(3)).

The Old VRBE contains a number of other operative provisions that are beyond the scope of this book, although in practice they would need to be considered by the legal adviser. In addition, the Commission has published a Notice, 'Guidelines on Vertical Restraints', which accompanies the Old VRBE and is an invaluable source of information (regularly consulted by practitioners) on its substance and interpretation. A copy of the Guidelines can be found on the Commission's website or in [2010] OJ C130/01. Extracts are also provided in the **Appendix** to this book.

Like the Old VRBE, the Guidelines on Vertical Restraints in the **Appendix** were replaced by an updated version on 1 June 2022. See **28.2.3.2** for a summary of the main change to the treatment of agency agreements in the revised Guidelines. The other changes to the Guidelines are generally beyond the scope of this book.

28.5.3 The New VRBE

The New VRBE is structured in the same way as the Old VRBE, with the same article numbers. The main changes in the New VRBE are:

(1) The definitions (Article 1) now include definitions of 'active' and 'passive' sales.

(2) The application of the block exemption is restricted where the supplier and the distributor are competitors, for example where the supplier sells its goods or services online in parallel to the distributor ('dual distribution'). This is becoming increasingly common, particularly where suppliers sell their products from their own websites. To the extent that the supplier makes direct sales, it is competing with the distributor, operating at the same level of the supply chain. The New VRBE therefore contains detailed provisions which set out exactly when it can still apply where the supplier and the distributor compete with one another (see Article 2).

The EU Commission is particularly concerned about competitors sharing information with one another, and so the New VRBE does not apply to the exchange of information between the supplier and the distributor when they are competitors, unless it is directly related to the implementation of the agreement or is necessary to improve the production or distribution of the goods or services to which the agreement relates.

(3)   Suppliers can appoint multiple exclusive distributors. The structure of Article 4 has changed as a result, but most of the essential points summarised above are not affected.

(4)   However, the supplier can restrict the distributor from making active sales into the exclusive territory of a maximum of five other distributors (or into territory reserved exclusively to the supplier).

(5)   A new Article 4(e) provides that a term preventing the distributor or its customers from using the internet to resell the supplier's goods or services is a hardcore restriction which will prevent the block exemption from applying. The Guidelines expressly state that a supplier can require a distributor to pay a different price for goods which are to be resold online (known as 'dual pricing'). For example, charging lower prices for offline sales may reflect the additional costs involved in selling from physical premises rather than over the internet. However, dual pricing is not allowed if it has the effect of discouraging the distributor from making online sales.

(6)   The rules on obligations which prohibit the distributor from competing with the supplier during the term of the agreement have been relaxed. A prohibition on competing which is limited to five years is not prohibited by Article 5(1)(a), even if it can be renewed.

(7)   Providers of online 'intermediation services' (such as booking platforms and price comparison sites) are not allowed to prevent the businesses whose goods or services they sell (for example, hotels or insurance companies) from selling their goods or services on more favourable terms on other platforms (sometimes known as 'parity' obligations). This is a new non-hardcore restriction under Article 5(1)(d).

Thus a booking platform cannot prevent a hotel listed on the platform from selling its rooms more cheaply via another platform. Including such a provision will not prevent the block exemption from applying to the rest of the agreement with the booking platform, as long as the parity obligation can be severed from it.

Like all EU block exemptions, the New VRBE has a finite period of validity. It will expire on 31 May 2034.

28.5.4   The UK's new block exemption: the VABEO

The VABEO is set out as a statutory instrument, and this means that its structure looks rather different from that of the New VRBE. It is divided into regulations with different numbering. However, most of its content is essentially the same. In a similar way to the European Commission's Guidelines on Vertical Restraints, the Competition and Markets Authority has issued guidance on the application of the VABEO. This can be accessed on the gov.uk website.

There are a few differences between the VABEO and the New VRBE:

(1)   The VABEO does not contain the same restriction on sharing information between parties who are competitors (see **28.5.3(2)**).

(2)   The VABEO does not list restrictions on reselling the goods or services online as a hardcore restriction (contrast **28.5.3(5)**). However, the CMA's guidance indicates that such restrictions will be treated in the same way under the VABEO as under the New VRBE.

(3)   Under the VABEO, there is no restriction on the number of distributors into whose exclusive territory the supplier can restrict active sales (the limit under the New VRBE is five: see **28.5.3(4)**).

(4)   The VABEO treats parity obligations rather differently. Under the VABEO, obligations which prohibit the distributor from competing with the supplier during the term of the agreement are still prohibited if they are automatically renewable beyond five years. This is similar to the treatment under the Old VRBE.

(5)   The VABEO also prohibits parity obligations which prevent a supplier from selling their goods or services on more favourable terms *whether directly to the customer or on other platforms*. Under the VABEO these obligations are hardcore restrictions.

      Thus a booking platform cannot prevent a hotel listed on the platform from selling its rooms more cheaply, either itself or via another platform. Including such a provision will prevent the block exemption from applying to the rest of the agreement with the booking platform.

The VABEO expires on 1 June 2028, six years earlier than the New VRBE.

28.5.5   Self-assessment

If the agreement cannot benefit from either NAOMI or a block exemption, self-assessment is the last resort open to the legal adviser. Self-assessment involves the parties and their advisers deciding whether the agreement qualifies for exemption under Article 101(3) TFEU or s 9 of the CA 1998.

Undertakings have to make their own assessment of the compatibility of their arrangements with competition law. It is for the undertaking or association of undertakings invoking Article 101(3) (or s 9) to prove that the exemption conditions have been satisfied.

The self-assessment criteria under the UK competition rules in s 9 of the CA 1998 are identical to those in Article 101(3) TFEU.

To obtain an exemption, an agreement must satisfy four conditions contained in Article 101(3), two positive and two negative. The two positive conditions are:

(a)   the agreement must contribute to an improvement in the production or distribution of goods, or to the promotion of technical or economic progress; and

(b)   consumers will get a fair share of the resulting benefit.

The two negative conditions are:

(c)   the agreement does not impose on the undertakings restrictions which are not indispensable; and

(d)   the agreement will not afford them the possibility of substantially eliminating competition.

It is theoretically possible for 'object' or hardcore restrictions to be exempted, in broad terms, where the anti-competitive effects are outweighed by pro-competitive effects. However, although the possibility exists, it is highly unlikely that a serious infringement could be justified in this way.

(Strictly speaking, block exemptions are granted pursuant to Article 101(3) TFEU. The purpose of the block exemptions is to identify the categories of agreement – including vertical agreements – which should automatically qualify for exemption under Article 101(3).)

28.5.6 Application

> **PRACTICAL EXAMPLE**
>
> Let us now look again at X's proposed agreement with Y (the facts of the scenario are at **28.3** above). As you will recall, we concluded that the agreement fell within Article 101(1). Now consider whether the agreement might take advantage of any of the ways in which an agreement that comes with Article 101(1) (and by implication the Chapter I prohibition) can be 'saved' and avoid liability being placed upon the parties.
>
> | | Application | Comment |
> |---|---|---|
> | NAOMI | This will not apply as X Ltd's market share is 20% (over the 15% limit under NAOMI). | In addition to the market share issue the proposed agreement contains hardcore infringements. |
> | Block exemption | The Old VRBE will clearly apply to the agreement. The arrangement is a vertical agreement and the market shares of X and Y appear to be within the thresholds contained in the VRBE. | Although the Old VRBE will potentially apply, the export ban and the price-fixing term are 'hardcore' restrictions as defined in Article 4, which would result in the agreement falling outside the Old VRBE. Clearly, a legal adviser would need to remove or adapt the offending terms so that the agreement could take advantage of the safe harbour afforded by the Old VRBE.

However, the grant of exclusive rights – which, as we saw, might breach Article 101(1) if it has an anti-competitive effect – could still be exempt as long as the Old VRBE applies. In order to obtain the benefit of this exemption, the 'hardcore' restrictions should be changed so that the Old VRBE will apply to the agreement. |
> | Exemption under Article 101(3) TFEU | Exemption under Article 101(3) TFEU is not subject to a market share threshold and is potentially open to all agreements. | Even if the agreement contained hardcore restrictions, in theory it could be exempt. However, the parties will have to show (in broad terms) that the pro-competitive effects of the arrangement outweigh the anti-competitive effects. |
>
> The treatment is likely to be the same under the New VRBE and the VABEO.

28.6 ARTICLE 102/CHAPTER II PROHIBITION

Thus far we have concentrated on the law relating to anti-competitive agreements. Here we briefly consider how competition law deals with abuses of market power. As an initial point, you should note that the rules on abuse of market power are additional to those on anti-competitive agreements and, as such, undertakings with a high market share will need to consider both sets of rules

Article 102 TFEU states:

Any abuse by one or more undertakings of a dominant position within the internal market or in a substantial part of it shall be prohibited as incompatible with the internal market in so far as it may affect trade between Member States.

Section 18 of the CA 1998 contains the UK prohibition on abuse by dominant undertakings. This is referred to as the 'Chapter II prohibition' and mirrors Article 102. As with Article 101, the only substantive difference between the two pieces of legislation is that the Chapter II prohibition relates to abusive conduct that 'may affect trade within the United Kingdom'.

Some terms are common to both Articles 101 and 102 (and by implication the Chapter I and II prohibitions) and will be interpreted in the same way. Accordingly, the types of business vehicles that fall within the term 'undertakings' will be the same as those outlined above at **28.2.3**. The important thing to note here, however, is that unlike under Article 101 there is no need for one or more separate undertakings, and abuse by *one* dominant undertaking (so-called unilateral behaviour) will be sufficient to impose liability.

In addition to 'undertakings', Article 102 also refers to 'trade between Member States'. We have already considered this concept, and the equivalent under UK competition law, above at **28.2.6**.

In order for there to be a breach of Article 102/the Chapter II prohibition, two elements must be present: a dominant position (or market power); and abuse.

28.6.1 Dominance

Establishing whether an undertaking has market power (or holds a 'dominant position' as it is referred to under European rules) is crucial to identifying the types of commercial activity that undertakings can enter into.

The ECJ laid down the legal test for dominance in Case 27/76 *United Brands v Commission* [1978] ECR 207:

> The dominant position thus referred to by Article [102] relates to a position of economic strength enjoyed by an undertaking which enables it to prevent effective competition being maintained on the relevant market by affording it the power to behave to an appreciable extent independently of its competitors, customers and ultimately of its consumers.

Indicative of an undertaking's ability to act independently is the market share that the undertaking enjoys on the market (although it is important to note that market share does not, in itself, establish dominance). Clearly, in order to ascertain market share, the market (or markets) on which the undertaking operates must be established. This will be done by consideration of both the relevant product market on which the undertaking operates as well as the relevant geographic market.

Once the relevant market (or markets) has been established, the undertaking's market share can be calculated. When assessing market share figures for the purpose of establishing dominance, the European Commission (and the UK competition authorities) does not apply rigid rules but considers that certain market share figures give rise to presumptions (which are capable of rebuttal). An outline of these presumptions is given below.

28.6.1.1 Market share of 50% or more – presumption of dominance

Clearly, any presumption is capable of being rebutted; however, the higher the market share, the less likely that the presumption will be rebutted. Accordingly, very high market share, of say 80%, would almost certainly result in a finding of dominance.

28.6.1.2 Market share between 40% and 50% – no presumption either way

Within roughly these market share figures, there is no presumption either way. Other factors would also need to be considered in order to establish dominance. For example, the market share of the undertaking's competitors on the market would also need to be assessed. It is less likely there will be a finding of dominance, for example, where the undertaking's two main competitors also held a significant share of the market.

28.6.1.3   Market share below 40% – presumption of non-dominance?

There have very rarely been findings of dominance below a 40% market share. Clearly, the lower the market share, the less likely it is that dominance will be established – a market share figure significantly lower than 40% is very unlikely to give rise to dominance.

28.6.1.4   Dominance – other factors

Although market share is an important element in establishing dominance, it should be noted that other factors will also be considered, for example the length of time the dominant position is held (the longer the time, the more likely the undertaking is dominant). In addition, how easily other undertakings can enter the market (so-called 'barriers to entry') will be considered: the more easily others can enter the market, the less likely dominance will be established.

28.6.2   Abuse

Occupying a dominant position in the relevant market will not of itself breach Article 102/the Chapter II prohibition. It is the abuse of that position that will impose liability.

Some examples of abusive conduct follow.

28.6.2.1   Charging excessive prices

Clearly, the most obvious way in which a dominant undertaking can abuse its position is by charging its customers an excessive price. Although this may appear to be an obvious abuse, in practice it raises some difficult questions, not least what amounts to an excessive price.

28.6.2.2   Predatory pricing

This type of practice aims to reduce prices to such a level that a competitor is forced to exit the market as it cannot match the very low prices being offered. In theory, once all competition is removed from the market, the dominant firm can then raise prices, in the knowledge that customers cannot turn to an alternative source of supply.

28.6.2.3   Refusal to supply

Competition may also be affected where a dominant firm refuses to supply its products. This can be particularly problematic where the dominant firm's refusal impacts on the ability of the potential buyer to compete in another market.

28.6.2.4   Tying

A typical example of a tying or 'bundling' abuse will involve placing a condition on a buyer that, in order to obtain supplies of one product (that the buyer requires), the buyer must also purchase a product that it does not want.

28.6.2.5   Price discrimination

This may arise where a dominant undertaking charges different prices to different customers for the same product, without justification on the grounds of quality, quantity or other characteristics.

28.6.3   Saving the arrangement

With regard to abuses of market power, there are no equivalent exception/exemptions similar to NAOMI, block exemptions or individual exemptions which apply to Article 101 (and the Chapter I prohibition) (see **28.5**). However, some limited ways in which the arrangement may be justified/exempted from penalty are set out below.

28.6.3.1 Objective justification

Certain types of behaviour carried out by a dominant undertaking may be commercially legitimate and not caught by Article 102. This will be the case if the conduct of the dominant firm can be justified as being objectively necessary (ie reasonably needed to protect its commercial interests) and proportionate to the objective (ie not more restrictive than necessary to achieve the objective). For example, a dominant supplier may refuse to supply (a potential abuse) on the basis that a buyer has a poor credit rating and/or history.

28.6.3.2 UK law

Section 40 of the CA 1998 provides for limited immunity for breaches of the Chapter II prohibition for conduct of minor significance. Broadly, an undertaking that has a turnover of under £50m a year may be immune from fines (but not from other sanctions).

SUMMARY

The competition law provisions most likely to apply to commercial agreements are Article 101 TFEU and the Chapter I prohibition in the UK Competition Act 1998. For there to be a breach of Article 101, there must be:

- an agreement between undertakings (or a decision by an association of undertakings or a concerted practice)
- which may affect trade *between Member States* and
- which has as its object or effect the prevention, restriction or distortion of competition *within the internal market*.

The Chapter I prohibition is almost identical, save only that the words italicised above should be replaced by the words '*within the United Kingdom*'.

Where an agreement breaches either of these provisions, the likely consequences are that:

- the parties may be fined (subject to limited immunity from fines for breach of the Chapter I prohibition)
- the parties may be ordered to cease their infringement
- the offending term will be void (and the remainder of the agreement will be void unless the offending term can be severed from it)
- aggrieved third parties may take action in the courts
- in the case of cartels taking effect within the UK, the UK competition authorities may seek to have individuals fined or imprisoned
- the UK competition authorities may seek to have directors of companies which breach the rules disqualified.

An agreement which would otherwise breach Article 101 TFEU or the Chapter I prohibition may be saved by reliance on either:

- the *de minimis* rules in the European Commission's Notice on Agreements of Minor Importance *or*
- a block exemption such as the Vertical Restraints Block Exemption (VRBE) (Regulation 330/2010/EU), the new VRBE (Regulation 2022/720/EU) or the VABEO *or*
- the exemption in Article 101(3) TFEU or s 9 of the CA 1998.

For an agreement to benefit from the VRBE:

- it must be a vertical agreement, as defined in Article 1(1)(a), and fulfil the other requirements in Article 2
- neither party's market share must exceed 30% (Article 3)
- the agreement must not contain any hardcore restrictions (Article 4)

The most important hardcore restrictions are retail price maintenance (Article 4(a)) and export bans and restrictions on customer groups (Article 4(b)). However, Article 4(b) does allow restrictions on *active sales* into territories and to customer groups which have been exclusively allocated to other exclusive distributors (up to five, under the New VRBE) or reserved to the supplier. Under the New VRBE, this list has been extended to include restrictions on online sales.

A term which is not a hardcore restriction may still be prohibited by Article 5. In that case, the term will not be exempt; the rest of the agreement will still be able to benefit from the exemption in the VBRE if the non-exempt term can be severed from it.

Where UK competition law applies, the approach under the VABEO is similar. There are differences of detail, particularly in relation to the treatment of sharing information between competitors, restrictions on online sales, and parity obligations, and there is no restriction on the number of exclusive distributors into whose territory the supplier may restrict active sales.

EU LAW AND INTELLECTUAL PROPERTY RIGHTS

LEARNING OUTCOMES

After reading this chapter you will be able to:

- appreciate the conflict between IP rights on the one hand and, on the other hand, the rules of EU law relating to competition and the free movement of goods

- describe how a licensing agreement may give rise to competition law concerns

- outline the structure of the Technology Transfer Block Exemption (Regulation (EU) 316/2014)

- advise, in the context of patents and trade marks, on the concept of exhaustion of rights and the extent to which the enforcement of those rights may be prevented by Article 34 TFEU.

29.1 INTRODUCTION

This chapter looks at the relationship between EU law and IP rights. It concentrates on the competition law problems which may arise in relation to the exploitation of IP rights (with particular reference to the licensing of patents), but also briefly considers the ways in which IP rights may come into conflict with the provisions of the Treaty on the Functioning of the European Union (TFEU) relating to the free movement of goods (Articles 34–36 TFEU, formerly Articles 28–30 EC).

The issues considered in this chapter are closely tied up with the EU's rules on free movement of goods. They will therefore be considered mainly from the point of view of EU law. The same issues can also arise under UK competition law, but the resulting problems tend to be less acute.

29.1.1 Exploiting intellectual property rights

CASE STUDY

Assume that Tecnici Carrera SpA ('Carrera'), a small Italian engineering company, has developed a revolutionary new machine, in respect of which it has obtained patents in Italy and other Member States, including France. Carrera's directors are now looking for ways to make money out of the monopoly right which Italian law has conferred on the company (not least so that it gets a return on the time and money spent in developing the machine; the directors see this as a just reward for the company's creativity and effort).

Carrera's two main options are:

(a)   make money by manufacturing and selling the machine itself; and/or
(b)   make money by licensing the right to other businesses to manufacture and sell the machine (ie, allowing other businesses to make use of the patent).

The advantages of licensing are covered briefly in **Chapter 34** of **Business Law and Practice**. It is possible here that Carrera may choose to license the patent because it is not geared up to manufacture the machine in sufficient quantities, or in other ways lacks the resources to exploit the patent fully, or because it finds a licensee with a better knowledge of the machine's target market.

29.1.2   How might the patent holder's actions cause competition law problems?

Italian law gives Carrera as patent holder a right which in itself might be thought to restrict trade and competition. Carrera can rely on the patent to stop anyone else making or selling the machine, or even developing a similar machine which comes too close to the patent. Even if Carrera allows other businesses to use the patent (by licensing it out), it could directly or indirectly restrict trade and competition by the terms which it includes in the licence; for example, it could grant a licensee exclusive territory, or stop a licensee exporting the machine from that territory.

29.1.3   The response of EU law

European Union law has a balancing act to perform in this situation. It must try to deal fairly with two potentially conflicting situations: on the one hand, the desire of the patent holder to be rewarded for its creativity (failure to permit this could stifle innovation and the development of new markets, and thus ultimately limit competition); and on the other hand, the need to stop IP rights granted under national law interfering with trade and competition within the common market.

The TFEU does not try to stop Member States passing laws which grant IP rights (although, increasingly, attempts are being made to harmonise national systems: see **Part III**). Article 345 TFEU (formerly Article 295 EC) provides that the Treaty 'shall in no way prejudice the rules in Member States governing the system of property ownership', which has led the EU competition authorities to take the view that EU law should not seek to control the mere existence of IP rights. What the law does seek to control, however, is the exploitation (or, as it is more commonly expressed, the 'exercise') of rights (see further **29.2**). The UK Competition Act 1998 is applied in accordance with Articles 101 and 102 TFEU, and so the distinction between the existence and exercise of IP rights is recognised in UK law as well as EU law.

29.1.4   Which rights may cause problems?

Many of the points covered by this chapter are relevant to all types of IP right. However, problems arise most often in relation to three of the rights because of their particular characteristics. Patents (on which this chapter concentrates) are particularly likely to pose problems because of their monopoly aspect. Trade marks may, if regularly re-registered, last for an indefinite period of time. Copyright cannot last indefinitely but has the longest periods of guaranteed validity of any IP right (ie, 70 years from the end of the year of the author's death in the case of most LDMA works).

29.2   ATTEMPTING TO RESOLVE THE CONFLICT

The distinction mentioned in **29.1.3** between the existence of an IP right and its exercise was developed by the ECJ as an attempt to reconcile Article 345 TFEU with other, possibly conflicting, Treaty provisions. Briefly, the ECJ's interpretation is that Article 345 TFEU is concerned with safeguarding the *existence* of national IP rights; other Articles (such as Articles 34–36 TFEU and Articles 101–102 TFEU) with controlling their *exercise*. As a basic rule, if the *exercise* of an IP right interferes with a Treaty provision (other than Article 345 TFEU), the Treaty provision will take precedence; the exercise of the right will be forbidden or restricted.

29.3 ARTICLE 101 TFEU AND THE EXPLOITATION OF INTELLECTUAL PROPERTY RIGHTS

If the holder of an IP right licenses it out, as Carrera is contemplating doing in the case study example, this will involve an agreement between the holder and the licensee (a licensing agreement, sometimes simply called a 'licence'). Broadly speaking, any IP right can be licensed in this way. In Carrera's case, the right happens to be a patent, and the agreement would be referred to as a patent licensing agreement, or patent licence. Because there is an agreement, Article 101 TFEU may apply (depending, of course, on the terms of the agreement). The existence of the IP rights which are being licensed will not, as such, infringe Article 101(1) TFEU. However, the licence agreement could infringe, if it might affect trade and competition within the internal market. In addition, bringing proceedings to stop infringement of an IP right may infringe Article 101(1) TFEU if the proceedings may affect trade within the internal market, and are brought as a result of an agreement. In other words, exercise of the right may be restricted if there is evidence that the exercise infringes Article 101(1) TFEU. Depending on the circumstances and the terms of the agreement, the licensing of any IP right may give rise to competition law problems. However, it is convenient to concentrate on patent licensing, in the light of the Carrera example.

Assume that Carrera is contemplating licensing the patent for the machine to Megaco, a French company. Megaco will use the patent to manufacture the machine. The parties have agreed the following licence terms in principle:

(a) Carrera has agreed that it will not appoint any licensees in France other than Megaco and will ensure that its licensees in other countries do not sell the machine in France; and

(b) Megaco will sell the machines at a price which Carrera will determine.

Would an agreement on these terms run into difficulties with Article 101(1) TFEU; and, if so, would it be possible to avoid this happening?

29.4 LICENSING AGREEMENTS AND COMPETITION LAW

29.4.1 Likely competition law problems

The terms outlined above could both give rise to some competition concerns. For example, term (a) concerns a territorial exclusion, and as such would prevent Carrera appointing another licensee in France. Clearly, the inability to appoint an alternative, competing licensee may have an impact on competition. However, looking at this from Megaco's perspective, it may have invested heavily in the manufacture of the machine and will want some protection. In the event that Megaco (or indeed other such potential licensees) is not afforded some protection by competition rules, it may simply not be prepared to take on such a commercial risk, and therefore no new product will be produced or sold in France.

In this simple example, it can be seen that competition rules have to be sufficiently flexible to give some protection to Megaco in these circumstances, whilst ensuring that any protection is limited so as to take into account competition concerns.

Conversely, there are other types of commercial behaviour that are highly unlikely to be excused from a competition law perspective. Term (b), by which Carrera is able to dictate the price at which Megaco can sell the machines, is unlikely to be justified on any grounds (you will have considered 'object' infringement – of which this is one example – in **Chapter 28**).

As we have seen at **28.5**, in the event that an agreement contains anti-competitive terms or arrangements, it may be justified in one of three ways:

(a)   the Notice on Agreements of Minor Importance (NAOMI);

(b)   a relevant block exemption; or

(c)   exemption under Article 101(3) TFEU.

As a general rule, hardcore restrictions cannot benefit from any of the three ways to justify an agreement outlined above. Consequently, a legal adviser would remove or reword any such restriction to ensure that it was capable of benefiting from one of these methods.

In terms of our approach here, although NAOMI could potentially apply, in practice it is rarely relied upon due to the very low market share thresholds. In addition, where there is a relevant block exemption, it is far more likely that any analysis of an agreement will ensure that it conforms with the terms of a block exemption in any event. Accordingly, we shall not consider NAOMI further here (however, for more information on how to apply NAOMI, see **28.5.1**).

29.4.2   Technology Transfer Block Exemption

The block exemption relating to IP licensing is now Commission Regulation (EU) No 316/2014 on the application of Article 101(3) TFEU to categories of technology transfer agreements. The Technology Transfer Block Exemption Regulation (TTBER), as it is more commonly known, is also accompanied by guidance published by the Commission. The TTBER is still in force in the UK as a 'retained exemption' under s 10 of the Competition Act 1998. The TTBER continues in force until 30 April 2026.

The TTBER adopts a broadly similar approach to many other block exemptions. The Preamble to the TTBER explains that technology transfer agreements 'will usually improve economic efficiency and be pro-competitive as they can reduce duplication of research and development, strengthen the incentive for the initial research and development, spur incremental innovation, facilitate diffusion and generate product market competition'.

'Technology transfer agreements' are defined in Article 1, para 1(c) of the TTBER as either: (i) a technology rights licensing agreement entered into between two undertakings for the purpose of the production of contract products by the licensee and/or its sub-contractor(s); or (ii) an assignment of technology rights between two undertakings for the purpose of the production of contract products where part of the risk associated with the exploitation of the technology remains with the assignor. The focus of the definition is on part (i) – licensing agreements. Part (ii) is about the more unusual situation where rights are assigned rather than licensed, but are subject to an ongoing relationship between the assignee and the assignor – for example, where the consideration for the assignment is payable over a period of time and is dependent on the volume of products sold, rather similar to a royalty payment.

'Technology rights' in turn means 'know-how' and other rights including patents, design rights and software copyright. 'Know-how' means 'a package of practical information, resulting from experience and testing', which is secret, substantial and identified.

As with vertical agreements, the presumption under the TTBER is broadly that technology transfer agreements will qualify for exemption from the prohibition in Article 101(1) TFEU where the parties' market shares do not exceed specified thresholds, and where the agreements do not contain certain severely anti-competitive ('hardcore') terms.

The structure and content of the block exemption are set out below in outline.

29.4.2.1   Competitors and non-competitors

There is one major difference between the operation of the TTBER and many other block exemptions. The difference arises because the Commission is concerned that IP licences can be used by businesses which would normally compete with one another, as a means of dividing markets up between themselves. The classic situation arises where competitors license technologies to each other, and in return agree not to compete with each other in other fields. What looks like a licence, designed to make technology more widely available, is therefore in fact little more than a cover for an agreement not to compete. The technology covered by the licences may even be relatively unimportant to the parties; what really matters to them is the non-compete agreement.

Because of this danger, the TTBER applies different rules to agreements between competitors and agreements between non-competitors. The market share thresholds are different, as are the lists of 'hardcore' anti-competitive terms. The TTBER makes a further distinction between two types of agreement between competitors. On the one hand there is the 'reciprocal' agreement, where each licenses technology to the other. This is seen as open to the sort of abuse described above. The other type of agreement between competitors is the 'non-reciprocal' agreement, where one competitor licenses technology to another. This is more likely to be a genuine licence and less likely to be used as a cover for an agreement dividing markets between the parties, and so is subject to fewer restrictions.

29.4.2.2   The structure of the TTBER

Like many modern block exemptions, the TTBER begins in Article 1 with a list of definitions. The exemption itself is contained in Article 2. Article 3 sets the market share thresholds.

Article 4 contains the 'hardcore' restrictions. The inclusion of such a 'hardcore' term will mean that the exemption provided for in Article 2 will not apply to the *entire agreement*. Here, there are two lists. Article 4, para 1 deals with restrictions in agreements between competitors; Article 4, para 2 deals with agreements between non-competitors.

Article 5 outlines the excluded restrictions. The exemption provided for in Article 2 will not apply to a particular *obligation* listed in Article 5, but the rest of the agreement may still benefit from the TTBER.

Article 6 allows the Commission and the national competition authorities of the Member States to withdraw the block exemption from any given agreement if they find that the agreement is anti-competitive and so does not qualify for exemption under Article 101(3) TFEU. Article 7 allows the Commission to disapply the block exemption from entire markets which are dominated by parallel networks of similar technology transfer agreements. Article 8 sets out detailed rules for the calculation of market share for the purposes of Article 3.

29.4.2.3   Does the Carrera–Megaco agreement fall within the TTBER?

The proposed agreement appears to fall within Article 2, in that it is a 'technology transfer agreement' (a patent licensing agreement) which contemplates the production of products made with the licensed technology, and which is between two undertakings, Carrera and Megaco (agreements between more than two undertakings are not covered). We do not know whether Carrera and Megaco are competing or non-competing undertakings, and we do not know whether their market shares fall within Article 3. However, there is definitely a hardcore restriction, in that Megaco cannot determine its prices when selling the machines to third parties. This is a hardcore restriction regardless of whether the parties to the agreement are competing or non-competing (Article 4(1)(a) and 4(2)(a)), and so, even if the market shares do fall within Article 3, the presence of this hardcore restriction will prevent the block exemption from applying.

Accordingly, the parties would need to remove term (b) from the agreement, or at the very least ensure that it is redrafted to conform with the TTBER. The TTBER does allow a licensor to impose a maximum or to recommend a sale price in certain circumstances (see Article 4(2)(a) – for example where the parties are non-competitors for the purposes of the TTBER). The legal adviser would need to discuss these points with their client.

Term (a) (territorial protection) may also be acceptable under the TTBER. There are two aspects to this term. First, by granting an exclusive licence to Megaco in France, Carrera is agreeing that it will not exploit the licensed technology, or grant other licences, in France. As long as the other conditions for the application of the TTBER are met, this restriction will be exempt under the block exemption.

The second aspect of term (a) is the proposal to prohibit Carrera's other licensees from selling the machine in France. It is necessary to consider whether the separate agreements between Carrera and its other licensees may be exempt under the TTBER. Where the agreement is between non-competitors, there is no prohibition on a term restricting active selling by the licensee (except in the case of a selective distribution system, which this is not – such arrangements are beyond the scope of this book). By Article 4(2)(b) of the existing TTBER, a non-competitor licensee can be restricted from making passive sales only in certain limited circumstances, none of which are applicable here. Therefore, if Carrera's other licensees are not its competitors then export restrictions imposed on them pursuant to term (a), if they are imposed at all, would need to be limited so as to apply only to active sales. If the other licensees are Carrera's competitors then the restrictions on sales permitted by the TTBER (Article 4(1)(c)) are even more limited, and include restrictions on active selling as well. (See **28.5.2.1** for an explanation of active and passive selling.)

29.5 ARTICLE 102 TFEU AND INTELLECTUAL PROPERTY RIGHTS

The ownership of IP rights may confer a dominant position on an undertaking within a particular geographic or product market. For example, a business may become dominant in a relevant product market by acquiring a patent; the patented item may form a market by itself if its novelty and inventiveness mean that consumers do not regard any other product as a substitute for it. However, this of itself (ie, the existence of the IP right) will not infringe Article 102 TFEU. Infringement requires abuse of a dominant position, which would mean improper exercise of the right in question. Not all exercises will be improper and, therefore, 'abusive'; it will depend on the circumstances, and in particular the effect on competition in the markets concerned. These general principles were confirmed by the ECJ in *Radio Telefis Eireann and Another v Commission of the European Communities and Another* (Cases C-241/91P and C-242/91P) [1995] ECR 1-801 (the 'Magill' case). However, some uncertainty still remains about the relationship between Article 102 TFEU and the exercise of IP rights; notably, exactly how far a right-holder's refusal to license its right to others amounts to abusive behaviour. For a more recent ECJ ruling on the matter, see *IMS Health GmbH and Co OHG v NDC Health GmbH and Co KG* (Case C-418/01) [2004] ECR I-5039.

29.6 ARTICLES 34–36 TFEU AND INTELLECTUAL PROPERTY RIGHTS

29.6.1 Introduction

The EU's competition authorities cannot resolve all the problems which arise from the existence and exercise of IP rights by using Articles 101–102 TFEU). For example, in many cases Article 101 TFEU does not apply because the situation does not involve a business arrangement of the type to which it can apply. It will then be necessary to control the exercise of IP rights by relying on the principles of free movement of goods (Articles 34–36 TFEU).

29.6.2 How Articles 34–36 TFEU may be relevant

Think again about the case study example. Assume that Tecnici Carrera SpA puts its patented machine on the market in Germany as well as in Italy. Market conditions in Germany mean that Carrera must sell the machine more cheaply there than in Italy. Gino, a businessman, realises that he can make money by (lawfully) buying the machine in Germany and reselling it in Italy at a price which still undercuts Carrera's Italian price. What if Carrera were to try to rely on its patent rights under Italian law to prevent Gino from importing the machines into Italy, claiming that those rights give it absolute control over what happens to the machines at all times?

Gino may try to argue that Italian patent law is a 'measure having equivalent effect' to a quantitative restriction on imports under Article 34 TFEU, as the patent holder is attempting to use the law to stop imports of patented goods into Italy. Article 34 TFEU prohibits such measures, so use of the Italian patent rights to stop the imports may not be justified, being incompatible with the free movement of goods around the common market.

However, Article 34 TFEU must be read subject to Article 36 TFEU. This permits derogations from Article 34 TFEU in certain circumstances, such as where the measure is necessary for 'the protection of industrial or commercial property rights', an expression which will cover IP rights such as patents. Thus, under Article 36 TFEU, the national measure (ie, the law on patents) may be justified if it protects something about the patent which needs protection.

However, in turn there are limits on the use of Article 36 TFEU. The Article itself provides that it cannot be invoked to justify a measure which amounts to 'arbitrary discrimination' or 'a disguised restriction on trade', and the ECJ has used this to ensure that any derogations from Article 34 TFEU do not go too far (the Court has also indicated that the measure must be proportionate). In particular, the Court has developed the doctrine that Article 36 TFEU can be invoked by the holder of an IP right only if the infringement action is necessary to protect the 'specific subject-matter' of the right. In other words, although EU law recognises that national IP rights need protection in certain circumstances, it also attempts to ensure that they do not interfere too much with trade within the common market.

29.6.3 Specific subject-matter

What constitutes the specific subject-matter of an IP right will vary according to the right concerned. The ECJ has held that the specific subject-matter of a patent is 'the guarantee that the patentee, to reward the creative effort of the inventor, has the exclusive right to use an invention with a view to manufacturing industrial products and putting them into circulation for the first time, either directly or by the grant of licences to third parties, as well as the right to oppose infringement' (*Centrafarm BV and Adrian de Peijper v Sterling Drug Inc* (Case 15/74) [1974] ECR 1147). For a trade mark, the specific subject-matter is 'the guarantee that the owner of the trade mark has the exclusive right to use that trade mark, for the purpose of putting products protected by the mark into circulation for the first time, and is, therefore, intended to protect him against competitors wishing to take advantage of the status and reputation of the trade mark by selling products illegally bearing that trade mark' (*Centrafarm BV and Adrian de Peijper v Winthrop BV* (Case 16/74) [1974] ECR 1183). The position in relation to copyright is less clear; this is at least partly because national systems of copyright law within the EU still vary quite considerably.

The specific subject-matter of an IP right may, therefore, be seen as a limit on the use of the principles relating to free movement of goods. The Court recognises that there is something central to each IP right which needs protection, but is reluctant to allow the right to be exercised in an uncontrolled manner; the Court will always be prepared to stop the use of IP rights if they are being used to restrict trade and competition within the common market.

29.6.4 Exhaustion of rights

This is further illustrated by the doctrine of 'exhaustion of rights', which the ECJ has applied to most IP rights, including patents, copyright and trade marks. It means that when goods which are subject to an IP right are lawfully put on the market for the first time in the EEA (either by the right holder, or with its consent), this 'exhausts' the right holder's opportunities to control what subsequently happens to the goods. In particular, the right holder cannot use the right to prevent the goods being imported into another Member State. However, note that this only applies to attempts by the right holder to control the movement of the goods around the EEA; it does not take away the holder's right to take action if the right has actually been infringed.

The case of *Silhouette International Schmied GmbH and Co KG v Hartlauer Handelsgesellschaft mbH* (Case C-355/96) [2000] All ER (EC) 769 showed the doctrine at work in relation to trade marks. The ECJ interpreted Article 7 of the Trade Marks Directive (89/104/EEC) to mean that exhaustion occurred only in the circumstances described above (lawful marketing in the EEA by the owner, or with the owner's consent). Thus, the owner of a trade mark would be entitled to stop products bearing the mark being imported into the EEA from outside that area (in this case, spectacle frames bearing Silhouette's mark being imported from Bulgaria, which was not then a Member State, into Austria). However, even after the *Silhouette* case, this area continued to prove problematic, particularly on the issue of the trade mark owner's consent. For example, how far could the owner's consent to imports of its goods into the EEA be implied when the owner had put its goods on the market outside the EEA without express restrictions as to where they could be re-sold?

The questions relating to consent appear to have been answered by the ECJ's ruling in the joined cases of *Zino Davidoff SA v A & G Imports Ltd; Levi Strauss & Co and Another v Tesco Stores Ltd and Another; Levi Strauss & Co and Another v Costco Wholesale UK* (Joined Cases C-414/99, C-415/99 and C-416/99) [2002] All ER (EC) 55. The Court in effect ruled that there had to be some positive expression of consent by the trade mark owner to its goods being imported into the EEA from outside. Consent cannot be implied from silence; there would have to be some unequivocal demonstration from the circumstances that the trade mark owner had given up its right to control the import into and marketing of the goods within the EEA. This ruling appears greatly to have strengthened the hand of trade mark owners: for example, it appears that there is now no need to state expressly in an agreement for goods which are to be sold outside the EEA that they must not be imported into and sold in the EEA.

The Court of Justice of the European Union has now held that the doctrine of exhaustion of rights also applies to software downloads. In *UsedSoft GmbH v Oracle International Corp* (Case C-128/11) (2012), it held that the right to distribute a downloaded copy of a computer program is exhausted if the rights holder permitting the download of the copy also granted a right to use that copy, for consideration, for an unlimited period of time. This allows the person who originally downloaded the program to resell it. However, the Court said that he must make his original copy unusable when reselling it. This important decision is expected to open up a new market in sales of second-hand software – to the obvious discomfort of the original rights holders – although the requirement to make the original download unusable should prevent the mass resale of copies of the software.

In contrast, in *Nederlands Uuitgeversverbond v Tom Kabinet Internet BV* (Case C-263/18), the Court held that different rules apply to e-books, because e-books are covered by the right of communication to the public rather than the distribution right. The fundamental differences between the two rights mean that the doctrine of exhaustion of rights does not apply to communication to the public. This decision means that authors/licensees and publishers can continue to prevent the copying of e-books after they have been sold.

This decision demonstrates the complexity of exhaustion of rights, and that, particularly with regard to copyright, it is necessary to consider precisely what type of right is relevant and how it is protected under the legislation.

Free movement of goods between the UK and the EU ceased at the end of the transitional period following the UK's departure from the EU. The UK is currently a 'unilateral participant' in the EU's exhaustion of rights regime. This means that the IP rights in goods which were first placed on the market in the EU were exhausted at that point, and can be imported into the UK without permission. By contrast, goods which have been placed on the market in the UK cannot be imported into the EU without the permission of the holders of the IP rights in those goods.

The United Kingdom government has completed a consultation on the regime which should apply in future to the exhaustion of rights within the United Kingdom. The majority view of respondents to the consultation was that the current rather one-sided regime should continue. The United Kingdom government is also considering the extent to which rights in goods which are placed on the market in the UK should be deemed to be exhausted for the purpose of trade within the UK.

29.7 ARTICLE 34 TFEU AND ARTICLES 101–102 TFEU: RELATIONSHIP

It seems clear that some attempts to use IP rights to prevent the import of goods from one Member State into another may be capable of infringing both Article 34 TFEU and Article 101 or 102 TFEU (*Nungesser (LC) and Kurt Eisle v Commission for the European Communities* (Case 258/78) [1982] ECR 2015: the 'Maize Seeds' case). Application of the rules on free movement of goods to a case does not necessarily preclude the application of the competition rules, although in practice it is comparatively rare for both to be argued actively in the same case.

> **SUMMARY**
> - By their nature, IP rights may be thought to conflict with competition law.
> - However, Article 345 TFEU expressly provides that EU law (from which both EU and UK competition law derive) cannot affect the ownership of property, including IP rights.
> - Because of this, competition law may regulate the *exercise* of IP rights but not their existence.
> - Restrictions in patent and know-how license agreements may be exempted from Article 101 TFEU/the Chapter I prohibition by the Technology Transfer Block Exemption, Regulation 316/2014/EU.
> - The use of IP rights to restrict trade between EU Member States may breach Article 34 TFEU.
> - Only the 'specific subject-matter' of a right is protected by the derogations in Article 36 TFEU; once a right is said to be 'exhausted', Article 34 will prevent the use of the right to restrict trade between EU Member States.

APPENDIX

LEGISLATION

Registered Designs Act 1949
1949 c. 88

An Act to consolidate certain enactments relating to registered designs

[16th December 1949]

Registrable designs and proceedings for registration

1.   Registration of designs

(1)   A design may, subject to the following provisions of this Act, be registered under this Act on the making of an application for registration.

(2)   In this Act "design" means the appearance of the whole or a part of a product resulting from the features of, in particular, the lines, contours, colours, shape, texture or materials of the product or its ornamentation.

(3)   In this Act—

"complex product" means a product which is composed of at least two replaceable component parts permitting disassembly and reassembly of the product; and

"product" means any industrial or handicraft item other than a computer program; and, in particular, includes packaging, get-up, graphic symbols, typographic type-faces and parts intended to be assembled into a complex product.

1B.   Requirement of novelty and individual character

(1)   A design shall be protected by a right in a registered design to the extent that the design is new and has individual character.

(2)   For the purposes of subsection (1) above, a design is new if no identical design or no design whose features differ only in immaterial details has been made available to the public before the relevant date.

(3)   For the purposes of subsection (1) above, a design has individual character if the overall impression it produces on the informed user differs from the overall impression produced on such a user by any design which has been made available to the public before the relevant date.

(4)   In determining the extent to which a design has individual character, the degree of freedom of the author in creating the design shall be taken into consideration.

(5)   For the purposes of this section, a design has been made available to the public before the relevant date if—

(a)   it has been published (whether following registration or otherwise), exhibited, used in trade or otherwise disclosed before that date; and

(b)   the disclosure does not fall within subsection (6) below.

(6)   A disclosure falls within this subsection if—

(a)   it could not reasonably have become known before the relevant date in the normal course of business to persons carrying on business in the geographical area comprising the United Kingdom and the European Economic Area and specialising in the sector concerned;

(b)   it was made to a person other than the designer, or any successor in title of his, under conditions of confidentiality (whether express or implied);

(c)   it was made by the designer, or any successor in title of his, during the period of 12 months immediately preceding the relevant date;

(d)   it was made by a person other than the designer, or any successor in title of his, during the period of 12 months immediately preceding the relevant date in consequence of information provided or other action taken by the designer or any successor in title of his; or

(e) it was made during the period of 12 months immediately preceding the relevant date as a consequence of an abuse in relation to the designer or any successor in title of his.

(7) In subsections (2), (3), (5) and (6) above "the relevant date" means the date on which the application for the registration of the design was made or is treated by virtue of section 3B(2), (3) or (5) or 14(2) of this Act as having been made.

(8) For the purposes of this section, a design applied to or incorporated in a product which constitutes a component part of a complex product shall only be considered to be new and to have individual character—

(a) if the component part, once it has been incorporated into the complex product, remains visible during normal use of the complex product; and

(b) to the extent that those visible features of the component part are in themselves new and have individual character.

(9) In subsection (8) above "normal use" means use by the end user; but does not include any maintenance, servicing or repair work in relation to the product.

1C. Designs dictated by their technical function

(1) A right in a registered design shall not subsist in features of appearance of a product which are solely dictated by the product's technical function.

(2) A right in a registered design shall not subsist in features of appearance of a product which must necessarily be reproduced in their exact form and dimensions so as to permit the product in which the design is incorporated or to which it is applied to be mechanically connected to, or placed in, around or against, another product so that either product may perform its function.

(3) Subsection (2) above does not prevent a right in a registered design subsisting in a design serving the purpose of allowing multiple assembly or connection of mutually interchangeable products within a modular system.

1D. Designs contrary to public policy or morality

A right in a registered design shall not subsist in a design which is contrary to public policy or to accepted principles of morality.

2. Proprietorship of designs

(1) The author of a design shall be treated for the purposes of this Act as the original proprietor of the design, subject to the following provisions.

(1B) Where a design is created by an employee in the course of his employment, his employer shall be treated as the original proprietor of the design.

(2) Where a design becomes vested, whether by assignment, transmission or operation of law, in any person other than the original proprietor, either alone or jointly with the original proprietor, that other person, or as the case may be the original proprietor and that other person, shall be treated for the purposes of this Act as the proprietor of the design.

(3) In this Act the "author" of a design means the person who creates it.

(4) In the case of a design generated by computer in circumstances such that there is no human author, the person by whom the arrangements necessary for the creation of the design are made shall be taken to be the author.

Effect of registration, etc

7. Right given by registration

(1) The registration of a design under this Act gives the registered proprietor the exclusive right to use the design and any design which does not produce on the informed user a different overall impression.

(2) For the purposes of subsection (1) above and section 7A of this Act any reference to the use of a design includes a reference to—

(a) the making, offering, putting on the market, importing, exporting or using of a product in which the design is incorporated or to which it is applied; or

(b) stocking such a product for those purposes.

(3) In determining for the purposes of subsection (1) above whether a design produces a different overall impression on the informed user, the degree of freedom of the author in creating his design shall be taken into consideration.

(4) The right conferred by subsection (1) above is subject to any limitation attaching to the registration in question (including, in particular, any partial disclaimer or any declaration by the registrar or a court of partial invalidity).

7A. Infringements of rights in registered designs

(1) Subject as follows, the right in a registered design is infringed by a person who, without the consent of the registered proprietor, does anything which by virtue of section 7 of this Act is the exclusive right of the registered proprietor.

(2) The right in a registered design is not infringed by—

    (a) an act which is done privately and for purposes which are not commercial;

    (b) an act which is done for experimental purposes;

    (c) an act of reproduction for teaching purposes or for the purpose of making citations provided that the conditions mentioned in subsection (3) below are satisfied;

    (d) the use of equipment on ships or aircraft which are registered in another country but which are temporarily in the United Kingdom;

    (e) the importation into the United Kingdom of spare parts or accessories for the purpose of repairing such ships or aircraft; or

    (f) the carrying out of repairs on such ships or aircraft.

(3) The conditions mentioned in this subsection are—

    (a) the act of reproduction is compatible with fair trade practice and does not unduly prejudice the normal exploitation of the design; and

    (b) mention is made of the source.

(4) The right in a registered design is not infringed by an act which relates to a product in which any design protected by the registration is incorporated or to which it is applied if the product has been put on the market in the United Kingdom or the European Economic Area by the registered proprietor or with his consent.

(5) The right in a registered design of a component part which may be used for the purpose of the repair of a complex product so as to restore its original appearance is not infringed by the use for that purpose of any design protected by the registration.

(6) No proceedings shall be taken in respect of an infringement of the right in a registered design committed before the date on which the certificate of registration of the design under this Act is granted.

7B. Right of prior use

(1) A person who, before the application date, used a registered design in good faith or made serious and effective preparations to do so may continue to use the design for the purposes for which, before that date, the person had used it or made the preparations to use it.

(2) In subsection (1), the "application date", in relation to a registered design, means—

    (a) the date on which an application for the registration was made under section 3, or

    (b) where an application for the registration was treated as having been made by virtue of section 14(2), the date on which it was treated as having been so made.

(3) Subsection (1) does not apply if the design which the person used, or made preparations to use, was copied from the design which was subsequently registered.

(4) The right conferred on a person by subsection (1) does not include a right to licence another person to use the design.

(5) Nor may the person on whom the right under subsection (1) is conferred assign the right, or transmit it on death (or in the case of a body corporate on its dissolution), unless—

    (a) the design was used, or the preparations for its use were made, in the course of a business, and

    (b) the right is assigned or transmitted with the part of the business in which the design was used or the preparations for its use were made.

8. Duration of right in registered design

(1) The right in a registered design subsists in the first instance for a period of five years from the date of the registration of the design.

(2)   The period for which the right subsists may be extended for a second, third, fourth and fifth period of five years, by applying to the registrar for an extension and paying the prescribed renewal fee.

(3)   If the first, second, third or fourth period expires without such application and payment being made, the right shall cease to have effect; and the registrar shall, in accordance with rules made by the Secretary of State, notify the proprietor of that fact.

(4)   If during the period of six months immediately following the end of that period an application for extension is made and the prescribed renewal fee and any prescribed additional fee is paid, the right shall be treated as if it had never expired, with the result that—

    (a)   anything done under or in relation to the right during that further period shall be treated as valid,

    (b)   an act which would have constituted an infringement of the right if it had not expired shall be treated as an infringement, and

    (c)   an act which would have constituted use of the design for the services of the Crown if the right had not expired shall be treated as such use.

8A.   Restoration of lapsed right in design

(1)   Where the right in a registered design has expired by reason of a failure to extend, in accordance with section 8(2) or (4), the period for which the right subsists, an application for the restoration of the right in the design may be made to the registrar within the prescribed period.

(2)   The application may be made by the person who was the registered proprietor of the design or by any other person who would have been entitled to the right in the design if it had not expired; and where the design was held by two or more persons jointly, the application may, with the leave of the registrar, be made by one or more of them without joining the others.

(3)   Notice of the application shall be published by the registrar in the prescribed manner.

(4)   If the registrar is satisfied that the failure of the proprietor to see that the period for which the right subsisted was extended in accordance with section 8(2) or (4) was unintentional, he shall, on payment of any unpaid renewal fee and any prescribed additional fee, order the restoration of the right in the design.

(5)   The order may be made subject to such conditions as the registrar thinks fit, and if the proprietor of the design does not comply with any condition the registrar may revoke the order and give such consequential directions as he thinks fit.

(6)   Rules altering the period prescribed for the purposes of subsection (1) may contain such transitional provisions and savings as appear to the Secretary of State to be necessary or expedient.

8B.   Effect of order for restoration of right

(1)   The effect of an order under section 8A for the restoration of the right in a registered design is as follows.

(2)   Anything done under or in relation to the right during the period between expiry and restoration shall be treated as valid.

(3)   Anything done during that period which would have constituted an infringement if the right had not expired shall be treated as an infringement—

    (a)   if done at a time when it was possible for an application for extension to be made under section 8(4); or

    (b)   if it was a continuation or repetition of an earlier infringing act.

(4)   If, after it was no longer possible for such an application for extension to be made and before publication of notice of the application for restoration, a person—

    (a)   began in good faith to do an act which would have constituted an infringement of the right in the design if it had not expired, or

    (b)   made in good faith effective and serious preparations to do such an act,

he has the right to continue to do the act or, as the case may be, to do the act, notwithstanding the restoration of the right in the design; but this does not extend to granting a licence to another person to do the act.

(5)   If the act was done, or the preparations were made, in the course of a business, the person entitled to the right conferred by subsection (4) may—

    (a)   authorise the doing of that act by any partners of his for the time being in that business, and

(b)   assign that right, or transmit it on death (or in the case of a body corporate on its dissolution), to any person who acquires that part of the business in the course of which the act was done or the preparations were made.

(6)   Where a product is disposed of to another in exercise of the rights conferred by subsection (4) or subsection (5), that other and any person claiming through him may deal with the product in the same way as if it had been disposed of by the registered proprietor of the design.

(7)   The above provisions apply in relation to the use of a registered design for the services of the Crown as they apply in relation to infringement of the right in the design.

Property in and dealing with registered designs and applications

15B.   Assignment, &c of registered designs and applications for registered designs

(1)   A registered design or an application for a registered design is transmissible by assignment, testamentary disposition or operation of law in the same way as other personal or moveable property, subject to the following provisions of this section.

(2)   Any transmission of a registered design or an application for a registered design is subject to any rights vested in any other person of which notice is entered in the register of designs, or in the case of applications, notice is given to the registrar.

(3)   An assignment of, or an assent relating to, a registered design or application for a registered design is not effective unless it is in writing signed by or on behalf of the assignor or, as the case may be, a personal representative.

(4)   Except in Scotland, the requirement in subsection (3) may be satisfied in a case where the assignor or personal representative is a body corporate by the affixing of its seal.

(5)   Subsections (3) and (4) apply to assignment by way of security as in relation to any other assignment.

(6)   A registered design or application for a registered design may be the subject of a charge (in Scotland, security) in the same way as other personal or moveable property.

(7)   The proprietor of a registered design may grant a licence to use that registered design.

(8)   Any equities (in Scotland, rights) in respect of a registered design or an application for a registered design may be enforced in like manner as in respect of any other personal or moveable property.

15C.   Exclusive licences

(1)   In this Act an "exclusive licence" means a licence in writing signed by or on behalf of the proprietor of the registered design authorising the licensee to the exclusion of all other persons, including the person granting the licence, to exercise a right which would otherwise be exercisable exclusively by the proprietor of the registered design.

(2)   The licensee under an exclusive licence has the same rights against any successor in title who is bound by the licence as he has against the person granting the licence.

Register of designs, etc.

19.   Registration of assignments, etc.

(1)   Where any person becomes entitled by assignment, transmission or operation of law to a registered design or to a share in a registered design, or becomes entitled as mortgagee, licensee or otherwise to any other interest in a registered design, he shall apply to the registrar in the prescribed manner for the registration of his title as proprietor or co-proprietor or, as the case may be, of notice of his interest, in the register of designs.

(2)   Without prejudice to the provisions of the foregoing subsection, an application for the registration of the title of any person becoming entitled by assignment to a registered design or a share in a registered design, or becoming entitled by virtue of a mortgage, licence or other instrument to any other interest in a registered design, may be made in the prescribed manner by the assign or, mortgagor, licensor or other party to that instrument, as the case may be.

(3)   Where application is made under this section for the registration of the title of any person, the registrar shall, upon proof of title to his satisfaction—

(a)   where that person is entitled to a registered design or a share in a registered design, register him in the register of designs as proprietor or co-proprietor of the design, and enter in that register particulars of the instrument or event by which he derives title; or

(b)   where that person is entitled to any other interest in the registered design, enter in that register notice of his interest, with particulars of the instrument (if any) creating it.

(3B)   Where national unregistered design right subsists in a registered design and the proprietor of the registered design is also the design right owner, an assignment of the national unregistered design right shall be taken to be also an assignment of the right in the registered design, unless a contrary intention appears.

(5)   Except for the purposes of an application to rectify the register under the following provisions of this Act, a document in respect of which no entry has been made in the register of designs under subsection (3) of this section shall not be admitted in any court as evidence of the title of any person to a registered design or share of or interest in a registered design unless the court otherwise directs.

Legal proceedings: general

24A.   Action for infringement

(1)   An infringement of the right in a registered design is actionable by the registered proprietor.

(2)   In an action for infringement all such relief by way of damages, injunctions, accounts or otherwise is available to him as is available in respect of the infringement of any other property right.

(3)   This section has effect subject to section 24B of this Act (exemption of innocent infringer from liability).

24B.   Exemption of innocent infringer from liability

(1)   In proceedings for the infringement of the right in a registered design damages shall not be awarded against a defendant who proves that at the date of the infringement he was not aware, and had no reasonable ground for supposing, that the design was registered.

(2)   For the purposes of subsection (1), a person shall not be deemed to have been aware or to have had reasonable grounds for supposing that the design was registered by reason only of the marking of a product with—

(a)   the word "registered" or any abbreviation thereof, or

(b)   any word or words expressing or implying that the design applied to, or incorporated in, the product has been registered,

unless the number of the design or a relevant internet link accompanied the word or words or the abbreviation in question.

(2A)   The reference in subsection (2) to a relevant internet link is a reference to an address of a posting on the internet—

(a)   which is accessible to the public free of charge, and

(b)   which clearly associates the product with the number of the design.

(3)   Nothing in this section shall affect the power of the court to grant an injunction in any proceedings for infringement of the right in a registered design.

24C.   Order for delivery up

(1)   Where a person—

(a)   has in his possession, custody or control for commercial purposes an infringing article, or

(b)   has in his possession, custody or control anything specifically designed or adapted for making articles to a particular design which is a registered design, knowing or having reason to believe that it has been or is to be used to make an infringing article,

the registered proprietor in question may apply to the court for an order that the infringing article or other thing be delivered up to him or to such other person as the court may direct.

(2)   An application shall not be made after the end of the period specified in the following provisions of this section; and no order shall be made unless the court also makes, or it appears to the court that there are grounds for making, an order under section 24D of this Act (order as to disposal of infringing article, &c).

(3)   An application for an order under this section may not be made after the end of the period of six years from the date on which the article or thing in question was made, subject to subsection (4).

(4)   If during the whole or any part of that period the registered proprietor—

(a)   is under a disability, or

(b)   is prevented by fraud or concealment from discovering the facts entitling him to apply for an order, an application may be made at any time before the end of the period of six years from the date on which he ceased to be under a disability or, as the case may be, could with reasonable diligence have discovered those facts.

(5)   In subsection (4) "disability"—

    (a)   in England and Wales, has the same meaning as in the Limitation Act 1980;

    (b)   in Scotland, means legal disability within the meaning of the Prescription and Limitation (Scotland) Act 1973;

    (c)   in Northern Ireland, has the same meaning as in the Statute of Limitations (Northern Ireland) 1958.

(6)   A person to whom an infringing article or other thing is delivered up in pursuance of an order under this section shall, if an order under section 24D of this Act is not made, retain it pending the making of an order, or the decision not to make an order, under that section.

(7)   The reference in subsection (1) to an act being done in relation to an article for "commercial purposes" are to its being done with a view to the article in question being sold or hired in the course of a business.

(8)   Nothing in this section affects any other power of the court.

24D.   Order as to disposal of infringing articles, &c

(1)   An application may be made to the court for an order that an infringing article or other thing delivered up in pursuance of an order under section 24C of this Act shall be—

    (a)   forfeited to the registered proprietor, or

    (b)   destroyed or otherwise dealt with as the court may think fit,

or for a decision that no such order should be made.

(2)   In considering what order (if any) should be made, the court shall consider whether other remedies available in an action for infringement of the right in a registered design would be adequate to compensate the registered proprietor and to protect his interests.

(3)   Where there is more than one person interested in an article or other thing, the court shall make such order as it thinks just and may (in particular) direct that the thing be sold, or otherwise dealt with, and the proceeds divided.

(4)   If the court decides that no order should be made under this section, the person in whose possession, custody or control the article or other thing was before being delivered up is entitled to its return.

(5)   References in this section to a person having an interest in an article or other thing include any person in whose favour an order could be made in respect of it—

    (a)   under this section;

    (b)   under section 19 of Trade Marks Act 1994; or

    (c)   under section 114, 204 or 231 of the Copyright, Designs and Patents Act 1988.

24E.   Jurisdiction of county court and sheriff court

(1)   In Northern Ireland a county court may entertain proceedings under the following provisions of this Act—

section 24C (order for delivery up of infringing article, &c),

section 24D (order as to disposal of infringing article, &c), or

section 24F(8) (application by exclusive licensee having concurrent rights),

where the value of the infringing articles and other things in question does not exceed the county court limit for actions in tort.

(2)   In Scotland proceedings for an order under any of those provisions may be brought in the sheriff court.

(3)   Nothing in this section shall be construed as affecting the jurisdiction of the Court of Session or the High Court in Northern Ireland.

24F.   Rights and remedies of exclusive licensee

(1)   In relation to a registered design, an exclusive licensee has, except against the registered proprietor, the same rights and remedies in respect of matters occurring after the grant of the licence as if the licence had been an assignment.

(2)   His rights and remedies are concurrent with those of the registered proprietor; and references to the registered proprietor in the provisions of this Act relating to infringement shall be construed accordingly.

(3)   In an action brought by an exclusive licensee by virtue of this section a defendant may avail himself of any defence which would have been available to him if the action had been brought by the registered proprietor.

(4)   Where an action for infringement of the right in a registered design brought by the registered proprietor or an exclusive licensee relates (wholly or partly) to an infringement in respect of which they have concurrent rights of action, the proprietor or, as the case may be, the exclusive licensee may not, without the leave of the court, proceed with the action unless the other is either joined as a claimant or added as a defendant.

(5)   A registered proprietor or exclusive licensee who is added as a defendant in pursuance of subsection (4) is not liable for any costs in the action unless he takes part in the proceedings.

(6)   Subsections (4) and (5) do not affect the granting of interlocutory relief on the application of the registered proprietor or an exclusive licensee.

(7)   Where an action for infringement of the right in a registered design is brought which relates (wholly or partly) to an infringement in respect of which the registered proprietor and an exclusive licensee have concurrent rights of action—

    (a)   the court shall, in assessing damages, take into account—

        (i)   the terms of the licence, and

        (ii)   any pecuniary remedy already awarded or available to either of them in respect of the infringement;

    (b)   no account of profits shall be directed if an award of damages has been made, or an account of profits has been directed, in favour of the other of them in respect of the infringement; and

    (c)   the court shall if an account of profits is directed apportion the profits between them as the court considers just, subject to any agreement between them;

and these provisions apply whether or not the proprietor and the exclusive licensee are both parties to the action.

(8)   The registered proprietor shall notify any exclusive licensee having concurrent rights before applying for an order under section 24C this Act (order for delivery up of infringing article, &c); and the court may on the application of the licensee make such order under that section as it thinks fit having regard to the terms of the licence.

24G.   Meaning of "infringing article"

(1)   In this Act "infringing article", in relation to a design, shall be construed in accordance with this section.

(2)   An article is an infringing article if its making to that design was an infringement of the right in a registered design.

(3)   An article is also an infringing article if—

    (a)   it has been or is proposed to be imported into the United Kingdom, and

    (b)   its making to that design in the United Kingdom would have been an infringement of the right in a registered design or a breach of an exclusive licensing agreement relating to that registered design.

(4)   Where it is shown that an article is made to a design which is or has been a registered design, it shall be presumed until the contrary is proved that the article was made at a time when the right in the registered design subsisted.

(5)   Nothing in subsection (3) shall be construed as applying to an article which may be lawfully imported into the United Kingdom by virtue of anything which forms part of retained EU law as a result of section 3 or 4 of the European Union (Withdrawal) Act 2018.

Unjustified threats

26.   Threats of infringement proceedings

(1)   A communication contains a "threat of infringement proceedings" if a reasonable person in the position of a recipient would understand from the communication that—

    (a)   a registered design exists, and

(b) a person intends to bring proceedings (whether in a court in the United Kingdom or elsewhere) against another person for infringement of the right in the registered design by—

    (i) an act done in the United Kingdom, or

    (ii) an act which, if done, would be done in the United Kingdom.

(2) References in this section and in section 26C to a "recipient" include, in the case of a communication directed to the public or a section of the public, references to a person to whom the communication is directed.

Unjustified threats

26A. Actionable threats

(1) Subject to subsections (2) to (5), a threat of infringement proceedings made by any person is actionable by any person aggrieved by the threat.

(2) A threat of infringement proceedings is not actionable if the infringement is alleged to consist of—

(a) making a product for disposal, or

(b) importing a product for disposal.

(3) A threat of infringement proceedings is not actionable if the infringement is alleged to consist of an act which, if done, would constitute an infringement of a kind mentioned in subsection (2)(a) or (b).

(4) A threat of infringement proceedings is not actionable if the threat—

(a) is made to a person who has done, or intends to do, an act mentioned in subsection (2)(a) or (b) in relation to a product, and

(b) is a threat of proceedings for an infringement alleged to consist of doing anything else in relation to that product.

(5) A threat of infringement proceedings which is not an express threat is not actionable if it is contained in a permitted communication.

(6) In sections 26C and 26D an "actionable threat" means a threat of infringement proceedings that is actionable in accordance with this section.

26C. Remedies and defences

(1) Proceedings in respect of an actionable threat may be brought against the person who made the threat for—

(a) a declaration that the threat is unjustified;

(b) an injunction against the continuance of the threat;

(c) damages in respect of any loss sustained by the aggrieved person by reason of the threat.

(2) It is a defence for the person who made the threat to show that the act in respect of which proceedings were threatened constitutes (or if done would constitute) an infringement of the right in the registered design.

(3) It is a defence for the person who made the threat to show—

(a) that, despite having taken reasonable steps, the person has not identified anyone who has done an act mentioned in section 26A(2)(a) or (b) in relation to the product which is the subject of the threat, and

(b) that the person notified the recipient, before or at the time of making the threat, of the steps taken.

Patents Act 1977
1977 c. 37

An Act to establish a new law of patents applicable to future patents and applications for patents; to amend the law of patents applicable to existing patents and applications for patents; to give effect to certain international conventions on patents; and for connected purposes   [29th July 1977]

Part I
New Domestic Law

Patentability

1.   Patentable inventions

(1)   A patent may be granted only for an invention in respect of which the following conditions are satisfied, that is to say—

(a)   the invention is new;

(b)   it involves an inventive step;

(c)   it is capable of industrial application;

(d)   the grant of a patent for it is not excluded by subsections (2) and (3) or section 4A below;

and references in this Act to a patentable invention shall be construed accordingly.

(2)   It is hereby declared that the following (among other things) are not inventions for the purposes of this Act, that is to say, anything which consists of—

(a)   a discovery, scientific theory or mathematical method;

(b)   a literary, dramatic, musical or artistic work or any other aesthetic creation whatsoever;

(c)   a scheme, rule or method for performing a mental act, playing a game or doing business, or a program for a computer;

(d)   the presentation of information;

but the foregoing provision shall prevent anything from being treated as an invention for the purposes of this Act only to the extent that a patent or application for a patent relates to that thing as such.

(3)   A patent shall not be granted for an invention the commercial exploitation of which would be contrary to public policy or morality.

(4)   For the purposes of subsection (3) above exploitation shall not be regarded as contrary to public policy or morality only because it is prohibited by any law in force in the United Kingdom or any part of it.

(5)   The Secretary of State may by order vary the provisions of subsection (2) above for the purpose of maintaining them in conformity with developments in science and technology; and no such order shall be made unless a draft of the order has been laid before, and approved by resolution of, each House of Parliament.

2.   Novelty

(1)   An invention shall be taken to be new if it does not form part of the state of the art.

(2)   The state of the art in the case of an invention shall be taken to comprise all matter (whether a product, a process, information about either, or anything else) which has at any time before the priority date of that invention been made available to the public (whether in the United Kingdom or elsewhere) by written or oral description, by use or in any other way.

(3)   The state of the art in the case of an invention to which an application for a patent or a patent relates shall be taken also to comprise matter contained in an application for another patent which was published on or after the priority date of that invention, if the following conditions are satisfied, that is to say—

(a)   that matter was contained in the application for that other patent both as filed and as published; and

(b)   the priority date of that matter is earlier than that of the invention.

(4)   For the purposes of this section the disclosure of matter constituting an invention shall be disregarded in the case of a patent or an application for a patent if occurring later than the beginning of the period of six months immediately preceding the date of filing the application for the patent and either—

(a)   the disclosure was due to, or made in consequence of, the matter having been obtained unlawfully or in breach of confidence by any person—

        (i)   from the inventor or from any other person to whom the matter was made available in confidence by the inventor or who obtained it from the inventor because he or the inventor believed that he was entitled to obtain it; or

        (ii)   from any other person to whom the matter was made available in confidence by any person mentioned in sub-paragraph (i) above or in this sub-paragraph or who obtained it from any person so mentioned because he or the person from whom he obtained it believed that he was entitled to obtain it;

    (b)   the disclosure was made in breach of confidence by any person who obtained the matter in confidence from the inventor or from any other person to whom it was made available, or who obtained it, from the inventor; or

    (c)   the disclosure was due to, or made in consequence of the inventor displaying the invention at an international exhibition and the applicant states, on filing the application, that the invention has been so displayed and also, within the prescribed period, files written evidence in support of the statement complying with any prescribed conditions.

(5)   In this section references to the inventor include references to any proprietor of the invention for the time being.

3.   Inventive step

An invention shall be taken to involve an inventive step if it is not obvious to a person skilled in the art, having regard to any matter which forms part of the state of the art by virtue only of section 2(2) above (and disregarding section 2(3) above).

4.   Industrial application

(1)   An invention shall be taken to be capable of industrial application if it can be made or used in any kind of industry, including agriculture.

4A.   Methods of treatment or diagnosis

(1)   A patent shall not be granted for the invention of—

    (a)   a method of treatment of the human or animal body by surgery or therapy, or

    (b)   a method of diagnosis practised on the human or animal body.

(2)   Subsection (1) above does not apply to an invention consisting of a substance or composition for use in any such method.

(3)   In the case of an invention consisting of a substance or composition for use in any such method, the fact that the substance or composition forms part of the state of the art shall not prevent the invention from being taken to be new if the use of the substance or composition in any such method does not form part of the state of the art.

(4)   In the case of an invention consisting of a substance or composition for a specific use in any such method, the fact that the substance or composition forms part of the state of the art shall not prevent the invention from being taken to be new if that specific use does not form part of the state of the art.

Property in patents and applications, and registration

30.   Nature of, and transactions in, patents and applications for patents

(1)   Any patent or application for a patent is personal property (without being a thing in action), and any patent or any such application and rights in or under it may be transferred, created or granted in accordance with subsections (2) to (7) below.

(2)   Subject to section 36(3) below, any patent or any such application, or any right in it, may be assigned or mortgaged.

(3)   Any patent or any such application or right shall vest by operation of law in the same way as any other personal property and may be vested by an assent of personal representatives.

(4)   Subject to section 36(3) below, a licence may be granted under any patent or any such application for working the invention which is the subject of the patent or the application; and—

    (a)   to the extent that the licence so provides, a sub-licence may be granted under any such licence and any such licence or sub-licence may be assigned or mortgaged; and

    (b)   any such licence or sub-licence shall vest by operation of law in the same way as any other personal property and may be vested by an assent of personal representatives.

(5)   Subsections (2) to (4) above shall have effect subject to the following provisions of this Act.

(6)   Any of the following transactions, that is to say—

     (a)   any assignment or mortgage of a patent or any such application, or any right in a patent or any such application;

     (b)   any assent relating to any patent or any such application or right;

   shall be void unless it is in writing and is signed by or on behalf of the assignor or mortgagor (or, in the case of an assent or other transaction by a personal representative, by or on behalf of the personal representative).

(6A)   If a transaction mentioned in subsection (6) above is by a body corporate, references in that subsection to such a transaction being signed by or on behalf of the assignor or mortgagor shall be taken to include references to its being under the seal of the body corporate.

(7)   An assignment of a patent or any such application or a share in it, and an exclusive licence granted under any patent or any such application, may confer on the assignee or licensee the right of the assignor or licensor to bring proceedings by virtue of section 61 or 69 below for a previous infringement or to bring proceedings under section 58 below for a previous act.

33.   Effect of registration, etc., on rights in patents

(1)   Any person who claims to have acquired the property in a patent or application for a patent by virtue of any transaction, instrument or event to which this section applies shall be entitled as against any other person who claims to have acquired that property by virtue of an earlier transaction, instrument or event to which this section applies if, at the time of the later transaction, instrument or event—

     (a)   the earlier transaction, instrument or event was not registered, or

     (b)   in the case of any application which has not been published, notice of the earlier transaction, instrument or event had not been given to the comptroller, and

     (c)   in any case, the person claiming under the later transaction, instrument or event, did not know of the earlier transaction, instrument or event.

(2)   Subsection (1) above shall apply equally to the case where any person claims to have acquired any right in or under a patent or application for a patent, by virtue of a transaction, instrument or event to which this section applies, and that right is incompatible with any such right acquired by virtue of an earlier transaction, instrument or event to which this section applies.

(3)   This section applies to the following transactions, instruments and events—

     (a)   the assignment or assignation of a patent or application for a patent, or a right in it;

     (b)   the mortgage of a patent or application or the granting of security over it;

     (c)   the grant, assignment or assignation of a licence or sub-licence, or mortgage of a licence or sub-licence, under a patent or application;

     (d)   the death of the proprietor or one of the proprietors of any such patent or application or any person having a right in or under a patent or application and the vesting by an assent of personal representatives of a patent, application or any such right; and

     (e)   any order or directions of a court or other competent authority—

         (i)   transferring a patent or application or any right in or under it to any person; or

         (ii)   that an application should proceed in the name of any person;

     and in either case the event by virtue of which the court or authority had power to make any such order or give any such directions.

(4)   Where an application for the registration of a transaction, instrument or event has been made, but the transaction, instrument or event has not been registered, then, for the purposes of subsection (1)(a) above, registration of the application shall be treated as registration of the transaction, instrument or event.

Employees' inventions

39.   Right to employees' inventions

(1)   Notwithstanding anything in any rule of law, an invention made by an employee shall, as between him and his employer, be taken to belong to his employer for the purposes of this Act and all other purposes if—

     (a)   it was made in the course of the normal duties of the employee or in the course of duties falling outside his normal duties, but specifically assigned to him, and the circumstances in either case were such that an invention might reasonably be expected to result from the carrying out of his duties; or

(b)   the invention was made in the course of the duties of the employee and, at the time of making the invention, because of the nature of his duties and the particular responsibilities arising from the nature of his duties he had a special obligation to further the interests of the employer's undertaking.

(2)   Any other invention made by an employee shall, as between him and his employer, be taken for those purposes to belong to the employee.

(3)   Where by virtue of this section an invention belongs, as between him and his employer, to an employee, nothing done—

(a)   by or on behalf of the employee or any person claiming under him for the purposes of pursuing an application for a patent, or

(b)   by any person for the purpose of performing or working the invention,

shall be taken to infringe any copyright or design right to which, as between him and his employer, his employer is entitled in any model or document relating to the invention.

40.   Compensation of employees for certain inventions

(1)   Where it appears to the court or the comptroller on an application made by an employee within the prescribed period that—

(a)   the employee has made an invention belonging to the employer for which a patent has been granted,

(b)   having regard among other things to the size and nature of the employer's undertaking, the invention or the patent for it (or the combination of both) is of outstanding benefit to the employer, and

(c)   by reason of those facts it is just that the employee should be awarded compensation to be paid by the employer,

the court or the comptroller may award him such compensation of an amount determined under section 41 below.

(2)   Where it appears to the court or the comptroller on an application made by an employee within the prescribed period that—

(a)   a patent has been granted for an invention made by and belonging to the employee;

(b)   his rights in the invention, or in any patent or application for a patent for the invention, have since the appointed day been assigned to the employer or an exclusive licence under the patent or application has since the appointed day been granted to the employer;

(c)   the benefit derived by the employee from the contract of assignment, assignation or grant or any ancillary contract ("the relevant contract") is inadequate in relation to the benefit derived by the employer from the invention or the patent for it (or both); and

(d)   by reason of those facts it is just that the employee should be awarded compensation to be paid by the employer in addition to the benefit derived from the relevant contract;

the court or the comptroller may award him such compensation of an amount determined under section 41 below.

(3)   Subsections (1) and (2) above shall not apply to the invention of an employee where a relevant collective agreement provides for the payment of compensation in respect of inventions of the same description as that invention to employees of the same description as that employee.

(4)   Subsection (2) above shall have effect notwithstanding anything in the relevant contract or any agreement applicable to the invention (other than any such collective agreement).

(5)   If it appears to the comptroller on an application under this section that the application involves matters which would more properly be determined by the court, he may decline to deal with it.

(6)   In this section—

"the prescribed period", in relation to proceedings before the court, means the period prescribed by rules of court, and

"relevant collective agreement" means a collective agreement within the meaning of the Trade Union and Labour Relations (Consolidation) Act 1992, made by or on behalf of a trade union to which the employee belongs, and by the employer or an employers' association to which the employer belongs which is in force at the time of the making of the invention.

(7)   References in this section to an invention belonging to an employer or employee are references to it so belonging as between the employer and the employee.

41.   Amount of compensation

(1)   An award of compensation to an employee under section 40(1) or (2) above shall be such as will secure for the employee a fair share (having regard to all the circumstances) of the benefit which the employer has derived, or may reasonably be expected to derive, from any of the following—

    (a)   the invention in question;

    (b)   the patent for the invention;

    (c)   the assignment, assignation or grant of—

        (i)   the property or any right in the invention, or

        (ii)   the property in, or any right in or under, an application for the patent,

    to a person connected with the employer.

(2)   For the purposes of subsection (1) above the amount of any benefit derived or expected to be derived by an employer from the assignment, assignation or grant of—

    (a)   the property in, or any right in or under, a patent for the invention or an application for such a patent; or

    (b)   the property or any right in the invention;

to a person connected with him shall be taken to be the amount which could reasonably be expected to be so derived by the employer if that person had not been connected with him.

(3)   Where the Crown, United Kingdom Research and Innovation or a Research Council in its capacity as employer assigns or grants the property in, or any right in or under, an invention, patent or application for a patent to a body having among its functions that of developing or exploiting inventions resulting from public research and does so for no consideration or only a nominal consideration, any benefit derived from the invention, patent or application by that body shall be treated for the purposes of the foregoing provisions of this section as so derived by the Crown, United Kingdom Research and Innovation or the Research Council (as the case may be).

In this subsection "Research Council" means a body which is a Research Council for the purposes of the Science and Technology Act 1965.

(4)   In determining the fair share of the benefit to be secured for an employee in respect of an invention which has always belonged to an employer, the court or the comptroller shall, among other things, take the following matters into account, that is to say—

    (a)   the nature of the employee's duties, his remuneration and the other advantages he derives or has derived from his employment or has derived in relation to the invention under this Act;

    (b)   the effort and skill which the employee has devoted to making the invention;

    (c)   the effort and skill which any other person has devoted to making the invention jointly with the employee concerned, and the advice and other assistance contributed by any other employee who is not a joint inventor of the invention; and

    (d)   the contribution made by the employer to the making, developing and working of the invention by the provision of advice, facilities and other assistance, by the provision of opportunities and by his managerial and commercial skill and activities.

(5)   In determining the fair share of the benefit to be secured for an employee in respect of an invention which originally belonged to him, the court or the comptroller shall, among other things, take the following matters into account, that is to say—

    (a)   any conditions in a licence or licences granted under this Act or otherwise in respect of the invention or the patent for it;

    (b)   the extent to which the invention was made jointly by the employee with any other person; and

    (c)   the contribution made by the employer to the making, developing and working of the invention as mentioned in subsection (4)(d) above.

(6)   Any order for the payment of compensation under section 40 above may be an order for the payment of a lump sum or for periodical payment, or both.

(7)   Without prejudice to section 12 or section 14 of the Interpretation Act 1978, the refusal of the court or the comptroller to make any such order on an application made by an employee under section 40 above

shall not prevent a further application being made under that section by him or any successor in title of his.

(8)   Where the court or the comptroller has made any such order, the court or he may on the application of either the employer or the employee vary or discharge it or suspend any provision of the order and revive any provision so suspended, and section 40(5) above shall apply to the application as it applies to an application under that section.

(9)   In England and Wales any sums awarded by the comptroller under section 40 above shall, if the county court so orders, be recoverable under section 85 of the County Courts Act 1984 or otherwise as if they were payable under an order of that court.

(10)   In Scotland an order made under section 40 above by the comptroller for the payment of any sums may be enforced in like manner as an extract registered decree arbitral bearing a warrant for execution issued by the sheriff court of any sheriffdom in Scotland.

(11)   In Northern Ireland an order made under section 40 above by the comptroller for the payment of any sums may be enforced as if it were a money judgment.

42.   Enforceability of contracts relating to employees' inventions

(1)   This section applies to any contract (whenever made) relating to inventions made by an employee, being a contract entered into by him—

(a)   with the employer (alone or with another); or

(b)   with some other person at the request of the employer or in pursuance of the employee's contract of employment.

(2)   Any term in a contract to which this section applies which diminishes the employee's rights in inventions of any description made by him after the appointed day and the date of the contract, or in or under patents for those inventions or applications for such patents, shall be unenforceable against him to the extent that it diminishes his rights in an invention of that description so made, or in or under a patent for such an invention or an application for any such patent.

(3)   Subsection (2) above shall not be construed as derogating from any duty of confidentiality owed to his employer by an employee by virtue of any rule of law of otherwise.

(4)   This section applies to any arrangement made with a Crown employee by or on behalf of the Crown as his employer as it applies to any contract made between an employee and an employer other than the Crown, and for the purposes of this section "Crown employee" means a person employed under or for the purposes of a government department or any officer or body exercising on behalf of the Crown functions conferred by any enactment or a person serving in the naval, military or air forces of the Crown.

Infringement

60.   Meaning of infringement

(1)   Subject to the provisions of this section, a person infringes a patent for an invention if, but only if, while the patent is in force, he does any of the following things in the United Kingdom in relation to the invention without the consent of the proprietor of the patent, that is to say—

(a)   where the invention is a product, he makes, disposes of, offers to dispose of, uses or imports the product or keeps it whether for disposal or otherwise;

(b)   where the invention is a process, he uses the process or he offers it for use in the United Kingdom when he knows, or it is obvious to a reasonable person in the circumstances, that its use there without the consent of the proprietor would be an infringement of the patent;

(c)   where the invention is a process, he disposes of, offers to dispose of, uses or imports any product obtained directly by means of that process or keeps any such product whether for disposal or otherwise.

(2)   Subject to the following provisions of this section, a person (other than the proprietor of the patent) also infringes a patent for an invention if, while the patent is in force and without the consent of the proprietor, he supplies or offers to supply in the United Kingdom a person other than a licensee or other person entitled to work the invention with any of the means, relating to an essential element of the invention, for putting the invention into effect when he knows, or it is obvious to a reasonable person in the circumstances, that those means are suitable for putting, and are intended to put, the invention into effect in the United Kingdom.

(3)   Subsection (2) above shall not apply to the supply or offer of a staple commercial product unless the supply or the offer is made for the purpose of inducing the person supplied or, as the case may be, the person to whom the offer is made to do an act which constitutes an infringement of the patent by virtue of subsection (1) above.

(5)   An act which, apart from this subsection, would constitute an infringement of a patent for an invention shall not do so if—

(a)   it is done privately and for purposes which are not commercial;

(b)   it is done for experimental purposes relating to the subject-matter of the invention;

(c)   it consists of the extemporaneous preparation in a pharmacy of a medicine for an individual in accordance with a prescription given by a registered medical or dental practitioner or consists of dealing with a medicine so prepared;

(d)   it consists of the use, exclusively for the needs of a relevant ship, of a product or process in the body of such a ship or in its machinery, tackle, apparatus or other accessories, in a case where the ship has temporarily or accidentally entered the internal or territorial waters of the United Kingdom;

(e)   it consists of the use of a product or process in the body or operation of a relevant aircraft, hovercraft or vehicle which has temporarily or accidentally entered or is crossing the United Kingdom (including the air space above it and its territorial waters) or the use of accessories for such a relevant aircraft, hovercraft or vehicle;

(f)   it consists of the use of an exempted aircraft which has lawfully entered or is lawfully crossing the United Kingdom as aforesaid or of the importation into the United Kingdom, or the use or storage there, of any part or accessory for such an aircraft;

(g)   it consists of the use by a farmer of the product of his harvest for propagation or multiplication by him on his own holding, where there has been a sale of plant propagating material to the farmer by the proprietor of the patent or with his consent for agricultural use;

(h)   it consists of the use of an animal or animal reproductive material by a farmer for an agricultural purpose following a sale to the farmer, by the proprietor of the patent or with his consent, of breeding stock or other animal reproductive material which constitutes or contains the patented invention.

(i)   it consists of—

(i)   an act done in conducting a study, test or trial which is necessary for and is conducted with a view to the application of paragraphs 1 to 5 of article 13 of Directive 2001/82/EC or paragraphs 1 to 4 of article 10 of Directive 2001/83/EC, or

(ii)   any other act which is required for the purpose of the application of those paragraphs;

(6)   For the purposes of subsection (2) above a person who does an act in relation to an invention which is prevented only by virtue of paragraph (a), (b) or (c) of subsection (5) above from constituting an infringement of a patent for the invention shall not be treated as a person entitled to work the invention, but—

(a)   the reference in that subsection to a person entitled to work an invention includes a reference to a person so entitled by virtue of section 55 above, and

(b)   a person who by virtue of section 20B(4) or (5) above or section 28A(4) or (5) above or section 64 below or section 117A(4) or (5) below is entitled to do an act in relation to the invention without it constituting such an infringement shall, so far as concerns that act, be treated as a person entitled to work the invention.

(6A)   Schedule A1 contains—

(a)   provisions restricting the circumstances in which subsection (5)(g) applies; and

(b)   provisions which apply where an act would constitute an infringement of a patent but for subsection (5)(g).

(6B)   For the purposes of subsection (5)(h), use for an agricultural purpose—

(a)   includes making an animal or animal reproductive material available for the purposes of pursuing the farmer's agricultural activity; but

(b)   does not include sale within the framework, or for the purposes, of a commercial reproduction activity.

(6C)   In paragraphs (g) and (h) of subsection (5) "sale" includes any other form of commercialisation.

(6D) For the purposes of subsection (5)(b), anything done in or for the purposes of a medicinal product assessment which would otherwise constitute an infringement of a patent for an invention is to be regarded as done for experimental purposes relating to the subject-matter of the invention.

(6E) In subsection (6D), "medicinal product assessment" means any testing, course of testing or other activity undertaken with a view to providing data for any of the following purposes—

    (a) obtaining or varying an authorisation to sell or supply, or offer to sell or supply, a medicinal product (whether in the United Kingdom or elsewhere);

    (b) complying with any regulatory requirement imposed (whether in the United Kingdom or elsewhere) in relation to such an authorisation;

    (c) enabling a government or public authority (whether in the United Kingdom or elsewhere), or a person (whether in the United Kingdom or elsewhere) with functions of—

        (i) providing health care on behalf of such a government or public authority, or

        (ii) providing advice to, or on behalf of, such a government or public authority about the provision of health care,

to carry out an assessment of suitability of a medicinal product for human use for the purpose of determining whether to use it, or recommend its use, in the provision of health care.

(6F) In subsection (6E) and this subsection—

"medicinal product" means a medicinal product for human use or a veterinary medicinal product;

"medicinal product for human use" has the meaning given by article 1 of Directive 2001/83/EC;

"veterinary medicinal product" has the meaning given by article 1 of Directive 2001/82/EC.

(6G) Nothing in subsections (6D) to (6F) is to be read as affecting the application of subsection (5)(b) in relation to any act of a kind not falling within subsection (6D).

(7) In this section—

"relevant ship" and "relevant aircraft, hovercraft or vehicle" mean respectively a ship and an aircraft, hovercraft or vehicle registered in, or belonging to, any country, other than the United Kingdom, which is a party to the Convention for the Protection of Industrial Property signed at Paris on 20th March 1883 or which is a member of the World Trade Organisation; and

"exempted aircraft" means an aircraft to which section 89 of the Civil Aviation Act 1982 (aircraft exempted from seizure in respect of patent claims) applies.

"Directive 2001/82/EC" means Directive 2001/82/EC of the European Parliament and of the Council on the Community code relating to veterinary medicinal products as amended by Directive 2004/28/EC of the European Parliament and of the Council;

"Directive 2001/83/EC" means Directive 2001/83/EC of the European Parliament and of the Council on the Community code relating to medicinal products for human use, as amended by Directive 2002/98/ EC of the European Parliament and of the Council, by Commission Directive 2003/63/EC and by Directives 2004/24/EC and 2004/27/EC of the European Parliament and of the Council.

61. Proceedings for infringement of patent

(1) Subject to the following provisions of this Part of this Act, civil proceedings may be brought in the court by the proprietor of a patent in respect of any act alleged to infringe the patent and (without prejudice to any other jurisdiction of the court) in those proceedings a claim may be made—

    (a) for an injunction or interdict restraining the defendant or defender from any apprehended act of infringement;

    (b) for an order for him to deliver up or destroy any patented product in relation to which the patent is infringed or any article in which that product is inextricably comprised;

    (c) for damages in respect of the infringement;

    (d) for an account of the profits derived by him from the infringement;

    (e) for a declaration or declarator that the patent is valid and has been infringed by him.

(2) The court shall not, in respect of the same infringement, both award the proprietor of a patent damages and order that he shall be given an account of the profits.

(3) The proprietor of a patent and any other person may by agreement with each other refer to the comptroller the question whether that other person has infringed the patent and on the reference the proprietor of the patent may make any claim mentioned in subsection (1)(c) or (e) above.

(4) Except so far as the context requires, in the following provisions of this Act—

(a)   any reference to proceedings for infringement and the bringing of such proceedings includes a reference to a reference under subsection (3) above and the making of such a reference;

(b)   any reference to a claimant or pursuer includes a reference to the proprietor of the patent; and

(c)   any reference to a defendant or defender includes a reference to any other party to the reference.

(5)   If it appears to the comptroller on a reference under subsection (3) above that the question referred to him would more properly be determined by the court, he may decline to deal with it and the court shall have jurisdiction to determine the question as if the reference were proceedings brought in the court.

(6)   Subject to the following provisions of this Part of this Act, in determining whether or not to grant any kind of relief claimed under this section and the extent of the relief granted the court or the comptroller shall apply the principles applied by the court in relation to that kind of relief immediately before the appointed day.

(7)   If the comptroller awards any sum by way of damages on a reference under subsection (3) above, then—

(a)   in England and Wales, the sum shall be recoverable, if the county court so orders, under section 85 of the County Courts Act 1984 or otherwise as if it were payable under an order of that court;

(b)   in Scotland, payment of the sum may be enforced in like manner as an extract registered decree arbitral bearing a warrant for execution issued by the sheriff court of any sheriffdom in Scotland;

(c)   in Northern Ireland, payment of the sum may be enforced as if it were a money judgment.

62.   Restrictions on recovery of damages for infringement

(1)   In proceedings for infringement of a patent damages shall not be awarded, and no order shall be made for an account of profits, against a defendant or defender who proves that at the date of the infringement he was not aware, and had no reasonable grounds for supposing, that the patent existed; and a person shall not be taken to have been so aware or to have had reasonable grounds for so supposing by reason only of the application to a product of the word "patent" or "patented", or any word or words expressing or implying that a patent has been obtained for the product, unless the number of the patent or a relevant internet link accompanied the word or words in question.

(1A)   The reference in subsection (1) to a relevant internet link is a reference to an address of a posting on the internet—

(a)   which is accessible to the public free of charge, and

(b)   which clearly associates the product with the number of the patent.

(2)   In proceedings for infringement of a patent the court or the comptroller may, if it or he thinks fit, refuse to award any damages or make any such order in respect of an infringement committed during the further period specified in section 25(4) above, but before the payment of the renewal fee and any additional fee prescribed for the purposes of that subsection.

(3)   Where an amendment of the specification of a patent has been allowed under any of the provisions of this Act, the court or the comptroller shall, when awarding damages or making an order for an account of profits in proceedings for an infringement of the patent committed before the decision to allow the amendment, take into account the following—

(a)   whether at the date of infringement the defendant or defender knew, or had reasonable grounds to know, that he was infringing the patent;

(b)   whether the specification of the patent as published was framed in good faith and with reasonable skill and knowledge;

(c)   whether the proceedings are brought in good faith.

67.   Proceedings for infringement by exclusive licensee

(1)   Subject to the provisions of this section, the holder of an exclusive licence under a patent shall have the same right as the proprietor of the patent to bring proceedings in respect of any infringement of the patent committed after the date of the licence; and references to the proprietor of the patent in the provisions of this Act relating to infringement shall be construed accordingly.

(2)   In awarding damages or granting any other relief in any such proceedings the court or the comptroller shall take into consideration any loss suffered or likely to be suffered by the exclusive licensee as such as a result of the infringement, or, as the case may be, the profits derived from the infringement, so far as it constitutes an infringement of the rights of the exclusive licensee as such.

(3)   In any proceedings taken by an exclusive licensee by virtue of this section the proprietor of the patent shall be made a party to the proceedings, but if made a defendant or defender shall not be liable for any costs or expenses unless he enters an appearance and takes part in the proceedings.

Unjustified threats

70.   Threats of infringement proceedings

(1)   A communication contains a "threat of infringement proceedings" if a reasonable person in the position of a recipient would understand from the communication that—

(a)   a patent exists, and

(b)   a person intends to bring proceedings (whether in a court in the United Kingdom or elsewhere) against another person for infringement of the patent by—

(i)   an act done in the United Kingdom, or

(ii)   an act which, if done, would be done in the United Kingdom.

(2)   References in this section and in section 70C to a "recipient" include, in the case of a communication directed to the public or a section of the public, references to a person to whom the communication is directed.

70A.   Actionable threats

(1)   Subject to subsections (2) to (5), a threat of infringement proceedings made by any person is actionable by any person aggrieved by the threat.

(2)   A threat of infringement proceedings is not actionable if the infringement is alleged to consist of—

(a)   where the invention is a product, making a product for disposal or importing a product for disposal, or

(b)   where the invention is a process, using a process.

(3)   A threat of infringement proceedings is not actionable if the infringement is alleged to consist of an act which, if done, would constitute an infringement of a kind mentioned in subsection (2)(a) or (b).

(4)   A threat of infringement proceedings is not actionable if the threat—

(a)   is made to a person who has done, or intends to do, an act mentioned in subsection (2)(a) or (b) in relation to a product or process, and

(b)   is a threat of proceedings for an infringement alleged to consist of doing anything else in relation to that product or process.

(5)   A threat of infringement proceedings which is not an express threat is not actionable if it is contained in a permitted communication.

(6)   In sections 70C and 70D "an actionable threat" means a threat of infringement proceedings that is actionable in accordance with this section.

70C.   Remedies and defences

(1)   Proceedings in respect of an actionable threat may be brought against the person who made the threat for—

(a)   a declaration that the threat is unjustified;

(b)   an injunction against the continuance of the threat;

(c)   damages in respect of any loss sustained by the aggrieved person by reason of the threat.

(2)   In the application of subsection (1) to Scotland—

(a)   "declaration" means "declarator", and

(b)   "injunction" means "interdict".

(3)   It is a defence for the person who made the threat to show that the act in respect of which proceedings were threatened constitutes (or if done would constitute) an infringement of the patent.

(4)   It is a defence for the person who made the threat to show—

(a)   that, despite having taken reasonable steps, the person has not identified anyone who has done an act mentioned in section 70A(2)(a) or (b) in relation to the product or the use of a process which is the subject of the threat, and

(b)   that the person notified the recipient, before or at the time of making the threat, of the steps taken.

Revocation of patents

72.   Power to revoke patents on application

(1)   Subject to the following provisions of this Act, the court or the comptroller may by order revoke a patent for an invention on the application of any person (including the proprietor of the patent) on (but only on) any of the following grounds, that is to say—

(a)   the invention is not a patentable invention;

(b)   that the patent was granted to a person who was not entitled to be granted that patent;

(c)   the specification of the patent does not disclose the invention clearly enough and completely enough for it to be performed by a person skilled in the art;

(d)   the matter disclosed in the specification of the patent extends beyond that disclosed in the application for the patent, as filed, or, if the patent was granted on a new application filed under section 8(3), 12 or 37(4) above or as mentioned in section 15(9) above, in the earlier application, as filed;

(e)   the protection conferred by the patent has been extended by an amendment which should not have been allowed.

Putting validity in issue

74.   Proceedings in which validity of patent may be put in issue

(1)   Subject to the following provisions of this section, the validity of a patent may be put in issue—

(a)   by way of defence, in proceedings for infringement of the patent under section 61 above or proceedings under section 69 above for infringement of rights conferred by the publication of an application;

(b)   in proceedings in respect of an actionable threat under section 70A above;

(c)   in proceedings in which a declaration in relation to the patent is sought under section 71 above;

(d)   in proceedings before the court or the comptroller under section 72 above for the revocation of the patent;

(e)   in proceedings under section 58 above.

(2)   The validity of a patent may not be put in issue in any other proceedings and, in particular, no proceedings may be instituted (whether under this Act or otherwise) seeking only a declaration as to the validity or invalidity of a patent.

(3)   The only grounds on which the validity of a patent may be put in issue (whether in proceedings for revocation under section 72 above or otherwise) are the grounds on which the patent may be revoked under that section.

Supplemental

125.   Extent of invention

(1)   For the purposes of this Act an invention for a patent for which an application has been made or for which a patent has been granted shall, unless the context otherwise requires, be taken to be that specified in a claim of the specification of the application or patent, as the case may be, as interpreted by the description and any drawings contained in that specification, and the extent of the protection conferred by a patent or application for a patent shall be determined accordingly.

(2)   It is hereby declared for the avoidance of doubt that where more than one invention is specified in any such claim, each invention may have a different priority date under section 5 above.

(3)   The Protocol on the Interpretation of Article 69 of the European Patent Convention (which Article contains a provision corresponding to subsection (1) above) shall, as for the time being in force, apply for the purposes of subsection (1) above as it applies for the purposes of that Article.

Copyright, Designs and Patents Act 1988
1988 c. 48

An Act to restate the law of copyright, with amendments; to make fresh provision as to the rights of performers and others in performances; to confer a design right in original designs; to amend the Registered Designs Act 1949; to make provision with respect to patent agents and trade mark agents; to confer patents and designs jurisdiction on certain county courts; to amend the law of patents; to make provision with respect to devices designed to circumvent copy-protection of works in electronic form; to make fresh provision penalising the fraudulent reception of transmissions; to make the fraudulent application or use of a trade mark an offence; to make provision for the benefit of the Hospital for Sick Children, Great Ormond Street, London; to enable financial assistance to be given to certain international bodies; and for connected purposes   [15th November 1988]

Part I
Copyright

Chapter I
Subsistence, ownership and duration of copyright

Introductory

1.   Copyright and copyright works

(1)   Copyright is a property right which subsists in accordance with this Part in the following descriptions of work—

    (a)   original literary, dramatic, musical or artistic works,

    (b)   sound recordings, films or broadcasts, and

    (c)   the typographical arrangement of published editions.

(2)   In this Part "copyright work" means a work of any of those descriptions in which copyright subsists.

(3)   Copyright does not subsist in a work unless the requirements of this Part with respect to qualification for copyright protection are met (see section 153 and the provisions referred to there).

2.   Rights subsisting in copyright works

(1)   The owner of the copyright in a work of any description has the exclusive right to do the acts specified in Chapter II as the acts restricted by the copyright in a work of that description.

(2)   In relation to certain descriptions of copyright work the following rights conferred by Chapter IV (moral rights) subsist in favour of the author, director or commissioner of the work, whether or not he is the owner of the copyright—

    (a)   section 77 (right to be identified as author or director),

    (b)   section 80 (right to object to derogatory treatment of work), and

    (c)   section 85 (right to privacy of certain photographs and films).

Descriptions of work and related provisions

3.   Literary, dramatic and musical works

(1)   In this Part—

"literary work" means any work, other than a dramatic or musical work, which is written, spoken or sung, and accordingly includes—

    (a)   a table or compilation other than a database,

    (b)   a computer program,

    (c)   preparatory design material for a computer program and

    (d)   a database;

"dramatic work" includes a work of dance or mime; and

"musical work" means a work consisting of music, exclusive of any words or action intended to be sung, spoken or performed with the music.

(2)   Copyright does not subsist in a literary, dramatic or musical work unless and until it is recorded, in writing or otherwise; and references in this Part to the time at which such a work is made are to the time at which it is so recorded.

(3)   It is immaterial for the purposes of subsection (2) whether the work is recorded by or with the permission of the author; and where it is not recorded by the author, nothing in that subsection affects the question whether copyright subsists in the record as distinct from the work recorded.

3A.   Databases

(1)   In this Part "database" means a collection of independent works, data or other materials which—

    (a)   are arranged in a systematic or methodical way, and

    (b)   are individually accessible by electronic or other means.

(2)   For the purposes of this Part a literary work consisting of a database is original if, and only if, by reason of the selection or arrangement of the contents of the database the database constitutes the author's own intellectual creation.

4.   Artistic works

(1)   In this Part "artistic work" means—

    (a)   a graphic work, photograph, sculpture or collage, irrespective of artistic quality,

    (b)   a work of architecture being a building or a model for a building, or

    (c)   a work of artistic craftsmanship.

(2)   In this Part—

"building" includes any fixed structure, and a part of a building or fixed structure;

"graphic work" includes—

    (a)   any painting, drawing, diagram, map, chart or plan, and

    (b)   any engraving, etching, lithograph, woodcut or similar work;

"photograph" means a recording of light or other radiation on any medium on which an image is produced or from which an image may by any means be produced, and which is not part of a film;

"sculpture" includes a cast or model made for purposes of sculpture.

5A.   Sound recordings

(1)   In this Part "sound recording" means—

    (a)   a recording of sounds, from which the sounds may be reproduced, or

    (b)   a recording of the whole or any part of a literary, dramatic or musical work, from which sounds reproducing the work or part may be produced,

regardless of the medium on which the recording is made or the method by which the sounds are reproduced or produced.

(2)   Copyright does not subsist in a sound recording which is, or to the extent that it is, a copy taken from a previous sound recording.

5B.   Films

(1)   In this Part "film" means a recording on any medium from which a moving image may by any means be produced.

(2)   The sound track accompanying a film shall be treated as part of the film for the purposes of this Part.

(3)   Without prejudice to the generality of subsection (2), where that subsection applies—

    (a)   references in this Part to showing a film include playing the film sound track to accompany the film,

    (b)   references in this Part to playing a sound recording, or to communicating a sound recording to the public, do not include playing or communicating the film sound track to accompany the film,

    (c)   references in this Part to copying a work, so far as they apply to a sound recording, do not include copying the film sound track to accompany the film, and

    (d)   references in this Part to the issuing, rental or lending of copies of a work, so far as they apply to a sound recording, do not include the issuing, rental or lending of copies of the sound track to accompany the film.

(4)   Copyright does not subsist in a film which is, or to the extent that it is, a copy taken from a previous film.

(5)   Nothing in this section affects any copyright subsisting in a film sound track as a sound recording.

6.   Broadcasts

(1)   In this Part a "broadcast" means an electronic transmission of visual images, sounds or other information which—

(a)   is transmitted for simultaneous reception by members of the public and is capable of being lawfully received by them, or

(b)   is transmitted at a time determined solely by the person making the transmission for presentation to members of the public,

and which is not excepted by subsection (1A); and references to broadcasting shall be construed accordingly.

(1A)   Excepted from the definition of "broadcast" is any internet transmission unless it is—

(a)   a transmission taking place simultaneously on the internet and by other means,

(b)   a concurrent transmission of a live event, or

(c)   a transmission of recorded moving images or sounds forming part of a programme service offered by the person responsible for making the transmission, being a service in which programmes are transmitted at scheduled times determined by that person.

(2)   An encrypted transmission shall be regarded as capable of being lawfully received by members of the public only if decoding equipment has been made available to members of the public by or with the authority of the person making the transmission or the person providing the contents of the transmission.

(3)   References in this Part to the person making a broadcast or a transmission which is a broadcast are—

(a)   to the person transmitting the programme, if he has responsibility to any extent for its contents, and

(b)   to any person providing the programme who makes with the person transmitting it the arrangements necessary for its transmission;

and references in this Part to a programme, in the context of broadcasting, are to any item included in a broadcast.

(4)   For the purposes of this Part, the place from which a wireless broadcast is made is the place where, under the control and responsibility of the person making the broadcast, the programme-carrying signals are introduced into an uninterrupted chain of communication (including, in the case of a satellite transmission, the chain leading to the satellite and down towards the earth).

(4A)   Subsections (3) and (4) have effect subject to section 6A (safeguards in case of certain satellite broadcasts).

(5)   References in this Part to the reception of a broadcast include reception of a broadcast relayed by means of a telecommunications system.

(5A)   The relaying of a broadcast by reception and immediate re-transmission shall be regarded for the purposes of this Part as a separate act of broadcasting from the making of the broadcast which is so re-transmitted.

(6)   Copyright does not subsist in a broadcast which infringes, or to the extent that it infringes, the copyright in another broadcast.

8.   Published editions

(1)   In this Part "published edition", in the context of copyright in the typographical arrangement of a published edition, means a published edition of the whole or any part of one or more literary, dramatic or musical works.

(2)   Copyright does not subsist in the typographical arrangement of a published edition if, or to the extent that, it reproduces the typographical arrangement of a previous edition.

Authorship and ownership of copyright

9.   Authorship of work

(1)   In this Part "author", in relation to a work, means the person who creates it.

(2)   That person shall be taken to be—

(aa)   in the case of a sound recording, the producer;

(ab)   in the case of a film, the producer and the principal director;

(b)   in the case of a broadcast, the person making the broadcast (see section 6(3)) or, in the case of a broadcast which relays another broadcast by reception and immediate re-transmission, the person making that other broadcast;

(d)   in the case of the typographical arrangement of a published edition, the publisher.

(3)   In the case of a literary, dramatic, musical or artistic work which is computer-generated, the author shall be taken to be the person by whom the arrangements necessary for the creation of the work are undertaken.

(4)   For the purposes of this Part a work is of "unknown authorship" if the identity of the author is unknown or, in the case of a work of joint authorship, if the identity of none of the authors is known.

(5)   For the purposes of this Part the identity of an author shall be regarded as unknown if it is not possible for a person to ascertain his identity by reasonable inquiry; but if his identity is once known it shall not subsequently be regarded as unknown.

11.   First ownership of copyright

(1)   The author of a work is the first owner of any copyright in it, subject to the following provisions.

(2)   Where a literary, dramatic, musical or artistic work, or a film, is made by an employee in the course of his employment, his employer is the first owner of any copyright in the work subject to any agreement to the contrary.

(3)   This section does not apply to Crown copyright or Parliamentary copyright (see sections 163 and 165) or to copyright which subsists by virtue of section 168 (copyright of certain international organisations).

Duration of copyright

12.   Duration of copyright in literary, dramatic, musical or artistic works

(1)   The following provisions have effect with respect to the duration of copyright in a literary, dramatic, musical or artistic work.

(2)   Copyright expires at the end of the period of 70 years from the end of the calendar year in which the author dies, subject as follows.

(3)   If the work is of unknown authorship, copyright expires—

(a)   at the end of the period of 70 years from the end of the calendar year in which the work was made, or

(b)   if during that period the work is made available to the public, at the end of the period of 70 years from the end of the calendar year in which it is first so made available,

subject as follows.

(4)   Subsection (2) applies if the identity of the author becomes known before the end of the period specified in paragraph (a) or (b) of subsection (3).

(5)   For the purposes of subsection (3) making available to the public includes—

(a)   in the case of a literary, dramatic or musical work—

(i)   performance in public, or

(ii)   communication to the public;

(b)   in the case of an artistic work—

(i)   exhibition in public,

(ii)   a film including the work being shown in public, or

(iii)   communication to the public;

but in determining generally for the purposes of that subsection whether a work has been made available to the public no account shall be taken of any unauthorised act.

(6)   Where the country of origin of the work is not the United Kingdom and the author of the work is not a national of the United Kingdom, the duration of copyright is that to which the work is entitled in the country of origin, provided that does not exceed the period which would apply under subsections (2) to (5).

(7)   If the work is computer-generated the above provisions do not apply and copyright expires at the end of the period of 50 years from the end of the calendar year in which the work was made.

(8)   The provisions of this section are adapted as follows in relation to a work of joint authorship or a work of co-authorship—

(a)   the reference in subsection (2) to the death of the author shall be construed—

    (i)   if the identity of all the authors is known, as a reference to the death of the last of them to die, and

    (ii)   if the identity of one or more of the authors is known and the identity of one or more others is not, as a reference to the death of the last whose identity is known;

(b)   the reference in subsection (4) to the identity of the author becoming known shall be construed as a reference to the identity of any of the authors becoming known;

(c)   the reference in subsection (6) to the author not being a national of the United Kingdom shall be construed as a reference to none of the authors being a national of the United Kingdom.

(9)   This section does not apply to Crown copyright or Parliamentary copyright (see sections 163 to 166D) or to copyright which subsists by virtue of section 168 (copyright of certain international organisations).

Chapter II
Rights of Copyright Owner

The acts restricted by copyright

16.   The acts restricted by copyright in a work

(1)   The owner of the copyright in a work has, in accordance with the following provisions of this Chapter, the exclusive right to do the following acts in the United Kingdom—

(a)   to copy the work (see section 17);

(b)   to issue copies of the work to the public (see section 18);

(ba)   to rent or lend the work to the public (see section 18A);

(c)   to perform, show or play the work in public (see section 19);

(d)   to communicate the work to the public (see section 20);

(e)   to make an adaptation of the work or do any of the above in relation to an adaptation (see section 21);

and those acts are referred to in this Part as the "acts restricted by the copyright".

(2)   Copyright in a work is infringed by a person who without the licence of the copyright owner does, or authorises another to do, any of the acts restricted by the copyright.

(3)   References in this Part to the doing of an act restricted by the copyright in a work are to the doing of it—

(a)   in relation to the work as a whole or any substantial part of it, and

(b)   either directly or indirectly;

and it is immaterial whether any intervening acts themselves infringe copyright.

(4)   This Chapter has effect subject to—

(a)   the provisions of Chapter III (acts permitted in relation to copyright works), and

(b)   the provisions of Chapter VII (provisions with respect to copyright licensing).

17.   Infringement of copyright by copying

(1)   The copying of the work is an act restricted by the copyright in every description of copyright work; and references in this Part to copying and copies shall be construed as follows.

(2)   Copying in relation to a literary, dramatic, musical or artistic work means reproducing the work in any material form.

This includes storing the work in any medium by electronic means.

(3)   In relation to an artistic work copying includes the making of a copy in three dimensions of a two-dimensional work and the making of a copy in two dimensions of a three-dimensional work.

(4)   Copying in relation to a film or broadcast includes making a photograph of the whole or any substantial part of any image forming part of the film or broadcast.

(5)   Copying in relation to the typographical arrangement of a published edition means making a facsimile copy of the arrangement.

(6)   Copying in relation to any description of work includes the making of copies which are transient or are incidental to some other use of the work.

18.   Infringement by issue of copies to the public

(1)   The issue to the public of copies of the work is an act restricted by the copyright in every description of copyright work.

(2)   References in this Part to the issue to the public of copies of a work are to the act of putting into circulation in the United Kingdom copies not previously put into circulation in the United Kingdom or the EEA by or with the consent of the copyright owner.

(3)   References in this Part to the issue to the public of copies of a work do not include—

(a)   any subsequent distribution, sale, hiring or loan of copies previously put into circulation (but see section 18A: infringement by rental or lending).

(4)   References in this Part to the issue of copies of a work include the issue of the original.

18A.   Infringement by rental or lending of work to the public

(1)   The rental or lending of copies of the work to the public is an act restricted by the copyright in—

(a)   a literary, dramatic or musical work,

(b)   an artistic work, other than—

(i)   a work of architecture in the form of a building or a model for a building, or

(ii)   a work of applied art, or

(c)   a film or a sound recording.

(2)   In this Part, subject to the following provisions of this section—

(a)   "rental" means making a copy of the work available for use, on terms that it will or may be returned, for direct or indirect economic or commercial advantage, and

(b)   "lending" means making a copy of the work available for use, on terms that it will or may be returned, otherwise than for direct or indirect economic or commercial advantage, through an establishment which is accessible to the public.

(3)   The expressions "rental" and "lending" do not include—

(a)   making available for the purpose of public performance, playing or showing in public or communication to the public;

(b)   making available for the purpose of exhibition in public; or

(c)   making available for on-the-spot reference use.

(4)   The expression "lending" does not include making available between establishments which are accessible to the public.

(5)   Where lending by an establishment accessible to the public gives rise to a payment the amount of which does not go beyond what is necessary to cover the operating costs of the establishment, there is no direct or indirect economic or commercial advantage for the purposes of this section.

(6)   References in this Part to the rental or lending of copies of a work include the rental or lending of the original.

19.   Infringement by performance, showing or playing of work in public

(1)   The performance of the work in public is an act restricted by the copyright in a literary, dramatic or musical work.

(2)   In this Part "performance", in relation to a work—

(a)   includes delivery in the case of lectures, addresses, speeches and sermons, and

(b)   in general, includes any mode of visual or acoustic presentation, including presentation by means of a sound recording, film or broadcast of the work.

(3)   The playing or showing of the work in public is an act restricted by the copyright in a sound recording, film or broadcast.

(4)   Where copyright in a work is infringed by its being performed, played or shown in public by means of apparatus for receiving visual images or sounds conveyed by electronic means, the person by whom the visual images or sounds are sent, and in the case of a performance the performers, shall not be regarded as responsible for the infringement.

20.   Infringement by communication to the public

(1)   The communication to the public of the work is an act restricted by the copyright in—

(a)   a literary, dramatic, musical or artistic work,

(b)   a sound recording or film, or

(c)   a broadcast.

(2)   References in this Part to communication to the public are to communication to the public by electronic transmission, and in relation to a work include—

(a)   the broadcasting of the work;

(b)   the making available to the public of the work by electronic transmission in such a way that members of the public may access it from a place and at a time individually chosen by them.

21.   Infringement by making adaptation or act done in relation to adaptation

(1)   The making of an adaptation of the work is an act restricted by the copyright in a literary, dramatic or musical work.

For this purpose an adaptation is made when it is recorded, in writing or otherwise.

(2)   The doing of any of the acts specified in sections 17 to 20, or subsection (1) above, in relation to an adaptation of the work is also an act restricted by the copyright in a literary, dramatic or musical work.

For this purpose it is immaterial whether the adaptation has been recorded, in writing or otherwise, at the time the act is done.

(3)   In this Part "adaptation"—

(a)   in relation to a literary work, other than a computer program or a database, or in relation to a dramatic work, means—

(i)   a translation of the work;

(ii)   a version of a dramatic work in which it is converted into a non-dramatic work or, as the case may be, of a non-dramatic work in which it is converted into a dramatic work;

(iii)   a version of the work in which the story or action is conveyed wholly or mainly by means of pictures in a form suitable for reproduction in a book, or in a newspaper, magazine or similar periodical;

(ab)   in relation to a computer program, means an arrangement or altered version of the program or a translation of it;

(ac)   in relation to a database, means an arrangement or altered version of the database or a translation of it;

(b)   in relation to a musical work, means an arrangement or transcription of the work.

(4)   In relation to a computer program a "translation" includes a version of the program in which it is converted into or out of a computer language or code or into a different computer language or code.

(5)   No inference shall be drawn from this section as to what does or does not amount to copying a work.

Secondary infringement of copyright

22.   Secondary infringement: importing infringing copy

The copyright in a work is infringed by a person who, without the licence of the copyright owner, imports into the United Kingdom, otherwise than for his private and domestic use, an article which is, and which he knows or has reason to believe is, an infringing copy of the work.

23.   Secondary infringement: possessing or dealing with infringing copy

The copyright in a work is infringed by a person who, without the licence of the copyright owner—

(a)   possesses in the course of a business,

(b)   sells or lets for hire, or offers or exposes for sale or hire,

(c)   in the course of a business exhibits in public or distributes, or

(d)   distributes otherwise than in the course of a business to such an extent as to affect prejudicially the owner of the copyright,

an article which is, and which he knows or has reason to believe is, an infringing copy of the work.

24.   Secondary infringement: providing means for making infringing copies

(1)   Copyright in a work is infringed by a person who, without the licence of the copyright owner—

(a)   makes,

(b)   imports into the United Kingdom,

(c)   possesses in the course of a business, or

(d)   sells or lets for hire, or offers or exposes for sale or hire, an article specifically designed or adapted for making copies of that work, knowing or having reason to believe that it is to be used to make infringing copies.

(2)   Copyright in a work is infringed by a person who without the licence of the copyright owner transmits the work by means of a telecommunications system (otherwise than by communication to the public), knowing or having reason to believe that infringing copies of the work will be made by means of the reception of the transmission in the United Kingdom or elsewhere.

25.   Secondary infringement: permitting use of premises for infringing performance

(1)   Where the copyright in a literary, dramatic or musical work is infringed by a performance at a place of public entertainment, any person who gave permission for that place to be used for the performance is also liable for the infringement unless when he gave permission he believed on reasonable grounds that the performance would not infringe copyright.

(2)   In this section "place of public entertainment" includes premises which are occupied mainly for other purposes but are from time to time made available for hire for the purposes of public entertainment.

26.   Secondary infringement: provision of apparatus for infringing performance, &c.

(1)   Where copyright in a work is infringed by a public performance of the work, or by the playing or showing of the work in public, by means of apparatus for—

(a)   playing sound recordings,

(b)   showing films, or

(c)   receiving visual images or sounds conveyed by electronic means,

the following persons are also liable for the infringement.

(2)   A person who supplied the apparatus, or any substantial part of it, is liable for the infringement if when he supplied the apparatus or part—

(a)   he knew or had reason to believe that the apparatus was likely to be so used as to infringe copyright, or

(b)   in the case of apparatus whose normal use involves a public performance, playing or showing, he did not believe on reasonable grounds that it would not be so used as to infringe copyright.

(3)   An occupier of premises who gave permission for the apparatus to be brought onto the premises is liable for the infringement if when he gave permission he knew or had reason to believe that the apparatus was likely to be so used as to infringe copyright.

(4)   A person who supplied a copy of a sound recording or film used to infringe copyright is liable for the infringement if when he supplied it he knew or had reason to believe that what he supplied, or a copy made directly or indirectly from it, was likely to be so used as to infringe copyright.

Designs

51.   Design documents and models

(1)   It is not an infringement of any copyright in a design document or model recording or embodying a design for anything other than an artistic work or a typeface to make an article to the design or to copy an article made to the design.

(2)   Nor is it an infringement of the copyright to issue to the public, or include in a film or communicate to the public, anything the making of which was, by virtue of subsection (1), not an infringement of that copyright.

(3)   In this section—

"design" means the design of the shape or configuration (whether internal or external) of the whole or part of an article, other than surface decoration; and

"design document" means any record of a design, whether in the form of a drawing, a written description, a photograph, data stored in a computer or otherwise.

Chapter IV
Moral Rights

Right to be identified as author or director

77.   Right to be identified as author or director

(1)   The author of a copyright literary, dramatic, musical or artistic work, and the director of a copyright film, has the right to be identified as the author or director of the work in the circumstances

mentioned in this section; but the right is not infringed unless it has been asserted in accordance with section 78.

(2)   The author of a literary work (other than words intended to be sung or spoken with music) or a dramatic work has the right to be identified whenever—

    (a)   the work is published commercially, performed in public or communicated to the public; or

    (b)   copies of a film or sound recording including the work are issued to the public;

and that right includes the right to be identified whenever any of those events occur in relation to an adaptation of the work as the author of the work from which the adaptation was made.

(3)   The author of a musical work, or a literary work consisting of words intended to be sung or spoken with music, has the right to be identified whenever—

    (a)   the work is published commercially;

    (b)   copies of a sound recording of the work are issued to the public; or

    (c)   a film of which the sound-track includes the work is shown in public or copies of such a film are issued to the public;

and that right includes the right to be identified whenever any of those events occur in relation to an adaptation of the work as the author of the work from which the adaptation was made.

(4)   The author of an artistic work has the right to be identified whenever—

    (a)   the work is published commercially or exhibited in public, or a visual image of it is communicated to the public;

    (b)   a film including a visual image of the work is shown in public or copies of such a film are issued to the public; or

    (c)   in the case of a work of architecture in the form of a building or a model for a building, a sculpture or a work of artistic craftsmanship, copies of a graphic work representing it, or of a photograph of it, are issued to the public.

(5)   The author of a work of architecture in the form of a building also has the right to be identified on the building as constructed or, where more than one building is constructed to the design, on the first to be constructed.

(6)   The director of a film has the right to be identified whenever the film is shown in public or communicated to the public or copies of the film are issued to the public.

(7)   The right of the author or director under this section is—

    (a)   in the case of commercial publication or the issue to the public of copies of a film or sound recording, to be identified in or on each copy or, if that is not appropriate, in some other manner likely to bring his identity to the notice of a person acquiring a copy,

    (b)   in the case of identification on a building, to be identified by appropriate means visible to persons entering or approaching the building, and

    (c)   in any other case, to be identified in a manner likely to bring his identity to the attention of a person seeing or hearing the performance, exhibition, showing or communication to the public in question;

and the identification must in each case be clear and reasonably prominent.

(8)   If the author or director in asserting his right to be identified specifies a pseudonym, initials or some other particular form of identification, that form shall be used; otherwise any reasonable form of identification may be used.

(9)   This section has effect subject to section 79 (exceptions to right).

Right to object to derogatory treatment of work

80.   Right to object to derogatory treatment of work

(1)   The author of a copyright literary, dramatic, musical or artistic work, and the director of a copyright film, has the right in the circumstances mentioned in this section not to have his work subjected to derogatory treatment.

(2)   For the purposes of this section—

    (a)   "treatment" of a work means any addition to, deletion from or alteration to or adaptation of the work, other than—

        (i)   a translation of a literary or dramatic work, or

(ii)   an arrangement or transcription of a musical work involving no more than a change of key or register; and

(b)   the treatment of a work is derogatory if it amounts to distortion or mutilation of the work or is otherwise prejudicial to the honour or reputation of the author or director;

and in the following provisions of this section references to a derogatory treatment of a work shall be construed accordingly.

(3)   In the case of a literary, dramatic or musical work the right is infringed by a person who—

(a)   publishes commercially, performs in public or communicates to the public a derogatory treatment of the work; or

(b)   issues to the public copies of a film or sound recording of, or including, a derogatory treatment of the work.

(4)   In the case of an artistic work the right is infringed by a person who—

(a)   publishes commercially or exhibits in public a derogatory treatment of the work, or communicates to the public a visual image of a derogatory treatment of the work,

(b)   shows in public a film including a visual image of a derogatory treatment of the work or issues to the public copies of such a film, or

(c)   in the case of—

(i)   a work of architecture in the form of a model for a building,

(ii)   a sculpture, or

(iii)   a work of artistic craftsmanship,

issues to the public copies of a graphic work representing, or of a photograph of, a derogatory treatment of the work.

(5)   Subsection (4) does not apply to a work of architecture in the form of a building; but where the author of such a work is identified on the building and it is the subject of derogatory treatment he has the right to require the identification to be removed.

(6)   In the case of a film, the right is infringed by a person who—

(a)   shows in public or communicates to the public a derogatory treatment of the film; or

(b)   issues to the public copies of a derogatory treatment of the film,

(7)   The right conferred by this section extends to the treatment of parts of a work resulting from a previous treatment by a person other than the author or director, if those parts are attributed to, or are likely to be regarded as the work of, the author or director.

(8)   This section has effect subject to sections 81 and 82 (exceptions to and qualifications of right).

False attribution of work

84.   False attribution of work

(1)   A person has the right in the circumstances mentioned in this section—

(a)   not to have a literary, dramatic, musical or artistic work falsely attributed to him as author, and

(b)   not to have a film falsely attributed to him as director;

and in this section an "attribution", in relation to such a work, means a statement (express or implied) as to who is the author or director.

(2)   The right is infringed by a person who—

(a)   issues to the public copies of a work of any of those descriptions in or on which there is a false attribution, or

(b)   exhibits in public an artistic work, or a copy of an artistic work, in or on which there is a false attribution.

(3)   The right is also infringed by a person who—

(a)   in the case of a literary, dramatic or musical work, performs the work in public or communicates it to the public as being the work of a person, or

(b)   in the case of a film, shows it in public or communicates it to the public as being directed by a person,

knowing or having reason to believe that the attribution is false.

(4)   The right is also infringed by the issue to the public or public display of material containing a false attribution in connection with any of the acts mentioned in subsection (2) or (3).

(5)   The right is also infringed by a person who in the course of a business—

  (a)   possesses or deals with a copy of a work of any of the descriptions mentioned in subsection (1) in or on which there is a false attribution, or

  (b)   in the case of an artistic work, possesses or deals with the work itself when there is a false attribution in or on it,

knowing or having reason to believe that there is such an attribution and that it is false.

(6)   In the case of an artistic work the right is also infringed by a person who in the course of a business—

  (a)   deals with a work which has been altered after the author parted with possession of it as being the unaltered work of the author, or

  (b)   deals with a copy of such a work as being a copy of the unaltered work of the author,

knowing or having reason to believe that that is not the case.

(7)   References in this section to dealing are to selling or letting for hire, offering or exposing for sale or hire, exhibiting in public, or distributing.

(8)   This section applies where, contrary to the fact—

  (a)   a literary, dramatic or musical work is falsely represented as being an adaptation of the work of a person, or

  (b)   a copy of an artistic work is falsely represented as being a copy made by the author of the artistic work,

as it applies where the work is falsely attributed to a person as author.

Right to privacy of certain photographs and films

85.   Right to privacy of certain photographs and films

(1)   A person who for private and domestic purposes commissions the taking of a photograph or the making of a film has, where copyright subsists in the resulting work, the right not to have—

  (a)   copies of the work issued to the public,

  (b)   the work exhibited or shown in public, or

  (c)   the work communicated to the public;

and, except as mentioned in subsection (2), a person who does or authorises the doing of any of those acts infringes that right.

(2)   The right is not infringed by an act which by virtue of any of the following provisions would not infringe copyright in the work—

  (a)   section 31 (incidental inclusion of work in an artistic work, film or broadcast);

  (b)   section 45 (parliamentary and judicial proceedings);

  (c)   section 46 (Royal Commissions and statutory inquiries);

  (d)   section 50 (acts done under statutory authority);

  (e)   section 57 or 66A (acts permitted on assumptions as to expiry of copyright, &c.).

Chapter V
Dealings with Rights in Copyright Works

Copyright

90.   Assignment and licences

(1)   Copyright is transmissible by assignment, by testamentary disposition or by operation of law, as personal or moveable property.

(2)   An assignment or other transmission of copyright may be partial, that is, limited so as to apply—

  (a)   to one or more, but not all, of the things the copyright owner has the exclusive right to do;

  (b)   to part, but not the whole, of the period for which the copyright is to subsist.

(3)   An assignment of copyright is not effective unless it is in writing signed by or on behalf of the assignor.

(4)   A licence granted by a copyright owner is binding on every successor in title to his interest in the copyright, except a purchaser in good faith for valuable consideration and without notice (actual or constructive) of the licence or a person deriving title from such a purchaser; and references in this Part to doing anything with, or without, the licence of the copyright owner shall be construed accordingly.

92.   Exclusive licences

(1)   In this Part an "exclusive licence" means a licence in writing signed by or on behalf of the copyright owner authorising the licensee to the exclusion of all other persons, including the person granting the licence, to exercise a right which would otherwise be exercisable exclusively by the copyright owner.

(2)   The licensee under an exclusive licence has the same rights against a successor in title who is bound by the licence as he has against the person granting the licence.

Moral rights

94.   Moral rights not assignable

The rights conferred by Chapter IV (moral rights) are not assignable.

Chapter VI
Remedies for Infringement

Rights and remedies of copyright owner

96.   Infringement actionable by copyright owner

(1)   An infringement of copyright is actionable by the copyright owner.

(2)   In an action for infringement of copyright all such relief by way of damages, injunctions, accounts or otherwise is available to the plaintiff as is available in respect of the infringement of any other property right.

(3)   This section has effect subject to the following provisions of this Chapter.

97.   Provisions as to damages in infringement action

(1)   Where in an action for infringement of copyright it is shown that at the time of the infringement the defendant did not know, and had no reason to believe, that copyright subsisted in the work to which the action relates, the plaintiff is not entitled to damages against him, but without prejudice to any other remedy.

(2)   The court may in an action for infringement of copyright having regard to all the circumstances, and in particular to—

(a)   the flagrancy of the infringement, and

(b)   any benefit accruing to the defendant by reason of the infringement,

award such additional damages as the justice of the case may require.

99.   Order for delivery up

(1)   Where a person—

(a)   has an infringing copy of a work in his possession, custody or control in the course of a business, or

(b)   has in his possession, custody or control an article specifically designed or adapted for making copies of a particular copyright work, knowing or having reason to believe that it has been or is to be used to make infringing copies,

the owner of the copyright in the work may apply to the court for an order that the infringing copy or article be delivered up to him or to such other person as the court may direct.

(2)   An application shall not be made after the end of the period specified in section 113 (period after which remedy of delivery up not available); and no order shall be made unless the court also makes, or it appears to the court that there are grounds for making, an order under section 114 (order as to disposal of infringing copy or other article).

(3)   A person to whom an infringing copy or other article is delivered up in pursuance of an order under this section shall, if an order under section 114 is not made, retain it pending the making of an order, or the decision not to make an order, under that section.

(4)   Nothing in this section affects any other power of the court.

100.   Right to seize infringing copies and other articles

(1)   An infringing copy of a work which is found exposed or otherwise immediately available for sale or hire, and in respect of which the copyright owner would be entitled to apply for an order under section 99, may be seized and detained by him or a person authorised by him.

The right to seize and detain is exercisable subject to the following conditions and is subject to any decision of the court under section 114.

(2)   Before anything is seized under this section notice of the time and place of the proposed seizure must be given to a local police station.

(3)   A person may for the purpose of exercising the right conferred by this section enter premises to which the public have access but may not seize anything in the possession, custody or control of a person at a permanent or regular place of business of his, and may not use any force.

(4)   At the time when anything is seized under this section there shall be left at the place where it was seized a notice in the prescribed form containing the prescribed particulars as to the person by whom or on whose authority the seizure is made and the grounds on which it is made.

(5)   In this section—

"premises" includes land, buildings, moveable structures, vehicles, vessels, aircraft and hovercraft; and

"prescribed" means prescribed by order of the Secretary of State.

(6)   An order of the Secretary of State under this section shall be made by statutory instrument which shall be subject to annulment in pursuance of a resolution of either House of Parliament.

Rights and remedies of exclusive licensee

101.   Rights and remedies of exclusive licensee

(1)   An exclusive licensee has, except against the copyright owner, the same rights and remedies in respect of matters occurring after the grant of the licence as if the licence had been an assignment.

(2)   His rights and remedies are concurrent with those of the copyright owner; and references in the relevant provisions of this Part to the copyright owner shall be construed accordingly.

(3)   In an action brought by an exclusive licensee by virtue of this section a defendant may avail himself of any defence which would have been available to him if the action had been brought by the copyright owner.

101A.   Certain infringements actionable by a non-exclusive licensee

(1)   A non-exclusive licensee may bring an action for infringement of copyright if—

    (a)   the infringing act was directly connected to a prior licensed act of the licensee; and

    (b)   the licence—

        (i)   is in writing and is signed by or on behalf of the copyright owner; and

        (ii)   expressly grants the non-exclusive licensee a right of action under this section.

(2)   In an action brought under this section, the non-exclusive licensee shall have the same rights and remedies available to him as the copyright owner would have had if he had brought the action.

(3)   The rights granted under this section are concurrent with those of the copyright owner and references in the relevant provisions of this Part to the copyright owner shall be construed accordingly.

(4)   In an action brought by a non-exclusive licensee by virtue of this section a defendant may avail himself of any defence which would have been available to him if the action had been brought by the copyright owner.

(5)   Subsections (1) to (4) of section 102 shall apply to a non-exclusive licensee who has a right of action by virtue of this section as it applies to an exclusive licensee.

(6)   In this section a "non-exclusive licensee" means the holder of a licence authorising the licensee to exercise a right which remains exercisable by the copyright owner.

102.   Exercise of concurrent rights

(1)   Where an action for infringement of copyright brought by the copyright owner or an exclusive licensee relates (wholly or partly) to an infringement in respect of which they have concurrent rights of action, the copyright owner or, as the case may be, the exclusive licensee may not, without the leave of the court, proceed with the action unless the other is either joined as a plaintiff or added as a defendant.

(2)   A copyright owner or exclusive licensee who is added as a defendant in pursuance of subsection (1) is not liable for any costs in the action unless he takes part in the proceedings.

(3)   The above provisions do not affect the granting of interlocutory relief on an application by a copyright owner or exclusive licensee alone.

(4)   Where an action for infringement of copyright is brought which relates (wholly or partly) to an infringement in respect of which the copyright owner and an exclusive licensee have or had concurrent rights of action—

    (a)   the court shall in assessing damages take into account—

(i)   the terms of the licence, and

(ii)   any pecuniary remedy already awarded or available to either of them in respect of the infringement;

(b)   no account of profits shall be directed if an award of damages has been made, or an account of profits has been directed, in favour of the other of them in respect of the infringement; and

(c)   the court shall if an account of profits is directed apportion the profits between them as the court considers just, subject to any agreement between them;

and these provisions apply whether or not the copyright owner and the exclusive licensee are both parties to the action.

(5)   The copyright owner shall notify any exclusive licensee having concurrent rights before applying for an order under section 99 (order for delivery up) or exercising the right conferred by section 100 (right of seizure); and the court may on the application of the licensee make such order under section 99 or, as the case may be, prohibiting or permitting the exercise by the copyright owner of the right conferred by section 100, as it thinks fit having regard to the terms of the licence.

Offences

107.   Criminal liability for making or dealing with infringing articles, &c.

(1)   A person commits an offence who, without the licence of the copyright owner—

(a)   makes for sale or hire, or

(b)   imports into the United Kingdom otherwise than for his private and domestic use, or

(c)   possesses in the course of a business with a view to committing any act infringing the copyright, or

(d)   in the course of a business—

(i)   sells or lets for hire, or

(ii)   offers or exposes for sale or hire, or

(iii)   exhibits in public, or

(iv)   distributes, or

(e)   distributes otherwise than in the course of a business to such an extent as to affect prejudicially the owner of the copyright,

an article which is, and which he knows or has reason to believe is, an infringing copy of a copyright work.

(2)   A person commits an offence who—

(a)   makes an article specifically designed or adapted for making copies of a particular copyright work, or

(b)   has such an article in his possession,

knowing or having reason to believe that it is to be used to make infringing copies for sale or hire or for use in the course of a business.

(2A)   A person ("P") who infringes copyright in a work by communicating the work to the public commits an offence if P—

(a)   knows or has reason to believe that P is infringing copyright in the work, and

(b)   either—

(i)   intends to make a gain for P or another person, or

(ii)   knows or has reason to believe that communicating the work to the public will cause loss to the owner of the copyright, or will expose the owner of the copyright to a risk of loss.

(2B)   For the purposes of subsection (2A)—

(a)   "gain" and "loss"—

(i)   extend only to gain or loss in money, and

(ii)   include any such gain or loss whether temporary or permanent, and

(b)   "loss" includes a loss by not getting what one might get.

(3)   Where copyright is infringed (otherwise than by reception of a communication to the public)—

(a)   by the public performance of a literary, dramatic or musical work, or

(b)   by the playing or showing in public of a sound recording or film, any person who caused the work to be so performed, played or shown is guilty of an offence if he knew or had reason to believe that copyright would be infringed.

(4)   A person guilty of an offence under subsection (1)(a), (b), (d)(iv) or (e) is liable—

    (a)   on summary conviction to imprisonment for a term not exceeding six months or a fine, or both;

    (b)   on conviction on indictment to a fine or imprisonment for a term not exceeding ten years, or both.

(4A)   A person guilty of an offence under subsection (2A) is liable—

    (a)   on summary conviction to imprisonment for a term not exceeding three months or a fine, or both;

    (b)   on conviction on indictment to a fine or imprisonment for a term not exceeding ten years, or both.

(5)   A person guilty of any other offence under this section is liable on summary conviction to imprisonment for a term not exceeding three months or a fine not exceeding level 5 on the standard scale, or both.

(6)   Sections 104 to 106 (presumptions as to various matters connected with copyright) do not apply to proceedings for an offence under this section; but without prejudice to their application in proceedings for an order under section 108 below.

107A.   Enforcement by local weights and measures authority

(1)   It is the duty of every local weights and measures authority to enforce within their area the provisions of section 107.

(3)   Subsection (1) above does not apply in relation to the enforcement of section 107 in Northern Ireland, but it is the duty of the Department of Economic Development to enforce that section in Northern Ireland.

(3A)   For the investigatory powers available to a local weights and measures authority or the Department of Enterprise, Trade and Investment in Northern Ireland for the purposes of the duties in this section, see Schedule 5 to the Consumer Rights Act 2015.

(4)   Any enactment which authorises the disclosure of information for the purpose of facilitating the enforcement of the Trade Descriptions Act 1968 shall apply as if section 107 were contained in that Act and as if the functions of any person in relation to the enforcement of that section were functions under that Act.

(5)   Nothing in this section shall be construed as authorising a local weights and measures authority to bring proceedings in Scotland for an offence.

108.   Order for delivery up in criminal proceedings

(1)   The court before which proceedings are brought against a person for an offence under section 107 may, if satisfied that at the time of his arrest or charge—

    (a)   he had in his possession, custody or control in the course of a business an infringing copy of a copyright work, or

    (b)   he had in his possession, custody or control an article specifically designed or adapted for making copies of a particular copyright work, knowing or having reason to believe that it had been or was to be used to make infringing copies,

order that the infringing copy or article be delivered up to the copyright owner or to such other person as the court may direct.

(2)   For this purpose a person shall be treated as charged with an offence—

    (a)   in England, Wales and Northern Ireland, when he is orally charged or is served with a summons or indictment;

    (b)   in Scotland, when he is cautioned, charged or served with a complaint or indictment.

(3)   An order may be made by the court of its own motion or on the application of the prosecutor (or, in Scotland, the Lord Advocate or procurator-fiscal), and may be made whether or not the person is convicted of the offence, but shall not be made—

    (a)   after the end of the period specified in section 113 (period after which remedy of delivery up not available), or

    (b)   if it appears to the court unlikely that any order will be made under section 114 (order as to disposal of infringing copy or other article).

(4)   An appeal lies from an order made under this section by a magistrates' court—

    (a)   in England and Wales, to the Crown Court, and

    (b)   in Northern Ireland, to the county court;

and in Scotland, where an order has been made under this section, the person from whose possession, custody or control the infringing copy or article has been removed may, without prejudice to any other form of appeal under any rule of law, appeal against that order in the same manner as against sentence.

(5)   A person to whom an infringing copy or other article is delivered up in pursuance of an order under this section shall retain it pending the making of an order, or the decision not to make an order, under section 114.

(6)   Nothing in this section affects the powers of the court under section 153 of the Sentencing Code, Part II of the Proceeds of Crime (Scotland) Act 1995 or Article 11 of the Criminal Justice (Northern Ireland) Order 1994 (general provisions as to forfeiture in criminal proceedings).

Supplementary

114.   Order as to disposal of infringing copy or other article

(1)   An application may be made to the court for an order that an infringing copy or other article delivered up in pursuance of an order under section 99 or 108, or seized and detained in pursuance of the right conferred by section 100, shall be—

    (a)   forfeited to the copyright owner, or

    (b)   destroyed or otherwise dealt with as the court may think fit,

or for a decision that no such order should be made.

(2)   In considering what order (if any) should be made, the court shall consider whether other remedies available in an action for infringement of copyright would be adequate to compensate the copyright owner and to protect his interests.

(3)   Provision shall be made by rules of court as to the service of notice on persons having an interest in the copy or other articles, and any such person is entitled—

    (a)   to appear in proceedings for an order under this section, whether or not he was served with notice, and

    (b)   to appeal against any order made, whether or not he appeared;

and an order shall not take effect until the end of the period within which notice of an appeal may be given or, if before the end of that period notice of appeal is duly given, until the final determination or abandonment of the proceedings on the appeal.

(4)   Where there is more than one person interested in a copy or other article, the court shall make such order as it thinks just and may (in particular) direct that the article be sold, or otherwise dealt with, and the proceeds divided.

(5)   If the court decides that no order should be made under this section, the person in whose possession, custody or control the copy or other article was before being delivered up or seized is entitled to its return.

(6)   References in this section to a person having an interest in a copy or other article include any person in whose favour an order could be made in respect of it—

    (a)   under this section or under section 204 or 231 of this Act;

    (b)   under section 24D of the Registered Designs Act 1949;

    (c)   under section 19 of Trade Marks Act 1994; or

    (d)   under regulation 1C of the Community Design Regulations 2005 (SI 2005/2339).

Part III
Design Right

Chapter I
Design Right in Original Designs

Introductory

213.   Design right

(1)   Design right is a property right which subsists in accordance with this Part in an original design.

(2)   In this Part "design" means the design of the shape or configuration (whether internal or external) of the whole or part of an article.

(3)   Design right does not subsist in—

    (a)   a method or principle of construction,

    (b)   features of shape or configuration of an article which—

        (i)   enable the article to be connected to, or placed in, around or against, another article so that either article may perform its function, or

        (ii)   are dependent upon the appearance of another article of which the article is intended by the designer to form an integral part, or

    (c)   surface decoration.

(4)   A design is not "original" for the purposes of this Part if it is commonplace in a qualifying country in the design field in question at the time of its creation; and "qualifying country" has the meaning given in section 217(3).

(5)   Design right subsists in a design only if the design qualifies for design right protection by reference to—

    (a)   the designer or the person by whom the designer was employed (see sections 218 and 219), or

    (b)   the person by whom and country in which articles made to the design were first marketed (see section 220),

or in accordance with any Order under section 221 (power to make further provision with respect to qualification).

(5A)   Design right does not subsist in a design which consists of or contains a controlled representation within the meaning of the Olympic Symbol etc. (Protection) Act 1995.

(6)   Design right does not subsist unless and until the design has been recorded in a design document or an article has been made to the design.

(7)   Design right does not subsist in a design which was so recorded, or to which an article was made, before the commencement of this Part.

214.   The designer

(1)   In this Part the "designer", in relation to a design, means the person who creates it.

(2)   In the case of a computer-generated design the person by whom the arrangements necessary for the creation of the design are undertaken shall be taken to be the designer.

215.   Ownership of design right

(1)   The designer is the first owner of any design right in a design which is not created in the course of employment.

(3)   Where a design is created by an employee in the course of his employment, his employer is the first owner of any design right in the design.

(4)   If a design qualifies for design right protection by virtue of section 220 (qualification by reference to first marketing of articles made to the design), the above rules do not apply and the person by whom the articles in question are marketed is the first owner of the design right.

216.   Duration of design right

(1)   Design right expires—

    (a)   fifteen years from the end of the calendar year in which the design was first recorded in a design document or an article was first made to the design, whichever first occurred, or

    (b)   if articles made to the design are made available for sale or hire within five years from the end of that calendar year, ten years from the end of the calendar year in which that first occurred.

(2)   The reference in subsection (1) to articles being made available for sale or hire is to their being made so available anywhere in the world by or with the licence of the design right owner.

Chapter II
Rights of Design Right Owner and Remedies

Infringement of design right

226.   Primary infringement of design right

(1)   The owner of design right in a design has the exclusive right to reproduce the design for commercial purposes—

    (a)   by making articles to that design, or

(b)   by making a design document recording the design for the purpose of enabling such articles to be made.

(2)   Reproduction of a design by making articles to the design means copying the design so as to produce articles exactly or substantially to that design, and references in this Part to making articles to a design shall be construed accordingly.

(3)   Design right is infringed by a person who without the licence of the design right owner does, or authorises another to do, anything which by virtue of this section is the exclusive right of the design right owner.

(4)   For the purposes of this section reproduction may be direct or indirect, and it is immaterial whether any intervening acts themselves infringe the design right.

(5)   This section has effect subject to the provisions of Chapter III (exceptions to rights of design right owner).

227.   Secondary infringement: importing or dealing with infringing article

(1)   Design right is infringed by a person who, without the licence of the design right owner—

(a)   imports into the United Kingdom for commercial purposes, or

(b)   has in his possession for commercial purposes, or

(c)   sells, lets for hire, or offers or exposes for sale or hire, in the course of a business,

an article which is, and which he knows or has reason to believe is, an infringing article.

(2)   This section has effect subject to the provisions of Chapter III (exceptions to rights of design right owner).

Remedies for infringement

229.   Rights and remedies of design right owner

(1)   An infringement of design right is actionable by the design right owner.

(2)   In an action for infringement of design right all such relief by way of damages, injunctions, accounts or otherwise is available to the plaintiff as is available in respect of the infringement of any other property right.

(3)   The court may in an action for infringement of design right, having regard to all the circumstances and in particular to—

(a)   the flagrancy of the infringement, and

(b)   any benefit accruing to the defendant by reason of the infringement,

award such additional damages as the justice of the case may require.

(4)   This section has effect subject to section 233 (innocent infringement).

230.   Order for delivery up

(1)   Where a person—

(a)   has in his possession, custody or control for commercial purposes an infringing article, or

(b)   has in his possession, custody or control anything specifically designed or adapted for making articles to a particular design, knowing or having reason to believe that it has been or is to be used to make an infringing article,

the owner of the design right in the design in question may apply to the court for an order that the infringing article or other thing be delivered up to him or to such other person as the court may direct.

(2)   An application shall not be made after the end of the period specified in the following provisions of this section; and no order shall be made unless the court also makes, or it appears to the court that there are grounds for making, an order under section 231 (order as to disposal of infringing article, &c.).

(3)   An application for an order under this section may not be made after the end of the period of six years from the date on which the article or thing in question was made, subject to subsection (4).

(4)   If during the whole or any part of that period the design right owner—

(a)   is under a disability, or

(b)   is prevented by fraud or concealment from discovering the facts entitling him to apply for an order, an application may be made at any time before the end of the period of six years from the date on which he ceased to be under a disability or, as the case may be, could with reasonable diligence have discovered those facts.

(5) In subsection (4) "disability"—

    (a) in England and Wales, has the same meaning as in the Limitation Act 1980;

    (b) in Scotland, means legal disability within the meaning of the Prescription and Limitation (Scotland) Act 1973;

    (c) in Northern Ireland, has the same meaning as in the Statute of Limitations (Northern Ireland) 1958.

(6) A person to whom an infringing article or other thing is delivered up in pursuance of an order under this section shall, if an order under section 231 is not made, retain it pending the making of an order, or the decision not to make an order, under that section.

(7) Nothing in this section affects any other power of the court.

231. Order as to disposal of infringing articles, &c.

(1) An application may be made to the court for an order that an infringing article or other thing delivered up in pursuance of an order under section 230 shall be—

    (a) forfeited to the design right owner, or

    (b) destroyed or otherwise dealt with as the court may think fit,

or for a decision that no such order should be made.

(2) In considering what order (if any) should be made, the court shall consider whether other remedies available in an action for infringement of design right would be adequate to compensate the design right owner and to protect his interests.

(3) Provision shall be made by rules of court as to the service of notice on persons having an interest in the article or other thing, and any such person is entitled—

    (a) to appear in proceedings for an order under this section, whether or not he was served with notice, and

    (b) to appeal against any order made, whether or not he appeared;

and an order shall not take effect until the end of the period within which notice of an appeal may be given or, if before the end of that period notice of appeal is duly given, until the final determination or abandonment of the proceedings on the appeal.

(4) Where there is more than one person interested in an article or other thing, the court shall make such order as it thinks just and may (in particular) direct that the thing be sold, or otherwise dealt with, and the proceeds divided.

(5) If the court decides that no order should be made under this section, the person in whose possession, custody or control the article or other thing was before being delivered up is entitled to its return.

(6) References in this section to a person having an interest in an article or other thing include any person in whose favour an order could be made in respect of it—

    (a) under this section or under section 114 or 204 of this Act;

    (b) under section 24D of the Registered Designs Act 1949;

    (c) under section 19 of Trade Marks Act 1994; or

    (d) under regulation 1C of the Community Design Regulations 2005 (SI 2005/2339).

233. Innocent infringement

(1) Where in an action for infringement of design right brought by virtue of section 226 (primary infringement) it is shown that at the time of the infringement the defendant did not know, and had no reason to believe, that design right subsisted in the design to which the action relates, the plaintiff is not entitled to damages against him, but without prejudice to any other remedy.

(2) Where in an action for infringement of design right brought by virtue of section 227 (secondary infringement) a defendant shows that the infringing article was innocently acquired by him or a predecessor in title of his, the only remedy available against him in respect of the infringement is damages not exceeding a reasonable royalty in respect of the act complained of.

(3) In subsection (2) "innocently acquired" means that the person acquiring the article did not know and had no reason to believe that it was an infringing article.

Chapter III
Exceptions to Rights of Design Right Owners

Infringement of copyright

236. Infringement of copyright

Where copyright subsists in a work which consists of or includes a design in which design right subsists, it is not an infringement of design right in the design to do anything which is an infringement of the copyright in that work.

Trade Marks Act 1994
1994 c. 26

An Act to make new provision for registered trade marks, implementing Council Directive No. 89/104/EEC of 21st December 1988 to approximate the laws of the Member States relating to trade marks; to make provision in connection with Council Regulation (EC) No. 40/94 of 20th December 1993 on the Community trade mark; to give effect to the Madrid Protocol Relating to the International Registration of Marks of 27th June 1989, and to certain provisions of the Paris Convention for the Protection of Industrial Property of 20th March 1883, as revised and amended; and for connected purposes   [21st July 1994]

Part I
Registered Trade Marks

Introductory

1. Trade marks

(1)   In this Act "trade mark" means any sign which is capable—

    (a)   of being represented in the register in a manner which enables the registrar and other competent authorities and the public to determine the clear and precise subject matter of the protection afforded to the proprietor, and

    (b)   of distinguishing goods or services of one undertaking from those of other undertakings.

A trade mark may, in particular, consist of words (including personal names), designs, letters, numerals, colours, sounds or the shape of goods or their packaging.

(2)   References in this Act to a trade mark include, unless the context otherwise requires, references to a collective mark (see section 49) or certification mark (see section 50).

Grounds for refusal of registration

3. Absolute grounds for refusal of registration

(1)   The following shall not be registered—

    (a)   signs which do not satisfy the requirements of section 1(1),

    (b)   trade marks which are devoid of any distinctive character,

    (c)   trade marks which consist exclusively of signs or indications which may serve, in trade, to designate the kind, quality, quantity, intended purpose, value, geographical origin, the time of production of goods or of rendering of services, or other characteristics of goods or services,

    (d)   trade marks which consist exclusively of signs or indications which have become customary in the current language or in the bona fide and established practices of the trade:

Provided that, a trade mark shall not be refused registration by virtue of paragraph (b), (c) or (d) above if, before the date of application for registration, it has in fact acquired a distinctive character as a result of the use made of it.

(2)   A sign shall not be registered as a trade mark if it consists exclusively of—

    (a)   the shape, or another characteristic, which results from the nature of the goods themselves,

    (b)   the shape, or another characteristic, of goods which is necessary to obtain a technical result, or

    (c)   the shape, or another characteristic, which gives substantial value to the goods.

(3)   A trade mark shall not be registered if it is—

    (a)   contrary to public policy or to accepted principles of morality, or

    (b)   of such a nature as to deceive the public (for instance as to the nature, quality or geographical origin of the goods or service).

(4)   A trade mark shall not be registered if or to the extent that its use is prohibited in the United Kingdom by any enactment or rule of law other than law relating to trade marks.

(4A)   A trade mark is not to be registered if its registration is prohibited by or under—

    (a)   any enactment or rule of law, or

    (c)   any international agreement to which the United Kingdom is a party,

providing for the protection of designations of origin or geographical indications.

(4B)   A trade mark is not to be registered if its registration is prohibited by or under—

    (a)   any enactment or rule of law, or

    (b)   any international agreement to which the United Kingdom is a party, providing for the protection of traditional terms for wine or traditional specialities guaranteed.

(4C)   A trade mark is not to be registered if it—

(a)   consists of, or reproduces in its essential elements, an earlier plant variety denomination registered as mentioned in subsection (4D), and

(b)   is in respect of plant varieties of the same or closely related species.

(4D)   Subsection (4C)(a) refers to registration in accordance with any—

(a)   enactment or rule of law, or

(c)   international agreement to which the United Kingdom is a party,

providing for the protection of plant variety rights.

(5)   A trade mark shall not be registered in the cases specified, or referred to, in section 4 (specially protected emblems).

(6)   A trade mark shall not be registered if or to the extent that the application is made in bad faith.

5.   Relative grounds for refusal of registration

(1)   A trade mark shall not be registered if it is identical with an earlier trade mark and the goods or services for which the trade mark is applied for are identical with the goods or services for which the earlier trade mark is protected.

(2)   A trade mark shall not be registered if because—

(a)   it is identical with an earlier trade mark and is to be registered for goods or services similar to those for which the earlier trade mark is protected, or

(b)   it is similar to an earlier trade mark and is to be registered for goods or services identical with or similar to those for which the earlier trade mark is protected,

there exists a likelihood of confusion on the part of the public, which includes the likelihood of association with the earlier trade mark.

(3)   A trade mark which—

(a)   is identical with or similar to an earlier trade mark,

shall not be registered if, or to the extent that, the earlier trade mark has a reputation in the United Kingdom and the use of the later mark without due cause would take unfair advantage of, or be detrimental to, the distinctive character or the repute of the earlier trade mark.

(3A)   Subsection (3) applies irrespective of whether the goods and services for which the trade mark is to be registered are identical with, similar to or not similar to those for which the earlier trade mark is protected.

(4)   A trade mark shall not be registered if, or to the extent that, its use in the United Kingdom is liable to be prevented—

(a)   by virtue of any rule of law (in particular, the law of passing off) protecting an unregistered trade mark or other sign used in the course of trade, where the condition in subsection (4A) is met,

(aa)   by virtue of any enactment or rule of law, providing for protection of designations of origin or geographical indications, where the condition in subsection (4B) is met, or

(b)   by virtue of an earlier right other than those referred to in subsections (1) to (3) or paragraph (a) or (aa) above, in particular by virtue of the law of copyright or the law relating to industrial property rights.

A person thus entitled to prevent the use of a trade mark is referred to in this Act as the proprietor of an "earlier right" in relation to the trade mark.

(4A)   The condition mentioned in subsection (4)(a) is that the rights to the unregistered trade mark or other sign were acquired prior to the date of application for registration of the trade mark or date of the priority claimed for that application.

(4B)   The condition mentioned in subsection 4(aa) is that—

(a)   an application for a designation of origin or a geographical indication has been submitted prior to the date of application for registration of the trade mark or the date of the priority claimed for that application, and

(b)   the designation of origin or (as the case may be) geographical indication is subsequently registered.

(5)   Nothing in this section prevents the registration of a trade mark where the proprietor of the earlier trade mark or other earlier right consents to the registration.

(6) Where an agent or representative ("R") of the proprietor of a trade mark applies, without the proprietor's consent, for the registration of the trade mark in R's own name, the application is to be refused unless R justifies that action.

Effects of registered trade mark

9. Rights conferred by registered trade mark

(1) The proprietor of a registered trade mark has exclusive rights in the trade mark which are infringed by use of the trade mark in the United Kingdom without his consent.

The acts amounting to infringement, if done without the consent of the proprietor, are specified in subsections (1) to (3) of section 10.

(1A) See subsection (3B) of section 10 for provision about certain other acts amounting to infringement of a registered trade mark.

(1B) Subsection (1) is without prejudice to the rights of proprietors acquired before the date of filing of the application for registration or (where applicable) the date of the priority claimed in respect of that application.

(2) References in this Act to the infringement of a registered trade mark are to any infringement of the rights of the proprietor such as is mentioned in subsection (1) or (1A).

(3) The rights of the proprietor have effect from the date of registration (which in accordance with section 40(3) is the date of filing of the application for registration):

Provided that—

(a) no infringement proceedings may be begun before the date on which the trade mark is in fact registered; and

(b) no offence under section 92 (unauthorised use of trade mark, &c in relation to goods) is committed by anything done before the date of publication of the registration.

10. Infringement of registered trade mark

(1) A person infringes a registered trade mark if he uses in the course of trade a sign which is identical with the trade mark in relation to goods or services which are identical with those for which it is registered.

(2) A person infringes a registered trade mark if he uses in the course of trade a sign where because—

(a) the sign is identical with the trade mark and is used in relation to goods or services similar to those for which the trade mark is registered, or

(b) the sign is similar to the trade mark and is used in relation to goods or services identical with or similar to those for which the trade mark is registered,

there exists a likelihood of confusion on the part of the public, which includes the likelihood of association with the trade mark.

(3) A person infringes a registered trade mark if he uses in the course of trade, in relation to goods or services, a sign which—

(a) is identical with or similar to the trade mark,

where the trade mark has a reputation in the United Kingdom and the use of the sign, being without due cause, takes unfair advantage of, or is detrimental to, the distinctive character or the repute of the trade mark.

(3A) Subsection (3) applies irrespective of whether the goods and services in relation to which the sign is used are identical with, similar to or not similar to those for which the trade mark is registered.

(3B) Where the risk exists that the packaging, labels, tags, security or authenticity features or devices, or any other means to which the trade mark is affixed could be used in relation to goods or services and that use would constitute an infringement of the rights of the proprietor of the trade mark, a person infringes a registered trade mark if the person carries out in the course of trade any of the following acts—

(a) affixing a sign identical with, or similar to, the trade mark on packaging, labels, tags, security or authenticity features or devices, or any other means to which the mark may be affixed; or

(b) offering or placing on the market, or stocking for those purposes, or importing or exporting, packaging, labels, tags, security or authenticity features or devices, or any other means to which the mark is affixed.

(4) For the purposes of this section a person uses a sign if, in particular, he—

(a) affixes it to goods or the packaging thereof;

(b)   offers or exposes goods for sale, puts them on the market or stocks them for those purposes under the sign, or offers or supplies services under the sign;

(c)   imports or exports goods under the sign;

(ca)   uses the sign as a trade or company name or part of a trade or company name;

(d)   uses the sign on business papers and in advertising; or

(e)   uses the sign in comparative advertising in a manner that is contrary to the Business Protection from Misleading Marketing Regulations 2008.

11.   Limits on effect of registered trade mark

(1)   A registered trade mark is not infringed by the use of a later registered trade mark where that later registered trade mark would not be declared invalid pursuant to section 47(2A) or (2G) or section 48(1).

(1B)   Where subsection (1) applies, the later registered trade mark is not infringed by the use of the earlier trade mark even though the earlier trade mark may no longer be invoked against the later registered trade mark.

(2)   A registered trade mark is not infringed by—

(a)   the use by an individual of his own name or address,

(b)   the use of signs or indications which are not distinctive or which concern the kind, quality, quantity, intended purpose, value, geographical origin, the time of production of goods or of rendering of services, or other characteristics of goods or services, or

(c)   the use of the trade mark for the purpose of identifying or referring to goods or services as those of the proprietor of that trade mark, in particular where that use is necessary to indicate the intended purpose of a product or service (in particular, as accessories or spare parts),

provided the use is in accordance with honest practices in industrial or commercial matters.

(3)   A registered trade mark is not infringed by the use in the course of trade in a particular locality of an earlier right which applies only in that locality.

For this purpose an "earlier right" means an unregistered trade mark or other sign continuously used in relation to goods or services by a person or a predecessor in title of his from a date prior to whichever is the earlier of—

(a)   the use of the first-mentioned trade mark in relation to those goods or services by the proprietor or a predecessor in title of his, or

(b)   the registration of the first-mentioned trade mark in respect of those goods or services in the name of the proprietor or a predecessor in title of his;

and an earlier right shall be regarded as applying in a locality if, or to the extent that, its use in that locality is protected by virtue of any rule of law (in particular, the law of passing off).

12.   Exhaustion of rights conferred by registered trade mark

(1)   A registered trade mark is not infringed by the use of the trade mark in relation to goods which have been put on the market in the United Kingdom or the European Economic Area under that trade mark by the proprietor or with his consent.

(2)   Subsection (1) does not apply where there exist legitimate reasons for the proprietor to oppose further dealings in the goods (in particular, where the condition of the goods has been changed or impaired after they have been put on the market).

Infringement proceedings

14.   Action for infringement

(1)   An infringement of a registered trade mark is actionable by the proprietor of the trade mark.

(2)   In an action for infringement all such relief by way of damages, injunctions, accounts or otherwise is available to him as is available in respect of the infringement of any other property right.

15.   Order for erasure, &c. of offending sign

(1)   Where a person is found to have infringed a registered trade mark, the court may make an order requiring him—

(a)   to cause the offending sign to be erased, removed or obliterated from any infringing goods, material or articles in his possession, custody or control, or

(b)   if it is not reasonably practicable for the offending sign to be erased, removed or obliterated, to secure the destruction of the infringing goods, material or articles in question.

(2)   If an order under subsection (1) is not complied with, or it appears to the court likely that such an order would not be complied with, the court may order that the infringing goods, material or articles be delivered to such person as the court may direct for erasure, removal or obliteration of the sign, or for destruction, as the case may be.

16.   Order for delivery up of infringing goods, material or articles

(1)   The proprietor of a registered trade mark may apply to the court for an order for the delivery up to him, or such other person as the court may direct, of any infringing goods, material or articles which a person has in his possession, custody or control in the course of a business.

(2)   An application shall not be made after the end of the period specified in section 18 (period after which remedy of delivery up not available); and no order shall be made unless the court also makes, or it appears to the court that there are grounds for making, an order under section 19 (order as to disposal of infringing goods, &c.).

(3)   A person to whom any infringing goods, material or articles are delivered up in pursuance of an order under this section shall, if an order under section 19 is not made, retain them pending the making of an order, or the decision not to make an order, under that section.

(4)   Nothing in this section affects any other power of the court.

19.   Order as to disposal of infringing goods, material or articles

(1)   Where infringing goods, material or articles have been delivered up in pursuance of an order under section 16, an application may be made to the court—

    (a)   for an order that they be destroyed or forfeited to such person as the court may think fit, or

    (b)   for a decision that no such order should be made.

(2)   In considering what order (if any) should be made, the court shall consider whether other remedies available in an action for infringement of the registered trade mark would be adequate to compensate the proprietor and any licensee and protect their interests.

(3)   Provision shall be made by rules of court as to the service of notice on persons having an interest in the goods, material or articles, and any such person is entitled—

    (a)   to appear in proceedings for an order under this section, whether or not he was served with notice, and

    (b)   to appeal against any order made, whether or not he appeared;

and an order shall not take effect until the end of the period within which notice of an appeal may be given or, if before the end of that period notice of appeal is duly given, until the final determination or abandonment of the proceedings on the appeal.

(4)   Where there is more than one person interested in the goods, material or articles, the court shall make such order as it thinks just.

(5)   If the court decides that no order should be made under this section, the person in whose possession, custody or control the goods, material or articles were before being delivered up is entitled to their return.

(6)   References in this section to a person having an interest in goods, material or articles include any person in whose favour an order could be made —

    (a)   under this section;

    (b)   under section 24D of the Registered Designs Act 1949;

    (c)   under section 114, 204 or 231 of the Copyright, Designs and Patents Act 1988; or

    (d)   under regulation 1C of the Community Design Regulations 2005 (SI 2005/2339).

Unjustified threats

21.   Threats of infringement proceedings

(1)   A communication contains a "threat of infringement proceedings" if a reasonable person in the position of a recipient would understand from the communication that—

    (a)   a registered trade mark exists, and

    (b)   a person intends to bring proceedings (whether in a court in the United Kingdom or elsewhere) against another person for infringement of the registered trade mark by—

        (i)   an act done in the United Kingdom, or

        (ii)   an act which, if done, would be done in the United Kingdom.

(2)   References in this section and in section 21C to a "recipient" include, in the case of a communication directed to the public or a section of the public, references to a person to whom the communication is directed.

21A.   Actionable threats

(1)   Subject to subsections (2) to (6), a threat of infringement proceedings made by any person is actionable by any person aggrieved by the threat.

(2)   A threat of infringement proceedings is not actionable if the infringement is alleged to consist of—

(a)   applying, or causing another person to apply, a sign to goods or their packaging,

(b)   importing, for disposal, goods to which, or to the packaging of which, a sign has been applied, or

(c)   supplying services under a sign.

(3)   A threat of infringement proceedings is not actionable if the infringement is alleged to consist of an act which, if done, would constitute an infringement of a kind mentioned in subsection (2)(a), (b) or (c).

(4)   A threat of infringement proceedings is not actionable if the threat—

(a)   is made to a person who has done, or intends to do, an act mentioned in subsection (2)(a) or (b) in relation to goods or their packaging, and

(b)   is a threat of proceedings for an infringement alleged to consist of doing anything else in relation to those goods or their packaging.

(5)   A threat of infringement proceedings is not actionable if the threat—

(a)   is made to a person who has done, or intends to do, an act mentioned in subsection (2)(c) in relation to services, and

(b)   is a threat of proceedings for an infringement alleged to consist of doing anything else in relation to those services.

(6)   A threat of infringement proceedings which is not an express threat is not actionable if it is contained in a permitted communication.

(7)   In sections 21C and 21D "an actionable threat" means a threat of infringement proceedings that is actionable in accordance with this section.

21C.   Remedies and defences

(1)   Proceedings in respect of an actionable threat may be brought against the person who made the threat for—

(a)   a declaration that the threat is unjustified;

(b)   an injunction against the continuance of the threat;

(c)   damages in respect of any loss sustained by the aggrieved person by reason of the threat.

(2)   It is a defence for the person who made the threat to show that the act in respect of which proceedings were threatened constitutes (or if done would constitute) an infringement of the registered trade mark.

(3)   It is a defence for the person who made the threat to show—

(a)   that, despite having taken reasonable steps, the person has not identified anyone who has done an act mentioned in section 21A(2)(a), (b) or (c) in relation to the goods or their packaging or the services which are the subject of the threat, and

(b)   that the person notified the recipient, before or at the time of making the threat, of the steps taken.

Registered trade mark as object of property

24.   Assignment, &c. of registered trade mark

(1)   A registered trade mark is transmissible by assignment, testamentary disposition or operation of law in the same way as other personal or moveable property.

It is so transmissible either in connection with the goodwill of a business or independently.

(1A)   A contractual obligation to transfer a business is to be taken to include an obligation to transfer any registered trade mark, except where there is agreement to the contrary or it is clear in all the circumstances that this presumption should not apply.

(2)   An assignment or other transmission of a registered trade mark may be partial, that is, limited so as to apply—

(a)   in relation to some but not all of the goods or services for which the trade mark is registered, or

(b) in relation to use of the trade mark in a particular manner or a particular locality.

(3) An assignment of a registered trade mark, or an assent relating to a registered trade mark, is not effective unless it is in writing signed by or on behalf of the assignor or, as the case may be, a personal representative.

Except in Scotland, this requirement may be satisfied in a case where the assignor or personal representative is a body corporate by the affixing of its seal.

(4) The above provisions apply to assignment by way of security as in relation to any other assignment.

(5) A registered trade mark may be the subject of a charge (in Scotland, security) in the same way as other personal or moveable property.

(6) Nothing in this Act shall be construed as affecting the assignment or other transmission of an unregistered trade mark as part of the goodwill of a business.

25. Registration of transactions affecting registered trade mark

(1) On application being made to the registrar by—

(a) a person claiming to be entitled to an interest in or under a registered trade mark by virtue of a registrable transaction, or

(b) any other person claiming to be affected by such a transaction,

the prescribed particulars of the transaction shall be entered in the register.

(2) The following are registrable transactions—

(a) an assignment of a registered trade mark or any right in it;

(b) the grant of a licence under a registered trade mark;

(c) the granting of any security interest (whether fixed or floating) over a registered trade mark or any right in or under it;

(d) the making by personal representatives of an assent in relation to a registered trade mark or any right in or under it;

(e) an order of a court or other competent authority transferring a registered trade mark or any right in or under it.

(3) Until an application has been made for registration of the prescribed particulars of a registrable transaction—

(a) the transaction is ineffective as against a person acquiring a conflicting interest in or under the registered trade mark in ignorance of it, and

(b) a person claiming to be a licensee by virtue of the transaction does not have the protection of section 30 or 31 (rights and remedies of licensee in relation to infringement).

(4) Where a person becomes the proprietor or a licensee of a registered trade mark by virtue of a registrable transaction and the mark is infringed before the prescribed particulars of the transaction are registered, in proceedings for such an infringement, the court shall not award him costs unless—

(a) an application for registration of the prescribed particulars of the transaction is made before the end of the period of six months beginning with its date, or

(b) the court is satisfied that it was not practicable for such an application to be made before the end of that period and that an application was made as soon as practicable thereafter.

(5) Provision may be made by rules as to—

(a) the amendment of registered particulars relating to a licence so as to reflect any alteration of the terms of the licence, and

(b) the removal of such particulars from the register—

(i) where it appears from the registered particulars that the licence was granted for a fixed period and that period has expired, or

(ii) where no such period is indicated and, after such period as may be prescribed, the registrar has notified the parties of his intention to remove the particulars from the register.

(6) Provision may also be made by rules as to the amendment or removal from the register of particulars relating to a security interest on the application of, or with the consent of, the person entitled to the benefit of that interest.

Licensing

28.   Licensing of registered trade mark

(1)   A licence to use a registered trade mark may be general or limited.

A limited licence may, in particular, apply—

(a)   in relation to some but not all of the goods or services for which the trade mark is registered, or

(b)   in relation to use of the trade mark in a particular manner or a particular locality.

(2)   A licence is not effective unless it is in writing signed by or on behalf of the grantor.

Except in Scotland, this requirement may be satisfied in a case where the grantor is a body corporate by the affixing of its seal.

(3)   Unless the licence provides otherwise, it is binding on a successor in title to the grantor's interest.

References in this Act to doing anything with, or without, the consent of the proprietor of a registered trade mark shall be construed accordingly.

(4)   Where the licence so provides, a sub-licence may be granted by the licensee; and references in this Act to a licence or licensee include a sub-licence or sub-licensee.

(5)   The proprietor of a registered trade mark may invoke the rights conferred by that trade mark against a licensee who contravenes any provision in the licence with regard to—

(a)   its duration,

(b)   the form covered by the registration in which the trade mark may be used,

(c)   the scope of the goods or services for which the licence is granted,

(d)   the territory in which the trade mark may be affixed, or

(e)   the quality of the goods manufactured or of the services provided by the licensee.

29.   Exclusive licenses

(1)   In this Act an "exclusive licence" means a licence (whether general or limited) authorising the licensee to the exclusion of all other persons, including the person granting the licence, to use a registered trade mark in the manner authorised by the licence.

The expression "exclusive licensee" shall be construed accordingly.

(2)   An exclusive licensee has the same rights against a successor in title who is bound by the licence as he has against the person granting the licence.

30.   General provisions as to rights of licensees in case of infringement

(1)   This section has effect with respect to the rights of a licensee in relation to infringement of a registered trade mark.

The provisions of this section do not apply where or to the extent that, by virtue of section 31(1) below (exclusive licensee having rights and remedies of assignee), the licensee has a right to bring proceedings in his own name.

(1A)   Except so far as the licence provides otherwise a licensee may only bring proceedings for infringement of the registered trade mark with the consent of the proprietor (but see subsections (2) and (3)).

(2)   An exclusive licensee may call on the proprietor of the registered trade mark to take infringement proceedings in respect of any matter which affects his interests.

(3)   If the proprietor mentioned in subsection (2)—

(a)   refuses to do so, or

(b)   fails to do so within two months after being called upon,

the exclusive licensee may bring the proceedings in his own name as if he were the proprietor.

(4)   Where infringement proceedings are brought by a licensee by virtue of this section or with the consent of the proprietor or pursuant to the licence, the licensee may not, without the leave of the court, proceed with the action unless the proprietor is either joined as a plaintiff or added as a defendant.

This does not affect the granting of interlocutory relief on an application by a licensee alone.

(5)   A proprietor who is added as a defendant as mentioned in subsection (4) shall not be made liable for any costs in the action unless he takes part in the proceedings.

(6)   In infringement proceedings brought by the proprietor of a registered trade mark any loss suffered or likely to be suffered by licensees shall be taken into account; and the court may give such directions as it thinks fit as to the extent to which the plaintiff is to hold the proceeds of any pecuniary remedy on behalf of licensees.

(6A)   Where the proprietor of a registered trade mark brings infringement proceedings, a licensee who has suffered loss is entitled to intervene in the proceedings for the purpose of obtaining compensation for that loss.

(7)   The provisions of this section apply in relation to an exclusive licensee if or to the extent that he has, by virtue of section 31(1), the rights and remedies of an assignee as if he were the proprietor of the registered trade mark.

31.   Exclusive licensee having rights and remedies of assignee

(1)   An exclusive licence may provide that the licensee shall have, to such extent as may be provided by the licence, the same rights and remedies in respect of matters occurring after the grant of the licence as if the licence had been an assignment.

Where or to the extent that such provision is made, the licensee is entitled, subject to the provisions of the licence and to the following provisions of this section, to bring infringement proceedings, against any person other than the proprietor, in his own name.

(2)   Any such rights and remedies of an exclusive licensee are concurrent with those of the proprietor of the registered trade mark, and references to the proprietor of a registered trade mark in the provisions of this Act relating to infringement shall be construed accordingly.

(3)   In an action brought by an exclusive licensee by virtue of this section a defendant may avail himself of any defence which would have been available to him if the action had been brought by the proprietor of the registered trade mark.

(4)   Where proceedings for infringement of a registered trade mark brought by the proprietor or an exclusive licensee relate wholly or partly to an infringement in respect of which they have concurrent rights of action, the proprietor or, as the case may be, the exclusive licensee may not, without the leave of the court, proceed with the action unless the other is either joined as a plaintiff or added as a defendant.

This does not affect the granting of interlocutory relief on an application by a proprietor or exclusive licensee alone.

(5)   A person who is added as a defendant as mentioned in subsection (4) shall not be made liable for any costs in the action unless he takes part in the proceedings.

(6)   Where an action for infringement of a registered trade mark is brought which relates holly or partly to an infringement in respect of which the proprietor and an exclusive licensee have or had concurrent rights of action—

(a)   the court shall in assessing damages take into account—

(i)   the terms of the licence, and

(ii)   any pecuniary remedy already awarded or available to either of them in respect of the infringement;

(b)   no account of profits shall be directed if an award of damages has been made, or an account of profits has been directed, in favour of the other of them in respect of the infringement; and

(c)   the court shall if an account of profits is directed apportion the profits between them as the court considers just, subject to any agreement between them.

The provisions of this subsection apply whether or not the proprietor and the exclusive licensee are both parties to the action, and if they are not both parties the court may give such directions as it thinks fit as to the extent to which the party to the proceedings is to hold the proceeds of any pecuniary remedy on behalf of the other.

(7)   The proprietor of a registered trade mark shall notify any exclusive licensee who has a concurrent right of action before applying for an order under section 16 (order for delivery up), and the court may on the application of the licensee make such order under that section as it thinks fit having regard to the terms of the licence.

(8)   The provisions of subsections (4) to (7) above have effect subject to any agreement to the contrary between the exclusive licensee and the proprietor.

Duration, renewal and alteration of registered trade mark

42.   Duration of registration

(1)   A trade mark shall be registered for a period of ten years from the date of registration.

(2)   Registration may be renewed in accordance with section 43 for further periods of ten years.

Surrender, revocation and invalidity

46.   Revocation of registration

(1)   The registration of a trade mark may be revoked on any of the following grounds—

    (a)   that within the period of five years following the date of completion of the registration procedure it has not been put to genuine use in the United Kingdom, by the proprietor or with his consent, in relation to the goods or services for which it is registered, and there are no proper reasons for non-use;

    (b)   that such use has been suspended for an uninterrupted period of five years, and there are no proper reasons for non-use;

    (c)   that, in consequence of acts or inactivity of the proprietor, it has become the common name in the trade for a product or service for which it is registered;

    (d)   that in consequence of the use made of it by the proprietor or with his consent in relation to the goods or services for which it is registered, it is liable to mislead the public, particularly as to the nature, quality or geographical origin of those goods or services.

(2)   For the purposes of subsection (1) use of a trade mark includes use in a form (the "variant form") differing in elements which do not alter the distinctive character of the mark in the form in which it was registered (regardless of whether or not the trade mark in the variant form is also registered in the name of the proprietor), and use in the United Kingdom includes affixing the trade mark to goods or to the packaging of goods in the United Kingdom solely for export purposes.

(3)   The registration of a trade mark shall not be revoked on the ground mentioned in subsection (1)(a) or (b) if such use as is referred to in that paragraph is commenced or resumed after the expiry of the five year period and before the application for revocation is made:

Provided that, any such commencement or resumption of use after the expiry of the five year period but within the period of three months before the making of the application shall be disregarded unless preparations for the commencement or resumption began before the proprietor became aware that the application might be made.

(4)   An application for revocation may be made by any person, and may be made either to the registrar or to the court, except that—

    (a)   if proceedings concerning the trade mark in question are pending in the court, the application must be made to the court; and

    (b)   if in any other case the application is made to the registrar, he may at any stage of the proceedings refer the application to the court.

(5)   Where grounds for revocation exist in respect of only some of the goods or services for which the trade mark is registered, revocation shall relate to those goods or services only.

(6)   Where the registration of a trade mark is revoked to any extent, the rights of the proprietor shall be deemed to have ceased to that extent as from—

    (a)   the date of the application for revocation, or

    (b)   if the registrar or court is satisfied that the grounds for revocation existed at an earlier date, that date.

47.   Grounds for invalidity of registration

(1)   Subject to subsections (2A) and (2G), the registration of a trade mark may be declared invalid on he ground that the trade mark was registered in breach of section 3 or any of the provisions referred to in that section (absolute grounds for refusal of registration).

Where the trade mark was registered in breach of subsection (1)(b), (c) or (d) of that section, it shall not be declared invalid if, in consequence of the use which has been made of it, it has after registration acquired a distinctive character in relation to the goods or services for which it is registered.

(2)   Subject to subsections (2A) and (2G), the registration of a trade mark may be declared invalid on the ground—

    (a)   that there is an earlier trade mark in relation to which the conditions set out in section 5(1), (2) or (3) obtain, or

    (b)   that there is an earlier right in relation to which the condition set out in section 5(4) is satisfied,

unless the proprietor of that earlier trade mark or other earlier right has consented to the registration.

(2ZA) The registration of a trade mark may be declared invalid on the ground that the trade mark was registered in breach of section 5(6).

(2A) The registration of a trade mark may not be declared invalid on the ground that there is an earlier trade mark unless—

    (a)   the registration procedure for the earlier trade mark was completed within the period of five years ending with the date of the application for the declaration,

    (b)   the registration procedure for the earlier trade mark was not completed before that date, or

    (c)   the use conditions are met.

(2B) The use conditions are met if—

    (a)   the earlier trade mark has been put to genuine use in the United Kingdom by the proprietor or with their consent in relation to the goods or services for which it is registered—

        (i)   within the period of 5 years ending with the date of application for the declaration, and

        (ii)   within the period of 5 years ending with the date of filing of the application for registration of the later trade mark or (where applicable) the date of the priority claimed in respect of that application where, at that date, the five year period within which the earlier trade mark should have been put to genuine use as provided in section 46(1)(a) has expired, or

    (b)   it has not been so used, but there are proper reasons for non-use.

(2C) For these purposes—

    (a)   use of a trade mark includes use in a form (the "variant form") differing in elements which do not alter the distinctive character of the mark in the form in which it was registered (regardless of whether or not the trade mark in the variant form is also registered in the name of the proprietor), and

    (b)   use in the United Kingdom includes affixing the trade mark to goods or to the packaging of goods in the United Kingdom solely for export purposes.

(2E) Where an earlier trade mark satisfies the use conditions in respect of some only of the goods or services for which it is registered, it shall be treated for the purposes of this section as if it were registered only in respect of those goods or services.

(2F) Subsection (2A) does not apply where the earlier trade mark is a trade mark within section 6(1)(c).

(2G) An application for a declaration of invalidity on the basis of an earlier trade mark must be refused if it would have been refused, for any of the reasons set out in subsection (2H), had the application for the declaration been made on the date of filing of the application for registration of the later trade mark or (where applicable) the date of the priority claimed in respect of that application.

(2H) The reasons referred to in subsection (2G) are—

    (a)   that on the date in question the earlier trade mark was liable to be declared invalid by virtue of section 3(1)(b), (c) or (d), (and had not yet acquired a distinctive character as mentioned in the words after paragraph (d) in section 3(1));

    (b)   that the application for a declaration of invalidity is based on section 5(2) and the earlier trade mark had not yet become sufficiently distinctive to support a finding of likelihood of confusion within the meaning of section 5(2);

    (c)   that the application for a declaration of invalidity is based on section 5(3)(a) and the earlier trade mark had not yet acquired a reputation within the meaning of section 5(3).

(3) An application for a declaration of invalidity may be made by any person, and may be made either to the registrar or to the court, except that—

    (a)   if proceedings concerning the trade mark in question are pending in the court, the application must be made to the court; and

    (b)   if in any other case the application is made to the registrar, he may at any stage of the proceedings refer the application to the court.

(4) In the case of bad faith in the registration of a trade mark, the registrar himself may apply to the court for a declaration of the invalidity of the registration.

(5) Where the grounds of invalidity exist in respect of only some of the goods or services for which the trade mark is registered, the trade mark shall be declared invalid as regards those goods or services only.

(5A)   An application for a declaration of invalidity may be filed on the basis of one or more earlier trade marks or other earlier rights provided they all belong to the same proprietor.

(6)   Where the registration of a trade mark is declared invalid to any extent, the registration shall to that extent be deemed never to have been made:

Provided that this shall not affect transactions past and closed.

The Paris Convention: supplementary provisions

56.   Protection of well-known trade marks: Article 6bis

(1)   References in this Act to a trade mark which is entitled to protection under the Paris Convention or the WTO agreement as a well known trade mark are to a mark which is well-known in the United Kingdom as being the mark of a person who—

(a)   is a national of a Convention country, or

(b)   is domiciled in, or has a real and effective industrial or commercial establishment in, a Convention country,

whether or not that person carries on business, or has any goodwill, in the United Kingdom.

References to the proprietor of such a mark shall be construed accordingly.

(2)   The proprietor of a trade mark which is entitled to protection under the Paris Convention or the WTO agreement as a well known trade mark is entitled to restrain by injunction the use in the United Kingdom of a trade mark which, or the essential part of which, is identical or similar to his mark, in relation to identical or similar goods or services, where the use is likely to cause confusion.

This right is subject to section 48 (effect of acquiescence by proprietor of earlier trade mark).

(3)   Nothing in subsection (2) affects the continuation of any bona fide use of a trade mark begun before the commencement of this section.

Competition Act 1998
1998 c. 41

An Act to make provision about competition and the abuse of a dominant position in the market; to confer powers in relation to investigations conducted in connection with Article 85 or 86 of the treaty establishing the European Community; to amend the Fair Trading Act 1973 in relation to information which may be required in connection with investigations under that Act; to make provision with respect to the meaning of "supply of services" in the Fair Trading Act 1973; and for connected purposes.

[9th November 1998]

The prohibition

2.   Agreements etc preventing, restricting or distorting competition

(1)   Subject to section 3, agreements between undertakings, decisions by associations of undertakings or concerted practices which—

(a)   may affect trade within the United Kingdom, and

(b)   have as their object or effect the prevention, restriction or distortion of competition within the United Kingdom,

are prohibited unless they are exempt in accordance with the provisions of this Part.

(2)   Subsection (1) applies, in particular, to agreements, decisions or practices which—

(a)   directly or indirectly fix purchase or selling prices or any other trading conditions;

(b)   limit or control production, markets, technical development or investment;

(c)   share markets or sources of supply;

(d)   apply dissimilar conditions to equivalent transactions with other trading parties, thereby placing them at a competitive disadvantage;

(e)   make the conclusion of contracts subject to acceptance by the other parties of supplementary obligations which, by their nature or according to commercial usage, have no connection with the subject of such contracts.

(3)   Subsection (1) applies only if the agreement, decision or practice is, or is intended to be, implemented in the United Kingdom.

(4)   Any agreement or decision which is prohibited by subsection (1) is void.

(5)   A provision of this Part which is expressed to apply to, or in relation to, an agreement is to be read as applying equally to, or in relation to, a decision by an association of undertakings or a concerted practice (but with any necessary modifications).

(6)   Subsection (5) does not apply where the context otherwise requires.

(7)   In this section "the United Kingdom" means, in relation to an agreement which operates or is intended to operate only in a part of the United Kingdom, that part.

(8)   The prohibition imposed by subsection (1) is referred to in this Act as "the Chapter I prohibition".

Exemptions

9.   Exempt agreements

(1)   An agreement is exempt from the Chapter I prohibition if it—

(a)   contributes to—

(i)   improving production or distribution, or

(ii)   promoting technical or economic progress,

while allowing consumers a fair share of the resulting benefit; and

(b)   does not—

(i)   impose on the undertakings concerned restrictions which are not indispensable to the attainment of those objectives; or

(ii)   afford the undertakings concerned the possibility of eliminating competition in respect of a substantial part of the products in question.

(2)   In any proceedings in which it is alleged that the Chapter I prohibition is being or has been infringed by an agreement, any undertaking or association of undertakings claiming the benefit of subsection (1) shall bear the burden of proving that the conditions of that subsection are satisfied.

10.   Retained exemptions

(A1)   An agreement is exempt from the Chapter I prohibition if it falls within a category of agreements specified as exempt in a retained block exemption regulation.

(3)   An exemption from the Chapter I prohibition under this section is referred to in this Part as a retained exemption.

(4)   A retained exemption—

    (b)   ceases to have effect—

        (i)   if the relevant retained block exemption regulation ceases to have effect; or

        (ii)   on being cancelled by virtue of subsection (5) or (7).

(5)   In such circumstances and manner as may be specified in rules made under section 51, the CMA may—

    (a)   impose conditions or obligations subject to which a retained exemption is to have effect in respect of an agreement;

    (b)   vary or remove any such condition or obligation;

    (c)   impose one or more additional conditions or obligations;

    (d)   cancel the exemption in respect of an agreement.

(6)   In such circumstances as may be specified in rules made under section 51, the date from which cancellation of an exemption is to take effect may be earlier than the date on which notice of cancellation is given.

(7)   Breach of a condition imposed by the CMA has the effect of cancelling the exemption.

(8)   In exercising its powers under this section, the CMA may require any person who is a party to the agreement in question to give it such information as it may require.

(12)   In this Part, "retained block exemption regulation" means the following regulations as amended from time to time—

    (a)   Council Regulation (EC) 169/2009 applying rules of competition to transport by rail, road and inland waterway;

    (b)   Commission Regulation (EC) 906/2009 on the application of Article 81(3) of the Treaty to certain categories of agreements, decisions and concerted practices between liner shipping companies (consortia);

    (c)   Commission Regulation (EU) 330/2010 on the application of Article 101(3) of the Treaty on the Functioning of the European Union to categories of vertical agreements and concerted practices;

    (d)   Commission Regulation (EU) 461/2010 on the application of Article 101(3) of the Treaty on the Functioning of the European Union to categories of vertical agreements and concerted practices in the motor vehicle sector;

    (e)   Commission Regulation (EU) 1217/2010 on the application of Article 101(3) of the Treaty on the Functioning of the European Union to certain categories of research and development agreements;

    (f)   Commission Regulation (EU) 1218/2010 on the application of Article 101(3) of the Treaty on the Functioning of the European Union to certain categories of specialisation agreements;

    (g)   Commission Regulation (EU) 316/2014 on the application of Article 101(3) of the Treaty on the Functioning of the European Union to categories of technology transfer agreements.

Enforcement

39.   Limited immunity in relation to the Chapter I prohibition

(1)   In this section "small agreement" means an agreement—

    (a)   which falls within a category prescribed for the purposes of this section; but

    (b)   is not a price fixing agreement.

(2)   The criteria by reference to which a category of agreement is prescribed may, in particular, include—

    (a)   the combined turnover of the parties to the agreement (determined in accordance with prescribed provisions);

    (b)   the share of the market affected by the agreement (determined in that way).

(3)   A party to a small agreement is immune from the effect of section 36(1) so far as that provision relates to decisions about infringement of the Chapter I prohibition; but the CMA may withdraw that immunity under subsection (4).

(4)   If the CMA has investigated a small agreement, it may make a decision withdrawing the immunity given by subsection (3) if, as a result of its investigation, it considers that the agreement is likely to infringe the Chapter I prohibition.

(5)   The CMA must give each of the parties in respect of which immunity is withdrawn written notice of its decision to withdraw the immunity.

(6)   A decision under subsection (4) takes effect on such date ("the withdrawal date") as may be specified in the decision.

(7)   The withdrawal date must be a date after the date on which the decision is made.

(8)   In determining the withdrawal date, the CMA must have regard to the amount of time which the parties are likely to require in order to secure that there is no further infringement of the Chapter I prohibition with respect to the agreement.

(9)   In subsection (1) "price fixing agreement" means an agreement which has as its object or effect, or one of its objects or effects, restricting the freedom of a party to the agreement to determine the price to be charged (otherwise than as between that party and another party to the agreement) for the product, service or other matter to which the agreement relates.

Enterprise Act 2002
(2002 c. 40)

An act to . . . to create an offence for those entering into certain anti-competitive agreements . . .

[7th November 2002]

Part 6
Cartel Offence

Cartel offence

188. Cartel offence

(1)   An individual is guilty of an offence if he agrees with one or more other persons to make or implement, or to cause to be made or implemented, arrangements of the following kind relating to at least two undertakings (A and B).

(2)   The arrangements must be ones which, if operating as the parties to the agreement intend, would—

(a)   directly or indirectly fix a price for the supply by A in the United Kingdom (otherwise than to B) of a product or service,

(b)   limit or prevent supply by A in the United Kingdom of a product or service,

(c)   limit or prevent production by A in the United Kingdom of a product,

(d)   divide between A and B the supply in the United Kingdom of a product or service to a customer or customers,

(e)   divide between A and B customers for the supply in the United Kingdom of a product or service, or

(f)   be bid-rigging arrangements.

(3)   Unless subsection (2)(d), (e) or (f) applies, the arrangements must also be ones which, if operating as the parties to the agreement intend, would—

(a)   directly or indirectly fix a price for the supply by B in the United Kingdom (otherwise than to A) of a product or service,

(b)   limit or prevent supply by B in the United Kingdom of a product or service, or

(c)   limit or prevent production by B in the United Kingdom of a product.

(4)   In subsections (2)(a) to (d) and (3), references to supply or production are to supply or production in the appropriate circumstances (for which see section 189).

(5)   "Bid-rigging arrangements" are arrangements under which, in response to a request for bids for the supply of a product or service in the United Kingdom, or for the production of a product in the United Kingdom—

(a)   A but not B may make a bid, or

(b)   A and B may each make a bid but, in one case or both, only a bid arrived at in accordance with the arrangements.

(7)   "Undertaking" has the same meaning as in Part 1 of the 1998 Act.

(8)   This section is subject to section 188A.

188A. Circumstances in which cartel offence not committed

(1)   An individual does not commit an offence under section 188(1) if, under the arrangements—

(a)   in a case where the arrangements would (operating as the parties intend) affect the supply in the United Kingdom of a product or service, customers would be given relevant information about the arrangements before they enter into agreements for the supply to them of the product or service so affected,

(b)   in the case of bid-rigging arrangements, the person requesting bids would be given relevant information about them at or before the time when a bid is made, or

(c)   in any case, relevant information about the arrangements would be published, before the arrangements are implemented, in the manner specified at the time of the making of the agreement in an order made by the Secretary of State.

(2)   In subsection (1), "relevant information" means—

(a)   the names of the undertakings to which the arrangements relate,

(b)   a description of the nature of the arrangements which is sufficient to show why they are or might be arrangements of the kind to which section 188(1) applies,

(c)   the products or services to which they relate, and

(d)   such other information as may be specified in an order made by the Secretary of State.

(3)   An individual does not commit an offence under section 188(1) if the agreement is made in order to comply with a legal requirement.

(4)   In subsection (3), "legal requirement" has the same meaning as in paragraph 5 of Schedule 3 to the Competition Act 1998.

(5)   A power to make an order under this section—

(a)   is exercisable by statutory instrument,

(b)   may be exercised so as to make different provision for different cases or different purposes, and

(c)   includes power to make such incidental, supplementary, consequential, transitory, transitional or saving provision as the Secretary of State considers appropriate.

(6)   A statutory instrument containing an order under this section is subject to annulment in pursuance of a resolution of either House of Parliament.

189. Cartel offence: supplementary

(1)   For section 188(2)(a), the appropriate circumstances are that A's supply of the product or service would be at a level in the supply chain at which the product or service would at the same time be supplied by B in the United Kingdom.

(2)   For section 188(2)(b), the appropriate circumstances are that A's supply of the product or service would be at a level in the supply chain—

(a)   at which the product or service would at the same time be supplied by B in the United Kingdom, or

(b)   at which supply by B in the United Kingdom of the product or service would be limited or prevented by the arrangements.

(3)   For section 188(2)(c), the appropriate circumstances are that A's production of the product would be at a level in the production chain—

(a)   at which the product would at the same time be produced by B in the United Kingdom, or

(b)   at which production by B in the United Kingdom of the product would be limited or prevented by the arrangements.

(4)   For section 188(2)(d), the appropriate circumstances are that A's supply of the product or service would be at the same level in the supply chain as B's.

(5)   For section 188(3)(a), the appropriate circumstances are that B's supply of the product or service would be at a level in the supply chain at which the product or service would at the same time be supplied by A in the United Kingdom.

(6)   For section 188(3)(b), the appropriate circumstances are that B's supply of the product or service would be at a level in the supply chain—

(a)   at which the product or service would at the same time be supplied by A in the United Kingdom, or

(b)   at which supply by A in the United Kingdom of the product or service would be limited or prevented by the arrangements.

(7)   For section 188(3)(c), the appropriate circumstances are that B's production of the product would be at a level in the production chain—

(a)   at which the product would at the same time be produced by A in the United Kingdom, or

(b)   at which production by A in the United Kingdom of the product would be limited or prevented by the arrangements.

190. Cartel offence: penalty and prosecution

(1)   A person guilty of an offence under section 188 is liable—

(a)   on conviction on indictment, to imprisonment for a term not exceeding five years or to a fine, or to both;

(b)   on summary conviction, to imprisonment for a term not exceeding six months or to a fine not exceeding the statutory maximum, or to both.

(2)   In England and Wales and Northern Ireland, proceedings for an offence under section 188 may be instituted only—

(a)   by the Director of the Serious Fraud Office, or

(b)   by or with the consent of the CMA.

(3)   No proceedings may be brought for an offence under section 188 in respect of an agreement outside the United Kingdom, unless it has been implemented in whole or in part in the United Kingdom.

(4)   Where, for the purpose of the investigation or prosecution of offences under section 188, the CMA gives a person written notice under this subsection, no proceedings for an offence under section 188 that falls within a description specified in the notice may be brought against that person in England and Wales or Northern Ireland except in circumstances specified in the notice.

Consumer Rights Act 2015
2015 c. 15

An Act to amend the law relating to the rights of consumers and protection of their interests; to make provision about investigatory powers for enforcing the regulation of traders; to make provision about private actions in competition law and the Competition Appeal Tribunal; and for connected purposes.

[26th March 2015]

2.   Key definitions

(1)   These definitions apply in this Part (as well as the definitions in section 59).

(2)   "Trader" means a person acting for purposes relating to that person's trade, business, craft or profession, whether acting personally or through another person acting in the trader's name or on the trader's behalf.

(3)   "Consumer" means an individual acting for purposes that are wholly or mainly outside that individual's trade, business, craft or profession.

(4)   A trader claiming that an individual was not acting for purposes wholly or mainly outside the individual's trade, business, craft or profession must prove it.

(5)   For the purposes of Chapter 2, except to the extent mentioned in subsection (6), a person is not a consumer in relation to a sales contract if—

(a)   the goods are second hand goods sold at public auction, and

(b)   individuals have the opportunity of attending the sale in person.

(6)   A person is a consumer in relation to such a contract for the purposes of—

(a)   sections 11(4) and (5), 12, 28 and 29, and

(b)   the other provisions of Chapter 2 as they apply in relation to those sections.

(7)   "Business" includes the activities of any government department or local or public authority.

(8)   "Goods" means any tangible moveable items, but that includes water, gas and electricity if and only if they are put up for supply in a limited volume or set quantity.

(9)   "Digital content" means data which are produced and supplied in digital form.

What statutory rights are there under a goods contract?

9.   Goods to be of satisfactory quality

(1)   Every contract to supply goods is to be treated as including a term that the quality of the goods is satisfactory.

(2)   The quality of goods is satisfactory if they meet the standard that a reasonable person would consider satisfactory, taking account of—

(a)   any description of the goods,

(b)   the price or other consideration for the goods (if relevant), and

(c)   all the other relevant circumstances (see subsection (5)).

(3)   The quality of goods includes their state and condition; and the following aspects (among others) are in appropriate cases aspects of the quality of goods—

(a)   fitness for all the purposes for which goods of that kind are usually supplied;

(b)   appearance and finish;

(c)   freedom from minor defects;

(d)   safety;

(e)   durability.

(4)   The term mentioned in subsection (1) does not cover anything which makes the quality of the goods unsatisfactory—

(a)   which is specifically drawn to the consumer's attention before the contract is made,

(b)   where the consumer examines the goods before the contract is made, which that examination ought to reveal, or

(c)   in the case of a contract to supply goods by sample, which would have been apparent on a reasonable examination of the sample.

(5)   The relevant circumstances mentioned in subsection (2)(c) include any public statement about the specific characteristics of the goods made by the trader, the producer or any representative of the trader or the producer.

(6)   That includes, in particular, any public statement made in advertising or labelling.

(7)   But a public statement is not a relevant circumstance for the purposes of subsection (2)(c) if the trader shows that—

   (a)   when the contract was made, the trader was not, and could not reasonably have been, aware of the statement,

   (b)   before the contract was made, the statement had been publicly withdrawn or, to the extent that it contained anything which was incorrect or misleading, it had been publicly corrected, or

   (c)   the consumer's decision to contract for the goods could not have been influenced by the statement.

(8)   In a contract to supply goods a term about the quality of the goods may be treated as included as a matter of custom.

(9)   See section 19 for a consumer's rights if the trader is in breach of a term that this section requires to be treated as included in a contract.

10.   Goods to be fit for particular purpose

(1)   Subsection (3) applies to a contract to supply goods if before the contract is made the consumer makes known to the trader (expressly or by implication) any particular purpose for which the consumer is contracting for the goods.

(2)   Subsection (3) also applies to a contract to supply goods if—

   (a)   the goods were previously sold by a credit-broker to the trader,

   (b)   in the case of a sales contract or contract for transfer of goods, the consideration or part of it is a sum payable by instalments, and

   (c)   before the contract is made, the consumer makes known to the credit-broker (expressly or by implication) any particular purpose for which the consumer is contracting for the goods.

(3)   The contract is to be treated as including a term that the goods are reasonably fit for that purpose, whether or not that is a purpose for which goods of that kind are usually supplied.

(4)   Subsection (3) does not apply if the circumstances show that the consumer does not rely, or it is unreasonable for the consumer to rely, on the skill or judgment of the trader or credit-broker.

(5)   In a contract to supply goods a term about the fitness of the goods for a particular purpose may be treated as included as a matter of custom.

(6)   See section 19 for a consumer's rights if the trader is in breach of a term that this section requires to be treated as included in a contract.

11.   Goods to be as described

(1)   Every contract to supply goods by description is to be treated as including a term that the goods will match the description.

(2)   If the supply is by sample as well as by description, it is not sufficient that the bulk of the goods matches the sample if the goods do not also match the description.

(3)   A supply of goods is not prevented from being a supply by description just because—

   (a)   the goods are exposed for supply, and

   (b)   they are selected by the consumer.

(4)   Any information that is provided by the trader about the goods and is information mentioned in paragraph (a) of Schedule 1 or 2 to the Consumer Contracts (Information, Cancellation and Additional Charges) Regulations 2013 (SI 2013/3134) (main characteristics of goods) is to be treated as included as a term of the contract.

(5)   A change to any of that information, made before entering into the contract or later, is not effective unless expressly agreed between the consumer and the trader.

(6)   See section 2(5) and (6) for the application of subsections (4) and (5) where goods are sold at public auction.

(7)   See section 19 for a consumer's rights if the trader is in breach of a term that this section requires to be treated as included in a contract.

12.   Other pre-contract information included in contract

(1)   This section applies to any contract to supply goods.

(2)   Where regulation 9, 10 or 13 of the Consumer Contracts (Information, Cancellation and Additional Charges) Regulations 2013 (SI 2013/3134) required the trader to provide information to the consumer before the contract became binding, any of that information that was provided by the trader other than information about the goods and mentioned in paragraph (a) of Schedule 1 or 2 to the Regulations (main characteristics of goods) is to be treated as included as a term of the contract.

(3)   A change to any of that information, made before entering into the contract or later, is not effective unless expressly agreed between the consumer and the trader.

(4)   See section 2(5) and (6) for the application of this section where goods are sold at public auction.

(5)   See section 19 for a consumer's rights if the trader is in breach of a term that this section requires to be treated as included in the contract.

13.   Goods to match a sample

(1)   This section applies to a contract to supply goods by reference to a sample of the goods that is seen or examined by the consumer before the contract is made.

(2)   Every contract to which this section applies is to be treated as including a term that—

(a)   the goods will match the sample except to the extent that any differences between the sample and the goods are brought to the consumer's attention before the contract is made, and

(b)   the goods will be free from any defect that makes their quality unsatisfactory and that would not be apparent on a reasonable examination of the sample.

(3)   See section 19 for a consumer's rights if the trader is in breach of a term that this section requires to be treated as included in a contract.

14.   Goods to match a model seen or examined

(1)   This section applies to a contract to supply goods by reference to a model of the goods that is seen or examined by the consumer before entering into the contract.

(2)   Every contract to which this section applies is to be treated as including a term that the goods will match the model except to the extent that any differences between the model and the goods are brought to the consumer's attention before the consumer enters into the contract.

(3)   See section 19 for a consumer's rights if the trader is in breach of a term that this section requires to be treated as included in a contract.

15.   Installation as part of conformity of the goods with the contract

(1)   Goods do not conform to a contract to supply goods if—

(a)   installation of the goods forms part of the contract,

(b)   the goods are installed by the trader or under the trader's responsibility, and

(c)   the goods are installed incorrectly.

(2)   See section 19 for the effect of goods not conforming to the contract.

16.   Goods not conforming to contract if digital content does not conform

(1)   Goods (whether or not they conform otherwise to a contract to supply goods) do not conform to it if—

(a)   the goods are an item that includes digital content, and

(b)   the digital content does not conform to the contract to supply that content (for which see section 42(1)).

(2)   See section 19 for the effect of goods not conforming to the contract.

17.   Trader to have right to supply the goods etc

(1)   Every contract to supply goods, except one within subsection (4), is to be treated as including a term—

(a)   in the case of a contract for the hire of goods, that at the beginning of the period of hire the trader must have the right to transfer possession of the goods by way of hire for that period,

(b)   in any other case, that the trader must have the right to sell or transfer the goods at the time when ownership of the goods is to be transferred.

(2)   Every contract to supply goods, except a contract for the hire of goods or a contract within subsection (4), is to be treated as including a term that—

(a)   the goods are free from any charge or encumbrance not disclosed or known to the consumer before entering into the contract,

(b)   the goods will remain free from any such charge or encumbrance until ownership of them is to be transferred, and

(c)   the consumer will enjoy quiet possession of the goods except so far as it may be disturbed by the owner or other person entitled to the benefit of any charge or encumbrance so disclosed or known.

(3)   Every contract for the hire of goods is to be treated as including a term that the consumer will enjoy quiet possession of the goods for the period of the hire except so far as the possession may be disturbed by the owner or other person entitled to the benefit of any charge or encumbrance disclosed or known to the consumer before entering into the contract.

(4)   This subsection applies to a contract if the contract shows, or the circumstances when they enter into the contract imply, that the trader and the consumer intend the trader to transfer only—

(a)   whatever title the trader has, even if it is limited, or

(b)   whatever title a third person has, even if it is limited.

(5)   Every contract within subsection (4) is to be treated as including a term that all charges or encumbrances known to the trader and not known to the consumer were disclosed to the consumer before entering into the contract.

(6)   Every contract within subsection (4) is to be treated as including a term that the consumer's quiet possession of the goods—

(a)   will not be disturbed by the trader, and

(b)   will not be disturbed by a person claiming through or under the trader, unless that person is claiming under a charge or encumbrance that was disclosed or known to the consumer before entering into the contract.

(7)   If subsection (4)(b) applies (transfer of title that a third person has), the contract is also to be treated as including a term that the consumer's quiet possession of the goods—

(a)   will not be disturbed by the third person, and

(b)   will not be disturbed by a person claiming through or under the third person, unless the claim is under a charge or encumbrance that was disclosed or known to the consumer before entering into the contract.

(8)   In the case of a contract for the hire of goods, this section does not affect the right of the trader to repossess the goods where the contract provides or is to be treated as providing for this.

(9)   See section 19 for a consumer's rights if the trader is in breach of a term that this section requires to be treated as included in a contract.

What remedies are there if statutory rights under a goods contract are not met?

19.   Consumer's rights to enforce terms about goods

(1)   In this section and sections 22 to 24 references to goods conforming to a contract are references to—

(a)   the goods conforming to the terms described in sections 9, 10, 11, 13 and 14,

(b)   the goods not failing to conform to the contract under section 15 or 16, and

(c)   the goods conforming to requirements that are stated in the contract.

(2)   But, for the purposes of this section and sections 22 to 24, a failure to conform as mentioned in subsection (1)(a) to (c) is not a failure to conform to the contract if it has its origin in materials supplied by the consumer.

(3)   If the goods do not conform to the contract because of a breach of any of the terms described in sections 9, 10, 11, 13 and 14, or if they do not conform to the contract under section 16, the consumer's rights (and the provisions about them and when they are available) are—

(a)   the short-term right to reject (sections 20 and 22);

(b)   the right to repair or replacement (section 23); and

(c)   the right to a price reduction or the final right to reject (sections 20 and 24).

(4)   If the goods do not conform to the contract under section 15 or because of a breach of requirements that are stated in the contract, the consumer's rights (and the provisions about them and when they are available) are—

(a)   the right to repair or replacement (section 23); and

(b)   the right to a price reduction or the final right to reject (sections 20 and 24).

(5)   If the trader is in breach of a term that section 12 requires to be treated as included in the contract, the consumer has the right to recover from the trader the amount of any costs incurred by the consumer as a result of the breach, up to the amount of the price paid or the value of other consideration given for the goods.

(6)   If the trader is in breach of the term that section 17(1) (right to supply etc) requires to be treated as included in the contract, the consumer has a right to reject (see section 20 for provisions about that right and when it is available).

(7)   Subsections (3) to (6) are subject to section 25 and subsections (3)(a) and (6) are subject to section 26.

(8)   Section 28 makes provision about remedies for breach of a term about the time for delivery of goods.

(9)   This Chapter does not prevent the consumer seeking other remedies—

(a)   for a breach of a term that this Chapter requires to be treated as included in the contract,

(b)   on the grounds that, under section 15 or 16, goods do not conform to the contract, or

(c)   for a breach of a requirement stated in the contract.

(10)   Those other remedies may be ones—

(a)   in addition to a remedy referred to in subsections (3) to (6) (but not so as to recover twice for the same loss), or

(b)   instead of such a remedy, or

(c)   where no such remedy is provided for.

(11)   Those other remedies include any of the following that is open to the consumer in the circumstances—

(a)   claiming damages;

(b)   seeking specific performance;

(c)   seeking an order for specific implement;

(d)   relying on the breach against a claim by the trader for the price;

(e)   for breach of an express term, exercising a right to treat the contract as at an end.

(12)   It is not open to the consumer to treat the contract as at an end for breach of a term that this Chapter requires to be treated as included in the contract, or on the grounds that, under section 15 or 16, goods do not conform to the contract, except as provided by subsections (3), (4) and (6).

(13)   In this Part, treating a contract as at an end means treating it as repudiated.

(14)   For the purposes of subsections (3)(b) and (c) and (4), goods which do not conform to the contract at any time within the period of six months beginning with the day on which the goods were delivered to the consumer must be taken not to have conformed to it on that day.

(15)   Subsection (14) does not apply if—

(a)   it is established that the goods did conform to the contract on that day, or

(b)   its application is incompatible with the nature of the goods or with how they fail to conform to the contract.

20.   Right to reject

(1)   The short-term right to reject is subject to section 22.

(2)   The final right to reject is subject to section 24.

(3)   The right to reject under section 19(6) is not limited by those sections.

(4)   Each of these rights entitles the consumer to reject the goods and treat the contract as at an end, subject to subsections (20) and (21).

(5)   The right is exercised if the consumer indicates to the trader that the consumer is rejecting the goods and treating the contract as at an end.

(6)   The indication may be something the consumer says or does, but it must be clear enough to be understood by the trader.

(7)   From the time when the right is exercised—

(a)   the trader has a duty to give the consumer a refund, subject to subsection (18), and

(b)   the consumer has a duty to make the goods available for collection by the trader or (if there is an agreement for the consumer to return rejected goods) to return them as agreed.

(8)   Whether or not the consumer has a duty to return the rejected goods, the trader must bear any reasonable costs of returning them, other than any costs incurred by the consumer in returning the goods in person to the place where the consumer took physical possession of them.

(9)   The consumer's entitlement to receive a refund works as follows.

(10)   To the extent that the consumer paid money under the contract, the consumer is entitled to receive back the same amount of money.

(11)   To the extent that the consumer transferred anything else under the contract, the consumer is entitled to receive back the same amount of what the consumer transferred, unless subsection (12) applies.

(12)   To the extent that the consumer transferred under the contract something for which the same amount of the same thing cannot be substituted, the consumer is entitled to receive back in its original state whatever the consumer transferred.

(13)   If the contract is for the hire of goods, the entitlement to a refund extends only to anything paid or otherwise transferred for a period of hire that the consumer does not get because the contract is treated as at an end.

(14)   If the contract is a hire-purchase agreement or a conditional sales contract and the contract is treated as at an end before the whole of the price has been paid, the entitlement to a refund extends only to the part of the price paid.

(15)   A refund under this section must be given without undue delay, and in any event within 14 days beginning with the day on which the trader agrees that the consumer is entitled to a refund.

(16)   If the consumer paid money under the contract, the trader must give the refund using the same means of payment as the consumer used, unless the consumer expressly agrees otherwise.

(17)   The trader must not impose any fee on the consumer in respect of the refund.

(18)   There is no entitlement to receive a refund—

    (a)   if none of subsections (10) to (12) applies,

    (b)   to the extent that anything to which subsection (12) applies cannot be given back in its original state, or

    (c)   where subsection (13) applies, to the extent that anything the consumer transferred under the contract cannot be divided so as to give back only the amount, or part of the amount, to which the consumer is entitled.

(19)   It may be open to a consumer to claim damages where there is no entitlement to receive a refund, or because of the limits of the entitlement, or instead of a refund.

(20)   Subsection (21) qualifies the application in relation to England and Wales and Northern Ireland of the rights mentioned in subsections (1) to (3) where—

    (a)   the contract is a severable contract,

    (b)   in relation to the final right to reject, the contract is a contract for the hire of goods, a hire-purchase agreement or a contract for transfer of goods, and

    (c)   section 26(3) does not apply.

(21)   The consumer is entitled, depending on the terms of the contract and the circumstances of the case—

    (a)   to reject the goods to which a severable obligation relates and treat that obligation as at an end (so that the entitlement to a refund relates only to what the consumer paid or transferred in relation to that obligation), or

    (b)   to exercise any of the rights mentioned in subsections (1) to (3) in respect of the whole contract.

23.   Right to repair or replacement

(1)   This section applies if the consumer has the right to repair or replacement (see section 19(3) and (4)).

(2)   If the consumer requires the trader to repair or replace the goods, the trader must—

    (a)   do so within a reasonable time and without significant inconvenience to the consumer, and

    (b)   bear any necessary costs incurred in doing so (including in particular the cost of any labour, materials or postage).

(3)   The consumer cannot require the trader to repair or replace the goods if that remedy (the repair or the replacement)—

    (a)   is impossible, or

    (b)   is disproportionate compared to the other of those remedies.

(4)   Either of those remedies is disproportionate compared to the other if it imposes costs on the trader which, compared to those imposed by the other, are unreasonable, taking into account—

    (a)   the value which the goods would have if they conformed to the contract,

(b)   the significance of the lack of conformity, and

(c)   whether the other remedy could be effected without significant inconvenience to the consumer.

(5)   Any question as to what is a reasonable time or significant inconvenience is to be determined taking account of—

    (a)   the nature of the goods, and

    (b)   the purpose for which the goods were acquired.

(6)   A consumer who requires or agrees to the repair of goods cannot require the trader to replace them, or exercise the short-term right to reject, without giving the trader a reasonable time to repair them (unless giving the trader that time would cause significant inconvenience to the consumer).

(7)   A consumer who requires or agrees to the replacement of goods cannot require the trader to repair them, or exercise the short-term right to reject, without giving the trader a reasonable time to replace them (unless giving the trader that time would cause significant inconvenience to the consumer).

(8)   In this Chapter, "repair" in relation to goods that do not conform to a contract, means making them conform.

24.   Right to price reduction or final right to reject

(1)   The right to a price reduction is the right—

    (a)   to require the trader to reduce by an appropriate amount the price the consumer is required to pay under the contract, or anything else the consumer is required to transfer under the contract, and

    (b)   to receive a refund from the trader for anything already paid or otherwise transferred by the consumer above the reduced amount.

(2)   The amount of the reduction may, where appropriate, be the full amount of the price or whatever the consumer is required to transfer.

(3)   Section 20(10) to (17) applies to a consumer's right to receive a refund under subsection (1)(b).

(4)   The right to a price reduction does not apply—

    (a)   if what the consumer is (before the reduction) required to transfer under the contract, whether or not already transferred, cannot be divided up so as to enable the trader to receive or retain only the reduced amount, or

    (b)   if anything to which section 20(12) applies cannot be given back in its original state.

(5)   A consumer who has the right to a price reduction and the final right to reject may only exercise one (not both), and may only do so in one of these situations—

    (a)   after one repair or one replacement, the goods do not conform to the contract;

    (b)   because of section 23(3) the consumer can require neither repair nor replacement of the goods; or

    (c)   the consumer has required the trader to repair or replace the goods, but the trader is in breach of the requirement of section 23(2)(a) to do so within a reasonable time and without significant inconvenience to the consumer.

(6)   There has been a repair or replacement for the purposes of subsection (5)(a) if—

    (a)   the consumer has requested or agreed to repair or replacement of the goods (whether in relation to one fault or more than one), and

    (b)   the trader has delivered goods to the consumer, or made goods available to the consumer, in response to the request or agreement.

(7)   For the purposes of subsection (6) goods that the trader arranges to repair at the consumer's premises are made available when the trader indicates that the repairs are finished.

(8)   If the consumer exercises the final right to reject, any refund to the consumer may be reduced by a deduction for use, to take account of the use the consumer has had of the goods in the period since they were delivered, but this is subject to subsections (9) and (10).

(9)   No deduction may be made to take account of use in any period when the consumer had the goods only because the trader failed to collect them at an agreed time.

(10)   No deduction may be made if the final right to reject is exercised in the first 6 months (see subsection (11)), unless—

    (a)   the goods consist of a motor vehicle, or

(b)   the goods are of a description specified by order made by the Secretary of State by statutory instrument.

(11)   In subsection (10) the first 6 months means 6 months beginning with the first day after these have all happened—

(a)   ownership or (in the case of a contract for the hire of goods, a hire-purchase agreement or a conditional sales contract) possession of the goods has been transferred to the consumer,

(b)   the goods have been delivered, and

(c)   where the contract requires the trader to install the goods or take other action to enable the consumer to use them, the trader has notified the consumer that the action has been taken.

(12)   In subsection (10)(a) "motor vehicle"—

(a)   in relation to Great Britain, has the same meaning as in the Road Traffic Act 1988 (see sections 185 to 194 of that Act);

(b)   in relation to Northern Ireland, has the same meaning as in the Road Traffic (Northern Ireland) Order 1995 (SI 1995/2994 (NI 18)) (see Parts I and V of that Order).

(13)   But a vehicle is not a motor vehicle for the purposes of subsection (10)(a) if it is constructed or adapted—

(a)   for the use of a person suffering from some physical defect or disability, and

(b)   so that it may only be used by one such person at any one time.

(14)   An order under subsection (10)(b)—

(a)   may be made only if the Secretary of State is satisfied that it is appropriate to do so because of significant detriment caused to traders as a result of the application of subsection (10) in relation to goods of the description specified by the order;

(b)   may contain transitional or transitory provision or savings.

(15)   No order may be made under subsection (10)(b) unless a draft of the statutory instrument containing it has been laid before, and approved by a resolution of, each House of Parliament.

Other rules about goods contracts

28.   Delivery of goods

(1)   This section applies to any sales contract.

(2)   Unless the trader and the consumer have agreed otherwise, the contract is to be treated as including a term that the trader must deliver the goods to the consumer.

(3)   Unless there is an agreed time or period, the contract is to be treated as including a term that the trader must deliver the goods—

(a)   without undue delay, and

(b)   in any event, not more than 30 days after the day on which the contract is entered into.

(4)   In this section—

(a)   an "agreed" time or period means a time or period agreed by the trader and the consumer for delivery of the goods;

(b)   if there is an obligation to deliver the goods at the time the contract is entered into, that time counts as the "agreed" time.

(5)   Subsections (6) and (7) apply if the trader does not deliver the goods in accordance with subsection (3) or at the agreed time or within the agreed period.

(6)   If the circumstances are that—

(a)   the trader has refused to deliver the goods,

(b)   delivery of the goods at the agreed time or within the agreed period is essential taking into account all the relevant circumstances at the time the contract was entered into, or

(c)   the consumer told the trader before the contract was entered into that delivery in accordance with subsection (3), or at the agreed time or within the agreed period, was essential,

then the consumer may treat the contract as at an end.

(7)   In any other circumstances, the consumer may specify a period that is appropriate in the circumstances and require the trader to deliver the goods before the end of that period.

(8)   If the consumer specifies a period under subsection (7) but the goods are not delivered within that period, then the consumer may treat the contract as at an end.

(9)   If the consumer treats the contract as at an end under subsection (6) or (8), the trader must without undue delay reimburse all payments made under the contract.

(10)   If subsection (6) or (8) applies but the consumer does not treat the contract as at an end—

(a)   that does not prevent the consumer from cancelling the order for any of the goods or rejecting goods that have been delivered, and

(b)   the trader must without undue delay reimburse all payments made under the contract in respect of any goods for which the consumer cancels the order or which the consumer rejects.

(11)   If any of the goods form a commercial unit, the consumer cannot reject or cancel the order for some of those goods without also rejecting or cancelling the order for the rest of them.

(12)   A unit is a "commercial unit" if division of the unit would materially impair the value of the goods or the character of the unit.

(13)   This section does not prevent the consumer seeking other remedies where it is open to the consumer to do so.

(14)   See section 2(5) and (6) for the application of this section where goods are sold at public auction.

29.   Passing of risk

(1)   A sales contract is to be treated as including the following provisions as terms.

(2)   The goods remain at the trader's risk until they come into the physical possession of—

(a)   the consumer, or

(b)   a person identified by the consumer to take possession of the goods.

(3)   Subsection (2) does not apply if the goods are delivered to a carrier who—

(a)   is commissioned by the consumer to deliver the goods, and

(b)   is not a carrier the trader named as an option for the consumer.

(4)   In that case the goods are at the consumer's risk on and after delivery to the carrier.

(5)   Subsection (4) does not affect any liability of the carrier to the consumer in respect of the goods.

(6)   See section 2(5) and (6) for the application of this section where goods are sold at public auction.

Can a trader contract out of statutory rights and remedies under a goods contract?

31.   Liability that cannot be excluded or restricted

(1)   A term of a contract to supply goods is not binding on the consumer to the extent that it would exclude or restrict the trader's liability arising under any of these provisions—

(a)   section 9 (goods to be of satisfactory quality);

(b)   section 10 (goods to be fit for particular purpose);

(c)   section 11 (goods to be as described);

(d)   section 12 (other pre-contract information included in contract);

(e)   section 13 (goods to match a sample);

(f)   section 14 (goods to match a model seen or examined);

(g)   section 15 (installation as part of conformity of the goods with the contract);

(h)   section 16 (goods not conforming to contract if digital content does not conform);

(i)   section 17 (trader to have right to supply the goods etc);

(j)   section 28 (delivery of goods);

(k)   section 29 (passing of risk).

(2)   That also means that a term of a contract to supply goods is not binding on the consumer to the extent that it would—

(a)   exclude or restrict a right or remedy in respect of a liability under a provision listed in subsection (1),

(b)   make such a right or remedy or its enforcement subject to a restrictive or onerous condition,

(c)   allow a trader to put a person at a disadvantage as a result of pursuing such a right or remedy, or

(d)   exclude or restrict rules of evidence or procedure.

(3)   The reference in subsection (1) to excluding or restricting a liability also includes preventing an obligation or duty arising or limiting its extent.

(4)   An agreement in writing to submit present or future differences to arbitration is not to be regarded as excluding or restricting any liability for the purposes of this section.

(5)   Subsection (1)(i), and subsection (2) so far as it relates to liability under section 17, do not apply to a term of a contract for the hire of goods.

(6)   But an express term of a contract for the hire of goods is not binding on the consumer to the extent that it would exclude or restrict a term that section 17 requires to be treated as included in the contract, unless it is inconsistent with that term (and see also section 62 (requirement for terms to be fair)).

(7)   See Schedule 3 for provision about the enforcement of this section.

Commercial Agents (Council Directive) Regulations 1993
(S.I. 1993 No. 3053)
Part I
General

1.   Citation, commencement and applicable law

(1)   These Regulations may be cited as the Commercial Agents (Council Directive) Regulations 1993 and shall come into force on 1st January 1994.

(2)   These Regulations govern the relations between commercial agents and their principals and, subject to paragraph (3), apply in relation to the activities of commercial agents in Great Britain.

(3)   A court or tribunal shall:

(a)   apply the law of the other member State concerned in place of regulations 3 to 22 where the parties have agreed that the agency contract is to be governed by the law of that member State;

(b)   (whether or not it would otherwise be required to do so) apply these regulations where the law of another member State corresponding to these regulations enables the parties to agree that the agency contract is to be governed by the law of a different member State and the parties have agreed that it is to be governed by the law of England and Wales or Scotland.

2.   Interpretation, application and extent

(1)   In these Regulations—

"commercial agent" means a self-employed intermediary who has continuing authority to negotiate the sale or purchase of goods on behalf of another person (the "principal"), or to negotiate and conclude the sale or purchase of goods on behalf of and in the name of that principal; but shall be understood as not including in particular:

(i)   a person who, in his capacity as an officer of a company or association, is empowered to enter into commitments binding on that company or association;

(ii)   a partner who is lawfully authorised to enter into commitments binding on his partners;

(iii)   a person who acts as an insolvency practitioner (as that expression is defined in section 388 of the Insolvency Act 1986) or the equivalent in any other jurisdiction;

"commission" means any part of the remuneration of a commercial agent which varies with the number or value of business transactions;

"EEA Agreement" means the Agreement on the European Economic Area signed at Oporto on 2nd May 1992 as adjusted by the Protocol signed at Brussels on 17th March 1993;

"member State" includes a State which is a contracting party to the EEA Agreement;

"restraint of trade clause" means an agreement restricting the business activities of a commercial agent following termination of the agency contract.

(2)   These Regulations do not apply to—

(a)   commercial agents whose activities are unpaid;

(b)   commercial agents when they operate on commodity exchanges or in the commodity market;

(c)   the Crown Agents for Overseas Governments and Administrations, as set up under the Crown Agents Act 1979, or its subsidiaries.

(3)   The provisions of the Schedule to these Regulations have effect for the purpose of determining the persons whose activities as commercial agents are to be considered secondary.

(4)   These Regulations shall not apply to the persons referred to in paragraph (3) above.

(5)   These Regulations do not extend to Northern Ireland.

Part II
Rights and Obligations

3.   Duties of a commercial agent to his principal

(1)   In performing his activities a commercial agent must look after the interests of his principal and act dutifully and in good faith.

(2)   In particular, a commercial agent must—

(a)   make proper efforts to negotiate and, where appropriate, conclude the transactions he is instructed to take care of;

    (b)   communicate to his principal all the necessary information available to him;

    (c)   comply with reasonable instructions given by his principal.

4.   Duties of a principal to his commercial agent

(1)   In his relations with his commercial agent a principal must act dutifully and in good faith.

(2)   In particular, a principal must—

    (a)   provide his commercial agent with the necessary documentation relating to the goods concerned;

    (b)   obtain for his commercial agent the information necessary for the performance of the agency contract, and in particular notify his commercial agent within a reasonable period once he anticipates that the volume of commercial transactions will be significantly lower than that which the commercial agent could normally have expected.

(3)   A principal shall, in addition, inform his commercial agent within a reasonable period of his acceptance or refusal of, and of any non-execution by him of, a commercial transaction which the commercial agent has procured for him.

5.   Prohibition on derogation from regulations 3 and 4 and consequence of breach

(1)   The parties may not derogate from regulations 3 and 4 above.

(2)   The law applicable to the contract shall govern the consequence of breach of the rights and obligations under regulations 3 and 4 above.

Part III

Remuneration

6.   Form and amount of remuneration in absence of agreement

(1)   In the absence of any agreement as to remuneration between the parties, a commercial agent shall be entitled to the remuneration that commercial agents appointed for the goods forming the subject of his agency contract are customarily allowed in the place where he carries on his activities and, if there is no such customary practice, a commercial agent shall be entitled to reasonable remuneration taking into account all the aspects of the transaction.

(2)   This regulation is without prejudice to the application of any enactment or rule of law concerning the level of remuneration.

(3)   Where a commercial agent is not remunerated (wholly or in part) by commission, regulations 7 to 12 below shall not apply.

7.   Entitlement to commission on transactions concluded during agency contract

(1)   A commercial agent shall be entitled to commission on commercial transactions concluded during the period covered by the agency contract—

    (a)   where the transaction has been concluded as a result of his action; or

    (b)   where the transaction is concluded with a third party whom he has previously acquired as a customer for transactions of the same kind.

(2)   A commercial agent shall also be entitled to commission on transactions concluded during the period covered by the agency contract where he has an exclusive right to a specific geographical area or to a specific group of customers and where the transaction has been entered into with a customer belonging to that area or group.

8.   Entitlement to commission on transactions concluded after agency contract has terminated

Subject to regulation 9 below, a commercial agent shall be entitled to commission on commercial transactions concluded after the agency contract has terminated if—

(a)   the transaction is mainly attributable to his efforts during the period covered by the agency contract and if the transaction was entered into within a reasonable period after that contract terminated; or

(b)   in accordance with the conditions mentioned in regulation 7 above, the order of the third party reached the principal or the commercial agent before the agency contract terminated.

9.   Apportionment of commission between new and previous commercial agents

(1)   A commercial agent shall not be entitled to the commission referred to in regulation 7 above if that commission is payable, by virtue of regulation 8 above, to the previous commercial agent, unless it is equitable because of the circumstances for the commission to be shared between the commercial agents.

(2)   The principal shall be liable for any sum due under paragraph (1) above to the person entitled to it in accordance with that paragraph, and any sum which the other commercial agent receives to which he is not entitled shall be refunded to the principal.

10.   When commission due and date for payment

(1)   Commission shall become due as soon as, and to the extent that, one of the following circumstances occurs:

(a)   the principal has executed the transaction; or

(b)   the principal should, according to his agreement with the third party, have executed the transaction; or

(c)   the third party has executed the transaction.

(2)   Commission shall become due at the latest when the third party has executed his part of the transaction or should have done so if the principal had executed his part of the transaction, as he should have.

(3)   The commission shall be paid not later than on the last day of the month following the quarter in which it became due, and, for the purposes of these Regulations, unless otherwise agreed between the parties, the first quarter period shall run from the date the agency contract takes effect, and subsequent periods shall run from that date in the third month thereafter or the beginning of the fourth month, whichever is the sooner.

(4)   Any agreement to derogate from paragraphs (2) and (3) above to the detriment of the commercial agent shall be void.

11.   Extinction of right to commission

(1)   The right to commission can be extinguished only if and to the extent that—

(a)   it is established that the contract between the third party and the principal will not be executed; and

(b)   that fact is due to a reason for which the principal is not to blame.

(2)   Any commission which the commercial agent has already received shall be refunded if the right to it is extinguished.

(3)   Any agreement to derogate from paragraph (1) above to the detriment of the commercial agent shall be void.

12.   Periodic supply of information as to commission due and right of inspection of principal's books

(1)   The principal shall supply his commercial agent with a statement of the commission due, not later than the last day of the month following the quarter in which the commission has become due, and such statement shall set out the main components used in calculating the amount of the commission.

(2)   A commercial agent shall be entitled to demand that he be provided with all the information (and in particular an extract from the books) which is available to his principal and which he needs in order to check the amount of the commission due to him.

(3)   Any agreement to derogate from paragraphs (1) and (2) above shall be void.

(4)   Nothing in this regulation shall remove or restrict the effect of, or prevent reliance upon, any enactment or rule of law which recognises the right of an agent to inspect the books of a principal.

Part IV
Conclusion and Termination of the Agency Contract

13.   Right to signed written statement of terms of agency contract

(1)   The commercial agent and principal shall each be entitled to receive from the other, on request, a signed written document setting out the terms of the agency contract including any terms subsequently agreed.

(2)   Any purported waiver of the right referred to in paragraph (1) above shall be void.

14.   Conversion of agency contract after expiry of fixed period

An agency contract for a fixed period which continues to be performed by both parties after that period has expired shall be deemed to be converted into an agency contract for an indefinite period.

15.   Minimum periods of notice for termination of agency contract

(1)   Where an agency contract is concluded for an indefinite period either party may terminate it by notice.

(2)   The period of notice shall be—

(a)   1 month for the first year of the contract;

(b)   2 months for the second year commenced;

(c)   3 months for the third year commenced and for the subsequent years;

and the parties may not agree on any shorter periods of notice.

(3)   If the parties agree on longer periods than those laid down in paragraph (2) above, the period of notice to be observed by the principal must not be shorter than that to be observed by the commercial agent.

(4)   Unless otherwise agreed by the parties, the end of the period of notice must coincide with the end of a calendar month.

(5)   The provisions of this regulation shall also apply to an agency contract for a fixed period where it is converted under regulation 14 above into an agency contract for an indefinite period subject to the proviso that the earlier fixed period must be taken into account in the calculation of the period of notice.

16.   Savings with regard to immediate termination

These Regulations shall not affect the application of any enactment or rule of law which provides for the immediate termination of the agency contract—

(a)   because of the failure of one party to carry out all or part of his obligations under that contract; or

(b)   where exceptional circumstances arise.

17.   Entitlement of commercial agent to indemnity or compensation on termination of agency contract

(1)   This regulation has effect for the purpose of ensuring that the commercial agent is, after termination of the agency contract, indemnified in accordance with paragraphs (3) to (5) below or compensated for damage in accordance with paragraphs (6) and (7) below.

(2)   Except where the agency contract otherwise provides, the commercial agent shall be entitled to be compensated rather than indemnified.

(3)   Subject to paragraph (9) and to regulation 18 below, the commercial agent shall be entitled to an indemnity if and to the extent that—

(a)   he has brought the principal new customers or has significantly increased the volume of business with existing customers and the principal continues to derive substantial benefits from the business with such customers; and

(b)   the payment of this indemnity is equitable having regard to all the circumstances and, in particular, the commission lost by the commercial agent on the business transacted with such customers.

(4)   The amount of the indemnity shall not exceed a figure equivalent to an indemnity for one year calculated from the commercial agent's average annual remuneration over the preceding five years and if the contract goes back less than five years the indemnity shall be calculated on the average for the period in question.

(5)   The grant of an indemnity as mentioned above shall not prevent the commercial agent from seeking damages.

(6)   Subject to paragraph (9) and to regulation 18 below, the commercial agent shall be entitled to compensation for the damage he suffers as a result of the termination of his relations with his principal.

(7)   For the purpose of these Regulations such damage shall be deemed to occur particularly when the termination takes place in either or both of the following circumstances, namely circumstances which—

(a)   deprive the commercial agent of the commission which proper performance of the agency contract would have procured for him whilst providing his principal with substantial benefits linked to the activities of the commercial agent; or

(b)   have not enabled the commercial agent to amortize the costs and expenses that he had incurred in the performance of the agency contract on the advice of his principal.

(8)   Entitlement to the indemnity or compensation for damage as provided for under paragraphs (2) to (7) above shall also arise where the agency contract is terminated as a result of the death of the commercial agent.

(9)   The commercial agent shall lose his entitlement to the indemnity or compensation for damage in the instances provided for in paragraphs (2) to (8) above if within one year following termination of his agency contract he has not notified his principal that he intends pursuing his entitlement.

18.   Grounds for excluding payment of indemnity or compensation under regulation 17

The indemnity or compensation referred to in regulation 17 above shall not be payable to the commercial agent where—

(a)   the principal has terminated the agency contract because of default attributable to the commercial agent which would justify immediate termination of the agency contract pursuant to regulation 16 above; or

(b)   the commercial agent has himself terminated the agency contract, unless such termination is justified—

   (i)   by circumstances attributable to the principal, or

   (ii)   on grounds of the age, infirmity or illness of the commercial agent in consequence of which he cannot reasonably be required to continue his activities; or

(c)   the commercial agent, with the agreement of his principal, assigns his rights and duties under the agency contract to another person.

19.   Prohibition on derogation from regulations 17 and 18

The parties may not derogate from regulations 17 and 18 to the detriment of the commercial agent before the agency contract expires.

20.   Restraint of trade clauses

(1)   A restraint of trade clause shall be valid only if and to the extent that—

   (a)   it is concluded in writing; and

   (b)   it relates to the geographical area or the group of customers and the geographical area entrusted to the commercial agent and to the kind of goods covered by his agency under the contract.

(2)   A restraint of trade clause shall be valid for not more than two years after termination of the agency contract.

(3)   Nothing in this regulation shall affect any enactment or rule of law which imposes other restrictions on the validity or enforceability of restraint of trade clauses or which enables a court to reduce the obligations on the parties resulting from such clauses.

Part V
Miscellaneous and Supplemental

21.   Disclosure of information

Nothing in these Regulations shall require information to be given where such disclosure would be contrary to public policy.

22.   Service of notice etc.

(1)   Any notice, statement or other document to be given or supplied to a commercial agent or to be given or supplied to the principal under these Regulations may be so given or supplied:

   (a)   by delivering it to him;

   (b)   by leaving it at his proper address addressed to him by name;

   (c)   by sending it by post to him addressed either to his registered address or to the address of his registered or principal office;

or by any other means provided for in the agency contract.

(2)   Any such notice, statement or document may—

   (a)   in the case of a body corporate, be given or served on the secretary or clerk of that body;

   (b)   in the case of a partnership, be given to or served on any partner or on any person having the control or management of the partnership business.

23.   Transitional provisions

(1)   Notwithstanding any provision in an agency contract made before 1st January 1994, these Regulations shall apply to that contract after that date and, accordingly any provision which is inconsistent with these Regulations shall have effect subject to them.

(2)   Nothing in these Regulations shall affect the rights and liabilities of a commercial agent or a principal which have accrued before 1st January 1994.

Copyright and Rights in Databases Regulations 1997
(S.I. 1997 No. 3032)

Part III
Database Right

12.   Interpretation

(1)   In this Part—

"database" has the meaning given by section 3A(1) of the 1988 Act (as inserted by Regulation 6);

"extraction", in relation to any contents of a database, means the permanent or temporary transfer of those contents to another medium by any means or in any form;

"insubstantial", in relation to part of the contents of a database, shall be construed subject to Regulation 16(2);

"investment" includes any investment, whether of financial, human or technical resources;

"jointly", in relation to the making of a database, shall be construed in accordance with Regulation 14(6);

"lawful user", in relation to a database, means any person who (whether under a licence to do any of the acts restricted by any database right in the database or otherwise) has a right to use the database;

"maker", in relation to a database, shall be construed in accordance with Regulation 14;

"Marrakesh beneficiary" has the meaning given by section 296ZE(1) of the 1988 Act;

"national of the United Kingdom" has the meaning given by section 178 of the 1988 Act;

"re-utilisation", in relation to any contents of a database, means making those contents available to the public by any means;

"substantial", in relation to any investment, extraction or re-utilisation, means substantial in terms of quantity or quality or a combination of both.

(2)   The making of a copy of a database available for use, on terms that it will or may be returned, otherwise than for direct or indirect economic or commercial advantage, through an establishment which is accessible to the public shall not be taken for the purposes of this Part to constitute extraction or re-utilisation of the contents of the database.

(3)   Where the making of a copy of a database available through an establishment which is accessible to the public gives rise to a payment the amount of which does not go beyond what is necessary to cover the costs of the establishment, there is no direct or indirect economic or commercial advantage for the purposes of paragraph (2).

(4)   Paragraph (2) does not apply to the making of a copy of a database available for on-the-spot reference use.

(5)   Where a copy of a database has been sold within the EEA, the United Kingdom or the Isle of Man by, or with the consent of, the owner of the database right in the database, the further sale within the EEA, the United Kingdom or the Isle of Man of that copy shall not be taken for the purposes of this Part to constitute extraction or re-utilisation of the contents of the database.

13.   Database right

(1)   A property right ("database right") subsists, in accordance with this Part, in a database if there has been a substantial investment in obtaining, verifying or presenting the contents of the database.

(2)   For the purposes of paragraph (1) it is immaterial whether or not the database or any of its contents is a copyright work, within the meaning of Part I of the 1988 Act.

(3)   This Regulation has effect subject to Regulation 18.

14.   The maker of a database

(1)   Subject to paragraphs (2) to (4), the person who takes the initiative in obtaining, verifying or presenting the contents of a database and assumes the risk of investing in that obtaining, verification or presentation shall be regarded as the maker of, and as having made, the database.

(2)   Where a database is made by an employee in the course of his employment, his employer shall be regarded as the maker of the database, subject to any agreement to the contrary.

(3)   Subject to paragraph (4), where a database is made by Her Majesty or by an officer or servant of the Crown in the course of his duties, Her Majesty shall be regarded as the maker of the database.

(4)   Where a database is made by or under the direction or control of the House of Commons or the House of Lords—

    (a)   the House by whom, or under whose direction or control, the database is made shall be regarded as the maker of the database, and

    (b)   if the database is made by or under the direction or control of both Houses, the two Houses shall be regarded as the joint makers of the database.

(4A)   Where a database is made by or under the direction or control of the Scottish Parliament, the Scottish Parliamentary Corporate Body shall be regarded as the maker of the database.

(5)   For the purposes of this Part a database is made jointly if two or more persons acting together in collaboration take the initiative in obtaining, verifying or presenting the contents of the database and assume the risk of investing in that obtaining, verification or presentation.

(6)   References in this Part to the maker of a database shall, except as otherwise provided, be construed, in relation to a database which is made jointly, as references to all the makers of the database.

15.   First ownership of database right

The maker of a database is the first owner of database right in it.

16.   Acts infringing database right

(1)   Subject to the provisions of this Part, a person infringes database right in a database if, without the consent of the owner of the right, he extracts or re-utilises all or a substantial part of the contents of the database.

(2)   For the purposes of this Part, the repeated and systematic extraction or re-utilisation of insubstantial parts of the contents of a database may amount to the extraction or re-utilisation of a substantial part of those contents.

17.   Term of protection

(1)   Database right in a database expires at the end of the period of fifteen years from the end of the calendar year in which the making of the database was completed.

(2)   Where a database is made available to the public before the end of the period referred to in paragraph (1), database right in the database shall expire fifteen years from the end of the calendar year in which the database was first made available to the public.

(3)   Any substantial change to the contents of a database, including a substantial change resulting from the accumulation of successive additions, deletions or alterations, which would result in the database being considered to be a substantial new investment shall qualify the database resulting from that investment for its own term of protection.

(4)   This Regulation has effect subject to Regulation 30.

18.   Qualification for database right

(1)   Database right does not subsist in a database unless, at the material time, its maker, or if it was made jointly, one or more of its makers, was—

    (a)   an individual who was a national of the United Kingdom or habitually resident within the United Kingdom,

    (b)   a body which was incorporated under the law of any part of the United Kingdom and which, at that time, satisfied one of the conditions in paragraph (2),

    (c)   a partnership or other unincorporated body which was formed under the law of any part of the United Kingdom and which, at that time, satisfied the condition in paragraph (2)(a),

    (d)   an individual who was habitually resident within the Isle of Man,

    (e)   a body which was incorporated under the law of the Isle of Man and which, at that time, satisfied one of the conditions in paragraph (2A), or

    (f)   a partnership or other unincorporated body which was formed under the law of the Isle of Man and which, at that time, satisfied the condition in paragraph (2A)(a).

(2)   The conditions mentioned in paragraphs (1)(b) and (c) are—

    (a)   that the body has its central administration or principal place of business within the United Kingdom, or

    (b)   that the body has its registered office within the United Kingdom and the body's operations are linked on an ongoing basis with the economy of the United Kingdom.

(2A)   The conditions mentioned in paragraphs (1)(e) and (f) are—

    (a)   that the body has its central administration or principal place of business within the Isle of Man, or

    (b)   that the body has its registered office within the Isle of Man and the body's operations are linked on an ongoing basis with the economy of the Isle of Man.

(3)   Paragraph (1) does not apply in any case falling within Regulation 14(4).

(4)   In this Regulation—

    (b)   "the material time" means the time when the database was made, or if the making extended over a period, a substantial part of that period.

19.   Avoidance of certain terms affecting lawful users

(1)   A lawful user of a database which has been made available to the public in any manner shall be entitled to extract or re-utilise insubstantial parts of the contents of the database for any purpose.

(2)   Where under an agreement a person has a right to use a database, or part of a database, which has been made available to the public in any manner, any term or condition in the agreement shall be void in so far as it purports to prevent that person from extracting or re-utilising insubstantial parts of the contents of the database, or of that part of the database, for any purpose.

20.   Exceptions to database right

(1)   Database right in a database which has been made available to the public in any manner is not infringed by fair dealing with a substantial part of its contents if—

    (a)   that part is extracted from the database by a person who is apart from this paragraph a lawful user of the database,

    (b)   it is extracted for the purpose of illustration for teaching or research and not for any commercial purpose, and

    (c)   the source is indicated.

(2)   The provisions of Schedule 1 specify other acts which may be done in relation to a database notwithstanding the existence of database right.

23.   Application of copyright provisions to database right

The following provisions of the 1988 Act apply in relation to database right and databases in which that right subsists as they apply in relation to copyright and copyright works—

    sections 90 to 93 (dealing with rights in copyright works)

    sections 96 to 102 (rights and remedies of copyright owner and exclusive licensee)

    sections 113 and 114 (supplementary provisions relating to delivery up)

    section 115 (jurisdiction of county court and sheriff court).

Electronic Commerce (EC Directive) Regulations 2002
(S.I. 2002 No. 2013)

2. **Interpretation**

(1) In these Regulations and in the Schedule—

"commercial communication" means a communication, in any form, designed to promote, directly or indirectly, the goods, services or image of any person pursuing a commercial, industrial or craft activity or exercising a regulated profession, other than a communication—

(a) consisting only of information allowing direct access to the activity of that person including a geographic address, a domain name or an electronic mail address; or

(b) relating to the goods, services or image of that person provided that the communication has been prepared independently of the person making it (and for this purpose, a communication prepared without financial consideration is to be taken to have been prepared independently unless the contrary is shown);

"consumer" means any natural person who is acting for purposes other than those of his trade, business or profession;

"coordinated field" means requirements applicable to information society service providers or information society services, regardless of whether they are of a general nature or specifically designed for them, and covers requirements with which the service provider has to comply in respect of—

(a) the taking up of the activity of an information society service, such as requirements concerning qualifications, authorisation or notification, and

(b) the pursuit of the activity of an information society service, such as requirements concerning the behaviour of the service provider, requirements regarding the quality or content of the service including those applicable to advertising and contracts, or requirements concerning the liability of the service provider, but does not cover requirements such as those applicable to goods as such, to the delivery of goods or to services not provided by electronic means;

"the Directive" means Directive 2000/31/EC of the European Parliament and of the Council of 8 June 2000 on certain legal aspects of information society services, in particular electronic commerce, in the Internal Market (Directive on electronic commerce);

"EEA Agreement" has the meaning given by Schedule 1 to the Interpretation Act 1978;

"enactment" includes an enactment comprised in Northern Ireland legislation and comprised in, or an instrument made under, an Act of the Scottish Parliament;

"enforcement action" means any form of enforcement action including, in particular—

(a) in relation to any legal requirement imposed by or under any enactment, any action taken with a view to or in connection with imposing any sanction (whether criminal or otherwise) for failure to observe or comply with it; and

(b) in relation to a permission or authorisation, anything done with a view to removing or restricting that permission or authorisation;

"enforcement authority" does not include courts but, subject to that, means any person who is authorised, whether by or under an enactment or otherwise, to take enforcement action;

"established service provider" means a service provider who is—

(a) a national of the United Kingdom or a member State, or

(b) a company or firm as mentioned in Article 54 of the Treaty,

and who effectively pursues an economic activity;

by virtue of which he is a service provider using a fixed establishment in the United Kingdom or a member State for an indefinite period, but the presence and use of the technical means and technologies required to provide the information society service do not, in themselves, constitute an establishment of the provider; in cases where it cannot be determined from which of a number of places of establishment a given service is provided, that service is to be regarded as provided from the place of establishment where the provider has the centre of his activities relating to that service; references to a service provider being established or to the establishment of a service provider shall be construed accordingly;

"information society services" (which is summarised in recital 17 of the Directive as covering "any service normally provided for remuneration, at a distance, by means of electronic equipment for the processing (including digital compression) and storage of data, and at the individual request of a recipient of a service") has the meaning set out in Article 2(a) of the Directive, (which refers to Article 1(2) of Directive 98/34/EC of the European Parliament and of the Council of 22 June 1998 laying down a procedure for the provision of information in the field of technical standards and regulations, as amended by Directive 98/48/EC of 20 July 1998);

"member State" includes a State which is a contracting party to the EEA Agreement;

"a national of the United Kingdom" means—

(a)   a British citizen;

(b)   a person who is a British subject by virtue of Part 4 of the British Nationality Act 1981 and who has a right of abode in the United Kingdom; or

(c)   a person who is a British overseas territories citizen by virtue of a connection with Gibraltar;

"recipient of the service" means any person who, for professional ends or otherwise, uses an information society service, in particular for the purposes of seeking information or making it accessible;

"regulated profession" has the meaning given in regulation 8(1) of the European Union (Recognition of Professional Qualifications) Regulations 2015;

"service provider" means any person providing an information society service;

"the Treaty" means the Treaty on the Functioning of the European Union.

(2)   In regulation 4 and 5, "requirement" means any legal requirement under the law of the United Kingdom, or any part of it, imposed by or under any enactment or otherwise.

(3)   Terms used in the Directive other than those in paragraph (1) above shall have the same meaning as in the Directive.

(4)   For the purposes of the definition of "established service provider" in paragraph (1), Article 54 of the Treaty is to be read as if the United Kingdom were a member State.

6.   General information to be provided by a person providing an information society service

(1)   A person providing an information society service shall make available to the recipient of the service and any relevant enforcement authority, in a form and manner which is easily, directly and permanently accessible, the following information—

(a)   the name of the service provider;

(b)   the geographic address at which the service provider is established;

(c)   the details of the service provider, including his electronic mail address, which make it possible to contact him rapidly and communicate with him in a direct and effective manner;

(d)   where the service provider is registered in a trade or similar register available to the public, details of the register in which the service provider is entered and his registration number, or equivalent means of identification in that register;

(e)   where the provision of the service is subject to an authorisation scheme, the particulars of the relevant supervisory authority;

(f)   where the service provider exercises a regulated profession—

(i)   the details of any professional body or similar institution with which the service provider is registered;

(ii)   his professional title and whether that title has been granted in the United Kingdom, or if not, the member State where that title has been granted;

(iii)   a reference to the professional rules applicable to the service provider in the United Kingdom or member State of establishment and the means to access them; and

(g)   where the service provider undertakes an activity that is subject to value added tax, the identification number referred to in Article 22(1) of the sixth Council Directive 77/388/EEC of 17 May 1977 on the harmonisation of the laws of the member States relating to turnover taxes— Common system of value added tax: uniform basis of assessment.

(2)   Where a person providing an information society service refers to prices, these shall be indicated clearly and unambiguously and, in particular, shall indicate whether they are inclusive of tax and delivery costs.

7.   Commercial communications

A service provider shall ensure that any commercial communication provided by him and which constitutes or forms part of an information society service shall—

(a)   be clearly identifiable as a commercial communication;

(b)   clearly identify the person on whose behalf the commercial communication is made;

(c)   clearly identify as such any promotional offer (including any discount, premium or gift) and ensure that any conditions which must be met to qualify for it are easily accessible, and presented clearly and unambiguously; and

(d)   clearly identify as such any promotional competition or game and ensure that any conditions for participation are easily accessible and presented clearly and unambiguously.

9.   Information to be provided where contracts are concluded by electronic means

(1)   Unless parties who are not consumers have agreed otherwise, where a contract is to be concluded by electronic means a service provider shall, prior to an order being placed by the recipient of a service, provide to that recipient in a clear, comprehensible and unambiguous manner the information set out in (a) to (d) below—

    (a)   the different technical steps to follow to conclude the contract;

    (b)   whether or not the concluded contract will be filed by the service provider and whether it will be accessible;

    (c)   the technical means for identifying and correcting input errors prior to the placing of the order; and

    (d)   the languages offered for the conclusion of the contract.

(2)   Unless parties who are not consumers have agreed otherwise, a service provider shall indicate which relevant codes of conduct he subscribes to and give information on how those codes can be consulted electronically.

(3)   Where the service provider provides terms and conditions applicable to the contract to the recipient, the service provider shall make them available to him in a way that allows him to store and reproduce them.

(4)   The requirements of paragraphs (1) and (2) above shall not apply to contracts concluded exclusively by exchange of electronic mail or by equivalent individual communications.

11.   Placing of the order

(1)   Unless parties who are not consumers have agreed otherwise, where the recipient of the service places his order through technological means, a service provider shall—

    (a)   acknowledge receipt of the order to the recipient of the service without undue delay and by electronic means; and

    (b)   make available to the recipient of the service appropriate, effective and accessible technical means allowing him to identify and correct input errors prior to the placing of the order.

(2)   For the purposes of paragraph (1)(a) above—

    (a)   the order and the acknowledgement of receipt will be deemed to be received when the parties to whom they are addressed are able to access them; and

    (b)   the acknowledgement of receipt may take the form of the provision of the service paid for where that service is an information society service.

(3)   The requirements of paragraph (1) above shall not apply to contracts concluded exclusively by exchange of electronic mail or by equivalent individual communications.

Privacy and Electronic Communications (EC Directive) Regulations 2003
(S.I. 2003 No. 2426)

2.   Interpretation

(1)   In these Regulations—

"bill" includes an invoice, account, statement or other document of similar character and "billing" shall be construed accordingly;

"call" means a connection established by means of a telephone service available to the public allowing two-way communication in real time;

"communication" means any information exchanged or conveyed between a finite number of parties by means of a public electronic communications service, but does not include information conveyed as part of a programme service, except to the extent that such information can be related to the identifiable subscriber or user receiving the information;

"communications provider" has the meaning given by section 405 of the Communications Act 2003;

"consent" by a user or subscriber corresponds to the data subject's consent in the UK GDPR (as defined in section 3(10) of the Data Protection Act 2018);

"corporate subscriber" means a subscriber who is—

(a)   a company within the meaning of section 735(1) of the Companies Act 1985;

(b)   a company incorporated in pursuance of a royal charter or letters patent;

(c)   a partnership in Scotland;

(d)   a corporation sole; or

(e)   any other body corporate or entity which is a legal person distinct from its members;

"the Directive" means Directive 2002/58/EC of the European Parliament and of the Council of 12 July 2002 concerning the processing of personal data and the protection of privacy in the electronic communications sector (Directive on privacy and electronic communications);

"electronic communications network" has the meaning given by section 32 of the Communications Act 2003;

"electronic communications service" has the meaning given by section 32 of the Communications Act 2003;

"electronic mail" means any text, voice, sound or image message sent over a public electronic communications network which can be stored in the network or in the recipient's terminal equipment until it is collected by the recipient and includes messages sent using a short message service;

"enactment" includes an enactment comprised in, or in an instrument made under, an Act of the Scottish Parliament;

"individual" means a living individual and includes an unincorporated body of such individuals;

"the Information Commissioner" and "the Commissioner" both mean the Commissioner appointed under the Data Protection Act 2018;

"information society service" has the meaning given in regulation 2(1) of the Electronic Commerce (EC Directive) Regulations 2002;

"location data" means any data processed in an electronic communications network or by an electronic communications service indicating the geographical position of the terminal equipment of a user of a public electronic communications service, including data relating to—

(f)   the latitude, longitude or altitude of the terminal equipment;

(g)   the direction of travel of the user; or

(h)   the time the location information was recorded;

"OFCOM" means the Office of Communications as established by section 1 of the Office of Communications Act 2002;

"personal data breach" means a breach of security leading to the accidental or unlawful destruction, loss, alteration, unauthorised disclosure of, or access to, personal data transmitted, stored or otherwise processed in connection with the provision of a public electronic communications service;

"programme service" has the meaning given in section 201 of the Broadcasting Act 1990;

"public communications provider" means a provider of a public electronic communications network or a public electronic communications service;

"public electronic communications network" has the meaning given in section 151 of the Communications Act 2003;

"public electronic communications service" has the meaning given in section 151 of the Communications Act 2003;

"subscriber" means a person who is a party to a contract with a provider of public electronic communications services for the supply of such services;

"traffic data" means any data processed for the purpose of the conveyance of a communication on an electronic communications network or for the billing in respect of that communication and includes data relating to the routing, duration or time of a communication;

"user" means any individual using a public electronic communications service; and

"value added service" means any service which requires the processing of traffic data or location data beyond that which is necessary for the transmission of a communication or the billing in respect of that communication.

(2) Expressions used in these Regulations that are not defined in paragraph (1) and are defined in the Data Protection Act 1998 shall have the same meaning as in that Act.

(3) Expressions used in these Regulations that are not defined in paragraph (1) or the Data Protection Act 1998 and are defined in the Directive shall have the same meaning as in the Directive.

(4) Any reference in these Regulations to a line shall, without prejudice to paragraph (3), be construed as including a reference to anything that performs the function of a line, and "connected", in relation to a line, is to be construed accordingly.

6.   Confidentiality of communications

(1) Subject to paragraph (4), a person shall not store or gain access to information stored, in the terminal equipment of a subscriber or user unless the requirements of paragraph (2) are met.

(2) The requirements are that the subscriber or user of that terminal equipment—

    (a)   is provided with clear and comprehensive information about the purposes of the storage of, or access to, that information; and

    (b)   has given his or her consent.

(3) Where an electronic communications network is used by the same person to store or access information in the terminal equipment of a subscriber or user on more than one occasion, it is sufficient for the purposes of this regulation that the requirements of paragraph (2) are met in respect of the initial use.

(3A) For the purposes of paragraph (2), consent may be signified by a subscriber who amends or sets controls on the internet browser which the subscriber uses or by using another application or programme to signify consent.

(4) Paragraph (1) shall not apply to the technical storage of, or access to, information—

    (a)   for the sole purpose of carrying out the transmission of a communication over an electronic communications network; or

    (b)   where such storage or access is strictly necessary for the provision of an information society service requested by the subscriber or user.

22.   Use of electronic mail for direct marketing purposes

(1) This regulation applies to the transmission of unsolicited communications by means of electronic mail to individual subscribers.

(2) Except in the circumstances referred to in paragraph (3), a person shall neither transmit, nor instigate the transmission of, unsolicited communications for the purposes of direct marketing by means of electronic mail unless the recipient of the electronic mail has previously notified the sender that he consents for the time being to such communications being sent by, or at the instigation of, the sender.

(3) A person may send or instigate the sending of electronic mail for the purposes of direct marketing where—

    (a)   that person has obtained the contact details of the recipient of that electronic mail in the course of the sale or negotiations for the sale of a product or service to that recipient;

    (b)   the direct marketing is in respect of that person's similar products and services only; and

    (c)   the recipient has been given a simple means of refusing (free of charge except for the costs of the transmission of the refusal) the use of his contact details for the purposes of such direct marketing, at the time that the details were initially collected, and, where he did not initially refuse the use of the details, at the time of each subsequent communication.

(4)   A subscriber shall not permit his line to be used in contravention of paragraph (2).

23.   Use of electronic mail for direct marketing purposes where the identity or address of the sender is concealed

A person shall neither transmit, nor instigate the transmission of, a communication for the purposes of direct marketing by means of electronic mail—

(a)   where the identity of the person on whose behalf the communication has been sent has been disguised or concealed;

(b)   where a valid address to which the recipient of the communication may send a request that such communications cease has not been provided;

(c)   where that electronic mail would contravene regulation 7 of the Electronic Commerce (EC Directive) Regulations 2002; or

(d)   where that electronic mail encourages recipients to visit websites which contravene that regulation.

Consumer Contracts (Information, Cancellation and Additional Charges)
Regulations 2013
(S.I. 2013 No. 3134)

4.   "Consumer" and "trader"

In these Regulations—

"consumer" means an individual acting for purposes which are wholly or mainly outside that individual's trade, business, craft or profession;

"trader" means a person acting for purposes relating to that person's trade, business, craft or profession, whether acting personally or through another person acting in the trader's name or on the trader's behalf.

5.   Other definitions

In these Regulations—

"business" includes the activities of any government department or local or public authority;

"business premises" in relation to a trader means—

(a)   any immovable retail premises where the activity of the trader is carried out on a permanent basis, or

(b)   any movable retail premises where the activity of the trader is carried out on a usual basis;

"CMA" means the Competition and Markets Authority;

"commercial guarantee", in relation to a contract, means any undertaking by the trader or producer to the consumer (in addition to the trader's duty to supply goods that are in conformity with the contract) to reimburse the price paid or to replace, repair or service goods in any way if they do not meet the specifications or any other requirements not related to conformity set out in the guarantee statement or in the relevant advertising available at the time of the contract or before it is entered into;

"court"—

(a)   in relation to England and Wales, means the county court or the High Court,

(b   in relation to Northern Ireland, means a county court or the High Court, and

(c)   in relation to Scotland means the sheriff court or the Court of Session;

"delivery" means voluntary transfer of possession from one person to another;

"digital content" means data which are produced and supplied in digital form;

"distance contract" means a contract concluded between a trader and a consumer under an organised distance sales or service-provision scheme without the simultaneous physical presence of the trader and the consumer, with the exclusive use of one or more means of distance communication up to and including the time at which the contract is concluded;

"district heating" means the supply of heat (in the form of steam or hot water or otherwise) from a central source of production through a transmission and distribution system to heat more than one building;

"durable medium" means paper or email, or any other medium that—

(a)   allows information to be addressed personally to the recipient,

(b)   enables the recipient to store the information in a way accessible for future reference for a period that is long enough for the purposes of the information, and

(c)   allows the unchanged reproduction of the information stored;

"functionality" in relation to digital content includes region coding, restrictions incorporated for the purposes of digital rights management, and other technical restrictions;

"goods" means any tangible moveable items, but that includes water, gas and electricity if and only if they are put up for sale in a limited volume or a set quantity;

"off-premises contract" means a contract between a trader and a consumer which is any of these—

(a)   a contract concluded in the simultaneous physical presence of the trader and the consumer, in a place which is not the business premises of the trader;

(b)   a contract for which an offer was made by the consumer in the simultaneous physical presence of the trader and the consumer, in a place which is not the business premises of the trader;

(c)   a contract concluded on the business premises of the trader or through any means of distance communication immediately after the consumer was personally and individually addressed in a place which is not the business premises of the trader in the simultaneous physical presence of the trader and the consumer;

(d)   a contract concluded during an excursion organised by the trader with the aim or effect of promoting and selling goods or services to the consumer;

"on-premises contract" means a contract between a trader and a consumer which is neither a distance contract nor an off-premises contract;

"public auction" means a method of sale where—

(a)   goods or services are offered by a trader to consumers through a transparent, competitive bidding procedure run by an auctioneer,

(b)   the consumers attend or are given the possibility to attend in person, and

(c)   the successful bidder is bound to purchase the goods or services;

"sales contract" means a contract under which a trader transfers or agrees to transfer the ownership of goods to a consumer and the consumer pays or agrees to pay the price, including any contract that has both goods and services as its object;

"service" includes—

(a)   the supply of water, gas or electricity if they are not put up for sale in a limited volume or a set quantity, and

(b)   the supply of district heating;

"service contract" means a contract, other than a sales contract, under which a trader supplies or agrees to supply a service to a consumer and the consumer pays or agrees to pay the price.

8.   Making information etc available to a consumer

For the purposes of this Part, something is made available to a consumer only if the consumer can reasonably be expected to know how to access it.

13.   Information to be provided before making a distance contract

(1)   Before the consumer is bound by a distance contract, the trader—

(a)   must give or make available to the consumer the information listed in Schedule 2 in a clear and comprehensible manner, and in a way appropriate to the means of distance communication used, and

(b)   if a right to cancel exists, must give or make available to the consumer a cancellation form as set out in part B of Schedule 3.

(2)   In so far as the information is provided on a durable medium, it must be legible.

(3)   The information referred to in paragraphs (l), (m) and (n) of Schedule 2 may be provided by means of the model instructions on cancellation set out in part A of Schedule 3; and a trader who has supplied those instructions to the consumer, correctly filled in, is to be treated as having complied with paragraph (1) in respect of those paragraphs.

(4)   Where a distance contract is concluded through a means of distance communication which allows limited space or time to display the information—

(a)   the information listed in paragraphs (a), (b), (f), (g), (h), (l) and (s) of Schedule 2 must be provided on that means of communication in accordance with paragraphs (1) and (2), but

(b)   the other information required by paragraph (1) may be provided in another appropriate way.

(5)   If the trader has not complied with paragraph (1) in respect of paragraph (g), (h) or (m) of Schedule 2, the consumer is not to bear the charges or costs referred to in those paragraphs.

(6)   If the contract is for the supply of digital content other than for a price paid by the consumer—

(a)   any information that the trader gives the consumer as required by this regulation is to be treated as included as a term of the contract, and

(b)   a change to any of that information, made before entering into the contract or later, is not effective unless expressly agreed between the consumer and the trader.

14.   Requirements for distance contracts concluded by electronic means

(1)   This regulation applies where a distance contract is concluded by electronic means.

(2)   If the contract places the consumer under an obligation to pay, the trader must make the consumer aware in a clear and prominent manner, and directly before the consumer places the order, of the information listed in paragraphs (a), (f), (g), (h), (s) and (t) of Schedule 2.

(3)   The trader must ensure that the consumer, when placing the order, explicitly acknowledges that the order implies an obligation to pay.

(4)   If placing an order entails activating a button or a similar function, the trader must ensure that the button or similar function is labelled in an easily legible manner only with the words 'order with obligation to pay' or a corresponding unambiguous formulation indicating that placing the order entails an obligation to pay the trader.

(5)   If the trader has not complied with paragraphs (3) and (4), the consumer is not bound by the contract or order.

(6)   The trader must ensure that any trading website through which the contract is concluded indicates clearly and legibly, at the latest at the beginning of the ordering process, whether any delivery restrictions apply and which means of payment are accepted.

16.   Confirmation of distance contracts

(1)   In the case of a distance contract the trader must give the consumer confirmation of the contract on a durable medium.

(2)   The confirmation must include all the information referred to in Schedule 2 unless the trader has already provided that information to the consumer on a durable medium prior to the conclusion of the distance contract.

(3)   If the contract is for the supply of digital content not on a tangible medium and the consumer has given the consent and acknowledgment referred to in regulation 37(1)(a) and (b), the confirmation must include confirmation of the consent and acknowledgement.

(4)   The confirmation must be provided within a reasonable time after the conclusion of the contract, but in any event—

(a)   not later than the time of delivery of any goods supplied under the contract, and

(b)   before performance begins of any service supplied under the contract.

(5)   For the purposes of paragraph (4), the confirmation is treated as provided as soon as the trader has sent it or done what is necessary to make it available to the consumer.

17.   Burden of proof in relation to off-premises and distance contracts

(1)   In case of dispute about the trader's compliance with any provision of regulations 10 to 16, it is for the trader to show that the provision was complied with.

(2)   That does not apply to proceedings—

(a)   for an offence under regulation 19, or

(b)   relating to compliance with an injunction, interdict or order under regulation 45.

18.   Effect on contract of failure to provide information

Every contract to which this Part applies is to be treated as including a term that the trader has complied with the provisions of—

(a)   regulations 9 to 14, and

(b)   regulation 16.

29.   Right to cancel

(1)   The consumer may cancel a distance or off-premises contract at any time in the cancellation period without giving any reason, and without incurring any liability except under these provisions—

(a)   regulation 34(3) (where enhanced delivery chosen by consumer);

(b)   regulation 34(9) (where value of goods diminished by consumer handling);

(c)   regulation 35(5) (where goods returned by consumer);

(d)   regulation 36(4) (where consumer requests early supply of service).

(2)   The cancellation period begins when the contract is entered into and ends in accordance with regulation 30 or 31.

(3)   Paragraph (1) does not affect the consumer's right to withdraw an offer made by the consumer to enter into a distance or off-premises contract, at any time before the contract is entered into, without giving any reason and without incurring any liability.

30.   Normal cancellation period

(1)   The cancellation period ends as follows, unless regulation 31 applies.

(2)   If the contract is—

(a)   a service contract, or

(b)   a contract for the supply of digital content which is not supplied on a tangible medium, the cancellation period ends at the end of 14 days after the day on which the contract is entered into.

(3)   If the contract is a sales contract and none of paragraphs (4) to (6) applies, the cancellation period ends at the end of 14 days after the day on which the goods come into the physical possession of—

(a)   the consumer, or

(b)   a person, other than the carrier, identified by the consumer to take possession of them.

(4)   If the contract is a sales contract under which multiple goods are ordered by the consumer in one order but some are delivered on different days, the cancellation period ends at the end of 14 days after the day on which the last of the goods come into the physical possession of—

(a)   the consumer, or

(b)   a person, other than the carrier, identified by the consumer to take possession of them.

(5)   If the contract is a sales contract under which goods consisting of multiple lots or pieces of something are delivered on different days, the cancellation period ends at the end of 14 days after the day on which the last of the lots or pieces come into the physical possession of—

(a)   the consumer, or

(b)   a person, other than the carrier, identified by the consumer to take possession of them.

(6)   If the contract is a sales contract for regular delivery of goods during a defined period of more than one day, the cancellation period ends at the end of 14 days after the day on which the first of the goods come into the physical possession of—

(a)   the consumer, or

(b)   a person, other than the carrier, identified by the consumer to take possession of them.

31.   Cancellation period extended for breach of information requirement

(1)   This regulation applies if the trader does not provide the consumer with the information on the right to cancel required by paragraph (l) of Schedule 2, in accordance with Part 2.

(2)   If the trader provides the consumer with that information in the period of 12 months beginning with the first day of the 14 days mentioned in regulation 30(2) to (6), but otherwise in accordance with Part 2, the cancellation period ends at the end of 14 days after the consumer receives the information.

(3)   Otherwise the cancellation period ends at the end of 12 months after the day on which it would have ended under regulation 30.

32.   Exercise of the right to withdraw or cancel

(1)   To withdraw an offer to enter into a distance or off-premises contract, the consumer must inform the trader of the decision to withdraw it.

(2)   To cancel a contract under regulation 29(1), the consumer must inform the trader of the decision to cancel it.

(3)   To inform the trader under paragraph (2) the consumer may either—

(a)   use a form following the model cancellation form in part B of Schedule 3, or

(b)   make any other clear statement setting out the decision to cancel the contract.

(4)   If the trader gives the consumer the option of filling in and submitting such a form or other statement on the trader's website—

(a)   the consumer need not use it, but

(b)   if the consumer does, the trader must communicate to the consumer an acknowledgement of receipt of the cancellation on a durable medium without delay.

(5)   Where the consumer informs the trader under paragraph (2) by sending a communication, the consumer is to be treated as having cancelled the contract in the cancellation period if the communication is sent before the end of the period.

(6)   In case of dispute it is for the consumer to show that the contract was cancelled in the cancellation period in accordance with this regulation.

33.   Effect of withdrawal or cancellation

(1)   If a contract is cancelled under regulation 29(1)—

(a)   the cancellation ends the obligations of the parties to perform the contract, and

(b)   regulations 34 to 38 apply.

(2)   Regulations 34 and 38 also apply if the consumer withdraws an offer to enter into a distance or off-premises contract.

34.   Reimbursement by trader in the event of withdrawal or cancellation

(1)   The trader must reimburse all payments, other than payments for delivery, received from the consumer, subject to paragraph (10).

(2)   The trader must reimburse any payment for delivery received from the consumer, unless the consumer expressly chose a kind of delivery costing more than the least expensive common and generally acceptable kind of delivery offered by the trader.

(3)   In that case, the trader must reimburse any payment for delivery received from the consumer up to the amount the consumer would have paid if the consumer had chosen the least expensive common and generally acceptable kind of delivery offered by the trader.

(4)   Reimbursement must be without undue delay, and in any event not later than the time specified in paragraph (5) or (6).

(5)   If the contract is a sales contract and the trader has not offered to collect the goods, the time is the end of 14 days after—

(a)   the day on which the trader receives the goods back, or

(b)   if earlier, the day on which the consumer supplies evidence of having sent the goods back.

(6)   Otherwise, the time is the end of 14 days after the day on which the trader is informed of the consumer's decision to withdraw the offer or cancel the contract, in accordance with regulation 32.

(7)   The trader must make the reimbursement using the same means of payment as the consumer used for the initial transaction, unless the consumer has expressly agreed otherwise.

(8)   The trader must not impose any fee on the consumer in respect of the reimbursement.

(9)   If (in the case of a sales contract) the value of the goods is diminished by any amount as a result of handling of the goods by the consumer beyond what is necessary to establish the nature, characteristics and functioning of the goods, the trader may recover that amount from the consumer, up to the contract price.

(10)   An amount that may be recovered under paragraph (9)—

(a)   may be deducted from the amount to be reimbursed under paragraph (1);

(b)   otherwise, must be paid by the consumer to the trader.

(11)   Paragraph (9) does not apply if the trader has failed to provide the consumer with the information on the right to cancel required by paragraph (l) of Schedule 2, in accordance with Part 2.

(12)   For the purposes of paragraph (9) handling is beyond what is necessary to establish the nature, characteristics and functioning of the goods if, in particular, it goes beyond the sort of handling that might reasonably be allowed in a shop.

(13)   Where the provisions of this regulation apply to cancellation of a contract, the contract is to be treated as including those provisions as terms.

35.   Return of goods in the event of cancellation

(1)   Where a sales contract is cancelled under regulation 29(1), it is the trader's responsibility to collect the goods if—

(a)   the trader has offered to collect them, or

(b)   in the case of an off-premises contract, the goods were delivered to the consumer's home when the contract was entered into and could not, by their nature, normally be returned by post.

(2)   If it is not the trader's responsibility under paragraph (1) to collect the goods, the consumer must—

(a)   send them back, or

(b)   hand them over to the trader or to a person authorised by the trader to receive them.

(3)   The address to which goods must be sent under paragraph (2)(a) is—

(a)   any address specified by the trader for sending the goods back;

(b)   if no address is specified for that purpose, any address specified by the trader for the consumer to contact the trader;

(c)   if no address is specified for either of those purposes, any place of business of the trader.

(4)   The consumer must send off the goods under paragraph (2)(a), or hand them over under paragraph (2)(b), without undue delay and in any event not later than 14 days after the day on which the consumer informs the trader as required by regulation 32(2).

(5)   The consumer must bear the direct cost of returning goods under paragraph (2), unless—

(a)   the trader has agreed to bear those costs, or

(b)   the trader failed to provide the consumer with the information about the consumer bearing those costs, required by paragraph (m) of Schedule 2, in accordance with Part 2.

(6)   The contract is to be treated as including a term that the trader must bear the direct cost of the consumer returning goods under paragraph (2) where paragraph (5)(b) applies.

(7)   The consumer is not required to bear any other cost of returning goods under paragraph (2).

(8)   The consumer is not required to bear any cost of collecting goods under paragraph (1) unless the trader has offered to collect the goods and the consumer has agreed to bear the costs of the trader doing so.

40.   Additional payments under a contract

(1)   Under a contract between a trader and a consumer, no payment is payable in addition to the remuneration agreed for the trader's main obligation unless, before the consumer became bound by the contract, the trader obtained the consumer's express consent.

(2)   There is no express consent (if there would otherwise be) for the purposes of this paragraph if consent is inferred from the consumer not changing a default option (such as a pre-ticked box on a website).

(3)   This regulation does not apply if the trader's main obligation is to supply services within regulation 6(1)(b), but in any other case it applies even if an additional payment is for such services.

(4)   Where a trader receives an additional payment which, under this regulation, is not payable under a contract, the contract is to be treated as providing for the trader to reimburse the payment to the consumer.

41.   Help-line charges over basic rate

(1)   Where a trader operates a telephone line for the purpose of consumers contacting the trader by telephone in relation to contracts entered into with the trader, a consumer contacting the trader must not be bound to pay more than the basic rate.

(2)   If in those circumstances a consumer who contacts a trader in relation to a contract is bound to pay more than the basic rate, the contract is to be treated as providing for the trader to pay to the consumer any amount by which the charge paid by the consumer for the call is more than the basic rate.

SCHEDULE 2   Regulations 10(1) and 13(1)

Information relating to distance and off-premises contracts

The information referred to in regulations 10(1) and 13(1) is (subject to the note at the end of this Schedule)—

(a)   the main characteristics of the goods, services or digital content, to the extent appropriate to the medium of communication and to the goods, services or digital content;

(b)   the identity of the trader (such as the trader's trading name);

(c)   the geographical address at which the trader is established and, where available, the trader's telephone number, fax number and e-mail address, to enable the consumer to contact the trader quickly and communicate efficiently;

(d)   where the trader is acting on behalf of another trader, the geographical address and identity of that other trader;

(e)   if different from the address provided in accordance with paragraph (c), the geographical address of the place of business of the trader, and, where the trader acts on behalf of another trader, the geographical address of the place of business of that other trader, where the consumer can address any complaints;

(f)   the total price of the goods, services or digital content inclusive of taxes, or where the nature of the goods, services or digital content is such that the price cannot reasonably be calculated in advance, the manner in which the price is to be calculated,

(g)   where applicable, all additional delivery charges and any other costs or, where those charges cannot reasonably be calculated in advance, the fact that such additional charges may be payable;

(h)   in the case of a contract of indeterminate duration or a contract containing a subscription, the total costs per billing period or (where such contracts are charged at a fixed rate) the total monthly costs;

(i)   the cost of using the means of distance communication for the conclusion of the contract where that cost is calculated other than at the basic rate;

(j)   the arrangements for payment, delivery, performance, and the time by which the trader undertakes to deliver the goods, to perform the services or to supply the digital content;

(k)   where applicable, the trader's complaint handling policy;

(l)   where a right to cancel exists, the conditions, time limit and procedures for exercising that right in accordance with regulations 27 to 38;

(m)   where applicable, that the consumer will have to bear the cost of returning the goods in case of cancellation and, for distance contracts, if the goods, by their nature, cannot normally be returned by post, the cost of returning the goods;

(n)   that, if the consumer exercises the right to cancel after having made a request in accordance with regulation 36(1), the consumer is to be liable to pay the trader reasonable costs in accordance with regulation 36(4);

(o)   where under regulation 28, 36 or 37 there is no right to cancel or the right to cancel may be lost, the information that the consumer will not benefit from a right to cancel, or the circumstances under which the consumer loses the right to cancel;

(p)   in the case of a sales contract, a reminder that the trader is under a legal duty to supply goods that are in conformity with the contract;

(q)   where applicable, the existence and the conditions of after-sale customer assistance, after-sales services and commercial guarantees;

(r)   the existence of relevant codes of conduct, as defined in regulation 5(3)(b) of the Consumer Protection from Unfair Trading Regulations 2008, and how copies of them can be obtained, where applicable;

(s)   the duration of the contract, where applicable, or, if the contract is of indeterminate duration or is to be extended automatically, the conditions for terminating the contract;

(t)   where applicable, the minimum duration of the consumer's obligations under the contract;

(u)   where applicable, the existence and the conditions of deposits or other financial guarantees to be paid or provided by the consumer at the request of the trader;

(v)   where applicable, the functionality, including applicable technical protection measures, of digital content;

(w)   where applicable, any relevant compatibility of digital content with hardware and software that the trader is aware of or can reasonably be expected to have been aware of;

(x)   where applicable, the possibility of having recourse to an out-of-court complaint and redress mechanism, to which the trader is subject, and the methods for having access to it.

Note: In the case of a public auction, the information listed in paragraphs (b) to (e) may be replaced with the equivalent details for the auctioneer.

SCHEDULE 3   **Regulations 10 and 13**

Information about the exercise of the right to cancel

A.   Model instructions for cancellation

Right to cancel

You have the right to cancel this contract within 14 days without giving any reason.

The cancellation period will expire after 14 days from the day [See Note 1].

To exercise the right to cancel, you must inform us [See Note 2] of your decision to cancel this contract by a clear statement (e.g. a letter sent by post, fax or e-mail). You may use the attached model cancellation form, but it is not obligatory. [See Note 3].

To meet the cancellation deadline, it is sufficient for you to send your communication concerning your exercise of the right to cancel before the cancellation period has expired.

Effects of cancellation

If you cancel this contract, we will reimburse to you all payments received from you, including the costs of delivery (except for the supplementary costs arising if you chose a type of delivery other than the least expensive type of standard delivery offered by us).

We may make a deduction from the reimbursement for loss in value of any goods supplied, if the loss is the result of unnecessary handling by you.

We will make the reimbursement without undue delay, and not later than—

(a)   14 days after the day we receive back from you any goods supplied, or

(b)   (if earlier) 14 days after the day you provide evidence that you have returned the goods, or

(c)   if there were no goods supplied, 14 days after the day on which we are informed about your decision to cancel this contract.

We will make the reimbursement using the same means of payment as you used for the initial transaction, unless you have expressly agreed otherwise; in any event, you will not incur any fees as a result of the reimbursement. [See Note 4].

[See Note 5]

[See Note 6]

Notes on instructions for completion:

1. Insert one of the following texts between inverted commas:
    (a) in the case of a service contract or a contract for the supply of digital content which is not supplied on a tangible medium: "of the conclusion of the contract.";
    (b) in the case of a sales contract: "on which you acquire, or a third party other than the carrier and indicated by you acquires, physical possession of the goods.";
    (c) in the case of a contract relating to multiple goods ordered by the consumer in one order and delivered separately: "on which you acquire, or a third party other than the carrier and indicated by you acquires, physical possession of the last good.";
    (d) in the case of a contract relating to delivery of a good consisting of multiple lots or pieces: "on which you acquire, or a third party other than the carrier and indicated by you acquires, physical possession of the last lot or piece.";
    (e) in the case of a contract for regular delivery of goods during a defined period of time: "on which you acquire, or a third party other than the carrier and indicated by you acquires, physical possession of the first good.".

2. Insert your name, geographical address and, where available, your telephone number, fax number and e-mail address.

3. If you give the option to the consumer to electronically fill in and submit information about the consumer's cancellation from the contract on your website, insert the following: "You can also electronically fill in and submit the model cancellation form or any other clear statement on our website [insert Internet address]. If you use this option, we will communicate to you an acknowledgement of receipt of such a cancellation on a durable medium (e.g. by e-mail) without delay.".

4. In the case of sales contracts in which you have not offered to collect the goods in the event of cancellation insert the following: "We may withhold reimbursement until we have received the goods back or you have supplied evidence of having sent back the goods, whichever is the earliest.".

5. If the consumer has received goods in connection with the contract
    (a) insert:
        — "We will collect the goods."; or,
        — "You shall send back the goods or hand them over to us or ... [insert the name and geographical address, where applicable, of the person authorised by you to receive the goods], without undue delay and in any event not later than 14 days from the day on which you communicate your cancellation from this contract to us. The deadline is met if you send back the goods before the period of 14 days has expired."
    (b) insert:
        — "We will bear the cost of returning the goods.";
        — "You will have to bear the direct cost of returning the goods.";
        — If, in a distance contract, you do not offer to bear the cost of returning the goods and the goods, by their nature, cannot normally be returned by post: "You will have to bear the direct cost of returning the goods, ... EUR [insert the amount]."; or if the cost of returning the goods cannot reasonably be calculated in advance: "You will have to bear the direct cost of returning the goods. The cost is estimated at a maximum of approximately ... EUR [insert the amount]."; or
        — If, in an off-premises contract, the goods, by their nature, cannot normally be returned by post and have been delivered to the consumer's home at the time of the conclusion of the contract: "We will collect the goods at our own expense."; and,
    (c) insert
            "You are only liable for any diminished value of the goods resulting from the handling other than what is necessary to establish the nature, characteristics and functioning of the goods."

6.   In the case of a service contract insert the following: "If you requested to begin the performance of services during the cancellation period, you shall pay us an amount which is in proportion to what has been performed until you have communicated us your cancellation from this contract, in comparison with the full coverage of the contract.".

B.   Model cancellation form

To [here the trader's name, geographical address and, where available, fax number and e-mail address are to be inserted by the trader]:

I/We [*] hereby give notice that I/We [*] cancel my/our [*] contract of sale of the following goods [*]/for the supply of the following service [*],

Ordered on [*]/received on [*],

Name of consumer(s),

Address of consumer(s),

Signature of consumer(s) (only if this form is notified on paper),

Date

[*] Delete as appropriate.

Treaty on the Functioning of the European Union

Article 101

1. The following shall be prohibited as incompatible with the internal market: all agreements between undertakings, decisions by associations of undertakings and concerted practices which may affect trade between Member States and which have as their object or effect the prevention, restriction or distortion of competition within the internal market, and in particular those which:

    (a) directly or indirectly fix purchase or selling prices or any other trading conditions;

    (b) limit or control production, markets, technical development, or investment;

    (c) share markets or sources of supply;

    (d) apply dissimilar conditions to equivalent transactions with other trading parties, thereby placing them at a competitive disadvantage;

    (e) make the conclusion of contracts subject to acceptance by the other parties of supplementary obligations which, by their nature or according to commercial usage, have no connection with the subject of such contracts.

2. Any agreements or decisions prohibited pursuant to this Article shall be automatically void.

3. The provisions of paragraph 1 may, however, be declared inapplicable in the case of:

    – any agreement or category of agreements between undertakings,

    – any decision or category of decisions by associations of undertakings,

    – any concerted practice or category of concerted practices,

    which contributes to improving the production or distribution of goods or to promoting technical or economic progress, while allowing consumers a fair share of the resulting benefit, and which does not:

    (a) impose on the undertakings concerned restrictions which are not indispensable to the attainment of these objectives;

    (b) afford such undertakings the possibility of eliminating competition in respect of a substantial part of the products in question.

Article 102

Any abuse by one or more undertakings of a dominant position within the internal market or in a substantial part of it shall be prohibited as incompatible with the internal market in so far as it may affect trade between Member States.

Such abuse may, in particular, consist in:

(a) directly or indirectly imposing unfair purchase or selling prices or other unfair trading conditions;

(b) limiting production, markets or technical development to the prejudice of consumers;

(c) applying dissimilar conditions to equivalent transactions with other trading parties, thereby placing them at a competitive disadvantage;

(d) making the conclusion of contracts subject to acceptance by the other parties of supplementary obligations which, by their nature or according to commercial usage, have no connection with the subject of such contracts.

Commission Regulation (EU) on the application of Article 101(3) of the Treaty on the Functioning of the European Union to categories of vertical agreements and concerted practices
No. 330/2010

THE EUROPEAN COMMISSION,

Having regard to the Treaty on the Functioning of the European Union,

Having regard to Regulation No 19/65/EEC of the Council of 2 March 1965 on the application of Article 85(3) of the Treaty to certain categories of agreements and concerted practices, and in particular Article 1 thereof,

Having published a draft of this Regulation,

After consulting the Advisory Committee on Restrictive Practices and Dominant Positions,

Whereas:

(1)   Regulation No 19/65/EEC empowers the Commission to apply Article 101(3) of the Treaty on the Functioning of the European Union by regulation to certain categories of vertical agreements and corresponding concerted practices falling within Article 101(1) of the Treaty.

(2)   Commission Regulation (EC) No 2790/1999 of 22 December 1999 on the application of Article 81(3) of the Treaty to categories of vertical agreements and concerted practices defines a category of vertical agreements which the Commission regarded as normally satisfying the conditions laid down in Article 101(3) of the Treaty. In view of the overall positive experience with the application of that Regulation, which expires on 31 May 2010, and taking into account further experience acquired since its adoption, it is appropriate to adopt a new block exemption regulation.

(3)   The category of agreements which can be regarded as normally satisfying the conditions laid down in Article 101(3) of the Treaty includes vertical agreements for the purchase or sale of goods or services where those agreements are concluded between non-competing undertakings, between certain competitors or by certain associations of retailers of goods. It also includes vertical agreements containing ancillary provisions on the assignment or use of intellectual property rights. The term 'vertical agreements' should include the corresponding concerted practices.

(4)   For the application of Article 101(3) of the Treaty by regulation, it is not necessary to define those vertical agreements which are capable of falling within Article 101(1) of the Treaty. In the individual assessment of agreements under Article 101(1) of the Treaty, account has to be taken of several factors, and in particular the market structure on the supply and purchase side.

(5)   The benefit of the block exemption established by this Regulation should be limited to vertical agreements for which it can be assumed with sufficient certainty that they satisfy the conditions of Article 101(3) of the Treaty.

(6)   Certain types of vertical agreements can improve economic efficiency within a chain of production or distribution by facilitating better coordination between the participating undertakings. In particular, they can lead to a reduction in the transaction and distribution costs of the parties and to an optimisation of their sales and investment levels.

(7)   The likelihood that such efficiency-enhancing effects will outweigh any anti-competitive effects due to restrictions contained in vertical agreements depends on the degree of market power of the parties to the agreement and, therefore, on the extent to which those undertakings face competition from other suppliers of goods or services regarded by their customers as interchangeable or substitutable for one another, by reason of the products' characteristics, their prices and their intended use.

(8)   It can be presumed that, where the market share held by each of the undertakings party to the agreement on the relevant market does not exceed 30%, vertical agreements which do not contain certain types of severe restrictions of competition generally lead to an improvement in production or distribution and allow consumers a fair share of the resulting benefits.

(9)   Above the market share threshold of 30%, there can be no presumption that vertical agreements falling within the scope of Article 101(1) of the Treaty will usually give rise to objective advantages of such a character and size as to compensate for the disadvantages which they create for competition. At the same time, there is no presumption that those vertical agreements are either caught by Article 101(1) of the Treaty or that they fail to satisfy the conditions of Article 101(3) of the Treaty.

(10)   This Regulation should not exempt vertical agreements containing restrictions which are likely to restrict competition and harm consumers or which are not indispensable to the attainment of the efficiency-enhancing effects. In particular, vertical agreements containing certain types of severe

restrictions of competition such as minimum and fixed resale-prices, as well as certain types of territorial protection, should be excluded from the benefit of the block exemption established by this Regulation irrespective of the market share of the undertakings concerned.

(11)   In order to ensure access to or to prevent collusion on the relevant market, certain conditions should be attached to the block exemption. To this end, the exemption of non-compete obligations should be limited to obligations which do not exceed a defined duration. For the same reasons, any direct or indirect obligation causing the members of a selective distribution system not to sell the brands of particular competing suppliers should be excluded from the benefit of this Regulation.

(12)   The market-share limitation, the non-exemption of certain vertical agreements and the conditions provided for in this Regulation normally ensure that the agreements to which the block exemption applies do not enable the participating undertakings to eliminate competition in respect of a substantial part of the products in question.

(13)   The Commission may withdraw the benefit of this Regulation, pursuant to Article 29(1) of Council Regulation (EC) No 1/2003 of 16 December 2002 on the implementation of the rules on competition laid down in Articles 81 and 82 of the Treaty, where it finds in a particular case that an agreement to which the exemption provided for in this Regulation applies nevertheless has effects which are incompatible with Article 101(3) of the Treaty.

(14)   The competition authority of a Member State may withdraw the benefit of this Regulation pursuant to Article 29(2) of Regulation (EC) No 1/2003 in respect of the territory of that Member State, or a part thereof where, in a particular case, an agreement to which the exemption provided for in this Regulation applies nevertheless has effects which are incompatible with Article 101(3) of the Treaty in the territory of that Member State, or in a part thereof, and where such territory has all the characteristics of a distinct geographic market.

(15)   In determining whether the benefit of this Regulation should be withdrawn pursuant to Article 29 of Regulation (EC) No 1/2003, the anti-competitive effects that may derive from the existence of parallel networks of vertical agreements that have similar effects which significantly restrict access to a relevant market or competition therein are of particular importance. Such cumulative effects may for example arise in the case of selective distribution or non compete obligations.

(16)   In order to strengthen supervision of parallel networks of vertical agreements which have similar anti-competitive effects and which cover more than 50% of a given market, the Commission may by regulation declare this Regulation inapplicable to vertical agreements containing specific restraints relating to the market concerned, thereby restoring the full application of Article 101 of the Treaty to such agreements,

HAS ADOPTED THIS REGULATION:

Article 1 Definitions

1.   For the purposes of this Regulation, the following definitions shall apply:

(a)   'vertical agreement' means an agreement or concerted practice entered into between two or more undertakings each of which operates, for the purposes of the agreement or the concerted practice, at a different level of the production or distribution chain, and relating to the conditions under which the parties may purchase, sell or resell certain goods or services;

(b)   'vertical restraint' means a restriction of competition in a vertical agreement falling within the scope of Article 101(1) of the Treaty;

(c)   'competing undertaking' means an actual or potential competitor; 'actual competitor' means an undertaking that is active on the same relevant market; 'potential competitor' means an undertaking that, in the absence of the vertical agreement, would, on realistic grounds and not just as a mere theoretical possibility, in case of a small but permanent increase in relative prices be likely to undertake, within a short period of time, the necessary additional investments or other necessary switching costs to enter the relevant market;

(d)   'non-compete obligation' means any direct or indirect obligation causing the buyer not to manufacture, purchase, sell or resell goods or services which compete with the contract goods or services, or any direct or indirect obligation on the buyer to purchase from the supplier or from another undertaking designated by the supplier more than 80% of the buyer's total purchases of the contract goods or services and their substitutes on the relevant market, calculated on the basis of the value or, where such is standard industry practice, the volume of its purchases in the preceding calendar year;

(e)   'selective distribution system' means a distribution system where the supplier undertakes to sell the contract goods or services, either directly or indirectly, only to distributors selected on the basis of specified criteria and where these distributors undertake not to sell such goods or services to unauthorised distributors within the territory reserved by the supplier to operate that system;

(f)   'intellectual property rights' includes industrial property rights, know how, copyright and neighbouring rights;

(g)   'know-how' means a package of non-patented practical information, resulting from experience and testing by the supplier, which is secret, substantial and identified: in this context, 'secret' means that the know-how is not generally known or easily accessible; 'substantial' means that the know-how is significant and useful to the buyer for the use, sale or resale of the contract goods or services; 'identified' means that the know-how is described in a sufficiently comprehensive manner so as to make it possible to verify that it fulfils the criteria of secrecy and substantiality;

(h)   'buyer' includes an undertaking which, under an agreement falling within Article 101(1) of the Treaty, sells goods or services on behalf of another undertaking;

(i)   'customer of the buyer' means an undertaking not party to the agreement which purchases the contract goods or services from a buyer which is party to the agreement.

2.   For the purposes of this Regulation, the terms 'undertaking', 'supplier' and 'buyer' shall include their respective connected undertakings.

'Connected undertakings' means:

(a)   undertakings in which a party to the agreement, directly or indirectly:

(i)   has the power to exercise more than half the voting rights, or

(ii)   has the power to appoint more than half the members of the supervisory board, board of management or bodies legally representing the undertaking, or

(iii) has the right to manage the undertaking's affairs;

(b)   undertakings which directly or indirectly have, over a party to the agreement, the rights or powers listed in point (a);

(c)   undertakings in which an undertaking referred to in point (b) has, directly or indirectly, the rights or powers listed in point (a);

(d)   undertakings in which a party to the agreement together with one or more of the undertakings referred to in points (a), (b) or (c), or in which two or more of the latter undertakings, jointly have the rights or powers listed in point (a);

(e)   undertakings in which the rights or the powers listed in point (a) are jointly held by:

(i)   parties to the agreement or their respective connected undertakings referred to in points (a) to (d), or

(ii)   one or more of the parties to the agreement or one or more of their connected undertakings referred to in points (a) to (d) and one or more third parties.

Article 2 Exemption

1.   Pursuant to Article 101(3) of the Treaty and subject to the provisions of this Regulation, it is hereby declared that Article 101(1) of the Treaty shall not apply to vertical agreements.

This exemption shall apply to the extent that such agreements contain vertical restraints.

2.   The exemption provided for in paragraph 1 shall apply to vertical agreements entered into between an association of undertakings and its members, or between such an association and its suppliers, only if all its members are retailers of goods and if no individual member of the association, together with its connected undertakings, has a total annual turnover exceeding EUR 50 million. Vertical agreements entered into by such associations shall be covered by this Regulation without prejudice to the application of Article 101 of the Treaty to horizontal agreements concluded between the members of the association or decisions adopted by the association.

3.   The exemption provided for in paragraph 1 shall apply to vertical agreements containing provisions which relate to the assignment to the buyer or use by the buyer of intellectual property rights, provided that those provisions do not constitute the primary object of such agreements and are directly related to the use, sale or resale of goods or services by the buyer or its customers. The exemption applies on condition that, in relation to the contract goods or services, those provisions do not contain

restrictions of competition having the same object as vertical restraints which are not exempted under this Regulation.

4.   The exemption provided for in paragraph 1 shall not apply to vertical agreements entered into between competing undertakings. However, it shall apply where competing undertakings enter into a non-reciprocal vertical agreement and:

(a)   the supplier is a manufacturer and a distributor of goods, while the buyer is a distributor and not a competing undertaking at the manufacturing level; or

(b)   the supplier is a provider of services at several levels of trade, while the buyer provides its goods or services at the retail level and is not a competing undertaking at the level of trade where it purchases the contract services.

5.   This Regulation shall not apply to vertical agreements the subject matter of which falls within the scope of any other block exemption regulation, unless otherwise provided for in such a regulation.

Article 3 Market share threshold

1.   The exemption provided for in Article 2 shall apply on condition that the market share held by the supplier does not exceed 30% of the relevant market on which it sells the contract goods or services and the market share held by the buyer does not exceed 30% of the relevant market on which it purchases the contract goods or services.

2.   For the purposes of paragraph 1, where in a multi party agreement an undertaking buys the contract goods or services from one undertaking party to the agreement and sells the contract goods or services to another undertaking party to the agreement, the market share of the first undertaking must respect the market share threshold provided for in that paragraph both as a buyer and a supplier in order for the exemption provided for in Article 2 to apply.

Article 4 Restrictions that remove the benefit of the block exemption — hardcore restrictions

The exemption provided for in Article 2 shall not apply to vertical agreements which, directly or indirectly, in isolation or in combination with other factors under the control of the parties, have as their object:

(a)   the restriction of the buyer's ability to determine its sale price, without prejudice to the possibility of the supplier to impose a maximum sale price or recommend a sale price, provided that they do not amount to a fixed or minimum sale price as a result of pressure from, or incentives offered by, any of the parties;

(b)   the restriction of the territory into which, or of the customers to whom, a buyer party to the agreement, without prejudice to a restriction on its place of establishment, may sell the contract goods or services, except:

(i)   the restriction of active sales into the exclusive territory or to an exclusive customer group reserved to the supplier or allocated by the supplier to another buyer, where such a restriction does not limit sales by the customers of the buyer,

(ii)   the restriction of sales to end users by a buyer operating at the wholesale level of trade,

(iii) the restriction of sales by the members of a selective distribution system to unauthorised distributors within the territory reserved by the supplier to operate that system, and

(iv)   the restriction of the buyer's ability to sell components, supplied for the purposes of incorporation, to customers who would use them to manufacture the same type of goods as those produced by the supplier;

(c)   the restriction of active or passive sales to end users by members of a selective distribution system operating at the retail level of trade, without prejudice to the possibility of prohibiting a member of the system from operating out of an unauthorised place of establishment;

(d)   the restriction of cross-supplies between distributors within a selective distribution system, including between distributors operating at different level of trade;

(e)   the restriction, agreed between a supplier of components and a buyer who incorporates those components, of the supplier's ability to sell the components as spare parts to end-users or to repairers or other service providers not entrusted by the buyer with the repair or servicing of its goods.

Article 5 Excluded restrictions

1.   The exemption provided for in Article 2 shall not apply to the following obligations contained in vertical agreements:

(a) any direct or indirect non-compete obligation, the duration of which is indefinite or exceeds five years;

(b) any direct or indirect obligation causing the buyer, after termination of the agreement, not to manufacture, purchase, sell or resell goods or services;

(c) any direct or indirect obligation causing the members of a selective distribution system not to sell the brands of particular competing suppliers.

For the purposes of point (a) of the first subparagraph, a non- compete obligation which is tacitly renewable beyond a period of five years shall be deemed to have been concluded for an indefinite duration.

2. By way of derogation from paragraph 1(a), the time limi- tation of five years shall not apply where the contract goods or services are sold by the buyer from premises and land owned by the supplier or leased by the supplier from third parties not connected with the buyer, provided that the duration of the non-compete obligation does not exceed the period of occupancy of the premises and land by the buyer.

3. By way of derogation from paragraph 1(b), the exemption provided for in Article 2 shall apply to any direct or indirect obligation causing the buyer, after termination of the agreement, not to manufacture, purchase, sell or resell goods or services where the following conditions are fulfilled:

(a) the obligation relates to goods or services which compete with the contract goods or services;

(b) the obligation is limited to the premises and land from which the buyer has operated during the contract period;

(c) the obligation is indispensable to protect know-how transferred by the supplier to the buyer;

(d) the duration of the obligation is limited to a period of one year after termination of the agreement.

Paragraph 1(b) is without prejudice to the possibility of imposing a restriction which is unlimited in time on the use and disclosure of know-how which has not entered the public domain.

Article 6 Non-application of this Regulation

Pursuant to Article 1a of Regulation No 19/65/EEC, the Commission may by regulation declare that, where parallel networks of similar vertical restraints cover more than 50% of a relevant market, this Regulation shall not apply to vertical agreements containing specific restraints relating to that market.

Article 7 Application of the market share threshold

For the purposes of applying the market share thresholds provided for in Article 3 the following rules shall apply:

(a) the market share of the supplier shall be calculated on the basis of market sales value data and the market share of the buyer shall be calculated on the basis of market purchase value data. If market sales value or market purchase value data are not available, estimates based on other reliable market information, including market sales and purchase volumes, may be used to establish the market share of the undertaking concerned;

(b) the market shares shall be calculated on the basis of data relating to the preceding calendar year;

(c) the market share of the supplier shall include any goods or services supplied to vertically integrated distributors for the purposes of sale;

(d) if a market share is initially not more than 30% but subsequently rises above that level without exceeding 35%, the exemption provided for in Article 2 shall continue to apply for a period of two consecutive calendar years following the year in which the 30% market share threshold was first exceeded;

(e) if a market share is initially not more than 30% but subsequently rises above 35%, the exemption provided for in Article 2 shall continue to apply for one calendar year following the year in which the level of 3 5% was first exceeded;

(f) the benefit of points (d) and (e) may not be combined so as to exceed a period of two calendar years;

(g) the market share held by the undertakings referred to in point (e) of the second subparagraph of Article 1(2) shall be apportioned equally to each undertaking having the rights or the powers listed in point (a) of the second subparagraph of Article 1(2).

Article 8 Application of the turnover threshold

1.   For the purpose of calculating total annual turnover within the meaning of Article 2(2), the turnover achieved during the previous financial year by the relevant party to the vertical agreement and the turnover achieved by its connected undertakings in respect of all goods and services, excluding all taxes and other duties, shall be added together. For this purpose, no account shall be taken of dealings between the party to the vertical agreement and its connected undertakings or between its connected undertakings.

2.   The exemption provided for in Article 2 shall remain applicable where, for any period of two consecutive financial years, the total annual turnover threshold is exceeded by no more than 10%.

Article 9 Transitional period

The prohibition laid down in Article 101(1) of the Treaty shall not apply during the period from 1 June 2010 to 31 May 2011 in respect of agreements already in force on 31 May 2010 which do not satisfy the conditions for exemption provided for in this Regulation but which, on 31 May 2010, satisfied the conditions for exemption provided for in Regulation (EC) No 2790/1999.

Article 10 Period of validity

This Regulation shall enter into force on 1 June 2010.

It shall expire on 31 May 2022.

This Regulation shall be binding in its entirety and directly applicable in all Member States.

Guidelines on Vertical Restraints
(2010/C 130/01)

Part II
Vertical Agreements Which Generally Fall Outside Article 101(1)

2. **Agency agreements**

2.1 *Definition of agency agreements*

(12) An agent is a legal or physical person vested with the power to negotiate and/or conclude contracts on behalf of another person (the principal), either in the agent's own name or in the name of the principal, for the:

- – purchase of goods or services by the principal, or
- – sale of goods or services supplied by the principal.

(13) The determining factor in defining an agency agreement for the application of Article 101(1) is the financial or commercial risk borne by the agent in relation to the activities for which he has been appointed as an agent by the principal. In this respect it is not material for the assessment whether the agent acts for one or several principals. Neither is material for this assessment the qualification given to their agreement by the parties or national legislation.

(14) There are three types of financial or commercial risk that are material to the definition of an agency agreement for the application of Article 101(1). First there are the contract-specific risks which are directly related to the contracts concluded and/or negotiated by the agent on behalf of the principal, such as financing of stocks. Secondly, there are the risks related to market-specific investments. These are investments specifically required for the type of activity for which the agent has been appointed by the principal, i.e. which are required to enable the agent to conclude and/or negotiate this type of contract. Such investments are usually sunk, which means that upon leaving that particular field of activity the investment cannot be used for other activities or sold other than at a significant loss. Thirdly, there are the risks related to other activities undertaken in the same product market, to the extent that the principal requires the agent to undertake such activities, but not as an agent on behalf of the principal but for its own risk.

(15) For the purposes of applying Article 101(1) the agreement will be qualified as an agency agreement if the agent does not bear any, or bears only insignificant, risks in relation to the contracts concluded and/or negotiated on behalf of the principal, in relation to market-specific investments for that field of activity, and in relation to other activities required by the principal to be undertaken in the same product market. However, risks that are related to the activity of providing agency services in general, such as the risk of the agent's income being dependent upon his success as an agent or general investments in for instance premises or personnel, are not material to this assessment.

(16) For the purpose of applying Article 101(1) an agreement will thus generally be considered an agency agreement where property in the contract goods bought or sold does not vest in the agent, or the agent does not himself supply the contract services and where the agent:

(a) does not contribute to the costs relating to the supply/purchase of the contract goods or services, including the costs of transporting the goods. This does not preclude the agent from carrying out the transport service, provided that the costs are covered by the principal;

(b) does not maintain at his own cost or risk stocks of the contract goods, including the costs of financing the stocks and the costs of loss of stocks and can return unsold goods to the principal without charge, unless the agent is liable for fault (for example, by failing to comply with reasonable security measures to avoid loss of stocks);

(c) does not undertake responsibility towards third parties for damage caused by the product sold (product liability), unless, as agent, he is liable for fault in this respect;

(d) does not take responsibility for customers' non-performance of the contract, with the exception of the loss of the agent's commission, unless the agent is liable for fault (for example, by failing to comply with reasonable security or anti-theft measures or failing to comply with reasonable measures to report theft to the principal or police or to communicate to the principal all necessary information available to him on the customer's financial reliability);

(e) is not, directly or indirectly, obliged to invest in sales promotion, such as contributions to the advertising budgets of the principal;

(f)   does not make market-specific investments in equipment, premises or training of personnel, such as for example the petrol storage tank in the case of petrol retailing or specific software to sell insurance policies in case of insurance agents, unless these costs are fully reimbursed by the principal;

(g)   does not undertake other activities within the same product market required by the principal, unless these activities are fully reimbursed by the principal.

(17)   This list is not exhaustive. However, where the agent incurs one or more of the above risks or costs, the agreement between agent and principal will not be qualified as an agency agreement. The question of risk must be assessed on a case-by-case basis, and with regard to the economic reality of the situation rather than the legal form. For practical reasons, the risk analysis may start with the assessment of the contract-specific risks. If contract-specific risks are incurred by the agent, this will be enough to conclude that the agent is an independent distributor. On the contrary, if the agent does not incur contract-specific risks, then it will be necessary to continue further the analysis by assessing the risks related to market-specific investments. Finally, if the agent does not incur any contract-specific risks and risks related to market-specific investments, the risks related to other required activities within the same product market may have to be considered.

2.2   *The application of Article 101(1) to agency agreements*

(18)   In the case of agency agreements as defined above, the selling or purchasing function of the agent forms part of the principal's activities. Since the principal bears the commercial and financial risks related to the selling and purchasing of the contract goods and services all obligations imposed on the agent in relation to the contracts concluded and/or negotiated on behalf of the principal fall outside Article 101(1). The following obligations on the agent's part will be considered to form an inherent part of an agency agreement, as each of them relates to the ability of the principal to fix the scope of activity of the agent in relation to the contract goods or services, which is essential if the principal is to take the risks and therefore to be in a position to determine the commercial strategy:

(a)   limitations on the territory in which the agent may sell these goods or services;

(b)   limitations on the customers to whom the agent may sell these goods or services;

(c)   the prices and conditions at which the agent must sell or purchase these goods or services.

(19)   In addition to governing the conditions of sale or purchase of the contract goods or services by the agent on behalf of the principal, agency agreements often contain provisions which concern the relationship between the agent and the principal. In particular, they may contain a provision preventing the principal from appointing other agents in respect of a given type of transaction, customer or territory (exclusive agency provisions) and/or a provision preventing the agent from acting as an agent or distributor of undertakings which compete with the principal (single branding provisions). Since the agent is a separate undertaking from the principal, the provisions which concern the relationship between the agent and the principal may infringe Article 101(1). Exclusive agency provisions will in general not lead to anti-competitive effects. However, single branding provisions and post-term non-compete provisions, which concern inter-brand competition, may infringe Article 101(1) if they lead to or contribute to a (cumulative) foreclosure effect on the relevant market where the contract goods or services are sold or purchased (see in particular Section VI.2.1). Such provisions may benefit from the Block Exemption Regulation, in particular when the conditions provided in Article 5 thereof are fulfilled. They can also be individually justified by efficiencies under Article 101(3) as for instance described below in paragraphs (144) to (148).

(20)   An agency agreement may also fall within the scope of Article 101(1), even if the principal bears all the relevant financial and commercial risks, where it facilitates collusion. This could for instance be the case when a number of principals use the same agents while collectively excluding others from using these agents, or when they use the agents to collude on marketing strategy or to exchange sensitive market information between the principals.

(21)   Where the agent bears one or more of the relevant risks as described in paragraph 16, the agreement between agent and principal does not constitute an agency agreement for the purpose of applying Article 101(1). In that situation the agent will be treated as an independent undertaking and the agreement between agent and principal will be subject to Article 101(1) as any other vertical agreement.

Part III

Application of the Block Exemption Regulation

3. **Hardcore restrictions under the Block Exemption Regulation**

(50) The hardcore restriction set out in Article 4(b) of the Block Exemption Regulation concerns agreements or concerted practices that have as their direct or indirect object the restriction of sales by a buyer party to the agreement or its customers, in as far as those restrictions relate to the territory into which or the customers to whom the buyer or its customers may sell the contract goods or services. This hardcore restriction relates to market partitioning by territory or by customer group. That may be the result of direct obligations, such as the obligation not to sell to certain customers or to customers in certain territories or the obligation to refer orders from these customers to other distributors. It may also result from indirect measures aimed at inducing the distributor not to sell to such customers, such as refusal or reduction of bonuses or discounts, termination of supply, reduction of supplied volumes or limitation of supplied volumes to the demand within the allocated territory or customer group, threat of contract termination, requiring a higher price for products to be exported, limiting the proportion of sales that can be exported or profit pass-over obligations. It may further result from the supplier not providing a Union-wide guarantee service under which normally all distributors are obliged to provide the guarantee service and are reimbursed for this service by the supplier, even in relation to products sold by other distributors into their territory. These practices are even more likely to be viewed as a restriction of the buyer's sales when used in conjunction with the implementation by the supplier of a monitoring system aimed at verifying the effective destination of the supplied goods, eg the use of differentiated labels or serial numbers. However, obligations on the reseller relating to the display of the supplier's brand name are not classified as hardcore. As Article 4(b) only concerns restrictions of sales by the buyer or its customers, this implies that restrictions of the supplier's sales are also not a hardcore restriction, subject to what is said below regarding sales of spare parts in the context of Article 4(e) of the Block Exemption Regulation. Article 4(b) applies without prejudice to a restriction on the buyer's place of establishment. Thus, the benefit of the Block Exemption Regulation is not lost if it is agreed that the buyer will restrict its distribution outlet(s) and warehouse(s) to a particular address, place or territory.

(51) There are four exceptions to the hardcore restriction in Article 4(b) of the Block Exemption Regulation. The first exception in Article 4(b)(i) allows a supplier to restrict active sales by a buyer party to the agreement to a territory or a customer group which has been allocated exclusively to another buyer or which the supplier has reserved to itself. A territory or customer group is exclusively allocated when the supplier agrees to sell his product only to one distributor for distribution in a particular territory or to a particular customer group and the exclusive distributor is protected against active selling into his territory or to his customer group by all the other buyers of the supplier inside the Union, irrespective of sales by the supplier. The supplier is allowed to combine the allocation of an exclusive territory and an exclusive customer group by for instance appointing an exclusive distributor for a particular customer group in a certain territory. This protection of exclusively allocated territories or customer groups must, however, permit passive sales to such territories or customer groups. For the application of Article 4(b) of the Block Exemption Regulation, the Commission interprets 'active' and 'passive' sales as follows:

    – 'Active' sales mean actively approaching individual customers by for instance direct mail, including the sending of unsolicited e-mails, or visits; or actively approaching a specific customer group or customers in a specific territory through advertisement in media, on the internet or other promotions specifically targeted at that customer group or targeted at customers in that territory. Advertisement or promotion that is only attractive for the buyer if it (also) reaches a specific group of customers or customers in a specific territory, is considered active selling to that customer group or customers in that territory.

    – 'Passive' sales mean responding to unsolicited requests from individual customers including delivery of goods or services to such customers. General advertising or promotion that reaches customers in other distributors' (exclusive) territories or customer groups but which is a reasonable way to reach customers outside those territories or customer groups, for instance to reach customers in one's own territory, are passive sales. General advertising or promotion is considered a reasonable way to reach such customers if it would be attractive for the buyer to undertake these investments also if they would not reach customers in other distributors' (exclusive) territories or customer groups.

(52)   The internet is a powerful tool to reach a greater number and variety of customers than by more traditional sales methods, which explains why certain restrictions on the use of the internet are dealt with as (re)sales restrictions. In principle, every distributor must be allowed to use the internet to sell products. In general, where a distributor uses a website to sell products that is considered a form of passive selling, since it is a reasonable way to allow customers to reach the distributor. The use of a website may have effects that extend beyond the distributor's own territory and customer group; however, such effects result from the technology allowing easy access from everywhere. If a customer visits the web site of a distributor and contacts the distributor and if such contact leads to a sale, including delivery, then that is considered passive selling. The same is true if a customer opts to be kept (automatically) informed by the distributor and it leads to a sale. Offering different language options on the website does not, of itself, change the passive character of such selling. The Commission thus regards the following as examples of hardcore restrictions of passive selling given the capability of these restrictions to limit the distributor's access to a greater number and variety of customers:

(a)   an agreement that the (exclusive) distributor shall prevent customers located in another (exclusive) territory from viewing its website or shall automatically re-route its customers to the manufacturer's or other (exclusive) distributors' websites. This does not exclude an agreement that the distributor's website shall also offer a number of links to websites of other distributors and/or the supplier;

(b)   an agreement that the (exclusive) distributor shall terminate consumers' transactions over the internet once their credit card data reveal an address that is not within the distributor's (exclusive) territory;

(c)   an agreement that the distributor shall limit its proportion of overall sales made over the internet. This does not exclude the supplier requiring, without limiting the online sales of the distributor, that the buyer sells at least a certain absolute amount (in value or volume) of the products offline to ensure an efficient operation of its brick and mortar shop (physical point of sales), nor does it preclude the supplier from making sure that the online activity of the distributor remains consistent with the supplier's distribution model (see paragraphs (54) and (56)). This absolute amount of required offline sales can be the same for all buyers, or determined individually for each buyer on the basis of objective criteria, such as the buyer's size in the network or its geographic location;

(d)   an agreement that the distributor shall pay a higher price for products intended to be resold by the distributor online than for products intended to be resold offline. This does not exclude the supplier agreeing with the buyer a fixed fee (that is, not a variable fee where the sum increases with the realised offline turnover as this would amount indirectly to dual pricing) to support the latter's offline or online sales efforts.

Communication from the Commission

Notice on agreements of minor importance which do not appreciably restrict competition under Article 101(1) of the Treaty on the Functioning of the European Union (*De Minimis* Notice)

(2014/C 291/01)

I.

1. Article 101(1) of the Treaty on the Functioning of the European Union prohibits agreements between undertakings which may affect trade between Member States and which have as their object or effect the prevention, restriction or distortion of competition within the internal market. The Court of Justice of the European Union has clarified that that provision is not applicable where the impact of the agreement on trade between Member States or on competition is not appreciable.[1]

2. The Court of Justice has also clarified that an agreement which may affect trade between Member States and which has as its object the prevention, restriction or distortion of competition within the internal market constitutes, by its nature and independently of any concrete effects that it may have, an appreciable restriction of competition.[2] This Notice therefore does not cover agreements which have as their object the prevention, restriction or distortion of competition within the internal market.

3. In this Notice the Commission indicates, with the help of market share thresholds, the circumstances in which it considers that agreements which may have as their effect the prevention, restriction or distortion of competition within the internal market do not constitute an appreciable restriction of competition under Article 101 of the Treaty. This negative definition of appreciability does not imply that agreements between undertakings which exceed the thresholds set out in this Notice constitute an appreciable restriction of competition. Such agreements may still have only a negligible effect on competition and may therefore not be prohibited by Article 101(1) of the Treaty.[3]

4. Agreements may also fall outside Article 101(1) of the Treaty because they are not capable of appreciably affecting trade between Member States. This Notice does not indicate what constitutes an appreciable effect on trade between Member States. Guidance to that effect is to be found in the Commission's Notice on effect on trade,[4] in which the Commission quantifies, with the help of the combination of a 5% market share threshold and a EUR 40 million turnover threshold, which agreements are in principle not capable of appreciably affecting trade between Member States.[5] Such agreements normally fall outside Article 101(1) of the Treaty even if they have as their object the prevention, restriction or distortion of competition.

5. In cases covered by this Notice, the Commission will not institute proceedings either upon a complaint or on its own initiative. In addition, where the Commission has instituted proceedings but undertakings can demonstrate that they have assumed in good faith that the market shares mentioned in points 8, 9, 10 and 11 were not exceeded, the Commission will not impose fines. Although not binding on them, this Notice is also intended to give guidance to the courts and competition authorities of the Member States in their application of Article 101 of the Treaty.[6]

6. The principles set out in this Notice also apply to decisions by associations of undertakings and to concerted practices.

7. This Notice is without prejudice to any interpretation of Article 101 of the Treaty which may be given by the Court of Justice of the European Union.

II.

8. The Commission holds the view that agreements between undertakings which may affect trade between Member States and which may have as their effect the prevention, restriction or distortion of competition within the internal market, do not appreciably restrict competition within the meaning of Article 101(1) of the Treaty:

    (a) if the aggregate market share held by the parties to the agreement does not exceed 10% on any of the relevant markets affected by the agreement, where the agreement is made between undertakings which are actual or potential competitors on any of those markets (agreements between competitors);[7] or

    (b) if the market share held by each of the parties to the agreement does not exceed 15% on any of the relevant markets affected by the agreement, where the agreement is made between undertakings which are not actual or potential competitors on any of those markets (agreements between non-competitors).

9.   In cases where it is difficult to classify the agreement as either an agreement between competitors or an agreement between non-competitors the 10% threshold is applicable.

10.   Where, in a relevant market, competition is restricted by the cumulative effect of agreements for the sale of goods or services entered into by different suppliers or distributors (cumulative foreclosure effect of parallel networks of agreements having similar effects on the market), the market share thresholds set out in point 8 and 9 are reduced to 5%, both for agreements between competitors and for agreements between non-competitors. Individual suppliers or distributors with a market share not exceeding 5%, are in general not considered to contribute significantly to a cumulative foreclosure effect.[8] A cumulative foreclosure effect is unlikely to exist if less than 30% of the relevant market is covered by parallel (networks of) agreements having similar effects.

11.   The Commission also holds the view that agreements do not appreciably restrict competition if the market shares of the parties to the agreement do not exceed the thresholds of respectively 10%, 15% and 5% set out in points 8, 9 and 10 during two successive calendar years by more than 2 percentage points.

12.   In order to calculate the market share, it is necessary to determine the relevant market. This consists of the relevant product market and the relevant geographic market. When defining the relevant market, reference should be had to the Notice on the definition of the relevant market.[9] The market shares are to be calculated on the basis of sales value data or, where appropriate, purchase value data. If value data are not available, estimates based on other reliable market information, including volume data, may be used.

13.   In view of the clarification of the Court of Justice referred to in point 2, this Notice does not cover agreements which have as their object the prevention, restriction or distortion of competition within the internal market. The Commission will thus not apply the safe harbour created by the market share thresholds set out in points 8, 9, 10 and 11 to such agreements.[10] For instance, as regards agreements between competitors, the Commission will not apply the principles set out in this Notice to, in particular, agreements containing restrictions which, directly or indirectly, have as their object: a) the fixing of prices when selling products to third parties; b) the limitation of output or sales; or c) the allocation of markets or customers. Likewise, the Commission will not apply the safe harbour created by those market share thresholds to agreements containing any of the restrictions that are listed as hardcore restrictions in any current or future Commission block exemption regulation,[11] which are considered by the Commission to generally constitute restrictions by object.

14.   The safe harbour created by the market share thresholds set out in points 8, 9, 10 and 11 is particularly relevant for categories of agreements not covered by any Commission block exemption regulation.[12] The safe harbour is also relevant for agreements covered by a Commission block exemption regulation to the extent that those agreements contain a so-called excluded restriction, that is a restriction not listed as a hardcore restriction but nonetheless not covered by the Commission block exemption regulation.[13]

15.   For the purpose of this Notice, the terms "undertaking", "party to the agreement", "distributor" and "supplier" include their respective connected undertakings.

16.   For the purpose of the Notice 'connected undertakings' are:

      (a)   undertakings in which a party to the agreement, directly or indirectly:

            i.   has the power to exercise more than half the voting rights, or

            ii.   has the power to appoint more than half the members of the supervisory board, board of management or bodies legally representing the undertaking, or

            iii. has the right to manage the undertaking's affairs;

      (b)   undertakings which directly or indirectly have, over a party to the agreement, the rights or powers listed in (a);

      (c)   undertakings in which an undertaking referred to in (b) has, directly or indirectly, the rights or powers listed in (a);

      (d)   undertakings in which a party to the agreement together with one or more of the undertakings referred to in (a), (b) or (c), or in which two or more of the latter undertakings, jointly have the rights or powers listed in (a);

      (e)   undertakings in which the rights or the powers listed in (a) are jointly held by:

            i.   parties to the agreement or their respective connected undertakings referred to in (a) to (d), or

ii.   one or more of the parties to the agreement or one or more of their connected undertakings referred to in (a) to (d) and one or more third parties.

17.   For the purposes of point (e) in point 16, the market share held by these jointly held undertakings is apportioned equally to each undertaking having the rights or the powers listed in point (a) in point 16.

NOTES

1. See Case C-226/11 Expedia, not yet reported, paragraphs 16 and17.

2. See Case C-226/11 Expedia, in particular paragraphs 35, 36 and 37.

3. See, for instance, Joined Cases C-215/96 and C-216/96 Bagnasco and Others [1999] ECR I-135, paragraphs 34 and 35.

4. Commission Notice – Guidelines on the effect on trade concept contained in Articles 81and 82 of the Treaty (OJ C 101, 27.4.2004, p. 81), in particular points 44 to 57.

5. It should be noted that agreements between small and medium sized undertakings (SMEs), as defined in the Commission Recommendation of 6 May 2003 concerning the definition of micro, small and medium-sized enterprises or any future recommendation replacing it (OJ L 124, 20.5.2003, p. 36), are also not normally capable of affecting trade between Member States. See in particular point 50 of the Notice on effect of trade.

6. In particular, in order to determine whether or not a restriction of competition is appreciable, the competition authorities and the courts of Member States may take into account the thresholds established in this Notice but are not required to do so. See Case C-226/11 Expedia, paragraph 31.

7. On the definition of actual or potential competitors, see the Communication from the Commission — Guidelines on the applicability of Article 101 of the Treaty on the Functioning of the European Union to horizontal cooperation agreements (OJ C 11, 14.1.2011, p. 1), point 10. Two undertakings are treated as actual competitors if they are active on the same relevant market. An undertaking is treated as a potential competitor of another undertaking if, in the absence of the agreement, in case of a small but permanent increase in relative prices it is likely that the former, within a short period of time, would undertake the necessary additional investments or other necessary switching costs to enter the relevant market on which the latter is active.

8. See also the Guidelines on Vertical Restraints (OJ C 130, 19.5.2010, p. 1, in particular points 76, 134 and 179. While in the Guidelines on Vertical Restraints in relation to certain restrictions reference is made not only to the total but also to the tied market share of a particular supplier or buyer, in this Notice all market share thresholds refer to total market shares.

9. Notice on the definition of the relevant market for the purposes of Community competition law (OJ C 372, 9.12.1997, p. 5).

10. For these agreements, the Commission will exercise its discretion in deciding whether or not to institute proceedings.

11. For supply and distribution agreements between non-competitors see in particular Article 4 of Commission Regulation (EU) No 330/2010 of 20 April 2010 on the application of Article 101(3) of the Treaty on the Functioning of the European Union to categories of vertical agreements and concerted practices (OJ L 102, 23.4.2010, p. 1) and for licensing agreements between non-competitors see in particular Article 4(2) of Commission Regulation (EU) No 316/2014 of 21 March 2014 on the application of Article 101(3) of the Treaty on the Functioning of the European Union to categories of technology transfer agreements (OJ L 93, 28.3.2014, p. 17). For agreements between competitors see in particular Article 5 of Commission Regulation (EU) No 1217/2010 of 14 December 2010 on the application of Article 101(3) of the Treaty on the Functioning of the European Union to certain categories of research and development agreements (OJ L 335, 18.12.2010, p. 36), and Article 4 of Commission Regulation (EU) No 1218/2010 of 14 December 2010 on the application of Article 101(3) of the Treaty on the Functioning of the European Union to certain categories of specialisation agreements (OJ L 335, 18.12.2010, p. 43) as well as Article 4(1) of Regulation (EU) No 316/2014.

12. For instance, trade mark licence agreements and most types of agreements between competitors, with the exception of research and development agreements and specialisation agreements, are not covered by any block exemption regulation.

13. For excluded restrictions see in particular Article 5 of Regulation (EU) No 330/2010, Article 5 of Regulation (EU) No 316/2014 and Article 6 of Regulation (EU) No 1217/2010.

Index

The Arabian Nights:
A Companion

===

BY THE SAME AUTHOR

Fiction:

The Limits of Vision
The Arabian Nightmare
Mysteries of Algiers

Non-fiction:

The Middle East in the Middle Ages:
The Early Mamluk Sultanate 1250–1382

ROBERT IRWIN

━━

The Arabian Nights:
A Companion

ALLEN LANE
THE PENGUIN PRESS

ALLEN LANE
THE PENGUIN PRESS

Published by the Penguin Group
Penguin Books Ltd, 27 Wrights Lane, London w8 5tz, England
Penguin Books USA Inc., 375 Hudson Street, New York, New York 10014, USA
Penguin Books Australia Ltd, Ringwood, Victoria, Australia
Penguin Books Canada Ltd, 10 Alcorn Avenue, Toronto, Ontario, Canada m4v 3b2
Penguin Books (NZ) Ltd, 182–190 Wairau Road, Auckland 10, New Zealand

Penguin Books Ltd, Registered Offices: Harmondsworth, Middlesex, England

First published 1994
1 3 5 7 9 10 8 6 4 2
First edition

Typeset by Datix International Limited, Bungay, Suffolk
Filmset in Monophoto Bembo
Printed in Great Britain by Clays Ltd, St Ives plc

A CIP catalogue record for this book is available from the British Library
ISBN 0–713–99105–4

Contents

═══

Introduction

Beneath English trees I meditated on that lost maze: I imagined it inviolate and perfect at the secret crest of a mountain; I imagined it erased by rice fields or beneath water; I imagined it infinite, no longer composed of octagonal kiosks and returning paths, but of rivers and provinces and kingdoms . . . I thought of a labyrinth of labyrinths, of one sinuous spreading labyrinth that would encompass the past and the future and in some way involve the stars.

Jorge Luis Borges, 'The Garden of the Forking Paths'

One feels like getting lost in *The Thousand and One Nights*, one knows that entering that book one can forget one's own poor human fate; one can enter a world, a world made up of archetypal figures but also of individuals.

Borges, '*The Thousand and One Nights*'[1]

According to a superstition current in the Middle East in the late nineteenth century when Sir Richard Burton was writing, no one can read the whole text of the *Arabian Nights* without dying. There have indeed been times (particularly when toiling through Burton's own distinctly unattractive translation of the *Nights*) when I thought that I might slit my throat rather than continue with this enterprise. However, I am still alive. It may be that I have acquired some sort of literary stamina from a youthful reading of Gibbon's *Decline and Fall of the Roman Empire* and Proust's *A la recherche du temps perdu*. The *Arabian Nights*, applying that title in its widest and loosest sense, is a very long book. Burton's own omnium-gatherum translation, based on an uncritical collation of a variety of Arabic printed texts and manuscripts, stretched to sixteen volumes and included 468 stories (give or take a few, depending on how one counts). Moreover, a critical study of the *Nights* cannot be based on a reading of Burton's translation alone. It was of course necessary to compare his version with those of rival translators and all of them with the original Arabic. Then there were the variant versions of the canonical tales to be read, the wider context of medieval Arab literature to be investigated, the secondary critical literature to be assessed and the multifarious offspring and influences of the *Nights* to be tracked down . . .

It will probably come as a shock to most people in the West today to learn that the *Nights* is longer than Proust. In the nineteenth century, Burton's, or it might be Payne's or Lane's, translation of the *Nights* was a standard work in gentlemen's libraries. In the twentieth century, however, its popularity has declined, and only garbled versions of a handful of stories ('Aladdin', 'Sinbad', 'Ali Baba' and the story of Sheherazade herself) survive in popular consciousness and in bowdlerized children's editions. Even professional Arabists, most of them, are shockingly ignorant of the contents of the *Nights*. It is commonly regarded as a collection of Arab fairy tales, the oriental equivalent of the *Märchen* (fairy tales or household tales) of the Brothers Grimm. But, while it is true that there are items in the *Nights* which might pass as fairy tales, the collection's compass is much wider than this. It also includes long heroic epics, wisdom literature, fables, cosmological fantasy, pornography, scatological jokes, mystical devotional tales, chronicles of low life, rhetorical debates and masses of poetry. A few tales are hundreds of pages long; others amount to no more than a short paragraph.

The title of the story collection in Arabic is *Alf Layla wa-Layla*, literally 'One Thousand Nights and a Night', but the eighteenth-century English translation of Galland's French version was called *The Arabian Nights Entertainments*. In this book I shall use the term 'the *Nights*' to refer to the story collection in any of its various early and late recensions. The one thing that all the collections have in common is that the stories in them are supposed to have been told by Sheherazade to King Shahriyar. We learn from the *Nights* that Shahriyar, a mythical king in ancient times, on discovering his wife's infidelity with a kitchen servant, had the wife put to death and, from that time on, fearing further sexual betrayals, he took virgins to his bed for one night only, invariably having them beheaded on the following morning. After this deflowering and slaughtering had gone on for some time, the vizier's daughter, who was called Sheherazade, volunteered herself, much against her father's will, as the next candidate for the king's bed. Brought before the king, she asked that her sister, Dunyazade, might attend her. She had already put Dunyazade up to asking for a story. Dunyazade, inconspicuously installed in Shahriyar's bedchamber, waited until he had deflowered her sister. Then, when she judged the moment was right, she asked her sister for a story. Sheherazade obliged her with 'The Story of the Merchant and the Demon'; but, since she did not relate all of it that night, Shahriyar was impelled to postpone her execution, so that he might hear the end of it on the following night. The following night, the story continued, but it did not conclude. Instead, Sheherazade began another story, inset within the first one, and broke off with this story also unfinished as dawn was breaking. And so things continued for several years (for two years and 271 days, if we are to take the 1,001 of the title literally), with Sheherazade, night by night, talking for her life. In the end, by the time her vast repertoire of stories was concluded, she had become mother to several of Shahriyar's children, and he had repented from his original determination to execute her.

The stories in the original manuscripts are interrupted every five pages or so by narrative breaks along the lines of 'But morning overtook Sheherazade, and she lapsed into silence. Then her sister said, "Sister, what an entertaining story!" Sheherazade replied, "What is this compared with what I shall tell you tomorrow night!"' But after a while, many compilers and transcribers of the *Nights* lose patience with this device, and thereafter one story follows another with no reference back to the frame of Sheherazade telling stories to Shahriyar and Dunyazade. Not only does Sheherazade tell stories, but some of the characters in her stories tell stories, and some of the characters in their stories also tell stories. The most notable example of this boxing, or framing, technique is the Hunchback cycle of stories; here, among other things, the tailor tells a tale told to him by a lame young man, and this lame young man's tale includes within it the tales of the barber and the barber's stories of his six unfortunate brothers.

In conversations in pubs (where much of my thinking on this subject has been done), after I have finished explaining all this, I have sometimes been asked, 'Well, when was it written?' This is a 'how-long-is-a-piece-of-string?' sort of question to which the only answer must be 'It all depends what you mean by the *Nights*.' A full answer to this question will be attempted in the pages which follow, but for the moment the short (and misleading) answer must be that there was certainly a version of the story collection circulating in the tenth century (though it was entitled *The Thousand Nights*, not *The Thousand and One Nights*), but we know very little about what may or may not have been in the story collection before the fifteenth century. Moreover, the tenth-century story collection drew on older collections of stories, and further stories went on being added to the original corpus until as late as the early nineteenth century. An even shorter answer to the inquisitive person in the pub might be that nobody knows when the *Nights* began – or when they will end.

Hitherto the *Nights* has received short and rather patronizing shrift in general histories of Arabic literature (for example, those of Nicholson and Gibb).[2] In the modern Middle East, with certain exceptions, the *Nights* is not regarded by Arab intellectuals as literature at all. It is true that the literary merit of the stories is variable – and to some extent a matter of taste anyway. Some of the tales in the *Nights* are naïve and vulgar, or even, at their worst, starkly incomprehensible in the form in which they have survived. However, the best stories are artfully constructed, highly sophisticated fictions; they are works of literature in the fullest sense. Though the authors are anonymous, they were not all unsophisticated. The comparative and structural approaches of folklorists may help to bring out the full significance of some of the stories in the *Nights*, but most of them deserve to be read as the products of a highly literary culture. Some knowledge of the complex background of this culture is therefore desirable. It is one of the aims of this *Companion* to sketch in that background, to make apparent to western readers the sheer strangeness of Arab literary culture, and to indicate the existence of whole genres of writing unknown in the western literary tradition. The *Companion* also investigates the aims of the authors of the stories, how these stories were listened to by audiences at the time, and how these same stories have been translated, interpreted, imitated and parodied in Europe and America.

However, the importance of the *Nights* is not just literary, and this *Companion* is not primarily a work of literary criticism. (Mia Gerhardt's *The Art of Story-Telling* may be recommended to those who are looking for a more narrowly literary approach.)[3] The *Nights* is also a valuable source on the social history of the Middle East in medieval and early modern times. Although I have tended to concentrate, in some of the chapters devoted to the stories' contents, on seedy and bizarre aspects of life in the medieval Near East, it must be borne in mind that the vast majority of the subjects of the Abbasid caliphs and Mamluke sultans were not sorcerers, snake-charmers, drug-takers or adulterers. The *Nights* itself contains a large number of pious and edifying stories about wonder-working holy men and virtuous sages, as well as improving fables which enjoin steadfastness, caution, generosity, and so on. However, there are many books about the heroes, scholars and saints of medieval Islam. Arab chronicles and biographical dictionaries have celebrated the achievements of the great and the good at considerable length. It is much more difficult to find out anything about the criminals, the incompetent, the clowns, the beggars and the rest of the humble folk in Baghdad and Cairo, those who were not so pompous or so pious. The *Nights* is an important source on such matters as the Islamic underworld and medieval private life (though certainly a source which has to be handled with caution).

In addition to treating the *Nights* as a source on the history of society and of *mentalités*, I have also sought to give an account of the various ways in which the *Nights* has been studied and, in so doing, to give some idea, however sketchy, of what it is that translators, textual editors, structuralist critics, social historians and folklorists are engaged in. The ramifications of this enterprise are endless, and, in giving the answer to one question, I have usually found that I have uncovered other questions which are even more perplexing. This *Companion* may serve as a guide into the labyrinth, but it offers no route out. But then, having entered the maze, why should one ever want to leave?

The potential scope of a companion to the *Nights* is vast. It is a matter of opening windows on to strange vistas and then rather swiftly closing them again. Subjects only alluded to, or not mentioned at all, in the body of this *Companion* include the poetry in the *Nights*, illustrators of the *Nights*, fables and wisdom literature in the *Nights*, political theory in the *Nights*, mysticism and religion in the *Nights*, plays, films and music inspired by the *Nights*, and the influence of the *Nights* on modern Arabic and Persian literature. This is not because I regard these topics as unimportant or uninteresting. On the contrary, I hope to tackle them in some future study, or studies. However, I did not want to produce a book as bulky as the *Nights* itself, a companion which was so long that no one could read it without dying.

I am treating every story published in the four nineteenth-century editions printed in Arabic (Calcutta I, Bulaq, Breslau and Calcutta II) as part of the *Nights*. Although I believe that these stories do constitute an intelligible unit of study, my procedure is admittedly a somewhat arbitrary one, and some scholars would argue that the real canon of stories which belong to the *Nights* should be narrowly defined as those which were included in the earliest manuscript version. They will object that I am confounding the genuine *Nights* stories with a later and much larger body of, as it were, *Nights* Apocrypha. This is an issue which will be dealt with in Chapter 2.

In 1984 Muhsin Mahdi published a critical edition of an Arabic manuscript of the *Nights* from the Bibliothèque nationale in Paris.[4] With the exception of a fragmentary page from a ninth-century version, the manuscript edited by Mahdi is the oldest surviving version of the opening stories of the *Nights*, and it was the one used by Antoine Galland for his translation. The appearance of Mahdi's edition puts scholarship on a new footing. In 1990 Husain Haddawy produced a very readable translation of the text as edited by Mahdi, and this translation is strongly recommended to anyone who wishes to taste the authentic flavour of those tales.[5] However, the Bibliothèque's manuscript edited by Mahdi contains only thirty-five and a half stories. For the first thirty-five stories in the *Nights*, then, I have quoted from Haddawy's translation. But there is no entirely satisfactory translation of the rest of the stories, hundreds of them, which at one time or another have been included in editions and translations of the *Nights*. After much hesitation and doubt, I have decided to use and quote from Burton's translation of these stories. (His *Arabian Nights Entertainments* with its supplemental volumes was first published in 1885–8.)[6] There are many problems with this translation, and the reasons for both my decision to use Burton and my reluctance to do so will be spelt out more fully in Chapter 1. Here it suffices to say that Burton's edition is a comprehensive one and, though there are quite a few errors in his translation, it is more accurate and scholarly than the later Mardrus/Powys Mathers version. Burton's transliteration of Arabic now seems archaic, and his use of the English language always was eccentric. I cite the titles of stories as they are given according to Burton, but elsewhere my transliteration more closely conforms to accepted academic usage. With the exception of certain Arabic names and words which have become familiar in an English form (among them Sheherazade, Aladdin, Mamluke and caliph), I have followed a simplified form of the transliteration used in the *Encyclopedia of Islam*; I have dispensed with diacriticals, as well as with most *ayns* and *hamzas*, and I have substituted *j* for *dj* and *q* for *k*. The English versions of the Koranic citations are from A.J. Arberry, *The Koran Interpreted* (London, 1955).

I should like to thank Helen Irwin, Dr Hugh Kennedy, Miles Litvinoff, Juri Gabriel, Professor Muhsin Mahdi, Dr Peter Caracciolo and Dr Abdullah al-Udhari for suggestions and advice, as well as Peter Carson for his patience and his faith that this book would eventually get written. Donald MacFarlan's enthusiasm got the book started in the first place. I am especially grateful to Dr Patricia Crone, who read and commented on the typescript and made many valuable criticisms. However, I must emphasize that any errors in the work are my own. I also benefited greatly from conversations with the late Martin Hinds. He is greatly missed.

I

Beautiful Infidels

As Jorge Luis Borges once observed, 'Nothing is as consubstantial with literature and its modest mystery as the questions raised by a translation.' Neglected until modern times in the Near East, the *Arabian Nights* has been so widely and frequently translated into western languages that, despite the Arab antecedents of the tales, it is a little tempting to consider the *Nights* as primarily a work of European literature. Yet there is no remotely satisfactory translation of the great bulk of the *Nights* into either English or French. As we shall see, Husain Haddawy's recent translation is both accurate and fluent, but it is a translation of the first 271 nights only. Earlier English translations have failings which were, to some extent, the product of the times in which they were made and, to some extent, the product of the quirks of the individual translators who made them. But all translation from Arabic poses a range of problems not encountered in translations from European languages, and translating the *Nights* poses quite specific difficulties.

Arabic is a difficult language.[1] The alien curlicued and dotted alphabet, which so bemuses the non-Arabist, is the least of the problems which translators of the language have to master. Only a few of the more serious problems will be listed here. First, one finds almost no punctuation at all in pre-modern Arabic manuscripts and texts. A sentence will run on until the end of the paragraph, if not until the end of the book, and there are no inverted commas to signal the opening and closing of direct speech. Secondly, the absence of capital letters can lead to proper names being mistranslated as things. Yet another feature of written

Arabic which makes it easy for readers to lose their way is the relatively heavy use of pronouns. One of the commonest problems that a translator from Arabic faces is working out whether a particular pronoun belongs to the subject, the object or some other given instrument in the passage – whether, for example, the *hu* ('he' or 'it') refers to the sultan, the unlucky porter or the whip with which the porter is being flogged. Translations from Arabic are peculiarly dependent upon judgements about context and plausibility. At its most obscure, the language has some of the features of a shorthand system. Moreover, some letters in the written language are distinguished from others by little dots, or diacriticals, placed above or beneath the main form of the letter. Thus the letter *za* is distinguished from the otherwise identical letter *ra* by having a little dot on top. But the writers and transcribers of manuscripts quite often carelessly omitted some of the dots, leaving the reader or translator to guess which word or words are intended.

There are also lexical problems. We still lack a really satisfactory dictionary of pre-modern Arabic. The scholar of the language has no access to anything remotely comparable to *The Oxford English Dictionary*, where the origins and changes in use of a word over the centuries are registered. One of the best dictionaries to have been produced so far is Edward Lane's massive but unfinished *Arabic–English Lexicon* (1863–93), a work which was based essentially on medieval Arab dictionaries of classical Arabic. Hans Wehr's *Arabisches Wörterbuch* (1952, English version by J.M. Cowan in 1960) is the standard reference work for modern vocabulary. However, the *Nights*, in the form in which it has come down to us, was written neither in classical Arabic nor in modern Arabic, but in what is known, rather vaguely, as Middle Arabic. Middle Arabic, the language of common usage from about AD 1200 to 1600, had its own distinctive grammatical peculiarities and, to some extent, its own vocabulary. Its peculiarities reflected the impact of spoken colloquial and regional dialects on the older 'high' or 'classical' language. The Arabic of the *Nights* also owed a little to Turkish and Persian vocabulary and syntax. Perhaps the most important and, for the translator, most taxing feature of Middle Arabic is its tendency to dispense with mood and case endings after verbs and nouns. Inspired guesswork can be as important as a good knowledge of grammar when decoding medieval texts. Since there are no comprehensive dictionaries or grammars devoted specifically to Middle Arabic, the scholar who undertakes to translate from the *Nights* lacks some of the most elementary aids to his work, and, of course, the early translators, such as Galland and Lane, had to work with even fewer guides.

A further range of problems stem from Arabic's rigid syntax and spelling, which make it difficult, though not absolutely impossible, to register colloquial and regional spoken usage. If one tampers with the spelling of a word, then one may be altering the word beyond recognition, changing its root form and therefore its meaning. Consequently, the *Nights* features no dialogue by the Middle Eastern equivalents of Sam Weller, Joe Gargery or Mrs Gamp. It has always been difficult for Arab writers to signal class or regional origin by distinctive forms of speech, though an Arab reader, familiar with the geographic or social environment, on being told that a character in a tale is an Egyptian peasant, or a black slave, or a Maghribi (North African) king, may well supply those forms for himself.

Arabic has a rich vocabulary, notoriously so perhaps. John Julius Norwich, in his entertaining *Christmas Crackers*, had gentle fun with the Arabic word *khal*, to which are assigned the following meanings in J.G. Hava's *Arabic–English Dictionary*: 'Huge mountain. Big camel. Banner of a prince. Shroud. Fancy. Black stallion. Owner of a th[ing]. Self-magnified. Caliphate. Lonely place. Opinion. Suspicion. Bachelor. Good manager. Horse's bit. Liberal man. Weak-bodied, weak-hearted man. Free from suspicion. Imaginative man.' Professor A.F.L. Beeston's *The Arabic Language Today* despondently notes that 'in Arabic of all periods, the semantic spectrum of many lexical items is apt to Europeans to seem unduly diffuse'.

In other ways, however, the Arabic vocabulary and syntax may appear to a European eye to be arid and restricted. For instance, it is conventional to translate *wa* as 'and' and *fa* as 'then', but these two conjunctions are regularly made to do far more work than their supposed English equivalents. In certain contexts the correct translation of *wa* will be not 'and', but 'therefore', or 'while', or 'yet', or 'now', or 'many a' or even an emphatic 'by' — as in 'by the beard of the Prophet!'. Additionally, in the absence of European-style punctuation, *wa* and *fa* can do the work of full stops and commas in breaking slabs of prose. Moreover, though medieval Arab writers were at least as fond of elegant variation as their European contemporaries, a somewhat similar problem arises with *qala*, which can be translated as 'he said'. The verb *qala*, in its various forms and tenses, is used far more frequently in Arabic than the English verb 'to say'. Where an English novelist will tend, in any extended piece of dialogue, to deploy such verbs as 'he asked', 'he interrupted', 'he replied', 'he sneered', 'he mumbled', and so on, the Arabic author will tend to stick monotonously with *qala*. One important implication of this lexical austerity is that a strict word-for-word translation of any work of Arabic literature will be both unattractive and, in a sense, seriously misleading. Therefore, only a half-wit or a liar would claim that it was possible to produce a complete and faithful word-for-word translation of the *Nights*, simply changing the Arabic letters into European ones; but, as we shall see below, Mardrus made this claim for his translation.

The restricted syntactical forms and the regular patterning of word forms make rhyme and metre relatively easy to achieve in Arabic, and both rhyme and metre are heavily used for moments of high emotion and for rhetoric in the *Nights*. Arabic rhymed prose (*saj'*) was used to evoke pompous ceremonies, fierce battles, extraordinary beauty, and so on. Any attempt to register this in

English is likely to appear bizarre. Richard Burton, however, did attempt it and consequently produced many unattractive passages like the following: 'But in the stress and stowre I got sundry grievous wounds and sore; and, since that time, I have passed on his back three days without tasting food or sleeping aught, so that my strength is down brought and the world is become to me as naught.' As for poetry, the closeness and profusion of rhyming and metrical patterns cannot be mimicked in English without serious strain. Of course, translating poetry from one language to another is always difficult, but translating Arabic poetry raises so many problems that is impossible even to list them here. Just one particularly obvious and pervasive problem should be noted and that is the Arab poet's penchant for punning and word-play. Again and again, a translator will find he can translate one sense of a couplet, but only at the cost of sacrificing a second sense which the author also intended and which gave force and wit to his verse. Although there is a lot of poetry in the *Nights* and its protagonists have little difficulty in spouting it, even when faced with shipwreck, rape or death, little of the poetry which features in the stories appears to have any direct bearing on the action. Understandably, then, some translators, notably Littmann, who produced the best German translation, and Dawood, who translated a selection of the stories for Penguin Books, took the decision to omit the poetry in the *Nights* altogether.

Although all translations from pre-modern Arabic have to face problems, translations of the *Nights* have to face special problems. For one thing, the sheer length of the collection has deterred most competent Arabists from even contemplating beginning a translation. Moreover, many of the tales, perhaps because they were written to be read aloud, are weighed down with repetition and recapitulation. Most important of all, the lack of a single established source text has created problems for all translators so far. When the texts printed in Calcutta, Bulaq and Breslau all give vaguely similar but significantly different versions of what is presumably the same tale, which text should the translator work from? None of the four versions of the *Nights* printed in Arabic in the nineteenth century was an edition in the scholarly sense of the word, and here and there in all the printed versions there are passages which, as they stand, are gibberish. Moreover, some of the stories are not all that well written; they are unpolished, and their grammar is imperfect. It follows that any translation into a fluent and grammatical English will be an improvement on the original – a misleading improvement. A 'good' translation of the *Nights* will not necessarily be a 'transparent' translation.

Antoine Galland (1646–1715), the first European translator of the *Nights*, played so large a part in discovering the tales, in popularizing them in Europe and in shaping what would come to be regarded as the canonical collection that, at some risk of hyperbole and paradox, he has been called the real author of the *Nights*.[2] Galland was born in Picardy and studied classical Greek and Latin at the Collège royal and the Sorbonne in Paris. It was Galland's excellent knowledge of Greek which induced the French ambassador, the Marquis de Nointel, to take him with him in 1670 as part of a French mission to the Ottoman Turkish Sultan. From 1670 until 1675 Galland was in the Levant, working as an interpreter and studying first Turkish and modern Greek, then Arabic and Persian. Galland also hunted out rare manuscripts, coins, statuettes and precious stones for the ambassador. Back in France, Galland was appointed a curator of the royal collection of coins and medals. He visited the Levant on two further occasions, for the purpose of copying inscriptions and collecting curios, as 'antiquary to the king'. He also produced a large number of translations and treatises on oriental matters, including *Paroles remarquables, bons mots et maximes des orientaux, De l'origine et progrès du café* and *Contes et fables indiennes de Bidpai et de Lokman*.

In 1692 Galland became assistant to Barthélemy d'Herbelot on his great work, the *Bibliothèque orientale ou Dictionnaire universal contenant généralement tout ce qui regarde la connaissance des peuples de l'Orient.*[3] This work, with over 8,000 entries, has been described as the first attempt at an encyclopaedia of Islam. It was a somewhat quirky compilation, designed to be consulted both for reference and for pleasure. The entries on Middle Eastern people, places and things drew heavily on illustrative anecdotes, culled from Arab, Turkish and Persian chronicles and encyclopaedias. The book was a treasure-house of oriental wisdom and wit. On d'Herbelot's death in 1695, Galland took over its compilation, and he published the completed work in 1697.

The *Bibliothèque orientale* is a work which stands at the beginning of orientalism, properly speaking. It was produced in an age when the Middle East was not perceived as being part of some underdeveloped Third World (for, after all, the Ottoman Turks had advanced to Vienna and put it under siege as recently as 1683). In the preface to the *Bibliothèque orientale*, Galland asks himself why Europeans are so interested in the Islamic world, while there is so little reciprocal interest on the part of Muslims in Christian Europe's civilization and society. Galland argued that Islamic literature was so rich and of such a high quality that it was self-sufficient. The *Bibliothèque* drew on some of the best of this literature; and on its publication, the collector of fairy tales Charles Perrault praised the book for introducing its readers to a new heaven and a new earth. The *Bibliothèque* was to introduce several generations of writers and scholars to the world of Islam. The notes to William Beckford's orientalist novel *Vathek* draw heavily on the *Bibliothèque orientale* for their recondite references to eastern manners and customs, and indeed the initial inspiration for Beckford's novel seems to have come from d'Herbelot's entry on the Abbasid Caliph Wathiq in the *Bibliothèque*. The notes to Robert Southey's epic poem *Thalaba* similarly draw on the *Bibliothèque*.[4]

However, the work which gave Galland his greatest fame was, of course, his translation of the *Nights*.[5] Some time in the 1690s Galland had acquired a manuscript of 'The Voyages of Sinbad' (there is no evidence that this story cycle ever formed part of the original Arab version of the *Nights*). Galland published the Sinbad stories in 1701, and later the same year, inspired by the success of this translation, he began work on a translation of the *Nights*, having had the manuscript sent to him from Syria. Volumes one and two of *Les Mille et une nuits* were published in 1704, the twelfth and final volume appearing in 1717. Galland used a three- or four-volume manuscript, dating from the fourteenth or fifteenth century, as the basis for his translation. One volume may or may not have been lost since, but the remaining three are to be found in the Paris Bibliothèque nationale (MSS arabes 3609–11). By chance, the manuscript Galland worked from is the oldest known surviving manuscript of the *Nights* (if we exclude a single fragmentary page dating from the tenth century).

The three-volume manuscript is unlikely to have been Galland's only source; for, even in the opening frame story, there are significant discrepancies between Galland's translation and the manuscript. For example, Galland begins the story of Shahriyar and his royal brother Shahzaman by referring to their fathers, but these fathers are not mentioned in the surviving manuscript. There is no obvious reason why Galland should have made up this detail. In some cases it is likely that Galland was inserting the extra details in order to clarify the narrative for his French audience. However, other details that Galland provided are sometimes confirmed in other surviving manuscripts of the *Nights*, so not all of the additional detail can be ascribed to Galland's own whims. He must have worked also from a second parallel manuscript which is now lost.

Moreover, Galland's translation, when it was completed, included many more stories than the Bibliothèque nationale manuscript contains or could have contained even if the hypothetical missing fourth volume were to turn up. In fact, we know that Galland did not rely entirely on manuscripts for his compilation. In 1709 Galland was introduced to Hanna Diab, a Maronite

Christian Arab from Aleppo who had been brought to Paris by Galland's friend the traveller Paul Lucas. Diab acted as Galland's informant and dictated from memory fourteen stories, seven of which later appeared in Galland's edition of the *Nights*. Comparing the notes which Galland took from dictation with the final printed versions of the stories, it is clear that Galland took extraordinary liberties with the stories he received from Diab. For example, when Galland came to transmit the story of 'Prince Ahmed and the Peri Banou', he added a great deal of additional picturesque material from a non-fictional account of a visit to India by a fifteenth-century Arab called Abd al-Razzaq. In the same story, he also slipped in a speech against the eighteenth-century French custom of arranged marriages.

Les Mille et une nuits introduced the stories of 'Aladdin', 'Ali Baba' and 'Prince Ahmed and his Two Sisters' to European audiences. The puzzling thing is that none of these stories has been found in any surviving Arabic manuscript written before Galland's translation of the *Nights* was published. The story of 'The Ebony Horse' does appear in manuscripts of the *Nights*, but only in ones written after Galland had produced his translation, which leaves open the possibility that the Arab version was actually based on Galland's French story. Indeed, some eighteenth-century readers and critics went so far as to accuse Galland of having made up all the *Nights* stories himself. In 'On Fables and Romance' (1783), James Beattie wrote:

whether the tales be really Arabick, or invented by Mons. Galland, I have never been able to learn with certainty. If they be Oriental, they are translated with unwarrantable latitude; for the whole tenor of the style is in the French mode: and the Caliph of Bagdat, and the Emperor of China, are addressed in the same terms of ceremony which are usual at the court of France.

In the case of some stories there are indeed grounds for suspicion; for, although Arabic manuscript versions of 'Aladdin' and 'Ali

Baba' have turned up, they post-date Galland's *Mille et une nuits* and may have been translations into Arabic of Galland's original French prose. To complicate the story of the making of *Les Milles et une nuits* still further, not all the stories in the collection were translated or chosen by Galland. The seventh volume included the stories of 'Zayn al-Asnam' and 'Khudad and his Brothers', as translated from a Turkish manuscript by another orientalist, Pétis de la Croix. This was done without Galland's knowledge or approval by the publisher, who was in a hurry to cash in on the extraordinary success of the stories.

Perrault's *Contes de la mère l'Oye*, or 'Mother Goose's Tales', had already introduced French readers to such stories as 'Little Red Riding Hood', 'Cinderella', 'Puss in Boots' and 'Bluebeard' and had helped to create a taste for fairy stories in sophisticated circles. As it happened, Charles Perrault (1628–1703) had been one of the most enthusiastic admirers of the *Bibliothèque orientale*, and he and Galland shared the same publisher. As the *Nights* stories started to appear, they were read and discussed in the salons, and, as with Perrault's stories, society ladies were Galland's most influential partisans. The publication of the *Nights* inaugurated a mania for oriental stories, whether translated or made up (and these rivals and imitations will be discussed in a subsequent chapter).

In the eighteenth and nineteenth centuries Homer's epics provided one of the two chief battle-grounds for debate about the theory and aims of translation. (The other was the Bible.) It was not thought ridiculous in the eighteenth century for a translator to claim that he had improved on the text he had translated from. Many conceived of the translator's job as being just that, and there were Englishmen who thought that Pope's or Chapman's translation of Homer was better than the interesting but barbarous original. (Intellectual fashion has changed, but even today there are people who judge Baudelaire's translations of Edgar Allan Poe, or Nabokov's translation of *Alice in Wonderland*, to be improvements on their originals.) During the French Renaissance, humanist translators of the literature of classical antiquity – the so-called 'beautiful infidels' – had argued that good taste took precedence over strict accuracy in translation. Galland's decorous aim in translating the *Nights* was not so much to transcribe accurately the real texture of medieval Arab prose, as to rescue from it items which he judged would please the salons of eighteenth-century France. Therefore, the barbarous and the overly exotic were toned down or edited out. The gallant and the pleasing were stressed or inserted. Much later, André Gide, determined to clear a space for his friend Mardrus's translation, was to stigmatize Galland's translation as graceful and charming, 'like the luke-warm steam room which precedes the hot room in the hammam'. Galland's way of working was indeed in stark contrast with that of Mardrus (or Burton), for where Burton and then Mardrus exaggerated the obscenity of the original, Galland censored it, though his pruning was less extreme than that carried out later by Lane. Besides excising most of the pornography, Galland also decided not to translate most of the poetry. Presumably he thought that it would not meet with the rather strict canons of eighteenth-century French literary taste. Galland, who made only occasional use of notes printed in the margins of his pages, did not hesitate to insert glosses explaining unfamiliar objects or institutions into the text itself. It is a device which many translators will judge to be acceptable. It is clear that Galland thought of *Les Mille et une nuits* as being, in a sense, an educational text, which continued the good work of the *Bibliothèque orientale*, in teaching his countrymen about the manners and customs of the Arabs – a graceful mingling of delight and edification.

The translations which followed immediately upon Galland's were translations of Galland rather than of any Arabic version of the *Nights*. Even before the last of Galland's volumes had been published in France, some of his stories had been translated into English and were circulating as cheap chap-books on the popular market.[6] Although many versions of the *Nights* claimed to be

independent translations made directly from the Arabic, few in fact
were. Rather, they were reworkings of Galland with occasional
additional material drawn from other sources.

Joseph von Hammer-Purgstall (1774–1856) was an Austrian
orientalist who eventually mastered ten languages and who served
as a dragoman, an interpreter and guide, in the Levant.[7] One of
his early commissions in Constantinople was to seek out a
manuscript copy of the *Nights* in 1799. In this he failed. He later
went on a mission to Egypt and there met the British naval
commander William Sidney Smith, whose service he entered.
Subsequently, back in Europe, von Hammer-Purgstall was
employed by Metternich and the Austrian Chancery until 1835,
when he retired from the diplomatic service to devote himself
to writing. It was possibly under Metternich's influence that he
developed an obsession with Freemasons and with conspiratorial
secret societies in general. His *The Mysteries of Baphomet Revealed*
(1818) sought to demonstrate that the Templars secretly
worshipped gnostic idols, including a certain Baphomet. In the
same year, he published *Geschichte der Assassinen* (1818) in which
he compared the medieval Shi'ite sect of the Assassins to the
Templars, the Jesuits and the regicides of the French Revolution.
He also published a translation of an early Arab treatise on secret
and occult alphabets. However, von Hammer-Purgstall is chiefly
remembered today (if he can be said to be remembered at all) for
his multi-volume history of the Ottoman Empire, which, though
it was published in 1827–35, is still not entirely superseded. He also
made a translation of the *Divan* of the fourteenth-century Persian
poet Hafiz of Shiraz, a translation which was to have a massive
influence on Goethe's *West-östliche Diwan* (1819).

Although von Hammer-Purgstall's quest for a manuscript of
the *Nights* in Constantinople had been unsuccessful, it seems that
he did find one in Cairo. This manuscript has since been lost, but
it appears to have been the first to have been discovered containing
a version of the ending of the *Nights*, in which Shahriyar at last

repents of his decision to have Sheherazade executed. Back in Constantinople, von Hammer-Purgstall set to work translating his text into French between the years 1804 and 1806. Both his manuscript and his translation have since been lost. However, a German translation of his French version was published in 1825 and still survives. He abridged the stories he translated, finding some of them wordy and boring. Suspiciously, his translation includes some of the stories which Galland included in his *Mille et une nuits*, but which are not known in any surviving manuscript of the *Nights* – so-called 'orphan stories'.

The publication of the earliest printed texts of the *Nights* – the Shirwanee text of 1814–18 (commonly known as Calcutta I), the Breslau text of 1824–43, the Bulaq text (printed in the Bulaq suburb of Cairo in 1835) and the Macnaghten text of 1839–42 (commonly known as Calcutta II) – gave a new impetus to the production of translations which were, or at least claimed to be, independent of Galland's. However, there are considerable problems regarding the sources and status of all these texts, and in particular with the Breslau text, the first eight volumes of which were printed under the direction of Maximilian Habicht.

Habicht, born in Breslau in 1775, had studied under the great French Arabist and philologist Sylvestre de Sacy in Paris. Habicht went on to teach Arabic in Breslau.[8] According to Habicht, he received a complete manuscript of the *Nights* sent from Tunisia by a certain Mordecai ibn al-Najjar. He began translating it into German in 1824 and published the results in 1825. Later that same year, he began publication of the Arabic manuscript he claimed to have been translating. Although he had published eight volumes by the time of his death in 1839, the edition was incomplete, and a student called Fleischer supervised the publication of the remaining four volumes (1842–3), 'improving' the Arabic as he went along. It is in fact very doubtful whether Habicht's Tunisian manuscript ever existed. What he seems to have done is patch together a collection of stories from various manuscripts of the *Nights* and from other Arabic story collections in European libraries, and when the Bulaq printed text appeared in 1835 he made use of its stories too. Habicht, like a number of his successors, was driven by a desire to produce a translation and edition substantial enough to embody the 1,001 nights promised by the title of the Arab story collection, and perhaps he dreamed of becoming rich in the process. Habicht's Tunisian manuscript is only one of a number of 'ghost manuscripts', whose alleged existence has bedevilled the study of what is in any case the complex story of the transmission of the *Nights*. As we shall see, similar frauds were perpetrated by Sabbagh, Chavis and Mardrus.

Gustav Weil (1808–89) had, like Habicht, studied under de Sacy in Paris, but he later improved his Arabic in Cairo. Early in his career as an orientalist, he made his mark by attacking the soundness of von Hammer-Purgstall's translation of the *Nights*. Weil himself produced a partial translation into German in 1837–41, which was based on the Bulaq and Breslau texts, plus manuscripts available in the Gotha library (the library of the Dukes of Saxe-Coburg-Gotha). It was not a full translation, for he omitted the rhymed prose and poetry in the stories. Weil was later to gain a great reputation for his monumental history of the Arab caliphate, but despite his status as a scholarly historian, his translation of the *Nights* has won little acclaim, even in Germany.

Jonathan Scott (1754–1829), like many other eighteenth-century Englishmen, picked up Arabic and Persian in India. (He worked for a while as Warren Hastings's Persian secretary.) Scott actually worked from Galland, making only occasional corrections and adding a few extra stories from other sources. Scott's translation, the *Arabian Nights Entertainments*, which appeared in 1811, was the first literary translation into English of Galland's work (as opposed to opportunistic translations by Grub Street hacks), and it was subsequently widely used as a basis for bowdlerized and popularized editions in English for children. The next Englishman to try his hand was Henry Torrens, who began work in Simla, translating the first fifty nights from Calcutta II, which he published in 1838. But Torrens found it hard going, for, despite his literary ambitions, his Arabic was not very good; and when he heard that E.W. Lane was beginning a rival translation, he readily ceded the field to Lane.

Edward William Lane, the son of a clergyman, was born in 1801.[9] In 1825 he went out to Egypt, intending to earn a living as a lithographer and looking for picturesque material to reproduce. On his return to England in 1828, he set to work to make a visual and written record of what he had observed during his time in Egypt. This was published in 1836 under the title *Manners and Customs of the Modern Egyptians* (revised edition 1842). This enormously influential book detailed the religious practices, domestic customs, superstitions, entertainments and material life of the citizens of Cairo. It deserves to be considered as an early work of anthropology. Although Lane had noted in *Manners and Customs* that manuscripts of the *Nights* were expensive and hard to come by, he also formed the view that its stories admirably reflected and illustrated a way of life that still continued in the city. Back in Cairo, he began work on a translation from the Arabic of the Bulaq printed text. Lane's translation appeared in monthly parts over the years 1838–41, before appearing in a three-volume bound version. Although his translation had been a considerable undertaking, he straight away began work on an even grander enterprise and from 1842 until 1849 he worked in Cairo on the *Arabic–English Lexicon*. This work entailed collecting a variety of manuscripts of the massive multi-volume dictionaries of Arabic compiled by the Arabs in the Middle Ages, collating them, arranging the Arabic root entries according to a logical system of his own devising and, of course, providing English equivalents for the words. In 1849 Lane returned to England and continued with the project there. He worked with intensity and became so steeped in this great work that he used to complain that reading English writing hurt his eyes. When he died in 1876, there were still eight letters of the Arabic alphabet on which he had done little or no work.

In the same way that Galland had intended his translation to be a continuation of the *Bibliothèque orientale*, so Lane's translation of the *Nights* was an extension of his earlier work of depicting and explaining the manners and customs of the modern Egyptians, which Lane considered to be more or less unchanged since the Middle Ages. Because he aimed to produce an instructional work, his translation carries an enormous baggage of footnotes – on cloves, graveyards, gypsum, chess, hippopotami, laws of inheritance, perspiration, polygamy, rubbish tips and much, much more. Indeed, it subsequently proved possible to publish the notes as a separate work under the title *Arabian Society in the Middle Ages: Studies from the Thousand and One Nights.*

Like most of those who followed him, Lane felt obliged to clear a space for his own translation by denigrating work that had been done before. He declared: 'I assert that Galland has excessively *perverted* the work. His acquaintance with Arab manners and customs was insufficient to preserve him always from errors of the grossest description.' Later, Lane's nephew and posthumous editor Stanley Lane-Poole was to pursue the charge, referring to the 'lameness, puerility and indecency' of Galland's translation. Lane took particular exception to Galland's style, which he felt was false to the spirit of the original. However, Lane was not a literary man, and, apart from Arabic literature, he had read little except the Bible. His own style tends towards the grandiose and mock-biblical. His text is full of people who 'sayeth' 'lo' and 'ye' and 'thou' and who 'conjure' and 'abjure' one another. Word order is frequently and pointlessly inverted. Where the style is not pompously high-flown, it is often painfully and uninspiringly literal (for example, Lane prefers to echo closely the Arabic usage by translating *ma zala* as 'ceased not', rather than as 'continued'). It is also peppered with Latinisms. True, Lane's translation is easier to read than Burton's, but that, as we shall see, is not saying very much.

Lane worked from the text printed at Bulaq in Cairo, cross-checking the text occasionally against those of Calcutta I and Breslau (though he took the unresearched view that the Bulaq text was clearly superior to its rivals and that discrepancies between the various versions were of little significance). One argument against plumping for Lane's as the best translation is that it is not a translation of the complete *Nights*. Lane designed his work for family reading. Therefore he expurgated or rewrote sections which he thought unsuitable for childish and virginal ears. In cases where he found whole tales to be obscene, he omitted them altogether. Not only did he prudishly censor his text, but in cases where he considered stories to be boring, repetitive or incomprehensible he omitted them too. A reader who has tried to wade through the whole lot, either in Arabic or in Burton's comprehensive translation, may have some sympathy with Lane's procedure, but the truth is that Lane's literary judgement was erratic and his editing arbitrary. Some very good stories have been cut from Lane's version. Nor did he always indicate where his cuts fell. He also discarded most of the poetry as irrelevant. Therefore Lane's translation should be regarded as a large selection from the original stories, rather than a comprehensive version of them.

Lane believed that the final version of the *Nights* as found in the Bulaq text was the work of a single author who lived in the seventeenth century. This betrays such insensitivity to matters of style and content in that certainly composite text as to raise questions about Lane's judgement in other questions. Nevertheless, Lane's translation was enthusiastically received. Leigh Hunt wrote in the periodical *London and Westminster* that 'Mr Lane's version is beyond all doubt a most valuable, praiseworthy, painstaking, learned and delightful work; worthy to be received with honour and thanks by all lovers of the "Arabian Nights" and to form an epoch in the history of popular Eastern literature.' Lane's fellow Scotsmen, headed by Andrew Lang, were particularly appreciative and they were to lead the opposition to Payne's subsequent rival translation of the *Nights*.

John Payne (1842–1906) showed an early aptitude for poetry and for foreign languages.[10] By the time he was nineteen, he had made translations of poetry from German, French, Italian, Spanish, Portuguese, Greek, Latin, Turkish, Persian and Arabic. Incredibly, it seems that Payne taught himself most of these languages – and he mastered Arabic, Persian and Turkish without ever having visited the Orient. (Although the East India Company sponsored the teaching of Arabic, and its employees who had passed an official examination in the language could qualify for higher pay, no comprehensive and accurate Arabic grammar was available in England until Thomas Wright published one in 1859–62.) Payne undertook various apprenticeships and had a short career as a solicitor. Eventually, however, he was able to earn a living as a translator and poet. He liked to work on his translations while riding around London on the top of a horse-drawn omnibus. As a young man of letters he enjoyed many literary friendships with Mallarmé, Swinburne and others. Two of his closest friendships were with Britain's leading collectors of and experts on pornography, Foster Fitzgerald Arbuthnot and H.S. Ashbee.[11] Arbuthnot was a Bombay civil servant with a strong interest in Indian pornography and oriental literature more generally. Ashbee compiled bibliographies of erotica under the pseudonym 'Pisanus Fraxi'. Some scholars believe that the latter may also have written the anonymous pornographic memoir, *My Secret Life*.

In 1877 Payne and a circle of friends set up a Villon Society, to publish in the first instance Payne's translations of Villon's medieval French verse. (The Victorian age was an age of massive scholarly publishing projects, stretching over many volumes and decades – among them Alexander Murray's *Oxford English Dictionary*, Sir Leslie Stephen's *Dictionary of National Biography* and the publications of the Hakluyt Society and the Early English Text Society. Subscription societies, like the Early English Text Society, which underwrote otherwise uneconomic publications, were a feature of the age.) It was the Villon Society which was to publish Payne's translation of the *Nights*. Not only did the society help fund the publication, it also afforded some measure of protection for Payne against charges of obscenity, as it could be pleaded that the society's publications were for subscribing members only. In the case of Payne's translation of the *Nights*, only 500 copies were printed, and all 500 were speedily taken up.

Payne began work on a translation of the Calcutta II edition in 1876 or 1877. Although Payne's translation was much fuller than Lane's, it was still not a full translation of the Arabic text, for he only included pornographic passages if they were also to be found in the Bulaq and Breslau versions. His friendship with Arbuthnot and Ashbee notwithstanding, Payne did not actually hunt out and exaggerate the obscenities he found in the original Arabic. Indeed, Payne tried to render the obscene passages in allusive paraphrases so as not to offend his readership. Payne made no attempt to render the 'doggerel' *saj'* into English rhyming prose. However, he took the poetry more seriously than his predecessors had done and he translated it all. Payne thought of his translation as a work of literature, and not as some kind of encyclopaedia of oriental manners and customs. Therefore he did not trouble to provide any annotations. It took Payne six years to complete his translation of the Calcutta II text. This was published in nine volumes over the years 1882–4. After he had completed it, he went on to translate additional stories found in the Breslau edition and Calcutta I. These he published in 1884 as *Tales from the Arabic*. When a copy of Zotenberg's manuscript of 'Zayn al-Asnam' and 'Aladdin' became available he translated these as well, publishing them in 1889.

Payne had consulted with and received help from many of the leading orientalists of the age – among them E.J.W. Gibb, author of *A History of Ottoman Court Poetry*, Dr F. Steingass, the compiler of what is still the best Persian–English dictionary, Yacoub Artin Pasha, an aristocratic orientalist of considerable eminence, and H. Zotenberg, the scholarly librarian who had made a special study of the manuscripts of the *Nights*. Nevertheless, partisans of Lane's translation, among them John Ruskin, Andrew Lang, William Robertson Smith and Stanley Lane-Poole, were fierce in their criticism of Payne's versions. On the matter of style, their criticism had some force. Payne had a passion for obscure and archaic words. The publications of the Early English Text Society and Alexander Murray's work on the *Oxford English Dictionary* had made more and more such words readily available, and Payne used them unstintingly in his translation. Though he worked hard on his translations of the Arabic poetry, little of it strikes the modern eye as satisfactory. His enthusiastic friend and biographer Thomas Wright was to claim that Payne 'as an original poet and translator was the greatest English man of letters of the late nineteenth and early twentieth centuries . . . He has given to Kilburn . . . a literary prominence that belongs to a Shiraz, an Avignon, a Weimar.'[12] This is not a judgement which has stood the test of time − even in Kilburn. Payne was opinionated and combative and replied to the criticisms levelled at his work by partisans of the Lane translation. He received powerful support in his combats from Sir Richard Burton.

Sir Richard Francis Burton (1821−90) was already famous as an author, adventurer and explorer.[13] He looked the part, and the young poet Swinburne, practically a disciple of his, said, 'Burton has the jaw of a devil and the brow of a god.' Burton acted the part too. According to his friend Lord Redesdale, he 'was the only man I knew who could fire the old fashioned elephant-gun from the shoulder without a rest; his powers of endurance were simply marvellous, and he could drink brandy with a heroism that would have satisfied Dr Johnson'. Burton had been British consul succes- sively in Santos (Brazil), Damascus and Trieste. He had written extensively on such subjects as swordsmanship, falconry, Indian brothels, mining techniques, Mormons and African geography. In 1864 he had engaged in fierce controversy with his erstwhile companion in exploration, John Hanning Speke, over the location of the source of the Nile. However, Burton was above all famous for his journey in disguise to the forbidden places of the Hejaz, an account of which he had published in 1855, under the title *Pilgrimage to Mecca and Medina*.

Burton first became aware that Payne was proposing to bring out a translation of the *Nights* through a letter by Payne in the *Athenaeum* of 5 November 1881, touting for subscriptions. At the time Burton read the letter, he had been engaged for almost ten years in the dull and insignificant task of representing British interests in Trieste. He straight away wrote to Payne, offering to correct his translation and to assist in any way that Payne might find useful. He claimed that he himself had been doing preparatory work on an independent translation of the *Nights* ever since 1852, when he and the explorer Steinhauser had discussed the project in Somaliland. In fact, there is little evidence that Burton had done any serious amount of translation from any of the versions of the *Nights* prior to the 1880s, though Lord Redesdale, who had visited Burton in 1871, when the latter was consul in Damascus, claimed that Burton had shown him the first two or three of his chapters of his translation then. Nevertheless, Payne welcomed Burton's assistance, both in advising on difficult passages of Arabic and later in giving support in the controversy that raged in the literary press about the respective merits of the translations by Payne and Lane.

Besides feeling bored and cheated of recognition in Trieste, Burton was short of money. Having made contact with Payne, he learned that Payne's translation had been four times oversubscribed, but that Payne had resolved nevertheless to publish no further editions of his work. (As it was, Payne made about £4,000 from his translation.) With Payne's approval, Burton decided to produce 'his own' translation, which he could market through a subscription list of 2,000. Burton's ten-volume edition of the main corpus of the *Nights* was published in 1885. Like Payne, Burton employed the device of a subscription society, both to raise money and to diminish the risk of being prosecuted for obscenity. Burton's edition appeared under the imprint of the Kama Shastra Society, Benares. The Kama Shastra Society had been set up by Burton and Arbuthnot, initially to publish classics of Indian erotica. It had already published the *Ananga Ranga* and the *Kama Sutra*. Later Burton's retranslation of the classic work of Arab erotica, the *Perfumed Garden*, would also be published by the same press. (Benares was, of course, a fiction. The books were printed in Stoke Newington.) After Burton had finished his rendering of the Calcutta II text, he, like Payne, went on to translate and publish stories found in other printed texts and manuscripts. These appeared in six supplementary volumes in 1886–8.

In fact, a very large part of Burton's 'translation' depends closely on Payne's earlier version, though Burton went to tiresome lengths to conceal this. Thus, for example, in the opening of 'The Tale of the Second Calender', where Payne has 'seven schools', Burton has 'seven readings', and where Payne has 'science of the stars', 'handwriting', 'Ind' and 'set out'. Burton has substituted 'star-lore', 'calligraphy'. 'Hind' and 'set forth'. Burton's quest for alternatives to Payne's vocabulary was systematic and at times desperate. However, this is not say that Burton was incapable of making an independent translation of the Arabic, for his translations of the poetry in the stories do not seem to depend on Payne to any significant extent. Moreover, Burton, unlike Payne, did attempt to echo the rhymed prose of *saj'*. Burton also translated some of the supplementary stories before Payne, among them 'Zayn al-Asnam' and 'Aladdin', and there Payne's translations which follow are very similar to Burton's. Burton also translated a number of stories which Payne did not attempt at all, though it is noticeable that Burton often experienced difficulties in translating some of these. Burton adopted such a catholic attitude that he strayed quite a distance into the *Nights* Apocrypha. Finding no Arabic originals for some of Galland's 'orphan tales', he adopted the bizarre procedure of retranslating them from Hindustani translations of Galland. In this way he hoped to recapture some of the original flavour of those tales.

Similarities in style between the Payne and Burton versions are to some extent accounted for by the fact that the two men shared similar literary tastes and friends. Swinburne, Ashbee and Arbuthnot were Burton's friends too, and they all traded books and dirty jokes. Burton shared Payne's enthusiasm for archaic and forgotten words. The style Burton achieved can be described as a sort of composite mock-Gothic, combining elements from Middle English, the Authorized Version of the Bible and Jacobean drama. Most modern readers will also find Burton's Victorian vulgarisms jarring, for example 'regular Joe Millers', 'Charleys' and 'red cent'. Burton's translation of the *Nights* can certainly be recommended to anyone wishing to increase their word-power: 'chevisance', 'fortalice', 'kemperly', 'cark', 'foison', 'soothfast', 'perlection', 'wittol', 'parergon', 'brewis', 'bles', 'fadaise', 'coelebs', 'vivisepulture', and so on. 'Whilome' and 'anent' are standard in Burton's vocabulary. The range of vocabulary is wider and stranger than Payne's, lurching between the erudite and the plain earthy, so that Harun al-Rashid and Sinbad walk and talk in a linguistic Never Never Land.

Burton shared Payne's enthusiasm for Rabelais's *Gargantua and Pantagruel*. More specifically, Burton had a passion for the first three books of that work, as translated in 1653 by the eccentric Scottish Cavalier and linguistic theorist Sir Thomas Urquhart.[14] Urquhart was an advocate of logopandocie – that is, readiness to admit words of all kinds into the language – and his translation of Rabelais took on the character of a verbal riot, something resembling a surrealist reworking of *Roget's Thesaurus*. Phrases and words that had been used by Urquhart in his Rabelais translation – such as 'close-buttock game', 'the two-backed beast', 'springal', 'shite-a-bed', 'tosspot' and 'looby' – resurfaced in Burton's *Arabian Nights*. Urquhart's 'English' rendering of Rabelais was generally wordier, more colourful and more obscene than the original French. Burton followed a similar procedure in trying to improve on his Arabic original. For instance, in the opening frame story, where, in the Arabic, Shahriyar's wife gives herself to 'a black slave', in Burton this man becomes 'a big slobbering blackamoor with rolling eyes which showed the whites, a truly hideous sight'. At its best, Burton's Urquhartian rendering produces flamboyant prose; but at its worst, it is turgid and obscure. Francesco Gabrieli, who later translated the *Nights* into Italian, wryly commented that it was often necessary to consult the original Arabic in order to understand Burton's English. However, Jorge Luis Borges, in his spirited essay 'The Translators of *The 1001 Nights*', did champion Burton's translation.[15] Borges provocatively argued that a translation which is limpid or neutral makes no contribution to literature. Burton's prose, on the other hand, should be valued for its cultural weight. 'In some way, the almost inexhaustible process is shadowed forth in Burton – the hard obscenity of John Donne, the gigantic vocabulary of Shakespeare and Cyril Tourneur, Swinburne's tendency to archaism, the gross erudition of the treatise-writers of the seventeenth century, the energy and vagueness, the love of tempests and magic.' Thus, Borges concluded that Burton's is the best of the English translations of the *Nights*. Not everyone would agree with Borges here, just as not everyone would accept Borges's contention that Robert Louis Stevenson and G.K. Chesterton are two of the greatest writers in English literature. But Burton's *Arabian Nights* is certainly one of the curiosities of English literature. In Husain Haddawy's phrase, it is 'a literary Brighton Pavilion'.[16]

One of the most curious features of this curiosity of English literature is the obstrusive and often supernumerary footnotes. Burton wished to achieve recognition in the world of learning as an anthropologist or scientist of sorts, but Lane's edition with its heavy annotation had more or less done all that was necessary in setting out what the lay reader needed to know about Muslim manners and material life. Indeed, Lane had perhaps explained rather more than any common reader would wish to know. However, out of rivalry with Lane, Burton seems to have been driven to annotate more and more recondite matters in his equally copious notes.

Burton was a man of many prejudices, and they were vigorous ones. He was racist (in an age when racism was acquiring pseudo-scientific pretensions). 'Niggers', Jews and Persians got rough treatment in the notes. He was also a misogynist with a particularly strong dislike for smart society women. He was anti-Christian and he considered Islam, for all the faults he believed it had, to be a better religion, because it was more rational and more useful as an instrument of social control. The indices to Burton's notes are extraordinary specimens of rostered bigotry: 'Blackamoors preferred by debauched women . . . Blind notorious for insolence, etc. . . . Blinding a common practice in the East, how done.' In 'The Tale of the Ensorcelled Prince', Burton has the king imitate 'blackamoor' speech – 'he keeps calling on 'eaven for aid until sleep is strange to me even from evenin' till mawnin', and he prays and damns, cussing us two', and so on. As has been indicated earlier in this chapter, it is hardly possible for Arabic to accommodate 'dis kine o' lordy lordy' speech, and in fact in the Calcutta II text the king speaks an uncoloured and correct Arabic.

Above all, Burton believed himself to be an expert on sex. Cumulatively his notes add up to an encyclopaedia of curious sexual lore. It easy to find Burton's notes on sex simply salacious or quaint, less easy to remember that he was a pioneer who wrote before Havelock Ellis and Sigmund Freud. In this area, Burton was able to draw on the intellectual and bibliographical resources of Fred Hankey and Monckton Milnes, Lord Houghton. Hankey, who lived in Paris, was a wealthy sadist and collector of the works of de Sade. Monckton Milnes had played a significant part in English politics and had been made a peer by Lord Palmerston, but he abandoned political ambitions to become one of England's leading society hosts and cultural patrons. He had long been Burton's friend, and it was through Monckton Milnes that Burton first met Swinburne. (The poet and the explorer rapidly discovered that they had common interests in flagellation and alcohol.) Sexual obsession and racism often came together in Burton's would-be scientific footnotes. It is clear that Burton believed in, and feared, the exceptional virility of the black man. He also claimed to believe that the Persians were born pederasts. More generally, one of his most cherished theories was that there was a 'sotadic zone', including the Mediterranean region and most of the Islamic lands, where homosexuality was the norm. Farting rivals sex as a favourite topic for digression in the notes – and not only in the notes. As far as I can tell, there is no Arab original for the story of 'How Abu Hasan Brake Wind' (which appears in volume five). It is a European story, which Burton naughtily smuggled into his translation of the *Nights*. Something very like it appears in John Aubrey's seventeenth-century *Lives*, though doubtless the story is much older.

Sex and farting apart, Burton's footnotes are a parade of barmy erudition, interspersed with snatches of autobiography. *Bab* is the Arabic word for 'door' or 'chapter'. It is naturally one of the commoner words in that language. Two-thirds of the way through his ninth volume, Burton is able to give this word his scholarly attention and point out that it has a rare, variant (and, in the context of the passage being annotated, utterly irrelevant) meaning of 'Coptic sepulchral chamber'. A note on *shaykh* in the first volume tells us that, in Islamic lore, Abraham was the first man to part his hair and to use a toothpick. In a note in the fifth supplementary volume, he cites Swedenborg on how there will be no looking at the back of people's heads in the afterlife. In other footnotes, he remembers how he was once attacked by a dog in Alexandria and reminisces about seances he has attended. Doubtless such excursuses enlivened the dull slog of transcribing his translation and collating it with Payne's work. Burton's notes are obtrusive, kinky and highly personal. It is tempting to speculate that they might have furnished one of the models for Kinbote's egocentrically deranged annotative scholarship in Nabokov's

marvellous novel, *Pale Fire*. (There is, however, no evidence that
Nabokov ever read Burton.)

It has become fashionable in recent years to discuss Burton, the
author, as if he were the spokesman for Victorian Britain and its
empire, one of those orientalists who provided a blueprint for
colonialism. From this sort of perspective, studies by Burton and
other nineteenth-century orientalists can be seen as amounting to
acts of cultural violation. According to Rana Kabbani, for
example, Burton bears a heavy responsibility for fostering the
myth of the erotic and exploitable East.[17] It is indeed true that
Burton attempted to justify his labours and peddle his edition by
pointing out that the British Empire, with its millions of Indian
and African Muslim subjects, was the largest Muslim empire the
world had ever known, and went on to claim that the stories of
the *Nights* gave an unrivalled insight into their customs and
institutions. It is also true that Burton seized on the racist and
sexist elements in the *Nights* and embroidered them. However, he
did not invent them. Moreover, it is obvious that Burton's *Nights*
was the work of an eccentric and embittered outsider, at odds
with the Foreign and Colonial offices, as well as with the Church
and with most of the literary and academic world. He had little
reward from the Empire and not much regard for it.

Predictably, Burton's work was attacked, as Payne's had been,
by partisans of Lane's translation. Burton had done quite a lot to
invite controversy. His notes and appendices were peppered with
corrections of and sneers at the work of Scott, Torrens and Lane.
The orientalists who had advised and supported Payne supported
Burton too in a new round of polemic on the subject. Swinburne
wrote (bad) verse celebrating the appearance of Burton's translation. Payne himself, while supporting Burton in public, had
private reservations about the new version. He thought that Burton
had a cloth ear for poetry. More important, Payne thought
Burton's concentration on the obscene passages excessive. It
amounted to a 'general rubbing of noses in the sewage of depravity'.

Henry Reeve, writing in the *Edinburgh Review*, characterized the then available translations as follows: 'Galland is for the nursery, Lane is for the library, Payne for the study and Burton for the sewers.'[18] Many agreed with him in preferring Lane's staider prose; for, as T.E. Lawrence put it much later, 'It doesn't matter missing if you don't aim; thereby Lane's *Arabian Nights* is better than Burton's.' Others criticized the Burton translation for being excessively literal, the word-for-word translation (noun for noun, and verb for verb) often giving rise to quaint and ugly effects. However, Burton's version survived these onslaughts fairly well, and his criticisms of Lane's selective procedures were on the whole justified. Burton had provided a full edition of the tales, even to the point of including in the supplementary volumes variants of tales he had already translated. His judgement of the respective merits and failings of individual tales was on the whole good, and he had a much saner view of the likely history of the formation of the corpus of the *Nights* than Lane had.

Unsurprisingly Galland's translation of the *Nights* retained a strong hold on the affections of his countrymen, and it was not until the eve of the twentieth century that a retranslation into French was attempted. However, the man who set out to do this was not French himself. Mardrus's grandfather was a Mingrelian, a native of the Caucasus, who had fought with the Muslims under Shamyl to resist the Russian annexation of the Caucasus. After the final defeat of Shamyl, the Mardrus family fled to Egypt, and the head of the Mardrus clan became head of the Mingrelian community there. Joseph Charles Mardrus was born in Cairo in 1868 and grew up in an Arabic-speaking environment, but, as will become obvious, Arabic can never have been his first language.[19] Subsequently, the young Mardrus moved to France and pursued a career in medicine. As a sanitary officer for the Ministry of the Interior, he did much of his work in the French colonies, especially in North Africa. His translation of the *Nights* came out in 1899–1904. (A very readable English translation of Mardrus's French by

Powys Mathers appeared in 1923.) Mardrus also produced a number of exotic and mystical effusions, quite forgotten today, among them *La Reine de Saba* and *L'Oiseau des hauteurs*. Mardrus's wife, Lucie Delarue-Mardrus, was a poet of some note and presided over a coterie of literary lesbians. Unsurprisingly, Proust in his last years was a frequent visitor to her circle, and there are several references to her husband's translation of the *Nights* in Proust's *A la recherche du temps perdu*. Although Lucie published her *Mémoires* in 1938, her husband and his work scarcely feature in those scrappy and egocentric jottings. Joseph Charles Mardrus died in 1949.

Mardrus's sixteen-volume translation, *Le Livre des mille nuits et une nuit*, has a brief preface which boasts of its stark, literal, word-for-word accuracy: 'Pour la première fois en Europe, une traduction complète et fidèle des *Mille nuits et une nuit* est offert au public. Le lecteur y trouvera le mot à mot pur, inflexible. Le texte arabe a simplement changé des caractères: ici il est en caractères français, voilà tout.' (There is something rather attractive about such presumption.) At the time of its appearance, it was hailed as a triumph. However, those who acclaimed its appearance were literary men, not scholars. Mardrus's translation (which was really more of a loose adaptation) caught the literary mood of the time. André Gide was a personal friend of Mardrus, and in an article devoted to '*Les Mille nuits et une nuit* du Dr Mardrus' he argued that Galland's shaping sensibility, his ever present *bon goût*, had so infused his translation that it really told us more about the world of Louis XV than about that of Harun al-Rashid. However, Gide had no access to the original Arabic, nor was he able to step outside the *bon goût* of his own time. He was unaware therefore how much Mardrus's translation spoke to and of its own time. Mardrus took elements which were there in the original Arabic and worked them up, exaggerating and inventing, reshaping the *Nights* in such a manner that the stories appear at times to have been written by Oscar Wilde or Stéphane Mallarmé. Mardrus's version of the Arabian tales was a belated product of *fin-de-siècle* taste, a portrait of a fantasy Orient, compounded of opium reveries, jewelled dissipation, lost paradises, melancholy opulence and odalisques pining in gilded cages.

When Mardrus began his translation, he claimed that he was translating from the 'best' version of the *Nights*, the Bulaq text. However, after some criticism from Arabists who noticed discrepancies between Mardrus's translation and the Bulaq version, Mardrus changed his story. Thereafter he claimed to be translating from a seventeenth-century North African manuscript of the *Nights*, which he alleged had served as the basis of the Bulaq printed text; but it is clear that Mardrus was lying and that this manuscript never existed. The new elements in Mardrus's translation derive from the translator's own fancies. Mardrus embroidered the original Arabic and inserted whole new stories. Many of Mardrus's interpolations were erotic ones, for he shared Burton's unspoken conviction that the *Nights* was not dirty enough and he seems to have thought that the stories would be improved if the erotic element in them could be heightened. At other points Mardrus added revolting little anti-Semitic embellishments of his own. More generally, he made all sorts of 'improvements' to the stories, his inventions often tending towards the fey or ironical. For example, Gide found a snatch of dialogue between Shahriyar and Sheherazade particularly charming. This was where Shahriyar asks Sheherazade what language the animals speak. 'In purest Arabic verse and prose,' replies Sheherazade, but this is really Mardrus having fun, for the exchange does not appear in any of the original Arabic manuscripts or texts. Additions apart, Mardrus also omitted some stories and rearranged others to suit his own taste.

Mardrus's translation of the actual Arabic, when he really was translating the Arabic, has also attracted criticism. At times it was painfully literal; at other times it was simply wrong. Mardrus's dogged literalism led him to turn perfectly ordinary Arabic into the most grotesque sort of French. For example, the Arabic word *ayn*, which means 'eye', can also mean 'well', 'spring' or 'essence'. But in contexts where *ayn* clearly means a well or other source of water, Mardrus translates it as 'the eye of water'. Then again *din* means both 'faith' and 'debt', but Mardrus regularly renders it as 'faith' regardless of whether it is correct in the context or not. It is just possible that for some readers such literalisms may help to give an air of exoticism to the text, but much of this exoticism is simply spurious, owing little to the original Arabic text, but much to the eccentricity of the translator. Moreover, quite apart from Mardrus's monocular practice of matching Arabic words with French words regardless of sense, there are also many simple errors of translation in his version. His translation was heavily criticized by academic Arabists. In response, Mardrus promised to produce a fat tome of learned commentary and justificatory pieces which would conclusively demonstrate his accuracy and scholarship. It is not surprising that this volume failed to materialize. D.B. MacDonald, possibly bending over backwards to be fair to Mardrus, was kind enough to point out that not all Mardrus's mistakes were his own; some of them were directly copied from Galland. However, MacDonald was forced to conclude that 'The Arabic scholarship of Dr Mardrus is beneath criticism.' Suhayr al-Qalamawi, author of one of the best studies in Arabic of the *Nights*, remarked of Mardrus's translation that 'With great regret, we cannot regard this translation as scholarly because of its vulgarity and distortions.'

In 1923 the publisher Jonathan Cape proposed to T.E. Lawrence that he translate Mardrus into English. Lawrence replied enthusiastically, describing the Mardrus version as 'Much the best version of the "Nights" in any language (not excepting the original which is in coffee-house talk!) and it's ambitious to make a still-better English version: and yet I think it's possible. Better, I mean, as prose. The correctness of Mardrus can't be bettered. The rivalry in English isn't high. Payne crabbed: Burton unreadable:

Lane pompous.'[20] T.E. Lawrence's breezy praise of Mardrus's translation calls his judgement into question (not for the first time, of course) and it makes one wonder how good Lawrence's knowledge of Arabic really was. For all his love of the Arabs of the desert, Lawrence showed little knowledge of or interest in Arabic literature. In the end, nothing came of the Lawrence/ Mardrus edition, and Mardrus's French was translated by E. Powys Mathers. Powys Mathers did a good job on Mardrus's French, but whether the job was worth doing in the first place is another matter.

Although the key translations of the *Nights* were into English and French, the stories have of course been translated into most of the world's written languages (though not often directly from the Arabic). In the twentieth century, German readers have been well served by Littmann's complete and very capable six-volume translation (1921–8). Enno Littmann (1875–1958) was an academic philologist with a good grasp of Arabic – and of Hebrew, Amharic, Syriac, Persian, Italian, Latin and Greek. He translated the whole of the *Nights*, except for the poetry, though he translated the most obscene bits not into German but into Latin. His translation was based on Calcutta II, and he seems to have made use of Burton as a crib for his rendering. Despite this partial dependence on Burton, Borges, while conceding that Littmann's translation was accurate and perfectly scholarly, still condemned it for its colourlessness: 'In Littmann, like Washington incapable of lying, there is no other thing than German probity. It is little, it is so little. The intercourse between the *Nights* and Germany should have produced something more.'[21] (German readers I have talked to tend to confirm Borges's judgement.)

In Italy, the distinguished Arabist Francesco Gabrieli presided over a team of anonymous translators who translated Bulaq collated with Calcutta II. Gabrieli took a bracingly critical view of the material which was being translated, criticizing the stories for their intellectual poverty, their puerility, their psychological shallowness, their lack of internal logic and their too easy resort to magic and marvels.[22] Gabrieli's view of the stories is excessively downbeat. However, both Gabrieli's introduction and his translation can be recommended to Italian readers. Russian readers too are apparently well served – in their case by a translation by M.A. Salier, which appeared in the years 1929–33. This translation was published by the Akademia publishing house in Moscow under the patronage of Maxim Gorky. The Akademia project was set up by Gorky in order to save writers and academics from starvation.

As has been noted in the Introduction, most recently we have a translation into English by Husain Haddawy of the Mahdi edition of the Galland manuscript. Published in 1990, Haddawy's translation covers only 271 nights, ending with 'The Story of Jullanar of the Sea', and of course it does not include any of the 'orphan stories' or any of the *Nights* Apocrypha. Some readers may therefore prefer the wider range of tales translated for Penguin from the second Calcutta edition by N.J. Dawood.[23] However, Haddawy's translation is both accurate and a pleasure to read. Moreover, the Mahdi text, from which Haddawy translates, contains many artful details which have been lost in the versions printed in Calcutta and Bulaq. For those wishing to sample the *Nights* and get a true impression of the style and art of the stories, Haddawy's translation cannot be too highly recommended.

The Book without Authors

Can textual criticism add anything to our pleasure in reading 'The Story of the Three Apples' or 'The Barber's Tale'? It seems doubtful. However, arguments about the oral or literary nature of the *Nights*, its folk sources and oriental prototypes, its narrative techniques, its social and political content and much else are arguments conducted in a vacuum unless one has some notion of what early versions of the *Nights* may have looked like and some notion too of how this corpus of tales came together in an Arab compilation. Besides, it will become apparent (I hope) that the arcanum of textual criticism and editorial technique has its own dry charm. Textual criticism is detective work, a mixture of routine foot-slogging and the occasional inspired deduction, at the end of which the suspects are narrowed down, identities are unmasked, and there are even 'criminals' to be apprehended; for, as we shall see further, the history of the textual transmission of the *Nights* has been muddied by forgers and compilers of pastiche manuscripts of the stories.

The very existence of the *Nights* was unknown in western Europe until Galland began to publish his translation in 1704 (even though, as we shall see, individual stories from the *Nights* had been included in medieval and Renaissance story collections). At first the stories were read for entertainment and studied only as a source for parodies and pastiches of eastern fairy tales. The investigation of such matters as the source or sources of the stories, the date of their compilation and the identity of their possible author only began in the early decades of the nineteenth century. That is to say, the serious study of the *Nights* coincided with the development

of orientalism as an academic discipline. Bonaparte's brief occupation of Egypt in 1798–9, the East India Company's need for good
linguists, the growing interest of theologians in Semitic languages
related to Hebrew, and the foundation of the Société Asiatique in
1821 and the Royal Asiatic Society in 1823 all helped to stimulate
a growing interest in the language and literature of the Arabs.[1]

It was European interest in the work that led to the production
of the first printed Arabic text of the *Nights*. This was printed in
two volumes in India in 1814–18 under the patronage of the East
India Company's College of Fort William.[2] The text, which
covered the first 200 nights, is known today as Calcutta I. Sheikh
Shirwanee, a teacher at the college and the compiler of Calcutta I,
did not indicate what his manuscript source was. Shirwanee was
not attempting to produce a scholarly text, but rather an entertaining text to be used by Englishmen and others learning Arabic.
Indeed, he believed the tales had originally been produced by a
Syrian Arab for the use of people learning Arabic. As we have
seen, the next printed version was produced in Breslau by Habicht
and Fleischer (1824–43).[3] The availability of these and yet later
printed versions of the Arabic stories helped fuel scholarly debate
about their origins.

Louis Mathieu Langlés was the founder, in 1795, of the Ecole
des langues orientales vivantes in Paris. In 1814, in a preface to a
text and translation of *Les Voyages de Sinbad le marin et la ruse des
femmes*, Langlés had suggested that the stories of the *Nights* had
ultimately an Indian origin, and he cited evidence from al-Mas'udi
to this effect. His suggestion was developed further by Baron von
Hammer-Purgstall (whose career and translation of the *Nights*
have been discussed in Chapter 1). In articles in the *Journal asiatique*
in 1826 and 1839, von Hammer-Purgstall stressed the role of
Persia and the Persian language as the conduit by which the Indian
stories had reached the Arab lands (no later than the tenth century).
Von Hammer-Purgstall's arguments did not impress Silvestre de
Sacy. Baron Antoine Silvestre de Sacy (1758–1838), Jansenist,

royalist, positivist, great linguist, expert editor of texts, author of the *Grammaire arabe* (1810) and successor to Langlés as director of the École des langues orientales vivantes, was the teacher of a whole generation of Arabists. (His protégés and pupils included Maximilian Habicht, Heinrich Fleischer, Jean Warsy and Michael Sabbagh.) In 1817 Silvestre de Sacy published a review of the Calcutta I edition. In the review, he rather offhandedly discounted the evidence from al-Mas'udi that the stories had a Persian and, ultimately, an Indian source. The stories seemed to him to be too Arab and too Islamic ever to have come from India. In a subsequent article published in the *Mémoires* of the Académie des inscriptions et belles-lettres, he argued that the work had been composed in Syria in the thirteenth century, but that its author had left the work unfinished.[4]

In 1835 a new recension of the *Nights* was printed in two volumes by the Bulaq press in Egypt.[5] Although an Arabic printing press had been set up briefly in Cairo by Bonaparte when the French invaded Egypt in 1798, the printing press set up under the direction of Muhammad Ali's regime in 1821 in the Bulaq suburb of Cairo was the first indigenous printing press in Egypt and one of the first in the Arab world. A certain Sheikh Abd al-Rahman al-Safti al-Sharqawi saw the *Nights* through the press. His edition of the stories gave no indication of its manuscript source, but the Bulaq text was to be the source of most subsequent printed versions of the *Nights* and was the basis of Lane's translation. Unlike the other printed versions of the *Nights*, the Bulaq text does not look like a composite one. Rather, it is thought to have been based on a single Egyptian manuscript of the eighteenth century, now lost. The Arabic of Bulaq's source was generally more correct than the garbled and semi-colloquial renderings given by the manuscripts used in the compilations of Calcutta I and Breslau. The Bulaq text was also used as a source for the fourth and last of the historically important printed versions. This was produced in Calcutta in four volumes (1839–42) and is usually referred to as Calcutta II.[6] Macnaghten, who compiled it, made use not only of the Bulaq edition, but also of the two other printed versions, as well as of an eighteenth-century Egyptian manuscript. Since it used more source manuscripts, Calcutta II appeared to be the 'fullest' version of the *Nights* and hence it was chosen by Torrens, Payne, Burton and Littmann as the basis for their translations. Although scholars of sorts were involved in the production of these printed texts, none of the editions were scholarly editions in any meaningful sense. Their 'editors' simply put the script into type, correcting what they judged to be errors of grammar and spelling, while adding new errors of their own.

The appearance in 1838–41 of Lane's abridged and expurgated translation of the Bulaq text provoked a new flurry of speculation about the provenance and nature of the tales. Lane's own opinion was that, while the collection may have had a Persian prototype, the work, as we now have it, was that of one or two authors writing in Egypt around the end of the Circassian Mamluke period – that is, around 1500. When Burton produced his translation, he denounced Lane's theory with characteristic vigour.[7] Burton argued that the original core of the stories had come into the Arab lands from Persia. The stories had no single author, but were the work of many hands over a long period of time, the last additions probably being made in the sixteenth century. Burton, who can now be seen to have had the better of the argument, in coming to the conclusions that he did, was greatly assisted by his friendship with Hermann Zotenberg. Zotenberg, who looked after oriental manuscripts in the Bibliothèque nationale in Paris, was the first scholar to attempt a comprehensive survey and comparison of the surviving manuscripts of the *Nights*.

At least twenty-two Arabic manuscripts of *Alf Layla wa-Layla* are known to have survived to the present day, and most of these were examined by Zotenberg.[8] The majority of the surviving manuscripts were identified by Zotenberg as having been written in Egypt, but a few were produced in Syria, and one manuscript seemed to be a copy of a Baghdadi prototype (and hence of particular importance, for most scholars were agreed that the first Arabic version of the *Nights* must have been put together in medieval Iraq). A large proportion of the manuscripts were of a late date and had ended up in European libraries. It is possible that many of those written in the eighteenth and early nineteenth centuries were produced to meet the demands of European manuscript-hunters in the Near East. (That relatively few manuscripts survived in the Near East might be taken as an indication that the work was not particularly popular there. On the other hand, one can argue that it was precisely the popularity of the work which led to the disintegration of its manuscripts in the hands of avid readers and hard-working professional storytellers.)

Zotenberg has many discoveries to his credit. Perhaps his most important achievement was to identify the main manuscript source used by Galland in his translation. This was a three-volume manuscript (though, as has been noted, there was perhaps once a fourth volume, now lost). These were the volumes which had been sent to Galland from Syria in 1701. Not only was this manuscript the main source for most of Galland's stories, but Zotenberg (correctly) judged it to be the oldest surviving manuscript of the *Nights*. The script, paper and language of the manuscript all pointed to it having been produced in Syria in the Mamluke period (mid-thirteenth to early sixteenth centuries). Furthermore, an inscription in the margin listed several of the work's owners. The earliest was a Sheikh Taj who had lived in Hama in (probably) the late fifteenth century. His grandson certainly possessed the manuscript in the Muslim year 943, corresponding to the Christian year AD 1536 or 1537. On the basis of the script, however, Zotenberg deduced that the manuscript was actually written in the late fourteenth century, and he later pushed this back to the early fourteenth century.

However, the three-volume manuscript in the Bibliothèque

nationale did not include all the stories that had appeared in Galland's translation, nor did it include more than a minority of the stories known to readers of Lane's or Burton's translations of the *Nights*. The Galland manuscript contained 281 nights or about forty stories (give or take a few, depending on what one judges to be a story unit), and the third volume of the manuscript broke off halfway through the story of 'Qamar al-Zaman'. The stories about Aladdin, Ali Baba, Sinbad, Crafty Dalilah and Prince Ahmed, and scores of others, are not included in it. It seems fairly clear that Galland also had access to another early manuscript which has since been lost. Galland's translation gives a fuller version of the opening frame story than the Bibliothèque nationale manuscript does, and the additional details furnished by Galland (such as the name of Shahriyar's father) are unlikely to have been invented by him (and in fact they also appear in later Egyptian manuscripts). John Richardson's *A Grammar of the Arabick Language . . . Principally Adapted for the Service of the Honourable East India Company* (1776) casually refers to Galland's work as 'an imperfect translation of not quite one half', before giving an Arabic text for 'The Tale of the Barber's Fifth Brother'. The manuscript which Richardson quoted from in his grammar, which once belonged to the notable orientalist Sir William Jones but is now lost, seems to have resembled the surviving Syrian group of manuscripts while being twice their length.

Other Syrian manuscripts, in the Vatican and the British government's India Office, break off where the Bibliothèque nationale manuscript does, and their texts are so similar to it that all three manuscripts must ultimately derive from a common manuscript source. Zotenberg also examined the more numerous Egyptian manuscripts. He found that they had many more stories, but that they tended to give more condensed versions of the story-line than did the Syrian manuscripts (though this is not always the case). Moreover, some of the stories were so garbled that they hardly made any sense at all. The Egyptian manuscripts (which are known collectively as Zotenberg's Egyptian Recension, or ZER) were mostly produced around 1800, almost a hundred years after Galland's translation. Zotenberg also discovered an Arabic version of 'Aladdin' in a manuscript copy of a Baghdadi version of the *Nights*. However, as we shall see, this discovery was not what it seemed.

In the 1880s and 1890s a lot of work was done on the *Nights* by Zotenberg and others, in the course of which a consensus view of the history of the text emerged. Most scholars agreed that the *Nights* was a composite work and that the earliest tales in it came from India and Persia. At some time, probably in the early eighth century, these tales were translated into Arabic under the title *Alf Layla*, or 'The Thousand Nights'. This collection then formed the basis of *The Thousand and One Nights*. The original core of stories was quite small. Then, in Iraq in the ninth or tenth century, this original core had Arab stories added to it – among them some of the tales about the Caliph Harun al-Rashid. Also, from perhaps the tenth century onwards, previously independent sagas and story cycles were added to the compilation, such as the epic of *Omar bin al-Nu'uman* and the *Sindibadnama* (or, as the latter cycle features in the Burton translation, 'The Craft and Malice of Women'). Then, from the thirteenth century onwards, a further layer of stories was added in Syria or Egypt, many of these showing a preoccupation with sex, magic or low life. In the early modern period yet more stories were added to the Egyptian collections so as to swell the bulk of the text sufficiently to bring up its length to the full 1,001 nights of storytelling promised by the book's title. At the same time older stories were modernized in small ways, so that one finds references to guns, coffee-houses and tobacco in some stories which certainly pre-date the invention or discovery of those things.

The debate about the origins and early form of the *Nights* was not dependent only on evidence found within the manuscripts themselves. Other medieval works referred to the existence of the

Nights or something very like the *Nights* in the Middle Ages. Al-Mas'udi (896–956) wrote a delightfully rambling history entitled *Muruj al-Dhahab*, or 'Meadows of Gold'. In a digression on stories, he had occasion to remark that there

are collections of stories which have been passed on to us translated from the Persian, Hindu and Greek languages. We have discussed how these were composed, for example the *Hazar Afsaneh*. The Arabic translation is *Alf Khurafa* ('A Thousand Entertaining Tales') ... This book is generally referred to as *Alf Layla* ('A Thousand Nights'). It is the story of a king, a vizier, the daughter of the vizier and the slave of the latter. These last two are called Shirazad and Dinazad. There are also similar works such as *The Book of Ferzeh and Simas* which contains anecdotes about the kings of India and their viziers. There is also *The Book of Sindibad* and other collections of the same type.[9]

Al-Mas'udi's observations are supported in general terms by Ibn al-Nadim (who died around the year 990). Ibn al-Nadim was a bookseller and the compiler of a catalogue of all the books that were known to have been written up to his own time, called the *Kitab al-Fihrist*. According to Ibn al-Nadim, the writing and collecting of entertaining stories (which it is clear he does not rate very highly) first became fashionable in pre-Islamic Sassanian Persia:

The first book to be written with this content was the book *Hazar Afsan* which means 'A Thousand Stories'. The basis for this [name] was that one of their kings used to marry a woman, spend a night with her and kill her the next day. Then he married a concubine of royal blood who had intelligence and wit. She was called Shahrazad and when she came to him she would begin a story, but leave off at the end of the night, which induced the king to ask for it the night following. This happened to her for a thousand nights, during which time he [the king] had intercourse with her until because of him she was granted a son, whom she showed to him, informing him of the trick played upon him. Then, appreciating her intelligence, he was well disposed towards her and kept her alive. The king had a head of the household named Dinar Zad who was in league with her in this matter.

Ibn al-Nadim says that, although *Hazar Afsan* means 'A Thousand Nights', there were only about 200 stories in the collection, and he adds that 'it is truly a coarse book, without warmth in the telling'.[10] Elsewhere in the *Fihrist*, when he lists the 'Names of the Books of the Byzantines about Evening Stories, Histories, Fables, and Proverbs', he includes 'Shahriyar the King and the Reason for his Marrying Shahrazad the Storyteller'.[11]

Then there is evidence from the Geniza (a medieval Egyptian Jewish archive to be discussed later). The Geniza contains a fragmentary record of loans made by a twelfth-century Jewish bookseller and notary in Cairo. One of the books lent out was *The Thousand and One Nights*.[12] (Here for the first time we get the title in its final form.) That these stories were circulating in Egypt at about this time is confirmed by al-Maqrizi, an Egyptian historian of the early fifteenth century, who quotes a thirteenth-century Spanish author, Ibn Said, who in turn quotes a certain al-Qurtubi ('the Cordovan'), to the effect that tales from *The Thousand and One Nights* were circulating in Fatimid times, that is, in the late eleventh century.[13]

Finally, in the preface to a late-eighteenth-century Turkish story collection, *Phantasms of the Divine Presence*, Ali Aziz Efendi the Cretan claims to be translating from, among other sources, *Elf Leyle* (i.e. 'The Thousand Nights') by al-Asma'i. Ali's story collection does indeed contain versions of stories that are common to the Arabic *Nights*, but he provides no supporting evidence that al-Asma'i, the distinguished ninth-century Basran philologist and companion of the Caliph Harun al-Rashid, did indeed compile such a collection; and in general, scholars have been chary of attributing the *Nights* to a single author.[14]

Although such external sources suggested that something like the *Nights* was circulating in the ninth or tenth century, it took scholars a long time to identify any text or fragment of the text which could have been written earlier than the thirteenth century. However, an important discovery was made after the Second World War. This was a couple of fragmentary sheets of paper, which had been preserved in Egypt's dry air, dating from the ninth century. The fragment was acquired by the University of Chicago and published by the distinguished papyrologist Nabia Abbott. It is one of the oldest surviving literary manuscripts from the Arab world, and by great good fortune the fragment which was preserved bears the title *Kitab Hadith Alf Layla*, or 'The Book of the Tale of the Thousand Nights', plus some fifteen lines of the opening of the book, in which Dinazad asks Shirazad, if she is not asleep, to tell her a story and give 'examples of the excellencies and shortcomings, the cunning and stupidity, the generosity and avarice, and the courage and cowardice that are in man, instinctive or acquired, or pertain to his distinctive characteristics or to courtly manners, Syrian or Bedouin'.[15] Obviously, the title is different, and there is no reference to the misfortunes of Shahriyar and Shahzaman in this opening fragment of the frame story; yet, equally obviously, here we have a prototype version of *The Thousand and One Nights*.

It seems probable from all the above that the Persian *Hazar Afsaneh* was translated into Arabic in the eighth or early ninth century and was given the title *Alf Khurafa* before being subsequently retitled *Alf Layla*. However, it remains far from clear what the connection is between this fragment of the early text and the *Nights* stories as they have survived in later and fuller manuscripts, nor how the Syrian manuscripts related to later Egyptian versions. In the absence of a critical text of the *Nights*, all opinions were at best speculative. Duncan Black Macdonald first formulated the project of producing a critical edition of the *Nights* in the earliest form which could be deduced from the surviving manuscripts.[16] Macdonald was born in Glasgow in 1863. He studied Semitic languages at Glasgow and Berlin and subsequently taught in the United States at the Hartford Theological College. His main academic interest was in Muslim theology and spirituality. His interest in the *Nights* really developed as a subsidiary to his main interest, for he believed that the stories could be used to illustrate the concerns and imagery of Muslim popular piety. Macdonald himself was particularly interested in the invisible world and in parapsychology.

Macdonald followed Zotenberg's trail, examining the manuscripts of the *Nights*, and he began to publish studies on the subject in 1908. Among his achievements in the field of *Nights* scholarship was the discovery in the Bodleian Library, Oxford, of a unique Arabic manuscript of the story of Ali Baba. ('Ali Baba' does not feature in the Bibliothèque nationale manuscript, and some had therefore speculated that Galland himself had made up the story.) Macdonald also demonstrated in devastating detail that Habicht's 'Tunisian manuscript', the basis for the Breslau edition, had never existed, the printed text being based on a variety of manuscript sources. Macdonald also planned to publish an edition of the Galland manuscript, collating it with another early manuscript of Syrian provenance which was preserved in the Vatican. However, this project does not seem to have got very far by the time he died in 1943.

The techniques involved in editing medieval texts, whether western or eastern, are based on those pioneered for the production of editions of the literature of classical antiquity.[17] These techniques depend heavily on what may be called the psychopathology of scribal error. The textual critic, working from a number of late and variant copies of a no longer extant original manuscript source, seeks to reconstruct as accurately as possible the appearance of the original manuscript. He does this by establishing a stemma, or hypothetical pedigree, in which some manuscripts are shown to descend from one or several earlier manuscripts. Common errors are crucial in helping to establish the mutual dependence of manuscripts upon a common source; for, while scribal mistakes which are shared between an early and a late manuscript of the same work may be the result of coincidence, this is not likely. It is much more likely that the later manuscript was directly copied from the earlier one (or from a copy of the earlier one), or that the two manuscripts had a common parentage and that they derive their shared errors from a manuscript from which both were copied. Common errors in scribal psychopathology include haplography (writing once what should have been written twice), dittography (writing twice what should have been written once) and *saut du même au même* (moving to the same word or phrase further down the page). Through the detection of shared errors, a family tree of manuscripts is established (curiously similar to the system devised by the eighteenth-century naturalist Linnaeus for classifying biological organisms).

The textual critic seeks, among other things, to establish which is the earliest manuscript. However, it is important to remember that the earliest manuscript is not necessarily the best, for a late manuscript might easily turn out to be a good copy of a now lost manuscript of an even earlier date. More importantly, the textual critic seeks to establish and date the archetype of the stemma, that is, the hypothetical manuscript from which all the surviving manuscripts with their different chains of transmission of error descend. According to the textual scholar Paul Maas, the archetype is defined as 'the exemplar from which the first split originated'. The archetype, however, is not necessarily and not often the same as the very first version of the manuscript, and the textual critic may attempt to go beyond the archetype, to divine what the source looked like when it was first written down, with all errors and deliberate interpolations removed (that is, to present a hypothetical *constitutio textus*).

A stemma gets a bit complicated if it can be demonstrated that cross-contamination has taken place – that is, if more than one manuscript has been consulted when making a copy of the work in question; with the result that one finds a confluence of readings (and scribal errors) deriving from two or more branches of the stemma. Textual criticism is, by its nature, a conjectural science, and the results it produces are often controversial. Several textual critics have noted the suspiciously frequent production by textual scholars of bipartite stemmata. E.J. Kenny has argued that what often happens in such cases is that one group of manuscripts has been treated as the chief chain of descent, while all the rest have been (unjustifiably) lumped together in a single divergent group, even though members of the divergent set are a miscellaneous residue rather than a genuine group with significant common characteristics.

It is worth noting finally that the great pioneers of textual criticism, among them Bentley, Pasquali and Lachman, worked on texts which had, or were presumed to have had, a single author and of which there was once in truth a single original manuscript (perhaps even an autograph written in the writer's own hand), from which all surviving manuscripts ultimately derived. Moreover, those scholars worked on authors like Homer, Callimachus and Lucretius, whose works were treated with reverence by later generations, with the consequence that copyists were often at considerable pains to transcribe them accurately. When faced with a problematic reading, reverentially careful scribes might even go so far as to compare the manuscript they were copying with another manuscript of the same work (and hence there was a possibility of cross-contamination).

Muhsin Mahdi, a professor of Arabic at Chicago and later at Harvard and at one time a colleague of Nabia Abbott, inherited the project – first conceived of by Macdonald – of editing the Galland manuscript and reconstructing the archetypal manuscript of the *Nights*, from which the Galland manuscript and all other surviving Syrian and Egyptian manuscripts derived. It involved him in years of back-breaking work, making a word-for-word, diacritical-point-by-diacritical-point comparison of widely dispersed and sometimes hard-to-read Arabic manuscripts. Mahdi began work in 1959, and the impressive outcome of his labours was published in 1984.[18]

Mahdi took as his base text the three-volume Syrian manuscript which had been used by Galland. He compared it with the other surviving Syrian manuscripts, paying attention to variants and errors. He compared the Syrian family of manuscripts with a parallel, though on the whole later, family of Egyptian manuscripts. Some of the Syrian manuscripts showed signs of contamination from the Egyptian branch; but, by relying mainly on the early versions, Mahdi was able to reconstruct the common ancestor of all the Syrian manuscripts (their archetype or, in Arabic, al-dustur), purged of all later additions and corruptions. He then carried out a similar though more cursory operation examining the mainly later Egyptian manuscripts and posited the existence of a common ancestor for this group too. Finally, he compared the two reconstructed manuscripts – the Syrian and the Egyptian – which were the sources of all surviving manuscripts of the Nights and deduced the form of their common ancestor, the ultimate archetype. It was not possible to go beyond the text of the archetype, but Mahdi was able to offer some plausible speculations about the circumstances of composition of the original or 'mother' source (in Arabic, al-nuskha al-umm) from which the archetype derived. According to Mahdi, the 'mother' source was produced in Syria, some time in the thirteenth or early fourteenth century, probably not many years before the archetype was in turn copied from it (and the Galland version followed on close behind the archetype). The 'mother' source manuscript was in turn based on an earlier version of the Nights, composed in Iraq, but Mahdi did not think it profitable to speculate on what form this Iraqi version would have taken.

For the first time, an authentic medieval text of the Nights has been made readily accessible to Arabists; and, for the first time, it is possible to make detailed criticism of the language, style and narrative technique of the *Nights*. The style of the *dustur* archetype (and of the Galland manuscript) displays a remarkable variety, ranging from dialect and common colloquial to a high-flown and very correct classical Arabic. Mahdi argues that this range is the product of design and that the 'author' adjusted his language according to the social context of the stories and the rank of his speakers. It is also possible that this variation in language merely reflects a haphazard and unintelligent compilation from diverse sources. Mahdi, however, does not believe that the compiler of the Syrian *Nights* was unintelligent or acted haphazardly. The stories in the Syrian recension were not thrown together, but have been linked to one another to fit an underlying design. In particular, Mahdi has argued that the exemplary tales that come framed within the main narrative are carefully placed to give a covert message about the fatuity of exemplary tales. In other words, the 'author' has used this genre of stories to undermine itself.[19]

It might also be added in support of Mahdi's thesis that, if one takes the first 270 to 280 nights as a unit (that is to say, the stories found in the Galland manuscript), it is possible to detect the recurrence of certain common devices and images in them. The crucial device is, of course, the framing one of a person talking to save a life. Sheherazade does it. So do the sheikhs who tell stories to a jinn (or genie) in order to save the merchant's life, and so do the guests in the house of the three ladies of Baghdad, and so do those who are arrested after the death of the hunchback. Then there is a preoccupation with mutilation (the three one-eyed dervishes; the young men who lost their hands in 'The Christian Broker's Tale' and 'The Jewish Physician's Tale'; and the various deformed brothers of the barber). The breaking of an interdiction often sets the story in motion or keeps it moving along. Underground spaces are associated with sex and danger. The 'author' has a playful, Shandyesque tendency to promise stories which are in fact never told (for example, the allusions to the *Sindibad* cycle and to 'the story of the crocodile' in 'King Yunan and Sage Duban'). Then there are the careful enumerations of things to be shopped for, something which features at the beginning of the story of 'The Porter and the Three Ladies of Baghdad' and at the beginning of the Hunchback cycle.

However, while it is possible that even more common themes and images can be found in this small core of stories, the existence of a common author or compiler is impossible to prove. Be that as it may, Mahdi contrasts the coherence of this early group of Syrian stories with the ragbag of tales which make up ZER and of which he has written that 'copyists who missed what [the Syrian compiler] was after and thought the book was like a hole in the ground in which one could dump one story after another regardless of their styles, structures or contradictory aims, disfigured the book'.[20] In Mahdi's opinion, the old idea that the *Nights* had no original designer and that its structure had always been fluid is based on nothing more than insufficient research.

Mahdi believes that the Galland manuscript incorporates all or very nearly all of what was available in the early Mamluke period, some forty stories related over 282 nights and written down in Syria. Subsequently in Egypt more and more stories were added to meet consumer demand and perhaps to match the number of nights to the title. While Mahdi's main achievement lies in his critical edition of the Galland manuscript, he has also made some interesting discoveries along the way. Mahdi shows that the Baghdad manuscript, which would have been the sole survivor of an Iraqi tradition of transmission and was allegedly copied by the Lebanese copyist Michael Sabbagh in the early nineteenth century, was a fake. What Sabbagh actually did was put his manuscript together by copying from various Egyptian and Syrian manuscripts of the *Nights* that he found lying around in Paris. Since he was a good writer, Sabbagh added little touches of his own, and, not having an Arabic original for 'Aladdin', he translated a French version of the tale back into Arabic. His 'discovery' of this alleged Baghdad manuscript earned him money as well as some academic fame. Similarly, Mahdi has shown that another manuscript, which purported to be the old continuation and completion of the Galland manuscript, was actually a fake perpetrated by a Syrian priest called Chavis, who in fact copied an eighteenth-century Egyptian manuscript. Chavis, like Sabbagh, also seems to have translated Galland's French version of 'Aladdin' into Arabic. A similar case arises with the manuscript of 'Ali Baba', which Macdonald had discovered in the Bodleian and which was in the hand of Jean Warsy, a French pupil of de Sacy's who had settled in Egypt as a merchant in the late eighteenth century. This too has been shown to be a retranslation back into Arabic of Galland's French version of the story.

Mahdi's meticulous editing and research have led him to some interesting conclusions. However, those conclusions, particularly with regard to the stemma and archetype, raise problems and doubts. He has employed a method pioneered by classicists for the study of highly regarded works of literature written by, for the most part, known authors (such as Manilius or Lucretius). Even in the Middle Ages, European scribal copyists took trouble to produce what they hoped would be accurate texts of Latin authors by comparing one manuscript with another and by correcting what seemed to them obvious errors in the manuscripts they were copying from. The case is perhaps a little different when we turn to a medieval Arab work of popular fiction. The *Nights* cannot have been seen as a canonical text which deserved special care or demanded accurate transmission; nor was it written to be read by scholars. It is unlikely that medieval copyists of manuscripts of the *Nights* had any great reverence for the text they were transcribing. Mahdi himself has noted the evidence, provided in the marginalia of a manuscript of the *Nights* now in the British Library, of a book dealer, Ahmad al-Rabbat, who traded in Aleppo in the late eighteenth century, who used to hire out copies of collections of stories and poetry – and when these collections began to suffer from wear, al-Rabbat would insert new pages, sometimes with new stories.

There was no reason for a scribal copyist of the *Nights* to take special pains to get the Arabic right, for it was never written in immaculate classical Arabic in the first place. Nor was there any reason to hesitate in adding or deleting stories, incidents or glosses. If there was no compelling reason for scribes to treat this anonymous work of popular fiction with reverence, then there was no reason for them to consult other manuscripts in order to ensure the accuracy of their copying. Yet Mahdi has argued that the later Syrian manuscripts show signs of cross-contamination, that readings from the Egyptian tradition appear in them. But why should Syrian scribes go to this sort of trouble?

In fact, it is likely that many copies of the *Nights* were written to be read aloud, whether by professional or amateur storytellers, and it may be that the storyteller had no need of the full text (never mind an accurate one!); he needed only an outline of a story on which he could embroider. Moreover, if storytellers themselves made copies of the text, they would very likely have added favourite elaborations of their own devising to stories in their repertoire. And, of course, while the Galland manuscript is the oldest surviving one, it is not possible to prove beyond any shadow of doubt that relatively late Egyptian versions of the *Nights* were not copied from an even older version of the tales. Classical text criticism tends to produce a stemma which leads back to a single source with a single author – and this is the result that Mahdi has achieved. However, the *Nights* are really more like the New Testament, where one cannot assume a single manuscript source, nor can one posit an original fixed canon. Stories may have been added and dropped in each generation. Mahdi's stemma suggests that there were very few thirteenth-century manuscripts of the *Nights*; for, in the end, the stemma narrows down to one single manuscript source. The references in the Geniza and in al-Maqrizi's topography of Cairo suggest, however, that the work was quite well known in the eleventh and twelfth centuries. Is it conceivable, then, that only one thirteenth-century manuscript served as the basis for all subsequent copies? It certainly seems unlikely.

Mahdi argues for a Syrian origin of the 'mother' manuscript, but the Galland manuscript, though it was written in Syria, seems to show a more detailed familiarity with Cairo than with anywhere in Syria. Moreover, Mahdi's stemma depends heavily on manuscripts in European libraries – for the most part the ones collected in Egypt and Syria by European travellers. Must the (longer) Egyptian manuscripts be judged inferior just because they are later? (While on the subject of Egyptian versions, why assume that Bulaq, alone of all the printed texts, was based on a single Egyptian manuscript source?) All the manuscripts, both Syrian and Egyptian, have three old men who offer to tell amazing stories to the jinn in order to save a merchant's life. However, none of the Syrian manuscripts give the third old man's story, while manuscripts in the Egyptian tradition do. Surely this suggests that the Egyptian tradition here was based on a fuller source? If the Egyptian manuscripts were right in including a third old man's tale, perhaps they were also right in including other material. It is also noteworthy that the Syrian group of manuscripts begin the story of 'Qamar al-Zaman' but break off at the 283rd night with the story barely begun. In completing the text of 'Qamar al-Zaman' for his edition of *Alf Layla wa-Layla*, Mahdi was obliged to make use of an Egyptian manuscript in the Bodleian. (This is the Wortley Montagu manuscript, brought to England in the late eighteenth century by the so-called 'Man in the Iron Wig', Edward Wortley Montagu, a notorious charlatan, necromancer and Arabist.)[21]

Although Mahdi's stemma suggests that everything comes from a single thirteenth- or early-fourteenth-century Syrian manuscript, it would appear that there was at least one other early Syrian version of the manuscript which was longer than the Galland manuscript and was available for Richardson to use when he prepared his Arabic grammar. Then again, can Mahdi be right in supposing that the Galland manuscript dates from the fourteenth century, and can the (now lost) source copy of the Galland manuscript be dated back to as early as the thirteenth century?[22] Most of the internal evidence suggests otherwise. It is true that a thirteenth-century dating might be suggested by an incident in 'The Barber's Tale', in which the barber uses his astrolabe to set up a horoscope in the Muslim year 653, that is, AD 1255.[23] However, notwithstanding this (and discounting Zotenberg's and Mahdi's impression of the date of the manuscript hand), other references in the Galland manuscript suggest that it cannot have been written any earlier than the fifteenth century. The Christian broker meets someone in Cairo at the Caravanserai of al-Jawli, which was founded only in the early fourteenth century.[24] In 'The Jewish Physician's Tale' there is reference to a large house in Damascus, known as the house of Sudun Abd al-Rahman. If this is a misrendering of Sudun min Abd al-Rahman, then the reference is to Sayf al-Din Sudun min Abd al-Rahman, who became Governor of Damascus in 1424 and died in 1438.[25] Finally, and most conclusively, in 'The Jewish Physician's Tale', a payment is made in the Ashrafi dinar, a coin which was first put in circulation in 1425 during the reign of the Sultan al-Ashraf Barsbay.[26]

From all the above, it must be apparent that complex problems remain to be resolved. There is still a great deal of work to be done. In particular, a number of manuscripts in Middle Eastern libraries need to be looked at. It would be useful if an edited version of the ZER recension could be produced (though that would certainly be a difficult and time-consuming task). It is also desirable that more research should be done on individual stories or story cycles, tracing their history prior to their incorporation in the corpus of the *Nights* and comparing their renderings in parallel and rival story collections. It is possible also that research into the history of Ottoman Turkish and Balkan popular fiction may produce interesting results. We have already had occasion to refer to Ali al-Effendi's story collection and his belief that the *Nights* were written by al-Asma'i. There seems also to be evidence that, by the seventeenth century at least, there was a version of the *Nights* in Romanian. The Romanian version had been translated from Greek and the Greek from Syriac, and the Syriac version was allegedly based on an Arabic translation made from Persian by Musa ibn Isa al-Kasrawi, a ninth-century scribe.[27]

Evidently, the issues raised in dating an anonymous, slowly evolving, composite work like the *Nights* are complex. The answer to the question how old is *The Thousand and One Nights* will depend, among many other things, on what one counts as the first version of the *Nights*. Should it be the Persian prototype, the *Hazar Afsaneh*? Or the ninth-century *Thousand Nights*, of which a few scrappy lines survive? Or *The Thousand and One Nights*, referred to in the twelfth century, but of which not even a few scrappy lines survive? Or the purely hypothetical thirteenth-century Syrian source manuscript? Or the Galland manuscript, which was written in either the fourteenth or the fifteenth century? Or the fuller versions of the *Nights*, translated by Lane and Burton, which were filled out with all sorts of ancient and recent stories (including 'Sinbad', 'The Ebony Horse', 'Ali Baba' and the rest) some time between the fifteenth and the early nineteenth centuries?

3

Oceans of Stories

====

Very deep is the well of the past. Should we not call it bottomless?

Thomas Mann, *Tales of Jacob*

Two rogues, pretending to be traders, attached themselves to a journeying merchant, having agreed to rob him of everything he had. However, each of the thieves had privately decided that he wanted all the spoils for himself, so each poisoned the other's food. Thus they perished, and the merchant proceeded on his way unharmed. This is how the tale features as 'The Merchant and the Two Sharpers' in the *Nights*. A more elaborate and more satisfyingly structured version of essentially the same story appears in *The Canterbury Tales* as 'The Pardoner's Tale', in which three rioters set out to find Death, who has killed the fourth man in their company. A mysterious old man tells them that they will find Death under a certain tree. But, instead of Death, they find treasure under the tree. Each man then plots to kill his fellows. The story ends with their success and the death of all three of them. An earlier and simpler version of this story-type is found in the ancient Indian story collection known as the *Jataka*. A more recent reworking can be found in John Huston's film *The Treasure of the Sierra Madre* (1947).[1]

A man approached an aged bawd and asked her to arrange an assignation with a woman in the town. The bawd had a certain woman in mind, but the trouble was that this woman was a virtuous wife. So the bawd devised a stratagem. She made cakes full of pepper and fed them to a bitch puppy, so that the dog's eyes were scalded with tears. Then the bawd took the bitch along with her when she went to visit the virtuous woman. When the woman asked why the dog was weeping, the bawd told her that this was a woman who had been transformed by sorcery into a dog for refusing the advances of a young man and so the dog wept as she remembered her previous state and the pleasures that she had so foolishly refused. In this way the hitherto virtuous wife was persuaded to let the bawd make an assignation for her with the man. When the hour of the assignation came, the wife's horror was great to discover that the man she had been brought face to face with was her own husband. But she kept her presence of mind and swiftly started abusing him, claiming that she had set this trap to test him and teach him a lesson. The husband promised to mend his ways and keep faithful to his wife thereafter. This story, which really consists of two linked story elements, the weeping puppy trick and the wife's quick-thinking stratagem, is found in the *Nights* as 'The Tale of the Woman who Wanted to Deceive her Husband', one of the *Sindibad* cycle of tales. But both halves of essentially the same tale are found elsewhere: in the eleventh-century Sanskrit *Katha Sarit Sagara*, in the twelfth-century Latin *Disciplina clericalis*, in the Middle English fabliau, or short tale in verse, of 'Dame Sirith', in the fourteenth-century Persian *Tutinameh* by al-Nakhshabi, in the fourteenth-century *Decameron* by Boccaccio, and in Thomas Mann's twentieth-century novel *Doctor Faustus*.[2]

Similar exercises can be performed on many other tales in the *Nights*. For example, the Ebony Horse in the *Nights* is unmistakably the same horse as the one featured in Chaucer's 'The Squire's Tale'. The same horse takes to the air again in the North African *One Hundred and One Nights*, in the thirteenth-century French romance of *Cleomades* and in the *Katha Sarit Sagara*.[3] Indeed, there is scarcely a tale in the whole of the *Nights* which does not have its precursors, derivatives or analogous versions. Tales evolve into other tales and they replicate, elaborate, invert, abridge, link and comment on their own structure in an endless play of transformation – but was there ever the first version of any story? It is almost always impossible to tell when a story was first told and when it was first written down, or how it was transmitted, and impossible too to say what the last telling and final version of a story will be. Good stories pay little attention to cultural or linguistic frontiers. The student of story collections finds himself adrift on an ocean of stories, an ocean which is boundless, deep and ceaselessly in motion.

What follows is a brief, all too brief, survey of those story collections which are *not* the *Nights* – as it were, the presentation of a jigsaw puzzle with its central piece missing. However, every one of the story collections to be discussed stands in some relation or another to the *Nights*, and the Arab collection can be better understood when it is placed in a global setting and compared with its Sanskrit, Greek, Latin and other rivals.

To begin where some scholars believe all great stories began, in India,[4] the *Jataka* is a Pali collection of 547 fables, stories, romances, maxims and legends that purportedly relate to previous incarnations of the Buddha. It is not known when this anthology was compiled. While it survives in a fifth-century version in Pali, it is probably much older. The tales are for the most part moral tales with an ethical purpose. 'The Tale of the Bull and the Ass' and the linked 'Tale of the Merchant and his Wife', in which a man knows the language of the beasts and takes warning from their conversation not to reveal the secret of his knowledge, are found in the *Jataka* and in the frame story of the *Nights*. (The vizier tells these stories to his daughter, Sheherazade, in the misguided belief that it will deter her from offering to become Shahriyar's next bride.) The same story, or one or other of its halves, is also found in the Sanskrit *Vetalapanchavinsati* and in the medieval Latin *Gesta Romanorum*, as well as in Estonian and Javanese folklore. Similarly, others of the *Jataka*'s tales can be found both in later Sanskrit story collections, like the *Panchatantra*, and in western collections like Aesop's *Fables*.

The *Panchatantra*, or 'Five Books', composed in Sanskrit no later than the sixth century, is a collection of stories in which the framing device is that of a wise brahmin who instructs three young princes in the wisdom that they must learn if they are ever to rule well.[5] It belongs, then, to the genre of 'mirrors for princes'. However, it is clear that the stories were aimed at a wider audience than one just composed of princes; and though, as in the case of the *Jataka*, it is claimed that the stories have been strung together for a moral purpose, it is clear that these were at least as often read for entertainment as for edification. The stories are concerned with losing and gaining friends, with war and peace, with the loss or gain of property and, finally, with ill-considered action. Animals form the cast of these stories – the lion who is the ruler, the two jackals who are his good and bad advisers, the stupid monkey, and so forth. The *Panchatantra* was a popular story cycle and it travelled far. In the sixth century it was translated into Pahlavi (Old Persian) as *The Fables of Bidpai*. In the eighth century Ibn al-Muqaffa translated it into Arabic as *Kalila wa-Dimna* (the title referring to the names of the two jackal viziers). From Arabic it was translated into Syriac, Hebrew and, ultimately, most of the European languages.

The stories of the *Panchatantra* were eventually incorporated in the *Katha Sarit Sagara*. This much grander compilation was translated from the Sanskrit into English by C.H. Tawney (published in 1880–84), and more accessibly republished by Norman Penzer under the title of *The Ocean of Story* (1928), and in this English version it runs to ten fat volumes.[6] It is perhaps because this extraordinary work was translated later than the *Nights* that it has found less fame in the West than the Arab stories. The Sanskrit collection of moral, humorous and horrific tales was originally compiled by Somadeva, a Kashmiri court poet, in the eleventh century. Bulky though the collection is, it seems that it is only the abridgement of a yet bulkier work, the *Brihat-Katha*, or 'Great Tale', by Gunadhya, which was put together some time before the seventh century but has since been lost. Taken as a whole, one of the most obvious features of the *Katha Sarit Sagara* is its misogyny. 'Woman has fickleness implanted in her by Nature like the flashings of lightning': murderous women, faithless women and shrewish women proliferate in its pages. (However, this is a general, almost invariable, feature of pre-modern story collections and their frame stories in particular. Why this should be so deserves further investigation.)

As the medieval Dutch proverb has it, 'Big fish eat little fish.' Individual stories are swallowed up in story collections, and these story collections in turn are swallowed up in yet larger collections of story collections. Besides the moral fables of the *Panchatantra*, the *Katha Sarit Sagara* also contains within it the *Vetalapanchavinsati*, or 'Twenty-Five Tales of a Vampire'.[7] A *vetala* is an evil spirit that haunts cemeteries. In this story collection within a story collection, the somewhat curious framing device is the story of a king who owes a beggar a favour. He agrees to fetch a corpse for the beggar. The corpse is hanging from a tree in a cemetery. As the king approaches the corpse, it emits a sinister laugh, for it is inhabited by a *vetala*, or vampire. The vampire-ridden corpse settles on the king's shoulder, and the vampire, knowing that the beggar plans to kill the king when he arrives, keeps telling the king stories with the aim of delaying his progress. Finally the vampire advises the king on how to outwit the sinister beggar. A version of some of these stories was translated from Hindu by Burton under the title *Vikram and the Vampire: or Tales of Hindu Devilry* (1870). Again – and this may have appealed to Burton – the misogynistic tenor of the tales is striking. This story collection contains the tale about the merchant who knew the language of animals, which eventually ended up in the frame story of the *Nights*. What is essentially an early form of the *Nights* tale of 'The King who Kenned the Quintessence of Things' is also found in this vampire's repertoire.

The *Sukasaptati*, or 'The Seventy Tales of the Parrot', was put together in India no later than the twelfth century. A parrot, by telling a string of stories, prevents a woman from committing adultery. Although the parrot is telling stories to preserve the wife's virtue, a large number of the tales it tells are of cunning, faithless women. This parrot collection reached the Middle East via a fourteenth-century translation from Sanskrit into Persian by al-Nakhshabi (d. 1350) entitled the *Tutinameh*.

The idea that the ultimate ancestor of the *Nights* was an Indian story collection has a long history. As we have seen, von Hammer-Purgstall argued that the *Hazar Afsaneh*, the presumed Persian original of the core of the earliest version of the *Nights*, was itself a translation or an adaptation of an Indian original. In the course of the nineteenth century the quest for the eastern, and usually Indian, origins of western culture continued to be an obsession in certain scholarly circles. Diffusionism – the notion that aspects of culture start from a single source and spread from there to other civilizations – was the fashion, and the theory tended to discount the possibility that things could be independently invented in several civilizations. The study of the history of language and of Sanskrit philology, of which Max Müller (1823–1900) was perhaps the most distinguished practitioner, provided a paradigm in which India was the fountain of culture. Theodor Benfey (1809–81), similarly a German Sanskrit scholar philologist, argued in the introduction to his translation of the *Panchatantra* (1859) that 'a great number of *Märchen* and other folk-tales have spread out from India over almost the entire world'. He went on to suggest that, prior to the tenth century, such stories were usually transmitted orally (although he believed the tales of the *Panchatantra* to be a rare exception). Thereafter, however, stories were commonly transmitted from India to Europe, via Persian and Arabic, in written texts. Benfey also believed that some Indian story collections reached the Mongols via Tibet and that the Mongols brought some of those stories to Europe in the thirteenth and fourteenth centuries. It seemed that stories, like the sun, always travelled in a westward direction. Since the stories of the

Panchatantra had been transmitted from Sanskrit to Persian, then to Syriac and Arabic and then to various European languages, Benfey believed that the same applied to the other stories that students of literature and folklore had found to be common to Europe and India. Benfey and his disciples also argued that the idea of framing stories within stories to provide a pretext for their telling was peculiarly Indian.

As far as the history of the study of the *Nights* is concerned, Emmanuel Cosquin (1841–1921) was the most important of Benfey's disciples, though he was not uncritical and he rejected the idea of the Mongols as the medieval bearers of Indian folk-tales to Europe. Also Cosquin did not believe in the Indian origin of almost everything. He preferred to think of the subcontinent, not as a fountain, but rather as a reservoir, a place which both supplied and received stories. However, Cosquin did believe in the Indian origin of the *Nights*. In 'Le Prologue-cadre des *Mille et une nuits*, les légendes perses et le Livre d'Esther' (*Revue biblique*, 1909), Cosquin first argued against the theory of a Persian origin for the frame story of the *Nights*, and against the idea that a lost ancient Persian tale had also been reworked in the biblical Book of Esther (in which Esther becomes the bride of King Ahasuerus and saves the Jews). Secondly and more importantly, Cosquin attempted to show that the frame story of the *Nights* derived from the reworking and stringing together of older Indian stories.[8] At least three elements from Indian sources were used in this manner: first the king who despairs of the possibility of woman's fidelity; secondly the woman who is guarded by a supernatural being in order to keep her faithful but who nevertheless eludes his guard to sleep with men; and thirdly the tireless telling of stories in order to delay an evil. The first two of these motifs were found in a Chinese Buddhist text of about AD 250, the *Kieou Tsa P'iyu King* of Seng-Houei, which Cosquin believed to have been translated from the Sanskrit. That text has the story of a prince who is unhappy because of the evil conduct of his mother; he is cheered up when he finds a brahmin magician who keeps his wife sealed in a pot which he can swallow or spit out at will; but the magician does not know that, when he sleeps, his wife, who has similar magical powers, can spit out a pot in which she keeps her secret lover. The affinity between this tale and the adventures of King Shahriyar is evident. As for the storytelling of Sheherazade, this had its precedent in the Jain legend of Kanakamanjari, who keeps the love of her king for six months by telling stories every night which have to be concluded on a following night.

Cosquin presumed that the Chinese story of Seng-Houei was based on a lost Sanskrit original, but there is no evidence for this. As Professor B.E. Perry has pointed out, the Chinese might just as well have taken it from an ancient Persian story, one which was later recycled in the *Hazar Afsaneh*.[9] The transformation of men and women in the *Nights* into animals has been held to be an indication of an Indian origin, a reminiscence of Buddhist and Hindu ideas on reincarnation. However, this motif is pervasive in the world's folklore, and such a basic fantasy as the transformation of a man into an animal does not need to have a single point of invention. After all, it even features in the myths of the North American Indians. When in the *Nights*, in 'The Second Dervish's Tale', the prince is transformed into a monkey, but a monkey who can write, the point of derivation may well be a reminiscence not of anything Hindu or Buddhist, but rather of the ape's form of the ancient Egyptian god of the scribes, Thoth. The theme of a man magically transformed into an animal is also at the heart of Apuleius' Latin novel *The Golden Ass*. One might refer also to Ovid's *Metamorphoses*, which, as its title suggests, is concerned with little else but the possibilities of shape-shifting. Moreover, going further back, when, in the Greek *Odyssey*, Circe transforms Odysseus' companions into beasts, must we look for some ancient Sanskrit model of inspiration?

India was in any case not the only possible source from which the Arabs could have derived the device of the framing story, for the frame story was also a familiar device in the western world. The insertion of smaller stories within the framework of a larger story is a basic technique. In the *Odyssey*, Homer has Odysseus telling tales at the court of King Alcinous, and Ovid's *Metamorphoses* also makes much play with stories within stories. Nor can Indian storytellers claim a monopoly on misogyny. Early Christian storytellers were also fond of tales with this theme. Since even Benfey thought that animal fables, of the Aesopic kind, originated in the West, in Greece, a western origin for other sorts of stories is also possible.

Here and there throughout the *Nights*, one comes across what seem to be survivals of stories and images from the literature of ancient Greece and Rome. Galland was the first to consider this question and he noticed that Sinbad's encounter, on his third voyage, with a giant, whom he blinds before making his escape, was an echo of the incident in the *Iliad* in which Odysseus encountered Polyphemus. Similarly, Galland found a reworking of Circe's enchantment of Odysseus' companions in the *Nights* story of 'Julnar the Sea-Born and her Son King Badr Basim', in which the sorceress Queen Lab uses a drug to transform her former lovers into birds. (The ninth-century translator, Hunayn ibn Ishaq, was able to recite sections of Homer by heart, presumably in Greek, yet he never translated him into Arabic. Although there are indications in the *Nights* and in the writings of al-Biruni, al-Shahrastani and others that the contents of Homer's epics were known to some, Homer was only a name to the cataloguer Ibn al-Nadim, and neither the *Iliad* nor the *Odyssey* was translated into Arabic until the present century.)[10]

Julnar the Sea-Born herself may owe something to Thetis, the sea deity and mother of Achilles. 'The Cranes of Ibycus' (the story of how a Greek poet of the sixth century BC was murdered and avenged) is recycled as 'The Sixteenth Constable's Story' in the cycle of tales told by Sultan Baybars's policemen. A prototype of the *rukh* (a huge mythical bird reputed to be able to carry a man through the skies) in 'The Voyages of Sinbad' may be found in Lucian's *True History* (second century AD). Images and incidents from *The Romance of Alexander* by Pseudo-Callisthenes crop up in a wide range of romances and adventures that were incorporated in the *Nights*.

In the third or second century BC, the Roman playwright Plautus wrote *Miles gloriosus*, or 'The Braggart Soldier', a play about two lovers in adjoining houses who make use of a hole in a common wall to meet. The resemblances of this story to the *Nights* story of 'Qamar al-Zaman and the Jeweller's Wife' are much too close for coincidence, and Gustave von Grunebaum argues that both the Roman play and the Arab story go back to an older Greek source. However, it may well be that an Arab author worked on a version of Plautus' play, transmitted via Greek and Syriac, and turned it into a story; and it is possible that more links between the dramatic tradition of classical antiquity and collections of stories in Arabic remain to be discovered. As we shall see in a later chapter, there is a certain family resemblance between the themes of plays acted out by classical mimes and the subject-matter of some of the stories of the *Nights*.

One could go on and on listing particular instances of potential Greek and Roman prototypes for the plot structures, themes and motifs of the later Arab stories.[11] Instead, one intriguing possibility should be considered. In the tenth-century *Fihrist*, or 'Catalogue', of the Iraqi bookseller Ibn al-Nadim, under the general heading 'The Names of the Books of the Byzantines about Evening Stories, Histories, Fables and Proverbs' is included a book called *Shatariyus the King and the Reason for his Marrying Shazad the Storyteller*.[12] What follows from this unique reference is that the frame story of King Shahriyar and Sheherazade the storyteller may be of Greek origin. While this is possible, it does not seem particularly likely. Even so, the alleged existence of a tenth-century, or earlier, Byzantine Greek version of the story is intriguing and it makes one wonder if a version of the *Nights* was not transmitted, via the Greek, to the various Balkan languages. Some at least of the *Nights* stories seem to have been known in Romania prior to Galland's translation of them.[13] Although it is improbable that the frame story of Sheherazade had a Byzantine origin, nevertheless, many of the romantic tales in the *Nights*, such as 'Uns al-Wujud and the Vizier's Daughter Rose-in-Hood', show signs of having borrowed from the conventions of Byzantine romance.

Of course, large areas of classical Greek and Latin literature were not imitated or reworked in the literature of the Arabs, and the works of Euripides, Aeschylus, Petronius and Marcus Aurelius have left, I think, no traces in the later literature of the Middle East. The question of why once popular stories or even whole genres of literature may fail and die out is an interesting one. For example, wisdom literature and fables were taken by the Arabs from their Hebrew, Greek, Roman and, above all, Persian precursors, and in turn medieval Christendom took much of that material from the Arabs. However, there is no market for such stuff now. La Fontaine and his seventeenth-century fables came very near the end of a line. While *The Seven Voyages of Sinbad* has survived to the present day and (even if in a highly mutated form) has made the leap on to celluloid, the once popular and highly improving discourse of the slave girl Tawaddud has been forgotten by all, save specialist scholars. We shall return to the survival of stories and the reason for their survival in the next chapter.

The Arabs became heirs by conquest not only to the storytelling lore of Greece and Rome, but also to that of the Copts, Hebrews, Berbers and Persians. Primitive prefigurations of some of the stories of the *Nights* have been found in the literature of Pharaonic Egypt, and it seems likely that some of those stories or parts of stories reached the Arabs via the folklore of the Coptic Christian inhabitants of Egypt. For example, the germ of 'The Tale of the Envious and the Envied' (narrated in the *Nights* by the second dervish to the wrathful jinn) is found in the ancient Egyptian story of 'The Blinding of Truth by Falsehood', which in its written form appears in the thirteenth century BC. Then again, the Twelfth Dynasty papyrus of 'The Tale of the Shipwrecked Man' anticipates some of the themes of *The Seven Voyages of Sinbad*. When Crafty Dalilah, in the *Nights*, gets a gang of her rivals drunk so that she may commit a theft, and then marks the success of her enterprise by shaving the right cheeks of the sleeping drunks, she repeats actions which Herodotus in his *Histories* ascribes to a thief in the reign of the Pharaoh Rhampsinitis (Rameses III). Finally, while on the topic of ancient Egyptian fiction, those who believe that only the Indians could have invented the frame story should consult *The Magical Stories Told to King Cheops* (the Westcar Papyrus, written between the eighteenth and sixteenth centuries BC) in which the king asks his sons for stories about the wonders worked by magicians.[14]

Other ancient civilizations of the Near East also made their contributions to the *Nights*. Most strikingly, there are many obvious echoes in 'The Adventures of Bulukiyya' (which is the tale of the quest of a pre-Islamic king for immortality) from the Babylonian *Epic of Gilgamesh* as it is known to us in a version of the first millennium BC.[15] Similarly, the Sumerian tale of 'The Poor Man of Nippur', in which a man who has been insulted avenges himself with three ingenious pranks, was passed on for over two millennia in a multitude of tongues and scripts to resurface in Arabic in the *Nights* as 'The Tale of the First Larrikin'.[16] It is also worth noting that 'The Say of Haykar the Sage', which Burton included in his *Nights* – though it really belongs to the *Nights* Apocrypha, since it comes from the manuscript put together by Chavis – is a medieval Arab version of the ancient Assyrian *Book of Ahigar*.[17]

The contribution of the pre-Islamic literature of Persia to the story lore of the medieval Arabs is both more obvious and more pervasive than the legacies of the ancient Semitic civilizations and of classical antiquity. Stories, fables and wisdom literature were much appreciated under the Parthians and the Sassanians, and it is unfortunate that (possibly because of the switch to Arabic script after the seventh-century Islamic conquest) relatively little has survived of early Persian fiction in its original form. The *Hazar Afsaneh*, or 'Thousand Stories', the presumed Persian prototype of the *Nights*, has already been discussed in the previous chapter. Ibn al-Nadim reported that that book was alleged to have been composed for Humai, daughter of King Bahram (a legendary ancient king of Persia). According to al-Mas'udi, Sheherazade was the mother of Bahram. The bookseller and cataloguer Ibn al-Nadim and the historian al-Mas'udi were always inclined to ascribe a Persian or an Indian origin to works of fiction. Often they were right to do so. However, in the case of the important *Sindibadnama* cycle of stories, al-Mas'udi's belief that they had an Indian origin led nineteenth-century scholars headed by Benfey to look in the wrong direction.

The *Sindibadnama*, or 'The Craft and Malice of Women', no longer survives in the pre-Islamic Persian version, and the oldest surviving manuscript is in Syriac.[18] From Syriac it passed into Hebrew and a wide variety of European languages. It was also translated into Arabic and incorporated into the *Nights*. In this compendium of moralizing tales (which have nothing to do with the cycle of stories concerning Sinbad the Sailor) the framing device is that of seven viziers who tell stories to a king in order to dissuade him from killing his son, Sindibad, on the insistence of his wicked wife. Meanwhile the son has to keep silent in the face of all accusations for seven days. The wicked stepmother who denounces the prince has a precedent in the ancient Buddhist *Jataka*. However, Professor Perry, an expert on ancient story collections, has discounted al-Mas'udi's vague claim that the collection had an Indian origin and has argued instead for a western origin in the Latin legend of Secundus the Silent.

Secundus the Silent is said to have been a philosopher living in the reign of the Emperor Hadrian. Having heard someone remark that there is no such thing as a faithful woman, he decided to test the truth of this statement by attempting to sleep with his mother. She, failing to recognize him after his many years' absence, proved ready enough to go to bed with him, but then he backed off. Since she pressed him hard for an explanation, he told her, whereupon she hanged herself. Horrified by the mischief his words had wrought, Secundus thereupon took an oath of silence. When asked by the Emperor Hadrian to answer some philosophic questions, Secundus refused, even though he was unaware that the emperor had secretly resolved to excute him if he broke his vow of silence. Secundus' silence saved him, and he was eventually able to answer the emperor's knotty questions in writing. This legend, with its message about the evils of fleshly pleasure and its stress on the virtue of silence, seems indeed to come from an authentic Pythagorean tradition. As a frame story, in various later and distorted forms, it was much imitated in Persian literature and then in Arab literature, so that the misogyny of the Pythagoreans came to mingle with that of the ancient Buddhists and Hindus in the Arabian tales of the *Nights*.

Another Persian story collection incorporated in the *Nights* is 'King Jali'ad of Hind and his Wazir Shimas', a cycle of stories with a frame story which loosely imitates that of the *Sindibadnama*. In the Jali'ad cycle, the king's viziers tell stories against a hostile woman, in order to preserve the life of the son of the sage Shimas.[19] As with the *Sindibadnama*, the original Persian version no longer survives. Again somewhat similar is the seventh-century Persian *Bakhtiyarnama*, which, since an Arabic version is included in the Breslau text, appears in the first of the supplementary volumes of Burton's translation of the *Nights* as 'The Ten Wazirs: or the History of King Azadbakht and his Son'. In this collection it is the viziers who are the villains, and Prince Bakhtiyar has to tell stories to save his life against the ten viziers, until a robber chief arrives with proof that Bakhtiyar is truly the king's son.

Mention has been made here of only a handful of Persian collections of stories which happened to be translated into Arabic and ended up in the *Nights*. The range of Persian storytelling was much wider than this, and it is tempting to explore and explain the plots of the *Marzubannama,* the *Haft Paykar* and the old Pahlavi romance of Vis and Rahmin (which may have furnished the original template for the European romance of Tristan and Isolde). But to do so would be to turn what should be a short and selective chapter into an ocean of summaries and theories. One can wander for ever, if one wishes, adrift on this sea of ancient stories, looking for Berber, Georgian, Syriac, Armenian, Turkish and Malay prototypes, analogues and derivations for one or other of the Arabian tales of the *Nights*. But it may be that a great weariness will come upon one, and then there is the temptation to ask, did the Arabs never invent a story? It is true that the Arabs were heavily indebted to their precursors and neighbours for their stories, but that is a universal cultural characteristic; and, as we shall see shortly, European literature, with its individual geniuses (among them Dante, Boccaccio and Chaucer), was in turn heavily indebted to the anonymous storytellers of the Arab world. The Arabs originated and exported at least as much story lore as they imported, and the Christians took their stories while often removing from them all their specifically Islamic features.

Evidently it is difficult, and usually it is impossible, to trace individual stories or collections of anonymous stories decisively to some single originating place or time. Attempts by folklorists to establish the rules by which stories migrate have not been successful. Much of their difficulty stems from the fact that, while they are dedicated to studying stories which were, more often than not, carried across the world by gypsies, sailors and merchants in oral versions, they nevertheless are reduced to studying the track of the migrating stories on the basis of the potentially very misleading evidence of surviving written versions. It has therefore been the argument of this chapter so far that there are no conclusive grounds for thinking that either the frame story of Sheherazade and Shahriyar or the original core of stories contained within that frame originated in India, and were then transmitted to the West via Persia; for India received stories as well as transmitted them.

It is also true, of course, that similar circumstances will give rise to similar stories. Certain basic plots will frequently occur to fiction-makers. Thus, essentially the same story may be created quite independently in different parts of the world (polygenesis). If sometimes the oldest surviving written version of a story is found in India or China, this does not necessarily mean that the story began life in the East. It is well to remember that the manufacture of paper was introduced to the Middle East from China in the ninth century, and its use seems to have become widespread only in the tenth century. As paper became more widely available, there was (or, at least, appears to have been, on the basis of what has survived) a corresponding explosion in the production of written collections of stories and other works of fiction in Arabic.

Writing some time in the 1950s, John Walsh, a lecturer in Turkish at the University of Edinburgh, observed that a 'society which does not paint pictures or carve images does not invent stories, and so the folk-tales and romances of Islam are all either pre-Islamic or borrowed from other peoples, and, like the looted portraits and statues, defaced of their specifically human features'.[20] Such crass orientalist theorizing betrays an ignorance of the achievements of Islamic art, which is only balanced by a corresponding unfamiliarity with the characteristics of Islamic literature. Admittedly, medieval Arab story collections plundered freely from Sanskrit and Persian precursors (and that is indeed one of the main themes of this chapter). But the transmission of folk-tales and similar materials across cultures is a global feature; and, as we shall see, European literature plundered Arab literature at least as ruthlessly as Arab writers had ransacked the writings of their neighbours.

Although the translation of works from other languages began under the Umayyad caliphs, Ibn al-Muqaffa, killed during the reign of the Abbasid Caliph al-Mansur (754–75), may have been the first to translate a work of fiction (the Persian version of *Kalila wa-Dimna*) into Arabic. Subsequently, the translation movement gathered momentum under the Caliph al-Mamun (reigned 813–17).[21] Al-Mamun, the son of Harun al-Rashid, founded the Bayt al-Hikma, or House of Wisdom. One of the main activities of that research-institute-cum-library was to translate books from Greek, Indian, Persian and other languages. However, the works given priority by al-Mamun's team of translators dealt with mathematics, medicine, chemistry, philosophy and other subjects which were perceived as being useful. Al-Mamun and his successors do not seem to have been interested in sponsoring translations of the world's great works of fiction, and the development of an Arab literature of entertainment seems to have owed little or nothing to caliphal patronage.

As has already been suggested, Ibn al-Nadim and al-Mas'udi were keen to ascribe Indian or Persian origins to the great story collections. However, Perry has concluded that the

proliferation of story-books in the Near East in the time of the Abbasid Caliphate (750–1258 AD) was not due to the importation of materials or models from India, as is too often supposed, but to the recognition of prose fiction on its own account as a legitimate form of literature, which came about with the new Persian–Arabian culture.[22]

Arab versions of Persian books were rarely slavish translations. When Ibn al-Muqaffa translated *Kalila wa-Dimna*, he made substantial additions and amendments of his own.[23] His translation, in turn, inspired many later Arab authors to try their hands at producing collections of animal fables with moral or political messages. The prestige of *Kalila wa-Dimna* was immense, and every courtier and court functionary was expected to be familar with its stories and adages. Throughout the Middle Ages it was widely recognized as one of the two great works of fiction in Arabic.

The second great work was undoubtedly the *Maqamat*, or

'Sessions', by al-Hariri (1054–1122). Al-Hariri's work was inspired by and loosely modelled on a similar work with the same title by al-Hamadhani, 'the Wonder of the Age' (968–1008).[24] Al-Hamadhani's *Maqamat* was probably the first entirely original work of prose fiction in Arabic (as opposed to an adaptation from another language), but, despite its great success with al-Hamadhani's contemporaries, its fame was to be eclipsed by al-Hariri's more elaborate and finished specimen of the genre. The *Maqamat* genre embraces episodic anecdotal works of fiction, written in rhymed prose, in which the sessions, or episodes, furnish pretexts for the display of wit and eloquence. In the case of al-Hariri's *Maqamat*, the protagonist is Abu Zayd, a wily, scrounging, hard-drinking rogue who makes his living by the swiftness of his wits and the fluency of his tongue. The fifty sessions in which Abu Zayd features are set-pieces of rhetorical eloquence and special pleading. As R.A. Nicholson put it in *A Literary History of the Arabs*, Abu Zayd offers his audience 'excellent discourses, edifying sermons, and plaintive lamentations mingled with rollicking ditties and ribald jests'.[25] As we shall see, the trickster enjoyed a high status in the culture of the medieval Arabs. Abu Zayd has much in common with the wily beggars, thieves, prostitutes and religious charlatans which fill the pages of other works of Arabic fiction, but his chief claim to distinction is that he is, before anything else, a grammatical trickster and master of linguistic artifice, making use of metaphors, puns, parallelisms, alliterations and *hapax legomena* to talk himself out of scrapes. Al-Hariri's work was the model for those who thought that high literature should be allusively obscure and complex.

Kalila wa-Dimna and the *Maqamat* were the two prose classics that every civilized Arab might be expected to have read. If a civilized Arab happened to have read the *Nights*, he probably kept quiet about it, since the vulgarity of that work's subject-matter, and even more the vulgarity of its style, rendered it unworthy of serious consideration.

Yet if the *Nights* was not regarded as a work of literature, neither in a sense were its more sophisticated rivals, for there was no word for 'literature' in medieval Arabic. The modern word for it, *adab*, is also used to refer in the more restricted sense to *belles-lettres*. But in the Middle Ages, *adab* referred neither to literature in general nor to *belles-lettres* in particular. It originally meant mental discipline, etiquette, polite accomplishments. In time and by extension, *adab* came to be applied to the literary and conversational culture of a gentleman and especially to the intellectual repertoire of the *nudama*, or cup-companions of the princes. Court scribes were also expected to have mastered an *adab* which encompassed, among other things, a knowledge of protocol, history, geography, poetry, proverbs, good jokes and entertaining stories.[26] However, although a knowledge of stories might form part of a courtier's *adab*, fiction had in general a very low status in the medieval Arab world. Stories, such as those found in the *Nights*, were classified as *khurafa*, lies or fantasies, tales fit for women and children, and only suitable for telling in the evenings when serious work had been done. Ibn al-Nadim gives a list of such stories of which nothing more was known than their names, including such intriguing titles as 'The Foot Bone of a Giant Lizard', 'Lover of the Cow' and 'Bird Droppings'. Ibn al-Nadim was generally contemptuous of prose fiction, regarding it as 'cold'.[27] He shared the common Arab prejudice in favour of poetry. Poetry was the most noble and challenging of literary forms and the one that attracted the most ambitious, sophisticated and enterprising practitioners.

The *Nights*, being full of *khurafa* and for the most part written in a fairly simple prose which was littered with colloquialisms, had a low status in medieval Arabic literature. It is almost certain that only the accident of its early translation into French and its finding favour with eighteenth-century European taste rescued this particular story collection from obscurity and possible oblivion. (Even today, with the exception of certain writers and academics, the *Nights* is regarded with disdain in the Arab world. Its stories are still regularly denounced as vulgar, improbable, childish and, above all, badly written.) However, despite the low status of the *Nights*, the story collection had several rivals in the Abbasid period.

As has been noted in Chapter 2, Ibn al-Nadim relates that a certain Muhammad ibn Abdus al-Jahshiyari (d. 942), a distinguished writer on politics and a vizier's aide, otherwise best known for his biographical dictionary of viziers,

began the compiling of a book in which he was to select a thousand tales from the stories of the Arabs, Persians, Greeks and others. Each section (story) was separate, not connected with any other. He summoned to his presence the storytellers (*musamirun*, literally the evening folk, or people who tell stories in the evening), from whom he obtained the best things about which they knew and what they did well. He also selected what pleased him from the books composed of stories and fables. As he was of a superior type, there were collected for him four hundred and eighty nights, each night being a complete story, comprising more or less than fifty pages. Death overtook him before he fulfilled his plan for completing a thousand stories. I saw a number of sections of this book.[28]

Alas, nothing seems to survive of al-Jahshiyari's mighty compilation, though some would identify it with the *Hikayat al-Ajiba wa'l-Akhbar al-Ghariba*, or 'Tales of the Marvellous and News of the Strange'.[29] This anonymous work survives in Istanbul in a single manuscript copy probably made in the fourteenth century. Although the surviving manuscript seems to be of a relatively late date, the content of the tales suggests that the collection was originally put together in Egypt some time in the tenth century. The title page lists forty-two stories, although only eighteen are still extant. Of these, several stories are common to the *Nights* collection, most notably the stories of the barber's six brothers and of 'Julnar the Sea-Born' (which appear in the Galland manuscript), as well as 'Abu Muhammad Called Lazy-Bones'. Among the tales which the *Hikayat* contains and which are not found in the *Nights*, perhaps the most striking is that of 'The Story of the Forty Girls' to be discussed later.

The *Hikayat al-Ajiba* also contains 'Su'l and Shumul', a strange story about the love of two Yemenis for one another and about how Shumul is spirited away and how Su'l travels through the Levant, seeking for her in one convent after another. Interestingly enough, this story also survives in an independent manuscript version dating from the sixteenth century. In that manuscript, the story is at first broken up into nights, with mornings overtaking Sheherazade, and her sister urging her to continue on the following evening. Evidently, the scribe intended to insert 'Su'l and Shumul' into the *Nights*, but, after the thirty-fifth page, he lost interest in this enterprise and continued the tale without breaks.[30]

Al-Tanukhi (939–94), a retired judge resident in Baghdad, was, like al-Jahshiyari, a collector of stories.[31] His most important work, *Al-Faraj ba'd al-Shidda*, or 'Relief after Distress', is a collection of stories on the theme promised by the title, and it draws on both literary and oral sources. From the ninth century onwards, books on the theme of 'joy after sorrow' came to constitute a sub-genre of Arabic literature, though al-Tanukhi's compilation is the best-known specimen of that sub-genre. These fictions of consolation deal with recovery after sickness, wealth after poverty, victory after defeat. Many of the tales in the *Nights* are on the theme of joy after sorrow (or 'all's well that ends well'), for example 'The Ruined Man who Became Rich Again through a Dream' and 'The Tale of the Envier and the Envied'. There are important comparisons to be made between *Al-Faraj ba'd al-Shidda* and the *Nights*, and it is unfortunate that the former work has not been translated. Part of one work by al-Tanukhi, the *Kitab Nishwar al-Muhadara wa-Akhbar al-Mudhakara*, has been translated into English (alas in an expurgated form) as *The Table Talk of a Mesopotamian Judge* (1922). Here again al-Tanukhi drew on oral sources, as emerges from his preface: 'It is my purpose to collect in this work such stories as are current on men's lips, and which have not hitherto been transferred from the custody of their memories to perpetuation in notebooks.' One important type of tale found in al-Tanukhi's *Table Talk*, in the *Nights* and in other story collections is the story of princely or vizieral generosity (for examples in the *Nights*, see 'Hatim of the Tribe of Tayy', 'Ma'an Son of Zaidah and the Three Girls' and 'Generous Dealing of Yahya Son of Khalid with a Man who Forged a Letter in his Name'). Many of these stories focused on the semi-legendary generosity of the Barmecide dynasty of viziers, in the service of the Abbasid caliphs. It seems that this sort of story was used by beggars to attract an audience and wheedle hand-outs from them. This sub-genre of stories therefore tended towards brevity. When Egyptian copyists and compilators set to swelling out the bulk of the *Nights*, they seem to have made liberal use of stories from al-Tanukhi's anthologies.

For reasons which are far from clear, the first wave of story collections were put together in Iraq in the ninth and tenth centuries, but then there was a renewed fashion for such anthologies in Syria and Egypt in the late Mamluke period. It is possible that in the latter period such collections of stories catered to the literary tastes of the Mamluke élite. Al-Ghuzuli (d. 1412) was a Berber who moved from North Africa to Mamluke Damascus and who wrote in Arabic.[32] His *Matali al-Budur fi Manazil al-Surur*, or 'Rising Places of Full Moons in the Places of Delights', is an *adab* treatise whose chapters are devoted to things that delight the senses, among them flowers, breezes, food, drink, parties, music, women and slave girls. One of his lengthy chapters is devoted to the *musamira*, or tales told by the night. Of the seven stories or 'nights' related in this chapter, at least four have parallel versions in the *Nights*; and elsewhere, embedded in other chapters of al-Ghuzuli's sprawling compendium, there are more tales to be found which are common to the *Nights*. Not only are the stories essentially the same, but sometimes there is a word-for-word correspondence, and it seems probable that compilers of later recensions of the *Nights* plundered al-Ghuzuli just as they had plundered al-Tanukhi.

Badr al-Din al-Ayni (1365–1451), a Turk born in Ayntab (a town in the Turkish-speaking part of Mamluke Syria), was a religious scholar and historian who found success in Cairo.[33] He became Cairo's market inspector and the court historian to a succession of sultans. Writing in both Turkish and Arabic, he was chiefly famous for his great Arabic chronicle, the *Iqd al-Juman*, but he also wrote an anthology of entertaining tales about different classes of people, the *Majmu Mushtamil ala Hikayat wa Ghayriha*.

After the sack of Damascus by the Turkish empire-builder Tamerlane in 1401, the young Ibn Arabshah (1392–1450) was taken as a captive to Tamerlane's Central Asian capital, Samarkand. Subsequently, he spent time at the court of the Ottoman Sultan Mehmed I, before returning to the Mamluke lands in the 1420s.[34] Ibn Arabshah is chiefly remembered today for his venomous life of Tamerlane (in which is embedded a tale also to be found in the *Nights*). He also translated a thirteenth-century collection of Persian beast fables, the *Marzuban-nama*. He later produced a greatly expanded and heavily reworked version of the Persian work, which he entitled *Fakihat al-Khulafa wa-Mufakihat al-Zurafa*, or 'The Caliph's Delicacies and Jests of the Refined', which, although it purports to be a 'mirror for princes', is full of entertaining tales which have no obvious educational value. The outer frame of the collection owes something to *Kalila wa-Dimna*, but, although the frame stories concern animals and birds, the stories the creatures tell are mostly about humans. Again, the *Fakihat* has stories in common with the *Nights*, among them the story of the slave who tells lies once a year and a variant of 'The Merchant and the Two Sharpers'.

Some of the stories found in the *Fakihat* are also to be found in yet another anthology of short fictions put together in Egypt during the Mamluke period, the *Mustatraf fi Kull Fann Mustazraf*. Its author, al-Ibshihi, who died some time after 1446, produced a vast rambling collection of improving stories, traditions, proverbs, fables and moralistic reflections.[35] Some of his tales are common to the *Nights*, and it is probable that he and the late Egyptian compilers of manuscripts of the *Nights* drew on a common source. Magic, marvels and adulterous liaisons featured prominently in the *Nights* and in rival story collections, but one should not lose sight of the fact that all these works contained a lot of edifying tales about virtuous deeds and holy men. Some anthologies were devoted exclusively to edifying themes. One such was *Rawd al-Riyahin fi Hikayat al-Salihin*, or 'Garden of the Breezes regarding Tales of Holy Men', by al-Yafi'i, a fourteenth-century Yemeni Sufi mystic.[36] His collection of improving and wondrous tales of the Sufis was plundered both by al-Ibshihi and by those who sought to swell up the bulk of the *Nights*.

After the end of the Mamluke period, there were few Arab writers of note in any genre until the late eighteenth century. Then al-Jabarti (d. 1825), one of the greatest Arab historians, began his masterful history of Egypt from the Ottoman conquest of 1517 until his own times. He also chronicled the French invasion of Egypt under Bonaparte in 1798. Al-Jabarti met with French scholars at their institute in Cairo. It may be that the French communicated some of their enthusiasm for the *Nights* to al-Jabarti. In any event, he later attempted to produce an expurgated version of the *Nights*. Alas, it has not survived.[37]

A curiosity, which has in the past been numbered among Arab story collections, perhaps deserves mention. This is the *Contes du Cheykh el-Mohdy* (1835), which purports to be a translation of an Arab collection of stories with the title 'The Present to the Awakened Bachelor for the Delight of the Somnolent Sleeper', by a certain Sheikh Muhammad al-Mahdi, a contemporary of al-Jabarti. This work was 'translated' by Jean-Joseph Marcel, an Arabist who accompanied Bonaparte to Egypt in 1798. The opening frame story is about a young man who keeps sending his audience to sleep with his stories. He irritates people so much that he ends up in the Cairo *maristan* or lunatic asylum, which becomes the bizarre setting for yet more storytelling. However, although there really was a Sheikh Muhammad al-Mahdi, there can be little doubt that the stories are fakes, European pastiches of the *Nights* tales; and it is all but certain that the motif of the storyteller who regularly sends his audience to sleep was plagiarized by Marcel from Cazotte's *Mille et une fadaises*.[38]

The above has been a somewhat haphazard sampling of once famous but now mostly forgotten writers of the 'Abbasid, Mamluke and Ottoman periods. However, what this fragmentary evidence suggests is that the stories contained in the *Nights* were not the exclusive property of anonymous storytellers. In many cases they were known and transmitted by scholars and belletrists of considerable distinction in anthologies which purported to do more than entertain idlers in coffee-houses. Despite the opinion generally held among educated Arabs that prose was inferior to poetry, and despite their frequently proclaimed contempt for prose fiction, it is evident that some members of the élite interested themselves in storytelling. It is possible that sometimes they took stories from the *Nights* and made use of them to convey political or religious messages. What is also apparent is that the scholars were well placed to introduce new and foreign items into the repertoire of Arab storytelling. Al-Ghuzuli was a Berber by origin, al-Ayni was a Turk, and Ibn Arabshah was a polyglot who had spent much of his life in Turkish- and Persian-speaking centres of culture. However, these writers 'wrote' their stories only in the sense of transcribing them (or at best adapting them). They did not invent stories – or, if they did, they kept quiet about it. In medieval Arab society, one did not boast of inventing stories: one claimed only to be transmitting them. (Sheherazade herself does not invent tales; she relates what she has heard. We should take it that she has been blessed with an excellent memory, rather than with a creative imagination.)

The stories edited by, say, al-Tanukhi or Ibn Arabshah would usually have been accessible only to a literate and sophisticated élite, though of course it is easy to imagine that there may sometimes have been public readings from their works. However, the taste for their works, and indeed even for the stories of the *Nights*, was eclipsed by the popularity of the great prose epics. It is clear that the latter appealed to quite unsophisticated audiences. The twelfth-century North African Jewish polygraph, Samwal ibn Yahya al-Maghribi, recorded his delight as a schoolboy in the popular epics:

At the age of between ten and thirteen, I was very much attracted by historical information and stories. I was very eager to read what happened in ancient times and to know what had taken place in past centuries. I read the different collections of stories and anecdotes. From that I transferred my predilection to the long fanciful tales, and then to the big novels, such as the stories of Antar, Dhu'l-Himmah, and al-Battal, the story of Alexander Dhu'l-Qarnayn ('the two-horned'), of al-Anqa' (the Phoenix), and Taraf ibn Ludhan, and others.[39]

Eventually, Samwal ibn Yahya moved on from these romantic pseudo-histories to the serious study of Islamic history, and, impressed by that history, he ended up by converting to Islam.

Although many of the popular folk-epics had a basis in history, that basis was invariably pretty shaky.[40] Centuries and wars were confounded in tales which tended to stray into fairyland at their topographical edges. The long rambling plots of these epics, in which crisis follows crisis, are characteristic of stories composed for serial delivery over a period of weeks and days (and have much in common with nineteenth-century European *feuilleton* literature). The straggling medieval sagas drew much of their inspiration, first, from the frontier wars with Byzantium from the mid-eighth century onwards and, secondly, from the struggle against the Crusaders from the 1090s onwards. 'The Tale of Omar bin al-Nu'uman', which started out as an independent work but eventually found its way into the *Nights*, is fairly typical of the genre. This sprawling epic (it occupies almost 250 pages in the Burton translation, not counting the stories framed within it) offers a pseudo-historical account of the seventh-century wars of the King of the Muslims and the Christian King of Constantinople against the Christian King of Caesarea. The career of the fictional hero may be very loosely based on the deeds of a historical Umar who was Emir of Malatya (a town in what is now eastern Turkey) in the ninth century, in a period of fierce frontier warfare between the Arabs and the Byzantines. Vague memories of his struggles and other Arab wars against the Byzantines were later conflated with the twelfth-to-thirteenth-century jihad against the Crusaders. The Franks feature prominently, and the villainous Jawfran is surely a distorted rendering of Godfrey – that is, Godfrey of Bouillon, one of the leaders of the First Crusade and the first of the Franks to rule over Jerusalem.

In this and similar epics, garbled and transposed reminiscences of events between the tenth and the thirteenth centuries are embedded in fantastic stories of high chivalry and sorcery. The taste for epic tales about superhuman heroes who undertake perilous journeys, fight battles against hopeless odds and survive the plots of evil wizards was not restricted to the Arabs. Indeed, it seems that various details in the Byzantine poem *Digenis Akrites* (which is difficult to date but was probably given clear literary form in the twelfth century) were taken from 'The Tale of Omar bin al-Nu'uman'. This poem about a heroic frontier warrior fighting for Byzantium strikingly resembles the Arab epic in many of its motifs and devices. (It also seems likely that Arab storytelling influenced similar works in other areas, such as the anonymous eleventh-century Armenian epic tales of *David of Sasun* and the Georgian Shota Rustaveli's twelfth-century *Knight of the Panther Skin*, but more research is needed in these areas.)

Returning to the *Nights*, the 'History of Gharib and his Brother Ajib' is, like 'The Tale of Omar bin al-Nu'uman', a preposterous and perfunctorily plotted farrago of magic, warfare and romantic intrigue. Like 'Omar Bin al-Nu'uman' too, it was originally an independent epic which was eventually incorporated as a bulky makeweight into the later Egyptian recensions of the *Nights*. However, many similar popular epics, which circulated in the medieval Arab world, were not included in the *Nights*, among them those of 'Dhat al-Himma' (or 'Delhemma') and 'Sayyid Battal'. These sagas, like those discussed above, are ostensibly set in the time of the early Arab–Byzantine wars; yet once again distorted but unmistakable reflections of the wars against the Crusaders appear.

In the chapter on storytelling in *Manners and Customs of the Modern Egyptians*, Lane observed that oral recitations from the *Nights* in early-nineteenth-century Cairo were rather rare; much more popular with the storytellers and their audiences were the epics devoted to the exploits of Abu Zayd, al-Zahir Baybars and Antar.[41] Abu Zayd, according to the storytellers, was the dark-skinned son of an Arab chief of the Hilali tribe. The romance of Abu Zayd (or rather romances, for there are several variant versions) is (are) devoted to the exploits of the Hilali Arabs and their victories over the Berbers in North Africa in the eleventh century. Although this cycle of stories probably first took shape in the eleventh century, it both drew on older plot motifs and devices and, as the centuries passed, added incidents and names which derived from the later Muslim jihad against the Crusaders. The exploits of Abu Zayd and the Hilali tribesmen were usually recited to a musical accompaniment.

The *Sira of al-Zahir Baybars* was the next most popular story cycle in nineteenth-century Cairo. This saga, which perhaps began to take shape in the fifteenth century, is ever so tenuously based on the exploits of the real-life Sultan al-Zahir Baybars I of Egypt (reigned 1260–77). Vague memories of that sultan's wars against the Crusaders and the Mongols are jumbled up with low-life adventures, mystical fantasies and marvels generally. (We shall have more to say about this *Sirat* when we come to examine how crime was treated in the *Nights* and in other works of medieval fiction.)

By contrast with these two epics, which were popular in every
sense, the *Sirat Antar*, a picturesque romance about a pre-Islamic
poet and warrior, half Arab and half Abyssinian, was not much in
demand. Lane says that the coffee-house audience found the poetry
a bit difficult. The *Sirat Antar* is mostly in rhymed prose, but
Antar's poems, amounting to about 10,000 verses, are embedded
within the rhymed prose. Another off-putting feature of this *Sirat*
may have been its length. The modern printed edition is in thirty-
two volumes. The Antariyya (who made a living from telling the
story of Antar) read the story from a book, and if there was not
much demand for the tale then they might read from another
book, for example the *Nights*.

Although *The Thousand and One Nights* could not compete with
the heroic epics in popularity, it retained a precarious hold on the
favour of nineteenth-century Egyptian café society. Further to the
west in the North African territories, however, a rival but similar
collection seems to have been more popular. This was *The Hundred
and One Nights* (in Arabic *Mi'at Layla wa-Layla*).[42] Although the
oldest surviving manuscript was transcribed in 1776, this collection
seems to have been put together in North Africa some time
during the Middle Ages. It contains stories which are similar or
occasionally identical to those found in the larger and more
famous story collection. In its frame story, 'Flower of the Gardens',
the eponymous young man is blessed with a luminously beautiful
face, but it loses its beauty when he discovers the adultery of his
wife. Flower of the Gardens' face only regains its former sheen
when Flower of the Gardens learns through later experience
(spying on a queen and her attendants) that all women are unfaith-
ful. Flower of the Gardens warns the king, his host, that he is
being cuckolded by the queen. The king promptly has his wife
slaughtered and thereafter takes a virgin to bed every night,
having them beheaded in the morning, until Sheherazade is
brought to his bed and succeeds in breaking the cycle. *The
Hundred and One Nights* also includes 'The City of Brass', 'The

Ebony Horse' and the *Sindibad* cycle, but some of its tales were unknown to the compilers of *The Thousand and One Nights*. This North African story collection is much shorter than its eastern prototype, for Sheherazade only has to tell stories for eight months, until it is obvious that she is pregnant (the Gaudefroy-Demombynes translation into French runs to less than 260 pages).

The great Arab epics borrowed from each other, threading their way through a great swamp of plot motifs, converging on and diverging one from another. They offered a vision of the Arab past which featured individual deeds of heroism undertaken by poetry-spouting warriors, as well as captive princesses, battles and single combats, enterprising gangsters, disguises and mistaken identities, marvellous poisons, Amazons, talismans and automata. The epics and shorter fictions found in the great story collections provided medieval Islam with a mythical past. However, as we have seen, plot motifs and incidents crossed cultural frontiers with considerable ease, and the Arabs borrowed from the Indians, among others, while lending to the Byzantines, among others. It is time now to consider medieval Europe's debt to Arab fiction and, more specifically, to investigate the possibility that all or part of the *Nights* may have been circulating in translation in one or other of the European languages centuries before the birth of Antoine Galland.

Although a certain amount of material was translated in Byzantium, Spain and Sicily were the main corridors for the translation and transmission of Arab learning – and the Arab literature of entertainment – into medieval Europe.[43] Arabic versions of Greek works of science and mathematics were being translated into Latin in Spain as early as the tenth century, but the translation movement really got under way in the twelfth century, with Toledo as one of its main centres. The translators continued to be interested mainly in Greek works of philosophy and mathematics which had been preserved in Arabic. Although the Koran was also translated into Latin in 1143, the translation was of course intended for use in anti-Muslim polemics. Probably the first Latin work to draw heavily on Arabic fiction was the *Disciplina clericalis*. This anthology was put together by Petrus Alfonsi in twelfth-century Toledo. Petrus Alfonsi was a Jew with a good knowledge of Arabic who had converted to Christianity in 1106. In the *Disciplina* he assembled thirty-four exemplary tales in a frame structure. In the prologue, Petrus Alfonsi announced that he had produced this work in order to give men a better knowledge of their Creator and to guide them to a virtuous life. However, he had broken up the book into small sections to prevent boredom setting in, and he claimed:

I have been mindful of the fact that in order to facilitate remembrance of what has been learnt, the pill must be softened and sweetened by various means ... For that reason then have I put together this book, partly from the sayings of wise men and their advice, partly from Arab proverbs, counsels, fables and poems, and partly from bird and animal similes.[44]

Not only did Petrus Alfonsi rely heavily on Arab fables and stories; his apologetic prologue also follows the pattern of his oriental sources. His compilation drew on a variety of works in Arabic, including *Kalila wa-Dimna* and the *Sindibad* cycle. Mention has already been made of the appearance of the 'weeping bitch' story in the *Disciplina clericalis*. The *Disciplina* was immensely popular. It was widely translated and became the vehicle for the transmission of many of the Arab tales found in later European story collections. For example, much of the *Disciplina*'s material was incorporated in the *Gesta Romanorum*, which was probably produced in thirteenth-century England and relates the mostly legendary lives of saints in Roman times.[45]

In the course of the thirteenth century and particularly at the court of Alfonso the Wise (reigned 1252–84) there was a partial shift to translating Arabic into vernacular Spanish.[46] Alfonso commissioned a translation of *Kalila wa-Dimna* into Spanish. (However, a rival Latin version made by John of Capua circulated more widely throughout Europe, being eventually translated into numerous other vernaculars.) The *Sindibad* cycle of stories was also translated into Spanish as *Sendebar* or *Libro de los enganos e los asayamientos de las mugeres* (1253) under the patronage of Alfonso's brother Prince Fadrique.

Alfonso the Wise's nephew, the Infante Don Juan Manuel (1282–1348), collected fifty-one exemplary tales under the title *Conde Lucanor*.[47] The rather naïve frame story is that of a tutor instructing the young pupil Lucanor. Juan Manuel knew Arabic and drew on Arab literature for many of his moral tales. One story in particular, about the sorcerer Don Illan and the Dean of Santiago (a story centred on the years-of-experience-in-an-instant-of-time motif), was subsequently rediscovered by the Argentinian short-story writer Jorge Luis Borges and retold by him under the title 'The Sorcerer Postponed'. It may be that, in the Borges tale, Don Illan stands in for the storyteller, who, just like the sorcerer, can unroll the whole of a man's life in less than an hour. (Nai-tung Ting, who has made a special study of this tale-type, points to a relatively recent example of it in C.S. Lewis's novel *The Lion, the Witch and the Wardrobe*.)[48] The *Nights* rendering of this motif is found in 'The Tale of the Warlock and the Young Cook of Baghdad'. Juan Manuel's story about the king who desired to test his three sons is also based on a famous oriental tale and is found both in the ninth-century chronicler al-Tabari's universal history and in the *Nights*, where it is called 'The Story of the Sultan of al-Yaman and his Three Sons'. The *Conde Lucanor* also contains a variant of the barber's story of his fifth brother.

The Catalan Ramón Lull (1233–1316) wrote poetry in the style of the troubadors and led a fairly dissolute life as a youth, but he later converted and became a Franciscan friar.[49] Thereafter, everything he wrote was intended to advance the faith. He produced a prodigious amount – according to one estimate, 243 books. He studied Arabic (with a view to converting the infidel) and came to know the language well enough to write books in it. *The Book of the Beasts* is a collection of animal fables, many of which seem to have an oriental origin. Lull certainly made use of *Kalila wa-Dimna* in either its Arabic version or its Spanish translation. More intriguingly Lull's book has a version of 'The Tale of the Merchant and his Wife' much like the one in the frame story of the *Nights*, where Sheherazade tells it to her father, the vizier. Then again, it is possible that the baroquely romantic *La vida es sueño*, or 'Life Is a Dream', by the great Spanish dramatist Calderón de la Barca (1600–81) may derive ultimately from 'The Sleeper and the Waker' (or 'The Sleeper Awakened' as it is often known). But where the *Nights* story is merely an entertaining farce, the play by Calderón examines the nature of human identity, as its protagonist Prince Segismondo learns to distinguish between dream and waking, between truth and reality. In prison, Segismondo meditates:

> I dream that I am here,
> Chained in these fetters. Yet I dreamed just now
> I was in a more flattering, lofty station.
> What is this life? A frenzy, an illusion,
> A shadow, a delirium, a fiction.
> The greatest good's but little, and this life
> Is but a dream, and dreams are only dreams.

(A much more lightweight reworking of the plot of 'The Sleeper Awakened' can be found in the first act of Shakespeare's *The Taming of the Shrew*. Shakespeare almost certainly took the gist of the plot from a sixteenth-century English collection of tales. Whether that collection took the story from an oral or a written source is not known.)[50]

The influence of Arabic literature on medieval European literature was not confined to Spain. Motifs and plots which look as though they must have been taken from stories in Arabic have been identified in twelfth- and thirteenth-century fabliaux (short

verse treatments of what are usually comic subjects), in the *Lais* of
Marie de France (1154–89), in *Tristram and Iseult*, in *Floire et
Blanchefor*, in *Aucassin and Nicolette*, in Adenet Le Roi's *Cleomades*
and in *Pierre de Provence et la belle Maguelonne*. (The resemblance
between the last and 'The Tale of Kamar al-Zaman' is particularly
striking; among other features, both the Arab and the French
stories make play with the motif of a female bird abandoned by a
male, a motif that was later to be picked up by Chaucer.) In
eleventh-century Germany the epic poem *Herzog Ernst* has details
which are curiously similar to those in the adventures of Sinbad
the Sailor. In the thirteenth century, the anonymous *Nibelungenlied*
and Wolfram von Eschenbach's *Parsifal* similarly drew on oriental
motifs.[51]

In England 'The Squire's Tale' in *The Canterbury Tales* by
Geoffrey Chaucer (*c.* 1345–1400) features a mechanical flying
horse of brass on which an Arabian knight travels to the court of
King Cambuscan. Chaucer may have been introduced to the
motif of the Ebony Horse by Adenet Le Roi's *Cleomades*. However, this is not the only element of Arab origin in 'The Squire's
Tale'; for the episode in which Princess Canacee (who has acquired
a magic ring that allows her to understand the language of birds)
eavesdrops on a female falcon which tells of its desertion by a
tercel, or male hawk, must derive ultimately from 'The Tale of
Taj al-Muluk and the Princess Dunya' in the *Nights* (possibly via
Pierre de Provence et la belle Maguelonne). Then again 'The
Merchant's Tale', the bawdy story about the cuckold, the lovers
and the pear-tree, has a Persian precursor in the *Mathnawi
Discourses*, mystical sermons delivered by Jalal al-Din al-Rumi, the
thirteenth-century Sufi master in Konya, as well as an Arab
precursor in 'The Tale of the Simpleton Husband' in the *Nights*.[52]

The story of the pear-tree and the lovers also features in that
other great collection of framed tales produced in fourteenth-
century Europe, Boccaccio's *Decameron* (1353).[53] This work hardly
pretends to originality in content. Of the stories – told by courtiers

who have fled from Florence to escape the Black Death – nine-tenths have identifiable precursors. The *Decameron* has many stories in common with the *Nights* and other Arab story collections. For example, Boccaccio's tale of how Calendrino was fooled into thinking that he was pregnant probably derives ultimately from the *Nights* story 'The Qadi who Had a Baby', just as the story about Federigo and the falcon has its precursor in the older Arab tale about legendary generosity, 'Hatim Tayyi'. Likewise, in the fifteenth century, Masuccio Salernitano's *Novellino*, a collection of fifty tales from southern Italy put together in loose imitation of the *Decameron*, contains 'The Tale of the Ill-Fated Corpse', which is in essence the same as the story of the hunchback which frames the Hunchback cycle in the *Nights*. (One should be a little cautious about assuming a genealogical relation between Salernitano's story and the *Nights* story. The story of the unlucky corpse also circulated among the North American Indians.)

So much material which is common to the *Nights* has been found in collections of stories put together in Europe in the centuries prior to Galland's translation that it has led some scholars to speculate that the *Nights* did circulate in Europe in an earlier translation – perhaps a translation into Latin made in Spain in, say, the twelfth century. However, no such translation has been found, and there is no reference to such a translation ever having been commissioned. Although there is plenty of evidence for items like parts of the *Sindibad* cycle and the odd individual story like 'The Ebony Horse' being recycled in Latin or one or other of Europe's vernacular languages, most of those stories were added to the *Nights* only in the later stages of its growth, from the fifteenth century onwards. European versions of stories which formed part of the early core of the *Nights*, such as 'The Tale of Kamar al-Zaman' or 'The Story of the Hunchback', are much rarer – though, as has been noted above, there seems to be a relation between the former and *Pierre de Provence et la belle Maguelonne* and between 'The Tale of the Hunchback' and one of Salernitano's tales. However, there was nothing to prevent either of these stories being imported to Europe, perhaps by oral transmission, as independent, free-standing tales.

It is perhaps more significant that something like the frame story of the *Nights* seems to have been known in medieval Italy. The *Novelle* by Giovanni Sercambi (1347–1424) comprises 155 tales told by characters who have left Lucca, fleeing from the plague of 1374. Evidently Sercambi took the idea of the frame story from the *Decameron*, and a few of his tales are also taken from Boccaccio and are not very interesting. However, the 'Novella d'Astolfo' should intrigue the student of Arabic literature. In this story, the king recovers from a melancholy, brought on by his being cuckolded, when he succeeds in making love to a woman kept in a casket by a Siennese merchant. After making love to her, the king gives her his ring. Here there are unmistakable echoes of the frame story of the *Nights* and the adventure of Shahriyar and Shahzaman with the lady kept in a casket by a jinn. (Since a similar version of this story exists in a Hungarian folk-tale, it is possible that it reached Italy via some Balkan version, rather than directly from an Arab text.)[54]

There seem to be further echoes of the adventures of Shahzaman and Shahriyar in Ariosto's sixteenth-century masterpiece, the epic poem *Orlando Furioso*. In Canto 28, an innkeeper tells Rodolfo the story of King Jocondo, who set out on a journey with his brother Astolfo to the latter's kingdom but, having forgotten something, returned unexpectedly to observe his beloved wife in the arms of a low-born page. With difficulty he restrained himself from killing the pair, slipped away and rejoined Astolfo on the road. Not long after arriving at Astolfo's court, Jocondo discovered that his brother's wife too was adulterous and delighted in the embraces of a humpbacked dwarf. Jocondo, cheered up by the discovery that he was not alone in his cuckolded state, revealed all to his brother. When the latter calmed down, he agreed to set out with his brother on a voyage of exploration in which it would be demonstrated that there is no such thing as a faithful woman. Thereafter the story-line diverges somewhat from that in the *Nights*, though the conclusion is still that, no matter what precautions are taken, it is impossible to guard a woman's chastity; and the moral is picked up by Rodolfo: 'I do believe that there is no limit to woman's wiles; not all the books in the world could record a fraction of them.'[55]

Other reflections of the *Nights* and of other Arab anthologies continued to appear in European story collections of the sixteenth and seventeenth centuries, such as the *Piacevoli notti* by Gianfrancesco Straparola, the *Heptameron* by Marguerite of Navarre and Giambattista Basile's *Pentamerone*. The *Pentamerone*'s fifty stories are mostly fairy stories and tales of wonder, divided into sessions of ten nights. Though Basile drew on the folklore of southern Italy, he was himself a highly literary nobleman in love with the fantastic. The twentieth-century novelist Italo Calvino wrote of the *Pentamerone* that 'it resembles the dream of an odd Mediterranean Shakespeare, obsessed with the horrible, for whom there were never enough ogres or witches, in whose far-fetched and grotesque metaphors the sublime was intermingled with the coarse and sordid.'[56] Basile was one of the pioneers of the fairy tale. In pre-modern times the genres of literary fiction and the folk-tale, or fairy tale, were not clearly separated. It is probable that many of the 'folk-tales' circulating in medieval and early modern Europe were really orally transmitted reminiscences of individual literary creations, while on the other hand compilers of works of literature (such as the *Decameron* and *The Canterbury Tales*) drew on both literary and oral folk sources. Generally, stories passed backwards and forwards between written and oral versions.

With the publication in 1697 of Charles Perrault's *Contes de la mère l'Oye* (or 'Tales of Mother Goose'), the fairy tale emerged more clearly as a distinct genre. This collection of eight stories, of the type that French peasants allegedly used to tell their children, created a vogue for such stories at court and in the salons of fashionable ladies. The vogue for tales about fairies and other marvels, created by the appearance of *Contes de la mère l'Oye*, was part of the background to the favourable reception accorded to Galland's translation of the *Mille et une nuits*. Perrault, D'Aulnoy, Galland and others aimed at cultivated adult audiences. (Of course, in the nineteenth and twentieth centuries, the tales collected by Perrault, Galland and the Brothers Grimm, which had been fashionable among intellectuals and society folk, sank in status to become the staple fare of children in the nursery. Why this happened remains mysterious, but part of the answer may be that science fiction has usurped the role of the fairy tale as the purveyor of marvels to adults.)

Although Perrault and his French imitators drew on peasant and oral source material, they did not hesitate to improve and write up that material to make it suitable for discerning literary tastes. The brothers Jacob and Wilhelm Grimm did similarly when they published their collection of folk-tales transcribed from oral informants, the *Kinder und Hausmärchen* (1812–22).[57] Most of the stories were subsequently further revised by the brothers in later editions. The Grimms' tales were a product of the age of Romanticism, in Germany the age of Wieland, Herder and the cult of medieval and folk poetry. The German cult of folk poetry had been stimulated in its turn by the success of James Macpherson's presentation of the ostensible works of a third-century Gaelic bard, Ossian, under the title *Fragments of Ancient Poetry Collected in the Highlands of Scotland and Translated from the Gaelic or Erse Language* (1760). The works of Ossian were a forgery of Macpherson's, but this was not at first detected.

In Germany the cult of the folk was more specifically the cult of the German *Volk* and its communal soul. Nineteenth-century German folklorists aimed to give Germany, divided as it was between hundreds of princely states and independent municipalities, a sense of cultural identity and a mythic past. The Brothers

Grimm claimed to have collected their stories from a wide area of Germany, to have sought out illiterate or at least ill-educated peasant informants and to have transcribed exactly what they were told without editing or improving them in any way. Although these precepts must have had a beneficial influence on later folklorists, the Brothers Grimm did not in fact practise what they preached. In recent times, careful study of their working methods suggests that they relied on rather few informants, and that these were mostly literate and middle class, residing in Kassel. The Grimms also reworked their tales to improve their readability and moral content. Two of their 'best' informants in Kassel had a French background, and their memories of childhood stories from Galland may account for the appearance of distorted but still recognizable versions of 'Aladdin' and 'Ali Baba' in the Grimms' collection of German folklore. The Grimms themselves identified the *Nights* as the ultimate source of eight of the tales they had been told. Additionally 'The Sea Rabbit' probably derives from 'The Story of Prince Calaf and the Princess of China' in the *Mille et un jours*, an oriental story collection produced by Pétis de la Croix. ('The Story of Prince Calaf' was also to inspire Gozzi's drama and Puccini's opera *Turandot*.)

Tales from the *Nights*, albeit stripped of their specifically Islamic and oriental features, circulated orally in Germany in pre-modern times, and for that matter in Italy, France and Spain too. In most cases it is impossible to determine whether those tales passed into Europe first by word of mouth or in manuscript form. The Grimm brothers were great admirers of the *Nights*, which for Jacob Grimm described 'the poetic geography of the East'. Hans Christian Andersen, who as a child was regularly read to from the *Nights*, was similarly devoted to its tales, but he made more deliberate use of its stories as a source of creative inspiration. His 'Tinder Box' certainly owes something to 'Aladdin', while his 'Little Mermaid' may be modelled on the story of 'Julnar the Sea-Born'. Similarly, his story of 'The Emperor's New Clothes' seems to be based on a story in the Turkish collection *The History of the Forty Viziers* (or a variant version in *Conde Lucanor*).

Deliberate literary plundering of the *Nights* by western novelists and short-story writers is the subject of a subsequent chapter. Returning to the main theme of this chapter, in Europe the rise of folklore studies and the new enthusiasm for collecting fairy tales (to which the works of the Brothers Grimm gave an enormous impetus) were concurrent with the rise of nationalism and the development of a science of philology. This is in marked contrast to what happened in the Middle East. As Ernest Gellner has put it: 'Arab nationalism defines itself and the limits of the nation in terms of the old literate High Culture and in opposition to its folk variants, whereas in Central and Eastern Europe it had been the other way around.'[58] That is to say, Arab intellectuals identify folk culture with regionalism and dialectal differences, whereas for the most part they conceive of the 'Arab nation' as transcending the national boundaries delimited by the European powers in the Near East in the twentieth century. The Arabs were slow to take an interest in the oral prose tale, though folklore institutes do now exist in Baghdad and Cairo. Hasan El-Shamy, director of archives at the Cairo Folklore Centre, has observed that 'Modern nationalistic ideologies have shunned local folk dialects and hold classical Arabic to be a major unifying force among the Arabic-speaking countries. It is not surprising that the novel and the short story emerged only in the late nineteenth century as a direct transplant from European literature.'[59] Yet, as this chapter may suggest and a future chapter will confirm, the paradox is that the way both the European novel and the short story developed owed an immense amount to the *Nights* and to other Arab works of fiction and folklore.

4

The Storyteller's Craft

===

They were words that held no meaning for me, hammered out with fire
and impact: to the man who spoke them they were precious and he was
proud of them. He arranged them in a rhythm that always struck me as
highly personal. If he paused, what followed came out all the more
forceful and exalted. I sensed the solemnity of certain words and the
devious intent of others. Flattering compliments affected me as if they
had been directed at myself; in perilous situations I was afraid. Everything
was under control; the most powerful words flew precisely as far as the
storyteller wished them to.

Elias Canetti, The Voices of Marrakesh¹

As Elias Canetti, the novelist, watches the storytellers at work in
the market-place of Marrakesh, he seems to be engaged in meditation on the mysterious origins of his own art. It is indeed tempting
to think of the storyteller in the market-place as a precursor or
primitive type of novelist. But the relationship between oral
narrative and written fiction is more complex than at first appears.

It has often been assumed that the stories collected in the *Nights*
derived from oral storytelling, but, as we have seen, this assumption is at best only partially true. Again, it has often been assumed
that the stories in the *Nights* formed part of the stock-in-trade of
the professional street-corner storyteller. As we shall see, this was
only occasionally the case. Little or no systematic research has been
carried out into the history of storytelling in the Middle East, and
indeed that history is very obscure. From the first, storytelling has
been rated as a low-grade and slightly disreputable activity. According to early Islamic tradition, one of the Prophet's contemporaries,

a man called Khurafa, from the tribe of Udhrah, was visited by the jinn and carried off by them. When he returned, he went around telling stories about his encounter with the jinn, but people disbelieved him, saying that his stories were impossible. Khurafa then allegedly gave his name to the Arabic word for a fable or silly story (*khurafa*), though it is obvious that this is a case of back-formation, the legendary fabulist having been invented to provide an etymology for the word.[2]

Although nothing certain is known about storytelling in the first two centuries of Islam, it is likely that the profession had a twofold ancestry, religious and secular. On the religious side, the popular preacher was certainly one of the precursors of the storyteller. The *khatib*, the man who preached the sermon in the main mosque on Fridays at noon, was usually a man noted for his piety and learning. But in the early centuries, besides the *khatibs*, there were also popular storytellers, *qussas*, who specialized in telling religious stories in the mosques. Many of the *qussas* were learned in the interpretation of the Koran and of irreproachable orthodoxy. However, they also included some less reliable narrators who specialized in telling tales from what may be reckoned to be the Muslim Apocrypha – marvellous and doubtful tales about the pre-Islamic prophets, about Muhammad and about the heroes of the early Islamic conquests. In the centuries which followed the initial preaching of Islam, Muslim scholars slowly reached some sort of consensus about what was fantastic and legendary in tales which purported to be religious. Eventually the *qussas* came to be looked on with suspicion by the religious establishment, both because of the doubtful orthodoxy of some of their edifying stories and because many of these storytellers cared less about edification than they did about increasing their personal income.

The *qussas* moved out from the mosques and into the market-places. The worst of them were not really distinguishable from buffoons or beggars. Alleged sayings of the Prophet were manufactured for profit and entertainment. 'He who can touch the tip of his nose with his tongue will not go to hell' was one such saying attributed to Muhammad by a popular preacher. While the preachers worked on their audiences with sob stories, confederates went among the people collecting money. Ibn al-Jawzi described the popular preachers in thirteenth-century Baghdad and commented that 'it is an evident way of making the stories a source of livelihood and of getting gifts from tyrannical princes and obtaining the like from the gatherers of unlawful imposts . . . Some of them go to the cemeteries where they dilate upon affection and parting with friends drawing tears from the women, but not exhorting them to take warning.' The *qussas* competed for pitches. Hence the saying 'One *qass* does not love another.'[3]

Islamic storytelling's second line of descent derives from acting. Until very recently it was thought that there was no live theatre in the Islamic world until the nineteenth century – apart, that is, from the Shi'ite passion plays which commemorated the martyrdom of Hasan and Hussein. The only known play scripts in Arabic to have survived from the Middle Ages are scripts for shadow plays. Therefore the scholarly consensus has been that the classical theatrical tradition was brought to an end by the Arab conquest of much of the Eastern Roman Byzantine Empire, or perhaps had withered away a century or two before the Arab invasions. However, the classical scholar Professor B.E. Perry has observed that

Put into narrative form, instead of dialogue, many of the mimes which were acted on the stage in late Alexandrian and early Roman imperial times would read very much like the clever stories of adulterous intrigue, the outwitting of husbands, the clever devices of women, the picaresque adventures of rogues, the tricks played by sharpers on simpletons, etc., which we find in the *Arabian Nights* and in *Sindbad*.[4]

What is implied here is that it is possible that some of the old classical farces continued to be played in Islamic times, and that some of the content of the *Nights* is based on the plots of those plays. In the last few years, moreover, the researches of an Israeli scholar, Dr Shmuel Moreh, have uncovered evidence of the survival of acting and specifically of classically derived performances of mime in the Arab lands.[5] Mime in its original Greek and Roman sense does not refer to a drama without words in which actors use only gestures and facial expressions to get over the drama's meaning; the classical mime was a short play, often about everyday life, or at least a farcical and bawdy version of everyday life, in which the actors did use speech. Indeed, they often entertained their audiences by mimicking the accents and speech patterns of certain stock types, such as doctors, peasants and barbarians.

Mimics and companies of actors did not actually disappear with the coming of the Arabs. The mimics merely added to their repertoire. *Hikaya* in modern Arabic means 'story', but originally the word meant mimicry, and the *hakiya* was a mimic. The *hakiya*'s art lay in his skill in imitating anything – birds, animals, natural disasters, famous people and social types. The ninth-century essayist al-Jahiz ('Goggle-Eyes') wrote a treatise on eloquence, the *Kitab al-Bayan wa'l-Tabyin*, in which he praises the expressive genius of mimics. They are

capable of producing in perfect detail the pronunciation of Yemenis; and they can equally well imitate Khurasanis, Ahwazis, Zanjis, Sindis or Ethiopians. They even seem more natural than the originals! When they imitate a man with a stammer, it is like all the peculiarities of all the world's stammerers rolled into one. They imitate blind men, making up their faces and eyes and affecting movements of their limbs such that not one blind man in a thousand exhibits all these peculiarities; the mimic seems able to catch all the characteristic movements of the blind man at the same time.[6]

Al-Mas'udi tells the tale of Ibn al-Maghazili, a ninth-century *hakiya* in Baghdad who was famous for his jokes, stories and imitations of 'Bedouin, grammarians, transvestites, judges, gypsies, Nabateans, Sindi, Zanj, eunuchs and Turks'. A eunuch in the service of the Abbasid court arranged to bring him before the Caliph al-Mu'tadid in return for a half-share in the reward that the *hakiya* would get for entertaining the caliph. When al-Maghazili came before al-Mu'tadid, it was agreed that he should receive 500 dirhams if he made the caliph laugh. However, it was stipulated that, if the caliph did not laugh, then the mimic would receive ten heavy blows on the neck. The mimic ran through his entire repertoire, but the unsmiling caliph kept his composure. The desperate mimic prepared to receive his punishment and in fact asked to have it doubled. Then, as soon as the beating had been administered, the sore and giddy mimic asked that the eunuch should receive his half-share too. Now indeed the caliph did burst into peals of laughter.[7]

Although the *hakiya* was not in the first instance a storyteller, it is easy to imagine how, as he developed the patter to go with imitations of ignorant bedouin or rich Persian merchants, this patter, designed to carry grotesque accents and mannerisms, might evolve into a full-blown story or series of stories. In the thirteenth century the distinguished Christian historian writing in Syriac, Barhebraeus, put together a collection entitled *Laughable Stories*, within which the fifteenth chapter is devoted to 'Amusing Stories of Mimics and Comedians'.[8] In fact, by the early fourteenth century at the latest, *hikaya* had come to mean 'story', and the storyteller had replaced the mimic in the market-places. Competing with the individual storyteller, small companies of actors continued to give open-air, street-corner performances of short comedies, just as they had done in Greek and Roman times. Although references to actors and live theatre are rare in the sober medieval chronicles, it seems that the shows which were put on were often bawdy farces somewhat similar to the Latin comedies of Plautus, though less sophisticated. Perhaps some performances were based on themes derived ultimately from Plautus. It is even possible that such *Nights* tales as 'The Tale of the Ugly Man and his Beautiful Wife' or 'The Tale of the Fuller, the Wife and the Trooper' (the plots of which have similarities with Plautus) may be the transcriptions of farces which had been acted out in medieval Baghdad or Cairo.

In the medieval Arab lands the professional Arab storyteller enjoyed (if that is the word) a very low status. He competed with snake-charmers, jugglers and pedlars of quack medicines for the attention and the money of the crowds. Like these other low-life entertainers, many of the storytellers in twelfth-century Cairo were to be found in the Bayn al-Qasrayn. The Bayn al-Qasrayn ('Between the Two Palaces') was originally the military parade ground between the two great Fatimid palaces in the heart of old Cairo. After the suppression of the Fatimid dynasty in the late twelfth century, the palaces fell into ruin, and by Mamluke times they had largely been built over, while the open space between them had become a market-thoroughfare and a place of popular entertainment. According to al-Qurti, the storytellers in the Bayn al-Qasrayn 'told stories of the Bedouin Girl and Ibn Mayyah and about al-Hakim bi-Amr Allah [a historical personage to whom many fantastic stories were attached]. These stories are comparable to the stories of al-Battal [a semi-legendary hero of the early Islamic conquests] and to *The Thousand and One Nights* and similar stories.'[9] The northern suburb of al-Husayniyya, an area settled by Kurds and Turks, was another favoured stamping ground of the storytellers. In medieval Fez, storytellers were normally found working close to the city's gates. Their stories were often accompanied by music, and the Moroccan storytellers sometimes supplemented their earnings by selling talismans.[10]

Because of their low status, individual storytellers were rarely noticed by the historians and compilers of biographical dictionaries. A rare passing mention of a storyteller comes in an obituary notice of a jurisprudent, Shams al-Din al-Fa'alati, in a fifteenth-century chronicle, whose author, Ibn Taghribirdi, notes that this man rose from humble and even disreputable origins, for one of his brothers was a geomancer and the other an astrologer, while his father earned his living by telling stories and by selling astrological predictions to professional wrestlers.[11]

The professional storyteller makes a rare appearance in the *Nights* itself. In 'The Tale of King Muhammad Bin Sabaik and the Merchant', the king has been criticized by his vizier for spending too much on his court poets, cup-companions and storytellers (*shu'ara wa'l-nudama wa arbab al-hikayat*); nevertheless he commissions Hasan the Merchant to seek out the most marvellous story ever. Hasan sends his mamluke slaves out on the quest. One of the mamlukes achieves success, for in Damascus he finds an old man who tells stories every day, seated on his storyteller's throne (*kursi*), and this old man knows the wondrous story of 'Sayf al-Muluk and Badia al-Jamal'. When the mamluke agrees to pay a fee of 110 dinars, the old man takes him to his home and allows him to make a copy of his book of the story. But the sale is on five conditions, which are as follows: 'that thou tell not this story in the beaten high road nor before women and slave-girls nor to black slaves nor feather-heads; nor again to boys; but read it only to Kings and Emirs and wazirs and men of learning, such as expounders of the Koran and others'.[12] The king is indeed pleased with the story, has his scribes copy it out in letters of gold and has it placed in the treasury. (The treasury, the *khizana*, was normally used as a book depository in Muslim palaces.) We need not take the old man's stipulations very seriously. An announcement that the story to come was fit only for crowned heads or for the very learned was a stock way of crying up one's wares. We may safely assume that the story of 'Sayf al-Muluk and Badia al-Jamal' was regularly listened to by the common people in the market-places, including slaves and women. A twelfth-century Andalusian Muslim market inspector's manual indeed warns of the dangers of unaccompanied women entering the booths or homes of story-tellers and fortune-tellers.[13]

The prelude to the story of 'Sayf al-Muluk' suggests that the professional storyteller commonly worked from written sources (and, as we shall see, Lane's testimony suggests the same). It also suggests that stories which were written had a higher status than those which continued to be transmitted orally. Remarkable stories deserved something better than oral transmission. That the story is so good that it must be written down is in fact a recurring topos in the *Nights*: 'Your story must be written down in books, and read after you, age after age.' Only writing guarantees survival, and writing makes the best claim on the attention of those who should marvel at or take warning from the stories.[14] A rather oddly phrased formulation of this recurs frequently: 'Verily my adventure is wondrous and were it graven with needle gravers on the eye corners it would be a warning to whoso would be warned and a matter of thought to whoso would think.'

With the Ottoman conquest of Egypt and Syria (1516–17), most crafts and trades in the cities of those provinces were organized into guilds.[15] (This was done mainly to facilitate the collection of taxes.) At about the same time, coffee drinking and coffee-houses spread through the Ottoman lands. The storyteller moved off the streets and into the coffee-house. The clientele of the Middle Eastern coffee-house was entirely male and often somewhat disreputable, numbering the unemployed, off-duty soldiers and drug addicts among its patrons. The most rigorous theologians held that coffee was an intoxicant and tried to get it banned, but learned opinion was divided, and coffee was rarely unavailable for very long in any Muslim city. From the seventeenth century onwards, coffee-houses were also where one went to smoke tobacco – another activity regarded with disapproval by religious rigorists. The seventeenth-century Turkish belletrist Katib Chelebi sourly remarked in an essay on the moral menace of coffee that 'Story-tellers and musicians diverted the people from their employ-ments, and working for one's living fell into disfavour.'[16] A list of guilds compiled in 1801 includes two corporations of storytellers who worked in cafés. Besides tips from the customers, the storyteller sometimes also received a small weekly fee from the proprietor of the café. In the early nineteenth century one of these guilds held weekly meetings in a coffee-house. The Madkhana, the 'Place for Laughing', was a particularly famous coffee-house in Cairo where the leading storyteller acted as a sort of president and chose other people to tell stories. Although most professional storytelling was done in coffee-houses, the storytellers were also summoned to the houses of the rich to perform at weddings or other important social functions.

Alexander Russell's *The Natural History of Aleppo* (1794) described a storyteller at work in a Syrian café in the mid-eighteenth century:

He recites walking to and fro in the middle of the coffee room, stopping only now and then, when the expression requires some emphatical attitude. He is commonly heard with great attention; and not unfrequently in the midst of some interesting adventure, when the expectation of his audience is raised to the highest pitch, he breaks off abruptly and makes his escape, leaving both his hero or heroine and his audience in the utmost embarrassment. Those who happen to be near the door endeavour to detain him, insisting upon the story being finished before he departs; but he always makes his retreat good; and the auditors suspending their curiosity are induced to return at the same time the next day to hear the sequel. He has no sooner made his exit than the company in separate parties fall to disputing about the characters of the drama or the event of an unfinished adventure. The controversy by degrees becomes serious and opposite opinions are maintained with no less warmth than if the fall of the city depended on the decision.

This 'Perils of Pauline' approach to storytelling may account for the rambling and crisis-punctuated narrative structure of some of the stories in the *Nights*. However, although Russell found that storytellers flourished in eighteenth-century Aleppo, he noted that the *Nights* collection was scarcely known to them.[17]

In Tangiers in the 1880s, Burton tracked down a storyteller weaving his enchantments in an extremely squalid suburb of the city: 'a foul slope; now slippery with viscous mud, then powdery with fetid dust, dotted with graves and decaying tombs, unclean booths, gargottes and tattered tents, and frequented by women, mere bundles of unclean rags, and by men wearing the haik or the burnus, a Franciscan frock, tending their squatting camels and chaffering over cattle for Gibraltar's beef eaters'. The storyteller, a disreputable-looking figure, carried a stick and an hourglass-shaped tom-tom. This man 'speaks slowly and with emphasis, varying the diction with breaks of animation, abundant action and the most comical grimace: he advances, retires and wheels about, illustrating every point with pantomime; and his features, voice and gestures are so expressive that even Europeans who cannot understand a word of Arabic divine the meaning of his tale'.[18] However, Burton never heard any stories from the *Nights* recited in Tangiers.

It is Edward Lane who, relying on his long sojourn in Cairo, gives the fullest and most useful information about the storyteller and his relationship to the *Nights*. Lane devoted three chapters of his *Manners and Customs of the Modern Egyptians* to the professional storytellers who worked in the Cairene coffee-houses, and the *Nights* features prominently in his account.[19] According to Lane, there were then few copies of the book to be found in Cairo, and, perhaps because of this, there were few reciters of its stories. Far more common were the *shu'ara* (literally, 'poets') who specialized in reciting the *Sira of Abu Zayd*, a popular romantic epic, half prose and half poetry. There were approximately fifty of these *shu'ara* who had memorized the book and who gave recitations from it, sometimes with a musical accompaniment on the viol. Some of them specialized in recitations of only part of the story (for it was very long). Next most numerous were the *muhaddithun* who specialized in telling stories from the *Sira of Baybars*. Finally, the smallest group specialized in chanted recitations from the *Sirat*

Antar, an epic celebration of Arab heroism and warfare in pre-Islamic times, most of which was put together between the eighth and the twelfth centuries. Lane observed that *Antar*, a distinguished example of rhymed prose in classical Arabic, was not really popular in the coffee-houses; and consequently there were only about half a dozen of the Antariyya in the whole of Cairo. It was the Antariyya who occasionally varied their repertoire by reading stories from the *Nights*. All these professional storytellers worked the Cairo coffee-houses and normally told their tales from the *mastaba*, or stone platform outside. The proprietor would pay them a small sum for the added custom which their stories brought, and the reciters could also hope to collect voluntary contributions from the audience.

The professional storyteller, or *hakawati*, did not always rely on memory, but often worked from a text. At the beginning of this century, the *Nights* scholar Duncan Black Macdonald purchased several scrappy manuscripts of prompt-texts that had belonged to a professional *hakawati* in Damascus. Macdonald also watched a professional storyteller at work in a Cairo coffee-house and noted how the audience preferred action and jokes to the poetry which the storyteller wished to insert into the narrative.[20]

Evidently the medieval *Nights* was a kind of cultural amphibian. Although the story collection should not be considered only in literary terms, it would be still less correct to consider it as merely oral folklore slapped down on paper. It is true that many of its stories first circulated as orally transmitted folk-tales, before being written down, but the point is that they *were* written down, and those who wrote them down almost invariably gave them a literary shaping. It is occasionally possible to detect the rhythms of oral delivery in the prose of the stories, and David Pinault (whose work will be discussed in a subsequent chapter) has identified the survival of the characteristics of verbal delivery in some parts of the text. However, there are only occasional traces in the *Nights* of such important features of oral transmission and delivery as steretoyped adjectives, mnemonic formulas and recurrent summaries of the plot so far. Therefore methods developed for the study of such things as the transmission of African tribal genealogies or the preservation of English country lore are not very useful when one turns to study the *Nights*.

It is true that most of the stories were told by storytellers (of a rather low social status) to illiterate audiences, but, as we have seen, the storytellers usually worked from a written text. Moreover, this was not the only way the stories continued in circulation, for some people borrowed the *Nights* and similar works from small private lending libraries. Anyway, it would be a mistake simply to equate oral transmission and delivery with some sort of 'low' culture. Poetry enjoyed the highest status in medieval Arabic culture, as it does in the modern culture, and poems were more often recited than read in private. People regularly committed enormous swaths of poetry to memory. Also, the only proper way that *hadiths*, traditions concerning the Prophet Muhammad and his contemporaries, could be passed on to students was by word of mouth, and it was not thought acceptable simply to mug up all that religious material from a book.

Turning to books, the normal way of 'publishing' a book in the early centuries of Islam was to take it along to the mosque and read it out loud there. Most people were familiar with such works of high literature as Ibn al-Muqaffa's *Kalila wa-Dimna* and al-Hariri's *Maqamat* from hearing them read out aloud. One might think that the lack of a fixed canonical text of the *Nights* in the Middle Ages was in itself a sign of its low status, but a great many important works had no fixed text, including *Kalila wa-Dimna*. It is very hard indeed to draw any sort of boundary between a 'high' Arabic culture and a 'low' culture; for example, vulgarly obscene stories, *mujun*, did not circulate exclusively among some sort of Arab lumpenproletariat, since the *nudama*, the drinking companions of the caliphs and sultans, were commonly expected to have a fund of such stories committed to memory and ready for use as after-dinner entertainment. Not only did street-corner storytellers gather some of their material from scholarly books, but scholars and literary men in their turn reworked much of the material that was the stock-in-trade of the storytellers. Al-Hariri's *Maqamat* deals with the low-life themes of begging and small-time confidence tricks, but it does this in an elaborate and technically brilliant high style. Such cultural cross-overs defeat attempts to draw a boundary between the culture of the literary élite and that of the masses. Finally, it must be remembered that the Arab literary élite was not co-extensive with the politico-military élite. Many of the sultans, emirs and governors who ruled over the Arab lands in the Middle Ages were Turks, who had grown up in a culture of the steppes in which legends and histories circulated orally. Members of this Turkish élite were often illiterate.

Although information about the professional Arab storyteller in pre-modern times is fairly sparse, the activities of his Turkish and Persian counterparts are better documented. The *ashiks* (literally 'lovers') were poet-minstrels who wandered through Turkey in early Ottoman times, singing or reciting poems about love and heroism. The *meddah*, or Turkish storyteller, may be a descendant of the *ashik*. *Meddah* literally means 'praise-giver', and the earliest *meddahs* specialized in heroic epics about Turkey's past. Only subsequently did they add fantastic, comic and bawdy tales to their repertoire. The *meddah* was a normal fixture at the courts of the Turkish princes. Lalin Kaha, the *meddah* of the Ottoman Sultan Mehmed III (reigned 1595–1603), was a particularly famous court storyteller.[21]

However, most Turkish storytellers were not part of a court establishment but, as in Egypt, were organized in a guild and normally told their stories in the coffee-houses. The *meddah* usually spoke from a chair in the café, using a handkerchief and wand as props. The handkerchief was sometimes used to muffle his voice for effect. The tales he told tended to be rich in dialogue and offered many opportunities for mimicry. The *meddahs* of Istanbul were renowned for their female impersonations. Some *meddahs* gave improvised performances, others read from texts. The story was told in an oddly stylized way, for first the *meddah* would announce that the story he was going to tell had a moral; next he would list the story's characters; then he would advertise the poetry and give the setting of the story; finally he would tell the story.

In medieval Persia, the *naqqal* (literally, the 'transmitter') used to recite from the great national epic, the *Shahnama*, produced by Firdawsi in the eleventh century. Since the *Shahnama* is over 50,000 couplets long and has claims to be the longest poem ever produced in world literature, most *naqqals* specialized in recounting different sections of the poem. (In serial form the *Shahnama* could take a whole year to recite). But as in Turkey, by the nineteenth century, if not earlier, these storytellers had added to their stock by telling folk-tales, as well as more recently coined stories. By the late nineteenth century, the *naqqals* had been organized into a guild headed by an imperial official, the *naqibolmalek*, who also doubled as the head of the official dervish order.[22] It was the *naqibolmalek*'s job to tell the Shah stories every evening until he fell asleep. (In much the same way, the Russian Tsar Ivan the Terrible used to employ three blind men to tell him stories until he drifted off.) Sir John Malcolm, who visited the court of Fath Ali Shah in 1801, reports Mullah Adeenah, the court storyteller, as saying: 'Besides my own invention, I have a great book, containing anecdotes on all subjects, and an infinite quantity of amusing matter, which I select at pleasure, and adapt my story to the circumstances of the moment, and to the characters of those who form the audience.'[23]

More generally, storytelling was closely associated with Sufism and the dervish orders. Jalal al-Din yal-Rumi, the thirteenth-century Persian Sufi who taught and preached in Konya (Anatolia), was steeped in Arabic and Persian poetry and prose. Rumi used familiar stories from, for example, *Kalila wa-Dimna* and recast them as mystical parables. He left the world a rich legacy of story lore in his *Mathnawi Discourses*, a great sprawling series of stories within stories, cast in poetic form, in which the inner stories comment on and indicate the mystical meanings of the outer stories.[24] C.J. Wills, a medical officer of the British Telegraph Department in nineteenth-century Persia, described the outlandish gear of the dervish storytellers – their short trousers of animal skin, their skull-caps and their huge axes or clubs: 'I frequently, on passing through the Maidan, or public square, of Shiraz, saw Aga Nusserulla surrounded by a gaping crowd of peasants, porters, and muleteers squatting in a circle, he striding up and down and waving his axe as he told his story of love or fairyland.'[25] A special sort of storyteller, the *pardadar*, made use of an additional prop, a large, gaudy painting featuring episodes from the story he was going to tell and which he pointed to as he progressed with his narrative.

In Persia the *naqqals* with their repertoire of entertainment and adventure tales sometimes had to compete with the *rowzeh khans*, who preached and told edifying stories. In particular, the *rowzeh khan* specialized in describing the martyrdom of Hasan and Hussein, the grandchildren of the Prophet Muhammad, and working on the audience's emotions to bring them to a state of repentance and religious fervour. However, sometimes the *naqqal* doubled as a *rowzeh khan*, telling secular stories most of the time, but switching to tales of martyrdom and piety on religious holidays. An American researcher, Mary Ellen Page, made a study of storytelling in Shiraz in the 1970s. She found that there were four professional *naqqals* working in the city. Each had his set rota of coffee-houses and could draw audiences of between 100 and 200 for performances which tended to go on for an average of an hour and a half, breaking off at a point of suspense. The stories they told were drawn from the *Shahnama*, large sections of which they had committed to memory. However, while the storyteller's apprenticeship consisted of rote memorization of a text, once embarked on his career he felt no obligation to stick closely to the text he had memorized. Rather, he embroidered and abbreviated at will to suit his personal style, as well as the tastes of his particular audience.[26]

Although professional storytelling still seems to flourish in modern Iran, it looks as though the profession has died out in all the Arab lands except Morocco, where tourism has helped keep it alive. In recent years Nacer Khemir, a Tunisian, has single-handedly revived the craft, telling tales from the *Nights* and from local Tunisian folklore to Arab and European audiences, building up a repertoire of about twenty-four hours of stories. But Khemir's performances are an individual creation rather than the perpetuation of a living tradition. Indeed, he has described how, some time around 1970, he hunted through the old part of Tunis for the last surviving practitioner of his chosen craft: 'It took us a long time before we eventually dug out an old, old storyteller, who, to earn his living, had had to take a job as a watchman at a charcoal depot. But we couldn't get him to talk of the past, and the mere mention of it threw him into agony.'[27]

The professional storyteller makes a unique appearance in 'The Tale of Sayf al-Muluk' and he is heavily outnumbered in the *Nights* by talented amateurs who tell tales in order to save their lives, make moral points, confuse suspicious husbands, win beautiful princesses or simply pass the time. Here fiction accurately models reality. Most storytelling has always been done by amateurs. Medieval Arab intellectuals, who espoused poetry and *belles-lettres* in opposition to prose fiction, often claimed that fanciful stories, or *khurafa*, were only suitable for women and children. In twentieth-century Egypt the researches of the folklorist Hasan El-Shamy have indeed revealed that fantastic stories are usually told by women to other women and to children.[28]

Storytelling is often regarded as a time-wasting activity and therefore as something which is rather sinful and may consequently attract the jinn. Therefore storytellers may begin their stories with some sort of evil-averting formula. (On the other hand, it is also common to finish with some ritually authenticating phrase such as 'I was there and just returned and I did not even have supper'.) Storytelling becomes less sinful when the day's work is over, and so wonder-stories were also known as *samar*, or 'things of the evening'. Also, at certain times of the year, there was less work to be done in the fields, and then again storytelling became a more respectable activity. El-Shamy notes that there is a particular demand for long stories in Egypt in July and August, when the flooding of the Nile means that the work-load is light. In Morocco, on the other hand, the winter months are the ones when one has some time to sit about and listen to stories. The novelist Richard Hughes, who resided in Tangiers in the 1920s, kept a cook who was an expert, if amateur, storyteller. Hughes transmitted some of his cook's narratives in a volume of short stories, *In the Lap of Atlas*, but he noted that each story was 'embellished with a wealth of detail that would have filled an ordinary-sized novel. The Arab story-teller excels at this long spinning-out of detail: he will begin the morning with a description of the hero's bridle as he starts out on the journey, and by the afternoon be still describing the horse's tail.'[29]

More recently the American novelist Paul Bowles has enjoyed a similar relationship with another amateur (in formal terms, that is) storyteller, Mohammed Mrabet. Mrabet's stories are tape-recorded and translated by Bowles before being published as books. Mrabet, who used to listen to the tales told by old men in cafés, comes almost at the end of a line. These days, according to Bowles,

practically every café has a television. The seats are arranged differently and no one tells any stories. They can't because the television is going. No one thinks of stories. If the eye is going to be occupied by a flickering image, the brain doesn't feel a lack. It's a great cultural loss. It's done away with the oral tradition of storytelling and whatever café music there was.[30]

5

Street Entertainments

===

There are more stories in the *Nights* about princes and sons of wealthy merchants than there are about street-corner layabouts and petty criminals. It could therefore be argued that it makes more sense to use the *Nights* as a source for the high life of the rich and powerful than for low life. However, when Arab storytellers described the world of the palace, its rituals, its intrigues and its fabulous wealth, whether in old Baghdad or Peking, they were conjuring up a fantasy vision of the lives of the great – a vision of ceremonies conducted behind high walls, of harems which could not be penetrated without the risk of being apprehended and executed and, above all, of days spent without having to do a hand's turn of work. They were describing a milieu which was no more familiar to them than it was to their audience. Such fantasies are gently mocked in the barber's story about the day-dream of his fifth brother. That brother, having invested what little capital he had in buying some glass, leaned against a balustrade and began to fantasize about selling the glass at a good profit, recycling the profits to buy more glass, using further profits to buy a great house and slaves and horses, then seeking and gaining the hand of the vizier's daughter. He saw himself making his new bride kiss his feet and subjecting her to various other humiliations; then, as she submissively presented herself to him once more in his reverie, he spurned her with his foot. Acting out what he was imagining, the barber's brother kicked out and smashed that small quantity of glass which he had acquired at such cost and which he had imagined would be the foundation of his fortune.

When storytellers talked about small shopkeepers, petty

criminals and beggars, however, they were able to draw on their own experience of life. Moreover and more important, modern students of the medieval Near East can find plenty of other sources to tell them about the lives of the princes, viziers, emirs and members of the merchant oligarchy.[1] High life is a matter of official record, of court panegyric and of pious chronicle. Such sources, of which there are thousands, offer an exhausting amount of detail on how great sultans, viziers, emirs and scholars lived. Very few sources shed any light on the lives of ordinary people (still less those of street-corner entertainers and criminals) in the pre-modern Islamic lands. The stories of the *Nights*, many of which deal with the lives of humble folk and were written down with that audience in mind, are an outstanding source, though not, as we shall see, a unique one. Of course, there are problems in mining fiction for facts; but, though the stories are fantasies, the settings – the buildings and their interiors, the costumes, the streetlife and the gestures – are, or rather were, facts faithfully transmitted. The small touches of background detail, such as the brokerage fees transmitted by the Christian broker, or the hunchback's 'tall green hat, with knots of yellow silk stuffed with ambergris', were used precisely to lend verisimilitude to the bizarre stories in which such details featured.

The stories of the *Nights* are urban stories, written for the most part by people in the cities about people in the cities for people in the cities. The urban nature of the collection as a whole is well illustrated by the themes of 'Abu Kir the Dyer and Abu Sir the Barber', a story about two wily Arab townsfolk who leave Alexandria and set sail from Egypt to seek their fortune. They end up penniless in a strange non-Islamic city, but after various twists and turns of the plot, Abu Kir, who has first made and lost a fortune by introducing different-coloured dyes to the city, finally finds favour with the king and makes his fortune by building the first *hammam* (public bath) in the place. Although the story is a fantasy (surely directed at an audience of Egyptian merchants) about the fortune that could be made using urban Muslim know-how in foreign parts, nevertheless it is a fantasy with some relationship to reality; for Muslim dyestuffs and other finished goods were successfully sold in markets throughout the known medieval world, from Britain to China; and wherever Muslims settled in any numbers, they invariably built *hammams*, as well as mosques and souks.

The peasant and the nomad feature only occasionally in the stories, and, when the nomadic Arab or Kurd does have a part in the stories, it is often an unflattering one. For example, in 'The Rogueries of Dalilah and her Daughter Zaynab', the guileless bedouin is persuaded by Dalilah to change places with her on the cross in the hope of thereby securing some honey fritters. The Kurd in 'Ali Shar and Zumurrud' is a villainous thief. In 'Ali the Persian' the Kurd is a rogue and a fool. It is true that in 'The Fellah and his Wicked Wife' we get a vivid picture of peasant life – ploughing, sowing, harvesting, milling and baking – but this story is almost unique and in any case is not one of the early core stories. The original core stories are pre-eminently set in Baghdad, Cairo and Damascus.

Baghdad, in the days of the Abbasid Caliph Harun al-Rashid (reigned 786–809), is the setting of 'The Story of the Porter and the Three Ladies' and of 'The Story of the Three Apples'. Although the Sinbad the Sailor cycle of stories was not added to the *Nights* until the early modern period, they were certainly composed in the Abbasid period, when Basra served as Baghdad's port on the Gulf. Many of the great love stories in the *Nights*, such as 'The Story of the Slave-Girl Anis al-Jalis and Nur al-Din Ali ibn Khaqan', show signs of having been composed in Abbasid Baghdad. Other shorter tales and anecdotes can also be shown to have originated in Baghdad, some time between the ninth and the eleventh centuries, for they feature in other works of that period such as al-Mas'udi's chronicle *The Meadows of Gold* or al-Isfahani's literary anthology *The Book of Songs*.

In the years 762–6 the Abbasid Caliph al-Mansur caused the perfectly round city of Baghdad to be built on the banks of the Tigris.[2] It was a planned city, and the essayist al-Jahiz remarked that 'It is as if it was poured into a mould and cast.' At the centre of the city was the caliph's residence, the Palace of the Golden Gate. The palace's dome was allegedly capped by a bronze horseman whose lance pointed in the direction from which enemy invasion might next be expected. (This bronze horseman may make one think of the brass horseman in 'The Third Dervish's Tale'.) Outside the palace compound, different concentric sectors of the city were at first reserved for the residences of specific functionaries, such as the palace guards, the water-carriers and the muezzins. It is hard to distinguish truth from legend in the earliest accounts of the city, and certainly no more remains of original Baghdad than of the mythical City of Brass. However, in the lifetime of al-Mansur, the Palace of the Golden Gate was abandoned in favour of the Palace of Eternity, which al-Mansur had founded beyond the walls of the original round city. Baghdad as a whole grew and spilt beyond those walls, and in time the formal layout at the centre of the city was eroded and built over, with the streets coming to assume the higgledy-piggledy layout that is characteristic of so many other medieval Islamic cities. In the centuries which followed, palaces proliferated, and so did suburbs, as the city drifted eastwards. In its heyday Baghdad had a population of at least half a million, making it the largest city west of China. The great slums which grew up came under the control of gangs of riff-raff (or *ayyarun*, of which more later). As for the inhabitants of the slums, lists have survived of the disapproved occupations in Abbasid Baghdad – disapproved of either because of their immorality or because of the noise and smells intrinsic to their practice: blacksmiths, butchers, conjurors, policemen, night-watchmen, tanners, makers of women's shoes, dung collectors, well diggers, bath stokers, masseurs, pigeon racers and chess players.

Few in the city had access to the palace. There, the caliphs conferred and caroused with their *nudama*, cup-companions or intimates, wits and virtuosi, experts on literature, art and human beauty. Beautiful page boys and singing girls waited on the caliph and his companions. The Abbasid palace was an enclosed world, to be fantasized about. Oleg Grabar has eloquently written of it that

the notion of a prince living in a separate world appears at its best in literature, where it is often connected with a secondary theme, that the interior of the forbidding and forbidden palace consists of a labyrinth of separate elements secretly and mysteriously related to each other. Such a world of courts, pavilions, baths, strange doors, and fantastically elaborate decorations appears in the story of the City of Brass from *The Thousand and One Nights*. It is from this kind of slightly immoral, if exciting, realm that Harun al-Rashid escapes for his forays into the living city. For ... the world of the prince – secluded, rich, and mysteriously complicated – was seen by the Muslim as an evil, and the just man, if called to it, never penetrated it without his own shroud.[3]

In 'Harun al-Rashid and Abu Hasan the Merchant of Oman', the latter is described as going to a brothel in Saffron Street in the quarter of Karkh.[4] However, whereas the storytellers often seem to know their way around Cairo or Damascus, it is rare to find even the pretence of any detailed knowledge of the topography of Baghdad. When one finds stories set in Baghdad during the caliphate of Harun al-Rashid, the notional setting should be read as an expression of nostalgia for a lost golden age, located in the early ninth century, when the Arabs still controlled their own destiny, before the Turks took control over the army and administration, and when almost all the Islamic lands were united under one ruler, the Abbasid caliph. Even though Baghdad is the setting for 'The Porter and the Three Ladies', and the story may well have been composed in that city in Abbasid times, it would be foolish to assume that this is the case; at the very least, the story shows signs of rewriting elsewhere; for it is suspicious how much of the lady's shopping bag, carried by the porter at the beginning of the story, consists of Syrian produce (Hebron peaches, Aleppo jasmine, Ba'albakk figs, Syrian cheese, etc.), and how almost none of the comestibles seem to come from Iraq or points further east.[5]

By the late twelfth century, Baghdad was in full decay. The Spanish Muslim traveller Ibn Jubayr, who visited the place in 1184, remarked: 'In comparison with its former state, before misfortune struck it and the eyes of adversity turned towards it, it is like an effaced ruin, a remain washed out or the statue of a ghost. It has no beauty that attracts the eye, or calls to him who is restless to depart to neglect his business and to gaze.'[6] The last Abbasid caliph to rule in Baghdad fell into the hands of the Mongols when they captured the city in 1258. He was executed by being wrapped up in carpet and trampled to death under the hoofs of the Mongol cavalry.

From the late thirteenth century, Cairo, governed by the Mamluke sultans, was effectively the religious and intellectual capital of Islam.[7] It is evident that many of the contributors to the *Nights* knew and loved this city, and they show detailed familiarity with its topography. For example, in 'The Christian Broker's Tale', in the Hunchback cycle of stories, it is told of the Broker how he lodged in the al-Jawli Caravanserai and how he came to hear the story of the man with the severed hand and how the latter had lodged at the Masrur Caravanserai. (The Masrur Caravanserai was a huge hostelry, chiefly for the use of visiting merchants, located on the Bayn al-Qasrayn, or broad central highway, that runs through the heart of old Fatimid Cairo.) He then walked up the Bayn al-Qasrayn to the Jerjes Market, where he attempted to sell his fabrics. Later this young man, having arranged an assignation with a mysterious lady, walked out through the Zuweyla Gate, heading towards the Habbaniyya Quarter, in search of the house of the Naqib Barqut Abu Shamah, which was close to the al-Tawqa Lane.[8] Most, though not all, of these places can be located with the help of old handbooks or maps of the city. The storyteller has ensured that his audience will have no difficulty in visualizing the setting of his tale by placing it in the urban environment with which they were probably all familiar. Again, in 'The Jewish Physician's Tale', the young man's kinsmen argue about which is the most beautiful city in the world. Someone suggests Baghdad, but the man's father is emphatic that there is nowhere to match Cairo and he recites verses in praise of the Nile and the Ethiopian Pleasure Pond, before concluding:

And what is this compared with the observatory and its charms, of which every approaching viewer says, 'This spot is full of wonders'; and if you speak of the Night of the Nile-Flooding Feast, open the floodgates of words and release the bow; and if you see al-Rauda Park in the shade of late afternoon, you will be thrilled with wonder and delight; and if you stand at the river bank, when the sun is sinking and the Nile puts on its coat of mail and shield, you will be refreshed by the deep and ample shade and gentle breeze.[9]

By the beginning of the fourteenth century, Cairo had a population of perhaps a quarter of a million. The city was a sprawling and poorly policed agglomeration of commercial and residential quarters. It has been calculated that over half its narrow and intricately twisting streets ended in cul-de-sacs.

Looming over the southern end of the city, the Citadel enclosed within its walls not only the sultan's palace but also the barracks of the élite mamluke slave soldiers. Beneath the Citadel there was a parade ground and arms market. Proceeding north, one came eventually to the Bab al-Zuweyla. According to local folklore, the Bab al-Zuweyla, one of the gates into the core of old Cairo, was the invisible seat of the Qutb, 'the Pole', a mystical figure who presided over a secret brotherhood of Sufi saints. The open space before the gate was also the place of public execution, and severed heads were set on spikes over the gate. Strangely this was no deterrent to the disreputable, and the Bab al-Zuweyla was one of their favourite meeting places. Here one could buy musical instruments, consult astrologers, take lessons in single-stick fighting and listen to stories from the *Nights* and similar collections. From 'The First Constable's History', one learns that the Zuweyla Gate was shut at night, thus protecting the greater part of commercial Cairo from night attacks by bandits. Ma'aruf the Cobbler had his shop in the Darb al-Ahmar, or 'Red Street', just outside the Zuweyla Gate.

The Zuweyla Gate was at the southern end of the Bayn al-Qasrayn. Bayn al-Qasrayn literally means 'Between the Two Palaces', and in earlier times this broad highway did indeed run between the palaces of the Fatimid caliphs. However, by the time the Christian broker's interlocutor went walking up this highway, it was lined by mosques, teaching colleges and shops. The great religious foundations provided an imposing backdrop to Mamluke ceremonial. The Bayn al-Qasrayn was Cairo's biggest shopping street, and, according to the fifteenth-century chronicler al-Maqrizi, storytellers and entertainers were to be found along its length. So were stalls serving cooked foods. Although restaurants were more or less unknown in medieval Cairo, many citizens availed themselves of take-away dinners which they either consumed as they continued walking or took back to their houses.

Smaller streets leading off the Bayn al-Qasrayn provided access to specialized markets, among them those of the sellers of knives, of books, of candles and of woodwork. Such markets are well described by Lane:

These streets are called, in Arabic, 'Sooks'; and are generally termed by us 'Bazars' [sic]. A whole street of this description, or a portion of such a street, commonly contains only or chiefly shops appropriated to that particular trade; and is called the Sook of that trade. In general, the shop is a small recess or cell, about six or seven feet high, and between three and four feet wide, the floor of which is even with the top of a raised seat of stone or brick, called 'mastabah', between two and three feet high and about the same in breadth; upon which the shopkeeper usually sits. The front of the shop is furnished with shutters; which when closed at night, are secured by a wooden lock.[10]

Such shops furnished the settings for what is a leitmotif in the *Nights*, the story which opens with the shopkeeper, who is minding his business in his shop, when a mysterious woman pauses to examine his stock. In 'The Christian Broker's Tale', the mysterious woman raises her veil to reveal a large pair of black eyes, before asking after a piece of silk fabric. In 'The Steward's Tale', she enters the young merchant's shop, raises her veil and begins a conversation. In 'The Story of Nur al-Din Ali Ibn-Bakkar and the Slave Girl', Nur al-Din was sitting with a friend in a shop when 'there came up ten full-bosomed virgins, looking like moons, with a young lady riding upon a gray she-mule with trappings of red silk set with gems and pearls'. Such commercial encounters are invariably the prelude to bizarre and wonderful adventures.

The slave market, or *suq al-raqiq*, usually took the form of a rectangular building with an open courtyard in the centre, with the stalls of the slaves ranged around the courtyard. Voyeurs were discouraged, and thus only those judged wealthy enough to be serious potential customers were admitted to this market. In 'The Tale of the Damsel Tuhfat al-Kulub', Harun al-Rashid goes to watch the buying and selling in the slave-dealers' quarters, which was 'a building tall of wall and large of lodgement, with sleeping-cells and chambers therein, after the number of slave-girls, and folk sitting upon the wooden benches'.[11] More public slave auctions, however, feature in 'Ali Shar and Zumurrud' and in 'Ali Nur al-Din and Miriam the Girdle-Girl'.

Shops and markets tended to be clustered close to the central axis of the Bayn al-Qasrayn, while residential quarters were located further out. Customarily the houses of the wealthy were closed in upon themselves, giving little evidence of wealth or even comfort to those who passed by on the street. Inside, however, was another matter, as the porter discovered in 'The Story of the Porter and the Three Ladies':

The shopper and the porter went in, and the doorkeeper locked the door and followed them until they came to a spacious, well-appointed, and splendid hall. It had arched compartments and niches with carved woodwork; it had a booth hung with drapes; and it had closets and cupboards covered with curtains. In the middle stood a large pool full of water, with a fountain in the center, and at the far end stood a couch of black juniper wood, set with gems and pearls, with a canopylike mosquito net of red silk, fastened with pearls as big as hazelnuts or bigger. The curtain was unfastened.[12]

As one moved away from the central highway of the Bayn al-Qasrayn, the streets became narrower. The narrow zigzag streets, the alleys going up in staircases and the frequent cul-de-sacs meant that the unwary traveller was always at risk from false guides and thieves. On the other hand, this pattern of street layout made it easier to barricade off parts of the city in times of civic disturbance and protect respectable neighbourhoods from the gangs of thugs and beggars which dominated the outer slums. The worst slums were located on the northern and western fringes of the city, beyond the old Fatimid walls. There the houses, or shanties, were made from sun-dried brick and palm-leaves. The quarters of al-Husayniyya and Bab al-Luq were dominated by criminal gangs and will be discussed later in that context.

The cemeteries, which in Cairo mostly lay to the east of the city, were places for pious meditation, amorous encounters and pickpockets. Lovers trysted in the underpoliced cemeteries. People who could find no homes elsewhere slept in the shelter of the tombs in the City of the Dead and begged or conducted their nefarious trades there. They shared their territory with ghouls. Also to the east of the city were the vast hills of rubbish which provided a living of sorts for scavengers, both animal and human.

A string of ponds, or pleasure pools, were to be found to the west of the city between the Nile and the Cairo Canal. The Ezbekiyya Pond, dug out in 1476 by a Mamluke emir called Ezbek, became the most popular place of entertainment in the late Middle Ages. People used to go there after the noon prayer on Fridays to relax. To the south of Ezbekiyya, the Elephant Pond was first dug out in Fatimid times, but it dried up subsequently and had to be re-excavated. Its surface is described as being covered with pleasure craft and yellow water lilies. It had a horse-racing track beside it, which is mentioned in story of 'Sayf al-Muluk and Badia al-Jamal'. The houses of the élite lined the edge of the pool. One of those buildings, the House of Kafur, was notorious as a haunted place to which the jinn fled to escape the conjurations of magicians. Further south was the Qarun Pond, noteworthy for the extraordinary adventures that Judar the Fisher-man had with three Maghribi sorcerers on its bank. Further to the south yet was the Ethiopian Pond. As has been noted, the delights of the Ethiopian Pond are extolled by the father in 'The Jewish Physician's Tale'. He even recites a series of verses, beginning with the couplet:

> O what a day by the Ethiopian Pond
> We spent between the shadows and the light

and concluding:

> Soft carpets made and spread for us to rest,
> As we sat passing the refreshing wine,
> Which of all drugs for sorrow works the best,
> Quaffing deep draughts from large and brimful cups
> For they alone can quench our burning thirst.

The pleasances and public spaces were thronged with entertain-ers, storytellers and their competitors. In his extraordinary treatise on the philosophy of history, the *Muqaddima*, the fourteenth-century thinker Ibn Khaldun suggested that entertainers flourished when a civilization decayed:

They become excessive when civilization develops excessively. Thus, we learn that there are Egyptians who teach dumb creatures like birds and domestic donkeys, who produce marvellous spectacles which give the illusion that objects are transformed, and who teach the use of a camel driver's chant, how to dance and walk on ropes in the air, how to lift heavy animals and stones, and other things.[13]

To those entertainers listed by Ibn Khaldun one might also add the storytellers, the snake-charmers, the contortionists, the shadow theatre players, the jugglers, the wrestlers and the *darrats* ('Pétomanes' or professional farters).[14] The storyteller's mode of working has already been discussed in the previous chapter. It is time now to turn to his rivals.

In the *Nights* 'Story of Woman's Wiles' (which is set in Damascus), the wily woman instructs a mamluke (a slave soldier) in the following terms: 'Arise and go straight away to the Takht al-Qala'a, seek out all the Banu Sasan, ape dancers, bear leaders, drummers, pipers.' The Takht al-Qala'a was an open space beneath the Damascus Citadel where people went to be entertained. For reasons which are mysterious, Banu Sasan, or 'Children of Sasan', was the term used to designate the loose community of low-life entertainers, spongers, beggars and thieves.[15] If the reference is to the Sassanian dynasty who ruled over Iran before the coming of Islam, the reference is still mysterious. Members of the Banu Sasan do not feature prominently in the texts on religion, law and history produced by Islam's clerical élite. However, a few long poems have survived which commemorate their achievements. Moreover, treatises were written to expose rogues' tricks. The most famous of these was the *Kashf al-Asrar*, or 'Unveiling of Secrets', by al-Jawbari, who wrote the work to a princely commission in thirteenth-century Iraq.[16] Although al-Jawbari's work was ostensibly written as a caution to the virtuous and a warning to the prudent, there can be little doubt that his retelling of famous confidence tricks, set-ups and practical jokes was written to entertain. Indeed, the genre he was writing in closely resembles the sixteenth- and seventeenth-century literature in English devoted to the exploits of coney catchers, bawdy baskets, Abraham men and other assorted rogues. Al-Jawbari himself, before he took to literature, had travelled and performed throughout the Islamic lands as a conjuror. In those days the conjuror's repertoire included acts which we would now regard as being the province of the juggler on the one hand and of the fraudulent occultist on the other. In the *Kashf al-Asrar*, al-Jawbari exposed not only the tricks of the conjuror, as broadly interpreted, but also the dodges of wonder-working monks, lasciviously pederastic Sufis, itinerant preachers, alchemists, fire-walkers, prostitutes, horse doctors and treasure-hunters.

In one chapter devoted to the frauds of the Banu Sasan, al-Jawbari relates how, when he was in the city of Harran, he saw an ape whose master had trained it to make the human gesture of salutation, to perform the ritual ablutions, to pray and to weep. The ape's master then brought the ape, accompanied by a retinue of servants in Indian costume, to the mosque, where the ape performed the ablutions and the prayer. When the curious in the congregation pressed him to explain this wonder, the ape's master replied that this was in truth no ape but an ensorcelled Indian prince. The king who was his father had married off the prince to a princess. All had gone well in the marriage, until the prince's wife became jealous, suspecting that he had fallen in love with a slave girl. His protestations were useless, and in a rage she used a spell to turn him into an ape. Ever since that moment, the prince had wandered the world in this unhappy form. The ape's master then took a collection on behalf of the 'prince'. Then he and his team scarpered from the town. Although al-Jawbari claims to have been an eyewitness to all this, it bears a certain affinity with 'The Second Dervish's Tale' in the *Nights*. It is an open question whether the *Nights* story inspired the confidence trickster or vice versa. We shall return to the conjuror, and to al-Jawbari's treatise, in the context of medieval Arab crime.

Conjuring, or *sha'badhah*, spawned a specialized literature of its own.[17] In the preface to his *Flowers of the Gardens Concerning Knowledge of Juggling*, the fifteenth-century street-corner conjuror al-Zakhruri writes of having seen many works on his craft. Al-Zakhruri's own treatise provided directions for the performance of an impressive range of tricks, some of which are quite elaborate. For example, he describes how a little wax model of a man clutching a scroll can be thrown into a basin of water by the conjuror, who claims that he has sent him as a messenger to the King of the Jinn. Then, when the manikin fails to reappear, the conjuror feigns annoyance and dispatches another wax figure, this one armed with a sword, to punish the messenger for his tardiness. In a little while the water in the basin is coloured red, the swordsman and the severed head of the messenger reappear on the surface, and everyone is amazed. Al-Zakhruri instructs the neophyte in the mechanics of the trick and the patter to go with it.[18]

Towards the end of his curious treatise, al-Zakhruri briefly describes the sort of competition that the street-corner conjuror had to face in medieval Cairo from fellow members of the Banu Sasan. First he mentions the professional treasure-hunters. Then there were the alchemists, who pretended to make gold from gypsum and had many other tricks up their sleeve. Then there were the fake ascetics, venerable sheikhs who pretended to go into isolation without food or water for forty days, so as to impress the piously credulous – whereas, in fact, food was being delivered to them by accomplices, who passed it up through a hidden trapdoor in the floor. Finally, there were the Saramitis, who travelled about with a great tabernacle covered with mystical signs, specialized in staging bogus manifestations of poltergeists and performed equally bogus exorcisms for a fee.[19]

Sometimes conjuring was put to pious purposes, as Sufi preachers might perform tricks in order to attract an audience, to whom they would then preach. Al-Hallaj, the great tenth-century Iraqi mystic, having produced an apple, seemingly out of the empty air, told the people around him that he had just plucked it from a tree in paradise. When one man, sharper-eyed than the rest, commented that the paradisal apple seemed to have worm holes in it, al-Hallaj's reply was swift: 'How could it be otherwise? I plucked the apple from a tree in the Mansion of Eternity and brought it into the House of Decay, and that is why it is touched with corruption!' Al-Hallaj is said to have travelled to India to study the rope trick and other magical feats. Hostile contemporaries accused al-Hallaj of having rigged up a special room, the 'Expanding Chamber', in which concealed pipes and partitions allowed him to fake the appearance of a living lamb from out of a flaming furnace, to conjure a fish out of thin air and to make his own body seem to swell until it filled most of the chamber.[20]

The word la'ab, which literally means 'play', was used to refer to both conjuring and juggling. According to those mysterious tenth-century encyclopaedists the Brethren of Purity, juggling 'is not anything real but just quickness of movement and concealment of the means (whereby the tricks are executed) ... The fools laugh, but the reasoning marvel at the skill of the performer.' The hawi, or snake-charmer, juggled with snakes. He also doubled as a kind of environmental health officer, getting rid of snakes from people's houses. According to Lane, members of certain dervish orders specialized in this activity. Maxime du Camp, Flaubert's travelling companion in Egypt in 1849, included a vivid account of the snake-charmer's modus operandi in the narrative of his travels. The young man, after letting the snake curl around his body several times, spat into its mouth and pressed upon its head, so that it became stiff (as stiff as the serpents conjured into rods by Pharaoh's sorcerers in the Old Testament). Then du Camp invited the snake-charmer into his room. The young man immediately divined the presence of a viper and, after stripping naked, he walked about the room whistling monotonously and tapping the walls. Then, invoking God, he conjured the snake to appear, ending with the words, 'If you are within, show yourself! I adjure you in the name of one so great that I dare not say it! If it is your will to obey, appear! If it is your will to disobey, die! die! die!' Sure enough, a snake did appear and come slithering towards the boy, who caught it. Du Camp, however, concluded that he had been fooled by sleight of hand.[21] The Rifaʿi dervishes, in particular, specialized in snake handling, going so far as to eat the snakes they handled. They also had a remunerative sideline in fire-walking (for all their 'miracles' were staged for money). In the early fourteenth century, the fundamentalist religious thinker Ibn Taymiyya mounted a campaign against them in which he revealed how they smeared frogs' fat, pieces of orange peel and talc on their feet to protect them from the burning coals.

Then there were the *bahluwans*. A *bahluwan* (literally, a champion) could be an acrobat, a tight-rope walker or a master of one or other of the martial arts. Wrestling was particularly popular in the Mamluke period. The Sultan al-Muzaffar Hajji (reigned 1346–7) loved the common people and common sports and he used to take part in wrestling matches, wearing only the leather trousers of the professional wrestler. (Hajji's other enthusiasms included single-stick fighting, pigeon racing and polo.) Fencers and the stagers of fights between animals also contended for the attention of pleasure seekers and loafers.[22]

Live theatre (*khayal*) was not entirely unknown in the Islamic lands, but shows seem to have been vulgar affairs, which were neither patronized by the élite nor treated as if they were part of Arab high culture.[23] (In the nineteenth century, Lane was particularly dismissive of the 'players of low and ridiculous farces, who are called "Mohabbazzen"'.) The little evidence that there is about live drama in the medieval Arab world suggests that many of the plays were crude farces, not very different from the stories of cuckoldry, roguery and low life that abound in the *Nights*; and, as we have seen, it is possible that some, at least, of both the plays and the stories derive from themes that were first developed in the

Hellenistic drama of late antiquity. One of the rare literary references to an actor occurs in a poem recited by Zumurrud in the story of 'Ali Shar and Zumurrud': 'You go with one beard and return with another / As if you were one of the performers of *khayal*.'[24] (Burton mistranslates the couplet in question, believing that *khayali* had to refer to a puppeteer.) Shadow plays (*khayal al-zill*) seem to have been staged more frequently than dramas using actors. Both types of presentation were staged by the disreputable for the vulgar and commonly comprised bawdy romps featuring buffoons, cuckolds, procuresses and hashish eaters. It was all closer in spirit to the music hall than to Molière. Shadow plays seem commonly to have been staged in *khans* or taverns.[25] Despite their bawdy nature, the pious head of Saladin's Chancery, al-Qadi al-Fadil, was able to perceive a mystical message in the performance of shadow plays: 'I have had a lesson of great significance. I have seen empires coming and empires going, and when the screen was folded up, I discovered that the prime mover was but one.' More generally, the illusory imagery of the shadow theatre often provided mystical poetry with a repertoire of metaphor.

The thirteenth-century texts of shadow plays written by Ibn Daniyal are an important source on entertainers and low life generally. Ibn Daniyal (1248–1311), by profession an ophthalmologist, had a reputation as a serious poet and was the friend of members of the mamluke élite in Cairo. However, there was another side to him; he wrote scripts (in colloquial Middle Arabic) for shadow plays, and three of these have survived. His play *Ajib wa Gharib* parades some of the seedier denizens of the marketplace. In it, the characters appear one after another in front of the Zuweyla Gate. Gharib (literally 'Strange') is a fraudulent occultist, who keeps body and soul together by selling bogus talismans, by faking epileptic fits to solicit charity, by gumming his eyelids together to feign blindness, by training performing apes and by other similarly dubious skills. He is followed by Ajib (literally 'Amazing'), a half-educated and fanciful preacher, the chief aim of whose sermons is to raise money for himself. Then come the snake-charmer, the seller of folk medicines, the herbalist, the surgeon, the tight-rope walker, the conjuror, the geomancer, the amulet seller, the lion tamer, the elephant handler, the man with the marvellous goat, the man who trains cats and mice to be friends, the dog trainer, the bear leader, the Sudanese clown, the sword-swallower, the ape dancer, the self-mutilator, the bogus pilgrim and the lamplighter who is also a beggar. They all make speeches, in which they reveal the tricks of their trade and lament the hardness of their lot. (Ibn Daniyal's collection of Banu Sasan types is not a comprehensive one, and al-Jawbari's *Kashf al-Asrar* lists many more, including stone-swallowers, thimble riggers, wrestlers, singers and galli-galli men.) A second play, *Tayf al-Khayal* ('Shadow of the Imagination'), actually has a plot, in which a soldier, the Emir Wisal, is trapped into an unsuitable marriage; but the plot is a vehicle for satire on contemporary manners and events – such as the Mamluke Sultan Baybars's much publicized (though ultimately ineffective) attempt to ban hashish, pubs and prostitution. The third of Ibn Daniyal's surviving plays, *Al-Mutayyam* ('The Love-Stricken One'), is a curious narrative dealing with the homosexual love of al-Mutayyam and a series of animal fights that he and his beloved stage.

Together with the works of Ibn Daniyal and al-Jawbari, some *adab* treatises and less well-known rival story collections, the *Nights* is one of few sources on the small-time and the seedy, and we have concentrated in this chapter on the disreputable street-corner rivals to the storyteller. However, the *Nights* has plenty to tell us about more ordinary trades. One only needs to think of the porter, the barber, Ma'aruf the Cobbler, Judar the Fisherman, Badr al-Basim the Blacksmith, the Ferryman of the Nile and a whole tribe of cuckolded *gadis* and foolish schoolmasters who crowd the pages of its stories. Such people furnished much of the subject-matter, as well as most of the audience, for the stories of the *Nights*. The real-life counterparts of these characters led lives which were largely ignored by the medieval Arab compilers of chronicles and biographical dictionaries, which focused rather narrowly on a military, administrative and religious élite.

It is fortunate that the *Nights* is not a unique source on the lives of humbler folk, for then one would have to be uneasy about using without corroboration a work of fantasy as a source about private life, commercial practice and *mentalités*. However, besides the literary sources already mentioned, there is also a vast and curious archive known as the Geniza. This huge hoard of documents, over 10,000 pieces of paper, was discovered in the sealed lumber-room of a synagogue in old Cairo in the 1890s. Because of the medieval Jewish reverence for the name of God, they were afraid to throw away anything that might bear his name. Therefore these papers and fragments of paper, written in the Arabic language but in the Hebrew alphabet, had been preserved, rather than being tossed out on to the rubbish heap. The Geniza, or store-room of papers, includes documents of all sorts – wills, laundry lists, letters, poems, deeds of sale, marriage contracts, prayers, legal contracts, and so on. As we have mentioned in Chapter 2, the Geniza even contains the earliest reference to the full title of the *Nights* (in a Jewish bookseller's record of books lent out). The Geniza has proved to be an extraordinarily rich historical source for everyday life in Egypt from the tenth to the thirteenth centuries. The evidence it provides has been brilliantly marshalled and interpreted by S.D. Goitein in his magisterial five-volume synthesis, *A Mediterranean Society: The Jewish Communities of the Arab World as Portrayed in the Documents of the Cairo Geniza* (1967–88). Goitein's study presents the world-view of a vanished society of merchants, shopkeepers, artisans and their families. (It is incidentally noteworthy that now and again Goitein drew on the *Nights* to supplement or confirm the data provided by the Geniza.)

The *Nights*, other literary sources and the Geniza documents offer us countless insights into the material life and *mentalité* of medieval Arab townsfolk: about eating, sleeping, child rearing and cooking. For the social historian, the detailed shopping lists provided at the beginning of both 'The Porter and the Three Ladies' cycle and the Hunchback cycle are as exciting as any fantasy about jinn and flying carpets. The stories are also a rich source for the proverbs and maxims which furnished the common currency of social intercourse: 'He broke his lance on the very first raid'; 'Be kind to him who wrongs you'; 'In love all are alike'; 'The jar cannot be saved every time'; 'A lie may save a man, but the truth is better and safer.' One also finds a range of slang and metaphor in the stories which is almost totally absent in the literature of officials and belletrists. The material contained in the *Nights* might further provide the basis for a study of the medieval Arab language of gesture. For example, to strike the left hand against the right signified regret (the Calcutta II version of 'The Jewish Physician's Tale'), while to bite one's hand signified repentance ('Abu'l-Husn and his Slave-Girl Tawaddud'). There is no space in the present study to explore this, or a thousand other tempting avenues, but, in the chapters which follow, we shall examine the themes of crime, sex and magic, as they feature in the *Nights* and in related sources.

6

Low Life

====

In pre-Islamic Arabia camel-raiding was not regarded as theft, and successful camel-raids were frequently celebrated in poetry. In general, theft was not considered to be a highly reprehensible crime. However, with the coming of Islam and the promulgation of the shari'a, or religious law, fixed penalties were instituted for theft; and a persistent thief, if he was caught, was liable to have one or both of his hands cut off. However, the attitudes persisted, and in certain circles thieves were admired and celebrated, so long as they were cunning and successful. The chronicles, biographical dictionaries and legal treatises which were produced by the medieval Arabs tell us little about the criminal underworld.[1] For that we are forced to turn to fiction. Tales about criminals and confidence tricksters abound in the *Nights*. Although Baghdad is occasionally the nominal setting of these stories, most of them seem to have been composed, or at least rewritten, in Egypt in the Mamluke and Ottoman periods.

Even so, though most 'Baghdadi' crime stories in the *Nights* are really about Cairo, Abbasid Baghdad did produce its own semi-legendary criminals. Many tales were told of the ingenious exploits of the ninth-century master-thief, al-Uqab ('the Eagle'), among them the story of a bet he had with a certain doctor that within a set period of time al-Uqab could steal something from the doctor's house. Although the house was closely guarded, al-Uqab drugged the guards. Then, posing as an apparition of Jesus and making use of hypnotism, he succeeded in stealing off with the doctor himself.[2]

Medieval treatises on crime recognized several categories of thief. One group of housebreakers, the burrowers, simply dug their way through the mud-dried bricks in order to force an entry into the house they wanted to burgle. Other thieves employed hooked poles and grappling irons to fish things out of windows. Others used to make use of a tortoise with a lighted candle placed on its back. They sent this creature ahead of them into the house they proposed to burgle. If the house was currently occupied, then the owner would surely exclaim in surprise on seeing the tortoise (something along the lines of, 'Oh, look! There's a tortoise with a candle on its back. I wonder what it's doing in my house'), and the thieves would be warned off. If, however, the house was unoccupied, then the candle on the tortoise's back would help to guide the thieves as they went about their work. The tortoise was not the only creature to be of use to the professional criminal. In the course of his bizarre and lengthy treatise that purported to discuss the respective merits of the cock and the dog, *Kitab al-Hayawan*, the ninth-century essayist al-Jahiz remarks that the stranglers, who always work in gangs, make use of dogs. Whenever they strangle a victim, at the same time they beat their dogs, so that the barking of the dogs drowns out the screams of the victim, and the suspicions of respectable people in the neighbourhood are not aroused.[3]

It seems that it was common in medieval Baghdad for retired thieves to join the police force as *tawwabun* or 'repentants'. According to the tenth-century historian al-Mas'udi, 'The Repentants are old thieves, who, as they get on in years, give up their profession. When a crime is committed, they know who did it and can point out the culprit. It does, however, often happen they share with the thieves the fruits of their thefts.'[4] What al-Mas'udi has to say about the *ayyarun* is no less curious. In Baghdad, *ayyarun* – gangs of ruffians and vagabonds – armed with cudgels collected protection money from shops and policed their neighbourhoods, controlling the local rackets and protecting them from rival gangs based in other quarters. These gangs were sufficiently organized and

armed to provide sizeable militias in times of civil strife. Al-
Mas'udi describes how the *ayyarun* 'went into battle almost naked,
wearing only short trousers or drawers. They had made themselves
a sort of helmet out of plaited palm-leaves, which they called
khudh. Their shields were made of these same leaves and of reed
mats covered with tar and stuffed with sand and gravel.' Bizarrely,
the leaders of the *ayyarun* went into battle riding on human
mounts, that is to say, the chiefs rode piggy-back on the shoulders
of lesser vagabonds who had decked themselves out as horses in
fancy harnesses. Gang warfare and factional strife, which plagued
Baghdad from the tenth century onwards, played a part in reducing the authority of the caliphate; and, for a while, the caliphs
removed themselves from Baghdad and settled in Samarra, in
order to bring the clashes between their soldiers and the city's
mobs to an end.[5]

The fame of some of the great criminals of Abbasid Baghdad
survived the fall of that city to the Mongols in 1258. In Mamluke
Egypt popular stories were produced about villains of both sexes
who were alleged to have flourished under the Abbasid caliphate,
and some of those stories eventually found their way into the later
compilations of the *Nights*. However, Cairo itself was the scene of
many spectacular crimes, crimes which were a cause of marvel and
the source of inspiration to storytellers. For example, some time in
the year 1264, in the reign of the Mamluke Sultan Baybars, a
dresser was summoned to a house at the Bab al-Sha'riyya on the
Khalij al-Masri (a canal that ran through Cairo into the Nile), on
the corner of the Husayniyya Quarter. There her assignment was
to dress and make up a woman called Ghazia, famed in the city
for her beauty and the extravagance of her apparel. The dresser
went into Ghazia's house, but never came out again. However,
unknown to the people in the house, the dresser had been accompanied by a female slave, who had been left to wait outside.
After waiting a long time, this slave girl went off to report her
mistress's disappearance to the Governor of Cairo. He promptly

had the place raided. Inside, they found not only the dresser's corpse, but a whole cellar full of corpses. The *shurta*, the police force, arrested the entire gang, and in a series of painful interrogations the gang's *modus operandi* was disclosed. Ghazia had made use of an old crone as a bawd or procuress. Ghazia used her beauty and the crone used encouraging words to lure gullible men back to the house. Inside the house, two male confederates would jump on the lusty and unsuspecting victims, killing them and stripping them of everything they had. A fifth confederate, a brickmaker, had a furnace, and at regular intervals the corpses would be taken along to be fed into the furnace. At the end of the investigation, the five were sentenced to death by crucifixion, and the house was confiscated. Somewhat incongruously the house was turned into a mosque, the Masjid al-Khanaqa, or Mosque of the Strangleress.[6]

In the case of Ghazia, robbery was the motive for murder. In times of famine, however, people were murdered in Cairo for the meat that was on their bodies. Abd al-Latif al-Baghdadi, an Iraqi physician who visited Cairo in the years 1200–1201, reported that small children were being boiled or roasted alive while he was there, despite the governor of the city's decree that any cannibals who were caught would be burned alive. Abd al-Latif's narrative abounds with tales calculated to make the flesh creep. 'One night after, a little after the sunset prayer, a young slave played with a newly weaned child which belonged to a wealthy person. While the child was at her side, a beggar, seizing a moment when the slave had her eyes turned from him, slit the child's stomach and began to eat its flesh raw.'[7] Similar stories of kidnap, body-snatching and cannibalism recurred in the 1290s when Egypt was again stricken by severe famine.[8]

At its best, a good crime was *ajib*, a marvel and something as wonderful to hear about as rain of blood or the birth of a two-headed calf. This fascination with crimes and their detection spawned a considerable literature, both factual and fiction. Al-Jawbari's thirteenth-century treatise, the *Kashf al-Asrar*, or

'Revelation of Secrets', has already been referred to.[9] It is one of our most important sources on criminal deceits. Al-Jawbari's book was ostensibly written to warn honest people of the dangers they faced from crooks and charlatans. (The unconvincing piety of this boast can be compared to that of the prologue to the *Nights*, in which it is claimed that the latter contains 'splendid biographies that teach the reader to detect deception and to protect himself from it'.) However, there can be little doubt that al-Jawbari's retelling of famous confidence tricks, set-ups and practical jokes was really put together for the sake of entertaining the reader rather than warning him. A considerable portion of the *Kashf al-Asrar* is devoted to criminal activities – among them the tricks of bogus holy men, bandits, fraudulent alchemists, horse fakers, muggers, body-snatchers, highwaymen and housebreakers.

'The Romance of Baybars', an anonymous late-medieval folk-epic about the legendary exploits of the thirteenth-century Mamluke Sultan Baybars, made only light use of the facts of Baybars's reign.[10] In their place a glorious farrago was conjured up concerning Baybars's youthful association in Syria and Egypt with all sorts of genial low-life types – wrestlers, grooms, cudgel-men, repentant thieves and, above all, the Isma'ilis. In historical reality, the Isma'ilis, Shi'ite heretics who came to use assassination to promote their aims, were among that Sultan's greatest enemies. In the 'Romance', however, the Isma'ilis are Baybars's greatest allies – and very valuable ones too, for they are expert cat burglars and skilled also in the use of drugs for overpowering enemies. The 'Romance' celebrates the cunning of the Isma'ilis and other semi-criminal friends of the Sultan in a struggle against corrupt officials and soldiers who are secret enemies of Islam.

More generally, a cult of cunning and tricks (*hiyal*) is pervasive in Arab literature, and tales of the cunning thieves or rogues constituted a sub-genre in the broader genre which celebrated the cunning of soldiers, women, uninvited guests and even animals. The celebration of artfulness or tricksiness, whether in the commission of crimes, in arguing points of law or in inserting puns in poems, is one of the most striking features of medieval Arab culture. The anonymous *Raqa'iq al-hilal fi Daqa'iq al-hiyal*, or 'Cloaks of Fine Fabric in Subtle Ruses', written in the Mamluke period, is a fairly typical example of the genre.[11] It includes sections on the cunning dodges of jinn, prophets, kings, viziers, lawyers, holy men, and so on. A further specialized sub-genre of the literature of cunning celebrated the disreputable though not exactly criminal activities of the *tufayli*, the uninvited guest or gate-crasher. In medieval Baghdad, gate-crashing was an organized way of earning a living, and the professional *tufaylis* formed a kind of guild under the direction of a sheikh, who each evening would allocate selected dinner parties to his following of gate-crashers.[12] In the *Nights* story of 'Isaac of Mosul and the Merchant', Isaac sees a singer in the street, falls in love with her and follows her into a house where a dinner is being held. The host, who has spotted that Isaac is a gate-crasher, merely remarks, 'This is a parasite [*tufayli*]; but he is a pleasant fellow, so treat him courteously.'

Whereas highwaymen and other robbers outside the towns were usually presented in the *Nights* tales and in other stories as pretty stupid (Jawan the Kurd, for example, in 'Ali Shah and Zumurrud') the urban criminal was generally reputed to be a cunning man. He was admired for his guile and the success which his guile brought him. (Robin Hood and Dick Turpin have comparable reputations in British culture.) Independent stories about real or legendary criminals, among them Mercury Ali, Crafty Dalilah and Ahmad the Sickness, circulated among the people prior to being gathered up into the *Nights* collection.[13] Ali Zaybak, or Mercury Ali, seems to have been a real brigand in eleventh-century Baghdad, before he became the hero of a loosely linked series of fictional exploits, some of which eventually found their way into the *Nights*. Similarly, Dalilah was already known of in Abbasid Baghdad, for al-Mas'udi refers to this 'famous female confidence trickster' in his tenth-century chronicle *Meadows of*

Gold. Al-Mas'udi, indeed, incorporated several allegedly true tales of crime and roguery in his chronicle.

Ahmad al-Danaf, or Ahmad the Sickness, like Ali Zaybak, may have been a historical figure. Inconsistent information is given by two Mamluke chroniclers. According to Ibn Taghribirdi, Ahmad the Sickness was the hero of a popular romance current in the fifteenth century, but his story was based on a certain criminal called Hamdi who lived in Cairo in the tenth century. According to Ibn Iyas, on the other hand, the bandit known as Ahmad the Sickness was captured by the Mamluke authorities in 1486 and executed by being sawn in half. Most likely the fifteenth-century criminal had taken to calling himself Ahmad the Sickness in reference to his legendary precursor in crime.

A brotherhood of crime flourished in medieval Cairo. With its own hierarchy and a code of honour (of sorts), the Cairene underworld presented a dark mirror to the ruling establishment. It would appear that gangsters sometimes messed and slept together in *tibaq*, or barracks. A hierarchy of respect among thieves is suggested in the story of 'The Sandalwood Merchant and the Sharpers', in which a merchant who has been swindled is advised to visit a certain Sheikh of Thieves, an old man 'versed in craft, magic and trickery', pre-eminent among the city's sharpers for his cunning, who adjudicated and delivered judgement on the exploits of his juniors.

The organization of criminals and rogues was not simply a fictional convention. It reflected elements of historical reality. Guilds were unknown in Mamluke Egypt, but when after the Ottoman occupation in the early sixteenth century guilds were established to regulate crafts and trades, the guilds of the thieves and the beggars were found among their number. In the Ottoman period (sixteenth to eighteenth centuries), Egyptian crime was organized and, to some extent at least, placed under state supervision. There were guilds for every craft in Cairo. Hence, thieves, prostitutes, entertainers, beggars and cheaters at cards had their recognized guilds. In most Ottoman cities it was possible for the victim of a robbery to go to the commander of the janissary regiment garrisoned in the town and report what had been stolen. The janissary commander would in turn contact the sheikh of the thieves' guild, and the stolen property might be returned – for a price. Thieves' guilds survived into the nineteenth century in Egypt. Edward William Lane, writing in the 1830s, informed his readers that 'Even the common thieves used, not many years since, to respect a superior who was called their sheykh. He was often required to search for stolen goods, and bring offenders to justice; which he generally accomplished.'[14]

In the Middle Ages a great deal of the criminal activity in the cities was controlled by the members of *futuwwa* lodges. *Futuwwa* is sometimes translated as 'chivalry', though it is more accurately translated as 'youngmanliness'. The history of *futuwwa* is somewhat obscure.[15] In tenth- or eleventh-century Iraq, lodges were formed initially at least by unmarried young men. These young men, perhaps because they were unemployed or underemployed, or perhaps because they had not accumulated enough capital to marry and therefore felt obliged to seek male companionship, came together in such associations. One was initiated into a *futuwwa* lodge by drinking a cup of salt water and donning a special pair of trousers, the trousers of *futuwwa*. Subsequently *futuwwa* lodges spread throughout the Middle East, and many of them were devoted to respectable and even idealistic purposes. They might help ensure high standards of artisanship and commercial practice; they might devote their resources to offering hospitality to passing strangers; or they might assemble to perform mystical exercises. In medieval Cairo, however, the lodges, or most of them at any rate, came under the control of criminal elements and provided the basis for the organization of protection rackets in the city's suburbs. Such gangsters proliferated in the Husayniyya, the north-eastern area of Cairo, and they congregated in special meeting places, 'the halls of *futuwwa*'. They organized themselves in lodges called 'villages'. The rogues who called themselves 'the sons of Husayniyya' feature prominently in 'The Romance of Baybars'. Moralists denounced the *futuwwa* groups for their assemblies during which wine was drunk and where it was suspected that sexual, especially homosexual, activities took place. Members of *futuwwa* groups carried knives, and having sworn always to help one another, if one of their number should be arrested, then they would mass outside the prison to enforce their fellow's release. According to one fourteenth-century critic of *futuwwa*, its members took their vows of brotherhood so seriously that a member of a lodge might force his wife into prostitution in order to support a fellow lodge member who had fallen upon hard times.[16]

Somewhat similar to the *futuwwa* lodges were the hunting lodges. *Shatir* (pl. *shuttar*) has a range of meanings. Most commonly it means a loose, immoral person, a cunning man, a sharper. The *Nights* abounds with tales of the 'sharpers' or 'larrikins'. However, in the Mamluke period *shatir* was also used to refer to archers who were members of hunting lodges. While members of *futuwwa* lodges tended to rely on the knife and the cudgel, the *shuttar* were specialists with the crossbow and expert hunters of birds. These hunting clubs, which effectively constituted a disreputable kind of militia, were regularly denounced by the *ulema* because of the criminal elements who tended to attach themselves to the *shuttar*. In one version of 'The Romance of Baybars', the young Baybars is inducted into a league of men who hunt birds with crossbows.[17]

In the *Nights*, *shatir* tends to be used in the wider sense of 'crafty rogue'; for example, the Egyptian Ali Zaybak is described as a *shatir*. Always one step ahead of the police, he is perhaps the greatest of all the *shuttar*. For Ali Zaybak stealing is an art, and he steals from fellow criminals simply to demonstrate to them his skill in this art. Ahmad al-Danaf, his rival in Baghdad, maintains a barracks in Baghdad from where he directs the activities of his forty *shuttar*. In a story outside the Ali Zaybak cycle, 'The tale of

Nur al-Din Ali and his Son', the benevolent pastry cook in Damascus, who takes in Badr al-Din Hassan, is a former *shatir* and thief: 'but Allàh had made him repent and turn from the evil of his ways and open a cook-shop'. Despite his repentance, it is evident from the story that he was still an intimidating figure and not the sort of person one would want to pick a fight with.

Fidawiyya are defined in Lane's *Arabic–English Lexicon* as 'those who undertake perilous adventures, more particularly for the destruction of enemies of their party; as though they offered themselves as ransoms or victims'. The expression was used to refer to religious devotees, in particular members of the Isma'ili Assassin sect who were prepared to use murder and to sacrifice their lives in order to further the interests of their particular Shi'ite sect.[18] Although the Isma'ili Assassins were reputed to carry out their murderous missions under the influence of hashish (and hence the derivation of the western word 'assassin' from *hashishin*), there is no good evidence that this was ever the case. It is more likely that the enemies of the heretical Isma'ilis, when they called them *hashishin*, meant that they were low-grade riff-raff. As has already been noted, in 'The Romance of Baybars' the sultan was assisted by Isma'ili heretics, called *fidawis*, who offered their criminal skills in the service of the Sultan and Islam. In medieval Arabic, however, *fidawi* could be used much more loosely to refer to any sort of desperado. In the *Nights* 'History of the First Larrikin', when the larrikin (or *shatir*) encounters forty *fidawis*, the sense is that he has encountered a gang of criminal vagabonds. In another tale, 'The History of the Lovers of Syria', a pirate crew are described as *fidawis*.

The *zu'ar* are a little difficult to distinguish from some of the more disreputable *futuwwa* lodges. In medieval Cairo, *zu'ar* referred to a loose association of criminal bands. They constituted a sort of organized criminal lumpenproletariat which 'protected' or controlled the slum areas of Cairo, such as al-Husayniyya, Bab al-Luq and Ard al-Tabala. Members of these bands used to hire themselves out to the emirs as cudgelmen and, like the *ayyarun* in earlier centuries, they could provide powerful armed militias to whoever was prepared to employ them. Sometimes *zu'ar* gangs played at a game called *shalaq*, or beggar's bag, a low-life form of rugby in which some of the players might die.[19]

Then there were the *harafish* (sing. *harfush*). Burton, in 'The Story of the Larrikin and the Cook' (a tale about one of the destitute whose wits are sharpened by hunger), translates the word *harfush* as 'larrikin' (nineteenth-century Australian slang for an urban layabout) and annotates it as 'blackguard'. This is a little inaccurate. The *harafish* were actually beggars who in Mamluke times lived on the patronage of emirs or on hand-outs from mosques. They were sturdy beggars and, like the criminal *zu'ar*, could provide powerful armed militias. In Mamluke Egypt there was a Sultan of the Harafish, a King of the Dregs, who spoke to the authorities on behalf of the mendicants and layabouts.[20] In Ottoman Egypt there was a guild for beggars, and its members paid tax on their income. Sometimes *ju'adiyya* ('curly-haired ones') replaces *harafish* as the word for beggars. In 'The Story of the Three Sharpers', the three destitute men who rummage around on rubbish heaps for salvageable scraps are called *ju'adiyya*.

The world of the beggar was a highly competitive one, and all sorts of dodges were adopted to stay alive in it. Al-Jawbari tells us that beggars used to take blood squeezed from camel ticks and mix it with gum arabic before smearing it over the eyelids in order to fake the appearance of congenital blindness. Al-Jawbari also gives a recipe for a peculiar concoction which those who wanted to fake the appearance of elephantiasis used to put in their bath. Other beggars pretended that they were mute, or insane, or had been wounded in the war against the infidel. Moralists deplored the habit of some beggars of solemnly cursing those who failed to give them alms. A literary genre developed, known as *adab al-kudyah* or the etiquette of mendicancy, in which beggars were instructed in how to go about their business and how to trick or wheedle money out of passers-by.[21] In al-Hariri's *Maqamat*, for example, the aged and wily rogue Abu Zayd preaches to his son on the merits of the beggar's way of life and exhorts his son to be alert, cunning and always on the move. Literary folk were rather inclined to romanticize the carefree raggle-taggle life of the professional mendicants. Al-Jahiz, who wrote a treatise on vagrants and their tricks, puts these words in the mouth of one old beggar:

Pray listen to me. Do you not know that vagrancy is a noble, enjoyable, pleasing calling? Vagrants enjoy boundless happiness; their task it is to rove the world by stages, and to pace out the earth; they need fear no harm. They go wherever they wish, getting the best there is to be had in every town . . . They are serene and content with their lot, and have no worries about families, possessions, houses or property.[22]

Lane gave an unsympathetic account of Cairo's beggars in *Manners and Customs of the Modern Egyptians*. According to him, there were 'many beggars, who spend the greater part of the day's gains to indulge themselves at night with the intoxicating hasheesh, which, for a few hours, renders them, in imagination, the happiest of mankind'.[23] Although opium, hashish and henbane (in Arabic *banj* can refer to either hashish or henbane) had long been used in the recipes of occultists as ingredients in medicines, poisons and aphrodisiacs, drug-taking does not seem to have become popular as a recreation among the common people until the twelfth or thirteenth century. The theologian and religious polemicist Ibn Taymiyya blamed the introduction of drugs into Syria on the entry of the Mongols into the Near East. In the centuries before the introduction of tobacco, drugs were either eaten or drunk in special cakes or decoctions, flavoured to remove the bitter taste of the drugs. In the *Nights* 'Tale of the Kazi and the Bhang-Eater', the Sultan enquires about hashish. His better-informed vizier replies: "Tis composed of hemp leaflets, whereto they add aromatic roots and somewhat of sugar: then they cook it and prepare a kind of confection which they eat.'

Drug-taking was regarded with abhorrence by the orthodoxly pious and the wealthy.[24] The consumption of hashish or opium was forbidden by most Muslim jurisprudents, since the effect of the drugs was held to be analogous with that of wine. However, the Hanafi law school tolerated their consumption. Moreover, hashish was very cheap and it was one of the few pleasures of the poor. According to the thirteenth-century historian Ibn Abd al-Zahir, hashish was so cheap that one silver dirham's worth of hashish had as much effect as one gold dinar's worth of wine. In fourteenth-century Damascus, it was low-grade occupations such as falconers and dog handlers who ran and profited from the hashish parlours. The stereotypical consumer of hashish is portrayed in 'The Rogueries of Dalilah and her Daughter Zaynab'; he is 'an ass-driver, a scavenger who had been out of work for a week and who was an Hashish-eater to boot'. In Mamluke Cairo, the area round the Bab al-Luq, an impoverished and disreputable quarter, was the best place to buy hashish. Opium, on the other hand, most of which was grown in Upper Egypt, was rather more expensive, and some respectable people indulged in it. Although drugs were always denounced by the pious and occasionally banned by the sultans, most of the time they were sold and consumed openly. In the *Nights* story of 'Ala al-Din Abu al-Shamat', when the Cairene merchant Shams al-Din seeks a drug to increase his fertility, he goes to the bazaar, where there was 'a man who was Deputy Syndic of the brokers and was given to the use of opium and electuary (*barsh*) and green hashish'. The deputy syndic then goes to a drug seller in order to buy opium and some other, more reputable substances in order to mix the wonder-working medicine.

'The wine of the *fuqara*' (that is, of the poor before God, i.e. the Sufis) was one of the nicknames of hashish. In some of the less respectable Sufi groups, poetry was written in praise of hashish or opium. The sixteenth-century Turkish poet al-Fuzuli wrote a treatise in praise of hashish. It was argued that drug-taking could provide an artificially induced taste of divine ecstasy, or that a temporary derangement of the mind might bring the drug-taker closer to a God, who transcends all rationality.[25] According to al-Jawbari, members of the Haydariyya dervish order took hashish before staging their performances of self-mutilation, in order to numb the pain.

Drugs feature in the *Nights* and other specimens of popular fiction in two contexts. First, *banj* (either henbane or hashish) and opium are rather naïvely called upon by the storyteller as a kind of Mickey Finn, or early form of chloroform, available for the use of villains. For example, in 'Ali Shar and Zumurrud', the sinister Nazarene uses *banj* (hashish) mixed with opium on Zumurrud in order to overpower her and steal her away. Then again, in 'The Rogueries of Dalilah and her Daughter Zaynab' the two women use *banj* to knock out Ahmad al-Danaf and his following and steal their clothes in a game of competitive cunning. In 'The Tale of the Enchanted King', the prince is knocked out night after night by *banj* which is secretly administered to him by his monstrous wife. Robbers who were supposed to use *banj* or other drugs to overpower their victims were known as *mubannij*, and al-Jawbari provides considerable detail about their activities. For example, in his supposedly factual compendium of rogues' tricks, he claims that hashish was used by the kidnappers of children to keep their little victims quiet. It is really very doubtful that henbane, hashish or opium can be used in this way, but plainly it was useful as a fictional convention.

Secondly, there was a sub-genre of *Nights* stories of the late Egyptian period devoted to the buffooneries of simple folk who have temporarily lost their wits on drugs. For example, in 'The Tale of the Kazi and the Bhang-Eater', the hashish-addicted poor fisherman mistakes the reflection of the moon on the ground for a river and a dog for a fish, whereupon he sets about trying to hook the dog, and then further absurdities ensue. In 'The Tale of the Hashish Eater', a beggar who has eaten a lump of hashish fancies that he has found his way into a palace where servants have washed and massaged him before he goes to bed with a beautiful girl ... but then suddenly he awakes to find himself surrounded by a small crowd, lying naked with an erection beside one of the public water troughs. Stories about hashish eaters in the *Nights* tend to be simple, crudely constructed tales, aimed at an audience which had a taste for bawdy or even lavatorial humour.

As has already been noted above, it was much cheaper to get intoxicated on hashish than on wine, and in the *Nights* it tends to be the princes and merchants who indulge in wine.[26] Alcohol is, of course, formally banned by Islam, but the ban was widely disregarded by the more easy-going believers. Some argued that only wine made from grapes was banned by the Koran, so it was all right to get drunk on alcohol made from, say, figs. Doctors, many of whom were Christians and Jews, regularly recommended wine to their patients for all sorts of ailments. In Egypt, the Turkish Mamluke élite used to get drunk on *qumiz*, a potent brew of fermented mare's milk. Drinking at court had a long ancestry. Although Harun al-Rashid features in the *Nights* as a genial and convivial lover of evening drinking sessions, in fact the historical Harun al-Rashid seems to have been a pious and austere figure, and there is no good evidence that wine ever touched his lips. However, other Abbasid caliphs were notorious for their evening drinking bouts. (Contrary to modern western practice, wine and conversation followed the meal, rather than accompanying it.) A class of courtly participants in these activities was the *nudama*, or cup-companions, who were expected to sing for their supper by entertaining their patron with poems, songs and witty anecdotes. Abu Nuwas, the ninth-century poet who was patronized by the Barmecid clan and later became the *nadim* of the Caliph al-Amin, was the greatest of the poets who celebrated both the joys of wine and the beauty of the boys who served that wine. Abu Nuwas also features in several of the *Nights* stories as the hero of a number of unedifying adventures, and several of his poems are inserted in the stories. Poems in praise of wine constituted a literary genre in their own right, *khamriyyat*. Examples of such poems abound in the *Nights*. In 'The Story of the Porter and the Three Ladies', the porter recites the following:

> Drink not the cup, save with a friend you trust,
> One whose blood to noble forefathers owes.
> Wine like the wind is sweet if o'er the sweet,
> And foul if o'er the foul it haply blows.

The porter follows this up with more verses in praise of wine. Then again, in the Hunchback cycle of stories, the Jewish physician's father recites verses in praise of idle pleasure and drinking wine beside the Ethiopian Pond in Cairo.

Poems were written in praise of intoxication, good fellowship and beautiful cup-bearers. Wine drinking and pederasty tended to go hand in hand – in literature at least. Sufi poets wrote poems in praise of wine and beautiful boys. Perhaps images of the cup of wine and of the beautiful boy were intended as metaphors for the intoxication of divine ecstasy and divine beauty, but many Muslims were doubtful, and controversy raged over whether the verses of Sufi poets like Umar ibn al-Farid (1181–1235), in particular his *Khamriyya*, or 'Hymn of Wine', were to be read literally or not. Often taverns (*khans*) were attached to Christian monasteries. Boys served the wine, and entertainments such as shadow plays might also be provided. In the *Maqamat*, al-Hariri describes the interior of a wine-hall in Damascus, where there was an 'old man in a gaily coloured dress among casks and wine-vats. There were around him cup-bearers of surpassing beauty, and lights that glittered, and the sweet scents of myrtle and jasmin, and pipe and lute.'[27] Despite the convivial scene evoked by al-Hariri, it was also possible to drink alone. In 'The Adventures of Mercury Ali of Cairo', Ali in a depressed state of mind goes to the wine shop and is given a room where he can get drunk alone.

Medieval Muslims gambled on many things, including horse-races, pigeon-races, backgammon, wrestling matches and egg-knocking.[28] Betting on how long a man could stand on one leg (*al-wuquf ala rijl wahidah*) attracted the disapproving attention of some Islamic jurists. In medieval Cairo there were sporting astrologers who specialized in predicting such things as the outcome of wrestling matches. The religious authorities prohibited gambling, because *maysir*, a pre-Islamic game of chance based on the flight of arrows and associated with pagan worship, was banned in the Koran. While some Muslims justified the game of chess on the grounds that it was good training in strategy (and hence something that could be put to the service of the jihad), other sterner Muslims disapproved, because it was customary to bet on the outcome of the game. In 'The Tale of King Ins bin Kays and his Daughter', for example, the prince, al-Abbas, and the merchant stake vast sums on the outcome of a series of games of chess.

It is possible that the cult of the criminal in popular literature was given additional impetus by the unpopularity of the judiciary and the police force.[29] In such *Nights* tales as 'The Lady and her Five Suitors', 'The Story of the Qadi and the Bhang Eater' and 'The Story of the Qadi who Had a Baby', the *qadis*, or judges, are relentlessly lampooned as corrupt, foolish, incompetent and lascivious. The police receive no better treatment in the *Nights*. Indeed, the police force was commonly known as *al-zalama*, or 'the tyrannous', and this is what the young man in 'The Christian Broker's Tale' calls them. (In that story the young man, who has been driven to theft in order to support his mistress, is apprehended and has his right hand cut off.) Arbitrary arrests, strippings, beatings and tortures inflicted by the police feature frequently in the *Nights*. So does police corruption. As has been mentioned already, many of the police in medieval Egypt and even as late as the early nineteenth century were pardoned thieves. The police force, or *shurta*, as it was officially called, was officered by a *wali*, who wrote regular reports for the sultan. In 'Al-Malik al-Zahir

Rukn al-Din Baybars and the Sixteen Captains of Police', and in 'Al-Malik al-Nasir and the Three Chiefs of Police', the police are regularly portrayed as corrupt and incompetent.

The *muhtasib*, or market inspector, supervised weights and measures as well as the quality of goods in the market, and he chased up debt defaulters. But he also had policing duties and was responsible for public morality. He tried to ensure that all Muslim men attended the noon Friday prayer at the main mosque and that the month-long Ramadan fast was observed. He also had to patrol secluded spots, lest they be used for adulterous assignations or frequented by drunks, beggars or prostitutes. Last but not least, the *muhtasib* levied commercial taxes on the markets. The opportunities for corrupt profit were immense, and in fact the office was often sold by the sultan. In 'Ali Nur al-Din and Miriam the Girdle-Girl', Miriam, who is being sold in the slave market, recklessly improvises verses which mock the *muhtasib*, who is a man of power in the town.

The *masha'ili*, or cresset-bearer, brings up the end of the procession in Ibn Daniyal's shadow play *Ajib wa Gharib* and boasts of his membership of the Banu Sasan. Historically, the *masha'ili*, who was under the supervision of the *muhtasib*, acted as night-watchman, lamplighter and town crier. He also collected night-soil, cleared the corpses of animals from the streets and escorted condemned criminals to execution. In the Hunchback cycle, it is the *masha'ili* who puts the rope round the neck of the Nazarene broker after the latter has been judged guilty of murdering the hunchback. In 'The Story of the Three Sharpers', the *masha'ili* again features as the executioner. In 'Ala al-Din Abu al-Shamat', the *masha'ili* is sent round the town to proclaim the elevation of the eponymous hero to the rank of Provost of the Merchants.

In the early Mamluke period, the Khizanat al-Bunud (literally Storehouse of Banners) was the main prison for common (i.e. non-political) prisoners. The Khizanat al-Bunud was also, incongruously, the officially sanctioned centre for licensed prostitution and the sale of wine and pork. It was then the custom (and it still is in some Middle Eastern countries) to make the prisoner chargeable for his upkeep. Those prisoners who could not find support from their own families were liable to be sent out in chain-gangs to beg for their sustenance in the streets. Alternatively they might be used on construction work or be entrusted with organizing the sale of wine at the Khizanat.

However, prison populations in pre-modern Muslim societies were usually small, and fines, floggings and amputations were also part of the armoury of social control. The young man in 'The Christian Broker's Tale' has his hand cut off at the Zuweyla Gate, the normal place for executions and amputations in Cairo, and is given a cup of wine after the operation has been carried out. One encounters many such unlucky one-handed men shuffling through the pages of the *Nights*. In Abbasid times, it had been common practice to pillory lesser offenders not deserving of death, and to tie them to a frame attached to the humps of a Bactrian camel which was then paraded around the city. The frame was known as a *lu'ba*, or manikin. The Mamlukes, more ruthless, used to crucify criminals and political failures on the backs of camels. Those criminals who had been condemned to be sawn in half were similarly displayed.[30] Executions were a form of street theatre and highly popular as such. When the Emir Qusun was condemned to be crucified, street vendors cashed in by selling lollipops in the shape of the crucified victim. After Tumanbay, the last Mamluke Sultan of Egypt, was hanged before the Zuweyla Gate in 1517, his execution was re-created by the masters of the shadow theatres, much to the delight of Egypt's new master, the Ottoman Sultan Selim the Grim.

7

Sexual Fictions

====

The stories from the *Nights* which have survived in popular memory, in the West at least, are stories like 'Aladdin' or 'Ali Baba', which have little or no sexual content. But sexual themes – incest, adultery, sadism, and so on – are pervasive in the *Nights*. Indeed, a series of sexual incidents furnishes the pretext for their narration. The two kings of the frame story, Shahriyar and Shahzaman, discover that their wives are adulterous and prefer black slaves and grooms to their husbands. Subsequently, the two kings set out on a quest for someone who has suffered the same kind of betrayal that they have. At length they approach and spy on a terrifying jinn who keeps his woman captive in a chest bound with seven padlocks. Yet even the jinn's precautions are of no avail; for, while he sleeps, the woman escapes from the casket and blackmails Shahriyar and Shahzaman into having sex with her. She takes their seal-rings as tokens and shows them the 570 seal-rings that she has already collected from men who have slept with her. Returning to his kingdom, Shahriyar decides that from now on, he will sleep only with virgins and that each virgin will be killed after he has spent a night with her. Sheherazade's never-ending tales are of course designed to delay her execution and abate the king's wrath. But the tales are designed also to teach, and it is striking how many of the tales feature adulterous women, virtuous women, dominant women and wily women. From some of the tales Shahriyar may learn that there can be such a thing as fidelity in love and marriage. From other tales he may conclude that women are infinitely lustful and will deceive their husbands if they can, and he may derive a melancholy sort of consolation from this. Then again, after listening to yet other stories, he may simply laugh and conclude that sex is not such a serious matter anyway. The sheer diversity of the stories can be seen as providing a therapy of a kind.[1]

In a study of the way western writers and artists have portrayed and usually travestied the Middle East, Rana Kabbani claimed that the *Nights* 'were originally recounted to an all male audience desiring bawdy entertainment'. As we have already seen, this account of the origins and audience of the tales is an oversimplification. However, Kabbani went on to claim that the women in the tales fall into two categories: on the one hand, the adulteresses, witches and prostitutes, a lascivious and devious lot; and, on the other, pious and prudent women 'who are not disturbingly sexual' and whose virtues 'are usually a decorative foil to the story-line but of no great dramatic value'.[2] Thus we are to understand that the stories were popular with the low fellows in the Cairo coffee-houses, because of the misogynistic stereotypes they promoted and because of the implication of feminine inferiority underlying the tales as a whole.

It is, however, possible to take a very different view. Mme Lally-Hollbecque's *Le Féminisme de Scheherezade* (1927) provides an extreme example of a different approach. Lally-Hollbecque argued that the collection of stories had a single author-compiler and, moreover, that the author was an ardent feminist. Lally-Hollbecque's Sheherazade teaches by stories, and what she teaches above all justifies and exalts women and their virtues. She initiates Shahriyar into love and civilizes him. Lally-Hollbecque's position seems as extreme and partial as that of Kabbani. (It is also somewhat undermined by her dependence on the thoroughly unreliable Mardrus translation of the *Nights*.)

In fact, it is difficult to argue that the story collection as a whole, with its diverse constituents, presents a case for either misogyny or feminism. It is even difficult to make deductions from the erotic content of the tales about actual sexual behaviour in the medieval Islamic lands, and anyone who wishes to make use of incidents in the stories as 'data' about Arab sexual practices faces serious problems. In the first place, obviously, many of the tales are not of Islamic origin. They have been translated into Arabic and lightly Arabized and Islamicized; characters have been given Arab names; the locale has been shifted to Baghdad or Cairo; but the structure of many of the stories and their inspiration come from elsewhere. For example, the nymphomaniac captive in the jinn's casket in the frame story of the *Nights* may derive from an earlier Indian prototype. Certainly, there are Indian precursors of 'The Woman who Wanted to Deceive her Husband' and of 'The Lady of Cairo and her Four Lovers'. Then again, the behaviour of the soldier in 'The Tale of the Fuller, the Wife and the Trooper' almost certainly owes more to a reworking, several times removed, of Plautus' Latin play *Miles gloriosus* than it does to scandalous goings-on in medieval Baghdad. At a more elevated level, romances concerning the separation of lovers, fidelity and heroic tests of lovers' prowess can often be traced back to Byzantine fictions. However, it remains true, of course, that the fact that such tales were translated and narrated in the Arab lands means that the attitudes and practices conveyed in those tales were not wholly alien to Arab knowledge and taste.[3]

In any case, the romantic and erotic fiction of any culture is always constructed from conventional plot motifs, literary stereotypes and stock themes. (Lovers often swooned in medieval fiction, but did they do so in medieval reality?) The way erotic fiction is put together makes it difficult to assign any hard documentary value to it; and, for example, a story that is overtly about a woman's scheme to get her husband out of the house, so that her lover may join her in bed, may be really a story about ingenuity, rather than female sexual needs. Adultery is often used as a plot mover in the stories of the *Nights* (rather like Uncle Tom's silver cow-creamer in the P.G. Wodehouse stories), and thus the incidence of adultery in the stories tells us little or nothing about the incidence of adultery in medieval society. The picture of Cairo's thriving bawdy low life, teeming with randy women, cuckolded husbands and lucky virile porters, may be as much a fantasy as the stories about the kingdoms of the jinn and the marvellous goings-on in caliphal palaces.

Even so, it is still likely that some of the tales, particularly those about low life in Cairo, composed in the Mamluke period, do reflect social and sexual practices of the time. A few of the stories may even be based on real incidents. Historical chronicles, legal judgements, records of table talk and satirical poems composed at the time all indicate that sexual scandals occurred frequently and that actual practice was often at odds with the religious ideal. The public face of Islam was austere and restrictive. Religious leaders and the sultans who sometimes listened to them sought to enforce a strict religious code. From time to time, particularly in years of famine or plague, when a need for public repentance was generally felt, women were banned from going out of doors unaccompanied, brothels were closed down, licentious festivals were suspended, and so on. In most years, though, an easy-going pragmatism prevailed. There were limits to what the regime could enforce or what the public would accept. Sultans tended to prefer to tax brothels and hashish concessions rather than to abolish them.

Puritanical Muslims urged that a woman should obey her husband and that she should be confined as much as possible to the harem, or women's part of the house. If a woman had to go out, she should be accompanied and wear a veil. But of course not all women did obey their husbands; some dominated them. The veil was not really practicable for women who worked in the fields and it seems rarely to have been worn in the countryside. Even in the cities the veil was not always worn (and Christian, Jewish and slave women were exempt from that prescription anyway). The seclusion of women in harem quarters was a pious or precautionary measure that only wealthy men could indulge in. As S.D. Goitein has observed: 'At the other end of the social spectrum [the lower end], the people who were not *mastur* – literally "not covered", not protected by their means, family or social standing, in short not respectable – had little power to seclude their wives, and no cause to restrain their tongues. Their voice is heard in the chronologically later parts of *The Arabian Nights*.'⁴ Moreover, much of Islam's teaching concerning sex and women is based not on the Koran but on *hadith*, the orally transmitted sayings and practices of the Prophet and his Companions. The vast number of *hadith* allowed both restrictive and permissive interpretations of Islam's social code to flourish. For example, *hadith* can be quoted both for and against the practice of coitus interruptus, so that the Prophet was quoted as approving of it, as in his reply to an enquiring companion, 'Practice coitus interruptus with her if you so wish, for she will receive what has been predestined for her', and yet disapproving of it, as in the statement, 'It is hidden infanticide.'⁵ Then again, while a misogynist might quote the Prophet's saying, 'Hell is mostly populated by women', a feminist might retort with his saying, 'Paradise is under the heels of the mothers.'

The *Nights* was not the only story collection with a strong sexual content. For example, the *Hikayat al-Ajiba wa'l-Akhbar al-Ghariba* ('Tales of the Marvellous and Information about the Strange'), which was probably put together in the tenth century, is a collection which includes several highly erotic tales.

The most notable of these is 'The Story of the Forty Girls', in which a prince, wandering across a desert, stumbles across a palace, which he enters. The place is deserted, though there are forty thrones and in the centre of the great chamber a golden table with food and water set out for forty people. The prince takes a little from the food and water of each setting. Then he is disturbed by the sound of horses' hoofs and, looking out of the window, he sees forty cavalry in full armour approaching. The prince conceals himself and spies on the warriors. It is only when they take off their armour that he discovers that these warriors are in fact women. They are all beautiful and *hur al-ayn*. (A woman who is *hur al-ayn* has eyes in which there is a strong contrast between the black and the surrounding white. To be *hur al-ayn* is one of the attributes of houris in paradise.) When the forty women sit to dinner they discover that their bread has been broken and they are disturbed by this; but, after one of their number promises to investigate the matter, they spend the night drinking, reciting and telling stories until the break of day. Then thirty-nine of the girls don their armour to set out hunting, while one of their number remains behind to solve the mystery. When the young man comes out to steal more food from the table, she pounces on him. She is at first uncertain whether he is human or a jinn, but eventually they eat and drink together and have sex. The following day the prince has essentially the same adventure, but with a different girl, and so it goes on until he has separately and secretly slept with all the women in the castle and made them all pregnant. 'The Story of the Forty Girls' is a joyous and graphic celebration of sex. It may be that stories about 'the castle of women' (and one finds this motif also in the *Nights*) were based ultimately on Muslim fantasies about what went on in convents. The *Hikayat al-Ajiba* certainly deserves to be translated into English.[6]

The *Nights* and the *Hikayat al-Ajiba* are mixed story collections, and many of their stories are perfectly proper; some are even edifying. However, the *Nights* had also to compete with the *kutub al-bah*, or books dedicted to pornography, in the form either of sex manuals or of collections of exclusively erotic tales.[7] The author of one such work was Ahmad ibn Yusuf al-Tayfashi, who was born in Tunisia but settled in Cairo and died there in 1253.[8] His *Nuzhat al-Albab* ('Delight of the Hearts') is an obscene collection of observations, stories and poems about debauchery. Al-Tayfashi was particularly interested in stories about homosexuals and pederasts, and some of his scabrous anecdotes concern named contemporaries. Al-Tayfashi's book, despite its obscenity, was intended as a work of *adab* – that is, a work of *belles-lettres* furnishing suitable material for table talk – and it was written at a time when homosexuality and homosexual mannerisms seem to have been fashionable in intellectual circles.

Unlike al-Tayfashi, Ali al-Baghdadi concerned himself exclusively with women.[9] Almost nothing is known of his life, but he seems to have been a hanger-on at the Mamluke court in the early fourteenth century. His *Kitab al-Zahr al-Aniq fi'l-Bus wa'l-Ta'hiq* ('The Book of the Delicate Flowers Regarding the Kiss and the Embrace') is a twenty-five-chapter compendium on the wiles of women (*ka'id al-nisa*) and deals with the tricks they use to deceive their husbands and lovers. The narrative is written in a vulgar Middle Arabic, and the sexual encounters are detailed with relish. Like al-Tayfashi, Ali included adventures which are ascribed to named contemporaries or to recently deceased personalities, usually men who were accustomed to receiving respect, like emirs and qadis. Though he provides a great deal of circumstantial detail about persons and places which serve to locate these stories firmly in Mamluke Egypt and Syria, nevertheless one should not take it for granted that all his stories can be used to provide documentary evidence about the sexual practices of Ali's time. Some at least of the stories are plainly fictions. (It is noteworthy that Ali's story of how the deputy governor of Bahnasa came to lose his clothes to a wily prostitute is found in the *Nights* in an abridged and less artful form as 'The Third Constable's History'.)

Al-Tayfashi and Ali al-Baghdadi were inventing or compiling fictions for entertainment. But the most famous of all pornographic manuals written in Arabic, the *Rawd al-Atir*, or 'Perfumed Garden', was primarily an instruction manual, with chapters on the various positions which can be used in copulation and advice on such matters as the treatment of sterility and impotence, increasing the size of the penis and getting rid of underarm odour. Its author, Sheikh al-Nafzawi (*c.* 1410), wrote in Arabic and prefaced the work with a pious Muslim's apologia which celebrated sex and women as wondrous works of God.[10] However, *The Perfumed*

Garden was clearly influenced by the notable Indian genre of sex manuals, of which the most famous example is the *Kama Sutra*; and, like its Indian precursors, *The Perfumed Garden* gives highly technical and sometimes intimidatingly athletic accounts of possible sexual positions. Nevertheless, even *The Perfumed Garden* carries a considerable freight of anecdotal and fictitious material (particularly in the inevitable chapter 'On the Deceits and Treacheries of Women'). Middle Eastern pornography is a field which has received little serious academic attention. Many works of Arab erotica have been falsely and mischievously ascribed to distinguished religious thinkers and philosophers. Some books which have the same title turn out to have different contents, or vice versa.

It is clear that the strong sensual, even pornographic, content of the *Nights* can be paralleled elsewhere in Arabic literature. Thus, drawing on rival works of erotic fiction and on sex manuals as well as on the *Nights*, one can get some sort of impression of the prevailing sexual practices and prejudices of the medieval Islamic world. In his excellent book *Arab Painting*, Richard Ettinghausen suggested that the medieval Arabs' image of the ideal woman can be reconstructed from early Arab poetry:

In these love lyrics one reads that the ideal Arab woman must be so stout that she nearly falls asleep; that she must be clumsy when rising and lose her breath when moving quickly; that her breasts should be full and rounded, her waist slender and graceful, her belly lean, her hips sloping and her buttocks so fleshy as to impede her passage through a door. Her legs are said to be like columns of marble, her neck like that of a gazelle, while her arms are described as well rounded, with soft delicate elbows, full wrists, and long fingers. Her face with its white cheeks must not be haggard, her eyes are those of a gazelle with the white of eye clearly marked.[11]

Essentially the same pneumatic image can be reconstructed from the *Nights*. When, in 'The Tale of Omar bin al-Nu'uman', the Muslim warrior Sharrkan wrestled with the Christian princess Abrizah, he found that his fingertips 'sank into the soft folds of her middle, breeding languishment'. Sharrkan was so overmastered by desire that he lost this wrestling bout, for Abrizah took advantage of his fainting passion, threw him and 'sat upon his breast with hips and hinder cheeks like mounds of sand'. Great attention was paid to women's bottoms. When Hasan of Basra spied upon the princesses in the pool, he saw that the most beautiful of them 'had thighs great and plump, like marble columns twain or bolsters stuffed with down from ostrich ta'en'. The male bottom too: Prince Kamar al-Zaman's waist 'was more slender than the gossamer and his back parts than two sand-heaps bulkier, making a babel of the heart with their softness'. The piously superstitious warned men against sitting on a place recently warmed by a female bottom, fearing that some sort of illicit sexual pleasure might be derived therefrom. The sixteenth-century Egyptian religious scholar Jalal al-Din al-Suyuti argued that in paradise people would have no behinds.[12] In some areas of the Middle East until quite recent times, women might choose to overeat systematically (the practice of *tasmina*) in order to acquire the sexually attractive fat.[13] A woman could draw attention to her bottom by adopting a distinctive waggling gait known as the *ghunj* – a term also used for the waggling of the hips during sexual intercourse. Sleepiness was also considered to be sexually attractive, and drowsy charms and languorous airs are frequently commended in the poems embedded in the *Nights*.

However, sexual tastes in the medieval Islamic world were not absolutely uniform, and rival ideals coexisted. The plump, panting languid woman faced plenty of competition from her more active sisters – in both fiction and fact. Indeed, one of the striking features of the *Nights* (especially if one compares it with western literature in the same period) is how active and vigorous the heroines of the stories are and, contrariwise, how passive and idle many of the nominal heroes are. How could Kabbani have missed

Tawaddud, who defeats the court sages in an intellectual form of strip-poker; Dunya, who kicks the vizier in the groin; Budur, who, having become a king (*sic*), revenges herself on her enemies and threatens her lover with sodomization; Marjana, who rescues Ali Baba and engineers the death of the forty thieves; or Miriam the Girdle-Girl, who rescued her lover from captivity in Christendom – not to mention such warrior-princesses as Princess al-Datma and Abriza, and the legions of Amazon warrior-women who troop through the pages of the *Nights*, as well as the special-ized variant the *kahramat* (armed female harem guards)? The taste for boylike women (*qhulumiyyat*) in fiction may have reflected the actual sexual tastes of Cairo men. According to the fifteenth-century historian and moralist al-Maqrizi, the women of his day, finding that they were having to compete with attractive young men, had themselves taken to dressing like boys in order to retain the affection of their husbands.[14]

Al-Maqrizi had been a student of the philosopher-historian Ibn Khaldun, who held that the spread of homosexuality was a sign of the decay of civilization.[15] Despite al-Maqrizi's almost apocalyptic dread of the spread of homosexuality in medieval Cairo, it is in fact difficult to gauge the degree of acceptance accorded to homosexuals.[16] Indeed, it may be a mistake to think of there being one reified condition, 'homosexuality', which has remained more or less constant in its characteristics from century to century and from culture to culture. There is some evidence to suggest that in medieval Arab society active homosexuality was regarded as an acceptable way of finding relief from sexual tension, but that passive homosexuals and those who cultivated effeminate traits were scorned.[17] However, the evidence does not all run in one direction, and there are indications in medieval texts that some Arabs thought of homosexuality as a single condition and even as a form of illness.

In chapter 6 of his *Nuzhat al-Albab*, al-Tayfashi deals with the characteristic features of homosexuals (*la'ita*) and of those who hire themselves out.[18] The homosexual should have a pleasant lodging, well furnished with books and wine, and made pleasanter yet by the presence of doves and singing birds. A homosexual can be recognized by the way he stares directly at one, this direct gaze often being followed by a wink. The typical homosexual has thin legs with hairy ankles and tends to wear robes which reach right down to the ground. When he walks, his hands and his legs sway. ('A man's second face is his leg' was a saying of the time.) A subsequent chapter is devoted to entertaining and funny stories about homosexuals. Al-Tayfashi is almost exclusively concerned with mature men who pursue beardless boys. However, he does note the existence of a minority group of men who went looking for sex with mature bearded men. He comments that these latter were known as 'men with short lives', because of the risks they ran of being mugged and murdered. As has already been noted, homosexuality seems to have been fashionable in literary circles in thirteenth-century Egypt and Syria. But homosexual practices (liwat, or the crime of Lot's people) were proscribed by the religious law, and those found guilty of a homosexual act might face the death penalty. In practice, while there were occasional instances of successful prosecutions, resulting in execution or castration, there is also evidence, at certain times and in certain places, of homosexuality being more casually accepted. Several of the Mamluke sultans were known to be homosexual, and the tastes of homosexual sultans and emirs were a factor behind the high prices paid for beautiful boys in the slave market.

Because the *Nights* is an omnium gatherum, one can use its texts, through selective quotation from the stories, to support the argument that homosexuality was widely approved of, or to argue that it was indifferently accepted, or to demonstrate that it was absolutely abominated. It was certainly openly discussed, and 'The Man's Dispute with the Learned Woman Concerning the Relative Excellence of Male and Female' in the *Nights* presents fiercely contrasted arguments. The (pederastic) man argues that it is better

to love men than women, since men are superior to women, and
the Koran itself declares that 'Men are the managers of the affairs
of women for that God has preferred in bounty one of them over
the other' (IV, 38). Man is active, woman passive. Somewhat
eccentrically, the man cites a saying of the Prophet that warns
against looking too long on young boys, because of their
resemblance to the houris of paradise. He also cites the poet Abu
Nuwas, to the effect that boys are better because they do not have
periods and they do not get pregnant. He points out how common
it is in poetry to praise women by comparing them to beautiful
boys.

However, the woman replies by describing the beauties of the
ideal girl, calling to her support the numbers of kings and rich
men who have squandered fortunes to acquire beautiful women.
She points out that, in the saying of the Prophet already quoted by
the man, boys are praised only by being compared to houris, who
are female. In any case, the Koran unequivocally condemns
homosexuality: 'What do you come to male beings, leaving your
wives that your Lord created for you? Nay, but you are a people
of transgressors' (XXXVI, 165). Also, a woman has more to offer
in the way of pleasure, since she can be taken both ways; and the
first wispy beards of young men are unattractive. The woman
quotes another saying of the Prophet: 'Three things I have valued
in this world, perfume, prayer and women.' Finally, she winds up
by reciting some rather explicit verses about the messiness of anal
intercourse.

Grosso modo, the debate reverberates throughout the Nights.
Some stories cheerfully celebrate homosexual seductions, particularly those in which Abu Nuwas features as the raffish hero.
Abu Nuwas was a historical figure, a familiar of the court of
Harun al-Rashid and a poet famous above all for his verses in
praise of wine (khamriyyat) and beautiful boys (mudhakkarat). He is
the hero of a number of (fictional) adventures in which his sexual
tastes may be sometimes a subject for teasing, but never for

vilification. On the other hand, some tales present the paedophile as a villain, and Ali Zaybaq, Nur al-Din Ali and Ala al-Din Abu Shamat, among others, are menaced by sinister male seducers. In 'The Rogueries of Dalilah', Hajj Muhammad, who as the slang had it loved 'to eat both figs and pomegranates' (i.e. he was a bisexual), is described as 'a man of ill-repute'. A leitmotif in the *Nights* is the seclusion of a beautiful boy by his parents in order to protect him from lascivious men. Although Princess Budur, disguised as a man, makes a stirring speech in favour of homosexuality to Kamar al-Zaman, whom she threatens to bugger, the interest of the story at this point lies in Kamar al-Zaman's fear and shame at the prospect of being homosexually raped. The pursuit of beardless boys by likeable or villainous rogues features fairly frequently in the *Nights* (just as it does in al-Tayfashi's work of literary erotica). However, love or buggery between two mature men is not, I think, dealt with anywhere in the *Nights*.

Lesbians do not seem to have been persecuted in medieval Islamic societies. However, lesbianism, or 'rubbing' (*musahaqa*), was associated with witchcraft in the popular mind. Leo Africanus reported that there was a notorious circle of lesbian witches operating in Fez at the end of the fifteenth century.[19] The anonymous storytellers of the *Nights* went along with popular prejudice, and the presentation of lesbianism in the stories is consistently hostile, with the lesbians usually doubling as witches. The dowager witch, poisoner and wrestler Zat al-Dawahi in 'The Tale of Omar bin al-Nu'uman and his Sons' is identified as a lesbian who used saffron to add spice to her masturbatory sessions. The description of her is not a flattering one: 'wanton and wily, deboshed and deceptious; with foul breath, red eyelids, yellow cheeks, dull brown face'. Unfortunately for Zat al-Dawahi, her smelly armpits made her unpopular among the young women of the harem. Shawahi, the 'lady of calamities' in the story of 'Hasan of Bassorah', is again a witch as well as a lesbian.

Although cross-dressing features in a number of stories, this is as a literary device and not as a statement of sexual preference. (Shakespeare, of course, used transvestism in the same way.) Budur disguised herself as a man, and Zumurrud did similarly, but they did so in order to travel in security and to advance their fortunes. Niama bin Rabia put on women's clothes, but he did so only in order to gain access to his beloved, who was immured in a harem. Bestiality features in a handful of the foulest and most vulgar tales. Necrophilia is something that ghouls indulge in, but the wide range of fetishes and perversions which feature commonly in western pornography seem to have been unknown to the Arab storyteller.

In 'The Story of the Porter and the Three Ladies', the women interrogate the porter about the correct name for their private parts; each time he gets the answer wrong, the porter is slapped and pinched. In the Barber cycle, in 'The Tale of the Second Brother, Babaqa the Paraplegic', Babaqa is led on and slapped about by the mysterious lady and her maidservants, before being thoroughly humiliated and cast out into the street. Al-Tayfashi devoted a chapter in his treatise to the subject of slapping, arguing, among other things, that it was good for the health of the recipient.

While there are a handful of stories in the *Nights* which focus on the joys of wedlock and domesticity, illicit sexual adventures, involving adulteresses, prostitutes, concubines and singing girls, furnish more of the staple fare of the *Nights*. In those stories it is often the singing girl (*qaina*, pl. *qiyan*) who is provided with the wittiest lines and most appropriate verses. The stories of 'Harun al-Rashid and the Two Slave-Girls' and 'Harun al-Rashid and the Three Slave-Girls' commemorate the bawdy wit of these accomplished entertainers. In historical fact, singing girls were much in demand at the court of the Abbasid caliphs and in the houses of other rich men, particularly as after-dinner entertainers and as a female counterpart to the learnedly witty *nudama*, or cup-companions. The most famous essayist of the Abbasid period, al-Jahiz, wrote a treatise sarcastically entitled *In Praise of Singing Girls* in which he warned against those wily, greedy, faithless seductresses, who stole first a man's senses and then his money: 'As soon as the observer notices her, she exchanges provocative glances with him, gives him playful smiles, dallies with him in verses set to music, falls in with his suggestions, is eager to drink when he drinks, expresses her fervent desire for him to stay a long while, her yearning for his prompt return, and her sorrow at his departure.'[20]

These accomplished courtesans, who may remind one of the ancient Greek *hetairai*, or of the Japanese geisha girls, might be free women or slaves. They usually accompanied their singing on the lute. The slave girl Tawaddud, at the end of a gruelling interrogation which ranged widely through the Muslim sciences, was presented with a lute by Harun al-Rashid: 'She laid her lute in her lap and, with bosom inclining over it, bent to it with the bending of a mother who suckleth her child; then she preluded in twelve different modes, till the whole assembly was agitated with delight, like a waving sea.' The annals of the Abbasid court abound with anecdotes illustrating the wit and learning of the singing girls, and though Tawaddud was a heroine of fiction her accomplishments can easily be paralleled by those of historical courtesans. For example, Mahbuba, before she was acquired by the Caliph al-Mutawakkil, had been trained by her first master. According to the chronicler al-Mas'udi, he 'had taken great care with her education, cultivated her mind and had enriched her with knowledge on the most varied subjects. She composed poetry which she sang to her own accompaniment on the lute and, in a word, she excelled in all those things which distinguish people of talent.'[21] Singing girls also flourished in the Mamluke period. Many of the songstresses were black, like Ittifaq, who started out as a concubine in the harem of the Egyptian Sultan al-Nasir Muhammad in the early fourteenth century. Ittifaq, who was famed not just for her beauty, but also for her intelligence and her singing voice, went on to marry successively four sultans and a vizier.[22] However, not many female singers enjoyed such distinguished careers, and in the Mamluke period there was an overlap between the profession of singer and that of prostitute. Both were taxed at the Daminat al-Maghani, or Tax Farm of the Singers.

In the early sixteenth century, any woman who wanted to become a prostitute registered her name at the above-mentioned office, and as long as she paid her taxes she could ply her trade undisturbed. Medieval Egypt knew three types of prostitute (or *baghiya*): the 'wild cow' who had her own room, the 'free cow' who went to the client's room and the 'milk cow' who had sex out of doors. Many of the Cairene prostitutes worked the *funduqs*, or travellers' hostels. However, a large group had their beat in and around the wax candle market, in the shadow of the Mosque of Aqmar. In 'The Story of the Chief of Police of Cairo', the policeman, seeking information about two criminals who frequent prostitutes, makes his enquiries among 'the taverners, and confectioners, and candle-makers and keepers of brothels and bawdy houses'. Prostitutes could be identified by their custom of wearing red leather trousers and carrying little daggers. They used to cough to attract the attention of clients. In the port of Alexandria many of the prostitutes were reported to be of European origin.[23] In 'The Tale of Harun al-Rashid and Abu Hasan, the Merchant of Oman', the latter visits a brothel in Baghdad, 'a tall and goodly mansion, with a balcony overlooking the river-bank and pierced with a lattice-window', and a standard tariff of between ten and forty dinars a night is quoted.[24]

Syphilis seems to have first appeared in Egypt in the first decade of the sixteenth century. The chronicler Ibn Iyas called it the *al-habb al-Franji*, or the European pimple. However, although coffee, tobacco and artillery feature in some of the later additions to the *Nights*, venereal disease does not, and its absence contributes to the sense of freedom and amorality in so many of the stories. Medieval

Muslims were none the less far from free of fear and superstition regarding sexual matters. It was believed that worms in the vagina caused nymphomania, that intercourse with a menstruating woman gave a man leprosy and that sex with old people was also dangerous. The beautiful young slave girl Tawaddud warned her audience on the danger of sex with 'old women, for they are deadly', and she was able to quote several authorities in support of this. Men travelling in the desert also feared the *udar*, a monstrous creature which raped men and left them to die of worm-infested anuses.[25] Only marginally more rational were the widespread fantasies on the part of medieval Arabs about the sexual powers of black men and their lusting after Arab women. Blacks were believed to be exceptionally virile, and fears of black virility are evident in the frame story of the *Nights* about the cuckolding of Shahriyar and Shahzaman. In *Race and Slavery in the Middle East*, Bernard Lewis comments that 'King Shahzaman and King Shahriyar were clearly white supremacists, with sexual fantasies, or rather nightmares, of a sadly familiar quality.'[26] Sexual and racist paranoia is fairly widespread throughout the *Nights* (see, for example, 'The Tale of the Enchanted King' and 'The Story of the Three Apples' among many others).

Turning away now from the perverse and fantastic, to consider more ordinary sexual practices, the well-off seem to have slept in separate beds. Wives in medieval Egypt were accustomed to demand money for coming to their husbands' beds and granting them sex – the *haqq al-firash*, or bed fee. Coitus interruptus was sanctioned by most Islamic jurists, but some also argued that the woman was entitled to financial compensation if early withdrawal was practised. People slept either naked or in their daytime clothes. Anal intercourse with women was vigorously disapproved of by the religious and therefore presumably sometimes practised by the less religious. More detailed information about normal copulation is hard to glean from the *Nights*, because of the linguistically ingenious and metaphorical modes of describing the sex act favoured by the storytellers, as they move smoothly from the description of foreplay to word-play. What we are offered are displays of rhetorical skill, not documentary accounts of fucking.

In the typical ideally romantic tale, the hero falls in love with a princess, merely by seeing her portrait, or just by hearing her name. They are predestined to love one another. Fate brings them together, and fate separates them. The hero, who swooned when he first saw the princess, swoons again when he discovers she has vanished. He will, or should, recite verses of lamentation. Then there are adventures, perhaps featuring storms, pirates, infidel armies and sorceresses. The princess may fall sick and begin to starve herself to death. The hero may think of suicide, but in the end fate reunites the lovers, and they live happily together until they are 'overtaken by the breaker of ties and the destroyer of delights'. It is all rather silly; but such stories, despite their patent lack of realism, may have served an educational purpose, and those who listened to these tales were instructed in the symbolic language of love – a surreptitious code devised to get round the proscriptions of society. In 'The Tale of Aziz and Azizah', for example, the woman's putting her finger into her mouth signifies that the man she gazes on is like her own body's soul to her; and when she strikes upon her breast with her palm and outstretched five fingers, it means that the man should come back in five days.

More generally, stories like 'The Tale of Taj al-Muluk and the Princess Dunya', 'The Tale of Ali bin Bakkar and Shams al-Nahar' and 'Masrur and Zayn al-Mawasif' set forth an *adab* of love, in which amorous young men and women were instructed in how to feel and behave.[27] Such stories not only provided a vocabulary of gestures, flowery compliments and verse couplets through which sexual attraction could be expressed, but they also gave guidance on how to dress and what gifts to offer the loved one. In 'Uns al-Wujud and the Vizier's Daughter Rose-in-Hood', Rose-in-Hood's nurse tells her that love is a sickness which can only be cured by passionate enjoyment:

'And how may one come by enjoyment?'

'By letters and messages, my lady; by whispered words of compliment and by greetings before the world; all this bringeth lovers together and makes hard matters easy.'

However, it was not always so easy to cure the sickness of love. In 'The Lovers of Banu Tayy', the pining and ill-starred bedouin drops dead even while he is running towards his beloved (who, like Juliet, belongs to the wrong tribe). Members of the pre-Islamic bedouin of the tribe of Banu Udhra, martyrs to chastity, espoused the cult of a platonic sort of thwarted love from a distance, even unto death, and a handful of stories in the *Nights* explore similarly gloomily romantic themes.[28] However, most of the romantic tales in the *Nights*, while they borrow plot motifs, gestures and postures from the old Udhrite literary tradition, tend to end happily, with the lovers brought together in the same bed after all their turbulent and improbable adventures.

8

The Universe of Marvels

=====

The pen is the most powerful sorcerer.

Balinus[1]

In an essay on 'Narrative Art and Magic', Jorge Luis Borges contrasted the slow-moving and realistic psychological novel with the adventure novel and the short story. The two latter, he argued, are ruled by a quite different sort of order, 'one based not on reason but on association and suggestion – the ancient light of magic'.[2] Certainly, the medieval storyteller and the sorcerer worked in parallel trades, manipulating words and phrases to achieve their effects, and the medieval Islamic sorcerer was pre-eminently a man with a book. In 'Judar and his Brethren', the Maghribi sorcerers dispute the possession of a volume entitled *Fables of the Ancients*, 'whose like is not in the world, nor can its price be paid of any, nor is its value to be evened with gold and jewels; for in it are particulars of all the hidden hoards of the earth and the solution of every secret'. In 'The Tale of the Wazir and the Sage Duban', the sage, who has been condemned to death by beheading on the orders of the foolish king, bequeaths to the king a book which, he claims, has the power to make his severed head speak. However, in reality, his legacy to the king is a poisoned book, and the king dies when he licks his ink-stained fingers. (Centuries later, the device of the poisoned book was to resurface in Umberto Eco's novel, *The Name of the Rose*.)

The storyteller and the sorcerer are professionals who know the power of the phrase, the word and the letter.[3] Knowledge of the name, the *mot juste*, can mean the difference between life and death. Ali Baba escapes from the perilous cave because he remembers the magical password 'Open sesame'; his brother does not and consequently perishes. The study and manipulation of words may confer knowledge of the future, as in 'The History of Mohammed, Sultan of Cairo', where the Maghribi sorcerer in the market-place has before him some leaves with writing on them which he uses to make predictions about the bystanders. Letter magic, *ilm al-huruf*, was one of the most important sub-sciences in Islamic occultism. In 'The Story of the Sage and the Scholar', for example, the sage controls the jinn and performs supernatural feats by virtue of his knowledge of the magical powers of letters. Finally, of course, the storyteller and the sorcerer, rivals in the market-place, are both traders in illusion. The sorcerer who has mastered the art of illusion, *ilm al-simiyya*, is able to offer his customers and victims visions of what is not – that is, he has become a creator of fictions.

Serious treatment of magic in the mainstream of modern European fiction is rare, and when magic does feature it often does so as a transparent metaphor. For example, Balzac's *The Ass's Skin* and Robert Louis Stevenson's *The Bottle Imp*, both tales which are ostensibly about the wish-conferring powers of a magical object, are really parables about the price paid for success and the diminishing options in life as one grows older. On the whole, stories about magic now seem to be considered to be most suitable for children. Edith Nesbit's cycle of stories about the Bastable children, C.S. Lewis's Narnia cycle and Ursula Le Guin's *Earthsea Trilogy* were all written for children (though adults may read them with guilty pleasure). Tanya Luhrmann in her penetrating and wide-ranging anthropological account of modern British witchcraft, *Persuasions of the Witch's Craft*, observes that 'Magical books encourage an embracing, dream-like absorption, a dissociated daydream of dragons, powers and higher realms. This sense of imaginative absorption, quite apart from any themes which it encompasses, is one of the most striking elements in magical fiction.'[4] Cardinal

Newman remarked in his autobiographical *Apologia pro Vita Sua* (1864): 'I used to wish the Arabian Tales were true: my imagination ran on unknown influences, magic powers and talismans.' It is a childhood dream of omnipotence. However, what also emerges from Luhrmann's survey of the modern witch is that novels about magic (by Dennis Wheatley, Dion Fortune and others) are widely read by practising occultists and enjoyed by them as fictions, yes, but as fictions about something that is real. For them, a story about magic is not *per se* purely fantasy.

Similarly, in the pre-modern Middle East, a story about magic and the supernatural may have had a double aspect; it may have been a wonderful piece of nonsense designed to enthral an audience of children, yet, at the same time, the adults listening to the same story could recognize social facts and aspects of everyday reality. There were, after all, practising sorcerers, alchemists and treasure-hunters in medieval Baghdad and Cairo. Geomancers were consulted regarding business trips and the outcome of sporting events. The powers of magic and the jinn were not to be doubted. They were attested to by the Koran:

> they follow what the Satans recited
> over Solomon's kingdom. Solomon disbelieved not,
> but the Satans disbelieved, teaching
> the people sorcery.
>
> (II, 96)

And again:

> Say: 'I take refuge with the Lord of the Daybreak
> from the evil of what he has created,
> from the evil of darkness when it gathers,
> from the evil of the women who blow on knots,
> from the evil of an envier when he envies.'
>
> (CXIII)

In this sort of social and intellectual context, the frontiers

between occult fiction and non-fiction were so weak as to be more
or less indistinguishable, and we find tales which would not be out
of place in the *Nights* embedded in such 'non-fictional' works as
sorcerers' manuals. For example, in an eleventh-century *grimoire*,
or sorcerer's manual, the *Ghayat al-Hakim* ('The Goal of the Sage',
later translated into Latin as *Picatrix*), the story is told of how in
old Harran, when the demon worshippers who dwelt there were
desirous of knowing what was to happen in the future, they
would hunt out a dark-complexioned man with eyebrows that
joined together and blue eyes. This man would be overpowered
and stripped. The unhappy victim was then plunged into a barrel
containing sesame oil with only his head remaining above the
surface of the oil. The head inhaled stupefying drugs which were
burnt before it while certain rituals were performed. The blue-
eyed man was then macerated in the oil for forty days until all the
flesh had fallen from his bones. After forty days it was possible to
detach the head from the rest of the body at the first vertebra. The
head (whose blue eyes no longer blinked) was set in a niche where
it gave out prophecies. The philosopher-historian Ibn Khaldun,
who gave a condensed account of the procedure, commented:
'This is detestable sorcery. However, it shows what remarkable
things exist in the world of man.'[5]

Even more striking, some tales of marvel included in the *Nights*
for the purpose of entertainment appear in other books as reports
of sober fact. 'The Caliph al-Maamun and the Pyramids of Egypt',
an account of the inaccessible treasures contained in the pyramids
and the magical guardians appointed by the ancients to protect
those treasures, is only a retelling of one of the standard wonder-
stories about the pyramids found elsewhere in medieval Arab
histories and topographies.[6] Again, in 'The Tale of the Warlock
and the Young Cook of Baghdad', a vizier enters a cauldron of
water at the urging of the warlock, and during the brief instant he
is in the water he experiences years of an alternative life. The
vizier's fictional ordeal is paralleled by the allegedly true experience

of the fifteenth-century Egyptian Sultan al-Ashraf Qaytbay. The sultan was visited by the famous Sufi Sheikh al-Dashtuti and fell into an argument with that great saint about whether it was possible for Muhammad to have visited all the heavens on a winged steed in a single night. Al-Dashtuti made the sultan plunge his head into a bowl of water for what seemed to onlookers to be only an instant. But when the sultan raised his head he declared that he had experienced several lifetimes of experience. It is most probable that this story, in its various forms, derives ultimately from an Indian fable, very likely Buddhist, about the illusory nature of time.[7]

The taste for the fantastic was so pronounced in the medieval Arab lands that it spawned a distinctive genre of literature, that of *aja'ib* (marvels), and books were written on the marvels of Egypt, of India and of the cosmos as a whole.[8] Such books were hugger-mugger compilations of improbable information about the stupendous monuments of antiquity, strange coincidences, the miraculous powers of certain plants, stones and animals, and feats of magic. Many of the marvels first found in 'non-fiction' works on cosmography eventually made their way into the *Nights*. The Sinbad cycle, which is a fictional reworking of mariners' yarns about the wonders to be found in the Indian and China seas (among them the wak-wak tree with its human-headed fruit, the Old Man of the Sea and the fish as large as an island), is the most obvious example of this process.[9]

Of course, readers and writers in medieval Christendom also had a taste for marvels and loved to read of monsters, of strange cities and of supernatural events. However, medieval Christendom and Islam did not share the same supernatural world. This is most strikingly apparent in the cases of the ghost and the witch. Ghosts and ghost stories feature prominently in medieval European culture.[10] This was not the case in the Islamic lands. In Christendom, ghosts were commonly conceived of as unshriven souls who sought revenge, absolution or Christian burial from the living. The Christian doctrine of purgatory implied that the prayers and acts of the living could aid the dead, and the restless souls who spoke to the living provided valuable testimony about the accuracy of the Catholic Church's vision of life after death. Purgatory does not feature in the orthodox Muslim's concept of the afterlife. However, though ghosts had no proper role in the Islamic vision of the world, native Christians in the Middle East believed in them, and it is possible that their fears sometimes infected their Muslim neighbours. In medieval Cairo it was customary to abandon a house where a murder or a suicide had occurred, and let the house fall to ruin, rather than run the risk of sharing the dwelling with a tormented spirit. Felix Fabri, a Christian pilgrim who visited Egypt in the fifteenth century, described a house on the banks of the Nile whose owner had been driven out by 'nymphs', nocturnal spirits, which threw out first the owner's furniture and then the owner and his companions. Despite subsequent attempts to let it, the haunted house had remained untenanted. However, these punctilious 'nymphs' did leave a monthly rent for the owner.[11] One is tempted to characterize such lodgers as ghosts, but this may be a mistake; for, as Burton observes: 'Haunted houses [in the Middle East] are there tenanted by Ghuls, Jinns and a host of supernatural creatures; but not by ghosts proper; and a man may live for years in Arabia before he ever hears of the "Tayf".'[12] *Tayf* may be translated as 'ghost'. So may *khayal*. But *tayf* also carries the sense of 'fantasy', and *khayal* that of 'shadow', both words implying that what is seen is not really there.

In the tales of the *Nights*, the title 'Ali the Cairene and the Haunted House of Baghdad' seems to promise a ghost story, but the story itself is no such thing. In the story, a young Egyptian, down on his luck in Baghdad, is offered temporary lodgings by a merchant. The merchant owns two houses, but Ali is warned that one of them 'is haunted, and none nigheth there but in the morning he is a dead man'. No one even dares enter the house to retrieve the corpses; instead they get the bodies out by hauling them on to another roof with ropes. As an opening for a traditional ghost story this seems promising, but, as the narrative makes clear, the locals believe the place to be haunted by jinn rather than by ghosts. As the story develops, the jinn who haunts the house is never seen. Only the voice of the jinn is heard, and, far from doing Ali harm, the jinn showers him with gold as the chosen one whose coming was expected.[13]

Medieval Christendom was haunted by fear of the witch. Witches were both numerous and dangerous. They flew by night, they destroyed cattle and livestock, they met in covens and they rendered obscene homage to the Devil. The Christian Inquisition devoted vast resources to hunting down, interrogating and burning witches. In the Middle East, however, there was no institution comparable to the Inquisition (although an *ad hoc* tribunal, a *mihna*,[14] might occasionally be established to try a heretic). Nor was there an obsessional fear of witches. Nevertheless, there were thought to be witches in the medieval Near East. (Instead of broomsticks, they flew about on jars.) Two types of witch feature in the tales of the *Nights*, and each type presents a sexual threat to men. First, there is the nymphomaniac man-killer (see, for examples, the sorceress-wife in 'The Ensorcelled Prince' or Jan Shah, the 500-year-old queen who forces men to sleep with her and then kills them in 'The History of Ghaib and his Brother Ajib'). The second type of witch was a lesbian, and as we have already seen, lesbians are several times maligned as witches in the pages of the *Nights*. Despite all the above, witches played a far smaller part in the demonology of the Arab lands than they did in the Christian West.

On the other hand, some occult pursuits were much more popular in the Middle East than in Europe. In Europe, magic was occasionally used to divine the whereabouts of buried treasure. The Elizabethan magus John Dee and his shady colleague Edward Kelley wasted a great deal of time in quest of the alleged ten great treasures buried in Britain by lords of King Arthur. In the Arab lands, however, treasure-hunting was both a sophisticated occult science and a popular obsession. The number of tales on the subject in the *Nights* bear witness to this. Of course, a treasure-hunt – the quest and the ordeals endured during the search for the goal – has been a popular theme in western storytelling. One only has to think of such books as *The High Quest of the Holy Grail*, Edgar Allan Poe's *The Gold Bug*, Robert Louis Stevenson's *Treasure Island* and J.R.R. Tolkien's *The Hobbit* and such films as *The Treasure of the Sierra Madre* and *Raiders of the Lost Ark*. What is striking about Arab fiction on the subject, however, is the central role of occult knowledge in the search for the treasure.

'Alaeddin, or the Wonderful Lamp', is surely the best known of all the *Nights* tales featuring a treasure-hunt. In the story, the Maghribi (i.e. North African) dervish, who is also a sorcerer, determines by astrology that the boy, Aladdin, is the only person who can bring a certain hoard of treasure out from its hiding place. The sorcerer brings the boy to the astrologically determined place and performs a ritual fumigation with incense in order to create a hole in the ground. Then the sorcerer consults his geomantic tablet. (Islamic geomancy will be discussed later in this chapter.) A copper ring attached to a marble slab is revealed by the cleaving open of the earth. The sorcerer bids Aladdin raise the slab (for it is the boy alone who can do this) and descend into the vaults below. The vaults are filled with treasures, but Aladdin is warned not to touch any of them or he will be turned into black stone – and in fact the sorcerer's quest is not for mere silver and gold, but for a magical lamp which confers power over a genie. There is no need here to follow the development of this famous story any further.[15]

The story of 'Judar and his Brethren', however, deserves to better known than it is. It is a more interesting story than 'Alaeddin' and succeeds better in creating an atmosphere of the uncanny. Judar is a young man who fishes to support his family.

One day he goes out to fish on Lake Karun, on the edge of Cairo, but before he can cast his net upon the waters he is approached by a Maghribi who salutes Judar by name and asks him to do him a service. He asks Judar to recite the first chapter of the Koran and to tie him up by his elbows and throw him into the lake. If and only if Judar subsequently sees the two hands of the Maghribi raised above the surface of the water is Judar to use his net to rescue him. If only the Maghribi's feet appear, then Judar will know that the Maghribi is dead. In that case Judar is to take the Maghribi's mule and precious saddle-bags to a certain Jew dwelling in Cairo and report to him, whereupon the Jew will give him 100 dinars. In the event, the Maghribi's bizarre escapological feat fails, and Judar sees the ill-fated man's feet rising above the surface of the water. So begins a long and complex story of Judar's involvement with four brother sorcerers from the Maghreb who are using a book known as *The Fables of the Ancients* to guide them in their quest for the magical treasures of al-Shamardal. Eventually it emerges that, like Aladdin, Judar is the appointed one, and only he can descend underground to retrieve the treasures of al-Shamardal.

Judar's ordeal is a curious one. In the wilderness, the Maghribi sorcerer (brother of the two magicians who have drowned in Lake Karun) conjures up two jinn who are enjoined to obey Judar and open up to him the treasures of al-Shamardal. Then he instructs Judar on what he must face when the door to the subterranean hoard is revealed. First, the man who opens the door will demand that Judar offers his neck for execution. Judar must agree to this, for only if he does so will the apparition vanish without doing any harm. Secondly, Judar must face a horseman with a lance and Judar must offer his chest to be run through, whereupon the horseman will disappear. At the third door, an archer will threaten Judar. At the fourth door, Judar must offer his hand to be bitten by a lion, and at the fifth he will be challenged by a black slave. At the sixth door, two dragons must be suffered to bite at Judar's hands. Finally, when he comes to the seventh door, he will see his mother welcoming him, but here he must draw his sword and force her to strip, for only by these means can this apparition be disarmed, and then Judar will able to proceed into the hall of treasures. Having received his instructions, Judar descends and outfaces all his ordeals until he comes to the seventh door, where he confronts the thing which appears to be his mother. Sword in hand, he forces her to strip down to her pants. At this point she (or should it be it?) cries out, 'O my son, is thy heart stone? Wilt thou dishonour me by discovering my shame?' Judar hesitates, and in his hesitation he is lost; the supernatural guardians of the treasures set upon him, flog him and expel him from the vaults. A year has to pass before the astrological conjunctions are once again favourable and Judar is able to make the attempt on the treasure again. This time he forces the vision of his mother to strip completely, and, as he does so, the thing turns into a body without a soul. The treasures are now his for the taking.[16]

Judar's subterranean ordeals seem vaguely reminiscent of an initiation rite into some sort of secret society, for which courage, readiness to die and a willingness to renounce both one's family and traditional social constraints are demanded. Alternatively, it is possible to read the story of Judar's ordeal as a thinly veiled psychodrama about descent into the unconsciousness to face the monsters waiting there before attaining the treasures of maturity. However, it is hard to say whether such subtexts could have been picked up by the story's medieval audience. There are many tales featuring treasure-hunts in the *Nights*, among them 'King Ibrahim and his Son', 'The City of Brass', 'The City of Labtayt', 'The Queen of the Serpents', 'Maamun and the Pyramids of Egypt', 'Zayn al-Asnam' and 'Hasan of Basra'. Most of these stories are of Egyptian origin; for Egypt, where tomb robbers had searched for thousands of years for the lost treasures of the Pharaohs, was pre-eminently the home of *mutalibun*, or professional treasure-hunters.

Treasure-hunts in medieval Egypt were not just the stuff of fantasy and fiction. In fact, treasure-hunting was both an occult science and a professional occupation. As a science, it demanded from its students a knowledge of ancient lore and sorcery. As a profession, it demanded courage. It was universally recognized that the *mutalib* (treasure-hunter) was engaged in a high-risk occupation. Al-Jawbari warned in his thirteenth-century treatise *Kashf al-Asrar* of the real perils that the treasure-hunter might face: 'Imagine you are in a long narrow passage descending into the deeps of the earth and the passage is lined by sword-bearing statues. Beware! Beat out the ground in front of you with a stick, so that the swords fall on emptiness.' Al-Jawbari went on to explain how the sword-wielding arms of the statues are activated by tubes of mercury attached to trip-wires. Readers of *Kashf al-Asrar* are instructed on how to avoid fire-traps by making magical fumigations, and to beat out the ground in front of one with a stick so as to avoid being pitched into a silo of sand by a revolving flagstone. A treasure-hunter needed patience, courage, occult knowledge and artisanal skill. Al-Jawbari spoke from personal experience. He and some friends excavating in a cemetery near Cairo found the gateway to a subterranean passage. They avoided the collapsing staircase by sounding it out with sticks, and they avoided the revolving flagstone by throwing a lump of lead on to it. Al-Jawbari does not say whether they found any treasure.[17]

While al-Jawbari was himself a *mutalib*, and respected the skills of the genuine treasure-hunter, he also warned of the dangers posed by confidence tricksters who posed as treasure-hunters, who used spurious maps and talismans, and salted away caches of 'treasure' and drugs for separating their clients from their money. In the *Nights*, 'The Tale of the Sharpers with the Shroff and the Ass' concerns a team of rogues who trick a shroff (money-changer) into believing that a donkey belonging to a confederate of theirs is the only creature which can guide them to a certain hoard of treasure. The shroff is persuaded to act on their behalf and offer their confederate a vast sum of money for the donkey, whereupon the sharpsters all disappear with the money.

While there were many frauds associated with treasure-hunting, nobody doubted that there were real fortunes to be won – and real perils to be encountered. Besides the threats posed by booby-traps and by jinn, the *mutalib* often had to encounter homicidal automata. A great deal of the ancient Greek expertise concerning ingenious mechanical devices (powered by wind, water, weights or springs) had been handed on to the medieval Arabs, and Arab engineers continued to develop and refine devices for telling the time, dispensing drinks and playing music.[18] However, in popular belief such automata – primitive robots – were powered by magic, and it was widely believed that ancient kings and wizards had set magically driven automata to guard over their hidden treasure hoards.

The automaton, a creature who is neither living nor dead, features frequently in the *Nights* as an uncanny accessory in its tales of wonder. The brass oarsman who bears a tablet of lead inscribed with talismanic characters on his breast and who rows the Third Dervish over to the Islands of Safety; the little manikin which a dervish fashions out of beeswax and which plunges into the river to retrieve the sultan's lost signet ring; the air-driven statues which seem to speak to Omar bin al-Nu'uman and his son in the palace of the Christian princess; and the Ebony Horse, which is powered by wind and, when the right lever is pulled, carries a man through the air: they all simulate life, but there is no life in them. Devised for the most part by masters long dead, they are remnants of a poorly understood and therefore dangerous past. In the idolatrous stone city in 'Abdullah bin Fazil and his Brothers', the idols are man-made, but, as the prophet sent by God points out, 'the Satans clad themselves therewith as with clothing, and they it is who spake to you from within the bellies of the images'.[19]

In order to find treasure, recourse might be had to oracles and divination. Treasure could be dowsed for, just as one dowsed for water, and the treasure-hunter might have recourse to the linked sciences of astrology and geomancy. In the course of her

examination by the sages of the caliph's court, the learned slave girl
Tawaddud, the heroine of the *Nights* story which bears her name,
gives an impromptu lecture on the mansions of the moon, the
benevolent and sinister aspects of the planets and the auspicious
and inauspicious days of the week. However, she is careful to
point out the limits of divination. Foreknowledge of certain things
is reserved for God alone. Tawaddud's reservations about the
powers of astrology were shared by many medieval thinkers. In
fiction, however, what is prophesied by the astrologers always
comes to pass. In 'The Third Dervish's Tale', the prince, hidden
on the island, tells Ajib ibn Khasib 'how the astrologers and wise
men, noting my birth date, read my horoscope' and then told his
father that 'Your son will live fifteen years, after which there will
be a conjunction of the stars, and if he can escape it, he will live.'[20]
But there is no escaping the doom of the astrologers; and, though
Ajib ibn Khasib has no wish to kill the prince, he still does kill
him, just as the astrologers have foretold.

In both Christian and Muslim lands, astrology was closely
linked with geomancy. In the Mamluke lands, diviners usually
made use of a combination of geomancy and astrology to
formulate their prophecies. 'I am the ready Reckoner; I am the
Scrivener; I am he who weeteth the Sought and the Seeker; I am
the finished man of Science; I am the Astrologer accomplished in
experience! Where then is he that seeketh?'[21] This is the cry of the
eponymous hero of 'The Tale of Kamar al-Zaman' when, to gain
access to the king's daughter, he dons the guise of a geomancer
and wanders through the streets, carrying the precious tools of his
trade: 'a geomantic tablet of gold, with a set of astrological
instruments and with an astrolabe of silver, plated with gold'. At
its least sophisticated level, geomancy involved the diviner in
nothing more than guessing the future from random marks in the
sand. In 'Ali Shar and Zumurrud', Zumurrud, who pretends to be
a geomancer, needs nothing more than a tray of sand and a brass
pen to allow her to divine the figure of a baboon from the

random markings made by her pen in the sand. However, as both Kamar al-Zaman's boasting and his impedimenta suggest, geomancy at a more sophisticated level involved complex astrological calculations. A geomantic figure was formed by making four random lines of dots. Then the number of dots in each row was counted to determine whether the row was even or odd. The combination of even and/or odd lines generated one of sixteen possible geomantic figures. The horoscope of the enquirer, the dominant planets at the time of enquiry and other astrological considerations all also played a part in determining the geomancer's final prognosis.[22] (Medieval Muslim and Christian geomancy is not to be confused with Chinese geomancy, which is concerned with 'the subtle currents in the earth' and the flow of the occult forces of *yin* and *yang* through landscapes and buildings.) In the *Nights*, geomancy is the most widely employed means of discovering the unknown. Crafty Dalilah casts a geomantic figure in order to discover Mercury Ali's true identity. Geomancers predict the future of Zayn al-Asnam. Geomancy reveals to the sorcerer that Aladdin is still alive.

Firasa, physiognomic divination, or divination from appearances, was a science or skill on the edge of the occult. Its practitioners might draw on occult lore to perform inexplicable feats of deduction, but they also used common sense and humdrum detective work. The word *firasa* comes from the same root as *faras*, meaning horse, and it may be that the skill of *firasa* was first developed by the bedouin to evaluate horses and see through the deceits of swindling horse-dealers. In later centuries, one of the chief practical uses of *firasa* was in the examination and assessment of slaves offered for sale in the market.[23] In a brilliant and wide-ranging essay, 'Clues, Roots of an Evidential Paradigm', the cultural historian Carlo Ginzburg has discussed the related techniques of art connoisseurship, psychoanalysis, detection and *firasa*. As Ginzburg observes: 'Ancient Arabic physiognomics was rooted on *firasa*, a complex notion which generally meant the capacity to leap from the known to the unknown by inference on the basis of clues.'[24]

'The King who Kenned the Quintessence of Things' and the 'Story of the Sultan of Al-Yaman and his Three Sons' are both tales about *firasa*. In the former tale, the king, who has lost his kingdom and has had himself sold as a slave, is able to amaze his successor on the throne by his ability to determine, just by looking, that a certain pearl is rotten inside, that, superficial appearances to the contrary, the older of a pair of horses offered for sale is a better buy, and that, finally, the king, his master, is the son of a baker. In 'The Story of the Sultan of Al-Yaman and his Three Sons', three gifted princes, wandering in the wilderness, are able to deduce that a one-eyed, tailless camel laden with halva and pickles has passed that way before them. This early detective story is of considerable antiquity. A variant version appeared in al-Tabari's tenth-century chronicle of Islamic history. Versions of essentially the same tale feature in Sercambi's fifteenth-century *Novelle*, in Voltaire's *Zadig* and, most recently, in Umberto Eco's *The Name of the Rose*. References to *firasa* abound elsewhere in the *Nights*. In 'The Night-Adventure of the Sultan Mohammed of Cairo', the sultan's disguise is penetrated by the youngest of the girls he visits, for she looks at him 'with the eye of the physiognomist'. To the ignorant such deductions must have seemed positively miraculous, but often it was only a matter of close observation coupled with logical reasoning. There was nothing necessarily occult about the process. However, certain Sufi sheikhs taught how interior truths might be deduced by occult intuition, a mystic might transform himself into a 'spy of the heart', and *firasa* might easily shade into thought-reading (*ilm al-mukashafa*). Outward appearances betrayed inner truths, and it is one of the commonplaces of the *Nights* that 'a man's destiny is written upon his forehead'.

The broad science of divination embraced some quite strange sub-specialisms, such as urinomancy (featured in 'The Tale of the

Weaver who Became a Leach', where the weaver pretends to skill as a urinomancer, but is actually using the broader skills of the physiognomist), divination from palpitations, divination from wounds, divination from beauty spots and *qiyafah* or divination of ancestry. Even predicting rainfall from examining the sky's appearance was classified as divination (perhaps rightly so, for modern attempts to turn meteorology into a fully fledged science are not entirely convincing).

However, astrology and geomancy apart, dream interpretation was probably the most commonly employed technique of unveiling the secrets of the future.[25] Despite the weirdly dreamlike quality of so many of the stories within the *Nights*, the dreams actually featured in the stories are rather simple ones and they are easily interpreted. It is a feature of popular stories that the dreams that the characters have always carry messages that are true. When, in 'The History of Gharib and his Brother Ajib', Gharib dreams that he and his companion are swept up from a valley by two ravening birds of prey, the dream's content is not that of a mystifying riddle with latent sexual content to be teased out and decoded. Rather, the following day Gharib and his companion are in a valley when two great birdlike creatures swoop down and carry them away. Medieval Arab storytellers did not make use of sophisticated dream symbolism. If a sultan in a story is warned of something, then the warning will come true. The dream in medieval Arab fiction was a storyteller's device, used to foreshadow what is going to happen – and, as such, a special form of literary adumbration or prolepsis. But dreams were not only used to prefigure what would happen later on in the story; as often as not, they also made the story happen. For example, in 'The Ruined Man who Became Rich Again through a Dream', the man in question is told to leave his native city of Baghdad and go to Cairo, where he will discover the whereabouts of some hidden treasure. In Cairo he experiences a series of misfortunes and ends up in gaol. There he tells his dream to the police chief. The police chief mocks the idea of veridical dreams and tells the man how he himself has dreamed of a certain house, a courtyard and a fountain in Baghdad and of treasure buried under that fountain. The imprisoned man recognizes that house as his own and, on his release from gaol, he goes back to Baghdad and digs up the treasure. (A variant of the same story in English folklore is known as the story of the Pedlar of Swaffham.)[26] In the above story and in numerous others, the dream not only predicts the future, it makes it happen. Most of the dreams in the *Nights* turn out to be self-fulfilling prophecies.

In medieval Islamic reality, as opposed to fiction, the science of dream interpretation was highly sophisticated, and not all dreams were regarded as being veridical. There were dreams which came from God and which were a portion of prophecy, and it was widely held by Muslims that no dream in which the Prophet appeared could be false or misleading. Then there were enigmatic dreams, which did not come directly from God but might nevertheless, if sensitively interpreted, give useful guidance about the present and future state of the one who had had the dream. Finally, there were very confused dreams, which were the product of nothing more than indigestion or a poor sleeping posture. Much depended on one's choice of dream interpreter, for the dream was not regarded as having any meaning until it had been assigned one by its interpreter. 'The dream follows his mouth.' Once the dream had been interpreted, however, its meaning was fixed. Thomas Mann made play with this ancient Semitic concept in his remarkable novel *Joseph the Provider*: 'For it may well be that dreaming is a single whole, wherein dream and interpretation belong together and dreamer and interpreter only seem to be two separate persons but are actually interchangeable and one and the same, since together they make up the whole.'[27] Dreams were also ranked according to the status of the dreamer. Thus, a king's dream was more to be believed than a commoner's, and a man's dream was more creditworthy than a woman's.

According to an ancient Arab tale (not included in the *Nights*), a man was walking down the street one morning when he saw Death looking at him strangely. In a panic, the man fled his native city, seeking to place as much distance between himself and Death as possible. In the evening he arrived in Samarra, but he found Death waiting for him there. The reason Death had looked so strangely on the man in the morning was that he was surprised to see him in that place, for Death knew that they had an appointment in Samarra that night. Here complementary actions combine to bring about the predestined fate. The structure of the story of 'The Appointment at Samarra' is essentially the same as that of 'The Ruined Man who Became Rich Again through a Dream', discussed above. Such tales offer perfect examples of the mysteriously satisfying symmetries of fate and fiction.

Qada and qadar play a determining role in the Muslim universe. Qada means decree, or fate in general (which is God's decree), while qadar is a particular application of qada. Although it has been contested by many Muslim thinkers and some sects, the notion of predestination, of the control of the lives of men and women by God's decree, has been fairly widely accepted by Sunni Muslims. If God's will is omnipotent, then human will counts for nothing – or rather, a man's will is determined by God's will, so that, somewhat subtly, a person of his or her free will chooses the fate that God has already predetermined for that person. The damned are damned because God has predetermined their damnation. 'God has set a seal on their hearts and on their hearing, and on their eyes is a covering, and there awaits them a mighty chastisement' (Koran, II, 7); and 'God leads astray whomsoever He will' (Koran, XIII, 27). According to Islamic folklore, when God made Adam, he took out all Adam's future descendants (they looked like little ants) and divided them into those with good futures and those with evil futures. The good were replaced on the right side of Adam's body and the evil on the left side.

The above is rather by way of an excursus, for the way that fate performed in medieval Arab fiction owed little to speculative theology. Al-Tanukhi's *Faraj ba'd al-Shidda*, or 'Relief after Distress', a tenth-century collection of stories to illustrate the workings of divine providence, was compiled with the aim of inspiring its audience to bear their tribulations with fortitude and pious resignation.[28] The *Nights* contains many stories and fables which share this 'you–can't–beat–fate' attitude and advocate a sort of religious quietism. In the fable of 'The Fishes and the Crab', the fishes, threatened by the drying up of their pool, go to the crab for advice. The crab urges resignation, for 'Know ye not that Allah (extolled and exalted be He!) provideth all His creatures without account and that He foreordained their daily meat ere He created aught of creation and appointed to each of His creatures a fixed term of life and an allotted provision, of His divine All-might?' And, as the trapped sparrow in one of the fables observes, 'It availed me not to beware of the stroke of fate and fortune, since even he who taketh precaution may never flee from destiny.' However, seeking to avoid fate makes for a better story than listening to the wise old crab and waiting for the rain to fall again. In most *Nights* stories, the protagonists refuse to heed the warnings of the wise old sages and astrologers, and they make their bids to beat fate.

To resign oneself to God's will is evidently laudable. Sometimes, however, one feels that the doctrine of predestination is being used to serve less laudable aims, and resignation to divine decree can serve as an apologia for idleness. Certainly, some of the stories in the *Nights* can be read in this way. 'The History of Khawajah Hasan al-Habbal', for example, is about the debate between two neighbours about whether hard work or luck makes man rich. Inevitably, it concludes that 'wealth cometh not by wealth; but only by the Grace of Almighty Allah does a poor man become a rich man'.[29] More generally, it is striking how many of the stories in the *Nights* (stories designed to entertain the idlers of Cairo's cafés) feature heroes who are idle and feckless, but who attain great fortunes through amazing good luck. Aladdin is perhaps the best-known example of these unimpressive heroes. Destiny is capricious and favours the humble, the talentless and the lazy. Consider also Ali Baba, Ma'aruf the Cobbler and a string of poor fishermen who haul up bottled jinn, talking fish and magic rings. What could be more chancy than casting one's net upon the waters? Fate, or destiny, under God, is the poor man's omnipotent ombudsman. 'Think not, O King, that thou art safe from the shifts of Time and the Strokes of Change which come like a traveller in the Night,' warns the wazir in 'The Tale of Kamar al-Zaman'. Destiny, like death, is a great leveller, and 'Death, the Destroyer of all Delights' is everybody's destiny. We are all eventually pulled through that dark and infinitely small hole.

'Character,' as the German poet Novalis cryptically observed, 'is destiny.' Novalis probably meant that each individual, through exercise of his particular qualities and in pursuit of his own particular ambitions, is the architect of his fortunes and misfortunes. In the *Nights*, however, the sense of this equivalence of character and destiny is reversed; for, as Todorov has observed in an essay on 'Les Hommes-Récits', 'characters' like Sinbad and Ali Baba seem to have no character, no inner depth and no psychological consistency. They are what they do, or, rather, they are what fate (working hard on behalf of the storyteller) makes them do.[30]

From the stories of the *Nights* we learn that fate is 'that which is written on the forehead'. Indeed, fate is written all over the place. *Mektub*, it is written. Fate is a thoroughly literary affair. Each man has his story, and it is written on him. The poet Zuhayr ibn Abi Salama once compared fate to 'a night-blind camel'. It may be true that in real life fate is blind. But when we turn to fiction, we find that the blindness of fate is a thoroughly misleading metaphor. As we shall see, fate is far from blind. It watches over everything and meticulously arranges it all. There is no random fumbling on the part of fate. Though fate is always omnipresent and active, it is discoverable only by certain clues, such as marks on the forehead or in the sand, or by the operation of amazing coincidence (*ittifaq*). Though largely invisible, Fate is a leading character in the *Nights*. As we have already seen, in 'The Second Dervish's Tale', Fate, helped along by the astrologers, is the architect of the misfortunes of Khasib and the prince he slays. Similarly, in 'The Story of King Ibrahim and his Son', the king is warned by his astrologers that his new-born son, when he reaches the age of seven, will be attacked by a lion, and moreover that, if the boy survives the lion's onslaught, he will grow up to slay his own father, the king. The king has his son secluded and carefully guarded against such an eventuality. But seven years later, 'the time of the Fate foreordered and the Fortune graven on the forehead' arrives. The son's nursemaid is slain by a lion, and the son vanishes. He reappears later inadvertently to slay his father. With his (rather prolix) dying breaths, the king forgives his son, for as he tells his courtiers, 'Know that what Allah hath writ upon the forehead, be it fair fortune or misfortune, none may efface, and all that is decreed to a man must perforce befall him.'

Again, in 'The Merchant's Daughter and the Prince of al-Irak', the merchant is warned by an invisible voice, first that 'Predestination overcometh Prudence and resignation to the trials sent by Allah is foremost and fairest', and secondly that his daughter will bear an illegitimate child to an Iraqi prince. In an (inevitable) attempt to avoid the decree of fate, the merchant takes steps to hide his daughter on a remote mountain. But the very steps that the merchant takes to secure his daughter's virtue ensure her fall; for the Iraqi prince goes out hunting one day and comes across a stallion which 'under decree of Destiny was influenced by the Lord and directed towards the Prince for the sake of that which was hidden from him in the World of Secrets', and this stallion eventually takes the prince to the maiden secluded on the mountain. And so the fate-laden story continues. In 'The Tale of Attaf' (also known as 'The Power of Destiny'), Harun visits a library, consults a volume at random, falls to laughing and weeping and dismisses the faithful vizier Ja'afar from his sight. Ja'afar, disturbed and upset, flees Baghdad and plunges into a series of adventures in Damascus, involving Attaf and the woman whom Attaf eventually marries. Returning to Baghdad, he reports back to Harun, who takes him into the library. Now Ja'afar is allowed to consult the book which caused his master such grief and mirth, and in it Ja'afar finds the story of his own adventures with Attaf, those same adventures which were provoked by Harun's reading of the story in the book. Even so was the doom of destiny fulfilled. A form of reverse causation operates in these stories, in which the prophecy gives birth to what is prophesied. C.S. Lewis has written of this type of tale (the legend of Oedipus comes in the same category):

Such stories produce (at least in me) a feeling of awe coupled with a certain sort of bewilderment such as one often feels in looking at a complex pattern of lines that pass over and under one another. One sees, yet does not quite see, the regularity . . . We have just had set before our imagination something that has always baffled the intellect: we have seen how destiny and free will can be combined, even how free will is the *modus operandi* of destiny.[31]

Fate is fond of symmetry and economy in stories, Fate standing here for the storyteller, of course. One way for the storyteller to achieve economy is through the canny deployment of coincidence, but what is coincidence? In Julian Barnes's novel *Flaubert's Parrot*, the narrator roundly denounces coincidences: 'There's something spooky about them: you sense momentarily what it must be like to live in an ordered, God-run universe, with Himself looking over your shoulder and helpfully dropping coarse hints about a cosmic plan.' And Barnes's curmudgeon continues: 'And as for coincidences in books – there's something cheap and sentimental about the device; it can't help seeming cheap and gimcrack. That troubador who passes by just in time to rescue the girl from a

hedgerow scuffle; the sudden but convenient Dickensian bene-
factors; the neat shipwreck on a foreign shore which reunites
siblings and lovers.' However, Barnes's narrator allows that
coincidence may have a proper place in picaresque narratives, and,
of course, the medieval Arab was quite sure that he was living in
'an ordered, God-run universe' and he had no objection to the
storyteller assuming similar powers over his fictional universe.[32]

In 'Julnar the Sea-Born and her Son', Princess Jauharah flees
from a palace coup to a certain island and hides up a certain tree.
Surely no one will discover her there? But, in fact, 'destiny from
eternity fore-ordained' drives Badr al-Basim, who is fleeing for his
life, to the very island where the princess has taken refuge, and
Badr lies down to rest under the very same tree. The coincidence
is ludicrous, and Barnes's spokesman would hate it, but without
the coincidence there would be no story. Without pattern, there is
no meaning. Coincidences, however, hint at a hidden meaning in
the world's ordering. Destiny promises – no, demands – adventures
and, having called up adventures, eventually resolves them. The
Italian film director Pier Paolo Pasolini, one of the most intelligent
of modern interpreters of the *Nights*, observed that

every tale in *The Thousand and One Nights* begins with an 'appearance of
destiny' which manifests itself through an anomaly, and one anomaly
always generates another. So a chain of anomalies is set up. And the
more logical, tightly knit, essential this chain is, the more beautiful the
tale. By 'beautiful' I mean vital, absorbing and exhilarating. The chain
of anomalies always tends to lead back to normality. The end of every
tale in the *The Thousand and One Nights* consists of a 'disappearance' of
destiny, which sinks back to the somnolence of daily life … The
protagonist of the stories is in fact destiny itself.[33]

Consciously or unconsciously, Pasolini's reflections on destiny
echo and elaborate on those of the social and cultural theorist
Walter Benjamin, who observed in an essay on 'Fate and
Character' that misfortune is a category of fate, but that 'happiness

is, rather, what releases a man from the embroilment of the Fates and from the net of his own fate'.[34] Pasolini's reflections may also remind one of Vladimir Propp's ideas about the functions of violation and resolution in Russian fairy tales (which will be discussed in the next chapter).

In *Chance and Necessity*, Jacques Monod, when considering which ideas are most likely to lodge themselves in people's heads and therefore survive, argues that 'What is very plain, however, is that the ideas having the highest invading potential are those that explain man by assigning him his place in an immanent destiny, a safe harbour where his anxiety dissolves.' As with ideas, so, surely, with stories. A story which has begun by conjuring up a problem (or an anomaly, or a violation), and which has ended by conjuring the problem away, will have commended itself to those in its audience who are worried about their own destiny and place in the universe. Fiction here has some of the same soothing powers as religion.[35]

Each man has his own fate, and one man's fate may conquer another. In 'The Adventures of Mercury Ali of Cairo', the sinister Jewish sorcerer, Azariah, discovers through geomancy that Ali's fortune conquers his, so he refrains from killing him and turns him into an ass instead. In the medieval Near East, Jews were often credited with magical powers, and, in fact, one can find features in surviving Arab magical texts from the Middle Ages which have obvious Jewish origins – the stress on letter-magic and the cabalistic manipulation of letters, the imagery of Solomon's seal, staff and ring, and Hebrew or at least Hebrew-sounding names of the spirits who could be conjured to do the sorcerer's bidding.

However, although Jews frequently featured as sorcerers in popular literature, the Maghribis – Arab or Berber Muslims from North Africa and Spain – were more commonly assigned roles as sorcerers in the *Nights* and in popular folklore. The best known of these Maghribi sorcerers must be the one who sought to make use and then dispose of Aladdin, but there are many others, among them the three brothers who make Judar tie them up and cast them into the Karun Pool and the Maghribi encountered by Sheikh Muhammad in 'The History of Mohammed, Sultan of Cairo', who had before him 'some written leaves and was casting omens for sundry bystanders' and who helps Muhammad against a deceitful jinn. It was not only the authors of fiction who assigned Maghribis a role as sorcerers. Ibn Iyas's history of Mamluke Egypt tells how a Maghribi sorcerer conjured up a garden which he sold to a citizen of Cairo, before vanishing, together with the garden. Of the two most important medieval Arab magical treatises, one, the *Ghayat al-Hakim*, or 'Goal of the Sage', was attributed to the tenth-century Spanish Muslim mathematician al-Majriti; while the other, *Shams al-Ma'arif*, or 'Sun of Gnosis', was attributed to al-Buni, a thirteenth-century North African Sufi who had settled in Alexandria. Al-Zannati, a key figure in the history of geomancy, was a Berber, and the Arabs thought, probably rightly, that geomancy came to them from the Berbers. Persians also occasionally feature as magicians. For example, there is the geomancer in 'Hasan of Bassorah', of whom Hasan's mother warns him: 'O my son, beware of hearkening to the talk of the folk, and especially of the Persians, and obey them not in aught; for they are sharpers and tricksters, who profess the art of alchemy.'[36] Bahram the Guebre (that is, the Zoroastrian) does indeed use the promise of teaching the alchemic arts to lure Hasan into his power (he really intends to sacrifice the youth to the fire which, as a Zoroastrian, he worships).

As has been noted above, there were no witch-hunts of any consequence in medieval Islamic history. The sorcerer, no matter how wicked he might be, was thought of not as the servant of the Devil, but rather as the master of the jinn. The sorcerer worked through books, swords, talismans and lamps to force the unseen legions to his will. In 'The Tale of the Warlock and the Young Cook of Baghdad', the warlock makes use of a metal flask, seven needles, a piece of aloes wood, some clay, a sheep's shoulder-blade, some felt and some silk. Having used these objects to make a curious bundle pierced through with needles, he recites over it: 'I have knocked, I have knocked at the hall doors of the earth to summon the Jann [a variant plural of Jinn], and the Jann have knocked for the Jann against the Shaytan.'

The jinn (sing. jinn or genie) were thought of as supernatural creatures with bodies of flame. They were normally invisible (and so it was that the merchant in the *Nights* inadvertently killed the son of a jinn by throwing away a date stone). However, they frequently make themselves visible in the *Nights*. Though they normally appear as human beings, this was not always the case. In 'The Tale of Zayn al-Asnam', Zayn al-Asnam is ferried across the lake by a jinn with the head of an elephant and the body of a lion. The hosts of jinn assembled on the other side of the lake are hideous to look upon; only the King of the Jinn has assumed the form of a handsome young man. Such accounts of meetings with the kings of the jinn and their legions can easily be paralleled in medieval Arab sorcerer's manuals which purported to be non-fiction. In the treatises of the thirteenth-century sorcerer Abu'l-Qasim al-Iraqi, for example, there are a variety of spells for summoning jinn, for learning their secrets and for using them as treasure-hunters. (Abu'l-Qasim also knew spells for flying, walking on water, mastering telepathy, giving people dogs' heads and giving women beards.) Another magician, writing under the name Ibn al-Hajj, produced a treatise called *Suns of the Lights*, which contains among other things a spell for having sex with the daughter of the White King of the Jinn. After twelve days' fasting and uttering of conjurations in the desert, first a dragon appears (which must be ignored) and then a very pale woman who approaches with an undulating walk and who is laden with gold and jewels. The trouble is, if you agree to marry her, this will make you impotent with ordinary women.[37]

The jinn were shape-shifters,[38] as emerges from the shape-shifting battle in 'The Second Dervish's Tale'. Very commonly jinn travelled about as whirlwinds. The society of the jinn was rather like human society. It had its own kings, courts and armies. In 'The Adventures of Bulukiya', Bulukiya comes before Sakhr, King of the Jinn, who is attended upon by lesser kings and princes of the jinn, as well as by counsellors, emirs and officers of state. There are good Muslim jinn, like Sakhr and his following, and there are evil, infidel jinn. (The evil jinn are sometimes character- ized as *shaytans*, or devils.) Since jinn often move about in the world of men and transact business with humans, a significant body of law was elaborated by religious jurisconsults, dealing with such matters as the property rights of jinn and cases of mixed marriages between jinn and women. Ritual hygiene was another potential issue. Although women have to perform the major ritual ablution (the *ghusl*) after having had sex with men before they can perform the prayers, according to the legal compilation *Al-Fatawa al-Hindiyya* there is no need for the ablutions after having had sex with jinn.[39]

Some considered Iblis, the Devil, to be a jinn; some thought of him as an angel.[40] (Angels are made of light, while jinn are made of fire.) The majority opinion appears to have been that he was a fallen angel and that he had been punished for his pride. Specifi- cally, he had refused God's command to bow down and venerate Adam. Though God cast him out of heaven for this, some Sufis venerated Iblis for his uncompromising refusal to bow down before anyone save God. The Devil rarely appears in the *Nights*, but (in an early Arab prefiguration of the story of Tartini and the Devil's trill), in the story of 'Ibrahim of Mosul and the Devil', the Father of Bitterness appears before Ibrahim and teaches him a new song. Iblis also appears in 'The Tale of the Damsel Tohfat al- Kulub'. In both stories he appears in the form of a handsome old man. In 'The Adventures of Bulukiya', we are told that the evil jinn are descendants of Iblis, while the good jinn are the offspring of the six angels who did not fall.

Jinn haunted lavatories, and so it is that in 'The Tale of Nur al-

Din Ali and his Son' the *ifrit* (powerful jinn) emerges out of the tank of the lavatory to persecute the hunchback. Tohfat al-Kulub was conducted by Iblis, 'Father of the Jinn', to the land of the jinn, via a magic exit concealed in one of the lavatories of the caliph's palace. Ruins, as in 'The King's Son and the Ogress' and 'Ma'aruf the Cobbler', and cemeteries were also favoured by the jinn, particularly by the sub-category of jinn known as ghouls. A ghoul is a malevolent jinn who lives in deserted places or cemeteries. He or she is fond of human flesh (and sometimes 'ghoul' was used as a synonym for human cannibal). A ghoul could be killed with a single blow, but if the killer inadvertently hit the ghoul again, then it would come back to life. According to the nineteenth-century desert explorer Charles Doughty, ghouls lured travellers from their paths by calling to them in the voice of their mother or sister.

When it comes to the vocabulary of teratology, Arab usage was neither precise nor consistent, but in general it seems that a *marid* was a more powerful sort of jinn and that an *ifrit* was an even more powerful one yet. *Ifrits* were usually malevolent (the verbal root from which the noun is derived means to roll in the dust, i.e. to bring low). Many of the jinn encountered in the *Nights* have been imprisoned in flasks or columns of stone by Solomon, who controlled the jinn through his seal-ring and his staff and punished them for their disobedience. In 'The City of Brass', the caliph in Damascus sends out an expedition to search for such flasks. The jinn are compelled by certain objects, such as the signet ring discovered by Ma'aruf the Cobbler in an underground cave. The notion that spirits could be controlled through correct manipulation of certain magical objects probably derives from a debased form of loosely Neoplatonic ideas popular in late antiquity concerning theurgy, or the practice of magic through the control of spirits. Whereas in the medieval West it was possible for some sceptical spirits to dismiss any story concerning fairies as an old wives' tale, the medieval Muslim could not dismiss the possibility of the existence of the jinn so easily, for they are repeatedly attested to in the Koran – for example, in a passage about Solomon's control of the jinn:

> And of the jinn, some worked before him
> by leave of his Lord; and such of them
> as swerved away from Our commandment,
> We would let them taste the chastisement of the Blaze.
>
> (XXXIV, 11)

Pagans in seventh-century Arabia seem to have held that the jinn were spirits related to God. This belief was denounced in the Koran (VI, 100):

> Yet they ascribe to God, as associates, the
> jinn, though he created them; and they impute
> to Him sons and daughters without any knowledge.

Subsequently, jinn in fiction borrowed aspects and powers both from the demons of late antiquity and from the Indian pantheon.

Some quite specialized types of jinn and monster are noticed in medieval Arab treatises. The *udar*, a spirit which raped men in the desert and left them with worm-infested anuses, is a homosexual ghoul. The *atra* is a devil which sends men to sleep during their prayers by pissing in their ears. The *qutrub* is the Arab werewolf. In popular belief the werewolf was a man or a woman who was transformed into a beast by night and who fed upon corpses. However, the great tenth-century physician al-Razi regarded lycanthropy as mental disorder. The victims of this affliction were melancholic, hollow-eyed, solitary folk who liked the night and cemeteries.[41] Kabikaj was the name of the jinn in charge of insects. Scribes sometimes wrote his name on their manuscripts to protect them from being eaten by worms. A *nasnas* is described by Lane as being 'half a human being; having half a head, half a body, one arm, and one leg, with which it hops with much agility'. In 'The Story of the Sage and the Scholar', the sage magically applies kohl (antimony, used for eye make-up) to one of the young man's eyes and turns the young man into a *nasnas*. A *diw* was a Persian spirit of evil and darkness. A *peri*, as in the story of 'Prince Ahmad and the Fairy Peri-Banu', is a beautiful female spirit and part of Persian mythology. They are usually virtuous and therefore persecuted by the *diws*. When the *diws* and *peris* feature in the *Nights*, they are to all intents and purposes identical with the jinn.

The *rukh* in Arab folklore was a bird of vast dimensions, very similar to the equally vast and mythical Persian *simurgh*. It was capable of carrying men and even elephants in its claws. The concept probably derives from images of the Indian garuda, the half-vulture, half-man, which is shown carrying Vishnu in Indian iconography. According to a cryptic tradition in Turkish folklore, the *rukh* was a bird with a name, but no body. The *rukh* appears in 'Abd al-Rahman the Maghribi's Story of the Rukh' and again in 'The Second Voyage of Sinbad'. To some extent, stories about this bird played on the wonder of scale. Abd al-Rahman the Maghribi described the *rukh*'s egg as being a great white dome one hundred cubits long. In part, however, stories such as the one in which Sinbad is carried by the bird into the Valley of Diamonds are fantasies about the possibility of human flight; and, together with the flying carpet and the Ebony Horse, the *rukh* must be conceded a role in the imaginative prehistory of aviation. Indeed, despite the technological naïvety of the wonders of the *Nights*, some of its stories must be included in the canon of proto-science fiction.

Coleridge, reflecting on childhood origins of his own poetic imagination, observed that 'from my early reading of Faery Tales, and Genii etc. etc. – my mind had been habituated *to the Vast*'. The fairy tale shares this imagination-enlarging function with science fiction, or speculative fantasy; for fantastic voyages, distortions of time and space, alien beings, strange technologies, alternative societies, post-holocaust societies and imaginary histories, all of which are the stock-in-trade of modern science fiction, can all

be found in the *Nights*. 'As one knows,' remarks the cultural
essayist Gilbert Adair (perhaps a little overconfidently),

science fiction bears exactly the same relation to the future, or to any of
the planet's foreseeable futures as fairy-tales do to the (crypto-medieval)
past. In both genres, for instance, animals (or robots and aliens) have
been invested with the at present exclusively human attributes of rational
thought and speech; the control systems, laser rays, microchips and
ultrasounds of science fiction – the whole dazzling cascade of what
might be called (after Dufy) *la fée electronique* – constitute a vertiginous
new alchemy, a Faustian near-infinite fund of knowledge and power;
and one immediately recognizes in both the same narrative structures,
the same Manichaean confrontations, the same elemental themes of
apprenticeship, quest and redemption.[42]

Brian Stableford (in *The Encyclopedia of Science Fiction*) has put
forward the claims of Mary Shelley's *Frankenstein* (1818) to be the
first true work of science fiction, because it is the first to be clear
on the distinction between science and magic, and the first to be
cast in the form of the novel.[43] Although one must respect the
purist's insistence that there could be no true genre of science
fiction until Mary Shelley, Edgar Allan Poe and Jules Verne had
established the ground rules of the genre, nevertheless the *Nights*
and science fiction stories treat of similar themes, draw on similar
techniques and share common aims. The medieval audience of
wonder-tales and the modern readers of science fiction, who
marvel at the scale and complexity of the universe and who
speculate about how it might be otherwise, share a state of mind.

The books on *aja'ib*, or marvels, constituted a distinct genre in
medieval Islamic literature.[44] The compilers of works on *aja'ib*
collected tales about the marvels of Greek, Roman, Pharaonic and
Sassanian antiquity. They recorded uncanny meteorological
phenomena (such as downpours of blood) and the birth of monsters
(such as three-headed calves). They collected details of bizarre
coincidences and they described the marvels of the known universe,

mingling truth and fable in their accounts of fantastic journeys. In their accounts of exotic parts of the world, Arab writers drew directly or indirectly on a pre-existing classical literature of marvels, by authors such as Lucian, Ctesias and Pseudo-Callisthenes, dealing with the wonders of India and the exploits of Alexander. (Those mendacious travellers Marco Polo and John de Mandeville also drew on this sort of material.)

The genre of the fantastic voyage goes back at least to the ancient Sumerian *Epic of Gilgamesh*. Ancient and pre-modern tales of fantastic journeys tended to be open or covert accounts of the voyage of the soul into the afterlife. In the *Nights* in 'The Adventures of Bulukiya' (which shows traces of deriving ultimately from the *Gilgamesh* epic), this aspect of the fantastic voyage is most evident.[45] Wonder is piled upon wonder. Bulukiya, in his quest for the herb of immortality, encounters speaking serpents as big as camels, captures the Queen of the Serpents, walks upon the surface of the sea, discovers the tomb of Solomon, visits strange and paradisal islands, discovers trees which bear clusters of human heads and birds on their branches as well as trees which laugh, watches mermaids sporting, enters the Garden of Eden and is expelled from it by a giant, has an audience with the King of the Jinn and is instructed by the latter as to the nature of the innumerable hells of Allah. In the least of these hells, Jahannam, there are 1,000 mountains of fire, on each mountain 70,000 cities of fire, in each city 70,000 castles of fire, in each castle 70,000 houses of fire, in each house 70,000 couches of fire and on each couch 70,000 manners of torment. This hellish image of infinity prefigures the vast imagination-stretching landscapes of galactic science fiction. Bulukiya is instructed further on the scale and structure of the cosmos when he encounters a vast angel seated on the peak of the cosmic mountain of Kaf. This angel instructs Bulukiya on the multiplicity of worlds beyond the one which Bulukiya knows (and which is encompassed within Mount Kaf). There are forty worlds, each more than forty times the size of

Bulukiya's world, lying beyond Mount Kaf, and each with its own strange inhabitants, colours and guardian angels. But the scale of these worlds is as nothing compared with the size of the angel who supports these worlds, and this angel stands on a rock which is supported by a bull which stands on a fish which swims in a mighty ocean. Bulukiya is allowed to see the fish, whose head takes three days to pass before his eyes. But the fish is small compared to the ocean, and the ocean is above an abyss of air which is above a realm of fire, and beneath all that is the cosmic serpent which can swallow up all that is above it and not notice the difference. The medieval Muslim conceived himself to be living in a universe that was vertiginous in its vastness. The grandeur of the vision of Bulukiya is the quintessence of the *aja'ib*, the astounding.

There is no space here to pursue the subject much further, but Bulukiya's cosmic journey can be compared to Islamic and gnostic speculations about alien life forms and life on other planets. For example, in the eleventh-century philosophical fantasy *Salaman wa-Absal* by Ibn Sina (better known in the West as Avicenna), Absal undertakes a journey across vast deserts and strange seas, like Bulukiya. He encounters bizarre creatures such as 'humans' who have acquired the skins of quadrupeds and on whom vegetation grows. However, Absal travels further than Bulukiya, and the reader of *Salaman wa-Absal* is introduced to the alien customs and appearances of the inhabitants of the moon and other planets. Absal even travels to the stars, to encounter the inhabitants of the zodiacal cities.[46]

While 'Sinbad' certainly draws on the (somewhat garbled) reports of real Arab seafarers in the Indian Ocean, the documentary element in the voyages of Sinbad should not be exaggerated.[47] Captain Buzurg, in his tenth-century compilation *The Book of the Wonders of India*, claimed that nine-tenths of the world's wonders were in the East. In his book Captain Buzurg did draw on real accounts by mariners and merchants of what they had seen in

India, China, Java and perhaps even Japan. However, the main impetus behind his and similar compilations was to collect instances of the *aja'ib*, so literary works were plundered to pad out these collections with tales of Amazon islands, cannibal societies, dog-headed men and human-headed trees. The further the traveller ventured from the heartlands of Islam, the stranger things became, until ultimately one came to the outermost ocean, the Green Sea. Nothing lives on or in this sea. No one has sailed in its waters. It is dark and stinking and extends for ever.

Not all science fiction takes place in space. The novels of Jules Verne and Edgar Rice Burroughs, for example, fantasized about the possibility of life under water. In this they were anticipated by the storytellers of the *Nights*. In 'Julnar the Sea-Born', King Shahriman learns from the mermaid Julnar about people who live underwater (the magic power of Solomon's seal-ring allows them to do so). Unfortunately no details are given of underwater society. However, this deficiency is remedied in 'Abdullah the Fisherman and Abdullah the Merman', where we find an alternative society portrayed. It is a utopia of sorts. Utopias are rare in Islamic fiction and non-fiction. After all, it was well known that rules and norms of the ideal society had been laid down in the Koran and its details elaborated in the sayings and practice of the Prophet Muhammad, and it was commonly held that strict observance of Islamic law and custom would be sufficient to bring about the ideal society. It is true that the tenth-century Arab philosopher al-Farabi, in his *Fi Mabadi ara ahl al-Madinat al-Fadila* ('On the Principles of the Views of the Inhabitants of the Good City'), set out the broad plan of an ideal society. Plato and the Koran were made to harmonize in a city-state directed by virtuous philosophers. (In Islamic thinking the ideal society is an urban one.) But the details of al-Farabi's ideal city were not fleshed out.[48]

However, the *Nights* story of 'Abdullah the Fisherman and Abdullah the Merman' does attempt to present an alternative society in some detail. At the invitation of Abdullah the Merman, Abdullah the Fisherman leaves his poor land to visit the seas of plenty. Having anointed his body with a certain miraculous fish oil, he finds that he is able to breathe underwater. Underwater society offers an inverted reflection of society on land. Everything is different; there is no buying and selling; jewels are commonplace baubles; people go about naked, clothes being unknown among them; free love is the rule; food is eaten raw; one rejoices at funerals. Or, rather, almost everything is different, for some of the merpeople are Muslims, just like Abdullah the Fisherman. However, the story is not really setting out a political programme. It offers something that is wonderful because it is strange, not something that is wonderful because it is a blueprint for the ideal of life in society. The primitive communism of submarine society is merely strange – and laughable. The same sort of point can be made about the Amazon societies which feature so frequently in the *Nights*. Stories about communities dominated by women were beguiling absurdities, but, even so, the descriptions of Amazon societies were not intended as satires on feminism. There was no feminism to satirize.

Predictions of a holocaust and speculations about what a post-holocaust society will be like have featured prominently in twentieth-century science fiction. Science fiction's imaginary societies are (usually) set in the future. In the *Nights*, however, they are located in the past, and the authors of its stories speculated about the lost technology of the ancients, vanished civilizations and the catastrophes which had overwhelmed them. The Koran abounds with examples of communities which went astray and which God destroyed, and this same theme is alluded to in the opening exordium of the *Nights* itself, in which praise is offered to God who 'destroyed the race of Thamud, Ad and Pharaoh of the vast domain'. The *Nights* offers a warning to those who will be instructed. Its audience should consider the hubris of those who sought to dwell in Iram of the Columns. King Shaddad spent 500 years building this city, but when he prepared to enter it, 'the Cry of Wrath' of the Angel of Death slew him and all his following. Or they should consider the city of Labtayt, whose king defied the ancient interdiction and opened the tower of treasures, thereby bringing about the sack of his city by the Arabs. Or the City of Brass, with its petrified inhabitants and their mummified queen (given a ghastly semblance of life by the quicksilver in her eye sockets). Or, in the cycle of 'The Porter and the Three Ladies of Baghdad', in 'The Tale of the First Lady', the city of fire-worshippers, who, all save one, failed to heed the mighty and invisible voice, did not turn to God and consequently were turned to stone. Such marvels are also warnings to those who would reflect, and a sense of wonderment is the beginning of philosophy.

9
Formal Readings

===

For he had been as instructive as Milton's 'affable archangel'; and with
something of the archangelic manner he told her how he had undertaken
to show (what indeed had been attempted before, but not with that
thoroughness, justice of comparison, and effectiveness of arrangement at
which Mr Casaubon aimed) that all the mythical systems or erratic
mythical fragments in the world were corruptions of a tradition
originally revealed. Having once mastered the true position and taken a
firm footing there, the vast field of mythical constructions became
intelligible, nay, luminous with the reflected light of correspondences.
But to gather in this harvest of truth was no light or speedy work.

George Eliot, *Middlemarch*

Enchanted castles, hands beckoning from dimly lit doors, can-
nibalistic ghouls, talking fish, flying horses, troglodytic bandits,
one-handed dervishes . . . the reader's first impression is likely to
be of the immense diversity of the stories in the *Nights* and of the
free-flowing imagination, or imaginations, which shaped them.
But, after a while, the reader starts to notice things – such as how
many of the heroes of the *Nights* are born to elderly couples who
pray for a child, how often the hero will be told, 'Whatever you
do, do not open that door' (but in vain, for he will certainly open
it) or how often disasters or opportunities come in threes. In time,
each story comes to resemble another story, and the reader begins
to recognize the patterns and permutations. Fantasy has its rules.
The imaginative universe of the Arab storyteller was subject to
invisible constraints.

There are peculiar problems in studying a body of fiction which is part literature and part folklore and partaking of the characteristics of both written and oral culture. We really know nothing about the authors of the tales gathered together in the *Nights*; yet many of those tales have unmistakable literary qualities, and the use of language in them precludes unthinking discussion of them as if they were all anonymous, composite, orally generated items of folk culture. Uncertainty about the status of the *Nights* and ignorance of the milieu in which it was composed have constituted a barrier to serious study of its stories both by literary critics and by folklorists. Literary verdicts used to be vague and effusive. According to the Victorian essayist Leigh Hunt: 'The *Arabian Nights* appeal to the sympathy of mankind with the supernatural world, with the unknown and the hazardous, with the possible and the remote. It fetches out the marvellous included in our common-places.'[1] Similar comments were made by other men of letters, such as William Hazlitt, Walter Bagehot and G.K. Chesterton. They tended to stress the wildness of these oriental stories, contrasting their exoticism with the drab realities of Europe in the age of the railway and the gas lamp.

Besides publishing fairy stories, the brothers Jacob and Wilhelm Grimm also pioneered the serious study of folklore in the early nineteenth century. The first folklore studies in Germany and France tended to be closely linked with philology and with theories about the Aryan sources of European languages and mythologies. Max Müller argued that mythology was 'a disease of language' and that folk-tales were the detritus of ancient myths, especially solar myths. The earliest folklorists to study the *Nights* seriously were chiefly concerned to trace the origins of its tales, and, as we have already seen, Müller's ideas strongly influenced Benfey and Cosquin in their attempts to find Indian (and therefore Aryan) sources for the *Nights*' tales. In Britain, however, the word 'folklore' developed under the overlapping shadows of antiquarianism and classical studies. (The term 'Folk Lore' was first used by W.J. Thoms, an editor of English medieval texts, in an article in the *Athenaeum* in 1846.) Continental theories about diffusionism and folklore as the degenerate descendant of myth were attacked by Andrew Lang (1844–1912). A Scottish man of letters, student of mythology and expert on the Homeric epics, Lang was able to point to potential sources for fairy tales and other items of folklore in the cultures of ancient Greece and Egypt. He also demolished the solar mythology theories of Müller and his school. Lang is chiefly known today for *The Blue Fairy Book* (1893) and its variously coloured successors. Lang also produced an edition of the *Nights* in 1898, based on Galland, but heavily and clumsily expurgated for its destined juvenile audience. Lang supported himself by his writing, and his edition of the *Nights*, like so many others, was produced to make money. More generally, folklore studies in the English-speaking world have until quite recent times been carried out by literary gentlemen and Sunday historians, and characterized by amateurism. Rituals, ballads, stories and jokes were unsystematically collected and recorded and then unsystematically compared with one another.

It was in nineteenth-century Finland that serious work on the classification of story-types began. Finland was the first country in the world to have a society devoted to its national folklore. National identity in Finland was closely identified with the national epic, the *Kalevala* (a collection of songs about the legendary hero Kaleva) and more generally with Finland's heritage of folklore. In the nineteenth century a vast mass of folk material was collected and classified by Elias Lönnrot and others. Taking the individual story as a unity, practitioners of what was known as the historic-geographic method sought to register the story's first appearance in different regions, its regional variations and sub-types, and the basic elements which came together to form it. Many Finnish scholars shared Lang's unhappiness with the tendency of Benfey and others to trace every story back to some hypothetical origin in India. However, the Finnish folklorists shared the diffusionists' preoccupation with discovering the starting-places of stories. Antti

Aarne (1867–1925) assembled a vast mass of tales, classified them in some sort of rough-and-ready order and assigned each item a number. His *Verzeichnis der Märchentypen* (1911) was a systematic catalogue of mainly Finnish items, but he included many references to parallel and earlier versions of the Finnish stories from Russia, Scandinavia, Germany and elsewhere. Subsequent revisions of the work after Aarne's death by the American folklorist Stith Thompson considerably expanded the scope of what is now known as *The Types of the Folktale*.[2] Items from all over Europe and India are included, and under some headings cross-references are occasionally made to African, North American Indian and Arab folklore, as well as reference to literary treatments of folklore themes by novelists or poets. However, though there is some overlap between Arab popular literature and the European folktale, Aarne's story-type classification was designed to trace relationships of borrowing and descent within European folklore. It was not designed to accommodate works of Arab literature.

A 'story-type' was defined by Stith Thompson as 'a narrative capable of maintaining an independent existence in tradition'. This is in contradistinction to a motif, which is 'any one of the parts into which an item of folklore can be analysed'. Thompson subsequently went on to extend the scope of the Finnish school's project by producing *The Motif-Index* (1932–6). This differed from the story-type index in that it was global in its coverage and also in that it regularly made reference to literary works such as Aesop's *Fables*, the *Katha Sarit Sagara* and the *Nights*. Unlike the story-type classification, the way the motif-index was compiled did not carry the built-in presupposition that any or all the items listed under a particular heading were genetically related. The motif-index just listed motifs in a sort of logical order, loosely analogous to the Dewey decimal system of library classification or to Roget's *Thesaurus*. *The Motif-Index* is an omnium gatherum in which magical and mythical people and things, marvels, riddles and taboo activities are all assigned numbers. For example, section

B is devoted to animals, B 0–99 to mythical animals, B 40 to bird-beasts; B 41.2 is the number of the flying horse. Under this heading we find reference, of course, to 'The Tale of the Ebony Horse' in Burton's edition of the *Nights*, but there are also references to flying horses in Sanskrit, Indo-Chinese, German and Norse folklore.

(It would be pleasant if something like the *The Motif-Index* existed for the modern novel. Then we could look up entries like 'N.P. (novel plot) Type A 493 Middle-aged adultery, 493a adultery of successful middle-aged man in Hampstead . . . see John Braine, Margaret Drabble . . .' But, alas, this sort of formal classification is really easier to apply to folklore than to the modern novel, for the anonymous folk-tale, unlike the novels of Henry James or John Fowles, does not normally seek to surprise or disappoint expectations, but to match them. Predictability and lack of ambiguity are even more important to the folk-tale than they are to television soap operas.)

However, returning to the story-type and motif-indices as they actually exist, their relevance to the study of the *Nights* is limited. First, the *Nights* is, at best, only partly a collection of folk-tales. It is to a significant extent a deliberate literary composition, drawing on other, older literary compositions. Secondly, the *Nights* was compiled in the Semitic culture area, and, as has been noted, Aarne's and Thompson's typology of stories was not intended to be used for the study of Semitic folklore. (Hasan El-Shamy in his *Folktales of Egypt* (1980) did try to assign story-type and motif numbers to his material whenever possible, but he commented that the 'type index is, however, seriously limited with regard to the treatment of Arabic and Berber folk-tales and especially Egyptian tales'.)[3] Moreover, other, more general and theoretical objections to the Aarne–Thompson approach have been raised by students of folklore. Some have queried aspects of the classificatory layout; others have gone further and challenged its underlying assumptions. For sure, one story may be a little like another story, but it will also be a little different. If one is going to adopt a comparative method, then it may be more important to focus on fundamental differences than on superficial likenesses (and, incidentally, it is not easy to see how one's understanding of anything is advanced by putting the eight-legged Norse flying horse Sleipnir in the same category as the Arabian Ebony Horse).

An earlier attempt to produce a motif-index by Arthur Christensen, a specialist in Persian legends and literature, was judged unsatisfactory by most critics in the field; but his *Motif et thème: Plan d'un dictionnaire des motifs des contes* (1925) served as the model for Nikita Elisséeff's *Thèmes et motifs des Mille et une nuits: Essai de classification* (1949), in which a fairly arbitrary selection of themes, motifs and epic accessories from the *Nights* was listed alphabetically in two tables. A motif was an element which constituted a complete episode in its own right within a story, such as a shipwreck or a fight with a jinn. A theme was the fundamental idea expressed by a motif. An epic accessory was an object made use of in the story, such as a flying horse or a sword. While Elisséeff's index does little to help one understand the *Nights*, it can be useful in locating stories or incidents within those stories.

Although the works of Aarne, Thompson and Christensen went some way towards satisfying the felt need to organize this vast mass of material, theirs was taxonomical work, and they made little attempt to study the deep, fiction-generating mechanisms and genre constraints or, finally, to formulate general rules deducible from the story lore. The criticisms of the taxonomic approach made by the Russian formalist folklore expert Vladimir Propp are of particular interest. In *Morfologija Skazki* ('The Morphology of the Folktale'), which was published in 1928, Propp criticized the arbitrariness of the categories in *The Types of the Folktale*, and criticized also the frequent confusion of story and motif found in its listings.[4] Preconceived categories had been imposed on the folklore materials from outside, rather than being derived from close study of the materials themselves. Propp argued that arbitrary distinctions were often made between stories that were essentially the same, on the basis of trivial external features. He also wondered why tales about animals were treated as if they were in a separate category from ordinary tales. Should a tale about a wonderful talking animal be treated as an animal tale or a wonder-tale? Aarne's categories were perhaps useful for reference, but they were not useful to think with.

Propp himself took a very different approach to his study of Russian folk-tales. He took as the basis for his research the *Narodnya Russkye Skazki* (1855–64), a collection of over 600 Russian folk-tales made by the great ethnographer Alexander Nicolaevich Afnasyev, and within Afnasyev's collection those stories which could be classified as wonder-tales. Propp aimed to put the study of folk-tales on a scientific basis and to become the Linnaeus or the Cuvier of these narratives. He held that the quest for the 'teeth' or 'vertebrae' of stories was the necessary precondition for the development of a soundly based theory of the origins of stories. Propp believed in the primacy of myth, that is, he believed that the folk-tales he studied were the distorted and degenerate descendants of earlier pagan myths and rites. In this, Propp had been influenced by the novelist and poet Goethe's strange attempt to develop a system of botanical morphology, based on analogical reasoning. Goethe hoped to demonstrate that there was once an *Urpflanze*, a primal plant of which all later plants were degenerate descendants. It can be seen that Goethe's bizarre taxonomy gave rise to a sort of Darwinism in reverse.

Propp used as his working sample a batch of Russian folk-tales (one hundred of them) which all fell between numbers 300 and 749 in Aarne and Thompson's *Types of the Folktale* – that is, they were marvel-tales, folk-tales which involved magic or the supernatural. The delimitation is important. Propp did not set out to cover animal tales, religious tales, romantic tales, jokes and anecdotes or formulaic tales, though these too are part of folklore (and for that matter find their place in the *Nights*).

In Propp's system, heroes, villains, epic accessories, settings and themes are merely external features of the wonder-story, and study of external features is of no assistance in understanding the true nature of the wonder-story. It is of little importance whether the villain has one or three heads, whether the action of the story takes place under water or up in the air, or whether the story features a house which walks about on chicken's legs. Rather, the story's functions are what matter and they provide the story with its vertebrae. There are thirty-one possible functions in the Russian marvel-tale. There is no space here to discuss all of them or even list them, but they begin: (1) one member of the family leaves home; (2) the hero encounters a ban; (3) he breaks the ban or commits a transgression; (4) the villain makes an attempt at reconnaissance; and so on. The list of functions ends with the hero marrying and coming to the throne. Not only were there a limited number of functions, but there were a limited number of ways that one function could be linked with another. For all their superficial wildness, the plots of wonder-stories developed in an ordered progression. Functions were what carried a story on from its beginning to its end. A function's only purpose for existence was to take a story to its conclusion.

Then, instead of characters, Propp preferred to think of spheres of action. A 'sphere of action' was likely to be a person, though it could be an animal or a thing. There were seven basic spheres of action: (1) the hero, (2) the false hero, (3) the aggressor, (4) the donator, (5) the sender, (6) the auxiliary, (7) the princess. Here one may query the means by which Propp has arrived at his lucky number of seven. Why distinguish between the aggressor and the false hero? Are the donator and the sender always different? It may also be objected that Propp's method privileges plot and devalues the inventiveness of imagery and dialogue. This formalistic reductiveness has its attractions, but, if plot is as predictable as Propp makes it out to be, then what can possibly be the pleasure in listening to the story?

Be that as it may, combining spheres of action and functions, it is possible, according to Propp, to set out the development of the marvel-tale in a kind of algebraic notation. Propp believed that 'All fairy tales are uniform in their structure.' The general pattern of all Russian wonder-stories is the move from equilibrium to adventure or instability and then back again to equilibrium. Propp's views on the fairy tale seem to have been shared by the film director Pier Paolo Pasolini, who, talking about the stories in the *Nights*, remarked that each tale begins with the appearance of anomaly and ends when that anomaly and any subsequent anomalies have been removed and we return 'to the happy somnolence of everyday life'.[5] Propp's views have been influential on a number of film critics who have used Proppian ideas about functions and spheres of action to bring out the underlying meaning of the story-lines of such films as *Kiss Me Deadly* and *Sunset Boulevard*.[6] Films apart, Alan Dundes has shown how Propp's categories could be used to study children's games as well as North American Indian legends.[7] Proppian analysis also lends itself easily to analysis of certain kinds of literary fiction, even when there is nothing supernatural in them. For example, in Robert Louis Stevenson's *Treasure Island*, Jim Hawkins is the hero, Long John Silver is the aggressor, Billy Bones is the donator, Benn Gunn is a helper. When Blind Pew comes after Billy Bones's map, that is f(unction) 4 (i.e. the villain tries to obtain information); when Hawkins sets sail for Treasure Island, that is f. 11 (the hero leaves home); and so on.

Propp's typology fits some *Nights* tales quite well. In *Sept contes des Mille et une nuits* (1981), the French Arabist André Miquel has shown that 'Abu Muhammad Hight Lazy Bones' is indeed an Arab tale of wonder which conforms to the pattern detected by Propp in the Russian ones. It begins with a lack (Zubaydah's need for a jewel) and proceeds through various functions before being brought to an end when the transgression has been healed, the villain punished, and the hero has returned home with his bride.

Moving on to 'Abu'l-Husn and his Slave-Girl Tawaddud', Miquel observed that, in its very broadest outlines, this story also conformed to Propp's structure, concluding with a happy marriage as the final function, but that this way of looking at the story concealed the real weight of tale as a didactic exposé of medieval Islamic scientific knowledge. Again, the first but not the second part of 'Abdullah the Fisherman and Abdullah the Merman' obeys Propp's rules. The second part of the story is full of marvels certainly, but it entirely fails to fit a structure of lack, damage or misdeed, and ultimate reparation. In a separate study, *Un conte des Mille et une nuits: Ajib et Gharib* (1977), André Miquel analysed the plot of this lengthy wonder-story and found that it did broadly obey Proppian rules, beginning with a misdeed (Ajib ordering the murder of Gharib's future mother) and continuing through the intermediate functions to end with a restoration to the throne and a marriage (that of Gharib); then a second round of Gharib's adventures led into a second cycle of Proppian functions. However, the story was more complex than any studied by Propp, and while it seems to conform in broad outline to Propp's typology of the wonder-tale, somehow the characterization is unsatisfactory.

David Pinault, in *Story-Telling Techniques in the Arabian Nights* (1992), notes that Muhammad's tale in the 'The Mock Caliph' follows precisely 'one of the traditional patterns examined by Vladimir Propp in his *Morphology of the Folktale*: interdiction / the interdiction violated / bodily injury-mutilation / expulsion / the misfortune or lack made known'. The *Nights* story runs like this: Muhammad is made to swear not to stir from his bed by his mistress Dunya / but Muhammad, summoned by Harun al-Rashid's wife Zubaydah, leaves the house / when Dunya discoves his disobedience she has him savagely beaten / and she casts him out of her house / Muhammad tells his tale to Harun al-Rashid.[8]

However, a dot-and-pick application of Propp to the *Nights* is not really very satisfactory. Some *Nights* tales resemble Russian stories, but others do not, and Propp's restricted range of functions and spheres of action cannot accommodate them. What about heroines who take active parts, even leading parts, in the *Nights* stories in which they function, among them Miriam the Girdle Girl, Marjana and Zumurrud? Another objection which may restrict the usefulness of Propp's interpretative system is that apparently all the Russian fairy tales featured in his sample end happily. This is not the case in the *Nights*. For example, the tales of the first, second and third dervishes are surely tales of wonder and magic, but they all end unhappily. In these stories, there is no return home, no happy marriage, no restitution of a lack: quite the contrary, the bearers of these stories are celibate mendicants, all of whom have lost an eye.

Propp's categories do not work for all types of story, nor were they intended to. Propp formulated his categories for a restricted range of Russian folklore material, and critics have pointed out that even within the range of the Russian marvel-tale there are all sorts of plots which do not conform to Propp's structural rules and are difficult to register in his symbolic notation. Nevertheless, literary theorists of a formalist or structuralist persuasion were attracted by the way Propp set about his task, and some were determined to apply his insights in broader literary fields. Attempts have been made in France, particularly by structuralists like Algirdas Greimas and Claude Bremond, as well as by the Bulgarian Tzvetan Todorov, to refine or extend Propp's categories.[9] They are fascinating if rather abstruse enterprises. Occasionally they make use of the stories of the *Nights* as testing grounds for their theories.

Claude Bremond, in his *Logique du récit* (1973), attempted to simplify Propp's categories and to apply them to, among other types of narrative, the stories of the *Nights*. Bremond considered that Propp's thirty-one plot functions were excessive and he substituted pivotal functions, points where a plot could go off in a variety of directions. Bremond also replaced Propp's seven spheres of action with agents, patients, influencers, ameliorators and beneficiaries. Bremond used pivotal functions and various types of active and passive figures, as well as moderators, to draw up abstract-looking plots, all numbered like propositions in Wittgenstein's *Tractatus*. Thus II.1.3.4 is 'Satisfaction or dissatisfaction experienced by the agent who judges himself to have succeeded in his task or failed in it'. One of the examples here is a robber in Galland's version of 'Ali Baba'. This robber tried to leave a mark of identification on Ali Baba's house, but he was outwitted by Marjana and he consequently submitted to execution by one of his fellow robbers. Bremond's methodology can be used to produce incredibly complicated diagrams of the plots of stories. However, it is not clear what else one can do with it. His pivotal functions allow so much flexibility that anything becomes possible, and Propp's 'vertebrae' seem to have been dissolved into jelly.

Tzvetan Todorov took a different approach. In both the *Grammaire du Decameron* and *The Fantastic*, Todorov sought to provide a generative grammar for restricted literary genres. The *Grammaire du Decameron* (1969) sets out to investigate the constituent parts of the 'language' of Boccaccio's stories. In the 'grammar' of storytelling, a 'noun' is a person or object in the story. A 'verb' is a form of action. Todorov posited three types of 'verb': first, change (a broad category including disguise/unmasking, attack/resistance, and so on); secondly, transgression; thirdly, punishment. 'Verbs' have modes – obligatory, optative, conditional and predictive. An 'adjective' is a state, quality or condition. Todorov's construing of the grammar of the *Decameron* led him to conclude that a large number of the tales dealt with unspoken codes of values or laws which were infringed by characters in the stories, but that these characters (often adulterers) commonly went unpunished. Thus Boccaccio's stories treated of the breakdown of the medieval moral code in fourteenth-century Italy; they were the harbingers of modern capitalist individualism.

It would be surprising if Todorov's conclusions regarding the *Decameron* were not relevant to the *Nights*, for here we are comparing like with like. Both are collections of tales, both have a frame story in which stories are told under the shadow of death, and both drew on folk-tale elements, while nevertheless giving them a literary form. In neither case were many, if any, of the stories invented by those who wrote them down. Moreover, as we have already seen, the *Decameron* and the *Nights* actually have a number of stories in common. It might also be argued that fourteenth-century Cairo and Florence belonged to a common Mediterranean culture area. However, in querying Todorov's thesis, one may object that, since some of Boccaccio's tales are essentially the same as those circulating in tenth-century Baghdad or seventh-century India, must we look for a disintegration of conventional morality in those times and places too?

Although Todorov has not attempted to produce a 'grammar' of the *Nights*, it is a text on which he has had a great deal of interest to say. In an important essay, 'Les Hommes-Récits', or 'Narrative Men' (published as an appendix in the *Grammaire du Decameron*),[10] he addressed himself to the 'thinness' of a certain type of fictional character and the lack of psychological depth in such works as the *Odyssey*, the *Decameron* and the *Nights*. Todorov argues that Sinbad the Sailor's personality cannot be separated from his story. He is a story-man. In the *Nights* (described by Todorov as a 'narrative machine'), all traits of character are immediately causal. We know that Sinbad loves to travel because he does travel; we know that he travels because he loves to travel. It is as if characters in the *Nights* only know who they are by seeing what they have done. In the naïve psychology of the *Nights*, motivation is directly wedded to action. The despotic sultan kills because he is cruel; he is cruel because he kills. Since personality is defined by action, it is natural that when a new character appears within a story, he establishes himself by telling his story (hence the embedding of tales which is so characteristic of the *Nights* and other story collections). People's stories are their lives, so it is entirely appropriate that again and again in the *Nights* they save their lives by telling stories.

Todorov's book *The Fantastic: A Structural Approach to a Literary Genre* (French version 1970) was an attempt to demarcate a genre and to discover its peculiar rules. Todorov wished to define the fantastic by its deep structure, rather than by its trappings – that is, not by ghosts, creaking castles, witches, jinn, magic rings, and so on. According to Todorov, fantastic tales are set in a world in which the laws of nature appear to be being broken. However, the reader is expected to ask himself if those laws are really being broken. Ambiguity is crucial to the fantastic story, and in the truest form of the fantastic tale, as in Henry James's *The Turn of the Screw*, the ambiguity is never resolved. (Are the children really being threatened by the ghost of Quint, or is the reader the victim of the governess's unreliable narration?) If a tale's ambiguity is resolved, then how it is resolved will determine whether a particular story is to be characterized as 'uncanny' or 'marvellous'. If at the end of the story we learn that no law of nature has actually been broken (for example, the ghosts were human impostors), then the story is uncanny. If, however, the laws of nature have been broken, then the story is marvellous.[11] Most of the fantastic tales in the *Nights* resolve themselves into marvel-tales. Wicked women turn out actually to have been transformed into dogs; Abdullah the Fisherman actually travels to the kingdom under the sea; and the Ebony Horse actually flies. The ambiguities characteristic of such writers as Cazotte, Potocki and Henry James are rarely present in the *Nights*. The stock-in-trade of the *Nights* is unambiguously the marvellous – a marvellous based on hyperbole (e.g. Sinbad and the great fish), on the exotic (e.g. Sinbad and the rhinoceros) and on the instrumental (e.g. the flying carpet).

Todorov's typology of the marvellous fits some stories well enough, but it is difficult to see how it fits, say, 'The Tale of the Hunchback', 'The Sleeper and the Wakened' or 'The Mock Caliph'. At times it is hard not to feel that Todorov gets results not so much from his methodology as from close readings intelligently conducted – as in his account of 'The Second Dervish's

Tale'. In this story, which Todorov characterizes as a story about metamorphoses and magical powers, Todorov interprets the jinn who turns the man into a monkey as the personification of that man's bad luck.[12] Supernatural beings often stand in for fate or happenstance in the *Nights* stories.

Todorov's observations on the *Nights* and on other select works of European fantasy fiction are unfailingly interesting. However, only a certain kind of fantastic fiction is covered, and it is hard to see how Todorov's restrictive theory of the fantastic genre might be stretched to encompass such works as George Macdonald's *Phantastes*, Mervyn Peake's *Gormenghast* or Tolkien's *Lord of the Rings*. What is needed is a formal system that not only can account for what has been written within a particular genre, but also can indicate what the limits of the genre are and what can or cannot be written in that genre. At present, however, each attempt to give a formal or structuralist basis to the analysis of fiction seems to begin from a new starting-point.

The influence of both Propp and Todorov is evident in the Egyptian writer Ferial Ghazoul's *The Arabian Nights: A Structural Analysis* (1980). Ghazoul argues that the *Nights* stories have rules, but within those rules it is possible to construct an almost infinite variety of stories (just as English grammar has rules, but by following those rules it is possible to construct an almost infinite variety of meaningful sentences). The stories are generated by a series of binary oppositions and through *bricolage* (a term taken from another structuralist, Claude Lévi-Strauss, meaning a cunning use of those materials which come readily to hand). Thus, in the case of the *Nights*, the redactors made use of old bits and pieces of stories in order to make new ones. It is unfortunate that Ghazoul's penetrating book, which was published in Cairo, is not easy to come by in the West.

David Pinault, in *Story-Telling Techniques in the Arabian Nights* (1992), has taken quite a different approach. One of his main preoccupations has been the detection of oral characteristics in the surviving literary versions of the *Nights*, and, like others who have explored the frontiers between orality and literacy, he has drawn on the work of Parry and Lord. From 1902 to 1935, Milman Parry studied the texts of the *Iliad* and the *Odyssey*. After his death, the work he began was completed by Albert B. Lord and published as *The Singer of Tales* (1978). This book studied the characteristic formulaic epithets used for the description of challenges, battles, ships, council meetings, men, and so on. Such epithets, Parry and Lord argued, served the early Greek bards as hand-me-down descriptions in the appropriate poetic metre. Such formulaic adjectives and phrases, which were easy to memorize, facilitated improvised performances by the bards. Parry and Lord found confirmation of their Homeric thesis in twentieth-century Yugoslavia. There they tape-recorded and analysed the performances of the illiterate Serbian *guslars*, or bards, and they also interviewed the *guslars* themselves. In this manner they acquired some understanding of how the bardic memory worked and how the *guslars* could recite long epics without having recourse to a text, by improvising (no two performances were exactly the same) and by making use of ready-made phrases. Parry and Lord argued that the two Homeric epics were formed by the stringing together of shorter ballads, which were originally created by the extempore performances of bards. Parry's and Lord's conclusions, though widely accepted, have been challenged in some quarters. The debate about the authorship of the Greek epics goes on, and, as a character in Aldous Huxley's *Those Barren Leaves* facetiously remarked: 'It's like the question of the authorship of the *Iliad* . . . The author of that poem is either Homer or, if not Homer, somebody else of the same name.'

Pinault argues, surely correctly, that in much the same way as the Greek bards made use of ready-made epithets and phrases, so those who composed the *Nights* drew on and rearranged pre-existing material and that 'a system of formulae is also at work in the *Arabian Nights*, though at the level of the story rather than the epithet or phrase'. Thus plot clichés served as building blocks for the orally transmitted stories. In 'The Story of the Fisherman and the Demon', 'the redactor . . . is clearly playing with the motif of the benevolent wish-granting genie familiar to us from other tales in this genre'. However, in this particular example, the redactor reverses the convention by making the demon, or jinn, very unbenevolent indeed. Pinault goes on to examine 'The Tale of King Yunan and the Sage Duban', which is framed within 'The Story of the Fisherman and the Demon'. Evidently the two tales are thematically linked, for just as the fisherman is threatened by the demon, so the sage is threatened by the ungrateful king; but Pinault shows how the two tales are linked by the careful use of the *Leitsatz* (key sentence) 'Spare me, and God will spare you!' Even more effective is the use made of the *Leitsatz* 'It is a warning to whoso would be warned' in 'The City of Brass'. Pinault also studies the use made of the *Leitwort*, or 'leading-word', by the redactors of the *Nights*. A *Leitwort* in the *Nights* is a triliteral word root which in its various forms generates words with cognate meanings. (Most Arabic words are formed by additions to a root form consisting of three consonants.) Such linked key-words can be used repeatedly to create a stylistic effect or to emphasize a story's message. (The notion of *Leitwortstil*, which was first deployed in biblical criticism, has also been used to analyse sections of the Koran by John Wansbrough in his *The Sectarian Milieu* (1978).) Pinault shows how, in 'The Story of the Porter and the Three Ladies', 'The Tale of the First Lady' plays with the root form *s-kh-t*, with the repetitive use of *maskhut* (meaning a man turned to stone by the wrath of God or more generally metamorphosed) and *sukht* (meaning displeasure or divine wrath). In this and other studies, Pinault seeks to derive pattern from the stories, rather than impose pattern on them. The implication here is that the pattern was chosen by the storyteller rather than imposed as an unconscious constraint upon him.[13]

Although this chapter is mostly concerned with structuralist approaches to the *Nights*, this should not be taken as implying that only disciples of Propp, Todorov or Lévi-Strauss have had anything of value to say about the *Nights*. Mia Gerhardt, unlike David Pinault, is no Arabist. Nevertheless, her book *The Art of Story-Telling* (1963) is one of the best literary studies of the *Nights*, as well as being the most readable. It is possible to detect the influence on her of André Jolles's essay in structuralism, *Einfache Formen* (1969) (which offered a morphology of what Jolles held to be the universal simple forms of the legend, the saga, the myth, the riddle, the proverb, the case, the memoir, the tale and the joke). However, Gerhardt's study is not methodology-driven, nor is its approach seriously constrained by morphological considerations. Patrice Coussonet, in *Pensée mythique, idéologie et aspirations sociales dans un conte des Mille et une nuits: Le Récit d'Ali du Caire* (1989) and in a number of shorter studies, has undertaken close readings with a view to dating individual stories and thus placing them in a correct social and ideological context. Each story has to be taken on its own merits, for it may happen that an old version of an old tale may survive only in a relatively recent text (for example, in the Bulaq or Habicht recensions). Andreas Hamori has produced a number of short but highly influential studies of individual stories, which serve to draw attention to aesthetic qualities (which are often neglected in the more austerely structuralist approaches to storytelling). Hamori's readings tend to discover hidden allegories in the stories. Finally, two general surveys, Suhayr al-Qalamawi's *Alf Layla wa-Layla* and Wiebke Walther's *Tausendundeine Nacht*, may also be recommended to readers of Arabic and German respectively.

Towards the end of *The Fantastic*, Todorov remarks that

psychoanalysis has replaced (and thereby made useless) the literature of the fantastic. There is no need today to resort to the devil in order to speak of an excessive sexual desire, and none to resort to vampires in order to designate the attraction exerted by corpses; psychoanalysis, and the literature which is directly or indirectly inspired by it, deal with these matters in undisguised forms.[14]

So far, publishers' lists hardly seem to confirm Todorov's thesis that fantasy is obsolete, and the idea that fantastic literature has to be useful may strike some readers as curious. Be that as it may, psychoanalysts take the utilitarian function of fantasies for granted. In *The Uses of Enchantment: The Meaning and Importance of Fairy Tales* (1976), its Freudian author, Bruno Bettelheim, assumes that children are the natural audience for fairy tales and he argues that the function of fairy tales is to educate children for adulthood, by dramatizing in disguised fictional forms the difficulties that they will eventually encounter in life. Very often, the various protagonists in the stories personify different aspects of the human personality. Fairy tales are interpreted by Bettelheim, as Freudians interpret dreams, as having a latent as well as a manifest content. Although most of his demonstration texts are taken from Grimm and Perrault, tales from the *Nights* are also drawn into the argument. Thus in 'Sinbad the Seaman and Sinbad the Landsman', the two Sinbads represent opposed parts of the human personality, for Sinbad the Landsman embodies the ego and Sinbad the Seaman the id, and, in a sense, Sinbad the Seaman's adventures are the fantasies of the hard-working, landbound ego. (It could be said in criticism here that Bettelheim gives too much prominence to Sinbad the Landsman, for in the Arab story he features only as the perfunctorily sketched-in audience for stories of his bolder namesake.)

As Bettelheim reads the frame story of the *Nights*, Sheherazade features as a medieval psychoanalyst and Shahriyar as her patient. She tells him a great many stories to bring about his cure, because 'no single story can accomplish it, for our psychological problems are much too complex and difficult of solution. Only a wide variety of fairy tales could provide the impetus for such a catharsis. It takes nearly three years of continued telling of fairy tales to free the king of his deep depression, to achieve his cure.' Shahriyar is a disturbed id, while Sheherazade is a 'superego-dominated ego'. Thus the nightly encounter of Sheherazade and Shahriyar becomes a parable of integration.[15] Many have read the frame story in the same way as Bettelheim. However, nowhere in the medieval text is Shahriyar described as 'mad', and nowhere is it said that Sheherazade 'cured' him. If we attend to what the frame story seems to be saying, it is that Shahriyar's perception of the world in general and of women specifically is broadly speaking correct; for, if one excepts that paragon Sheherazade, it would appear that all women are indeed sexual betrayers. More generally, Bettelheim's interpretation of the stories as little dramas starring the id, ego and superego seems depressingly claustrophobic and reductive. It is hard to believe that the secrets of any medieval Arab tale can only be unlocked with the help of a twentieth-century western psychological theory.

Like the Freudians, the Jungians are eager when studying myths, legends and fairy tales, to elide the differences that separate one culture from another and one historical period from another. Thus Joseph Campbell, the Jungian mythographer, seems always to be more concerned with resemblances than differences. In his preface to a selection of stories from the *Nights* published in the United States, he remarked:

The battle scenes might comfortably appear in the *Morte d'Arthur;* the tales of enchanted castles, miraculous swords, talismanic trophies, and quest in the realms of the Jinn are reminiscent in numerous features of the favourites of Arthurian romance; the pattern of romantic love is in essence identical with that of twelfth-century Provence; the pious tales breathe the same odor of spiritual childhood and the misogynistic exempla the same monastic rancor as those of Christian Europe.

In his well-known study *The Hero with a Thousand Faces*, Campbell treated Qamar al-Zaman in 'The Tale of Kamar al-Zaman' as a hero conforming to the same essential type as Cuchulain, Moses and Krishna. The Jungian formation apart, the influence of Propp on Campbell is perhaps also detectable. The jinn who bring Qamar al-Zaman and Budur together are recognizably helpers of the Proppian sort. In Campbell's eyes, the encounter of the two young people, engineered by the jinn, and Qamar al-Zaman's reception of a ring from Budur signify Qamar al-Zaman's recognition of his unconscious deeps and of the equal validity of its truths with those of ordinary waking life. 'Not everyone has a destiny: only the hero who has plunged to touch it, and has come up again – with a ring.'[16] (Pasolini's filmed treatment of the same story in his *Arabian Nights* may be recommended as a counter-weight to Campbell's unhealthily obsessive preoccupation with heroes and heroic destiny.)[17]

Propp has remarked that the 'folktale, like any living thing, can only generate forms that resemble itself'. Although the formalist or structuralist approach strips a story of style, setting, characterization and imagery – of almost everything that might make it pleasing to the reader – the dissection of the bare bones of plot nevertheless may be useful in providing a framework for the study of the generation and survival of stories. Moreover, Propp's regular recourse to biological metaphors is striking. In a passage on the survival of ideas, in *Le Hazard et la nécessité* (1970, translated 1971), the French biologist Jacques Monod observed that ideas, like biological organisms, 'tend to perpetuate their structures and to multiply them; they too can fuse, recombine, segregate their contents; in short they can evolve, and in this evolutionary selection certainly plays an important role'.[18] It is a commonplace to speak of the modern novel as 'evolving' from stories, such as those found in the *Decameron* or *The Canterbury Tales*. But surely it is time to move beyond the unconsidered use of the word 'evolving' and time to speculate on the laws that might possibly govern the evolution of literary forms.

Taking a lead from the geneticist Richard Dawkins, it may be useful to think of the story as a 'selfish word-string', on the lines of the selfish gene.[19] This word-string has no volition of its own, but it is nevertheless unconsciously engaged in a blind struggle for survival through replication. I use the word 'replicate' advisedly. Word-strings are carried from coffee-house to coffee-house, and from library to library. At present, however, many problems remain to be resolved. How does a story's 'generation' take place? And what is the unit of replication? Is it the story? Or is it the story-motif? In the latter case, would the story be merely a way for the story-motif to reproduce itself? If stories compete with one another for the attention of audiences and thus survival, what forms of adaptation will enhance a story's memorability and assist its transmission and survival? Stories must offer something to their human hosts in order to make the crucial leap from memory to memory or page to page. One way a story may commend itself to its host is if the host can make a living by telling it (and here Arab beggars' tales of legendary generosity are a particularly cogent case in point). Alternatively, a story may promote the survival of a group by promoting its cohesion and sense of common history (a saga like that of Omar bin al-Nu'uman might serve as an example). Two stories may link together in order to improve their chance of survival (as we have seen the 'weeping bitch' story-type link up with 'The Wife's Clever Response' to form 'The Tale of the Woman who Wanted to Deceive her Husband'). Similarly, by inserting themselves within a framing story, if the frame story survives, then the stories are likely to survive too. A number of quite dull and insipid tales thus survived under the umbrella of Sheherazade's narration. Stories have to adapt to the culture in which they find themselves (thus the specifically Indian features of tales taken from *Katha Sarit Sagara* – for example, Indian names and references to the Hindu pantheon – have been weeded out in the *Nights* versions). As in genetics proper, so in storytelling, error, or mutation, may occasionally enhance the viability of stories (for example, the error of transmission which caused Cinderella's fur slippers eventually to become glass ones).

The *Nights* story of 'Sinbad the Seaman and Sinbad the Landsman' is a more complex and sophisticated tale than its (hypothetical) Pharaonic prototype, 'The Tale of the Shipwrecked Sailor'. It is plausible that blind word-strings, or stories, acquire more complex forms because these complex forms have more survival value in the complex societies of today in which old stories precariously circulate. By contrast, simpler forms, such as exempla, fables and anecdotal wisdom literature, are all but extinct in modern western society; and although the adventures of Aladdin have survived fairly well in modern popular consciousness, the story of Tawaddud with its heavy freight of Islamic lore and outdated scientific theory retains only a precarious place in the memories of a few academics. In the *Nights*, stories are the vehicle for saving lives – for example, the tales told by Sheherazade, or the tales told by the old men in order to save the life of the merchant who killed a jinn's son with a carelessly discarded date stone. In the *Nights*, knowledge of a story and the ability to tell it may assure the survival of an individual. Analogously it may be that in real life too knowledge of stories assists the survival of communities or of individuals within those communities. Monod himself believes that stories which reassure man about his destiny have a particular survival value. To engage in literary biology is, of course, only to play with a metaphor. Still, it is perhaps a fruitful metaphor.

10

Children of the Nights

From the eighteenth century onwards, translations of the *Nights* circulated so widely in Europe and America that to ask about its influence on western literature is a little like asking about the influence on western literature of that other great collection of oriental tales, the Bible. An answer to the latter question might include reference to *The Divine Comedy*, *The Private Memoirs and Confessions of a Justified Sinner*, *Middlemarch*, *Apologia pro Vita Sua*, *Anna Karenina*, *Joseph and his Brothers*, *Ben Hur* and *Boating for Beginners*, to suggest only a few obvious titles. In some cases, the Bible has been a stylistic influence. In others it has provided characters and props for a good yarn. In yet others, the authors' study of the text has set them moral and intellectual problems which they have then sought to resolve in fictional or poetic form. In countless cases, early and repeated exposure to the Bible has shaped the mentality and temperament of a writer. The Bible is so deeply embedded in western culture that there are many people today who, though they have never opened the book, still have an extensive knowledge of the Bible's teachings and stories. In the same way, people who have never sat down to read the *Nights* may know, or at least know of, the stories of Ali Baba, Aladdin and Sinbad. As Jorge Luis Borges (in characteristically paradoxical vein) observed of the *Nights*: 'It is a book so vast that it is not necessary to have read it.'[1] If one asks what was the influence of the *Nights* on western literature, then one is asking not for a single answer, but rather for a series of answers to a group of questions which relate to one another in complex ways.

Antoine Galland produced his translation of *Les Mille et une nuits* in the course of the years 1704–17. Even before his translation was completed, cheap versions and extracts from the early volumes were circulating in France and England. In France the instant success of Galland's work was marked by a rush of imitations and parodies. Thomas Simon Guellette (1683–1766) produced volumes of Tartar, Moghul and Chinese tales in mock-oriental vein. He even produced a collection of wholly bogus Peruvian tales. Popular at the time, they are rightly neglected now.[2]

Sex and satire were the staples of the pseudo-oriental story in the early eighteenth century. Anthony Hamilton (1646–1720), an Irish Cavalier and one of Charles II's courtiers, writing in French, produced such light fictions, which were highly acclaimed at the time. Hamilton's stories, which simultaneously imitate and mock his model, are characteristic examples of the impact of the *Nights* in the first few decades after their publication. Readers of the *Nights* in early-eighteenth-century France found in its pages a form of liberation, a flight from solemnity and a disregard of plausibility. *Histoire du Fleur d'Epine*, 'The Story of May-Flower', was written in parody of the *Nights* in a style which Hamilton claimed was 'more Arab than that of the Arabs'. In that work Sheherazade narrates a preposterously silly tale involving a questing sage, Pooh Pooh, as well as a musical mare, a luminous hat and a beautiful maiden who kills with a glance. Hamilton has Dunyazade criticize Sheherazade for the prolixity and confusion of her tale. (In Hamilton's case the reader may well feel that Dunyazade has right on her side.) Hamilton's *Les Quatre Facardins* was similarly silly. The four princes, who are all called Facardin (Facardin is Hamilton's rendering of the Arabic name Fakhr al-Din), attempt to give a coherent account of their magical and amorous adventures. They are not very successful, as their tales are regularly interrupted by other tales and only rarely concluded. The oriental touches in Hamilton's fabulous farrago are perfunctory, and Perrault's French fairy tales were at least as much the target of Hamilton's parody as were the stories of the *Nights*.[3]

The frivolous tone of Hamilton's stories was echoed in the pastiches of Crébillon *fils*. (His father, a weightier but dimmer figure, was also a writer.) Although he perversely worked as a government censor, Crébillon *fils* (1707–77) also specialized in the writing of erotic fictions. *Le Sopha* (1742) makes use of a frame story device and oriental settings. In the frame story, a sultan, whose grand passions are embroidery and patchwork, commands Amanzei, one of his courtiers, to entertain him with stories. The sultan works away at his patchwork and as he listens comments on Amanzei's tales. Amanzei has had a remarkable and lengthy past. He is able to recall previous lives, in particular a period when he was condemned to be incarnated as a series of sofas, until such time as he should bear the weight of two people consummating their love for the first time. Amanzei tells the sultan six stories of lovers of whose dalliances he has been an intimate witness and support. Crébillon's use of the oriental tale as a vehicle for a cynical and satirical presentation of the *amours* of contemporary libertines must have influenced Denis Diderot (1713–84). Diderot allegedly wrote *Les Bijoux indiscrets* (1748) in a fortnight for a bet, to show how easy it was to write a story in the manner of Crébillon. In Diderot's pornographic satire on the manners and pleasures of the French aristocracy, Cucufa, a genie, gives the sultan a magic ring which has the power to make his subjects' sexual organs speak and reveal what they have been up to. Hamilton, Crébillon and Diderot produced brittle fictions which made only trivial use of oriental settings, names and magical devices. The novelist's Orient was as yet only a playground and not to be taken seriously.

The deployment of oriental motifs in weightier moral tales was equally perfunctory. *Les Lettres persanes*, published by Montesquieu in 1721, is an epistolary novel in which the author uses the device of letters passing to and from two Persians travelling in Europe, Usbek and Rica, in order to expound his own views on religion, politics and law. Usbek's and Rica's accounts of the strange things they have seen in Europe alternate with letters from Persia giving an account of the increasingly tragic intrigues in Usbek's harem. Though later and dimmer readers may not always have realized this, Montesquieu was not attempting to present a serious picture of family life in Persia; the letters from the harem are really as much about France as the letters that are sent from France. However, to trap out his oriental harem, Montesquieu mainly made use of the seventeenth-century French narratives of travels in Persia by Chardin and Tavernier as sources for oriental matters. At the same time, when he presented contemporary France through the eyes of the Persians as a land of marvels and strange superstitions, Montesquieu seems to have been deliberately and playfully attempting to invest his own society with the illusory charms of one of the Arabian kingdoms, made popular by Galland's recently published translation. There is no evidence, however, that Montesquieu was an admirer of Galland's work, and the genuine oriental tales are criticized by Rica in the 137th letter for their tedium and implausibility: 'I am sure that you would not approve of an army being conjured out of the ground by a sorceress, or of another, a hundred thousand strong, being destroyed single-handed by the hero. However that is what our novels are like. The frequent repetition of these insipid adventures is boring, and the nonsensical miracles are repellent.'

Voltaire pretended to a similarly low opinion of the genuine oriental tale, though he was prepared to make use of its conventions for his own purposes. 'Enchanter of Eyes, Disturber of Hearts, Light of the Mind, I kiss not the dust from your feet, because you rarely walk, or walk only upon Iranian carpets or on roses.' This opening sentence of the dedicatory epistle to *Zadig* sets the light-hearted tone of his philosophic romance. *Zadig ou la destinée* (1748) was set in Babylon on the Euphrates in a vaguely pre-Islamic Orient. It tells of the adventures of the wise young man Zadig, of his quest for happiness and of the misfortunes he experiences through the fickleness of monarchs and of woman. Voltaire's fantasy is a satire on religious bigotry and contemporary mores, telling us much more about France in the age of the Enlightenment than it does about ancient Iraq, but it is above all a treatise in fictional form on the nature of chance and destiny. Zadig experiences the sudden reversals of fortune that are so frequently encountered by the heroes of the tales of the *Nights*. In the end, after many turns of fate and fortune and after having been instructed by an angel, Zadig concludes that, behind the appearance of chance and misfortune in the world, a divine providence does in fact rule over all things: 'there is no such thing as accident. All is either trial or punishment, reward or foresight.'[4] However, the conclusion of *Zadig* is perhaps a little ambiguous; it was certainly provisional, and Voltaire was later ruthlessly to satirize providential explanations of evil and misfortune in his even more widely acclaimed philosophical romance, *Candide*.

Although Voltaire was steeped in the stories of the *Nights* (he claimed to have read them fourteen times) and though he lifted themes and motifs from them for use in several of his fictions, this did not prevent him from mocking the contemporary craze for them. In *Zadig* he has the Sultan Ouloug question the sultanas on their preference for such tales. '"How can you prefer stories," asked the wise Ouloug, "which have neither sense nor reason?" "But that is just why we do like them," replied the Sultanas.' Moreover, though Voltaire was perfectly familiar with Galland's tales, he was later to tell William Beckford that the chief inspiration for *Zadig* had come from the romances of Anthony Hamilton. In the hands of Hamilton, Diderot and numerous lesser figures, the mock-oriental tale had acquired a life of its own, more or less independent of its Arabian prototype.

It has been estimated that almost 700 romances in the oriental mode were published in France in the eighteenth century. Guellette, Hamilton, Crébillon and other French writers who wrote in this vein were all translated and eagerly read in eighteenth-century England, and Galland's rendering of the *Nights* was at least as popular in England as in France.[5] An anonymous English translation of 'Aladdin' appeared, probably in 1708, and circulated as a chap-book. More translations of selections from Galland followed in chap-book form, and very soon English writers were engaged in reworking, imitating and parodying the Arabian tales. It would be a mistake, however, to regard *Les Mille et une nuits* as the only source behind the mania for the Orient in France and England. A taste for Galland and his imitators and parodists was only part of a wider fashion for chinoiserie, turquerie, oriental silks and ceramics, and architectural follies in the Egyptian or Chinese mode. The increased consumption of opium in the eighteenth century seems to have gone hand in hand with an interest in oriental imagery. The translations of Sir William Jones (1746–96) from Hindu, Persian and Arabic classics were widely read. The travel narratives of Chardin, Tavernier, Tournefort, Sherley and Bernier were also popular. The commercial and military ventures of Britain and France in India stimulated an interest in Indo-Muslim culture. Towards the very end of the century, in 1798, Bonaparte and the French landed in Egypt, and, as Edward Said remarks, this 'invasion was in many ways the very model of a truly scientific appropriation of one culture by another'.[6]

In general, English writers working in the oriental mode failed to match the wit and the licentiousness of their French contemporaries.[7] Indeed, most English oriental tales tended to be leadenly moral. Caliphs, princesses, jinn, calender dervishes and sorcerers become fodder for what are mostly pompous and dreary sermons. The essayist Joseph Addison (1672–1719) held the enlightened view that every child should be encouraged to fantasize. However, if one is to judge by his own retelling of tales from the *Nights*, fantasy is strictly subservient to moral ends. In 'The Story of the Graecian King and the Physician Douban', Addison strove to civilize and Christianize his exotic materials, and as he remarked of his version of 'Nuschar's Daydream': 'The virtue of compliance in friendly discourse is very prettily illustrated by a little wild Arabian tale' (only it is not so very wild in Addison's retelling). Addison's characteristic tone in his moral tales is politely sceptical, though certainly never to the point of questioning Christian truths. Indeed, his finest essay in the oriental genre, 'The Vision of Mirza', is an allegory of the Christian view of life. Though he claimed that this story, first published in the *Spectator*, was a translation from an eastern tale, the pretence was not very serious. In this grandiose allegory (which may remind some readers of the spectacular canvases of catastrophe painted by 'Mad' John Martin), Mirza looks down on the great bridge of life over which humanity must travel. Sooner or later, all who travel on the bridge lose their footing and fall, either to damnation on the rocks or to salvation in a current which carries them to the islands of the blessed. Mirza is told that he is looking on 'that Portion of Eternity which is called Time, measured out by the Sun, and reaching from the Beginning of the World to its Consummation'. Addison blends oriental fantasy with Christian preaching: '"Surely," said I, "man is but a shadow and a dream."'

Samuel Johnson's *Rasselas: Prince of Abyssinia* (1759) resembles Voltaire's *Zadig* in its use of a fabulous Orient as a field of philosophical enquiry. But its philosophical preoccupations are closer to Voltaire's other masterpiece, *Candide* (and curiously the two works were published within weeks of one another). In *Rasselas*, the eponymous Prince leaves the Happy Valley in Abyssinia, declaring that 'I shall long to see the miseries of the world, since the sight of them is necessary to happiness', and he embarks on a pilgrimage of enquiry into the meaning of life and a search for a lasting and worthwhile happiness. Johnson's melancholy temperament did not allow him to offer his readers a conclusive answer to Rasselas's enquiry. The heavy freight of moralizing and social satire in both Johnson and Voltaire is quite alien to the original Arabian tales. Johnson, like Voltaire, mocked what he perceived to be the lush ornateness of the Arabian originals. He had no real interest in Islam, the Middle East or Arab literature, but this did not stop him from pandering to the taste of the times and publishing separately sixteen oriental tales in the *Rambler* and the *Idler*, which were really sermons tricked out in oriental fancy dress.

It would seem that in the eighteenth century the English could not get enough of being preached at. Otherwise, it is hard to explain the success both of Addison's and Johnson's little tales and of Hawkesworth's rather longer *Almoran and Hamet* (1761). John Hawkesworth (1715–73), an essayist and journalist, was a friend of and collaborator with Johnson. Hawkesworth influenced Johnson, and vice versa. *Almoran and Hamet*, a Johnsonian parable about how true happiness may be found, is set in Persia.[8] Almoran is a vicious prince, and Hamet is his virtuous brother. Almoran is aided in his vile schemes by a jinn who presents him with a ring which allows him to change shape with anyone he thinks of. 'I will quench no wish that nature kindles in my bosom,' declares Almoran. The premise may be promising, but Hawkesworth throws away his opportunities. Almoran fails to deflower the blushfully virtuous Almeida, and the story turns into a dour lecture on the worthlessness of a quest for pleasure unrestrained by any considerations of morality. In the end the despotic Almoran is turned into a rock. He and the reader have learned their lessons.

Similarly boring, if improving, stuff was produced by many other hands – among them the Reverend James Ridley (*Tales of the Genii, or the Delightful Lessons of Horan, the Son of Asmar*, 1764), Hugh Kelly (*Orasmin and Elmira*, 1767) and Maria Edgeworth ('Murad the Unlucky', 1804). Though tedious, such works were popular at the time. Charles Dickens, for example, loved Ridley's stories as a child, making several allusions to them in later novels. Although Frances Sheridan's *Nourjahad* (1767) is a moral tale in the same exasperating genre, it is redeemed by the strangeness and originality of its conceit. Nourjahad is promised immortality and almost limitless riches by his guardian genius (or jinn), but at the same time he is told that these gifts carry with them a penalty.

The genius warns him that he will sometimes and without warning fall asleep for long periods of time – for several years or decades. However, Nourjahad is undeterred, and thus it is that he sleeps through the birth of his son and the death of his wife. Then again, he plans a blasphemous party in which youthful and ravishing members of his harem are to impersonate the wives of the Prophet, but, when he wakes up on what seems like the folowing morning, he finds that the ladies of his harem, who were to have danced before him with roses in their hair, have become stooped and withered hags. Nourjahad continues to fall asleep at inappropriate times and for inappropriate lengths of time, until Sheridan's novelette concludes with a surprise moralizing twist in the tail. *Nourjahad* offers an interesting variant of the 'years-of-experience-in-a-moment-of-time' motif; and setting the moralizing twist aside, Sheridan's story can be read as a parable on the theme of time as the destroyer of all man's hopes. As the sagacious Cozro remarks to Nourjahad: 'What have all thy misfortunes been . . . that are not common to all the race of man?'[9]

Clara Reeve took an ancient Arab legend as the basis for an oriental-cum-biblical novel, *The History of Charoba, Queen of Aegypt* (1785). This tale of a King Gebirus who invades Egypt, but who is subsequently defeated by magic and by women's wiles, was later to inspire Walter Savage Landor's epic poem *Gebir* (1798). Besides producing a novel in the oriental mode, Clara Reeve had also tried her hand at the Gothic novel, with *The Champion of Virtue: A Gothic Story* (1777). However, it was left to William Beckford to unite the two genres in a single work.

It is possible to discuss Beckford's *Vathek* as if it too was a moral tale, but, as we shall see, its conformity to the conventions of the genre was purely formal, and this novel is the first oriental tale to have any real and lasting literary worth.[10] William Beckford (1760–1844) was the son of one of England's wealthiest merchants. His father had made his fortune in Jamaican sugar and went on to become Lord Mayor of London and a leading Whig politician.

Alderman Beckford had hoped that his son would follow him into politics, but William was to achieve fame in other, less edifying areas. As a child, he had been fascinated by the *Nights* and he had begun to collect oriental paintings. His godfather, William Pitt, Lord Chatham, concerned at the boy's unhealthy interest in things oriental, wrote to his tutor instructing him to ensure that the boy have no further access to the *Nights*. Beckford's Indian paintings were burnt, but tales of oriental vice and despotism had already worked upon the boy's imagination, and Beckford's early interest in the Near East was to be reinforced later by his drawing master, the painter Alexander Cozens. Cozens (1717?–86), who claimed to be the illegitimate son of Tsar Peter the Great, had grown up in Russia, where he had met many Persians and acquired oriental interests. He was consequently nicknamed 'the Persian' by his pupil.

Beckford's parents died while he was a child. Thereafter, under the faltering guidance of tutors, he became accustomed to having his extravagant and arbitrary tastes gratified without demur. In 1781 a three-day party was held to mark his coming of age. The stage designer, painter, spy and occultist Philippe de Loutherbourg assisted in preparing the setting for one of the most magnificent masquerades to be held in eighteenth-century England. Loutherbourg's magical lighting effects transformed the family home at Fonthill in Wiltshire, and behind closed shutters and curtains Beckford's party of revellers and gilded youths wandered through an exotic dreamscape. As Beckford later put it:

The solid Egyptian Hall looked as if hewn out of a living rock – the line of apartments and apparently endless passages extending from it on either side were all vaulted – an interminable stair case, which when you looked down on it – appeared as deep as the well in the pyramid – and when you looked up was lost in vapour, led to suites of stately apartments gleaming with marble pavements – as polished as glass – and gawdy ceilings . . . Through all these suites – through all these galleries –

did we roam and wander – too often hand in hand – strains of music swelling forth at intervals.

Stagecraft helped to confer a labyrinthine *Nights* complexity upon Fonthill House:

The glowing haze investing every object, the mystic look, the vastness, the intricacy of this vaulted labyrinth occasioned so bewildering an effect that it became impossible for anyone to define – at the moment – where he stood, where he had been, or to whither he was wandering – such was the confusion – the perplexity so many illuminated storeys of infinitely varied apartments gave rise to.[11]

Beckford was later to acknowledge that it was this masquerade which inspired his novel, one of the strangest in English literature. In turn, Beckford's work on this novel, *Vathek*, inspired a further party in 1782 in which Fonthill was transformed into the Palace of Alkoremi and the Hall of Iblis. Beckford claimed that he wrote *Vathek* in three days and two nights, which may be true, but it took longer to produce a final version; and during the early 1780s, while he polished and revised the novel, he also worked with the assistance of a Turk, Zemir, on a rather loose translation into French of some stories in a manuscript of the *Nights*, which had been brought to England by Edward Wortley Montagu. (This translation, including 'The Tale of the Envier and the Envied' and 'Uns al-Wujud', was published for the first time in 1992.) There were rumours that William and his cousin Louisa Beckford had dabbled in black magic in these years. The rumours were perhaps unfounded, but in 1784 another scandal became public knowledge. It was reported in the London journals that Beckford had been discovered in bed with his young cousin, William Courtenay. Beckford was forced to travel abroad until the scandal died down, returning to England only in 1796.

Though Beckford was to publish accounts of his travels and other short pieces, from then on he concentrated on collecting books and paintings and he became an architectural patron. He had his father's mansion, Fonthill House, pulled down and used his rapidly dwindling fortune to build a palace to house his treasures. James Wyatt was commissioned to build the mock-Gothic Fonthill Abbey, described by Pevsner as 'the most prodigious romantic folly in England'. The frantic pace of building went on by day and night. As Beckford wrote to a friend: 'I listen to the reverberating voices in the stillness of the night and see immense buckets of plaster and water ascending, as if they were drawn up from the bowels of a mine, amid shouts from the depths, oaths from Hell itself, and chanting from Pandemonium or the synagogue.' Fonthill Abbey was built in the form of a cross, the arms of that cross meeting in the stucco vaulted great hall. The whole construction was overlooked by a 276-foot tower. Twelve miles of twelve-foot-high walls secluded the master of this place from the gaze of the curious, and there he ruled, like a secluded oriental despot, as 'the Caliph of Fonthill'. But debts forced him to sell the place in 1822, and the great tower, built without proper foundations, collapsed in 1825. Beckford spent the last years of his life as an increasingly eccentric and misanthropic recluse. Although he left a body of travelogues and miscellaneous writing, *Vathek* is the masterpiece for which he is remembered.

Written in French originally, in or around the year 1782 (and published in English in 1786), William Beckford's *Vathek* has become a classic of English literature. Its author announced in the preface that it was a 'story so horrid that I tremble while relating it, and have not a nerve in my frame but vibrates like an aspen'. Vathek, a young Abbasid prince, grows up bored and dissolute under the influence of his sorcerer mother, Carathis. He recognizes no good other than the achievement of his desires. 'His figure was pleasing and majestic; but when he was angry, one of his eyes became so terrible, that no person could bear to behold it; and the wretch upon whom it was fixed instantly fell backwards, and sometimes expired.' A sinister Indian *giaour* (Turkish for 'infidel')

appears, acting as emissary for Eblis, the Devil. The *giaour* offers
Vathek the treasures of the pre-Adamite sultans, but first Vathek
must slaughter fifty innocent children. Vathek makes the atrocious
sacrifice and sets out for the ruined city of Istakar where, he has
been told, the treasures are to be found. On the way, Vathek rests
with the Emir Fakreddin, one of his most loyal subjects. Fakreddin
has a daughter, Nouronihar, who has been betrothed to her effete
harem-raised cousin, Gulchenrouz:

Nouronihar loved her cousin, more than her own beautiful eyes. Both
had the same tastes and amusements; the same long languishing looks;
the same tresses; the same fair complexions; and, when Gulchenrouz
appeared in the dress of his cousin, he seemed to be more feminine than
even herself. If at any time, he left the harem, to visit Fakreddin, it was
with all the bashfulness of a fawn, that consciously ventures from the lair
of its dam.

Despite Fakreddin's attempts to hide Nouronihar and
Gulchenrouz from Vathek, the latter abuses his hospitality by
seducing the daughter and stealing away with her. Together,
Vathek and Nouronihar complete the last stage of the journey:
'they advanced by moonlight till they came within view of the
two towering rocks that form a kind of portal to the valley, at the
extremity of which rose the vast ruins of Istakar.' Descending steps
of marble and passing through ebony gates, they enter the Palace
of Subterranean Fire:

The Caliph and Nouronihar beheld each other with amazement, at finding
themselves in a place, which, though roofed with a vaulted ceiling, was so
spacious and lofty, that, at first, they took it for an immeasurable plain. But
their eyes, at length, growing familiar to the grandeur of the surrounding
objects, they extended their view to those at a distance; and discovered rows
of columns and arcades, which gradually diminished, till they terminated in
a point as radiant as the sun, when he darts his last beams athwart the ocean.

The treasures of the pre-Adamite sultans are indeed heaped up all around, but amidst these treasures 'a vast multitude was incessantly passing, who severally kept their right hands on their hearts, without once regarding anything about them: they had all the livid paleness of death. Their eyes, deep sunk in their sockets, resembled those phosphoric meteors that glimmer by night in places of interment.' After three days of this gloomy contemplation, they are brought before Eblis: 'His person was that of a young man, whose noble and regular features seemed to have been tarnished by malignant vapours. In his large eyes appeared both pride and despair: his flowing hair retained some resemblance to that of an angel of light.' Eblis condemns Vathek and Nouronihar to wander through his halls for all eternity with their hearts in flame.

Additional episodes for *Vathek* were written but never published in Beckford's lifetime. Two and a half episodes – tales told by sufferers encountered by Vathek in the halls of Eblis – were only rediscovered in the twentieth century. These tales of the damned reveal Beckford's characteristic preoccupations. 'Histoire des deux princes amis, Alasi et Firouz' features homosexual love. 'The Story of Prince Barkariokh' includes scenes of what is effectively necrophiliac rape. 'The Story of the Princess Zulkais and Prince Kalilah' treats of incest. In this story, Zulkais joins her twin brother, who is also her lover, in hell, and she tells Vathek how

at last, I reached a chamber, square and immensely spacious, and paved with a marble that was of flesh colour, and marked as with the veins and arteries of the human body. The walls of this place of terror were hidden by huge piles of carpets of a thousand kinds and a thousand hues, and these moved slowly to and fro, as if painfully stirred by human creatures beneath their weight. All around were ranged black chests, whose steel padlocks seemed encrusted with blood.

Vathek is a weird fantasy, but since it was written by a weird man it is not difficult to see it as an autobiographical fantasy – or not wholly fantasy at all. In this *roman à clef*, Beckford's grim

Calvinist mother has been transformed into the sorceress Carathis. His father's fierce rages and intimidating gaze have been transferred to Vathek, but that caliph's quest for illicit knowledge and forbidden pleasures are based on the author's own desire to dedicate his life to unbridled pleasure and on his interest in exotic things. Nouronihar is surely based on Beckford's cousin Louisa. The effete Gulchenrouz bears more than a passing resemblance to William Courtenay. The *giaour* is perhaps, in part, a portrait of the sinister artist Alexander Cozens. The Palace of Subterranean Fires has features in common with Fonthill.

Beckford's assistant and collaborator, the Reverend Samuel Henley, took the uncorrected draft of *Vathek* to Paris, where he laboured to provide the fantasy with footnotes which had the dual purpose of establishing the fantasy's basis in genuine oriental lore and instructing the reader in the manners and customs of the Orient (in much the same way as Lane's annotations to the *Nights* were later to do). D'Herbelot's encyclopaedic *Bibliothèque orientale* was referred to frequently in the notes. It was indeed in the *Bibliothèque orientale* that Beckford had first read of the historical Abbasid Caliph Vathek (or Wathiq) and learned that 'le Khalife Vathek avoit l'oeil si terrible, qu'ayant jetté un peu avant sa mort, une oeillade de colère sur un de ses Domestiques qui avoit fait quelque manquement, cet homme en perdit contenance, & se renversa sur un autre qui étoit proche de luy'. The Koran, *The Tales of Inatuulla* (in Dow's translation) and travellers to the East such as Chardin and Thevenot are frequently cited in the notes.

The notes also suggest that Beckford was indeed indebted to the *Nights* for certain details and motifs in his novel, and the episodes certainly draw on stories from the *Nights*. 'The Story of Princess Zulkais and Prince Kalilah' borrows an episode from 'The Second Dervish's Tale', and 'The Story of Prince Barkariokh' is in part adapted from 'The Second Shaykh's Story'. But, although Beckford had some competence in Arabic and had laboured on a translation of some of the stories in the *Nights*, most of his knowledge of those stories seems to have come via Galland, and there is little or no sign of any wider influence of Arabic literature on *Vathek*. Henley's mock-learned glosses to Beckford's fantasy started a fashion for annotating oriental fictions, and *Vathek*'s example was to be followed by Southey in *Thalaba* and Moore in *Lalla Rookh*.

Vathek was the most richly realized of all oriental tales to appear in English or French up to that date and the most accurate in its details about life in the Islamic lands. Even so, it was not very accurate, and much of the erudition suggested by the footnotes was really rather bogus. The work almost certainly owes more to pseudo-oriental fictions in English and French than to Arabic sources. The Caliph Vathek in his unbridled pursuit of selfish desires and exercise of arbitrary power certainly owes something to Hawkesworth's despot, Almoran. When Almoran proclaimed, 'If I must perish, I will at least perish unsubdued. I will quench no wish that nature kindles in my bosom; nor shall my lips utter any prayer, but for new powers to feed the flame', he anticipated Vathek's carefully tended cult of the arbitrary will. Many of *Vathek*'s most striking images were borrowed from Guellette's pseudo-oriental tales. Even more pervasively, the tones of deflationary irony and mocking exaggeration which Beckford employed from time to time to punctuate a narrative of sombre terror and atrocity were surely modelled on those of his distant kinsman, the urbane and witty romancer Anthony Hamilton.

Despite the exotic detail and parade of Islamic lore, the grandiose and horrific depiction of the hellish domains of Eblis owes very little to the *Nights*, but a great deal to European literature. Vathek's temptation and his quest for the forbidden surely owes something to the Faust legend, and his interrogations of the damned must, in part, have been inspired by similar episodes in Dante's *Inferno*. Then again, Beckford's youthful but ruined Eblis recalls Milton's description of Lucifer in *Paradise Lost*:

His form had yet not lost
All her original brightness, nor appeared
Less than archangel ruined and th'excess
Of glory obscured.

Since the novel ends with Vathek and Nouronihar consigned to
hellish suffering for all eternity, it might be argued that Beckford's
fantasy is a moral tale in the tradition of such earlier orientalist
writers as Guellette and Hawkesworth. However, such an argument can carry little conviction, for the author's intense enjoyment
both of his protagonists' vices and of their punishment is not really
consistent with a genuinely Christian sensibility. *Vathek*'s sombre
tones, morbid themes and sinister imagery suggest affinities with
such early examples of the Gothic novel as Horace Walpole's *The
Castle of Otranto* (1765) and M.G. Lewis's *The Monk* (1796).
Admittedly, the tone is not uniformly serious, and exaggeration
and excess are at times pushed to parodic extremes. Many of
Beckord's touches of Gothic horror may originally have been
intended as parody; but by the time Vathek and Nouronihar reach
Istakar, their creator has allowed himself to be betrayed into
conviction, and private nightmares have assumed an oriental garb.
Despite Beckford's multifarious borrowings from earlier tales in
western and eastern languages, *Vathek* had no real precursors.
However, it was to have many imitators and admirers, among
them Byron, Disraeli, Poe, Melville and Lovecraft.

'Read Sinbad and you will be sick of Aeneas,' the Gothic
novelist Horace Walpole had urged. Beckford's choices in reading
and writing had been part of his revolt against the classics of Greek
and Roman literature which 'fell flat upon his mind'. The oriental
and the Gothic were closely allied in the eighteenth-century revolt
against classical canons in literature. The origins of the Gothic
novel in English literature should probably be sought chiefly in
the growing interest in the old English ballads, in the institutions
of chivalry, in the architecture of the Middle Ages and in the

growing interest in antiquarianism generally. Nevertheless, Reeve and Beckford were not the only Gothic writers to have fallen under the spell of the Orient. There are traces (albeit fainter traces) of the influence of the *Nights* and other collections of genuine or pseudo-oriental tales on almost all the writers in the Gothic genre. Horace Walpole, who produced a collection of *Hieroglyphic Tales* (1785) in imitation of Anthony Hamilton, was a great enthusiast for the stories of the *Nights*, proclaiming that 'there is a wildness in them that captivates'. It is surely significant that when he produced his famous novel in the Gothic mode, *The Castle of Otranto*, he described that too as 'so wild a tale'. Familiarity with the oriental storytelling tradition had a liberating effect on writers in the late eighteenth century, freeing them from the constraints of plausibility and encouraging them to experiment with supernatural effects (as when, in *The Castle of Otranto*, Bianca rubs her ring and a giant figure appears). Matthew Gregory Lewis translated Anthony Hamilton into English and was a great admirer of *Vathek*. 'Monk' Lewis's novel *The Monk* is set in eighteenth-century Spain and is devoid of obvious oriental trappings. However, this dubiously edifying Gothic schlock-horror novel, a tale of a lascivious and murderous monk who misguidedly sells his soul to the Devil in order to escape human justice, is a romantic reworking of the story of 'Barsisa', from the old Turkish story collection *The Forty Viziers*.

The tale of the spectral bleeding nun is framed within Lewis's story of the damned monk Ambrosio, and it may be that Lewis was influenced by oriental storytelling conventions in his employment of the framing device. This same device of story-within-story was used to greater effect and more elaborately in Charles Robert Maturin's *Melmoth the Wanderer* (1820). (In this story, Melmoth, who has sold his soul to the Devil, seeks to find someone who will change places with him. Though he finds many people in horrific predicaments and learns all their stories, no one will take on his burden of damnation.) However, whatever debt the Gothic novelist may owe to the medieval Arab storyteller, the spirit of the Gothic novel, with its chain-rattling, blood-curdling horrors and its cult of the grandiose and the antique, is quite alien to the Arab sensibility. The absence of the ghost story in Arabic has already been noted, and, though there are horrors in the *Nights*, those horrors are not milked, nor did the authors of the Arabian tales interest themselves in the psychology (or psychopathology) of extreme states.

There are a number of curious resemblances between Maturin's *Melmoth the Wanderer* and Potocki's great work of fiction, *The Saragossa Manuscript*. Both open with the reading of a discovered manuscript; in each case the manuscript's contents turn out to be a series of interactive boxed stories (that is to say, of boxed stories of which developments in some stories have consequences in others); and both books feature a hero unjustly condemned by the Spanish Inquisition. It is possible that Maturin read parts at least of Potocki's remarkable masterpiece and was impressed by them. The life of the author of the *The Saragossa Manuscript* was hardly less remarkable than his fiction.[12] Jean Potocki was born in 1761, a member one of one of Poland's most distinguished families. He was educated in Switzerland and later at the Vienna Academy of Military Engineering. He proved himself to be an accomplished linguist and knew at least eight languages. (At some point in his life, he mastered Arabic.) As a young man, he travelled widely in western Europe, as well as visiting Tunisia, Constantinople, Egypt and Morocco. In 1779 he was made a Knight of Malta and he joined the Knights on a pirate hunt against Barbary corsairs. (He was later to draw on his experiences as a Knight of Malta in *The Saragossa Manuscript*.) In Constantinople in 1784, he observed the professional storytellers at work in the cafés and experimented himself in composing tales in the oriental manner. Later, in Morocco in 1791, he hunted without success for a manuscript of the *Nights*. He was told, however, that the only story collection available there went under the title of *The Three Hundred and Fifty-*

Four Nights, but there was not even any manuscript of this available for purchase. On the way back from Morocco, he passed through Spain, observing the traces of Muslim culture in Andalusia, and he crossed the desolate and bandit-ridden Sierra Morena *en route* for Madrid. Potocki was fascinated by Islamic culture. It is possible that this fascination pre-dated his visits to the Near East, for Poland in the late eighteenth century harboured substantial communities of Muslims (indeed, there are still some today), and Persian costumes and fashions were the rage among the Polish nobility.

Potocki's travels in western Europe provided as much material for his future novel as did his travels in the Islamic world. In Paris in the 1780s, he frequented the salons and met leading spokesmen of the Enlightenment. He also investigated the secret aims of the Illuminists, studied cabalism and attended spiritualist seances (this was the age of Cagliostro, Mesmer and Swedenborg). Potocki was intrigued by the occult strain in eighteenth-century rationalism. He was also, at first, sympathetic to the aims of the Enlightenment and of the reformers who were to play a leading role in the French Revolution. In 1788 he returned to Poland, filled with ideas about progress and reform. In the same year, he became the first Pole to go up in a balloon, ascending over Warsaw with M. Blanchard. They were accompanied by Osman, a Turkish valet Potocki had brought back with him from Istanbul, and by his dog Lulu. Though Potocki was later to become disillusioned with the bloody progress of the Revolution in France, as late as 1791 he still had friendly contacts with the Jacobin Club in Paris.

In 1798 Potocki travelled through the Caucasus. He was a pioneer in the study of the ancient cultures and languages of that region. In particular, he learned the secret language reserved for the use of the Circassian nobility. Potocki wrote volumes on the ethnography and archaeology of the Slavic and Caucasian peoples. Among his non-fiction were such imposing works of scholarship as the *Essai sur l'histoire universelle et recherches sur la Sarmatie* and the *Principles of Chronology for the Ages Anterior to the Olympiads*. In 1805 he was sent by Tsar Alexander on an embassy to Peking. Though the mission was turned back by the Chinese in Mongolia, he made many valuable observations on the manners and customs of the Siberian and Mongol peoples. In his last years he retired to his estate in Podolia and succumbed to acute boredom and melancholia. It seems that one of his fantasies was that he had become a werewolf, and it is said that when he finally decided to commit suicide he melted down a samovar to obtain silver for the fatal bullet. He shot himself on 20 November 1815.

During the 1780s and 1790s, Potocki had written some short fictions in the oriental mode. (Like Gérard de Nerval later, he embedded them in his travel narratives.) He began work on his masterpiece *Le Manuscrit trouvé à Saragosse* (*The Saragossa Manuscript*) in 1797. Although the work was, in a superficial sense, completed by the time of his death in 1815, the ending is somewhat rushed and perfunctory; and it is possible that, if its author had been able to persuade himself to live a little longer, then *The Saragossa Manuscript* might have had quite a different ending.

Potocki's narrative is divided into days, perhaps on the model of the *Nights*. The story begins in 1739, when a young Walloon officer, Alphonse Van Werden, is travelling across the Sierra Morena, hoping to reach Madrid. However, he is foolish enough to spend the night in a haunted inn, and thereafter he plunges into a series of mysterious and nightmarish adventures. In the course of the first night he becomes entangled with the sweetly seductive Moorish sisters Emina and Zubeida, who claim to be his cousins, but who may be emissaries of the Devil at work to persuade Alphonse to renounce his chance of Christian salvation. Whoever they may be, Alphonse drifts off to sleep in their bed, dreaming of the charms of the seraglio, but when he awakes he finds that he is not in bed in the inn with the bewitching sisters, but is instead lying under a gibbet, which has been used to hang two bandits. Moreover: 'The bodies of Zoto's brothers were not strung up, they were lying by my side. I had apparently spent the night with them. I was lying on pieces of rope, bits of wheels, the remains of human carcasses and on the dreadful shreds of flesh that had fallen away through decay.' As strange encounter follows strange encounter and mystery is piled on mystery, Alphonse wonders if he may not be the victim of dreams, impostures or, perhaps, hallucinations brought on by drugs. He is never sure what to believe, and neither is the reader.

The perplexing adventures of Alphonse serve as a frame for other tales told by people he encounters, including a demoniac, a cabalist, a gypsy chief, a mathematician, a bandit and the Wandering Jew. Their tales in turn serve as frames for yet other stories – of love, honour, revenge, adultery and magic, featuring soldiers, lovers, Inquisitors and supernatural apparitions. The labyrinthine complexity of Potocki's story collection outdoes even such set pieces in the *Nights* as the boxed tales of the Hunchback cycle, for Potocki's tales interlock and overlap, the plot of one story determining the outcome in another. Somewhere, buried in all these stories, is the promise of secret knowledge. Alphonse Van Werden's interlocutors introduce him to a world of mysteries, initiatic secrets and buried treasure. Emina and Zubeida are subterranean creatures, first encountered in a cellar. Their father, the Sheikh of the Gomelez, masterminds a vast plot, which mirrors and parodies the alleged and real conspiracies of the Illuminists and other politico-occult groups of the late eighteenth century.

Some of the mysteries confronted by Alphonse are sexual ones. In particular, the dangerous delights of troilism are dangled before Alphonse and his companions, first in one form and then in another, in a long series of eerie doublings. Both Emina and Zubeida declare their wish to marry Alphonse (but perhaps their charms are deceitful and their bodies the reanimated corpses of the Zoto brothers). Alphonse is tempted and he will later find his temptation echoed when he hears the story of Pacheco the demoniac about his ill-fated love for the sisters Camille and

Inesille; and Pacheco's story is in turn echoed on a higher plane by Rebecca's tale of the cabalistic raising of two mystical entities known as the Celestial Twins. And so on. Thus doubles are redoubled in a series of uncanny distorting mirrors. What is going on? Just as in Cazotte's *Le Diable amoureux* (to be discussed shortly), the horror lies in the ambiguity. Potocki's treatment of this ingredient of the fantastic is masterly, and for most of the narrative Alphonse, like Abu al-Hasan in 'The Sleeper and the Wakened', is never sure whether he is awake or dreaming.

Oriental themes, Gothic horrors and occult doctrines and practices fascinated Potocki, but they also repelled him. His mysterious horrors are not entirely serious, and at times mystification gives way to pure comedy, as in the tale of the man in Madrid who wished to contribute to literature but, lacking the talent to write himself, dedicated his life to making ink to serve the literati. Potocki the *philosophe* kept an ironic distance from his materials and used the props of Romanticism (gypsies, succubi, cabalists and bandits) in the service of Enlightenment values. *The Saragossa Manuscript* is to some extent a tract on the virtues of tolerance and a satire on outmoded feudal codes of honour. Potocki wished to instruct as well as to entertain, and there is space in over 800 pages for an encyclopaedic collection of discourses on strange customs, ethical systems and contemporary philosophy.

The story of the writing and publication of Potocki's tales is, if anything, more confusing than the tales themselves. According to a contemporary source, the origins of the work lay in Potocki's reading of the *Nights* and his wish to entertain his sick wife by telling stories in the same vein. He started to put the stories on to paper in 1797. In 1804–5 he had the first part of the work (the first thirteen days) printed on his own printing press for distribution among friends. The second section of the work was subsequently commercially published in Paris as *Avadoro, histoire espagnole* in 1813. Then the two printed versions were joined together in a three-volume edition produced in St Petersburg in 1814. (Pushkin toyed with the idea of a verse translation into Russian.) The last part of the work seems to have been written before his abortive journey to China. The collection of stories had not been fully revised by the time of his death. *The Saragossa Manuscript* was written in French. In 1847 a complete version was discovered by Edmund Chojecki and translated by him into Polish. Subsequently the original French manuscript was lost, and the integral French edition published in Paris only in 1989 is, for the most part, a retranslation from the Polish into French. Printed versions of Potocki's tales were only fragmentarily available in western Europe in the nineteenth century. They were nevertheless ruthlessly plagiarized by Maurice Cousin in his *Memoirs of Cagliostro*, by Washington Irving in *Wolfert's Roost and Other Stories*, by Jean Nodier in *Ines de las Sierras* and by Gérard de Nerval in *Les Infernales*.

Beckford and Potocki are two of the founding fathers of modern fantasy literature. It is time now to consider a third key figure, Jacques Cazotte (1719–92).[13] Cazotte has already been mentioned in an earlier chapter as the collaborator with the Syrian priest Dom Chavis on an early translation of the *Nights* into French. Cazotte was educated by Jesuits and subsequently employed by the French Ministry of the Marine. In Martinique he landed himself in all sorts of trouble and ended up in prison, broken in health and financially ruined. He returned to France in 1759 and began a new career as a writer. Perrault, D'Aulnoy and Galland had popularized the fairy tale in France, and Cazotte followed the trend. In his *La Patte du chat* (1741), Armadil, a courtier, is banished by the queen for stepping on the paw of her cat. He subsequently encounters a siren, is lured by her into a lake and travels in strange regions, before he returns to court and, forgiven by the queen, marries the princess. A year later, Cazotte produced a parody of the *Nights*, *Les Mille et une fadaises*, in which an abbot is required to cure a society lady's insomnia by telling her stories. He is very successful in this, as the stories he tells are so dull that they invariably send his audience to sleep. The tales which Cazotte has the abbot tell are light-hearted and gallantly sentimental in the manner of Guellette and Hamilton. Indeed, pseudo-oriental fabulists are one of the targets of Cazotte's parody. *Les Mille et une fadaises* and the later and rather similar work *Le Lord impromptu* (1767) were immensely popular at the time, but are of only historic interest now.

The same cannot be said of Cazotte's masterpiece, *Le Diable amoureux* ('The Devil in Love') (1772). Some critics have argued that this book is the first fantasy novel to have been written in France. The young hero, Alvaro, after practising cabalistic rituals to raise the Devil in a graveyard, is confronted by an apparition of a camel which cries out in a terrrible voice, 'Che vuoi?' ('What do you want?) A little later Alvaro becomes acquainted with a young woman, Biondetta, whose sole apparent desire is to serve him. Entering Avadoro's service, she clings devotedly to him. She is never anything but slavishly devoted and sweetly loving, but Alvaro is tormented by doubts. Is she what she seems or is she the Devil in human form? After two months with her, Alvaro is still not sure. In an echo of 'The Sleeper and the Waker' theme in the *Nights*, he muses: 'But what could I make of my entire adventure? It all seems a dream, I kept telling myself; but what else is human life? I am dreaming more extravagantly than other men, that is all.' Everything is cast in doubt, everything ambiguous almost to the very end of the novel. Even if Alvaro, and we, could be certain that Biondetta was the Devil, it would be the Devil in a new and unusual light: 'I am a woman by choice, Alvaro, but still I am a woman, and subject to all the weaknesses of one.' It may be that *Le Diable amoureux* was intended as a strange parable on the vulnerability of evil.

Cazotte's text warned of the dangers of dabbling in the occult. After the book's publication, he was contacted by Martinists and Illuminists who thought that they could detect elements of genuine occult lore in the fantasy. Martinists followed the teachings of the obscure eighteenth-century visionary Martinez de Pasqually (1727–74). Organized in secret lodges on masonic lines throughout France, they believed in a world of unseen spirits and in the possibility of making these spirits visible and having contact with them. They held that all men were spirits once, but that since the Fall their souls have been trapped in the world of matter. In performing magical rituals, Martinist initiates sought to raise man's status by contact with the spirit world and to secure the help of good spirits in combating evil ones. They strove to redeem the fallen state of man since his expulsion from Eden and through psychic reintegration to return to man's original godlike status. In the late eighteenth century, the success of cults such as Martinism and Swedenborgianism, as well as the careers of figures like Casanova and Cagliostro, can, to some extent, be seen as evidence of a revolt against the values of the Enlightenment. But the more one investigates the links between Enlightenment thinking and occult philosophy, the less appropriate does any crudely drawn contrast between reason and superstition seem. (European Free-masons, for example, combated the superstitions of the Catholic Church, while inventing new myths and rituals of their own.) In the latter part of his life Cazotte acquired a reputation as a visionary, and stories circulated about his prophetic powers. His friend La Harpe relates that at a dinner in 1788 Cazotte predicted the execution of Louis XIV and Marie Antoinette, as well as the fates of those who sat around the table, including also the execution of the Marquis de Condorcet and himself. In 1792 Cazotte, who had become a mystical monarchist, was arrested and guillotined as a counter-revolutionary.

Presumably it was Cazotte's taste for the supernatural and the erotic which drew him to the *Nights*. As has been noted, Chavis and Cazotte's *Suite des mille et une nuits* (which was published as volumes 38 to 41 of the fairy tale anthology *Cabinet des fées*, 1788–90) is, in part, a genuine translation of Arab tales (being based on the Paris Bibliothèque nationale MS arabe 1723). Chavis provided a crude word-for-word translation which Cazotte then turned into elegant French, modelled on the style of Galland. However, Cazotte also reworked the authentic tales to turn them into mystical Martinist allegories. Moreover, it seems that four of the stories in the Chavis and Cazotte collection were composed by Cazotte himself: 'The Story of Xailoun the Idiot', 'The History of Alibengiad, Sultan of Herak, and of the False Birds of Paradise', 'The History of the Family Schebanad of Surat' and 'The History of Maugraby, or the Magician'. The last of these stories is the most impressive and the most mystical. In it, Habed-il-Kalib, King of Tadmur, engages in spiritual combat with Maugraby, an agent of Satan. Maugraby specializes in kidnapping children, whom he takes to the caverns of Domdaniel under the roots of the sea where they may be brainwashed and trained in the evil arts of sorcery. Habed receives guidance in dreams, studies magic and undergoes ordeals of initiation, in preparation for his battle with the shape-shifting Maugraby. This weird and grim tale was unmistakably intended by Cazotte to serve as a parable about the Martinist programme for spiritual reintegration and salvation.

Chavis and Cazotte's work was translated into English by Robert Heron as *The Arabian Tales, or a Continuation of the Arabian Nights* in 1792, and it was from the translated text of 'Maugraby the Magician' that the poet Robert Southey took the story-line for his epic poem *Thalaba the Destroyer* (1800).[14] Southey, having read Galland (or perhaps indeed Cazotte), had declared: 'The Arabian tales certainly abound with genius, they have lost their metaphorical rubbish in passing through the filter of a French translation.' The poet, who thought that Arab literature, and for that matter the art and the religion of the Arabs, was worthless, turned the fantastic story into an allegory of Christian duty and endeavour. Cazotte's Habed-il-Kalib is christened Thalaba by Southey, and Thalaba sets out to battle with the sorcerers who dwell in the submarine domain of Domdaniel, 'under the Roots of ocean', encountering all sorts of *Nights*

marvels, before his final triumph and apotheosis. Despite the
strong story-line and the vivid imagery, the poetry is not actually
very good. Imitating Beckford's procedure with *Vathek*, Southey
equipped his romance with a massive quantity of orientalist
footnotes – they take up more space than the poem. Despite his
hostility to Islam and his contempt for Arab literature, Southey
remained fascinated by oriental themes and in *The Curse of Kehama*
(1810) replanted the Wandering Jew theme in a Hindu setting.

Southey's poetic renderings of oriental stories were much
criticized when they were published and did not sell well. By
contrast, Thomas Moore's *Lalla Rookh* (1817) was immensely
popular and went through repeated reprintings in the decades after
its first appearance.[15] In Moore's book, the eponymous princess is
being escorted by a certain Feramorz on her way to an undesired
marriage with the King of Bukharia. In order to while away the
journey, Feramorz tells the princess stories. This prose story frames
four tales told by Feramorz in verse. (Moore took as his model
here Inayat Allah's *Bahari Danish*, or 'Garden of Knowledge', an
Indo-Persian story collection, which was also cited in the footnotes
of Beckford's *Vathek* and Southey's *Thalaba*.) The tales are 'The
Veiled Prophet of Khorassan' (which furnished the main source
for Borges's 'The Masked Dyer, Hakim of Merv'), 'Paradise and
the Peri', 'The Fire Worshippers' and 'The Light of the Haram'.
Lalla Rookh, in the course of listening to these tales, which are
saturated with lush oriental imagery, has fallen in love with
Feramorz, and fortunately when they arrive in Bukharia she
discovers that he is none other than the King of Bukharia, so they
are happily wed.

Certainly, Moore was to some extent inspired by the wildness
and the imagery of the *Nights*. However, *Lalla Rookh* owes a
heavier debt to translations of such medieval Persian poets as Sadi
and Hafiz of Shiraz. By the early nineteenth century, an increasing
amount of Persian and Arabic literature was being made available
in English, French and German translations, and writers were no

longer so dependent on the *Nights* as their source of oriental inspiration. As can be seen by the foregoing discussion, besides authentic works of Middle Eastern literature, novelists and poets were also finding inspiration in the burgeoning body of pseudo-oriental literature, by Anthony Hamilton, Frances Sheridan, Jacques Cazotte, William Beckford and others. Moreover, the Middle East was now more open to western travellers than ever before. Although the poet Lord Byron deployed imagery from the *Nights* in a number of his poems, most notably in *Don Juan*, *Vathek*, which he reverenced, was probably a greater influence on him: 'For correctness of costume, beauty of description, and power of imagination, it far surpasses all European imitations' (and Byron also imitated the *Vathek*ian footnote).[16]

However, Byron's own travels in the eastern Mediterranean lands were yet more important still in shaping such poems as *The Giaour* (1813) and *The Corsair* (1814). In the nineteenth century, English works of 'orientalist' literature, such as Thomas Hope's *Anastasius* (1819), James Morier's *Hajji Baba of Isfahan* (1824), Alexander Kinglake's *Eothen* (1844), William Makepeace Thackeray's *Notes of a Journey from Cornhill to Grand Cairo* (1845) and Benjamin Disraeli's *Tancred* (1847), drew on their authors' travels in the Ottoman lands. Contemporary realities there often disappointed those whose image of the Levant had been formed by Galland's courtly version of the *Nights*. (Kinglake, who travelled through Syria and Egypt, decided that the *Nights* 'cannot have owed their conception to a mere oriental, who, for creative purposes, is a thing dead and dry – a mental mummy that may have been a live king just after the Flood, but has since lain balmed in spice'. Kinglake decided that the *Nights* must have been written by Greeks instead.) Some writers now thought of the *Nights* as something that should be put away with other childish things when they attained maturity.

Children take unpredictable things away from what they have read, and not all of them found unalloyed delight in the *Nights*.

Coleridge and De Quincey found sinister things there. According to Samuel Taylor Coleridge (1772–1834):

One tale . . . (the tale of a man who was compelled to seek for a pure virgin) made so deep an impression on me (I had read it in the evening while my mother was mending stockings) that I was haunted by spectres, whenever I was in the dark – and I distinctly remember the anxious and fearful eagerness, with which I used to watch the window, in which the books lay – & whenever the sun lay upon them, I would seize it, carry it by the wall & bask & read –. My Father found out the effect, which these books had produced – and burnt them.[17]

Coleridge claimed to have read the *Nights* at the age of six. Coleridge was not always the most reliable witness about his own life, but, at whatever age he read the stories, it is hard to know what it was that so terrified him in the story of 'Zayn al-Asnam' (one of Galland's 'orphan stories'), in which the Lord of the Jinn, who has taken the form of a beautiful young man, orders Zayn al-Asnam to find a beautiful girl, who has never lusted after a man, and bring her to him.[18]

More generally, Coleridge saw dark things in the oriental tales. In 1800 he had an opium-laced dream of 'a Woman whose features were blended with darkness catching hold of my right eye & attempting to pull it out – I caught hold of her arm fast – a horrid feel . . . the Woman's name Ebon Ebon Thalud – When I awoke, my right eye swelled.' This nightmare vampire seems to derive partly from Ebn Thaher, a drug dealer in one *Nights* story, and partly from a female ghoul in another.[19] The *Nights* was associated in Coleridge's mind with acts of justice so cruel and arbitrary that they can hardly be seen as acts of justice at all. Challenged about the frightfulness of the ordeal of the Ancient Mariner and his companions which began with the killing of the albatross, he compared their fate to that of the merchant who tosses away a date stone and then finds himself condemned to death by a jinn.

Though steeped in the *Nights*, Coleridge also found inspiration in pseudo-oriental literature. 'The Adventures of Abduah the Merchant', in James Ridley's *Tales of the Genii*, presented 'Kubla Khan' with the key image of a houri separated from her lover by a dismal chasm from the bottom of which rose 'Wild notes of strange uncouth warlike music'. The Orient was for Coleridge a repository of weird and nightmarish images and, beyond imagery, the source of something grander and more impalpable. From reading the *Nights*, his mind had 'been habituated to the Vast – and I never regarded *my senses* in any way as the criteria of my belief'. But the influence of the *Nights* went even wider yet. In John Livingston Lowes's fine study of the sources of Coleridge's imagination, *The Road to Xanadu* (1927), Lowes wrote that 'to attempt to trace the prints of the *Arabian Nights* . . . in "The Rime of the Ancient Mariner," and "Christabel," and "Kubla Khan," were like seeking the sun and the rain of vanished yesterdays in the limbs and foliage of the oak. But the rain and sun are there.'[20]

Like Coleridge, Thomas De Quincey (1785–1859) had been terrorized as a child by the *Nights*. De Quincey was not an admirer of the *Nights* in general, considering the stories to be lacking in psychological depth and artistic unity, and he remarked of Sinbad, for example, that 'it is not a story at all, but a mere series of adventures, having no unity of interest whatsoever'. However, in his *Autobiography*, he made an exception for 'Aladdin' and for one particular incident in that story which had terrified him when young and was to exercise a complex and rather sinister influence over the patterns of his adult thinking. The magician in the depths of Africa seeks the child Aladdin, the one fated child who can lead him to the treasure:

Where shall such a child be found? Where shall he be sought? The magician knows: he applies his ear to the earth; he listens to the innumerable sounds of footsteps that at the moment of his experiment are tormenting the surface of the globe; and amongst them all, at a distance of six thousand miles, playing in the streets of Baghdad, he distinguishes the peculiar steps of the child Aladdin.

For the magician 'has the power, still more unsearchable, of reading in that hasty moment an alphabet of new and infinite symbols . . . The pulses of the heart, the motions of the will, the phantoms of the brain, must repeat themselves in secret hiero-glyphics uttered by the flying footsteps.'[21]

De Quincey found in this passage an allusion to the notion (common to Arab diviners and physiognomists) that everything has grammar and meaning and that 'the least things in the universe must be secret mirrors to the greatest'. It is a remarkable passage in De Quincey's memoirs – not least because a description of the sorcerer, such as he recalls, listening to the myriad footsteps of the world is not to be found in any surviving edition of the *Nights*. It is perhaps a false memory, deriving from one of the writer's opium reveries (which were always rich in sinister oriental imagery), and so this reminiscence of De Quincey's may be reckoned to be his own contribution to the corpus of the *Nights* and part of its disconcertingly large pseudepigrapha. De Quincey consistently associated the *Nights* with images of horror and despair-ing inevitability. In *Suspiria de Profundis*, he reveals how (slightly distorted) memories of 'The Second Dervish's Tale' – in which the young man who has slept with the jinn's woman is tracked down by the jinn – were for ever associated in his own mind with the guilty sensation of being found out: 'It appeared, then, that I had been reading a legend concerning myself in the *Arabian Nights*. I had been contemplated in types a thousand years before on the banks of the Tigris. It was horror and grief that prompted that thought.'

In a brief discussion of the impact of the *Nights* on English literature, Edward Said observed (somewhat sourly) that 'the *Arabian Nights*, for example, are regularly associated with child-hood, beneficent fantasies, it is true, but ones occurring in a sense

so that they may be left behind'.[22] Said was surely thinking of
such passages as that which occurs in the fifth book of
Wordsworth's *The Prelude*:

> I had a precious treasure at that time,
> A little, yellow canvas-cover'd book,
> A slender abstract of Arabian Tales;
> And when I learn'd, as now I first did learn,
> From my Companions in this new abode,
> That this dear prize of mine was but a block
> Hewn from a mighty quarry; in a word,
> That there were four large Volumes, laden all
> With kindred matter, 'twas, in truth, to me
> A promise scarcely earthly.

Tennyson evoked similar childhood delights in his 'Recollections
of the *Arabian Nights*':

> When the breeze of a joyful dawn blew free
> In the silken sail of infancy,
> The tide of time flow'd back with me,
> The forward-flowing tide of time;
> And many a sheeny summer-morn,
> Adown the Tigris I was borne,
> By Bagdat's shrines of fretted gold,
> High-walled gardens green and old;
> True Mussulman was I and sworn,
> For it was in the golden prime
> Of good Haroun Alraschid.

In Dickens, too, the linkage between the stories of the *Nights*
and the lost delights of innocent childhood is strong indeed. In *A
Christmas Carol*, the Ghost of Christmas Past introduces Scrooge
to the forgotten delights of infancy:

'Why it's Ali Baba!' Scrooge exclaimed in ecstasy. 'It's dear old honest

Ali Baba . . . And what's his name who was put down in his drawers, asleep, at the Gate of Damascus; don't you see him! And the Sultan's Groom turned upside-down by the Genii; there he is upon his head! Serve him right. I'm glad of it. What business had *he* to be married to the Princess!'

In *Hard Times*, the soulless and materialistic Gradgrind confronts Sissy Jupe and asks her what she has been reading to her father: ' "About the fairies, sir, and the Dwarf, and the Hunchback, and the Genies," she sobbed out . . . "Hush!" said Mr Gradgrind, "that is enough. Never breathe a word of such destructive nonsense any more." '

But though it is not difficult to find *pièces justicatives* for Said's observation, it is still a selective reading. Even in Dickens, imagery from the *Nights* is not always used to summon up the innocent and the childlike. The first paragraph of the first chapter of *The Mystery of Edwin Drood* presents an opiate vision of the city of Cloisterham, in which the spire of Cloisterham's cathedral loses its Englishness and becomes old Baghdad:

What IS the spike that intervenes, and who has set it up? Maybe, it is set up by the Sultan's orders for the impaling of a horde of Turkish robbers, one by one. It is so, for cymbals clash, and the Sultan goes by to his palace in long procession. Ten thousand scimitars flash in the sunlight, and thrice ten-thousand dancing girls strew flowers.

The orientalizing transfiguration of an English provincial town prefigures the part played by crime and opium in this mystery novel.[23]

Not all those who read the *Nights* as children were inspired to become novelists or poets. Some became bank clerks or grocers; and, if they found inspiration or consolation in the stories, it was a private matter and is now forgotten. For many readers the *Nights* offered the first introduction to ancient and alien cultures. Edward Gibbon (1737–94) was introduced to the *Nights* at an early age. He found it to be a book 'which will always please by the moving picture of human manners and specious miracles'. In the words of his biographer G.M. Young: 'his imagination moved most freely in the East, and the work of his manhood is shot with a child's vision of grave and bearded Sultans who only smiled on the day of battle, the sword of Alp Arslan, the mace of Mahmoud, Imaus and Caf, and Altai, and the Golden Mountains, and the Girdle of the Earth'. It is probably due to Gibbon's childhood reading of the *Nights* that his account of the medieval Near East, and especially of the court of the Abbasids, in the later volumes of *The Decline and Fall of the Roman Empire*, glows with an imaginative sympathy, something which is often lacking in his portrayal of feudal Europe.[24] In much the same way as a reading of Homer's *Iliad* inspired Schliemann to look for the historical ruins of Troy, so Sir Henry Layard's childhood reading of tales about the Ebony Horse and the City of Brass led him as an adult in the 1840s to uncover the ruins of ancient Nineveh. (Those same fantastic dead Arabian cities are, of course, the ghostly precursors of such morbidly poetic Victorian necropolises as Christina Rossetti's 'The Dead City' (1847) and James Thomson's 'The City of Dreadful Night' (1874).)

No two people ever read the same book, and the stories which led Layard to archaeology hinted to Newman of divine mysteries. Cardinal Newman, looking back on his childhood in *Apologia pro Vita Sua* (1864), remembered that he 'used to wish the Arabian Tales were true: my imagination ran on unknown influences, magic powers and talismans'. It seems that the numinous and the miraculous qualities of the Arabian fairy tales left an imprint on the youthful mind of John Henry Newman that was to lead him as an adult to accept the Catholic faith, a faith in which the numinous and the miraculous are indeed true for its believers. (In a similar manner, in the next century, C.S. Lewis's childhood enthusiasm for Norse myths and legends was to lead him as an adult to accept the Incarnation of Christ as God as a myth, but a myth which had the advantage of being true.) Mock-oriental literature also had a part in setting Newman on the spiritual path that he was to follow. Southey's epic poem on the theme of spiritual testing, *Thalaba*, impressed Newman greatly and influenced his spiritual mission: '*Thalaba* has ever been to my feelings the most sublime of English poems – I mean *morally* sublime.'

While the *Nights* continued to exercise a sway over the imaginations of poets, novelists and others in the Victorian period, the writing of oriental tales, in the manner of Hamilton or Beckford, had quite gone out of fashion in Britain. The only full-length mock-oriental novel of note to be published in this period was the eccentric and now little-read *Shaving of Shagpat: An Arabian Entertainment* (1855).[25] George Meredith (1828–1909) read the *Nights* as a child. It was his favourite book, and *The Shaving of Shagpat*, his first novel, was modelled on it. In the preface, he told his readers that his book was an attempt to reproduce 'the style and manner of Oriental Story-tellers'. (As far as style is concerned, it was of course more closely modelled on Lane's translation of the *Nights*, which had been published in 1838–41.) Meredith used to make up Arabian tales to tell to his young stepdaughter, and it may be that elements in *The Shaving of Shagpat* derive from these nightly inventions. However, the novel was really written for adults:

Now, the story of Shibli Bagarag, and of the ball he followed, and of the subterranean kingdom he came to, and of the enchanted palace he entered, and of the sleeping king he shaved, and of the two princesses he released, and of the Afrite held in subjection by the arts of one and bottled by her, is it not known as 'twere written on the finger-nails of men and traced in their corner-robes . . .?

Bagarag, the humble barber, finds himself engaged in a heroic series of quests and ordeals in his struggle to shave an enchanted hair from the head of Shagpat the clothier and so free the city, also called Shagpat, from subjection to the man.

The telling of the story is parodically prolix and extended by the insertion of framed stories and inserted fragments of verse. Though Shibli Bagarag is a humble barber, his speech is grandiose indeed. Faintly ludicrous mock-oriental similes abound, and high sentence is played off against low comedy. Humble Bagarag is both assisted and hindered in his ordeals by high-born women. Meredith's Asian queens are *femmes fatales*. In the framed 'Story of Bhanavar the Beautiful', Bhanavar possesses a jewel which gives her power over the serpents and, alone in her chamber,

she arose, and her arms and neck and lips were glazed with the slime of the serpents, and she flung off her robes to the close-fitting silken inner vest looped across her bosom with pearls, and whirled in a mazy dance-measure among them, and sang melancholy melodies, making them delirious, fascinating them; and they followed her round and round, in twines and twists and curves, with arched heads and stiffened tails; and the chamber swam like an undulating sea of shifting sapphire lit by the moon of midnight.

Rabesqurat is Mistress of Illusions, 'surrounded by slaves with scimitars, a fair Queen, with black eyes, kindlers of storms, torches in the tempest, and with floating tresses, crowned with a circlet of green-spiked precious stones and masses of crimson weed with flaps of pearl'. Similarly, the Princess Goorelka is a poisoner and sorceress who keeps men in enchanted captivity as birds and torments them when they displease her. Noorna bin Noorka, on the other hand, is the barber's guiding good spirit and the woman he will eventually marry.

Today *The Shaving of Shagpat* is a forgotten novel by an unfashionable novelist. In some respects, the novel deserves its neglect. If it is taken as a pastiche or parody of the *Nights*, it is not a very good one. As an adventure story, it is confused and rambling. Many current sword-and-sorcery romances have a better grip on narrative. If one reads *The Shaving of Shagpat* as an allegory, as many critics have done, then the allegory is obscure.

In general terms, it is plain that Shagpat, with his magical hair, stands for oppression based on the power of illusion, but whether the oppression is social and class-based or whether it rests on some form of intellectual deceit, or clinging to outmoded ideas, is unclear, and further details of the allegory are impenetrable. However, some of the imaginative imagery in the book, such as Rabesqurat's mirror made from human eyes, or the bridge of eggs, is brilliant.

Meredith's novel of Arabian sword and sorcery was inspired by Lane's translation. Curiously, though, the appearance first of Lane's and then of Burton's translations coincided with a decline in the grip of the *Nights* on the English literary imagination. It may be that those translations, stylistically unattractive and bottom-heavy with annotation, were actually responsible for that decline. Paradoxically, a fuller and more accurate knowledge of the *Nights* led to a closing of the gates of imagination. From the late nineteenth century onwards, the *Nights* ceased to be part of the common literary culture of adults. As for children, they now read selected and heavily expurgated versions of the stories. 'Sinbad', 'Ali Baba', 'Aladdin', 'The Ebony Horse' and a handful of other stories continued to be read, but it was a much reduced corpus, and the *Nights* had increasingly to compete for attention with books written specifically for children by Dean Farrar, George MacDonald, Frederick Marryat, E. Nesbit and many others. (Of course, the *Nights* was often a major influence on this new breed of writer; for example, Nesbit's Psammead stories obviously owe a great deal to the Arab tales.)

Robert Louis Stevenson wrote both for children and for adults, and it is often difficult to determine whom his stories were intended for. Meredith's books were a strong influence on him, and like *The Shaving of Shagpat*, Stevenson's *New Arabian Nights* (1882) pastiched the style of the *Arabian Nights Entertainments* – that is, the style of the commonly available English translation of Galland. Stevenson's book also has a frame story of sorts, in which

Prince Florizel and Colonel Geraldine wander the streets of nineteenth-century London in disguise, as Harun al-Rashid and Jafar had done in old Baghdad. Their wanderings frame six rather good stories of adventure, murder and suicide. In the *New Arabian Nights* and in its sequel *More New Arabian Nights: The Dynamiter*, the stress is on plot and on colourful settings, rather than psychological or social verisimilitude (and this was indeed what late-nineteenth-century readers found in the medieval *Nights*). A later story by Stevenson, 'The Bottle Imp', in *Island Nights Entertainments* (1893), reverses the quest formula, in that the wonder-working bottle is something which must be got rid of, a curse which must be lifted, rather than sought. This inversion of the quest formula echoes the frame story of the Hunchback cycle in the *Nights* (and it also has affinities with the frame of Maturin's *Melmoth the Wanderer*).[26]

In the nineteenth century, merchants in the United States carried on a surprisingly extensive commerce with Muslim Zanzibar. Later, American shipping in the Mediterranean was to suffer from the depredations of the Barbary corsairs, prompting the United States government to action. However, unlike Britain, the United States did not rule over an empire of Muslims. It is not surprising, then, that the influence of the *Nights* on nineteenth-century American literature was relatively slight. Though the influence was slight, however, it was there.[27]

Washington Irving (1783–1859) has already been mentioned as one of the plagiarists who made use of Potocki. *The Conquest of Granada* (1829) and *Legends of the Alhambra* (1832, revised and expanded 1857) are based on his three-month sojourn in Spain in 1829. *Legends of the Alhambra* is a scrapbook compilation of travel reminiscences, inconsequential encounters and framed stories. Irving was enchanted by the Old World and the vestiges of vanished civilizations. In particular, the Moors of Spain, mysterious and forgotten as the inhabitants of the City of Brass, haunted his imagination. The moonlit ruins of the Moorish palace of the

Alhambra served as the setting for moralistic and melancholy reflections that are rich in atmosphere and cliché. The framed tales are of ghosts, hidden treasures, sorcerers, bandits and gypsies. In Irving (as with Cazotte, Potocki, Maturin and Richard Burton) a cult of the Orient went hand in hand with a fascination with gypsies.

'The Legend of the Moorish Astrologer' is perhaps the best thing in the book. This is a retelling of a story found in al-Maqqari's *Nafh al-Tibb* (a romantic history of the lost Muslim realm of Andalusia written in Damascus in the early seventeenth century). An earlier version of al-Maqqari's story is found in the *Nights*. A Muslim Spanish ruler employs an astrologer to use his magic powers to defend the kingdom. The astrologer uses his occult lore to construct a bronze talismanic statue of an armoured horseman as well as armies of miniature figurines. The astrologer's operation of these miniature figures in the tower secures victories for the king's armies in the field. When the astrologer seeks his reward, the king is unresponsive, but the astrologer has his revenge, and the kingdom is ruined. 'The Legend of Prince Ahmed el Kamel or the Pilgrim of Love' borrows motifs from the *Nights*, including such stock features as the young prince who is secluded to protect him from a prophesied evil fate, learning the language of birds, falling in love with birds, a magic carpet and a flying horse.[28]

Although Edgar Allan Poe published a collection entitled *Tales of the Grotesque and Arabesque* in 1840, the influence of the *Nights* on his writing appears decidedly superficial. In characterizing some of his tales as 'Arabesque', Poe intended no specific reference to the Arab manner of telling stories. He only used the term to refer to intricately patterned tales (intricate as the design of an oriental carpet) in which the centre of interest lay in the cunningly crafted plot, rather than in the exploration of the characters in the tales. (More generally, words like 'arabesque', 'carbuncle', and 'talisman' and phrases like 'Barmecide feast' and 'Aladdin's cave' were part of the age's common stock of literary bric-à-brac from a cultural attic.)

Poe's short story 'The Thousand-and-Second Tale of Scheherezade' is a lightweight, though heavily laboured, sketch in which Sheherazade starts to tell Shahriyar a story, one of the hitherto untold adventures of Sinbad, featuring an ironclad steamship, an automaton chessplayer, Babbage's Calculating Machine, the telegraph, the daguerreotype, and so forth. Shahriyar finds her account of the technological wonders of nineteenth-century civilization so preposterous that he loses patience and gives orders for her to be strangled. 'She derived, however, great consolation (during the tightening of the bowstring) from the reflection that much of the history remained still untold, and that the petulance of her brute of a husband had reaped for him a most righteous reward, in depriving him of many inconceivable adventures.' It is possible that Poe, as an early writer of science fiction, found similar difficulties in interesting his audience in stories about future marvels of science.

On the face of it, it is improbable that Arabian or pseudo-Arabian themes should play much part in a novel about a whaling ship out of Nantucket. However, it is fairly clear that Herman Melville's *Moby Dick* (1851) does draw heavily on such material. Like every other educated westerner in the nineteenth century, Melville read the *Nights* as a child. He also travelled in the East and read widely both in other accounts of oriental travel and in such novels as *Vathek* and *Anastasius*. In particular, the two despots, Captain Ahab and the Caliph Vathek, share the terrible and intimidating eye, and Ahab's damned hunt for the thing which should not be sought has a certain affinity with Beckford's caliph's quest for forbidden treasure. The seas across which Ahab roams teem with marvels, spirits and omens. Ahab's favoured harpoonist and familiar, the turbaned Fedallah, is 'such a creature as civilized, domestic people in the temperate zone only see in their dreams, and that but dimly; but the like of whom now and then glide among the unchanging Asiatic communities, especially the Oriental isles to the east of the continent'. It is hinted that Fedallah may be a descendant of the jinn. The text of *Moby Dick* is enriched by covert embedded references to the *Nights* and other sources of nineteenth-century culture. In an earlier novel, *Mardi and a Voyage Thither* (1849), the influence of the *Nights* is more obvious and more superficial. The book draws heavily on story-motifs that Melville had encountered in his reading of Lane's translation of the stories. *Mardi* tells of a quest for an abducted princess in a fantastic archipelago in the South Seas and of the strange societies that are found on those islands. It is a modern version of the voyages of Sinbad, but in Melville political, social and religious allegory takes precedence over wonder.[29]

In the nineteenth century English and French writers plundered the *Nights* for oriental props and knick-knacks. The engagement of twentieth-century writers has been more cerebral, and the *Nights*, containing as it does early and exotic examples of framing, self-reference, embedded references, hidden patterns, recursion and intertextuality, has become a source book for modernist fiction in its playful mode. It has also served as an advertisement for grand pretensions on the part of modern writers.

James Joyce (1882–1941), horribly well read, owned a copy of the translation of the *Nights* by Burton (or 'Old Bruton' as he is called in *Finnegans Wake*). His masterpiece, *Ulysses* (1922) gives an account of a single day (Bloomsday, 16 June 1904) in the lives of Stephen Dedalus and Leopold and Molly Bloom. Although Joyce's narrative is set in Dublin, it is obvious that both the novel's structure and many of its more detailed allusions derive from Homer's *Odyssey*. But behind the wanderings of Odysseus, there is a second range of reference to another tempest-driven, roving seafarer – Sinbad. (It may be recalled that already at the beginning of the eighteenth century Galland had speculated that the Sinbad cycle of stories might have taken some of its details from the Homeric epic.) In Joyce's novel, mirages of old Baghdad and

Basra are discernible in twentieth-century Dublin. In the 'Proteus' chapter, a chapter of transformations and disguises, Stephen awakes groggy from sleep and dreaming. One thought he manages to catch at: 'Remember. Haroun al Raschid.' It is a prefiguration of Stephen's encounter with Bloom, who like Haroun al-Rashid wanders round the streets of his city incognito. Will Stephen Dedalus, like Sinbad, return safely to port? Eventually, yes. Towards the end of the book, in the 'Ithaca' chapter, Leopold Bloom, who has offered Stephen safe haven, reflects on Stephen's current sleeping state:

He rests. He has travelled.

    With?

Sinbad the Sailor and Tinbad the Tailor and Jinbad the Jailor and Whinbad the Whaler and . . . [and so on].

Finnegans Wake (1939), a linguistically rich and notoriously taxing phantasmagoria, treats, among other things, of the cyclical nature of history and myth. The dreams of Humphrey Chimpden Earwicker frame stories, in the same way as does one of the novel's models and sources, 'the 'unthowsent and wonst nice' or, as it is also known, the 'arubyat knychts, with their tales within wheels and stucks between spokes' or, again, 'this scherzarade of one's thousand and one nightinesses'. In alluding to the omnium-gatherum richness of the *Nights*, Joyce was laying claim to the same quality for his *Finnegans Wake* and he was setting himself up in competition with the medieval Arab storytellers: 'Not the king of this age could richlier eyefeast in oriental longuardness with alternate nightjoys of a thousand kinds but one kind. A shahryar cobbler on me when I am lying!' By the time Joyce wrote *Finnegans Wake*, he had become familiar with the translation of Mardrus, who appears as 'the Murdrus dueluct', and Joyce tells us elsewhere that 'the author was in fact mardred'. And so the teasing references continue, 'until there came the marrer of mirth'.[30]

'Prost bitte!' *Finnegans Wake* also contains many allusions to

Proust, and Proust's masterpiece, *A la recherche du temps perdu* (translated in English as *Remembrance of Things Past*) is also studded with references to the *Nights*. Early in the first chapter of its first volume, *Swann's Way*, the narrator speculates that if his great-aunt had learned of the secret amatory life of the outwardly eminently respectable Charles Swann, whom she used to entertain to dinner, then she might have found it as extraordinary 'as the thought of having had to dinner Ali Baba, who as soon as he finds himself alone and unobserved, will make his way into the cave, resplendent with its unsuspected treasures', a scene she was familiar with, 'for she had seen it painted on the plates we used for biscuits at Combray'. Towards the very end of the last chapter of the last volume, *Time Regained*, the narrator broods on his approaching death and the possible termination of his storytelling task:

If I worked, it would be only at night. But I should need many nights, a hundred perhaps, or even a thousand. And I should live in the anxiety of not knowing whether the master of my destiny might not prove less indulgent than the Sultan Shahriyar, whether in the morning, when I broke off my story, he would consent to a further reprieve and permit me to resume my narrative the following evening.

Like the *Nights*, Proust's novel is a story told against death.

In between Proust's commencement and his conclusion runs a skein of allusions and comparisons which conduct the narrator's memory inevitably back to childhood. Comparisons with characters and incidents in the *Nights* are also used to make the otherwise familiar bizarre and exotic. Thus, to those who do not know her, the Princesse de Guermantes seems as fantastic as the Princess Badroul Boudour. The narrator, wandering at a loss by night in the strange city of Venice, compares himself to a character in the *Nights*. Paris defamiliarized by wartime and the presence of Senegalese troops and Levantine taxi-drivers similarly appears like old Baghdad. Contrariwise, Bassorah of the *Nights* has become the Basra from which British troops in Mesopotamia are conducting their campaign against the Ottoman Turks. Then again, the narrator compares his glimpse of Baron de Charlus being flogged in a homosexual brothel to a tale in the *Nights*, 'the one in which a woman who has been turned into a dog willingly submits to being beaten in order to recover her former shape' (that is, 'The Porter and the Three Ladies of Baghdad').

As noted above, the *Nights* first appears in Proust's novel in a non-literary form, as images on the cake plates in his childhood home in Combray. The plates feature scenes from 'Ali Baba', 'Aladdin', 'Sinbad' and 'The Sleeper and the Waker'. Subsequently the much loved plates are irretrievably lost. Although the oriental images displayed on the cake plates are less famous than the madeleine dipped in tea, they too play a recurring role in conducting the narrator back to his lost past. Later, in mid-life, his mother talks to him of his childhood in Combray and of his childhood reading there, and the narrator expresses the wish to reread the *Nights*. His mother sends him copies of the translations by Galland and by Mardrus, though she is hesitant about including the Mardrus version; for not only do the older generation disapprove of the licentiousness of Mardrus, but also Mardrus's new-fangled manner of transliteration (one can hardly call it a system of transliteration) has a defamiliarizing effect. Even the title is different – not *The Thousand and One Nights*, as in Galland, but *The Thousand Nights and One Night*.

Proust loved the *Nights*, but he was emphatic that *Remembrance of Things Past* was not intended as a pastiche or some other form of reworking of the *Nights* in modern dress. In the final sequence of meditations on his end and the end of the book, he argues that 'you can make a new version of what you love only by renouncing it. So my book, though it might be as long as the *Thousand and One Nights*, would be entirely different.' And yet it may be that, in renouncing the beloved fictions of childhood in favour of the truth, the narrator has indeed (and paradoxically) written a *Thousand and One Nights* for his own times.

If the length of Proust's novel challenges comparison with the story collection of the *Nights*, the brevity of Borges's fictions matches that of most of the stories in that collection. The views of the Argentinian short-story writer and poet Jorge Luis Borges (1899–1986) on the merits of the various translations of the *Nights* have already been discussed. Apart from his essay on its translators, he also wrote an essay on the stories themselves. '*The Thousand and One Nights*' (published in *Siete noches*, or 'Seven Nights', in 1980). The *Nights* is a key text, perhaps the key text, in Borges's life and work. At an early age Borges discovered the Burton translation in his father's library and devoured it, together with the works of Thomas De Quincey, Robert Louis Stevenson, G.K. Chesterton and others. (The key authors and texts which influenced this famous modernist writer are, for the most part, curiously old-fashioned ones.) Later on, in Spain in 1919, Borges met and was befriended by Rafael Cansinos-Assens, the polyglot poet and translator of the *Nights* into Spanish. Borges's stories, like most of the stories in the *Nights*, are extremely short; and like the *Nights* stories they are strong in plot and aim to provoke a sense of wonder in the reader, but they usually have little psychological depth. To borrow Edgar Allan Poe's terminology, Borges wrote 'Arabesques'.

Borges's version of the *Nights* is an anglophile and anglophone one. Not only did he approach the *Nights* through Burton's translation, but his responses to the stories were almost certainly conditioned by the responses of his beloved Stevenson and Chesterton. (G.K. Chesterton, who wrote a critical study of Stevenson, was, like Stevenson, a master of short and highly coloured fictions.) Of course, the *Nights* furnished Borges with a treasure-house of oriental props on which he drew for stories like 'The Search of Averroes', 'The Ascent of al-Mutasim' and 'The Masked Dyer of Merv'. Occasionally, Borges restricted himself to the retelling of stories from the *Nights* – for example, the stories in *A Universal History of Infamy* of 'The Chamber of Statues' and

'The Tale of the Two Dreamers'. However, stories that have one meaning in the context of an anonymous medieval Arab story collection acquire another meaning when related by a twentieth-century modernist and Argentinian fabulist. (In the same way, *Don Quixote* when narrated by Borges's invention, the twentieth-century littérateur Pierre Menard, is not at all the same book as the one written by Cervantes, even though the two versions are word for word identical.) The *Nights* tale of 'The City of Labtayt' is a tale of *aja'ib*, of the wonders of pre-Islamic Spain; Borges's version of it is essentially a story about the recursive nature of destiny. It is possible to discover one's fate, but one would not have encountered that fate if one had not enquired about it in the first place. The paradox is there in the Arab version, but Borges's version, because it is by Borges, makes the paradox the central feature of the story. Again, 'The Ruined Man who Became Rich Again through a Dream' is an Arab story about prophecy fulfilled; but when essentially the same story appears in Borges's *A Universal History of Infamy*, it becomes a parable about recursion. Thus the cultural attic of the *Nights* furnished Borges with metaphysical themes, and Borges found in the *Nights* precisely what he was hoping to find – *doppelgängers*, self-reflexiveness, labyrinthine structures and paradoxes, and especially paradoxes of circularity and infinity.

The night on which Sheherazade started to tell Shahriyar the story of herself and her storytelling particularly fascinated Borges. He has Albert refer to this passage in 'The Garden of the Forking Paths'. Albert, meditating on the ways in which books could be infinite, 'remembered that night which is at the middle of the Thousand and One Nights when Scheherezade (through a magical oversight of the copyist) begins to relate word for word the story of the Thousand and One Nights, establishing the risk of coming once again to the night when she must repeat it, and thus on to infinity'. The same horrifying problem is discussed in 'Partial Magic in *Quixote*'. Italo Calvino, failing to find the episode in the *Nights*, later accused Borges of making it up – a plausible charge, given Borges's penchant for playful literary forgery. In fact, Sheherazade does tell 'The Tale of the Two Kings and the Wazir's Daughters' in the Breslau version of the *Nights* (and it is translated by Burton in the second of his supplementary volumes), but Borges's reading of what is going on was a misreading and perhaps a wilful misreading, though a fruitful one. Although 'The Tale of the Two Kings and the Wazir's Daughters' is followed by more stories in the Burton translation, in the original Breslau text Sheherazade's telling of her own story is her last story and it brings the story cycle to an end; it was not intended to plunge its audience into a new and potentially infinite sequence of stories within stories. But Borges may have the last word on the subject of misreadings: 'I think that the reader should enrich what he is reading. He should misunderstand the text; he should change it into something else.'

The function of the 'frame' in literature fascinated Borges. It is not merely that one tale may frame another tale, which in turn may frame another, suggesting the possibility of an infinitely prolonged descent through tales within tales. Borges also argued that the fascination of framing stems from the possibility that the reader, as he reads a story framed within another story, may become himself uneasily aware that he too may be framed, that is, part of a story that someone else is telling. The reader as he reads may suspect that he is as much a fiction as the characters in the *Nights* who tell stories but are themselves inventions of Sheherazade.

'The South' is one of several of Borges's stories in which the *Nights* plays a overt role, albeit an enigmatic one. It begins with the protagonist, Dahlmann, buying an imperfect copy of Weil's translation of the *Nights*. His purchase of this volume sets in train a mysterious series of events, beginning with an assault on a staircase during which Dahlmann is injured by some unknown thing. Apparently recovered, Dahlmann sets out by train, heading south. He carries with him the first volume of *The Thousand and One*

Nights, 'which was so much a part of the history of his ill-fortune, was a kind of affirmation that his ill-fortune had been annulled; it was a joyous and secret defiance of the frustrated forces of evil'. Dahlmann seems to die in a knife duel on the Argentinian pampas, but the early appearance of the fantastic Arabian text is perhaps a warning that all of Dahlmann's experiences on the pampas may be a fantasy.

Again, in 'Doctor Brodie's Report' the fact that that report is discovered in the pages of one of the volumes of Lane's translation of the *Nights* – a translation which was lavishly furnished by Lane with annotations on Muslim manners and customs – warns the reader that the Borges story which follows is an ethnographic fantasy. Similarly, it is not by chance that in 'Tlon Uqbar, Orbis Tertius', among the volumes of the encyclopaedia devoted to the strange alternative world of Tlon Uqbar, the eleventh volume has 1,001 pages. For Borges, as for the medieval Arabs, 1,001 is the number of infinity. Thus the non-existent encyclopaedia opens the way into infinite alternative possibilities. (But though the *Nights* may be considered to be a literary labyrinth, its anonymous authors did not share Borges's preoccupation with mazes, and there is no word in medieval Arabic for a maze.)

Besides drawing on the *Nights* itself, Borges also reworked western stories which derived from the *Nights* or pastiched it in the pseudo-oriental manner. Borges's 'The Sorcerer Postponed' in *A Universal History of Infamy* is a treatment of the years-of-experience-in-a-moment motif. Although the same motif is found in the *Nights* 'Tale of the Warlock and the Young Cook of Baghdad', Borges did not take his inspiration from there but from 'The Tale of Don Illan' in the medieval story collection *Conde Lucanor* by Don Juan Manuel. (Don Juan Manuel reworked his originally Arab material to tell a moral tale, warning against the sin of ingratitude, but the same tale told by Borges becomes a paradoxical parable about the nature of storytelling; for however long it takes a man to live his life, that life may be recounted as a story in ten minutes or so.) Similarly, in the same collection, 'The Masked Dyer of Merv' takes its story from the first framed tale in Moore's poem *Lalla Rookh*.

Borges read the *Nights* as a child and many times subsequently as an adult. He quotes the *Nights*, he rewrites tales from the *Nights* and he often strives for the same imaginative effects as the medieval authors of the *Nights* achieved. Clearly, in several senses (all of them naïve) Borges has been influenced by the *Nights*, but what does this mean? Influence does not just pass down from ancient writers to more modern writers, like a stream running downhill. Writers are not passive receptacles. Being influenced is an active process, and writers actually hunt for the books they wish to be influenced by, making choices among the thousands of books that they might be influenced by. Sometimes they are seeking the retrospective authorization of past precedent for something they were going to write anyway – or, if not that, then an ancient set of references to provide a familiar form for something new. Writers choose those whom they will be influenced by and they also choose how they will be influenced.

Not only do writers find their influences; in doing so, they modify our vision of the works they have been influenced by. When Borges read the *Nights*, he did not read what a medieval Egyptian had read; instead he read the stories that Stevenson and Chesterton read. As Borges himself remarks in 'Kafka and his Precursors' (in *Other Inquisitions*): 'The word "precursor" is indispensable in the vocabulary of criticism, but one should try to purify it from every connotation of polemic or rivalry. The fact is that each writer *creates* his precursors. His work modifies our conception of the past, as it will modify the future.'[31] In his novel *Small World* (1984), David Lodge has some gentle but serious fun with this notion. Persse, Lodge's questing knight in academia, announces that he has been doing a thesis on Shakespeare and T.S. Eliot:

'It's about the influence of T.S. Eliot on Shakespeare.'

'That sounds rather Irish, if I may so,' said Dempsey, with a loud guffaw. His little eyes looked anxiously around for support.

'Well, what I try to show,' said Persse, 'is that we can't avoid reading Shakespeare through the lens of T.S. Eliot's poetry. I mean, who can read *Hamlet* today without thinking of "Prufrock"? Who can hear the speeches of Ferdinand in *The Tempest* without being reminded of "The Fire Sermon" section of *The Waste Land*?'[32]

So it is that those of us who have read Borges find ourselves reading quite a different *Nights* from the text that admirers of *Vathek* or of *The Shaving of Shagpat* used to read. John Barth (b. 1930) is the American author of long, ambitious and somewhat chaotic novels, such as *The Sot-Weed Factor* and *Giles Goat-Boy*. Barth's intertextual games-playing with the *Nights* would certainly have baffled Addison or Hawkesworth. (Even Borges might have found him a bit difficult.) In 1974 Barth's novel *Chimera* appeared. In part a reworking of the Greek legends about Pegasus and Bellerophon, it is also a meditation on the nature of storytelling, a meditation in which the author inserts himself in his narrative and, masquerading as a time-travelling genie, communes with Sheherazade ('Sherry') and her sister Dunyazade ('Doony'). Barth shares Borges's preoccupation with problems of literary self-reference. According to Barth, the *Nights* is a book which begins by quoting itself: 'There is a book which is called *The Thousand and One Nights*.' In Barth's book, the Genie's message to Sheherazade is that 'the key to the treasure is the treasure'. It is not entirely clear what the Genie, or Barth, intends by this cryptic formulation, but perhaps the sense is that the story of the telling of the story is itself the story – or that the solution to writer's block is to write fiction about fiction. The former formulation is somewhat reminiscent of Tzvetan Todorov's observation that, in the thirteenth-century work *The Quest of the Holy Grail*, the quest for the Grail is in the deepest sense the quest for the story of that quest.[33] Barth pursues his own quest for the narrative of narrative in a series of dizzying spirals.

In the first part of *Chimera*, the 'Dunyazadiad', Barth is much preoccupied with the ways in which framed stories can operate on the stories which frame them. Sheherazade and the Genie speculate on whether one might go beyond the normal conventions of framed stories to create something more dynamic 'and conceive a series of, say, *seven* concentric stories-within-stories, so arranged that the climax of the innermost would precipitate that of the next tale out, and that of the next, et cetera, like a string of firecrackers or the chains of orgasms that Shahriyar could sometimes set my sister catenating'. In fact, the Genie has already suggested a limited precedent for all this in the *Nights* tale of 'The Ensorcelled Prince', which is framed within 'The Fisherman and the Jinni', but whose outcome determines the outcome of the story which frames it. In the latter parts of the book, the 'Perseid' and the 'Bellerophoniad', Barth goes on to execute this programme suggested by the Genie. The results are spectacularly bewildering.

The pervasive imagery of the spiral signifies the self-reflexive nature of the book. However, Barth's sense of the erotic nature of fiction prevents the 'Perseid' and the 'Bellerophoniad' from becoming excessively cerebral. Barth works through climaxes and orgasms to adumbrate feminist themes (in what is perhaps a conscious echo of Lally-Hollebecque's vision of the *Nights* as feminist document). In these later sections of the book, where Perseus and Bellerophon are centre stage, there is also some playful exploration of the folklore classification systems of Vladimir Propp and Stith Thompson. The tone of *Chimera* is throughout slangy and breezy.

The breeziness continues in Barth's volume of essays, *The Friday Book, or Book-Titles Should Be Straightforward and Subtitles Avoided* (1984). In this volume, Barth offers snippets of autobiography, such as the fact that he discovered the *Nights* and *The Ocean of Story* while a student doing library work at Johns Hopkins University. He also comments on both the *Nights* and *Chimera* and devotes a separate essay to *The Ocean of Story*. As far the *Nights* are concerned, he was particularly exercised by two problems: why does Sheherazade's storytelling take precisely 1,001 nights, and what is the significance of her three pregnancies? The fruits of his meditations on the sexual nature of Sheherazade's storytelling emerged in yet another fictional cat's cradle, *Tidewater Tales* (1987). In this complex farrago of tales within tales, Sheherazade belatedly returns the Genie's call, turns up to join a boating and storytelling party on Chesapeake Bay and then finds herself trapped in the twentieth century. 'Good readers read the lines and better readers read the spaces.' Prior to her time-travelling appearance, Barth, picking up on the question he had asked in *The Friday Book*, rather implausibly deduces from hints and silences in the *Nights* that the limit of 1,001 nights is tightly and directly linked to the sequence of Sheherazade's pregnancies and to her menstrual cycle. *Tidewater Tales* as a whole is playful and clever, but by comparison with *Chimera* really rather shallow. Barth's parasitic procedures may have sucked his literary host-body dry.

Salman Rushdie, asked on the BBC radio programme *Desert Island Discs* what book (apart from the Bible and Shakespeare) he would have with him on his island, chose the *Nights*, but Rushdie has discovered in this, his favourite book, something different again from what Borges and Barth found. Rushdie's *Nights* represents an alternative tradition in Islamic literature, something to set against the dour decrees of the mullahs of the Middle East and the dictators of the Indian subcontinent. References to the *Nights* abound in all of Rushdie's books. In *Midnight's Children* (1981), Saleem Sinai, one of 1,001 children born on the night of India's independence, at an early age immerses himself in the stories of Sinbad, Aladdin and the Genie of the Lamp, before embarking on his own magical adventures. In *The Satanic Verses* (1988) the stories of his protagonists, Gibreel Farishta and Saladin Chamcha, frame yet other stories of wonder and magic, and images from the *Nights* are given a surrealistic reworking – as for example the glass genie who is his own bottle. Finally, Rushdie's intertextual children's book, *Haroun and the Sea of Stories* (1990), sports with both the *Nights* and *The Ocean of Story*. But ultimately the question he asks, though sarcastically phrased, is a serious one and it is addressed to adult holders of power: 'What's the use of stories which aren't even true?'

Barth and Rushdie are unusual now in their knowledge of and involvement with the text of the *Nights*. Most people in the West today encounter a few bowdlerized versions of stories from the *Nights* as children. Later, as adults, they are likely to forget even those few stories. Borges observed: 'All great literature becomes children's literature.' This observation has some truth, and doubtless Borges was thinking of such classics as *Gulliver's Travels* and *Robinson Crusoe*: equally certainly, he had conveniently forgotten such works as *The Brothers Karamazov* and *Remembrance of Things Past*, which show no signs of becoming popular with children. In order for the *Nights* to regain some of the status it once held in European intellectual life, it will probably be necessary to commission a new translation of all or most of the stories in the fullest recension (so that Burton's version can at last be relegated to the repository shelves). Obviously, further studies of both the content and the influence of the *Nights* would also be helpful. In this chapter, a highly selective and idiosyncratic look has been taken at selected instances of various types of influence exerted by the *Nights* on a heterogeneous body of writers. In place of the writers discussed above, one might have substituted Goethe, Walter Scott, Thackeray, Wilkie Collins, Elizabeth Gaskell, Nodier, Flaubert, Stendhal, Dumas, Gérard de Nerval, Gobineau, Pushkin, Tolstoy, Hofmannsthal, Conan Doyle, W.B. Yeats, H.G. Wells, Cavafy, Calvino, Georges Perec, H.P. Lovecraft, A.S. Byatt and Angela Carter, for all these writers too have been influenced in one way or another by the *Nights*. Indeed, it might have been an easier, shorter chapter if I had discussed those writers who were not influenced by the *Nights*. A discussion of the lack of influence of the *Nights* on, say, William Blake, Evelyn Waugh and Vladimir Nabokov might have been just as rewarding. But enough . . .

Although better and fuller translations of the *Nights* may well be produced in the next hundred years, it still seems unlikely that the *Nights* will regain all of the status and the popularity it enjoyed in Britain and Europe in the eighteenth and nineteenth centuries. In part, this is because, as has been indicated above, the *Nights* has had an important role in engendering its own competition. In England, for example, translations of the *Nights* started to circulate at the beginning of the eighteenth century. The first novels only started to appear somewhat later – Defoe's *Robinson Crusoe* in 1719, Richardson's *Pamela* in 1741 and Fielding's *Joseph Andrews* in 1742. From the late eighteenth century onwards, as we have seen, the *Nights* influenced the development of the novel in many important ways. Any edition of the *Nights* published today faces competition from science fiction, sword-and-sorcery fantasy, horror, romance, crime and thrillers. These are mass-market genres which had not been thought of when the first English versions of the *Nights* began to circulate, but in their origins all these types of the literature of entertainment surely owe something to the ancient oriental story collection. To quote John Livingston Lowes (on Coleridge) again and to give his words a more general application: 'to attempt to trace the prints of the *Nights* . . . were like seeking the sun and rain of vanished yesterdays in the limbs and foliage of the oak. But the rain and sun are there.'

Today, of course, any edition of the *Nights* also has to compete with film and television for the public's attention. However, the 'selfish word-strings' which comprise the stories of the *Nights*, in continuing to mutate, have made the successful transition on to film. As early as 1905 the pioneer film-maker Georges Méliès drew on the pantomime tradition to present in *Le Palais des Mille et une nuits* an opulent, if now quaintly dated, vision of the gorgeous East. Other films have followed, with such titles as *A*

Tale of the Harem, *The Cobbler and the Caliph*, *Kismet* and *The Seventh Voyage of Sinbad*. Most filmed adaptations of stories from the *Nights* are frankly trashy, but a few, including the two versions of *The Thief of Baghdad* (1924 and 1940) and Pasolini's *Il fiore delle Mille e una notte* (1974), rank high among the masterpieces of world cinema. Thus the *Nights* continues to adapt, increasing in bulk and replicating its stories in new and strange forms. As much a cultural amphibian in the modern West as it was in the medieval Near East, the inspiration of the *Nights* flourishes not only in novels by intellectuals but also in films aiming at mass entertainment. Pier Paolo Pasolini's epigraph for his wonderful film will serve for this book as well:

La verità non sta in un solo sogno, ma in molti sogni.

(One does not find truth in a single dream, but rather in many dreams.)

Chronology

869	The essayist al-Jahiz dies.
910	Fatimid caliphate founded in North Africa.
942	Al-Jahshiyari, compiler of a no-longer-extant rival story collection, dies.
956	The cosmographer and historian al-Mas'udi dies.
969	Fatimid occupation of Egypt and foundation of Cairo. *Rasa'il Ikhwan al-Safa* ('Letters of the Brethren of Purity') written.
987	Ibn al-Nadim's *Fihrist*, a catalogue of books, completed.
994	Al-Tanukhi, compiler of the story collection *Faraj ba'd al-Shidda*, dies.
1085	Somadeva's *Katha Sarit Sagara*.
early 12th century	Heroic epic *Sirat Antar* put together.
1110	Petrus Alfonsi, compiler of the *Disciplina clericalis*, dies.
1122	Al-Hariri dies.
1143	Koran translated into Latin.
1171	Saladin brings to an end Fatimid caliphate in Egypt and founds Ayyubid dynasty.
1200	Ibn al-Jawzi dies.
early 13th century	Al-Jawbari's exposé of rogues' tricks, the *Kashf al-Asrar*, written.
1250–60	Collapse of Ayyubid principalities in Egypt and Syria and their replacement by Mamluke sultanate.

1252–84	Alfonso the Wise reigns in Castile.
1253	The pornographer al-Tayfashi dies. *Sindibad* translated into Spanish.
1258	Mongols sack Baghdad. Execution of last Abbasid caliph of Baghdad.
1260–77	Mamluke Sultan al-Zahir Baybar reigns over Egypt and Syria.
1311	Shadow-play author Ibn Daniyal dies.
1330	Nakhshabi's *Tutinameh*.
1353	Boccaccio's *Decameron* written.
1367	Al-Yafiʻi, collector of Sufi tales, dies.
1384	Don Juan Manuel dies.
1387	Chaucer begins *Canterbury Tales*.
c. 1410	The pornographer al-Nafzawi *floruit*.
1412	Al-Ghuzuli, compiler of the *belles-lettres* collection *Matali al-Budur*, dies.
1424	Sercambi dies.
1486	Ahmad al-Danaf, notorious Egyptian criminal, executed.
1516	Ottoman Turkish occupation of Mamluke Syria. Ariosto's *Orlando Furioso* published.
1517	Ottoman Turkish occupation of Mamluke Egypt. Execution of Tumanbay, last of Mamluke sultans.
1549–59	*Heptameron* compiled by Margaret of Navarre.
1634–6	Basile's *Pentamerone*.
1646	Birth of Antoine Galland.
1697	D'Herbelot's *Bibliothèque orientale* posthumously published under Galland's supervision. Perrault's *Contes de la mère l'Oye* published.

1704	Galland begins publishing his translation, *Les Mille et une nuits*. (The last volume appears in 1717.)
1708	Probable date of first chap-book edition of Galland in English translation.
1715	Death of Galland.
1721	Montesquieu's *Lettres persanes*.
1742	*Le Sopha* by Crébillon *fils*. *Les Mille et une fadaises*.
1748	Diderot's *Les Bijoux indiscrets*. Voltaire's *Zadig*.
1759	Johnson's *Rasselas*.
1761	Hawkesworth's *Almoran and Hamet*.
1764	Ridley's *Tales of the Genii*.
1765	Walpole's *Castle of Otranto*.
1767	Sheridan's *Nourjahad*.
1772	Cazotte's *Le Diable amoureux*.
1776	Richardson's *Grammar of the Arabick Language*.
1786	English edition of Beckford's *Vathek*.
1792	Cazotte guillotined.
1794	Alexander Russell's *Natural History of Aleppo*.
1795	Foundation of the Ecole des langues orientales vivantes, Paris.
1796	Death of the orientalist Sir William Jones. M.G. Lewis's *The Monk*.
1798–1801	French occupation of Egypt.
1799	Von Hammer-Purgstall in Istanbul.
1800	Southey's *Thalaba*.
1804	Maria Edgeworth's 'Murad the Unlucky'.

1804–5	First part of Potocki's *Saragossa Manuscript*.
1810	Silvestre de Sacy's *Grammaire arabe*. Southey's *The Curse of Kehama*.
1811	Jonathan Scott's translation of the *Nights*.
1812–22	Grimms' *Kinder und Hausmärchen*.
1812–32	Byron's *Giaour*.
1813	Brothers Grimm publish their *Märchen*.
1814–18	Calcutta I edition of the *Nights*.
1815	Suicide of Potocki.
1817	Moore's *Lalla Rookh*.
1820	Maturin's *Melmoth the Wanderer*.
1824–43	Breslau edition of the *Nights*.
1825	Al-Jabarti dies. Habicht begins to publish his version of the *Nights*. German version of von Hammer-Purgstall's translation of the *Nights* published.
1832	Washington Irving's *Legends of the Alhambra*.
1835	Bulaq edition of the *Nights*.
1836	Lane's *Manners and Customs of the Modern Egyptians*.
1837	Weil begins his translation of the *Nights*.
1838	Torrens's translation of the *Nights*.
1838–41	Lane's translation of the *Nights*.
1839–42	Calcutta II edition of the *Nights*.
1840	Poe's *Tales of the Grotesque and Arabesque*.
1844	Kinglake's *Eothen*.

1851	Nerval's *Voyage en Orient*. Melville's *Moby Dick*.
1855	Meredith's *The Shaving of Shagpat*.
1863–93	Lane's *Arabic–English Lexicon*.
1882	Stevenson's *New Arabian Nights*.
1882–4	Payne's translation of the *Nights*.
1885–8	Burton's translation of the *Nights*.
1899–1904	Mardrus's translation of the *Nights*.
1911	Aarne's *Verzeichnis der Märchentypen*.
1921–8	Littmann's German translation of the *Nights*.
1928	Vladimir Propp's *Morfologija Skazki*.
1943	Death of D.B. Macdonald.
1974	John Barth's *Chimera*.
1978	Albert B. Lord's *The Singer of Tales*.
1984	Mahdi's edition of *Alf Layla wa-Layla*.

Notes

Introduction

1 Jorge Luis Borges, 'The Garden of the Forking Paths', in *idem, Labyrinths* (London, 1970), p. 48; *idem, 'The Thousand and One Nights'*, in *idem, Seven Nights* (London, 1980), p. 50.
2 R.A. Nicholson, *A Literary History of the Arabs* (London, 1907), pp. 456–9; H.A.R. Gibb, *Arabic Literature: An Introduction* (2nd revised edn, Oxford, 1963), pp. 148–9.
3 Mia I. Gerhardt, *The Art of Story-Telling: A Literary Study of the Thousand and One Nights* (Leiden, 1963).
4 Muhsin Mahdi, *Alf Layla wa-Layla* (Leiden, 1984), 2 vols.
5 Husain Haddawy, *The Arabian Nights* (London and New York, 1990). For famous tales (such as 'Sinbad', 'Aladdin' and 'Ma'aruf the Cobbler') which are not found in the oldest manuscript and therefore do not feature in Haddawy's translation, the reader may wish to consult the modern translation, in Penguin Books, by N.J. Dawood, *Tales from the Thousand and One Nights* (London, 1973).
6 Richard Burton, *A Plain and Literal Translation of the Arabian Nights Entertainments, Now Entitled the Book of the Thousand Nights and a Night* (Benares = Stoke Newington, London, 1885), 10 vols; and *Supplemental Nights to the Book of the Thousand Nights and a Night* (Benares = Stoke Newington, London, 1886–8), 6 vols. (In later reprints of the *Supplemental Nights* it is common to find that the third volume has been split into two. However, the pagination in supplemental volumes 3 and 4 is continuous.)

1 Beautiful Infidels

1 On the Arabic language in general, see A.F.L. Beeston, *The Arabic Language Today* (London, 1970); and *Encyclopedia of Islam* (2nd edn), s.v. 'Arabiyya'.
2 On the life and work of Galland, see Mohamed Abdel-Halim, *Antoine*

Galland, sa vie et son ouevre (Paris, 1964); Georges May, *Les Mille et une nuits d'Antoine Galland* (Paris, 1986); Claude Hagège, 'Traitement du sens et fidelité dans l'adaptation classique: Sur le texte arabe des *Mille et une nuits* et la traduction du Galland', *Arabica*, 27 (1980), pp. 114–39.

3 On the life and work of d'Herbelot, see Henry Laurens, *Aux sources de l'orientalisme: La Bibliothèque orientale de Barthélemi d'Herbelot* (Paris, 1978).

4 On Beckford and Southey, see Chapter 10.

5 On translations of the *Nights* in general, see D.B. Macdonald, 'On Translating the *Nights*', *The Nation* (1900), pt 1, pp. 167–8, and pt 2, pp. 185–6; *idem*, 'A Bibliographical and Literary Study of the First Appearance of the *Arabian Nights* in Europe', *Library Quarterly*, 2 (1932), pp. 387–420; Nikita Elisseef, *Thèmes et motifs des Mille et une nuits* (Beirut, 1949), pp. 69–84; Hagège, 'Traitement du sens et fidelité'; Jorge Luis Borges, 'The Translators of *The 1001 Nights*', in *Borges: A Reader*, ed. E.R. Monegal and A. Reid (New York, 1981), pp. 73–86; Wiebke Walther, *Tausendundeine Nacht* (Munich, 1987), pp. 36–53.

6 On English translations of Galland, see especially C. Knipp, 'The *Arabian Nights* in England', *Journal of Arabic Literature*, 5 (1964), pp. 44–74.

7 On the life and works of von Hammer-Purgstall, see Baher Mohammed Elgohary, *Joseph Freiherr von Hammer-Purgstall, 1774–1856: Ein Dichter und Vermittler orientalischer Literatur* (Stuttgart, 1979); Bernard Lewis, *The Assassins* (London, 1967), pp. 12–13; Peter Partner, *The Murdered Magicians: The Templars and their Myth* (Oxford, 1982), pp. 138–45.

8 On Habicht's translation, see D.B. Macdonald, 'Maximilian Habicht and his Recension of *The Thousand and One Nights*', *Journal of the Royal Asiatic Society* (1909), pp. 685–704.

9 On the life and works of Lane, see Leila Ahmed, *Edward W. Lane: A Study of his Life and Works and of British Ideas of the Middle East* (London, 1978); A.J. Arberry, *Oriental Essays* (London, 1960), pp. 87–121; R. Irwin, 'The Garden of Forking Paths', *Times Literary Supplement* (26 April, 1985), p. 474.

10 On the life and work of John Payne, see Thomas Wright, *The Life of John Payne* (London, 1919).

11 On nineteenth-century British pornographers, see Steven Marcus, *The Other Victorians* (London, 1966), esp. ch. 2.

12 Wright, *Life of John Payne*, p. 269.

13 There are four modern biographies of Burton in English worthy of consideration (each has its own slant and its particular problems): Byron Farewell, *Burton* (London, 1963); Fawn M. Brodie, *The Devil Drives* (New York, 1967); Edward Rice, *Captain Sir Richard Francis Burton* (New York, 1990); Frank McLynn, *Burton: Snow upon the Desert* (London, 1990). For reviews of the latter two books, see R. Irwin, 'The Many Lives of Ruffian Dick',

Washington Post Book World (20 May, 1990), pp. 3, 6; and *idem*, 'A Passion for the Unknowable', *Times Literary Supplement* (12 October, 1990), pp. 1089–90. Richard Francois Gournay's *L'Appel du Proche-Orient: Richard Francis Burton et son temps* is a more penetrating study than any of the English biographies. James A. Casada's *Sir Richard F. Burton: A Bibliographical Study* (London, 1990) is excellent.

14 On Urquhart, see Sir Thomas Urquhart, *The Jewel*, ed. R.D.S. Jack and R.J. Lyall (Edinburgh, 1983); Richard Boston (ed.), *The Admirable Urquhart: Selected Writings* (London, 1975).

15 Borges, 'The Translators of *The 1001 Nights*', pp. 73–86.

16 Husain Haddawy, *The Arabian Nights* (London and New York, 1990), p. xxv.

17 Rana Kabbani, *Europe's Myths of Orient* (London, 1986), pp. 45–66; cf. Edward W. Said, *Orientalism* (London, 1978), pp. 194–7.

18 Henry Reeve, '*The Arabian Nights*', *Edinburgh Review*, 164 (1886), p. 184.

19 On the life and works of Mardrus, see Emile-François Julia's (to all intents and purposes unreadable) *Les Mille et une nuits et l'enchanteur Mardrus* (Paris, 1935); and cf. Rana Kabbani, 'Turkish Delight', *Observer* (13 July 1986), p. 53. For less rhapsodic views of Mardrus and his translation, see Macdonald, 'On Translating the *Nights*', pt 2, pp. 185–6; V. Chauvin, '*Les Mille et une nuits* de M. Mardrus', *Revue des bibliothèques et archives de Belgique*, 3 (1905), pp. 290–95; I. Cattan, 'Une traduction dite "littérale": *Le Livre des mille et une nuits* par le docteur J.-C. Mardrus', *Revue tunisienne*, 13 (1906), pp. 16–23; Abdel-Halim, *Antoine Galland*, pp. 208–13; Suhayr al-Qalamawi, *Alf Layla wa-Layla* (Cairo, 1976, in Arabic), p. 23; Hagège, 'Traitement du sens et fidelité', pp. 129–32.

20 Jeremy Wilson, *Lawrence of Arabia* (London, 1989), p. 719.

21 Borges, 'Translators', p. 86.

22 Francesco Gabrieli, 'Le *Mille e una notte* nella cultura europeana', in *idem*, *Storia e civiltà Musulmana* (Naples, 1947), pp. 99–107.

23 N.J. Dawood (trans.), *Tales from the Thousand and One Nights* (London, 1973). Michael Beard, in a review of Haddawy's translation in the *Journal of the American Oriental Society*, 112 (1992), pp. 144–5, while praising Haddawy's work, contrasted it with the Dawood translation in the following terms: 'in general, Dawood is nimbler, choosing to frame clusters of action between strong pauses which allow the reader to stand back from the action. Haddawy's tendency is to accumulate actions in small unsorted units, sometimes confusingly'. Of course, it must be borne in mind that the two translators are working from different texts; and, in the end, it all depends what you are looking for in a translation.

2 The Book without Authors

1 On the rise of orientalism, see Raymond Schwab, *La Renaissance orientale* (Paris, 1950) (though Schwab concentrates mainly on India). Also: Maxime Rodinson, *Europe and the Mystique of Islam* (Seattle and London, 1987); Albert Hourani, *Islam in European Thought* (Cambridge, 1991). Edward W. Said's *Orientalism* (London, 1978) is a stimulating book. For some of the criticism it has stimulated, see B. Lewis, 'The Question of Orientalism', *New York Review of Books* (24 January 1982), pp. 49–56; R. Irwin, 'Writing about Islam and the Arabs: A Review of E.W. Said, *Orientalism*', *I & C* (formerly *Ideology and Consciousness*), 9 (Winter 1981–2), pp. 103–12; E. Sivan, 'Edward Said and his Arab Reviewers', in *idem, Interpretations of Islam, Past and Present* (Princeton, 1985), pp. 133–54.

2 *The Arabian Nights Entertainments in the Original Arabic: Published under the Patronage of the College of Fort William by Sheykh Uhmud bin Moohummud Sheerwanee ool Yumunee* (Calcutta, 1814, 1818), 2 vols. On the early printed editions in general, see Nikita Elisseef, *Thèmes et motifs des Mille et une nuits* (Beirut, 1949), pp. 65–8; Muhsin Mahdi, *Alf Layla wa-Layla* (Leiden, 1984), vol. 1, pp. 14–22.

3 *Tausend und Eine Nacht Arabish: Nach einer Handschrift aus Tunis Herausgegeben von Dr Maximilian Habicht* (Breslau, 1825–38), 8 vols. Four further volumes were published by R. Fleischer in 1842–3.

4 Silvestre de Sacy, 'Compt-rendu du tome 1er de la première edition de Calcutta', *Journal des savants* (November 1817), pp. 667–86; *idem*, 'Mémoire sur l'origine du recueil de contes intitulés les *Mille et une nuits*', *Mémoires de l'Académie des inscriptions et belles-lettres*, 10 (1829), pp. 30–64.

5 *Alf Layla wa-Layla* (Bulaq, Cairo, 1835), 2 vols.

6 *Book of the Thousand and One Nights Commonly Known as the 'Arabian Nights Entertainments' Now for the First Time Published Complete in the Original Arabic*, ed. W.H. Macnaghten (Calcutta, 1839–42).

7 Richard Burton, *A Plain and Literal Translation of the Arabian Nights Entertainments, Now Entitled the Book of the Thousand Nights and a Night* (Benares = Stoke Newington, London, 1885), vol. 10, pp. 66–94 (pt 1 of the 'Terminal Essay').

8 On the manuscripts of the *Nights*, see H. Zotenberg, 'Notice sur quelques manuscrits des *Mille et une nuits* et la traduction de Galland', *Notices et extraits des manuscrits de la Bibliothèque nationale de Paris*, 28 (1888), pp. 167–320; D.B. Macdonald, 'Lost Manuscripts of the *Arabian Nights* and a Projected Edition of Galland', *Journal of the Royal Asiatic Society* (1911), pp. 219–26; *idem*, 'A Preliminary Classification of Some Mss of the *Arabian Nights*', in *Volume of Oriental Studies Presented to E.G. Browne* (Cambridge,

1922), pp. 304–21; *idem*, 'The Earlier History of the *Arabian Nights*', *Journal of the Royal Asiatic Society* (1924), pp. 355–97; Elisseef, *Thèmes et motifs*, pp. 55–64; Mahdi, *Alf Layla wa-Layla*, vol. 1, pp. 25–36 (in Arabic).

9 Al-Mas'udi, *Les Prairies d'or*, ed. and trans. C. Barbier de Meynard (Paris, 1861–77), vol. 4, pp. 89–90.

10 Ibn al-Nadim, *The Fihrist of al-Nadim*, trans. Bayard Dodge (New York, 1970), vol. 2, pp. 713–14.

11 Ibid., p. 718; cf. R. Irwin, 'The Image of the Byzantine and the Frank in Arab Popular Literature of the Late Middle Ages', in Benjamin Arbel, Bernard Hamilton and David Jacoby (eds), *Latins and Greeks in the Eastern Mediterranean after 1204* (London, 1989), p. 230.

12 S.D. Goitein, 'The Oldest Documentary Evidence for the Title *Alf Laila wa-Laila*', *Journal of the American Oriental Society*, 78 (1959), pp. 301–2.

13 Al-Maqrizi, *Kitab al-Khitat* (Cairo, 1854), vol. 1, p. 485.

14 Richard Burton, *Supplemental Nights to the Book of the Thousand Nights and a Night* (Benares = Stoke Newington, London, 1886–8), vol. 3, pp. 41–2; Nabia Abbott, 'A Ninth-Century Fragment of the *Thousand Nights*', *Journal of Near Eastern Studies*, 8 (1949), p. 157n.

15 Abbott, 'A Ninth-Century Fragment', pp. 129–64.

16 On the career of Macdonald, see William Douglas Mackenzie, 'Duncan Black Macdonald: Scholar, Teacher and Author', in *The Macdonald Presentation Volume* (Princeton, London and Oxford, 1933), pp. 3–10; Jean-Jacques Waardenburg, *L'Islam dans le miroir de l'Occident* (The Hague, 1962), pp. 132–5. For some of his writings on the *Nights*, see note 8 above.

17 On textual criticism and the editing of manuscripts, see Paul Maas, *Textual Criticism* (Oxford, 1958); M.L. West, *Textual Criticism and Editorial Technique* (Stuttgart, 1973); E.J. Kenny, *The Classical Text: Aspects of Editing in the Age of the Printed Book* (Berkeley and Los Angeles, 1974); Sebastiano Timpanaro, *The Freudian Slip* (London, 1976). On the editing of Arabic manuscripts (including the *Nights*), see Jan Just Witkam, 'Establishing the Stemma: Fact or Fiction?', *Manuscripts of the Middle East*, 3 (1988), pp. 88–101.

18 Mahdi, *Alf Layla wa-Layla*. Although the text, introduction and critical apparatus are all in Arabic, Mahdi has provided a very brief statement in English of his aims and conclusions at the end of the first volume.

19 *Idem*, 'Exemplary Tales in the *1001 Nights*', in *The 1001 Nights: Critical Essays and Annotated Bibliography/Mundus Arabicus*, 3 (1983), pp. 1–24.

20 Ibid., p. 23.

21 For the unedifying life of this adventurer, see Jonathan Curling, *Edward Wortley Montagu, 1713–1776* (London, 1954). On the manuscript, see Fatma Moussa-Mahmoud, 'A Manuscript Translation of the *Arabian Nights* in the Beckford Papers', *Journal of Arabic Literature*, 7 (1976), pp. 7–23.

22 On dating the *Nights*, see Macdonald, 'The Earlier History of the *Arabian Nights*', pp. 353–97; W. Popper, 'Data for Dating a Tale in the *Nights*', *Journal of the Royal Asiatic Society* (1926), pp. 1–14; Wiebke Walther, *Tausendundeine Nacht* (Munich, 1987), pp. 16–18.

23 Mahdi, *Alf Layla wa-Layla*, vol. 1, p. 235; Husain Haddawy, *The Arabian Nights* (London and New York, 1990), p. 255.

24 Mahdi, *Alf Layla wa-Layla*, vol. 1, p. 290; Haddawy, *The Arabian Nights*, p. 215.

25 Mahdi, *Alf Layla wa-Layla*, vol. 1, p. 319; Haddawy, *The Arabian Nights*, p. 241. On the career of Sudun, see Gaston Wiet, *Les Biographies du Manhal safi* (Cairo, 1932), p. 162 (no. 1133).

26 Mahdi, *Alf Layla wa-Layla*, vol. 1, p. 319. Haddawy in his translation of *The Arabian Nights* renders the key phrase (on p. 241) as 'two dinars', rather than as 'two Ashrafi dinars'. It is one of the rare trivial blemishes in a fine translation.

27 H.T. Norris, review of Haddawy's *Arabian Nights*, *Bulletin of the School of Oriental African Studies*, 55 (1992), pp. 330–31.

3 Oceans of Stories

1 Richard Burton, *A Plain and Literal Translation of the Arabian Nights Entertainments, Now Entitled the Book of the Thousand Nights and a Night* (Benares = Stoke Newington, London, 1885), vol. 3, p. 158; E.L. Ranelagh, *The Past We Share: The Near Eastern Ancestry of Western Folk Literature* (London, 1979), pp. 205–7.

2 Burton, *Nights*, vol. 6, pp. 152–5; Eberhard Hermes (trans. and ed.), *The Disciplina Clericalis of Petrus Alfonsi* (London, 1977), pp. 124–5; Dorothee Metzliki, *The Matter of Araby in Medieval England* (New Haven and London, 1977), pp. 97–103; Ranelagh, *The Past We Share*, pp. 182–8.

3 Burton, *Nights*, vol. 5, pp. 1–32; M. Gaudefroy-Demombynes, *Les Cent et une nuits* (Paris, 1982), pp. 182–98, 299–302; Metzliki, *The Matter of Araby*, pp. 140–41.

4 On the Sanskrit story collections, see A.B. Keith, *History of Sanskrit Literature* (Oxford, 1928).

5 On the *Panchatantra* and *Kalila wa-Dimna*, see T. Benfey, *Pantschatantra* (Leipzig, 1859), 2 vols; Ion G.N. Falconer, *Kalilah and Dimnah, or the Fables of Bidpai* (Cambridge, 1885); *Encyclopedia of Islam* (2nd edn), s.v. 'Kalilah wa-Dimnah'.

6 Somadeva, *The Ocean of Story*, trans. C.H. Tawney, ed. N. Penzer (London, 1924–8), 10 vols.

7 Louis Renou (trans.), *Contes du vampire* (Paris, 1963), is a complete translation with notes.

8 Emmanuel Cosquin, *Etudes folkloriques: Recherches sur les migrations des contes populaires et leur point du départ* (Paris, 1920).

9 B.E. Perry, 'The Origin of the Book of Sindbad', *Fabula*, 3 (1960), pp. 26–7n.

10 On Homer and the *Nights*, see Armand Abel, *Les Enseignements des Mille et une nuits* (Brussels, 1939), p. 113; Mohamed Abdel-Halim, *Antoine Galland, sa vie et son ouevre* (Paris, 1964), p. 296; Gustave E. von Grunebaum, 'Greece in the *Arabian Nights*', in *idem, Medieval Islam: A Study in Cultural Orientation* (Chicago, 1953), pp. 303–4.

11 On the possible legacy of classical literature generally (and of Plautus specifically) on the *Nights*, see Edward Rehatsek, 'A Few Analogies in the *Thousand and One Nights* and in Latin Authors', *Journal of the Bombay Branch of the Royal Asiatic Society*, 14 (1880), pp. 74–85; Abel, *Les Enseignements*, pp. 111–3; von Grunebaum, 'Greece in the *Arabian Nights*', pp. 294–319; *idem*, 'Greek Form Elements in the *Arabian Nights*', *Journal of the American Oriental Society*, 62 (1942), pp. 277–92; Perry, 'The Origin of the Book of Sindbad'; *idem*, 'Two Fables Recovered', *Byzantinische Zeitschrift*, 54 (1961), pp. 4–14; *idem*, 'Some Traces of Lost Medieval Story Books', in *Humaniora: Essays in Literature, Folklore, Bibliography, Honouring Archer Taylor* (Locust Valley, NY, 1960), pp. 150–60.

12 Ibn al-Nadim, *The Fihrist of al-Nadim*. trans. Bayard Dodge (New York, 1970), vol. 2, p. 718.

13 See Chapter 2, note 27.

14 On the survival of Pharaonic stories, see Hasan El-Shamy, *Folktales of Egypt* (Chicago, 1980), pp. 248, 259, 275, 281; *Encyclopedia of Islam* (2nd edn), s.v. 'Alf Layla wa-Layla'. On ancient Egyptian literature in general, see Gaston Maspero, *Popular Stories of Ancient Egypt* (London and New York, 1915); Ernest A.W. Budge, *Egyptian Tales and Romances: Pagan, Christian, and Muslim* (London, 1931); W.K. Simpson (ed.), *The Literature of Ancient Egypt* (New Haven, 1972); Stith Thompson, *The Folktale* (Berkeley and Los Angeles, 1977), pp. 273–6.

15 Stephanie Dalley, '*Gilgamesh* in the *Arabian Nights*', *Journal of the Royal Asiatic Society* (1991), pp. 1–17.

16 O.R. Gurney, 'The Tale of the Poor Man of Nippur and its Folktale Parallels', *Anatolian Studies*, 22 (1972), pp. 149–58.

17 Nikita Elisseef, *Thèmes et motifs des Mille et une nuits* (Beirut, 1949), p. 48.

18 On the *Sindibadnama*, see Perry, 'The Origin of the Book of Sindbad'; S. Belcher, 'The Diffusion of the Book of Sindbad', *Fabula*, 28 (1987), pp. 34–58.

19 H. Zotenberg, 'Histoire de Gal'ad et Chimas, roman arabe', *Journal asiatique*, 6 (1885), p. 551, and 7 (1886), pp. 97–123; Perry, 'The Origin of the Book of Sindbad', pp. 1–94, *passim*.

20 J.R. Walsh, 'The Historiography of Ottoman–Safavid Relations in the Sixteenth and Seventeenth Centuries', in Bernard Lewis and P.M. Holt (eds), *Historians of the Middle East* (London, 1962), p. 197.

21 On the translation movement, see L.E. Goodman, 'The Translation of Greek Materials into Arabic', in M.L.J. Young, J.D. Latham and R.B. Serjeant (eds), *Religion, Learning and Science in the Abbasid Period* (Cambridge, 1990), pp. 477–97.

22 Perry, 'Some Traces', pp. 156–7.

23 On Ibn al-Muqaffa and *Kalila wa-Dimna*, see Esin Atil, *Kalila wa Dimna: Fables from a Fourteenth-Century Arabic Manuscript* (Washington, 1981); J.D. Latham, 'Ibn al-Muqaffa and Early Abbasid Prose', in Julia Ashtiany, T.M. Johnstone, J.D. Latham, R.B. Serjeant and G. Rex Smith (eds), *Abbasid Belles-Lettres* (Cambridge, 1990), pp. 48–77; *Encyclopedia of Islam* (2nd edn), s.v. 'Ibn al-Muqaffa' and 'Kalilah wa-Dimnah'; R. Irwin, 'The Arabic Beast Fable', *Journal of the Warburg and Courtauld Institutes*, 55 (1992), pp. 36–50.

24 On the *Maqamat* of al-Hamadhani and al-Hariri, see R.A. Nicholson, *A Literary History of the Arabs* (Cambridge, 1930), pp. 328–36; Abdelfattah Kilito, *Les Séances* (Paris, 1983); A.F.L. Beeston, 'Al-Hamadhani, al-Hariri and the *Maqamat* Genre', in Ashtiany *et al.* (eds), *Abbasid Belles-Lettres*, pp. 125–35; Shmuel Moreh, *Live Theatre and Dramatic Literature in the Medieval Arab World* (Edinburgh, 1992), pp. 104–22.

25 R.A. Nicholson, *A Literary History of the Arabs* (London, 1907), p. 332.

26 On the origins and development of *adab*, see Barbara Daly Metcalf (ed.), *Moral Conduct and Authority: The Place of Adab in South Asian Islam* (Berkeley and Los Angeles, 1984) (esp. chapters by Peter Brown, Ira M. Lapidus and Gerhard Bowering); S.A. Bonebakker, '*Adab* and the Concept of Belles-Lettres', in Ashtiany *et al.* (eds), *Abbasid Belles-Lettres*, pp. 16–30.

27 Al-Nadim, *The Fihrist of al-Nadim*, vol. 2, pp. 712–24, 734–5.

28 Ibid., p. 714; cf. *Encyclopedia of Islam* (2nd edn), s.v. 'Djashiyari'.

29 Hans Wehr (ed.), *Al-Hikayat al-Ajibah wa'l-Akhbar al-Gharibah* (Wiesbaden, 1956).

30 F.C. Seybold (ed.), *Geschichte von Sul und Schumul. Unbekannte Erzahlungen aus Tausend und Einer Nacht* (Leipzig, 1920).

31 On al-Tanukhi, see D.S. Margoliouth, *Table Talk of a Mesopotamian Judge* (London, 1922); *Encyclopedia of Islam* (1st edn), s.v. 'Tanukhi'; Wiebke Walther, *Tausendundeine Nacht* (Munich, 1987), pp. 19, 24.

32 On al-Ghuzuli, see C. Torrey, 'The Story of el-Abbas and his Fortunate Verses', *Journal of the American Oriental Society*, 16 (1896), pp. 43–70; *idem*,

'A Story of a Friend in Need: The Arabic Text Edited from the Vienna Manuscript of al-Ghuzuli and Translated for the First Time', *Journal of the American Oriental Society*, 26 (1905), pp. 296–305; *Encyclopedia of Islam* (2nd edn), s.v. 'Ghuzuli'.

33 On al-Ayni, see *Encyclopedia of Islam* (2nd edn), s.v. 'Ayni'.

34 On Ibn Arabshah, see Freytag (ed.), *Fakihat al-Khulafa wa Mafakihat al-Zurafa* (Bonn, 1832), 2 vols, reviewed by Sylvestre de Sacy in *Journal des savants* (1835), pp. 602–12, 652–67; Clement Huart, *A History of Arabic Literature* (London, 1903), pp. 363–4; El-Shamy, *Folktales of Egypt*, pp. 263, 275–6; *Encyclopedia of Islam* (2nd edn), s.v. 'Ibn Arabshah'.

35 On al-Ibshihi, see *Encyclopedia of Islam* (2nd edn), s.v. 'Ibshihi'.

36 On al-Yafi'i, see Mia I. Gerhardt, *The Art of Story-Telling: A Literary Study of the Thousand and One Nights* (Leiden, 1963), pp. 369, 372n., 374, 465; *Encyclopedia of Islam* (1st edn), s.v. 'Yafi'i'.

37 D. Ayalon, 'The Historian al-Jabarti and his Background', *Bulletin of the School of Oriental and African Studies*, 23 (1960), p. 246.

38 Huart, *A History*, pp. 425–6; Ayalon, 'The Historian al-Jabarti'.

39 Franz Rosenthal, *A History of Muslim Historiography* (Leiden, 1962), pp. 42–3.

40 On the medieval Arab folk-epics, see R. Paret, *Die Geschichte des Islams im Spiegel der Arabischen Volksliteratur* (Tübingen, 1927); *idem, Der Ritter-Roman von Umar an-Numan und seine Stellung zur Sammlung von 1001 Nacht* (Tübingen, 1927); R. Goossens, 'Autour du *Digenis Akritas*: La "Geste d'Omar" dans les *Mille et une nuits*', *Byzantion*, 7 (1932), pp. 303–16; M. Canard, 'Delhemma: Epopée arabe des guerres arabo-byzantines', *Byzantion*, 10 (1935), pp. 283–300; N. Christides, 'An Arabo-Byzantine Novel: *Umar B. al-Nu'man* compared with *Digenis Akritas*', *Byzantion*, 22 (1962), pp. 549–604; U. Steinbach, *Dhat al-Himma. Kulturgeschichteliche Untersuchungen zu einem arabischen Volksroman* (Wiesbaden, 1972); G. Canova, 'Gli studi sull'epica popolare araba', *Oriente moderno*, 57 (1977), pp. 211–26; P. Heath, 'A Critical Review of Modern Scholarship on *Sirat Antar* ibn Shaddad and the Popular Sira', *Journal of Arabic Literature*, 15 (1984), pp. 19–44; B. Connelly, *The Arab Folk Epic and Identity* (Berkeley, Los Angeles and London, 1986).

41 Edward William Lane, *An Account of the Manners and Customs of the Modern Egyptians. Written in Egypt during the Years 1833–1835* (London, 1836), chs 21–3. (See also Chapter 4 for more detail on Lane's observations.)

42 M. Gaudefroy-Demombynes, *Les Cent et une nuits* (Paris, 1982).

43 On medieval European translations from Arabic generally, see R.W. Southern, *Western Views of Islam in the Middle Ages* (Cambridge, Mass., 1962); James Kritzek, *Peter the Venerable and Islam* (Princeton, 1964); Norman

Daniel, *The Arabs and Mediaeval Europe* (London, 1975); Juan Vernet, *Ce que la culture doit aux Arabes d'Espagne* (Paris, 1978); Maxime Rodinson, *Europe and the Mystique of Islam* (Seattle, 1987), pp. 3–37.

44 Hermes, *The Disciplina Clericalis of Petrus Alfonsi*, p. 104.

45 On the influence of the *Disciplina*, see Metzliki, *The Matter of Araby*, pp. 95–106.

46 On translation from Arabic in Spain, see Angel Gonzalez Palencia, *Historia de la literatura arabigo-española* (Barcelona, 1928); Vernet, *Ce que la culture doit aux Arabes d'Espagne*.

47 On Don Juan Manuel, see Palencia, *Historia*, pp. 313–4; Vernet, *Ce que la culture doit aux Arabes d'Espagne*, pp. 320–1; T. Montgomery, 'Don Juan Manuel's Tale of Don Illan and its Revision by Jorge Luis Borges', *Hispania*, 47 (1964), pp. 464–6.

48 Nai-tung Ting, 'Years of Experience in a Moment: A Study of a Tale Type in Asian and European Literature', *Fabula*, 22 (1981), pp. 210–11 (and cf. pp. 190–19 on Don Juan Manuel).

49 On Lull, see E. Allison Peers, *Ramón Lull: A Biography* (London, 1929).

50 Ferial J. Ghazoul, '*The Arabian Nights* in Shakespearean Comedy: "The Sleeper Awakened" and *The Taming of the Shrew*', in *The 1001 Nights: Critical Essays and Annotated Bibliography/Mundus Arabicus*, 3 (1983), pp. 58–70.

51 On the diffusion of Arab tales and motifs in Europe, see Metzliki, *The Matter of Araby*; Ranelagh, *The Past We Share*.

52 On some Arab sources for *The Canterbury Tales*, see Chaucer Society, *Originals and Analogues of Chaucer's Canterbury Tales* (London, 1872–88); W.F. Bryan and Germaine Dempster, *Sources and Analogues of Chaucer's Canterbury Tales* (Chicago, 1941); Metzliki, *The Matter of Araby*.

53 On the *Decameron*, see A.C. Lee, *The Decameron: Its Sources and Analogues* (London, 1909).

54 On Sercambi, see Cosquin, *Etudes folkloriques*, pp. 286–8; Bryan and Dempster, *Sources*, pp. 21–2; *Encyclopedia Iranica*, s.v. 'Alf Layla wa-Layla'. Quite a few of Sercambi's stories seem to derive from oriental sources, including the *Nights*.

55 Ariosto, *Orlando Furioso*, trans. Guido Waldman (Oxford, 1974), pp. 339–51.

56 Italo Calvino, *Italian Folktales* (London, 1980), p. xv.

57 On the Brothers Grimm and their sources, see Otto Spies, *Orientalische Stoffe in den Kinder – und Hausmärchen der Bruder Grimm* (Waldorf-Hessen, 1952); J.M. Ellis, *One Fairy Story Too Many* (Chicago, 1983).

58 Ernest Gellner, in *Times Literary Supplement* (22 August 1986), p. 903.

59 El-Shamy, *Folktales of Egypt*, p. xlii.

4 The Storyteller's Craft

1 Elias Canetti, *The Voices of Marrakesh* (London, 1978), p. 77.
2 On *khurafa*, see E.W. Lane, *Arabic–English Lexicon* (Cambridge, 1984, reprinted from edn of 1863), vol. 1, p. 726; D.B. Macdonald, 'The Earlier History of the *Arabian Nights*', *Journal of the Royal Asiatic Society* (1924), pp. 362–76; Nabia Abbott, 'A Ninth-Century Fragment of the "Thousand Nights": New Light on the Early History of the *Arabian Nights*', *Journal of Near Eastern Studies*, 8 (1949), pp. 155–8.
3 On preaching, see *Encyclopedia of Islam* (2nd edn), s.v. 'khatib' and 'khutba'. On popular preachers, see Ibn al-Jawzi, *Kitab al-Qussas wa'l-Mudhakkirun*, ed. and trans. M.L. Swartz (Beirut, 1986); Adam Mez, *The Renaissance of Islam* (London, 1937), pp. 326–7, 351; Ignaz Goldziher, 'The Hadith as a Means of Edification and Entertainment', in *idem, Muslim Studies* (London, 1971), vol. 2, pp. 145–63; Johannes Pedersen, 'The Criticism of the Islamic Preacher', *Die Welt des Islams*, n.s. 2 (1953), pp. 215–31; Khalib Athamina, 'Al-Qasas: Its Emergence, Religious Origin and Socio-Political Impact on Early Muslim Society', *Studia Islamica*, 76 (1992), pp. 53–74; *Encyclopedia of Islam* (2nd ed), s.v. 'kass'.
4 B.E. Perry, 'The Origin of the Book of Sindbad', *Fabula* 3 (1960), p. 11.
5 On live theatre in the pre-modern Arab world, see Shmuel Moreh, *Live Theatre and Dramatic Literature in the Medieval Arab World* (Edinburgh, 1992); cf. Peter J. Chelkowski (ed.), *Taziyeh: Ritual and Drama in Iran* (New York, 1979).
6 Charles Pellat (ed. and trans.), *The Life and Works of Jahiz* (Berkeley and Los Angeles, 1969), p. 101; cf. Moreh, *Live Theatre*, pp. 87–9; cf. *Encyclopedia of Islam* (2nd edn), s.v. 'hikaya'.
7 Al-Mas'udi, *The Meadows of Gold: The Abbasids*, trans. and ed. Paul Lunde and Caroline Stone (London, 1989), pp. 352–4.
8 Barhebraeus, *The Laughable Stories: The Syriac Text*, ed. and trans. E.A.W. Budge (London, 1897).
9 Al-Maqrizi, *Kitab al-Khitat* (Cairo, 1854), vol. 1, p. 485.
10 Roger Le Tourneau, *Fez in the Age of the Marinides* (Norman, Okla, 1961), p. 71.
11 Ibn Taghribirdi, *Al-Nujum al-Zahira* (Cairo, n.d.), vol. 7, pp. 813–14.
12 Richard Burton, *A Plain and Literal Translation of the Arabian Nights Entertainments, Now Entitled the Book of the Thousand Nights and a Night* (Benares = Stoke Newington, London, 1885), vol. 7, pp. 308–14.
13 E. Lévi-Provençal (ed. and trans.), *Seville Musulmane au début du XIIe siècle: Le Traité d'Ibn Abdun sur la vie urbaine et les corps des métiers* (Paris, 1947), pp. 60–61 and cf. p. 147n.

14 On this theme of *ibra*, or warning, in the *Nights*, see Abdelfattah Kilito, *L'Oeil et l'aiguille*, (Paris, 1992); David Pinault, *Story-Telling Techniques in the Arabian Nights* (Leiden, 1992), pp. 148–239.

15 On the guild of storytellers, see André Raymond, 'Une liste des corporations au Caire en 1801', *Arabica*, 4 (1957), p. 158; Gabriel Baer, *Egyptian Guilds in Modern Times* (Jerusalem, 1964), p. 116.

16 Katib Chelebi, *The Balance of the Truth* (London, 1957), p. 61. On the Middle Eastern coffee-house generally, see Antoine Galland, *De l'origine et du progrès du café: Sur un manuscrit arabe de la Bibliothèque du Roy* (Paris, 1699); Ralph S. Hattox, *Coffee and Coffee Houses: The Origins of Social Beverage in the Medieval Near East* (Seattle and London, 1985).

17 Alexander Russell, *The Natural History of Aleppo* (London, 1794), pp. 148–9.

18 Burton, *Nights*, vol. 10, pp. 164–6.

19 Edward William Lane, *An Account of the Manners and Customs of the Modern Egyptians: Written in Egypt during the Years 1833–1835* (London, 1836), chs 21–3.

20 Macdonald, 'The Earlier History of the *Arabian Nights*', p. 370.

21 On storytelling in Turkey, see Wolfram Eberhard, *Minstrel Tales from South Eastern Turkey* (Berkeley and Los Angeles, 1955); Ahmet O. Evin, *Origins and Development of the Turkish Novel* (Minneapolis, 1983), pp. 26, 30–39; Metin And, *Culture, Performance and Communication in Turkey* (Tokyo, 1987), pp. 74–5, 110–14; *Encyclopedia of Islam* (2nd edn), s.v. 'maddah'.

22 On storytelling in Persia, see Jiri Cepek, 'Iranian Folk-Literature', in Jan Rypka (ed.), *History of Iranian Literature* (Dordrecht, 1968), pp. 608–61; Elwell Sutton, 'Collecting Folklore in Iran', *Folklore*, 93 (1982), pp. 98–104; Peter Chelkowski, 'Popular Entertainment, Media and Social Change in Twentieth-Century Iran', in Peter Avery and Gavin Hambly (eds), *The Cambridge History of Iran* (Cambridge, 1991), vol. 7, pp. 766, 782–3.

23 John Malcolm, *Sketches of Persia* (London, 1845), p. 175.

24 Annemarie Schimmel, *The Triumphal Sun: A Study of the Works of Jalaloddin Rumi* (London and The Hague, 1978), esp. pp. 40–41; cf. Marshall S.G. Hodgson, *The Venture of Islam* (Chicago, 1974), vol. 2, pp. 244–9.

25 C.J. Wills, *In the Land of the Lion and the Sun, or Modern Persia: Being Experiences of Life in Persia from 1866 to 1881* (London, 1891), pp. 44–5.

26 Mary Ellen Page, 'Professional Storytelling in Iran: Transmission and Practice', *Iranian Studies*, 12 (1979), pp. 195–215.

27 M. Akar, 'The Arab Story-Teller: Nacer Khemir and the Revival of a Tradition', in *The Arab Cultural Scene* (*Literary Review*, special supplement, London, 1982), pp. 105–9.

28 Hasan El-Shamy, *Folktales of Egypt* (Chicago, 1980), p. xlviii.

29 Richard Hughes, *In the Lap of Atlas* (London, 1979), p. 41.
30 Iain Finlayson, *Tangier: City of the Dream* (London, 1992), p. 167.

5 Street Entertainments

1 For general histories of Islamic societies in pre-modern times, see M.G.S. Hodgson, *The Venture of Islam* (Chicago, 1974), 3 vols; Ulrich Haarmann, *Geschichte der arabischen Welt* (Munich, 1987); I.M. Lapidus, *A History of Muslim Societies* (Cambridge, 1988); Albert Hourani, *A History of the Arab Peoples* (London, 1991).

2 On Abbasid history, see Hugh Kennedy, *The Prophet and the Age of the Caliphates: The Islamic East to the Eleventh Century* (London, 1986). On Baghdad and social life in the eighth, ninth and tenth centuries, see Adam Mez, *The Renaissance of Islam* (London, 1937), an exceptionally lively book, full of recondite snippets and anecdotes; Gaston Wiet, *Baghdad: Metropolis of the Abbasid Caliphate* (Norman, Okla, 1974); M.M. Ahsan, *Social Life under the Abbasids* (London, 1979); Jacob Lassner, *The Topography of Baghdad in the Early Middle Ages* (Detroit, 1970); Louis Massignon, *The Passion of al-Hallaj, Mystic and Martyr of Islam* (Princeton, 1982), vol. 1, esp. pp. 224–94.

3 Oleg Grabar, *The Formation of Islamic Art* (New Haven and London, 1973), p. 173.

4 Richard Burton, *A Plain and Literal Translation of the Arabian Nights Entertainments, Now Entitled the Book of the Thousand Nights and a Night* (Benares = Stoke Newington, London, 1885), vol. 9, pp. 193–4.

5 Husain Haddawy, *The Arabian Nights* (London and New York, 1990), p. 66.

6 Ibn Jubayr, *The Travels of Ibn Jubayr*, trans. R.J.C. Broadhurst (London, 1952), p. 226.

7 On the history of the Mamlukes of Egypt and Syria, see Robert Irwin, *The Middle East in the Middle Ages: The Early Mamluk Sultanate 1250–1382* (Beckenham, Kent, 1986); P.M. Holt, *The Age of the Crusades: The Near East from the Eleventh Century to 1517* (London, 1986); U. Haarmann, 'Der arabische Osten im späten Mittelalter 1250–1517', in *idem* (ed.), *Geschichte der arabischen Welt* (Munich, 1987), pp. 217–63. On medieval Cairo, see Gaston Wiet, *Cairo: City of Art and Commerce* (Norman, Okla, 1964); S.D. Goitein, 'Cairo: An Islamic City in the Light of the Geniza Documents', in I.M. Lapidus (ed.), *Middle Eastern Cities* (Berkeley and Los Angeles, 1969), pp. 80–96; I.M. Lapidus, *Muslim Cities in the Later Middle Ages* (Cambridge, Mass., 1967).

8 Haddawy, *The Arabian Nights*, pp. 215–18, 221–2.

9 Ibid., pp. 239–41.

10 Edward William Lane (trans.), *The Thousand and One Nights, Commonly Called, in England, the Arabian Nights Entertainments* (London, 1877), vol. 1, p. 67; cf. *idem, An Account of the Manners and Customs of the Modern Egyptians: Written in Egypt during the Years 1833–1835* (London, 1836), pp. 291–2.

11 Richard Burton, *Supplemental Nights to the Book of the Thousand Nights and a Night* (Benares = Stoke Newington, London, 1886–8), vol. 2, p. 72.

12 Haddawy, *The Arabian Nights*, p. 69.

13 Ibn Khaldun, *The Muqaddimah: An Introduction to History*, trans. Franz Rosenthal (London, 1958), vol. 2, p. 348.

14 On the strangely neglected topic of the professional farter in the Middle Ages, see now Shmuel Moreh, *Live Theatre and Dramatic Literature in the Medieval Arab World* (Edinburgh, 1992), pp. 65–6. It is odd that Burton, for all his immense interest in the subject in general, restricts himself in his annotations to commenting on amateurs.

15 On the Banu Sasan, see Clifford Edmund Bosworth's marvellous book, *The Mediaeval Islamic Underworld* (Leiden, 1976), 2 vols.

16 There is as yet neither a decent edition of al-Jawbari's bizarre masterpiece, nor a scholarly translation. However, in the meantime, al-Jawbari, *Kashf al-Asrar* (Cairo, 1918?), and Abd al-Rahmane al-Djawbari, *Le Voile arraché: L'Autre Visage de l'Islam*, trans. René R. Khawam (Paris, 1979), 2 vols, may be used with caution. On al-Jawbari, see S. Wild, 'Jugglers and Fraudulent Sufis', in *Proceedings of the VIth Congress of Arabic and Islamic Studies* (Stockholm, 1975), pp. 58–63; Bosworth, *Mediaeval Islamic Underworld*, vol. 1, pp. 106–18; *Encyclopedia of Islam* (supplementary fascicule), s.v. 'Djawbari'.

17 On medieval Arab conjuring, see Wild, 'Jugglers and Fraudulent Sufis'; *idem*, 'A Juggler's Programme in Medieval Islam', in *La Signification du bas moyen age dans l'histoire et la culture du monde musulman: Actes du 8ième congrés de l'union européenne des arabisants et islamisants* (Aix-en-Provence, 1976), pp. 161–72.

18 Muhammad ibn Abu Bakr al-Zakhruri, 'Zahr al-Basatin fi Ilm al-Mashatin', British Library, Supp. MS 1210, f. 42a–b.

19 Ibid., ff. 92b–93b.

20 Massignon, *Passion of al-Hallaj*, vol. 1, pp. 155–61.

21 Du Camp is cited in Francis Steegmuller (trans. and ed.), *Flaubert in Egypt* (London, 1972), pp. 87–9.

22 On al-Muzaffar Hajji, see Irwin, *Middle East*, pp. 133–4.

23 On live theatre, see Moreh, *Live Theatre, passim*.

24 Burton, *Nights*, vol. 4, p. 193.

25 On shadow plays, see P. Kahle, 'The Arabic Shadow Play in Medieval

Egypt (Old Texts and Old Figures)', *Journal of the Pakistan Historical Society*
(1954), pp. 85–115; *idem*, 'The Arabic Shadow Play in Egypt', *Journal of the
Royal Asiatic Society* (1940), pp. 21–34; M.M. Badawi, 'Medieval Arabic
Drama: Ibn Daniyal', *Journal of Arabic Literature*, 13 (1982), pp. 83–107;
Shmuel Moreh, 'The Shadow Play (*Khayal al-Zill*) in the Light of Arabic
Literature', *Journal of Arabic Literature*, 18 (1987), pp. 46–61; *Three Shadow
Plays by Ibn Daniyal*, ed. Paul Kahle, Derek Hopwood and Mustafa Badawi
(Cambridge, 1992); Moreh, *Live Theatre, passim.*

6 Low Life

1 There is very little secondary literature on crime in the medieval Near East.
However, see Clifford Edmund Bosworth, *The Mediaeval Islamic Underworld*
(Leiden, 1976), 2 vols; Muhammad Rajab al-Najjar, *Hikayat al-Shuttar wa'l-
Ayyarun fi'l-Turath al-Arabi* (Kuwait, 1981); *Encyclopedia of Islam* (2nd edn),
s.v. 'liss'. On crime fiction, see Fadwa Malti-Douglas, 'Classical Crime
Narratives: Thieves and Thievery in *Adab* Literature', *Journal of Arabic
Literature*, 19 (1988), pp. 108–27; and cf. *idem*, 'The Classical Arabic Detec-
tive', *Arabica*, 35 (1988), pp. 59–81. There are also some extremely interesting
remarks about the medieval Arab origins of certain detection techniques in
Carlo Ginzburg's 'Clues: Roots of an Evidential Paradigm', in his *Myths,
Emblems, Clues* (London, 1986), pp. 96–125.
2 Al-Mas'udi, *The Meadows of Gold: The Abbasids*, trans. and ed. Paul Lunde
and Caroline Stone (London, 1989), pp. 356–7.
3 Charles Pellat (ed. and trans.), *The Life and Works of Jahiz* (Berkeley and Los
Angeles, 1969), p. 145.
4 Al-Mas'udi, *Meadows*, pp. 348; cf. pp. 350, 356.
5 Ibid., pp. 150, 154–5, 156–7, 160–61. On urban militias and related groups,
see Claude Cahen, 'Mouvements populaires et autonomisme urbain dans
l'Asie musulmane du moyen âge', *Arabica*, 5 (1958), pp. 225–50, and 6
(1959), pp. 25–56, 223–65.
6 For this and other criminal scandals, see Ulrich Haarmann, *Quellenstudien
zür fruhen Mamlukenzeit* (Freiburg im Breisgau, 1970), pp. 172–3.
7 Abd al–Latif al-Baghdadi, *The Eastern Key: Kitab al-Ifadah wa'l-Itibar*, trans.
Kamal Hafuth Zand and John A. and Ivy E. Videan (London, 1965),
pp. 223–79. One learns from the introduction to this edition (Arabic and
English on facing pages) that, centuries after his death, Abd al-Latif, desperate
to get his book into circulation again, contacted the Videans at a London
seance presided over by a Mrs Ray Welch.

8 Al-Maqrizi, *Le Traité des famines de Magrizi*, trans. Gaston Wiet (Leiden, 1962), p. 37.

9 See Chapter 5.

10 On the *Sira* or 'Romance' of al-Zahir Baybars, see E.W. Lane, *An Account of the Manners and Customs of the Modern Egyptians: Written in Egypt during the Years 1833–1835* (London, 1836), pp. 367–80; H. Wangelin, *Das arabische Volksbuch vom Konig Azzahir Baibars* (Stuttgart, 1936); M.C. Lyons, 'The Sirat Baybars', in *Orientalia hispanica*, 1 (Leiden, 1974), pp. 490–503. The *Sira* was printed in forty-eight parts in Cairo, 1908–9. *Les Enfances de Baibars*, trans. Georges Boulas and Jean-Patrick Guillaume (Paris, 1985), is the first volume of an ongoing translation of a modern Syrian manuscript.

11 *The Subtle Ruse: The Book of Arabic Wisdom and Guile* (London and The Hague, 1980).

12 On *tufaylis* and the science of gate-crashing, see Ahmad ibn Ali al-Khatib al-Baghdadi, *Al-Tatfil wa Hikayat al-Tufaylyyin* (Damascus, 1927); al-Mas'udi, *Meadows*, pp. 303–5; *idem, Les Prairies d'or*, ed. and trans. C. Barbier de Meynard (Paris, 1874), vol. 8, pp. 13–19; *Encyclopedia of Islam* (1st edn), s.v. 'tufaili'. Abu Zayd, the picaresque protagonist of al-Hariri's *Maqamat*, was of course a *tufayli par excellence*.

13 On the cycle of crime stories incorporated into the *Nights*, see Nikita Elisseef, *Thèmes et motifs des Mille et une nuits* (Beirut, 1949), p. 51; Mia I. Gerhardt, *The Art of Story-Telling* (Leiden, 1963), pp. 167–90; André Miquel, *Sept contes des Mille et une nuits, ou Il n'y a pas de contes innocents* (Paris, 1981), pp. 51–78.

14 On thieves' guilds in medieval and in Ottoman times, see Lane, *Modern Egyptians*, p. 113; Bernard Lewis, 'The Islamic Guilds', *Economic History Review*, 8 (1937–8), p. 35; Gabriel Baer, *Egyptian Guilds in Modern Times* (Jerusalem, 1964), pp. 9, 13, 35, 81; *idem, Fellah and Townsman in the Middle East* (London, 1982), p. 151.

15 On *futuwwa*, see Cahen, 'Mouvements populaires'; *Encyclopedia of Islam* (2nd edn), s.v. 'futuwwa'. However, academic interest so far has concentrated almost exclusively on the respectable side of *futuwwa*.

16 For hostile accounts of *futuwwa*, see e.g. I. Goldziher, 'Eine Fetwa gegen die Futuwwa', *Zeitschrift der Deutschen morgenlandischen Gesellschaft*, 73 (1919), pp. 127–8; Joseph Schacht, 'Zwei neue Quellen zur Kenntnis Futuwa', in *Festschrift Georg Jacob* (Leipzig, 1932), pp. 276–87; al-Turkomani, *Kitab al-Luma*, ed. S.Y. Labib (Stuttgart, 1986), pp. 54–62, 113–19.

17 On *shuttar*, see Louis Massignon, *The Passion of al-Hallaj, Mystic and Martyr of Islam* (Princeton, 1982), vol. 1, pp. 270–71; I.M. Lapidus, *Muslim Cities in the Later Middle Ages* (Cambridge, Mass., 1967), p. 272; al-Turkomani, *Kitab al-Luma*, pp. 63–8, 125–33; al-Najjar, *Hikayat al-Shuttar wa'l-Ayarrun*.

18 On the sect, see Bernard Lewis, *The Assassins* (London, 1967).

19 On the *zu'ar*, see Lapidus, *Muslim Cities*, pp. 153–64, 173–7.

20 On the *harafish*, see ibid., pp. 177–83.

21 On the etiquette of mendicancy, see M.L.J. Young, J.D. Latham and R.B. Serjeant (eds), *Religion, Learning and Science in the Abbasid Period* (Cambridge, 1990), p. 506.

22 Pellat, *Life and Works of Jahiz*, p. 255.

23 Lane, *Manners*, p. 299.

24 On drug-taking, see Franz Rosenthal, *The Herb: Hashish versus Medieval Muslim Society* (Leiden, 1971); Sami-Ali, *Le Haschisch en Egypte: Essai d'anthropologie psychoanalytique* (Paris, 1988); Michael Dols, *Majnun: The Madman in Medieval Islamic Society* (Oxford, 1982), pp. 101, 105–8.

25 On the Sufi use of drugs, see J. Spencer Trimmingham, *The Sufi Orders in Islam* (Oxford, 1971), p. 199n.; Annemarie Schimmel, *Mystical Dimensions of Islam* (Chapel Hill, NC, 1975), pp. 335–6; Peter Lamborn Wilson, *Scandal: Essays in Islamic Heresy* (New York, 1988), pp. 195–213.

26 On wine and its celebration in the Middle East, see Wilson, *Scandal*, pp. 123–151; F. Harb, 'Wine Poetry (*Khamriyyat*)', in Julia Ashtiany, T.M. Johnstone, J.D. Latham, R.B. Serjeant and G. Rex Smith (eds), *Abbasid Belles-Lettres* (Cambridge, 1990), pp. 219–34; Dols, *Majnun*, pp. 104–5; *Encyclopedia of Islam*, (2nd edn), s.v. 'khamr'.

27 *The Assemblies of al-Hariri Retold by Amina Shah* (London, 1980), p. 51.

28 On gambling, see Franz Rosenthal, *Gambling in Islam* (Leiden, 1975); *Encyclopedia of Islam* (2nd edn), s.v. 'kimar'.

29 On the police and law enforcement, see Reuben Levy, *The Social Structure of Islam* (Cambridge, 1969), pp. 331–8; Lapidus, *Muslim Cities*, p. 270.

30 On executions, see Adam Mez, *The Renaissance of Islam* (London, 1937), pp. 367–74; Max Meyerhof and Joseph Schacht, *The Theologus Autodidactus of Ibn al-Nafis* (Oxford, 1968), pp. 81–2; Boaz Shoshan, *Popular Culture in Medieval Cairo* (Cambridge, forthcoming).

7 Sexual Fictions

1 On the alleged madness of Shahriyar, and on Sheherazade as a medieval psychoanalyst, see Chapter 9. Although, in *Majnun: The Madman in Medieval Islamic Society* (Oxford, 1992), p. 172, Michael Dols has adduced one eighteenth-century French source which suggests that inmates of Cairo's lunatic asylum were told stories, evidence for the therapeutic use of storytelling in the medieval Near East is extremely slight.

2 Rana Kabbani, *Europe's Myths of Orient: Devise and Rule* (London, 1986), p. 48.

3 The secondary literature on sex in Islamic societies is quite extensive. See, in particular, Afaf Lutfi al-Sayyid-Marsot (ed.), *Society and the Sexes in Medieval Islam* (Malibu, 1979); B.F. Musallam, *Sex and Society in Islam: Birth Control before the Nineteenth Century* (Cambridge, 1983); Abdelwahab Bouhdiba, *Sexuality in Islam* (London, 1985); Fedwa Malti-Douglas, *Woman's Body, Woman's Word: Gender and Discourse in Arabo-Islamic Writing* (Princeton, 1991); Nikkie R. Keddie and Beth Baron (eds), *Women in Middle Eastern History: Shifting Boundaries in Sex and Gender* (New Haven and London, 1991). Salah al-Din Munajjid's *Al-Hayat al-jinsiyya ind al-Arab* [Sexual Life among the Arabs] (Beirut, 1958) deserves to be translated into English.

4 S.D. Goitein, *A Mediterranean Society* (Berkeley and Los Angeles, 1988), p. 308.

5 On this issue, see Musallam, *Sex and Society*.

6 On the *Hikayat al-Ajiba*, see Chapter 3.

7 On erotica, see Manfred Ullman, *Die Medizin im Islam* (Leiden, 1970), pp. 193–8; Munajjid, *Al-Hayat*, esp. pp. 149–72; Bouhdiba, *Sexuality*, pp. 140–58. Luce López-Baralt, *Un Kama Sutra español* (Madrid, 1992), offers both the text of an erotic treatise written by a seventeenth-century Spanish Muslim exile in Tunisia, and what is now the most important survey of Arabic erotic literature, as well as of knowledge of that literature in the medieval West.

8 On al-Tayfashi, see Ahamad al-Tayfashi, *Surur al-Nafs*, ed. Ihsan Abbas (Beirut, 1980); Ahmad al-Tifachi, *Les Délices des coeurs*, trans. René R. Khawam (Paris, 1981); Musallam, *Sex and Society*, pp. 91–3; Munajjid, *Al-Hayat*, p. 161.

9 Ali al-Baghdadi, *Les Fleurs éclatantes dans les baisers et l'accolement*, trans. René R. Khawam (Paris, 1973). Although Khawam does not say so, he appears to be translating the Paris Bibliothèque nationale MS arabe 3671 of *Kitab al-Zahr al-Aniq*.

10 For al-Nafzawi, see *The Perfumed Garden of the Shaykh Nefzawi*, trans. Sir Richard Burton, ed. Alan Hull Walton (London, 1963); al-Nafzawi, *The Glory of the Perfumed Garden: The Missing Flowers* (London, 1975). Burton's translation of al-Nafzawi was a really a plagiaristic rendering of an earlier French translation. The older literature misdates al-Nafzawi. For the correct century, see Robert Brunschvig, *La Berberie orientale sous les Hafsides* (Paris, 1947), pp. 372–3.

11 Richard Ettinghausen, *Arab Painting* (New York, 1977), p. 32.

12 Bouhdiba, *Sexuality*, pp. 75, 171, 202–3. Bottoms also feature prominently in the Nobel Prize-winning novelist Naguib Mahfouz's *Cairo Trilogy*.

13 On *tasmina*, see Bouhdiba, *Sexuality*, p. 202; Huda Lutfi, 'Manners and Customs of Fourteenth-Century Cairene Women: Female Anarchy versus Male Shar'i Order in Muslim Prescriptive Treatises', in Keddie and Baron, *Women*, p. 110.

14 On *qhulumiyyat*, see Ahmad Abd ar-Raziq, *La Femme au temps des Mamlouks en Egypte* (Cairo, 1973), p. 183; Bouhdiba, *Sexuality*, p. 201.

15 Ibn Khaldun, *The Muqaddimah: An Introduction to History*, trans. Franz Rosenthal (London, 1958), vol. 2, pp. 295–6.

16 On homosexuality in the medieval Near East, see *Encyclopedia of Islam* (2nd edn), s.v. 'liwat'. Burton's theories about the 'sotadic zone' (found in the *Nights*, 'Terminal Essay', vol. 10) tell one a lot about Burton's phobias and nothing about anything else.

17 On the distinction between active and passive homosexuality, and on the latter considered as an illness in the Middle Ages, see Franz Rosenthal, 'Ar-Razi on the Hidden Illness', *Bulletin of the History of Medicine*, 52 (1978), pp. 45–60; Dols, *Majnun*, pp. 95–9, 106. For a similar distinction in a pre-Islamic culture, see K.J. Dover, *Greek Homosexuality* (London, 1979).

18 A translation exists by René R. Khawam; see note 8 above. However, as Khawam refrains from revealing what manuscript he is translating, it is impossible to assess the translation's accuracy; cf. Munajjid, *Al-Hayat*, p. 161.

19 Leo Africanus, *The History and Description of Africa of Leo Africanus* (London, 1896), vol. 2 (Hakluyt Society, vol. 93), p. 458. On lesbianism more generally, see Bouhdiba, *Sexuality*, pp. 44–5.

20 Al-Jahiz, *The Epistle on Singing Girls* (Oxford, 1980), p. 32.

21 Al-Mas'udi, *The Meadows of Gold*, trans. Paul Lunde and Caroline Stone (London, 1989), p. 264.

22 Robert Irwin, *The Middle East in the Middle Ages: The Early Mamluk Sultanate 1250–1382* (Beckenham, Kent, 1986), pp. 130, 133.

23 On prostitution, see Abd ar-Raziq, *La Femme*, pp. 45–8; Bouhdiba, *Sexuality*, pp. 189–95; *Encyclopedia of Islam* (2nd edn), s.v. 'bigha'.

24 Richard Burton, *A Plain and Literal Translation of the Arabian Nights Entertainments, Now Entitled the Book of the Thousand Nights and a Night* (Benares = Stoke Newington, London, 1885), vol. 9, p. 194.

25 On the *udar*, see *Encyclopedia of Islam* (2nd edn), s.v. 'liwat'.

26 Bernard Lewis, *Race and Slavery in the Middle East* (Oxford, 1990), p. 20.

27 On the *adab* of love, see Lois Anita Giffen, *Theory of Profane Love among the Arabs* (London and New York, 1972).

28 On the Banu Udhra, see Burton, *Nights*, vol. 2, p. 304n.; Giffen, *Theory*, pp. 29, 33, 75; J.C. Burgel, 'Love, Lust and Longing: Eroticism in Early Islam as Reflected in Literary Sources', in Marsot, *Society and the Sexes*, pp. 91–6; A. Hamori, 'Love Poetry (*Ghazal*)', in Julia Ashtiany, T.M.

Johnstone, J.D. Latham, R.B. Serjeant and G. Rex Smith (eds), *Abbasid Belles-Lettres* (Cambridge, 1990), pp. 205–6. See also Burton, *Nights*, vol. 7, pp. 117–24, for the story of 'The Lovers of Banu Uzrah'.

8 The Universe of Marvels

1 *Encyclopedia of Islam* (2nd edn), s.v. 'Balinus'.
2 Jorge Luis Borges, 'Narrative Art and Magic', in *Borges: A Reader*, ed. E.R. Monegal and A. Reid (New York, 1981), pp. 34–8.
3 Useful literature on Islamic occultism is not easy to come by. Even readers of Arabic are not well served. However, see Edmond Doutté, *Magie et religion dans l'Afrique du nord* (Algiers, 1908); Paul Kraus, *Jabir Ibn Hayyan: Contribution à l'histoire des idées scientifiques dans l'Islam* (Cairo, 1942–3), 2 vols; Toufic Fahd, *La Divination arabe* (Strasburg, 1966); Manfred Ullman, *Die Natur-und Geheimwissenschaften im Islam* (London, 1972); Sylvie Matton (ed.), *La Magie arabe traditionelle* (Paris, 1977); *Encyclopedia of Islam* (1st edn), s.v. 'sihr'. Armand Abel's 'La Place des sciences occultes dans la décadence', in R. Brunschvig and G.E. von Grunebaum (eds), *Classicisme et déclin culturel dans l'histoire de l'Islam* (Paris, 1957), pp. 291–311, is an exceptionally stimulating *tour d'horizon*.
4 Tanya Luhrmann, *Persuasions of the Witch's Craft* (Oxford, 1989), p. 87.
5 [Pseudo-] al-Majriti, *Ghayat al-Hakim*, ed. H. Ritter (Leipzig and Berlin, 1933), pp. 139–40; David Pingree (ed.), *Picatrix: The Latin Version of the Ghayat al-Hakim* (London, 1986). The medieval Latin translation omits this anecdote, contenting itself with remarking: 'eorum tanta fuere mirabilia que si narrare vellemus essent auditoribus et narrantibus difficilia'. See also Ibn Khaldun, *The Muqaddimah: An Introduction to History*, trans. Franz Rosenthal (London, 1958), vol. 1, p. 221; Ibn al-Nadim, *The Fihrist of al-Nadim*, ed. Bayard Dodge (New York, 1970), vol. 2, p. 753. For some interesting ideas on the background to parts of pseudo-al-Majriti's strange and extremely sinister text, see J. Hjarpe, *Analyse critique des traditions arabes sur les Sabeens harraniens* (Uppsala, 1972).
6 On al-Mamun and the pyramids, see Richard Burton, *A Plain and Literal Translation of the Arabian Nights Entertainments, Now Entitled the Book of the Thousand Nights and a Night* (Benares = Stoke Newington, London, 1885), vol. 5, pp. 105–7; Ulrich Haarmann (ed.), *Das Pyramidenbuch des Abu Ga'far al-Idrisi* (Beirut, 1991) (Arabic text), pp. 128–9.
7 Richard Burton, *Supplemental Nights to the Book of the Thousand Nights and a Night* (Benares = Stoke Newington, London, 1886–8), vol. 6, pp. 135–42;

A. Schimmel, 'Some Glimpses of the Religious Life in Egypt during the Later Mamluk Period', *Islamic Studies* (Rawlapindi), 7 (1965), pp. 373–4; cf. Nai-tung Ting, 'Years of Experience in a Moment: A Study of a Tale Type in Asian and European Literature', *Fabula*, 22 (1981), pp. 183–211.

8 A book on *aja'ib* by Roy Mottahedeh is forthcoming. It should be good. In the meantime, see Mohammed Arkoun, Jacques Le Goff, Tawfiq Fahd and Maxime Rodinson (eds), *L'Etrange et le merveilleux dans l'Islam médiéval* (Paris, 1978).

9 On the Sinbad the Sailor cycle and related Islamic nautical yarns, see Francesco Gabrieli, 'I viaggi di Sinbad', in *idem, Storia e civiltà Musulmana* (Naples, 1947), pp. 83–9; Jean Sauvaget (ed. and trans.), *Akhbar as-Sin wa l-Hind: Relation de la Chine et de l'Inde* (Paris, 1948); Mia I. Gerhardt, *The Art of Story-Telling: A Literary Study of the Thousand and One Nights* (Leiden, 1963), pp. 236–63; Michel Gall, *Le Secret des Mille et une nuits* (Paris, 1972), pp. 17–72; Captain Buzurg ibn Shahriyar of Ramhormuz, *The Book of the Wonders of India* (London and The Hague, 1981); André Miquel, *Sept contes des Mille et une nuits, ou Il n'y a pas de contes innocents* (Paris, 1981), pp. 79–109.

10 On medieval European ghosts, see M.R. James, 'Twelve Medieval Ghost-Stories', *English Historical Review*, 37 (1922), pp. 413–22; Keith Thomas, *Religion and the Decline of Magic* (London, 1971), pp. 701–2; R.C. Finucane, *Appearances of the Dead: A Cultural History of Ghosts* (London, 1982), pp. 29–89.

11 Fabri, *Le Voyage en Egypte de Felix Fabri, 1483*, trans. J. Masson (Paris, 1975), vol. 2, pp. 445–6.

12 Burton, *Nights*, vol. 3, p. 252n.

13 Ibid., vol. 5, pp. 166–86.

14 On the *mihna*, see *Encyclopedia of Islam* (2nd edn), s.v. 'mihna'.

15 On Aladdin considered as a tomb robber, see C.R. Long, 'Aladdin and the Wonderful Lamp', *Archaeology*, 9 (1956), pp. 210–14. On Islamic treasure-hunting, see G. Maspero, 'L'Abrégé des merveilles', *Journal des savants* (1899), pp. 69–81, 155–72; Doutté, *Magie*, pp. 265–70; Haarmann, *Pyramidenbuch, passim*.

16 Burton, *Nights*, vol. 6, pp. 213–56; cf. Gerhardt, *Art of Story-Telling*, pp. 328–33.

17 Abd al-Rahmane al-Djawbari, *Le Voile arraché: L'Autre Visage de l'Islam*, trans. R. Khawam (Paris, 1979), pp. 243–54.

18 On Arab automata, see Banu-Musa, *The Book of Ingenious Devices*, trans. Donald R. Hill (Dordrecht, 1979); al-Jazari, *The Book of Knowledge of Ingenious Mechanical Devices*, trans. Donald R. Hill (Dordrecht, 1974). However, the Banu Musa and al-Jazari provided specifications for machines

which could actually have worked. There is, as far as I know, no literature on their fictional counterparts.

19 Burton, *Nights*, vol. 9, p. 324.

20 Husain Haddawy, *The Arabian Nights* (New York and London, 1990), p. 119.

21 Burton, *Nights*, vol. 3, pp. 269–70.

22 On Islamic geomancy, see Stephen Skinner, *Terrestrial Astrology: Divination by Geomancy* (London, 1980), pp. 30–52; E. Savage-Smith and Marion B. Smith, *Islamic Geomancy and a Thirteenth-Century Divinatory Device* (Malibu, 1980); *Encyclopedia of Islam* (2nd edn), s.v. 'khatt'.

23 On *firasa*, see Yasin Mourad, *La Physiognomie arabe* (Paris, 1939); Fahd, *Divination*, pp. 369–429; *Encyclopedia of Islam* (2nd edn), s.v. 'firasa'.

24 Carlo Ginzburg, *Myths, Emblems, Clues* (London, 1990), p. 125.

25 On dreams and dream interpretation in the Middle East, see N. Bland, 'On the Muhammedan Science of Tabir or Interpretation of Dreams', *Journal of the Royal Asiatic Society* (1856), pp. 118–71; G.E. von Grunebaum and R. Caillois (eds), *The Dream and Human Societies* (Berkeley, 1966); K. Brackertz (trans.), *Das Traumbuch des Achmet ben Sirin* (Munich, 1986); Fadwa Malti Douglas, 'Dreams, the Blind and the Semiotics of the Biographical Notice', *Studia Islamica*, 51 (1980), pp. 137–62; cf. Peter Burke. 'L'Histoire sociale des rêves', *Annales: Economies, sociétés, civilizations*, 28 (1973), pp. 329–42.

26 Burton, *Nights*, vol. 4, p. 289. Essentially the same story features as non-fiction in a fourteenth-century chronicle by Ibn al-Dawadari; see Ulrich Haarmann, 'Der Schatz im Haupte des Gotzen', in U. Haarmann and P. Bachmann (eds), *Die Islamische Welt zwischen Mittelalter und Neuzeit* (Beirut, 1979), pp. 198–229, esp. pp. 208–9n.

27 Thomas Mann, *Joseph and his Brothers*, trans. H.T. Lowe-Porter (London, 1959), pp. 892–3. More generally, Mann's great fictional tetralogy is an excellent guide to many aspects of old Semitic culture.

28 On al-Tanukhi, see Chapter 3.

29 Burton, *Supplemental Nights*, vol. 4, pp. 341–66. Maria Edgeworth's schoolmistressy *Murad the Unlucky* (1804) reads as if it was written specifically in opposition to this *Nights* tale.

30 On Todorov, see Chapter 9.

31 C.S. Lewis, 'On Stories', in *idem, Of This and Other Worlds* (London, 1982), p. 39.

32 Julian Barnes, *Flaubert's Parrot* (London, 1984), pp. 66–7.

33 Paul Willemen (ed.), *Pier Paolo Pasolini* (London, 1977), p. 74.

34 Walter Benjamin, 'Fate and Character', in *idem, One Way Street* (London, 1979), p. 126.

35 Jacques Monod, *Chance and Necessity* (London, 1972), pp. 154–5.

36 Burton, *Nights*, vol. 8, p. 9.

37 Most of the works of Abu'l-Qasim remain in mauscript only. However, on him, see P. Casanova, 'Alphabets magiques arabes', *Journal asiatique*, ser. 11, 18 (1921), p. 38; E.J. Holmyard, 'Abu'l-Qasim al-Iraqi', *Isis*, 8 (1926), pp. 403–26; Stefan Wild, 'A Juggler's Programme in Mediaeval Islam', in *La Signification du bas moyen âge dans l'histoire et la culture du monde musulman: Actes du 8me congrès de l'union européenne des arabisants et islamisants* (Aix-en-Provence, 1976), pp. 353–60; Ullman, *Die Natur- und Geheimwissenschaften*, pp. 125, 237, 412.

38 On the jinn, see Toufy Fahd, 'Anges, démons et djinns en Islam', in D. Bernot *et al.* (eds), *Génies, anges et démons* (Paris, 1971), pp. 153–214; *Encyclopedia of Islam* (2nd edn), s.v. 'djinn'.

39 Abdelwahab Bouhdiba, *Sexuality in Islam* (London, 1985), p. 50.

40 *Encyclopedia of Islam* (2nd edn), s.v. 'Iblis'.

41 On lycanthropy as mental illness, see Michael W. Dols, *Majnun: The Madman in Medieval Islamic Society* (Oxford, 1992), pp. 61, 64–6, 84, 87, 89.

42 Gilbert Adair, *Myths and Memories* (London, 1986), p. 75.

43 Brian Stableford, 'Proto Science Fiction', in Peter Nicholls and John Clute (eds), *The Encyclopedia of Science Fiction* (London, 1979), pp. 476–8. However, Pierre Versins took the view that science fiction is not a genre to be narrowly defined and dated, but is rather 'a state of mind'. See his magnificent *Encyclopédie de l'utopie, des voyages extraordinaires et de la science fiction* (Paris, 1972), esp. s.v. 'Arabe (culture)'.

44 See note 8 above.

45 Stephanie Dalley, '*Gilgamesh* in the *Arabian Nights*', *Journal of the Royal Asiatic Society* (1991), pp. 1–17.

46 Ibn Sina's visionary tale survives only fragmentarily in a thirteenth-century commentary on it by the Persian philosopher Nasir al-Din al-Tusi, *Hall Mushkilat al-Isharat* (Tehran, 1926). On *Salaman wa-Absal*, see Henry Corbin, *Avicenna and the Visionary Recital*, trans. W.R. Trask (Princeton, 1960), pp. 223–41; Hossein Nasr, *An Introduction to Islamic Cosmological Doctrines: Conceptions of Nature and Methods Used for its Study by the Ikhwan al-Safa, al-Biruni and Ibn Sina* (Cambridge, Mass., 1964), pp. 181, 263n., 265–6, 274; I. Strousma, 'Avicenna's Philosophical Stories: Aristotle's *Poetics* Reinterpreted', *Arabica*, 39 (1992), pp. 183–206.

47 See note 9 above.

48 On al-Farabi, see E.I.J. Rosenthal, *Political Thought in Medieval Islam* (Cambridge, 1962), pp. 122–42.

9 Formal Readings

1 *Leigh Hunt's Literary Criticism*, p. 246, cited in Muhsin Jassim Ali, *Scherezade in England: A Study of Nineteenth-Century English Criticism of the Arabian Nights* (Washington, 1981), p. 83.
2 Stith Thompson, *The Types of the Folktale: Antti Aarne's Verzeichnis der Marchentypen Translated and Enlarged* (Helsinki, 1932–6).
3 Hasan M. El-Shamy, *Folktales of Egypt* (Chicago, 1980), p. 237.
4 Vladimir Propp, *The Morphology of the Folktale* (Austin and London, 1968). See also *idem, Theory and History of Folklore* (Manchester, 1984).
5 Paul Willemen (ed.), *Pier Paolo Pasolini* (London, 1977), p. 74.
6 On Proppian approaches to film, see Pam Cook (ed.), *The Cinema Book* (London, 1985), pp. 234–8.
7 Alan Dundes, *The Morphology of North American Indian Tales* (Helsinki, 1964); *idem*, 'On Game Morphology', *New York Folklore Quarterly*, 20 (1964).
8 David Pinault, *Story-Telling Techniques in the Arabian Nights* (Leiden, 1992), p. 131.
9 On the response of literary theorists to Propp, see Robert Scholes, *Structuralism in Literature*, (New Haven and London, 1974), pp. 59–69, 91–117; Jonathan Culler, *Structuralist Poetics: Structuralism, Linguistics and the Study of Literature* (London, 1975), pp. 207–9, 212–13, 232–4.
10 An English translation of 'Les Hommes-Récits' appears in Tzvetan Todorov, *The Poetics of Prose* (Ithaca, 1977), pp. 66–79.
11 Tzvetan Todorov, *The Fantastic: A Structural Approach to a Literary Genre* (Ithaca, 1975), pp. 107–10.
12 Ibid., pp. 160–61.
13 Pinault, *Story-Telling Techniques, passim*.
14 Todorov, *The Fantastic*, pp. 160–61.
15 Bruno Bettelheim, *The Uses of Enchantment: The Meaning and Importance of Fairy Tales* (New York, 1976), pp. 86–90.
16 Joseph Campbell, *The Hero with a Thousand Faces* (London, 1975), p. 197.
17 Pasolini's film *Il fiore delle Mille e una notte / The Arabian Nights* was released in 1974. Despite the merits of various other film adaptations of the *Nights*, notably that of Powell and Pressburger, Pasolini's is the only version made for adults.
18 Jacques Monod, *Chance and Necessity* (London, 1971), p. 154.
19 Dawkins's ideas about selfish genes are found in *The Selfish Gene* (Oxford, 1976).

10 Children of the Nights

1 Jorge Luis Borges, 'The Thousand and One Nights', in idem, Seven Nights (London, 1984), p. 57.

2 On Thomas Guellette and his rivals and imitators, see M.-L. Dufrenoy, L'Orient romanesque en France 1704–1789 (Montreal and Amsterdam, 1946–7, 1975), 3 vols; Martha Pike Conant, The Oriental Tale in England in the Eighteenth Century (New York, 1908).

3 See note 2 above.

4 See W.H. Trapnell, 'Destiny in Voltaire's Zadig and the Arabian Nights', International Journal of Islamic and Arabic Studies, 4 (1987), pp. 1–15.

5 On the early appearance of Galland in English versions, see Sheila Shaw, 'Early English Editions of the Arabian Nights: Their Value to Eighteenth-Century Literary Scholarship', Muslim World, 49 (1959), pp. 232–8; C. Knipp, 'The Arabian Nights in England: Galland's Translation and its Successors', Journal of Arabic Literature, 5 (1974), pp. 44–54.

6 Edward W. Said, Orientalism (London, 1978), p. 42.

7 On Addison and other 'orientalist' writers in England in this period (Samuel Johnson, John Hawkesworth, Joseph Crabtree, etc.), see Conant, The Oriental Tale.

8 Hawkesworth's Almoran and Hamet has recently been reprinted, together with Frances Sheridan's The History of Nourjahad, Clara Reeve's The History of Charoba, Queen of Egypt and Maria Edgeworth's Murad the Unlucky, in Robert L. Mack (ed.), Oriental Tales (Oxford, 1972).

9 See note 8 above.

10 The literature on Beckford is vast, but André Parreaux, William Beckford, Auteur de Vathek [1760–1844]: Etude de la création littéraire (Paris, 1960), is fundamental. See also Fatma Moussa-Mahmoud (ed.), William Beckford of Fonthill 1760–1844: Bicentenary Essays (New York, 1960); Boyd Alexander, England's Wealthiest Son: A Study of William Beckford (London, 1962); Fatma Moussa-Mahmoud, 'A Manuscript Translation of the Arabian Nights in the Beckford Papers', Journal of Arabic Literature, 7 (1976), pp. 7–23. Vathek has appeared in innumerable editions. Beckford's Suite de contes arabes, ed. Didier Girard, was published for the first time in Paris in 1992.

11 J.W. Oliver, The Life of William Beckford (London, 1932), pp. 89–90, 91.

12 Very little has been written about Potocki (except perhaps in Polish). However, see Edouard Krakowski, Le Comte Jean Potocki: Un témoin de l'Europe des Lumières (Paris, 1963); Czeslaw Milosz, The History of Polish Literature (London, 1969), pp. 192–4; 'Jean Potocki et le Manuscrit trouvé à

Saragosse', in *Actes du colloque organisé par le Centre de civilisation française de l'Université de Varsovie, Avril, 1972* (Warsaw, 1974); Franz Rottensteiner, *The Fantasy Book* (London, 1978), pp. 21–2; Tzvetan Todorov, *The Fantastic: A Structural Approach to a Literary Genre* (Ithaca, 1975), *passim*; Marcel Schneider *Histoire de la littérature fantastique en France* (Paris, 1985), pp. 114–19. A complete version of the novel has only recently been published: *Manuscrit trouvé à Saragosse*, ed. René Radrizzani (Paris, 1989). An English translation of this edition is forthcoming. In the meantime, see *Tales from the Saragossa Manuscript (Ten Days in the Life of Alphonse Van Worden)*, trans. Christine Donougher, ed. Brian Stableford (Sawtry, Cambs., 1991). Some of his travel writings have been published as Jean Potocki, *Voyages* (Paris, 1980), 2 vols. Dominic Triaire, *Potocki* (Arles, 1991), came to hand too late for me to use it here.

13 Jacques Cazotte, *The Devil in Love*, trans. Judith Landry, ed. Brian Stableford (Sawtry, Cambs., 1991). On Cazotte, see Richard Burton, *Supplemental Nights to the Book of the Thousand Nights and a Night* (Benares = Stoke Newington, London, 1868–88), vol. 6, pp. i–xii; Edward Pease Shaw, *Jacques Cazotte (1719–1792)* (Cambridge, Mass., 1942); Schneider, *Histoire*, pp. 99–107;

14 On Southey, see Byron Porter Smith, *Islam in English Literature* (2nd edn, New York, 1975), pp. 179–87; Peter L. Caracciolo, 'Introduction', in *idem* (ed.), *The Arabian Nights in English Literature: Studies in the Reception of the Thousand and One Nights into British Culture* (London, 1988), p. 9. Caracciolo's book, and particularly its introduction, is fundamental to the study of the influence of the *Nights* on British literature.

15 On Moore, see Smith, *Islam*, pp. 195–201; M. Asfour, 'Thomas Moore and the Pitfalls of Orientalism', *International Journal of Arabic and Islamic Studies*, 4 (1987), pp. 75–92.

16 On Byron, see Smith, *Islam*, pp. 127–8, 189–95; Wallace Cable Brown, 'Byron and English Interest in the Near East', *Studies in Philology*, 34 (1937), pp. 55–64; Harold S.L. Wiener, 'Byron and the East: Literary Sources of the *Turkish Tales*', *Nineteenth-Century Studies* (1940), pp. 89–129; Caracciolo, 'Introduction', p. 20.

17 Samuel Taylor Coleridge, *Collected Letters*, vol. 1, p. 347, cited in John Beer, *Coleridge's Poetic Intelligence* (London, 1977).

18 Burton, *Supplemental Nights*, vol. 3, pp. 3–38. On Coleridge and the *Nights*, see Allan Grant, 'The Genie and the Albatross: Coleridge and the *Arabian Nights*', in Caracciolo (ed.), *The Arabian Nights*, pp. 111–29.

19 Aletha Hayter, *Opium and the Romantic Imagination* (London, 1968), p. 207.

20 John Livingston Lowes, *The Road to Xanadu* (Boston, 1927), p. 416.

21 Thomas De Quincey, *Autobiography* (Edinburgh, 1889), pp. 128–9; cf. Hayter, *Opium*, p. 128. On De Quincey and the Orient, see John Barrell, *The Infection of Thomas De Quincey: A Psychopathology of Imperialism* (New Haven and London, 1991).

22 Edward W. Said, 'Islam, Philology and French Culture', in *idem*, *The World, the Text and the Critic* (London, 1984), p. 271.

23 On Arabian themes in Dickens, see Harry Stone, *Dickens and the Invisible World: Fairy Tales, Fantasy and Novel-Making* (London, 1979), pp. 21–5; Michael Slater, 'Dickens in Wonderland', in Caracciolo (ed.), *The Arabian Nights*, pp. 130–42.

24 G.M. Young, *Gibbon* (London, 1932), pp. 13–14.

25 On *Shagpat*, see Cornelia Cook, 'The Victorian Scheherazade: Elizabeth Gaskell and George Meredith', in Caracciolo (ed.), *The Arabian Nights*, pp. 201–17.

26 On Stevenson, see Leonee Ormond, 'Cayenne and Cream Tarts: W.M. Thackeray and R.L. Stevenson', in Caracciolo (ed.), *The Arabian Nights*, pp. 178–96.

27 On 'orientalist' literature in the United States, see Luther S. Luedtke, *Nathaniel Hawthorne and the Romance of the Orient* (Bloomington and Indianapolis, 1989).

28 On Washington Irving, see E.L. Ranelagh, *The Past We Share* (London, 1979), pp. 247–58; M.M. Obeidat, 'Washington Irving and Muslim Spain', *International Journal of Islamic and Arabic Studies*, 4 (1987), pp. 27–44.

29 On oriental themes in *Moby Dick*, see Dorothee Finkelstein, *Melville's Orienda* (New Haven, 1961).

30 On oriental themes in Joyce, see Robert G. Hampson, 'The Genie out of the Bottle: Conrad, Wells and Joyce', in Caracciolo (ed.), *The Arabian Nights*, pp. 229–43.

31 Jorge Luis Borges, *Other Inquisitions, 1937–1952* (New York, 1966), p. 113.

32 David Lodge, *Small World* (London, 1984), pp. 51–2.

33 Tzvetan Todorov, 'The Quest of Narrative', in *idem*, *The Poetics of Prose* (Ithaca, 1977), pp. 120–42.

Index